COGNITION

Sixth Edition

COGNITION

Scott Sinnett | Daniel Smilek | Alan Kingstone

OXFORD

UNIVERSITY PRESS

OXFORD
UNIVERSITY PRESS

Oxford University Press is a department of the University of Oxford.
It furthers the University's objective of excellence in research, scholarship,
and education by publishing worldwide. Oxford is a registered trade mark of
Oxford University Press in the UK and in certain other countries.

Published in Canada by
Oxford University Press
8 Sampson Mews, Suite 204,
Don Mills, Ontario M3C 0H5 Canada

www.oupcanada.com

Third Edition published in 2007
Fourth Edition published in 2010
Fifth Edition published in 2013

Library and Archives Canada Cataloguing in Publication
Smilek, Daniel, 1974–
[Cognition]
Cognition / Scott Sinnett, Daniel Smilek, Alan Kingstone.
— Sixth edition.

Revision of: Cognition / Daniel Smilek, Scott Sinnett, Alan
Kingstone. — Fifth edition. — Don Mills, Ontario, Canada
: Oxford University Press, [2013]
Includes bibliographical references and index.

ISBN 978–0–19–901970–0 (hardback)

1. Cognition—Textbooks. 2. Cognitive psychology—Textbooks.
I. Kingstone, Alan, 1941–, author II. Sinnett, Scott, author III. Title.
IV. Title: Smilek, Daniel, 1974 . Cognition

BF311.S65 2016   153   C2016-900328-0

Cover image: Tom Barrick, Chris Clark, SGHMS/Science Photo Library

Oxford University Press is committed to our environment.
Wherever possible, our books are printed on paper which comes from
responsible sources.

Printed and bound in the United States of America

3 4 5 — 20 19 18

Brief Contents

Contents

Contents   vii

From the Publisher

What do we know, and how do we know it? What is the relation between the mind and the brain? How does memory work? What is intelligence? How do we learn language, acquire concepts, and solve problems?

These are just a few of the fundamental questions that frame the sixth edition of *Cognition*, the essential text for introductory courses in cognitive psychology. Building on the strengths of previous editions, the sixth edition maintains its clear, straightforward style and continues to provide fascinating research examples; in addition, it offers a student-friendly reorganization of key material and a new chapter on consciousness. Accompanied by a robust suite of ancillaries, *Cognition* is a well-rounded, current, and comprehensive text that is both accessible to students and a pleasure to teach from.

***Cognition,* sixth edition, retains all the hallmarks of previous editions:**

- broad, balanced treatment of major theories and controversies;
- clear, focused writing that makes even the most difficult concepts accessible without oversimplifying;
- historical perspectives on key issues and phenomena; and
- abundant citations of both classic and current research from Canada and around the world.

Highlights of the Sixth Edition

A new chapter on consciousness focuses on the distinction between the mind and the brain and covers an array of theories and disorders related to consciousness.

The Physiology of Visual Perception

In this chapter we are going to focus primarily on visual perception (multimodal perception will be discussed at the end of the chapter), and so it is worthwhile to begin with a brief overview of the physiology of the visual system. This overview will help us understand the perception deficits described in the Case Study, and it will also provide a useful foundation for understanding some of the findings described later in this chapter.

Visual perception involves the processing of information conveyed by light energy that enters the eye. As such, it seems reasonable to begin with a brief look at how the eye works. A simplified schematic of the eye is shown in Figure 3.1.

Light energy enters the eye through the cornea, which is the outer transparent tissue of the eye against which contact lenses are placed. After passing through the cornea, the light makes its way through a small opening called the pupil. The size of the pupil is controlled by the iris, the coloured tissue that surrounds it and makes the eye look blue, hazel, brown, etc. Next, light is refracted through the lens, which focuses the light on the tissue at the back of the eye known as the retina. The retina contains light receptors called photoreceptors, which are most densely packed in the small region of the retina known as the fovea. These photoreceptors capture light energy and through a chemical process transduce it into a neural signal that is transmitted by neurons through the optic nerve to the brain.

The neurons that carry signals from the eyes connect to several regions of the brain (see Weiskrantz, 1996). One of those regions is the primary visual cortex, located in the back of the brain. This region is responsible for the early processing of the visual signal and is also involved in visual consciousness. Because visual information falling on adjacent areas of the retina is processed in adjacent areas of the primary visual cortex, this region is said to be retinotopic. If a part of the primary visual cortex is damaged, the result is blindness in the corresponding area of the visual field.

Early on, the visual cortex was believed to be responsible for all visual processing:

> The view was trenchantly held that the visual image on the retina, encoding the many attributes of the visual scene, was transmitted to, and passively analyzed

cornea
The outer tissue of the eye and the first layer that light passes through on its way to the back of the eye.

pupil
The space through which light passes on its way to the back of the eye, adjusted in size by the iris, to an observer the pupil appears black.

iris
The tissue that surrounds the pupil and is responsible for the distinct colour of the eye.

lens
The transparent tissue in the eye that refracts light and focuses it on the back of the eye.

retina
The tissue at the back of the eye that contains light receptors.

photoreceptors
Cells that transduce light energy into a neural signal.

fovea
The region of the retina where photoreceptors are most densely packed.

primary visual cortex
The area at the back of the brain that is primarily responsible for the basic processing of visual information.

retinotopic
A principle of organization of the primary visual cortex, whereby information falling on adjacent areas of the retina is processed in adjacent areas of the cortex.

FIGURE 3.1 | The basic anatomy of the eye
The blue arrow represents light energy coming into the eye.

Major revisions include a new ordering of the chapters on memory (chapters 5 and 6), a revised approach to explaining memory systems (in Chapter 5), and an enhanced discussion of the physiology of visual perception (in Chapter 3).

occurs when you "look" at something "from the corner of your eye." To experience this, just look straight ahead and, without moving your eyes, try to see what a person in the periphery of your vision is doing. In this case, overt attention is focused straight ahead and covert attention is focused to the side of your line of sight. You will probably find that this is hard to keep up; after a few minutes, it's likely to take you some effort to maintain the dissociation between your covert and overt attention. Even if the eyes and covert attention can operate separately, then, this is more the exception than the rule.

Findlay and Gilchrist (2003) maintain that overt and covert attention in most cases move together, and that researchers should focus on studying overt attention because of its critical role in everyday attending. They argue that the importance of overt attention is related to the physical constraints of the eye. As we saw in Chapter 3, a high-resolution image of the world is available only for the small amount of information that falls on the foveal region of the retina. This means that if you want to see something clearly, you have to move your eyes so that information falls on that specific location at the back of your eye. In what follows, we will discuss how overt attention shifts (i.e., how the eyes move) during several everyday tasks such as reading and viewing objects and scenes.

Overt Attention During Reading

Are your eyes moving smoothly from letter to letter as you read this text? To accurately measure the behaviour of the eyes, researchers use complicated eye-tracking technology. An example of a modern eye-tracking device is shown in Figure 4.13. This device works by aiming a camera and a small infrared light at the eye and then locating (a) a reflection of this light off the cornea and (b) the location of the pupil, which is the point where the most

FIGURE 4.13 | A modern eye-tracking system
The EyeLink II system, developed by Canadian-based SR Research. The device is placed on the head and two cameras positioned below the eyes track the location of eye gaze.

Discussions of recent research, with new and expanded coverage of attention, auditory imagery, cognitive control, and other essential topics, detail the latest developments in the field.

every time we count our change we rely on our knowledge of how to add and subtract. To many people, these everyday activities—attending, comprehending, remembering, manipulating numerical information—fall under the general heading of "thinking." To psychologists, they are aspects of information processing—the subject matter of cognitive psychology.

Information Theory

Basic to the concept of information processing is the idea that information reduces uncertainty in the mind of the receiver. The amount of information provided by a given message is proportional to the probability that that particular message will occur. If you greet a friend with the query "How are you?" and receive the reply "Absolutely awful—I must have picked up a flu bug" rather than a standard "Fine, thanks," the former reply is much more informative than the latter because it is much less probable. The idea underlying information-processing theory is that the information provided by a particular message is not determined solely by its content, but rather by the whole array of possible messages of which this

FIGURE 1.2 | There is a lot of information in our world

An outstanding art program—featuring over 200 photos, figures, and tables as well as a lively four-colour design—invites students to engage with the text and helps them visualize key concepts and theories.

Engaging Pedagogy

Themed boxes draw attention to important points and encourage students to reflect actively on what they are learning.

"Cognition in Action" boxes showcase the real-life significance of key concepts discussed in the text.

COGNITION IN ACTION
BOX 8.2 | Do Experts Embody Information Differently?

Have you ever tried to learn a difficult skill such as shooting a puck or serving a tennis ball? If you have, you most likely had a friend, parent, or coach who gave you a visual demonstration of what you were supposed to do. Seeing a motor action performed correctly seems to have an effect on how well you perform it yourself. Indeed, many amateur athletes consciously try to emulate professional players or Olympic champions. This is a clever strategy, as a growing body of evidence suggests that action and perception are intimately linked. It seems that perceiving a particular motor action, or even just an object that could be acted upon, such as a puck or a ball, leads to activation in premotor areas of the brain, as if you were somehow preparing to perform a related action.

For example, imagine that you are looking at a frying pan with the handle facing to the right. If you were asked to press a key in response to some feature of the pan (e.g., its colour or size), you would be faster if you delivered your response with your right hand than with your left, presumably because the handle was facing to the right and activated a right-hand grasping response; this would be the case even if you were left-handed (Tucker & Ellis, 1998). It's important to note that the direction of the handle has nothing to do with a task involving colour or size. Nevertheless, response times are faster with the hand that the handle is pointing towards. This type of embodiment has been observed across a variety of experimental paradigms, stimuli, and even species: non-human animals also show embodiment effects (see, for example, Bach & Tipper, 2006; Beilock & Holt, 2007; Dipellgrino et al., 1992).

You might wonder how the link between perception and action plays out with experts in different types of motor skills (e.g., highly skilled athletes or dancers). Do they have a stronger embodiment response to motor actions in their expert repertoire than to actions they are less familiar with? Do people who become experts in a particular domain of motor skills have a greater ability to embody the action involved in that domain? To address this question, Calvo-Merino and colleagues (2005, 2006) explored how expert ballet and capoeira dancers responded to dancers performing skilled moves that they either would perform themselves or would only see performed by other dancers (e.g., a capoeira dancer watching a ballet dancer or a female dancer watching a male-specific move). Measurement of the viewers' brain activity, using fMRI, revealed more activity in response to motor actions that the experts had been trained to perform than to actions that they did not perform themselves. These results suggest that motor expertise can modulate how we perceive action.

Watching professional sports will not make you a professional athlete. Even so, aspiring athletes should probably watch the experts as closely as they can.

FIGURE 8.4 | Capoeira

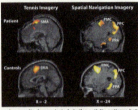

CONSIDER THIS
BOX 13.5 · Brain Imaging Reveals Consciousness in a Patient Diagnosed as Being in a Vegetative State

In the disorders of consciousness discussed so far—spatial neglect, split-brain, phantom limb—consciousness has been equated with our ability to communicate that we are self-aware through a behavioural response. But what if the ability to speak, mouth a word, smile, move a hand, or just blink one's eyes was absent? If you were conscious but unable to communicate this fact to others, then by definition you would not be considered conscious. In short, if the opportunity to self-report awareness is lost, it is impossible to determine if consciousness exists. Until now, patients with "locked-in syndrome" following acute brain injury or disease have been considered to be in a vegetative state in that they show "no evidence of awareness of environment or self." However, this positive diagnosis (vegetative state) is dependent on a negative finding (no signs of consciousness) and therefore is vulnerable to a false-negative result (what scientists call a Type II error).

Professor Adrian Owen, a researcher formerly at Cambridge University in the UK, now at the University of Western Ontario, has recently used some of the neuroimaging techniques discussed in Chapter 2 to solve this problem. Owen reasoned that if a measurable brain response could be used as a proxy for a motor response, then locked-in patients would have the opportunity to communicate to others that they were conscious. In his original paper, published in *Science* (Owen et al., 2006), he studied a 23-year-old woman, Sharleen, who had suffered a severe brain injury in a traffic accident. Because she was unresponsive to outside stimulation and did not exhibit any spontaneous intentional behaviours, Sharleen was diagnosed as being in a vegetative state. Using fMRI, however, Owen and his team asked Sharleen to engage in two mental imagery tasks: (1) walking around rooms in her home, and (2) playing tennis. Each task produced a classic pattern of brain activity that was indistinguishable from that produced by conscious control subjects. Imagining walking around her house yielded brain activations in the navigation network (the parahippocampal gyrus and parietal cortex), and imagining playing tennis resulted in activations in brain regions that control motor responses (supplementary motor areas). Owen et al.

FIGURE 13.15 | Brain imaging results demonstrated similar activity patterns between Sharleen and conscious controls when instructed to imagine walking around the house or playing tennis

From Owen, A. M., Coleman, M.R., Boly, M., Davis, M.H., Laureys, S, & Pickard, J.D. (2006). Detecting awareness in the vegetative state. *Science, 313*, 1402.

"Consider This" boxes highlight major findings from classic and current research.

"Think Twice" boxes invite students to engage personally with ideas and issues raised in the chapter.

THINK TWICE
BOX 4.3 · Do You Make Errors?

Have you ever started walking down the street and noticed that you still had your slippers on? Or absent-mindedly tried to fit a plastic coffee lid on your porcelain mug? Or put the cereal box in the fridge and the milk in the cupboard? According to James Reason (1979; 1984, see also Norman, 1981) these *action slips* are quite common, especially when we are engaged in some "parallel mental activity" (Reason, 1979, p. 76)—a fancy term for "mind wandering."

FIGURE 4.10 | An action slip: putting a plastic coffee lid on a porcelain mug

Reason (1979; 1984) described a series of diary studies in which participants were asked to keep a record of every silly (and not so silly) error they made. Interestingly, Reason found that these errors are often attention- and memory-related, and that they tend to occur more at certain times of the day than at others. To keep track of your own everyday mistakes, use a diary or your smart phone to record the error, the circumstances surrounding it, and the time of day. After doing this for several weeks, look to see if there are any patterns.

action slips
The kind of behavioural errors that often occur in everyday life

parallel mental activity
Thinking about something other than the task at hand

second letter. Since awareness of the letters requires that you allocate sufficient attentional resources to them, you are aware of the first one but completely unaware of the second.

Olivers and Nieuwenhuis (2005) have reported some very counterintuitive findings, which suggest there is something you can do to reduce the attentional blink. They presented participants with a rapid stream of roughly 15 letters and 2 numbers. The letters were to be ignored and the two numbers were targets. While this procedure might seem very similar to the SART task described earlier, the AB task is quite different with regard to the speed of presentation. In the SART the items are presented every 2 seconds and each item is considered to be a single trial. By contrast, in the AB task the items are presented about every 120 ms and each stream of 17 items constitutes a single trial. The quick presentation of successive stimuli is often referred to as rapid serial visual presentation (RSVP). An example of an RSVP stream is shown in Panel A of Figure 4.11. After the RSVP stream, participants are asked to report the first number and then the second number.

Olivers and Nieuwenhuis varied the number of letters intervening between the two target digits. When there is one intervening item between the first digit (Target One: T1) and the second digit (Target Two: T2), T2 is said to be presented at Lag 2 because T2 is the second item after T1. At Lag 3 there are two intervening letters between T1 and T2, and so on. Because the attentional blink typically occurs only when two targets are presented in close temporal proximity, one would expect the most blinking to occur at short lags and for performance to improve at longer lags.

More important, Olivers and Nieuwenhuis also included a condition in which participants completed the AB task in silence, and a condition in which they listened to music

rapid serial visual presentation (RSVP)
The presentation of a series of stimuli in quick succession

CASE STUDY

When Memory Fails

The previous chapter highlighted some basic ideas about the various systems of memory. In this chapter we will focus on different types of long-term memory, but first let's turn our attention to a case study that highlights the importance of memory and the dire consequences that can follow when memory fails.

In July 1984 a college student named Jennifer Thompson woke up and saw a man with a knife beside her bed. When she screamed, he held the knife to her throat and said he would kill her if she didn't keep quiet. She offered him her wallet, even her car, but he told her he didn't want those things. Realizing what he was there for, she made a conscious effort to study his face, looking for details she could remember later and use to identify him. Eventually she escaped to a neighbour's by persuading the rapist to let her get him a drink.

Thompson worked closely with the police to create a composite sketch. When she was shown a photo lineup she studied it carefully before deciding the man the police had identified as the suspect. She picked out the same man, Ronald Cotton, in a physical lineup, and when the case went to court she swore that he was the one who had raped her, Cotton, 22, was sentenced to life.

In prison Cotton met someone who looked so much like him that other prisoners sometimes mistook one for the other. Bobby Poole had been living in the same North Carolina town as Cotton and Thompson, and was serving time for a series of rapes. When Cotton asked if he had raped Thompson he denied it, but another inmate informed Cotton that Poole told him he had. Finally, in 1995 a DNA test confirmed Poole's guilt. Cotton was exonerated, and

FIGURE 6.1 | Jennifer Thompson and Ronald Cotton

Case studies at the beginning of each chapter introduce real-world situations that illustrate one or more of the concepts to be explored in the chapter that follows.

CASE STUDY

Case Study Wrap-Up

Kim Ung-Yong, the child prodigy who was the subject of the case study that opened this chapter, was estimated by the Stanford–Binet test to have an IQ of 210. How Kim would score on the Raven test of *g* (general intelligence) we don't know, but according to Spearman's two-factor theory of intelligence (Figure 12.2) he would probably have a very high *g*. We can likely make the same assumption with respect to Sternberg's concept of analytical intelligence, since it has been argued that *g* and analytical intelligence are largely the same. Where Kim would score on Spearman's variable *s* (specific ability: the variable ability within an individual for different abilities) or Sternberg's practical intelligence is not clear. However, we may find a partial answer in Kim's own reflections on his life.

As we saw, Kim completed his PhD in the US at the age of 15 and then went to work for NASA. But by 1978 the loneliness of his life there led him to move back to Korea. Although he eventually established a successful career in business planning, the choice to return attracted considerable attention, and some media critics judged him a failure. In 2010 Kim told the *Korea Herald* that "People expected me to become a high-ranking official in the government or a big company, but I don't

think just because I chose not to become the expected it gives anyone a right to call anyone's life a failure."

Fortunately, Kim now says he is happy. Although his exceptional intelligence has helped him in life, he feels that too much importance is attached to a high IQ: "If there is a long spectrum of categories with many different talents, I would only be a part of the spectrum. I'm just good in concentrating on one thing, and there are many others who have different talents." Thus by his own assessment it seems likely that Kim would have a relatively high *g*, but varying specific abilities.

As you have probably noticed, one of the messages of this chapter is that there are many kinds of intelligence. Kim's story may lend credence to Gardner's theory of multiple intelligences. But a high *g* does not necessarily mean that someone will be intelligent across all domains, or act in the most intelligent manner in all situations. There could be many supposed geniuses who don't have a creative bone in their bodies. In any event, Kim's modest appraisal of his own abilities may give hope to the rest of us. Even if you aren't an expert in calculus, as he was, there are likely some other types of intelligence in which you excel.

Case study wrap-ups at the end of each chapter revisit and expand on chapter-opening case studies in the light of the chapter discussion.

In the Know: Review Questions

1. What is insight? What is responsible for its occurrence? What can be done to facilitate it?
2. What is functional fixedness? Why does it occur?
3. Outline the basic features of GPS, using the Tower of Hanoi problem to illustrate your answer.
4. Discuss methods for studying problem-solving in science.

Key Concepts

algorithms
analysis of the situation
artificial intelligence
BACON
chunk decomposition
cognitive history of science
computational models
constraint relaxation
distributed reasoning
Einstellung effect (Luchins)
evaluation function
face validity
feeling of knowing
feeling of "warmth"
functional fixedness (Duncker)
General Problem Solver (GPS)
Gestalt switch
goal stack
heuristic
hints (Maier's view)
historical accounts

insight problem
in vivo/in vitro method (Dunbar)
laboratory studies
means–end analysis
mindfulness vs mindlessness (Langer)
negative transfer
observation of ongoing scientific investigations
problem space
production rules
productive thinking (Wertheimer)
progress monitoring theory
representational change theory
search tree
strong but wrong routines
structurally blind/reproductive thinking
subgoal
thinking aloud
toy problems
unexpected findings
Zeigarnik effect

Links to Other Chapters

feeling of knowing
Chapter 5 (butcher-on-the-bus phenomenon)

Gestalt switch
Chapter 2 (isomorphism)

heuristics
Chapter 8 (commitment heuristic)
Chapter 11 (heuristics and biases, representativeness, availability, recognition)

insight
Chapter 12 (creativity and problem-finding)

metacognition
Chapter 6 (elaboration and distinctiveness)

problem space
Chapter 11 (importance of the problem space)
Chapter 12 (creativity and problem-finding)

sleep
Chapter 6 (sleep, memory, and false memory)

End-of-chapter learning resources—including "In the Know" review questions, lists of key concepts, links to other chapters, and discussions of further readings—help students review what they have learned and identify reliable starting points for further study.

Further Reading

Gick and Lockhart (1995) proposed a simple technique for constructing insight problems that you might like to try yourself. They noted that the key to composing a riddle is to get the problem-solver to initially interpret information incorrectly. One way to do this is to use a word that can be interpreted in more than one way. For example, most people interpret the word *lake* to refer to a liquid body of water, but a lake can also be frozen. A riddle can be constructed by requiring the problem-solver to come up with the less common meaning in order to make sense of the situation that the riddle describes. An example of a riddle solution given by Gick and Lockhart is "The stone rested on the surface of the lake for three months, after which it sank to the bottom some 10 metres below." Only when the problem-solver realizes that the lake was initially frozen does the solution to the riddle become clear.

Some criticisms of computer simulation approaches to thinking go even further than the Gestalt critique, arguing that the activities of computer programs don't count as thinking. People who express this belief often ally themselves with the German philosopher Heidegger (1968). For Heidegger, the ability of computer programs to represent the chain of inferences leading from one state to another would not have been the essence of thinking. Computer programs are good at simulating processes such as reasoning and calculation. However, the essence of thinking lies *behind* these processes; it is not reducible to them. Computer programs don't capture the subjective origin of thinking—the concern with the fundamental problem of being alive in the world. Although Heidegger is often difficult to follow, and even more difficult to paraphrase, his ideas about thinking may resonate with many people who have reservations about artificial intelligence.

Computer simulation approaches to psychological processes have often been criticized for what they appear to leave out. Even some cognitive psychologists have suggested that to design a computer program that would simulate emotion would not be a very meaningful exercise; among them is Neisser (1964). Although Simon (1967) attempted to deal with this problem, most work in this area has specialized in cognition, and it is perhaps fair to say that the role of emotion in mental life has been neglected. See also Simon (1995).

For a wonderful example of the cognitive history of science see Netz (1999).

Gick, M., & Lockhart, R.S. (1995). Cognitive and affective components of insight. In R.J. Sternberg & J.E. Davidson (Eds.), *The nature of insight* (pp. 197–228). Cambridge, Mass.: MIT Press.
Heidegger, M. (1968). *What is called thinking?* (J. Glen Gray, Trans.). New York: Harper & Row.
Neisser, U. (1964). The multiplicity of thought. *British Journal of Psychology, 54*, 1–14.
Netz, R. (1999). *The shaping of deduction in Greek mathematics: A study in cognitive history.* Cambridge: Cambridge University Press.
Simon, H.A. (1967). Motivational and emotional controls of cognition. *Psychological Review, 74*, 29–39.
Simon, H.A. (1995). The information-processing theory of mind. *American Psychologist, 50*, 507–508.

Marginal definitions of key terms, which also appear in the end-of-text glossary, help students fully understand important discussions and build their discipline-specific vocabularies.

The Building Blocks of Language

The branch of cognitive psychology that studies the acquisition, production, comprehension, and representation (in the mind) of language is called psycholinguistics. Psycholinguists have a rich history in exploring how language is structured. To begin with, it is important to emphasize that language is hierarchical in nature. That is, a series of components can be combined to form larger components, which in turn can be combined, as long as each combination follows certain rules. While languages obviously vary widely, there are components that all of them share. One example is the phoneme. Phonemes are the smallest units in language, and can be combined with other phonemes to form morphemes. Morphemes are the smallest meaningful units of language. For instance, the phonemes /d/, /o/, and /g/ can be combined to form the morpheme /dog/, which also happens to be a word. Note that not all morphemes are words: some are word elements that do not necessarily form words on their own. For example, /s/ by itself is a phoneme, but it becomes a morpheme (i.e., a unit carrying meaning) when it is combined with /dog/ to form the plural /dogs/.

Different languages are composed of different numbers of phonemes. For example, whereas English has approximately 44 phonemes (24 consonant and 20 vowel),

psycholinguistics
The branch of cognitive psychology interested in how we comprehend, produce, acquire, and represent (in the mind) language.

phoneme
The smallest unit in language. Phonemes are combined to form morphemes.

morpheme
The smallest unit in language that carries meaning.

Supplements

Cognition, sixth edition, is supported by an outstanding array of ancillary materials, all available on the companion website: **www.oupcanada.com/Cognition6e**.

For the Instructor

- **An instructor's manual** includes comprehensive chapter overviews, topics for classroom discussion and debate, recommended readings, web links, media suggestions, homework assignments with sample answers, suggestions for research paper topics, and a sample syllabus.
- **A test generator** offers a comprehensive set of multiple-choice, true/false, short-answer, and fill-in-the-blank questions classified according to skill level, with page references that indicate where to find relevant material in the text.
- **PowerPoint slides** summarize key points from each chapter and incorporate figures, tables, and images from the textbook.
- **An image bank** provides access to all photos, figures, and tables found in the text, so that they may be incorporated into classroom materials.

For the Student

- **A student study guide** offers additional review questions linked to each chapter; self-grading practice quizzes, including a practice mid-term exam and final examination quiz; an answer key for review questions and quizzes with page references to help students find the answers in the text; key terms and definitions; and study tips for mid-terms and final exams.

Dashboard for Cognition

Cognition, sixth edition, includes access to Dashboard, an online learning and assessment platform that delivers a simple, informative, and textbook-specific experience for instructors and students. Dashboard includes tools to track student progress in an intuitive, web-based learning environment. It features a streamlined interface that connects students and instructors with the functions used most frequently, simplifying the learning experience to save time and put student progress first.

Dashboard includes *Discovery Lab,* created by Carolyn Ensley, Department of Psychology, Wilfrid Laurier University, which offers a wide variety of interactive experiments, exercises,

and animations—including five experiments new to this edition—designed to help students understand important concepts and principles. *Discovery Lab* brings cognition topics to life, allowing students to act as researchers and test subjects by giving them the ability to participate in experiments and to analyze and share results. Throughout the text, students will find icons that direct them to visit *Discovery Lab* online, where they will find activities related to what they are learning about in the text.

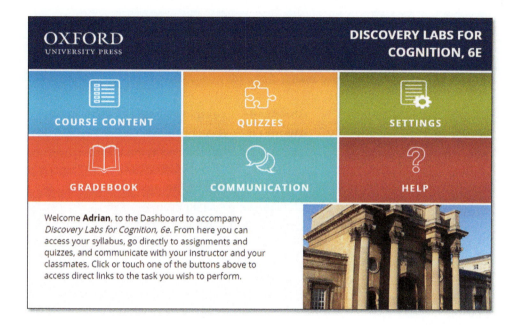

A Final Word of Thanks

We gratefully acknowledge the contributions of the following individuals whose efforts and thoughtful review comments and suggestions have helped to shape this book and its ancillaries:

Kelly Arbeau, University of Alberta
Robert Cassidy, Concordia University
Gillian Dale, Brock University
Todd Ferretti, Wilfrid Laurier University
Deanna Friesen, York University
Sandra Hessels, Concordia University
Dan Hufnagle, University of Calgary
Karin Humphreys, McMaster University
Jason Ivanoff, Simon Fraser University
Patricia McMullen, Dalhousie University
Harvey H.C. Marmurek, University of Guelph
Jean Paul Minda, Western University
Penny M. Pexman, University of Calgary
Michael Picard, University of Victoria
Catherine Plowright, University of Ottawa
Gillian Rowe, University of Toronto

List of Boxes

THINK TWICE

COGNITION IN ACTION

CASE STUDY WRAP-UP

List of Figures

List of Tables

Preface to the Sixth Edition

With this sixth edition of *Cognition* we believe we have written a textbook that will please students and instructors alike. In response to feedback from the community, we have introduced a new chapter on consciousness and made significant changes to both the structure and the presentation of the memory chapters. In addition, after combing the text for outdated or non-essential material, we have incorporated a number of recent studies that will bring readers up to speed on the latest developments in the study of human cognition.

Acknowledgements

We are supremely grateful to Oxford University Press in general, and to our developmental editor, Tamara Capar, and editor, Sally Livingston, in particular. We would also like to thank the reviewers whose thoughtful comments and suggestions helped to shape this edition.

Finally, and most importantly, we thank our wives, Cindy Sinnett, Shelley Smilek, and Erica Levy, for their incredible support and encouragement. Without their efforts, this book would not have been possible, and without their patience, we might all now be single. We dedicate this book to them and to our children.

Scott Sinnett, Daniel Smilek, and Alan Kingstone
January 2016

COGNITION

1

Introduction

Chapter Contents

Chapter Objectives

- To identify the concepts associated with the field of cognition, beginning with information processing.
- To outline the essentials of information theory.
- To distinguish among different models of the information-processing approach to cognition.
- To explain the advantages and limitations of the information-processing approach.
- To review experimental evidence for the information-processing approach.
- To identify different research methods in cognitive psychology.

What Is Cognition?

The year is 2054, and you are sleeping peacefully when suddenly, out of nowhere, Captain John Anderton and three associate members of the "PreCrime" police force crash through your skylight, yank you out of your bed, put you in handcuffs, and place you under arrest. Why? A small group of "PreCogs"—mutated individuals with pre-cognitive abilities—working for the PreCrime Unit have looked into the future and witnessed you committing a horrific murder later that morning. For the past six years, the PreCogs' visions have allowed the PreCrime Unit to arrest "killers" before they have had the chance to kill. And directly as a result of these PreCog visions, depicted in the futuristic movie thriller *Minority Report*, the city of Washington, DC, has been homicide-free for six years.

Even though it has no basis in reality, the *Minority Report* scenario raises a number of fundamental questions, including the classic philosophical question of free will vs. determinism: do people have the freedom to choose what they do, or are they fated to carry out certain actions? With respect to cognition, the scenario also raises the question of whether any one person's perception—whether a PreCog's vision of the future or an ordinary human's perception of the present or memory of the past—can be accepted as an accurate and truthful (i.e., veridical) reflection of the world.

But we are getting ahead of ourselves. First we should consider why the mutant visionaries are called "PreCogs." Well, *pre* obviously means "before" or "prior to." And *cog* is short for "cognitive," the adjective formed from the noun *cognition*—a word that, as we shall see, has an extraordinarily rich and wonderfully complex set of meanings.

As a starting point, let's look at the way the word *cognition* is understood in everyday life. Although scientific psychology usually seeks to refine the "common-sense" assumptions of **folk psychology**, a quick look at the concepts typically associated with cognition may give us an idea of the range of topics that cognitive psychology might cover.

folk psychology
An umbrella term for various assumptions and theories based on the everyday behaviour of ourselves and others.

FIGURE 1.1 | A "PreCog" from *Minority Report*

For example, *The New Oxford American Dictionary* defines *cognition* as "the mental action or process of acquiring knowledge and understanding through thought, experience, and the senses." This definition underscores a key point: that cognition is the mental *action* of knowing. How we come to know is the domain of cognition and the focus of this textbook.

Cognitive Psychology and Information Processing

The study of human cognition has advanced in three stages (Van Kleeck & Kosslyn, 1991). The first stage, from the late 1950s to the early 1960s, was one of rapid progression propelled by the methods of traditional psychophysics (the scientific investigation of the relationship between sensation and **stimulus**) and experimental psychology. The second stage, under way by the mid-1970s, was fuelled by computational analysis and marked the arrival of cognitive science. The third phase, which began in the mid-1980s, has incorporated evidence from neuropsychology and animal neurophysiology, and most recently an ever-increasing array of imaging techniques that allow us to observe the brain in action.

Foundational to all of cognitive psychology is the idea that the world contains information that is available for humans to process. The importance of this idea cannot be overstated. Cognitive psychology sees humans not as passive receivers and transformers of signal information, but as active selectors of information from the environment. Only some of the information is selected for processing because our nervous systems are able to handle only so much information at any one time, and only some of the information is responded to because our head, eyes, hands, feet, etc., cannot be in two places at the same time. Because information theory plays a central role in cognitive psychology, it's essential to have a firm grounding in it. We'll begin with an introduction to the basic concept and the classic models.

The amount of information provided by a given event can be quantified in terms of **bits** (short for "binary digits"). Imagine a situation in which one of two equally likely events is about to occur: a coin toss, for instance. You are uncertain of the outcome until the coin falls, but when it does it gives you one bit of information: either heads or tails. Every time the number of equally likely outcomes doubles, the number of information bits you receive increases by one. A common illustration of this process is the old guessing game in which I think of a number and you try to guess it by asking me questions (Garner, 1962, p. 5). The number of information bits in play corresponds to the number of questions you need to ask. Your best strategy is to reduce the number of possibilities by half with each question. For example, if the number I'm thinking of is between 1 and 8, you need to ask at most three questions. First, ask if it's above 4. If the answer is "yes," then ask if it's above 6. If the answer is "yes" again, then ask if it's above 7. If the answer is "yes," then the number is 8; if it's "no," then the number is 7.

Every day we take in and act on information in countless ways. As we drive down the street we take in information about location, direction, the traffic, the weather, the people on the sidewalk. When we're learning a new computer system we try to understand and remember the procedures and commands that we'll need to use later. And

---

stimulus
An entity in the external environment that can be perceived by an observer.

bit
Short for "binary digit"; the most basic unit of information. Every event that occurs in a situation with two equally likely outcomes provides one "bit" of information.

every time we count our change we rely on our knowledge of how to add and subtract. To many people, these everyday activities—attending, comprehending, remembering, manipulating numerical information—fall under the general heading of "thinking." To psychologists, they are aspects of information processing—the subject matter of cognitive psychology.

Information Theory

Basic to the concept of information processing is the idea that information reduces uncertainty in the mind of the receiver. The amount of information provided by a given message is proportional to the probability that that particular message will occur. If you greet a friend with the query "How are you?" and receive the reply "Absolutely awful—I must have picked up a flu bug" rather than a standard "Fine, thanks," the former reply is much more informative than the latter because it is much less probable. The idea underlying information-processing theory is that the information provided by a particular message is not determined solely by its content, but rather by the whole array of possible messages of which this

FIGURE 1.2 | There is a lot of information in our world

particular message is just one. To put it more succinctly, the amount of information a message conveys is an increasing function of the number of possible messages from which that particular message could have been selected. In other words, information theory posits that the information provided by a particular message is inversely related to the probability of its occurrence: the less likely it is, the more information it conveys.

Limitations on Information Processing

The classic experiments by Hick (1952) and Hyman (1953; illustrated in Figure 1.3) demonstrate that it takes time to translate a visual signal to either a key-press or a verbal response. The amount of time it takes for information to flow through the nervous system is one limitation on information-processing capacity (see Figure 1.4), but the amount of visual information that a person can process at any one time has limits as well. The more information a visual signal conveys, the longer it takes for the viewer to make an appropriate response. Thus, in addition to a time limitation, the nervous system has a capacity limitation for the amount of information that it can handle within a fixed period of time.

Experimental paradigms using simultaneous auditory messages suggest a similar conclusion. In an early experiment, Webster and Thompson (1953) had airport control-tower operators listen to recorded voice transmissions simulating messages from pilots. A pilot-to-tower communication consisted of the aircraft's call signal and a sequence of three unrelated words. For example, a typical message might be "Tower, this is BA 427, Pencil, Beard, Camera, over" or "Tower, this is WW 618, Rage, Wire, Coffee, over." The call signals (BA 427, WW 618) were drawn from a set of 10 possible signals, whereas the word messages (e.g., "Pencil, Beard, Camera)" were drawn from a set of 1152 possibilities. Clearly, the amount of information (in a technical sense) conveyed by each call signal was much less than that contributed by each word message because the traffic controllers had a fairly good idea of what the call signal would be, but almost no idea of what the word message would be. Although they were able to identify the call signals from two airplanes arriving simultaneously, they could not identify more than one of two simultaneous word messages (Figure 1.5).

information theory
The theory that the information provided by a particular event is inversely related to the probability of its occurrence.

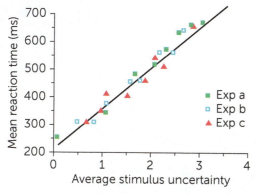

FIGURE 1.3 | Hyman's data showing mean reaction times for one subject

Hyman used small lights as stimuli, and subjects gave vocal responses. The three experiments varied stimulus uncertainty by using (a) different numbers of stimuli, (b) different stimulus frequencies, and (c) different stimulus sequences.

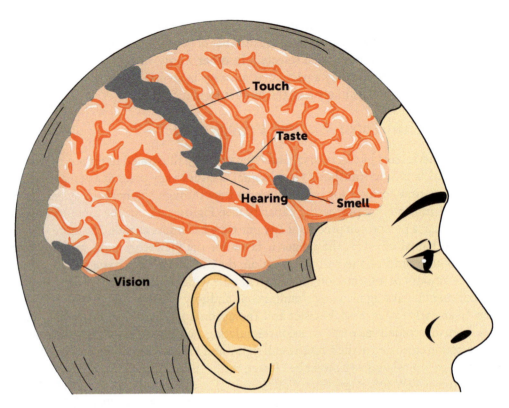

FIGURE 1.4 | The flow of information to the brain takes time to occur

Based on: research.yale.edu/ysm/images/77.4/articles-synesthesia-brain.jpg.

FIGURE 1.5 | Dichotic listening

In dichotic listening, as in the instance of an air traffic controller, two different messages are received simultaneously.

Based on: http://penta.ufrgs.br/edu/telelab/2/dochotic.jpg.

This finding suggests that there are limits to the nervous system's capacity for information processing. When two messages arrive simultaneously, the amount of interference between them depends on the amount of information they convey. The limit is, as Broadbent (1957) would say, one of information rather than stimulation. For example, Hyman showed that people respond faster to an expected stimulus than to one that is unexpected.

Models of Information Processing

Cognitive psychologists have suggested several models of the relationships between different cognitive processes. We will consider two classic models here.

Broadbent's Filter Model

Studies of human attention have focused on the limitations of the capacity to process information and the selective processes that are used to deal with those limitations. How much control do we have over which information we select and which we reject? What are the costs and the benefits of expecting one particular type of information rather than another? The first complete theory of attention was Broadbent's (1958) filter model (Figure 1.6). The idea behind it—that information processing is restricted by channel capacity—was originally suggested by Shannon (1948) and Shannon and Weaver (1949).

Broadbent (1958) argues convincingly that the whole nervous system can be regarded as a single channel with limits to the rate at which it can transmit stimulus information. Overloading of this limited capacity channel is prevented by a selective device or filter, which allows only some of the available incoming information to enter the system. Preceding the filter is a capacity-free sensory buffer or temporary store.

When two or more signals or messages occur at one time, they enter the sensory buffer together. The buffer then extracts such simple stimulus characteristics as colour (vision), voice (hearing), or spatial location. The filter operates by selecting messages that share some basic physical characteristic (e.g., location in space) and passing them along to the limited capacity system that is responsible for the analysis of "higher-order" stimulus attributes, such as form and meaning. Meanwhile, any messages that were not selected are held, in parallel (i.e., simultaneously), in the sensory buffer, where they are subject to decay with the passage of time.

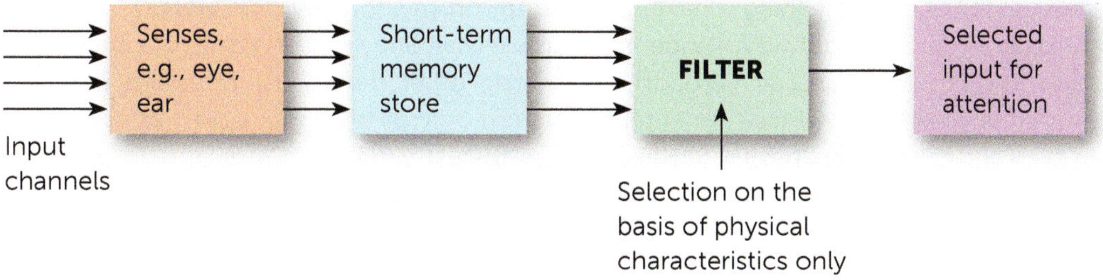

filter model
A theory based on the idea that information processing is restricted by channel capacity.

channel capacity
The maximum amount of information that can be transmitted by an information-processing device.

Input channels → Senses, e.g., eye, ear → Short-term memory store → **FILTER** → Selected input for attention

Selection on the basis of physical characteristics only

FIGURE 1.6 | Broadbent's filter model

This filter theory represented a strong account of the data on attention that were available at the time (cf. Broadbent, 1956; Cherry, 1953; Hick, 1952; Hyman, 1953; Webster & Thompson, 1953, 1954). A classic example comes from Broadbent (1954), who asked his participants to listen to three pairs of digits. One member of each pair arrived at one ear at the same time that the other member of the pair arrived at the other ear. For instance, if the sequence was "73–42–15" the participant would hear "7, 4, 1" in the left ear, and simultaneously "3, 2, 5" in the right ear. The pairs were separated by a half-second interval, and the participants were asked to recall the digits in whatever order they wished. They were able to recall 65 per cent of the lists correctly, and in almost every case the correct responses followed the same pattern: participants would recall all the digits presented to one ear, followed by all the digits presented to the other ear (e.g., "741–325" or "325–741"). In a second condition, participants were asked to recall the items in the sequence in which they were presented. Since the participants were hearing two digits at

---

THINK TWICE | Distracted Driving
BOX 1.1

Are you a good driver? Can you manoeuvre your vehicle through traffic while drinking a coffee and listening to the radio? We suspect that most of you would say "yes" (many people overestimate their driving skills). Are you also aware that many jurisdictions have recently made it illegal to use a cell phone while driving? Do you think such legislation is needed?

Before you answer, let's consider another question. Is it safe to drive with a blindfold over your eyes? Every time you take your eyes off the road, whatever the reason, you are essentially putting a blindfold on. That's why texting while driving is so dangerous. You might think that just talking on your phone would be no problem, since you can still keep your eyes on the road, but you would be wrong. Obviously, reading a text requires you to physically move your eyes away from the road to look at the screen; this is an overt attention shift. But the same thing happens when a conversation directs your attention away from the road, even if your eyes don't move. The only difference is that this attention shift is covert (we will discuss the distinction between overt and covert attention in more detail in Chapter 4). The truth is that any distraction can compromise your ability to use the information that your eyes take in: you might look but fail to see.

To demonstrate this, Strayer, Drews, and Johnston (2003) placed participants in a driving simulator and asked them to complete a driving course, keeping pace with the traffic, staying in their own lanes, and braking for obstacles. What they found was that conversing on a cell phone led to significantly poorer driving performance. Amazingly, it made no difference if the phone was hands-free (Strayer & Johnston, 2001)! In a subsequent experiment the same authors (2003) used an eye tracker to register where the eyes were looking and for how long. It showed that drivers who were engaged in a cell phone conversation were roughly half as likely as the phone-less control group to remember details from the course (e.g., billboards), even though their eyes had rested on those details for the same length of time. In the past 10 years, literally hundreds of studies have followed up on this foundational work. For two sobering examples see Strayer et al. (2013, 2014), who report on, among other things, the profound detrimental effects not only of texting but even of using a Siri-like speech-to-text system while driving. In short, using a cell phone while driving can be deadly even if you never take your eyes off the road, because it can affect what you see.

the same time, one in each ear, they were allowed to report either member of the pair first, but were required to report both digits before continuing through the sequence (e.g., either "73–42–15" or "37–24–51"). In this condition participants were able to report only 20 per cent of the lists correctly.

Broadbent interpreted this difference in recall performance to mean that the ears function as separate channels for information input. The different physical locations for the two messages are initially entered and preserved in the short-term sensory buffer. Selective attention, represented by the filter, operates to determine which channel is recalled first. Switching attention between ears requires time. Performance is poorer for recall by presentation order because more attentional switching is required. Meanwhile, as attention is switching between locations (ears), the information in the sensory buffer continues to decay, and thus becomes less and less available with the passage of time. In the first condition, where participants recalled all the items from one ear and then all the items from the other ear, only one switch of attention was required—from one input location to the other. In the second condition, where participants had to recall the items in the order of presentation, at least three switches of attention were required—for example, from left to right, from right to left, and once more from left to right.

Waugh and Norman's Model of Information Processing

Figure 1.7 comes from an early but still important paper by Waugh and Norman (1965). The flow of information is indicated by the arrows. Upon being stimulated, we may have an experience called a primary memory, a concept derived from the highly influential American psychologist William James (1890/1983). This is noteworthy because the approach that James relied on for many of his major insights and hypotheses was one that few if any cognitive psychologists today would use: **introspection** (see Box 1.2). **Primary memory** consists of the "immediately present moment" (James, 1890/1983, p. 608), and is thus also known as "immediate memory." The arrow labelled "rehearsal" refers to the fact that primary memories tend to be quickly forgotten unless they are repeated, as you might repeat a telephone number to yourself after looking it up. Whereas primary memory belongs to the present, **secondary memory** belongs to the past.

introspection
"Looking inward" to observe one's own thoughts and feelings.

primary memory
What we are aware of in the "immediately present moment"; often termed "immediate memory" or "short-term memory."

secondary memory
Knowledge acquired at an earlier time that is stored indefinitely, and is absent from awareness; also called "long-term memory."

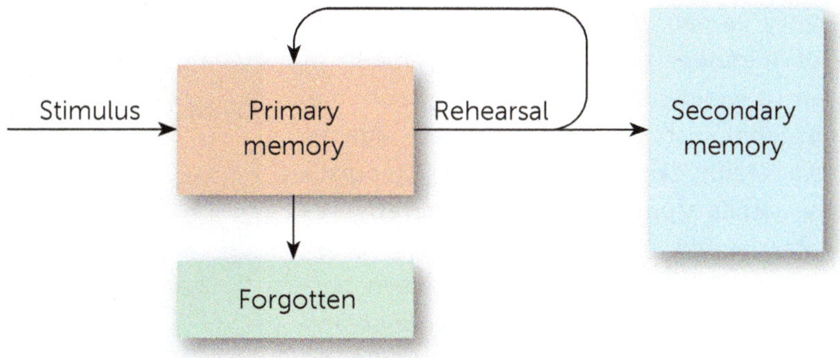

FIGURE 1.7 | Waugh and Norman's model of information processing

Copyright © 1965 by the American Psychological Association. Adapted with permission. Waugh, N.C., & Norman, D.A. (1965). Primary memory. *Psychological Review, 72*, pp. 89–104. Use of APA information does not imply endorsement by APA.

INTROSPECTION	EXPERIMENTAL
Subjective	Objective
Individual thoughts/ perspectives	Group data averaged
Non-statistical	Statistical

FIGURE 1.8 | Introspection vs experimental method

Brown–Peterson task

An experimental paradigm in which subjects are given a set of items and then a number. Subjects immediately begin counting backward by threes from the number and, after a specific interval, are asked to recall the original items.

DISCOVERY LAB

Waugh and Norman (1965) noted that James's distinction between primary and secondary memory was based on introspective evidence. Such evidence is seldom treated as definitive in cognitive psychology. However, the subjective reports of participants are often used in conjunction with more objective evidence such as that provided by well-designed experiments (Jack & Shallice, 2001; see Figure 1.8). Experimental evidence for the primary–secondary memory distinction came from analysis of the **Brown–Peterson task** (J. Brown, 1958; Peterson & Peterson, 1959)—one of the most widely used experimental tasks in memory research. In the typical Brown–Peterson experiment, participants are given a set of items to remember (e.g., the letters B, Q, R), and then a number from which they immediately begin counting backward by threes. Thus a participant given the number "107" would start counting ("104, 101, 98, . . ." and so on) and after a specific interval (say, 6, 9, 12, 15, or 18 seconds), would be asked to recall the specified items (in this case, the letters B, Q, R). Because the interval is filled with the counting exercise, the participant is presumably prevented from rehearsing the letters and therefore unable to retain them in his or her primary memory. An unfilled interval, by contrast, would allow the participant to rehearse the items and keep them in primary memory. Waugh and Norman's analysis showed that participants' ability to recall letters declined as the number of interfering items increased (Figure 1.10).

CONSIDER THIS
BOX 1.2

William James (1842–1910)

Students of literature might know of William James as the older brother (by a year) of Henry James, the famous American realist novelist of manners and personal psychology, yet today William is widely recognized as one of the most eminent psychologists the world has known. Born in New York to a wealthy family with liberal ideals and wide interests, James studied medicine at Harvard, where he later taught. His two-volume, 1200-page masterwork, *The Principles of Psychology* (1890), exemplifies James's holistic thinking, embracing not only psychology, physiology, and philosophy, but a wealth of personal observation, introspection, and opinion. For example, James described the infant's perception of the observed world "as one great blooming, buzzing confusion" (is that your recollection of earliest infancy?); introduced the idea of "the stream of consciousness"; pointed out the importance of habit in human life; and warned against the "psychologist's fallacy" whereby researchers too often allow their own personal experience and views to intrude on their rational understanding of the phenomena they are analyzing.

FIGURE 1.9 | William James

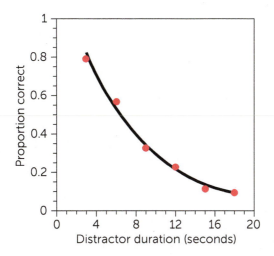

FIGURE 1.10 | Brown–Peterson classic result

Copyright © 1959 by the American Psychological Association. Adapted with permission. Peterson, L.R., & Peterson, M.J. (1959). Short-term retention of individual verbal items. *Journal of Experimental Psychology*, 58, 193–8. Use of APA information does not imply endorsement.

Waugh and Norman (1965) pointed out that primary memory makes it possible for us to immediately and accurately recall our most recent experiences. For example, we are able "to recall verbatim the most recent few words in a sentence [we are] hearing or speaking" (p. 102), provided that no distraction intervenes. Although we take primary memory for granted, it is extremely important to us.

Ecological Validity

In standard information-processing models such as Broadbent's or Waugh and Norman's, a lot of interest is focused on the processing required to make a stimulus meaningful. However, such models may not say very much about the information available in the stimulus itself. Other psychologists, such as J.J. Gibson (1904–79) (Figure 1.11), took more interest in the richness of the information provided by the environment in which people find themselves. Gibson (1950, 1966) argued that the stimuli used by information-processing psychologists in their experiments were often impoverished in comparison with the information available in the real world. He argued for the development of an **ecological approach** to perception that would describe environmental stimulation at the appropriate level. Gibson believed that the meaning of objects and events can be perceived through what he called their **affordances**, which he defined as "simply what things furnish, for good or ill" (1966, p. 285): thus food affords the possibility of eating, stairs afford the possibility of climbing, ice affords the possibility of skating, and so on. Of course, knowledge of those affordances is not innate: we have to learn what can (and can't) be done with items in the world. Thus Gibson's theory is one of **information pickup**, in which learning means becoming progressively more attuned to what the environment affords us.

By contrast, Neisser (1976, p. 21) proposed a cyclical model of cognition in which the perceiver possesses a **schema** that represents what he or she expects to find in the environment and that directs his or her exploration of it. In the course of that exploration,

ecological approach
A form of psychological inquiry that reflects conditions in the real world.

affordances
The potential functions or uses of stimuli (i.e., objects and events) in the real world.

information pickup
The process whereby we perceive information directly.

schema
An expectation concerning what we are likely to find as we explore the world (plural *schemas* or *schemata*).

however, the perceiver encounters not only the expected information but also some that is unexpected (Figure 1.12). This unexpected information is capable of modifying the schema so as to increase the accuracy with which it represents the environment. Thus the **perceptual cycle** (Figure 1.13) begins with a schema that brings the perceiver into contact with new information that he or she can use to correct the schema, and so on.

To see how this perceptual cycle might work, consider Figures 1.14a and 1.14b. Halper (1997) noticed a building in Manhattan with balconies that appeared to tilt upward. Obviously, it would be absurd to build balconies like that, so what was going on? In terms of the perceptual cycle, we might describe the process as follows. Our schema is our cognitive model of the environment, constructed over time through our interactions with that environment. Our schema provides us with a set of general expectations and assumptions regarding what we are likely to find in the environment, although we need not be aware of them. One of our expectations is that balconies will be either square or rectangular (i.e., bounded by right angles). We automatically impose this expectation on the buildings in Figures 1.14a and 1.14b. As a consequence we perceive the balconies of the building in the foreground to be tilting upward, as they would have to be if they were rectangular. When we explore this building from a different angle, our expectations may even lead us to perceive the balconies as tilting downward, as in Figure 1.14c. If we continue to explore the situation, however, we can come to understand it. In fact, "the balconies are parallelograms vertically perpendicular to the face of the building" (Halper, 1997, p. 1322), as can be seen in Figure 1.14d. Now

FIGURE 1.11 | J.J. Gibson (1904–79)

Gibson's theory of visual perception emphasized an ecological perspective on stimuli that was missing from other accounts of the way perception and attention function (e.g., Broadbent's filter theory).

perceptual cycle

The process whereby our schemas guide our exploration of the world and in turn are shaped by what we find there.

FIGURE 1.12 | Darth Vader vs Luke Skywalker

Unexpected events force us to adjust our expectations of the environment. As expectations change, we must change our schemas. Here's one small example: Darth Vader never said "Luke, I am your father" (perhaps the most famous line associated with the *Star Wars* series). What he actually said was "No, I am your father." Time for a schema adjustment?

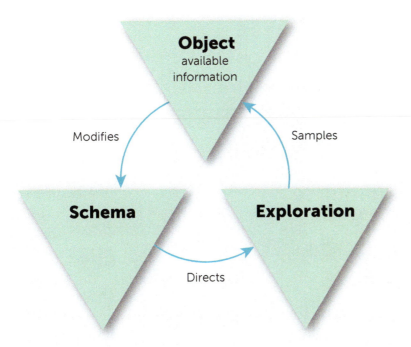

FIGURE 1.13 | Neisser's perceptual cycle

Based on: huwi.org/images/image001.gif.

our schema for buildings has been modified to include the possibility that some balconies will be built at angles that are other than right. In general, the perceptual cycle allows us to become increasingly sophisticated in our dealings with the environment.

The relative virtues of laboratory-based and ecological approaches to cognitive research have been hotly debated (e.g., Anderson & Bushman, 1997; Chayter & Schmitter-Edgecomb, 2003; Loftus, 1991; Neisser, 1978; Schmuckler, 2001; Kingstone, Smilek, Ristic, Friesen, & Eastwood, 2003). Kingstone, Smilek, and Eastwood (2008) have recently outlined an approach that may resolve this dispute. **Cognitive ethology** (see Box 1.3) offers concrete and specific suggestions for carrying out studies in the real world in a way that will complement laboratory-based research.

Metacognition and Cognitive Psychology

Metacognition is the term for knowledge about knowledge—that is, knowledge about the way that cognitive processes work. The study of cognitive psychology can be seen as a process of developing our metacognition (Rebok, 1987). We all begin in pretty much the same place, with a common-sense understanding of cognition, and our goal in studying cognitive psychology is to develop this understanding further. Sometimes that means changing our beliefs about how cognition takes place, or giving them up altogether. Often it means accepting some uncertainty regarding what we can assert about cognition at a particular point. Cognitive psychology is not a complete body of knowledge, but an actively developing

cognitive ethology
A new research approach that links real-world observations with laboratory-based studies.

metacognition
Knowledge about the way that cognitive processes work; understanding of our own cognitive processes.

FIGURE 1.14 | Balconies on *The Future*, a building in New York City

area of inquiry (see Figure 1.15). What it offers is not so much a set of definitive answers as a series of hypotheses about the way the mind works. The next chapter will review some of the better-known approaches to the field.

The biggest challenge for beginners in cognitive psychology may be to get over the feeling that thinking about thinking is an impossibly abstract skill. In fact, you probably already have a pretty elaborate way of thinking about thinking. As you work through this book, try to relate the concepts and hypotheses you encounter to the ones you already have. Of course, this means that you will need to work out what you think at this point. You may discover that some of your own ideas offer interesting alternatives to the theories that cognitive psychologists have already developed. When that happens, you are becoming a cognitive psychologist yourself. Try to think of ways of testing your hypotheses. As many

---

COGNITION IN ACTION
BOX 1.3

Cognitive Ethology

Research into human cognition, like research in general, often begins when cognitive researchers notice something interesting in the world. They then design and run lab-based experiments that control for everything except the factor or variable in question. When all the experiments have been done, they conclude that they have a fundamental explanation of the mental process that causes the real-world phenomenon they wanted to understand.

A new research approach, called cognitive ethology, recognizes that this standard research approach operates on the flawed assumption that cognitive processes, like off-the-shelf tools, always do the same job regardless of the situation (Kingstone, Smilek, & Eastwood, 2008). This is patently untrue. By the mid-1970s it had become very clear that most statements about cognition were true only if particular laboratory conditions were met; when those conditions were not met, the relationships between factors became unpredictable. **"If A then B" in the lab does not necessarily mean "If A then B" in the world.**

So, for example, memory experiments found that what research subjects remembered depended on factors such as (a) what processing they performed on the stimulus materials, (b) what stimulus materials they expected to receive, (c) what materials were actually presented, (d) what they were doing before their memory was measured, and (e) how their memory was measured. The take-home messages were multiple: that cognitive processes vary; that they are affected by what is happening elsewhere within the cognitive system; and therefore that they depend critically on the specific situational context in which the subject is embedded.

The fact that cognitive processes are fluid, adapting to the situation and goals of each individual, means that many of our psychological theories could be flawed if not downright wrong. It also means that the justification behind traditional lab-based cognitive research—the assumption that we can isolate and test the same mental process in different environments—may no longer hold, and that we need to broaden the ways in which we do our work.

Cognitive ethology proposes the following alternative approach:

1. Carefully observe and describe behaviour as it naturally occurs.
2. Then move it into the laboratory and gradually simplify relevant factors.
3. Test to find out whether lab findings predict, as well as explain, real-world phenomena.

psychologists have observed (e.g., Kuhn, 1989), testing of hypotheses based on personal observation is one of the ways in which scientific knowledge develops.

The Range of Cognitive Psychology

Cognitive psychology provides tools for the analysis of many problems. Throughout this book you will find both concrete, practical examples of the application of cognitive psychology and discussions of the social and emotional aspects of cognition. The study of those topics has been greatly influenced by cognitive psychology, but they have not always been covered in cognition texts. Now cognitive psychology has developed to the point that it is integral to most other forms of psychology, and it's important to be aware of how it may be applied, both in other areas of psychology and in life generally.

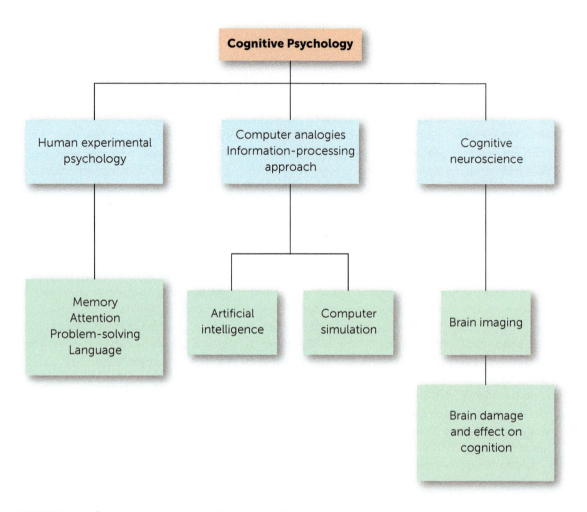

FIGURE 1.15 | Some examples of the range of cognitive psychology

Summary

In this chapter we have introduced several of the key concepts covered by the term *cognition*, beginning with information processing. Central to the information-processing approach to cognition is the idea that the information provided by a particular message is not determined solely by the message itself, but rather by the whole array of possible messages of which this particular one is just one instance. The less likely it is that a particular signal will occur, the more information it will convey and the more time it will take to process. Hick and Hyman have produced experimental evidence using visual stimuli to support the notion that people respond more slowly to less likely signals. The slow reaction times suggest that there are limits to the amount of information that the nervous system can handle within a fixed period of time, whether the information signal is visual or auditory. To prevent overloading of our capacity to process information, we select only some of the available signal information to process, respond to, and remember. In other words, we are not merely passive receivers of information from our perceptual world: we are *active selectors* of information.

Several classic models dominate the study of information processing. First, Broadbent's *filter model* is based on the idea that information processing is restricted by the *capacity* of the *channel* that is the nervous system. When multiple messages arrive at the same time, Broadbent's model suggests that a filtering device chooses among them on the basis of common physical characteristics. By contrast, Norman and Waugh's model distinguishes between primary and secondary memory. Primary memories are created in the immediately present moment and tend to be quickly forgotten unless they are rehearsed or repeated. We will extend our exploration of memory to more recent concepts in Chapter 6.

Also noteworthy is Gibson's ecological approach to information processing. His theory of *information pickup* focuses on the wealth of information available through the stimulus itself, rather than the processing required to make a stimulus meaningful. In this model, learning is less about the processing of information and more about becoming attuned to what the environment affords us.

One thing these varied models have in common is their reliance on the standard lab-based research approach, which assumes that the same mental processes can be isolated and tested in different environments. An alternative research approach is *cognitive ethology*, which acknowledges that cognitive processes are fluid, adapting to the situation and goals of an individual. Whichever approach is employed, the study of cognitive psychology can be understood as a matter of *metacognition*—in other words, "thinking about thinking."

CASE STUDY

Case Study Wrap-Up

We began this chapter with a scenario in which the PreCogs' perceptions of the future led to your arrest for a murder that you had yet to commit. In the context of that scenario we raised the question of how veridical cognition can be. Can the PreCogs' vision be taken as an accurate reflection of something that was actually going to occur? Or is there some uncertainty in play? Based on what we have seen in this chapter, and what we will see in the chapters that follow, it seems that cognition always involves some element of uncertainty. Indeed, much of the research discussed in this chapter was designed to come to grips with this apparent fact. From the beginning, researchers recognized that there was a connection between the amount of information conveyed by any given event

and the probability of that event: the less likely the event, the more information it conveys. Furthermore, because people are limited in the amount of information they can process at any one moment in time, a lot of information is going to be lost.

And there's the rub. There is no single reality for any of us. What we see, what we attend to, what we think about, and what we remember is a complex combination of the situation within which we receive information and the actions that we perform on the basis of that information; and those actions of course will reflect who we are. Thus my cognition in a given situation will almost certainly be different from yours. So, can the PreCogs' visions be trusted? Could the PreCrime Unit have made a grave error when they arrested you?

In the Know: Review Questions

1. Cognitive psychology draws heavily on the idea that humans are information processors. What are some advantages of this approach? What are some limitations?
2. Folk psychology and introspection are two possible sources of knowledge about cognition, based on everyday observation and personal reflection, respectively. How valuable do you think they are? How does the knowledge derived from those sources relate to the knowledge produced by the controlled studies of researchers like Hick, Hyman, and Broadbent?

Key Concepts

What follows here is a list of some of the most influential ideas in the area we have just reviewed, which made their first appearance above in boldface; a similar list will be included in each of the chapters to follow. Some concepts are quite general and not associated with any particular psychologist. Others are accompanied by the names of the psychologists with whom they are identified. If any of the names or concepts seem unfamiliar, reread the appropriate section of the chapter. You should be able to define each concept and discuss the research that is relevant to it. Brief definitions are included in the margins where the terms are introduced, as well as in the Glossary at the end of the book.

affordances

bit

Brown–Peterson task

channel capacity

cognitive ethology

ecological approach

filter model (Broadbent)

folk psychology

information pickup

information theory

introspection

metacognition

perceptual cycle

primary memory (Waugh and Norman)

schema

secondary memory (Waugh and Norman)

stimulus

Links to Other Chapters

affordances

Chapter 8 (prototypicality)

ecological approach and ecological validity

Chapter 4 (inattentional blindness)

Chapter 5 (involuntary semantic memories)

Chapter 6 (ecological approaches to memory)

Chapter 8 (criticisms of classical concept research)

Chapter 10 (*in vivo* and *in vitro* methods)

Chapter 11 (ecological rationality)

Chapter 12 (practical intelligence)

metacognition

Chapter 6 (elaboration and distinctiveness)

Chapter 10 (feeling of knowing)

perceptual cycle

Chapter 4 (attention capture and inattentional blindness)

Chapter 7 (images as anticipations)

primary memory
Chapter 3 (pattern recognition)
Chapter 6 (levels of processing)

schema
Chapter 4 (task switching)
Chapter 13 (schema theories, Bartlett, body schema, phantom limbs, scripts)

Further Reading

A history of early developments in cognitive psychology can be found in Chapter 14 of Benjafield (2005). For a particularly well-informed analysis of those developments, see Mandler (2002).

Analyses of folk psychology—people's beliefs about how the mind works—include Rips and Conrad (1989) and Fellbaum and Miller (1990). Additional elaboration on folk psychology can be found in D'Andrade (1987) and Vendler (1972). Stich (1983) is a classic critique of folk psychology. For a more appreciative survey of the pervasiveness and variability of folk psychology see Lillard (1998).

We review the large literature on metacognition at various places in this book. Flavell (1979) is a good place to start; he was one of the pioneers in this area. For a more recent perspective see Sternberg (1998).

Winograd, Fivush, and Hirst (1999) is a collection of papers presented in appreciation of Neisser's contribution to ecologically valid studies.

Benjafield, J. (2005). *A history of psychology.* Toronto: Oxford University Press.

D'Andrade, R. (1987). A folk model of the mind. In D. Holland & N. Quinn (Eds.), *Cultural models in language and thought* (pp. 112–148). Cambridge: Cambridge University Press.

Fellbaum, C., & Miller, G.A. (1990). Folk psychology or semantic entailment? *Psychological Review 97*: 565–570.

Flavell, J. (1979). Metacognition and cognitive monitoring. *American Psychologist 34*: 906–911.

Lillard, A. (1998). Ethnopsychologies: Cultural variations in theories of mind. *Psychological Bulletin 123*: 3–32.

Mandler, G. (2002). Origins of the cognitive (r)evolution. *Journal of the History of the Behavioral Sciences 38*: 339–353.

Rips, L.J., & Conrad, F.G. (1989). Folk psychology of mental activities. *Psychological Review 96*: 187–207.

Sternberg, R.J. (1998). Metacognition, abilities, and developing expertise. *Instructional Science 26*: 127–140.

Stich, S. (1983). *From folk psychology to cognitive science: The case against belief.* Cambridge, Mass.: MIT Press.

Vendler, Z. (1972). *Res cogitans: An essay in rational psychology.* Ithaca, NY: Cornell University Press.

Winograd, E., Fivush, R., & Hirst, W. (Eds.). (1999). *Ecological approaches to cognition.* Mahwah, NJ: Erlbaum.

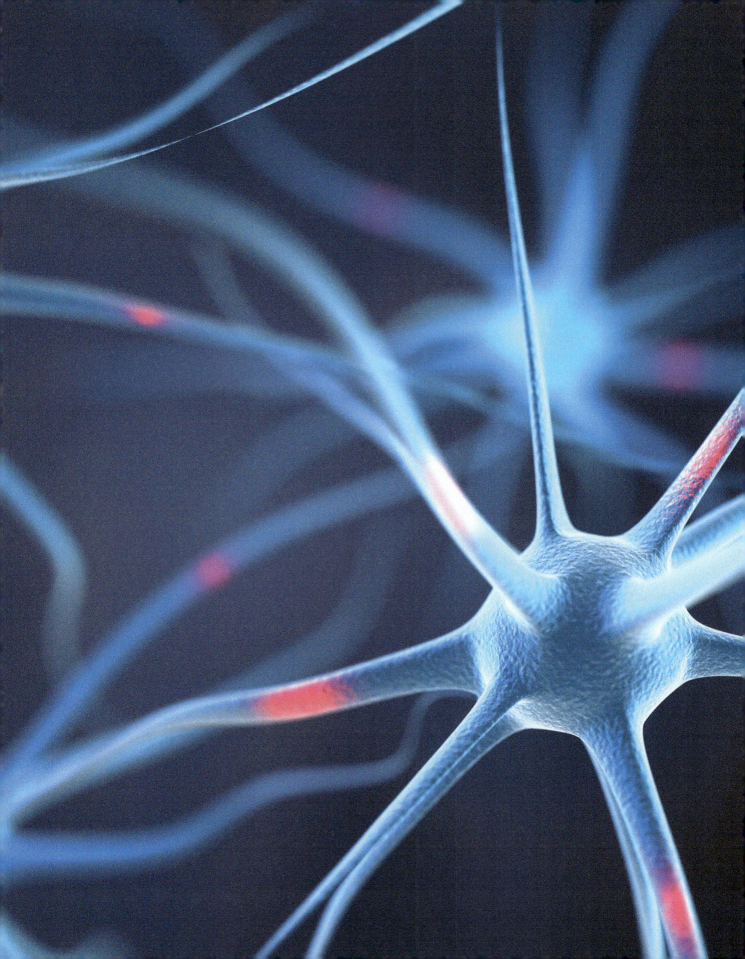

2

Cognitive Neuroscience

Chapter Contents

Chapter Objectives

- To examine the key issues in the localization of function debate.
- To outline the theoretical issues surrounding the relationship between the mind and the brain.
- To explain approaches to studying that relationship.
- To identify the advantages and limitations of the various methods used to localize cognitive processes in the brain.

Head Office

Let's take a moment to think about our heads and all they do for us. First of all, the head houses the nose and mouth, both of which are crucial to life itself. For the purposes of cognitive psychology, however, eyes and ears are equally important, for they are what enable us to see and hear the world around us. The simple fact that the head is centred at the top of the body means that it is ideally situated for the reception of information from the environment, which ultimately leads to perception and behaviour. These are all fairly obvious observations. Less obvious, perhaps, is the significance of the fact that your head is hard—really hard. Why is that so important? Your brain knows why: because it is the star of the show that is your life, and it needs all the protection it can get.

Although it accounts for only about 2 per cent of your body weight, your brain manages to claim about 20 per cent of all the blood supply in your body. If you didn't have a brain you wouldn't have a thought, and without thought there is no cognition. Yet we often take the brain for granted—at least until something goes wrong.

You may know someone whose life has been changed profoundly because of a brain disease or injury. If not, you almost certainly know of some prominent person who has suffered a brain injury, whether as a result of a stroke, a tumour, or some kind of trauma.

For instance, consider the boxer Muhammad Ali. One of the most famous athletes in the world, as a fighter he would "float like a butterfly and sting like a bee" (to borrow his own phrase), and he commanded as much respect for his quick intelligence and verbal skills as for his abilities in the ring. Now this most beloved and dignified man is barely able to move or speak. Or consider Ronald Reagan and Margaret Thatcher, the two most powerful people in the Western world in the 1980s (Figure 2.1). By the time of his death in 2004, Reagan had lived with Alzheimer's disease for a decade. Similarly, Thatcher fought a decade-long battle with dementia before her death in 2013.

Virtually everyone who has ever taken an introductory psychology course will know the name of Phineas Gage, a young railroad foreman who in 1848 survived an explosion that drove an iron bar through his head. Although he was said to have suffered bouts of depression, drinking problems, and a general change in personality, it now seems that in fact his cognitive abilities and character were remarkably unaffected (Macmillan, 2002). As amazing as the Gage story is, it appears to have been replicated in Brazil in August 2012. Eduardo Leite was working on a construction site when a falling 1.8-metre iron bar pierced his hard hat, entered his skull, and came out between his eyes (see Figure 2.2).

FIGURE 2.1 | **Muhammad Ali, Ronald Reagan, and Margaret Thatcher**

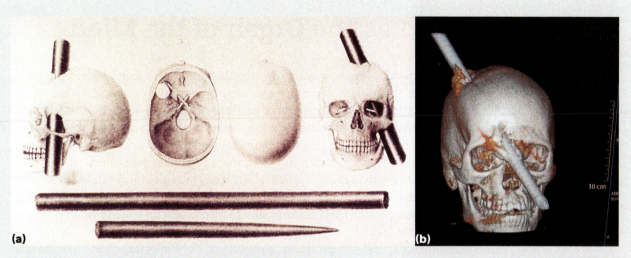

(a)
(b)

FIGURE 2.2 | (a) Lithograph of Phineas Gage's injury; (b) Tomography scan of Eduardo Leite's injury

The surgery to remove the bar took five hours. Although it is still too soon to be certain, doctors report that Leite shows few if any cognitive deficits.

Almost as recent is the story of US Congresswoman Gabrielle Giffords. On the morning of 8 January 2010 she was holding a "Congress on your corner" session, meeting and answering questions from members of her Arizona constituency, when suddenly a gunman appeared and shot her along with more than a dozen other people. The bullet entered Giffords' head just above her ear and ripped through her brain. But she was not killed. Surgeons removed part of her skull to allow the injured brain to swell without pressure on the regions that are critical for life functions.

Fast forward to five months after the shooting. As the swelling subsided, the surgeons replaced the part of the skull that had been removed, and 180 days after the shooting Giffords was released from hospital. Her cognitive abilities are not yet what they were before she was shot: in particular, she still has some difficulty speaking. Walking is also difficult, and her right arm is paralyzed. Nevertheless, she marked the third anniversary of the shooting by going skydiving.

Let's pause here for a moment and ask why it was Giffords' language abilities that were compromised rather than, say, her ability to remember past events. What might this tell us about the relationship between forms of cognition and the brain? One thing it suggests is that specific cognitive mechanisms are associated with specific brain areas. The area of research concerned with this relationship is cognitive neuroscience: a combination of cognitive psychology and neuroscience that seeks to discover the brain mechanisms that give rise to mental functions such as language, memory, and attention. This is an ambitious goal, and one that cannot be reached via any single research approach. In fact, cognitive neuroscience is both defined and fuelled by its interdisciplinary emphasis.

FIGURE 2.3 | Gabrielle Giffords

The Brain as the Organ of the Mind

modules
Different parts of the brain, each of which is responsible for particular cognitive operations.

phrenology
The study of the shape, size, and protrusions of the cranium in an attempt to discover the relationships between parts of the brain and various mental activities and abilities.

localization of function
The idea that there is a direct correspondence between specific cognitive functions and specific parts of the brain.

This chapter will introduce several ways of investigating the relationship between the brain and behaviour. First, though, it's important to note that cognitive neuroscientists assume that the brain is composed of specific parts or **modules** (Fodor, 1983), each of which is responsible for particular cognitive operations. Whether it is completely modular is a matter of debate, and there have been differences of opinion over the number of modules that may exist (e.g., Pinker, 1997; Sperber, 2002). However, there is general agreement on the basic principle, and once we begin to speculate about how many modules there might be, it's only a short step to wondering which cognitive functions each of them might be responsible for.

Efforts to determine which parts of the brain are specialized for which cognitive operations go back at least as far as Franz Joseph Gall (1758–1828) and his student J.G. Spurzheim (1776–1832). Gall and Spurzheim promoted **phrenology**. Phrenological charts like the one in Figure 2.4 purport to show where various psychological functions are located in the brain. Although Gall and Spurzheim's theories are not taken seriously today, their underlying premises still deserve consideration:

> Their argument reduced to three basic principles: (1) The brain is the sole organ of the mind. (2) Basic character and intellectual traits are innately determined. (3) Since there are differences in character and intellectual traits among individuals as well as differences in various intellectual capacities within a single individual, there must exist differentially developed areas in the brain, responsible for these differences! Where there is variation in *function* there must be variation in the controlling *structures* (Krech, 1962, p. 33).

Gall and Spurzheim's method for locating functions in the brain was highly speculative. They believed that the more highly developed a function was, the larger it would be, and that the larger the function, the more clearly it would manifest itself as a protrusion on the skull. On the basis of these assumptions they reasoned that they could divine a person's strengths and weaknesses by examining the shape of his or her skull. Their theory had a powerful impact on nineteenth-century cultural practices, and many people were willing to pay for phrenological advice (Sokal, 2001). The weakness of the phrenologists' method is now obvious. Still, their underlying hypothesis—that specific functions are localized in specific parts of the brain—has guided much subsequent research (e.g., Gardner, 1983; Sarter, Berntson, & Cacioppo, 1996), even though not all those involved have agreed that there is a direct correspondence between specific cognitive functions and specific parts of the brain.

A landmark in the history of the **localization of function** debate was the work of Shepherd Ivory Franz (1874–1933). Franz was an expert in the technique of ablation, whereby parts of the cortex

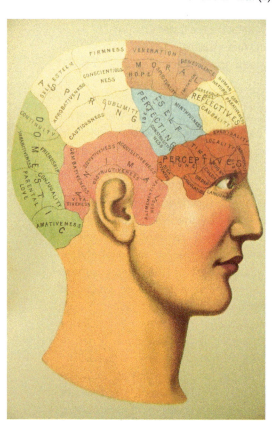

FIGURE 2.4 | A phrenological chart

(the outer layer of the brain, which plays a significant role in cognitive functions such as memory, attention, perception, and language) of an animal are destroyed and the consequences for behaviour are observed. If functions were localized in the cortex, then the effect of ablation should depend on the area destroyed. However, this was not what his observations showed.

Franz and his student Karl Lashley (1890–1958) studied the effects of ablation of the frontal lobes in rats. Instead of opening up the animal's skull, they would make small holes in it and then observe the effect of the lesions on the retention of a simple learned maze habit; only later would they examine the animal's brain to see "precisely where the lesions had occurred" (Bruce, 1986, p. 38). Their results persuaded them that as long as sufficient tissue remained after the operation, the location of that tissue was irrelevant. Franz (1912) concluded that "mental processes are not due to the independent activities of individual parts of the brain, but to the activities of the brain as a whole" and that "it would appear best and most scientific that we should not adhere to any of the phrenological systems" (p. 328).

Lashley subsequently published a work that became a classic in the area of localization of function, called *Brain Mechanisms and Intelligence* (1929). This research developed further the procedures he had learned from Franz. Lashley lesioned the cortex of rats in different places and to different degrees. He reasoned that "if there were reflex paths transversing the cortex . . . then surgery would destroy them" (Weidman, 1994, p. 166). Lashley (1929, p. 74) observed the ability of rats to learn or remember tasks such as finding their way through mazes of differing difficulty, and found that performance in simple mazes was not greatly affected by limited brain damage (Figure 2.5). However, performance declined as

FIGURE 2.5 | Rat in a maze

the difficulty of the task and/or the amount of brain damage increased. Lashley (1930/1978) summarized the implications of his results as follows:

> Small lesions either produce no symptoms or very transient ones, so that it is clear that the mechanisms for habits are not closely grouped within small areas. When larger areas are involved, there are usually amnesias for many activities.... After injuries to the brain, the rate of formation of some habits is directly proportional to the extent of the injury and independent of the position within any part of the cortex (p. 271).

There was no evidence in the brain for specialized connections developed as a result of learning. Neither learning nor memory was "dependent upon the properties of individual cells"; rather, both were functions of "the total mass of tissue" (Lashley, 1930/1978, p. 271). These results came to be formulated as two laws: the **law of mass action** (learning and memory depend on the total mass of brain tissue remaining) and the **law of equipotentiality** (although some areas of the cortex may become specialized for certain tasks, any part of an area can, within limits, do the job of any other part of that area). To explain his findings, Lashley (1930, p. 271) compared the cortex to an electric sign: the "functional organization plays over" cortical cells "just as the pattern of letters plays over the bank of lamps in an electric sign." A single bank of lights can be used to display any number of messages; similarly, the cortex can be organized in any number of ways, depending on circumstances.

The Relationship between Mind and Brain

Cognitive neuroscience draws on several disciplines, including biology, linguistics, philosophy, and psychology, in its efforts to arrive at an integrated understanding of the mind and the brain (Gold & Stoljar, 1999). We will begin this section by examining four classic efforts toward that end: interactionism, epiphenomenalism, parallelism, and isomorphism. First, however, it's important to note that, although the brain is often considered the "organ of the mind," specifying the exact relationship between mind and brain is far from easy, and debate on this issue is ongoing (e.g., Noë & Thompson, 2004). It's also important to distinguish between "consciousness" and "mind." Consciousness is the narrower concept, often taken to mean what we are aware of at any point in time. Mind is the broader concept. It includes consciousness, but also encompasses processes that may take place outside our awareness. Both of these concepts are the focus of intense research activity, and consequently neither of them has a universally accepted definition.

Interactionism is associated with Descartes (1596–1650), who believed mind and brain to be separate substances that interacted and influenced each other. He even specified the particular place in the brain where he thought this interaction took place—an organ in the centre of the brain called the pineal gland (Finger, 1994, p. 26). Ingenious though it was, Descartes' dualistic answer to the mind/brain problem was not widely adopted by subsequent investigators (Finger, 2000, p. 80). More recently, though, some eminent psychologists have taken interactionist positions. Among them was Nobel Prize winner

---

law of mass action
Learning and memory depend on the total mass of brain tissue remaining rather than the properties of individual cells.

law of equipotentiality
Although some areas of the cortex may become specialized for certain tasks, any part of an area can (within limits) do the job of any other part of that area.

interactionism
Mind and brain are separate substances that interact with and influence each other.

Roger Sperry, whose work will be discussed later in this chapter. Although some argued that Sperry's position was a form of dualism, he insisted that it was monistic (i.e., that a mind cannot exist apart from a functioning brain).

Epiphenomenalism maintains that the mind is simply a by-product of brain processes and has no causal role in determining behaviour. T.H. Huxley (1825–95) used an analogy to illustrate the epiphenomenal position: the mind is to the brain as the steam from a steam whistle is to a coal-powered locomotive. Just as you would not discover much about the locomotive by studying the steam from the whistle, so you would not discover much about the brain by examining what goes on in the mind. Many twentieth-century psychologists adopted positions similar to epiphenomenalism, believing that consciousness was irrelevant to an understanding of behaviour (e.g., Skinner, 1989). Indeed, studies suggesting that action can precede conscious experience of the decision to act (e.g., Libet et al., 1983) have been taken as evidence in support of epiphenomenalism.

Parallelism found its purest expression in the work of G.T. Fechner (1801–87), whose studies of the relationships between events in the external world and the mind and brain have not lost any of their relevance (Dehaene, 2003; Link, 1994; Murray, 1993). For the parallelist, mind and brain are two aspects of the same reality, and every event in the mind is accompanied by a corresponding event in the brain. If this is the case, then studying mental events might reveal something of value about the brain. For example, one might ask research subjects to introspect and then record events in their brains as they do so (Jack & Roepstorff, 2002).

Isomorphism can be traced to Gestalt psychologists such as Wolfgang Köhler (1887–1967); the term *Gestalt* means form or configuration. These psychologists argued that consciousness tends to be organized into a coherent whole. Some still maintain that this is a fundamental property of consciousness (e.g., Searle, 2000, p. 9). The doctrine of isomorphism holds that an experience and its corresponding neural process share the same pattern (e.g., Lehar, 2003). The difference between parallelism and isomorphism is that the latter envisions more than a simple point-for-point correspondence between mental events and brain events: as Köhler put it, "psychological facts and the underlying events in the brain resemble each other in all their structural characteristics" (Köhler, 1969, p. 64).

To illustrate this hypothesis, a Necker cube (Figure 2.6) is often used; it was named after Louis Albert Necker (1832/1964), who was the first to remark on this psychologically interesting phenomenon. When you focus on the cube face labelled ABCD, then that face seems to be in the foreground. However, the figure can reverse itself in your focus so that the face labelled EFGH comes to the foreground. This is an important example of isomorphism because it illustrates how the "external stimulus is constant but . . . the internal subjective experience varies" (Searle, 2000, p. 15). For each subjective experience the parts of the cube are organized differently. When the cube switches from one organization to the other, there must be a corresponding change in the structure of the underlying brain process. Köhler's idea was that such alterations were produced as a result of prolonged inspection of a figure. The area in the brain that is responsible for processing and creating a representation of the figure becomes fatigued, or only weakly capable of supporting electrical fields,

epiphenomenalism
"Mind" is a superfluous by-product of bodily functioning.

parallelism
"Mind" and brain are two aspects of the same reality, and they operate in parallel.

isomorphism
Mental events and neural events share the same structure.

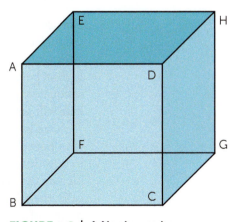

FIGURE 2.6 | A Necker cube

and so another part of the cortex then begins to take over the task. As the cortical representation changes, so too does one's perception of it. Although Köhler's specific hypothesis was discredited, the relationship between such "Gestalt switches" and the underlying brain organization remains the focus of considerable research interest (e.g., Kornmeier & Bach, 2004; Long & Toppino, 2004; Parker, Krug, & Cumming, 2003; Toppino, 2003).

Numerous alternatives to and variations on the preceding formulations have appeared more recently (e.g., Baars, 2002), and we will consider some of them as we go along. However, we should not expect solutions to such a longstanding and difficult problem to come easily. The following quotation from the neuroanatomist Larry Swanson (2003) underlines what we are up against:

> Gram for gram, the brain is far and away the most complex object we know of in the universe, and we simply haven't figured out its basic plan yet—despite its supreme importance and a great deal of effort. There is nothing equivalent to the periodic table of the elements, relativity, or the theory of evolution for organizing and explaining a large (but still woefully incomplete and often contradictory) body of information about brain structure and function. No Mendeleyev, Einstein, or Darwin has succeeded in grasping and articulating the general principles of its architecture; no one has presented a coherent theory or model of its functional organization (p. 2).

In Chapter 13 we consider in detail the mind–brain relationship and its bearing on consciousness. Given the magnitude of the challenge, it's fortunate that there is no need to decide the mind/brain issue in order to discover extremely interesting and suggestive correlations between psychological functions and brain activity. The next section will outline some of the ways in which the study of the brain can facilitate the inquiries of cognitive psychologists.

Methods in Cognitive Neuroscience
Animal Models

The use of non-human animals in research—whether other primates, cats, pigeons, or mice—is a subject that many people take very seriously. It touches on core issues in both science and ethics, and it is only right that those wishing to conduct research on animals be held to the highest possible standards. We have no illusions that such a complex issue can be addressed adequately in a couple of paragraphs, and so we trust that our failure to discuss it in depth here will not be taken to mean that we do not believe it to require serious reflection.

One basis for determining whether it is appropriate to use an animal model has to do with how closely it resembles a human, either genetically or in terms of the phenomenon in question (e.g., the structure or function of a particular organ). Other key considerations include the existing literature on the animal model, the cost, the space required, and, critically, the ethical concerns associated with the research. The fundamental question for supporters of animal rights (the question of suffering aside) is whether conducting research on a particular animal model can provide meaningful information about the human condition that could not be obtained in any other way—the implication being that if that is not the case, then the research is unethical and invalid.

Almost everything we currently know about the micro-organization of brain structure and function is derived from the study of animal brains, largely because the research methods involved are considered too invasive to be used on humans. Experiments that track the response of cell units as an animal is required to change the focus of its attention show how attention may control the processing of some visual stimuli (Moran & Desimone, 1985; Spitzer, Desimone, & Moran, 1988) or enhance the processing of others (cf. Colby, 1991, for a review). The use of carefully controlled lesions, including reversible lesions produced by procedures such as cooling, makes it possible to specify the relationship between cognition and different brain regions. A complete description of human brain structure and function may ultimately depend on our understanding of animal neuroanatomy and physiology.

However, even a full understanding of brain operations in another organism will not lead us to a complete understanding of human brain operations. A mouse brain is not a monkey brain, and a monkey brain is not a human brain (Figure 2.7). Differences in structure and function limit our ability to generalize from one species to another and from animal models to humans. Homologous structures can be very difficult to identify across species, and the specializations of different animals lead to large differences in their neuroanatomy and neurophysiology. For example, much of the rat brain is dedicated to olfactory

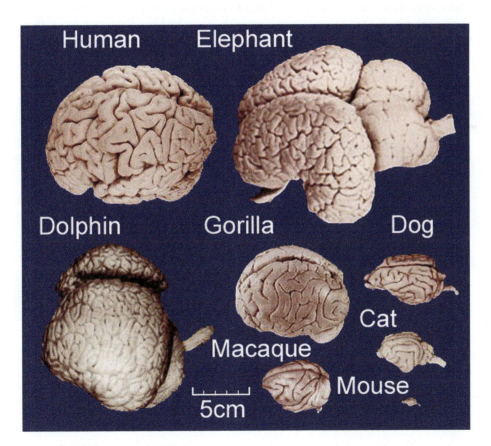

FIGURE 2.7 | Different brain sizes

input, while much of the human brain is dedicated to visual input. Understanding human psychological states of mind ultimately requires study of the human brain at work.

Behavioural Studies

Behavioural investigations of healthy human subjects can tell us a lot about the structure and function of the human brain. This second approach combines our knowledge of normal sensory systems with precise stimulus presentation and response recording. A **sensory system** is a part of the nervous system, composed of sensory receptors, neural pathways, and distinct regions of the brain preferentially dedicated to the perception of information, that translates the physical world into perceptual experiences. There are six main sensory systems: vision, audition, taste, smell, somatosensory (touch as well as other perceptions, such as muscle and joint movement), and vestibular (balance and spatial orientation). However, behavioural studies alone cannot identify a specific link between behaviour and underlying brain mechanisms. For example, many experiments have shown that we move our eyes from point A to point B faster when the item fixated at point A disappears from view. Through careful behavioural research involving the timing of when points A and B disappear and appear, researchers such as Saslow (1967) and Kingstone and Klein (1993) concluded that the disappearance of an item at point A triggers a disinhibition of the eye movement system, and that a small midbrain structure called the superior colliculus (SC) plays a critical role in this response. Importantly, they had no direct evidence that the SC was involved, but had to rely on studies (cf. Munoz & Wurtz, 1992) of non-human primates. The study of eye movements is illustrated in Figure 2.8.

sensory system

A system that links the physical and perceptual worlds via the nervous system; composed of sensory receptors, neural pathways, and distinct regions of the brain preferentially dedicated to the perception of information.

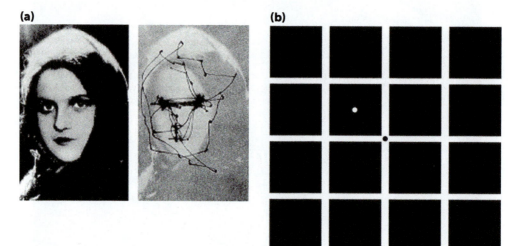

FIGURE 2.8 | Eye movements

(a) An observer views a picture (left) while eye positions are monitored (right) for one minute. The eyes jump and then seem to fixate or rest momentarily, producing a small dot on the trace, before jumping to a new region of fixation. Even during the fixation or "rest" times, however, the eyes are continuously moving, never still. (b) Pattern for showing fixational eye movements. Look at the central black dot for about a minute, then look at the white dot in the adjacent dark square. The dark after-image of the white line pattern should be seen in constant motion owing to fixational eye movements.

(a) Yarbus, A.L. (1967). With kind permission from Springer Science+Business Media B.V. (b) Verheijen, F. J. A simple after image method demonstrating the involuntary multidirectional eye movements during fixation. *Optica Acta* (London) 8, 309–312 (1961), reprinted by permission of the publisher (Taylor & Francis Ltd, http://www.tandfonline.com).

The Study of Brain Injuries

Brain injuries can serve as a kind of substitute for experiments that provide evidence for the localization of one or more functions. It may be possible to relate the symptoms displayed by brain-injured patients to the parts of the brain that have been damaged. The study of cases involving brain injury is seldom straightforward, and it is difficult for such studies to yield definitive evidence concerning localization of function. Even so, they are certainly more informative than the phrenological studies of the early nineteenth century.

A classic example is Paul Broca's (1824–80) study of the loss of the ability to speak. Most of us know how it feels to be momentarily dissatisfied with our ability to put our thoughts into words; imagine how frustrating it would be to lose the ability to express yourself more or less entirely. This condition is often called **Broca's aphasia**. Broca (1861/1966) described a patient who was unable to speak, but apparently was still able to understand what was said to him. An autopsy showed severe damage to a part of the left hemisphere that has since come to be known as **Broca's area** (Figure 2.9). Broca and others observed similar damage in similarly aphasic patients at autopsy.

Another class of patients, who are able to speak but unable to comprehend what is said to them or to produce coherent speech, was identified by Karl Wernicke (1848–1905). In extreme cases, these patients may ramble incoherently, their words bearing no obvious relationship to thought. Wernicke studied 10 such cases and found that the lesions apparently responsible for their symptoms were located in the left hemisphere in the area

Broca's aphasia
A deficit in the ability to produce speech as a result of damage to Broca's area.

Broca's area
The area of the brain's left hemisphere that is responsible for how words are spoken.

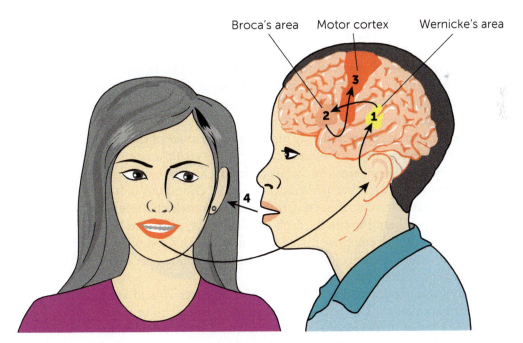

FIGURE 2.9 | Traditional illustration of language comprehension and production

The meaning of words is processed in Wernicke's area (1). That information is then passed to Broca's area (2), which determines how words will be spoken. That information in turn is passed to the motor cortex (3), which controls the movement of the mouth and tongue, ultimately resulting in the production of speech (4).

Based on: www.gazzaro.it/g/Language%20in%20the%20brain_file/broca_wernicke_speak.gif

Wernicke's area

Area of the brain's left
hemisphere that is
responsible for processing
the meaning of words.

Wernicke's aphasia

A deficit in the ability to
comprehend speech as
a result of damage to
Wernicke's area.

that became known as Wernicke's area (Figure 2.9). The corresponding disorder is called Wernicke's aphasia.

Although Broca and Wernicke made lasting contributions to the study of localization of function, discoveries such as theirs cannot be interpreted in any straightforward way. It may be tempting to believe that Broca's area is responsible for speech production and Wernicke's area for speech comprehension, but such a simple conclusion is not justified. For one thing, the aphasias are not particularly well defined, and it is recognized "that clinical aphasic syndromes are comprised of variable clusters of symptoms" (Poeppel & Hickok, 2004, p. 4). It's difficult to see how such ill-defined phenomena could be regulated by a precisely located part of the brain. More important, the exact location of (for example) Wernicke's area is difficult to determine on the basis of anatomy alone (Cacioppo et al., 2003, p. 654). Even more important, "modern work has identified areas outside of the classical regions that are implicated in language processing" (Poeppel & Hickok, 2004, p. 5). Together, Broca's and Wernicke's areas form "an image with iconic status in neuroscience, . . . the basis of a neurolinguistic model that has informed research for almost 150 years and constitutes the canonical model of brain and language taught across disciplines" (Poeppel & Hickok, 2004, p. 1); however, they cannot bear the full weight of explanation. The general lesson to be learned from studies of the relationship between the loss of psychological functions and brain damage is that such studies can be very suggestive, but are seldom definitive or complete (Marshall & Fink, 2003).

Surgical Intervention

We discussed earlier in this chapter how Lashley used ablation to investigate localization of function. Roger Sperry (1913–94) also used surgical techniques, but in a more precise manner. Sperry received the Nobel Prize in 1981, in part for his research on interhemispheric transfer. This work was conducted on cats and initially involved severing the optic chiasm (the area in the brain where the optic nerves that transmit information from the eyes to the visual cortex cross), with the result that information coming from the right eye was projected only onto the visual areas of the right hemisphere, and information from the left eye projected only onto the visual areas of the left hemisphere. Eventually Sperry also severed the corpus callosum, and in so doing showed that it "plays the dominant role in interhemispheric interaction" (Hoptman & Davidson, 1994, p. 2). When the corpus callosum is severed, information transfer between the hemispheres is disrupted. Under these conditions, each hemisphere appeared to be "a separate mental domain operating with complete disregard—indeed with a complete lack of awareness—of what went on in the other. The split brain animal behaved . . . as if it had two entirely separate brains" (Sperry, 1964, p. 43).

Sperry's work broadened considerably when he was able to study human patients whose corpus callosum had been severed by neurosurgeons in the hope of alleviating epilepsy. In a series of clever experiments, Sperry and his associates claimed to have shown not only that "the two hemispheres of the brain had unique capabilities" but also that "the combination of both hemispheres working together produced a unified state of consciousness that amounted to more than the simple additive effects of the two hemispheres alone" (Puente, 1995, p. 941). Sperry's work led to an avalanche of research seeking to discover the "unique capabilities" of each hemisphere. As we have already seen, the work of Broca

interhemispheric transfer

Communication between
the brain's hemispheres,
enabled in large part by
the corpus callosum.

split brain

A condition created by
severing the corpus
callosum.

and Wernicke suggested that the left hemisphere was typically associated with linguistic functions. Split-brain research led many to the general conclusion that the left hemisphere managed "analytic" (e.g., verbal, rational) tasks and the right hemisphere, "holistic" (e.g., non-verbal, intuitive) tasks (e.g., Jaynes, 1976, pp. 100–125; Martindale, 1981, pp. 286–287). However, it later became clear that there was no simple division of labour between the two hemispheres in an intact brain (e.g., Gardner, 1982, pp. 278–285; Hoptman & Davidson, 1994). Indeed, "because of their complexity, the actual organization of intracerebral connections may well lie beyond the limits of human comprehension" (Swanson, 2003, p. 166). While the split brain (Figure 2.10) is a fascinating object of study, there are limits to the conclusions that can be drawn from such atypical cases.

In the final phase of his career, Sperry turned his attention to broad issues such as the nature of consciousness (Erdmann & Stover, 1991/2000; Stover & Erdmann, 2000). He argued that consciousness is an **emergent property** of the brain, meaning that it is neither reducible to nor a product of other features of the brain. Once consciousness emerges, then, it can have an influence on lower-level functions, a process that may be termed **emergent causation** (Erdmann & Stover, 1991/2000, p. 50). Sperry (1987, p. 165) recognized a "mutual interaction between neural and mental events" such that "the brain physiology determines the mental events" but is in turn "governed by the higher subjective properties of the enveloping mental events." Describing the mind as **supervenient**, he argued that mental states may "exert downward control over their constituent neuronal events—at the same time that they are being determined by them" (Sperry, 1988, p. 609). Although Sperry's speculations on the mind/brain relationship

emergent property (Sperry)

In Sperry's sense, a property that "emerges" as a result of brain processes, but is not itself a component of the brain. In the case of the mind, this means that consciousness is neither reducible to, nor a property of, a particular brain structure or region.

emergent causation

In Sperry's sense, causation brought about by an emergent property. Once the "mind" emerges from the brain, it has the power to influence lower-level processes.

supervenient

In Sperry's sense, describes mental states that may simultaneously influence neuronal events and be influenced by them.

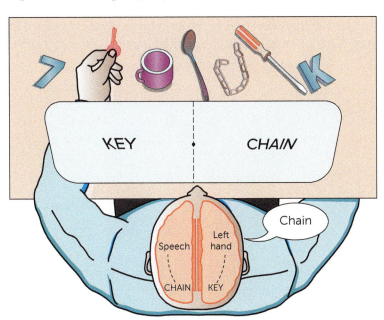

FIGURE 2.10 | Split-brain operations

There is no way to communicate between the right and left hemispheres once the corpus callosum has been severed. For this reason, patients who have undergone such operations provide scientists with valuable information about the lateralization of the human brain: in particular, the dominance of the left hemisphere for language and the right hemisphere for visual–spatial tasks.

Based on: erraticwisdom.com/images/38.gif

were greeted with skepticism, they were an important part of the discussion that led to a more open consideration of the problem of consciousness.

Event-Related Potentials

The earliest imaging technique, computed tomography (CT), provided detailed anatomical data that revolutionized neurology and experimental neuropsychology. Magnetic resonance imaging (MRI) provides similar images but with higher spatial resolution. Both produce high-quality "snapshots" of human brain structures and thus make it possible to localize brain lesions, tumours, and developmental abnormalities. However, neither provides images of brain activity. To measure the time course of the flow of sensory information and response-related processes, the electrical signals emitted by the brain can be recorded using electrodes placed on the scalp (electroencephalography, or EEG). The electrical signals that occur after the onset of a stimulus, such as a word, make up a pattern of electrical activity called an **event-related potential (ERP)** and can be represented by waveforms such as those shown in Figure 2.11. A single trial is not enough to provide unambiguous information, but when the electrical responses to a stimulus are averaged over many trials, interesting patterns may emerge. One such pattern can be seen in Figure 2.11, which shows the results of studies reviewed by Rugg (1995). In these studies, participants were initially presented with a series of items (e.g., words, labelled S1, S2, S3, and S4 in Figure 2.11) and the ERP associated with each one was recorded. Note the waveform arising after each of the items in Figure 2.11. Subsequently, the participants were asked to recall the items. The experimenter then sorted the items into those that were recalled and those that were not, and looked for differences in the ERPs for each class of item. Figure 2.11 suggests that the waveform for items that will be remembered is different from the waveform

event-related potential (ERP)

An electrical signal emitted by the brain after the onset of a stimulus.

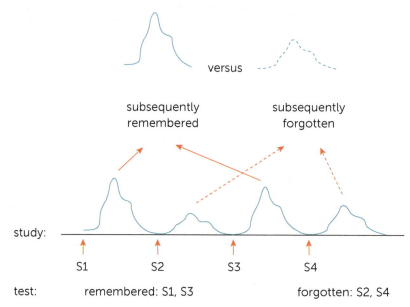

FIGURE 2.11 | Event-related potentials: Differences in neural activity for remembered versus forgotten items

From: Rugg, M.D., Otten, L.J., & Henson, R.N.A. (2003). Fig. 10.1, p.213. By permission of Oxford University Press.

for items that will be forgotten. So far, so good: it looks as if the ERP can predict the subsequent recall of items. However, it's not easy to interpret ERPs in terms of the cognitive processes that underlie them. In this case, perhaps the different waveforms simply indicate that the participants paid attention to some items and ignored others (Rugg, Otten, & Henson, 2003, p. 213); or perhaps they represent more complex processes. In general, although event-related potentials can provide suggestive information, additional techniques must be used in order to gain a more complete picture of brain processes.

Positron Emission Tomography (PET)

One assumption underlying **positron emission tomography (PET)** is that when a specific psychological function is engaged, then only those parts of the brain responsible for that function will also be engaged (Papanicolaou, 1998, p. 23). If a participant is given a specific cognitive task, the parts of the brain responsible for that task will "work harder" than when the participant is not performing that task. When a part of the brain is active in this way, it will use up oxygen at a faster rate than when it is inactive, and the need to replenish that oxygen in turn will lead to an increase in blood flow to the area. PET takes advantage of this chain of events. The participant in a PET study is first given a radioactive substance that mingles with the blood and thus circulates to the brain. This procedure allows for the detection of blood flow to particular areas of the brain and makes it possible to construct images showing which parts of the brain are particularly active in relation to the performance of different tasks (Figure 2.12).

positron emission tomography (PET)
An imaging technique in which a participant is injected with a radioactive substance that mingles with the blood and circulates to the brain. A scanner is then used to detect the flow of blood to particular areas of the brain.

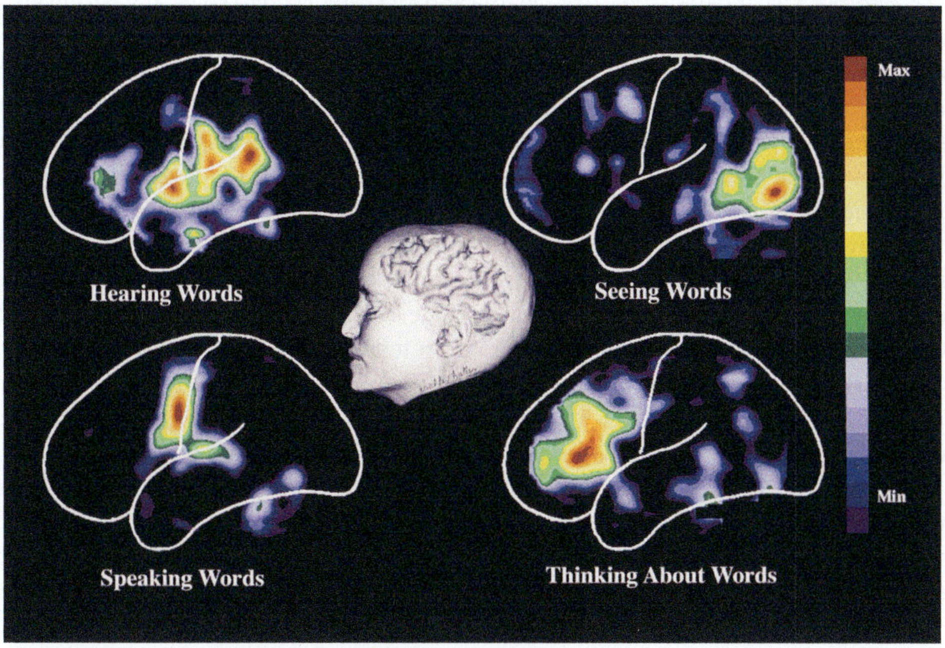

FIGURE 2.12 | Positron emission tomography (PET)

Positron emission tomography showing activity in different parts of the brain related to different language functions.

One problem with PET methodology is that there are limits to the amount of radiation to which a participant may be exposed, and therefore limits to the amount of information that can be obtained from each participant. Although PET was extremely popular until the mid-1990s, functional magnetic resonance imaging has now replaced it as the method of choice (Rugg, 2002, p. 59).

Functional Magnetic Resonance Imaging (fMRI)

functional magnetic resonance imaging (fMRI)

A non-radioactive, magnetic procedure for detecting the flow of oxygenated blood to various parts of the brain.

While standard MRI can be extremely useful in viewing the structure of the brain, it does not indicate what areas of the brain are involved in any specific behaviour. However, **functional magnetic resonance imaging (fMRI)** does measure blood flow (actually, the flow of oxygen in the blood) while the subject completes some sort of task, and is capable of correlating the location of brain activity with the cognitive behaviour. One advantage of fMRI is that it does not depend on a radioactive signal. Another is that data can be acquired

CONSIDER THIS
BOX 2.1

"Mind Reading"

Can brain imaging be used to read minds? Some scientists believe that it can. In 2007, for instance, Dr Marco Iacoboni of the University of California, Los Angeles, and colleagues published an article in *The New York Times* called "This Is Your Brain on Politics." Accompanying the article was a series of images of the brains of swing voters recorded as they responded to photos and videos of several potential candidates for the presidency in the 2008 US election. Iacoboni and colleagues said the findings were clear-cut. Activity in the amygdala in response to Mitt Romney revealed voter anxiety; activity in the insula indicated disgust with John Edwards, while the patterns of brain activity elicited by photos of Barack Obama and John McCain suggested no powerful reaction, either positive or negative.

Unfortunately, Iacoboni and colleagues (2007) made a mistake that many consumers of science make: they assumed a one-to-one correlation between brain regions and mental states: in this case, that amygdala activation meant anxiety, that activity in the insula meant disgust, and so on. In fact, such one-to-one mapping is simply not possible. For instance, we know that the amygdala is activated not only by anxiety but also by anger, arousal, happiness, and sexual excitement. And

activation of the insula may just as easily indicate a sense of unfairness, or pain, or pleasure as disgust. As for Obama and McCain failing to spark any strong emotions, we now know that this was not the case.

Overly simplistic interpretations of brain-imaging results are far too common. For instance, a difference in brain activation for faces that differ in attractiveness is taken to indicate the activation of a neural mechanism that computes attractiveness; yet the same effect might be caused by mechanisms associated with feelings of familiarity, or the assessment of social status. A difference in brain activation for white and black faces is interpreted to mean that certain brain regions are associated with racism when it could just as well indicate feelings of social injustice or inequality. These fundamental limitations aside, there remains the issue of whether brain activations generated in a lab-based environment can tell us anything about behaviour in real-world settings; currently there is no evidence whatsoever that brain activations are predictive of performance in everyday life. These are important points to keep in mind whenever a study claims to have found that a particular brain region is associated with a specific mental state or behaviour.

more rapidly using fMRI than is possible using PET (Rugg, 1999, p. 22). The fMRI technique involves placing the subject's head inside a very large magnetic field and having him or her view some sort of stimuli, or perform some sort of cognitive task. This allows for neurological measurement of activity associated with the functioning of some aspect of cognition. The magnetic field of the machine causes atoms in the brain to become aligned with it (Papanicolaou, 1998, p. 49). Changes in the flow of oxygenated blood can then be picked up as alterations in the magnetic field, and this information can be used to construct an image of cortical activity.

An experiment conducted by Bavelier et al. (1997) is an example of an fMRI study involving Broca's and Wernicke's areas. The tasks used in that study were sentence reading and the viewing of consonant strings. Sentence reading "invoke[s] many different aspects of language processing," while viewing "consonant strings is believed to activate only basic visual recognition routines. . . . The comparison of these two conditions should reveal brain areas concerned with . . . language processing" (Bavelier et al., 1997, p. 667). The results revealed wide individual differences in the patterns of activation shown by each of the eight participants. Examination of the pattern of activation that best characterized the entire group of participants did show that Broca's and Wernicke's areas were more activated by the sentence-reading task than by the viewing of consonant strings. However, other areas were also consistently more activated by sentence reading than by consonant viewing. Bavelier et al. (1997, p. 678) concluded that language is not simply localized "in a few cortically well-circumscribed areas" (see Figure 2.13).

Sentences vs Consonant Strings

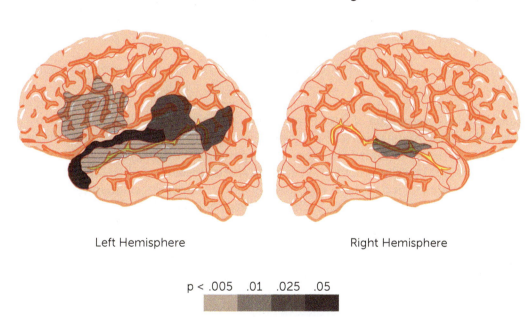

Left Hemisphere · Right Hemisphere

p < .005 .01 .025 .05

FIGURE 2.13 | Functional magnetic resonance imaging (fMRI)

Showing the difference in activity of language processing in the left and right hemispheres between sentence reading (the darker shaded areas in Broca's and Wernicke's areas of the left hemisphere) and the viewing of consonant strings (the fine lines throughout both hemispheres).

From: Bavelier, D., et al. (1997). Reprinted by permission of MIT Press Journals.

It's tempting to wish for a "magic bullet" technique that would reveal the precise cortical locations for all psychological functions. If brain-imaging techniques did constitute such a "magic bullet," however, they would be "no more than a modern and extraordinarily expensive version of 19th century phrenology" (Raichle, 2003, p. 3959). In fact, the view of the brain that seems to be emerging is not at all phrenological (Zago, Stefano, et al., 2011). According to Marshall and Fink (2003), "recent work [suggests] that functional localization is not such a fixed property of brain regions as either lesion studies or early neuroimaging work might have suggested" (p. 56). They illustrate this point with respect to Broca's area. Neuroimaging studies have found that it plays "a role in natural language syntactic processing (Caplan, Alpert, Waters, & Olivieri, 2000; Heim, Opitz, & Freiderichi, 2003), in processing musical syntax (Maess, Koelsch, Gunter, & Friederichi, 2001), in the perception of rhythmic motion (Schubotz & von Cramon, 2001), in imaging movement trajectories (Binkofski et al., 2000)," and so on (see Raichle, 2008, 2010 for excellent recent reviews). Marshall and Fink conclude that "it is difficult to see how a single common function (localized in Broca's area) could underlie such a disparate collection of effects" (p. 56), and suggest that, at least to some extent, the interaction of different areas of the brain determines their function on a particular occasion. This point is reinforced by Cabeza and Nyberg (2003, p. 241), who observe that "the vast majority of functional neuroimaging studies have investigated a single cognitive function. Yet, with the accumulation of functional neuroimaging data, it has become obvious that . . . the neural correlates of cognitive functions overlap considerably, with most brain regions being involved in a variety of cognitive functions." Marshall and Fink (2003, p. 56) anticipate the development of "new methods of measuring the functional integration of different brain regions" that will improve our current models of the brain.

Magnetoencephalography (MEG)

magnetoenceph-alography (MEG)

A non-invasive brain imaging technique that directly measures neural activity.

While the spatial resolution of fMRI is very good, the temporal resolution is quite poor compared to ERP. Magnetoencephalography (MEG) is a noninvasive brain imaging technique that seeks to marry the significant spatial resolution of fMRI with the outstanding temporal resolution of ERP. While the spatial resolution of MEG might not be quite as good as fMRI, it does have significantly better temporal resolution (10 milliseconds or faster vs hundreds of msecs for fMRI) because MEG measures the magnetic fields produced by electrical activity in the brain. An additional advantage of MEG is that it provides a direct measurement of neural activity rather than the indirect measurement offered by fMRI and PET, which are intimately tied to changes in blood flow in the brain. A third advantage of MEG is that irregularities in the head itself (e.g., the skull) do not have much effect on the magnetic fields produced by neural activity, unlike the electrical fields used by ERP. Nevertheless, MEG has two limitations. First, the decay of signal as a function of distance is pronounced for magnetic fields (as anyone who has tried to push two magnets together will know) and therefore MEG is really good only for detecting activity near the cortical surface of the brain. Second, MEG devices are not widely available (unlike fMRI) and therefore their cost effectiveness is relatively poor (see Figures 2.14 and 2.15).

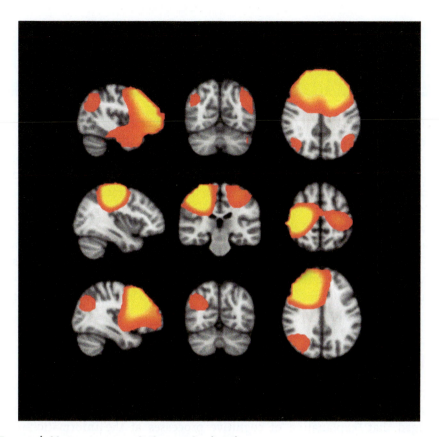

FIGURE 2.14 | Magnetoencephalography (MEG)

Scans of the magnetic fields produced by the networks of electrical currents resulting from neuronal activity within the brain. The gradient of activity runs from low (red) to high (yellow). The top row shows the network involved when the brain is at rest; this network disappears when the subject is performing a task. The second row shows the sensory–motor network, which appears when the subject performs a motor task (e.g., tapping fingers). The bottom row shows the right lateral frontoparietal network.

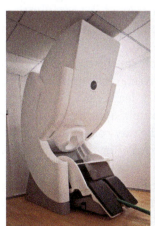

FIGURE 2.15 | Magnetoencephalograph scanner

THINK TWICE / The Ethics of Brain Imaging

Let's make the reasonable assumption that you're a good person—that you don't cheat or steal, that you recycle as best you can, and that you believe in treating everyone equally, regardless of skin colour. Yet you have recently taken part in a brain imaging study that suggested you could be an unconscious racist. What does this mean? Do you accept that brain imaging has advanced to the point where it can detect your unconscious attitudes, even if those attitudes are in direct conflict with what you consciously believe and do? Even if imaging had advanced to that point, do interior, unconscious attitudes matter more than overt actions? These are the types of issues that neuroscientists, specifically those in the field of neuroethics, are now grappling with. Do people who have never behaved in a racist manner but who show brain activation that suggests racial prejudice deserve to be treated as racists? Do people who have never stolen anything but who show heightened activation in regions of the brain associated with the need to exert cognitive control deserve to be treated as if they were predisposed to steal? What do you think? The "Cognition in Action" box on p. 44 may help you to work through this issue.

---

connectionism
A theory that focuses on the way cognitive processes work at the physiological/neurological (as opposed to information-processing) level. It holds that the brain consists of an enormous number of interconnected neurons and attempts to model cognition as an emergent process of networks of simple units (e.g., neurons) communicating with one another.

diffusion tensor imaging (DTI)
An MRI-based neuroimaging technique that makes it possible to visualize the white-matter tracts within the brain.

DISCOVERY LAB ✳

neural network
Neurons that are functionally related or connected.

Connectionist Models

It's not intuitively obvious that the information-processing flow-chart models we have looked at so far could also be models of how the brain works. For instance, Herbert Simon acknowledged that "explanation of cognitive processes at the information-processing (symbolic) level is largely independent of explanation at the physiological (neurological) level that shows how processes are implemented" (Simon, 1992, p. 153). **Connectionism** is an example of the latter: an alternative to the more traditional approaches focused on information-processing (Schneider, 1987) that focuses on the physiological/neurological level. Connectionist theory holds that the brain consists of an enormous number of interconnected neurons, and that a model of the networks formed by these neurons might help us to understand how cognitive processes work. Using modern brain imaging techniques such as **diffusion tensor imaging (DTI)**, researchers can understand the organization of the neural interactions within the brain (e.g., how information flows between and within brain regions; see Figure 2.16).

The two basic connectionist ideas are that (a) information can be broken down into elementary units (neurons) and (b) there are connections between these units. These connections can have different strengths, and a **neural network** learns by modifying the strength of connections between elements so that the proper output occurs in response to a particular input. Among the assumptions made concerning the way connections between neurons are formed and strengthened is the **Hebb rule**, named after the Canadian D.O. Hebb, one of the founders of neuropsychology. The Hebb rule states that "when an axon of cell A is near enough to excite a cell B and repeatedly or persistently takes part in firing it, some growth process or metabolic change takes place in one or both cells such that A's efficiency, as one of the cells firing B, is increased" (Hebb, 1949, p. 62). This "idea that a connection between two neurons takes place only if both neurons are firing at about the same time" has greatly influenced subsequent theorizing (Milner, 2003, p. 5).

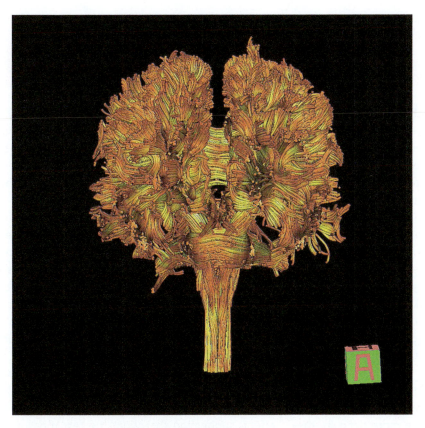

FIGURE 2.16 | Diffusion Tensor Imaging (DTI)

Coloured 3D DTI scan of the brain, showing the bundles of white matter nerve fibres that transmit nerve signals between brain regions and between the brain and the spinal cord. DTI scans show the diffusion of water along white matter fibres, making it possible to map their orientations and the connections between brain regions.

Another assumption of connectionist models is that many connections can be active at the same time. This is an example of **parallel processing** as opposed to **serial processing**, in which only one connection operates at a time. Thus connectionist models may also be described as *parallel distributed processing* models (McClelland & Rumelhart, 1986a, 1988).

A big difference between connectionism and older information-processing approaches is that knowledge is embodied in the connections that make up the network rather than in a series of information-processing stages. Connectionist models are quite good at simulating many cognitive processes; we will examine some of these models in succeeding chapters.

Combining Methods

At its best, cognitive neuroscience melds theories and methods from all the approaches described in this chapter. Hypotheses about brain mechanisms in animal models are constructed through careful control of behaviour using paradigms developed through research on both animals and humans. Data from human behavioural studies can be interpreted in

Hebb rule

A connection between two neurons takes place only if both neurons are firing at approximately the same time.

parallel processing

Many neural connections may be active at the same time.

serial processing

Only one neural activity may take place at any one time.

COGNITION IN ACTION
BOX 2.3
The Implicit Association Test

In a ground-breaking study, Richeson and colleagues (2003) found that some people need to exert additional cognitive control to avoid behaving in a racist manner. They also found that the same people showed a unique pattern of brain activation when presented with pictures of black faces. Participants first completed a task called the implicit association test (IAT). The IAT seeks to measure hidden biases by requiring participants to respond to two categories of words with a single button press, for instance, press the left key if a word is positive (e.g., LOVE) or a name typically associated with white people; and press the right key if the word is negative (e.g., HATE) or a name typically associated with black people. In a separate run of trials the positive–negative and black–white associations were reversed. The IAT effect is the difference between the two conditions (e.g., longer response times for the positive–black pairing than for the positive–white pairing). Richeson et al. found that the more racial bias participants showed on the IAT, the more difficulty they had on a cognitive control task that they were asked to perform after interacting with a black experimenter. According to the researchers' interpretation, the participants with the higher IAT scores had to make a special effort to exercise cognitive control when interacting with the black experimenter, and this strain affected their ability to perform the task (specifically, the Stroop task; see Chapter 4). Critically, fMRI revealed that those participants also showed greater activity in brain regions associated with cognitive control when looking at pictures of black faces that were irrelevant to their task.

Does this mean that the IAT is a valid measure of racial bias and prejudice, or that people must be prejudiced if, when presented with pictures of black faces, they show heightened activation in the areas of the cortex associated with cognitive control? Both conclusions must be treated with caution, for two reasons. First, the IAT measures a relative difference, so even if we accept that it taps into unconscious attitudes toward whites and blacks, a large effect could be observed in people who have positive associations with blacks if their associations with whites are *more* positive. Second, most blacks (and all whites) show an IAT effect, suggesting that what the test measures is environmental associations with whites and blacks (i.e., familiarity with stereotypes) rather than the individual's personal endorsement of those associations. Either of these alternative scenarios would produce the same pattern of results that Richeson et al. reported.

the context of findings provided by animal studies, allowing direct observation of neural functioning at a local level. Data from either or both of these sources can be used when designing and interpreting experiments using functional imaging methods or looking at patients who have had some sort of brain lesion. For instance, by combining behavioural measures with *static* brain-imaging techniques such as CT or MRI, strong links can be established between behaviour and brain structure. With *dynamic* imaging techniques such as ERP, PET, fMRI, or MEG, these links can be expanded to map the connections between behaviour and function.

Fendrich, Wessinger, and Gazzaniga (1992) used the latter approach to study a patient with a condition known as "blindsight." As we will see in Chapter 13, some people who have suffered lesions to the primary visual cortex are able to make accurate judgments about the location of visual stimuli that they claim they cannot see. This "blindsight" has been attributed to visual pathways that bypass the primary cortex (for reviews, see

Weiskrantz, 1990; Cowey & Stoerig, 1991). However, others have argued that it could be the result of spared functioning in the primary cortex (Poppel, Held, & Frost, 1973; Campion, Latto, & Smith, 1983). Using psychophysical tests and an image stabilizer that allows for extended and repetitive stimulus presentations to a very small area of the retina, Fendrich, Wessinger, and Gazzaniga (1992) discovered a small and isolated island of blindsight in a hemianopic patient (i.e., one who was functionally blind on one side of the visual field). This behavioural result suggested that a region of cortex within the lesioned area had been spared. MRI images confirmed that there was indeed cortical sparing, and a subsequent PET investigation revealed that the spared cortex was metabolically active. Based on this combination of behavioural and neuroimaging data, Fendrich et al. (1992) were able to conclude that blindsight can result from cortical sparing within a lesioned area (see also Gazzaniga, Fendrich, & Wessinger, 1994).

DISCOVERY LAB

One final comment on the methods of cognitive neuroscience is in order. This section has looked at various methods of localizing cognitive processes in the brain. As researchers we generally operate as if our task were simply to find the brain correlates of those processes. If we're thoughtful, however, we have to admit that there is no universal agreement even on what the basic cognitive processes are (Fodor, 2000; Marshall & Fink, 2003, p. 54; Uttal, 2001). One of our most important goals in this text is to present current perspectives on cognitive processes. We should expect that our understanding of cognitive processes and their relationship to the brain may never be set once and for all. It is in the nature of science that our theories are always evolving and hence always provisional.

DISCOVERY LAB

Summary

In this chapter we have introduced cognitive neuroscience, the field that studies the brain mechanisms that give rise to human cognition and behaviour. A major research question for this field is which parts of the brain are specialized for specific cognitive operations. From the speculative methods of phrenology to the lesion studies of Lashley (*law of mass action*; *law of equipotentiality*) to the behavioural work of Gauthier, Skudlarski, Gore, and Anderson (2000), research has explored the strictness of the correspondence between specific cognitive functions and specific parts of the brain (*localization of function*).

Another major research question in cognitive neuroscience is the relationship between the mind and the brain. Some traditional approaches to the mind/brain problem include *interactionism*, *epiphenomenalism*, *parallelism*, and *isomorphism*. A significant distinction emerging from these approaches is that between "consciousness" and "mind." "Consciousness" refers to what we are aware of at any point in time. "Mind" is a broader phenomenon that includes consciousness but also a number of other processes that may take place outside our awareness. These concepts and their meaning are the subject of continuing research and debate.

Interestingly, the fact that the mind/body question has not been resolved has not prevented the discovery of either correlations between psychological functions and brain activity or methods for localizing cognitive processes in the brain. An indirect route to investigating brain mechanisms in humans is through the study of animal neuroanatomy and physiology using invasive techniques that cannot be used on humans. However, even a full understanding of another organism's brain operations will not lead us to a complete understanding of human brain operations.

A second approach focuses on behavioural investigations of healthy human subjects. This approach combines our knowledge of normal sensory systems with precise stimulus presentation and response recording. The shortcoming of this approach is that it can only infer a relationship between behaviour and underlying brain mechanisms: it cannot establish a specific link.

A third approach is based on case studies of brain-injured patients. By relating patients' symptoms to the parts of the brain that have been damaged, these studies can provide evidence of localization of function (Broca's aphasia; Wernicke's aphasia). However, because individual cases differ, brain injuries can at best provide only incomplete evidence. In some cases of brain injury, surgical intervention is necessary. One outcome of such intervention can be greater understanding of the relationship between brain function and behaviour (*interhemispheric transfer*; *split brain*).

Recent technological advances have enabled us to observe the brain structures directly through both *static* brain-imaging techniques such as CT or MRI and *dynamic* imaging techniques such as ERP, PET, fMRI, and MEG. Each has its own specific strengths and limitations. Generally, dynamic or functional neuroimaging studies provide images not only of brain structures but also of brain activity. However, many of these investigations focus on a single cognitive function and thus do not capture the overlap of brain regions involved in a variety of functions. Furthermore, it is questionable whether brain activations generated in a lab-based environment can tell us anything about behaviour in real-world settings.

Finally, a fourth approach to understanding cognitive processes reflects the theory known as *connectionism*: that cognition can be modelled as a network of interconnected units (e.g., neurons). Connectionist models operate on a set of specific assumptions (*Hebb rule*, *serial processing*, *parallel processing*) about the formation and strengthening of neural network connections.

CASE STUDY

Case Study Wrap-Up

We began this chapter by considering how easy it is to take the brain for granted, even though it is indispensable to all thought and behaviour. The life-altering consequences of brain injury were recently driven home by the case of Congresswoman Giffords, who survived a bullet in the head but then faced significant difficulties in understanding and producing speech. Based on what you have read in this chapter, which side of her brain do you think was injured?

We have considered three convergent lines of evidence suggesting that the injury must have been in the left hemisphere: brain lesion studies (e.g., the research conducted by Broca and Wernicke), surgical intervention (e.g., the split-brain work of Sperry and colleagues), and the fMRI studies involving healthy individuals. In fact, it was the left hemisphere of Giffords' brain that was damaged (see Figure 2.17).

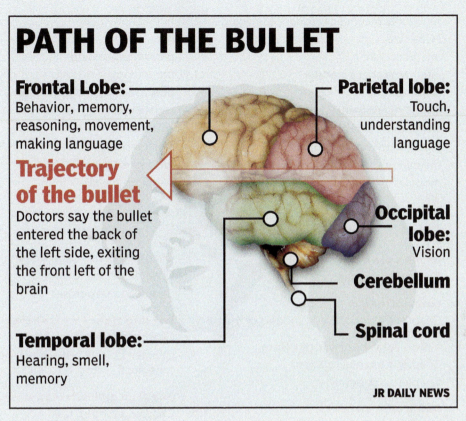

FIGURE 2.17 | Lesions in left hemisphere of Gabrielle Giffords' brain

In the Know: Review Questions

1. How important do you think the physical localization of cognitive processes is to the study of human cognition?
2. Review the approaches to the mind/brain issue outlined in the text (including Sperry). Which of these approaches (if any) do you prefer? If you don't favour any of them, what is your alternative?
3. Explain the major differences between ERP, PET, MRI, fMRI, MEG, and DTI. How do they differ functionally? What are their limitations?

Key Concepts

Broca's aphasia
Broca's area
connectionism
diffusion tensor imaging (DTI)

emergent causation
emergent property (Sperry)
epiphenomenalism
event-related potential (ERP)

functional magnetic resonance imaging (fMRI)

Hebb rule

interactionism

interhemispheric transfer

isomorphism

law of equipotentiality

law of mass action

localization of function

magnetoencephalography (MEG)

modules

neural networks

parallelism

parallel processing

phrenology

positron emission tomography (PET)

serial processing

split brain

supervenient

Wernicke's aphasia

Wernicke's area

Links to Other Chapters

Broca's area
Chapter 9 (evolution of language)

connectionism
Chapter 5 (connectionist models of memory)

event-related potential (ERP)
Chapter 7 (mental rotation)
Chapter 10 (insight)

functional magnetic resonance imaging (fMRI)
Chapter 4 (Stroop task)

Chapter 6 (levels of processing)
Chapter 7 (dual coding)
Chapter 12 (expertise)

left and right hemispheres
Chapter 7 (mental rotation)
Chapter 13 (split brain, visual hemispatial neglect)

positron emission tomography (PET)
Chapter 4 (Stroop task)

Further Reading

Three excellent histories of the emergence of cognitive psychology are Baars (1986), Gardner (1985), and Hilgard (1987).

Searle (1980) includes a famous critical discussion of computer simulation. For a very readable account of some of his views, see Searle (1999). Green (1996) offers a sophisticated analysis of many of the issues surrounding computer simulation.

For a basic introduction to neural networks see Hinton (1992). Smith (1996) is another introduction to connectionism that also shows some of its broader implications.

An influential book by an enthusiast of connectionism is Churchland (1996). Rock and Palmer (1990) is a suggestive review of the contributions of Gestalt psychology that shows its similarity to some aspects of connectionism.

For overviews of the mind/brain issue by four eminent scientists and one philosopher see Crick and Koch (2003), Edelman (2004), LeDoux (2002), and Chalmers (1996).

Not everyone is enthusiastic about the achievements of cognitive neuroscience. For a well-informed critique see Bennett and Hacker (2003). They argue that, as Wittgenstein (1953, p. 232) put it, "problem and method pass one another by" in cognitive neuroscience: in other words, that neuroscience is not addressing the problems it thinks it is addressing. To appreciate their line of argument, you might want to become acquainted with Wittgenstein, although understanding him is no mean achievement.

For a basic introduction to event-related potentials, see Begleiter (1977). Finally, Logothetis (2003) is a demanding but worthwhile discussion by one of the most highly respected researchers in the field of fMRI.

Baars, B.J. (1986). *The cognitive revolution in psychology*. New York: Guilford Press.

Begleiter, H. (1977). *Evoked brain potentials and behavior*. New York: Plenum.

Bennett, M.R., & Hacker, P.M.S. (2003). *Philosophical foundations of neuroscience*. Oxford: Blackwell.

Chalmers, D.J. (1996). *The conscious mind: In search of a fundamental theory*. New York: Oxford University Press.

Churchland, P.M. (1996). *The engine of reason, the seat of the soul*. Chichester: Wiley.

Crick, F., & Koch, C. (2003). A framework for consciousness. *Nature Neuroscience, 6*, 119–126.

Edelman, G.M. (2004). *Wider than the sky: The phenomenal gift of consciousness*. New Haven: Yale University Press.

Gardner, H. (1985). *The mind's new science*. New York: Basic Books.

Green, C.D. (1996). Fodor, functions, physics, and fantasyland: Is AI a Mickey Mouse discipline? *Journal of Experimental and Theoretical Artificial Intelligence, 8*, 95–106.

Hilgard, E.R. (1987). *Psychology in America: An historical survey*. New York: Harcourt Brace Jovanovich.

Hinton, G.E. (1992). How neural networks learn from experience. *Scientific American, 267* (Sept.), 144–151.

LeDoux, J. (2002). *Synaptic self: How our brains become who we are*. New York: Penguin.

Logothetis, N.K. (2003). The neural basis of the blood-oxygen-level-dependent functional magnetic resonance imaging signal. In A. Parker, A. Derrington, & C. Blakemore (Eds.), *The physiology of cognitive processes* (pp. 62–116). Oxford: Oxford University Press.

Rock, I., & Palmer, S. (1990). The legacy of Gestalt psychology. *Scientific American, 263* (December), 84–90.

Searle, J.R. (1980). Minds, brains, and programs. *Behavioral and Brain Sciences, 3*, 417–424.

Searle, J.R. (1999). I married a computer. *New York Review of Books* (Apr. 8), pp. 34–38.

Smith, E.R. (1996). What do connectionism and social psychology have to offer each other? *Journal of Personality and Social Psychology, 79*, 893–912.

3

Perception

Chapter Contents

Chapter Objectives

- To describe the basic physiology of visual perception.
- To outline basic facts about perception learned from the visual deficits of patients with brain damage.
- To describe how objects are consciously perceived and recognized.
- To illustrate the importance of context and observer knowledge in theories of perception.
- To examine the relation between perception and action.
- To explore the nature of multimodal perceptions.

CASE STUDY

An Unusual Perceptual Experience

Imagine for a moment that you have just woken up in a hospital bed after suffering a head injury or a stroke that has blocked the blood flow to a part of your brain. As the scene around you slowly comes into focus, you are horrified to realize that you can't attach a name to any of the things you see. Someone comes over to your bed and holds up a series of objects, which she asks you to identify. You can't do it. Finally you reach out and grab one of the objects, and on feeling it you immediately recognize it as a hairbrush and name it correctly. But you still can't identify any of the objects that you haven't touched.

A very similar situation was described more than a century ago by H. Lissauer (1888/2001). An 80-year-old patient who was experiencing perceptual deficits as a result of damage to the brain was presented with a number of simple visual objects and asked to identify them. His responses are reported in quotation marks here, interspersed with the interviewer's questions and comments:

visual agnosia

An inability to identify objects visually even though they can be identified using other senses (e.g., touch).

perception

The processing of sensory information in such a way that it produces conscious experiences and guides action in the world.

Object Presented	Patient's Response
A lamp containing a light:	"A figure." What does it represent? "That, I can't guess." After a pause: "It could be a man. But the figure only goes up to there" (shows the length of the light). "The other (shows the lamp) is something fixed, a base." Is it really a man and not perhaps a column? "No, here are his head and his legs." "Here is even (shows the bent wick of the light) a bent leg."
Clothes brush:	"That is the earlier figure which was a cat." What was it really? "I have forgotten." The movement of brushing is demonstrated on his jacket. "Oh, of course, a brush."
A large wall mirror:	"That is a lamp made of glass I think." "A lamp." He steps close up to it. Where does the light go? "Here." He points to a corner of the mirror. What is inside it? (the reflection of the patient himself): "Seems to have a horse in it."
Umbrella (2 feet long):	"A lamp." How large do you estimate it to be? "8 inches." Shows on request both ends of the umbrella correctly. How long is 8 inches? Marks with his hands approximately the length of the umbrella. The umbrella is put up. Is it really a lamp? "Yes, yes, there (near the top) the light is put there."(. . .)
A sheet of paper with illustrations of animals is shown (not in colour):	
Donkey:	"That's Napoleon." Is it a picture? "Yes, it's a painting of Napoleon."
Horse:	"Horse." Shows head and tail correctly.
Parrot:	"Seems to be a donkey."
Swan:	"A giraffe."
Cat:	"Cat or monkey." The sheet of paper is turned over so that its reverse is shown: Do you see any pictures here? "No."

Amusing as it is to imagine mistaking a donkey for Napoleon, it's worth noting that the patient did identify some of the objects correctly, including the horse and (after briefly second-guessing himself) the cat. This condition, characterized by impairment in visual identification of objects, is known as visual agnosia.

How can this fascinating condition be explained? In this chapter we will take a closer look at some of the major ways in which cognitive psychologists have studied and theorized about perception. At the most general level, researchers investigate how sensory information is processed, how we become conscious of information received through the senses, and how information from the environment guides action in the world. One of the exciting aspects of visual perception from a student's perspective is that it's so easy to test: you can learn a lot about visual perception by "seeing" how it works for yourself.

The Physiology of Visual Perception

In this chapter we are going to focus primarily on visual perception (multimodal perception will be discussed at the end of the chapter), and so it is worthwhile to begin with a brief overview of the physiology of the visual system. This overview will help us understand the perception deficits described in the Case Study, and it will also provide a useful foundation for understanding some of the findings described later in this chapter.

Visual perception involves the processing of information conveyed by light energy that enters the eye. As such, it seems reasonable to begin with a brief look at how the eye works. A simplified schematic of the eye is shown in Figure 3.1.

Light energy enters the eye through the cornea, which is the outer transparent tissue of the eye against which contact lenses are placed. After passing through the cornea, the light makes its way through a small opening called the pupil. The size of the pupil is controlled by the iris, the coloured tissue that surrounds it and makes the eye look blue, hazel, brown, etc. Next, light is refracted through the lens, which focuses the light on the tissue at the back of the eye known as the retina. The retina contains light receptors called photoreceptors, which are most densely packed in the small region of the retina known as the fovea. These photoreceptors capture light energy and through a chemical process transduce it into a neural signal that is transmitted by neurons through the optic nerve to the brain.

The neurons that carry signals from the eyes connect to several regions of the brain (see Weiskrantz, 1996). One of those regions is the primary visual cortex, located in the back of the brain. This region is responsible for the early processing of the visual signal and is also involved in visual consciousness. Because visual information falling on adjacent areas of the retina is processed in adjacent areas of the primary visual cortex, this region is said to be retinotopic. If a part of the primary visual cortex is damaged, the result is blindness in the corresponding area of the visual field.

Early on, the visual cortex was believed to be responsible for all visual processing:

> The view was trenchantly held that the visual image on the retina, encoding the many attributes of the visual scene, was transmitted to, and passively analyzed

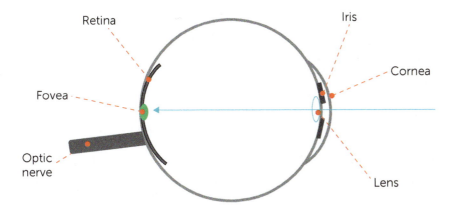

FIGURE 3.1 | The basic anatomy of the eye

The blue arrow represents light energy coming into the eye.

---

cornea

The outer tissue of the eye and the first layer that light passes through on its way to the back of the eye.

pupil

The space through which light passes on its way to the back of the eye; adjusted in size by the iris; to an observer the pupil appears black.

iris

The tissue that surrounds the pupil and is responsible for the distinct colour of the eye.

lens

The transparent tissue in the eye that refracts light and focuses it on the back of the eye.

retina

The tissue at the back of the eye that contains light receptors.

photoreceptors

Cells that transduce light energy into a neural signal.

fovea

The region of the retina where photoreceptors are most densely packed.

primary visual cortex

The area at the back of the brain that is primarily responsible for the basic processing of visual information.

retinotopic

A principle of organization of the primary visual cortex, whereby information falling on adjacent areas of the retina is processed in adjacent areas of the cortex.

by, a single region of visual cortex . . . It was argued that if a single region were responsible for processing the many attributes of the visual scene then damage to this region would compromise the perception of all of them. (Heywood and Zihl, 1999, p.1)

However, later work revealed that the processing of visual information does not stop at the primary visual cortex: in fact, the latter both transmits information to and receives information from several other areas of the brain.

One of the central principles of visual processing in the brain is that it is highly modular: distinct regions of the brain process different aspects of the visual input. For instance, there are specific areas that are involved in processing colour (McKeefry & Zeki, 1997; Zeki & Marini, 1998), and other areas that process object motion (Beckers & Zeki, 1995). We know this in part because neuroimaging studies consistently isolate specific brain areas that correspond to aspects of perceptual experience such as colour and motion, and also because studies have shown that damage to specific areas of the brain has very specific effects on visual experience. For instance, damage to one particular area can result in severe deficits in the person's experience of colour while leaving other perceptional experiences relatively intact. This deficit in colour perception as a result of selective brain damage is known as achromatopsia (Bouvier & Engel, 2006; Zeki, 1990). In his book *An Anthropologist on Mars*, Oliver Sacks (1995), a gifted neurologist and writer, provides a wonderful description of an artist who lost the ability to see colour after suffering a head injury in a car accident ("The Case of the Colorblind Painter," pp. 3–41). Achromatopsia can be contrasted with **akinetopsia** (also known as **motion blindness**: Marcer, Zihl & Cowey, 1997; Zeki, 1991): a condition involving a profound inability to perceive objects in motion. Here is an excerpt from a case study reported by Zihl, Von Cramon and Mai (1983, p. 315):

> The visual disorder complained of by the patient was a loss of movement vision in all three dimensions. She had difficulty, for example, in pouring tea or coffee into a cup because the fluid appeared frozen, like a glacier. In addition, she could not stop pouring at the right time since she was unable to perceive the movement in the cup . . . when the fluid rose.

Over the years researchers have identified a number of specific brain areas that are responsible for processing specific components of visual information. These areas can be organized into two relatively distinct visual processing streams or pathways (see de Haan & Cowey, 2011), depicted in Figure 3.2 (the back of the brain, containing the primary visual cortex, is located on the right). What the figure shows is that visual information processed in the primary visual cortex is then propagated along two paths. One pathway projects towards the inferior temporal lobe of the brain, and is responsible both for processing the visual characteristics of objects, such as their shape and colour, and for assigning meaning to objects; it is often referred to as the ventral or "what" pathway. The other pathway projects to the parietal lobe of the brain and is responsible for processing the spatial aspects of visual information, including object movement and object location, and is involved in guiding action in the world; it is known as the dorsal or "where" pathway. As you might have guessed, people with visual agnosia (one of the conditions described in the opening

achromatopsia

A visual deficit characterized by inability to perceive colour because of damage to the area of the brain that processes colour information.

akinetopsia (motion blindness)

An inability to perceive the motion of objects.

ventral ("what") pathway

The stream of visual processing in the brain that is responsible for determining object shape, colour, and meaningful identity.

dorsal ("where") pathway

The stream of visual processing in the brain that is responsible for determining object location and motion, and which guides action.

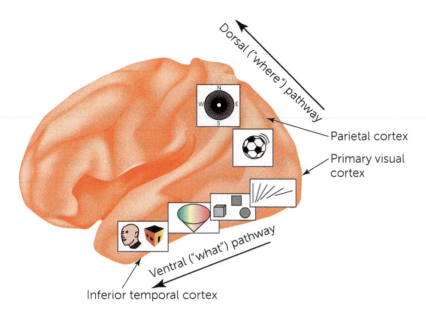

FIGURE 3.2 | The ventral ("what") and dorsal ("where") pathways involved in visual processing

Image adapted from: de Haan, E.H.F., & Cowey, A. (2011), On the usefulness of "what" and "where" pathways in vision, *Trends in Cognitive Neuroscience, 15,* 460–466.

case study) have damage to the ventral ("what") pathway, whereas people with akinetopsia have damage to the dorsal ("where") pathway.

One additional principle of the physiology of vision that we should highlight here is that the connections between visual brain areas are bi-directional. By this we mean that information not only flows from the primary visual cortex to areas in the ventral and dorsal pathways that process more complex aspects of vision, but it also flows in reverse, from the higher level areas back to the primary visual cortex. Lamme and Roelfsema (2000) reviewed a large amount of evidence and concluded that information from the primary visual cortex first propagates down the ventral and dorsal pathways in an initial "**feedforward sweep**" that might take roughly 100 milliseconds. Immediately following this feedforward sweep, and even as information continues to feed forward, regions at the ends of the ventral and dorsal pathways send information back to the primary visual cortex through **re-entrant (feedback) connections** (see also Enns & Di Lollo, 2000). Why is this important? Well, re-entrant pathways allow an observer's expectations and knowledge to influence the early visual processing and bias what is ultimately perceived. The effects of feedforward processing on perceptual experiences are often referred to as "**bottom-up influences**"; those of feedback processing, as "**top-down influences**." According to Pashler, Johnston and Ruthruff (2001), it is probably rare for perception to be determined solely by either bottom-up or top-down processing. Rather, perception, like "[m]ost human behavior[,] would seem to lie in between these two extremes, reflecting the joint impact of high-level goals (so-called top-down influences) and recent stimuli (so-called bottom-up influences)" (Pashler, Johnston, & Ruthruff, 2001, p. 630). In the next section we will discuss various views on how object identification takes place in the ventral stream, the role of feedback connections, and the relation between perception and action involving the dorsal pathway.

feedforward sweep
The propagation of visual information from the primary visual cortex down the "what" and "where" pathways.

re-entrant (feedback) connections
Connections between brain areas that allow the propagation of visual information from the endpoints of the "what" and "where" pathways back to the primary visual cortex.

bottom-up influences
The feedforward influence of the external environment on the resulting perceptual experience.

top-down influences
The feedback influence of context and the individual's knowledge, expectations, and high-level goals on perceptual experience.

The Ventral Pathway and Object Recognition

fusiform face area (FFA)

An area in the inferior temporal cortex that is responsible for the conscious recognition of faces.

prosopagnosia

A selective deficit in the ability to consciously recognize faces resulting from damage to the FFA.

percept

The visual experience of sensory information.

parahippocampal place area (PPA)

An area in the ventral stream that is responsible for the conscious recognition of places.

extrastriate body area (EBA)

An area in the ventral stream that is involved in processing non-facial body parts.

pattern recognition

The ability to recognize an event as an instance of a particular category of event.

memory trace

The trace that an experience leaves behind in memory.

Höffding function

The process whereby an experience makes contact with a memory trace, resulting in recognition.

As we mentioned earlier, the ventral visual pathway is involved in processing the identity of objects. The available neuropsychological evidence suggests that the primary visual cortex processes the basic features of objects (e.g., the orientation of line segments: Hubel & Wiesel 1962) while cells in the ventral stream process more complex aspects, and areas of the inferior temporal cortex are involved in identifying entire objects. For instance, there is considerable evidence that specific areas in the inferior temporal cortex respond selectively to faces. The area specifically responsive to faces is known as the fusiform face area (FFA) because it is located in the fusiform area of the inferior temporal cortex (Kanwisher, McDermott & Chun, 1997). Damage to this area leads to a selective impairment in the recognition of faces known as prosopagnosia (Barton, Press, Keenan, & O'Connor, 2002). People with prosopagnosia can recognize other people by relying on clues such as a unique piercing or distinctive glasses, but cannot combine the features of the face to form a complete percept. Other areas of the temporal lobe are involved in recognizing places (the parahippocampal place area, or PPA; Epstein, Harris, Stanley & Kanwisher, 1999), and body parts other than faces (extrastriate body area, or EBA: Downing, Jiang, Shuman & Kanwisher, 2001; Urgesi, Berlucchi & Aglioti, 2004). While we know that certain brain areas along the ventral pathway are involved in different aspects of object recognition, the details of the process remain something of a mystery.

Researchers in cognitive psychology have explored the way people recognize objects by focusing on pattern recognition. The term pattern recognition comes from computer science, where it refers to a computer's ability to identify configurations such as the account numbers on bank cheques. Humans appear to have a similar ability to identify many of the configurations they encounter. For example, you recognize the components of this sentence as words rather than meaningless squiggles; and when you are confronted with a small cylindrical object with a handle, you recognize it as a *coffee mug*. Currently, machines outperform humans in "highly constrained" situations such as ensuring the alignment of printed labels on medicine bottles, but humans outperform machines in "real-world tasks" such as face recognition (Sinha, 2002).

Recognizing a configuration involves contact between the emerging percept and memory. This process is sketched in Figure 3.3. We can imagine that at some point in your early childhood you were shown the letter *A*. At that time you would have formed first a percept of *A* and then a memory trace of that experience. The phrase "memory trace" simply refers to the trace of an experience that is left in memory (Rock & Ceraso, 1964). In order to *recognize* the letter *A* on some later occasion, your emerging perception of *A* must somehow make contact with its memory trace. The process whereby an emerging perception makes contact with a memory trace is called the Höffding function, named after a nineteenth-century Danish psychologist (Neisser, 1967, p. 50).

Cognitive psychologists have proposed several general theories to understand pattern recognition. Among them are feature detection theory, recognition by components theory, and template matching theory.

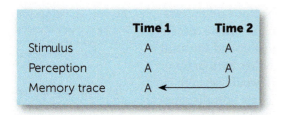

	Time 1	Time 2
Stimulus	A	A
Perception	A	A
Memory trace	A	

FIGURE 3.3 | The Höffding function

From: Asch, S. (1969). A reformulation of the problem of associations. *American Psychologist, 24*, pp. 92–102. Copyright 1969 by the Americal Psychological Association.

Feature Detection

One approach to pattern recognition had its origin in the **feature detection theory** of Selfridge (1959; Neisser, 1967, p. 71). A simple version of this model is called **pandemonium**. It consists of three levels and has a whimsical quality. At the bottom level is the image, or cluster of data, in which a pattern of features is represented. These **features** might include properties such as size, colour, shape, and so on. The next level consists of so-called **cognitive demons** who examine the pattern of features in the image. Each demon is looking to detect a particular pattern. Thus there might be a demon for detecting apples, one for detecting oranges, one for detecting baseballs, and so on. If a cognitive demon thinks that it detects the pattern it has been waiting for, then it shouts. The more similar the pattern in the image is to the one it is looking for, the louder the demon shouts. All the demons may be shouting at the same time with different levels of intensity, depending on the similarity of what they have found to the data in the image. It's because of the ruckus these shouting demons create that the model is called "pandemonium." Sitting above all the hullabaloo is the **decision demon**, who selects the cognitive demon that is shouting loudest. This choice constitutes the pattern that is recognized.

In practice, of course, the process would be much more complicated than this. However, the basic ideas behind Selfridge's model, and others like it, have been very influential. The notion that objects and events are made up of clusters of features, and that we use those clusters to identify them, has been embedded in many theories of pattern recognition.

A study by Pelli, Farell, and Moore (2003) is relevant to the feature detection stage of models such as Selfridge's. They investigated the effect of the contrast between the letters in a word and the background on which they are printed. For example, a grey letter printed on a grey background would be unreadable, a grey letter printed on a white background would be readable, and a black letter on a white background would be more readable still. As Pelli et al. put it, black letters on a white background have more **contrast energy** than grey letters on the same background do. Pelli et al. reported a study in which they varied both contrast energy and word length (the number of letters in a word). Participants were shown common English words varying in length between 2 and 16 letters. Each word was shown on a screen for 200 milliseconds. After each word was shown, the participants were presented with a list of 26 words of the same length as that word and asked to pick out the one they had just seen. All told, the participants were exposed to 26 words for each word length between 2 and 16 letters. Within each set of 26 words, contrast energy was varied, allowing the experimenters to determine how much contrast energy was required for each word length. They found that the contrast energy required for a participant to identify a word was closely related to the length of the word: the more letters it contained, the greater the contrast energy required.

According to Pelli et al., their results showed that letters (as opposed to overall patterns) are crucial features that the visual system attempts to detect during the process of word recognition. Remember that participants were shown a word for only 200 milliseconds. The longer the word, the more letters had to be detected per unit of time. For high contrast-energy words, the signal presented by each letter was strong enough to enable detection even when the presentation was very brief. However, if the contrast energy of individual letters was too low, identifying a large number of them in a short time became too difficult, and the process of word recognition ground to a halt. Letters with low contrast energy are weak signals that the visual system will tend to "squelch," preventing any further processing of features that

feature detection theory
Detecting patterns on the basis of their features or properties.

pandemonium
A model of pattern recognition consisting of three levels: data, cognitive demons, and decision demon.

feature
A component or characteristic of a stimulus.

cognitive demon
A feature detector in the pandemonium model that decides whether the stimulus matches its pattern.

decision demon
A feature detector in the pandemonium model that determines which pattern is being recognized.

contrast energy
The relative ease with which a stimulus can be distinguished from the background against which it is displayed.

are not clearly present. **Squelching** is a reflection of the visual system's preference for rigour in the detection of figures. In refusing to "guess" when it is not sure, the system "achieves reliability at the expense of efficiency.... The human visual system has a vast number of feature detectors, each of which can raise a false alarm, mistaking noise for signal. Squelching blocks the intrusion of countless false features that would besiege us if weak features were not suppressed" (Pelli, Farell, & Moore, 2003, p. 754).

Recognition by Components

A critical issue that feature detection theories must consider is the precise size of the finite set of features from which all objects can be put together. It's relatively easy to compile a list of basic features for letters or words, but what are the fundamental elements for complex three-dimensional objects such as people or automobiles?

To explain how feature analysis could apply to such real-world objects, Biederman (1987) proposed the **recognition by components (RBC)** theory: "when an image of an object is painted on the retina, RBC assumes that a representation of the image is segmented—or parsed—into separate regions at points of deep concavity, particularly at cusps where there are discontinuities in curvature" (p. 117). Biederman hypothesized that this parsing ultimately breaks the object down into its most basic components: a set of three-dimensional shapes that he called "**geons**." Figure 3.4 shows how just two of the set of 36 fundamental geons (a rectangle and a cylinder) can be used to create an image of an object as complex as a tractor. Once objects are reduced to their constituent geons, the theory states that the resulting geons are compared with existing geon configurations stored in memory. When a reasonable match is made between input and memory, you recognize the object.

Biederman and his colleagues hypothesized that if objects are parsed into geons, then object recognition should be a function of the number of geons available to perceive. To verify

FIGURE 3.4 | **A tractor made from two geons (a cylinder and rectangle) for an annual fall fair near Fergus, Ontario**

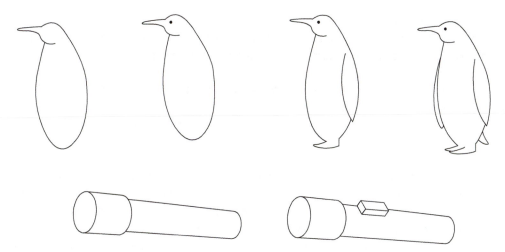

FIGURE 3.5 | Objects with different degrees of complexity represented by a varying number of geons

Adapted from: Biederman, I. (1987). Recognition-by-components: A theory of human image understanding. *Psychological Review, 24*, 2, pp. 122–3. Copyright © 1987 the American Psychological Association.

this hypothesis they conducted an experiment in which they varied the *number* of geons used to depict a given object. Figure 3.5 shows two of the objects they constructed (a penguin and a flashlight) from different numbers of components. In addition, they varied the *complexity* of the objects. More complex objects, such as the penguin on the right, needed more geons (nine, in this case) than less complex ones, such as the three-geon flashlight. The objects were flashed for only 100 milliseconds and then covered up to interrupt perceptual processing. Participants were then asked to name the object as quickly and accurately as possible.

Overall, the results showed that people were quite good at recognizing objects represented by only two or three geons; accuracy was around 80 per cent at the worst. It also turned out that recognition ability improved progressively when more geons were used to add detail. Thus accuracy increased for the more detailed penguin images. In addition, contrary to what intuition might suggest, Biederman found that more complex objects (e.g., penguin) were recognized more efficiently than less complex ones (e.g., flashlight). It seems reasonable that more complex objects, since they contain more information, should require more processing and hence more time, but obviously this is not the case. What complexity and detail provide is more geons, and more geons lead to better recognition. With this and many other studies, Biederman and his colleagues made a strong case that deconstructing objects into geons is a critical component of object recognition.

Template Matching

According to the *Oxford English Dictionary*, the word *template* originally meant a "gauge or a guide to be used in bringing a piece of work to its desired shape." Such a guide might have edges corresponding to the outline of the finished product. For example, if you were painting a sign, you might make a cut-out, or stencil, of the letters you wanted to use. The cut-out is a template. It's possible that we store templates in memory that correspond to the standard forms of the configurations we see. The process of template matching would involve comparing the current configuration with the standard or **prototypical** forms that we have in memory. Thus a letter can take any one of many different forms. Here is the first letter of the alphabet, in lower-case, printed in several different fonts:

$$a \quad a \quad \textbf{\textit{a}} \quad a \quad \textup{a} \quad a$$

According to **template-matching theory**, we would *compare* each *a* with the prototypical *a* that we have in memory; then, if the match is good enough, we would recognize the letter.

Although superficially plausible, template matching is a difficult process to spell out in detail (e.g., Hofstadter, 1982). The prototypical pattern must differ somewhat from the particular patterns we perceive, just as each *a* in the example above differs from the others. As Uhr (1966, pp. 372ff.) observed, the problem is to specify how a template can match not only patterns that are identical to it, but also patterns that are *similar enough* to it. It's not easy to spell out the characteristics that a pattern must have to qualify as a "similar enough" match to a template. For this reason template models have often been criticized. Nevertheless, the hypothesis that we see things as similar to one another because they resemble an underlying prototype is one that, in various forms, has been extensively investigated.

One approach to the role of prototypes in recognition comes from Hintzman (1986; Hintzman, Curran, & Oppy, 1992), who proposed a **multiple-trace memory model** that accounts for prototype effects in an interesting way. Hintzman's multiple-trace model assumes that traces of each individual experience are recorded in memory. No matter how often a particular kind of event is experienced, a memory trace of the event is recorded every time it is experienced.

Hintzman's approach distinguishes between primary and secondary memory. As we saw in Chapter 1, primary memory is what we are aware of at any point in time, whereas secondary memory refers to all the memory traces created out of all the experiences we have had. Secondary memory can be activated by means of a **probe** from primary memory. According to Hintzman (1986, p. 412), "The probe is an active representation of an experience" in primary memory. When a probe goes out from primary to secondary memory, memory traces are activated to the extent that they are similar to the probe. The activated memory traces are said to return an **echo** to primary memory. The echo is made up of contributions from all the activated memory traces.

Hintzman suggested that one way to understand what he meant by the term *echo* would be to think of listening to a choir. Instead of hearing only one voice in response to a probe of memory, we may hear an entire chorus of voices if many memory traces are similar to the current experience. In such a chorus, the properties of individual memory traces will tend to be lost, and only a general impression of what they all have in common will remain.

Hintzman used his theory to explain the results of classic studies by Posner and various colleagues (Posner, Goldsmith, & Welton, 1967; Posner & Keele, 1968, 1970). In these experiments, participants were shown distortions of several prototypical patterns (for examples

prototypical

Representative of a pattern or category.

template-matching theory

The hypothesis that the process of pattern recognition relies on the use of templates or prototypes.

multiple-trace memory model

Traces of each individual experience are recorded in memory. No matter how often a particular kind of event is experienced, a memory trace of the individual event is recorded each time.

probe

A "snapshot" of information in primary memory that can activate memory traces in secondary memory.

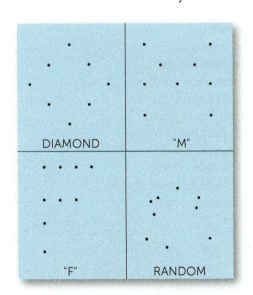

FIGURE 3.6 | Prototypical patterns

From: Posner, M.I., Goldsmith, R., & Welton, K.E. (1967). Perceived distance and the classification of distorted patterns. *Journal of Experimental Psychology, 73*, 28–38. Copyright 1967 by the American Psychological Association.

of the prototypes see Figure 3.6). These distortions were formed by randomly moving the dots away from their positions in the prototype (Figure 3.7). Posner and Keele (1968, p. 359) referred to each set of the distortions derived from a given prototype as a "concept." Participants were shown the "concepts" (i.e., the distortions of the various prototypes) but did not see the prototypes themselves. Later they were required to classify another set of patterns into the various "concepts." This time, however, the patterns consisted of the prototypes, the original distortions, and some new distortions of the prototypes. The interesting result was that the prototypical patterns were quite well classified, even though they had never been seen before. In another experiment, Posner (1969) showed that participants sometimes misidentified the prototype as a pattern they had seen before, even though they had previously seen only distortions of it.

Hintzman explained Posner's findings as follows. The memory traces of the set of distorted patterns produce an echo based on what the different distortions have in common, rather than the peculiarities of each individual distortion. Therefore the prototype is recognized even though it has never been seen before. An interesting implication of this approach is that once an echo has been experienced in primary memory, it can leave a memory trace of itself in secondary memory. In this way, relatively abstract experiences can later be directly remembered as "echoes of echoes" (cf. Goldinger, 1998).

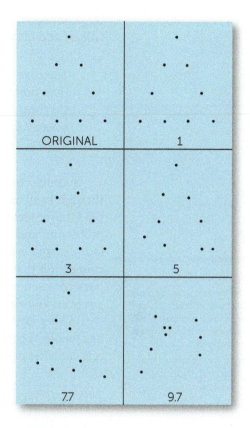

FIGURE 3.7 | A set of distortions of a prototype

From: Posner, M.I., Goldsmith, R., & Welton, K.E. (1967). Perceived distance and the classification of distorted patterns. *Journal of Experimental Psychology, 73*, 28–38. Copyright 1967 by the American Psychological Association.

Context and Feedback Effects in Perception

Thus far we have considered how percepts might be formed from the combination of specific perceptual components (e.g., features, geons). The implied assumption in the views we have discussed thus far has been that the processing of perceptual components is independent of the context in which the components appear. However, there is considerable evidence now that the context in which an object appears is critically important for determining the final conscious percept of it. Bar (2004) suggests that context effects are likely very common:

> Recognizing someone's hand, for instance, significantly limits the possible interpretations of the object on that person's wrist to either a watch or a bracelet; it is not likely to be a chair or an elephant. This *a priori* knowledge allows the visual system to sensitize the corresponding visual representations of a watch and a bracelet so that it is easier to recognize the surrounding objects when we attend to them (p. 617).

There are at least two ways in which context effects can occur in the visual system. First, the perception of a visual component can be influenced by its neighbours through

echo
When a probe goes out from primary to secondary memory, memory traces are activated to the extent that they are similar to the probe.

context effects
The change in perception of a visual component of a scene based on the surrounding information in the scene and the observer's prior knowledge.

interconnections among neighbouring neurons in primary visual cortex. According to Gilbert and Li (2013, p. 351):

> There is an emerging view that in the early stages of visual … processing, rather than doing a local analysis of simple features, neurons can integrate information over large parts of the visual field and that neurons in these areas can show selectivity for complex stimulus configurations. The integrative properties of cortical neurons are reflected in their selectivity for stimulus context.

Second, contextual information can influence perception of a visual component through feedback connections between later processing areas in the ventral stream (e.g., the inferior temporal cortex) that are sensitive to broader aspects of a scene and the early processing area (the primary visual cortex) that processes image features. Gilbert and Li (2013, p. 350) note that "for every feedforward connection, there is a reciprocal feedback connection that carries information about the behavioral context." Through these feedback connections, our perception of the elements of a visual scene can be influenced by our prior knowledge and expectations.

In this section we consider several classic demonstrations of the impact that context and feedback connections can have on perception. One interesting example of the way context can alter perception is the phenomenon known as the **moon illusion** (Box 3.1).

Perceptual Grouping and Gestalt Psychology

If the context in which the visual components of a scene are embedded influences the way they are perceived, then perception of the scene cannot be predicted simply by considering those components in isolation. This general observation was highlighted by the Gestalt school of psychology (e.g., Koffka, 1922; Köhler, 1969), which we encountered in Chapter 2 in our discussion of the Necker cube and the concept of isomorphism. According to Gaetano Kanizsa (1979, p. 56), a later member of the movement:

> "Gestalt" ought to be translated as "organized structure," as distinguished from "aggregate," "heap," or simply "summation." When it is appropriately translated, the accent is on the concept of "organization" and of a "whole" that is *orderly, rule-governed, nonrandom*.

As Kanizsa's definition suggests, the Gestalt movement believed that perception is **holistic** (focusing on whole objects) in nature rather than **atomistic** (focusing on features or elements), and that the **grouping** of visual features to form a whole follows certain fundamental **organizational principles** (i.e., rules or laws; see also Wagemans et al., 2012). Because of its focus on the idea that the whole of an object cannot be predicted by the individual features from which it is composed, Gestalt psychology can be thought of as highlighting the importance of context on perception.

We will discuss a few of the Gestalt organizational principles, focusing on those reviewed by Katz (1951) and Wagemans et al. (2012, p. 1180). Although early Gestalters put less emphasis on it than later ones did, let's begin with the **principle of experience**. According to this principle, we organize components into whole objects based on our prior experience

moon illusion
The tendency for the moon to appear different in size depending on whether it is near the horizon or high in the night sky.

holistic
Focusing on the entire configuration of an object.

atomistic
Focusing on the components of objects.

grouping
The combination of individual components to form a percept of a whole object.

organizational principles
The rules (or laws) that govern the perception of whole objects or events from a collection of individual components or features.

principle of experience
Visual components are grouped together based on the prior experience and knowledge of the observer.

COGNITION IN ACTION
BOX 3.1

The Moon Illusion

Children are often amazed at how large the moon can look at times. When parents are asked to explain why sometimes the moon looks larger than other times, many are caught off guard and make up explanations—that the atmosphere somehow distorts the size of the moon, or that the moon moves closer and farther away from the earth in the course of an elliptical orbit. You can prove to yourself that these explanations are incorrect simply by taking photos of the moon at moments in its orbit. When you look at the photos you will find that the moon is always the same size (see Enns, 2004, p. 303; Rock & Kaufman, 1962). And don't be tricked by professional photos with large-looking moons: those are created by overlaying a zoomed shot of the moon onto a photo of a landscape taken with a lens that has a wider angle. It turns out that the notion of a moon that changes size is a perceptual error referred to as the moon illusion.

One promising explanation of the moon illusion takes into account the visual context in which the moon appears (see Enns, 2004; Rock & Kaufman, 1962; Kaufman & Kaufman, 1999). The moon typically looks larger when it is near the horizon than when it is high in the sky. When it's near the horizon, the moon is close to various objects that we can use to judge its distance from us. When the horizon moon is compared to the objects on the earth, the visual system assumes that it is very far away—much farther than when it is high in the sky. The visual system further assumes that if the moon at the horizon is farther away than the moon when it is high in the sky, but the images projected into your eye (as on the sensor of a camera) are the same size, the horizon moon must in reality be substantially bigger. With these assumptions in mind, your visual system compensates and makes the moon close to the horizon seem a lot bigger. This explanation is known as the **apparent-distance theory** (see Kaufman & Rock, 1962; Kaufman & Kaufman, 1999) and is illustrated in Figure 3.8 (for a similar depiction see Enns, 2004, p. 304). There is a quick experiment you can do that may convince you the apparent-distance theory is likely correct (see Kaufman & Rock, 1962; Kaufman & Kaufman, 1999). The next time you see a large moon at the horizon, just occlude the objects on the earth from view and you will likely see the moon illusion disappear. The moon illusion is an excellent example of how context affects perception.

apparent-distance theory

An explanation for the moon illusion based on the idea that the perceived size of the moon depends on the assumptions the visual system makes about the distance of the moon from the observer.

✦ DISCOVERY LAB

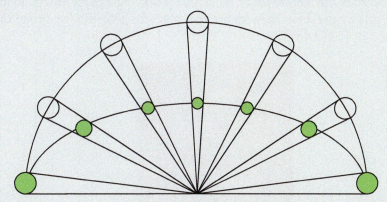

FIGURE 3.8 | The real (white circles) and perceived (green circles) distance and size of the moon according to the apparent-distance theory

From: Kaufman, L., & Kaufman, J.H. (1999). Explaining the moon illusion. *Proceedings of the National Academy of Sciences, 97,* 1, 500–5. Copyright 1999, National Academy of Sciences, USA.

FIGURE 3.9 | Do you see a face, or just a bunch of fruit, vegetables, and flowers?

with objects in the world. This principle is at play when you view the painting entitled "Vertumnus," created around 1590 by Giuseppe Arcimbaldo (see Figure 3.9). As you can see, the image is composed entirely of fruit, vegetables, and flowers. However, our prior experience with faces leads us to interpret the organization of those components into a face (albeit a funny looking one). In modern terms, the principle of experience likely operates through feedback connections from areas in the inferior temporal cortex responsible for face perception to the area responsible for parsing the visual components of the painting.

Although the early Gestalters acknowledged the role of prior experience, they quite often downplayed its role. As Köhler (1928, p. 208) observed more than 80 years ago:

That meaning automatically produces a form where beforehand there is none, has not been shown experimentally in a single case, as far as I know. It may be that in a very *unstable* constellation, in which a certain form can be seen or organized, past experience of such a form will tend to produce it really, whereas without that previous experience, this would not happen. Even in this case, however, we would still have to explain what factors produced that form in previous life.

Gestalters such as Köhler were interested in much more *fundamental* laws of perceptual organization, ones that ultimately give rise to recognizable objects. To illustrate these, they often used very simple and meaningless visual components and showed that their grouping depends on how they are arranged, with even subtle changes in the arrangement of the components leading to vastly different perceptions of them as a whole (Katz, 1951; Palmer, 1999; Wagemans et al., 2012). For example, in Figure 3.10a you likely perceive the pattern as consisting of groups of four letters (Xs and Os) making a checkerboard pattern. This demonstrates the **principle of similarity**, according to which "all else being equal, the most similar elements (in colour, size, and orientation . . .) tend to be grouped together" (Wagemans et al., 2012, p. 1180). It's easy to find examples of this principle in everyday life. For instance, when you're leaving a party and go to look for your shoes in the pile by the door, chances are that you will perceptually group the similar-looking shoes

principle of similarity
Visual features that have a high degree of visual similarity are combined.

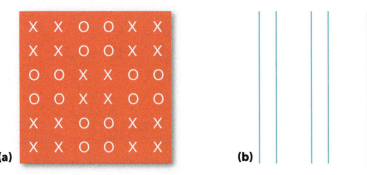

FIGURE 3.10 | The principles of similarity (a) and proximity (b)

Panel B adapted from: Katz, D. (1951). *Gestalt psychology: Its nature and significance.* London: Methuen.

together. As another example, Figure 3.10b illustrates our tendency to combine visual components based on how close they are to each other in space; this is known as the **principle of proximity**. Thus in the figure the lines that are close to one another seem to be paired, whereas the lines spaced more widely apart do not.

Some of the Gestalt rules apply to "the perceptual grouping of more complex elements, such as lines and curves" (Wagemans et al., 2012, p.1180). These include the principles of **symmetry**, whereby lines that are symmetrical in nature are combined to form a single percept, and **parallelism**, whereby lines that undulate in a parallel or similar fashion are perceived as going together (see Wagemans et al., 2012; Palmer, 1999). These principles are illustrated in Figures 3.11a and 3.11b respectively.

In general, the Gestalt demonstrations of the basic principles of organization show that the context of visual components of a scene play an important role in how the scene is perceived. Many of these organizational principles likely involve the interaction between neighbouring neurons (even distant neighbours) in the primary visual cortex, though some (like the principle of experience) would likely involve feedback from later visual areas in the ventral stream to the primary area (i.e., the primary visual cortex).

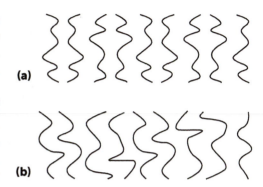

FIGURE 3.11 | The principles of symmetry (a) and parallelism (b)

From Wagemans, J., Elder, J.H., Kubovy, M., Palmer, S.E., Peterson, M., Singh, M., & von der Heydt, R. (2012), A century of Gestalt psychology in visual perception: I, Perceptual grouping and figure-ground organization, *Psychological Bulletin, 138*, 1172–1217, Figure 1 (p.1180).

Figure–Ground Segmentation

Feedback connections from later to earlier processing areas in the ventral stream also seem to play an important role in our ability to segment a scene into a figural object and a backdrop or ground on which it is superimposed (Poort et al., 2012; Roelfsema et al., 2002). This **figure–ground segmentation (segregation)** (Poort et al., 2012) is illustrated in the images shown in Figure 3.12, which for most people lead to perception of objects placed against a backdrop.

How does this figure–ground segmentation occur? The Gestalt psychologists "found that small, convex, and symmetric image regions are usually perceived as figures whereas large, concave and asymmetric regions are often perceived as background" (Poort et al., 2012). However, these characteristics do not always define a figure: the stimuli shown in Figure 3.12, for instance, were designed so that the two regions in each panel were roughly equal in visual characteristics such as size, curvature and symmetry. Rather, Peterson and Gibson (1993) found that the regions usually perceived as the objects in those images are the ones with higher **denotivity**—that is, those that appear more familiar and meaningful to the observer. The results of Peterson and Gibson's study strongly suggest that the way we segment a visual scene into figural object and background is influenced by our knowledge of and familiarity with objects in the world.

To explain all the available findings regarding figure–ground segmentation, Roelfsema and colleagues (2002) proposed a model that relies on feedback connections in the brain. According to their model, the primary visual cortex contain neurons that respond to specific features of the visual array. These neurons are interconnected with each other, and their interconnections allow them to change their activity so that the edges (discontinuities in textures) are emphasized. This information about features and edges is then fed forward to later visual areas in the ventral stream, which code for broader object information,

principle of proximity
Visual components that are close to one another are grouped to form a whole.

principle of symmetry
Symmetrical lines are perceived as going together.

principle of parallelism
Lines that are parallel or similar in orientation are perceived as going together.

figure–ground segmentation (segregation)
The separation of a scene such that one component of the scene becomes a figural object and the other component(s) become(s) the backdrop.

denotivity
The degree to which an object is meaningful and familiar to an individual observer.

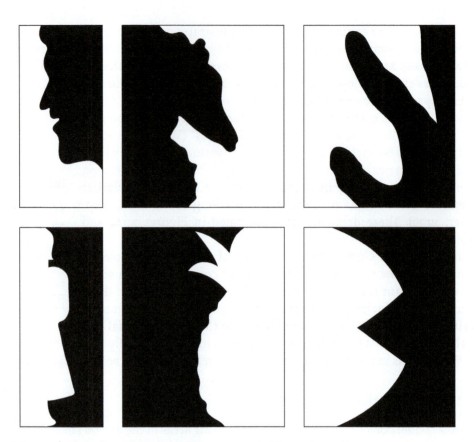

FIGURE 3.12 | The stimuli used by Peterson and Gibson (1993)

The top three panels show stimuli in which the black regions are high in denotivity and the bottom three panels show stimuli in which the white regions are high in denotivity.

From: Peterson, M.A., & Gibson, B.S. (1993).

responding to specific regions in an image. The later visual areas then send information back to the primary visual area through feedback pathways. "The feedback pathway ensures that responses to the entire figural region are enhanced relative to responses from the background" (Roelfsema et al., 2002, p. 529). In many cases, this process may not include the very late areas in the ventral stream such as the inferior temporal cortex; however, when denotivity is used for segmentation, feedback from the inferior temporal cortex (which codes for object meaning) likely plays an important role.

Letters in Context

Let us now move away from simple patterns and consider the role of context in perceiving letters and words. A profound example of the effect of context on word and letter perception is the **jumbled word effect** (Grainger & Whitney, 2004). Conisder soemhting lkie tihs senetnece. Even though the letters are mixed up within the words, you can easily make sense of the sentence. (Does this mean that all the time you spent learning to spell was wasted?) How is this possible? One of the reasons may already have occurred to you: your expectations help you to determine what the words actually are.

jumbled word effect
The ability to raed wdors in steentnces evne wnhe smoe of the ltteers rea mexid up.

Another well-documented example of how letter perception is affected by context is the **word superiority effect** (Reicher, 1969): the finding that it is easier to perceive a letter correctly when it appears in a real word than when it appears in a non-word. Remarkably, it is even easier to perceive a letter in a word than a letter alone. This effect might occur because after "years of fast reading" we are able to "more efficiently map strings of tentatively identified letters to real words" (Pelli, Farell, & Moore, 2003, p. 755).

word superiority effect
It's easier to identify a letter (e.g., *p*) if it appears in a word (e.g., *warp*) than if it appears alone.

Colour in Context

✦ **DISCOVERY LAB**

Colour vision is another domain where context influences perception. It's tempting to think that when we look at the world, the colours we see are determined only by the wavelengths of light that are reflected from surfaces. Contrary to this intuition, however, what you see can depend on the context.

An interesting recent example involves a photograph (Figure 3.13) that was posted online with this plea: "guys please help me—is this dress white and gold, or blue and black? Me and my friends can't agree and we are freaking the f*** out" (http://swiked.tumblr.com). The photo went viral, and so did the debate. Why was there so much disagreement?

Part of the answer can be found in a comic about the dress at the website xkcd.com (Figure 3.14). As you can see, the dress on the left looks white and gold, whereas the one on the right looks blue and black (to most people). However, if you were to occlude everything in the image except for the two dresses, you would realize that the two versions are exactly the same colour (and both match the colours of the original dress shown in the middle of the cartoon). What makes them look different is the fact that they are displayed against different

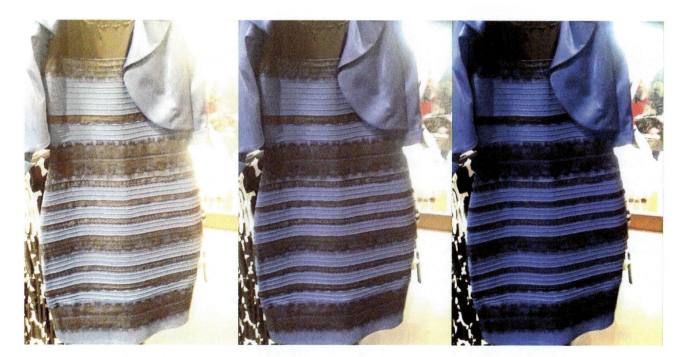

FIGURE 3.13 | Does this dress look white and gold or blue and black?

background colours: blue on the left and light beige on the right. These different background colours give the visual system two different ideas of the type of light that might be illuminating the two dresses, and the visual system adjusts the colour it perceives on the dresses accordingly. Critically, this shows that your perception of colour depends not only on the wavelengths of light reflecting from objects and entering your eye, but also on the colour information provided by the context. Even so, there is one more factor that comes into play, and the dress mystery underlines its importance.

Purves and Lotto (2003) provide many examples of similar colour illusions (available at www.purveslab.net/see-for-yourself/). To explain them, they developed a theory that they call an **empirical theory of colour vision**. The basic idea is that our perception of colour depends on our prior experience with how objects look when they are viewed among different objects and under various lighting conditions. This implies that colour perception is not solely the result of the patterns of light reflected from objects; context and, crucially, prior experience are part of the equation as well, and all these factors together create the final percept. So, the differences in perception of the dress colour in the viral photo are likely due to individual differences in (a) prior experience with the way different illuminations affect colour perception, and (b) the inferences that the visual system makes as a result. For another example of how prior experience influences our perception, see Box 3.2.

FIGURE 3.14 | Do the two dresses in this comic look different?

Image source: http://xkcd.com/1492/

empirical theory of colour vision

The theory that colour perception is influenced by prior experience with the way different illuminations affect colour.

CONSIDER THIS
BOX 3.2

Perceiving Causes in Object Movement

Take a moment to examine the displays shown in the four panels of Figure 3.15. The panels are meant to depict a sequence of images taken from various moments of a continuous movie used in a study reported by White and Milne (1999). The movie shows a horizontal bar starting on the left side of the display and a circle of balls sitting statically in the middle (Panel A). The bar then begins to move to the right until it makes contact with the circle of balls in the middle of the screen (Panel B). The bar stops and the balls begin to disperse (Panel C), moving from the centre of the display to the periphery (Panel D). In a series of conditions, White and Milne (1999) varied the relative movement speeds of the bar before contact and of the balls after contact.

As you can see, the objects in the displays are very simple and the sequence could just be showing a series of objects moving independently of each other. However, the evidence suggests that people favour a causal interpretation. To demonstrate this preference, White and Milne (1999, p. 503) asked participants to rate the extent to which each of the following descriptions captured the sequence of events they had seen:

(1) the bar "smashes" the circle of balls "to pieces by hitting it";
(2) the circle of balls "explodes or pops when contacted by" the bar; or
(3) the circle of balls "disintegrates of its own accord."

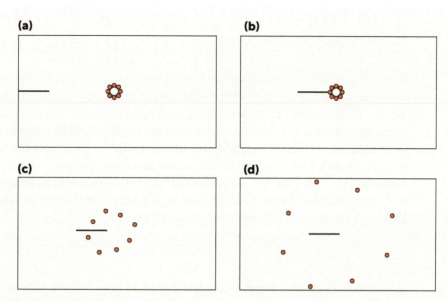

FIGURE 3.15 | A sequence of computer displays showing a bar moving from left to right and then hitting a circle of balls, which disperse

From White, P.A., & Milne, A. (1999), Impressions of enforced disintegration and bursting in the visual perception of collision events, *Journal of Experimental Psychology: General, 128*, 499–516.

Participants rated their experience on a scale ranging from "completely disagree" (a rating score of "0") to "completely agree" (a rating score of "100"). The results showed that participants' ratings depended on the relative speeds of the bar and the balls after contact. Interestingly, in some conditions, the participants favoured a causal interpretation. For instance, when the speed of the bar was slow (5.4 cm/s) and the speed of the balls was medium (13.5 cm/s), participants generally agreed that the circle of balls exploded or popped when it was contacted by the bar, with average agreement of about 71 on the rating scale. The ratings for the other options in this condition were significantly lower: the idea that the circle disintegrated of its own accord received an average rating of 25, and the idea that it was "smashed" averaged only about 18. White and Milne (1999) described the impression people have of this sequence of events as *"bursting."*

Interestingly, White and Milne's (1999) study was just one in a rapidly growing body of literature, largely motivated by the early work of Michotte (1963), which showed that people were quick to infer causality from simple events and also to attribute animacy to inanimate objects depending on the movements of the objects

(see Scholl & Tremoulet [2000] for a review). For example, Scholl and Tremoulet (2000, p. 299) had participants view the following sequence of events:

Two small squares are sitting in a line, separated by several inches. The first square (A) begins moving in a straight line towards the second square (B). As soon as A gets close to B, B begins moving quickly away from A in a random direction, until it is again several inches from A, at which point it stops. A continues all the while to move straight towards B's position, wherever that is at any given moment. This pattern repeats several times.

When viewing this sequence of events, participants reported a strong sense that the two objects were "alive" and that square A was pursuing square B, which (who?) was trying to get away. That is, the viewers inferred that the squares had intentions! That we would perceive causation in the movements of inanimate objects and attribute intentions to them further supports the notion that knowledge and expectations influence our perception of the world.

The Dorsal Pathway and the Relation between Perception and Action

According to the Canadian vision researcher Melvyn Goodale (Western University), one key function of the dorsal ("where") pathway is to support the individual's visually guided actions in the world. This idea makes sense given the aspects of visual stimuli that this pathway is involved in processing, such as the location and movement of objects in the environment, since this is the kind of information that we need in order to take action. In this section we will first consider several cases involving patients with brain damage, which compellingly illustrate the involvement of the dorsal pathway in perception for action. We will then consider the views of J.J. Gibson, a perception researcher who is well known for making a strong link between perception and action.

Patient Studies

In a seminal research paper published in the journal *Nature*, Goodale, Milner, Jakobson and Carey (1991) reported a study of a woman suffering from visual agnosia. This patient, referred to as DF, was unable to identify objects visually as a result of damage in the ventral stream of perception, but was nevertheless able to act on objects (e.g., reach for them) with considerable precision because her spared dorsal stream of perception was intact. To demonstrate this, Goodale and colleagues had DF and two other people without brain damage (control participants referred to as CG and CJ) complete a set of tasks that tested their perception for the orientation of objects. In one task, participants were given a card and shown a slot roughly an arm's length away. Each participant was asked to keep the card close to her body (away from the slot) and to tilt it to match the orientation of the slot. The orientation of the slot was varied over successive trials.

Figure 3.16A shows the performance of each participant. The columns in the figure correspond to slots of different orientations, ranging from 0 degrees (horizontal) to an angle of 150 degrees. The triangle beside each circle shows the correct orientation of the slot, and the lines within the circle show the orientations of the various attempts made by the participant at matching the orientation of the slot. As you can see, the two control participants were able to match the orientation of every slot almost perfectly. By contrast, DF's accuracy was very poor, highlighting her visual agnosia.

Based on her performance in Figure 3.16A, you might think that DF had a fundamental problem with her overall ability to perceive objects. However, part B of the figure shows that when she was asked to place the card into the slot, her ability to match the orientation was almost equal to that of the two control participants. Based on these results, Goodale and

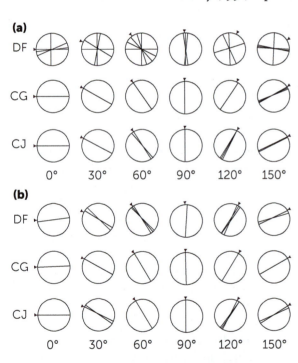

FIGURE 3.16 | Judgment of the orientation of a slot simulated close to the body (Panel A) and the orientation of a card as it is moved towards the slot in an act of placing the card into the slot (Panel B)

The data are for patient DF and two control participants (CG and CJ).

From Goodale, M.A., Milner, A.D., Jakobson, L.S., & Carey, D.P. (1991), A neurological dissociation between perceiving objects and grasping them, *Nature, 349*, 154–156.

his colleagues (1991, p. 155) concluded that DF's "difficulty" was limited to "using visual orientation information for perceptual or cognitive purposes" and that she was able to use such information "accurately . . . in visuomotor action."

Goodale and his colleagues noted that DF's visual agnosia could be contrasted with a fascinating condition known as optic ataxia, which is an inability to properly reach for objects, particularly those in the periphery of vision, accompanied by unimpaired ability to identify them visually (see Jakobson, Archibald, Carey & Goodale, 1991). For instance, Jakobson and colleagues (1991) reported a case study of a patient identified as VK, who was able to identify objects correctly, but was unable to properly modulate the grip aperture (the distance between the thumb and index figure) when attempting to grasp them. Figure 3.17 shows the grip aperture corresponding to the grasping movements of VK and two control participants (LK and BS) as they reached for a block that was 100 mm in width. The horizontal axis in the figure depicts the

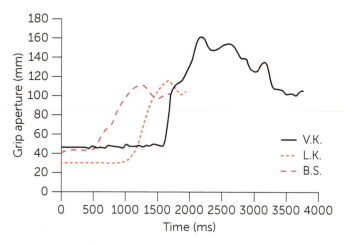

FIGURE 3.17 | **Changes in grip aperture over time as patient VK and two control participants (LK and BS) reached to take hold of an object**

From Jakobson, L.S., Archibald, Y.M., Carey, D.P., & Goodale, M.A. (1991), A kinematic analysis of reaching and grasping movements in a patient recovering from optic ataxia, *Neuropsychologia, 29*, 803–809: Figure 2 (p. 808).

unfolding of time over the course of the reaching movement. Notice that VK's maximum grip aperture is much greater than that of the control participants, and the reduction of the aperture as the patient is about to grip the object takes longer and includes many small adjustments. These results confirm that VK's grasping movements were impaired relative to those of the control participants. As you might have guessed, VK's optic ataxia was caused by damage to the dorsal visual pathway. Patients with optic ataxia are able to identify and describe objects correctly because their ventral visual pathway is unimpaired.

J.J. Gibson's Ecological Optics: Perception for Action

Long before the ventral and dorsal pathways were identified, the pre-eminent perception researcher J.J. Gibson (1961, 1966) proposed that a primary role of perception is to drive action. Gibson's (1961) theory of ecological optics focused on the idea that in real-world situations, the sensory organs are stimulated by energy coming from the environment, and that this energy contains systematic information which can be used to guide action. We first encountered Gibson in Chapter 1, when we discussed his concept of affordances—opportunities for action provided by objects in the environment. For instance, a small rock affords throwing but a large boulder does not (the small rock is the right size for your hand, while the large boulder is not). Gibson's views in this regard imply a tight coupling between perception and action; in fact, he argued that a key purpose of perception is to allow and guide action.

In a series of influential studies, Tucker and Ellis (1998, 2001, 2004) had participants respond to images that afforded a particular type of action (e.g., using the right hand as opposed to the left hand to grasp an object that is facing to the right, such as the handle of a hammer). They observed faster response times and fewer errors when

optic ataxia

A condition characterized by a deficit in the ability to successfully reach for objects, especially when they are presented in the periphery of vision, with unimpaired ability to identify them.

theory of ecological optics

The proposition that perception results from direct contact of the sensory organs with stimulus energy emanating from the environment and that an important goal of perception is action.

participants were instructed to respond with the afforded effector (e.g., the right hand for a hammer that has the handle facing to the right), even though the tasks (e.g., to determine which objects are manufactured vs. natural) were completely unrelated. In fact, other research has demonstrated that action affordances can be observed even when participants are shown still photos of well-known athletes who are associated with a particular action (e.g., hitting a tennis ball or kicking a soccer ball), but not actually performing it (Sinnett, Hodges, Chua, & Kingstone, 2011). For instance, responses to tennis and soccer players are faster when participants are instructed to respond using the effector associated with each sport (i.e., the hand or foot respectively).These effects, and others, have led to an emerging viewpoint in cognitive psychology that the mind's representation of objects might be rooted in action (see, for example, Beilock & Holt, 2007; Clark, 1999; di Pellegrino, Rafal, & Tipper, 2005; Stanfield & Zwaan, 2001; Zwaan, 2004; Zwaan, Madden, Yaxley, & Aveyard, 2004).

Gibson believed that the energy coming into the visual system was all that was needed to guide action, and that complex processing of this stimulation into conscious experience was not necessary. Gibson expressed the relationship between external stimulation and perception as follows: "perception is the function of stimulation and stimulation is a function of the environment; hence perception is a function of the environment" (Gibson, 1959, p. 459). He also believed that "all processes for explaining the conversion of sensory data into percepts are superfluous. No process of conversion is assumed" (Gibson, 1959, p. 460). In other words, Gibson believed perception to be accomplished mainly by the sensory organs themselves, without any extensive internal processing of the incoming information. The point is captured in the title of his influential book *The Senses Considered as Perceptual Systems* (Gibson, 1966). Of course, we now know (through neuroimaging and patient studies like the ones described earlier) that the sensory information that comes in through the eyes is processed as it is propagated down the two visual streams. So in some ways Gibson's theory is incorrect. However, in drawing attention to the critical role that perception plays in supporting action, it continues to be very influential.

As an example of the information in the environment that can be directly used to drive action, Gibson pointed to the patterns in light that are reflected from surfaces and the objects around us. He referred to the panorama of visual information available as we look out at the world from any given position as the **ambient optical array (AOA)**, or the ambient array (see Gibson, 1966). Gibson noted that from every individual viewing point, the pattern of light that enters the eyes is unique because it is reflected from and emitted by a unique combination of surfaces. Furthermore, as we move through the environment, the pattern of light hitting our eyes is continually changing and guiding action (e.g., further movement) in the world. The change in the way all surfaces project light on the retina as the individual moves through space is referred to as a **transformation** of the optic array (Gibson, 1966). The focus on movement led to the concept of the **optic flow field**—the continually changing (i.e., transforming) pattern of information in the AOA that results from the movement of either objects or the observer through an environment (see Lee, 1980).

For example, consider what happens when you walk on a brick road (see Figure 3.18). If you stand on a brick road and look down at your feet, you will see that the bricks are

---

ambient optical array (AOA)

All the visual information that is present at a particular point of view.

transformation

Gibson's (1966) term for the changes in the optical information hitting the eye that occur as the observer moves through the environment.

optic flow field

The continually changing (i.e., transforming) pattern of information that results from the movement of either objects or the observer through the environment.

FIGURE 3.18 | Brick walkway, Distillery District, Toronto

rectangles of roughly equal size. If you looking down the road, however, you will see that the rectangles gradually morph into progressively smaller parallelograms. As Gibson (1950) noted, the density of the components (in this case bricks) increases. The incremental changes in the density of the bricks are **gradients of texture density** (Gibson, 1950, see also Rosenholtz & Malik, 1997; Pike & Edgar, 2005). As you walk along the road, the dense parallelograms that were some distance in front of you now appear as larger, less dense rectangles under your feet. This tells your visual system that the bricks are actually equal in size. At the same time, the density gradient conveys important information regarding the slant of the surface, helping you to navigate it safely. Gibson also noted that when two different textures intersect, they create a discontinuity in the pattern, which he called a **topological breakage** (see Figure 3.19). Topological breakage gives us useful information about the edges of objects (Gibson, 1966)—information that helps us act in the world (e.g., helping us avoid stubbing our toes on the curb).

To directly evaluate whether the slant of a surface could be judged on the basis of gradients of texture density, Gibson (1950) compared how well different people were able to judge the slants of surfaces consisting of irregular and regular textures. The two types of textures used are shown in Figure 3.20. As you can see, the irregular texture consists of elements that are not clearly defined, whereas the regular texture is composed of clearly discernible repeating elements. Participants were shown photographs of these surfaces at different slants and asked to judge the angle of each slant. Gibson conjectured that if people

gradient of texture density
Incremental changes in the pattern on a surface, which provide information about the slant of the surface.

topological breakage
The discontinuity created by the intersection of two textures.

FIGURE 3.19 | Topological breakage at the intersection of two converging textures

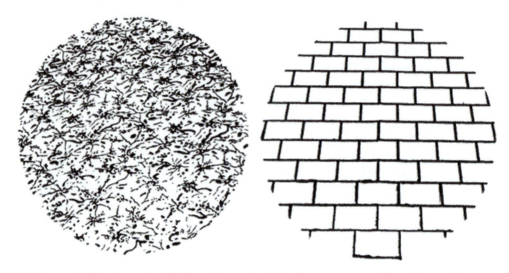

FIGURE 3.20 | The irregular (left) and regular (right) textures used by Gibson (1950)

use the gradients of texture density to judge the slant of surfaces, then (1) they should be able to judge the slants of these surfaces quite well based only on texture information, and (2) their judgments should be more accurate with regularly textured surfaces, as these would provide clearer information about the gradient of texture density at various slants. The results showed that participants were able to judge the relative slants of all the surfaces reasonably well. However, the assessments were more accurate for the regularly textured surface than for the irregular one.

As another example, consider the view you see from a moving car. Figure 3.21 shows a photograph taken (by the passenger, not the driver!) from the side window of a car travelling on the highway. The car was moving quite fast (though within the speed limit) and the camera was set at a relatively slow shutter speed, which caused the objects in the scene to appear blurred in the photograph. However, if you look closely you will see that the bushes in the foreground are more blurred than the trees in the background. This is because objects that are relatively close to the moving camera (i.e., the observer) appear to be moving faster than objects that are farther away. Thus the perceived speed of object motion can be used as a guide to judge the relative distance between the object and the observer. McLean and Hoffman (1973) have shown that drivers use this information when navigating bends in the road. See Box 3.3 for another example of the useful information contained in the AOA.

DISCOVERY LAB

FIGURE 3.21 | **Photo taken from the side window of a car travelling on a highway**

CONSIDER THIS
BOX 3.3

Gibson's Views on the Perception of Surfaces

J.J. Gibson also argued that the roughness of surfaces can be discerned from the information in the ambient optic array. Gibson (1966) observed that different textures reflect light in different ways and thus that the nature of the light reflected from a surface provides useful information about the smoothness of the surface. For instance, a rough surface reflects light more widely than a smooth surface. This is illustrated in Figure 3.22, where the solid lines indicate rays coming from a light source and the dashed lines indicate rays that have been reflected from two surfaces that differ in smoothness. The degree of **scatter-reflection** (i.e., how widely light scatters) from an object tells us a lot about the nature of its surface.

scatter-reflection
The degree to which light scatters when reflected from a surface.

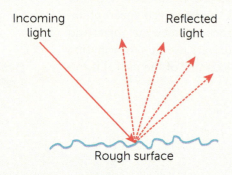
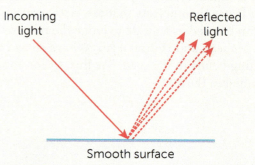

FIGURE 3.22 | Light is reflected differently from rough and smooth surfaces

Adapted from: Gibson, JJ. (1966).

Interactions Between the Ventral and Dorsal Pathways

Thus far we have treated the ventral and dorsal pathways as distinct visual pathways. However, there is considerable evidence that these two pathways, though dissociable, can nevertheless interact with each other (see Goodale & Westwood, 2004). While these interactions are clearly bidirectional, here we will focus on the influence of visually guided action (processed primarily in the dorsal pathway) on how an object is perceived (a process that involves the ventral pathway).

As an example, let's consider how performance in sports might influence how athletes perceive sport-related objects. In 2001, after the basketball superstar Vince Carter—then with the Toronto Raptors—had played a monster game, sinking shot after shot from three-point land, he told reporters that "The basket looked like a lake" (http://www.nydailynews.com/archives/sports/carter-answers-50-article-1.900596). Was he just using a figure of speech, or did he really perceive the basket to be larger than usual during his shooting streak? More generally, is increased performance in sports associated with perceptual distortions of the critical game-related objects such as baskets, nets, and balls?

FIGURE 3.23 | **The circles that participants in the study by Witt and Proffitt (2005) had to choose from when judging actual baseball size**

From Witt, J. K. (2011), Action's effect on perception, *Current Directions in Psychological Science, 20*, 201–206: Figure 1, p. 202.

This question was addressed by Witt and Proffitt (2005) in a study inspired by reports such as this one from the famous baseball player Mickey Mantle, following a great performance: "I never really could explain it. I just saw the ball as big as a grapefruit" (see Witt and Proffitt, 2005, p. 937). To verify these reports, Witt and Proffitt showed softball players a sheet of circles of different diameters, ranging from 9 cm to 11.8 cm (see Figure 3.23) and asked them which one best matched the actual diameter of a softball (10 cm).

In addition, Witt and Proffitt collected information about the players' batting averages, to see whether their judgments of softball size were related to their skill level. Figure 3.24 shows the sizes of the circles from which participants made their choices on the vertical axis, and the range of batting averages on the horizontal axis. As you can see, there is a positive correlation between perceived baseball size and batting average (shown by the line), whereby players with higher batting averages perceive the baseball as larger than less-successful players do. These results indicate that "perceived dimensions of the environment are affected by the perceiver's behavioral potential" (Witt & Proffitt, 2005, p. 937). These findings can be construed as another

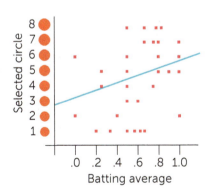

FIGURE 3.24 | **The relation between players' perceptions of softball size (y-axis) and their batting averages**

From Witt, J.K., & Proffitt, D.R. (2005), See the ball, hit the ball: Apparent ball size is correlated with batting average, *Psychological Science, 16*, 937–938: Figure 1 (p. 938).

example of the way perception is influenced by contextual factors, in this case the individual's "behavioural potential" in the context of playing ball.

Another example of the way action can influence the conscious experience of objects is the intentional binding effect, first reported by Haggard, Clark and Kalogeras (2002; see also Moore & Obhi, 2012, for a review): the perception of events that occur after one has performed an action as occurring closer in time to the action than was actually the case. As a participant in a study of intentional binding, you might be asked to press a button (that is, to perform an action), then listen for a tone and report the exact time when it was presented by noting the location of a hand on a clock that you were watching as you pressed the button and the tone was presented. The general finding is that intentionally pressing the button will lead you to perceive the tone as occurring sooner than it actually did. In fact, participants in some studies perceived the tone as occurring about 50-ms earlier than it did (Haggard et al., 2002). This experience can be contrasted with situations in which you don't have to press a button, or your finger is made to twitch involuntarily before the onset of the tone. In those situations, you typically do not judge the tone to have occurred earlier than it did. According to Haggard et al. (2002, p. 384) these results strongly suggest that "intentional actions elicit perceptual attraction," which "binds together awareness of the voluntary action with awareness of its sensory consequences, bringing them closer in perceived time." Thus the intentional binding effect provides another example of how action influences perception.

intentional binding effect
Events that take place after one has taken some action are perceived as occurring sooner than they actually did.

CONSIDER THIS
BOX 3.4 | Identifying Objects by Common Movement

Recall that the dorsal pathway is involved in the processing of object movement. It turns out that object movement can also be used to group scene components together to isolate objects from their backgrounds. The role of movement in object identification was first noted by the Gestalt psychologists in the principle of common movement, according to which we tend to group together items that are "moving simultaneously and in a similar manner" (Katz, 1951, p. 27). A good example of this principle in action has recently been reported by a team of researchers from the Western University, led by Susanne Ferber (Ferber, Humphrey, & Vilis, 2003). They showed participants images such as the one in Figure 3.25b, which looks like a jumble of random line elements. However, embedded among the random line segments was a meaningful shape, such as the bear shown in Figure 3.25a. After participants had looked at the composite image (as in Figure 3.25b), the elements forming the object (e.g., the bear) were rotated around the centre of the image while the random elements remained in their place. This separated the components of the object from the random components, grouping them together and making the object readily identifiable (see also Regan, 2000). This grouping reflects the principle of common movement. Interestingly, the percept of the object remained for some time *after* the components ceased to move. By measuring brain activation as the participants viewed the images, Ferber and colleagues were able to show that parts of the brain associated with object recognition in the ventral stream were active when the critical object could be segregated from the random elements both during the movement, when they were grouped by the principle of common

principle of common movement
Visual features that move simultaneously and follow the same path are perceived to form a whole entity.

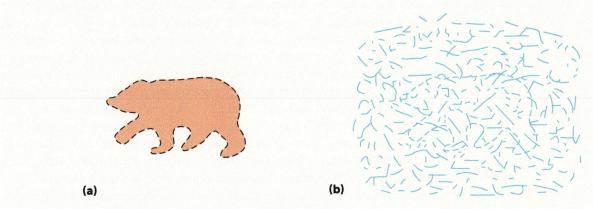

FIGURE 3.25 | The principle of common movement

This example of the stimuli used by Ferber, Humphrey, and Vilis (2003) shows an object made of broken line segments (a) and the object placed in a display of random line elements (b) so that the object is no longer recognizable.

Adapted from: Ferber, S., Humphrey, G.K., & Vilis, T. (2003).

movement, and for a short while after the movement had stopped. These findings also lend credence to one of the assumptions underlying the Gestalt movement: that the principles of grouping are fundamental, rooted in basic neural functions (see Kanizsa, 1979; Katz, 1951). In showing how object movement (which is processed primarily by the dorsal stream) can influence object identification (which involves the ventral stream), Ferber et al.'s study provides a good example of the interaction between the two streams of visual processing.

Multimodal Perception

Before we continue, take a moment to try this small exercise. Pay close attention to your surroundings and think about what you perceive. At first you might think that all you perceive are the words printed on this page, but chances are that there are several other streams of information arriving at your senses. If you're reading in a coffee shop, for instance, there may be music and conversation in the background, the smell of coffee and muffins, and the feeling of either warm or cool air blowing on your skin. In fact, if you think about it, your sensory system is almost always receiving information, though much of it fades into the background so that you consciously perceive only the most important and goal-relevant information (we will discuss unconscious perception in Chapter 13). Given this fact, it is important to note that historically the study of perception has not taken multimodal sensory experience into account: instead, most research has focused on a single sensory modality at a time. While a deep understanding of how individual senses function, both physiologically and in relation to perception, is obviously important, the lack of multimodal research may point to a disconnection between laboratory research and actual cognitive experience. Fortunately, the past two decades have seen a surge in research investigating multimodal perception. In this section we will briefly explore some of the major findings in this burgeoning field.

As we noted above, most of the time at least two of our senses are actively processing information at any given moment: for example, speech perception typically involves both hearing sounds and seeing mouth movements (Alsius, Navarra, Campbell, & Soto-Faraco, 2005;

Massaro, 1998). In some situations, information arriving at multiple sensory modalities is easily integrated even when the messages are incongruent (McGurk & MacDonald, 1976). However, in other situations multisensory messages can compete, and when this happens the most appropriate modality tends to dominate (Welch & Warren, 1980). That is, according to the **modality appropriateness hypothesis**, the fact that certain stimuli are better processed by specific senses means that one modality or another will be dominant at different times. For example, it has been proposed that the visual modality is superior to the auditory modality for processing spatial information (Howard & Templeton, 1966; O'Connor & Hermelin, 1972; Shimojo & Shams, 2001), whereas the reverse has been theorized for temporal information (Shams, Kamitani, & Shimojo, 2002; Stein, London, Wilkenson & Price, 1996). Accordingly, which sense (visual or auditory) emerges as dominant can depend on the conditions in which the stimuli are presented; however, examples of visual dominance are more prevalent in the literature (see Koppen, Alsius, & Spence, 2008; Ngo, Sinnett, Soto-Faraco, & Spence, 2010; Ngo, Cadieux, Sinnett, Soto-Faraco, & Spence, 2011; Sinnett, Soto-Faraco, & Spence, 2008; see Spence, 2009 for a review). One explanation of this **visual prepotency effect** suggests that we may place more importance on attending to visual stimuli in order to compensate for the fact that the visual system is less effective than the auditory and tactile systems at processing alerting stimuli (e.g., you can hear events that are happening behind you; see, for example, Posner, Nissen, & Klein, 1976; Spence, Nicholls, & Driver, 2001).

One of the challenges of multimodal research is to determine how the different sensory modalities influence perceptual processing in other senses. In some cases (e.g., the visual prepotency effect) one sense may be dominant. In other cases the signals arriving at each sense may be integrated and interpreted to mean something qualitatively different from the message carried by any of the constituent parts. In the next few pages we will briefly explore how different senses interact to create our perceptions.

Vision and Audition

The **McGurk effect** (McGurk & MacDonald, 1976; see also Shams, Kamitani, and Shimojo, 2004, for a description) is an excellent example of how visual input can change auditory perception, such that the resulting percept is something that was never actually presented. You can easily simulate the McGurk effect by asking two friends to stand one behind the other so that you see only the one in front. You then have the person in front (the one you can see) make mouth movements corresponding to the syllable "ga" but without actually making any sound. Simultaneously (you can synchronize your actors by counting to three) you have the occluded person clearly say the syllable "ba." What do you hear? Since your perception could be biased by your knowledge of what the actors are doing, you might want to ask someone else to observe with you and report what he or she hears. Chances are that what either or both of you hear will be neither "ga" (mouthed by the actor you see) nor "ba" (spoken by the actor you don't see), but "da." If so, your perception of the sound was altered by the visual cues provided by the mouth movements of the visible actor. Because the closing of the mouth needed to initiate the sound "ba" is inconsistent with the open mouth required to make the sound "ga," your perceptual system creates the experience of something in between—a syllable that sounds like "ba" but can be created with an open mouth.

In other cases sound can modulate how we perceive visual events. For instance, Sekuler, Sekuler, and Lau (1997) demonstrated that the addition of a simple sound can greatly change how we perceive visual motion. To do this they presented participants

---

modality appropriateness hypothesis

The hypothesis that different senses are better at processing different stimuli, and therefore that different sensory modalities dominate at different times, depending on circumstances.

visual prepotency effect

The hypothesis that the visual system dominates the other senses when it comes to perceptual processing.

McGurk effect

The auditory experience of the syllable "da" when seeing a mouth silently saying "ga" while at the same time hearing a voice say "ba."

with two discs that moved towards each other, coincided for a brief moment, and then moved away from one another (see Figure 3.26). There are two possible ways of perceiving this movement: either the discs collided and bounced off each other, or they simply passed one another and continued moving in their own direction. When shown this visual event, only about 20 per cent of participants perceived the discs to bounce off each other. However, if a simple sound was played at the moment when the discs coincided, three times as many participants perceived them to collide and bounce. As you can see, understanding exactly how vision and audition interact can be elusive, as the characteristics of both the situation and the stimulus characteristics can often change the resulting perception.

Vision and Touch

The perception of temporal order in the presentation of stimuli can be dramatically changed depending on the modalities involved and how the stimuli are presented. This can be demonstrated quite easily. Close your eyes and put your hands directly in front of you. Now have a friend tap each of your hands in quick succession, once only, while you judge which hand was touched first. You will be amazed at how closely in succession your hands can be tapped while you maintain a high degree of accuracy. Now try the exact same thing but now with your hands crossed. You should notice that the task is much harder. Yamamoto and Kitizawa (2001) showed that people are very accurate at this task as long as their hands are not crossed, but that accuracy falls dramatically when they are.

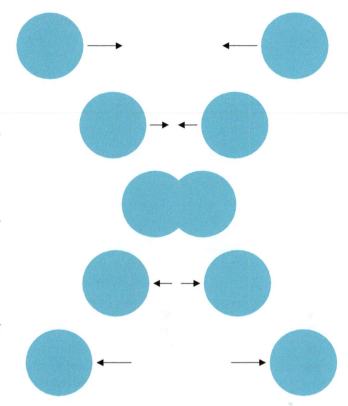

FIGURE 3.26 | Participants were shown two discs moving towards each other and crossing paths

When no sound was played at the moment when they coincided, only about 20 per cent of participants perceived the discs as colliding and bouncing back. When a sound was played at that moment, more than 60 per cent perceived them as colliding.

In follow-up research, Yamamoto and Kitizawa (2001) were able to replicate this effect, but this time without any actual crossing of arms. In this clever experiment, participants were given drumsticks and were asked to determine which stick was touched first. When the sticks were crossed, performance was worse than in the uncrossed condition, as in the earlier study. As you can see in panel C in Figure 3.27, the slope of the line with solid green circles (the crossed condition) is not as steep as the line with open circles (the uncrossed condition). What this means is that the participants had a much harder time judging the temporal order of the touches (the steeper the slope, the more accurate the performance). What is perhaps more interesting is the finding from the "double-crossed" position. Here the arms are crossed, but so are the sticks: thus the tip of each stick is actually on the same side of the body as the hand holding it (panel D of Figure 3.27). In this case performance was nearly as good as in the control condition (uncrossed arms and uncrossed sticks, see panel A).

It's important to note that the participants' eyes were closed during this experiment: this shows that the spatial position of the sticks was processed before the temporal order

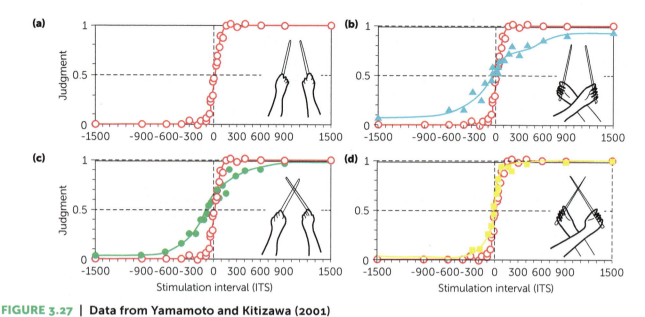

FIGURE 3.27 | Data from Yamamoto and Kitizawa (2001)

From Yamamoto, S., and Kitizawa, S. (2001), Reversal of subjective temporal order due to arm crossing, *Nature Neuroscience, 4(7)*, 759–765.

of actual touches was perceived. The *drumstick* study is important in advancing our knowledge of how proprioception (the sense of the position of our limbs), touch, and vision interact in our perception.

Multimodal Perception and Taste

One of the most interesting areas of multimodal perception research looks at the influence of other senses on flavour perception—a subject that may not only deepen our understanding of multisensory integration in general, but may also have potential applications in the food and beverage industry. Charles Spence is a world renowned experimental psychologist who has helped lead the field of multimodal perception and attention, and has recently sought to explore how the other senses can affect our sense of taste (see Spence, 2015, for a review).

You've probably noticed that food doesn't taste as good as usual when you have a cold. Laboratory research supports this well-known effect (see, for example, Stevenson, Prescott, & Boakes, 1999). The influence of vision on food perception has also been widely demonstrated. For example, Hoegg and Alba (2007) added food colouring to orange juice and found that the participants in their study reported non-existent differences in the taste. In some cases, the visual influence on taste can even make people ill. As Schlosser (2001) explains in his book *Fast Food Nation*, participants did not have any problems with taste when eating steak and fries that looked normal under special lights. However, some actually became ill when the lights were changed and they saw blue steak and green fries!

It may be obvious that our senses of smell and vision can affect what we taste; but what about our sense of touch or hearing? Most of us would likely agree that the texture of food will affect flavour perception. In fact, some researchers have suggested that we should think of all the receptors in the mouth as forming a single somatosensory system (see Green, 2001). This is not far-fetched: recent fMRI work has demonstrated that taste stimuli sensed on the tongue and somatosensory stimuli from the mouth activated common areas of the brain (Cerf-Duscatel et al., 2001). Finally, you might think that hearing would be highly unlikely to influence flavour perception, but you would be wrong. When Zampini and Spence (2004) enhanced the crispy sound that potato chips made when eaten, participants perceived flavour differences in the chips that simply were not there. Thus it seems that even flavour perception is much less straightforward than it seems: nearly all the senses can come into play.

Summary

Visual information is processed by multiple areas of the brain, each specialized to process particular aspects of visual information (e.g., colour). The ventral pathway is responsible for processing "what" information (e.g., identifying objects), while the dorsal pathway is responsible for processing "where" information (e.g., location and movement), and plays an important role in coordinating action.

Focusing first on the ventral stream, we considered several theories of pattern recognition—including feature detection, recognition by components and template matching—that focus on how perception is driven by feedforward (bottom-up) information. Noting that the perception of objects is also influenced by feedback connections in the visual system, we next explored the various ways in which context and prior knowledge influence perception. Notable examples of context effects are figure–ground segmentation, Gestalt principles of organization, the jumbled word effect, the word superiority effect, and contextual colour perception.

Focusing next on the dorsal stream of visual processing, we explored evidence from patient studies (visual agnosia and optic ataxia) suggesting that the dorsal stream is heavily involved in the perception required for action. We then explored J.J. Gibson's theory of ecological optics, according to which visual perception does not require any significant internal processing, but is a direct function of the information provided by the environment: cues such as topological breakage give us all the information we need in order to act on them appropriately.

Although most of the chapter focused on visual perception, in the last section we considered multimodal perception. Specifically, we explored how what we perceive from one modality can be influenced by information we receive from the others. In some cases (e.g., the visual prepotency effect) one modality (vision) dominates over another (e.g., audition). In other cases, the information from two sensory modalities is combined to produce a perception that differs from what either sense alone perceives. An example of this is the McGurk effect.

CASE STUDY

Case Study Wrap-Up

The case study that started this chapter pointed to several concepts central to the study of perception. First, Lissauer's case of visual agnosia nicely illustrates the difference between perception for the purpose of conscious identification (conducted by the ventral stream) and perception for the purpose of action (conducted by the dorsal stream). As we noted, Melvyn Goodale and his colleagues (Goodale et al., 1991; Milner & Goodale,

Continued

1995) conducted extensive studies of a patient who, like Lissauer's patient, suffered from visual agnosia. While she was unable to identify the orientation of an object, she was able to correctly orient her hand when reaching for the object. Thus her capacity for conscious object identification was impaired (visual agnosia), but her perception for the purpose of action remained intact. We can relate this phenomenon to Gibson's *theory of ecological optics*, which focuses on the way humans use the complex array of visual stimuli provided by the environment to guide their action in the world. Some patients with visual agnosia are apparently able to use information in the *ambient optic array* to guide action even when they can't identify the object they are acting on.

Second, the case study highlights the distinction between the processing of visual features and the perception of meaningful whole objects. Specifically,

Lissauer's patient had a particular subtype of *visual agnosia* in which he was able to perceive visual *features* but unable to use *Gestalt grouping principles* to group the features together into meaningful wholes. This suggests that different mechanisms might be responsible for feature detection and Gestalt grouping.

Third, although Lissauer's patient was unable to recognize objects using his vision, he was able to recognize them quite quickly using his other senses, such as touch. This is typical of patients with visual agnosia, and points to the importance of multimodal perception.

Finally, the case study underlines how complex perception actually is. Before taking this course you probably never imagined that visual perception would involve so many distinct cognitive processes. Even today, researchers are only beginning to scratch the surface of this fascinating topic.

In the Know: Review Questions

1. Describe several different brain areas responsible for different aspects of visual perception.
2. Compare and contrast the feature-detection and template-matching approaches to pattern recognition.
3. How does Gibson's theory of vision fit with the distinction between the ventral and dorsal visual pathways?
4. What contributions did Gestalt psychologists make to our understanding of how visual perception of the components of scenes is influenced by contextual factors?
5. Discuss two examples of multimodal perception.

Key Concepts

achromatopsia

akinetopsia (motion blindness)

ambient optical array (AOA)

apparent-distance theory

atomistic

bottom-up influences

cognitive demon

context effects

contrast energy

cornea

decision demon

denotivity

dorsal ("where") pathway

echo

empirical theory of colour vision

extrastriate body area (EBA)

feature

feature detection theory

feedforward sweep

figure–ground segmentation (segregation)

fovea

fusiform face area (FFA)

geons

gradient of texture density

grouping

Höffding function

holistic

intentional binding effect

iris

jumbled word effect

lens

McGurk effect

memory trace

modality appropriateness hypothesis

moon illusion

multiple-trace memory model

optic ataxia

optic flow field

organizational principles

pandemonium

parahippocampal place area (PPA)

pattern recognition

percept

perception

photoreceptors

primary visual cortex

principle of common movement

principle of experience

principle of parallelism

principle of proximity

principle of similarity

principle of symmetry

probe

prosopagnosia

prototypical

pupil

re-entrant (feedback) connections

recognition by components (RBC)

retina

retinotopic

scatter-reflection

squelching

template-matching theory

theory of ecological optics

topological breakage

top-down influences

transformation

ventral ("what") pathway

visual agnosia

visual prepotency effect

word superiority effect

Links to Other Chapters

memory trace
Chapter 5 (consolidation)
Chapter 5 (encoding specificity)

bottom-up processing
Chapter 4 (Stroop task)
Chapter 10 (flexibility–rigidity and the brain)

template matching
Chapter 8 (prototypicality)

direct perception
Chapter 11 (perception and intuitive concepts)

Further Reading

Palmer (1999) is an excellent and comprehensive overview of vision science that deals with all aspects of perception from the time that light energy hits the retina to the time when a visual object is fully recognized.

Purves and Lotto (2003) is a detailed account of the empirical theory of colour vision that includes discussions of numerous fascinating and provocative illusions.

For a comprehensive description of visual agnosia see Farah (1990).

Farah, M.J. (1990). *Visual agnosia: Disorders of object recognition and what they tell us about normal vision.* Cambridge, MA: MIT Press.

Palmer, S.E. (1999). *Vision science: Photons to phenomenology.* Cambridge, MA: MIT Press.

Purves, D., & Lotto, R.B. (2003). *Why we see what we do: An empirical theory of vision.* Sunderland, MA: Sinaur Associates, Inc.

4

The Varieties of Attention

Chapter Contents

Chapter Objectives

- To distinguish between theories of early and late attentional selection and review experimental evidence for each.
- To discuss endogenous and exogenous shifts of spatial attention and how attention capture and inattentional blindness are complementary aspects of cognition.
- To review experimental studies investigating divided attention.
- To explain why mind wandering reduces attention to a primary task.
- To discuss the vigilance decrement and explain why performance on some tasks declines over time.
- To distinguish between covert and overt visual attention.

CASE STUDY

A Total Wreck

In September 2013 a double-decker public transit bus in Ottawa crashed into a moving passenger train, killing six of the people on the bus, including the driver, and injuring 33. Thankfully, everyone aboard the train emerged unscathed. Photos of the accident scene (see Figure 4.1) show the bus with its front almost completely demolished, and the derailed train sitting just a stone's throw away from the railway crossing. It was not long before the media began to speculate about possible causes of the shocking accident.

According to passenger reports, the bus had not slowed down as it approached the crossing, even though the barriers were in place and the lights were flashing. The driver had seemed oblivious as the bus crashed through the barriers and, seconds later, into the moving train. In the final moments some of the passengers called out to alert the driver, who tried to apply his brakes seconds before impact, but it was too late (Stone & Lindell, 2013).

Federal Transportation Safety Board investigators could find no mechanical problems with either the bus or the railway crossing equipment. And after interviewing passengers and examining various event recorders, they concluded that the driver should have been able to stop before hitting the train, even though the bus was going slightly over the speed limit. There was no evidence of drug or alcohol use on his part, he had not been using his cell phone, there were no previous cases of negligence on his record, and the reports of his family members indicated that he had enjoyed his work. So what caused the ghastly crash? As of 2015, the most recent theory is that the driver might have been distracted by a video monitor—located above the front windshield—that tracked activity on the upper deck. There is some evidence that the driver might have been "glancing towards [the monitor] intermittently while looking towards the road ahead" as he approached the railway crossing (www.bst-tsb.gc.ca/eng/

FIGURE 4.1 | After the Ottawa bus–train collision

medias-media/sur-safe/letter/rail/2014/r13t0192/
r13t0192-617-10-14-20140924.asp).

Transportation safety expert Randall Jamieson believes that a fair number of rule violations in the railway and public transportation industries can be attributed to attention failure (personal communication). According to his calculations, in some situations as many as 60 per cent of rule violations could be related to distractions other than cell phones, including radio chatter and absorption in internal thoughts. Yet many people in the transportation industry seem to be unaware of the critical role that human attention plays in the safety of their operations.

In this chapter we will explore cognitive theories and studies of human attention. As you read it, ask yourself how these theories and studies might apply to real-world situations such as the Ottawa accident.

James's Description of Attention

At the turn of the twentieth century, William James was the leading psychologist in North America (Cattell, 1903). His great textbook *Principles of Psychology* (1890/1983) contains a chapter on attention that many psychologists still cite (e.g., Johnston & Dark, 1986; LaBerge, 1990; Fernandez-Duque & Johnson, 2002). Here is one of James's (1890/1983) most famous passages on the subject:

> Everyone knows what attention is. It is the taking possession by the mind, in clear and vivid form, of one out of what seem several simultaneously possible objects or trains of thought. . . . It implies withdrawal from some things in order to deal effectively with others, and is a condition which has a real opposite in the confused, dazed, scatterbrained state which . . . is called distraction (pp. 381–382).

A century later, not all of us are so confident when it comes to defining attention. Harold Pashler (1998), an eminent contemporary cognitive psychologist, has gone so far as to say that "No one knows what attention is, and . . . there may even not be an 'it' there to be known about (although of course there might be)" (p. 1). Pashler's statement exemplifies the complexity of studying attention today. We no longer think that just because we have a word like *attention* there must be one particular phenomenon that it corresponds to. In fact, *attention* has a variety of meanings. Even James acknowledged this when he called a section of his chapter "The Varieties of Attention." Among the variations on the theme of attention that we will address in this chapter are selecting what to attend to; not attending to what we could attend to; involuntary attention; attempting to attend to more than one thing at a time; and switching our attention between tasks.

Selective Attention

Early research on attention was driven by practical problems experienced by armed forces personnel. One of those problems arose "in communication centers, where many different streams of speech reached the person at the same time" (Broadbent, 1980, p. 54). Investigation of this problem led to the development of an experiment in which the participant was

DISCOVERY LAB ✦

required to "answer one of two messages which start at the same point in time, but one of which is irrelevant" (Broadbent, 1952/1992, p. 125). The experimental technique that Broadbent used, which we introduced in Chapter 1, is called **dichotic listening**. Participants were presented with two previously recorded verbal messages simultaneously and were required to answer questions posed in only one of the messages. When participants knew in advance which of two different voices contained the required message, then performance on this task was very good. In other words, they were good at **selective attention**—able to select the information that was relevant to their task and ignore the information that was not.

Broadbent also worked closely with Colin Cherry (1953), who identified what came to be known as the cocktail party phenomenon and invented a seminal technique for investigating attention (Wood & Cowan, 1995). The **cocktail party phenomenon** occurs when you are able to attend to one conversation in a crowded room where many other conversations are going on. Cherry studied the ability to attend to one message while ignoring another by using a **shadowing task**, in which participants wear headphones and are given two messages, one in each ear. The participants shadow one of the two messages by repeating it as they hear it. Early information-processing theories suggested that people must *filter out* information they do not wish to attend to (Treisman, 1969). Thus one of the stages of information-processing might involve a kind of **filter** that would admit some messages and block others.

A study by Neisser and Becklen (1975) used a visual analogue of dichotic listening called **selective looking**. Suppose you take videotapes of two different sequences of events, such as a hand-slapping game and a game involving throwing a basketball. What happens if you show the two videotapes overlapping? This would be like watching two television channels on the same screen. In the Neisser and Becklen study, people were able to attend to either sequence quite easily. They saw only the sequence they were attending to, and were not distracted by the unattended sequence.

The studies of dichotic listening and selective looking both produced results consistent with what is called the **early selection** view of attention. This view holds that "attention can effectively prevent early perceptual processing of irrelevant distractors" (Lavie, Hirst, Fockert, & Viding, 2004). On this account, the participant literally does not see or hear the irrelevant information. However, other tasks have produced results that appear to be more consistent with a **late selection** view of attention, according to which both relevant and irrelevant stimuli are perceived and participants must actively ignore the irrelevant stimuli in order to focus on the relevant ones. Late selection is often illustrated by the Stroop task.

The Stroop Task

Consider the following sequence of colour names: red, green, blue, green, red, yellow, blue, yellow, blue, green. It's easy to read those names in black and white. But suppose they were printed in colours different from the colours they name. For example, suppose the word *red* was printed in *blue*; the word *green* in *yellow*, and so on. This is called a **Stroop task** (Stroop, 1935/1992), after John R. Stroop (1897–1973), the psychologist who invented it. (There are several demonstrations of the Stroop task on the Internet: you should try at least one of them. You'll find that naming the colours of the words takes longer than reading the colour words themselves.) Reading the colour names and naming the colours are strikingly different experiences. When you try to name the colours, it's as if you are constantly being distracted by the tendency to read the names. We could say that the tendency to read the names interferes with the attempt to name the colours. There are several variants of this task. For example, suppose you show someone a picture of a bird that is labelled "camel": if you then ask the person to name the picture, the tendency to say "camel" will interfere with the correct response, "bird" (MacLeod & MacDonald, 2000, p. 384).

One of the most useful research tools ever invented, the Stroop task has been employed in thousands of experiments (MacLeod, 1991, 1992; MacLeod & MacDonald, 2000). A typical Stroop experiment compares performance in an incongruent condition (e.g., the word *red* is printed in green and the participant's task is to name the colour that the word is printed in) with control conditions (e.g., the letters XXX are printed in green and the participant's task is to name the colour of the letters). It is reliably found that the incongruent condition takes more time than the control condition does.

If a process has been overlearned, there is often a tendency to carry it out whether we wish to or not. For example, if you have learned how to read and you are presented with a list of words, you will find it hard not to read them. This may help to explain what happens in a Stroop task, which requires the participant to deliberately inhibit the reading of the words in order to accomplish the goal of naming the colours.

The results of Stroop experiments have often been taken to illustrate **controlled versus automatic processes**. Some processes may pick up information more or less automatically. A truly *automatic process* is autonomous; it runs itself without requiring us to pay attention to it. By contrast, with other processes we must pay attention if we are to execute them properly. Such processes are often called *controlled processes* (Shiffrin & Schneider, 1977). Although the distinction between automatic and controlled processes is still widely recognized (Birnboim, 2003; Schneider & Chein, 2003), there is another family of constructs that captures similar distinctions. Thus so-called automatic processes may also be described as bottom-up, stimulus-driven, or involuntary, while so-called controlled processes may also be called top-down, goal-directed, or voluntary (cf. Pashler, Johnston, & Ruthruff, 2001, p. 641). In the Stroop situation, an incongruent condition requires you to keep the goal of naming colours in mind even though you have an involuntary tendency to read the words.

Some intriguing investigations of the Stroop phenomenon have used hypnosis (MacLeod & Sheehan, 2003; Raz et al., 2003). People vary in their susceptibility to hypnosis. A standard test used to measure suggestibility is the Stanford Hypnotic Susceptibility Scale (Weitzenhoffer & Hilgard, 1962; available on the Internet). Raz and his colleagues gave English-speaking participants who scored high on the scale two post-hypnotic suggestions: first, that any letter strings they saw would appear to be in an unknown foreign language, and, second, that the participants would "not attempt to attribute any meaning to them" (Raz et al., 2003, p. 337). The participants' sole task was to name the colours in which the "meaningless" letter strings were displayed. Of course, they were actually given a standard Stroop task using English words. The interesting result was that the highly suggestible participants did not show the typical Stroop effect, whereas those who were less suggestible did.

This result has been replicated both by Raz and by MacLeod and Sheehan (2003). One possible explanation is that the reading of words is suppressed in those who are highly suggestible, allowing them to name the colour in which the word is printed with ease. This would mean that even an apparently automatic process such as word reading can be controlled by means of hypnosis. More generally, it suggests that cognitive processes normally

Stroop task
A naming task in which colour names are printed in colours other than the colours they name.

controlled vs automatic processes
Processes that demand attention if we are to carry them out properly versus processes that operate without requiring us to pay attention to them.

considered to be automatic are nonetheless susceptible to "top-down influences exerted by suggestion at the neural level" (Raz et al., 2003, p. 343).

Several PET and fMRI studies have been designed to shed light on the brain processes underlying Stroop task performance (MacLeod & MacDonald, 2000, pp. 386–390). These studies compare blood flows to different regions of the brain for performance in incongruent and control conditions. Among the brain regions most often identified in these studies are the dorsolateral prefrontal cortex (DLPFC) and the anterior cingulate cortex (ACC). The relative locations of these areas are shown in Figure 4.2. The DLPFC is called *dorso* (short for *dorsal*), meaning that it is towards the top of the cortex as opposed to the bottom (*ventral*). *Lateral* refers to the outside as opposed to the inside (*medial*) part of the cortex. *Prefrontal* means that it is located at the front of the frontal lobes. So the *dorsolateral prefrontal cortex* is located towards the top, outside part of the front of the frontal lobes (Harrison, 2001, p. 160). The ACC is called *anterior*, meaning towards the front as opposed to the back (*posterior*). *Cingulate* means "arch-shaped."

In general, the prefrontal areas are thought to exert "a top-down bias that favours the selection of task-relevant information. . . . [S]uch a bias is especially important for exerting control when task-irrelevant information can effectively compete with task-relevant information for priority in processing" (Milham, Banich, & Barad, 2004, p. 212). Both the DLPFC and the ACC may be "activated among some tasks that require processes to resolve among competing responses. We also know that these brain regions are not necessarily involved in all such tasks, but that other regions may be recruited instead" (Jonides, Badre, Curtis, Thompson-Schill, & Smith, 2002, p. 243).

dorsolateral prefrontal cortex (DLPFC)

An area of the brain that may exert a top-down bias that favours the selection of task-relevant information.

anterior cingulate cortex (ACC)

An area of the brain that may detect conflicting response tendencies of the sort that the Stroop task elicits.

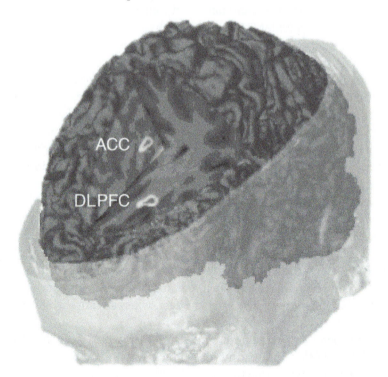

FIGURE 4.2 | **The dorsolateral prefrontal cortex and the anterior cingulate cortex**

From: MacLeod, C.M., & MacDonald, P.A. (2000). Reprinted by permission of Elsevier.

A great deal of speculation has centred on the role of the ACC. One possibility is that it detects conflicting response tendencies of the sort that the Stroop task elicits. It's also possible that heightened ACC activity is accompanied by heightened awareness of such conflicts (U. Mayer, 2004). However, the precise role of the ACC may change depending on the specific task with which the person is dealing (Kéri, Decety, Roland, & Gulyás, 2003, p. 31). The ACC should probably be seen as one part of a network responsible for attentional control, "communicating with other equally essential components within this network … [and having] multiple functions depending on the content and origin of the signals from other components in the attentional network" (Tibbetts, 2001, p. 329).

Endogenous and Exogenous Spatial Attention

The issue of attentional selection also applies when considering objects in different spatial locations. As you look around, you will notice that there are numerous objects around you; yet as we learned in Chapter 3, on perception, we are not aware of all these objects at the same time. We have to use attention to select a subset of objects in space for conscious perception. This aspect of selective attention is often referred to as **spatial attention** (see Posner, 1980).

One popular way to understand spatial attention is to think of it as a spotlight that shines on a certain location in space, bringing the objects it shines on into conscious awareness as whole objects, in much the same way that a spotlight in a theatre makes the objects it shines on perceptible relative to other objects that remain in the darkness. This is commonly referred to as the **spotlight metaphor** of spatial attention (see Fernandez-Duque & Johnson, 1999, pp. 93–98, for a theoretical review). Of course this spotlight notion is only a metaphor, intended to help us think about how attention might work; no one really believes that there is a spotlight in our heads.

Early work on spatial attention focused on understanding how the spotlight of attention can be moved in visual space (Posner, 1978; 1980). The available evidence suggests that spatial attention can be moved in at least two ways. **Endogenous shifts** of attention are volitional, determined by our goals and intentions (see Ristic & Kingstone, 2006; Peelen, Heslenfeld & Theeuwes, 2004). By contrast, **exogenous shifts** of attention are involuntary, determined by an external stimulus that grabs our attention regardless of our goals and intentions (see Ristic & Kingstone, 2006; Peelen et al., 2004). Researchers also call this latter type of attention shift **attention capture**. Attention capture is the diversion of attention by a stimulus so powerful that it compels us to notice it even when our attention is focused on something else. Intuitively, attention capture would appear to be "ecologically useful … [because it enables] attention to be drawn to new objects in the field [that] may well represent either an important threat to be avoided (like a predator) or an important opportunity to be sought out (like prey)" (Pashler, Johnston, & Ruthruff, 2001, p. 632). It's possible that we are "tuned" to pick up useful information even when our attention is directed elsewhere. When we discuss shifts of attention, it's important to keep in mind that we are not talking about shifts of the eyes, but shifts in the focus of attention while the eyes remain fixed on the same position in space. We will return to the relationship between eye movements and spatial attention later in this chapter.

Exogenous shifts of attention are typically demonstrated using the **peripheral cueing paradigm** (see Jonides, 1981). The sequence of displays presented to participants on each

spatial attention
The process of selecting visual information for conscious awareness in specific regions of space.

spotlight metaphor
The idea that spatial attention is like a spotlight that we shine on an object when we select it for more complex and conscious processing.

endogenous shifts
Voluntary movements of attention.

exogenous shifts
Involuntary movements of attention triggered by external stimuli.

attention capture
The diversion of attention by a stimulus so powerful that it compels us to notice it even when our attention is focused on something else.

peripheral cueing paradigm
A test in which a light (i.e., the cue) flashes in the periphery and is followed by a target either in the same (cued) location or a different (uncued) one.

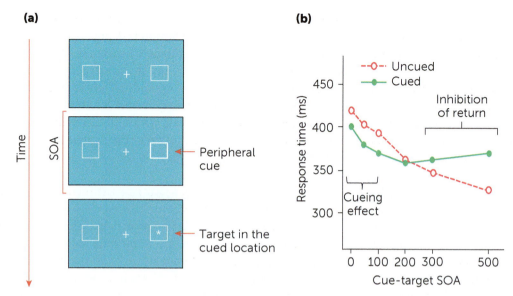

FIGURE 4.3 | **The sequence of displays in the peripheral cueing paradigm (Panel A) and the pattern of response time data (Panel B)**

SOA refers to the cue-target stimulus onset asynchrony. Panel A shows the target appearing in the cued (valid) location. Panel B shows the cueing effect at short SOAs and inhibition of return at longer SOAs.

Adapted from Posner, M.I., & Cohen, Y. (1984), Components of visual orienting, in Bouma, H. and Bouwhuis, D., eds., *Attention and Performance, X*, pp. 531–556 (Hillsdale, NJ: Erlbaum). See also Klein (2000) for a similar figure.

trial of the peripheral cueing task is shown in Panel A of Figure 4.3. As you can see, on each trial participants are first presented with a fixation cross in the center of the screen and two boxes, one on each side of the fixation. Participants are asked to keep their eyes focused on the central fixation cross throughout the trial. The boxes on either side of the fixation are meant to serve as placeholders, indicating the possible locations in which the target will appear. Next, one of the boxes brightens for a brief moment. The brief brightening of one of the boxes is the critical "peripheral cue" because it occurs some distance away from the centre of the participant's visual field. Finally, a target appears in one of the two boxes. Participants are required to press a button as soon as they see the target appear. The key measure is the time it takes to detect the target, which is measured from the moment the target appears to the moment when the response button is pressed. To discourage random button pressing, on a small subset of the trials the target is not presented. Trials on which a target does not appear are called **catch trials**, because if participants are responding without paying attention to the target, they will respond on these trials, allowing the experimenter to "catch" them not doing the task properly.

Importantly, in the standard version of the peripheral cueing paradigm, the peripheral cue is completely non-predictive of the location in which the target will appear on that trial. In other words, the target appears in the same location as the peripheral cue (the cued location or valid location) half the time and in the opposite location (uncued or invalid location) the other half of the time. This means that attending to the cue will not help the participant maximize performance on all trials.

catch trials

Trials of a detection task in which a target is not presented.

Even though the peripheral cue is non-predictive of target location, the results show that people are faster at detecting the target when it appears in the cued (valid) location than when it appears in the uncued (invalid) location. This is taken to mean that the cue captures the spotlight of attention, allowing the observer to quickly detect the target if it appears in the cued location. Responses to targets that appear in the uncued location are slower because the spotlight of attention has been captured by the cue and must be shifted to the target location in order for the target to be detected, and this shift takes time. Shorter response times on cued as compared to uncued trials are known as the *cueing effect*. The fact that a non-predictive cue captures attention suggests that the shift in attention is involuntary, or independent of the observer's intentions.

Experimenters often add another twist to these studies, varying the interval between the onset of the cue and the onset of the target. The length of this interval, referred to as the *stimulus onset asynchrony (SOA)*, can vary from 25 to 1200 ms. Panel B of Figure 4.3 shows response times plotted as a function of cued and uncued trials across a set of SOAs. As you can see, the cueing effect is present even at very short SOAs, which means that the peripheral cue attracts attention very rapidly. Notice also that the cueing effect diminishes as the SOA increases, and at long SOAs the effect is actually reversed, so that responses are faster at the uncued location than the cued location. Why does this reversal occur? The evidence suggests that at long SOAs, when attention is initially captured by the peripheral cue but no target appears, attention than disengages and shifts to the uncued location. This makes target detection faster at the uncued location than at the cued location, because the delay in the appearance of the target has led attention to shift to the uncued location, and now it has to disengage from that location and shift back to the cued location if that is where the target happens to appear. The reversed cueing effect at long intervals between the cue and target is called *inhibition of return (IOR)* (Klein, 2000).

Endogenous shifts of attention are typically demonstrated using the *central cueing paradigm* (see Jonides, 1981); see Panel A of Figure 4.4. Each trial again begins with a central fixation cross and two boxes. However, in this paradigm the fixation cross in the centre is replaced by a directional cue, such as an arrow pointing to either the left or the right box. After a variable SOA, a target is presented in one of the two boxes. Another key difference between this and the peripheral cueing paradigm is that in this case the cue reliably predicts the location of the target. For instance, the target will appear in the location at which the arrow is pointing (cued or valid location) 80 per cent of the time and in the other location (uncued or invalid) 20 per cent of the time. Typically, response times are faster when targets are presented in the cued rather than in the uncued location. In this case, participants are able to strategically and intentionally shift the spotlight of attention to the cued location. Central cueing normally does not lead to IOR (see Figure 4.4, Panel B).

Taken together, initial studies using the peripheral and central cueing paradigms suggested that exogenous shifts of attention (triggered by peripheral flashes of light) are ballistic (rapid) and reflexive (occurring independently of intention), while endogenous shifts of attention (in response to arrows) are a little slower and depend on volition. However, more recent studies suggest that the story is a bit more complicated. It turns out that even putatively "volitional" central cues such as arrows can lead to cueing effects when they are non-predictive of the target location (Ristic & Kingstone, 2006), which was initially thought to only occur for reflexive, exogenous cues. Apparently, even very familiar directional cues, such as arrows, can shift the spotlight of attention in a reflexive manner.

cueing effect
Faster responses on cued compared to uncued trials in the cueing task.

stimulus onset asynchrony (SOA)
The time difference between the onset of one stimulus and the onset of a subsequent stimulus.

inhibition of return (IOR)
Slower responses to cued than to uncued trials in the cueing paradigm.

central cueing paradigm
An experimental method in which a central cue (e.g., arrow) points to a location in which a target might subsequently appear.

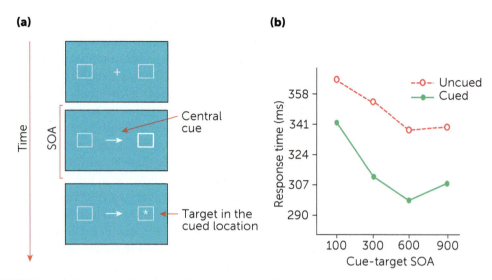

FIGURE 4.4 | An example of the displays typically employed in the central cueing paradigm, showing the target appearing in the cued (valid) location (Panel A) and the pattern of response time data for cued and uncued trials as a function of cue-target SOA (Panel B)

Adapted from Ristic, J. & Kingstone, A. (2006), Attention to arrows: Pointing to a new direction, *Quarterly Journal of Experimental Psychology, 59,* 1921–1930.

Comparing Attention Capture and Inattentional Blindness

If you're walking down the hall and someone behind you says your name, chances are that you will attend to that voice and turn around. As we have discussed, this is an example of attention capture. The reverse of attention capture is **inattentional blindness**: failure to attend to events that we might be expected to notice. "Imagine an experienced pilot attempting to land an airplane on a busy runway. He pays close attention to his display console, carefully watching the airspeed indicator on his windshield to make sure he does not stall, yet he never sees that another airplane is blocking his runway" (Mack, 2003, p. 180). According to Mack, Haines (1991) found that some experienced pilots using flight simulators did just that, failing to notice the second plane until it was too late to abort the landing. A great many accidents may be due to inattentional blindness.

Although attention capture and inattentional blindness may appear to be contradictory, they actually go hand in hand. Let's begin with inattentional blindness. Recall the Neisser and Becklen (1975) experiment on selective looking that we discussed earlier in the section on selective attention. Participants who were shown two overlapping videos of different sequences of events were able to attend to one sequence without being distracted by the other. In a subsequent study using the selective looking paradigm, Simons (2000; Simons & Chabris, 1999) showed participants overlapping videos of two teams playing basketball and asked them to count the passes made by one of the teams. Accordingly, the participants paid close attention to one or the other of the teams, and 73 per cent of them failed to notice a gorilla walk across the screen. Even when the gorilla stopped and pounded its chest, only 50 per cent of the participants noticed it!

inattentional blindness

Failure to attend to events that we might be expected to notice.

Mack and Rock (1998; Mack, 2003) used a different experimental paradigm to investigate inattentional blindness. Participants were shown a series of asymmetrical crosses and on each trial were asked to judge which arm of the cross was longer. On the fourth trial the display included a new feature: a small black square located in one of the quadrants defined by the cross. Thus the critical fourth trial looked something like Figure 4.5. When the participants were asked if they had seen anything other than the cross, many said they had not. Paying attention to the cross, they had failed to perceive the unexpected intrusion.

Mack and Rock's (1998) paradigm has also been used to find out what types of stimuli capture attention. In one variation of the experiment, Mack and Rock (1998) used a happy cartoon face rather than small black squares. The happy faces were detected 85 per cent of the time. Other stimulus categories such as simple circles were detected as rarely as 15 per cent of the time. This result suggests that faces may be special. Indeed, Lavie and her colleagues (Lavie, Ro, & Russell, 2003; Ro, Russell, & Lavie, 2001) have provided evidence for the hypothesis that faces are more likely to attract attention than other classes of stimuli. In one experiment they used a version of a so-called **flanker task**: participants had to search the computer screen for the name of a famous person and then indicate whether that person was a show-business personality (e.g., Michael Jackson) or a politician (e.g., Bill Clinton). The name might appear in any of several locations on the screen, sometimes by itself and sometimes within a list of letter strings (e.g., Csiprmy Qhplrt). Meanwhile, on the periphery of the screen was a picture of either the person whose name was being sought (congruent condition) or a person from the opposite category (incongruent condition). One screen from this task is presented in Figure 4.6. Thus a congruent condition would be to search for Bill Clinton's name while his picture was being shown, while an incongruent condition would be to search for Michael Jackson's name while Clinton's picture was shown. Participants were told to ignore the face and, when they found the name, to press a key indicating whether it belonged to a celebrity or to a politician. Of course, it took longer to identify the name correctly as the number of alternatives on the name list increased from 1 to 2 to 4 to 6 (because participants had to search through more alternatives). Incongruent conditions also took longer than congruent ones, indicating that the faces were not ignored but in fact interfered with

FIGURE 4.5 | Asymmetrical crosses and inattentional blindness

The participant judges the relative line lengths of the cross and may fail to see the black square.

flanker task

An experiment in which participants may be influenced by an irrelevant stimulus beside the target.

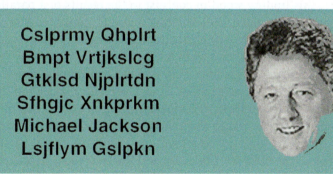

FIGURE 4.6 | Example of a flanker task

This example shows an incongruent condition. The target name (Michael Jackson) could appear in any of the six positions in the list of names, and the face could appear on either the left or the right.

Adapted from Watson, J.M., & Strayer, D.L. (2010).

COGNITION IN ACTION | Déjà Vu
BOX 4.1

Have you ever had the feeling that you have lived through the current moment or experience before, accompanied by the sense that this may not in fact be the case? If so, you have lots of company. **Déjà vu** (French for "already seen") has been studied by psychologists for at least 100 years. As Brown (2003) observed, it's unfortunate that déjà vu has typically been associated with paranormal and pathological experiences, because this has hindered its investigation as a common experience for "ordinary" people. In fact, the results of more than 41 surveys together suggest that approximately two-thirds of us have had at least one déjà vu experience (Brown, 2003, p. 397).

Déjà vu

The impression that you have already experienced the situation in which you find yourself, accompanied by the sense that this is not actually the case.

Interesting demographics are associated with the experience of déjà vu. For one thing, people over the age of 60 are less likely to report having had a déjà vu experience than are people in their twenties. As Brown observes, this pattern is illogical, since everyone who reaches the age of 60 was once 20. The explanation seems to be that social attitudes have changed, so that people today are more willing to report déjà vu experiences than they might have been in the 1960s (Brown, 2003, p. 400). Although there are no reliable gender differences in the frequency of déjà vu experiences, there are differences related to socio-economic circumstances, education, and travel: those who are higher on the socio-economic scale, better-educated, and more widely travelled are more likely than others to report déjà vu experiences, perhaps because they are more likely to have experienced novel situations.

Brown reviews several possible explanations of déjà vu. One possibility involves inattentional blindness. As we have seen, Mack and Rock's studies showed that we often fail to perceive something right in front of them, "hiding in plain sight" as it were; yet, as we will learn later (Chapter 13), sometimes what we don't see can still register below the level of awareness and influence the way we structure subsequent experience. "For example, one may enter a room talking on a cell phone while looking directly at a particular stimulus, and moments later this same stimulus is consciously perceived and elicits a déjà vu" (Brown, 2003, p. 407).

reaction time. Importantly, the size of this distractor effect was the same regardless of the number of names on the list.

This finding stood in contrast to the results of a parallel study in which participants searching for the names of either musical instruments or fruits were presented with pictures of fruits or musical instruments as distractors. Here again, there were both list length and congruence effects, with incongruent trials generally taking longer. However, the congruence effect was reduced and eventually disappeared as the list got longer. If we compare the two studies, we see that as task difficulty increased, faces continued to distract the participants, but fruits and musical instruments did not. In other words, faces were always attended to, no matter what else the participants were supposed to be doing. By contrast, participants "gave up" on attending to fruit and musical instruments when the overall task became too difficult. Lavie, Ro, and Russell (2003, p. 510) concluded that "face processing may be mandatory." In other words, attention to faces seems to be involuntary: we can't help noticing them, even when we try to ignore them.

Faces are not the only things that capture our attention: so do representations of the human body. Downing, Bray, Rogers, and Childs (2004) used the same technique that Mack and Rock (1998) did in their attentional blindness study, placing silhouettes of whole human bodies as well as other objects in different quadrants of the cross. The bodies were detected at a much higher rate than were the other objects (telephones, guns, even human hands).

Downing and his colleagues discussed their findings in relation to the suggestion that there may be **domain-specific modules** in the brain that automatically process faces (e.g., Farah, 1996; Kanwisher, McDermott, & Chun, 1997). The existence of such a module would mean that in the presence of a face we can't help but attend to it. Does the finding that human bodies capture attention mean that there may also be a module specialized for detecting bodies? Downing and colleagues conclude that there may indeed be "independent neural systems for a few object types" (2003, p. B28). However, such modules need not be innate. Rather, it may be that over time we gain expertise in dealing with particular categories of stimuli, such as faces and bodies. If modules for faces and bodies are not innate, it's possible that certain brain areas may be recruited to process stimuli of this kind (Gauthier, Skudlarski, Gore, & Anderson, 2000). This issue is likely to be a focus of research for some time (Gauthier, Curran, Curby, & Collins, 2003; Rhodes, Byatt, Michie, & Puce, 2004).

> **domain-specific modules**
> The hypothesis that parts of the brain may be specialized for particular tasks, such as recognizing faces.

A related issue involves the heightened ability of particular stimuli to capture attention. For example, it has been known for decades that a person's own name has the power to capture that person's attention (e.g., Moray, 1959). Mack and his colleagues (Mack, Pappas, Silverman, & Gay, 2002, p. 504), who considered this finding in conjunction with other studies of attention capture, have suggested that highly meaningful stimuli are able to capture our attention; this would explain why a mother will awake to her child's cry while others remain asleep. "[M]eaning is the primary determinant of selective attention and therefore of the content of perceptual consciousness. We see what interests us, what we are looking for and what we are expecting."

Finally, Horstmann (2002) has placed the discussion of attention capture in the context of the perceptual cycle (Neisser, 1976). As we noted in Chapter 1, this is the cycle in which our expectations (i.e., schemata) guide our exploration of the environment, but the environment itself can also influence our experience of it. "If attentional capture were always conditional on an intention, organisms would perceive only what they intended to see; other events would rarely be recognized, and threats would be frequently overlooked" (Horstmann, 2002, p. 504). Although we often see only what we are looking for, if something meaningful happens that we were not expecting, we recognize it very quickly. What examples from your own experience can you think of?

Dual Tasks and the Limits of Attention

One obvious question about attention concerns its capacity. How many things can we attend to at once? The answer to this question may depend on what sorts of things we are trying to do and how skilled we are at doing them. Although it's easy to see how we are able to perform a voluntary task in conjunction with an automatic one, such as carrying on a conversation while walking, it's not so easy to imagine doing two goal-directed things at once. We can do more than one simple task at a time, but as the tasks become more complex they begin to interfere with one another. A common example involves driving a car (e.g., C.D. Wickens, 1984). If you are a skilled driver and you are driving a route you know well, you may also be able to carry on a lively conversation as you drive. However, should something out of the ordinary happen—if it starts snowing heavily, for example—then driving is likely to become a more complex task.

As Hirst (1986; Hirst & Kalmar, 1987) pointed out, the notion that attention is limited can be conceptualized in various ways. One possibility is that attention is like a power supply (Kahneman, 1973) or a reservoir of fuel. If you try to do too much, you will simply run out of gas. Performance on a task has a limit imposed by the capacity of the fuel tank that powers attention. For obvious reasons, this model of attention is called a capacity model.

Another possibility is that attention has **structural limits**. If two tasks require the same kind of activity, then they may interfere with one another more than they would if they required two different kinds. For example, we can make a distinction between auditory and visual processes. You might very well be able to have a visual image of your living room and describe it in words at the same time. However, suppose you were asked to think of (without writing down) the sentence "A bird in the hand is worth two in the bush" and then categorize each word as either a noun or not a noun by saying yes or no (L.R. Brooks, 1968). The correct sequence would be "no, yes, no, no, yes, no, no, yes, no, no, yes."

This task turns out to be quite hard. Try it yourself with this sentence: "Wise men make proverbs and fools repeat them." The problem is that you are trying to do two highly verbal tasks at the same time: imagining a sentence may require you to say it to yourself, and categorizing the words requires you to say yes and no. Saying two things at once is not easy. If you perform the same task by tapping with your left hand for a noun and tapping with your right hand for a non-noun, then it's easier. This is because the two tasks are quite different: tapping is a non-verbal process and therefore interferes less with a verbal task. From this viewpoint, interference between tasks is more likely to occur if they both draw on the same processing resources (e.g., both visual or both verbal) (Kahneman & Treisman, 1984).

Some theories see attention as requiring a central processor (e.g., Broadbent, 1984). If that is the case, then we can't pay attention to more than one thing at a time. This is because the central processor will be able to handle only one task at a time, and if another task is added, then the processor will have to switch from one task to another. It's as if there is a central bottleneck through which information relevant to only one task at a time can pass (Pashler, 1994). Doing two things at once will require you to alternate your attention between the two tasks and selectively attend to only one at a time. Can we learn to attend to more than one thing at a time? If so, we would have mastered the skill of **divided attention**. If we were able to successfully divide our attention, then perhaps with practice our attention could improve beyond normal limits.

An influential study of divided attention was conducted by Spelke, Hirst, and Neisser (1976). Few students would attempt to read and take lecture notes at the same time. Yet this is essentially what these researchers taught their participants to do. In their first study, they trained two participants, named Diane and John, to read short stories while copying dictated words; the participants were then given comprehension tests regarding what they had read while taking dictation. This dual task was very difficult at first, but after roughly six weeks of practice their comprehension was as good as it had been for reading stories alone. However, at this stage Diane and John were not picking up information about the words being dictated to them; for instance, they did not notice that some of the words in the lists came from the same category (e.g., vehicles). They were then told to try to notice any special characteristics of the dictated words. The two participants were soon able to recognize the

capacity model
The hypothesis that attention is like a power supply that can support only a limited amount of attentional activity.

structural limits
The hypothesis that attentional tasks interfere with one another to the extent that they involve similar activities.

central bottleneck
The hypothesis that there is only one path along which information can travel, and it is so narrow that the most it can handle at any one time is the information relevant to one task.

divided attention
The ability to attend to more than one thing at a time.

relationships between the dictated words even while reading with comprehension. In another experiment with new participants, comprehension and speed of reading did not suffer even when the difficulty of the material to be read was increased; performance when doing both tasks was equal to performance when reading alone.

In a follow-up study, Hirst, Spelke, Reaves, Caharack, and Neisser (1980) trained two participants, Arlene and Mary, to simultaneously read and copy complete sentences. Here are examples of some of the dictated sentences:

> The rope broke.
> Spot got free.
> Father chased him.

The participants were tested to see if they could recognize sentences that had been dictated to them. Here are examples of some of the test sentences:

> Father chased him.
> Spot chased Father.
> Spot's rope broke.

The first of the test sentences should be recognized as one of the originally dictated sentences. The second sentence should not be recognized. The third sentence might be falsely recognized if the participants were paying attention to the dictated sentences. The reason for this is that people will often make inferences on the basis of what they hear (Bransford & Franks, 1971). They will then often falsely recognize these inferences as sentences they actually heard. This is in fact what happened in the study by Hirst et al. This result can be taken as demonstrating that the participants genuinely understood the sentences they were writing while they were reading. In other words, they were not taking the dictation mechanically, without paying attention, any more than they were reading mechanically, without paying attention.

Perhaps people can learn to genuinely divide their attention between two tasks, rather than just switch it rapidly back and forth between two tasks. Perhaps so-called "simultaneous" translators, who listen to a speaker in one language and very quickly translate that speech into another language, have perfected this skill as well (Hirst, Neisser, & Spelke, 1978, p. 61). However, the studies we have just reviewed do not disprove the hypothesis that people who seem to be doing two things at once are actually switching very rapidly from one to the other. "It is quite possible that critical mental operations on the two tasks never proceed at the same time, but [participants] are nonetheless able to smoothly switch back and forth between the two tasks" (Pashler, Johnston, & Ruthruff, 2001, p. 644).

Do bottlenecks still exist with highly practised tasks? Experiments on this subject typically involve figuring out what response goes with what stimulus; this is called "stimulus response mapping." For example, participants might be presented with one of three tones—low, middle, or high—and asked to say "one" for the low, "two" for the middle, and "three" for the high tone. This task maps auditory stimuli onto verbal responses. Another task might map visual stimuli onto manual responses. For example, the participant might see a stimulus appear in one of three locations on a computer screen and respond by pressing a key with one of three fingers (index, middle, or ring). We can think of these tasks as consisting

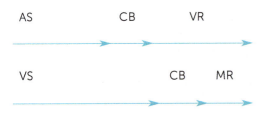

FIGURE 4.7 | A latent bottleneck

AS = auditory stimulus; VS = visual stimulus; CB = central bottleneck; VR = verbal response; MR = motor response. The processing stages for AS and VS end at different times, allowing each to be processed separately by the central bottleneck.

of three stages (Hazeltine, Teague, & Ivry, 2002, p. 532). The first stage is identification of the stimulus, the second would be use of a central processor to select the appropriate response (this is where the attentional bottleneck comes in), and the third would be the execution of the response.

One of the experiments reported by Hazeltine, Teague, and Ivry (2002) used the tasks described in the previous paragraph. Participants were trained on each task separately and then asked to execute them simultaneously. That is, the visual and auditory stimuli were presented at the same time, and participants were instructed to execute both tasks as fast as they could. The conclusion was that "participants were able to achieve levels of performance under dual task conditions that were similar to those obtained under single task conditions" (Hazeltine, Teague, & Ivry, 2002, p. 530). The experimenters found no evidence of a central bottleneck that could not be overcome through practice. They also pointed out that the ability to perform two tasks simultaneously without interference (i.e., to perform them as well together as separately) may require that the stimulus and response phases of each process involve different modalities (e.g., auditory and visual stimuli, verbal and motor responses).

You might think that would be the end of the matter, but Ruthruff, Johnston, Van Selst, Whitsell, and Remington (2003) observed that it is still logically possible for a "latent" bottleneck to exist even with highly practised tasks. This possibility is represented in Figure 4.7. Notice that the "pre-bottleneck" stages finish at different times. This allows each task to pass through the bottleneck separately. You can see how many logical possibilities there are even in an apparently simple situation such as the dual-task experiment. That is one reason why research in cognition seldom progresses rapidly. Since it's necessary to examine all the logical possibilities before definitive conclusions can be drawn, the process is both labour-intensive and time-consuming.

Mind Wandering and Dual Tasks

Typically, when we talk about "dual task" situations, we are referring to conditions under which an individual is given two tasks that must be performed at the same time, as when Spelke and colleagues (1976) had participants read stories and take dictation at the same time. Another example would be a bus driver who has to perform at least one additional task while operating the vehicle. Remember the apparent cause of the bus crash discussed in the case study: the driver was trying simultaneously to watch the road and to monitor the video display. Since both tasks draw on the same limited pool of attentional resources, they simply cannot be done effectively at the same time (see Box 4.2).

But let's consider for a moment a different kind of "dual task" situation, illustrated by a near-accident involving two commuter trains. In another case outlined by railway safety investigator Randall Jamieson (personal communication), a veteran engineer with a perfect performance record ran a red light and almost smashed his train right into an oncoming train (personal communication). Fortunately, the engineer noticed the red signal in time to radio an emergency call to the oncoming train and engage his emergency brakes. Onboard cameras from the cab of the offending engineer's train show that as it left the preceding station, he was agitated, pacing around the cab and audibly talking to himself.

CONSIDER THIS
BOX 4.2
Are You Resistant to Dual-Task Interference?

There is considerable evidence that using a cell phone while driving can impair performance, even if the phone is hands-free (see Strayer & Drews, 2007, for a review). As we saw in Chapter 1, using a cell phone not only slows driving-related responses (Strayer & Johnston, 2001) but impairs memory for signs on the side of the road (Strayer, Drews & Johnston, 2003). Yet it seems there are some people for whom performing a secondary task while driving does not measurably reduce driving performance. Could you be one of those people, the ones Watson and Strayer (2010) call "supertaskers"? Watson and Strayer (2010) had a larger number of university students do a driving task in a simulator either as a single task, or while solving math problems (a dual-task situation). The driving performance of most of the participants suffered when they had to simultaneously complete a secondary task. Strikingly, however, 2.5 per cent of the participants seemed to be completely unaffected by the secondary task. Figure 4.8 shows this pattern of results for the time it takes to initiate braking when an obstacle appeared; the only people who weren't affected by the dual task were the supertaskers. If you're tempted to think that you might be one of them, don't be surprised if you find out you're not: remember, only about 2.5 per cent of the people in any population fall into that category.

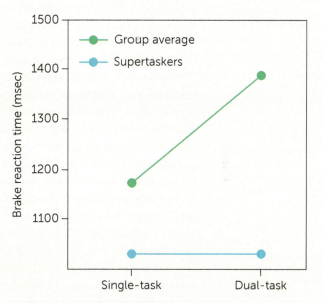

FIGURE 4.8 | The dual task impairs brake reaction time for most people, but not for supertaskers

Adapted from: Watson, J.M. & Strayer, D.L. (2010).

At times he was shaking his head and moving his fingers as if counting something. Between these agitated behaviours, the engineer followed the rule that required him to signal acknowledgment of both the yellow lights that preceded the red light. Yet instead of slowing his train, he sped up. The train was moving quite quickly when the red light came into view, at which point the engineer stopped the train just in time. A post-incident interview with the engineer revealed that he had been having problems with the train and had got into an argument with his supervisor at the preceding station. As he left that station, therefore, he was preoccupied, thinking about the mechanical problems he had experienced and replaying the argument with his supervisor over and over in his mind. In Mr Jamieson's opinion, the engineer's attentional resources had been absorbed in his thoughts and so diverted away from the safe operation of the train. In effect, it was as if the engineer's mental preoccupation were an internally imposed secondary task that distracted him from his primary task. Could this be the case? Can **mind wandering** take attention away from the task at hand?

mind wandering
A shift of mental resources away from the task at hand and towards internal thoughts.

sustained attention to response task (SART)

A continuous response task in which digits (e.g., 0 to 9) are sequentially presented on a computer screen and participants are asked to press a button in response to all but one of them (e.g., the infrequent digit 3); response to this infrequent digit is supposed to be withheld (see Robertson et al., 1997).

commission error

Failure to withhold a response to the infrequent digit in the SART.

default network

A set of brain areas that are active when an individual does not have a specific task to do and is absorbed in internal thought.

attentional blink (AB)

Failure to notice the second of two stimuli presented within 550 milliseconds of each other.

The answer appears to be a resounding "yes." According to a recent study by a research group at the University of British Columbia, both task performance and brain activity clearly showed that mind wandering was associated with reduced attention to the primary task (Christoff, Gordon, Smallwood, Smith & Schooler, 2009). The participants in this study were required to perform a version of the **sustained attention to response task (SART)**, which involves pressing a response button (e.g., the spacebar) when a digit is presented on a computer screen and withholding a response when an infrequent "critical digit" is presented (see Robertson, Manly, Andrade, Baddeley & Yiend, 1997). In this particular case, the digits 0 to 9 were presented every two seconds and the critical digit requiring a non-response was 3, which occurred roughly five per cent of the time. Since withholding a response to the infrequent critical digit requires attention, failure to do so is a good indicator that attention is disengaged from the task; thus **commission errors** are the primary measure of attention lapses in this task. A sample sequence of trials is illustrated in Figure 4.9. As you can imagine, this simple, repetitive task is very boring, and thus people tend to start thinking about other things after only a short time. Importantly, the researchers interrupted the task every now and then to ask participants whether they were attending to the SART task (i.e., on task) or thinking about something else (i.e., mind wandering). The task was done in an fMRI scanner so that the experimenters could measure the brain activity in each case.

Christoff and colleagues (2009) compared brain activity and SART behaviour in the 10 seconds preceding moments of mind wandering and the 10 seconds before moments of on-task performance. They found that people made more commission errors on the SART prior to mind wandering than prior to on-task performance. Furthermore, mind wandering was more likely than on-task performance to be associated with increased activity in the **default network** of the brain: a set of areas that are known to be active when people don't have a task to do and are simply absorbed in their thoughts (see Raichle & Snyder, 2007). Taken together, these results suggest that when the mind wanders, attention is removed from the task at hand and turned inward. Apparently, mind wandering does require some of our limited attentional resources, leading us to perform more poorly on concurrent tasks. This is how the mental ruminations of the railway engineer led him to disengage his attention from the operation of the train and run a red light. Box 4.3 describes how bouts of mind wandering can lead to all sorts of everyday action errors.

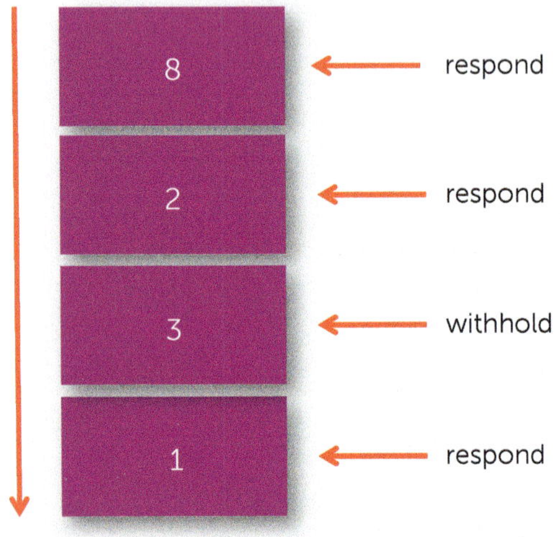

FIGURE 4.9 | An example of a sequence of displays in the sustained attention to response task (SART)

Adapted from Olivers, N.L. & Nieuwenhuis, S. (2005).

The Attentional Blink

Another fascinating demonstration of the limits of human attention is known as the **attentional blink** or **AB** (Shapiro, Arnell, & Raymond, 1997). Suppose you present a series of letters in the centre of a screen and ask participants to identify them. The attentional blink occurs when two of these stimuli are presented within 550 milliseconds of each other. During that very short interval, the probability that the second letter will be reported is much less than it would be for a longer interval. In such cases it's as if participants' attention "blinks" and leaves them with nothing to report. One interpretation of these results is that participants apply their attentional resources to the first letter and then don't have enough attentional resources left to apply to the

Do You Make Errors?

FIGURE 4.10 | An action slip: putting a plastic coffee lid on a porcelain mug

Have you ever started walking down the street and noticed that you still had your slippers on? Or absent-mindedly tried to fit a plastic coffee lid on your porcelain mug? Or put the cereal box in the fridge and the milk in the cupboard? According to James Reason (1979; 1984; see also Norman, 1981) these **action slips** are quite common, especially when we are engaged in some "**parallel mental activity**" (Reason, 1979, p. 76)—a fancy term for "mind wandering."

Reason (1979; 1984) described a series of diary studies in which participants were asked to keep a record of every silly (and not so silly) error they made. Interestingly, Reason found that these errors are often attention- and memory-related, and that they tend to occur more at certain times of the day than at others. To keep track of your own everyday mistakes, use a diary or your smart phone to record the error, the circumstances surrounding it, and the time of day. After doing this for several weeks, look to see if there are any patterns.

action slips
The kind of behavioural errors that often occur in everyday life.

parallel mental activity
Thinking about something other than the task at hand.

second letter. Since awareness of the letters requires that you allocate sufficient attentional resources to them, you are aware of the first one but completely unaware of the second.

Olivers and Nieuwenhuis (2005) have reported some very counterintuitive findings, which suggest there is something you can do to reduce the attentional blink. They presented participants with a rapid stream of roughly 15 letters and 2 numbers. The letters were to be ignored and the two numbers were targets. While this procedure might seem very similar to the SART task described earlier, the AB task is quite different with regard to the speed of presentation. In the SART the items are presented every 2 seconds and each item is considered to be a single trial. By contrast, in the AB task the items are presented about every 120 ms and each stream of 17 items constitutes a single trial. The quick presentation of successive stimuli is often referred to as **rapid serial visual presentation (RSVP)**. An example of an RSVP stream is shown in Panel A of Figure 4.11. After the RSVP stream, participants are asked to report the first number and then the second number.

Olivers and Nieuwenhuis varied the number of letters intervening between the two target digits. When there is one intervening item between the first digit (Target One: T1) and the second digit (Target Two: T2), T2 is said to be presented at Lag 2 because T2 is the second item after T1. At Lag 3 there are two intervening letters between T1 and T2, and so on. Because the attentional blink typically occurs only when two targets are presented in close temporal proximity, one would expect the most blinking to occur at short lags and for performance to improve at longer lags.

More important, Olivers and Nieuwenhuis also included a condition in which participants completed the AB task in silence, and a condition in which they listened to music

☀ DISCOVERY LAB

rapid serial visual presentation (RSVP)
The presentation of a series of stimuli in quick succession.

while completing the AB task. We will refer to these two conditions as the No Music and Music conditions, respectively. The music in the Music condition was meant to function as a concurrent, though irrelevant, task that might engage some attentional resources. How would this secondary task influence performance in the AB? Based on the studies we have discussed thus far, you might think that the music would deplete attentional resources, making the attentional blink larger.

The results of the Olivers and Nieuwenhuis study are shown in Panel B of Figure 4.11. The figure shows the accuracy with which participants were able to identify the second digit (T2) as a function of Lag between T1 and T2, as well as whether or not participants listened to music while doing the task. Strikingly, the results showed that playing music actually reduced the magnitude of the attentional blink, leading to very high accuracy of T2 identification! Olivers and Nieuwenhuis (2005, p. 268) concluded that "performance on an attentionally demanding visual detection task may improve when the task is accompanied by task-irrelevant mental activity." So at least in some cases, it appears that allocating some attention to a secondary task may actually improve performance in the primary task.

The attentional blink has also been used to address other issues related to attention and perception. Shapiro, Arnell, and Raymond (1997) explored whether the second target— which is not perceived consciously because it occurs shortly after the first target (i.e., T2 is in the attentional blink)—could nevertheless be processed unconsciously and still have a priming effect. Suppose you presented three targets in a row, with the second and third being semantically related words (e.g., *lawyer, judge*). Suppose further that the second word (*lawyer*) is "blinked." It turns out that the third word (*judge*) is more likely to be correctly identified than it would be if the second word had been semantically unrelated to it (e.g., *tree*) (Shapiro, Arnell, & Raymond, 1997, pp. 291–292). This elegant evidence for perception in the absence of attention supports the existence of subliminal perception (see Chapter 13.)

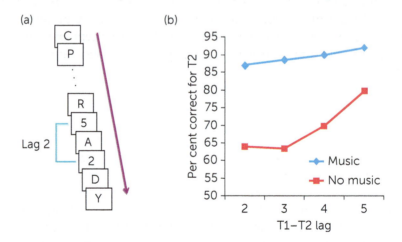

FIGURE 4.11 | An example of a sequence of displays and the results of an attentional blink study reported by Olivers and Nieuwenhuis (2005)

Panel A: A sequence of displays illustrating T1 and T2 separated by a Lag of 2. The dots illustrate other intervening letter displays. *Panel B*: The accuracy with which T2 is identified. Notice that there is a substantial attentional blink in the No Music condition, which is largely absent in the Music condition.

Adapted from Olivers, N.L. & Nieuwenhuis, S. (2005).

Barnard, Scott, Taylor, May, and Knightley (2004) have used the attentional blink to reinforce the connection between attention and meaning. In one study they presented

> lists of 35 words . . . at a rate of 110 ms/item, with one word replacing another with no interstimulus interval. Most words referred to things or events occurring in natural environments (e.g., *island*, *snowstorm*). Participants were instructed to report a single target, a word that referred to a job or profession that people engage in for pay (e.g., *banker*, *shepherd*). On test trials, targets were preceded . . . by a potential distractor word and the semantic relationship between distractor and target was varied (p. 179).

One class of distractor items included words referring to activities for which people are not paid, such as *shopper*, *coward*, and *witness*. Because these distractors are also properties of people, they are semantically related to the target. Another class of distractor was inanimate (e.g., *freezer*, *cupboard*, *wireless*), and thus less closely related to the target. When a semantically related word preceded a target word, there was a greater likelihood of an attentional blink than when an inanimate word preceded the target. That is, people were less likely to report the target when it followed a semantically related word than when it followed an inanimate word.

One important feature of this study was that the targets and distractors differed only in meaning, not in characteristics such as colour (Barnard et al., 2004, p. 179). The participants were set to attend to *jobs that people do for pay*. The more meaningfully the item was related to the target, the more it was attended to. Barnard et al. (2004, p. 185) conceived of this process as involving an initial "glance" at an item, followed by a closer "look" if it seemed to be a possible target. The more time was spent looking at an item, the less likely it was that the next item would receive even a "glance." The result was an attentional blink. This account of the attentional blink harks back to Mack's point that highly meaningful stimuli capture our attention. It also recalls the notion that much of cognition involves what Bartlett (1932) called an "effort after meaning." We will consider this point in detail in Chapter 5.

Task Switching

The term **set** (or mental set) refers to the way "an individual often prepares to act before beginning the overt effective action," as when sprinters take their marks on the starting line (Woodworth, 1940, p. 29). Woodworth (1869–1962) argued that there are many different kinds of sets. For example, in addition to the sprinter's preparatory set there are executive sets that guide us through a sequence of responses, as when driving a car; and goal sets that represent what we aim to achieve. Woodworth described sets as temporary organizations in the brain that act "by facilitating some responses, while preventing or inhibiting others. . . . While looking eagerly for a lost object you do not notice sounds that at other times would surely attract your attention. Readiness for one act is at the same time unreadiness for other acts" (Woodworth, 1940, p. 33). In the context of the distinctions we have been using throughout this chapter, a set is a top-down process that organizes our action to meet a particular goal.

set
A temporary, top-down organization in the brain that facilitates some responses while inhibiting others in order to achieve a certain goal; also referred to as a "mental set."

The concept of the "set" played an important role in the initial research into **task switching** (Jersild, 1927). Suppose you are at your computer, trying to finish an essay, when an email arrives from the registrar's office, reminding you that today is the deadline for paying the remainder of your fees. You are annoyed at the interruption, but recognize the importance of the message. You look around for your bank card, find it, and head off to the registrar's office. Along the way, you stop and talk with some friends. Each of these tasks—writing an essay, reading an email, finding your bank card, going to the registrar's office, talking to friends—"requires an appropriate configuration of mental resources, a procedural 'schema' . . . or 'task-set.' . . . We exercise intentional 'executive' control to select and implement the task-set, or the combination of task-sets, that are appropriate to our dominant goals . . . , resisting temptations to satisfy other goals" (Monsell, 2003, p. 134).

Closely associated with task switching is the phenomenon known as **switch cost** (Monsell, 2003, p. 135). This cost is a reflection of the fact that performance on a task immediately after a switch is worse than typical performance on the same task. To continue with the example from the previous paragraph, when you return from the registrar's office and start working on your essay again, you may not be able to pick up smoothly where you left off. You may need to reconstruct exactly what you were doing before you switched to the task of reading the email from the registrar. Sometimes switching back to a task can lead you to feel as if you need to start all over again. This may be due to the time required to reset the cognitive system so that the behaviours appropriate to the current task are engaged once again and behaviours appropriate to the previous task are inhibited (Yeung & Monsell, 2003, p. 919).

Most experiments on this topic require participants to switch tasks when given a certain cue by the experimenter. For example, they may be shown a series of letter–number pairs, such as "H 3" (Yeung & Monsell, 2003, p. 923). Participants are required to perform one of two tasks on each trial. In the "alphabet arithmetic" task, they must "add" the number to the letter. In this case the participant would say *K* because *K* is the third letter in the alphabet from *H*. In the "perceptual comparison task" the participant must say "yes" if the letter and the number both contain curved lines or both contain only straight lines. For a pair such as "H 3" the answer would be "no" because the letter has only straight lines while the number has only curved lines (Yeung & Monsell, 2003, p. 922). When cued to do so, participants must switch from whatever task they are currently doing to the other task. A switch cost is reliably observed under such conditions.

Arrington and Logan (2004) did a clever experiment that shed light on task switching when the participant, rather than the experimenter, controls precisely when the task switch occurs. Voluntary task switching was initiated by telling the participants that they had to decide which tasks to perform on each trial. The participants' goal was to perform each task about half the time and to try to switch randomly between them, without either counting the number of times they had performed each task or simply alternating between them (Arrington & Logan, 2004, p. 611). On each trial the participants were shown a single digit between 1 and 9. The two tasks consisted of indicating whether the digit was even or odd and indicating whether it was larger or smaller than 5.

Even though the task switching was voluntary, there was still a switch cost for each task. The participants did perform each task approximately half the time. However, although the participants had been instructed to try to switch randomly, they did not in fact do so. Rather, they tended to produce a series of runs on one task, then switch to a series of runs on the other task, then switch back to a series of runs on the first task, and so on. This suggests that once participants are used to one task they may be reluctant to incur the cost of switching to the other. Notice that these participants were not completely free to choose which task to perform but were constrained to try to perform each task about half the time. It's possible that, in a situation where we are completely free to choose which task to perform, we may persist with one task until boredom sets in and we are prepared to pay the switch cost. We will consider the important role that boredom plays in directing our attention in Chapter 13, on personal cognition.

Like other topics we have examined in this chapter, task switching research suggests that top-down processes play an important role in regulating our attention. Indeed, Pashler, Johnston, and Ruthruff (2001) have concluded that one of the "main themes to emerge from" recent research "is the idea that the effects of mental set are more pervasive than had been previously thought" (p. 648). It is also true that recent research has reached "a rather broad consensus that higher level control operations—those operations that implement task sets by selecting, ordering, and chaining lower level task execution processes—are intimately linked to conscious awareness" (Meiran, Hommel, Bibi, & Lev, 2001, p. 10). Task switching requires us to change our set—just the sort of operation that might be expected to show a correlation with awareness. Thus we might assume that people are aware of achieving a preparatory set and know when they are ready to perform the next task. Meiran et al. (2001) tested this assumption by asking participants in a task-switching experiment to indicate for each trial when they were ready. The fact that longer preparation times were not associated with better performance suggested that they were *not* actually aware of whether they were ready or not. All of this is consistent with earlier research, reviewed by Humphrey (1951/1963, Ch. 2), suggesting that people may be aware of the goal they are trying to achieve, but not of the operations required to achieve it.

Sustained Attention

Recall the last time you had to sit through a very long and perhaps boring presentation or lecture. Did you find that as time went by you were paying less attention? The act of paying attention to a task over a prolonged period of time is referred to as sustained attention. When the requirement to sustain attention is externally imposed (e.g., when it is part of your job), we refer to this activity as vigilance (see Hancock, 2013).

Much of the research on sustained attention and vigilance was motivated by a very practical problem that became apparent during the Second World War (Mackworth, 1948). The introduction of the radar to military operations meant that operators had to monitor the device for extended periods of time in order to detect brief signals (i.e., blips on the radar indicating possible enemy vessels) that occurred very rarely.

In designing experimental tasks to study vigilance, researchers tried to closely model the radar operator's task. Here is the thinking behind one such task, which became known as the "Mackworth Clock Task":

> Laboratory studies were therefore started, initially for this wholly practical reason, to determine over what length of time accuracy could be maintained in work of this sort. It was arbitrarily decided that the synthetic laboratory

sustained attention
The act of maintaining attention focused on a single task for a prolonged period of time.

vigilance
Sustained attention as an externally imposed requirement.

situation need attempt to reproduce only the more general features of watch-keeping duties. It therefore seemed necessary to provide a series of visual signals which were all difficult to perceive because the subject had no more than a glimpse of each of these barely visible stimuli. It was also thought important to ensure that the signals were presented only occasionally, so that the lengthy searching nearly always drew a blank, although many rather similar signals of no importance at all were constantly being encountered and having to be disregarded. Isolation of the watcher seemed a significant factor in the situation, and care was taken to ensure that the subject had no reliable objective yardstick by which he could gauge his own performance (Mackworth, 1948, p. 7).

The Mackworth Clock Task involves having participants monitor a line, much like a clock hand, moving in discrete steps around an imaginary circle. There are numerous variations on this task, but consider a case (Mackworth, 1948) in which the clock hand jumps roughly 1/30 of the clock circle every second, but very infrequently (less than 0.5 per cent of the movements; see Mackworth, 1964), the clock hand would "skip" one position and move about 2/30 of the clock in one jump. Participants were asked to watch for the infrequent "skips" and to press a button when they occurred.

When participants were asked to perform the Mackworth Clock Task for a two-hour period, their performance showed a considerable decline over time (see Mackworth, 1948). The average incidence of missed stimuli over a two-hour watch period is shown in broken lines in Figure 4.12. As you can see, performance dropped substantially from the first half-hour to the second half-hour of the task, and then continued to decline at a slightly more modest rate all the way to the fourth half-hour. This performance decline is referred to as the **vigilance decrement**.

The vigilance decrement has been documented in many everyday tasks and contexts. For instance, recent studies have shown that students' attention to lecture material tends to decline over time in a class. This seems to be the case both when lectures are viewed online on a computer screen (e.g., Risko, Anderson, Sarwal, Engelhardt, & Kingstone, 2012) and when they are experienced live in a real classroom (e.g., Young, Robinson & Alberts, 2009). Vigilance decrements have also been demonstrated in safety-critical contexts, such as driving. Yet even though drivers tend to respond more slowly to critical stimuli as driving time increases, they actually report becoming more vigilant over time (Schmidt et al., 2009). This finding led Schmidt and colleagues (2009, p.1091) to conclude "that drivers in a reduced state of vigilance following a prolonged and monotonous drive are vulnerable to a misjudgment of their objective vigilance state in terms of performance. . . ."

At present there are two dominant views of the cognitive mechanisms underlying the vigilance decrement (see Pattyn, Neyt, Henderickx & Soetens, 2008). Advocates of the **overload view** focus on the high attentional demands imposed by vigilance tasks (Warm, Parasuraman, & Matthews, 2008; Grier, Warm, Dember, Matthews, Galinsky, Szalma, & Parasuraman, 2003). For example, the **resource depletion account** (see Grier et al., 2003) posits that the pool of attentional resources is limited to begin with and becomes depleted over time, as the vigilance task progresses. By contrast, advocates of the **underload view** argue that vigilance situations are typically under-stimulating, and that the resulting boredom leads people to decouple their attention from the vigilance task and shift it elsewhere,

vigilance decrement
The decline in performance over time in vigilance tasks.

overload view
The view that performance on vigilance tasks declines over time because such tasks are so demanding.

resource depletion account
A version of the overload view according to which performance declines over time as attentional resources become depleted.

underload view
The view that performance on vigilance tasks declines over time because such tasks are not stimulating enough to hold people's attention.

embodied
Existing within a body; the term reflects the general view that cognition depends not only on the mind but also on the physical constraints of the body in which the mind exists.

often to internal thoughts that are unrelated to the task (see Pattyn et al., 2008; Robertson et al., 1997).

So which of these accounts is correct? The jury is still out. On the one hand, participants report that vigilance tasks are difficult and stressful (e.g., Warm et al., 2008), and vigilance decrements are often exacerbated by the addition of another resource-demanding task (e.g., Helton & Russell, 2011; 2013); this evidence supports the overload view. On the other hand, physiological measures (e.g., heart rate) showing that people become progressively under-aroused during vigilance tasks (Pattyn et al., 2008), and subjective reports revealing that thoughts unrelated to the task increase over time (Thomson, Seli, Besner & Smilek, 2014) suggest that the underload account might be correct.

Overt Visual Attention

Based on what we have learned about attention so far, you may be tempted to think that attention has been conceived of only as an internal mental process. Indeed, many models of visual attention construe it as a mental capacity or limited resource. In this section we will see that attention can also be understood as something that is embodied and therefore constrained by the nature and limitations of our physical body. In the case of visual attention, this suggests that attention should be considered in the context of the physical nature of the eyes,

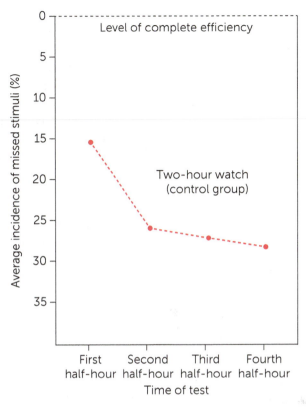

FIGURE 4.12 | Performance in a vigilance task over four segments of a two-hour watch period

From Mackworth (1948), p. 9.

the light receptors in the eye, the nature of the primary visual cortex of the brain, and how the eyes move. The process of attending to objects by moving the eyes to look at them is referred to as overt attention and can be contrasted with the process of attending to an object while holding the eyes stationary, which is referred to as covert attention (see Findlay & Gilchrist, 2003; Klein & Pontefract, 1994).

The available evidence suggests that the two forms of attention often work closely together. If you choose to attend to another person in the room, for instance, you will likely shift your eyes to wherever that person is. First, however, it's likely that your covert attention will already have moved to that location. Studies using controlled laboratory stimuli have suggested that when new objects are about to be viewed, covert attention shifts to the location first and then is followed by the eyes. This has been referred to as the sequential attention hypothesis (Henderson, Pollatsek, & Rayner, 1989; see Findlay & Gilchrist, 2003, for a review). This hypothesis suggests a tight connection between covert and overt attention (Findlay & Gilchrist, 2003).

But the two forms of attention are not always so tightly coupled (Findlay & Gilchrist, 2003). Recall, for instance, the studies of inattentional blindness discussed earlier. In these studies, an object was presented exactly where the person was looking but the latter failed to notice it. If covert attention was focused exactly where the person was looking, how could this happen? Another example of a separation between the two forms of attention

DISCOVERY LAB

overt attention
Attending to something with eye movement.

covert attention
Attending to something without eye movement.

sequential attention hypothesis
The hypothesis about the relationship between overt and covert attention that posits a tight relationship between the two, whereby covert attention is shifted first and overt eye movement follows.

occurs when you "look" at something "from the corner of your eye." To experience this, just look straight ahead and, without moving your eyes, try to see what a person in the periphery of your vision is doing. In this case, overt attention is focused straight ahead and covert attention is focused to the side of your line of sight. You will probably find that this is hard to keep up; after a few minutes, it's likely to take you some effort to maintain the dissociation between your covert and overt attention. Even if the eyes and covert attention can operate separately, then, this is more the exception than the rule.

Findlay and Gilchrist (2003) maintain that overt and covert attention in most cases move together, and that researchers should focus on studying overt attention because of its critical role in everyday attending. They argue that the importance of overt attention is related to the physical constraints of the eye. As we saw in Chapter 3, a high-resolution image of the world is available only for the small amount of information that falls on the foveal region of the retina. This means that if you want to see something clearly, you have to move your eyes so that information falls on that specific location at the back of your eye. In what follows, we will discuss how overt attention shifts (i.e., how the eyes move) during several everyday tasks such as reading and viewing objects and scenes.

DISCOVERY LAB ✳

Overt Attention During Reading

Are your eyes moving smoothly from letter to letter as you read this text? To accurately measure the behaviour of the eyes, researchers use complicated eye-tracking technology. An example of a modern eye-tracking device is shown in Figure 4.13. This device works by aiming a camera and a small infrared light at the eye and then locating (a) a reflection of this light off the cornea and (b) the location of the pupil, which is the point where the most

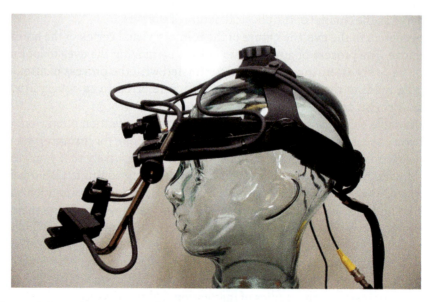

FIGURE 4.13 | A modern eye-tracking system

The EyeLink II system, developed by Canadian-based SR Research. The device is placed on the head and two cameras positioned below the eyes track the location of eye gaze.

light is absorbed. By tracking the bright corneal reflection and dark pupil from moment to moment, the system is able to determine precisely how the gaze moves over time.

If you feel that your eyes are moving smoothly from left to right across the page, you're mistaken. Studies using eye-tracking devices have shown that in fact eye movement while reading is a series of rapid, seemingly chaotic movements called saccades interspersed by moments of relative stillness, known as fixations (see Findlay & Gilchrist, 2003; Palmer, 1999; and Rayner, 1998, for reviews). During fixation the eye is relatively stationary in order to optimize the transmittal of visual information to the brain, while during saccades the eyes move very rapidly and visual information is essentially cut off. The typical fixation duration is between 200 and 300 milliseconds, but times can vary widely depending on the word being fixated, the position where the eye falls within the word, and how well the word has been interpreted (see Rayner, 1998). It's worth keeping in mind that during fixations the eyes are not perfectly stationary. In fact, they are in a state of constant but minute movement known as nystagmus (Rayner, 1998; Palmer, 1999). Typically, eye-tracking programs have an algorithm that uses the velocity and distance of the eye movements to determine whether they represent fixation (very small movements) or saccade (larger movements).

Figure 4.14 shows the eye movements made by someone reading a passage from the book *A Short History of Nearly Everything* by Bill Bryson (2003). The number "1" just below the last word of the first paragraph marks the first place the reader looked on this page; and the line running up to the second word of the second line of text represents the first saccade. The circles show the locations of the reader's eye fixations, and their sizes indicate the

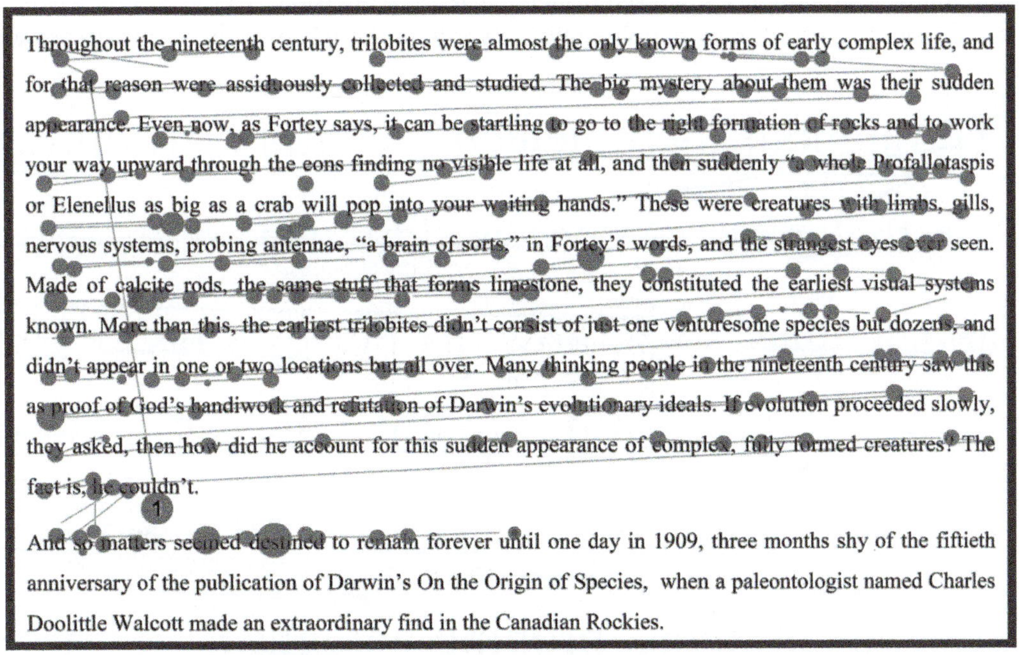

saccades
The rapid, jerky movements made as the eye scans an image.

fixation
Holding the eye relatively still in order to maintain an image on the fovea.

nystagmus
Small but continuous eye movements during fixation.

FIGURE 4.14 | An example of eye movement behaviour when reading an extended passage

Fixations are indicated by circles (circle size reflects fixation duration) and lines indicate the saccades that connect successive fixations.

From: Yarbus, A.L. (1967). With kind permission from Springer Science+Business Media B.V.

duration. As this example shows, in most cases the eyes fixate on a word only once, and for a consistent period, before moving on to the next word perhaps six or more letters on down the line. At other times, though, fixations come in clusters, and a small section of text may receive multiple fixations of varying duration until the reader has understood it well enough to move on. That all of this goes on without our conscious awareness of it—indeed, without any particular intentional control—is quite remarkable.

Figure 4.14 shows that the motion of the reading eye is anything but smooth. However, it doesn't show the direction of all the saccades. If it did, it would reveal a further illusion in our subjective experience of reading: the feeling that our eyes are moving consistently from left to right. If this impression were true and we put arrows on the saccade lines, nearly all the arrows would point to the right, with the exception of the one long saccade back from the end of one line to the beginning of the next. But this is not the case. Figure 4.15 shows an enlarged portion of the left half of a page so that you can see the eye movements in more detail. Inspection of the figure reveals a large number of leftward saccades, most of which represent reorientations within or between words while reading. These are referred to as **regressions** (Rayner, 1998). In addition, notice that some leftward saccades terminate to the left of the vertical dotted line; these are primarily the result of expected transitions from the end of one line to the beginning of the next. Interestingly, in every case this transition requires two saccades, not one: the first, longer saccade does the majority of the work in transitioning between lines, but it stops short of the beginning of the line, and a second, smaller saccade is necessary to reach the desired starting point.

One question that emerged early in the study of overt attention during reading was how much information is processed from the periphery of vision. In other words, when the eye fixates on a word, how many letters or words to the left or right are processed and

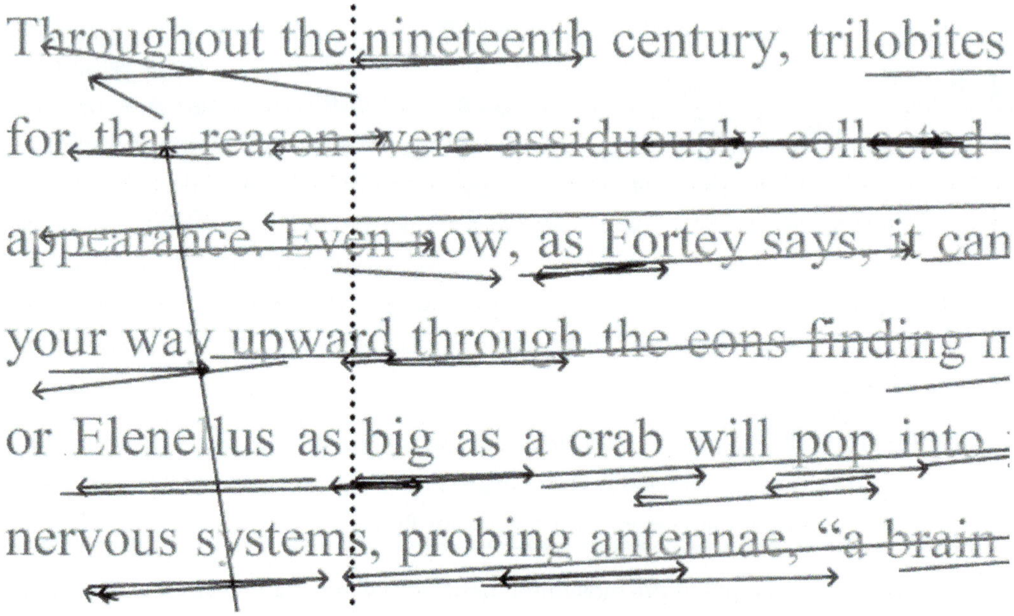

regressions

Right to left movements of the eyes during reading, directing them to previously read text.

FIGURE 4.15 | A sample of saccades from Figure 4.14 with direction of motion identified by arrows

influence what is understood? McConkie and Rayner (1975; see Rayner, 1998, and Findlay & Gilchrist, 2003, for reviews) developed a clever method called the **moving window technique** to answer this question. This technique involves narrowing the window of text that is visible to the reader by obscuring all but (say) six letters to either side of the person's current fixation (for example, by changing all the letters outside that small area to *Xs*), Then, every time the eyes move to a different location, another six letters on either side of the fixation would be visible, but all letters farther away would again be obscured. This is done with sophisticated eye-tracking technology that changes the reading material on the fly, depending on where the reader is looking. The results showed that reading is hindered when the person sees fewer than 17 to 20 characters; as long as that much is visible, reading seems to be unaffected.

Thus far we have considered how people move their eyes while reading printed text. However, a growing body of research is now considering more complex situations, such as reading a page that contains both text and images. For instance, Rayner and colleagues (2001) studied how the eyes move when people are asked to evaluate visual advertisements. You can imagine how informative such research would be for the advertising industry! Consistent with what we have discussed thus far, the eyes move in very systematic ways in the context of advertisement viewing. Specifically, we tend to look first at the words and then at the images. Overall, more fixations are made on the text than on the picture. However, the average fixation on pictures is longer than the average fixation on the words.

Eye movements have even been measured while people engage with more complex material such as newspapers. Newspapers are an interesting medium because each page contains a number of articles, which often include large headings and pictures. Recently, Holmberg, Holsanova, and Holmqvist (2006) studied how people view newspaper pages. As you might expect, the results showed that most people begin by searching for places—**entry points**—to start reading. An entry point might be either a heading or a picture. After finding an entry point, people will often read a section of text for some period of time and then begin looking for another entry point. This research also found individual differences with regard to (1) how much of an article people will read before moving on and (2) the extent to which people look at the pictures. At present, researchers are only scratching the surface of how overt attention is deployed when viewing complex reading materials. It's quite possible that studies of eye movements during reading will change the way text is formatted and laid out, so that it allows for faster reading and optimal comprehension.

Object and Scene Viewing

One of the main conclusions drawn from the research on the movement of overt attention during reading is that the eyes move in very systematic ways. You might say that this makes sense, given that the visual organization of text is so systematic: words are organized in horizontal lines, and to extract meaning we have to read from left to right. But how do our eyes move when we are viewing more complex objects and scenes? Some of the initial work addressing this question was conducted by Alfred L. Yarbus (1967). At a time when eye-tracking technology was still in its infancy, Yarbus was able to measure eye movements with relatively high accuracy as his participants viewed pictures of objects and natural scenes.

You have already encountered one example of the sorts of eye-tracking records that Yarbus collected. Figure 2.8 showed that when we look at a face, whether of a person or an

moving window technique
A method of determining how much visual information can be taken in during a fixation, in which the reader is prevented from seeing information beyond a certain distance from the current fixation.

entry points
The locations to which we direct our eyes before starting to read a section in a piece of complex material such as a newspaper.

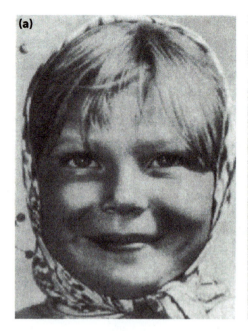

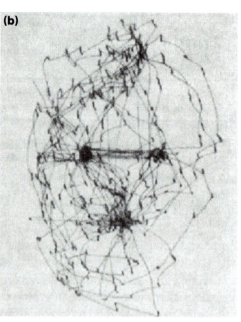

FIGURE 4.16 | **Recorded eye movements (b) while viewing a photograph of a face (a) over a three-minute period**

Compare these tracings with those shown in Figure 2.8.

From: Yarbus, A.L. (1967). With kind permission from Springer Science+Business Media B.V.

animal, for one minute, we tend to focus primarily on the eyes and mouth. The face in Figure 4.16 was viewed for three minutes. In this case we can see that this tendency to fixate on the eyes and mouth is especially pronounced at the beginning of the viewing process, while other areas are explored somewhat later. Based on his research, Yarbus (1967, p. 190) concluded that an "observer's attention is usually held only by certain elements of the picture." That is, the eye fixations are not just randomly or evenly spaced but seem to focus on important information. As Yarbus noted, the eyes and mouth tell us a lot about an individual and so it makes sense that people focus on those parts of the face.

The eye-tracking record shown in Figure 4.16 also makes another interesting point about the nature of eye movements. The record is not just a combination of dots (fixations) and straight lines (eye movements). In addition, there are some lines that are curved in various ways with dot-like discontinuities. This is because the eyes don't always move in perfectly straight lines. Yarbus drew the moment-to-moment positions of the eyes during ballistic (rapid) movement to give a better idea of what the eyes are actually doing when they move quickly. The discontinuities in Yarbus's eye-tracking records are fixations, and, as we noted, these discontinuities seem to aggregate in certain meaningful locations of the image.

As an aside, we should mention that the eyes can be made to move smoothly, without interrupting fixations, when they are following a smoothly moving target. You can observe this by having a friend face you and follow your finger with her or his eyes as you move it from left to right. As you look at the person's eyes you will notice that the movements are not jerky but smooth. These are called **smooth pursuit movements** (Robinson, 1965). Interestingly, according to Robinson (1965, p. 569), these "[s]mooth pursuit movements . . . constitute a large portion of ocular activity."

Yarbus also conducted numerous studies of how people shift their gaze when looking at scenes. From them he drew some important conclusions, which we will illustrate using more recently collected eye movement records. Take a look at the photo in the upper half of Figure 4.17. As you can see, it shows a number of people sitting outside a coffee shop. Below it is the eye-tracking record of a viewer who was asked to look at that image for 15 seconds and then *describe the people* in it. In this instance, the viewer's eyes

smooth pursuit movements

Movements of the eye that, because they are not jerky, enable the viewer to maintain fixation on a moving object.

FIGURE 4.17 | A scene from the Distillery District, Toronto (a), and the eye fixations (black dots) of a participant (b) asked to view the image and describe the people

The participant's objective was to be able to describe the people in the image.

fixated almost exclusively on the people. When the same experiment was conducted with a different viewer (results not shown here), most of the fixations again fell on the people, although the background also received a few. This evidence of similarity in the way different individuals move their eyes when given the same viewing task is consistent with one of the conclusions reached by Yarbus. Finding these commonalities across individuals performing the same tasks is exciting for researchers because they indicate that eye movements are systematic behaviours that generalize across individuals.

Another important conclusion drawn by Yarbus (1967) is illustrated in Figure 4.18, which shows the eye fixation pattern of an individual who was asked to view the image in Figure 4.17a with the purpose of describing the *location* rather than the people. In this case the eyes fixated not only on the people, but also on the sign beside the door and on items in the window and on the wall. Looking back at Figure 4.17b you will see that the sign on the coffee shop was never fixated on when the participant's task was to describe the people in the scene. This illustrates that the deployment of overt attention depends not only on the nature of the image viewed, but also on the *goals* of the viewer. This conclusion, originally drawn by Yarbus, is consistent with a large body of scene-viewing literature reviewed by Henderson (2003). Henderson refers to eye guidance based on the task goals of the observer as guidance by **task-related knowledge**. Of course, it's worth noting that salient visual features, such as bright or uniquely coloured portions of an image, may also influence how overt attention is deployed in a scene (see Henderson, 2003). However, our prior knowledge, our goals, and our biases seem to account for a substantial portion of our viewing behaviour.

Studies of eye movement during real-world tasks such as reading and scene viewing have substantially improved our understanding of how visual attention is deployed in more complex situations (see Box 4.4 for another example). With the advent of portable eye-tracking technology, it is now possible to study the ways in which attention operates in everyday life as well as in lab-based paradigms (see Kingstone et al., 2008).

task-related knowledge

An observer's knowledge of the goals and the task at hand as it guides the eyes during a visual task.

FIGURE 4.18 | The eye fixations of an individual asked to view the image in order to later describe the location of the scene

The fixations are depicted by black circles.

COGNITION IN ACTION
BOX 4.4

Eye Movements in Sports: The Quiet Eye

Have you ever marvelled at the professional basketball player as he effortlessly makes his free-throw shot or the golf pro who putts with incredible precision? Anyone who has played these sports will be familiar with the conventional wisdom of "picking your spot" (i.e., concentrating on the spot where the ball will land), or drawing an imaginary line between the ball and the target destination. But exactly how do the experts direct their overt visual attention when playing sports? How does vision guide the body's movements to achieve the necessary hand–eye coordination? Recent research suggests that expert athletes use their gaze differently than non-experts do. It appears that the key to an expert's success lies in the ability to keep the gaze on a critical location for just the right amount of time, a technique known as the **quiet eye** (Vickers, 1996, 2004; Harle & Vickers, 2001).

Joan Vickers, a researcher at the University of Calgary, and her colleagues explored the gaze behaviour of basketball players who varied in their shooting ability (Vickers, 1996; Harle & Vickers, 2001). The players were divided into two groups based on their free-throw performance. Here we will refer to them as experts of high and moderate proficiency. While each of the players performed free throws, Vickers and her colleagues recorded (1) the scene the player was looking at, (2) his eye position in relation to the objects in the scene, and (3) his body posture and movement. The recording equipment used was specially designed for these studies. The results of the study were striking. Among other things, they showed that, compared to moderately proficient experts, the highly proficient experts gazed at the rim of the basket sooner and for a longer period of time before beginning the body movements associated with the free throw. In other words, they appeared to use the quiet eye. The best players also tended to direct their eyes away from the front of the hoop while shooting, to effectively suppress further processing of relevant visual cues so that, once initiated, the shot process would not be disrupted. By contrast, moderately proficient players tended to keep looking at the hoop during the action, leaving open the possibility of modifying their shots as they released the ball. The fact that outstanding players benefit by not looking at the hoop while shooting may explain why they can often make shots even when their view is blocked by members of the opposing team. In fact, by preventing the shooter from seeing the basket during the shot, the defender may inadvertently be helping the shooter! The idea that free-throw performance is improved by (1) using the quiet eye to effectively locate the target and (2) looking away from the basket while actually shooting the ball to suppress unwanted cues is known as the **location-suppression hypothesis**.

Perhaps you're asking yourself whether you could score more often in basketball if you mimicked the eye movements of experts. Harle and Vickers (2001) conducted a fascinating study to answer this very question. They found that training a basketball team in how to use the quiet eye improved free-throw performance substantially, and that the improvement was greater than that shown by other teams not trained in the technique.

If you're interested in sports such as volleyball, hockey, or golf, you may also be interested to know that variants of the quiet eye have been shown to operate in those sports as well. Overall, it seems that the quiet eye involves:

> **quiet eye**
> Sustained and steady eye gaze prior to an action or behaviour.

> **location-suppression hypothesis**
> A two-stage explanation for the quiet eye phenomenon: in the preparation stage, the quiet eye maximizes information about the target object; then, during the location stage, vision is suppressed to optimize the execution of an action or behaviour.

DISCOVERY LAB

1. Focusing the eyes on the optimal location of the critical target(s) in the sport.
2. Beginning and ending the quiet eye at the optimal times, corresponding to action initiation.

Continued

3. Holding the eyes on the optimal location for an extended period of time.

Of course, the details differ across sports. For example, an accurate putt in golf requires, among other things, that the golfer coordinate the position of the ball and the position of the hole. The eye movements of good and poor putters are shown in Figure 4.19. As you can see, good putters (1) focus their gaze on the back of the ball for several seconds, (2) then move their eyes quickly and accurately to the front of the hole, and (3) hold their gaze on the resting location of the ball even after the ball leaves that spot. The good news for aspiring amateurs is that training the quiet eye can substantially improve performance in many sports (Harle & Vickers, 2001). Try it for yourself: next time you're playing golf or shooting baskets, apply the quiet eye and see if your performance improves.

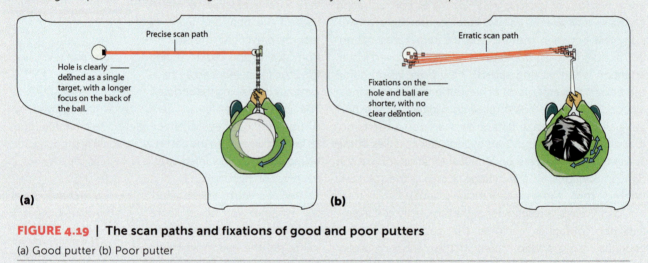

Precise scan path

Hole is clearly defined as a single target, with a longer focus on the back of the ball.

Erratic scan path

Fixations on the hole and ball are shorter, with no clear defintion.

(a)   (b)

FIGURE 4.19 | The scan paths and fixations of good and poor putters

(a) Good putter (b) Poor putter

Summary

"Attention" is a sophisticated concept encompassing a number of processes, including selective attention and inattention, involuntary attention, divided attention, task switching, sustained attention and overt attention.

Early studies of selective attention suggested that people must filter out information to which they do not wish to attend. Dominating the *filter* theory literature is an important distinction between early and late selection. With early selection, attention prevents the perception of irrelevant information, as evidenced by dichotic listening and selective looking tasks. In late selection, both relevant and irrelevant stimuli are perceived, so that the person must actively ignore the irrelevant stimuli in order to focus on the relevant ones (e.g., Stroop task). Another distinction identified in the early information-processing theories is the one between automatic and controlled processes. Automatic processes can unfold without our having to pay attention to them. By contrast, activities using controlled processes require that we pay attention to the activities in order to execute them properly.

Automatic and controlled processes are also involved in directing attention to different spatial locations. Exogenous shifts of attention occur when stimuli automatically capture our attention and exogenous shifts occur when we voluntarily move our attention to a location in space. Attention capture, which occurs when our environment influences our experience of it, making us suddenly aware of meaningful events that we did not expect, is an example of an exogenous shift of attention. A contrasting phenomenon is inattentional blindness, or failure to attend to events that we might be expected to notice (demonstrated by the flanker task).

How many things we can attend to at once? The central bottleneck theory suggests that attention requires a central processor to handle the relevant information, and that this processor is unable to handle the information for more than one task at a time. In turns out that even mind wandering requires the central processor. Studies on divided attention and task switching have explored the bottleneck theory by examining whether people can learn to divide their attention between two tasks, as opposed to simply switching rapidly back and forth between them.

Tasks that are performed over an extended period of time require sustained attention. However, performance on such tasks tends to decline over time; this phenomenon is referred to as the vigilance decrement. Some researchers believe that the vigilance decrement occurs because tasks requiring vigilance are excessively demanding of attentional resources—in effect, over-stimulating. Other researchers believe that the vigilance decrement occurs because vigilance tasks are under-stimulating and thus lead us to decouple our attention from the task and focus on something else, like internal thoughts.

Researchers have distinguished between covert and overt shifts of spatial attention. Overt shifts of attention involve movement of the eyes to fixate attended regions of the visual field so that they can be processed by the high-resolution section of the retina in the back of the eye (the fovea). Studies of eye movement in the contexts of reading, scene viewing, and sports suggest that the eyes are guided not only by the nature of the visual stimuli but also by the goals of the observer.

CASE STUDY

Case Study Wrap-Up

How can we apply the contents of this chapter to the bus accident described in the case study? Well, one central point is that the concept of attention is relevant for almost everything that we do. This is especially the case in settings where errors can have drastic consequences. Public transportation operations are excellent examples of such safety-critical settings. And as these industries are beginning to find out, many previously unexplained accidents could have been caused by failures of attention.

Bus drivers may be prone to making mistakes in situations where they are required to juggle multiple tasks at the same time—answering the radio, monitoring intersections, looking for yellow or red signals or adjusting their speed. In these moments of *divided attention*, drivers could make mistakes because their attentional *capacity* is insufficient to successfully perform one or more of the critical tasks (e.g., looking for yellow or red signals). And since the evidence also suggests that *task switching* entails a *switch cost*, even if they do see the flashing light, their response to it could be delayed.

Bus drivers may also be at risk of making errors in situations that are relatively uneventful and thus conducive to *mind wandering*. In such situations, drivers may rely on *automatic processes* rather than *controlled processes*. Just as word reading interferes with colour naming in the *Stroop task*, so automatic processes can cause serious problems when they conflict with the controlled processes that the bus driver actually wants to carry out. During mind wandering (and multi-tasking, for that matter), engineers could suffer from *inattentional blindness*, and therefore completely miss important signals. Episodes of inattention might also increase over the course

Continued

of a long shift, leading to the decline in performance known as the *vigilance decrement*.

Finally, there are the limits of *overt attention* to consider. If a bus driver becomes tired and stops regularly scanning the road ahead, she or he might fail to *fixate* important information and thus completely miss it. Given the many limits that attention is subject to, it's surprising that major accidents don't happen more often.

In the Know: Review Questions

1. What is the vigilance decrement and why does it occur?
2. Discuss the ways in which inattentional blindness and attention capture reveal complementary aspects of cognition.
3. How can mind wandering influence performance on a task that requires primary attention?
4. What is the difference between overt and covert shifts of attention?

Key Concepts

action slips
anterior cingulate cortex (ACC)
attentional blink
attention capture
capacity model
catch trials
central bottleneck
central cueing paradigm
cocktail party phenomenon
commission error
controlled vs automatic processes
covert attention
cueing effect
default network
déjà vu
dichotic listening
divided attention
domain-specific modules
dorsolateral prefrontal cortex (DLPFC)
early selection
embodied
endogenous shifts
entry points
exogenous shifts
filter
fixation
flanker task
inattentional blindness

inhibition of return (IOR)
late selection
location-suppression hypothesis
mind wandering
moving window technique
nystagmus
overload view
overt attention
parallel mental activity
peripheral cueing paradigm
quiet eye
rapid serial visual presentation (RSVP)
regressions
resource depletion account
saccades
selective attention
selective looking
sequential attention hypothesis
set
shadowing task
smooth pursuit movements
spatial attention
spotlight metaphor
stimulus onset asynchrony
Stroop task
structural limits
sustained attention
sustained attention to response task (SART)

switch cost
task-related knowledge
task switching

underload view
vigilance
vigilance decrement

Links to Other Chapters

anterior cingulate cortex (ACC)
Chapter 10 (insight and the brain)
Chapter 13 (cognition and emotion)

domain specificity
Chapter 5 (teaching domain-specific knowledge)
Chapter 8 (folk biology)
Chapter 11 (the selection task and domain-specific reasoning, training in statistical reasoning)

Chapter 12 (evolution of *g*)

dorsolateral prefrontal cortex (DLPFC)
Chapter 5 (working memory)
Chapter 10 (flexibility–rigidity and the brain)

selective attention
Chapter 8 (perceptual symbol systems)

subliminal perception
Chapter 13 (unconscious perception)

Further Reading

People are able to discriminate between human and computer voices very early in the process of attention, according to Lattner et al. (2003).

A connectionist model of Stroop performance can be found in Cohen, Dunbar, and McClelland (1990).

Attention is sometimes characterized as a limited resource; for a discussion see Norman and Bobrow (1975). However, it's not easy to specify precisely what kind of resource it is, as Allport (1980) shows.

For more on inattentional blindness, see Most et al. (2001).

Finally, some preliminary findings in the neuropsychology of task switching are reviewed by Gurd, Weiss, Amunts, and Fink (2003).

Allport, D.A. (1980). Attention and performance. In G. Claxton (Ed.), *New directions in cognitive psychology* (pp. 26–64). London: Routledge & Kegan Paul.

Cohen, J.D., Dunbar, K., & McClelland, J.L. (1990). On the control of automatic processes: A parallel distributed processing account of the Stroop effect. *Psychological Review, 97,* 332–361.

Gurd, J.M., Weiss, P.H., Amunts, K., & Fink, G.R. (2003). Within-task switching in the verbal domain. *NeuroImage, 20,* S50–S57.

Lattner, S., Maess, B., Wang, Y., Schauer, M., Alter, K., & Friederici, A.D. (2003). Dissociation of human and computer voices in the brain: Evidence for a pre-attentive Gestalt-like perception. *Human Brain Mapping, 20,* 13–21.

Most, S.B., Simons, D.J., Scholl, B.J., Jimenez, R., Clifford, E., & Chabris, C.F. (2001). How not to be seen: The contribution of similarity and selective ignoring to sustained inattentional blindness. *Psychological Science, 12,* 9–17.

Norman, D.A., & Bobrow, D.G. (1975). On data limited and resource limited processes. *Cognitive Psychology, 7,* 44–64.

Memory Systems

Chapter Contents

Chapter Objectives

- To distinguish between various memory systems.
- To explore sensory and short-term memory.
- To distinguish between short-term and working memory.
- To outline Tulving's approach to memory.
- To look at various models of semantic memory.
- To review experimental evidence for the role of spreading activation in semantic memory.
- To examine the concept of working memory.
- To identify what the study of older individuals and people with memory deficits tells us about the nature of memory.

What Was That Movie . . . ?

Quick! What was the movie with Drew Barrymore and Adam Sandler where Adam's character (Henry) fell in love with Drew's (Lucy), even though she woke up every day with no recollection of the previous day's events? Lucy was effectively trapped in time, unable to retain any new memories after suffering brain damage in a car accident.

Although the plot line is obviously far-fetched, it brings up many questions about how human memory operates. Is memory just a big black box where all the information we have ever taken in is stored? Are there different types of memory? If so, are there different areas in the brain dedicated to each type? Are they distinct from one another neurologically? Is it possible that one type of memory can be damaged while other types are spared? These are just some of the questions that will be discussed in this chapter.

Before we start, were you able to remember the film's title? If you said *50 First Dates*, you were right. This simple exercise is actually a good introduction to the subject of memory. If you were able to answer the question, you must have had the information stored in long-term memory. But how did you access it? Was there a mechanism that selected this information and effectively "pulled" it from memory so that you could answer the question? As we will see later in this chapter, this may in fact be the way we access an accurate memory.

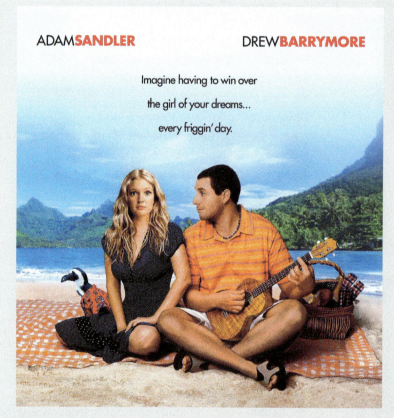

FIGURE 5.1 | **Drew Barrymore (Lucy Whitmore) and Adam Sandler (Henry Roth) in** *50 First Dates*

Understanding Memory Systems

The ability to accurately recall information—that is, to remember—is one of the most important faculties that humans possess. Simply remembering that red means "stop" and green means "go" could make the difference between life and death, and the same is true of a doctor's ability to recall knowledge stored in long-term memory. The ability to commit information to memory and access it quickly is fundamental both to everyday existence and to long-term survival. This chapter and the next will describe many different ideas about how memory functions and how it can fail, along with numerous approaches, past and present, to investigating and modelling this crucial cognitive process.

The study of memory has a rich history of scientific inquiry (as well as its fair share of philosophical and pseudoscientific supposition). Memory is of great interest to cognitive psychologists for many reasons. For instance, all of us rely on our past experiences (now memories) to create our identity. But it doesn't end there: much of our future behaviour will be based on information stored in memory. Another reason for interest in memory research is its potential for practical application (in fact, the next chapter will discuss some studying techniques that you may find useful in this course).

Finally, the scope for the study of memory systems is vast, simply because there are multiple types, each of which is the subject of a separate subfield of research. While most researchers agree that there are at least three major memory systems, some have suggested that there may be as many as five in all (Schacter & Tulving, 1994; Schacter, Wagner, & Buckner, 2000): working, episodic, semantic, and procedural memory (the oldest from an evolutionary perspective), and the perceptual representation system. Memory theorists, like all scientists, try to divide their subject matter (as Plato advised) "along its natural joints," without "splinter[ing] any part, as a bad butcher might do" (Plato, *Phaedrus*, 265). However, the process of identifying those "natural joints" is far from complete. Figure 5.2 shows some of the memory systems that have been investigated.

A General Framework

If you were to ask people on the street to tell you about memory, you would almost certainly get a wide variety of responses. Nevertheless, most of them would probably include some reference to *long-term memory*, *short-term memory*, and perhaps *working memory*. These familiar terms reflect the rich history of memory research. By now you will recognize the name William James. As we saw in our discussion of Waugh and Norman's (1965) model of information processing in Chapter 1 (Figure 1.7), James can be credited with the first strong distinction between what are commonly referred to as short-term memory (STM) and long-term memory (LTM). James considered **primary memory** to be the area where information is initially stored so that it can be available for conscious inspection, attention, and introspection. This can be contrasted with **secondary memory**, which he saw as a long-term storage unit for all other memories. In this framework primary memory can be seen as STM, and secondary memory as LTM, with information being shared between them. That is, in order to be available for use, information stored in secondary memory must be brought to consciousness (i.e., placed in primary memory).

primary memory
A memory system proposed by William James (1890); thought to be the area where information is initially stored so that it is available for consciousness, attention, and general use.

secondary memory
A memory system proposed by William James (1890); thought to be the long-term storage area for memories.

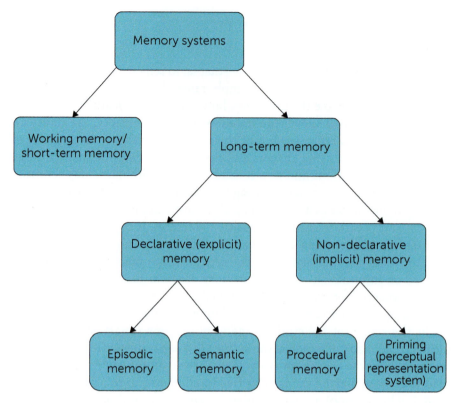

FIGURE 5.2 | Some of the many memory systems that memory researchers investigate

modal model of memory

A memory model proposed by Atkinson and Shiffrin (1968), consisting of sensory memory, short-term memory, and long-term memory.

iconic and echoic sensory memory

The visual and auditory sensory memory systems, respectively. Sensory memory has the ability to register a large amount of information, although it typically decays quickly: iconic memory has an upper limit of one second; echoic memory has a limit of two seconds.

decay

The term used to refer to the time course of forgetting.

The Modal Model of Memory

Sensory Memory

Although they are now outdated, the memory systems proposed by James (1890) provided an excellent framework for later research. Atkinson and Shiffrin's (1968) **modal model of memory** was so influential that most people probably know of it even if they haven't studied psychology. In its most basic form, the modal model contains three interconnected memory systems: sensory, short-term, and long-term. Information from the outside world is initially processed by our senses. For example (as you may recall from Chapter 3), light enters through the lens of the eye and is then transduced by cells in the retina before the information it carries is sent to the occipital lobe for further processing. In the visual modality, this information is stored for a very brief moment (likely less than a second) in the form of a visual or **iconic memory**; the auditory equivalent is known as **echoic sensory memory**. Essentially, sensory memory can be understood as a buffer system for stimuli received through the senses. You have probably had the experience of seeing (or hearing) something for only a moment and yet being able to remember exactly what it was and where it was located (or where it came from). This experience is exemplified in seminal research by George Sperling (1960, 1963), in which participants were flashed a matrix of nine letters (in rows of three) for a brief moment (50 ms). As Figure 5.3 shows, in a *partial report task* participants were required to immediately

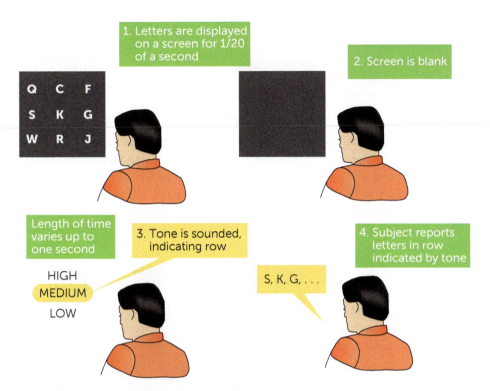

FIGURE 5.3 | Participants in Sperling's (1960) sensory memory experiment were briefly flashed a matrix of nine letters

In the whole report condition they were required to recall all the letters. In the partial report condition a tone indicated which row of letters they should report. The tone could occur at the moment when the matrix of letters disappeared, or after some predetermined delay (i.e., stimulus onset asynchrony, or SOA; see Chapter 4).

recall only one row of letters, and they did so with surprising accuracy. By contrast, performance in a *whole report task*—where participants were required to recall all nine letters—was very poor. Of crucial interest to memory research, Sperling was also able to use this paradigm to determine the time course of sensory memory, essentially asking how long it lasted. To do so he would wait until the matrix had disappeared before indicating which of the three rows participants were to recall, varying the length of the delay. As you can see in Figure 5.4, the rate of decay for visual sensory memory is relatively fast: after merely a second's delay, participants' ability to recall three letters was no better than their ability to recall all nine letters immediately.

These seminal findings are important for several reasons. First, they show that our sensory system has the ability to store a large amount of information at a single glance. Although Sperling's experiments involved only the visual modality, an analogous sensory memory system appears to

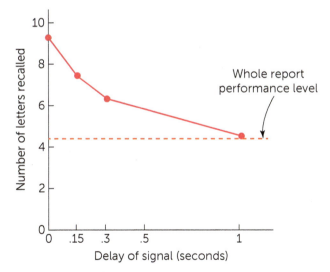

FIGURE 5.4 | Typical results from Sperling's experiment

Notice that performance is relatively good when the stimulus (tone) is presented immediately; however, it quickly declines when the stimulus is delayed.

The Battle of the Species

Is your memory better than a chimpanzee's? If you are confident that it is, you might want to reconsider. Ayuma (the chimp in Figure 5.5) is part of a project led by Japanese researcher Tetsuro Matsuzawa at Kyoto University's Primate Research Institute. The Ai Project (named after Ayuma's mother) is designed to explore chimpanzee cognition as a way of improving our understanding of human cognitive capabilities.

It's true that you would be much better than Ayuma at remembering the answers to questions on a cognitive psychology exam, but his memory is also capable of some impressive feats. The first step in this intriguing research project was to teach Ayuma how to count from 1 to 9. This was accomplished by rewarding him each time he touched the correct order of numbers on a touch screen. Starting with easy arrays of only two numbers (1 and 2), he gradually learned to count all the way to 9. At this point in the experiment the researchers used a limited-hold memory task that involved flashing all nine digits in random locations on the screen: then the numbers were replaced by white boxes, and Ayuma was required to tap the boxes in the correct order. When the numbers were displayed for around 700 ms and then removed from the screen, there were no performance differences between Ayuma and the university students who also participated in the experiment: everyone scored around 80 per cent. However, when the display time was decreased to about 200 ms, human performance plummeted to about 40 per cent, while Ayuma still scored around 80 per cent. Thus it appears that chimps' visual sensory memory (at least Ayuma's) is vastly superior to ours (see Inoue & Matsuzawa, 2007).

FIGURE 5.5 | Tetsuro Matsuzawa and Ayuma, one of the participants in this intriguing sensory memory experiment

Ayuma performed much better than his human counterparts when recalling the locations of the digits on the screen in the correct numerical order.

DISCOVERY LAB

exist for all six senses. For example, auditory or echoic sensory memory lasts approximately two seconds: most people are able to repeat something they have just heard nearly word for word. Despite its very short duration, sensory memory may help us to see the world in a continuous manner, without interruptions, each time we blink or make a saccade (a quick eye movement). While sensory memory can register a large amount of information, not all of it enters short-term memory—the second stage of the modal model of memory.

Short-Term Memory

The second major component of Atkinson and Shiffrin's (1968) modal model of memory is short-term memory, which receives information from both sensory memory and long-term memory. As previously discussed, sensory memory is capable of registering a large quantity of information. However, most of that information fades from memory (decays) unless it is given attention. In its simplest form, the modal model claims that attended information enters short-term memory and is retained there for a short time, typically no more than 18 seconds (Peterson & Peterson, 1959). Beyond this upper limit, information once again decays unless it is adequately rehearsed.

Suppose someone told you a phone number to call and you didn't have a smart phone (a situation the authors of this book lived with for most of their lives). You would probably rehearse (repeat) the number over and over until you were sure you had it stored in your long-term memory. Interestingly, the development of the phone number dovetails with seminal research conducted by Harvard psychologist George Miller. Miller (1956) demonstrated that the capacity of human short-term memory is somewhere between five and nine items. In fact, you might know that when it comes to memorizing items, the "magical number" is "seven plus or minus two" That saying comes from Miller, and it means that holding more than nine items in short-term memory is a very tough task. The introduction of the seven-digit phone number is often credited to the fact that Bell Laboratories looked to Miller for advice in the 1950s.

While rehearsal is one common way of promoting the consolidation of long-term memories, there are other strategies for increasing the span of short-term memory. One of them, called chunking, reflects the idea that you can increase the capacity of your short-term memory by grouping pieces of information together. Thus you can remember a seven-digit sequence (say, 5-6-4-3-2-4-7) much more easily if you *chunk* it into two groups (564–3247). There are many ways of reducing the total number of items to be remembered. Just think of acronyms such as NHL for the National Hockey League, or ROYGBIV for the colours of the spectrum of light.

Despite the influence that Miller's (1956) work has had, both in the scientific world and in the public realm, recent research suggests that seven might not be the magic number after all. Determining exactly how much information can be stored in a single chunk is a challenge. However, given its limited capacity, it seems unlikely that the short-term memory system can handle much more than four chunks of information at a time (see Cowan, 2001).

Long-Term Memory

The final component of the modal model is long-term memory: information that is stored and brought back to short-term memory for immediate usage. There are many different divisions of long-term memory, and we will explore them in detail shortly. First, however, it is important to introduce a concept that the modal model does not take into account: working memory.

Working Memory

Before we begin to discuss working memory, try this quick exercise: read the rest of this paragraph while keeping in mind the numbers 0 - 5 - 2 - 1 - 4. The concept of working memory has been at the centre of Alan Baddeley's (1986, 1989, 2000a, 2001, 2002a, 2002b; Baddeley & Hitch, 1974; N. Morris & Jones, 1990; Parkin & Hunkin, 2001) influential research program. Working memory "involves the temporary storage and manipulation of information that is assumed to be necessary for a wide range of complex cognitive activities"

rehearsal
The process through which information in short-term memory is maintained.

consolidation
The process through which memory traces are stabilized to form long-term memories. See Chapter 6 for a full discussion.

chunking
A strategy used to increase the capacity of STM by arranging elements in groups (chunks) that can be more easily remembered.

working memory
The system that allows for the temporary storage and manipulation of information required for various cognitive activities.

(Baddeley, 2003a, p. 189). While this may sound similar to short-term memory, there are many differences. In fact, the short-term memory model turns out to have a number of shortcomings. Now, without returning to the beginning of this section, what were the numbers that you were supposed to keep in mind?

Chances are you were right, or nearly so. Yet according to the modal model, the capacity limitations of short-term memory would have made it impossible to store the number and at the same time read the text. Baddeley recognized this and concluded that, under some circumstances, the short-term memory system must in fact be capable of carrying out two tasks at once.

As conceptualized by Baddeley and Hitch (1974), working memory is the system that pulls all the other memory systems together, enabling us to work with different types of information in a dynamic fashion. It consists of four distinct subsystems (Figure 5.6), one of which (the **central executive**) coordinates information from the other three (the phonological loop, the visuo-spatial sketchpad, and the episodic buffer). The **phonological loop** represents the entirety of short-term memory as conceptualized by the modal model of memory. Quite simply, anything that is auditory in nature or language-related is said to have obligatory access to the phonological loop (i.e., it must be processed and temporarily held in the phonological loop). However, not all the information that we keep in memory is auditory or language-based. If you've ever moved from one home to another, you will have faced the problem of manoeuvring a large piece of furniture down a staircase or through a narrow doorway. In that situation, most of us would first step back and try to imagine how to navigate without damaging anything. This example highlights the **visuo-spatial sketchpad**: a separate component of working memory that we use for non-verbal information. Both the phonological loop and the visuo-spatial sketchpad interact with long-term memory, while the **episodic buffer** is used to move information to and from long-term memory. Its most important function is to organize information "from the phonological and visuo-spatial subsystems of [working memory] with information from [long-term memory]" (Baddeley, 2001, p. 1349). All three of these subsystems have limited capacities and hold information only temporarily (Baddeley, 2000b, p. 421).

The central executive selects and integrates information from across the three subsystems. It is intimately associated with consciousness, constituting a workspace within which solutions are formulated (Baars, 2002). Finally, notice the distinction in Figure 5.6 between **fluid systems** and **crystallized systems**. The former are cognitive processes that manipulate information but are "themselves unchanged by learning," while the latter are "cognitive systems capable of accumulating long-term knowledge" (Baddeley, 2000b, p. 421).

To illustrate how some of the components of working memory interact, Baddeley (1989, p. 36) used a simple example (previously used by Shepard, 1966, and Neisser, 1970). Suppose you were asked to recall the number of windows in your house or apartment. You would probably form a mental image of the building, using the visuo-spatial sketchpad, and imagine walking around it, counting the windows as you go. The counting is done by the phonological (or articulatory) loop, and the entire process is coordinated by the central executive.

Baddeley (2003b) suggested that the phonological loop evolved as an aid in the acquisition of language, facilitating the learning of words by allowing us to temporarily store and rehearse them. Once learned, speech becomes a powerful tool, capable of influencing the behaviour both of others and of ourselves. Sub-vocal speech can be used to articulate our plans and is an important aspect of self-control. Baddeley (2003b) also suggested that

central executive
The component of working memory that coordinates information from the three subsystems.

phonological loop
Temporary store of linguistic information.

visuo-spatial sketchpad
Temporary store of non-linguistic (visual) information.

episodic buffer
The mechanism that moves information to and from long-term memory.

DISCOVERY LAB

fluid systems
Cognitive processes that manipulate information.

crystallized systems
Cognitive systems that accumulate long-term knowledge.

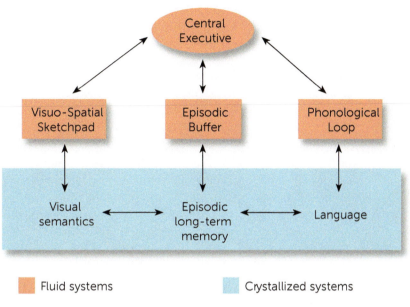

FIGURE 5.6 | Working memory model

Source: Donald T. Stuss and Robert T. Knight. (2002) Principles of Frontal Lobe Function. Oxford: Oxford University Press; Alan Baddeley. "The episodic buffer: a new component of working memory?" *Trends in Cognitive Sciences,* Vol. 4, Issue 11, pp. 417–23.

the visuo-spatial sketchpad evolved in order to facilitate the representation of things and their relations. Thus it aids in tasks as diverse as planning a route (e.g., how to get to a novel location) or figuring out how to put the parts of something together (e.g., assembling furniture components). Processes of this kind will be explored in the chapters on imagery (7), problem-solving (10), reasoning (11), and creativity (12).

Working Memory and the Brain

Baddeley (2002a) observed that working memory is a complex system and hence

> unlikely to map in a simple way onto an anatomical structure such as the frontal lobes. However, it is clear that the frontal lobes play an important role in integrating information from many other areas of the brain, and are crucially involved in its manipulation for purposes such as learning, comprehension, and reasoning. . . . [T]hese are precisely the roles attributed to working memory (p. 258).

One frontal area that has been singled out as particularly important for working memory (Figure 5.7) is the dorsolateral prefrontal cortex (DLPFC). When we reviewed Stroop research in Chapter 4, on attention, we noted that the DLPFC was believed to play a role in selecting between alternative response tendencies. This is an important function of working memory, in particular of the central executive. Curtis and D'Esposito (2003) have suggested that the DLPFC is an integral part of working memory, acting to monitor and control alternative courses of action.

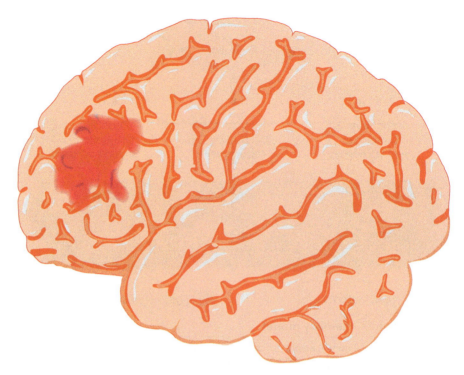

FIGURE 5.7 | The dorsolateral prefrontal cortex

The DLPFC is thought to play an especially important role in working memory.

Divisions of Long-Term Memory

Ken Jennings holds the record for the longest winning streak on the television game show *Jeopardy!* He won an amazing 74 games in a row, amassing more than 3 million dollars along the way. Apparently his ability to access information in long-term memory is vastly superior to the average person's.

Research has determined that long-term memory, like working memory, consists of several subsystems. To begin with, there are two main divisions of long-term memory: declarative and non-declarative.

Declarative Memory

Declarative memory (also known as explicit memory) is the system in which knowledge that can be stated (e.g., factual information) is stored. According to Endel Tulving (1972), who played a major role in this research, it has two subdivisions: episodic memory handles "temporally dated, spatially located, and personally experienced events or episodes," while semantic memory handles "knowledge about words and concepts, their properties and interrelations" (Tulving & Thomson, 1973, p. 354). In short, episodic memory deals with events that are personally experienced, while semantic memory is concerned with general knowledge.

declarative memory
One of two major divisions of memory, also known as explicit memory; the memory system that contains knowledge that can be stated.

episodic memory
The subdivision of declarative memory concerned with personal experience.

semantic memory
The subdivision of declarative memory concerned with general knowledge (e.g., facts, words, and concepts).

The Episodic–Semantic Distinction

Among the examples of episodic memories given by Tulving (1972) are the following:

> I remember seeing a flash of light a short while ago, followed by a loud sound a few seconds later.

> Last year, while on my summer vacation, I met a retired sea captain who knew more jokes than any other person I have ever met.

> I remember that I have an appointment with a student at 9:30 tomorrow morning (Tulving, 1972, p. 386).

By contrast, examples of semantic memories include the following (Tulving, 1972):

> I remember that the chemical formula for common table salt is NaCl.

> I know that the name of the month that follows June is July (p. 387).

As Tulving (1972) observed, memories of this kind differ from episodic memories in that they are general knowledge, not "personally experienced unique episodes" (p. 387). However, it's important to note that episodic and semantic memories are not mutually exclusive. For example, you might remember the day in grade two when Mrs Butterworth taught you that Ottawa is the capital of Canada. It was only after rehearsing your episodic memory of the lesson that you were able to store the fact in your semantic memory. In other words, episodic memory can serve as a gateway for the formation of semantic memory.

Neuropsychological Evidence for the Episodic–Semantic Distinction

Studies of people with brain injuries have provided compelling evidence for the theory that episodic and semantic memory are independent systems. A good example is a study by Klein, Loftus, and Kihlstrom (1996) of a patient known as WJ, who suffered retrograde amnesia—inability to recall events prior to the injury—following a closed head injury (one in which the skull remains intact) that impaired her episodic memory. The issue that this case addresses is whether episodic memory is necessary in order to have a sense of personal identity. "Is it possible for someone who cannot recall any personal experiences—and therefore cannot know how he or she behaved—to know what he or she is like?" (Klein, Loftus, & Kihlstrom, 1996, p. 250).

Distinguishing between these two types of personal knowledge is actually quite simple. For instance, semantic personal knowledge "might include the facts that the person is kind, outgoing or lazy. . . . Episodic personal knowledge, by contrast, consists of memories of specific events involving the self [and] could include memories of instances in which one was kind, outgoing or lazy" (Klein, Loftus, & Kihlstrom, 1996, pp. 250–51). If semantic personal memory and episodic personal memory were truly independent of one another, then damage to one system should not affect the other system. Thus someone might recall her personality as outgoing without being able to recall personal instances demonstrating this trait.

WJ was an 18-year-old undergraduate who had sustained a concussion in a fall. When she was initially tested, about five days after the injury, she had no episodic memories for the preceding six or seven months. However, her general knowledge was good. She knew which classes she was enrolled in, although she could not remember attending any of them. She also knew the names of teachers and friends, although she could not recall any personal experiences involving them. Essentially, her semantic memories for that time period were more or less intact: only her episodic memories were absent. In most cases retrograde amnesia resulting from closed head injury is temporary and the patient recovers within a few weeks. Fortunately, three weeks after the event, WJ's memory for events prior to the accident had returned to normal.

A technique invented by Crovitz and Schiffman (1974) was used to evaluate WJ's episodic memory during her amnesia. She was given a list of 24 nouns, each of which could easily be represented by a picture (e.g., *alarm clock*), and asked to recall a personal event in relation to each word from any time in the past, and then date the memory in terms of when it occurred. Thus someone might recall hitting the snooze button repeatedly on the *alarm clock* this morning. When tested five days after her injury, WJ produced a very different pattern of results than did a control group of three undergraduate women of approximately her age. As Figure 5.8 shows, the control participants had a **recency bias** in that they tended to recall experiences from the previous 12 months. By contrast, WJ showed a **primacy bias** in that she tended to recall experiences in the relatively distant past. Four weeks later, however, after she had recovered, her pattern of episodic memory was similar to that of the control group.

To test her semantic personal memory while she was still amnesic, WJ was asked to rate herself in terms of 80 personality traits (i.e., to indicate the extent to which she was *agreeable*, *dominant*, and so on). She then repeated this exercise after her amnesia had lifted. There was strong agreement between the two sets of ratings—a level of consistency similar to that of control participants. While amnesic, WJ was also asked to rate her personality as if she were in high school. The fact these ratings differed from her current ratings indicated awareness that she had changed since starting college. "WJ knew something about what she had been like at college, which was different from what she was like in high school; but she knew this despite the fact that she could not recall anything from her time in college" (Klein, Loftus, & Kihlstrom, 1996, p. 256). These results are consistent with the hypothesis that episodic and semantic memory are two distinct systems, and that we can have access to semantic knowledge without having access to episodic memory.

Another case of amnesia, which Tulving (1985, 2002) reported on, also supports the dissociation between episodic and semantic memory. The patient known at the time as NN (KC in later

recency bias vs primacy bias

A tendency to recall experiences from the recent past versus a tendency to recall experiences from the relatively distant past.

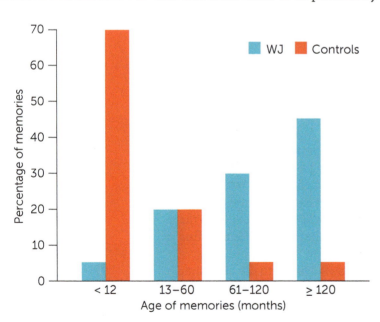

FIGURE 5.8 | Percentage of personal memories for different time periods

Data from: Klein, S.B., Loftus, J., & Kihlstrom, J.F. (1996). p. 255. Copyright © 1996 by the American Psychological Association. Adapted with permission. The use of APA information does not imply endorsement by APA.

Earlier we discussed the tragic story of Lucy, who fell in love with Henry in the movie *50 First Dates*. While the type of memory loss that Lucy was said to suffer was a bit far-fetched, there was a scene at the end of the movie (spoiler alert) in which she did seem to have some memory of Henry, based on the numerous paintings that she had made of him. Is it possible for someone with severe amnesia to actually learn some form of declarative memory? Recent research suggests that this might in fact be the case, albeit in a very limited sense.

Much of what we know about amnesia comes from Henry Molaison, who until his death in 2008 was known only as HM (Figure 5.9). As a young man he had a severe form of epilepsy, which was alleviated by a bilateral medial lobectomy. The surgery removed a number of brain structures in the medial temporal lobe strongly associated with memory, including most of the **hippocampus** (Figure 5.10). Without a functioning hippocampus, Henry was unable to form new semantic memories: you could spend hours with him, but if you left the room for a couple of minutes and then returned, he would have no recollection that he had ever met you. At the time it was widely thought that people with severe amnesia, like Henry, were completely unable to form any type of declarative memory, semantic or episodic. However, more recent research suggests that it may be possible for such people to retain some form of declarative memory after all. Henry was the participant in one of these studies (O'Kane, Kensinger, & Corkin, 2004).

Henry underwent his surgery in 1953. Thus in theory he should not have any memory, semantic or episodic, of anything after that date. However, when O'Kane et al. (2004) used recall and recognition tasks to test whether he had been able to acquire knowledge about 35 people who became famous after 1953, Henry was able to recall the last names for 12 of them. For example, when given the name "Billie Jean" he supplied the last name "King" (Billie Jean King was a famous tennis player in the 1970s). And he performed nearly twice as well when he was given semantic cues about the people in question—although still much worse than someone with an intact hippocampus would. This pointed to the existence of a network of semantic knowledge despite the absence of the brain structures thought necessary to form such memories.

So what might account for Henry's ability to form new semantic memories, however limited, about certain people when he consistently failed to form such memories about other things? One possibility is simple repetition: in the case of John F. Kennedy, for instance, he would almost certainly have heard many discussions of the 1963 assassination, both on the news and in his presence. In any event, the results of this study, and others like it, suggest that brain structures other than the hippocampus may have the capacity (albeit limited) to encode long-term semantic memories.

> **hippocampus**
> A site in the brain that plays a crucial role in the consolidation of memory traces.

FIGURE 5.9 | Henry Gustav Molaison (HM, 1926–2008)

FIGURE 5.10 | A hippocampus looks like a sea horse

FIGURE 5.11 | Patient KC/NN

publications; see Tulving, 2002a) was born in 1951 and suffered a closed head injury when he was 30 as a result of a motorcycle accident (Figure 5.11). With "extensive brain lesions in multiple cortical and subcortical brain regions" (Tulving, 2002, p. 130), he never recovered his episodic memory. However, his other intellectual skills remained intact. For example, he was able to outline a standard restaurant script (scripts will be discussed in the next chapter)—evidence that his semantic memory was still functioning. However, he could neither recall individual events from his past nor imagine what he might do in the future. Tulving (1985) reported a fragment of an interview that he (ET) conducted with NN:

> ET: Let's try the question again about the future. What will you be doing tomorrow?
> (There is a 15-second pause)
> NN: smiles faintly, and says, "I don't know."
> ET: Do you remember the question?
> NN: About what I'll be doing tomorrow?
> ET: Yes. How would you describe your state of mind when you try to think about it?
> (A 5-second pause)
> NN: A blank I guess (p. 4).

At various points NN described his blank state of mind as resembling "being asleep," "being in a room with nothing there and having a guy tell you to go find a chair, and there's nothing there," or "swimming in the middle of a lake [with] nothing there to hold you up or do anything with" (Tulving, 1985, p. 4). While NN retained his semantic memory systems, then, his episodic memory system was drastically impaired.

Non-Declarative Memory

non-declarative memory
The other major division of memory, also known as implicit memory; the memory system associated with behaviour that does not require conscious thought.

The other major division of long-term memory is **non-declarative memory**, also known as implicit memory. Unlike declarative memories (episodic and semantic), non-declarative memories do not require conscious thought and are often difficult to put into words.

THINK TWICE
BOX 5.3

The Sense of Smell

Many people believe that their sense of smell is intimately connected with memory. In this case the people are right: even though our perceptual experiences tend to be dominated by sight and sound, smell can often trigger a memory that is decades old. It's likely that many of you have had the experience of a distinctive scent sparking a memory (fond or otherwise) of something from years past. Perhaps, for instance, the smell of apple pie takes you back to your grandmother's kitchen.

How is it that smell can trigger a memory? Addressing this question is relatively easy. After an odour molecule enters your nose and is recognized by olfactory sensors, this information is sent first to the olfactory bulb and ultimately to the cortex and limbic system of your brain. As you may have learned in other classes, the limbic system includes a number of structures associated with memory. The hippocampus is especially important for the consolidation of long-term memories.

On the other hand, the sensory neurons in the epithelium (where smells are first registered) survive for only about 60 days. So how can a smell trigger a memory of something that happened years ago? It turns out that once a particular connection has been established between neuronal units in the epithelium and the hippocampus, it remains in place even as new olfactory neurons are generated to replace those that have died. Because the connections of the neurons always go to the same place in the hippocampus, the memories associated with a particular smell survive.

There are many situations in which we may remember something without being aware of doing so (e.g., Jacoby & Dallas, 1981; Jacoby & Witherspoon, 1982). "It is possible to distinguish the effects of memory for prior episodes or experiences on a person's current behaviour from the person's awareness that he or she is remembering events of the past" (Eich, 1984, p. 105). Schacter (1987, 1992) proposed the term "implicit memory" for such phenomena. Implicit memory comes into play when "information that was encoded during a particular episode is subsequently expressed without conscious or deliberate recollection" (Schacter, 1987, p. 501).

A demonstration of the practical consequences of participating in priming experiments is a study by Jacoby and Hollingshead (1990) in which participants read incorrectly spelled words. This experience subsequently increased the likelihood that the participants would unintentionally make the same spelling mistakes themselves. As Jacoby and Hollingshead observed, this kind of research may be unethical, because it can impair participants' performance in an important area (spelling) without their knowing it; in the same way, reading students' poor spelling "may be hazardous" to professors (p. 345). Jacoby and Hollingshead (1990) also noted that the latter herself "lost confidence in her spelling accuracy [and could] no longer judge spelling accuracy on the basis of a word 'looking right.' The word might look right because it was one of our incorrectly spelled words" (p. 356). (This finding also makes us wonder about the wisdom of relying on all the texting shortcuts we use today.)

Implicit memory has also been studied using a famous name paradigm (Jacoby & Kelley, 1992; Kelley & Jacoby, 2000). Participants were divided into two groups and given a series of non-famous names (e.g., *Sebastian Weisdorf*) to read. As the names appeared on a computer screen, one group read them with full attention (i.e., no distractions) and one with divided attention (achieved by adding a task such as listening to a series of numbers and pressing

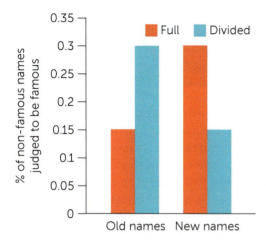

FIGURE 5.12 | Fame judgment task (full versus divided attention)

Data from: Jacoby, L.L., & Kelley, C.M. (1994).

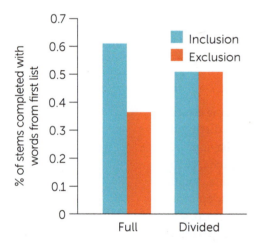

FIGURE 5.13 | Inclusion versus exclusion task (full versus divided attention)

The simplest way to understand non-declarative memory is in terms of its two major subtypes: the perceptual representation system (e.g., priming) and procedural memory.

Data from: Jacoby, L.L., & Kelley, C.M. (1994), p. 175. Copyright © 1994 by (SAGE) Reprinted by Permission of SAGE Publications, Inc.

method of opposition

Pits conscious (explicit) and unconscious (implicit) tendencies against one another.

a key if there were three odd numbers in a row). Then names from the first trial (old non-famous names) were mixed with new names, some famous and some not, and the participants were asked to judge whether or not they were famous. Participants were also told that all the names on the first list were non-famous. Consequently, anyone who recognized a name as coming from the first list was aware that it was not famous. Now examine Figure 5.12, in which the vertical axis is the percentage of non-famous names judged to be famous. The higher the number, the more non-famous names that group judged to be famous. Under conditions of full attention people tended to recognize names from the first list, and to say that fewer names from the first list were famous. However, participants from the divided attention group had implicit memories of the old names without explicitly recognizing them as coming from the first list. Thus they were more likely to categorize names from the first list as famous because they seemed familiar. It was as if they said to themselves, "Oh, I've heard that name before, but I don't remember where—it must be famous." In this way *Sebastian Weisdorf* became famous.

Another way of showing unconscious influences in memory is through studies using the **method of opposition** (Curran, 2001), which pits conscious (explicit) and unconscious (implicit) tendencies against one another (e.g., Jacoby, 1998; Jacoby & Kelley, 1992; Toth, 2000). Participants are shown a number of words (e.g., *motel*) under conditions of either full or divided attention. They are then given a number of word stems (e.g., *mot– –*). Half the participants in each condition (full and divided attention) are asked to complete the word stems using either a word from the list previously seen or, if they could not remember one, the first word they thought of. The other half are asked to complete the word stems by *not* using a word from the list previously seen. Thus if *motel* was on the previous list, they should choose an ending other than *-el* to complete the stem (e.g., *-or*, to form *motor*). The first instruction is the *inclusion* condition, while the second is the *exclusion* condition.

Now examine Figure 5.13. The vertical axis is the percentage of stems completed with words from the first list. Under the full attention condition, participants performed well on both the inclusion and exclusion tasks. When told to include words from the first list, they completed the word stems with words from the first list 61 per cent of the time. When they were told to exclude words from the first list, the number of stem completions using words from the first list dropped to 36 per cent. This difference indicates that the participants had some degree of conscious control over the process of stem completion. However, in the divided attention condition there was no difference between the inclusion and exclusion tasks. These participants completed the stems with words from the first list equally often, whether they were trying to do so or trying not to. Thus they did not demonstrate any conscious control over their behaviour in these tasks.

Conscious control is reflected in differences between performance when one is trying to do something, and performance when one is trying *not* to do it (Jacoby & Kelley, 1992, p. 177). A good analogy to the memory experiments we have been reviewing might be the various real-world attempts we make *not* to do something. For example, when we diet we try *not* to eat as much as usual, or when we quit smoking we try *not* to smoke. If there is a difference between our behaviour when we are trying *not* to do something and our "ordinary" behaviour, then we are demonstrating that we can consciously control that behaviour. However, if our behaviour when we are trying *not* to do something is the same as it always was, then we are demonstrating that we are unable to consciously control that behaviour.

The Perceptual Representation System

The results of experiments on implicit memory are consistent with the notion that there is a memory system called the **perceptual representation system** or PRS (Hayman & Tulving, 1989; Tulving & Schacter, 1990; Schacter, Wagner, & Buckner, 2000) that is responsible for priming effects (discussed below). The important distinction is between "systems concerned with explicit recollection of past events" as opposed to "primed identification of previously encountered objects" (Tulving & Schacter, 1990, p. 302). The PRS contains very specific representations of previously encountered events. Thus if you had been shown the word fragment M–S–OU–I, only that fragment would be in your PRS: the complete word (*MISSOURI*) would not. The episodic memory system and the PRS would be driven by different processes. The episodic memory system operates with a deeper understanding of information, whereas the PRS deals with information on a more superficial level. Amnesiacs have an impaired episodic memory system, but their PRS may be relatively intact. Precisely how the PRS relates to other memory systems, such as semantic memory, is still unclear. As Berry and Dienes (1991) observed, there may be similarities between the processes responsible for implicit memory and those underlying implicit learning—a topic we will consider in Chapter 8, on concepts.

Priming is the unconscious process through which our response to a given stimulus is facilitated by previous exposure to a related (or identical) stimulus, making our response both quicker and more accurate than it would otherwise be. Priming can be considered as a process that occurs in the PRS: that is, one that functions without conscious awareness (i.e., implicit).

Experiments conducted by Dehaene et al. (1998) demonstrated that implicit presentations (below the threshold for awareness) nonetheless facilitated participants' responses to related information. This finding, and others demonstrating the effects of priming, can be inferred by certain testing paradigms, resting on the assumption that prior exposure does indeed facilitate processing. Specifically, the experimentation requires both a **prime** (i.e., the item that is presented first) and a **probe or target** (i.e., an item presented after the prime that may be identical, related, or unrelated to it). Response rates are faster when the prime and target are related than when they are not.

One means of testing the effects of priming is a **lexical decision task (LDT)**, in which participants are presented with a letter string and asked to indicate whether or not it constitutes a word (e.g., *house* or *boesu*). Studies (e.g., Meyer & Schvaneveldt, 1971; Tweedy, Lapinski, & Schvaneveldt, 1977) have found that the recognition of lexically correct words was faster when participants had already been exposed to words typically associated with the target. For example, the target *doctor* would be recognized as an actual word much faster if it had been preceded by the prime *nurse*. Similarly robust priming effects are found with word fragment completion tasks, where participants are exposed to an incomplete word and asked to complete it (see for example, Sloman, Hayman, Ohta, Law, & Tulving, 1988; Tulving, Schacter, & Stark, 1982); image completion tasks, in which

---

perceptual representation system (PRS)
A memory system containing very specific representations of events that is hypothesized to be responsible for priming effects.

priming
The unconscious process through which recognition of a particular item is facilitated by previous exposure to an identical or related item.

prime
The item that is presented first in a priming experiment. Later response times to this or related items are generally faster.

probe or target
The second item presented in a priming experiment; may be identical, related, or unrelated to the prime.

lexical decision task (LDT)
A task requiring participants to determine whether a presented string of letters is a word or not.

DISCOVERY LAB

participants are asked to name an incomplete image that slowly becomes more and more complete over time (see for example, Matsukawa, Snodgrass, & Doniger, 2005); and decision-making paradigms (see for example, Klein, 1993). Whatever the task, such experiments consistently show that primes are stored in memory and facilitate processing of the related items without the participant's awareness.

Procedural memory

procedural memory
The memory system concerned with knowing how to do things.

tacit knowledge
Knowing how to do something without being able to say exactly what it is that you know.

Another type of non-declarative memory, procedural memory (J.R. Anderson, 1976), underlies rote skills, such as riding a bicycle. Like priming, it operates without our conscious awareness. One way of thinking about the distinction between procedural and other forms of memory is in terms of the distinction between explicit and tacit knowledge. Polanyi (1958) pointed out that "the aim of a skilled performance is achieved by the observance of a set of rules which are not known as such to the person following them" (p. 49).

Even if you don't remember learning to balance on a bicycle, you still know how to do it; and even if you haven't ridden for years, you have no problem doing it (though your legs may tire out fast). However, you would likely find it difficult to explain what you're doing. Indeed, most procedural skills are very hard to put into words, regardless of a person's expertise. An expert pianist or golfer would have similar trouble explaining their complex motor skills; and their performance would suffer if they had to think consciously about what they were doing.

Physical skills are not the only ones stored in procedural memory: so are many cognitive skills, including the ability to read. The fact that you can read this sentence without (we hope!) any conscious mental effort demonstrates that reading is a type of procedural memory.

If you were to outline the principles that underlie reading, or riding a bike—that is, to convert your tacit knowledge into explicit knowledge—you would be using your semantic memory. And if you were to recall a particular experience of reading or bicycling—as in "Remember that time we rode from Vancouver to Abbotsford and it rained all day, and we ran out of food . . . ?"—you would be drawing on episodic memory. Procedural knowledge is tacit (implicit) in that we aren't necessarily aware of what it is that we know.

Further Developments in Memory Systems Theory

Tulving's distinction between episodic and semantic memory has continued to stimulate research for more than four decades, and the field has developed in response to this work. Tulving himself published a number of modifications to his basic theory (e.g., Tulving, 1983, 1984, 1985, 1986, 2000, 2001a, 2001b, 2002a, 2002b), and many other researchers have explored directions suggested by his findings. We will look at some of their studies now.

Episodic Memory and Development

According to Tulving (1985), children acquire episodic memory relatively late compared with other kinds of memory. In this connection, Tulving cited the work of authors as diverse as Neisser (1978a) and K. Nelson and Gruendel (1981), who suggested that very young children do not experience anything that adults would call episodic memory. The hypothesis is that episodic memory develops out of semantic memory (Kinsbourne & Wood, 1975). Although small children are prodigious learners, most of their learning seems to involve the acquisition of general knowledge, rather than the accumulation of individual experience.

Perner (2000, p. 301) suggested that episodic memory does not emerge until roughly four to six years of age. It is then that children are able to discriminate between things they have known for a long time and things they have learned recently. In a similar vein, four-year-olds are able to discriminate between events they have observed and events they have been told about, while younger children can seldom make that distinction. Wheeler, Stuss, and Tulving (1997, p. 345) conclude that "the self-knowledge necessary for episodic remembering is not reached until around age 4 or later."

The Butcher-on-the-Bus Phenomenon

As we have seen, Tulving distinguished between episodic "remembering" and semantic "knowing." Thus "even when a person does not remember an event, she may know something about it" (1985, p. 6). For example, I may know that I have eaten at a particular restaurant without remembering the experience of eating a specific meal on a specific occasion. The feeling of knowing in the absence of episodic memory has been called the **butcher-on-the-bus phenomenon** (Yovel & Paller, 2004). The term refers to the experience of running into someone who looks familiar (the butcher) in an unexpected place (on the bus) and not being "able to remember the circumstances of any previous meeting or anything else about" him (Yovel & Paller, 2004, p. 789).

Tulving's distinction has been made in various forms by other memory researchers (e.g., Gardiner, 2001; Gardiner & Richardson-Klavehn, 2000; Squire, 2004) and has stimulated quite a bit of ingenious research.

Tip-of-the-Tongue Phenomenon

As we have seen, Tulving (1972) compared semantic memory to a mental thesaurus containing words, concepts, and their relations, but basically the term refers to general knowledge—a category that includes names. When (as often happens) you can't quite come up with a particular name, you experience the **tip-of-the-tongue phenomenon (TOT)**. James (1890), who described this experience as a "gap," noted that it is highly specific: when incorrect names are suggested, they are immediately rejected because "[t]hey do not fit into its mold." Further, the "gap of one word does not feel like the gap of another. . . . When I try vainly to recall the name of Spalding, my consciousness is far removed from what it is when I vainly try to recall the name of Bowles" (p. 251).

R. Brown and McNeill (1966) famously gathered data on the properties of TOT. First, they observed this state when it occurred in themselves. For example, one of them was trying to remember the name of the street on which a relative lived. He kept coming up with names like *Congress, Corinth,* and *Concord*. When he looked up the street name, it turned out to be *Cornish*. This example illustrates several properties of the TOT state that Brown and McNeill subsequently observed in an experiment.

butcher-on-the-bus phenomenon

The feeling of knowing a person without being able to remember the circumstances of any previous meeting or anything else about him or her.

tip-of-the-tongue phenomenon (TOT)

Knowing that you know something without quite being able to recall it.

Participants in that experiment were given the definitions of 49 low-frequency (i.e., uncommon) words, such as *apse, nepotism, cloaca, ambergris,* and *sampan,* and asked them to identify the words. When participants found themselves in a TOT state, they were often able to identify some aspects of the target word, such as its first letter or the number of syllables it contained. In addition they were often able to make judgments about words that came to mind while they searched for the target word. Sometimes they knew that their incorrect guesses were similar to the target either in sound or in meaning. For example, while searching for *sampan,* some participants knew that *Siam* and *sarong* had a similar sound, and that *barge* and *houseboat* had a similar meaning. Thus they had access to quite a bit of information about the target word before they were actually able to recall it. *Generic recall* is the term used by Brown and McNeill for this ability to recall parts and attributes of a word without explicitly recalling the word itself.

If you want to experience a TOT state yourself, try naming the seven dwarfs from the film *Snow White and the Seven Dwarfs* (Meyer & Hilterbrand, 1984). In a study exploring the connection between TOTs and stress, A.S. Brown (1991) surveyed 79 undergraduate psychology majors and found that 75 per cent of them said they experienced TOTs more often under stress (e.g., during exams). Studies of the frequency with which TOTs occur find that adults generally experience about one a week, although the frequency tends to be somewhat greater in older people.

Several studies have replicated Brown and McNeill's finding that when people are experiencing a TOT, they are likely to recall words that are similar either in sound or in meaning. They are often able to guess the first letter of the desired word with a high degree of accuracy (e.g., Rubin, 1975). They may also know the last letter, though to a lesser extent than the first (A.S. Brown, 1991, p. 212). One of the most intriguing aspects of the TOT phenomenon is the often-reported experience of recalling the desired word only after we have stopped trying to recall it: "1 hour and 39 minutes after the start of the recall attempt, the word came . . . hours prior to the solution, there was no recollection of thought on the topic" (Norman and Bobrow, 1976, p. 116).

Burke, McKay, Worthley, and Wade (1991) believe that TOTs occur mainly with words that the person concerned has not used very often or has not used very recently, with the result that the link between its meaning and its pronunciation may have atrophied because of disuse. Consequently, other words that have a similar sound and/or meaning may be elicited along with the correct word. For example, consider *charity* and *chastity.* These words not only sound similar but may be considered related in that both are associated with virtue; furthermore, neither of them is used very often. Thus they may interfere with one another, causing a TOT state. Burke et al. (1991) also reported the interesting result that the names of famous people are particularly likely to lead to TOTs in older people. It's possible that this effect comes about because older people learned these names longer ago than younger people did. As a result, the names may be fresher in the memory of younger people and less prone to interference.

Brown and McNeill (1966) suggested that memory for words and their definitions (usually considered a central part of semantic memory) is organized like a dictionary. However, they realized that the structure of a mental dictionary was unlikely to be the same as that of a standard dictionary. Since the 1960s a great deal of work has gone into trying to determine how the mental store of words is organized and how we go about searching through it to find the information we need.

Spreading Activation

An important notion to emerge from the study of semantic memory is the concept of **spreading activation**. Spreading activation was proposed by Quillian (1969) and elaborated by Collins and Loftus (1975). The idea is that when you search a semantic network, you activate the paths where the search takes place. This activation spreads from the node at which the search begins. "The spread of activation constantly expands, first to all the nodes linked to the first node, then to all the nodes linked to each of these nodes, and so on" (Collins & Loftus, 1975, p. 408). The more active a node is, the more easily its information can be processed. Thus information from active nodes can be retrieved more quickly than information from less active ones. Now let's see how the idea of spreading activation can help to explain how priming works.

Several experiments on priming have been done within the framework of the study of semantic memory; for a review of some of the best-known, see Meyer and Schvaneveldt (1976). One experiment on word recognition followed the procedure outlined in Figure 5.14. Participants looked at a screen with two fixation points, one above the other. Then a string of letters appeared at the top point. Sometimes the string was an English word such as *wine* and sometimes a non-word such as *plame*. The participants were required to complete a lexical decision task—that is, to decide whether or not the letter string was a word—and to respond "yes" if it was a word and "no" if it was a non-word. The time it took to make this response was recorded. Then another string of letters appeared and participants had to decide if this second string of letters was a word.

Sometimes the two letter strings were semantically related words: for example, *bus* and *truck*, or *sunset* and *sunrise*. These are pairs of words that you might expect to be close together in a semantic network. By contrast, if the first word was *sunset* and the second word was *truck*, then this pair would be semantically unrelated. You would not expect these two words to be close together in a semantic network.

This study found that the time it took to correctly recognize the second word was partly determined by the nature of the first word. If the second word was semantically related to the first, then the time it took to recognize it was less than if it was semantically unrelated. That is, if the two words were semantically related (*sunset–sunrise*), then the first word primed recognition of the second. This priming effect did not occur if the two words were semantically unrelated (*sunset–truck*).

DISCOVERY LAB

DISCOVERY LAB

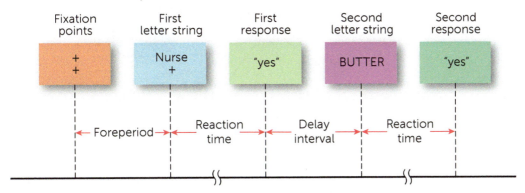

FIGURE 5.14 | Meyer, Schvaneveldt, and Ruddy's priming procedure

Meyer, D.F., Schvaneveldt, R.W., and Ruddy, M.G. (1975). Loci of contextual effects on visual recognition. In P.M.A. Rabbitt & S. Dornie (Eds.), *Attention and performance V* (p. 100). London: Academic Press.

One way of understanding this finding is in terms of the spreading activation theory outlined above. Consider the fragment of a semantic network in Figure 5.15. In this diagram, the greater the distance between any two concepts, the less closely they are related to one another. Thus *cherries* and *apples* are directly connected, but the connection between *street* and *flowers* is indirect, running through several paths. The closer together concepts are, the more easily activation will spread from one concept to another. If *clouds* is activated, it will in turn activate (or prime) *sunrises* and *sunsets*, but several more activations would be required to prime *vehicle*.

Now let's consider Meyer and Schvaneveldt's results in relation to Figure 5.15. Suppose that *bus* and *truck* and *sunset* and *sunrise* are connected in a semantic network in the way depicted in that figure. When the word *bus* is seen, activation quickly spreads to the *truck* node. The nodes for *sunrise* and *sunset* are much farther away in the network and so will be less activated. Consequently, *truck* will be primed by *bus* much more than by either *sunset* or *sunrise*. Conversely, if the participant sees *sunset* first, then *sunrise* will be primed much more than either *bus* or *truck*. In this way, the semantic network model can explain the priming effect.

The precise mechanisms governing spreading activation still need to be worked out (Bodner & Masson, 2003; Chwilla & Kolk, 2002; McRae & Boisvert, 1998). However, the concept of spreading activation has proven to be quite durable (McNamara, 1992), and continues to be a useful explanatory tool for studies of semantic memory. A good example is a study of **involuntary semantic memory** by Kvavilashvili and Mandler (2004).

involuntary semantic memory ("mind popping")
A semantic memory that pops into your mind without episodic context.

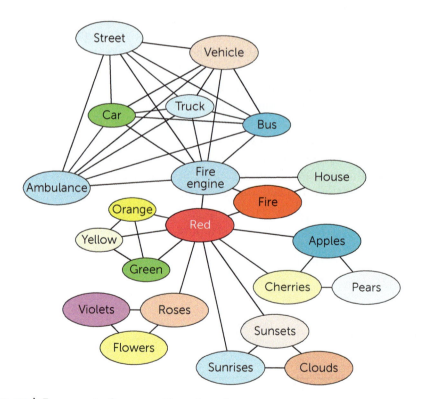

FIGURE 5.15 | Fragment of a semantic network

Collins, A.M., and & Loftus, E.F. (1975). Copyright 1975 by the American Psychological Association. Reprinted with permission. Use of APA information does not imply endorsement by APA.

Involuntary Semantic Memories

An involuntary semantic memory occurs whenever a semantic memory (e.g., a tune) pops into your mind without any episodic context. That is, you don't recall any autobiographical information that might have triggered the semantic memory; it just pops up by itself and appears to be irrelevant to what you are currently thinking about. Kvavilashvili and Mandler (2004) call this *mind popping*. Kvavilashvili and Mandler (2004) reported on diary and questionnaire studies designed to probe the mind-popping phenomenon. Kvavilashvili kept two diaries of her semantic "mind pops": the first for 19 weeks, at the age of 35, and the second for 18 weeks, two years later. She logged a total of 428 memories, which tended to be either words (e.g., *rummage*) or images (e.g., *a view of a road and a small church in Cardiff*). She had no episodic information accompanying these involuntary semantic memories. Most of the mind pops occurred while she was engaged in routine activities not requiring a lot of attention, and at first they appeared unrelated to the current activity. In retrospect, however, Kvavilashvili was often able to find cues that had triggered the memories without her awareness. For example, one pop-up was *Itchy and Scratchy*, the names of two characters from *The Simpsons* television show. Kvavilashvili recalled she was scratching her back when the pop-up occurred. Examples like this suggest that involuntary semantic memories are primed by events of which we are typically unaware. Kvavilashvili and Mandler's (2004) study shows how ecologically valid research can complement and extend laboratory work.

Connectionist Models of Memory

When we introduced connectionist models in Chapter 2, we noted that they were designed to represent neural networks as they might exist in the brain. McClelland (2000, p. 583) observed that from a connectionist viewpoint individual items are not "stored in memory": rather, memories consist of certain patterns of activity. Nor are copies of particular experiences stored as memory traces; rather, neuron-like units representing each of the properties of an experience are connected to other neuron-like units. McClelland et al. (1986) pointed out that some experiences will have the same properties, and so the unit for a particular property will tend to be connected with several different experiences. Every time one property is activated, all the units to which it is connected will tend to be activated as well. In order to accurately recall previous experiences, therefore, the system needs to **excite** some connections and **inhibit** others.

McClelland (1981) and McClelland et al. (1986, pp. 27ff.) have demonstrated how a simple connectionist system might work. Figure 5.16 lists the members of two gangs, the Jets and the Sharks, with some of their properties: name, gang affiliation, age, education, marital status, and occupation. Some of the units that would be required to represent these individuals in memory are then presented in Figure 5.17. In the centre of the diagram are units representing shared properties for each of the persons listed in Figure 5.16. These individual units are connected to the appropriate property units. For convenience, the property units are grouped within different "clouds," and units within a particular cloud inhibit each other. Thus an individual cannot be called both *Lance* and *Art* at the same time.

excitatory and inhibitory connections
Connections that either enhance or diminish the associations between the units that make up a neural network.

\multicolumn{6}{c}{The Jets and the Sharks}
Name	Gang	Age	Edu.	Mar.	Occupation
Art	Jets	40s	J.H.	Sing.	Pusher
Al	Jets	30s	J.H.	Mar.	Burglar
Sam	Jets	20s	J.H.	Sing.	Burglar
Clyde	Jets	40s	J.H.	Sing.	Bookie
Mike	Jets	30s	J.H.	Sing.	Bookie
Jim	Jets	20s	J.H.	Div.	Burglar
Greg	Jets	20s	H.S.	Mar.	Pusher
John	Jets	20s	J.H.	Mar.	Burglar
Doug	Jets	30s	H.S.	Sing.	Bookie
Lance	Jets	20s	COL.	Mar.	Bookie
George	Jets	20s	J.H.	Div.	Burglar
Pete	Jets	20s	H.S.	Sing.	Bookie
Fred	Jets	20s	H.S.	Sing.	Pusher
Gene	Jets	20s	COL.	Sing.	Pusher
Ralph	Jets	30s	J.H.	Sing.	Pusher
Phil	Sharks	30s	COL.	Mar.	Pusher
Ike	Sharks	30s	J.H.	Sing.	Bookie
Nick	Sharks	30s	H.S.	Sing.	Pusher
Don	Sharks	30s	COL.	Mar.	Burglar
Ned	Sharks	30s	COL.	Mar.	Bookie
Karl	Sharks	40s	H.S.	Mar.	Bookie
Ken	Sharks	20s	H.S.	Sing.	Burglar
Earl	Sharks	40s	H.S.	Mar.	Burglar
Rick	Sharks	30s	H.S.	Div.	Burglar
Ol	Sharks	30s	COL.	Mar.	Pusher
Neal	Sharks	30s	H.S.	Sing.	Bookie
Dave	Sharks	30s	H.S.	Div.	Pusher

FIGURE 5.16 | Some properties of gang members

Adapted from McClelland, J.L., Retrieving general and specific knowledge from stored knowledge of specifics, Proceedings of the Third Annual Conference of the Cognitive Science Society, Berkeley, Calif., p. 27. Copyright 1981 by J.L. McClelland.

Imagine that you have met all these individuals at one time or another. Imagine also that you find yourself in a conversation about the individual whose name is *Art*. When you try to remember what *Art* is like, what happens? Initially, when you hear the name *Art*, the name unit for *Art* will be activated. This name unit is connected to the individual unit for *Art*. The individual unit for *Art* is connected to all the property units that *Art* possesses. Activation of all of these property units corresponds to remembering *Art*. This model can be seen as an extension of the spreading activation model.

Of course, the act of remembering is not always so straightforward. If you hear someone talking about a gang member who is single, that information is not enough to enable you to identify the person in question, since several individual units are connected to the "single" property. However, a combination of properties might serve to specify the individual more or less completely. Thus if you also hear that the *single* person in question is

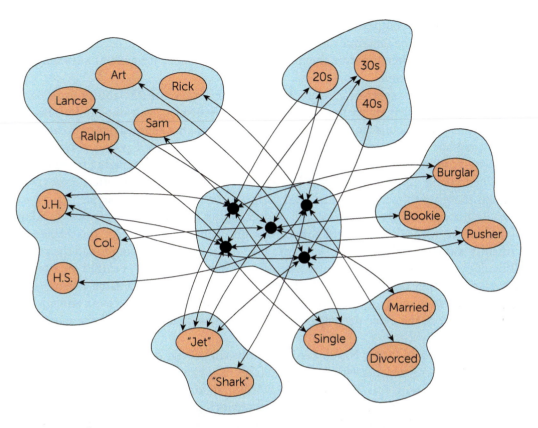

FIGURE 5.17 | A connectionist model of the information in Figure 5.16

From: McClelland, J.L. (1981). p. 28. Copyright © 1981 by J.L. McClelland. Reprinted by permission.

a *burglar* in his *twenties* with only a *junior-high* education, all four of those properties will point to the *Sam* unit, causing more activation there than in any of the other units. Activating the *Sam* unit will also activate the property units associated with *Sam*, and make you think that the person being talked about is a member of the *Jets*.

In this memory model, information about individual experiences is derived from the state of the entire system at a particular time. The pattern of excitation and inhibition in the system as a whole determines what you will remember.

Aging and Memory Disorders

Memory and Aging

Folk wisdom says that memory declines with age, but in fact some forms of memory are relatively unscathed by advancing years. It is episodic memory in particular that shows a strong age effect (Craik & Grady, 2002, p. 529). A good illustration can be found in a study by Mitchell (1989) that explored differences in the ways episodic and semantic memories decline with age. Remembering that *I put salt on my food at lunch yesterday* is an episodic memory; remembering that *the formula for salt is NaCl* is a semantic memory. When Mitchell tested the memories of two groups of people, one aged 19–32 and the other aged 63–80, the young people clearly outperformed the older ones on the episodic memory tasks, but this was not the case on the semantic memory tasks. Although older people may sometimes have trouble recollecting recent personal experiences, their memory for general knowledge can continue to function well.

One frustrating aspect of getting older is a deterioration in the ability to recognize people and/or recall their names. In one study by Schweich, van der Linden, Bredart, Bruyer, Nelles, and Schils (1992), three groups of participants kept diaries of occasions on which they had experienced such difficulties. Group 1 contained young university students (19–25 years old) who reported no previous difficulties in recognizing faces; Group 2 contained young university students (19–25) who claimed they were often embarrassed by their inability to recognize faces; and Group 3 consisted of older people (54–73) also attending university. Over a one-month period, Group 2 reported the greatest incidence of difficulties, while Groups 1 and 3 reported significantly fewer; in fact, the incidence of difficulty was identical for the two latter groups. Group 2, not surprisingly, had the greatest difficulty with recognizing faces, while most of Group 3's problems centred on attaching names to faces they recognized. The inability to consciously retrieve a name, given the face, is similar to the inability to directly remember episodic associations. Given enough time, however, most of the older participants in this study were able to recall the names they were looking for.

Naveh-Benjamin (2000; Naveh-Benjamin, Hussain, Guez, & Bar-on, 2003) has shown that older people's problems with names and faces may have the same source as their more general difficulty with episodic memory. According to his associative deficit hypothesis, older adults have a "deficiency in creating and retrieving links between single units of information" (Naveh-Benjamin, Guez, Kilb, & Reedy, 2004, p. 541). In one experiment, the ability to recall face–name associations was examined for two groups of men, one with a mean age of about 21 and the other with a mean age of about 72. All participants were shown 40 pairs of names and faces for three seconds per pair and were told to try to learn not only the faces and names, but also their pairings. They were then given a name recognition test, a face recognition test, and a face–name association test. In the first test, they were shown a name they had seen in the first part of the experiment, paired with one they had not seen, and were asked to identify the one they had seen before. They were shown 16 such pairs in all. The face recognition test was the same, except that the pairs were faces. Finally, in the face–name association test participants were shown eight names they had seen before, each one paired with two faces, one they had seen previously and one they had not. They were also shown eight faces they had seen before, each paired with two names, one seen previously and one not. The task was to identify the names and faces they had seen before.

In general, the older participants were less able than the younger ones to correctly identify names or faces when they were presented by themselves; however, the difference was quite small. The big difference associated with age became apparent when participants had to correctly identify the name that went with a face, or the face that went with a name (Figure 5.19). In this task the older participants were considerably less successful than the younger ones. Thus the problem was not so much that older people don't recognize names or faces as it was that they don't bind them together as easily as younger people do. Older adults have trouble in situations requiring the "merging of different aspects of an episode into a cohesive unit" (Naveh-Benjamin, Guez, Kilb, & Reedy, 2004, p. 541). Recalling

associative deficit hypothesis
The hypothesis that older adults have a deficiency in creating and retrieving links between single units of information.

Memory and the Internet

Many readers will be too young to remember it, but there was a time not too long ago when humans' access to information was much more limited than it is today. When the authors of this book were growing up they had to resort to books, libraries, or experts with specific knowledge just to complete homework or figure out which movie won the Oscar for Best Picture in 1976 (Google says it was *Rocky*—which demonstrates the point). Today information is never farther away than the nearest computer or smart phone. Indeed, the company name Google is now an official word in the dictionary, and is regularly used as a verb. However, recent research has suggested that even though it is virtually indispensable in our daily lives, the ability to "google" whatever information we need could have consequences for our memory.

Sparrow, Liu, and Wegner (2011) devised an interesting experiment to explore whether having easy access to information could have an impact on how such information is encoded. In one of the experimental conditions participants were given a number of trivia statements that they had to type into a computer to verify. For example, a participant would read "An ostrich's eye is bigger than its brain" and then make that statement the subject of an Internet search. The key manipulation was that half of the participants believed the computer was saving whatever they typed, whereas the other half were led to believe it was not,

and therefore that the statements would not be accessible at a later time. In a subsequent test of their ability to remember the trivia statements, participants performed better if they had thought that their search queries were being deleted.

This could indicate that we will put less effort into encoding and storing information if we think we will have easy access to it at a later date than we will if we think we won't have that access. In fact, in another experiment Sparrow, Liu, and Wegner found that memory for where to find the information (e.g., which website was best) was better than memory for the information itself. By extension, although "googling it" can often give us instant answers, we may not remember those answers as well as we might wish.

FIGURE 5.18 | Google search engine

previous episodes becomes difficult because the parts of a previous experience have not been bound together to form a coherent whole.

While older people may have difficulty consciously recalling recently experienced events, Howard, Fry, and Brune (1991, Experiment 2) found that they can still demonstrate knowledge of those events when tested more subtly. Younger (18–24 years) and older (62–75) people were asked to learn new associations. They were shown pairs of words (e.g., *queen–stairs, author–project*) and asked to make up a sentence containing them. When participants were given the first member of a pair and asked to recall the

FIGURE 5.19 | **Young and old meeting**

Which one is better at remembering names?

second member, the younger people tended to do better than the older ones. However, older people did just as well as the younger ones on a more indirect test of memory. The indirect test was a word fragment completion task similar to those we mentioned earlier in the section on implicit memory. Participants were shown the first word of a pair plus a fragment of the second. Sometimes the word-fragment pairs corresponded to pairs shown in the first phase of the experiment (e.g., *queen–sta—, author–pro—*) but sometimes the pairs were mixed up (e.g., *queen–pro—, author–sta—*). Participants were asked to complete the stem with the first word that came to mind. Notice that in each case there are several words that could come to mind besides the one given (*star, process*, etc.). However, if the pair–stem combination corresponded to one they had seen before (e.g., *queen–sta—*), then both younger and older participants tended to choose the word originally shown (*stairs*), an effect that was not present if the word fragment pair had not been seen before (e.g., *queen–pro—*). This demonstrated that the older participants had implicitly learned the new associations, even though they may not have realized it. Howard and colleagues concluded that you *can* teach old dogs new tricks—though only if they are given as much time as they want to learn those tricks. Self-pacing appears to be very important.

In a review of studies such as that of Howard, Fry, and Brune (1991), Mitchell and Bruss (2003) confirmed that older adults do seem to be able to form implicit memories just as easily as younger people. They also respond to priming just as readily as younger people. Implicit memory appears to be stable across age.

Thus memory deficits in older people tend not to be general (Rabbitt, 1990). Not only may there be great individual differences in the rate at which memory declines, but the extent of a deficit may depend on the context in which it is tested. Rabbitt (1990, p. 230) suggested that repeated testing may improve the performance of older people to the point that age differences are eliminated.

The Amnesic Syndrome

Both Schacter (1987) and Baddeley (1987a) pointed out the relevance of **Korsakoff's syndrome** for the study of memory. A form of amnesia affecting the ability to form new long-term memories (see Figure 5.20), Korsakoff's syndrome is attributed to the atrophy of brain tissue resulting from malnutrition, particularly thiamine deficiency (Brokate, Hildebrandt, Eling, Fuchtner, Runge, & Timm, 2003) and is often (though not exclusively) seen in chronic alcoholics. Edouard Claparède (1873–1940) was a pioneer in the investigation of this syndrome (Kihlstrom, 1995). Here is Claparède's (1911/1951) famous description of a 47-year-old Korsakoff's patient:

> Her old memories remained intact. She could correctly name the capitals of Europe, make mental calculations, and so on. But she did not know where she was, though she had been at the asylum five years. She did not recognize the doctors whom she saw every day, nor her nurse who had been with her

for six months. When the latter asked the patient whether she knew her, the patient said: "No Madame, with whom have I the honor of speaking?" She forgot from one minute to the next what she was told, or the events that took place. She did not know what year, month, and day it was, though she was being told constantly (p. 68).

Schacter (1987) also reviewed research on the so-called *amnesic syndrome*. This is a disorder produced by brain lesions, and is seen in patients with Korsakoff's syndrome, as well as Tulving's patient NN, whose case we mentioned earlier in this chapter. Amnesic patients may be able to operate normally in many areas, but unable to remember events that have occurred since the beginning of their affliction. Talland (1968) described this kind of patient:

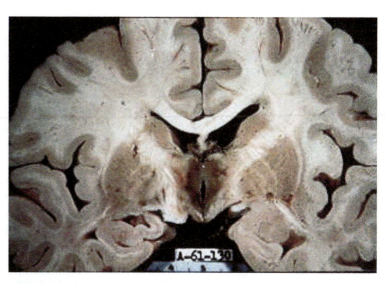

FIGURE 5.20 | Korsakoff's syndrome, or Wernicke-Korsakoff encephalopathy

Note the pigmentation of grey matter, which occurs with thiamine (vitamin B_1) deficiency, most often in chronic alcoholics.

University of Texas (Houston)

> If time has come to a stop for the amnesic patient it is because he remembers virtually none of the events that he has witnessed since the onset of his illness. The days go by and none seems to be different from the others. Staff members and fellow patients reappear looking no more familiar than complete strangers. A story gives as much satisfaction on the tenth as it did on the first reading, its novelty never seems to wear off. If the patient recognizes a new figure in his environment, his doctor for example, as someone familiar, he may easily confuse him with another figure encountered in the same environment or name him correctly but as diffidently as if it were a wild guess. In the literature there are several accounts of the medical examination that had to be interrupted for a few minutes, in which the patient greeted the doctor on his return as someone he had not met for a long time (p. 123).

Warrington and Weiskrantz (1982) suggest that these amnesic patients have a **disconnection syndrome**: they may be able to acquire new information and yet not be aware that learning has taken place. It's as if there are at least two memory systems (Tulving, 1985) that normally interact but have become disconnected. This interpretation is reinforced by studies using the *famous name paradigm* described earlier. Squire and McKee (1992) showed lists of names to people with amnesia and a control group. Some of the names were famous (e.g., *Olga Korbut*, a celebrated Olympic gymnast) while others were not (e.g., *Emia Lekovic*). Then all participants were shown another set of famous and non-famous names, some of which had been on the previous list and some of which had not, and asked to rate them as famous or non-famous. Both the control group and the people with amnesia tended to rate a name as famous if it had appeared on the first list, even if it was not actually famous. Thus simply having been exposed to a name tends to influence participants' judgments.

disconnection syndrome
Amnesic patients may be able to acquire new information and yet not be aware that learning has taken place.

However, while the participants in the control group were usually able to recognize a name as one that had appeared on the first list, people with amnesia were much less able to do so. They could judge a non-famous name to be famous because they had just seen it on the previous list, and yet not know that they had seen it.

Together, several studies reviewed by Warrington and Weiskrantz (1982) strongly suggest that amnesic patients do poorly on tasks requiring explicit memory, but much better on those requiring implicit memory. Graf and Schacter (1985) were able to further demonstrate this by giving a word-fragment completion test to both people with amnesia and a control group. Participants were presented with pairs of words, some of which were related by existing associations (e.g., *buttoned–shirt*) and some of which were not (e.g., *window–shirt*). In one part of the experiment, participants were required to make up a sentence that related the words "in a meaningful manner." Thus, given the word pair *ripe–apple*, a participant might generate the sentence "He ate the ripe apple." Participants were then allowed to study each pair of words once.

Each participant was given two tests: a word completion test for implicit memory, and a cued recall test for explicit memory. In the former, participants were shown the first member of a word pair and the first three letters of the second member of the pair (the "word fragment") and asked to complete the word. The interesting question was whether they would complete the fragment with the word they were shown initially. Both groups tended to do so. However, on the cued recall test, in which participants were given the first half of a word pair and had to recall the second, the people with amnesia were much less successful than the control group.

Levy, Stark, and Squire (2004) also observed that people with amnesia showed similar performance to the control group on an implicit memory task, even though their performance on an explicit memory task was far below the control level. People with amnesia may be able to form associations, and thus learn new material (Schacter & Graf, 1986; Kihlstrom, Schacter, Cork, Hurt, & Behr, 1990). However, this learning would be available to them only in implicit, not explicit, form. Korsakoff himself (1899, pp. 512, 518, cited in Schacter, 1987, p. 503) described this phenomenon as follows:

> Although the patient was not aware that he preserved traces of impressions that he received, those traces . . . probably existed and had an influence in one way or another on the course of ideas, at least in unconscious intellectual activity.
>
> We notice that a whole series of traces which could in no way be restored to consciousness, neither actively or passively, continue to exist in unconscious life, continue to direct the course of ideas of the patient, suggesting to him some or other inferences and decisions. That seems to me to be one of the most interesting peculiarities of the disturbance about which we are speaking.

Alzheimer's Disease

Alzheimer's disease is among the most feared memory disorders (see Figure 5.21). In an American survey conducted in 2002, 95 per cent of respondents agreed that Alzheimer's was a "serious problem facing the whole nation," and 64 per cent of those between 35 and 49 years of age said they were afraid of getting it themselves (Halpern, 2002, p. 16). "Four

Although a definitive diagnosis of Alzheimer's still requires an autopsy, the symptoms are better understood today than they were when this form of dementia was first identified, more than a century ago.

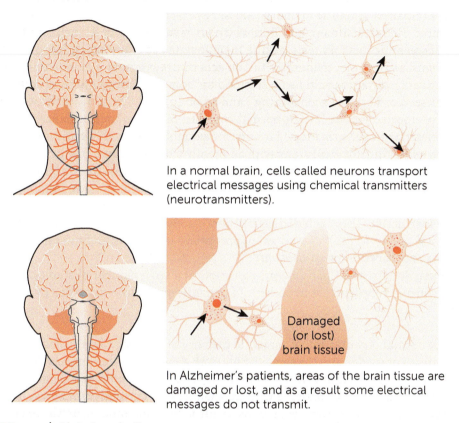

In a normal brain, cells called neurons transport electrical messages using chemical transmitters (neurotransmitters).

Damaged (or lost) brain tissue

In Alzheimer's patients, areas of the brain tissue are damaged or lost, and as a result some electrical messages do not transmit.

FIGURE 5.21 | Alzheimer's disease

From: www.alzheimersmemoryloss.info/alzheimers-disease.jpg

million Americans already have the disease, a number that is expected to grow to fourteen million by mid-century" (Halpern, 2002, p. 16). Similar rates are likely in other industrialized countries (Di Carlo et al., 2002).

The criteria for diagnosis of Alzheimer's disease have become much clearer since the first case was recorded by Alois Alzheimer in 1907. The disease is progressive, beginning with a deterioration of episodic memory. A decline in the ability to retain recently acquired information is characteristic of the early stages (Hodges, 2000, p. 443). An example given by Jacoby (1999) illustrates how frustrating Alzheimer's can be for caregivers. He describes a woman diagnosed with Alzheimer's who was taken to visit a nursing home before moving there. She was introduced to the customs of the nursing home, one of which was that there was no tipping in the dining room. This fact was repeated several times. Later, however, when the prospective resident was asked if she had any questions, she asked if she should tip in the dining room. "[R]epeated asking of questions is one of the most striking and frustrating symptoms of memory impairment resulting from Alzheimer's disease" (Jacoby, 1999, p. 3).

Not everyone who is unable to learn new material will go on to develop Alzheimer's. "It is . . . necessary to follow such patients for years in order to determine that they do indeed have" it (Hodges, 2000, p. 445). As the disease progresses, Alzheimer's patients will show impaired semantic memory (Glosser & Friedman, 1991; Hodges, 2000, p. 445). For example, Hodges, Salmon, and Butters (1992) gave a group of Alzheimer's patients a battery of semantic memory tests: asking them to name as many exemplars of a category (e.g., *animals*) as possible; to identify the objects in drawings; to generate definitions of words (e.g., *alligator*) that could be understood by "someone from a different country who has never seen or heard of such a thing"; and so on (p. 305). On all tests the Alzheimer's patients performed less well than normal controls. Moreover, performance on one test was correlated with performance on others: for example, failure to identify the animal in a drawing as an alligator went along with an inability to define an alligator. This suggests that what Alzheimer's disease involves is not so much the inability to retrieve existing knowledge as the deterioration of knowledge that once existed. Hodges, Salmon, and Butters (1992, p. 312) observe that the definitions given by the Alzheimer's patients were particularly instructive. They included very general, non-specific characteristics (defining a *land animal* as *four-legged*), as well as inappropriate intrusions (defining a *rhinoceros* in terms more appropriate for an *elephant*).

Salmon, Butters, and Chan (1999), in a review of a large number of studies, concluded that the evidence supported the hypothesis of semantic memory deterioration in Alzheimer's patients:

> The normal organization of semantic memory is disrupted by this loss of semantic knowledge and the semantic network appears to deteriorate as the disease progresses. Although the neuroanatomical basis of the deterioration of semantic memory in patients with [Alzheimer's] is currently unknown, it is likely that it results from synapse loss, neuron loss, and other neurodegenerative changes in the association cortices that presumably store semantic representations (p. 115).

The Retraining of Memory

Efforts to rehabilitate memory have usually been based on intuition rather than adequate theories of memory disorders. B.A. Wilson and her colleagues (Kapur, Glisky, & Wilson, 2002; Wilson, 2002; Wilson & Moffat, 1984; Wilson & Patterson, 1990) have tried to identify treatment approaches that have a history of working and/or are based on a sound theoretical foundation.

Environmental Adaptations

Minimizing the number of situations requiring memory can be helpful. A written timetable, located where the patient can't miss it, can serve as a guide, helping him or her move from one activity to another. Simply posting signs that tell patients which room they are in can be valuable (Giles & Clark-Wilson, 1988). In general, environments should be designed so that they elicit the desired behaviour.

External Memory Aids

Prospective memory comes into play when we need to remember to do something at some future time. Older people in general, as well as those with memory disorders specifically, may forget not only when to do something, but also whether or not they have done it. For example, in addition to forgetting to take their medication on time, they may forget that they have done so and thus take it again (Einstein, McDaniel, Smith, & Shaw, 1998). An electronic diary that sounds an alarm when it's time to perform a particular task and keeps track of the patient's behaviour may help with this problem (Harris, 1984). Electronic organizers such as a smart phone may be useful too, serving as "prosthetic memories" with "a built in camera, handwriting recognition system and diary" (Abraham, 2004). The patient can take pictures of people as an aid to future recognition. These devices can also be programmed with a week's "to do" list and prompt the user to "remember" on each occasion. Of course, teaching patients how to use the device is a long and painstaking process, because most must rely on implicit rather than explicit memory. Sheer repetition makes a difference, and it's important that the teacher help the patient avoid errors. **Errorless learning** is widely believed to maximize patients' ability to use whatever memory resources they still have. Patients learn to do only what should be done and never learn to do things incorrectly (Wilson, 2002, p. 667).

Teaching Domain-Specific Knowledge

Learning in amnesiacs is unlikely to be generalizable to contexts very different from the one in which the original learning took place. Indeed, there is no evidence that attempting to restore "general memory ability" through practice actually accomplishes anything for the patient (Kapur, Glisky, & Wilson, 2002, p. 772). A more realistic goal is to teach amnesiacs specific skills that might be useful to them. To this end, Glisky and Schacter (1989) reported on what they called the **method of vanishing cues**. Amnesic participants were taught the meaning of computer commands by being presented with definitions of the commands and fragments of their names (e.g., S——for the command SAVE). Additional letters were presented until the participant guessed the word. Then letters were progressively removed until the patient was able to give the name of the command upon being presented with its definition. Glisky and Schacter report that this technique allowed amnesic patients to successfully perform basic computer operations. In such situations it's important that the material to be learned be concrete and specific and that the patient not be required to generalize very far from the original learning context.

Summary

In this chapter we have examined memory systems. The modal model of memory has been especially influential in the study of memory. This approach to memory outlines how information arriving at our senses is first stored in sensory, and then by short-term memory, eventually being transferred to long-term memory should sufficient processing be conducted. The classification of the various systems of long-term memory reflects the influential work of Endel Tulving, who was a pioneer in distinguishing between episodic and semantic memory. *Episodic memory* provides long-term storage for personal experiences and events, whereas *semantic memory* stores factual information and general knowledge about the world.

prospective memory
The intention to remember to do something at some future time.

errorless learning
Participants in a learning situation are taught in such a way that they never have the opportunity to make errors.

method of vanishing cues
A way of teaching amnesic patients the meaning of computer commands by presenting them with definitions of the commands and fragments of the commands' names. Additional letters are presented until the patient guesses the word. Then letters are progressively removed until the patient is able to give the name of the command when presented with its definition.

The independence of these two memory systems is supported by studies of brain-injured persons, especially those with amnesia. Tulving's distinction between *remembering* and *knowing* is reflected in the *butcher-on-the-bus phenomenon*. The last 40 years have seen a lot of research on phenomena associated with semantic and episodic memory, including tip-of-the-tongue phenomenon, spreading activation, and involuntary semantic memory. The more recent literature suggests that there may be as many as five memory systems in all. *Procedural memory* contains our knowledge of how to do things that involve a sequence of operations, such as riding a bicycle. Such knowledge is *tacit* (implicit) rather than *explicit* because we aren't necessarily aware of how we perform those operations. The *perceptual representation* system (the system associated with priming) contains specific representations of previously encountered events. It is responsible for priming *implicit memory*—that is, unintentional or unconscious recollection of a prior episode (for example, experiments by Jacoby and Hollingshead). *Working memory*—the system that allows for temporary storage and manipulation of the information necessary for many cognitive activities—pulls all the other memory systems together. Baddeley's working memory model has four components: the *central executive*, the *phonological loop*, the *visuo-spatial sketchpad*, and the *episodic buffer*.

The *connectionist model* of memory provides an alternative to the idea of memory as a stored memory trace. In this model neuron-like units representing the various properties of an experience are connected to other neuron-like units. The excitation or inhibition of specific connections between units creates a pattern of activity that constitutes memory.

In evolutionary terms, procedural memory is considered the oldest system and episodic the most recent. In terms of development, Tulving argues that we begin to develop episodic memory relatively late, at around 4–6 years. Do all forms of memory decline with age? A large body of research suggests that they do not. Studies by Howard, Fry, and Brune (1991) and Mitchell and Bruss (2003) show that even though older adults often have difficulty recalling recent events, they form implicit memories just as readily as younger people do. Similarly, amnesic patients do not differ from control participants on implicit memory tasks; however, their performance on explicit memory tasks is below normal. Patients with Alzheimer's disease experience a loss of semantic knowledge and a disruption in the organization of semantic memory. For the elderly and some amnesiacs, the rehabilitation of memory typically involves environmental adaptation, external memory aids, and instruction in domain-specific knowledge.

CASE STUDY

Case Study Wrap-Up

At the beginning of this chapter we briefly discussed the strange memory deficit of Lucy Whitmore, the young woman played by Drew Barrymore in the movie *50 First Dates*. After reading this chapter you should have a better idea of what Lucy's problem was. If you recall, a car accident had supposedly left her unable to retain new memories from one day to the next; however, all the memories she had formed before the accident were intact, and she was able to form new memories from moment to moment. In fact, all the forms of memory discussed in this chapter (semantic, episodic, tacit, explicit, implicit) appeared to operate normally for Lucy throughout any particular day: the only problem was that the new semantic and episodic memories disappeared overnight. Presumably Lucy would have been able to retain new implicit memories, as patients with disconnection syndrome do, although this wasn't demonstrated in the movie.

What type of real-world amnesia most closely resembles Lucy Whitmore's memory deficit? Earlier in the chapter we discussed Korsakoff's syndrome, a severe form of anterograde amnesia in which the individual is unable to form new memories. While this appears to describe exactly the deficit suffered by Drew Barrymore's character, there is a key difference that separates fact from fiction.

Someone who suffers from Korsakoff's syndrome (or an equivalent anterograde amnesia) is unable to form new long-term memories. The components of working memory can often be intact, in which case the individual may be able to retain new information for 30 seconds or so. However, as soon as that information leaves working memory it is lost, apparently forever. Thus the real-life equivalent of Lucy Whitmore's memory problem is much more severe than the movie suggests. While the fictional character's memory functions normally until she falls asleep, in real life people with Korsakoff's syndrome (or an equivalent anterograde amnesia) have no normal moment-to-moment memory function. If you introduced yourself to a Korsakoff's patient and then left the room for 30 seconds, he or she might not recognize you when you came back.

If you enjoyed *50 First Dates* you might want to check out *Memento*, which presents a much more accurate (though still embellished) picture of this particular memory dysfunction.

In the Know: Review Questions

1. Outline Tulving's approach to memory, emphasizing the distinctions between different memory systems.
2. Discuss the role of spreading activation in semantic memory, using relevant experiments to illustrate.
3. What do older people, people with the amnesic syndrome, and people with Alzheimer's disease tell us about the nature of memory? What are the most effective ways of helping such people? Why?

Key Concepts

associative deficit hypothesis
butcher-on-the-bus phenomenon
central executive
chunking
consolidation
crystallized systems
decay
declarative memory
disconnection syndrome
episodic buffer
episodic memory (Tulving)
errorless learning
excitatory and inhibitory connections
fluid systems

hippocampus
iconic and echoic sensory memory
involuntary semantic memory ("mind popping")
Korsakoff's syndrome
lexical decision task (LDT)
method of opposition
method of vanishing cues
modal model of memory
non-declarative memory
perceptual representation system (PRS)
phonological loop
prime
prime memory

priming

probe or target

procedural memory

prospective memory

recency bias vs primacy bias

rehearsed

secondary memory

semantic memory (Tulving)

spreading activation

tacit knowledge

tip-of-the-tongue phenomenon

visuo-spatial sketchpad

working memory

Links to Other Chapters

episodic memory
Chapter 13 (memory and consciousness)

semantic memory
Chapter 7 (synesthesia)

working memory
Chapter 6 (Are memory traces permanent?)

Chapter 9 (social context of language, evolution of language)
Chapter 10 (flexibility–rigidity and the brain)
Chapter 11 (natural deduction systems)
Chapter 12 (working memory and *g*)

fluid and crystallized systems
Chapter 12 (fluid intelligence and *g*)

Further Reading

For additional angles on memory systems see Gaffan (2003), Moscovitch (2000), Roediger (1990), and Roediger and Blaxton (1987).

Evidence from functional neuroimaging studies illustrating the variety of areas in the brain involved in semantic memory is discussed in Maguire and Frith (2004) and Thompson-Schill (2003). Tulving and his colleagues have presented a model suggesting that the left prefrontal cortex is more involved than the right prefrontal cortex in acquiring episodic memories, but that the reverse is true for recalling episodic memories. See Nyberg, Cabeza, and Tulving (1996) and Habib, Nyberg, and Tulving (2003). For a critique of this model see Owen (2003).

It's difficult for "normals" to imagine what learning is like for amnesiacs. An analogy might be the kind of learning that takes place while a normal person is unconscious. For example, Kihlstrom, Schacter, Cork, Hurt, and Behr (1990) investigated memory for events that occur while a (non-amnesic) patient is anesthetized. They pointed out that following surgical anesthesia, patients are typically not able to recall anything that took place while they were unconscious. However, there is also some evidence suggesting that events that take place during surgery can affect patients' subsequent behaviour, although these findings are controversial.

For a thorough review that supplements our discussion of the rehabilitation of cognitive deficits see Park and Ingles (2001).

Gaffan, D. (2003). Against memory systems. In A. Parker, A. Derrington, & C. Blakemore (Eds.), *The physiology of cognitive processes* (pp. 234–51). Oxford: Oxford University Press.

Habib, R., Nyberg, L., & Tulving, E. (2003). Hemispheric asymmetries of memory: The HERA model revisited. *Trends in Cognitive Science, 7,* 241–244.

Memory Traces and Memory Schemas

Chapter Contents

Learning Objectives

- To distinguish between memory traces and memory schemas.
- To outline the concept of flashbulb memories.
- To examine schema theory and review experimental evidence supporting it.
- To understand the concept of encoding specificity.
- To review research into eyewitness testimony and false memories.
- To identify the strengths and weaknesses of the "levels of processing" framework.

When Memory Fails

The previous chapter highlighted some basic ideas about the various systems of memory. In this chapter we will focus on different types of long-term memory, but first let's turn our attention to a case study that highlights the importance of memory and the dire consequences that can follow when memory fails.

In July 1984 a college student named Jennifer Thompson woke up and saw a man with a knife beside her bed. When she screamed, he held the knife to her throat and said he would kill her if she didn't keep quiet. She offered him her wallet, even her car, but he told her he didn't want those things. Realizing what he was there for, she made a conscious effort to study his face, looking for details she could remember later and use to identify him. Eventually she escaped to a neighbour's by persuading the rapist to let her get him a drink.

Thompson worked closely with the police to create a composite sketch. When she was shown a photo lineup she studied it carefully before deciding she recognized the man that the police had identified as the suspect. She picked out the same man, Ronald Cotton, in a physical lineup, and when the case went to court she swore that he was the one who had raped her. Cotton, 22, was sentenced to life.

In prison Cotton met someone who looked so much like him that other prisoners sometimes mistook one for the other. Bobby Poole had been living in the same North Carolina town as Cotton and Thompson, and was serving time for a series of rapes. When Cotton asked if he had raped Thompson he denied it, but another inmate informed Cotton that Poole told him he had. Finally, in 1995 a DNA test confirmed Poole's guilt. Cotton was exonerated, and

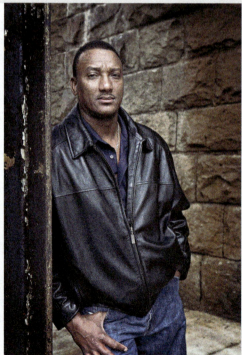

FIGURE 6.1 | Jennifer Thompson and Ronald Cotton

Thompson was overwhelmed with remorse. How could she have made a mistake that cost an innocent man more than 10 years of his life?

In fact, eyewitnesses are very often mistaken. As of September 2015, DNA tests have led to the exoneration of 330 convicted men in the US alone, and in approximately 75 per cent of those cases faulty eyewitness testimony had been involved (Innocence Project, 2015). Why are eyewitnesses so often wrong? How are false memories created? How is it that the people who hold them believe them to be true? These are among the many questions that this chapter will explore.

We may not know everything there is to know about how memory operates, but one thing we do know is that memory doesn't work the way a video camera does. You can't turn it on and off, it doesn't simply record whatever is going on in front of its lens, and it can't be rewound and replayed at will. Rather, it seems that we capture the gist of incoming messages, assimilate that information with schemas that are already stored in our long-term memory, and then use those schemas to "fill in the blanks" when we're missing important bits and pieces of information.

Introduction

We will begin this chapter by considering the distinction between a memory trace (a concept introduced in Chapter 3) and a memory schema. Both Paul (1967) and Erdelyi (1985) suggest that Freud's (1925/1961) **mystic writing pad model** might be a good place to start.

The mystic writing pad is a common children's toy consisting of a sheet of waxed paper sandwiched between a layer of black wax and a sheet of clear plastic (celluloid). When you write on the plastic with a stylus, you can see what you've written because the waxed paper sticks to the wax wherever you have pressed on it. When you lift the waxed paper and plastic, the writing disappears from the overlay, but the imprint of the stylus remains visible on the black wax.

The overlay is like our perception of an event. Such perceptions are transitory; we pass from one experience to the next. Memory traces are similar to what remains on the wax tablet after we lift the plastic—after-effects of perception. The problem is that over time they tend to run together. Thus if you examine the black wax layer after using the pad for a while, you will see numerous lines overlapping, as in Figure 6.2. How can you tell what was originally written? You can't: all you can do is reconstruct it on the basis of whatever evidence is available. In this case, given the traces that you can make out—a clear *p* followed by a slightly less clear *e*, two straight descending lines, what looks like another *e*, and a clear *r*—you would probably decide that the word written was *pepper*.

Although the mystic writing pad analogy is imperfect—it's highly unlikely that memory has the truly haphazard structure of the fragments that remain on a wax tablet—it may help to clarify the significance of the schema-based theories that we will examine a little later in this chapter. First, however, we will take a look at how the trace theory has evolved.

mystic writing pad model

A model of memory based on a toy writing tablet that retains fragments of old messages even after they have been "erased." In time, these fragments accumulate and begin to overlap, so that they become increasingly hard to read.

FIGURE 6.2 | The mystic writing pad

From: Erdelyi, M.H. (1985). p. 119. Copyright 1985 by Matthew Hugh Erdelyi. Used with permission.

DISCOVERY LAB

The Trace Theory

For a long time, memory traces were assumed to be permanent and complete copies of past events, and remembering was thought to be like re-experiencing the past; a modern analogy might be a video recording that can be preserved indefinitely and replayed over and over. This notion is what Neisser—who rejected it—called the **reappearance hypothesis**: "that the same 'memory' . . . can disappear and reappear over and over again" (1967, p. 282). To the contrary, he followed Bartlett (1932) in arguing that there are no "stored copies of finished mental events," and that memory is schematic, relying on "fragments . . . to support a new construction" (p. 286). Today, as we will see, virtually all memory theorists agree. It now seems clear that even the most vivid memories are subject to change.

reappearance hypothesis

Neisser's term for the now rejected idea that the same memory can reappear, unchanged, again and again.

Flashbulb Memories

Even as the idea of the schema was gaining ground, some psychologists argued that one particular type of memory was in fact permanent. For example, a great many people who were of school age or older in 1963 still claim to remember exactly how they learned of John F. Kennedy's assassination. These memories were first investigated by R. Brown and Kulik (1977), who in the mid-1970s asked 80 Harvard undergraduates to recall the circumstances under which they heard the news. In addition to writing a "free recall" account of what they remembered, they estimated how consequential they felt the event was at the time, and how frequently they had talked about it. A similar procedure was used to study memories of the assassinations or attempted assassinations of several other prominent figures, such as Martin Luther King, Jr.

The students' accounts typically included information on five specific subjects:

1. Where they were when they learned of the assassination;
2. What they were doing at the time;
3. The person who told them;
4. Their affect (how they felt at the time); and
5. The aftermath: what they did immediately after hearing the news.

Almost every participant had what appeared to be vivid, detailed memories not only of the Kennedy assassination, but often of the others, and the more consequential they felt the event to have been, the more often they had rehearsed it (i.e., discussed it with others).

The term that Brown and Kulik (1977) coined to refer to such unusually vivid and detailed accounts was **flashbulb memories**. To explain how such memories are produced, they expanded on Livingston's (1967) **Now Print! theory** to create the model illustrated in Figure 6.3. The Now Print! theory, as originally envisioned by Livingston (1967), resembled the production of a photocopy: just press the Print button and your brain will store a faithful reproduction of everything in the scene, including the context in which the experience occurred. In short, flashbulb memories would be examples of highly detailed memory traces.

The sequence that Brown and Kulik proposed has five stages. First, the stimulus event is tested for "surprisingness." If it's completely ordinary, we will pay no attention to it. However, if the event is extraordinary (as assassinations generally are), then we will pay very close attention. In the second stage the event is tested for consequentiality. Events that fail this test will be forgotten, but those that we consider important as well as surprising will move on to the third stage, in which flashbulb memories are formed. Flashbulb memories will vary in vividness and completeness depending on how surprising and consequential the events are.

flashbulb memories

Vivid, detailed memories of significant events.

Now Print! theory

The theory that especially significant experiences are immediately "photocopied," preserved in long-term memory, and resistant to change.

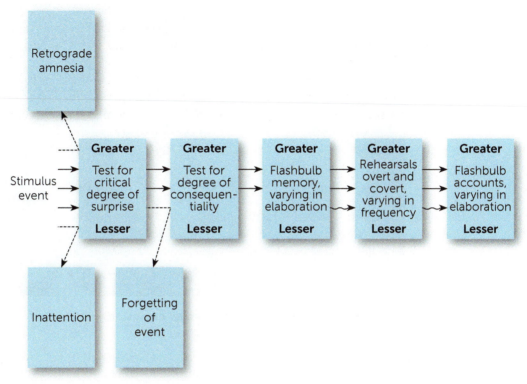

FIGURE 6.3 | Brown and Kulik's model of flashbulb memories

From: Brown, R., & Kulik, J. (1977). Copyright 1977 by Elsevier Science Publishers. Reprinted by permission.

The fourth stage is rehearsal, in which we think about those memories and develop verbal accounts of them. Finally, in the fifth stage we tell and retell those accounts to other people.

Investigating the Flashbulb Hypothesis

Brown and Kulik's work attracted a great deal of attention, and a number of historically important events were eventually investigated as possible sources of "flashbulbs." Among them was the *Challenger* space shuttle explosion (Figure 6.4) in January 1986 (Bohannon, 1988; Bohannon & Symons, 1992; McCloskey, Wible, & Cohen, 1988). Three days after the disaster, McCloskey and colleagues asked 45 people the following questions:

1. Where were you when you first learned of the *Challenger* explosion?
2. What were you doing?
3. Did you see the event as it was actually happening, or did you learn about it later?
4. What were your first thoughts on hearing the news?

Then, approximately nine months later, they had 27 of the original participants, along with 31 new people, complete the same questionnaire.

All participants remembered something about the circumstances in which they had heard about the disaster. However, comparison of the immediate and nine-month

FIGURE 6.4 | Flashbulb memories: The *Challenger* explosion

questionnaire data showed that quite a bit of information had been lost over the interval, and that the details were not always consistent. Although seven of the nine-month accounts were more specific than the immediate accounts, 20 were more general (less specific). For example, someone who had initially named the person he heard the news from might only refer to "a friend" nine months later. In addition, seven of the nine-month accounts were inconsistent with the original reports on matters such as where the respondents were when they heard the news (e.g., sitting at the desk versus walking out the office door).

Even so, it's important to note that none of the nine-month accounts were wildly inconsistent with the earlier versions. Rather, the inconsistencies were "the same sort of reconstructive errors that seem to occur frequently for 'ordinary' memories." In both cases, "inaccuracies may be introduced when information that cannot be retrieved from memory is filled in through inference or guesswork" (McCloskey et al., 1988, p. 175).

In addition, McCloskey et al. concluded that there is no need for any special mechanism to account for so-called flashbulb memories: if such memories seem easier to recall in vivid detail than ordinary memories, it's only because we have replayed them so often and thought about them so much. Recall that in Brown and Kulik's model, flashbulb memories are associated with events that are sufficiently significant not only to attract intense attention, but also to become the subject of frequent rehearsal, both in the media and in discussions with others. These factors in themselves could explain why we might feel that our own flashbulb memories are particularly strong.

A number of studies have explored flashbulb memories concerning the destruction of the World Trade Center in New York City on 11 September 2001 (see Figure 6.5) (e.g., Greenberg, 2004; Neisser, 2003). Talarico and Rubin's (2003) study was particularly well designed. On 12 September 2001, they had 54 Duke University students complete an open-ended questionnaire (similar to Brown and Kulik's) asking for descriptions not only

Imagine that you have just been attacked on the street by three people. Fortunately, in the midst of the attack you see a police officer racing towards you. But he runs right past! The officer later says he was chasing someone else and did not recall seeing what was happening to you. Do you believe him? Remember your answer.

This very scenario played out in Boston in 1995. Around 2:00 a.m. police officer Kenneth Conley responded to a call about a shooting and ultimately gave chase to the suspect. During the chase he ran right past three fellow police officers who were beating a man they mistakenly believed to be the suspect (in fact, he was an undercover police officer). Conley claimed he never saw the attack, but the jury rejected his story. He was later convicted of perjury and obstruction of justice and sentenced to 34 months in jail. As unlikely as this scenario seems, it raises a serious question: could Conley really not have seen a brutal assault that was taking place right in front of his eyes?

This real-world example should remind you of our earlier discussions of the use of cell phones while driving (Chapter 1) and inattentional blindness (Chapter 4). In both cases, the point was that people whose attention is distracted can sometimes fail to consciously perceive things that are right in front of their eyes. This obviously has a direct impact on their ability to remember things. If Conley never had any conscious perception of the assault, how could he have had any recollection of it?

Conley's conviction was eventually overturned on technical grounds. Recently, though, a group of researchers at Union College in New York set out to determine if his story could in fact have been true (see Chabris, Weinberger, Fontaine, & Simons, 2011). In their study they asked participants to run behind a confederate (someone helping with the experiment), while three other confederates staged a fight along the route. Amazingly, a post-experiment questionnaire revealed that only 35 per cent of the participants recalled noticing the fight when the experiment was conducted at night (the Conley incident took place in the dead of night). And although the percentage jumped to 56 per cent in daylight, almost half the participants still failed to notice the fight! This experiment highlights the importance of attention and conscious perception for memory. If the event was not consciously perceived, then memories of it (if they exist at all) will be degraded. After reading the previous three chapters you should be aware of how interconnected many cognitive processes are. That is, it should be apparent that sensation, perception, and attention all play significant roles in how and what we remember. Now recall your answer to the question we asked in the first paragraph above. Would you have believed Conley? Do you think he should have been convicted?

of the momentous events of the previous day, but also of an ordinary event, such as a party, that each participant had recently experienced. In addition, Talarico and Rubin used other measures to test additional aspects of the flashbulb phenomenon, such as the intensity of the emotion felt when the events were recalled. They then divided the 54 participants into three groups of 18 each and re-tested each group once. The first group was tested 1 week later; the second, 6 weeks later; and the third, 32 weeks later. The major variable of interest was the consistency of the accounts given at the three different intervals. For example, if a participant said on 12 September that "Fred" was with him when the event occurred and later said that "Alice" was with him, but not "Fred," that response was scored as inconsistent. Each participant's recall was given a consistency

FIGURE 6.5 | Flashbulb memories: Terrorist attacks on the World Trade Center, New York City

score based on the number of details consistently recalled, as well as an inconsistency score. Figure 6.6 shows the change in consistency and inconsistency scores as a function of time. Notice that both flashbulb and everyday memories show a decline in consistency and an increase in inconsistency. Although the flashbulb memories had more emotion associated with them, in terms of their actual content they were no more accurate than "ordinary" memories. However, participants erroneously believed that their flashbulb memories were more accurate than their "ordinary" memories. Talarico and Rubin concluded that although a flashbulb event "reliably enhances memory characteristics such as vividness and confidence," people should not put too much faith "in the accuracy of their flashbulb memories" (2003, p. 460).

Are Memory Traces Permanent?

consolidation theory
The classic theory that memory traces of an event are not fully formed immediately after that event, but take some time to consolidate.

These flashbulb memory experiments have led many to question the idea that memory traces persist unchanged over time. As a result, the trace theory has undergone considerable modification (Dudai, 2004; Nader, 2003; Wixted, 2004a). According to the classic **consolidation theory** (Woodworth, 1938, p. 51), memory traces of an event are not fully

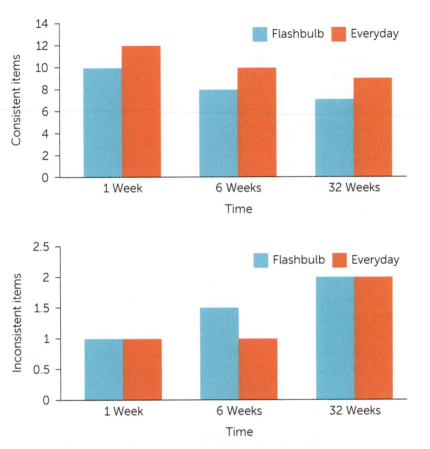

FIGURE 6.6 | Properties of flashbulb memories

Notice that the y-axes of the two graphs are not to the same scale.

Data from: Talarico, J.M., & Rubin, D.C. (2003).

formed immediately after that event, but take some time to consolidate. This process of consolidation can be disrupted by events that occur after the event to be remembered; such disruption is called **retroactive interference**. Woodworth's (1938, p. 227) review of the classic literature (e.g., Jenkins & Dallenbach, 1924) concluded that "rest immediately after learning . . . allows for full consolidation of the traces, while strenuous mental work just at this time . . . leaves the traces weak." This conclusion is echoed in the recent literature. For example, Wixted (2004a, p. 247) argued that "even if the intervening study material is not related to the original learning in any obvious way, the new learning draws on a limited pool of resources that may have otherwise been available to consolidate the original learning. As a result, memory for the original material suffers." Not surprisingly, sleep deprivation has also been associated with deficits in memory (see Box 6.5, later in this chapter).

It is known that the hippocampus is a crucial site for the consolidation of memory traces, converting immediate memories into long-term memories. "If the hippocampal formation is damaged before the consolidation process is complete, recently formed memories that are still undergoing the consolidation process will be impaired" (Wixted, 2004a, p. 242). It is likely that retroactive interference occurs because "ordinary mental exertion

retroactive interference

A decline in recall of one event as a result of a later event.

and memory formation" detract from an ongoing process of [hippocampal] consolidation" (Wixted, 2004a, p. 264).

It was long believed that once the consolidation process was complete, then the memory trace in question was fixed and permanent. However, it now appears likely that when the stored trace is re-activated, it becomes labile (i.e., changeable) (Dudai, 2004; Nader, 2003). Thus recalling a previous experience places it in working memory (see Chapter 5), where it comes into contact with other experiences. For example, the context in which you recall a flashbulb event may be quite different from the context in which you originally experienced it. This provides an opportunity for revision of the memory trace, although the *extent* of such revision is controversial. In any case, the revised trace would then undergo **reconsolidation** in the hippocampus (Nader, 2003, p. 66). Furthermore, there is nothing to say that this process cannot become a cycle whereby a memory trace is reactivated and reconsolidated indefinitely. Thus we have no reason to believe that a memory trace is necessarily a faithful rendition of the original experience.

Nader (2003, p. 70) reviewed the memory reconsolidation literature, and his conclusion is extremely important: "There can be no doubt at this point that memories are fundamentally dynamic processes, as first explicitly demonstrated by Bartlett (1932). They are not snapshots of events that are passively read out but, rather, are constructive in nature and always changing" (Loftus & Yuille, 1984; Tulving & Thomson, 1973; Schacter, 1999). In reaching this conclusion, Nader paid tribute to Frederic Bartlett (1886–1969) and in particular his 1932 book *Remembering*. It is to an examination of that work and its influence on cognitive psychology that we will now turn.

Schema-based Theories of Memory

Probably no idea is more important in cognitive psychology generally, and in theories of memory in particular, than the idea of the schema. When we first encountered the schema, in Chapter 1, we defined it in terms of what we expect to find as we explore the world. However, we could also say that a schema is something that helps us to organize and categorize the information we receive.

Bartlett and the Concept of the Schema

It was Bartlett who made the schema concept central to the psychology of memory (Roediger, 1997; Thompson, 1997; Weiskrantz, 2000; Zangwill, 1972). His best-known experimental techniques were the **method of repeated reproduction** and the **method of serial reproduction**. In the former, a participant, A, is given a story to read and then attempts to reproduce it, first 15 minutes later and then at longer intervals. The latter begins the same way, but A's version is then given to a second participant, B, who reads it and then writes down what he or she can recall of it. B's version in turn is given to C, and so on (if you ever played "telephone" in elementary school, you'll recognize the principle). Thus each participant tries to reproduce the previous participant's version of the original story based solely on what he or she can recall. The results showed the same pattern in both cases, but were particularly dramatic with the method of serial reproduction. The story to be reproduced was the following North American folktale:

reconsolidation
The hypothetical process whereby a memory trace is revised and reconsolidated.

method of repeated reproduction
One participant is given multiple opportunities to recall a story over time.

method of serial reproduction
One participant, A, writes down what he or she can recall of a previously read story. A's version is given to a second participant, B, who reads it and then tries to reproduce it. B's version in turn is given to C, and so on.

The War of the Ghosts

One night two young men from Egulac went down to the river to hunt seals, and while they were there it became foggy and calm. Then they heard war-cries, and they thought: "Maybe this is a war party." They escaped to the shore and hid behind a log. Now canoes came up, and they heard the noise of paddles and saw one canoe coming up to them. There were five men in the canoe, and they said:

"What do you think? We wish to take you along. We are going up the river to make war on the people."

One of the young men said: "I have no arrows."

"Arrows are in the canoe," they said.

"I will not go along. I might get killed. My relatives do not know where I have gone. But you," he said, turning to the other, "may go with them."

So one of the men went, but the other returned home.

And the warriors went on up the river to a town on the other side of Kalama. The people came down to the water, and they began to fight, and many were killed. But presently the young man heard one of the warriors say: "Quick, let us go home: that Indian has been hit." Now he thought: "Oh, they are ghosts." He did not feel sick, but he said he had been shot.

So the canoes went back to Egulac, and the young man went ashore to his house and made a fire. And he told everybody and said: "Behold I accompanied the ghosts, and we went to fight. Many of our fellows were killed, and many of those who attacked us were killed. They said I was hit, and I did not feel sick."

He told it all, and then became quiet. When the sun rose he fell down. Something black came out of his mouth. His face became contorted. The people jumped up and cried.

He was dead (Bartlett, 1932, p. 65).

To test your own recall, stop reading now and wait 15 minutes; then try to reproduce the story.

In Bartlett's serial experiment, successive reproductions became increasingly different from the original. By the tenth person the story had become the following:

The War of the Ghosts (2)

Two Indians were out fishing for seals in the Bay of Manpapan, when along came five other Indians in a war canoe. They were going fighting.

"Come with us," said the five to the two, "and fight."

"I cannot come," was the answer of the one, "for I have an old mother at home who is dependent upon me." The other also said he could not come, because he had no arms. "That is no difficulty," the others replied, "for we have plenty in the canoe with us"; so he got into the canoe and went with them.

In a fight soon afterwards this Indian received a mortal wound. Finding that his hour was come, he cried out that he was about to die. "Nonsense," said one of the others, "you will not die." But he did (Bartlett, 1932, p. 124).

Bartlett believed that this experiment showed what happens to memory over time. Obviously, several parts of the original were dropped along the way, so that the story was simplified. Although the title was reported correctly in reproduction 10, there was no longer any mention of ghosts. Participants tended to select some material to remember and omit other material. These omissions reflect a process of **rationalization** as each participant tried to make the story as coherent and sensible as possible, from his or her viewpoint. Material that did not seem to fit tended to drop out of the narrative. Recall the death of the Indian in the original version: "When the sun rose he fell down. Something black came out of his mouth. His face became contorted." Over successive reproductions this passage changed substantially—a "black thing rushed from his mouth," "his soul fled black from his mouth," "his spirit fled"—until finally, by version 10, these details had disappeared altogether. Bartlett noted that unfamiliar material was transformed over time to conform to more familiar patterns.

On the basis of his experiments, Bartlett concluded that

> remembering is not the re-excitation of innumerable fixed, lifeless and fragmentary traces. It is imaginative reconstruction, or construction, built out of the relation of our attitude towards a whole active mass of organized past reactions or experience, and to a little outstanding detail which commonly appears in image or in language form (1932, p. 213).

This "active mass of organized past reactions" is what Bartlett meant by the term **schema**. Thus a schema in Bartlett's sense is an organized setting that guides our behaviour and memory, a standard that can be adjusted to fit changing circumstances.

As an example Bartlett used the ability to make the proper stroke in a sport such as tennis. You must adjust your position, posture, and bodily movements (swing) to fit the current situation. You don't simply repeat a stroke that you have performed before, because the ball is not likely to be in exactly the same place twice, and neither are you.

Over the years many studies have employed the schema concept in the same general way that Bartlett did. Several reviews (e.g., Alba & Hasher, 1983, p. 204; Koriat, Goldsmith, & Pansky, 2000, pp. 494–495) suggest that most schema theories discuss memory in terms of four processes: **selection**, **abstraction**, **interpretation**, and **integration**. The schema selects information consistent with our interests at the time. We then convert that information into a more abstract form. In other words, instead of trying to preserve the specifics of the event in its entirety, we extract its gist, or meaning. We then interpret that information in terms of other information in our memory. Finally, we integrate the information in such a way as to make it consistent with the schema. Koriat, Goldsmith, and Pansky (2000) add a fifth process, reconstruction, whereby the act of recall blends general knowledge and individual experiences in order to "imaginatively reconstruct" the past.

Thus after you've finished reading this chapter, it's unlikely that you will remember every word of it (though we certainly hope you'll remember some of it). You will probably have selected some points to remember and let others go, depending on your interests and concerns at the time of reading. If someone asks you what the chapter is about, you're more likely to provide a selective abstract than a literal recap. Over time, you may realize that you did not simply interpret the ideas in this chapter: you also

rationalization

The attempt to make memory as coherent and sensible as possible.

DISCOVERY LAB

schema (Bartlett)

An active mass of organized past reactions that provides a setting that guides our behaviour.

selection

The hypothesis that we select information both as we receive it and as we recall it.

abstraction

The hypothesis that we tend to remember only the gist, not the specifics, of what we experience.

interpretation

The hypothesis that we interpret information by making inferences, and then remember the inferences as part of the original information.

integration

The hypothesis that we abstract the meaning of an event and then put that meaning together with the rest of our knowledge to form a coherent, consistent whole.

integrated them with other ideas that you had already taken in. For example, the idea that the schema is selective may remind you of a similar point about attention that you read in Chapter 4. Moreover, the processes we are now discussing may reflect the way information is encoded—another process mentioned in Chapter 4. Of course, these connections may seem somewhat vague (i.e., schematic), and you may need to reread those sections in order to fully remember the concepts discussed earlier. Finally, years from now, if you set out to reconstruct what you learned from this chapter, you may have only fragmentary clues to work with. You may have trouble remembering when you took this course, what grade you got for it, who was in your class at the time, or even which textbook you used.

In sum, a schema is a flexible organization, and that is what makes it useful. If our memory were just a collection of traces, it would too rigid to be useful. A schema is a more abstract and general setting within which memory traces have meaning. It's important to note that Bartlett never denied the existence of memory traces (Ost & Costall, 2002). The case of Professor Aitken (Hunter, 1977) is a very good example of the way memory traces and memory schemas can work together; see Box 6.2.

Eyewitness Testimony

A classic study by Loftus and Palmer (1974) investigated how eyewitness testimony can be affected by the way questions are phrased. All participants were shown the same film of a traffic accident and then asked to estimate the cars' speed. For some the question was phrased "About how fast were the cars going when they hit each other?" For others the basic question was the same, but the word *hit* was replaced by *smashed, collided, bumped,* or *contacted.* The results are given in Figure 6.8. Notice that the estimate of the cars' speed is a function of the intensity of the verb in the question. If the question used the word *smashed,* then the cars were reported to have been going faster than if they had merely come into "contact" with one another.

In another experiment, participants were also shown a film of a collision and then asked one of two questions: either "How fast were the cars going when they hit each other?" or "How fast were the cars going when they smashed into each other?" One week later, the same participants were asked some additional questions about the accident they had seen on film the week before. One of the questions was "Did you see any broken glass?" The participants who had earlier been asked if the cars "had smashed into each other" were more likely to report seeing broken glass than were the participants who had been asked if the cars "had hit each other" (Figure 6.9). Loftus and Palmer (1974) interpreted these results as follows:

> We would like to propose that two kinds of information go into one's memory for some complex occurrence. The first is information gleaned during the perception of the original event; the second is external information supplied after the fact. Over time, information from these two sources may be integrated in such a way that we are unable to tell from which source some specific detail is recalled. All we have is one "memory" (p. 588).

In several subsequent publications, Loftus and others provided a great deal of evidence that misleading post-event information often becomes integrated with the original

COGNITION IN ACTION
BOX 6.2

An Exceptional Memory

Professor A.C. Aitken (1895–1967) (Figure 6.7) was a "brilliant mathematician . . . and an accomplished violinist" whose phenomenal memory was studied for decades by psychologists (Hunter, 1977). Often people with an extraordinary memory are said to have a correspondingly poor ability to think abstractly, but that was not the case with Aitken. In fact, it was precisely because of his ability to rapidly schematize information that his memory was so prodigious. According to Hunter (1977, p. 157), Aitken would take even the most mundane events and weave them into an "unusually rich densely structured gestalt of properties" that still preserved the uniqueness of each event—a process that exemplified what Bartlett (as we noted in Chapter 4) called "effort after meaning." Typically, Aitken's ability to remember was an unintended consequence of his desire to make things meaningful. He never wanted to "memorize" anything merely by rote.

Aitken felt that the most important thing was to relax and become absorbed in the material to be learned. Once you allow yourself to become interested in it, then you will begin to comprehend it in deeper and deeper ways. The more deeply you understand something, the better you will remember it. (This is a theme that will recur towards the end of this chapter, when we discuss the "levels of processing" approach to memory.) Aitken observed that "the thing to do is to learn by heart, not because one has to, but because one loves the thing and is interested in it" (Hunter, 1977, p. 158).

Because he was interested in his own mental processes, Aitken agreed to be a participant in a variety of experiments. In 1933 he was asked to memorize 25 unrelated words. Twenty-seven years later, in 1960, he attempted to recall them, and succeeded. However, Aitken did not repeat even this "meaningless" list of words by rote. Rather, he proceeded by inference to reconstruct the list. Aitken's memory operated in a schematic way even for a list of words. (We will examine some very different techniques for memorizing large amounts of material in our discussion of imagery, in Chapter 7.)

More typical of Aitken's memory was his knowledge of music. He believed that musical memory could be both rich and precise because music has so many different aspects, including "a metre and a rhythm, a tune, . . . the harmony, the instrumental colour, a particular emotion, . . . a meaning, . . . perhaps a human interest in the composer" (Hunter, 1977, p. 157). All these elements combine to create a framework within which the act of recall can take place. You may be reminded of Aitken's musical memory later in this chapter, when we discuss how actors learn their lines.

FIGURE 6.7 | Professor A.C. Aitken

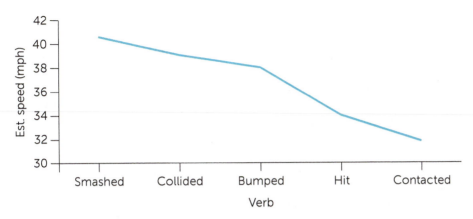

FIGURE 6.8 | **Results of Loftus and Palmer's experiment**

From: Loftus, E.F., & Palmer, J.C. (1974). Reprinted with permission from Elsevier.

FIGURE 6.9 | **One-week follow-up of Loftus and Palmer's experiment**

From: Loftus, E.F., & Palmer, J.C. (1974). Reprinted with permission from Elsevier.

information (e.g., Cole & Loftus, 1979; Loftus, 1992, 2003; Loftus & Loftus, 1980). This has been termed the **misinformation effect** (Loftus, 2004, p. 868; Loftus & Hoffman, 1989). According to Loftus (2004, p. 145), recent research strongly suggests that more can be changed than "a detail in memory for a previously experienced event." Indeed, it appears quite possible to "plant an entirely false memory into the mind."

misinformation effect
The hypothesis that misleading post-event information can become integrated with the original memory of the event.

False Memories

A key aspect of Loftus and Palmer's original argument was that we may integrate information from different sources into our memory of an event. If we experience an event and are later given misleading information about it, we may not recognize that the source of that information is something other than the event itself. In the same way, we may fail to discriminate between memories of real events and memories of imagined events (Johnson, Hashtroudi, & Lindsay, 1993; Johnson & Raye, 1981; Lindsay, 1993). If we imagine an event in a particularly vivid way, we may later have the illusion that it actually happened. The idea that people can fail to identify the true source of their memories was investigated by D.S. Lindsay and Johnson (1989).

Lindsay and Johnson's experiment was typical of studies of source monitoring. Participants were shown a picture of four people in an office containing a variety of objects (e.g., coffee cup, pencil holder). After seeing the picture some participants also read a text describing the office. Sometimes the text contained misleading descriptions (e.g., "There is a filing cabinet behind the women on the right," when there was no filing cabinet). Participants were tested in two ways. One test simply asked them to read a list of items and indicate whether or not each item (e.g., filing cabinet) had appeared in the picture. This was called the recognition test. Another test asked participants to indicate whether or not each item was in the picture, in the text, or in both. This last test was called the source-monitoring test.

The results of the recognition test showed evidence of suggestibility, as had been found in similar experiments of this type. That is, participants attributed suggested items to the picture when they had in fact appeared only in the text. However, the source-monitoring test resulted in fewer errors of this sort. On the basis of these data Lindsay and Johnson argued that the mistakes people make when they try to recall an event are often due to faulty source monitoring. In general, the theoretical framework within which Johnson and others have investigated such phenomena is called the source monitoring framework (e.g., Johnson & Raye, 1998; Lindsay & Johnson, 2000; Mitchell & Johnson, 2000).

source monitoring framework
The theory that some errors of memory are caused by mistaken identification of the memory's source.

DISCOVERY LAB

Loftus on Bartlett

The aspects of memory that we have examined here are often explained using a general schema theory. The last word on this subject should go to Elizabeth Loftus, who has done more than anyone else to expose the vagaries of memory:

> A half century ago, Frederic C. Bartlett ... posited that remembering is "imaginative reconstruction, or construction," and "it is thus hardly ever exact" (Bartlett, 1932, p. 213). His insights link up directly with contemporary research on memory distortion, although even he might have been surprised to find out just how inexact memory can be. ... Bartlett died in 1969, just missing the beginning of a vast effort to investigate the memory processes that he so intelligently foreshadowed, and that show unequivocally how humans are the authors or creators of their own memories. They can also be the authors or creators of someone else's memory (Loftus, 2004, p. 147).

Encoding Specificity

Early experimental work by Tulving suggested that the type of schema from which we recall memories can influence their content. Thus Tulving and Thomson (1973) proposed the **principle of encoding specificity**: that a cue is more likely to lead to the recall of a particular item if the cue was initially encoded along with that item: "a critical condition for effective retrieval is the extent to which the processing that occurs during retrieval re-instates the processing that took place during encoding" (Koriat, 2000, p. 337). For example, the word *poker* can be understood, or encoded, as either a metal rod or a card game, and if it's encoded as a metal rod, it is less likely to be recalled by a cue such as *card game* than by a cue such as *prod* (Brown & Craik, 2000, p. 99).

As this example demonstrates, information can be stored in different ways, and Tulving and Thomson's (1973) classic experiments exploited this fact. Participants learned a list of 24 pairs of words. The words that made up the pairs were only weakly associated, and they were printed differently, one of them in lower case and the other in upper case. For example, *plant* might be paired with BUG. The fact that a BUG is unlikely to be among the first things you think of when you think of a plant means that the two words are weakly associated. The same is true for a pair such as *ground* and COLD. The first word of each pair is called the weak cue word, and the second word of each pair is called the target word.

After learning a list of these weakly associated pairs, participants were given a series of tasks. In one case they were shown a list of 24 words, each of which was strongly associated with one of 24 target words on the original list. For example, *insect* was strongly associated with BUG, and *hot* was strongly associated with COLD. The words on this new list can be called *strong cue words*. Participants were asked to free-associate to the entire set of strong cue words and write up to six words that came to mind for each of the strong cue words. On average, participants came up with about 18 of the original 24 target words in this way. Participants were then asked to examine the lists of words they had generated. The question was: How many of those words would they recognize as target words from the original list? If they were able to recognize all of them, they would have recognized about 18 words on average. However, they were only able to recognize about four of the words they had generated. In other words, participants came up with target words without recognizing them as target words. Finally, participants were given the original 24 weak cue words and asked to recall the target words. This time they were able to recall about 15 of the target words.

There are several interesting points to be made about these results. First, and most important, the words generated in response to the strong cues were the same words that the participants had learned in response to the weak cues. However, the participants in many cases were not able to recognize those words. Thus "conditions can be created in which information about a word event is available in . . . memory . . . in a form sufficient for the production of the appropriate response and yet a literal copy of the word is not recognized" (Tulving & Thomson, 1973). This phenomenon is called "recognition failure of recallable words," and has been extensively investigated (e.g., Tulving & Wiseman, 1975).

Tulving argued that the ability to remember a given item depends on how that item was encoded at input. In other words, the nature of the encoding will influence the memory trace. In the Tulving and Thomson experiments, participants learned the target words in the context of the weak cues. This meant that, as retrieval tools, the weak cues were more effective than the strong cues because the latter were not present when the participant

DISCOVERY LAB

COGNITION IN ACTION
BOX 6.3

Context-Dependent Learning

The principle of encoding specificity is related to the concept of context-dependent learning: the idea that we are most likely to recall something we have learned if the environment in which that information was encoded is replicated during retrieval. You may have experienced this yourself. Have you ever completely forgotten about a homework assignment, only to remember it the moment you walked into the classroom? There are many intriguing experimental findings that demonstrate this phenomenon. An extreme example was a study conducted by Godden and Baddeley (1975) in which scuba divers had to learn lists of words either underwater or on the shore. Memory recall was then tested in either a congruent or incongruent condition. That is, half the divers who had learned the words underwater were tested underwater (congruent) and half on shore (incongruent). As you can probably imagine, the divers' ability to recall the words was best in the congruent condition. Could you incorporate this principle into your own studying? Studying in the same room where the exam will be held might help you score a few extra points.

A closely related concept is known as state-dependent learning: the idea that recall is best when the mental (Eich, 1995) or physiological (Goodwin, Powell, Bremer, Hoine, & Stern, 1969) state of the learner is consistent across encoding and retrieval. The idea that retrieval can be facilitated when the learner is in the matching physiological state has even been borne out in an experiment involving marijuana (Eich, Weingartner, Stillman, & Gillin, 1975). In other circumstances, however, drug use has been observed to reduce overall learning by half (Rickles, Cohen, Whitaker, & McIntyre, 1973). Thus we strongly recommend keeping a clear head both in class and in exams.

There are other areas for which this research could have important implications. For instance, Wong and Read (2011) had participants view a video of a theft and then return a week later to identify the culprit in either the same or a different environment. Their findings suggested that accuracy was greater in the congruent than the incongruent condition. However, the improvement in accuracy came with another, more concerning finding. While recall was indeed better for many participants in the congruent condition, confidence levels were also much higher, even among those who were wrong.

---

learned the original list of word pairs: only the weak cues were present and therefore became part of the memories formed at that time. By contrast, the strong cues are associated with the target words only because those relationships are part of people's general knowledge about words. Because general knowledge is not very helpful in remembering specifically what was learned in the experiment, one might conclude that it involves a different kind of memory than the memory trace formed by the experiment.

As Box 6.3 shows, many studies have found that recall is better when the context in which it takes place is similar to the context in which the information to be recalled was learned; this phenomenon is known as *context-dependent recall* (Baddeley, 1987b). A related hypothesis suggests that recall can be facilitated by mood congruence between learning and recall sessions. In fact, although the effect does not always occur, several studies have found evidence to support this **mood-dependent recall** hypothesis (Blaney, 1986; Eich & Forgas, 2003, pp. 70–72).

Another phenomenon that has been extensively studied is the effect of **mood congruence** on "learning of affective material" (Gilligan & Bower, 1984, p. 557). For example,

mood-dependent recall
The hypothesis that mood congruence between learning and recall sessions should facilitate recall.

mood congruence
The idea that mood might cause selective learning of affective material.

if you are in a sad mood and listen to a story containing both happy and sad elements, will you later remember more of the latter than someone who was happy when listening to the story? Gilligan and Bower reported that mood does in fact appear to affect the kind of material that we learn. Blaney (1986, p. 236) summarized the results of 29 studies that generally supported the effect of mood congruence.

Depression and Memory

Understanding how mood affects memory is important because of its relevance to phenomena such as depression (Ellis, 1990). A series of experiments by Hertel and Hardin (1990) investigated the relationship between depressed mood and memory. Briefly, they presented participants with homophones—words that sound alike but have different meanings (e.g., *pear* and *pair*). In the Hertel and Hardin studies, participants heard homophones embedded in questions (*What colour is a pear?*). The context in which the homophone was presented always favoured the less common spelling of the homophone (*pear* rather than *pair*). Then participants were asked to spell a series of words that included some of the homophones they had heard in the previous phase of the experiment, as well as some homophones they had not heard before and some non-homophones. Finally, they were given a recognition test, in which they were read all the homophones used in the questions, mixed with other words, including some that had been included in the spelling test but had not been part of the original set used in the questions. Participants were asked to indicate for each word whether or not it had been heard in the questions asked in the first phase of the experiment.

In all their experiments Hertel and Hardin used a mood-induction procedure. A depressed mood was induced in some participants by having them read a set of depressive statements (e.g., *I am feeling sad today*). Other participants read a set of neutral statements (e.g., *There are 26 breeds of cats*). Hertel and Hardin found that the initial exposure to homophones led participants to adopt the less common spelling on the spelling test, regardless of mood. This meant that the questions did lead all participants to learn something about the homophones used in the questions. Importantly, however, the mood-induction procedure also had an effect on the number of words recognized: participants in a depressive mood recognized fewer words than did those in a neutral mood.

Scripts

As we have seen, the schema concept has been used to explain a great deal. Some other approaches are quite similar to it, but are sufficiently distinctive to merit separate discussion. The concept of the script, for example, can explain many of the same phenomena that the schema concept does.

A script has been defined as a "structure that describes an appropriate sequence of events in a particular context," or "a predetermined stereotyped sequence of actions that defines a well-known situation" (Schank, 1982a, p. 170). The use of this concept in memory research can be traced to the work of Schank and Abelson (1975, 1977; Schank, 1982a, 1982b), who focused on scripts for particular situations, such as going to a restaurant. If people are asked to describe what typically happens when they go to a restaurant, their

script
A set of expectations concerning the actions and events that are appropriate in a particular situation.

stories will usually include a common sequence of events: ordering food, eating it, paying the bill, and so on. Although the particulars of the stories will vary, there will still be quite a bit of common ground across situations and people (Bower, Black, & Turner, 1979). Thus one feature that distinguishes a script from a schema is that a script refers to a particular *sequence* of events or actions.

CONSIDER THIS
BOX 6.4

Implanting False Memories

A particularly effective demonstration of the implanting of false memories was conducted by Lindsay, Hagen, Read, Wade, and Garry (2004). It was based on the assumption that viewing photographs from our childhood can lead us to give vivid accounts of events from our lives that may or may not have actually happened. The participants in the study were undergraduates whose parents had supplied the researchers with a class photo from Grade 1 or 2 and a description of a true episode from Grade 3–5. Each participant was then presented with two written accounts: one true, describing the actual episode from his or her life, and one false, describing "putting Slime, a brightly colored gelatinous compound manufactured by Mattel as a toy, on the teacher's desk" in either Grade 1 or Grade 2 (p. 150). In addition, approximately half the participants were given the photos of their Grade 1 or 2 class. The participants were encouraged to try to remember the earliest of the episodes (i.e., the fictional "Slime" event), and a week later they were asked if they had remembered it. Amazingly, two-thirds of the students who had seen their class photos "remembered" the "Slime" event, compared with 23 per cent who had not looked at photos.

The fact that even the no-photo condition elicited a fair number of false memories is worth noting. However, the photos stimulated significantly more of them. As the authors observe, it's common for psychotherapists to suggest that patients seeking to recover lost childhood memories look at pictures from their youth while ruminating about their past. The "Slime" study suggests that this practice may encourage false memories.

Lindsay et al. (2004) note that their results may be understood in the framework of source monitoring theory. If looking at a childhood photo encourages active imagining of what might have been, it may lead to confusion between what actually happened and what never did.

COGNITION IN ACTION
BOX 6.5

Sleep, Memory, and False Memory

Have you ever stayed up all night studying for an exam, only to find that you couldn't remember the answers to questions you know you reviewed? One reason that all-night cramming is not recommended is that we need sleep to consolidate new memories. In fact, more than a century of research has demonstrated that sleep plays an important role in memory retention.

For a long time researchers thought that sleep helped memory by limiting interference from competing stimuli. While it's obvious that we can't encode new information if we're asleep, recent research has nevertheless demonstrated that sleep does play a critical role in memory consolidation. As Rasch and Born (2013) note in their review of the literature, the frequent association of memory deficits with the interruption of REM (rapid eye movement) sleep, in particular, suggests that sleep's role in memory consolidation must be something other than simply preventing interference (since it's unlikely that we are *more* susceptible to interference at different sleep stages). One hypothesis that has recently attracted considerable support focuses on the notion of active systems consolidation. It proposes that newly encoded memories are repeatedly activated during sleep, and that through this repeated activation, more stable memory traces are formed that can be further integrated with existing long-term memories.

Could sleep deprivation also play a role in the formation of false memories? Recent evidence seems to suggest that this is the case. Frenda and colleagues (2014) demonstrated that susceptibility to false-memory formation increased for participants who were already sleep-deprived when they encoded the original (accurate) information and then were exposed to false information; by contrast, sleep deprivation did not have a significant effect if it occurred after the memory had been encoded. Still not convinced that it's important to get a full night's rest? Maybe you should at least sleep on the idea.

Autobiographical Memory

Autobiographical memory is the story of a person's life made up of memories of the events of which he or she has been a part. **Autobiographical memories** are episodic memories of events recalled in terms of the time in our lives when each one occurred. Research into autobiographical memory benefited from the technique invented by Crovitz and Schiffman (1974). They gave participants a list of 20 words and asked them to attach a personal memory to each one, with an estimate of how long ago the remembered event occurred. The words were common nouns such as *ball* and *oven*, which occur frequently in English and easily elicit a mental image in most people. The units that the participants in the Crovitz and Schiffman experiment used to date their memories were the usual categories of minutes, hours, days, weeks, months, and years. The procedure was similar to one devised by Galton (1879a, 1879b), who used to take note of the personal memories cued by each object he came across in the course of a walk. (This is a very simple task, and we encourage you to try it. Make a list of the memories that come to mind as you walk; then later work out when the remembered events occurred.)

Crovitz and Schiffman (1974) found that the frequency of autobiographical memories declined steadily as the length of time since the remembered events increased. Eventually, with Apter, they analyzed the findings from that study in an effort to determine how many such memories would be available to an individual, given a time span of 20 years. The answer they arrived at was 224—a figure they called **Galton's number** (Crovitz, Schiffman, and Apter, 1991).

autobiographical memories
Episodic memories of events recalled in terms of the time in our life when they occurred.

Galton's number
The number of autobiographical episodes available to participants from the preceding 20 years, as calculated by Crovitz, Schiffman, and Apter (1991): 224.

childhood amnesia
The general inability to retrieve episodic memories from before the age of about 3.

Childhood Amnesia

One factor that may have an effect on autobiographical memory is **childhood amnesia**. There appear to be fewer memories from the first few years of life than would be expected if memory decayed smoothly over time. Wetzler and Sweeney (1986) examined a series of studies of early memories and concluded that childhood amnesia sets in sometime before age five. Rubin (2000) reviewed 10 studies that used four different methods to sample early childhood memories. In addition to the Crovitz and Schiffman technique, there was the *exhaustive search technique*, in which participants spent several hours trying to recall childhood memories; the *focused method*, in which people were asked to recall events from a particular period of childhood; and the *intensive personal interview method*. Combining data from all these studies, Rubin (2000) found that the first three years accounted for only 1.1 per cent of all memories from the first ten years of life. After age three, the percentage of childhood memories in each year begins to increase rapidly. Rubin noted that these data were collected from Americans, and that children in other cultures may show a different pattern (cf. Fivush & Nelson, 2004).

Studies by Usher and Neisser (1993) and Eacott and Crawley (1998) found that not all memories formed before the age of three are necessarily lost. The accuracy of such memories (e.g., being told that your mother was going to have a baby) was often confirmed by the mothers of the participants. This led Neisser (2004) to conclude that there may be no definite age before which autobiographical memories cannot exist.

Nevertheless, it seems clear that the way children experience events will change as they develop the ability to describe them using language (Neisser, 1962; Fivush & Nelson, 2004), and this change may cause them to lose contact with early memories (Schactel, 1947). Neisser (1962) suggested that any discontinuity in development will tend to produce amnesia for events prior to the change. The rapid acquisition of language is surely a profound discontinuity in a child's development, and memories formed before and after it should be expected to differ radically. A similar discontinuity would occur for people who learned one language as children and then learned a second after moving to another country. For example, Marian and Neisser (2000) studied Cornell students who had immigrated to the United States from Russia around the age of 14. Two sets of English cue words (e.g., *summer, neighbours*) were constructed. Half the participants were given the first list, followed by a Russian translation of the second list. The other half were given a Russian translation of the second list, followed by the first list. The participants were then asked to recall autobiographical memories associated with each cue word. Russian cue words elicited more "Russian memories" (i.e., memories in which everyone involved spoke only Russian), while English cue words elicited more "English memories." That is, each language tended to elicit autobiographical memories originally experienced in the context of that language. As Shrauf and Rubin (2003, p. 141) put it, "insofar as memory is language specific, it makes sense to think of the bilingual immigrant as inhabiting different worlds and having the experience of language-specific selves."

The Memory Bump

Rubin, Wetzler, and Nebes (1986) examined data from several studies that employed the Crovitz and Schiffman technique with a wide range of age groups. They summarized the data concerning autobiographical memory as follows. First, childhood amnesia makes very early memories largely inaccessible. Second, there is a general tendency for memories to become increasingly unavailable as time passes: thus things that happened many years ago are generally less recallable than things that happened just a short time ago. Third, despite this general tendency for memories to decay with time, people over the age of about

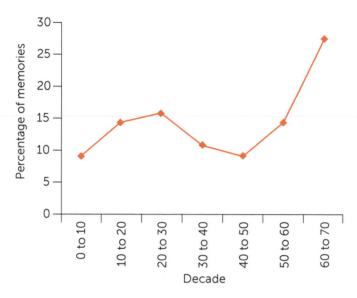

FIGURE 6.10 | **Percentage of autobiographical memories in different decades**

Data from: Chu, S., & Downes, J.J. (2000), p. B43.

50 tend to have significantly more memories from their teens and twenties than would be expected if memories decayed smoothly over time (Rubin, 2000). These three tendencies combine to produce the curve shown in Figure 6.10, in which the years between the ages of 10 and 30 show a distinct **memory bump**.

Although the bump is a reliable phenomenon, its magnitude depends to a certain extent on the way autobiographical memories are elicited. Usually such cues are verbal. However, Chu and Downes (2000) showed that using odours as cues produced a different pattern of recall. The novelist Marcel Proust is famous for describing the power of taste and smell as autobiographical memory cues, so this could be called a **Proust effect**. Chu and Downes demonstrated the Proust effect with participants ranging in age from 65 to 83. Some were asked to sniff various substances (e.g., cloves, mint, coffee, whisky, paint, baby powder) and report any autobiographical events that occurred to them. These participants had their eyes closed and were not told the name of the substance. Other participants were given only the name of the substance and did not sniff it. The verbal cue condition produced the expected bump in autobiographical memories. However, the odour cue produced more memories from between ages 6 and 10 than did the verbal cue. Thus odours may bypass verbally encoded memories and make contact with memories formed so early in life that they were not encoded in words.

Theories of the Bump

Although the magnitude of the bump depends to some extent on the method used to elicit autobiographical memories, it is still a sufficiently robust phenomenon to require an explanation. One theory (Erikson, Erikson, & Kivnick, 1986) is based on Erik Erikson's (1959) theory concerning the role of identity in the life cycle. People who are now over 50 probably made their most important choices (marriage, career, etc.) several decades earlier, in late

memory bump

An increase in the number of memories between 10 and 30 years of age over what would be expected if memories decayed smoothly over time.

Proust effect

The power of odours as autobiographical memory cues.

adolescence and young adulthood. Therefore it's not surprising that when they reflect on what they have done with their lives, they tend to focus on the periods when they were making formative decisions (Boylin, Gordon, & Nehrke, 1976; Mackavey, Malley, & Stewart, 1991, p. 52).

As a test of this theory, Mackavey, Malley, and Stewart (1991) did a content analysis of the autobiographies of 49 well-known psychologists (31 men and 18 women) written at various ages between 54 and 86 years; the average age was 72. They found that approximately 80 per cent of the **autobiographically consequential experiences (ACEs)** reported in these accounts occurred between the ages of 18 and 35. This result is consistent with the hypothesis that experiences between the ages of 10 and 30 are particularly memorable because of their importance in the formation of a person's identity (Conway & Pleydell-Pearce, 2000, p. 280).

Erikson's theory is not the only possible explanation for the memory bump, however (Rubin, Rahhal, & Poon, 1998). Rubin & Berntsen (2003) emphasize the importance of what they call **life scripts**: "culturally shared expectations as to the order and timing of life events in a prototypical life course" (Berntsen & Rubin, 2004, p. 427). Whereas the scripts studied by Schank and Abelson describe situations such as going to a restaurant, life scripts prescribe the age norms that each society uses to "structure expectations and regulate behavior" (p. 429). That is, instead of simply describing an individual's life, they prescribe what the sequence of important events in that life should be. A life script is not abstracted from personal experiences, as a restaurant script is, but is "handed down from older generations, from stories, and from observations of the behavior of other, typically older, people within the same culture" (p. 429). When Berntsen and Rubin (2004) asked Danish undergraduates to list the seven most important life events they would expect a person to experience, the ten most commonly predicted events were these: start school, fall in love, leave home, college, first job, marriage, first child, death of others, death of parents, and retirement. The students expected six of these ten events to take place between the ages of 18 and 30.

One reason for thinking that life scripts may play a role in the memory bump is that it becomes evident when older people are asked to recall their most positive and important memories—not when they are asked for their saddest or most negative ones (Berntsen & Rubin, 2002); as you might expect, memories of the latter kind—the deaths of loved ones, for instance—tend to occur later in life. Since life scripts are structured mainly around positive events, such as falling in love and getting a job, the life script schema favours the recall of events that took place during the bump period. The net result is that when older people recall their lives, most of the stories they tell are relatively happy; the more difficult times are often excluded (Rubin & Berntsen, 2003, p. 12).

Yet another theory of the bump is based on the action of basic cognitive processes (Rubin, 2005). *Distinctiveness* (discussed below) is the notion that relatively novel events will tend to be remembered better than events that are similar to one another. The second and third decades of life are a period when people are likely to experience a number of distinctive events (Rubin, 2000, p. 173): falling in love for the first time, having their first child, and so on. The first time an event occurs, it is distinctive not only because of its novelty but because we pay more attention to details that we will have learned to ignore by the time it occurs again (Rubin, Rahhal, & Poon, 1998, p. 14).

Of course, all these explanations are compatible with one another. Autobiographically consequential experiences and those prescribed by life scripts are distinctive

---

autobiographically consequential experiences (ACEs)
Pivotal experiences in a person's life, typically occurring between the ages of 18 and 35.

life script
A cultural narrative that prescribes the age norms for important events in an individual's life.

almost by definition. Each explanation simply highlights different aspects of what may very well be the same underlying process of development during a particularly important period of life.

Levels of Processing

Think back to our discussion of the information-processing tradition in Chapter 1. Craik (1980) noted that the early models were more concerned with the *structure* of cognition than with the *process* of cognition. That is, early information-processing approaches were preoccupied with the various components of the cognitive system. As we have already seen, these components were identified by labels such as "primary memory" and "secondary memory" (Waugh & Norman, 1965), or "short-term memory" and "long-term memory" (Atkinson & Shiffrin, 1971). To remind yourself of the sort of model that Craik criticized, look again at the diagram of the Waugh and Norman model in Figure 1.7 (p. 11). Waugh and Norman emphasized the structure of memory, dividing it into "primary" and "secondary" components.

Craik criticized models such as Waugh and Norman's because they don't tell us very much about the processes that determine what will be remembered (i.e., what exactly it is that leads us to remember certain kinds of information better than others). The capacity of structures such as primary memory depends on the process used to deal with the information to be remembered, and the process in turn depends on the nature of the information. As Craik pointed out, if the items to be remembered are unrelated (e.g., a random group of digits), primary memory will be unable to retain more than four or five of them. However, that capacity will be much higher if the items are related in some way. Thus if I ask you to remember 10 words that form a sentence—say, "The lazy brown dog ran over the energetic green turtle"—you will have no problem doing it. This suggests that it would be more fruitful to focus on the *process* of remembering, rather than the structures that might underlie memory. Primary memory, as Lockhart and Craik (1990) conceived of it, is a "processing activity and not a structure"; it is not located in any one place, but is a way of "paying attention to different types of information" (p. 105).

Craik and Lockhart (1972) presented an approach to memory research that did indeed focus on the processes that influence memory. This approach begins by distinguishing between shallow and deep **levels of processing**. For example, consider the word *TRAIN*. A relatively shallow way of processing that word is to observe that it is printed in capital letters. This is shallow because it deals only with the word's physical characteristics. A deeper way of processing the word would be to observe that it refers to a form of transportation. Now you are processing the word in terms of its semantic meaning. The more meaning you extract from an event, the more deeply you are processing it. In other words, according to Craik and Lockhart, cognition is a system designed for perception and understanding. The more deeply we process an event, the more thoroughly we will comprehend it. The more important an event is to us, the more effort we will put into comprehending it, and thus the more likely we are to recall it accurately. Thus depth of processing is a continuum that ranges from registering an event purely in terms of its physical characteristics to analyzing it in terms of its meaning and relationship to other things that you know. These relationships are illustrated in Figure 6.11.

levels of processing
A continuum that ranges from registering an event purely in terms of its physical characteristics to analyzing it in terms of its relationship to other things that you know.

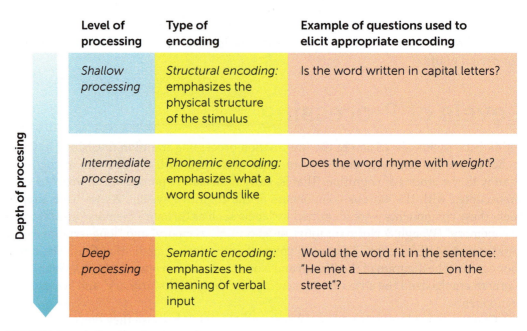

Level of processing	Type of encoding	Example of questions used to elicit appropriate encoding
Shallow processing	*Structural encoding:* emphasizes the physical structure of the stimulus	Is the word written in capital letters?
Intermediate processing	*Phonemic encoding:* emphasizes what a word sounds like	Does the word rhyme with *weight*?
Deep processing	*Semantic encoding:* emphasizes the meaning of verbal input	Would the word fit in the sentence: "He met a _____ on the street"?

(Depth of processing — vertical axis label)

FIGURE 6.11 | Depth of processing

Elaboration and Distinctiveness

elaboration
Adding to or enriching information by relating it to other information.

distinctiveness
The precision with which an item is encoded.

As Lockhart and Craik (1990; Craik, 2002) observed, the notion that there are different levels of processing has been refined with development of the concepts of elaboration and distinctiveness, both of which involve a deeper level of processing. **Elaboration** has been defined as "extra processing . . . that results in additional, related or redundant" material (Reder, 1980, p. 7), while **distinctiveness**, in a broad sense, refers to the precision with which an item is encoded; for example, to encode *cabbage* as a "food" is less distinctive than to encode it as a "vegetable" (Frase & Kamman, 1974).

There is evidence that the more distinctively an item is elaborated, the better it will be remembered. For example, Stein et al. (1982) compared the elaborations produced by two groups of students, one academically successful and the other less so. In one experiment the students were given short statements on the model of "The hungry man got into his car" (in which the fact that the man is hungry has no obvious bearing on the fact that he got into his car) and had to write continuations for them. The academically successful students tended to write precise elaborations that connected the formerly unrelated elements: for example, "The hungry man got into his car to go to the restaurant." This elaboration is precise because the information it adds is directly related to the fact that the man is hungry. By contrast, the elaborations produced by the less academically successful students tended to be less precise: for example, "The hungry man got into his car and drove away." This is a less precise elaboration because the additional material doesn't explain why the man got into his car. It also turned out that the academically successful students were able to recall more statements than were their less successful colleagues.

The authors concluded that, unlike the more academically successful students, the less successful ones did not spontaneously use precise elaboration on the material they were attempting to learn. They also suggested that academically successful students may have a better understanding of the importance of elaborating information in a meaningful way. Knowing what strategies to use in order to facilitate cognitive processes is another example of metacognition (Chapter 1). Training students how to use elaboration may be an important way of improving their performance. In Chapter 7, on imagery, we will review additional research into the role of distinctiveness in facilitating memory.

The importance of elaboration in memory has been further demonstrated in a series of studies of the way professional actors learn their lines. Noice (1991, 1992, 1993) showed that professional actors do not memorize scripts by rote. In a study comparing the strategies used by professional actors and novices to learn a six-page scene, Noice (1991) found that the professionals made many more elaborations of the material they needed to learn. These elaborations included considering the perspective of the character and asking questions about motivation. In another study (1992) she had professional actors describe their strategies for learning a part. They said they did not use rote memory, and stressed the importance of "finding reasons why [a] character says each line and performs each action." Noice concluded that when people talk about an actor "creating" a character, "it is literally true. The author supplies the words but the actor ferrets out the meaning" (Noice, 1992, p. 425). A by-product of actors' relentless search for meaning is that they end up memorizing the part without rote repetition. This should remind you of Aitken's musical memory, discussed in Box 6.2.

Levels of Processing and Aging

Craik (2002) has suggested that it may be helpful to distinguish between **specific and general levels of representation**, particularly in connection with age-related changes in memory performance. Among those changes is a loss of the ability to remember specifics such as names, even when the people concerned are close acquaintances. Another change is a tendency to retell the same stories to the same audience. Craik argues that names are relatively superficial details and that, even if you forget someone's name, you may still have a deep knowledge and understanding of that person. Similarly, the importance of remembering the occasions on which you have told a particular story pales in comparison to the importance of the story itself. With advancing age, the specific details of events may be forgotten, but their deeper meaning may still be retained.

> **specific and general levels of representation**
> As people age they tend to forget specific details but to remember deeper, more general meanings.

Levels of Processing and the Brain

As Roediger, Gallo, and Geraci (2002) observed, one implication of the "levels of processing" approach is that there is no particular place in the brain where memories are stored. Rather, the same parts of the brain used to comprehend an event will be activated when the event is recalled. They describe an MRI study done by Wheeler, Petersen, and Buckner (2000) in which participants were shown a word (e.g., *dog*) and then presented with either a compatible sound (e.g., barking) or a compatible picture (e.g., of a dog). Subsequently, participants were shown the word and asked to recall what went with it. When recall was successful, the predicted area of the brain was activated. Thus if the person had heard a dog barking, then at recall the auditory cortex was more activated, while if the person had seen a picture, then the visual cortex was more activated. The conclusion was that "the type of processing during test recruits the same brain regions as engaged during study" (Roediger, Gallo, & Geraci, 2002, p. 328; see also Nyberg, 2002 for similar findings).

Evaluation of the Levels of Processing Approach

The "levels of processing" approach has had an enduring influence on memory research. This influence was reviewed by Lockhart and Craik (1990) and in a set of papers looking back over 30 years of levels of processing research (Clifford, 2004). A persistent criticism has been that the concept of levels of processing is too vague (Baddeley, 1978). Although there is general agreement on what constitutes deep as opposed to shallow processing, there is still no objective measure of depth (Craik, 2002, p. 308). At its most superficial, research into levels of processing has simply extended Bartlett's point that the effort after meaning is a crucial determinant of what is remembered (Craik, 2002, p. 312). However, as Lockhart and Craik (1990; Craik, 2002) pointed out, the levels of processing framework has continued to generate important research. Its heuristic value is undeniable.

Two Approaches to Memory Research

There are two contrasting approaches to memory research. Both seek to uncover the general principles regulating memory, but one is lab-based and emphasizes experimental control, while the other incorporates real-world complexities.

The Lab-Based Approach

For several decades, most memory research has focused on laboratory experiments. This lab-based approach to memory research, which Bruce (1985) called the general principles tradition, goes back at least to Ebbinghaus (1885/1964), whose work has been enormously influential (Gorfein & Hoffman, 1987; Slamecka, 1985).

Ebbinghaus pioneered the use of nonsense syllables—a consonant followed by a vowel followed by a consonant, such as *pib* or *wol*—in memory research. In one experiment he read and re-read lists of 13 nonsense syllables each until he could recite them perfectly twice from memory. He then determined how long it took him to relearn a list after various intervals. Naturally, the longer the time since the original learning, the longer it took to relearn a list. On the basis of these experiments he was able to estimate how much he had forgotten after different periods of time. In general, memory loss was greatest immediately after learning; then the rate of decline became more gradual. Ebbinghaus's results were replicated by other experimenters, and can be summarized in the famous forgetting curve, an example of which is shown in Figure 6.12.

One general principle that has fared very well over time is Jost's law of forgetting, which was first published in 1897. This law states that of two memory traces of equal strength, the younger trace will decay faster than the older one (Wixted, 2004b). In other words, the rate at which forgetting occurs becomes slower over time. Figure 6.12 illustrates this nicely. Notice that more than 70 per cent of the material is lost in the first two days, but that there is only a very slow decline over the subsequent four days. Although the specific amount of forgetting that takes place during a particular interval will depend on many

lab-based approach to memory research
An approach that emphasizes controlled laboratory (as opposed to real-world) research in the search for general principles.

nonsense syllables
Nonsense "words" consisting of a consonant followed by a vowel followed by a consonant.

forgetting curve
Ebbinghaus's finding that the rate at which information is forgotten is greatest immediately after the information has been acquired, and declines more gradually over time.

Jost's law of forgetting
Of two memory traces of equal strength, the younger trace will decay faster than the older one.

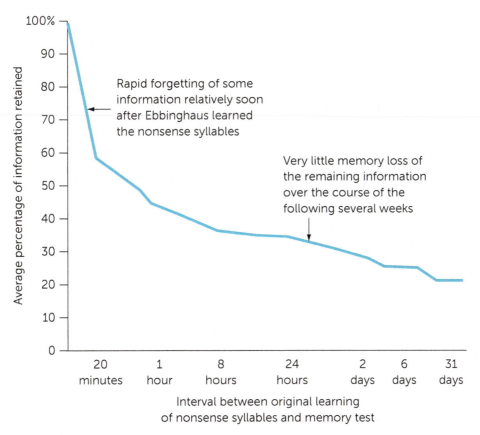

Rapid forgetting of some information relatively soon after Ebbinghaus learned the nonsense syllables

Very little memory loss of the remaining information over the course of the following several weeks

FIGURE 6.12 | Ebbinghaus's forgetting curve

factors, including the nature of the material learned, the general finding that the rate of forgetting slows with the passage of time is extremely robust.

A likely explanation of Jost's law involves the process of consolidation, which we referred to earlier in this chapter. We noted that over time memories tend to become more resistant to interference from more recently acquired information. This suggests that "as a result of the process of consolidation . . . forgetting functions would be expected to exhibit an ever-decreasing rate of decay and Jost's law of forgetting would follow naturally" (Wixted, 2004b, p. 877). Another implication of Jost's law is **Ribot's law of retrograde amnesia**: that older memories are less likely to be lost as a result of brain damage than are newer memories. Ribot's law illustrates a very general tendency that R. Brown (1958, p. 297) called the **law of progressions and pathologies**. This is a "last in, first out" principle suggesting that the last system to develop is the first to show the effects of degeneration. Whether this law is truly general remains unclear.

The Ecological Approach

The lab-based approach to the study of memory can be contrasted with the **ecological approach** (Loftus, 1991; see also the discussion in Chapter 3). Proponents of the latter have often argued that lab-based approaches do not come to grips with the complexity of memory

Ribot's law of retrograde amnesia

Older memories are less likely to be lost as a result of brain damage than are newer memories.

law of progressions and pathologies

A "last in, first out" principle referring to the possibility that the last system to emerge is the first to show the effects of degeneration.

ecological approach to the study of memory

An approach that emphasizes real-world complexities in its investigations to discover general principles.

as it operates in everyday life (Neisser, 1978b, 1982b). An ecological approach would examine memory in natural settings (Neisser, 1985) and explore how it functions in complex real-world situations (Hirst & Levine, 1985).

For its part, the ecological approach has been criticized precisely because it can sacrifice experimental control in its search for general principles. Proponents (e.g., Neisser, 1991) have replied that the kinds of field studies done by those with an ecological orientation are an important part of other sciences, such as biology, and should be central to the scientific study of memory as well.

Neisser (1997a) sounded a conciliatory note in this dispute (see Banaji & Crowder, 1989). Drawing on Koriat and Goldsmith (1996), he recast the issue as a debate between those who investigate how memory is stored (e.g., Ebbinghaus) and those who investigate how it is used (e.g., Bartlett). "Memories are not so much retrieved as they are constructed, usually with a specific goal in mind" (Neisser, 1997a, p. 1697). If the goal changes, the memory that is reconstructed may change as well.

Neisser described those who study how memory is used as "ecologically oriented" because they are concerned with the way it operates in the real world. However, he noted that lab-based approaches can help us understand "the neural systems that preserve information in the brain," and that both types of studies are necessary "if we are ever to understand the exquisitely human activity of remembering in an adequate way" (Neisser, 1997a, p. 1701).

Bahrick and the Permastore

Studies of flashbulb memories, which we reviewed earlier in the chapter, are often cited as models of ecologically valid research. Also singled out in this regard are Bahrick's (1984, 2000; Bahrick & Hall, 1991) studies of long-term memory focusing on the practical question of how long we remember what we learned in school. Because Bahrick's studies focus on retention of real material, as opposed to nonsense words, they stand in sharp contrast to Ebbinghaus's lab-based studies. Writing in 1984, Bahrick pointed out that while there had been many laboratory studies of learning, few studies had investigated how well people remember what they actually learned in school. In the late 1970s Neisser (1978b, p. 5) had questioned why, since higher education "depends heavily on the assumption that students remember something valuable from their educational experience," psychologists had not taken "the opportunity to study a critical memory problem so close to hand, but they never do." Thanks in large part to Bahrick's work, we now know much more than we did about what we remember from our schooling.

Bahrick (2000, p. 347) observed that since the 1980s a consensus had gradually developed according to which "important questions about memory should not be ignored just because they are not amenable to laboratory exploration." Although there are serious methodological problems involved in studying long-term retention of school learning, researchers simply must do the best they can under the constraints of real-world environments. In studying learning in school, the investigator needs to know such things as how well something was originally learned, and how often it has been rehearsed in the interval. Acquiring this kind of information is difficult and very time-consuming. Bahrick (1984) attempted to overcome these problems in a naturalistic study of Spanish learned in school.

With 773 participants, Bahrick's study was very large. Some participants were current students of Spanish at the high school or college level. Others had studied it in the past, anytime between 1 and 50 years earlier. All participants were classified in terms of the number and level of Spanish courses they had taken in high school and college.

Participants were asked for information concerning the grades they had received in their Spanish courses and how often they had been able to use Spanish since they had last studied it. They also took a comprehensive test of their knowledge of Spanish, which included measures of reading comprehension, vocabulary, grammar, and knowledge of idioms and word order. In the reading comprehension test, participants were asked to read a passage in Spanish and then answer questions about it. The vocabulary test, in part, required participants to write the English meaning of a Spanish word, and vice versa. Grammar items required the participants to write the proper form of a verb to use in a sentence. Knowledge of idioms was tapped by asking participants to identify the English meaning of Spanish idioms such as *desde luego* ("of course"), and knowledge of Spanish word order was measured by giving participants a random sequence of Spanish words to reorder in a proper sentence.

The first point to note is that the absolute level of performance varied with the number of Spanish courses taken and the grade level obtained. The more Spanish participants had studied and the higher their grades, the better they performed when their knowledge was tested later on. Responses to the question about rehearsal indicated that very few participants had spoken, read, written, or listened to Spanish after the end of their studies. The most striking finding was the consistency of the pattern of language loss over time. For the first three to six years after stopping the study of Spanish, there was a continuous loss of knowledge. However, after that initial period there was a period of roughly 25 years during which no further loss occurred. The general shape of the curve describing levels of knowledge at different times is shown in Figure 6.13. Of course, the absolute level of knowledge will vary with the amount and quality of prior learning, but the shape of the curve tends to be similar for everyone.

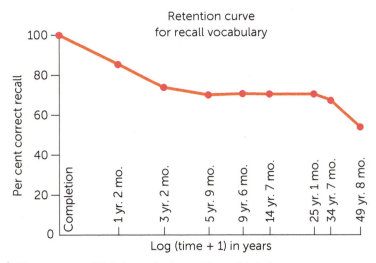

FIGURE 6.13 | The rate at which knowledge of Spanish is lost

Bahrick, H.P. (1984). Copyright 1984 by the American Psychological Association. Used with permission. The use of APA information does not imply endorsement by APA.

permastore
Bahrick's term for the state of relative permanence in which he found that some kinds of memory can be retained over very long periods of time.

Bahrick argued for the existence of what he called a **permastore**. It's important to note that by "permastore" Bahrick did not mean a particular place where memories are stored, but the state of relative permanence in which some kinds of memory may continue to exist after the initial period of decay comes to an end. Because Bahrick's study found so little evidence of Spanish rehearsal after studies had ended, it appears that rehearsing material after it is learned does not affect the transfer of information to permastore. Whether material ends up in permastore appears to be determined at the time when the material is learned. However, the precise mechanism through which the transferral of information to permastore takes place remains unclear.

Additional Demonstrations of Long-Term Retention of Educational Material

Bahrick and Hall (1991) also looked at long-term retention for mathematics, in a study involving 1726 participants. They sampled items from standardized tests of algebra and geometry from high-school mathematics courses taught between 1937 and 1986. Participants ranged in age from 19 to 84, and their mathematical training ranged from no algebra or geometry courses at all to university-level studies.

It turned out that long-term retention of knowledge from participants' first algebra course was influenced most by their subsequent exposure to or practice with algebra. "When exposure to mathematics is extended over several years, performance levels remain stable for half a century without the further benefit of practice"; and participants who had taken "three or more college-level math courses, with the highest of these above calculus," showed virtually no loss of high-school algebra knowledge over 50 years, even if there was no measurable rehearsal in the interim (Bahrick & Hall, 1991, p. 24). Whether a student got As or Cs mattered less than how many courses were taken. There were similar findings for geometry knowledge. In short, the study suggested that subsequent learning reinforced and consolidated prior learning.

Practical Implications of Long-Term Memory Research

Bahrick (2000; Bahrick & Hall, 1991) argued that his work had several practical implications. For example, since retention seemed to be "much more influenced by . . . variables pertaining to the curriculum and schedule of instruction" than by "individual differences [in] aptitude and achievement," the "life span of knowledge" could be extended by introducing "[c]hanges that increase the duration of acquisition or exposure and require maintenance and relearning of content during an extended period" (Bahrick & Hall, 1991, p. 32). Among the "curricular interventions [that] could produce such changes" were a longer course duration (so that the same number of hours were spread out over a longer time); "cumulative re-examinations at the end of a program of several years; and . . . capstone review courses at the end of programs" (Bahrick & Hall, 1991, p. 32).

Bahrick's studies suggest that how well students do in a subject is not the only thing that determines how much they will remember in the long run. Rather, any student who takes several courses in a discipline will forget less of the material, even after several years have gone by, than a student who has taken only one intensive course. To retain your knowledge of a particular subject, you should spread your studies out over several years, with lots of repetition of central concepts. Apparently it is entirely possible to learn at least some aspects of a subject so well that you will never forget them. They would be permanently stored in memory, and recallable when required. (If you were to look at some of your old exams, you might be surprised to see at how much you can still remember.) In fact, Conway, Cohen, and Stanhope (1991) found that students in a cognitive psychology course may retain general factual knowledge from the course for at least 12 years.

Summary

In this chapter we have considered the development of our understanding of memory as a cognitive process. Central to this understanding are the concepts of the memory trace and the memory schema. *Memory traces* were initially thought to be complete and permanent copies of past mental events that, when recalled, enabled us to re-experience those events (the *reappearance hypothesis*). However, research has suggested that memory traces are (at best) fragments of information that must be reconstructed every time we recall them. The organizational frameworks that are hypothesized to support these new constructions are called *memory schemas.*

Both concepts have given rise to interesting research questions. To investigate the accuracy of memory traces, R. Brown and J. Kulik (1977) looked at what they called *flash-bulb memories*: unusually clear, detailed, and enduring memory traces that would appear to lay down enduring records of experience. They theorized that flashbulb memories were produced by a unique sequence of information-processing events (*Now Print! theory*). However, when McCloskey et al. (1988) tested people's memories of the *Challenger* explosion—an event that might be expected to produce flashbulb memories—over time, they found that those memories were no more consistent than ordinary memories and that their formation did not require any special mechanism. The dominant idea in the memory literature today is that memory is a dynamic process. Memory traces of an event are not fully formed immediately after that event, but take some time to become complete (*consolidation theory*). The consolidation process (which appears to take place in the hippocampus) can be disrupted by events occurring immediately after the event-to-be-remembered (*retroactive interference*), and even after it has been completed, the memory trace is still susceptible to revision through *reconsolidation*.

The concept of the memory schema originated with Bartlett, whose experiments with *serial* and *repeated reproduction* demonstrated that memory production involves both the selection of some elements and the omission of others to conform to the abstract setting provided by a particular schema. Most of the memory schema literature today assumes that memory involves four processes: *selection*, *abstraction*, *interpretation*, and *integration*. Loftus and Palmer showed how eyewitness testimony can be distorted when misleading post-event information becomes integrated with information from the original event (the *misinformation effect*). Lindsay and Johnson's study of false memory investigated the failure to monitor the sources of memories.

Tulving and Thomson (1973) proposed the principle of encoding specificity, which suggests that the way something was stored in memory will affect how it is retrieved. For instance, matching the physical setting of encoding and retrieval will lead to superior memory performance. Likewise, the mood-dependent memory hypothesis suggests that memory retrieval will be better if you can match the mood you were in when you first learned something with the mood you are in when retrieving that memory.

We also considered the concept of the *script* as a standard sequence of events that structures our memories of certain types of activity (e.g., going to a restaurant), before looking at Berntsen and Rubin's (2004) study of *life scripts*: cultural narratives that outline the most important events in the life course (first job, marriage, etc.) and prescribe the approximate ages when they should occur. Life scripts may help to account for the fact that *autobiographical memory* typically shows a distinct increase or *bump* for the ages between 10 and 30, although several other explanations have also been proposed. Crovitz, Schiffman, and Apter (1991) calculated that participants in an earlier study would have had access to 224 autobiographical memories from the preceding 20 years; they called this figure *Galton's number*. A less traditional approach to memory research focuses not on the structures of memory but on levels of processing. Craik and Lockhart (1972) distinguished between *shallow* and *deep processing*, as well as *general* and *specific* levels of processing. Their approach also accounted for extra processing of related material (*elaboration*) and how precisely an item is encoded (*distinctiveness*). However, with no objective measure of depth, the "levels of processing" concept of memory has been criticized for being too vague.

Finally, *ecological approaches* focus on memory in real-world situations. Researchers such as Bahrick (2000; Bahrick & Hall, 1991) study the complexity of memory in everyday life by looking at the long-term retention of educational experiences (the *permastore*).

CASE STUDY

Case Study Wrap-Up

Jennifer Thompson was devastated to realize how her mistaken testimony had harmed Ronald Cotton, and eventually she arranged to meet with him. To her amazement, he not only forgave her but became her friend and, eventually, co-author. Their joint memoir, *Picking Cotton* (co-written with Erin Torneo), was published in 2009. Thompson is now an advocate for the wrongfully convicted, calling for legal reform and, in particular, better understanding of why eyewitness testimony is so unreliable.

Several elements of the Cotton case can be related to the material in this chapter. Loftus and Palmer demonstrated how easily memory for an event can be modified by post-event information. Furthermore, Thompson appears to have had a particular script or schema in mind when she picked Cotton out of the photo lineup. She told NBC she was "consciously . . .

trying to figure out the person in the photographic lineup that most closely resemble[d] the [police] sketch, as opposed to the actual attacker" (NBC News, 2009), and in an interview with CBS she explained how her expectations influenced her behaviour: "When you're sittin' in front of a photo lineup, you just assume one of these guys is the suspect" (CBS News, 2009). For their part, the police had already chosen Cotton as a suspect, so their bias was confirmed when Thompson chose him out of the photo lineup, and this initial confirmation may have led them to disregard other evidence. It's possible that Thompson would have identified Bobby Poole if she had seen his picture early enough in the investigation. Unfortunately for Ronald Cotton, she did not: by the time the case went to trial, his face was the only one she remembered.

Finally, the Cotton case highlights one of the most important take-home messages from this chapter. To put it simply, memory is far from perfect. Eyewitnesses are not the only ones whose testimony may be fallible: all of us are prone to errors of memory, whether because of post-event misinformation, decay, or interference. This is not necessarily a bad thing. After all, if we were required to remember every detail of every daily encounter, our thoughts might well be preoccupied with them, severely limiting our ability to function in the present.

In the Know: Review Questions

1. Discuss the differences between memory traces and memory schemas. How might they be related?
2. What are flashbulb memories? Discuss alternative explanations of their nature. Do you have any memories that fall into this category? Is there any way for you to check on their accuracy?
3. Discuss research relevant to the general form of schema theory as outlined by Alba and Hasher, as well as Koriat, Goldsmith, and Pansky.
4. Review the research on eyewitness testimony and false memories discussed in this chapter. How does the misinformation effect work?
5. Summarize the strengths and weaknesses of Craik and Lockhart's "levels of processing" framework.

Key Concepts

abstraction
autobiographical memory
autobiographically consequential experiences (ACEs)
childhood amnesia
consolidation theory
distinctiveness
ecological approach to the study of memory
elaboration
flashbulb memories
forgetting curve
Galton's number
integration
interpretation
Jost's law of forgetting
lab-based approach to memory research
law of progressions and pathologies
levels of processing
life scripts
memory bump
method of repeated reproduction (Bartlett)

method of serial reproduction (Bartlett)
misinformation effect (Loftus)
mood congruence
mood-dependent recall
mystic writing pad model (Freud)
nonsense syllables
Now Print! theory
permastore (Bahrick)
principle of encoding specificity (Tulving)
Proust effect
rationalization (Bartlett)
reappearance hypothesis
reconsolidation
retroactive interference
Ribot's law of retrograde amnesia
schema (Bartlett)
script
selection
source monitoring framework
specific and general levels of representation

Links to Other Chapters

consolidation theory
Chapter 10 (insight and the brain)

hippocampus
Chapter 7 (cognitive maps and the hippocampus)
Chapter 10 (insight and the brain)
Chapter 12 (expertise)

levels of processing
Chapter 9 (literacy)

distinctiveness
Chapter 7 (imagery and distinctiveness)

working memory
Chapter 5

Tulving's contributions to memory research
Chapter 5

Further Reading

For a useful collection of papers on so-called flashbulb memories, see Winograd and Neisser (1992).

Arbib and Hesse (1986) argue that schema theory may be applied to just about everything.

Bartlett's emphasis on the social nature of remembering is discussed in Weldon and Bellinger's (1997) study of collective memory.

For a fascinating review of the factors that influence eyewitnesses' identification of suspects in contexts such as police lineups, see Wells and Olson (2003). On the importance of interviewing witnesses as close to the time of the crime as possible, see Tuckey and Brewer (2003).

There has been a great deal of additional work with the script concept. If you are interested in deepening your knowledge of this topic, you should read Mandler (1984) and Mandler and Murphy (1983). See also Thorndyke (1984).

For more on forgetting curves, see Rubin and Wenzel (1996). Noice and Noice (2002) studied long-term memory retention among professional actors and reached conclusions similar to those of Bahrick.

Ecological approaches to memory are well-illustrated by Herrmann and Neisser (1979). In the same edited volume, Hunter (1979) discusses memory in everyday life. Perhaps the tour de force on ecological approaches to memory is Rubin (1995).

Arbib, M.A., & Hesse, M.B. (1986). *The construction of reality*. Cambridge: Cambridge University Press.

Herrmann, D.J., & Neisser, U. (1979). An inventory of everyday memory experiences. In M.M. Gruneberg & P.E. Morris (Eds.), *Applied problems in memory*. London: Academic Press.

Hunter, I.M.L. (1979). Memory in everyday life. In J.R. Anderson & S.M. Kosslyn (Eds.), *Tutorials in learning and memory* (pp. 167–191). San Francisco: Freeman.

Mandler, J.M. (1984). *Stories, scripts and scenes*. Hillsdale, NJ: Erlbaum.

Mandler, J.M., & Murphy, C.M. (1983). Subjective judgements of script structure. *Journal of Experimental Psychology: Learning, Memory, and Cognition 9*, 534–543.

Noice, T., & Noice, H. (2002). Very long-term recall and recognition of well-learned material. *Applied Cognitive Psychology 16*, 259–272.

Rubin, D.C. (1995). *Memory in oral tradition: The cognitive psychology of epic, ballads, and counting out rhymes.* New York: Oxford University Press.

Rubin, D.C., & Wenzel, A.E. (1996). One hundred years of forgetting: A quantitative description of retention. *Psychological Review 103,* 734–760.

Thorndyke, P.W. (1984). Applications of schema theory in cognitive research. In J.R. Anderson & S.M. Kosslyn (Eds.), *Tutorials in learning and memory* (pp. 167–191). San Francisco: Freeman.

Tuckey, M.R., & Brewer, N. (2003). The influence of schemas, stimulus ambiguity, and interview schedule on eyewitness memory over time. *Journal of Experimental Psychology: General 9,* 101–118.

Weldon, M.S., & Bellinger, K.D. (1997). Collective memory: Collaborative and individual processes in remembering. *Journal of Experimental Psychology: Learning, Memory, and Cognition 23,* 1160–1175.

7

Imagery

Chapter Contents

Chapter Objectives

- To review experimental evidence for Paivio's dual-coding theory.
- To examine how synesthesia and eidetic imagery relate to ordinary imagery.
- To outline the role of distinctiveness in memory.
- To distinguish mental rotation, mental scanning, and egocentric perspectives.
- To identify the basic properties of cognitive maps.
- To explore auditory imagery and the brain areas involved in auditory imagery.

CASE STUDY

Time–Space Synesthesia and Number Forms

When we need to remember the time and date of an appointment or special occasion, most of us rely on our trusty day planners or smartphones. But imagine for a moment that instead of recording appointments in a book or electronic device, you could visualize a virtual calendar, with each month, day, and hour in a specific location in space, and you could simply place an appointment in the "right spot" there. In fact, there are people who experience this kind of **time space**. When they hear, see, or even just think of the names of various units of time such as days of the week (Monday, etc.), weeks, and months (January, etc.), they see them in spatial patterns external to themselves. Cases of this kind were described by several early investigators, including Sir Francis Galton (1908/1973). An example of one person's time space is shown in Figure 7.1. She experiences the months of the year in an oval form, which appears about 30 cm in front of her face. Other individuals experience their time spaces as surrounding their bodies at about waist height. Some find that when they rotate their torso the space rotates with them; in fact, it goes with them wherever they go. An interesting aspect of these experiences is that they seem to occur automatically, which means that they cannot be consciously inhibited. People with time spaces often report using them as calendars to store important dates such as birthdays and due dates.

time spaces
The visual experience of time units such as days of the week or months of the year as occupying spatial locations outside the body.

number forms
Automatically generated images of numbers in various spatial layouts external to an individual.

Some people also seem to be able to create vivid picture-like images of number sequences. Those who experience **number forms** see numbers organized in various geometric forms in front of them. Figure 7.2 shows a bird's eye view of the number form experienced by a woman known as "L" (see Jarick et al., 2009). She experiences single-digit numbers as if they were located to her left, the numbers from 10 to 20 in front of her, and higher numbers to her right. As with time spaces, number forms are often experienced automatically: a number will simply appear, like a virtual picture, whenever it is thought of. Of course, it isn't really there: it's just a very vivid image.

Time spaces and number forms are relatively unusual forms of imagery. However, most of us can picture things in our minds, which is to say that we experience imagery of some sort or another. It's not easy to define precisely what an image is. The similarity between images and pictures has often been noted; in fact, *The Oxford English Dictionary* gives "To form a mental image of, to imagine" as one of the meanings of the verb *to picture*. Although a mental image can be defined as a "picture in the head," a number of qualifications must be added to this simple definition (Reber, 1985). This chapter is about those qualifications. In it we will examine how images arise, how they operate, and how they influence other psychological processes. At the end of the chapter we will also consider auditory imagery (i.e., "sounds in your head").

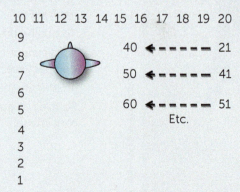

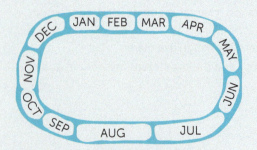

FIGURE 7.1 | An example of a time space

From: Smilek, D., Callejas, A., Dixon, M.J., & Merikle, P.M. (2007). Reprinted with permission from Elsevier.

FIGURE 7.2 | An example of a number form

Adapted from: Jarick, M., Dixon, M. J., Maxwell, E.C., Nicholls, M.E.R. and Smilek, D. (2009).

Memory and Imagery
Paivio's Dual-Coding Theory

Images seem to be very subjective phenomena, and for a while during the twentieth century many psychologists considered them too subjective to be studied scientifically. However, interest in imagery began to revive during the 1960s. This revival was to an important extent sparked by Allan Paivio's (1971, 1986, 1991; Paivio & Begg, 1981) research into what came to be known as **dual-coding theory**. Paivio postulated that humans have two systems for representing events, verbal and non-verbal, each of which has its own code (Johnson, Paivio, & Clark, 1996, p. 115). For example, an event can be described in words using the verbal system, or it can be imagined without words, using the non-verbal system. Which system is used depends on the nature of the information.

The relationships between the two systems are outlined in Figure 7.3. If you follow the diagram from the top down, you'll see that information arrives in either verbal or non-verbal form. After being picked up by the sensory systems, verbal information is represented in the verbal system and non-verbal information in the non-verbal system. The units that make up the verbal system are called **logogens** (a term borrowed from Morton, 1969). A logogen contains the information underlying our use of a particular word. The units that make up the non-verbal system are called **imagens** and contain the information that

dual-coding theory
The theory that there are two ways of representing events, verbal and non-verbal.

logogens
The units containing the information underlying our use of a word; the components of the verbal system.

imagens
The units containing information that generate mental images; the components of the non-verbal system.

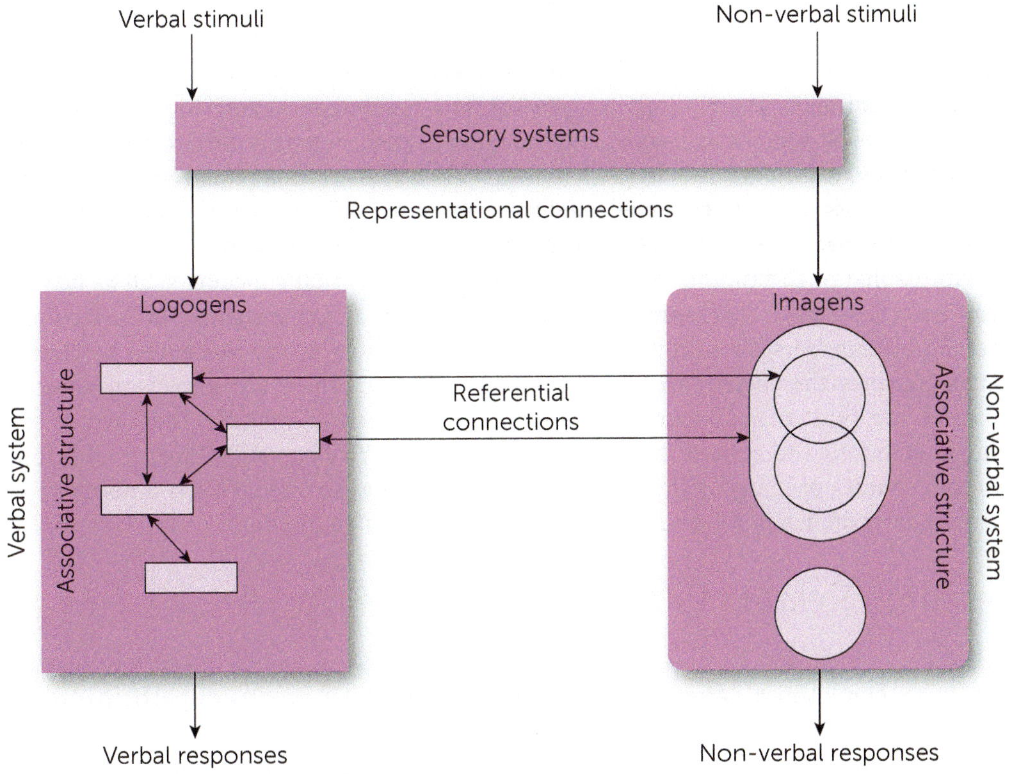

FIGURE 7.3 | Paivio's dual-coding theory

From: Paivio, A. (1986). Fig 4.1, p. 67. By permission of Oxford University Press.

generates mental images. Imagens "correspond to natural objects, holistic parts of objects, and natural groupings of objects" (Paivio, 1986, p. 60). Imagens operate synchronously: the parts they contain are available for inspection simultaneously. This means that a variety of related mental images can be generated from imagens. For example, you can imagine a group of people, one person from the group, the face of that person, the nose on the face of that person, and so on. By contrast, logogens operate sequentially. When you listen to a sentence, for example, the words are not present all at once, but come one after the other.

Information contained in one system can give rise to a process in the other system. As an example, Paivio (1986, p. 62) used the experience of describing your dining-room table. If you are somewhere other than your dining room, you can probably still experience a mental image of the table. What you then describe is that image. This means that the two systems are linked by what Figure 7.3 calls "referential connections." A verbal description of something can elicit an image of it, and an image in turn can elicit a description. Paivio used the term **imagery** to refer to the ease with which something such as a word can elicit a *mental image*—that is, "a mental picture, or sound" (e.g., Toglia & Battig, 1978, p. 4).

According to Paivio's (1971) theory, words that easily elicit a mental image—that is, words with a high degree of *imagery*—tend to be concrete (e.g., *table*), whereas words that don't easily elicit a mental image tend to be abstract (e.g., *purpose*). **Concreteness** is defined as the degree to which a word refers to "concrete objects, persons, places, or things that can be heard, felt, smelled or tasted" (Toglia & Battig, 1978). In other words, *concreteness* is the degree to which a word refers to something that can be experienced by the senses. The notion that ideas have their origin in concrete sensory experience has a long tradition in the history of Western thought (see, for example, R. Brown, 1968; J.M. Clark & Paivio, 1989).

To measure imagery and concreteness, Paivio would give participants the definitions of those terms outlined above and have them rate words on seven-point scales anchored either with "low imagery" and "high imagery" or "low concreteness" and "high concreteness." In most cases he found imagery and concreteness to be very highly correlated (e.g., Paivio, Yuille, & Madigan, 1968). This led Paivio (e.g., Paivio & Begg, 1981) to argue that imagery and concreteness measure two aspects of the same process because our experience of concrete events is necessarily saturated with images.

Notice that one of the implications of the foregoing is that concepts such as *pain* and *love* are not concrete. If this seems puzzling, remember that "concreteness" in Paivio's sense refers to objects, persons, and places. Pain and love can certainly be caused by concrete things, but they themselves are not concrete events. Thus there are some words, such as *pain* and *love*, that are not concrete but still elicit vivid mental imagery. These words often refer to emotions (Benjafield, 1987; Paivio, 1971, p. 83; Yuille, 1968). Thus in addition to external sources of imagery there are internal, emotional sources. This is a point we will return to later on, when we discuss the effects of imagery on memory.

Research Related to Dual-Coding Theory

One of Paivio's earliest studies (Paivio, 1965) focused on the role of imagery in learning. This study employed a paired-associate learning task. Four groups of participants each learned 16 pairs of words.

Each group learned a different kind of stimulus–response pair. For the first group, both words were concrete (e.g., *coffee/pencil*); for the second, the first word in each pair was concrete and the second abstract (e.g., *string/idea*); for the third, the first word was abstract and the second concrete (e.g., *virtue/chair*); and for the fourth, both words were abstract (e.g., *event/theory*). In the first learning trial, participants listened to the list of words, after which they were given the first (stimulus) word of each pair and asked to write down the second word. After four such trials, examination of the total number of correct responses revealed clear differences between the groups. These data are presented graphically in Figure 7.4.

Notice that learning was best when both words were concrete and worst when both were abstract. Notice also that the greatest difference in recall was between concrete and abstract stimuli: a concrete stimulus led to much better recall of the response than an abstract stimulus. Paivio also had participants rate the image-ability of each word, and found that the concrete words were rated higher than the abstract ones. These results have been replicated many times (Marschark, Richman, Yuille, & Hunt, 1987; Paivio, 1983; Paivio, Khan, & Begg, 2000; Paivio, Walsh, & Bons, 1994).

According to dual-coding theory (Paivio, 1969, 1971), these results can be explained as follows. A concrete word can be coded by both the verbal and non-verbal systems, whereas an abstract word will tend to be coded only by the verbal system because it is not likely to elicit much of an image. The

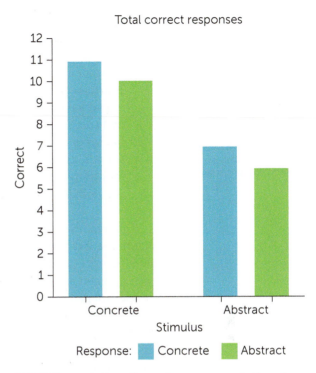

FIGURE 7.4 | Recall performance of the four groups in Paivio's (1965) study

Data from: Paivio, A. (1965). Reprinted with permission from Elsevier.

fact that a concrete word is coded in two systems means that it is more easily available to memory than an abstract word that is coded in only the verbal system.

Paivio hypothesized that stimulus concreteness would be particularly important in learning pairs of words. Suppose you are given the stimulus–response pair *coffee/pencil* to learn. You might imagine a coffee cup with a pencil in it. Thus both words may give rise to a single image, and this imaginal code may be stored in memory. When the stimulus word *coffee* is later presented by itself, "its image arousing value would be particularly important, for the stimulus member must serve as a cue that reinstitutes the compound image from which the response component can be retrieved" (Paivio, 1969, p. 244). Abstract words would be less effective cues because they are not coded imaginally.

Paivio's dual-coding theory has been applied to various phenomena. For example, in addition to the findings on the relationship between memory and imagery that we have already reviewed, dual-coding theory has been extended to the investigation of figurative language, such as metaphor (Katz, Paivio, Marschark, & Clark, 1988). It has also been used as a framework for understanding the mental processes involved in reading and writing (Sadoski & Paivio, 2001; Whitehead, 2003).

Dual-Coding Theory and the Brain

As we noted in Chapter 2, before the 1990s many researchers understood split-brain research to imply that the left hemisphere manages "analytic" (e.g., verbal, rational) tasks and the right hemisphere "holistic" (e.g., non-verbal, intuitive) tasks. Consistent with this viewpoint, Paivio (1991) argued that the verbal and non-verbal systems are

> dependent on different parts of the brain. The **left hemisphere** of most people controls speech and is more efficient than the **right hemisphere** at processing verbal material in such tasks as perceptual recognition, episodic memory, and comprehension. The right hemisphere has the advantage in such nonverbal tasks as face identification and discrimination, recognition of nonverbal sounds, and memory for faces and spatial patterns. The generalization holds for different sensory modalities, justifying the conclusion that the distinction is a verbal/nonverbal symbolic one that cuts across sensory modalities (p. 272).

The hypothesis that imagery is mainly a right-hemisphere activity and verbal representation a left-hemisphere activity has been challenged by fMRI work done by Fiebach and Friederici (2003). A clear implication of dual-coding theory is that concrete words will trigger greater activity in the right hemisphere than will abstract words. After a review of the relevant neuroimaging research, Fiebach and Friederici (2003, p. 66) concluded that the evidence "does not fully support the assumption of a specific right-hemispheric involvement during the processing of concrete relative to abstract words."

Fiebach and Friederici (2003) conducted an fMRI study of their own in which participants were shown concrete words (e.g., *bike, church, basket*), abstract words (e.g., *norm, feature, status*), and pseudo words (words in which one or two letters have been randomly replaced). The participants were given a lexical decision task (see Chapter 5) in which they had to indicate by a manual response whether or not each stimulus was a word. This task allows the experimenter to compare images of the brain activity triggered by abstract and concrete words even though the participants' response should be the same to both (i.e., both are words). Since the participants were not intentionally processing abstract and concrete words differently, any differences in brain activation could be attributed solely to the different properties of abstract and concrete words. The results showed that abstract and concrete words elicited different patterns of activity in the left hemisphere, but that concrete words did not elicit heightened activity in the right hemisphere. Thus the hypothesis that concrete words elicit greater right-hemisphere activation than abstract words was not supported (Fiebach and Friederici, 2003, p. 68). Commenting on these results, Scott (2004) suggested that linking imagery strongly with the right hemisphere is one example among many of "simplistic right brain/left brain attributions of cognitive functions, which in reality are supported by rather more complex bilateral systems" (p. 152).

Imagery and Mnemonics

Yates's *The Art of Memory* (1966) is a history of **mnemonic techniques**: techniques used to aid memory. According to Yates, imagery has been used as a mnemonic technique since ancient times. A second-century document called the *Ad Herennium*, for example, gave instructions for memorizing a great many items. This technique, usually called the **method of loci**, basically had two parts: places (*loci*) and images. The idea was to establish a cognitive map of a large building and place in each of its various *loci* an image representing one of the things to be remembered; then recalling those things would simply be a matter of mentally strolling through the building and collecting the images. It was recommended that the images be as distinctive as possible, even bizarre. For example, if you wanted to remember someone whose name was *Gorden* you might form an image of a garden and then "choose a prominent feature of the person's face and link the image of the name to it. Thus if Gorden has a large nose, an image could be formed of a garden growing over his nose" (P.E. Morris, Jones, & Hampson, 1978, p. 335). Yates reported that great feats of memory were accomplished using this technique; one adept was able to recite 2000 names in the order in which they were given, after hearing the list only once.

Yates's account of ancient mnemonic techniques stimulated quite a bit of contemporary research. Are these old methods really effective? There is some reason to believe that they are. Not only are similar methods promoted by professional teachers of mnemonic techniques (e.g., Lorayne & Lucas, 1976), but psychologists have shown that they really do aid memory. In an important account of the psychological principles behind mnemonics, Bower (1970a, 1970b) pointed out how you could use the method of *loci* to create a mental shopping list. First you would form images of various locations around the house, such as the living room and the bedroom; then you would form vivid images of the items to be bought (say, milk and bread) and relate those images to specific locations: for example, you might imagine someone milking a cow in the living room, and a loaf of bread tucked into the bed. At the store you would remember what to buy by imagining each place and recalling the images located there.

Items interrelated to form units are easier to remember than individual items (Asch, 1969). The fact that imagery can be used to organize disparate items into meaningful units may be part of the reason it is so useful. However, a mental image can also make information distinctive (Begg, 1982). We have already observed, in our discussion of levels of processing in Chapter 6, that **distinctiveness** is an important aid to memory. The relationship between imagery and distinctiveness has been the subject of some interesting research, to which we now turn.

Imagery and Distinctiveness

The author of the *Ad Herennium* recommended that the images used as memory aids be as striking as possible: "active, [with] exceptional beauty or singular ugliness," "ornamented 'with crowns or purple cloaks,'" "stained with blood or soiled with mud or smeared with red paint" (Yates, 1966, p. 10). The possibility that memory is facilitated by bizarre images has been extensively investigated. Initially, experiments did not demonstrate any effect of bizarreness (e.g., Nappe & Wollen, 1973). However, subsequent research showed that bizarreness can have an effect under certain circumstances (e.g., D. Anderson & Buyer, 1994; O'Brien & Wolford, 1982; Richman, 1994).

The specific conditions under which bizarreness has an effect have been explored in some detail (e.g., Einstein & McDaniel, 1987; Einstein, McDaniel, & Lackey, 1989; McDaniel, DeLosh, & Merritt, 2000; McDaniel, Einstein, DeLosh, May, & Brady, 1995). One of the more reliable findings has been that people remember bizarre items better when they occur along with common items. Thus if participants were given a list of sentences to learn, some of which were bizarre (e.g., *the maid licked ammonia off the table*) and some of which were not (e.g., *the maid spilled ammonia on the table*), then the bizarre items were remembered better. However, if the list consisted solely of bizarre items, then recall was generally no better than for a list composed entirely of common items.

distinctiveness hypothesis
The hypothesis that the more distinctive the item is, the easier it will be to recall.

von Restorff effect
If one item in a set is different from the others, it is more likely to be recalled.

The finding that bizarre items are memorable when they occur together with common items is reminiscent of a long-standing phenomenon called the **von Restorff effect** (von Restorff, 1933; Hunt, 1995), which holds that if one item in a set is different from the others then it is more likely to be recalled. It's important to realize that "being different" is a relative and not an absolute property (Hunt & Lamb, 2001). In a list of bizarre and common items, the bizarre items are more distinctive than the common items. This distinctiveness makes them memorable in a way that they are not when they appear in a list composed entirely of bizarre items. If a list is composed entirely of bizarre items, none of them will be distinctive.

Humour and Distinctiveness

Schmidt (2002; Schmidt & Williams, 2001) has observed that humour can have an effect similar to that of bizarreness. In a series of experiments, he used as humorous items a set of cartoons by a well-known cartoonist; a set of literal items created by eliminating incongruous information in the cartoons, rendering them humourless; and a set of weird cartoons created by adding irrelevant elements to the original cartoons. In one study, participants were shown a set of cartoons and then unexpectedly asked to provide a brief description of each cartoon. When the cartoons shown were a mixture of the three types, the participants' descriptions of the humorous items were more accurate than those of either the literal or the weird ones. However, when all the items shown were humorous, the descriptions were generally no better than for all-literal or all-weird sets. These results paralleled those described above for bizarre items: the humorous items became more memorable only when contrasted with non-humorous items (both literal and weird). However, humorous items were apparently more memorable than weird items, and this raised the possibility of a connection with the effect of bizarreness: although bizarreness is less memorable than humour, the fact that it often strikes people as funny might help to explain why bizarre items can, under some circumstances, be easier to remember than common ones. Humour in itself may be a strong aid to memory, especially in situations where humorous material stands in contrast to neutral material (Schmidt, 2002, p. 135).

The Problem of Distinctiveness

E. Winograd and Soloway (1986) noted that people often believe they can remember things better if they make the material to be remembered distinctive in some way. One strategy is to store things in special places. If we have something valuable to store, and we want to make sure we remember where it is, we will often put it in some special place. The problem with this strategy is that when you want to recover the item, you can't remember where that special place was. Winograd and Soloway (1986) pointed out that at first glance the special-place strategy may look similar to the method of loci that Yates (1966) described. However, there are important differences between the two.

Winograd and Soloway (1986) began with the observation that a special place to store an item is an unlikely place in which to find it. Some special places are chosen specifically to make sure that no one else, especially not a burglar, will find the item. Winograd and Soloway (1986, p. 371) commented that this is presumably why so many people store valuables such as cash in unlikely places, such as the freezer.

In one of Winograd and Soloway's experiments, participants were given sentences describing the locations of objects, such as "The milk is in the refrigerator" or "The tickets are in the freezer." Some participants rated these sentences for likelihood: how likely was it that somebody would store that particular object in that location? Some other participants also rated these sentences for memorability: how memorable would that location be as a place to store that item? A final group of participants were told to imagine putting each item in the location described, and then to rate each location for memorability. All groups were administered a recall test in which participants were given the name of the item and then asked to recall its location (e.g., "Where is the milk?" or "Where are the tickets?").

Winograd and Soloway compared recall for items of different levels of likelihood and memorability. It turned out that items from item-location pairings that were rated low in likelihood were remembered less well than items from item-location pairings that were rated high in likelihood, regardless of the level of rated memorability. To put this result a slightly different way: no matter how memorable we think a location will be, we will in fact remember it less well if it is unlikely than if it is likely. So the next time you decide to store your spare credit card in the medicine cabinet, perhaps you should think again.

Winograd and Soloway agreed with Begg's (1982) suggestion that distinctiveness is an effective aid for remembering individual items, but is not so useful for remembering the association between items. Consider why this difference is so important when you store an item in an unlikely place. When you want to retrieve it, you need to remember where you stored it: that is, you need to come up with an association between the object and the location. The problem is that the stored object is not an effective cue for remembering the location, and the distinctiveness of the location is irrelevant to the process of remembering.

This is where we can see how the "special places" storage method differs from the method of loci. When you use the method of loci, you begin with a set of places and then store items in them by forming an imaginative relationship between the two. Later, when you want to remember the item, you first recall the locus and then the object stored there. The process of recall goes from place to object. By contrast, when you store an object in a special place, the process of recall has to go from object to location, and there is usually no imaginative relationship between the two to serve as a memory cue.

Brown, Bracken, Zoccoli, and Douglas (2004, p. 650) have observed that the special places strategy is similar to a strategy that many of us use when creating passwords. We want a password that we can easily remember, but that others will be unable to discover. As we have just seen, it's very difficult to satisfy both these requirements simultaneously. Brown et al. (2004, p. 650) suggest using easily remembered (and therefore easily discovered) passwords in situations not requiring security, and creating distinctive passwords only when necessary. Finally, although you should certainly keep a written record of your passwords in a secure location, you should probably make sure the place you choose is not too special.

Putting things in special places or creating unique passwords means relying on distinctiveness alone to be a sufficient aid to recall. Winograd and Soloway (1986) suggested that this is an example of a mistaken belief about the way memory works. Metamemory is the name for our beliefs about how memory works. The decision to squirrel something away in an unusual location is an instance of metamemory failure.

special places strategy
Choosing a storage location that other people will not think of; the problem is that when the time comes to retrieve the item, you may not think of it either.

metamemory
Beliefs about how memory works.

Synesthesia and Eidetic Imagery

synesthesia

The condition in which a stimulus appropriate to one sense (e.g., a sound) triggers an experience appropriate to another sense (e.g., a colour).

chromesthesia

Coloured hearing.

inducer

The cue that elicits a synesthetic experience.

concurrent

The synesthetic response itself.

One of the most intriguing psychological states is synesthesia: a condition in which a stimulus appropriate to one sense (e.g., a sound) triggers an experience appropriate to another sense (e.g., a colour). Here is a report of an extreme synesthetic experience from a participant under the influence of mescaline (Werner, 1948/1961). "I think that I hear noises and see faces, and yet everything is one and the same. I cannot tell whether I am seeing or hearing. I feel, I taste, and smell the sound. It's all one. I, myself, am the tone" (p. 92). People who routinely have such experiences in everyday life are called *synesthetes*, and the most common experience that they report is chromesthesia, or *coloured hearing* (Harrison, 2001, p. 182). This is the experience of colour in response to an auditory stimulus. For example, a synesthete may experience a colour when hearing someone's name. The cue that elicits a synesthetic experience is called an inducer, and the synesthetic response itself is called the concurrent (Grossenbacher & Lovelace, 2001).

As many as one in 200 people may be synesthetes (Ramachandran, 2004, p. 19). Synesthesia appears to run in families, and occurs more often in women than in men (Bailey & Johnson, 1997). Perhaps the most famous synesthete was the novelist Vladimir Nabokov, who routinely experienced coloured hearing, as did his wife and his mother (Harrison, 2001, p. 131).

Cytowic (2002) described several cases of synesthetes who believed that synesthesia improved their memory. Smilek, Dixon, Cudahy, and Merikle (2002) provided evidence that this may indeed be the case. They reported on a synesthete, known as C, who is possessed of an extraordinary memory. For example, when asked to remember four lists of nine digits each, she could recall them all, and after an interval of two months she could recall all but two of the digits. In C's case each digit consistently induces a particular colour. Thus the number 2 printed in black always induces the colour *red*, which is projected onto the number. Smilek et al. (2002) compared C's digit memory with that of a control group of non-synesthetes. Each participant was asked to memorize three displays of 50 numbers each. The first display had numbers printed in black. The second display had numbers printed in colours that were different from C's concurrents. For example, 2 induces *red* in C, but was printed in *purple*. This is called the *incongruent display*. The third display was composed of numbers printed in C's concurrents (e.g., 2 was printed in *red*). This is called the *congruent display*. C outperformed all other participants in the first, black-digit display. However, the incongruent display caused C's performance to plummet from 66 per cent correct in the first display to only 4 per cent correct in the second (see Figure 7.5). By contrast, the performance of other participants was similar on both displays. C found the incongruent display discombobulating, saying that she "had never had this happen" to her before, and that she had "all these numbers swirling around" in her head. It seems reasonable to think that the colours of the digits in the incongruent display interfered with the colour she projected onto them. This interpretation is particularly likely since the congruent display did not adversely affect her performance (see Figure 7.5). Although C typically remembered digits extremely well, her memory for other kinds of material was similar to that of control participants. Thus it seems reasonable to conclude that synesthesia is an aid to memory in C's case, and perhaps in other synesthetes as well. In fact, recent

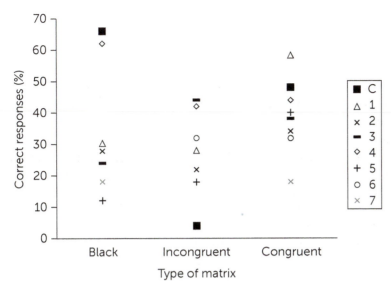

FIGURE 7.5 | The results of an experiment on synesthesia: congruent and incongruent number–colour matching and memory

From: Smilek, D., Dixon, M.J., Cudhay, C., & Merikle, P.M. (2002).

studies of other synesthetes have shown very similar results (see Radvansky, Gibson, & McNerney, 2011). In his book *Embracing the Wide Sky: A Tour Across the Horizons of the Mind*, the synesthete Daniel Tammet (2009, 73–74) describes a study examining how his condition affected his memory performance:

> For me, the numbers 0 to 9 have different sizes ranging from 6 (the smallest) to 9 (the largest). The researchers [Shai Azoulai and Ed Hubbard] presented me with two 100-digit number matrices (each for three minutes); one that presented the numbers in sizes that conformed to my synesthetic perception of them, and another that did not. . . . Three days later I was able to remember 68 digits from the first but barely any from the second. I found the experience of being asked to read and later recall the numbers presented in "wrong" sizes extremely dizzying and uncomfortable—rather like asking someone to read and recite in a language he does not know!

Theories of Synesthesia

A traditional explanation of synesthesia is that it reveals the underlying unity of the senses (e.g., Werner, 1948/1961, p. 93). The idea is that our five senses evolved out of one primordial sense, and that synesthetic phenomena reflect this common origin. A more recent version of this theory was advanced by Maurer (1997), who suggested that "the newborn's senses are not well differentiated but are instead intermingled in a synesthetic confusion" (p. 227). This lack of differentiation could be due to inborn connections between different areas of the infant's brain, such as between "the visual and auditory areas of the immature cortex" (Kennedy, Batardière, Dehay, & Barone, 1997, p. 253). These are called *transient connections* because they are not permanent: over time they are gradually pruned, much as surplus branches are pruned from a tree. The pruning process, which allows the senses to become differentiated from each other, is called **apoptosis**, and is a form of programmed cell death. Perhaps adult synesthesia occurs when this pruning process fails to run its course, and what were supposed to be transient connections end up being permanent. It has been suggested that, in the case of synesthetes, "the 'pruning' gene is defective," resulting "in cross-activation between areas of the brain" (Ramachandran, 2004, p. 68).

Failure to weed out inter-sensory connections can't be the whole story, however. It turns out that synesthetic responses can be elicited by concepts as well as percepts. Thinking about the number 7 is different from seeing the number 7 printed on a page. If simply thinking of a number can induce the same synesthetic response as perceiving the number, then cross-activation between sensory areas cannot be all there is to synesthesia. Dixon, Smilek, Cudahy, & Merikle (2000), in another study of C, had her perform the following task. After being shown two numbers (e.g., 5 + 2), she was shown a colour and asked to name it. It turned out that if the colour shown was incongruent with the sum of the two numbers, then C took longer to name the colour than if the colour shown was congruent with that sum. For example, suppose C was shown 5 + 2. For C, 7 is the inducer for *yellow*. Thus C could then name the colour *yellow* faster than she could name the colour *red*. However, 2 is the inducer for *red*. When shown 1 + 1, therefore, C could name the colour *red* faster than she could name the colour *yellow*. Incongruent colours interfered with C's ability to name the concurrent induced by the sum of the two numbers. Notice that this sum was not shown to C: she had to calculate it herself. The fact that C's synesthesia did not depend on an external sensory stimulus, but could be induced by the sum of two numbers, is evidence that synesthesia need not be the result of connections between sensory systems, but can also be the outcome of a conceptual process.

Ward and Simner (2003) have further explored linguistic and conceptual factors in synesthesia. They reported on a man named JIW, who was a lifelong synesthete. In his case, the sounds of specific words induced particular tastes. For example, the word *Chicago* induces an *avocado* taste. Notice that *Chicago* sounds a bit like *avocado*, and some of the inducer words have this relationship to the taste concurrents. Thus *Virginia* induced *vinegar* and *Barbara* induced *rhubarb*. Some other word–taste links involved the meaning of the word. For example, *bar* induced *milk chocolate*. In general, the foods that JIW tasted on hearing words that recalled their names were ones he had known as a child. More recently acquired tastes, such as *coffee*, were rarely induced. Since the links between the names of foods and their tastes are obviously acquired, not inborn, they may properly be said to belong to semantic memory. These results "suggest a strong role for language and conceptual factors in the development of this type of synesthesia" (Ward & Simner, 2003, p. 254). In at least some cases, the experiences of synesthetes may be "entirely mediated by neural connections that exist in normal adult human brains" (Grossenbacher & Lovelace, 2001, p. 40).

Strong and Weak Synesthesia

Martino and Marks (2001) have distinguished between *strong* and *weak* forms of synesthesia. Strong forms are the "classic" instances involving an inducer in one sensory modality (e.g., a sound) and a concurrent image in another sensory modality (e.g., a colour).

THINK TWICE
BOX 7.1
Can Anyone Become a Synesthete?

Non-synesthetes who wish they could experience synesthesia themselves often ask whether it is possible to induce the condition. If we were to train them on various letter and colour pairings, then perhaps over time they could begin to experience synesthesia. Although there is no solid evidence that such training would be effective, there is some evidence that synesthetic experiences can be induced through hypnosis. In a fascinating study reported by Cohen Kadosh and colleagues (2009), non-synesthetes were hypnotized and then told that each digit was associated with a particular colour: for instance, "2" with yellow and "4" with blue. Following the hypnotic session, these "posthypnotic suggestion" participants were interviewed and asked what they saw when they were shown a black digit. Promisingly, their responses were similar to those offered by synesthetes: they experienced the black digits as having coloured overlays. To objectively test these reports, Cohen Kadosh and colleagues (2009) showed participants brief displays of a black digit against a background that was either congruent or incongruent with the colour hypnotically associated with the digit. Participants then had to name the digit. Strikingly, the participants with the hypnotically induced synesthesia actually made many errors when the background colour of the display matched the colour associated with the digit. By contrast, they made very few errors when the digit and background colour were incongruent. Apparently the digits did elicit the hypnotically induced colour associations, and as a result they stood out from the background on incongruent trials, but blended in with the background on congruent trials. These results can be seen in Figure 7.6, which shows the error rate of digit identification on congruent and incongruent trials for two participants,

one of whom received a posthypnotic suggestion (PHS) and one of whom (the control) did not (No PHS). Notice that the control group made virtually no errors in either the congruent or incongruent conditions because the black letters on a coloured background were easily perceptible. So it seems that synesthesia can be hypnotically induced. Still, before you run off to get yourself hypnotically induced with synesthesia, you should know that this method would work only for the small subset of the population who are highly hypnotizable; those of us who resist hypnotic suggestions are out of luck.

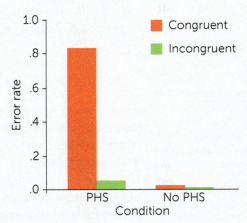

FIGURE 7.6 | The effects of hypnotically induced synesthesia

Errors of digit identification on congruent and incongruent trials for two groups of participants: the PHS group had synesthesia induced through posthypnotic suggestion, while the No PHS group did not receive any posthypnotic suggestion.

From: Kadosh, R. C., Henik, A., Catena, A., Walsh, V., & Fuentes, L. J. (2009). Copyright © 2016 by SAGE. Reprinted by permission of SAGE, Inc.

Martino and Marks give the example of Carol, who experienced colour (e.g., orange) in response to pain (e.g., as a result of a leg injury). The people we have discussed in the preceding section are **strong synesthetes**.

Even people who are not strong synesthetes may still show similar **cross-modal effects**. L.E. Marks (1982) observed that most people will judge *sneezes* to be brighter

cross-modal effects
The ability to appreciate that the sensations of one modality can be similar to those in another modality.

than *coughs*, and *sunlight* to be louder than *moonlight*. These and similar phenomena demonstrate that visual and auditory sensations share certain qualities for most people. For example, brightness and loudness seem to go together. Most of us are **weak synesthetes** in that we can appreciate these cross-modal associations without having strong synesthetic experiences. Martino and Marks (2001) suggested that these synesthetic associations "develop over childhood from experience with percepts and language" (p. 64).

Synesthesia can influence the way we label our experiences. McManus (1983) showed that some colour words are used more frequently than others in modern English novels, popular literature, and both English and Chinese poetry. The colour words used most frequently are those that emerged earliest in the language (such as *black*). A word such as *black* has great synesthetic power; it can be used to describe a wide variety of experiences, while labels such as *pink* have emerged later in the history of the language and have a more restricted range of synesthetic meanings.

The fact that one sense can represent information from another sense facilitates the use of figurative language such as metaphor. Consider this line from Keats's "Isabella": "Taste the music of that pale vision." Because it unites three senses (taste, audition, and vision), the line is especially memorable (Pollio, Barlow, Fine, & Pollio, 1977, p. 60; Ullmann, 1957). We will discuss some additional properties of colour words in Chapter 9, on language.

Eidetic Imagery

An **icon** is a snapshot of the information contained in a visual stimulus. This information persists briefly even after the stimulus itself is no longer present. The icon's occurrence seems to depend on the eye's being stationary, a situation that seldom happens naturally (Haber, 1983). However, it's useful to compare the icon with a related phenomenon known as **eidetic imagery**. Like iconic images, eidetic images persist even after the stimulus (e.g., a picture) is removed. Unlike the icon, which decays rapidly, eidetic images may persist for a minute or more. Eidetic imagery is similar to synesthesia in that both are examples of **cognitive dedifferentiation** (Glicksohn, Steinbach, & Elimalac-Malmilyan, 1999), in which processes that typically function independently are fused instead. "For example, synesthesia entails the dedifferentiation of sense modalities, while eidetic imagery entails the dedifferentiation of imagery and perception" (Cytowic, 2002, p. 109). An eidetic image is a fusion of imagery and perception, such that the image is experienced as a percept.

Here are some of the features of eidetic images as identified by Haber (1979):

- Experiencing an eidetic image is not the same as having a vivid mental image: the image is perceived as being located "out there" rather than inside one's head.
- The image can be scanned and its parts described.
- Descriptions of an eidetic image are quicker and more assured than reports from memory.
- Eidetic imagery is much more common in children than in adults.

---

weak synesthetes
People who can appreciate cross-modal associations without having strong synesthetic experiences.

icon
The initial, brief representation of the information contained in a visual stimulus.

eidetic imagery
Images projected onto the external world that persist for a minute or more even after a stimulus (e.g., a picture) is removed.

cognitive dedifferentiation
Fusion of perceptual processes that typically function independently.

Here is an excerpt from an 11-year-old's description of the eidetic image she experienced after viewing a picture for 30 seconds (Haber, 1979). Depicting a feast and containing many people, objects, and actions, the picture was no longer in front of her:

Experimenter: Tell me what you "see."

Participant: Up above it looks like stairs coming down and then there's a bench and a boy, then a girl and a couple of boys sitting on it, and then there's a very long table it looks like more plates without anything on them than food. There's a lady serving behind the table and then by the doorway it looks like children just gushing in and there's a clock by that—up in the left hand corner there's a china cabinet and a big hefty woman is putting dishes in there (p. 587).

This excerpt represents only about one-quarter of the child's description. Despite the quantity of detail, however, it appears that descriptions of eidetic images are generally no more accurate than are ordinary memories collected from non-eidetic viewers of the same scene. Thus eidetic images are not *photographic* images, since they are not literal copies of the scene.

Jaynes (1979) made the intriguing suggestion that paleolithic cave paintings, such as those in France and Spain, are "tracings of eidetic images" (p. 606). That is, Cro-Magnon artists may have experienced eidetic images of significant objects, such as animals, and then drawn these images on cave walls. Among the factors that led Jaynes to this hypothesis was the fact that each image appeared to have been painted all at once (there is no evidence of repeated attempts at representation). Jaynes believed that describing an eidetic image may cause it to fade, and that Cro-Magnon eidetic images may have lasted longer than the images experienced in contemporary lab experiments partly because they were images of objects and events of great significance to the viewer and partly because they did not have to be put into words.

An excellent test for people who claim to have a photographic memory for pages in a text is to ask them to recall a page from the last word to the first. If they are actually "looking" at an image of the page, then they should be able to read it backwards as well as forwards. Most people are unable to do this; recall is much better in the forward direction (Neisser, 1967). However, Strohmeyer (1970/1982) reported the case of Elizabeth, an accomplished artist who claimed that she could write out a poem in a foreign language that she did not understand, and had seen only once, years before, from the last line to the first. Elizabeth's method was similar to the one used to create old-fashioned stereograms. In one test she was shown two dot patterns—one for each eye—that combined to form a three-dimensional image. Elizabeth would look at one pattern with one eye and form an eidetic image of it. Then she would look at the second pattern with the other eye and project an eidetic image of the first pattern onto the second. The result was an in-depth image. If you have an old stereoscope around the house, you could try using it this way; however, this kind of eidetic imagery ability is quite rare. In fact, there has not been another documented case resembling Elizabeth's, so although the results of Strohmeyer's experiment are suggestive, we should be cautious not to base any general conclusions on his findings.

Vividness of Visual Imagery

Eidetic imagery seems to be an extraordinary form of imagery (Neisser, 1979), but it may only be an extreme form of an ability that is present in everyone (Paivio, 1986, p. 119). People vary in their experience of ordinary visual memory images (Harshman & Paivio, 1987). For example, **vividness of visual imagery** varies widely. This can be measured using the Vividness of Visual Imagery Questionnaire or VVIQ (D.F. Marks, 1972, 1999). Vividness is defined in terms of "clarity and liveliness" as well as similarity to an actual percept (D.F. Marks, 1999, p. 570). A clear and lively image is one in which colour is bright, form is well-defined, and so on. The current version of the VVIQ (D.F. Marks, 1999, p. 583) asks participants to imagine a series of people (e.g., relatives or friends) and scenes. Participants then rate the vividness of parts of the resulting image (e.g., the colours of a friend's clothes) on a scale ranging from "perfectly clear and as vivid as normal vision" to "No image at all." On the basis of these ratings, participants receive a VVIQ score.

The VVIQ has been used in a large number of studies, of which McKelvie (1995) reviewed more than 250. One obvious question is whether people who score high on the VVIQ are better able to learn and remember than low scorers. The answer is that vividness of visual imagery does not appear to be a good predictor of superior performance on memory tasks. Baddeley and Andrade (2000) noted that the relationship between vivid imagery and memory is complex. Participants examined pictures taken from a book of British and European birds after having judged their prior knowledge of birds as either "poor," "moderate," or "good." Participants were also given the name of each bird as it was presented. Then they were given the names again in the same order. Participants were asked to form an image of each bird as they heard its name and to rate the vividness of their image on a scale ranging from 0 (no image at all) to 10 (image as clear and vivid as normal vision). Those who rated their prior knowledge of birds as either "moderate" or "good" had higher vividness ratings than those who rated their prior knowledge as "poor." Baddeley and Andrade speculate that vividness of visual imagery is proportional to familiarity with the object envisioned. However, vividness is not an index of the accuracy of memory, only of its richness. It's possible to have very vivid imagery associated with events that are untrue (Gonsalves, Reber, Gitelman, Parrish, Mesulam, & Paller, 2004).

Another important issue is the relationship between the vividness of imagery and perception. Can vivid imagery influence perception of external stimuli? This issue has been addressed in an interesting study reported by Cui, Jeter, Yang, Montague, and Eagleman (2007). On each trial of their study, participants were shown a sequence of displays depicted in Panel A of Figure 7.7. The critical display in the sequence contained a colour word (e.g., *orange*) presented in black against a coloured background that was either the same as (congruent with) or different from (incongruent with) the colour expressed by the colour word. The display was presented very briefly and followed by a pattern mask (a sequence of Xs) that made the colour word difficult to see. Participants were required to name the word on the display as accurately as possible. In addition, Cui et al. (2007) measured vividness of imagery using a version of the VVIQ in which low scores represent a high degree of vividness of imagery. Critically, they measured the difference in word identification accuracy between congruent and incongruent trials and related this to the participant's vividness of imagery as measured by the VVIQ. The results are shown in Panel B of Figure 7.7. Clearly, the difference in performance on congruent and incongruent trials correlated quite

(a)

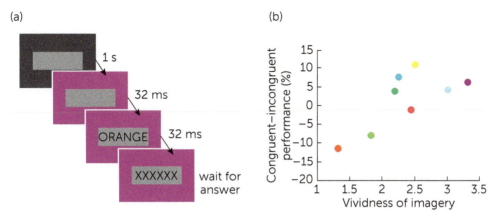

(b)

FIGURE 7.7 | The sequence of displays in the study reported by Cui et al. (2007) and the relationships between colour word identification and vividness of imagery

Cui, X., Jeter, C.B., Yang, D., Montague, P.R.,& Eagleman, D.M. (2007). P. R.,& Eagleman, D.M. (2007). Reprinted with permission from Elsevier.

strongly with vividness of imagery scores. Interestingly, participants with a high degree of vividness of imagery (i.e., low VVIQ scores) were actually more accurate on incongruent trials than congruent ones. Cui et al. (2007, p. 477) suggest that "for more visual subjects, incongruent colors make it easier to see a color word. These findings imply an increased interaction between brain areas that code for color perception and color naming in highly visual individuals."

Mental Rotation

Thus far we have considered mental images only as static mental pictures. But of course we can also imagine objects in motion.

A canonical demonstration of the dynamic nature of mental images was conducted by Shepard and Metzler (1971). In their experiment, participants were presented with 1600 pairs of line drawings like those in Figure 7.8. Half the pairs showed the same object (as in Figures 7.8a and 7.8b) and half showed different objects (as in Figure 7.8c). The pairs of drawings of the same object varied in the angular rotation that would be required in order to bring the two images into alignment. The angular rotation required varied from 0° to 180° through 20° intervals. Some of the correct pairs required an angular rotation in the picture plane (as in Figure 7.8a), whereas others required an angular rotation in depth (Figure 7.8b).

For each pair, the participants had to decide whether the drawings depicted the same object or a different one and indicate their decision by pulling a lever with either the right hand or the left. Shepard and Metzler (1971) also measured the length of time it took to make each decision.

The most interesting findings concerned the relationship between angular rotation and reaction time for correct responses to drawings of the same object. This relationship is shown in Figure 7.9. For both picture-plane and depth pairs, the relationship between the two variables is almost perfect. The greater the angular rotation required, the longer it takes the participant to make a decision. Shepard and Metzler (1971) concluded that

DISCOVERY LAB

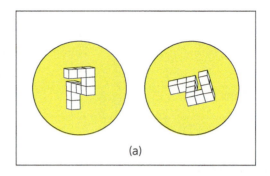

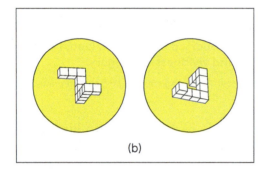

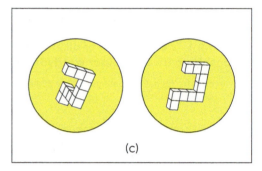

FIGURE 7.8 | **Which pairs are drawing the same object?**

Based on Shepard, R.N., & Metzler, J. (1971).

mental rotation

Imagining an object in motion and viewing it from different perspectives.

participants determined whether or not the drawings depicted the same object by means of a process called **mental rotation**. Perhaps participants were imagining the rotation of one of the pairs to determine if it matched the other member of the pair. The greater the angular rotation required, the longer it would take to imagine the rotation of one of the pairs until it came into alignment with the other. On the basis of Shepard and Metzler's (1971) data, it appears that the speed of mental rotation in this task was 60° per second.

There have been several subsequent demonstrations of the accuracy with which people are able to imagine the rotation of objects (Shepard, 1978; Shepard & Cooper, 1982). Shepard (e.g., 1984) has noted that the process of imagining an object seems quite similar to the process of perceiving an object. "What we imagine, as much as what we perceive, are external objects; although in imagining, these objects may be absent or even nonexistent" (Shepard, 1984, p. 420). As we shall see, considerable research has examined the apparent similarity between the processes of imagining and perceiving. Box 7.2 looks at some recent research related to video games and the perception of imagery.

Is mental rotation a right-hemisphere process?

When we considered Paivio's theory, we concluded that imagery was not confined to the right hemisphere. However, mental rotation is a more dynamic process than static imagining of the sort elicited by concrete words. Mental rotation is a non-linguistic process, and for that reason may tend to be localized in the right hemisphere. However, the existing evidence is not decisive (Corballis, 1997). In an event-related potentials (ERP) study,

Milivojevic, Johnson, Hamm, and Corballis (2003) further investigated the lateralization of mental rotation. They had participants perform two different tasks. One was a simple letter rotation task, in which letters were presented in normal or mirror-reversed orientation at varying degrees of tilt. For example, participants might see the letter *R* like this:

The participants' task was to say whether the letter was normal or mirror-reversed. What would you conclude about the letter above? How did you do it? The second task involved more complex folding tasks. For example:

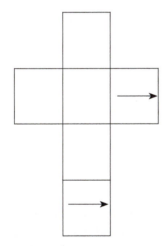

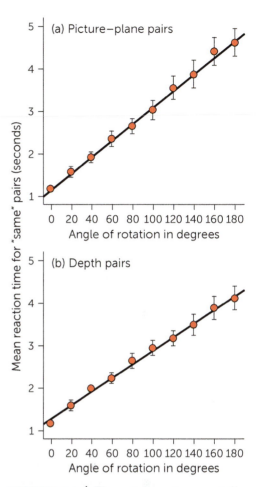

FIGURE 7.9 | Time taken to mentally rotate an object as a function of angular rotation

From: Shepard, R.N., & Metzler, J. (1971). Copyright 1971 by the American Association for the Advancement of Science. Reprinted by permission.

Participants had to decide whether or not the arrowheads would be aligned if the squares were folded to make a box. Again, what's your conclusion? How did you come to it? The first task required one mental transformation, while the second required a series of transformations. The second task took longer than the first, reflecting its greater difficulty. The ERP analysis showed that the mental rotation task tended to be carried out in the right hemisphere. However, the mental folding task was not lateralized, and both hemispheres were equally involved. Milivojevic et al. (2003, p. 1359) concluded that "the right hemisphere may be preferentially engaged when the task is simple" but "the left hemisphere is also engaged as the task becomes more complex."

Scanning Mental Images

In a series of experiments Kosslyn and his colleagues explored the relationship between imagery and perception (e.g., Kosslyn, 1980, 1983; Denis & Kosslyn, 1999). In one such study (Kosslyn, Ball, & Reiser, 1978) participants were asked to memorize a map of an island that contained seven different locations (a tree, a beach, a hut, and so on; Figure 7.10). Some of the distances between the various locations were longer than others: for example, the distance from the hut to the beach was longer than the distance from the hut to the tree. The time it would take you to scan from one location to another on the real map would depend

If you are an avid video game player, you may have wondered whether all the hours you've spent playing amount to anything. Researchers at the University of Toronto (Feng, Spence and Pratt, 2007) reported a fascinating study exploring how action video games influence imagery abilities, and whether they affect males and females differently. The study tested two groups of participants. One group was asked to play a well-known violent game named "Medal of Honor." The second group, which served as the control group in this case, played a non-violent game named "Balance." The violent game was chosen because it demanded much more attention than the non-violent game. Importantly, the researchers tested participants' mental rotation abilities (see Shepard and Metzler, 1971) both before and after 10 hours of playing the video games. They also looked at the performance of males and females separately. Initially, males performed better than females on the mental rotation task, but after 10 hours of play, the performance of all those playing the violent game improved, and the improvements were greater for females than males. The performance of those who had played the non-violent game did not show any enhancement. Thus playing action video games seems to improve spatial imagery and reduce pre-existing gender differences in this ability (for related results see De Lisi & Wolford, 2002).

on the real distance: thus it would take longer to scan from the hut to the beach than from the hut to the tree.

What about the participant's memory image of the map? Does it take longer to scan between parts of the memory image that are far apart than between the parts that are close together? To answer this question, Kosslyn and his colleagues asked participants to imagine one of the locations on their memory image of the map. Then they were to imagine "a little black speck zipping in the shortest straight line" (Kosslyn et al., 1978, p. 52) from that location to another location. Sometimes they were asked to scan to locations that were not on the map. For example, they might imagine the hut and then be asked to scan from the hut to the beach (which is on the map) or from the hut to a location that is not on the map. If they could find the location, they pressed one button, and if they could not find it they pressed another button. The results showed that, for places actually on the map, the farther apart the two objects were, the longer it took to scan between them (Figure 7.11). This was interpreted by Kosslyn and his co-workers to mean that **objective distances** are preserved in our mental images of perceived scenes.

Rinck and Denis (2004) have shown that objective distance is not the only feature that determines how long it takes to scan from one part of a mental image to another. Another important variable is **categorical distance**: "the number of units that are traversed during mental scanning, for instance, landmarks on an island map, rooms in a building, or counties in a state" (Rinck & Denis, 2004, p. 1212). To investigate the relative influences of objective and categorical distances, participants were given a map of a museum floor to memorize. The floor was divided into rooms of different sizes, and each room contained paintings by various well-known artists, such as Van Gogh and Leonardo da Vinci (Figure 7.12). (At this point, in order to visualize the task, imagine the floor plan of your own dwelling, and imagine paintings by different artists in each room. Now

objective distances
The true distances between objects in the real world, which are preserved in our mental images.

categorical distance
The number of units traversed during mental scanning: for instance, landmarks on an island map, rooms in a building, or counties in a state.

FIGURE 7.10 | The map of the island used in a mental image scanning experiment

Participants mentally travelled over the locations on the island.

From: Kosslyn, S.M., Ball, T.M., & Reiser, B.J. (1978). Copyright © 1978 by the American Psychological Association. Reproduced with permission. The use of APA information does not imply endorsement by APA.

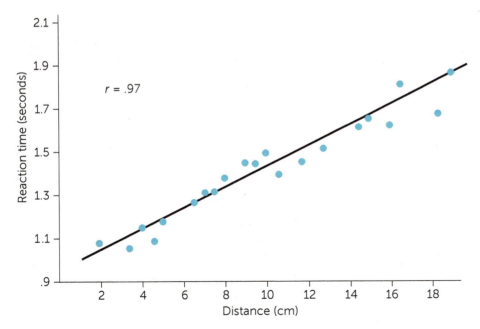

FIGURE 7.11 | Results from the mental image scanning experiment of Kosslyn et al.

From: Kosslyn, S.M., Ball, T.M., & Reiser, B.J. (1978). Copyright © 1978 by the American Psychological Association. Reproduced with permission. The use of APA information does not imply endorsement by APA.

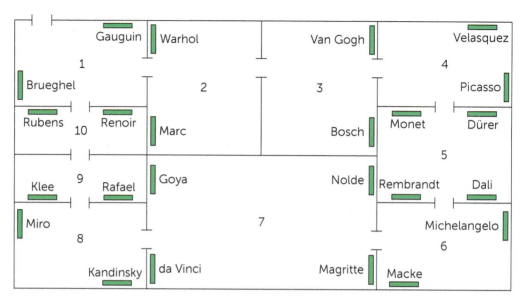

FIGURE 7.12 | The museum floor plan used in the 2004 experiment of Rinck and Denis

Participants mentally travelled between paintings

From: Rinck, M., & Denis, M. (2004). Copyright © 1978 by the American Psychological Association. Reproduced with permission. The use of APA information does not imply endorsement by APA.

imagine walking across a room from one painting to another. This would be an objective distance. Now imagine walking from a painting in one room to a painting in another room. This would involve not only an objective distance but also a categorical distance. This was the sort of task given to participants in this experiment.) Both the objective distance travelled and the categorical distance affected the amount of time it took to travel mentally between one painting and another. This result suggests that images may be structured hierarchically, with objective distances nested within categorical differences. We will return to this possibility in our discussion of cognitive maps, next.

Images as Anticipations

image as anticipation hypothesis

The hypothesis that an image is a readiness to perceive something.

Podgorny and Shepard (1978) conducted an experiment using grids like those in Figure 7.13. The participants' task was to imagine a letter superimposed on a grid, such as the letter F in Figure 7.13a. To try it yourself, imagine the F superimposed on the grid in Figure 7.13b. If you were a participant in this experiment, then a dot probe would appear in one of the squares in the grid, as in Figure 7.13c. Your task would be to decide, as quickly as possible, whether or not the dot was in a square covered by your imaginary F. It turns out that this is a task that people can do both rapidly and accurately. In fact, performance on this particular task with imaginary letters is strikingly similar to performance when letters are actually present in the grid.

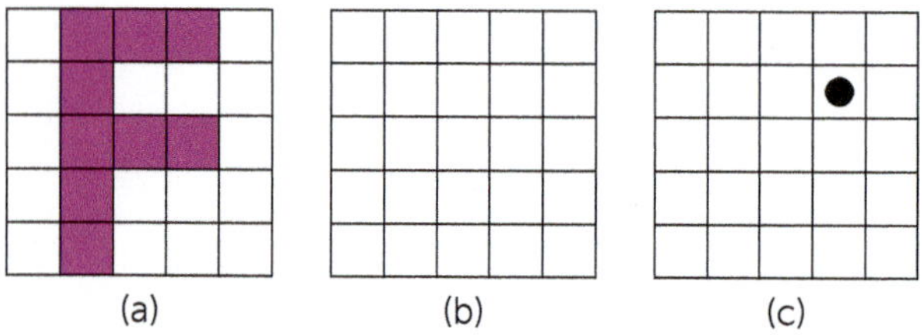

Farah (1989) used a similar task to demonstrate the role of **images as anticipations**. Participants imagined a letter superimposed on a grid, as in the Podgorny and Shepard

FIGURE 7.13 | Grid used in the Podgorny and Shepard experiment

From: Shepard, R.N. (1978). Reproduced with permission. The use of APA information does not imply endorsement by APA.

experiment. However, the probe stimulus, an asterisk (*), was presented only for a very brief interval, and the participants had to detect its occurrence. The asterisk could fall either in a square covered by a participant's image, or in a square not covered by the participant's image. Probes were detected more often in the former case.

Farah also reported evidence suggesting that imagery lowers the participant's criterion for detecting a stimulus. It was not so much that participants were more sensitive to stimuli falling within the imaged region as it was that they were better prepared to pick up stimuli falling within the area of a projected image. Farah characterized this process in terms used by Ryle (1949) and Neisser (1976). Neisser defined an image as a readiness to perceive something (1976, p. 130; cited by Farah, 1989).

To understand what "a readiness to perceive something" means, remember our discussion of perceptual organization in Chapter 3. At any point in time, we anticipate picking up certain kinds of information and not others. When we anticipate something, the perceptual cycle is ready to pick up the information, but the information is not there yet. These anticipations are mental images (Neisser, 1978a). For example, if I imagine what is inside my desk drawer, I am anticipating what I would see if I opened the drawer. We pick up information that we anticipate more readily than information that we don't anticipate. In Farah's experiment, when participants projected an image onto the grid, they were anticipating seeing something in the squares covered by the image. That is, they were prepared to pick up a target that occurred in those squares.

Farah (1989) also described another experiment that elaborated on the anticipatory nature of images. Participants were shown a pattern of shaded squares that could be seen as either an H or a T, as in Figure 7.14. They were told to attend to one letter or the other. Try this yourself. You can see the configuration in Figure 7.14 as an H if you attend only to those squares in the grid that make up an H; or you can see it as a T if you attend only to those squares that make up a T. Attending to one pattern or the other facilitates the pick-up of probes in that area, just as projecting an image does. That the results are the same for

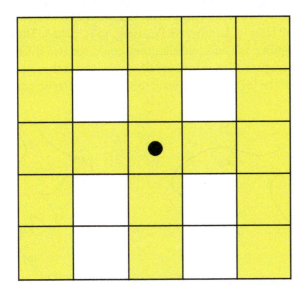

FIGURE 7.14 | The pattern of squares used in Farah's experiment

From: Farah, M. (1989). Copyright 1989 by the American Psychological Association. Reproduced with permission. The use of APA information does not imply endorsement by APA.

projecting and attending suggests that imagery is an active process that prepares you for perceiving information, and not just a passive representation of information.

Brockmole, Wang, and Irwin (2002) conducted a detailed investigation of the conditions under which images and percepts may be combined. They presented participants with a 4 × 4 grid in which several squares were filled with a dot. That grid disappeared and was replaced by another grid with dots in several other squares. One square only was not filled with a dot on either occasion, and the participant's task was to identify that square. Performance on this task was best when the interval between the first and second grid was about 1300 milliseconds. It's likely that participants required about that long to form an image of the first grid. The percept of the second grid could then be integrated with the image of the first grid to yield a representation that combined both grids and allowed the participant to identify the empty square. This integration of images and percepts shows that perception and imagery must share many of the same mechanisms (Kosslyn, Ganis, & Thompson, 2001). Box 7.3 explores how we construct real pictures out of what we see and imagine.

Images and Ambiguous Figures

Farah's H or T figure is an example of an ambiguous figure. Some very interesting properties of images can be explored further using ambiguous drawings like the ones in Figure 7.15, which may be interpreted in two ways (Shepard, 1978, p. 129). The drawing on the left can be seen as either a duck or a rabbit; the one on the right, as either a chef or a dog. An interesting question is whether ambiguous figures can be imagined as ambiguous. If imagining something is a bit like perceiving it, then it might be possible to shift from seeing one thing in an imaginary ambiguous figure to seeing something else. That is, perhaps I could imagine Figure 7.15a as a duck, and then imagine it as a rabbit, and then return to imagining it as a duck, and so on.

Chambers and Reisberg (1985) investigated this possibility. Participants were first shown some ambiguous figures, and the experimenter made sure that each participant was able to see them reverse from one view to another. Then participants were shown a slide of the duck/rabbit in Figure 7.15a and asked to form a "mental picture of the slide so that they would be able to draw it later" (Chambers & Reisberg, 1985, p. 320). They were then shown the chef/dog picture in Figure 7.15b and told that they could see two different things by looking at different parts of the figure. (Try this yourself. If you look at the upper right you tend to see a dog, but if you look at the lower left you tend to see a chef.) Participants were asked to try to

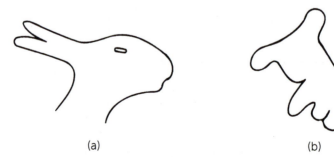

(a)   (b)

FIGURE 7.15 | The duck/rabbit and chef/dog stimuli

Chambers, D. & Reisberg, D. (1985). Copyright 1985 by the American Psychological Association. Reprinted with permission.

Mental Images and Real Pictures

As we noted at the beginning of this chapter, when we imagine a scene, the experience is a bit like looking at a picture. That partly explains why it's so tempting to define images as mental pictures. Pinker and Finke (1980) compared the properties of images with the properties of actual pictures. Although images seem to be accurate representations of a scene as it appears from a particular viewpoint, the pictures that people actually make of scenes don't always have this property. Look at the drawing at the left in Figure 7.16. There is no way that such a scene could actually be seen. The picture appears to us to be a distorted representation of an actual scene, because there is more in the picture than you could possibly see from one vantage point. The drawing at the right in Figure 7.16 more accurately represents what would actually be seen from a single vantage point. Nevertheless, many people make drawings that are more like the drawing on the left than the one on the right. How can we explain the apparent discrepancy between the accurate images we experience and the inaccurate drawings we so often produce?

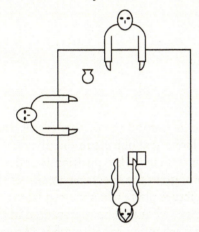 

FIGURE 7.16 | Viewpoint

Arnheim, R. (1974). *Art and visual perception: A psychology of the creative eye.* Berkeley: University of California Press, Figures 86 and 87. Copyright 1974 by the Regents of the University of California.

reverse their mental image of the duck/rabbit slide in the same way. None of the participants could do so. However, all of them were able to draw the duck/rabbit figure from memory.

There are at least three possible explanations for this discrepancy, according to Pinker and Finke (1980). One is that even if you can accurately imagine how something will look, you may not be able to draw your image. It's not always easy to translate the image in your mind into a sequence of arm movements that will reproduce that image on the page. Another possibility is that you don't actually try to draw your image, but instead try to draw the object as you know it really is. This is a critical drawing error, as art historians have frequently observed (e.g., Edgerton, 1975). When you draw something the way you think it should be, the result will be a distorted representation that does not look at all like the object you actually see. This point is illustrated in Figure 7.17. What the artist represents on the picture plane is a projection of the surface of an object. The result is that

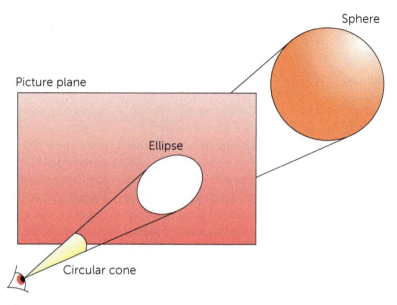

FIGURE 7.17 | The picture plane

From: *The Oxford Companion to the Mind* by Richard L. Gregory (2004); fig. 7, p. 722. By permission of Oxford University Press.

objects depicted in a picture appear to lie behind the picture plane. The picture plane is like a window through which you are looking at objects in the distance. The eye can only be at one place when the picture is constructed. That position is called the station point (Sedgwick, 1980, p. 40). The station point gives the spectator a point of view. Notice that a circle will appear as an ellipse on the picture plane when viewed from a particular station point. Changing the station point changes what will be represented in the picture, just as moving in relation to a window changes what you see through it. "As we approach a window we see more of the scene; as we move to the left, a portion of the scene on the left side becomes hidden by the window frame while more is revealed on the right, etc." (Sedgwick, 1980, p. 41). An artist using classical rules of perspective eliminates the third source of error mentioned by Pinker and Finke, which is attempting to draw parts of the scene from different vantage points, so that there is no consistent point of view.

Chambers and Reisberg (1985) argued that these and similar results from other studies suggest that mental images are not ambiguous: a mental image appears to be only one thing. If Chambers and Reisberg are right, then this would be one of the ways in which images differ from perceptions. However, Finke, Pinker, and Farah (1989) questioned the generality of Chambers and Reisberg's results. To test it, they had participants construct images in stages. For example, , participants would be asked to imagine a capital letter *H*, and then to imagine a capital letter *X* on top of the *H*. Follow these instructions yourself, and then inspect your image and see if you can detect any familiar forms in it. Participants often reported geometric shapes and letters such as *M* and *N*. This result is important because it means that more can be found in a mental image than whatever went into its construction (Shepard, 1978a). In the process of constructing an image, new properties may emerge. These are often referred to as **emergent properties** (e.g., Finke, 1996; Pinker & Finke, 1980).

emergent properties
New properties that emerge when a mental image is constructed.

Other researchers (e.g., Brandimonte & Gerbino, 1993; Hyman & Neisser, 1991; Peterson, Kihlstrom, Rose, & Glisky, 1992) have also found that images can be reinterpreted. An insightful study by Mast and Kosslyn (2002; Lyddy, 2002) shows how mental rotation can lead to a new interpretation of an image. They constructed the configuration shown in Figure 7.18, which can be seen as a young woman when upright and an older woman when rotated 180 degrees. Participants were first shown the figure in one of the two orientations and memorized it so that they would be able to draw it from memory. Participants were not told that the figure was reversible. They then imagined the figure rotated to different angles. Several participants discovered the alternate figure when their image had been rotated 180 degrees. The conclusion was that "at least some people can detect a previously unrecognized interpretation" of a mental image (Mast & Kosslyn, 2002, p. 69).

Young Woman   Old Woman

FIGURE 7.18 | A reversible figure

From: Mast, F.W., & Kosslyn, S.M. (2002). Copyright 2002. Reprinted by permission of Elsevier.

It has often been argued that imagery is an **analog form of representation** (e.g., Shepard, 1978, p. 135). An analog embodies the essential relationships of the thing it represents. Spence (1973) gave the following example of an analog device. A carpenter who is building a picket fence wants to make sure that the spaces between the pickets are equal. The best way to do this is to cut a stick as long as the desired space. Then put up the first picket and use the stick to place the next one. The stick is an analog of the distance. Similarly, mental images may be analogs of situations in the external world, useful not only for capturing essential relationships between things in the external world, but also for discovering new relationships.

analog form of representation hypothesis
The hypothesis that a mental image embodies the essential relationships of the thing it represents.

Egocentric Perspective Transformations

As Franklin and Tversky (1991) observed, reading a story produces a lot of mental imagery. To make their point, they quoted the following passage from Ernest Hemingway's 1927 story "The Snows of Kilimanjaro":

> Out of the window of the hospital you could see a field with tumble weed coming out of the snow, and a bare clay butte. . . . From the other window, if the bed was turned, you could see the town, with a little smoke above it, and the Dawson mountains looking like real mountains with the winter snow on them.

Did you experience any mental imagery while reading that passage? Did you imagine yourself located in the narrative? Could you locate the objects described relative to yourself?

In the Shepard and Metzler mental rotation task discussed earlier, participants were shown an image and then performed imaginary operations on it. By contrast, when we read a story, we typically construct an imaginary representation of the environment that it describes. In such a representation, some things are in front of you, some behind, some above, some below, some to the right, some to the left. Does it matter where things are located? For example, could you imagine something behind you as quickly as something ahead of you? Such tasks require egocentric perspective transformations, in which your point of view changes. Rather than imagining an object rotated in space, as in the Shepard and Metzler task, you must imagine yourself moving while the objects in the environment remain still (Zacks, Mires, Tversky, & Hazeltine, 2000).

In one of their experiments, Franklin and Tversky (1991) had participants read different narratives. Here is a fragment of one of the stories:

> You are . . . at the opera. . . . you are standing next to the railing of a . . . balcony, overlooking the first floor. Directly behind you, at your eye level is . . . a lamp . . . mounted on a nearby wall beyond the balcony, you see a large bronze plaque . . . sitting on a shelf directly to your right is a beautiful bouquet of flowers. . . (p. 65).

The story goes on quite a bit further, but you get the idea. If you had been a participant in this experiment, you would then have answered questions about the locations of the objects described. For example, was the lamp ahead of you, behind you, above you, below you, to your right, or to your left? Then you would have been asked to imagine yourself turned to face a different direction (e.g., 90 degrees to your left), and to answer the same questions.

All participants reported that they relied on mental imagery to recall the scene. Moreover, some questions are easier to answer than others. You can locate something quickly if it is above or below you. It takes longer to locate something behind you, perhaps because you have to imagine yourself turning around. Locating something that is to the right or left of you is also a relatively slow process. These results may reflect the fact that normally we imagine ourselves as being upright in a spatial framework that has one vertical (*above–below*) and two horizontal dimensions (*ahead–behind* and *left–right*) (Tversky, 2003). With respect to our bodies, *above–below* and *ahead–behind* are asymmetrical: our head is different from our feet, and our front is different from our back. However, our bodies are bilaterally symmetric: the left half of our body is the mirror image of the right half. Thus the two asymmetric dimensions are easily distinguished, but the symmetric dimension (*right–left*) is not. This symmetry may explain why we sometimes have so much difficulty remembering our right from our left (Bryant, Tversky, & Franklin, 1992; Franklin & Tversky, 1990, p. 74).

Controversy Over the Nature of Mental Imagery

An enormous amount of research has been done on mental imagery, and some critics (beginning with Pylyshyn, 1973) have argued that the subject does not warrant so much attention. At the centre of this long-standing controversy is the question of how knowledge about the world is represented in the mind. One view is that such knowledge is represented and stored in the form of propositions. If we accept this argument regarding propositional knowledge just to see where it leads, then what role might images play in cognition?

One possibility would be that images are *epiphenomenal*. As we noted in our discussion of the mind–brain issue in Chapter 2, an epiphenomenon is a by-product, or symptom, of something else. An example is the smoke that comes from a steam locomotive. The smoke is a by-product of the locomotive's operation and serves no function itself. Similarly, imagery may serve no function. Images might be merely decorative, like pictures on the wall of your room, and not essential aspects of the mind's functioning.

Pylyshyn (2002, 2003a, 2003b) argued that it is a mistake to believe that images are "two-dimensional moving pictures" on "the surface of your visual cortex" (Pylyshyn, 2003a, p. 114), which we scan in order to extract information. Rather, you imagine something by "considering what it would look like if you saw it" (p. 114). The process of imagining how objects would look from other viewpoints requires inference and is susceptible to error. A similar argument was made by Rock, Wheeler, and Tudor (1989), who presented evidence that mental rotation is accurate only in highly practised tasks. When the task requires the rotation of unfamiliar objects, such as twisted wire shapes, then inaccuracy is the norm. Perhaps people find it harder to make the correct inferences concerning what an unfamiliar object will look like when it is rotated. Deciding how things will look from different perspectives requires thought, and can be difficult in unfamiliar situations.

Naturally, those who are particularly intrigued by imagery find such criticisms unwarranted. They point out that imagery is interesting in its own right, regardless of its function (e.g., Kosslyn, 1980, p. 21; Kosslyn, Ganis, & Thompson, 2003; Kosslyn, Thomas, & Ganis, 2002, p. 201). Indeed, there is evidence that scores on the vividness of visual imagery questionnaire reflect the degree to which people consider vividness of visual imagery to be worth investigating (Reisberg, Pearson, & Kosslyn, 2003). The more vivid your own imagery, the more interested in imagery you're likely to be. The debate over the nature and function of imagery is sure to continue.

Cognitive Maps and Mental Models
Basic Properties of Cognitive Maps

It was Tolman (1948) who put cognitive maps on the map, so to speak. He believed that information from the environment was "worked over and elaborated . . . into a tentative, cognitive-like map of the environment. And it is this tentative map, indicating routes and paths and environmental relationships" (p. 193), that determines our behaviour. Tolman thought that broad and comprehensive cognitive maps were more useful than narrow maps. Narrow, overspecialized cognitive maps cannot contain information about more than a few routes through the environment. They may facilitate adaptation to specific environments, but they don't transfer well to new circumstances. For Tolman, a cognitive map was more useful if it gave its user a big picture of the environment and could be employed in a variety of situations.

The partial nature of our cognitive maps means that we are capable of making several interesting errors. For example, which of the following statements are true?

- Madrid (Spain) is farther north than Washington (District of Columbia).
- Seattle (US) is farther north than Montreal (Canada).
- The Pacific entrance of the Panama Canal is east of the Atlantic entrance.

In fact, *all* these statements are true (Stevens & Coupe, 1978, p. 423). The reason they may seem to be false can be seen by comparing the statements above with the following:

- Spain is farther north than the District of Columbia.
- The US is farther north than Canada.
- The Pacific Ocean is east of the Atlantic Ocean.

cognitive map
Information from the environment that is "worked over and elaborated . . . into a tentative, cognitive-like map . . . indicating routes and paths and environmental relationships" (Tolman).

All the preceding statements are untrue. Large geographic units (e.g., countries, states, counties) can, in general, have one relationship to one another, while some of their members (e.g., cities) can bear the opposite relationship to one another. Because our cognitive maps are simplified, we may assume that *all* members of a large geographic unit have the same relationship to *all* members of other large geographic units. Some people will totally reject the statement about the Atlantic and Pacific entrances of the Panama Canal until they have verified it for themselves on a map. Our cognitive maps are partly convenient fictions, designed to represent reality in a way that we think is useful but that may not be very accurate.

To illustrate this last point, draw a cognitive map of your campus showing the main *landmarks* (e.g., important buildings), *paths* (e.g., roads), and *boundaries* (e.g., streams), and get some classmates to do the same (Lynch, 1960). You may be surprised at how widely the maps they produce differ. What might account for the differences? For example, has one person been at your campus for several years and another for only a few months?

Cognitive Maps and the Hippocampus

Cognitive maps have been linked with hippocampal activity at least since the classic work of O'Keefe and Nadel (1978; Nadel & Hardt, 2004). Among the most direct sources of evidence for hippocampal involvement are studies relating the relative size of the hippocampus to the amount of knowledge required to successfully navigate in a complex environment. A particularly dramatic example of this relationship has been observed in London taxi drivers. To qualify for a licence, drivers are required to learn the routes that connect thousands of places in London—a task that takes two years on average. Every London taxi driver has a highly complex, detailed cognitive map of the city. Maguire et al. (2000) compared MRI brain scans of licensed London taxi drivers with those of non-taxi drivers. Not only was the posterior part of the hippocampus larger in taxi drivers than in the control group, but the increase varied with the number of years spent on the job. This finding indicated that it was the experience of driving a taxi that had led to the enlargement of the hippocampus, not an unusually large hippocampus that enabled the individual to become a taxi driver. In order to store the immense cognitive map required for the job, the posterior part of the hippocampus of taxi drivers becomes enlarged.

Egocentric Frames of Reference

There are at least two ways of finding our way through the environment. One is to use a cognitive map of the environment just as we use a real map, by locating our position on it and then figuring out how to proceed from there. This appears to be what London taxi drivers do. Another approach is to use an **egocentric frame of reference** (McNamara, Rump, & Werner, 2003). This means taking the sort of egocentric perspective discussed above: you imagine yourself at the centre of the action and use information available from your current perspective to orient yourself.

egocentric frame of reference
Using information available from our current perspective to orient ourselves.

Some aspects of egocentric frames of reference can be illustrated as follows. Draw the following situation, which is taken from Hutchins (1983, p. 209): "Go at dawn to a high place and point directly to the centre of the rising sun. That defines a line. Return to that same high place at noon and point again to the centre of the sun. That defines a second line." Your drawing probably will look something like Figure 7.19. Notice that this drawing defines the position of the sun relative to your position on the earth. The drawing suggests that you stay still while the sun moves overhead. We both know better, of course. Yet it's natural to represent the situation that way. It corresponds to the situation as it appears from our egocentric perspective and allows us to think about it easily.

Wang and Spelke (2000, 2002) suggest that we often use egocentric frames of reference when we navigate. This process does not require an enduring cognitive map that you consult as you travel. All it requires is a temporary representation that is continuously updated. One example is a process known as **path integration**, whereby our position in relation to an important location (e.g., home) is continuously updated as we move through the environment. Other animals and insects also appear to use egocentric forms of navigation. For example, "desert ants forage by traveling on new and apparently random routes and then return home on a direct path once food is found" (Wang & Spelke, 2002, p. 376). Similarly, in principle you can explore a novel environment (e.g., a city you are visiting as a tourist) while keeping track of where you are in relation to some important landmark (e.g., your hotel).

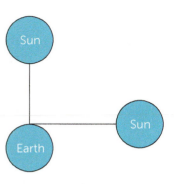

FIGURE 7.19 | Is this the relationship between the sun and an observer at dawn and at noon?

Cognitive Maps as Mental Models

A **mental model** is a representation of a situation that enables us to understand and reason about it (Gentner, 2002, p. 9683). We have mental models for a very wide range of situations, and we use them to describe, explain, and predict events (Rouse & Morris, 1986). For example, people often have mental models of the way a machine such as a vacuum cleaner works. DiSessa (1983) asked participants to "think of a vacuum cleaner whose nozzle you hold in your hand. If you put your hand over the nozzle, will the pitch of the sound you hear from the motor go up or down?" (p. 23). Ordinary people come up with different answers to this question. Some people think that the pitch will go down, and the speed of the motor will be reduced. This is because their mental model of the way a vacuum cleaner works suggests to them that placing a hand over the nozzle will interfere with the working of the motor and make it harder for the motor to run. Other people correctly say that the motor speed and the pitch will go up. The explanation they give is that, because the motor is being interfered with, it must put out more effort to overcome the resistance.

Notice that the vacuum cleaner models described above are quite anthropomorphic, attributing human characteristics to the machine (for example, the machine was represented as responding to interference by working harder). Mental models are often like this—"unscientific" and even "superstitious" (D.A. Norman, 1983, p. 8). However, they may still be useful for representing the world. One of their functions is to permit us to draw analogies between different domains (Gentner, 1983). Here is one person's mental model of how electricity works:

Question: When you plug in a lamp and it lights up, how does it happen?

Answer: . . . basically there is a pool of electricity that plug-in buys for you . . . the electricity goes into the cord for the appliance, for the lamp and flows up to—flows—I think of it as flowing because of the negative to positive images I have, and also because . . . a cord is a narrow contained entity like a river (Gentner & Gentner, 1983, p. 99).

path integration
The process whereby our position in relation to an important location is continuously updated as we move through the environment.

mental model theory
The theory that we construct a mental model of a given situation, on the basis of which we understand, reason, and draw conclusions about it.

The virtue of mental models is that they give us a way of representing and drawing inferences about the behaviour of things in a wide range of contexts. Of course, our mental models do not always lead us to draw the correct inference about what will happen in a particular situation. The mental model in Figure 7.19, for example, is based on an erroneous assumption. Mental models can be a source of error as well as of insight. We will explore mental models further in Chapter 11, when we look at reasoning.

Auditory Imagery

Although this chapter has focused primarily on visual imagery, it is possible to experience imagery in other sensory modalities, including audition (the sense of hearing; see Hubbard, 2010 for a review) and olfaction (the sense of smell; see Stevenson & Case, 2005a, for a review). In this section we will briefly consider auditory imagery.

Have you ever been listening to a familiar song when the sound switched off, but the song continued to "play" in your mind? If so, you've experienced auditory imagery, which is the experience of sound in your mind that is not caused by stimulation of the receptive cells in your ears (see Hubbard, 2010).

In an interesting study of auditory imagery, Kraemer, Macrae, Green, and Kelley (2005) had participants listen to different songs—familiar and unfamiliar, with lyrics and without—while lying in the fMRI machine, so that their brain activity could be recorded. Critically, segments of the songs were replaced with silence at various points. Kraemer et al. (2005) wanted to investigate whether participants would experience auditory imagery during the moments of silence, and if they did, how this would be reflected in their brain activity. Not surprisingly, when the songs were familiar, participants reported consciously continuing to "play" the song in their minds during the silent segments, but not when they were unfamiliar. This suggests that auditory imagery can occur spontaneously.

Auditory imagery during the familiar selections also showed different patterns of brain activation depending on whether or not they contained words. Specifically, imagery experienced during silent moments in familiar tunes that included words activated the auditory association area located on the superior temporal sulcus (STS), depicted in green in Figure 7.20. By contrast, imagery during silent moments in familiar music without words showed activation in the auditory association area that also "extended into the left primary auditory cortex" (PAC; Kraemer et al., 2005, p. 158), shown in red in Figure 7.20. These findings are interesting because these brain areas are normally involved in the perception of external auditory sounds. That is, the primary auditory cortex is typically associated with processing the basic ("low-level") aspects of external sound, such as pitch and timbre, whereas the auditory association cortex processes more elaborate aspects of sound. In the words of Kraemer et al. (2005, p. 158):

> . . . the extent of neural activity in the primary auditory cortex was determined by the linguistic features of the imagined experience. When semantic knowledge (that is, lyrics) could be used to generate the missing information, reconstruction terminated in auditory association areas. When this meaning-based route to reconstruction was unavailable (as in instrumentals), activity extended to lower-level regions of the auditory cortex, most notably the primary auditory cortex.

auditory imagery
The experience of sound in your mind that is not caused by stimulation of the receptive cells in your ears.

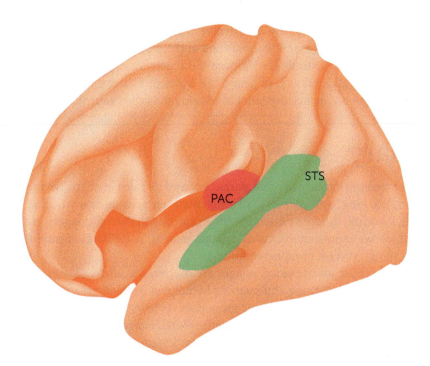

FIGURE 7.20 | Brain areas active during auditory imagery

PAC = primary auditory cortex; STS = superior temporal sulcus.

Reprinted by permission from Macmillan Publishers Ltd: *Nature*, 158 (10 March 2005), copyright (2005).

It seems, then, that auditory imagery uses the same neural apparatus that auditory perception does. And this isn't the only similarity between the two. In another study (Zatorre & Halpern, 1993) participants were shown a phrase from a familiar song on a computer screen with only two of the words presented in capital letters and the rest of the words shown in lowercase letters: for example: "dashing through the SNOW in a one-horse open SLEIGH, o'er the fields we go, laughing all the way" (Zatorre & Halpern, 1993, p. 224). The task was to judge whether the second capitalized word is sung at a higher or lower pitch than the first capitalized word. The researchers assumed that to make this judgment, participants would need to use their auditory imagery and imagine singing the song. Critically, the number of beats between the capitalized words (when they are sung) was varied. The results showed that participants' response times increased with the number of beats between the capitalized words. This result was consistent with the idea that participants were "playing" the song in their heads, pretty much in "real time." In other words, in both imagined and real ones, the more beats there are between two words, the longer it takes to get from one to the other. As you might have noticed, this experiment on auditory imagery is very similar to Kosslyn et al.'s (1978) experiments with mental imagery.

A particularly intriguing form of auditory imagery is the phenomenon known as an "earworm" (Halpern & Bartlett, 2011). An earworm is a conscious experience of sound—typically a short phrase of music—that seems to get stuck on replay in your head. Have you ever had this experience? According to a set of diary studies conducted by Halpern and Bartlett (2011), earworms are very common; they occur most often in the morning (about

earworm
A conscious experience of sound—typically a short phrase of catchy music—that seems to get stuck on replay in your head.

34 per cent of the time); almost always involve familiar songs (about 96 per cent of the time); and (despite the unpleasant connotations of the word "earworm") are usually enjoyable (about 83 per cent of the time; see Halpern & Bartlett, 2011, p. 426). So what triggers an earworm? Apparently all it takes is to hear a few notes of a catchy tune. To make the most of your auditory imagery, make sure you have happy music on your iPod!

Summary

In this chapter we have examined mental imagery and its roles in cognitive processes such as perception, learning, and memory. Behind much current research in this area is the influential dual-coding theory of Allan Paivio. According to Paivio, imagery is a non-verbal system by which we represent events as mental images. It exists alongside and often in reference to a verbal system of representation.

The defining properties of mental images are *concreteness*, *distinctiveness*, and *vividness*. These properties support learning and memory by helping us to organize incoming information into meaningful units. Sometimes the common ability to form mental images takes extraordinary forms, as with individuals who experience *eidetic imagery* or *synesthesia*. People with one common form of synesthesia associate particular letters or digits with particular colours.

Unlike static pictures, mental images are dynamic. They can be *mentally rotated*, moved, or scanned, often within an egocentric frame of reference. Mental images differ from perceptions in that they are unambiguous, appearing to be only one thing. Nevertheless, that one thing may contain emergent properties, resulting from the very process of constructing the mental image.

The functional importance of mental images has been hotly debated. Some research supports the *anticipatory* use of mental images to ready us for perceiving certain kinds of information. Other studies suggest that we use imagery in the form of *cognitive maps* as a way of working out environmental relationships and aiding memory. Another point of contention is the idea that image-processing is primarily a right hemisphere activity. To date, the evidence points to varied levels of engagement in both right and left hemispheres.

Finally, we considered auditory imagery. Earworms, in which part of a song plays over and over in your head, are a common example of auditory imagery. Auditory imagery involves the same areas of the brain that are typically active during auditory perception of external sounds.

CASE STUDY

Case Study Wrap-Up

In this chapter we have encountered several varieties of the condition known as synesthesia. We began with a description of time–space synesthesia, a subtype in which concepts of time take on external spatial locations. Later we described a subtype in which letters and numbers are associated with colour experiences (grapheme–colour synesthesia). At first glance, many of us may find these and other synesthetic experiences—like perceiving numbers in geometric forms or digits in very specific sizes (recall Daniel Tammet's experiences)—somewhat odd.

But if you think further about the intricacies of human imagery discussed in this chapter, perhaps synesthesia isn't so strange after all. The available evidence suggests that many people are able not only to create very *vivid* images in their minds, but even to *scan* them (recall Kosslyn's image scanning studies) and rotate them mentally (recall Shepard and Metzler's findings). Furthermore, just as synesthetes can use their synesthetic images to help them remember, say, a list of digits, most people can use image-based *mnemonic techniques* as memory aids. Finally, like time-spaces and number-forms, the *cognitive maps* that virtually all of us use have a clear spatial component.

Among the most striking characteristics of time–space synesthesia is the way some people with the condition experience time units as revolving around the body. But even that experience may not be so odd after all. As we have seen, projection of an image onto external space is also characteristic of *eidetic imagery*, and may occur in people with a high degree of *vividness of visual imagery*. Finally, think about this: when you look out onto the world, you experience your visual perceptions as though they are "out there in space." How can that be? In Chapter 3 we learned that light information comes into our eyes and then is processed by the visual areas of our brain. If that is the case, why don't we experience what we perceive as being "in our heads" rather than "out there in space"? It seems that our brains fashion an internal model or "image" of the world and "project" it "out there." Could that mean that the projection of images is not odd at all, but rather an inherent part of perception?

In the Know: Review Questions

1. Critique Paivio's dual-coding theory, paying attention to relevant experimental and neuropsychological evidence.
2. When it comes to memory, is distinctiveness always a good thing? Have you ever used the special places strategy? Have you ever failed to find something you hid in a special place?
3. What do synesthesia and eidetic imagery have in common? How do they differ from ordinary imagery?
4. Discuss the similarities and differences between mental rotation, mental scanning, and egocentric perspective transformations.
5. Compare and contrast cognitive maps and egocentric frames of reference.
6. Give an example of auditory imagery. What areas of the brain are active in such experiences?

Key Concepts

analog form of representation hypothesis

apoptosis

auditory imagery

categorical distance

chromesthesia

cognitive dedifferentiation

cognitive map

concreteness (Paivio's sense)

concurrent

cross-modal effects

distinctiveness hypothesis

dual-coding theory

earworm

egocentric frame of reference

egocentric perspective transformations

eidetic imagery

emergent properties

icon

image as anticipation hypothesis

imagens

imagery (Paivio's sense)
inducer
left and right hemispheres theory
logogens
mental model theory
mental rotation
metamemory
method of loci
mnemonic techniques
number forms
objective distance

path integration
propositional knowledge
    hypothesis
spatial framework
special places strategy
strong synesthetes
synesthesia
time spaces
vividness of visual imagery
weak synesthetes
von Restorff effect

Links to Other Chapters

distinctiveness
Chapter 6 (levels of processing)

emergent properties
Chapter 2 (Sperry)
Chapter 11 (mental models)

mental models
Chapter 11 (mental models and deductive
    reasoning)

vividness of visual imagery
Chapter 8 (perceptual symbol systems)

Further Reading

Halpern (1988) investigated mental scanning for the auditory imagery we associate with familiar songs. As she pointed out, an auditory image has different locations, just as a visual image does, and (like the songs you actually hear) imagined songs have a beginning, middle, and end. Try imagining the song *Happy Birthday to You*. You start at the beginning ("Happy birthday to you, Happy birthday to you . . ."), move to the next line ("Happy birthday, dear . . ."), and finish with the last line ("Happy birthday to you"). In other words, auditory imagery is extended in time just as visual imagery is extended in space. This point is developed further in Cupchik, Philips, and Hill (2001).

Another fascinating history of mnemonic techniques is Carruthers (1990). Eskritt, Lee, and Donald (2001) explore how the development of literacy has changed our strategies for remembering.

Under certain circumstances, our ability to recall things we have learned can actually improve as we attempt to recall them on successive occasions. This phenomenon is called *hypermnesia*. Defined by Payne (1987) as "improvements in net recall levels associated with increasing retention intervals," hypermnesia was discovered many years ago (Ballard, 1913), but M.H. Erdelyi rekindled interest in it. Erdelyi argued that imagery leads initially to better recall and later to hypermnesia. See, for example, Erdelyi and Becker (1974) and Erdelyi and Kleinbard (1978). However, the role of imagery in hypermnesia has also been called into question. See, for example, Mulligan (2002).

Shepard (1978) explores mental imagery as an aid to creativity. For an autobiographical note on the convergence of the author's interests in drawing and the mind, see Shepard (1990).

Grasping a New Concept

It was January 2010 and the hype had reached a fever pitch. Rumours had been circulating for weeks that Steve Jobs, founder and CEO of Apple Inc., was going to introduce a new product at a press event in San Francisco. Or was he? No one could be sure with Steve. And that was a big part of the appeal. Steve Jobs loved to surprise people with his revolutionary devices—from the original Apple 1 personal computer way back in 1976 to all the iPods, iPhones, and iPads that are now part of everyday life—often introducing them just before the end of a show with a tantalizing "Oh, and one more thing . . ."

Still, the excitement in 2010 felt different. It wasn't just that no one knew *if* Jobs would introduce the new product—a similar uncertainty had existed for the iPod and the iPhone. No, the difference was that in the past people had known what the product, if it was indeed

introduced, *would* be. That's not to say that they knew exactly how it would look—not at all. But they knew how to conceptualize it. They had known that the iPod would be an MP3 player, for instance, and the iPhone a smartphone. But the new device—rumoured to be something between an iPhone and a laptop—had people flummoxed. What was it exactly? How should they *conceive* of it? Should they think of it as a laptop? Or as something more along the lines of a writing tablet, like the Microsoft Tablet PC, or the Newton MessagePad 100, which Apple had introduced many years before, and which had failed terribly?

Fast forward to the moment when Steve Jobs steps onstage. He introduces the iPad as offering the most extraordinary web browsing experience possible, better than any smart phone or laptop. Without a hint of exaggeration, he claims that it's like holding the Internet in your own hands. There is extensive coverage both in the mainstream media and in online blogs and reviews. But as the dust begins to settle, it seems that people are still unsure what the iPad is. Some hail it as the successor to the laptop, some think of it as an eReader for books. Others say it's for watching movies and playing games that pit angry birds against pigs, or plants against zombies. Others still predict that it is doomed to fail because people don't know what it is—that is, they don't know how to *conceptualize* it.

As you will see in this chapter, there are many theories about how people acquire new concepts. While you're reading it, ask yourself what these theories might have to say about the iPad. How would they go about conceptualizing it? Would they have predicted the uncertainty that surrounded its introduction?

FIGURE 8.1 | Steve Jobs

The Classical Approach

A milestone in the study of cognition was the publication, in 1956, of Bruner, Goodnow, and Austin's book *A Study of Thinking*, in which they described a series of experiments exploring how people acquire concepts. A concept is a general category into which we can sort any number of particular instances. The object you're looking at now, for example, is

8

Concepts

Chapter Contents

Chapter Objectives

- To review and evaluate classical approaches to the study of concept attainment.
- To review experiments used to study complex rules.
- To describe vertical and horizontal dimensions of concept organization.
- To outline how cognition is embodied.
- To examine and provide evidence for the theory of idealized cognitive models.
- To consider how folk biology relates to concept attainment.

Getty Images/Yamanda Taro

A fascinating study of the ways in which blind people represent space can be found in Kennedy (1993).

Carruthers, M. (1990). *The book of memory: A study of memory in medieval culture.* New York: Cambridge University Press.

Cupchik, G.C., Philips, K., & Hill, D.S. (2001). Shared processes in spatial rotation and musical permutation. *Brain and Cognition, 46*, 373–382.

Erdelyi, M.H., & Becker, J. (1974). Hypermnesia for pictures: Incremental memory for pictures but not for words in multiple recall trials. *Cognitive Psychology, 6*, 159–171.

Erdelyi, M.H., & Kleinbard, J. (1978). Has Ebbinghaus decayed with time? The growth of recall (hypermnesia) over days. *Journal of Experimental Psychology: Human Learning and Memory, 4*, 275–289.

Eskritt, M., Lee, K., & Donald, M. (2001). The influence of symbolic literacy on memory: Testing Plato's hypothesis. *Canadian Journal of Experimental Psychology, 55*, 39–41.

Halpern, A.R. (1988). Mental scanning in auditory imagery for songs. *Journal of Experimental Psychology: Learning, Memory, and Cognition, 14*, 434–443.

Kennedy, J.M. (1993). *Drawing & the blind: Pictures to touch.* New Haven: Yale University Press.

Mulligan, N.W. (2002). The emergent generation effect and hypermnesia: Influences of semantic and nonsemantic generation tasks. *Journal of Experimental Psychology: Learning, Memory, and Cognition, 28*, 541–554.

Payne, D.G. (1987). Hypermnesia and reminiscence in recall: A historical and empirical review. *Psychological Bulletin, 101*, 5–27.

Shepard, R.N. (1978). The externalization of mental images and the act of creation. In B.S. Randhawa & W.E. Coffman (Eds.), *Visual learning, thinking and communication* (pp. 133–187). New York: Academic Press.

Shepard, R.N. (1990). *Mind sights.* New York: Freeman.

an instance of the concept *book*. It qualifies as a book because of the basic *attributes* it has in common with other instances of the concept *book* (pages, print, a cover), regardless of differences in the *values* of those attributes: size of pages, colour of print, type of cover (hard or paper), and so on.

Bruner et al. (1956) were concerned with the different ways in which attributes define concepts. A *conjunctive concept* is one defined by a simple conjunction of two or more attributes, but there are two other types that are more complex. A *disjunctive concept* is defined by one of two or more possible sets of attributes. For example, Canadian citizenship is a disjunctive concept in that there are three ways of acquiring it: by being born in Canada, *or* by being born abroad to a Canadian parent, *or* by becoming a naturalized citizen. Similarly in baseball, a strike is *either* "a pitch that is across the plate and between the batter's knees and shoulders *or* it is any pitch at which the batter strikes but fails to send the ball into the field" (Bruner et al., 1956, p. 43). The third type of concept is *relational*. Here it is the relationship between attributes that determines the class to which an event will be assigned. The concept of marriage, for example, is a relationship between two people (Holloway, 1978).

A study of thinking inspired many researchers to design experiments exploring how people acquire concepts based on the attributes that define membership in a category. The original experiments conducted by Bruner et al. made use of the cards shown in Figure 8.2. Suppose each card either is or is not an instance of a particular concept. If it *is* an instance of a particular concept, then it is a *positive instance*. Thus a simple *conjunctive concept* might be *black* and *square*. Any card with these two attributes would be a positive instance. This means that all the cards in column 6 in Figure 8.2 are positive instances. If a card does *not* contain the right attributes, then it is a *negative instance*. Thus the top leftmost card is a negative instance. In this example, attributes such as the number of figures on a card are irrelevant.

To understand why something is a positive instance of a simple conjunctive concept like the one in the preceding example, you need to know which attributes are critical for membership in the concept and which ones are not. You might try to figure this out by noting which attributes recur in positive instances. If an attribute is present in all positive

DISCOVERY LAB

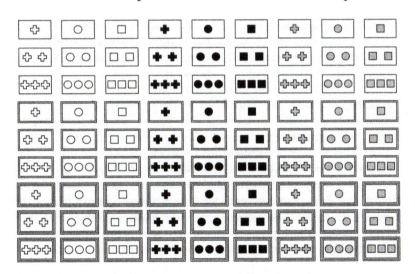

FIGURE 8.2 | The Bruner cards

From: Bruner, J.S., Goodnow, J., & Austin, G.A. (1956). p. 42. Copyright 1956 by John Wiley & Sons, Inc. Reprinted by permission of the author.

criterial attribute

An attribute that is required in order for something to qualify as an instance of a concept.

instances, then you might conclude that it is a **criterial attribute**: its presence is required if something is to be considered a member of the concept. All attributes that do not recur in positive instances would be irrelevant.

The process of including recurring attributes and excluding non-recurring ones is the process of *abstraction*. According to *The Oxford English Dictionary*, *to abstract* originally meant "to take away from." When you abstract the recurrent attributes from a set of positive instances you take them away from all the others. The recurrent attributes form a set that defines the concept.

Sometimes the process of abstraction is likened to a *composite photograph* (e.g., Galton, 1883). Imagine that you had negatives of photographs of everyone in your family for several generations and laid them one on top of the other. Then, if you held the pile of negatives up to the light, the recurrent attributes or features of the individual family members would stand out because they would be darker than the non-recurrent features. In this way you could abstract the recurrent features. This abstract set of features would not belong to any one person. Rather, it would define the concept of what a member of your family looks like. (Incidentally, composite photographs were quite popular in the nineteenth century. It was believed that a composite image showed what a "typical" family member would look like.) The notion that concepts are like composite photographs is somewhat problematic, however. Think of your own family: do all members share some physical attributes, or are there some who don't look anything like the others? What does the idea of "family resemblance" really mean?

Concept Formation Tasks

In their experiments Bruner et al. used two contrasting tasks to find out what strategies participants would use to acquire a simple conjunctive concept (e.g., "one black square"). In the first kind, known as a selection task, the experimenter would give you, the participant, one of the cards shown in Figure 8.2 (e.g., a card with one black square and a single border), tell you it was a positive instance of the concept, and challenge you to figure out what that concept was. Then you would be invited to choose any card you liked and the experimenter would tell you whether that card was a positive or a negative instance of the concept. This is called a **selection task**, because the participants select the instances they will use to figure out the concept that the experimenter has in mind. Which card would you choose next? What reason would you give for your choice?

selection task

A concept formation task in which the participant selects instances from those presented by the experimenter.

One way of approaching this task is to choose an instance that differs from the first positive instance by only one feature. Thus you might choose a card with one white square and a single border. If the experimenter told you that your choice was a positive instance, what would you conclude? It must be that the attribute that has changed from the first positive instance is not included in the concept, because when it changes the instance remains positive. By contrast, if the experimenter told you that your choice was a negative instance, what would you know? Because the card you have chosen differs from the first positive instance in only one value of one attribute, that attribute must be criterial and "black" must be part of the concept. The colour of the figure is important because, when it changes, the instance changes from positive to negative.

Notice that the process we are describing is not a passive one in which the attributes that make up the concept are automatically abstracted after you have seen enough instances. Rather, you are actively formulating hypotheses and selecting instances to see if your hypotheses are correct. That is, you are using a strategy to try to discover what the concept is. The particular strategy we have been describing here is called conservative focusing because, when you use it, you focus on one attribute at a time and select instances that vary only in that particular attribute.

This was not the only strategy that Bruner et al.'s participants used in this task. Among the others were focus gambling, simultaneous scanning, and successive scanning. In the case of focus gambling, you select instances that differ from the first positive instance in more than one attribute. You may get lucky and be able to eliminate a number of hypotheses quickly. Thus if, after being shown a card with one black square and one border, you choose two black squares with two borders and it turns out to be a positive instance, then you know that the number of squares and the number of borders are irrelevant. Simultaneous scanning involves keeping in mind all possible hypotheses and trying to eliminate as many as possible with each instance selection. This places a very great load on memory, because you must always keep in mind which hypotheses could be correct and which have been proven incorrect. Successive scanning is less demanding. The participant formulates a single hypothesis and tests it by selecting instances until the correct hypothesis emerges. Thus if "black square" was your hypothesis, you would keep selecting cards consistent with that hypothesis until it was disconfirmed. Then you would formulate another hypothesis and carry on as before.

Reception Strategies

The second task used by Bruner et al. is called a reception task. Here the order in which instances are presented is controlled by the experimenter. Under this condition many of the participants in their study appeared to adopt one of two strategies, either wholist or partist.

With a wholist strategy, your first hypothesis is that all attributes in the first positive instance are included in the concept. If the next instance confirms that hypothesis, then you retain it. However, if the next positive instance is inconsistent with that hypothesis, then you form a new one that is consistent with whatever the old hypothesis and the current instance have in common.

With a partist strategy, your initial hypothesis includes only a part of the first positive instance. Then you maintain that hypothesis until you receive some disconfirming evidence. At that point you change your hypothesis to make it consistent with all the instances you have previously seen. This strategy, in its ideal form, places a heavy load on memory, because you must recall all previous instances in order to successfully revise your hypothesis.

The Bruner et al. study stimulated a great deal of research. Some of this work was concerned with the logical relations between different types of concepts (e.g., Hunt & Hovland, 1960; Neisser & Weene, 1962). There are some excellent reviews of this period of concept research (e.g., Bourne, 1966; Pikas, 1966). Nevertheless, psychologists gradually began to have doubts about the legitimacy of this kind of research.

Criticisms of Classical Concept Research

Experiments like the ones Bruner et al. conducted are reminiscent of certain kinds of games. In fact, there is a real similarity between the Bruner task and the popular game Mastermind (Best, 2001; Laughlin, Lange, & Adamopoulos, 1982). In Mastermind one player uses coloured pegs to create a code that another player must guess by proposing

conservative focusing
A concept formation strategy of actively formulating hypotheses and selecting instances to see if your hypotheses are correct by focusing on one attribute at a time and by selecting instances that vary only in that attribute.

focus gambling
The concept formation strategy of selecting instances that vary from the first positive instance in more than one attribute.

simultaneous scanning
The concept formation strategy of keeping in mind all possible hypotheses and trying to eliminate as many as possible with each instance selection.

successive scanning
The concept formation strategy of formulating a single hypothesis and testing it by selecting instances until the correct hypothesis emerges.

reception task
A concept formation task in which the instances presented to the participant are chosen by the experimenter.

wholist strategy
A concept formation strategy, used in reception tasks, in which you initially hypothesize that all attributes are members of the concept.

partist strategy
A concept formation strategy, used in reception tasks, in which you initially hypothesize that only some attributes are members of the concept.

possible solutions (recorded with pegs on a board) and receiving feedback on their accuracy. Similarly, in the Bruner task the experimenter is the code-maker and the participants are the code-breakers. The participants try to read the experimenter's mind and guess the code; then the experimenter provides feedback that the participants can use to tell how "warm" or "cold" their guesses are.

When the Bruner task is described in these terms, it begins to sound rather artificial, and by the early 1970s many psychologists had begun to question this kind of laboratory study of concepts. Aren't real-world concepts more complex than the ones studied in a Bruner-type task? We saw in Chapter 4 that some techniques for studying attention have greater ecological validity than the kind that rely on contrived laboratory contexts. If you want to understand how people actually acquire and use concepts, perhaps there is a better way to go about it.

One way might be to continue studying artificial concepts (because that gives you more experimental control over their properties) but to try to make those concepts resemble real-world concepts in important ways. Another would be to give up studying artificial concepts and concentrate on studying concepts that people actually use.

Learning Complex Rules

Consider the diagram in Figure 8.3. It is an example of a *finite state grammar*. Such diagrams may also be called *railroad diagrams*. The reason for the latter name becomes clear if you imagine that each number in the diagram is a railroad station and each arrow is a track that you can follow from one station to another. The tracks go only one way, so you have to travel in the direction indicated by the arrow. All journeys begin at 1 and end at 4, 5, or 6. Each track is labelled by a particular letter, and some are even called by the same letter. Finally, some tracks are recursive: they go back to the place where they started.

The finite state grammar in Figure 8.3 is really a set of rules for generating strings of letters. It's capable of generating all the strings of letters listed below the diagram (and several

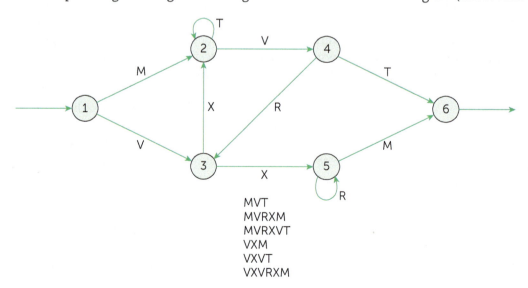

MVT
MVRXM
MVRXVT
VXM
VXVT
VXVRXM

FIGURE 8.3 | A finite state grammar

From: Reber, A.S., & Allen, R. (1978). Copyright 1978 by Elsevier Science Publishers. Reprinted by permission.

others as well). These are letter strings that are consistent with this particular grammar. However, a string like VXRT would be inconsistent with this particular grammar.

Suppose you were asked to distinguish between those strings of letters that are consistent with the grammar (positive instances) and those that are inconsistent with it (negative instances). This concept task would require you to know the grammar in order to be able to make the proper distinctions.

As part of their investigation into the way people acquire knowledge about artificial grammars, Reber and his associates (1967; Allen & Reber, 1980; Reber & Allen, 1978; Reber, Allen, & Regan, 1985; Reber & Lewis, 1977) explored the distinction between implicit and explicit learning. For an illustration of implicit learning, suppose you show one group of participants some letter strings like those in Figure 8.3 and ask them to memorize as many of them as possible, but don't tell them that the strings follow certain rules. This group would represent the implicit learning condition. Now suppose you do tell a second group of participants that the letter strings follow certain rules and ask them to figure out what those rules are. This group would represent the explicit learning condition.

Which group do you think would do better at telling grammatical from non-grammatical letter strings? One way of finding out would be to show both groups a set containing both grammatical and ungrammatical letter strings and then ask them to identify the strings with the same structure as the first set of strings they had seen. It turns out that the implicit learning condition leads to a significant amount of rule-learning. Sometimes implicit learning even leads to better performance than explicit learning does.

This result is surprising because it suggests that people who are not trying to learn the rule structure can learn it at least as well as those who are consciously trying to learn it. Rather than actively forming and testing hypotheses, the people in the implicit learning group are unconsciously abstracting the structure of the grammar. Perhaps the implicit learning group is acquiring knowledge unconsciously and more efficiently than the explicit learning group.

According to Reber, people who learn implicitly have a vague sense of what is grammatical and what is not without being able to say specifically what the grammatical structure is. The higher the level of performance, the better the participants' ability to say what they have learned tends to be. However, implicit learners' knowledge of what they have learned is largely *tacit*: they know it without necessarily being able to say exactly what it is.

According to Reber (1989, 1990; Reber, Walkenfeld, & Hernstadt, 1991), his work shows that the **cognitive unconscious** plays an important role in cognition; he has also suggested that "implicit and unconscious cognitive processes appeared early in our evolutionary history; consciousness is a late arriver on the phylogenetic scene" (Reber, 1990, p. 342). One implication of Reber's analysis is that conscious mental processes are associated with relatively recent forms of cognition. Reber, Walkenfeld, and Hernstadt (1991) argued that what we call "academic intelligence" is a form of cognition that has evolved relatively recently. Examples would include the ability to solve arithmetic problems and answer vocabulary questions of the kind used in standard IQ tests. These tests measure explicit, as opposed to implicit, cognitive abilities. Reber, Walkenfeld, and Hernstadt hypothesized that explicit cognitive abilities would predict performance on a task requiring explicit cognition, but not performance on a task requiring implicit cognition. To test this hypothesis, they gave participants a standard IQ test, as well as tests of implicit and explicit cognition. The implicit task was similar to the finite state grammar task we looked at

implicit vs explicit learning
Learning that takes place unintentionally versus learning that takes place intentionally.

cognitive unconscious hypothesis
The hypothesis that implicit learning represents an evolutionarily primitive form of unconscious cognition.

above. The explicit task involved choosing the correct letter to complete a series of letters such as ABCBCDCDE (you can probably figure out that the right answer is D). As predicted, the correlation between scores on the IQ test and scores on the explicit task was much higher than the correlation between IQ scores and the implicit task. Moreover, there was only a small correlation between scores on the implicit and explicit tasks.

Reber concluded that the implicit cognitive system is very old in evolutionary terms and has not changed for a long time. "Once an adaptive, functional system evolves, and . . . the system is broadly operational in diverse environments, there is no adaptive value in change" (Reber, Walkenfeld, & Hernstadt, 1991, p. 894; see also Reber, 1997; Reber, Allen & Regan, 1985). Explicit cognition is more recent and less fixed by evolutionary processes. Consequently, although people differ widely in terms of explicit cognitive abilities, they do not differ very much in terms of implicit cognitive processes. Implicit cognition is a process in which we all share equally, according to Reber.

However, Dulany, Carlson, and Dewey (1984, 1985) argued that this interpretation was not justified. In a replication of an implicit learning experiment, they found that participants who had learned an artificial grammar implicitly were indeed able to formulate hypotheses about its underlying rules. Although their hypotheses were not perfect, the novel rules they consciously generated were in fact correlated with the actual rules. If their behaviour was under the control of those informal but nevertheless conscious rules, then Reber's emphasis on unconscious processes was mistaken.

Dulany, Carlson, and Dewey's argument has been refined and extended by others (e.g., Cleeremans, Destrebecqz, & Boyer, 1998). In a series of studies, Shanks and his colleagues (e.g., Kinder, Shanks, Cock, & Timney, 2003; Shanks, 2004; Tunney & Shanks, 2003) have presented additional evidence that implicit learning is accompanied by awareness (i.e., it is not unconscious). In one study, Tunney and Shanks (2003) had participants learn an artificial grammar implicitly, following a procedure similar to the one that Reber used. However, in addition to judging whether a letter string was grammatical or ungrammatical, participants had to indicate how confident they were that their judgment was correct. If they were more confident of correct judgments than incorrect ones, that would suggest that they had some awareness of the basis for their decisions; or, to put it another way, if they were aware of the reason for a particular decision, they would express confidence in it, but if they were unsure, they would not. If confidence ratings were unrelated to the correctness of their judgments, that would indicate that participants were unaware of what they had learned. As it turned out, the confidence ratings were related to the accuracy of the judgments, suggesting that participants did indeed have some conscious awareness of the basis for their decisions.

This discussion of implicit learning may remind you of *implicit memory* (Chapter 5); you will also hear echoes of it in Chapter 13's discussion of *implicit perception* and the boundary between conscious and unconscious processes. Deciding whether a process is conscious or unconscious remains an extremely difficult methodological problem.

Wittgenstein's Analysis of Concepts

Up to this point we have considered concepts that have a definite rule structure. But is that the case with the concepts we use in everyday life? The philosopher Wittgenstein (1953) was interested in this question, and his approach to it was very influential both in philosophy and in psychology. In the following quotation, Wittgenstein is speaking to the question, "What do all members of a category have in common?" For example, what do all vegetables have in common that makes them all vegetables? Or what do all pieces of furniture have in common that makes them all furniture? Read his answer carefully:

> I am saying that these phenomena have no one thing in common which makes us use the same word for all—but that they are related to one another in many different ways. Consider for example the proceedings we call "games." I mean board-games, card-games, ball-games, Olympic games, and so on. What is common to them all? Don't say: "There must be something common, or they would not be called 'games'"—but look and see whether there is anything common to all.
>
> And the result of this examination is: we see a complicated network of similarities overlapping and criss-crossing: sometimes overall similarities, sometimes similarities of detail.
>
> And I can think of no better expression to characterize these similarities than "family resemblances"; for the various resemblances between members of a family: build, features, color of eyes, gait, temperament, etc. etc. overlap and criss-cross in the same way.—And I shall say: "games form a family" (Wittgenstein, 1953, pp. 31–32).

Several ideas in this passage are worth noting. The most important is that the members of a category may not share any common features. Rather, their attributes may constitute a complicated network of overlapping features. This is a part of what we mean when we say that the members of a category bear a **family resemblance** to one another. Individual instances of a concept may shade into one another without any clearly definable boundary to the concept itself. Wittgenstein's example of the game concept illustrates this point nicely. Even if there were some activities that could not be considered games, it would still be difficult to say precisely where the concept of *game* begins and ends.

> *family resemblance*
> Instances of concepts that possess overlapping features, without any features being common to all.

Wittgenstein's philosophical analysis is open to the criticism that it is based only on his intuitions and may not be true for everyone (Nichols, 2004). However, Wittgenstein held his philosophical observations to be a reflection of the way ordinary people use concepts. For that reason, some psychologists have wanted to explore Wittgenstein's insights by examining the way ordinary people use concepts. Eleanor Rosch is well known for having taken this next step.

Rosch and Prototypicality

In some of her earliest studies, Rosch (formerly Heider) (Heider, 1971a, 1971b; Heider & Olivier, 1972) was interested in the structure of colour categories. Colour is a fascinating topic, and we will consider it again in Chapter 9, in relation to language. For now, we'll just note that some hues are better examples of a particular colour category than others. For example, some hues to which English-speakers apply the word *red* seem "redder" than others. In other words, some reds are more **prototypical** than others. Colour is not the only category in which this is true. Some breeds of dog (such as retrievers) are more representative of the

> *prototypical*
> Representative of a pattern or category.

category "dog" than others (such as Pekingese). Notice that, in this respect, natural concepts are unlike the artificial concepts with which we began this chapter. In the case of the Bruner cards, all cards with the attributes "black" and "square" are equally acceptable as examples of the concept "black square."

Rosch went on to develop a highly influential view of the nature of concepts. In doing so, she formulated two principles that she believed underlie the way we use concepts (Rosch, 1978): cognitive economy and perceived world structure.

Rosch's principle of cognitive economy refers to the constant effort to balance two opposing tendencies: towards differentiation and simplification. On one hand, we want to maximize the amount of information available to us by organizing it in as many categories as possible. The more categories we have, the more distinctions we can make. Taken to its logical conclusion, this principle would lead to the creation of a separate category for every event in the world. Of course, if that were the case, why have any categories at all?

On the other hand, one key reason for creating categories is to reduce the amount of information that we have to deal with. Although we want to be able to discriminate between events in the world, we also want to be able to group them together. In general, people try to make concepts as simple as possible (Feldman, 2003). We can promote simplicity by ignoring differences between events and focusing on similarities. That way, many events that are different in some respects but similar in others can be treated as members of the same class. However, this tendency towards simplification has to be balanced against the necessity for differentiation. This tension between simplicity and complexity can create problems, as described in Box 8.1.

Rosch's second principle, perceived world structure, refers to the fact that some combinations of attributes tend to occur more frequently than other combinations. For example, animals that have wings also tend to have feathers and tend not to be covered with fur. Rosch contrasted this example with the sort of attribute relations used in artificial concept experiments. The Bruner cards in Figure 8.2, for example, do not have **correlated attributes**. Rather, the attributes of colour, form, number, and so on are orthogonal, or uncorrelated. Thus a black object is just as likely to be a square as it is to be a circle. This is another way in which artificial concepts differ from natural concepts. In the real world, attributes tend to cluster.

correlated attributes
The hypothesis that some combinations of attributes tend to occur more frequently than other combinations.

Vertical and Horizontal Dimensions

Rosch suggested that the principles of *cognitive economy* and *perceived world structure* lead us to organize concepts in a system that has both vertical and horizontal dimensions. The vertical dimension refers to the level of inclusiveness of the category: for example, *furniture* is a more inclusive category than *chair*, which is a more inclusive category than *kitchen chair*. Thus the vertical dimension refers to how general the concept is. By contrast, the horizontal dimension distinguishes between different concepts at the same level of inclusiveness: for example, *dog* and *cat* are concepts at roughly the same level of generality.

The Vertical Dimension

It's no accident that the example given above (*furniture, chair, kitchen chair*) has three levels of inclusiveness. This is just what Rosch found in her studies of concepts. The three levels are

CONSIDER THIS
BOX 8.1
The Downside of Categories

Suppose that at the beginning of the baseball season the Toronto Blue Jays are favoured to win the World Series. However, since there will also be a number of strong American-based teams with an excellent chance to win, and since Toronto is the only Canadian city with a team in the league, it would also be true that a team from an American city is likely to win the World Series. The reason for this apparent contradiction is that there are two different levels of category in this example, and the prediction we make will depend on the level we choose: the subordinate level of individual teams or the superordinate level of the countries to which these teams belong. If you're betting on which team will win, then Toronto is the best pick. However, if you're betting on which *country* will win, then you should put your money on an American team. This is an example of what Lagnado and Shanks (2003, p. 158) call **misaligned hierarchies**, in which a "judgment made with respect to one level of hierarchy" (Toronto will probably win) "may suggest one conclusion" (bet on Toronto) "whereas a . . . judgment made at a different level of hierarchy" (an American team will probably win) "may suggest a contrasting conclusion" (bet on an American team). Lagnado and Shanks (2003, p. 173) conclude that people

> do not just consider the most probable category, but commit in some way to its truth. We believe that this generalizes to many real world situations. Faced with uncertain information

about multiple categories, people adopt a shortcut strategy that focuses on just the most probable pathway, and neglects the less probable alternatives. This can empower their inferential capabilities, but will sometimes lead to error.

The title of this box is taken from an article by Murphy (2003), who drew out some of the implications of the Lagnado and Shanks study. He suggested that we may habitually use what Lagnado and Shanks call the **commitment heuristic** because we so often need to make decisions rapidly. Suppose you're speeding along the highway and see a car behind you in the distance. You think it may be a police car, but you aren't sure. If you decide that it is a police car and slow down, then you may avoid the ticket that you would have received if you'd waited until you knew for sure. Although the commitment heuristic may lead us into error in some situations, it may be of value in others. "One does not overuse a heuristic that is useless; one overuses one that has proved invaluable in the past" (Murphy, 2003, p. 514).

misaligned hierarchies
Judgments made at one level suggest one conclusion while judgments made at another level suggest a contrasting conclusion.

commitment heuristic
A strategy in which we commit ourselves to the belief that something is true when it is only likely to be true.

called **superordinate**, **basic**, and **subordinate**. For examples, see Table 8.1. There is considerable evidence to support the idea of three levels. For example, in one experiment, Rosch, Mervis, Gray, Johnson, and Boyes-Braem (1976) asked participants to list all the attributes for concepts such as those in Table 8.1. Basic-level concepts had more attributes in common than did those at the superordinate level. In another experiment, participants were asked to describe their body movements when interacting with objects. Objects in superordinate categories showed fewer common movements than did categories at the basic level. For example, what can you say about actions that go with clothing? Not much, right? But how about pants? You can probably imagine a fairly clear sequence of actions associated with

superordinate, basic, and subordinate levels (Rosch)
Levels of inclusiveness of a concept, as in *tree*, *oak*, and *live oak*.

TABLE 8.1 | Different Levels of Concept of Objects

Superordinate	Basic Level	Subordinates
musical instrument	guitar	bass guitar, classical guitar
	piano	grand piano, upright piano
	drum	kettle drum, bass drum
fruit	apple	Delicious apple, McIntosh apple
	peach	freestone peach, clingstone peach
	grape	Concord grape, green seedless grape
tool	hammer	ball-peen hammer, claw hammer
	saw	hack hand saw, cross-cutting hand saw
	screwdriver	Phillips screwdriver, flat-head screwdriver
clothing	pants	Levi's, double-knit pants
	socks	knee socks, ankle socks
	shirt	dress shirt, knit shirt
furniture	table	coffee table, dining-room table
	lamp	floor lamp, desk lamp
	chair	kitchen chair, living-room chair
vehicle	car	sports car, four-door sedan
	bus	city bus, cross-country bus
	truck	pick-up truck, tractor-trailer truck

Adapted from: Rosch, E.H., Mervis, C.B., Gray, W.D., Johnson, D.M., & Boyes-Braem, P. (1976). Basic objects in natural categories. *Cognitive Psychology, 8*, 382–439. Copyright 1976 by Academic Press. Reprinted by permission of Elsevier.

pants. Subordinate categories, such as Levi's, have common movements as well, but they do not constitute an important difference over basic-level categories. Interestingly, Rosch also showed that children name basic-level categories accurately before they name superordinate categories. Thus words like *chair* are acquired earlier than words like *furniture*.

Basic-level concepts strike an important balance between the highly inclusive superordinate concepts and the highly differentiated subordinate concepts. Yet Rosch often noted that the level of a particular concept could change, depending on the sophistication of the person assigning the category. Thus *piano* is a basic-level object for most people. But what about musicians? Perhaps they perceive more differences among pianos, so that what is a basic-level object for a non-musician may be a superordinate-level object for a musician. Palmer, Jones, Hennessy, Unze, and Pick (1989) showed that something like this is, in fact, the case. When musicians and non-musicians were asked to list all the attributes they could think of for several instruments (e.g., *flute, violin, trumpet, piano, drum*), musicians tended to give more distinctive descriptions. This suggests that our ability to perceive differences in the properties of individual objects becomes more refined as our experience of them increases.

J.J. Gibson's (1977; E.J. Gibson & Spelke, 1983) theory of *affordances* (Chapter 3) is relevant here. Particular objects afford particular actions. Thus a piano and an organ afford playing in different ways. The more experience you have with a particular class of objects, the more aware you will be of its affordances. One consequence, as Palmer et al. suggest, is that the more expertise we have, the more subtle the distinctions we will make between categories.

The Horizontal Dimension

Within each category level, some category members are more prototypical than others. This is the horizontal dimension of category structure. Rosch (1975) asked participants to rate category members according to how well they exemplified their categories. The results probably won't surprise you. For example, in the furniture category *chair* is a better example than *telephone*; a *car* is a better example of a vehicle than an *elevator* is; and a *gun* is better than *shoes* as an example of the weapon category. People tend to have similar intuitions about how well a particular instance fits a particular category.

Rosch and Mervis (1975) showed that the more prototypical category members have more attributes in common than do atypical ones. Prototypical members also have the fewest attributes in common with members of other categories. This suggests that prototypical category members are the most representative of their own category and the least representative of other categories. Rosch and Mervis argued that this is what is meant by the phrase *family resemblance*. A category member has a strong family resemblance to the extent that it is a good example of the category to which it belongs and a poor example of any other category.

These findings with respect to the horizontal dimension of category structure can be summarized by saying that concepts have a **graded structure**. A concept is usually said to have a graded structure if some members of the category are better examples of it than others, and the boundaries of the category are unclear. However, Armstrong, Gleitman, and Gleitman (1983) showed that even some well-defined concepts show prototypicality effects. Consider the concept of *odd number*. It does not have a fuzzy boundary: a number is either odd or even. However, when Armstrong et al. asked participants to rate examples of odd numbers for prototypicality, they judged *three* to be a better example of odd-numberedness than *fifty-seven*. Similarly, *four* was deemed better than *eight-hundred and six* as an example of even-numberedness. Thus even a clearly defined concept can have members that are "more prototypical" than others. This test showed that prototype effects are generalized subjectively and show up even in places where you might not expect them.

graded structure
Describes a concept in which some members of the category are better examples of it than others.

Embodied Cognition

In an important paper, Glenberg (1997) suggested that concepts should not be seen as disembodied abstract representations. Rather,

> the world is conceptualized (in part) as patterns of possible bodily interactions, that is, how can we move our hands and fingers, our legs and bodies, our eyes and ears, to deal with the world that presents itself? That is, to a particular person, the meaning of an object, event, or sentence is what that person can do with the object, event or sentence (p. 3).

Have you ever tried to learn a difficult skill such as shooting a puck or serving a tennis ball? If you have, you most likely had a friend, parent, or coach who gave you a visual demonstration of what you were supposed to do. Seeing a motor action performed correctly seems to have an effect on how well you perform it yourself. Indeed, many amateur athletes consciously try to emulate professional players or Olympic champions. This is a clever strategy, as a growing body of evidence suggests that action and perception are intimately linked. It seems that perceiving a particular motor action, or even just an object that could be acted upon, such as a puck or a ball, leads to activation in premotor areas of the brain, as if you were somehow preparing to perform a related action.

FIGURE 8.4 | Capoeira

For example, imagine that you are looking at a frying pan with the handle facing to the right. If you were asked to press a key in response to some feature of the pan (e.g., its colour or size), you would be faster if you delivered your response with your right hand than with your left, presumably because the handle was facing to the right and activated a right-hand grasping response; this would be the case even if you were left-handed (Tucker & Ellis, 1998). It's important to note that the direction of the handle has nothing to do with a task involving colour or size. Nevertheless, response times are faster with the hand that the handle is pointing towards. This type of embodiment has been observed across a variety of experimental paradigms, stimuli, and even species: non-human animals also show embodiment effects (see, for example, Bach & Tipper, 2006; Beilock & Holt, 2007; Dipelligrino et al., 1992).

You might wonder how the link between perception and action plays out with experts in different types of motor skills (e.g., highly skilled athletes or dancers). Do they have a stronger embodiment response to motor actions in their expert repertoire than to actions they are less familiar with? Do people who become experts in a particular domain of motor skills have a greater ability to embody the action involved in that domain? To address this question, Calvo-Merino and colleagues (2005, 2006) explored how expert ballet and capoeira dancers responded to dancers performing skilled moves that they either would perform themselves or would only see performed by other dancers (e.g., a capoeira dancer watching a ballet dancer or a female dancer watching a male-specific move). Measurement of the viewers' brain activity, using fMRI, revealed more activity in response to motor actions that the experts had been trained to perform than to actions that they did not perform themselves. These results suggest that motor expertise can modulate how we perceive action.

Watching professional sports will not make you a professional athlete. Even so, aspiring athletes should probably watch the experts as closely as they can.

We often ignore the fact that the brain/mind is situated in a body, and the "body requires a mind to make it function" (M. Wilson, 2002, p. 625). Cognition is embodied, and this means that its role is to facilitate successful interaction with the environment. Concepts must be understood as a part of the process whereby possible action patterns are determined. At any particular time, the environment affords many different actions. Concepts provide the bridge between our goals on the one hand, and the environmental possibilities on the other. For example, suppose I need a vase to put a flower in. I look around the environment for an object that would meet that need, see an empty Coke bottle, and decide that it will do (Glenberg, 1997, p. 18). In this case, a Coke bottle would become a positive instance of the concept *vase* because it allows me to act in accordance with my current goal. If my goals change, then the meaning of a Coke bottle can change too. It can be a *doorstop* or even a *weapon*. "The meaning of a Coke bottle (how we interact with it) is not fixed, but infinitely varied depending on the context of use" (Glenberg, 1997, p. 18).

embodied cognition
The role of cognition is to facilitate successful interaction with the environment.

Goal-Derived Categories

If your house caught fire, what would you try to save first? Presumably your list would include children, pets, computers, and so on. But suppose you had never thought of making such a list before. In fact, it is possible to construct on the spot a category of *things to save from home during a fire*. Such a concept is called an *ad hoc* or goal-derived category (Barsalou, 1983, 1987, 1999). A goal-derived category may contain members with no attributes in common, and may be something that most people have never thought of.

goal-derived category
A category invented for a specific purpose on a particular occasion.

Barsalou (1983) showed that goal-derived categories have a graded structure. In one experiment, participants were asked to judge items in terms of how well they exemplified a particular category. For example, consider the concept *ways to escape being killed by the mob*. How well do each of the following fit in that category?

Change your identity and move to the mountains of South America.

Stay where you are presently living in New Jersey.

Barsalou (1983) found substantial agreement among participants concerning good and poor instances of goal-derived categories; this suggests that such categories have a graded structure. What determines how typical an item in a goal-derived category is? Barsalou suggested that the important determinant is how relevant the item is to the goal that the category serves. For example, imagine a category of *things not to eat on a diet*. The attribute "high in calories" is relevant to this category, but many other properties of foods that would ordinarily matter to us are irrelevant.

As Rosch suggested, people may initially prefer to classify an object using basic-level category names. Thus if you were asked to categorize a chair, your first response might be *furniture*. However, as poverty-stricken aristocrats have occasionally discovered, when you run out of firewood you can burn a chair to keep warm, even if it is a priceless antique. As Barsalou (1983) noted, the goal-derived category of *emergency firewood* allows you to cross-classify a chair. The ability to cross-classify an object both in terms of its basic-level name and in terms of other goal-derived categories may be an important aspect of the ability to think creatively. "Perceiving these new organizations may be necessary to achieving new goals or to approaching old ones in novel ways" (Barsalou, 1983, p. 226).

A study by Ratneshwar, Barsalou, Pechmann, and Moore (2001) showed how a change in goals affects the extent to which objects are viewed as similar or different. People often construct categories based on personal goals: thus the category *healthy lunch substitutes* might include *sliced melon*, *green salad*, and *tuna sandwich*. But these personal goals will also be shaped by particular situational goals. For example, the situational goal of finding *things to eat while driving a car* should probably exclude *green salad*. In Ratneshwar et al.'s study participants were asked to judge the similarity of different pairs of food products (e.g., *apple–orange*). Their judgments were made as a function of different situational goals (e.g., *things to eat as snacks when in a hurry*). Notice that in this example the two foods (*apple–orange*) are similar with respect to nutritional value, but dissimilar in relation to the situational goal of *things to eat as snacks when in a hurry* (it takes some time to peel an orange). In the Ratneshwar et al. study, the judged similarity between foods was reduced (i.e., they were seen as more different) when one was consistent with the situational goal but the other was not. One advertising strategy that this research suggests would be to make situational goals more salient for consumers. Perhaps *soup* could come to be seen as a *breakfast food* if it were presented as satisfying the goal of *eating a hot and nutritious breakfast* (cf. Ratneshwar et al., 2001, p. 155).

Perceptual Symbol Systems

In the previous section we saw the enormous flexibility of the conceptual process. Barsalou (2003) argued that "there are no permanent or complete abstractions of a category in memory. Instead, abstraction is the skill to construct temporary . . . interpretations of a category's members" (p. 1177). This is why it is usually not possible to list all the criterial attributes that define a concept. As we saw when we discussed Wittgenstein, no matter how one defines a concept (e.g., *games*) there will be some members of the category to which that definition does not apply. Once we realize that concepts are usually temporary constructions designed to satisfy a specific goal in a particular situation, then their variability is no longer puzzling.

For Barsalou (1999, 2003), understanding how concepts are formed means studying the skills that enable us to construct temporary categories. These skills are rooted in perceptual experience. In the last chapter we observed that imagery and perception shared common mechanisms. Barsalou goes further, suggesting that perception and concept formation also have much in common. Recall our discussion of *selective attention* in Chapter 4, in which we noted that we perceive only a subset of all the information available. What perception delivers to memory are schematic instances of particular categories. For example, on many separate occasions we perceive different *cars*. Over time, these instances become integrated across all our senses and become a categorical representation. "For cars, such knowledge includes not only how they look but also how they sound, smell and feel, how to operate them, and emotions they arouse" (Barsalou, Simmons, Barbey, & Wilson, 2003, p. 88).

When knowledge of a particular category is distributed across all our senses it enables us to re-experience perceptual memories; for this reason such knowledge is called a *simulator*. The activity of conceptualization involves simulating sensory experiences. When we simulate sensory experiences we do not reconstruct all our previous perceptions. Rather, the simulation we conduct on a specific occasion is sensitive to the situation in which we find ourselves and our momentary goals. "On one occasion the ... simulator might produce a simulation of travelling in a car, whereas on others it might produce simulations of repairing a car, seeing a car park and so forth" (Barsalou, 2003, p. 1180). We have no invariant concept of a *car*: rather, we construct different versions of *cars* on different occasions, each version focusing on different aspects of *cars*. Not every simulation of a car will include a *seatbelt*, or a CD *player*, or an *airbag*. Simulations represent those properties that are relevant for the task at hand.

The act of conceptualizing engages perceptual symbols: aspects of perceptual memories that "function symbolically, standing for referents in the world" (Barsalou, Solomon, & Wu, 1999, p. 210). Studies requiring participants to list the features of category members provide evidence for the perceptual nature of conception. For example, ask yourself what the features of a *watermelon* are. Now ask yourself what the features of a *half watermelon* are. Repeat this exercise for *computer* and *open computer*. If you are like the participants in the study conducted by Barsalou et al. (1999), the simulation of a *watermelon* or a *computer* is different from the simulation of a *half watermelon* or an *open computer*. The former brings to mind external properties, such as *surface colour*, while the latter reveals internal properties such as *seeds* or *wires*. It's likely that the object you imagine changes as its description changes. However, as we saw in the last chapter, people vary widely in the vividness of their visual imagery. Consequently, Barsalou made the point that we need not be aware of the activity of perceptual symbols, although we often will be. In essence, perceptual symbols represent brain states. "Most importantly, the basic definition of perceptual symbols resides at the neural level: unconscious neural representations—not conscious mental images—constitute the core content of perceptual symbols" (Barsalou, 1999, p. 583).

Perceptual Symbol Systems and the Brain

Like other approaches to embodied cognition (Wilson, 2003), the theory of perceptual symbol systems understands conceptualization as a process that connects our perceptions and our actions. In this respect the perceptual symbol systems theory has much in common with other approaches to categorization that are collectively called *sensory–funtional theories* (Cree and McRae, 2003, p. 168). Such approaches have their roots in a study by Warrington and Shallice (1984) of category-specific deficits due to brain damage. The four patients they studied had partially recovered from encephalitis and were able to correctly identify inanimate objects. For example, one patient defined a *submarine* as a *ship that goes underneath the sea*. However, they were unable to provide satisfactory definitions for living things; one patient defined *ostrich* as simply *unusual* (Farah & McClelland, 1991, p. 340). To account for this selective impairment, Cree and McRae (2003) proposed that *living things* are understood primarily in terms of their sensory features, while *inanimate objects* are understood primarily in terms of their functions. Thus a *moose* might have *antlers* as one of its most salient features, whereas a *knife* might be defined as something that is *used for cutting* (Cree & McRae, 2003, p. 199). Sensory-functional theories assume that "knowledge of a specific category is located near the sensory-motor areas of the brain that process its instances. ... Consequently, a deficit for living things may arise from damage to brain regions that process sensory information,

perceptual symbols
Aspects of perceptual memories that stand for events in the world and enter into all forms of symbolic activity.

category-specific deficits
Selective deficits in knowledge, resulting from brain damage.

whereas a deficit for manipulable artefacts may arise from damage to regions that implement functional action" (Simmons & Barsalou, 2003, p. 452). The sensory-functional theory accounts for some cases, but not all. It predicts that objects that are equally "sensory" should all be equally affected by a conceptual deficit. For example, a conceptual deficit for *living things* should span all *living things*. Yet some patients with a deficit for *fruits* and *vegetables* show no deficit for *animals* (Martin & Caramazza, 2003, p. 199; Samson & Pilon, 2003). Findings such as these mean that a simple sensory-functional theory can't be the whole story, and that complementary viewpoints need to be taken into account to provide a fuller account of conceptual deficits (Simmons & Barsalou, 2003, p. 454). We will become acquainted with some of these alternative viewpoints in the remainder of this chapter.

Concepts as Metaphors

A simile is a figure of speech in which we use the word *like* to draw an analogy between two otherwise unrelated things. A metaphor is much the same, except that it doesn't use *like*: instead, it makes the connection directly, either by stating that one thing *is* the other, or by referring to one thing in language normally associated with the other. Some of the most famous literary metaphors come from Shakespeare: "the world's a stage," "love is blind," "a sea of troubles." As Lakoff and Johnson (1999, p. 46) have argued, however, metaphor is not only or even primarily a literary device. Rather, it arises naturally as a result of connections between sensory-motor and other forms of experience. For example, every time a child pours water into a glass, he or she will see the level of liquid rise. Over time, repetition of this experience leads to the formation of connections between those areas of the brain responsible for representing quantity and those representing verticality. Eventually "more is up" becomes a **primary metaphor**, "pair[ing] subjective experience and judgment with sensorimotor experience" (Lakoff & Johnson, 1999, p. 49). We can then understand and use expressions such as "Prices are down" or "The stock market is high" without thinking the metaphors through.

Another example given by Lakoff and Johnson (1999, p. 50) is the connection between *friendliness* or *affection* and *warmth*. They suggest that this pairing reflects the literal warmth we experience in an affectionate embrace. They also observe that "we first acquire the bodily and spatial understanding of concepts and later understand their metaphorical extensions in abstract concepts" (Johnson & Lakoff, 2002, p. 254). This is a point first made by Asch (1955, 1958; Asch & Nerlove, 1960), who described the process whereby words are initially applied to physical events and only later used metaphorically to describe persons. Asch (1955) called terms such as *warm* and *cold* **double-function words**. Essentially they refer to physical properties such as temperature, but secondarily they have been paired with the properties of people. Asch and Nerlove (1960) showed that children initially use these words to refer to physical objects, and only later use them psychologically. Thus children may have difficulty answering the question "Is your teacher a warm person?" unless they are able to use the word *warm* metaphorically. Lakoff and Johnson (1999, p. 50) list a number of primary metaphors, such as "Bad is Stinky" and "Help is Support." It would be a useful exercise to work out the sensorimotor basis for these metaphors yourself; you might also come up with some of your own.

primary metaphor
A pairing of subjective experience with sensorimotor experience.

double-function words
Words that refer to both physical and psychological properties (e.g., *warmth*).

If you were asked to categorize another person's personality, would you use Asch's (1955) approach and focus on "warm" and "cold" words? Perhaps a more interesting question is whether the direction of this relationship can be reversed. That is, can actual physical "warmth" or "coldness" influence the way you would describe another person? To test this idea, Williams and Bargh (2008) had several participants each take a short elevator ride with a confederate of the experiment who was carrying several things, including a cup of coffee that was either hot or iced. The confederate would then ask the participant to lend a hand and carry the coffee. Amazingly, those who had held the hot coffee later rated a hypothetical person as having a warmer personality than did those who had carried the iced coffee.

Is it really that easy to influence another person's judgment of you? Should you give a hot coffee to everyone you want to have warm feelings for you? And what about countries that naturally have warmer or colder climates? Although anecdotal evidence suggests that people in tropical countries do tend to be very friendly, most Canadians would probably like to think that they have warm personalities too, even if they are cold for several months of the year. If you think more research is needed in this area, you aren't alone. In fact, three high-powered independent studies have recently attempted to replicate Williams and Bargh's (2008) finding and failed, disconfirming the original result (Lynnott et al., 2014).

This example underlines the importance of research replication in science in general, and psychology in particular. In fact, a recent spate of failed replications in social psychology have brought into question not only the data behind some classic studies, but in several cases the ethics of the scientists who conducted them. If you're interested in learning more about this important issue, a good place to start is at http://retractionwatch.com.

Conceptual Modules

We suggested in Chapter 2 that the mind is composed of specific parts or *modules*, each of which is responsible for particular cognitive operations. As we noted, there are differences of opinion concerning the numbers and kinds of modules that may exist (e.g., Fodor, 1983; Pinker, 1997; Sperber, 2002). However, one school of thought holds that there are conceptual modules dedicated to domain-specific knowledge (i.e., that deal exclusively with particular subject areas) (Hirschfeld & Gelman, 1994). In this section we will look at the evidence for one such module, dedicated to what has been called folk biology (Medin & Atran, 2004): the concepts that ordinary people use to understand living things.

Discussions of folk biology are often introduced by a quotation from Darwin (1859, p. 431) (e.g., Atran, 2005, p. 43):

> From the most remote period in the history of the world organic beings have been found to resemble each other in descending degrees, so that they can be classed into groups under groups. This classification is not arbitrary like the grouping of stars in constellations.

Darwin's hypothesis that people invariably classify living things hierarchically has been borne out in research, beginning with the work of Berlin, Breedlove, and Raven (1974).

conceptual modules
Modules responsible for domain-specific knowledge.

folk biology
The concepts that ordinary people use to understand living things.

folk taxonomy

A classification system composed of a hierarchy of groups.

All cultures have a folk taxonomy, or classification system, "composed of a stable hierarchy of inclusive groups of organisms, or taxa, which are mutually exclusive at each level of the hierarchy" (Atran, 1999, p. 316). These levels can be compared to the levels identified by Rosch et al. in Table 8.1, in that there is a superordinate level (*tree*, *bird*), followed by a basic generic species level (*oak*, *robin*), and then a subordinate level (*white oak*, *mountain robin*) (Medin & Atran, 2004, p. 962). The generic species level plays the same role in folk biology that basic-level concepts play in Rosch et al.'s classification.

Folk Biology and the Brain

We saw earlier that some brain-damaged patients display a category-specific deficit in that they are unable to provide satisfactory definitions for living things. Although this does not necessarily mean that there is a conceptual module responsible for folk biology, advocates of the domain-specific module theory point to such findings in support of their position (e.g., Medin & Atran, 2004, p. 963). For example, Farah and Rabinowitz (2003) reported on a case of a young man who suffered brain damage as a result of meningitis when he was only one day old. Adam (a pseudonym) attended public school and had a normal verbal IQ. However, at age 16, when he was asked to name pictures of living and non-living things, he showed "a relatively selective impairment in knowledge of living things" (p. 404). In another test, he was given a questionnaire consisting of four item types:

1. Visual knowledge of living things (e.g., Do ducks have long ears?)
2. Non-visual knowledge of living things (e.g., Are roses given on Valentine's day?)
3. Visual knowledge of non-living things (e.g., Is a canoe widest in the centre?)
4. Non-visual knowledge of non-living things (e.g., Were wheelbarrows invented before 1920?)

Of a total of 380 questions, Adam correctly answered half in each category *yes*, the rest *no*. Control participants got roughly 80–90 per cent correct in each category. Adam's performance on the non-living things questions was not different from that of the controls. However, for both sets of questions on living things, his performance was only 40–45 per cent (Figure 8.5). Farah and Rabinowitz concluded that Adam's deficit was specific to knowledge of living things. They also drew out the implications of the fact that his brain damage had been present virtually since birth, arguing that "prior to any experience . . . we are destined to represent our knowledge of living and non-living things with distinct neural substrates" (p. 408).

Summary

We use concepts to organize and categorize the events we experience based on their *attributes*. Attributes can define concepts in several ways, as seen in examples of *conjunctive*, *disjunctive*, and *relational* concepts. To understand what makes something an instance of a particular concept, we need to determine the attributes that are critical for membership in it.

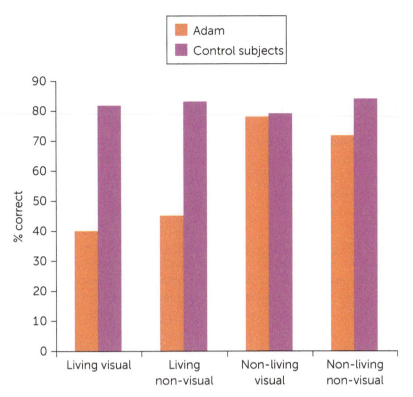

FIGURE 8.5 | Biological concepts and the brain: results from the Farah & Rabinowitz (2003) experiment involving a brain-damaged individual

From: Farah, M.J., & Rabinowitz, C. (2003). Reprinted by permission of the publisher (Taylor & Francis Ltd, http://www.tandfonline.com).

The processes by which we acquire and use concepts have been studied extensively. Classical research by J.S. Bruner used selection and reception tasks to observe and test different strategies used in concept acquisition, such as abstraction, conservative focusing, and successive and simultaneous scanning. However, the classical approach has been criticized for studying artificial concepts constructed in a lab rather than real-world concepts that people actually do acquire and use.

CASE STUDY

Case Study Wrap-Up

The irrelevance of the classical approach to real-world concept formation becomes clear when we consider the challenge of categorizing the iPad. Bruner et al. were concerned with the relations between attributes and concepts, where the concepts can be complex but are ultimately rather clear-cut. The problem is that the iPad's attributes cut across many different types of technologies. Those who consider the iPad to be a kind of laptop note it's a light, portable computer about the size of a textbook. However, if you are going to call an iPad a laptop, then your concept of the latter must be extended to include attributes not normally associated with laptops (e.g., a touch screen for typing instead of physical keys). This would be an example of a disjunctive concept. Unfortunately, those other attributes are central to other concepts, such that of the eReader. And there lies the problem.

Eleanor Rosch has taken a different tack, using the natural concept of colour categories to explore the idea that members of a category share a family resemblance. She finds that with natural concepts there are prototypical instances that are unusually good examples of a particular category. Furthermore, she identifies two principles that govern the way we use natural concepts: cognitive economy and perceived world structure. These principles lead us to organize concepts along two dimensions: vertical (superordinate, basic, subordinate)

and horizontal. These ideas may help us to understand why the iPad was so difficult to categorize. For instance, Rosch's notion of cognitive economy recognizes a tension between two opposing tendencies. On one hand, the desire to make things as simple as possible leads us to ignore differences between specific objects or events so that we can lump them all into the same category: thus many devices that differ in terms of size, colour, or brand can all be conceived of as "laptops." On the other hand, we need to be able to discriminate accurately between things that are not in fact identical. After all, there are many critical features that make the iPad unique and valuable that are not captured by the standard attributes of the laptop category. The key is balance: thus the desire to increase the complexity of the category of laptop or portable computer is balanced by the desire to keep things as simple as possible.

In the Know: Review Questions

1. Outline the procedure that Bruner, Goodnow, and Austin used to study concepts. What were their major conclusions? Briefly criticize their approach.
2. Outline the procedure used by Reber and his colleagues to study complex rules. What was his major conclusion? Criticize Reber's work from the viewpoint of Dulany, Carlson, and Dewey.
3. What innovations did Rosch introduce to the study of concepts? Outline the horizontal and vertical dimensions of the system she used to understand concepts.
4. In what sense is cognition "embodied"?

Key Concepts

category-specific deficits
cognitive unconscious hypothesis
commitment heuristic
conceptual module
conservative focusing
correlated attributes
criterial attribute
double-function words (Asch)
embodied cognition
family resemblance (Wittgenstein)
focus gambling
folk biology
folk taxonomy
goal-derived categories

graded structure
implicit vs explicit learning
misaligned hierarchies
partist strategy
perceptual symbol
primary metaphor
prototypical
reception task
selection task
simultaneous scanning
successive scanning
superordinate, basic, and subordinate levels (Rosch)
wholist strategy

Links to Other Chapters

domain-specific knowledge
Chapter 4 (attention capture)
Chapter 11 (social contract theory)

implicit vs explicit learning
Chapter 13 (implicit perception)

tacit knowledge
Chapter 5 (procedural memory)

embodied cognition
Chapter 3 (Gibson's theory of ecological optics)

Further Reading

Many experimental paradigms other than Reber's have been used to investigate implicit or incidental learning. A good example is Lacroix, Giguère, and Larochelle (2005).

Perruchet and Vinter explore alternative approaches to the cognitive unconscious.

Do current events have an effect on what we consider to be a typical exemplar of a category? This question is examined in Novick (2003).

Two good examples of neural network approaches to classical concept formation problems are Carbonaro (2003) and Dawson, Medler, McCaughan, Willson, and Carbonaro (2000).

For a clever experiment designed to demonstrate a weakness of embodied cognition theories see Markman and Brendl (2005).

Geary and Huffman (2002) offer an evolutionary perspective on modularity.

Carbonaro, M. (2003). Making a connection between computational modeling and educational research. *Journal of Educational Computing Research, 28*, 63–81.

Dawson, M.R.W., Medler, D.A., McCaughan, D.B., Willson, L., & Carbonaro, M. (2000). Using extra output learning to insert a symbolic theory into a connectionist network. *Minds and Machines, 10*, 171–201.

Geary, D., & Huffman, K. (2002). Brain and cognitive evolution: Forms of modularity and functions of mind. *Psychological Bulletin, 128*, 667–698.

Lacroix, G.L., Giguère, G., & Larochelle, S. (2005). The origin of exemplar effects in rule-driven categorization. *Journal of Experimental Psychology: Learning, Memory, and Cognition, 31*, 272–288.

Markman, A.B., & Brendl, C.M. (2005). Constraining theories of embodied cognition. *Psychological Science, 16*, 6–10.

Novick, L.R. (2003). At the forefront of thought: The effect of media exposure on airplane typicality. *Psychonomic Bulletin & Review, 10*, 971–974.

Perruchet, P., & Vinter, A. (2002). The self-organizing consciousness. *Behavioral and Brain Sciences, 25*, 297–388.

Igor Plotnikov/Shutterstock.com

9

Language

Chapter Contents

Chapter Objectives

- To explore the structure of language.
- To outline Chomsky's approaches to language.
- To review evidence for the innateness hypothesis and identify the "poverty of the stimulus" argument.
- To examine the process of communication and comprehension.
- To evaluate evidence for linguistic relativity.

CASE STUDY

Reading in the "Olden Days"

First published in 1836 (and revised substantially over the years), *McGuffey's First Eclectic Reader* was for many decades one of the most popular reading textbooks in North America. Whether at school or at home, children learned to read using the McGuffey series, which included a Primer and a Spelling Book as well as five progressively more difficult readers.

diacritical marks
Symbols that indicate the correct pronunciation of letters in a particular word.

The McGuffey's series was characterized by a rigour that is rarely seen in contemporary reading material for children. For example, by lesson 228 in the Spelling Book students were learning words such as *corymb* and *terpsichorean*. (If you want to develop a truly "erudite" vocabulary, you can look them up.) As for the complexity of the readers, take a look at the excerpt from the *Second Eclectic Reader* (p. 8) in Figure 9.1. Students were encouraged to learn how to interpret **diacritical marks**: symbols above letters that indicate their correct pronunciation in a particular word. According to the reader's preface,

> If the pupil is not familiar with the diacritical marks, he should be carefully drilled . . . until the marked letter instantly suggests the correct sound. He is then prepared to study his reading lessons without any assistance from the teacher (p. iii).

With the help of the diacritical marks, students could teach themselves how to read almost from the

ECLECTIC SERIES.

SHORT SOUNDS.

ă, as in ăm.	ŏ, as in ŏdd.
ĕ, " ĕlm.	ŭ, " ŭp.
ĭ, " ĭn.	ŏŏ, " lŏŏk.

DIPHTHONGS.

oi, as in oil.	ou, as in out.

TABLE OF SUBVOCALS.

b, as in bĭb.	v, as in vălve.
d, " dĭd.	th, " this.
g, " gĭg.	z, " zine.
j, " jŭg.	z, " ăzure.
n, " nīne.	r, " râre.
m, " māim.	w, " wē.
ng, " hăng.	y, " yĕt.

l, as in lŭll.

TABLE OF ASPIRATES.

f, as in fīfe.	t, as in tärt.
h, " hĭm.	sh, " shē.
k, " cāke.	ch, " chăt.
p, " pīpe.	th, " thĭck.
s, " sāme.	wh, " whȳ.

FIGURE 9.1 | A page from *McGuffey's Second Eclectic Reader*

Note the diacritical marks and the proper pronunciation of various letters and letter combinations.

16 *ECLECTIC SERIES.*

LESSON IV.

a bŏve′	wõrld	därk	ŏft
nĕv′er	spärk	dew	tĭll
dī′a mond	twĭn′kle	blāz′ing	

THE LITTLE STAR.

1. Twinkle, twinkle, little star;
How I wonder what you are,
Up above the world so high,
Like a diamond in the sky!

2. When the blazing sun is set,
And the grass with dew is wet,
Then you show your little light;
Twinkle, twinkle, all the night.

3. Then, if I were in the dark,
I would thank you for your spark.
I could not see which way to go,
If you did not twinkle so.

4. And when I am sound asleep,
Oft you through my window peep;
For you never shut your eye,
Till the sun is in the sky.

FIGURE 9.2 | Reading Lesson IV from *McGuffey's Second Eclectic Reader*

From: *McGuffey's Second Eclectic Reader*, Revised Edition. John Wiley & Sons, Inc. p. 8.

start, when learning easy words such as *mine*, *soap*, *was*, and *red*. In a given lesson, such as Lesson IV shown in Figure 9.2, students would be shown a set of new words with the diacritical marks indicating the correct pronunciation. A short reading passage containing the new words would follow. Students would be required to practise the passage on their own until they had mastered it and then to read the passage to the teacher.

By the sixth reader students would be learning more complex aspects of reading, such as proper intonation. Intonation was diagrammed as shown in Figure 9.3, with lines set at angles to show how the voice should rise and fall as the sentence is read. Throughout the course of study, students would also be learning the correct interpretation and use of punctuation, as well as **articulation**, defined as the "utterance of the elementary sounds of a language, and of their combinations" (*McGuffey's Sixth Eclectic Reader*, p. 11). To "acquire the power of uttering those sounds with *distinctness*, *smoothness*, and *force*,"

students were urged to practise until they had gained "perfect control of [their] organs of speech" (p. 11, italics in the original).

The McGuffey method was quite different from the methods used to teach reading today. Chances are that you were never taught how to interpret diacritical marks, or the art of articulation, and you might wonder how children in the second grade could have managed it, mostly on their own. You might also wonder whether teaching such complex skills ultimately led to better results than modern methods.

In this chapter we will discuss some of the main concepts in the cognitive psychology of language. One of the questions we will address is whether the complexity of a teacher's speech can influence the development of speech in children. Before we get there, however, we will begin by considering how language is structured.

articulation
The production of a language's sounds.

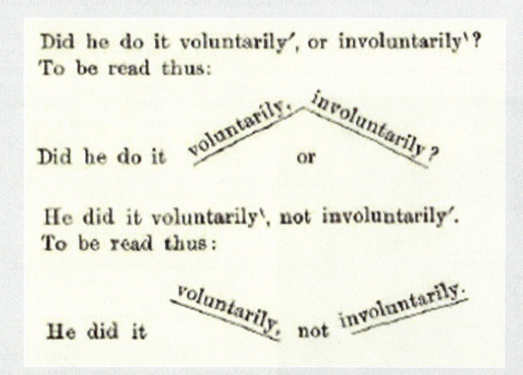

FIGURE 9.3 | A lesson on intonation from *McGuffey's Sixth Eclectic Reader*

From: *McGuffey's Sixth Eclectic Reader*, John Wiley & Sons (1997), p. 20.

The Structure of Language

It is undeniable that language plays an important role not only in our ability to communicate but in human cognition in general. But what exactly is language? Is it just a form of communication? If that is the case, what makes human language different from the communication systems that other animal species use? Even if it is possible that some non-human animals share certain elements of human language (an idea that has been heavily debated), it is obvious that human language is far more rich and creative than any other animal communication system.

> "Humans are so innately hardwired for language that they can no more suppress their ability to learn and use language than they can suppress the instinct to pull a hand back from a hot surface" (Pinker, 1994).

There are currently more than 7,000 languages in the world (Lewis, Simons, & Fennig, 2015). While the most common (Mandarin) has nearly a billion speakers, many others are in critical danger. For example, at the time of writing this chapter (2015) Chamicuro was spoken by at most 10 people in Peru, all of them elders (the children have switched to Spanish), and is almost certain to disappear. In fact, UNESCO has identified more than 200 languages that have died since 1950, and another 3,000 that are on the verge of becoming extinct—with cultural implications that go far beyond the scope of this textbook. What we can discuss here are the characteristics that all languages, whether spoken by hundreds of millions or only a handful, share.

Perhaps the most important of the characteristics that human languages share is their capacity for **recursion**: that is, the capacity of any one component (e.g., phrase or sentence) to contain any number of similar components. In theory (if not in practice) it's possible to construct a sentence that has an infinite number of other sentences embedded in it, like nesting dolls. The following verse, attributed to the Victorian mathematician Augustus de Morgan, is often used to illustrate the concept:

> Great fleas have little fleas,
> upon their backs to bite 'em,
> And little fleas have smaller fleas,
> and so ad infinitum.
> And the great fleas, themselves, in turn
> have greater fleas to go on;
> While these again have greater still,
> and greater still, and so on.

As this verse suggests, language's capacity for recursion—like the problem of fleas—is arguably infinite. We will return to the concept of recursion later in this chapter.

recursion
The capacity of any one component (e.g., phrase or sentence) to contain any number of similar components.

FIGURE 9.4 | Native speakers of Chamicuro

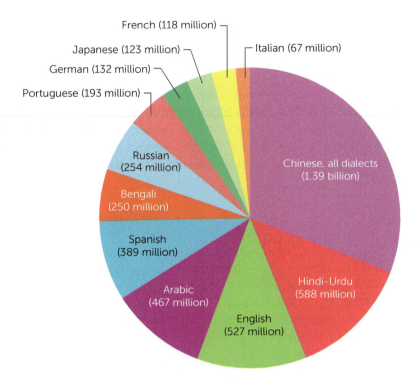

FIGURE 9.5 | Widely spoken languages of the world.

Sources: Ulrich Ammon, University of Dusseldorf, Population Reference Bureau.

The Building Blocks of Language

The branch of cognitive psychology that studies the acquisition, production, comprehension, and representation (in the mind) of language is called **psycholinguistics**. Psycholinguists have a rich history in exploring how language is structured. To begin with, it is important to emphasize that language is hierarchical in nature. That is, a series of components can be combined to form larger components, which in turn can be combined, as long as each combination follows certain rules. While languages obviously vary widely, there are components that all of them share. One example is the **phoneme**. Phonemes are the smallest units in language, and can be combined with other phonemes to form morphemes. **Morphemes** are the smallest meaningful units of language. For instance, the phonemes /d/, /o/, and /g/ can be combined to form the morpheme /dog/, which also happens to be a word. Note that not all morphemes are words: some are word elements that do not necessarily form words on their own. For example, /s/ by itself is a phoneme, but it becomes a morpheme (i.e., a unit carrying meaning) when it is combined with /dog/ to form the plural /dogs/.

Different languages are composed of different numbers of phonemes. For example, whereas English has approximately 44 phonemes (24 consonant and 20 vowel), Spanish has only 24 (19 consonant and 5 vowel). It's important to note that newborn infants have the capacity to learn all the phonemes in all the languages of the world, although babies lose this ability after about a year, as they begin to focus on the phonemes of the language(s) spoken around them. This explains why learning

psycholinguistics
The branch of cognitive psychology interested in how we comprehend, produce, acquire, and represent (in the mind) language.

phoneme
The smallest unit in language. Phonemes are combined to form morphemes.

morpheme
The smallest unit in language that carries meaning.

a language with unfamiliar phonemes can be so difficult. A well-known example is the tendency of native Japanese speakers to have difficulty distinguishing between /l/ and /r/, because the particular distinction that English makes is not part of the Japanese language.

From phonemes and morphemes we create words, which can then be combined to form sentences. The process of combination is subject to two sets of rules. The rules that govern how words are arranged in sentences are known as syntax. For example, to say "the tennis player the ball hit" would be an error of syntax. However, a syntactically correct sentence can still be deficient in terms of semantics (meaning): for example, "the tennis player hit the potato."

Early Work on Language

Wilhelm Wundt (1832–1920) is often credited with founding the first laboratory in psychology, but he was also one of the first to do important research into the psychology of language (Blumenthal, 1970; Carroll, 1953). Wundt's view anticipated many contemporary theories regarding the structure of language. One of his most interesting discussions concerned the relationship between experience and the words used to describe it. Let's briefly reconsider the structure of our experience.

As we saw in Chapter 4, we are able to attend to "one out of what seem several simultaneously possible objects or trains of thought" (James, 1890/1983, p. 403). Our attention is like a spotlight that highlights some aspects of a situation and leaves others in the background (Treisman, 1986). Nevertheless, all the aspects of a situation to which we could pay attention are available simultaneously. We can shift our attention from one aspect to another, and consider the relationships between the various parts of a situation.

Wundt (1890/1970; Blumenthal, 1970, p. 17) used tree diagrams to describe the relationships between different parts of our overall experience of a situation. For example, suppose you are listening to some music. Your experience includes relationships between elements that you can put into words and could be diagrammed as in Figure 9.6. Thus the music can be described as the subject of a sentence and its loudness as the predicate, as in "The music is loud." The process of speech proceeds from one level at which a number of relationships are simultaneously present to another level at which they are ordered serially as a succession of words in a sentence (e.g., subject, predicate). The person who hears "The music is loud" can then reconstruct the speaker's experience by reversing the process and moving from the level of words in succession to the level where the two elements are present simultaneously. Wundt's model of sentence production is similar to more modern notions—in particular, some of Noam Chomsky's early formulations. Although Chomsky's linguistic theories have undergone many changes over the years, his earlier ideas have had a profound impact on many cognitive psychologists' thinking about language. Thus we will begin with some of them before we explore some of his more recent approaches.

syntax

The rules that govern how words and sentences are structured.

semantics

The meaning of words and sentences.

tree diagram

A description of a process that proceeds from one level at which a number of relationships are simultaneously present to other levels at which those relationships are ordered serially.

FIGURE 9.6 | A tree diagram of the relationship between two elements experienced while listening to music

Transformational Grammar

According to Pinker, Chomsky is "among the ten most-cited writers in all of the humanities (beating out Hegel and Cicero and trailing only Marx, Lenin, Shakespeare, the Bible, Aristotle, Plato, and Freud) and the only living member of the top ten" (1994, p. 23). His fame was not immediate, however. In fact, his doctoral dissertation was considered so unusual that he had difficulty getting it published.

In a condensed version, published as *Syntactic Structures* (1957), Chomsky pointed out that because language is recursive, the set of possible sentences is infinite. **Language** is open-ended and consists of all possible sentences, whereas **speech**, which consists of those sentences that are actually spoken, is only a small subset of language (de Saussure, 1916). This is a very important point, because it means that there must be a set of rules—a *grammar*—that is capable of producing all possible sentences in the language. From a finite set of rules, the grammar is in principle able to generate an infinite number of sentences. This is what enables you to create a sentence that may never have been uttered in the past. In order to understand the structure of language, we need to understand the structure of this grammar.

As Chomsky pointed out, a grammatical utterance need not be a meaningful utterance. As an example he famously proposed the nonsense sentence "Colourless green ideas sleep furiously" (Chomsky, 1957, p. 15). Although meaningless, that combination of words is still grammatical, at least when compared to the combination "Furiously sleep ideas green colourless." This observation, and others like it, led Chomsky to make a sharp distinction between *grammar* and *semantics*, the study of meaning. He argued that the processes that make a sentence grammatical are different from the processes that make a sentence meaningful.

Chomsky went on to consider the nature of a grammar for a natural language such as English. He rejected the notion that a finite state grammar (see Chapter 8) could generate all the sentences in such a language. For the purposes of the present discussion, a critical feature of a finite state grammar is that every word in a sentence is produced in a sequence starting with the first word and ending with the last. We have already seen one example of a finite state grammar (or railroad diagram) in Figure 8.3; for another, see Figure 9.7. This grammar generates sentences such as *The man comes*, *The old man comes*, *The men come*, and *The old men come*. These are only a few of the possible sentences in English. Can you imagine how vast a railroad diagram would have to be in order to be able to generate 1000 sentences? 10,000? 100,000? There are a great many more possible sentences than these in English. If we had to learn them all using a finite state grammar, we would need to listen to several sentences a second for more than 100 years before we had learned enough sentences to allow us to speak and understand a significant portion of English (G.A. Miller, Galanter, & Pribram, 1960, p. 147).

Chomsky (1957, p. 21) argued that no finite state grammar could generate all (and only) the grammatical utterances of a natural language. Finite state grammars are too simple to underlie the complexity of natural languages. As an illustration of this complexity, consider the fact that natural languages contain sentences that are embedded within other sentences. This example comes from Chomsky (1957): *The man who said that S is arriving today* (p. 22). The symbol *S* can stand for an unlimited number of possible sentences that could be inserted at that point in the example. *The man who*

language
Open-ended verbal communication that consists of all possible sentences.

speech
Those sentences that are actually spoken; only a small subset of language.

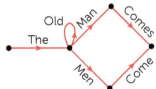

FIGURE 9.7 | A finite state grammar

From: Chomsky, N. (1957). p. 19. Copyright 1957 by Mouton de Gruyter. Reprinted by permission.

said that the bank will renew our mortgage is arriving today and *The man who said that Roscoe will become a star is arriving today* are just two out of an indefinite number of possibilities. A grammar must be able to generate such sentences, and Chomsky believed it was impossible for a finite state grammar to do so.

One of the problems with finite state grammars is that they operate at only one level. They generate sentences by a process that moves only from left to right, as it were. The alternative proposed by Chomsky (1957) is a top-down process that uses phrase structure rules and grammatical transformations. **Phrase structure rules** consist of symbols and rewrite rules. Here is a small set of such rules, adapted from Chomsky (1957, p. 26) and J. Greene (1972, p. 35):

1.   Sentence (S) → Noun Phrase (NP) + Verb Phrase (VP)
2.   NP → Article (*art*) + Noun (N)
3.   VP → Verb (V) + NP
4.   *art* → *a, the*
5.   N → *girl, car, boy*, etc.
6.   V → *drives, likes, helps*, etc.

phrase structure rules
Rules describing the way symbols can be rewritten as other symbols.

These rules, which describe the way symbols such as S can be rewritten as other symbols, such as NP and VP, are capable of generating an infinite number of sentences. The derivation of a sentence can be represented using a tree diagram, as in Figure 9.8. Each stage in the process yields a different string (such as NP + VP), and the final sequence of words generated is called a terminal string.

Rewrite rules operate on single symbols, such as NP and VP. However, Chomsky (1957, p. 44) proposed that there are also rules that operate on entire strings to convert them to new strings. He called these rules **grammatical transformations**. An example is the *passive transformation*. Take a sentence with the following underlying form:

grammatical transformations
Rules operating on entire strings of symbols to convert them to new strings.

$$NP_1 + V + NP_2$$

An example is the sentence *Boswell admired Johnson*. The passive transformation, *Johnson was admired by Boswell*, converts the string underlying the terminal string to produce something like the following (Deese, 1970, p. 26):

$$NP_2 + to\ be + V + by + NP_1$$

This transformation reverses the order of the two noun phrases and inserts a form of the verb *to be* and the word *by* in their proper places. Instead of *Boswell admired Johnson* we now have *Johnson was admired by Boswell*. The passive transformation is an example of an *optional transformation*. It's not necessary for optional transformations to be applied in order to make a sentence grammatical. Chomsky (1957, p. 45) defined *kernel sentences* as those that are produced without optional transformations. This suggests that kernel sentences might be easier to understand and remember because they require fewer transformations. Much psychological research was stimulated by this notion (e.g., Mehler, 1963). However, it was difficult to demonstrate that it was the number of transformations—rather than variables such as sentence

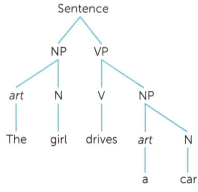

FIGURE 9.8 | Derivation of a sentence using a tree diagram

length—that determined ease of understanding and recall (J. Greene, 1972, pp. 157ff.). For example, the passive sentence *Johnson was admired by Boswell* has more words than its active counterpart, and may be more difficult to process for that reason.

In the end, interest in the concept of kernel sentences declined as Chomsky revised his theory. Chomsky (1965, 1966, 1967, 1968, 1972) went on to introduce several concepts that became very influential. Among the important distinctions he introduced were those between *competence* and *performance* and between *deep structure* and *surface structure*.

Competence and Performance

Chomsky (e.g., 1967, p. 397) considered what it means to say that a person "has a command" of a language. On the one hand, it means that the person has internalized a system of rules that relates sound to meaning. This internalized system of rules constitutes a basic linguistic **competence**—the basis on which the person is able to understand and to use the language. This competence is not always reflected in the person's actual use of the language. Linguistic **performance** is determined not only by the person's basic linguistic competence, according to Chomsky, but also by cognitive factors such as memory. In principle, therefore, we can generate extremely long sentences, but such sentences cannot be easily understood because they exceed the attentional capacities of listeners. To take another example, the form that utterances take often depends on the age of the speaker: the same thing might not be said in the same way by an adult and by a young child. Thus even though the grammar of a language is a model of linguistic competence, observing someone's linguistic performance will not always give us a completely accurate picture of that person's competence. An analogous example can be seen in second-language learners, who quite often claim to understand or know more than they are actually able to produce.

Chomsky (1967, p. 399) argued that a central problem for psychology is to discover the characteristics of linguistic competence. This would involve specifying the idealized grammar that constitutes this competence. A theory of linguistic performance would specify not only the nature of linguistic competence but also the psychological processes that go into the production of actual sentences.

Deep and Surface Structures

Chomsky believes that linguistic competence has a largely innate internal structure. This highly debated innate structure is called *universal grammar*. One aspect of universal grammar is universal syntax, which provides the rules that enable us to transform meaning into words. The meaning is at one level, called the **deep structure**, whereas the words are at another level, called the **surface structure**. The distinction between deep and surface structure allows us to understand a number of interesting linguistic phenomena, including ambiguous sentences.

The reason ambiguous sentences are interesting is often illustrated by sentences like the following (e.g., Bigelow, 1986, p. 379):

1. *Time flies like an arrow.*
2. *Fruit flies like a banana.*

competence vs performance
We may have an internalized system of rules that constitutes a basic linguistic competence, but this competence may not always be reflected in our actual use of the language (performance).

DISCOVERY LAB

deep and surface structure
The sequence of words that make up a sentence constitutes a surface structure that is derived from an underlying deep structure.

DISCOVERY LAB

Sentence 1 is usually interpreted as a comparison in which *flies* is a verb and *like* is a preposition: time passes as quickly as an arrow flies through the air. A similar interpretation could be imposed on sentence 2 as well. However, in this case we're more likely to read *flies* as a noun and *like* as a verb.

These examples may seem a bit silly, but they help to make a serious point. From Chomsky's perspective, the existence of ambiguity in language illustrates why we need to make a distinction between deep and surface structure. The same surface structure can be derived from different deep structures. The different meanings of the above sentences, for example, are carried by two different deep structures. *Meaning* is not given on the surface of a sentence: it is given by the *deep structure* interpretation of the sentence. When we understand a sentence, we transform a surface structure into a deep structure. When we produce a sentence we work the other way: from a deep structure to the construction of a surface structure.

The Innateness Hypothesis
The "Poverty of the Stimulus" Argument

innateness hypothesis
The hypothesis that children innately possess a language acquisition device that comes equipped with principles of universal grammar.

"poverty of the stimulus" argument
The argument that the linguistic environment to which a child is exposed is not good enough to enable language acquisition on its own.

language acquisition device (LAD) and universal grammar hypothesis
The hypothesis that children possess a language acquisition device containing general principles that apply to any natural language (universal grammar).

As we noted above, Chomsky believes that linguistic competence is largely innate. Among the arguments for this innateness hypothesis is the belief that the speech to which a small child is exposed is an inadequate database from which to abstract the structure of language (e.g., Chomsky, 1972, pp. 13–160). The typical linguistic performance of an adult is too full of errors and too incomplete a sample of language to give children the data they need to generate a natural language grammar on their own. This is called the "poverty of the stimulus" argument (Chomsky, 1980a, 1980b; Lightfoot, 1982) because it claims that the apparent stimulus for language (i.e., other people's language) is not good enough to enable children to use it effectively. On a side note, the fact that small children will often come up with words that they would never hear from an adult—for instance, "goed" instead of "went"—lends credence to the idea that language competence is not simply learned from other people (i.e., their environment). Given this tendency, and the fact that children acquire their first language much more rapidly than seems possible if they started from scratch, they must possess a language acquisition device, or LAD (McNeill, 1970), that contains principles of universal grammar. These are very general principles that apply to any natural language, be it English or Chinese. Among the things that the LAD "knows" are the facts that languages contain things such as noun phrases and verb phrases, and that they are arranged in particular ways, such as subject followed by predicate (McNeill, 1970, p. 71). In a sense, the LAD is a theory of language that children use to discover the structure of the particular language community in which they happen to be living. This is why you could place a baby in any geographic region around the world and s/he would easily learn the local language, with the help of the LAD. Children come equipped with the tools necessary to enable them to rapidly acquire a facility in their first language (or multiple languages, if their parents are bilingual, or they live in a part of the world where more than one language is used consistently, e.g., Catalan and Spanish in Catalonia, Spain).

Support for the innateness hypothesis came in part from the findings of a classic study by R. Brown and Hanlon (1970). According to Pinker (1988), Brown and Hanlon's findings "may be one of the most important discoveries in the history of psychology" (p. 104). The reason Brown and Hanlon's study is so important is that it bears directly on one of the alternatives to the innateness hypothesis. That alternative is usually identified with B.F. Skinner (1957).

Skinner's approach, and others like it, implied that children must learn a language by receiving informative feedback on their utterances. Perhaps language learning takes place when children are given approval for generating grammatical sentences and disapproval for generating ungrammatical ones (R. Brown & Hanlon, 1970, p. 46). However, Brown and Hanlon found no evidence to support that idea. Observing the interactions of mothers and their children, Brown and Hanlon found that mothers not only allowed ungrammatical sentences to go uncorrected, but responded to such utterances in the same way that they responded to grammatical utterances. Approval seemed to depend on whether or not the statement the child was trying to make was true; its grammatical quality was irrelevant. Thus to a child who says *Mama isn't boy, he a girl* the parent says *That's right.* However, to a child who says *And Walt Disney comes on Tuesday* the parent says *No, he does not* (R. Brown & Hanlon, 1970, p. 49).

One implication of studies such as Brown and Hanlon's is that children do not typically receive information that would tell them when they are making an ungrammatical sentence (Rice, 1989, p. 150). In the absence of such feedback, it's not easy to see how the child could learn to eliminate ungrammatical utterances. Yet from the perspective of the innateness hypothesis this does not seem such a big problem. That is because the innateness hypothesis maintains that children come equipped with the kind of knowledge that will ultimately allow them to produce grammatical sentences and avoid ungrammatical ones. As we shall see, however, not everyone accepts the innateness hypothesis. Moreover, even if we accept some version of the innateness hypothesis, we still need to spell out precisely what it is that must be innate in order for children to acquire language, and that is not at all easy.

Minimalism

As we noted earlier, Chomsky's theory has undergone considerable modification over time (e.g., Chomsky, 1981, 1995, 2005). The current version is called **minimalism** (Uriagereka, 1998). As the name suggests, the minimalist approach is parsimonious (Atran, 2005, p. 58): it assumes that linguistic competence has only those characteristics that are absolutely necessary, with no added frills. The working hypothesis of minimalism is that "the human language faculty might be a computationally perfect solution to the problem of relating sound to meaning" (Lasnik, 2002, p. 434). The main criticisms of minimalism are that it is not driven by empirical findings, and is so vague that it is not falsifiable (Lappin, Levine, & Johnson, 2000). Like many ideas in cognitive psychology, it continues to be debated.

A key minimalist hypothesis is that the acquisition of a particular language involves **parameter setting** (Piatelli-Palmarini, 1989). Chomsky (1981, 1995) proposed that universal grammar contains several switches, which can be set to turn various possible parameters on and off. As an example Hyams (1986, p. 3) points to the placement of verbs and their objects. In English the verb always comes before the object: "take the cheese." In German, however, the positions are reversed: "the cheese take." The position of the verb

minimalism
The belief that linguistic competence has only those characteristics that are absolutely necessary.

parameter-setting hypothesis
The hypothesis that language acquisition involves the setting of various parameters contained within a universal grammar (e.g., position of verb in relation to object). A parameter is a universal aspect of language that can take on one of a small set of possible values.

is a parameter set for a specific language. Chomsky (1995) described parameter-setting as follows:

> A plausible assumption today is that the principles of language are fixed and innate, and that variation is restricted. . . . Each language, then, is . . . determined by a choice of values for lexical parameters: with one array of choices, we should be able to deduce Hungarian; with another Yoruba. . . . The conditions of language acquisition make it plain that the process must be largely inner-directed, as in other aspects of growth, which means that all languages must be close to identical, largely fixed by initial state (p. 17).

As Piatelli-Palmarini (1989) pointed out, the parameter-setting approach implies that children are not trained to speak a specific language: they do not receive any explicit training on the position of verbs, for example. Rather, a language is selected out of the many possible ones that are supported by universal grammar. Through exposure to a particular language, such as English or German, the switches get set to the specific values that characterize that language (Yang, 2004).

Of course, the need for parameter-setting arises because of the variety of languages that children must be prepared to acquire as their native tongues. But why do different languages exist at all? It's possible that different languages arose and developed through a series of historical accidents:

> We find different languages because people move apart and lose touch, or split into factions that hate each other's guts. People always tinker with the way they talk, and as the tinkerings accumulate on different sides of the river, mountain range, or no-man's land, the original language slowly splits into two. To compare two languages is to behold the histories of two peoples, their migrations, conquests, innovations, and daily struggles *to make themselves understood* (Pinker, 1997, p. 213, italics added).

concealing function hypothesis

The hypothesis that language is a kind of code, and that the parameters set for one language serve to conceal its meanings from the speakers of another language.

Like Pinker, most theorists assume that the goal of every speaker, regardless of language, is to be able to communicate with others. But what if the goal was to facilitate communication with some people *and not with others*? In other words, what if "the language faculty [had] a **concealing function** as well as a revealing function" (Baker, 2003, p. 351)? In that case, the parameters that are set for one language would serve to conceal its meanings from the speakers of another language, and vice versa. This would mean that language could usefully be seen as a kind of code. Baker (2003) points out that the US successfully used the Navajo language as a code in the Second World War. In general, it would be advantageous for the members of a particular group to be able to pass information to one another while keeping it secret from the members of another group with whom they were at war, or competing for resources. Since conflict between groups is extremely common, it may be that linguistic parameters evolved precisely in order to keep open the possibility of creating and learning new languages. This example illustrates the extremely broad range of possible evolutionary explanations for the various features that language possesses. Different theories of the psychology of language are intimately associated with specific theories of the evolution of language. In fact, it's virtually impossible to disentangle the psychology of language from the story of its evolution. Box 9.1 explores some of the theories that psychologists have proposed regarding the evolution of language (you might want to review the material on Broca's area in Chapter 2 before reading it).

Is the Stimulus for Language Really Impoverished?

The "poverty of the stimulus" argument rests on the premise that the data a child would need in order to acquire a language from scratch are unavailable (Pullum and Scholz 2002; Scholz & Pullum, 2002). If that is true, then language cannot be acquired solely by means of data-driven learning. However, this argument would be undermined if one could "identify a set of sentences such that if the learner had access to them, [then] the claim of data driven-learning . . . would be supported" (Pullum & Scholz, 2002, p. 19). Since the Brown and Hanlon (1970) study discussed above, an enormous amount of information has accumulated concerning the kinds of sentences to which children may be exposed (e.g., MacWhinney, 2000). Consequently, investigators now have much richer samples against which to test the "poverty of the stimulus" argument. By examining large samples of sentences, Pullum and Scholz (2002, pp. 24–26) were able to document the existence of many constructions that had been assumed to be either infrequent in or absent from the language to which infants would be exposed. For example, consider how children understand irregular constructions such as plurals in noun–noun compounds. The sentence *I put my books on the book shelf* is fine as an English sentence. However, *I put my books on the books shelf* sounds strange, and we can surmise that children are unlikely to hear it. Nevertheless, children understand that *a new books shelf* means *a shelf for new books*. They don't think it means *a new shelf of books*. Where does this understanding come from? It has been claimed that children understand constructions like this as "another demonstration of knowledge despite 'poverty of the input'" (Pinker, 1994, p. 147). However, the child's knowledge should not be surprising, given the number of constructions such as *rules committee, publications catalogue, letters policy,* or *complaints department* that they will be able to overhear in the speech of adults. Perhaps exposure to these constructions provides all the information a child needs in order to use this grammatical form properly.

Pullum and Scholz (2002) render what is called a "Scottish verdict" on the "poverty of the stimulus" argument: not proven. Indeed, Hoff (2004) makes the useful point that it is difficult if not impossible to disprove the argument. No one has given, or perhaps ever can give, a complete account of all the data available to a child that would make language acquisition possible without any innate contribution. Nevertheless, there is now considerable evidence that children are given much more data in support of their language acquisition efforts than was previously suspected (MacWhinney, 2004). We have space here to consider only two examples. First, it now appears that children do receive and make use of corrective feedback on their ungrammatical constructions. Second, the complexity of the speech to which the child is exposed is significantly related to the complexity of the speech that the child then produces. We will now briefly examine representative studies illustrating these findings.

The Evolution of Language

Psychologists have speculated endlessly about the evolution of language. At times the speculation is so rampant that it almost seems reasonable to ban discussion of the topic. Indeed, the French Academy of Sciences did exactly that in 1866. Like most prohibitions, it proved ineffective, and now, once again, theories abound. However, one theory in particular is currently attracting more attention than any other. It should come as no surprise that this theory is associated with Noam Chomsky.

Hauser, Chomsky, and Fitch (2002) made a distinction between broad and narrow conceptions of the faculty of language. In its broad sense, the faculty of language has three parts. There is a sensory–motor system that allows us both to perceive and to produce patterns of speech. There is also a conceptual–intentional system that allows us to grasp the meaning of speech. Finally, there is a uniquely human system that mediates between the first two. Let's consider each of these systems in turn.

Sensory–Motor Systems

Other animals share our ability to perceive and produce speech sounds. For example, vocal imitation occurs in dolphins, parrots, crows, and songbirds. Songbirds are particularly interesting examples because they acquire their songs only by listening to other birds of the same species, and this input must come during a critical period or their songs will not develop properly. It's much the same with human language acquisition. After a certain age people can still learn a second language, but they will never be able to speak it exactly the way a native speaker does. This, along with other similarities between human and animal sensory–motor systems, suggests that there is nothing uniquely human about this aspect of language.

Conceptual–Intentional Systems

The ability of other animals to represent the world and their place in it may not be as rich as that of humans. However, they are still capable of formulating and acting on relatively complex plans. For example, Clayton and Dickinson (1998) conducted an experiment with scrub jays. These birds stored both larvae (which they value highly as food but which spoils quickly) and peanuts (which they value less highly as food, but which remain edible for a long time), but in different locations. When the birds were allowed to retrieve stored food, their choice depended on the length of the interval between storage and retrieval. If the interval was short, then they retrieved the larvae, but if it was long they went for the peanuts instead. "Individuals often search for food by an optimal strategy, one involving minimal distances, recall of locations searched, and kinds of objects retrieved" (Hauser, Chomsky, & Fitch, 2003, p. 1578). This suggests that that conceptual–intentional systems are not unique to humans.

A Uniquely Human System?

What may be unique to humans is the ability to use symbols recursively. Recall the earlier discussion of recursion and the examples of sentences embedded within other sentences. Another way to think about recursion is as a process that *refers to* itself. Consider the following examples, adapted from Uriagereka (1999, pp. 3–4):

S → You are saying that S
S → You are saying that you are thinking that S
S → You are saying that you are thinking that you are talking to someone that S

In these examples S refers to itself, so that each successive example becomes longer. In principle this recursive process could go on indefinitely, but in practice it is limited by what we can keep in working memory (as well as the capacity of listeners to attend to what we are saying).

Morton (1976) gave a witty example of recursion in an article titled "On recursive reference." The body of the paper consists of one sentence: "Further details of this paper may be found in Morton (1976)." In other words, the paper refers to itself, inviting the reader to go back to the beginning and read it over again, and then again, and so on. The paper is not only about recursion, but is an example of a recursive loop in itself.

Hauser, Chomsky, and Fitch (2002) realized that recursive behaviour may yet be found in animals, but they could find no good examples in existing research. They concluded that recursion may be the uniquely human property of the language faculty. Hence the narrow conception of the faculty of language is that it consists of the ability to recursively combine symbols. It enables the construction of an infinite number of possible expressions of the conceptual–intentional system to be realized as sentences produced by the sensory–motor system (Hauser, Chomsky, & Fitch, 2002, p. 1578). In short, it enables us to translate thought into speech.

Chomsky (2005) describes the evolutionary appearance of this narrow faculty of language as follows:

> The simplest account of the "Great Leap Forward" in the evolution of humans would be that the brain was rewired, perhaps by some slight mutation. . . . Perhaps . . . the Great Leap Forward was effectively instantaneous, in a single individual, who was instantly endowed with intellectual capacities far superior to those of others, transmitted to offspring and coming to predominate. . . (p. 12).

Despite the influence that Chomsky has had in this area, it is important to note the special case of Pirahã, the language spoken by the Pirahã people of Amazonas state in Brazil. Pirahã is the only surviving dialect of the Mura language, and is thought to be a finite language, without recursion. If that is the case, its existence would seem to undermine Chomsky's notion that recursion plays a central role in universal grammar. Although Chomsky has argued that recursion is an innate characteristic that need not be manifested in every language, some believe that the defining difference between human and non-human cognition does not lie in language, but rather in humans' ability to reason relationally, which includes the capacity for recursion (Penn, Holyoak, & Povinelli, 2008). We will return to relational reasoning in Chapter 11.

From Gesture to Speech

An alternative account of the evolution of language presents much more specific hypotheses about its emergence. Corballis (2003, 2004a, 2004b) argues that humans, like other primates, originally communicated by means of gesture. This argument is based on the following facts:

- Other primates do not have speech, but they do have a relatively sophisticated system of gestural communication.
- The area corresponding to Broca's area in monkeys contains **mirror neurons** that fire not only when the animal makes grasping movements, but also when the monkey observes other animals making those movements.
- A mutation on a gene called FOXP2 can cause a severe speech disorder. Functional MRI studies suggest that this disorder may be due to a problem in Broca's area that prevents it from handling speech.
- Around 40,000 years ago there was a rapid increase in the production of tools, decorations, and cave art.

mirror neurons
Neurons that fire not only when performing an action, but also when observing an action. Broca's area in monkeys contains mirror neurons that fire not only when the animal makes grasping movements, but also when it observes other animals making those movements.

Indeed, people still make meaningful gestures while speaking (McNeill, 1980, 1985a, 1985b, 1989). However, at one time we communicated primarily through gesture supplemented by simple vocalizations bearing little resemblance to modern speech. Broca's area was responsible for gestural communication, enabling us not only to regulate our gestures, but also to interpret the gestures of other people. A mutation on FOXP2 enabled the recruitment of Broca's area for speech. That is why any further mutation on FOXP2 causes a speech disorder. The emergence of speech took the pressure off gesture as a channel of communication, freeing the hands for other tasks. This in turn allowed the development of elaborate tools, decorations, and works of art.

There are other evolutionary narratives, of course (e.g., Pinker & Jackendoff, 2005). All of them are open to debate. However, there is no denying the reciprocal influence between the search for the evolutionary origins of language and the development of the psychology of language.

Adult Reformulations of Child Errors

parental reformulations
Adult reformulations of children's speech. They are negative in that they inform children that they have made a mistake and positive in that they provide examples of correct speech.

"Children produce many errors during acquisition, and the issue is how they manage to get rid of them" (Chouinard & Clark, 2003, p. 638). Perhaps parental reformulations of a child's erroneous utterances play a role. For example, consider the following exchange:

Child: I want butter mine.
Father: OK give it here and I'll put butter on it.
Child: I need butter *on it* (Chouinard & Clark, 2003, p. 656).

The fact that he takes up his father's reformulation suggests that the child realizes two things: that the reformulation means the same thing as his initial erroneous formulation, and that in order to speak correctly he must emulate his father. In general, adult reformulations are negative in that they inform children that they have made a mistake. At the same time they are positive in that they provide models of correct speech.

Chouinard and Clark sampled utterances of five children between the ages of two and four years, the parental responses to these utterances, and the children's next utterances. Their data came from a standard archive called the "Child Language Data Exchange System" (MacWhinney, 2000). The data set they analyzed was quite large, varying from 730 items for one child to 9187 for another. Chouinard and Clark discovered that reformulations of erroneous utterances occurred between 50 and 70 per cent of the time when the child was about two years old. They also found that the children repeated these reformulations up to 50 per cent of the time, as shown by their subsequent repetition of the reformulation. Thus these interactions provide occasions for the child to learn how to speak correctly, and the child takes advantage of them. Reformulations become less frequent as children get older, presumably because of ongoing improvements in their speech.

The Impact of Teachers' Speech

syntactic development
Development of the ability to organize words into grammatical sentences.

Huttenlocher, Vasilyeva, Cymerman, and Levine (2002, p. 338) note that "there are substantial variations in the language environments children encounter and . . . these variations may be correlated with differences in development." For example, children's syntactic development—their ability to organize words into grammatical sentences—may be influenced by input from speakers other than parental caregivers. Language development is an ongoing process, and after a certain age, much of the speech that children are exposed to comes from teachers. The fact that the complexity of kindergarten and first-grade children's syntax develops more between October and April than between April and October (Huttenlocher et al., 2002, p. 343)—the period that includes the summer vacation—suggests that exposure to speech at school is the important factor. In order to test this hypothesis, Huttenlocher and her co-workers recorded samples of different preschool teachers' speech during a typical class day. Then they analyzed these recordings to determine the extent to which individual teachers presented children with challenging examples of speech. A particularly important example is the multi-clause sentence (e.g., *The lamp broke because it fell off the table*). Consequently, Huttenlocher et al. calculated the proportion of multi-clause sentences in each teacher's speech, which turned out to vary between 11 and 32 per cent (Figure 9.9). The children were roughly four years old, attended three different preschools, and came from families that together represented a range of incomes from high to low. The children were tested by means of a comprehension task (illustrated in Figure 9.10) that required them to match each sentence with the correct picture. The test included both multi-clause sentences and sentences with varying numbers of noun phrases.

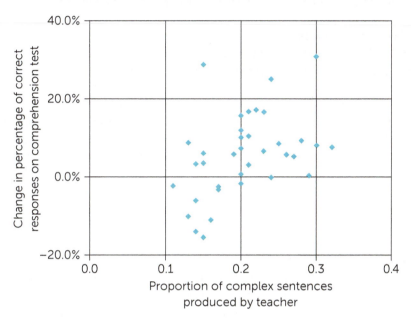

FIGURE 9.9 | The relationship of the proportion of complex sentences in teacher speech to comprehension scores

From: Huttenlocher, J., Vasilyeva, M., Cymerman, E., & Levine, S. (2002). Copyright 2002. Reprinted by permission of Elsevier.

The boy is looking for the girl behind a chair, but she is sitting under the table.

The baby is holding the big ball and the small block.

FIGURE 9.10 | The comprehension task

From: Huttenlocher, J., Vasilyeva, M., Cymerman, E., & Levine, S. (2002). P. 363. Copyright 2002. Reprinted by permission of Elsevier.

Each class had the same primary teacher throughout the study. Children were tested at both the beginning and the end of the school year, and an average comprehension score for each class was calculated for each test. Then the average scores on the first test were subtracted from the average scores on the second, to measure how much syntactic growth had taken place *in each class*. This measure was found to be significantly related to the complexity of teacher speech: the more complex the teacher's speech, the greater the syntactic growth in that class. Importantly, "teacher speech was *not* significantly related to children's skill levels at the start of the school year, but *was* significantly related to growth in children's skill levels over the school year" (Huttenlocher et al., 2002, p. 370). Simply put, greater improvements in syntactic understanding were seen in children whose teachers used more complex speech.

One benefit of exposure to complex speech may be that the child learns more complex ways of thinking about things. In this context, Huttenlocher et al. (2002, p. 371) cite Vygotsky's (1934/1986) work on the interaction between language and thought—a topic that we will take up later in the chapter.

Evaluation of Chomskian Theories

If the value of theories is measured by the amount of research they generate, then Chomsky's various theories have been a smashing success. The degree to which they are true or false has still to be determined. However, two complementary trends seem to have been established. First, innate processes are now believed to play a lesser role in language acquisition than was formerly thought (Pinker & Jackendoff, 2005, p. 204). Second, the linguistic environment of the child is much richer than had been believed. Language acquisition is increasingly acknowledged to be dependent on learning.

Communication and Comprehension

Obviously, an important field of inquiry in the psychology of language is the way listeners comprehend spoken and/or written speech. When you comprehend spoken or written language, you understand what it means. The context in which listeners or readers receive language is extremely important in determining what interpretations they will extract from the message. As a consequence, speakers or writers must take the audience's context into account.

A useful distinction is made between *given* and *new information* (H.H. Clark & E. Clark, 1977, pp. 32, 92). Speakers and listeners are said to enter into **a given–new contract** (H.H. Clark & Haviland, 1977) whereby the speaker tacitly agrees to connect new information to what the listener already knows. Thus, for example, a sentence may consist of a part that is given, or shared between speaker and listener, and a part that is known to the speaker but new to the listener (Bruner, 1985, p. 31). Suppose there is a howling winter storm outside, and you say, "A cold front from Alberta is causing this storm." You are introducing a new piece of information (*a cold front from Alberta*), and relating it to something your listener and you already know (*the storm*). Comprehension would be difficult if not impossible if we simply introduced new information without connecting it to something of which the listener already has some knowledge.

given–new contract
A tacit agreement whereby the speaker agrees to connect new information to what the listener already knows.

Sperber and Wilson's (1986/1995; 2002) theory of the way conversation is conducted and comprehended has been very influential. They contrasted two approaches to communication: the code model and the inferential model. The code model derives from information-processing theories such as those we reviewed in Chapter 2. According to this model, the initial stage of communication is a process whereby a speaker's thoughts are encoded in words. When spoken, these words are an acoustic signal that passes through the air and impinges on the listener. The listener must decode the signal to arrive at the thought that the speaker intended to communicate. According to Sperber and Wilson, the code model assumes that speaker and listener have a great deal of knowledge in common: otherwise the listener would not be able to decode the signal properly and arrive at the correct interpretation. As an example, Sperber and Wilson imagined a speaker who says: *Coffee would keep me awake.* This sentence is open to at least two interpretations: that the speaker wishes to stay awake, and so wants some coffee, and that the speaker does not wish to stay awake, and so does not want any coffee. To successfully interpret this sentence the listener must share the speaker's understanding of the situation. Sperber and Wilson point out that a drawback of the code model is the difficulty of spelling out how people could come to have enough shared knowledge to guarantee successful communication.

The inferential model derives from the work of Grice (1957/1971, 1975), who analyzed communication in terms of *intentions* and *inferences*. A speaker intends to inform a listener, and the listener infers what the speaker intends. Suppose you're sitting in a room with another person. It's the middle of winter, but you think the room is stuffy and so you open a window. What would you infer if the other person then said, "Were you raised in a barn?" Would you decode this utterance as a simple request for information, and reply sincerely, "No, I was raised in a two-bedroom semi-detached house"? Or would you interpret the utterance as a request that the window be closed, because the speaker is implying that only people raised in primitive conditions would open the window in winter? The meaning of the utterance depends critically on the inferences you make concerning the meaning that the speaker intends. Grice (1957/1971) suggested that to say someone "meant something" by a particular utterance is to say that the speaker intended "to produce some effect in an audience by means of the recognition of this intention" (p. 58). In the example above, when you recognize that your companion "meant something" by asking if you were raised in a barn, you're expected to respond appropriately, most likely by closing the window.

To facilitate the process of communication, most of us follow what Grice called the co-operative principle: speakers try to be concise, truthful, relevant, and unambiguous, and listeners take it for granted that this is the case. From this principle Grice derived four rules or conversational maxims (Paprotte & Sinha, 1987, p. 205):

1. Say no more than is necessary (*maxim of quantity*);
2. Be truthful (*maxim of quality*);
3. Be relevant (*maxim of relation*); and
4. Avoid ambiguity and be clear (*maxim of manner*).

In turn, according to Grice, listeners assume that speakers are following those maxims, and they interpret whatever *implicatures* they perceive on the basis of the same assumption.

To illustrate how the inferential model might work in ordinary conversation, let's return to Sperber and Wilson's example of the person who says, "Coffee will keep me awake."

code model of communication
A model of communication based on the information-processing theory.

inferential model of communication
A model of communication based on Grice's inferential theory.

co-operative principle
The assumption that the speaker intends to say something concise, truthful, relevant, and unambiguous.

conversational maxims
Say no more than is necessary (*maxim of quantity*); be truthful (*maxim of quality*); be relevant (*maxim of relation*); and avoid ambiguity (*maxim of manner*).

Suppose that the speaker and listener are on a road trip, driving nonstop from Winnipeg to Vancouver, and it's the speaker's turn to drive. If both parties are following the co-operative principle, the listener can easily infer that the speaker wants coffee. There's nothing mysterious about this process: it simply involves taking the four conversational maxims for granted and drawing the inferences that make sense in the circumstances. On the other hand, Grice was writing more than half a century ago. Do the people you know follow the co-operative principle? Is the inferential model valid today?

For Sperber and Wilson (1986), communication sometimes follows the coding model and sometimes follows the inferential model. People communicate in ways that blend coding and inference. Under all circumstances, however, the goal of communication is *relevance*. An utterance is relevant to the extent that it is both true and easy to understand (Van der Henst, Carles, & Sperber, 2002, p. 458). Truthfulness and relevance are not always the same. For example, when they are asked the time, many people will round the answer to the nearest five minutes: thus if your watch says 2:18, you might say it's 2:20. In one study, Van der Henst et al. (2002) found that 97 per cent of speakers with analog watches rounded their replies to the nearest five minutes. Perhaps this is because the precise time is more difficult to see on a wrist watch, or is not relevant; or perhaps a rounded time is simply easier for both speaker and listener to process.

Comprehension may require inferences of the sort Grice proposed, but the inferential process need not be a conscious chain of reasoning. Sperber and Wilson (2002) refer to comprehension as "intuitive," meaning that it is an "unreflective process which takes place below the level of consciousness" (p. 9). It's possible that most people have an implicit theory of how other people's minds work, and that they use this theory when they attempt to comprehend what others are saying (Perner, 2000; Sperber & Wilson, 2002, p. 275).

Figurative Language

figurative language
Various figures of speech, such as metaphor and irony.

Insight into the way communication works can be gained from the study of **figurative language**, which consists of figures of speech such as metaphor and irony (Roberts & Kreuz, 1994). Figurative language may at first seem to be an unusual form of communication. However, it is commonly used in ordinary discourse (Pollio, Smith, & Pollio, 1990), as we saw in Chapter 8, on concepts. In what follows we will focus on *irony* because a great deal of research has been devoted to it. We will see that irony illustrates many facets of communication in everyday life.

Irony

Irony belongs to a family of concepts that includes *satire* and *sarcasm*. A satirical remark holds something up to ridicule. Sarcasm and irony are vehicles for satire. *The Oxford English Dictionary* defines sarcasm as a "sharp, bitter or cutting remark" and *irony* as "a figure of speech in which the intended meaning is the opposite of that expressed by the words used." Irony is sometimes considered to be a form of sarcasm, and ordinary speakers of the language consider the two to be quite similar (Gibbs, 1986).

An ironic statement is intended to communicate the opposite of what it says. Thus you might say of someone you find particularly cold and unfeeling, "He's such a warm person." Given the right context and tone of voice, you can communicate exactly how you feel, even though you are saying the opposite. What are the conditions under which a listener perceives the ironic intent of a speaker?

H.H. Clark and Gerrig (1984, p. 121) followed Grice (1978) in arguing that irony involves the use of pretense: the speaker is only pretending to mean what he says. They quoted Fowler (1965):

> Irony is a form of utterance that postulates a double audience, consisting of one party that hearing shall hear and shall not understand, and another party that, when more is meant than meets the ear, is aware both of that more and of the outsiders' incomprehension. . . . [It] may be defined as the use of words intended to convey one meaning to the uninitiated . . . and another to the initiated, the delight of it lying in the secret intimacy set up between the latter and the speaker (pp. 305, 306).

As Clark and Gerrig noted, irony usually involves a particular tone of voice. It's difficult to spell out, but when someone says something like "What a terrific movie" ironically, the tone is unmistakably different from the one that would be used if the speaker really meant the words.

Several authors have described (without necessarily accepting) what is sometimes called the *standard theory of irony* (e.g., Gibbs, 1986; Jorgenson, Miller, & Sperber, 1984; Kreuz & Glucksberg, 1989). According to this theory, listeners initially take the ironic utterance literally, but soon realize that the speaker can't mean it literally. Then the listener reaches the conclusion that the speaker means the opposite of what he or she has just said. Grice's *co-operative principle* (that listeners normally expect speakers to be truthful and relevant) could help to explain the way the listener arrives at this conclusion (Kreuz & Glucksberg, 1989, p. 374). The listener realizes that the speaker cannot be both truthful and relevant and literally mean what he or she says. Thus the listener can infer that the speaker must mean the opposite.

A recurrent issue in the study of irony in particular and of figurative language in general is whether or not the listener must understand the literal meaning of an utterance first before extracting the figurative meaning. Gibbs (1986) presented evidence that people comprehend ironic utterances as quickly as literal ones. Glucksberg (2003) reported that metaphorical utterances (e.g., *My job is a jail*) are also apprehended "as quickly and as automatically as we apprehend literal meanings." Results such as these imply that we don't need to extract the literal meaning of an utterance first. This may be particularly true if speakers and listeners share enough common ground (H.H. Clark & Gerrig, 1984, p. 124) to enable the latter to comprehend the ironic utterance more or less directly (Gibbs, 1986, p. 13). However, when figurative language is unexpected, we may take longer to process it. For example, in many cultures people expect men to make more sarcastic utterances than women. Consequently, comprehension of a sarcastic utterance made by a woman is "delayed as people attempt to integrate" the statement with their expectations (Katz, Blasko, & Kazmerski, 2004, p. 187).

Speech Disfluency

It's very common for speakers to pause at various points while they speak. Such hesitation pauses have been extensively researched (e.g., Goldman-Eisler, 1968; Deese, 1984). Stanley Schachter and his colleagues (Schachter, Christenfeld, Ravina, & Bilous, 1991; Schachter,

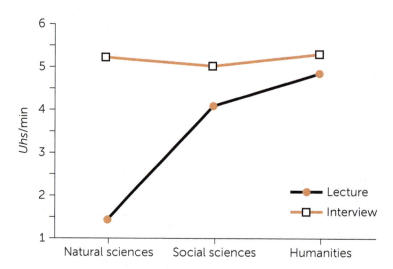

FIGURE 9.11 | Speech disfluencies of lecturers in the natural sciences, humanities, and social sciences

From: Schachter, S., Christenfeld, N., Ravina, B., & Bilous, F. (1991). Copyright © 1991 by the American Psychological Association. Reproduced with permission. The use of APA information does not imply endorsement by APA.

Rauscher, Christenfeld, & Crone, 1994) explored hesitation pauses made by university lecturers, focusing on pauses filled by *ums, ers, uhs*, and *ahs*. No doubt you have heard many such *speech disfluencies*. Schachter and his colleagues counted the number of filled pauses in the speech of 47 lecturers in 10 departments at Columbia University. Collected unobtrusively by a trained observer sitting in the class, the data showed that speech disfluencies were more common among lecturers in the humanities and social sciences than among their counterparts in the sciences (Figure 9.11).

Schachter et al. (1991) attributed the difference in hesitation pauses between the disciplines to a difference in vocabulary between the sciences and the arts. Science lecturers are speaking about a subject that is much more clearly defined than the subject matter of arts lecturers. As Schachter et al. (1994) observed, there are fewer synonyms for scientific terms than there are for concepts in the humanities and social sciences. "There are, for example, no synonyms for *molecule*, or *atom* or *ion*. . . . In contrast, consider the alternatives for *love, beauty, group structure, prejudice*, or *style*" (p. 37). This vocabulary difference means that lecturers in the arts have many more possible words to choose among than do lecturers in the sciences. Hesitation pauses represent points at which the lecturers are choosing among the various possibilities afforded by their respective disciplines. Since science lecturers have fewer choices to make, they produce fewer hesitation pauses.

Schachter et al. (1994) suggested that the differences they uncovered are not unique to lecturers, but can be found in speech generally. Someone who produces many speech disfluencies when talking about subjects in the arts or humanities is likely to produce many fewer when talking about a scientific topic.

Clark and Fox Tree (2002) suggested that *uh* and *um* should be seen as English words with specific uses in spontaneous speech. They hypothesized that *uh* is used to signal a short delay in speaking, while *um* is used to signal a longer delay. Clark and Fox Tree examined speech from a variety of sources, ranging from conversations to messages recorded on answering machines. The results were in line with their predictions. Pauses after *um* were longer than pauses after *uh*. The implication of this finding is that speakers are doing two things at the same time. On the one hand, they are planning what they are going to say. On the other, they are monitoring the planning process itself. When they detect an upcoming delay, they insert *uh* or *um*, depending on how long they think the delay will be. Of course, this monitoring process may not be fully or even partly conscious. The following example (Clark & Fox Tree, 2002, p. 84) comes from a study in which participants were asked questions that could be answered in one word (Smith & Clark, 1993).

> Questioner: In which sport is the Stanley Cup awarded?
> Participant: (Pauses for 1.4 s) Um (Pauses for 1.0 s) hockey.

Not only were pauses after *um* significantly longer than pauses after *uh*, but the length of time from the end of the question until the beginning of the answer was longer with *um* than with *uh*. Participants "were able to estimate how long it would take them to retrieve the answer even before they had retrieved it" (Clark & Fox Tree, 2002, p. 84).

All this leads to the conclusion that *uh* and *um* are not merely speech disfluencies, but also serve a communicative function. They notify the listener that the speaker has detected either a minor (*uh*) or a major (*um*) problem while attempting to produce the appropriate output.

The Social Context of Language

Although L.S. Vygotsky died in the first half of the twentieth century, his ideas have become more influential as time has gone by. One reason is that Vygotsky "provides the still needed provocation to find a way of understanding [the person] as a product of culture as well as a product of nature" (Bruner, 1986, p. 78). As a noted Vygotsky scholar (Wertsch, 1985, p. 231) remarked, "It may strike many as ironic that Vygotsky's ideas should appear so fruitful to people removed from him by time and space. . . . Instead of viewing this as paradoxical, however, it should perhaps be seen as a straightforward example of how human genius can transcend historical, social and cultural barriers."

Originally published in the 1930s, Vygotsky's book *Thought and Language* was not translated into English until 1962 (a newer translation has since become available). Vygotsky (1934/1986, p. 83) was particularly interested in the interaction between thought and speech. Of course, thought and speech can function independently of each other: we can think without speaking just as surely as we can speak without thinking! However, Vygotsky believed that children begin to think about what they say in their second year, and that at that point thought and speech begin to influence each other. Children show a marked increase in curiosity about word meanings around the age of two (Wertsch, 1985, pp. 99ff.), and vocabulary begins to grow quite rapidly (G.A. Miller, 1986, p. 174).

Vygotsky (1986, p. 226) reanalyzed what Piaget called egocentric speech. Piaget observed that young children's speech often does not take the listener's viewpoint into account. Egocentric speech declines as the child becomes socialized, and social speech develops in its place. Egocentric speech might be described as speech for oneself, whereas social speech might be described as speech for others (Werner & Kaplan, 1963, p. 318; Vygotsky, 1986, p. 225). Vygotsky argued that egocentric speech does not disappear but

egocentric speech
Speech that does not take the listener's perspective into account.

becomes **inner speech** (as opposed to external speech) and as such comes to play an important role in regulating thought.

The structure and function of inner speech were summarized by Werner and Kaplan (1963, pp. 322ff.) as follows. Because inner speech is silent, it's a rapid medium for thought. It's also a condensed form of representation. Vygotsky (1986, pp. 236ff.) observed that inner speech typically consists of predicates: because it is addressed to oneself, there is no need to specify the subject. In this respect, inner speech resembles the speech that takes place between people who know each other well. Have you ever been part of a three-way conversation in which the other two people know each other intimately and you are barely acquainted with either of them? The two who know each other well can communicate with a single word or gesture, but you need to spell everything out.

In inner speech, one word can contain a great many meanings. Inner speech conveys the personal meaning of words rather than the conventional meaning. This makes inner speech a very rich medium. Sometimes the richness of inner speech can be observed, especially when speech occurs under unusual conditions. Vygotsky (1986) made this point by way of an entry from Dostoyevsky's *Diary of a Writer* for 1873. It told of

> a conversation of drunks that entirely consisted of one unprintable word . . . :
> "One Sunday night I happened to walk for some fifteen paces next to a group of six drunken young workmen, and I suddenly realized that all thoughts, feelings and even a whole chain of reasoning could be expressed by that one noun, which is moreover extremely short" (Vygotsky, 1986, p. 241).

Dostoyevsky then went on to illustrate how the same word can be used to express contempt, doubt, anger, insight, delight, disapproval. (Can you imagine other contexts in which a word might take on many different senses?) In inner speech all these senses are available, allowing thought to proceed along multiple avenues (Werner & Kaplan, 1963, p. 322).

Although inner speech in adults is usually silent, it is occasionally externalized. Goffman (1978) suggested several situations in which people may produce audible speech that is ostensibly for themselves but is actually intended for others. For example, people coming in from the cold sometimes say *brr*. How often have you said *brr* when no one else was around? Isn't it your intention to implicitly communicate your inner state to others? How about saying *oops* when you make a mistake? Do you say *oops* if there's nobody there to hear you? Perhaps the most compelling of Goffman's examples involves people who are reading something in the presence of someone else and suddenly let out an exclamation—*amazing!* or *incredible!* or *unbelievable!* Their eyes may never leave the printed page, but they are still attempting to communicate with the other person. Instead of saying *I've just read something really interesting that I'd like to share with you*, they try to attract the other person's attention without explicitly asking for it. Try not responding the next time you're with someone who says *Interesting!* while reading in your presence; then see what happens.

One function of inner speech that Vygotsky (1986, p. 242) believed to be especially important was the planning of cognitive operations. He compared inner speech to a mental draft that we use to plan and organize our thinking. While we are engaged in a task, whether planning a meal or changing a car tire, inner speech directs us through the operations necessary to complete the task (Benjafield, 1969a; Luria, 1961; Wertsch & Stone, 1985). Switching between tasks is also under the control of inner speech. Emerson and Miyake (2003) found that when participants' inner speech was suppressed by forcing them to repeat the letters *a-b-c*, then their ability to switch between an addition and a subtraction task was impaired. Baddeley (2003a, p. 199) suggested that one way inner speech may be articulated is by means of the phonological loop part of working memory (discussed in Chapter 5).

The Zone of Proximal Development

Vygotsky (1935/1978) defined the **zone of proximal development** as "the distance between the actual developmental level as determined by independent problem-solving and the level of potential development as determined through problem-solving under adult guidance or in collaboration with more capable peers" (p. 86). The concept of a zone of proximal development draws our attention to the social aspects of cognitive development. "What is in the zone of proximal development today will be the actual developmental level tomorrow—that is, what a child can do with assistance today she will be able to do herself tomorrow" (Vygotsky, 1978, p. 87). As Berk (1994) observed, there is a close relationship between the zone of proximal development and the development of inner speech. "When a child discusses a challenging task with a mentor, that individual offers spoken directions and strategies. The child incorporates the language of those dialogues into his or her private speech and then uses it to guide independent efforts" (p. 80).

zone of proximal development
Defined by Vygotsky as "the distance between the actual developmental level as determined by independent problem-solving and the level of potential development as determined through problem-solving under adult guidance or in collaboration with more capable peers."

Literacy

Literacy means a great many different things to different people (e.g., Heath, 1986, 1989). Before we try to settle on a definition of literacy, it may be useful to consider some work by one of the prominent contemporary literacy researchers, David Olson (e.g., Olson, 1977, 1985, 1986, 1996). We'll begin our consideration of literacy as Olson and Astington (1986b, p. 8) began theirs, by quoting a famous interview of an illiterate man from Uzbekistan by Luria (1976, p. 108). Luria was a student of Vygotsky, and among the most influential of Russian psychologists.

Luria began by presenting the man with a syllogism:

> "In the Far North, where there is snow, all bears are white. Novaya Zemlya is in the Far North and there is always snow there. What colour are the bears there?"
> The illiterate participant replied, "There are different sorts of bears."
> Luria then repeated the syllogism.
> The illiterate participant responded with this: "I don't know; I've seen a black bear, I've never seen any others. . . . Each locality has its own animals: if it's white, they will be white; if it's yellow, they will be yellow."
> Luria then asked directly, "But what kind of bears are there in Novaya Zemlya?"
> The illiterate participant said, "We always speak of what we see; we don't talk about what we haven't seen."
> Finally, Luria asked, "But what do my words imply?" and repeated the syllogism.
> The illiterate participant had the last word: "Well, it's like this: Our tsar isn't like yours, and yours isn't like ours. Your words can be answered only by someone who was there, and if a person wasn't there he can't say anything on the basis of your words."

The illiterate participant was not willing to draw any conclusions from what Luria said. As Olson and Astington noted, he wanted to talk about real bears, whereas Luria wanted to talk about hypothetical ones. In refusing to discuss the implications of Luria's words, he made it clear that, for him, words were nothing without the reality they referred to. By contrast, in talking about language without worrying about what it referred to (Cazden, 1976; Yaden & Templeton, 1986), Luria was demonstrating **metalinguistic awareness**. Sometimes metalinguistic awareness is described in terms of the ability to make language opaque (Cazden, 1976); that is, "difficult to see through." Usually the language we read or hear is transparent: we don't focus on the words themselves entirely literally, but rather see through the words to the meaning they convey.

Ordinarily we use language to talk about other things, but we can also use language to talk about language itself. When we do that, we are using *metalanguage*. For example, to use the word *simile* to refer to a comparison between two things using *like* or *as* is to employ metalanguage. Thus literacy can mean the ability to talk or write about text—to discuss a play by Shakespeare or to write an essay about Whitman's use of language, for example. It can also mean the ability to use metalanguage to discuss the performers in a play or the speech of a politician.

As Olson and Astington (1986b) pointed out, **literacy** in this sense is much broader than the simple ability to read and write. It means "being competent to participate in a certain form of discourse. . . . [Literacy means] competence in talking about talk, about questions, about answers, in a word, competence with a metalanguage" (p. 10). As such, literacy has sometimes been described as a kind of cognitive steroid, enabling us to think in a way that we could not otherwise. Some people experience deficiencies in this regard for a variety of reasons, as discussed in Box 9.2.

Literacy makes it possible to distinguish between a text (oral or written) and interpretations of it (Olson, 1986, p. 113). Someone who is literate is able to discuss different possible interpretations of a variety of texts: plays, poetry, and novels; biographies and histories; laws and regulations; and so on. As Olson pointed out, such

metalinguistic awareness

The ability to talk about language itself, without worrying about what it refers to.

literacy

The ability to read and write; sometimes extended to include the metalinguistic ability to talk or write about text.

COGNITION IN ACTION | Deficits in Reading
BOX 9.2

dyslexia

A reading disorder, ranging from difficulty learning to read and spell to the loss of those abilities.

Reading is an integral part of human communication. This has become even more true with the advent of blogs, text messaging, and text-based forums such as Twitter. What are the processes that underlie reading? A simple model of word reading is shown in Figure 9.12. According to this model, when a reader sees a printed word, he or she processes it as a complete unit and compares it to a mental dictionary (also known as a "lexicon") that contains all the words he or she knows. Once a match is made, the reader recognizes the word and is able to utter it.

Although this simple model seems reasonable, studies of people with dyslexia suggest that it is not the whole story. The term **dyslexia** covers a wide range of conditions, from difficulty learning to read and spell to the

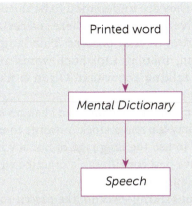

FIGURE 9.12 | A simple model of word reading

loss of those abilities (usually as a result of brain injury or stroke). For example, people with a subtype known as surface dyslexia have trouble pronouncing irregular words such as *yacht* (see Castles & Coltheart, 1993) because they cannot match a word to a mental dictionary to come up with the right pronunciation. Instead, they have to sound out the word letter-by-letter using a set of rules that convert graphemes (letter shapes) to phonemes (sounds), and then stitch the sounds together in order to speak the word. This means that people with surface dyslexia use a different pathway when reading, one that involves translating letters to sounds (see Figure 9.13). Because surface dyslexics can pronounce words by stringing the adjacent letters together, they are able to read non-words such as *blost*, even though they have never seen them before (see Castles & Coltheart, 1993).

Thus it is not always the case that reading involves access to a mental dictionary, as our simple model suggests. Nevertheless, that model is at least partly supported by another subtype of dyslexia. People with **phonological dyslexia** cannot read letter-by-letter, and therefore must rely on their mental dictionaries (see Castles & Coltheart, 1993). Phonological dyslexics are able to read irregular words by accessing their mental dictionaries, but have difficulty with non-words that are not in their dictionaries.

The differences between surface and phonological dyslexia have led researchers to postulate a **dual route theory** of word reading (Castles & Coltheart, 1993; Coltheart et al., 2001). Essentially, the theory suggests that we are able to read either by accessing a mental dictionary (the lexical route), as in Figure 9.12, or by reading letter-by-letter through a process of assigning phonemes to graphemes (the non-lexical route), as in Figure 9.13. The "dual route" model is shown in Figure 9.14.

surface dyslexia
A form of dyslexia affecting only the ability to recognize words as entire units; the ability to read words letter-by-letter remains intact.

phonological dyslexia
A form of dyslexia affecting only the ability to read letter-by-letter; the ability to recognize words as entire units remains intact.

dual route theory
The theory there are two separate pathways for reading, one for comparing words to a mental dictionary and another for converting letters to sounds and stringing the sounds together to make words.

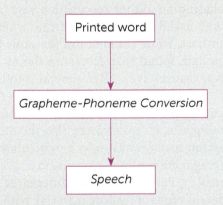

FIGURE 9.13 | A grapheme–phoneme conversion path to reading

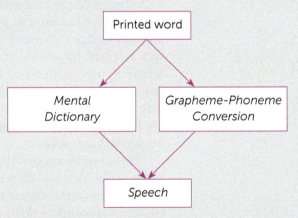

FIGURE 9.14 | A dual route model of word reading

Adapted from: Coltheart, M., Rastle, K., Perry, C., Ziegler, J., & Langdon, R. (2001). Copyright © 2001 by the American Psychological Association. Reproduced with permission. The use of APA information does not imply endorsement by APA.

interpretations are seen as subjective. That is, they are understood to be the outcomes of mental processes, rather than objectively given by the text. There is a certain kind of language that is used to describe this kind of mental process. This language includes words such as *interpret* and *infer* (Olson, 1986, p. 120). Such words are a part of the language of literacy: they are used for talking about text (Olson & Astington, 1986b, p. 12).

One implication of the preceding discussion is that our language changes when we become literate. It's likely that a literate person has learned a stock of words to use when talking about text. Not surprisingly, our ability to use the language of literacy improves with age, and we may not master it until we have had considerable practice with meta-linguistic words (Olson & Astington, 1986a, p. 191).

Most of the words people use to talk about talking—words like *assert*, *contradict*, and *remark*—came into the English language relatively late in its history. Olson and Astington (1986a, 1986b) reported that these words typically emerged during or after the sixteenth century. By contrast, words such as *know* and *think*, which are used to describe mental states but are not used to talk about text, are usually much older. Thus the emergence of literacy coincided with the use of a special language designed to refer to language itself.

The Consequences of Print Exposure

Stanovich and Cunningham (1992) pointed out that literacy is not an all-or-nothing state of affairs. Even people who are literate differ widely in their exposure to printed materials and in the degree to which they develop metalanguages. It's possible that this variation may be correlated with cognitive skills such as vocabulary and verbal fluency. To assess the strength of the relationship between print exposure and cognitive skills, Stanovich and Cunningham studied 300 undergraduate students from American state universities. These students were given several tests, including a test of general intelligence as well as tests of cognitive skills such as vocabulary, verbal fluency, spelling, and knowledge of history and literature. In addition, the students' exposure to print was assessed by several measures, including an author recognition test (ART) and a magazine recognition test (MRT). The ART asked students to indicate whether or not they were familiar with a list of book authors, while the MRT did the same for a list of magazine titles. Stanovich and Cunningham found that scores on the ART and MRT predicted scores on the cognitive skills measures even after general intelligence had been taken into account.

These results suggest that print exposure makes an independent contribution to cognitive skills, over and above general intelligence. It's noteworthy that the ART—an indirect measure of the degree to which a person reads books—was a particularly powerful predictor of cognitive skills. "Relative to magazine reading, exposure to books appears to be more related to positive verbal outcomes. . . . Perhaps there are differences in depth of processing typically associated with different types of reading material, with magazines being more likely to elicit shallow processing" (p. 63).

THINK TWICE
BOX 9.3

An Exercise in Writing

Before you read the rest of this box, take a few minutes to write a paragraph about why you decided to go to university and what you plan to do after you graduate. Then ask several friends to do the same.

Now that you and your friends have written your paragraphs, consider the following findings reported by David Snowdon in his fascinating book *Aging with Grace: What the Nun Study Teaches Us About Leading Longer, Healthier and More Meaningful Lives* (2001). In it Snowdon describes how 678 elderly nuns opened their lives and (after death) their brains to science for what is now known as "the Nun Study." Snowdon and his colleagues were interested in understanding what sorts of factors, measured early in life, could predict the onset of cognitive decline (i.e., dementia) later in life. Among the best predictors they found were the short autobiographical essays that all the nuns had written just before entering the convent. Snowdon and his colleagues analyzed these essays and scored them on their "**idea density**"—a measure based on the number of distinct ideas present in a sentence or paragraph.

Here are two examples of sentences written approximately 60 years earlier by two nuns who joined the study in the early 1990s (Snowdon, 2001, p. 110):

I was born in Eau Claire, Wis., on May 24, 1913 and was baptized in St. James Church—Sister Helen.

It was about a half hour before midnight between February twenty-eighth and twenty-ninth of the leap year nineteen-hundred-twelve when I began to live and to die as the third child of my mother, whose maiden name is Hilda Hoffman, and my father, Otto Schmitt—Sister Emma.

No formal coding is required to see that the second of these examples is much higher in idea density than the first. By 1992 Sister Helen had been diagnosed with dementia. The initial assessment of her cognitive function showed it to be severely impaired, and when she died, a year later, examination of her brain confirmed the diagnosis of Alzheimer's disease. On the same test Sister Emma received the maximum score, and she showed no sign of decline a year later.

In short, the idea density of the autobiographies they wrote as young women predicted which of the nuns would show evidence of dementia in their eighties: "Somehow, a one-page writing sample could, fifty-eight years after pen was put to paper, strongly predict who would have cognitive problems" (Snowdon, 2001, p. 112).

idea density
The number of distinct ideas present in a sentence or paragraph.

Now take a look at the paragraphs you and your friends wrote. Are some more densely packed with ideas than others? It could be that whoever wrote the paragraph with the highest idea density will be least likely to develop dementia later in life.

Language, Cognition, and Culture

Linguistic Relativity

In addition to being one of the most influential linguists of the twentieth century, Benjamin Lee Whorf (1956, p. 135) worked for a fire insurance company. He was responsible for investigating the causes of many fires and explosions, and in the course of his work he observed that many fires were the result of the way people perceived a situation. Moreover, people's perception of that situation was determined by the way it was described. That is, the words used to label objects shaped their behaviour in relation to those objects. Here is one of Whorf's examples:

> People will exercise great caution around a set of containers labelled "gasoline drums." Because they know that gasoline is flammable, they will be careful about smoking in the vicinity. However, if the containers are labelled "empty gasoline drums," then people will be less cautious. This is because the word *empty* not only suggests that there is no gasoline, but also that the containers are inert and not dangerous. In fact, as Whorf pointed out, empty gasoline drums are very dangerous because they contain gasoline vapour and are extremely flammable. However, the way the drums are labelled may make people perceive them as safe when they are not.

Notice the relationship between words and the interpretation of those words that this example brings out. The word *empty* determines that a dangerous situation will be perceived as safe. Whorf gave many other examples of this sort, demonstrating that the way we judge a situation is determined by the words used to describe it. These examples show how a particular language conditions the way we analyze a situation. Suppose we spoke another language with a different way of describing the very same situation. Might not the way we perceive that situation be different because the language used to describe it leads us to perceive it differently? This kind of question led to the formulation of what is often called the **Sapir–Whorf hypothesis**. Sapir was a linguist with whom Whorf studied, and whose ideas greatly influenced him. Whorf began one of his papers by quoting Sapir (1949) on the relationship between language and experience. This quotation nicely gives the flavour of the Sapir–Whorf hypothesis:

> Human beings do not live in the objective world alone, nor alone in the world of social activity as ordinarily understood, but are very much at the mercy of the particular language which has become the medium of expression for their society. It is quite an illusion to imagine that one adjusts to reality essentially without the use of language and that language is merely an incidental means of solving specific problems of communication or reflection. The fact of the matter is that the "real world" is to a large extent unconsciously built up on the language habits of the group. . . . We see and hear and otherwise experience very largely as we do because the language habits of our community predispose certain choices of interpretation (p. 162).

The Sapir–Whorf hypothesis is not limited to the way individual words shape our experience of the world. The hypothesis is much more general. Whorf (1956) argued that different languages have different "grammatical categories, such as plurality, gender, and similar classifications (animate, inanimate, etc.), tenses, voices and other verb forms, classifications of the type of parts of speech" (p. 137), which combine to create a particular system of categories that organizes our experience of the world. Whorf's view leads to **linguistic relativity**: the notion that two languages may be so different from each other as to make their native speakers' experience of the world quite different from each other (e.g., Black, 1962, p. 244). Whorf (1956) put it this way: "The linguistic relativity principle . . .

Sapir–Whorf hypothesis
The hypothesis that two languages may be so different from one another as to make their native speakers' experience of the world qualitatively different.

linguistic relativity
The notion that two languages may be so different from each other as to make their native speakers' experience of the world quite different from each other.

means, in informal terms, that users of markedly different grammars are . . . not equivalent as observers but must arrive at somewhat different views of the world" (p. 221).

Whorf grouped European languages, such as English, French, and German, together as standard average European (SAE) languages and contrasted them to Amerindian languages such as Hopi, which he believed to have a fundamentally different structure. The following example illustrates the sorts of basic differences between these languages that Whorf (1956, p. 141) thought were important. In SAE we have a pattern of description that follows the formula *form + substance*. We have names for substances such as *water*, *coffee*, and *meat*. These are called mass nouns. In our system, mass nouns denote formless substances. The word *bread*, for example, does not by itself convey anything about the size or shape of the bread. Bread is a substance existing independently of any particular case. Mass nouns refer to unbounded, or limitless, categories. When we describe a particular case using a mass noun, we must also include a description of its limits. Thus we say *a loaf of bread*, or *a cup of coffee*, or *a glass of water*. We describe a form (e.g., *a glass of*) plus a substance (e.g., *water*). This way of describing things corresponds to the way we think about the world. We believe that the world consists of formless substances that are given a specific form on particular occasions. After describing this pattern of thought, which he said is common to speakers of SAE, Whorf went on to claim that Hopi speakers experience the world differently. In Hopi, all nouns refer to particular occurrences: "'water' means one certain mass or quantity of water, not what we call the substance water" (Whorf, 1956, p. 141). The Hopi speaker experiences the world in terms of specific events. This goes along with a different conception of time. Time is not thought of as existing independent of specific occurrences. Instead of talking about "this summer"—in which the current season, or the one just passed, is to the unbounded category "summer" what "a loaf of" is to "bread"—the Hopi talk only about specific occasions: "summer now" or "summer recently" (Whorf, 1956, p. 143).

Whorf famously cites the number of words that Inuit use for snow. The Inuit, many of whom live in Nunavut, used to be called "Eskimos" but are now called by their own name for themselves: "Inuit" means "the people" in their language, Inuktitut. Whorf claimed that the Inuit have many different words for *snow*, indicating that their perception of snow is more finely differentiated than ours. This example of the "Whorfian hypothesis" is very widely accepted. According to a document from Canada's Department of Indian and Northern Affairs (2000), there are at least 14 words for snow in Inuktitut, ranging from *apigiannagaut* ("the first snowfall of autumn") to *qiqumaaq* ("snow whose surface has frozen after a light spring thaw"), which would seem to support the Whorfian hypothesis.

Drawing on research by Martin (1986), Pullum (1991) attempted to debunk the more-words-for-snow hypothesis. He approached this project in two ways. First he looked carefully at what some researchers have claimed are Inuit words for snow. For example, *igluksaq* is supposed to be "snow for igloo-making." However, it is actually formed from *iglu* (meaning "house"), and *ksaq* (meaning "material for"). Thus Pullum argued that *igluksaq* really means "house-building material," and "would probably include plywood, nails, perhaps bricks or roofing tiles" (Pullum, 1991, p. 169). However, "would probably" sounds more like a hypothesis than a rigorously researched fact. Furthermore, Pullum's claim assumes adaptation to the post-contact era: if the term was originally part of the pre-contact Inuktitut lexicon, *ksaq* could not have referred to anything but snow suitable for the building of the *iglu*. Second, Pullum pointed out that Whorf may have been aware of how many words English-speakers can use to refer to snow: consider *slush*, *sleet*, *blizzard*, *hardpack*, *powder*, *flurry*, *dusting*, and so on. Pullum claims that the Inuit may perceive many different kinds of snow, but that it's probably not because they have more words for it. Instead he suggests that if the Inuit do indeed perceive more varieties of snow, it's because of their expertise with snow. In this respect they are like other kinds of specialists: "Horse breeders have various names for breeds, sizes, and ages of horses; botanists have names for leaf shapes; interior decorators have names for shades of mauve; printers have many different names for different fonts" and so on (Pullum, 1991, p. 165). In other words, the names are the result of their expertise, not its cause. In fact, though, while knowledge of snow creates language about snow, that language in turn preserves and even enhances the knowledge of it within a culture or society.

Despite the controversial nature of the Whorfian hypothesis, a milder version of it has attracted favourable attention from some psychologists. For example, Hunt and Agnoli (1991) reviewed evidence suggesting that differences between languages may have effects on cognitive processes that are at least as important as the individual differences in cognitive processes found within a particular language community. That is, not only are there differences in cognitive processes between individuals who speak the same language, but there are equally large differences in cognitive processes between people who speak different languages. For example, there are cases in which two different languages "cause speakers . . . to structure the same experience in different ways" (p. 379). One example of this possibility concerns polysemy. A polysemous word has more than one meaning. English words are significantly more polysemous than Italian words. Hunt and Agnoli (1991) pointed out that the English sentence "I went out to buy the pot" is ambiguous because we don't "know whether the speaker spends leisure time in gardening or recreational pharmacology" (p. 382). But the corresponding Italian sentence (*"Uscii a comprare il vaso"*) is not ambiguous. Consequently, it's likely that a native English speaker will need more time to disambiguate such a sentence than a native Italian speaker would. On the basis of examples such as this, Hunt and Agnoli concluded that differences between languages can affect performance, even if it is the case that every sentence in any one language can be translated into a sentence in any other language.

Other lines of investigation are reviving a stronger form of the hypothesis of linguistic relativity (Bloom & Keil, 2001, pp. 356–358). It is to these that we now turn.

> **polysemy**
> The existence of multiple meanings for one word.

Colour Words

Another focus for the study of the relationships between language, thought, and culture has been the relationship between colour perception and colour naming (Rosch, 1988, pp. 374ff.). On the one hand, colour names provide distinctive categories such as *red* and *green*. On the other hand, the physical stimulus for colour is continuous: different colours, or *hues*, are elicited by different wavelengths of light. The term *visible spectrum* refers to those wavelengths of light that we can see. Within the visible spectrum, *blue* is elicited by relatively short wavelengths, whereas *red* is elicited by relatively long wavelengths (Ratliff, 1976, p. 313). Do colour names refer to the same parts of the visible spectrum regardless of culture, so that the same wavelength corresponds to *blue* for everyone? Or do different cultures carve up the visible spectrum differently, so that the wavelength for *blue* in one culture is not the same as the wavelength for *blue* in another? Perhaps what we call *blue* strikes people from another culture as more *bluish green* because in their colour-naming system a true blue is located at a different place on the visible spectrum (R. Brown, 1968, p. 238).

A very influential study of the importance of colour names was that of R. Brown and Lenneberg (1956; R. Brown, 1968, pp. 239ff.). They had a group of judges select 24 colours that were representative of the entire range of colours. Of the 24 colours, 8 were judged to be "ideal" examples of *red, green, yellow, blue, orange, purple, brown,* and *pink*. With these as the central colours, the others that were not judged to be such good exemplars became the *peripheral* members of their respective colour categories. Brown and Lenneberg then asked their participants, all of whom spoke English as their native language, to name the 24 different colours. There were several differences between responses to the central and peripheral colours. For example, the central colours were named more rapidly. Moreover, when participants were shown an assortment of colours they had seen earlier and colours they had not been exposed to, they recognized the central colours as ones they had seen before. This finding, that colours that can be easily named are also more easily remembered, appeared to be quite reliable (Rosch, 1988, p. 376).

To find out whether a culture with different colour names also remembers colours differently, Heider [Eleanor Rosch] and Olivier (1972) studied the Dani, an Indonesian New Guinea people whose language appeared to have only two terms for colour. Heider and Olivier reported that the Dani's memory for colours was nevertheless similar to that of the American participants. Having a colour name available in the language did not seem to be a prerequisite for remembering the colour. Moreover, the Dani appeared to remember central colours better than peripheral ones, just as the American participants did. These results implied that, in terms of perception, the structure of colour was similar for everyone. It's possible that central, or focal, colours are more perceptually salient than peripheral colours, and that colour names refer to those aspects of the spectrum that are most readily noticed. Heider and Olivier's findings complemented the results of cross-cultural research conducted by Berlin and Kay (1969), whose remarkable theory we will now discuss.

Berlin and Kay argued that there are 11 **basic colour terms**, and that there appears to be an invariant sequence regulating the emergence of these colour terms in any language. This sequence is diagrammed below and can be described as follows. Although different languages may have different numbers of colour terms, there is a particular order in which those terms emerge in the history of a given language. If a language has only two colour terms, they will be *black* and *white*; if three, they will be *black, white,* and *red*; if five, they will be *black, white, red, green,* and *yellow*; and so on:

black	red	green	blue	brown	purple
white		yellow			pink
					orange
					grey

This invariance was claimed to be a consequence of the nature of the visual system (Kay & McDaniel, 1978; Ratliff, 1976; Rosch, 1988). The model of colour perception that was used to explain the Berlin–Kay order derives from Hering (1878/1961). Hering argued that red, green, blue, and yellow are *primary colours*, meaning that they are not experienced as blends of other colours. Hering's theory also attempted to capture the distinction between *achromatic* and *chromatic* colours. Achromatic colours cover the range from black through grey to white,

basic colour terms hypothesis (Berlin–Kay order)
The hypothesis that there is an invariant sequence regulating the emergence of colour terms in any language.

opponent process theory of colour vision

The hypothesis that colour vision is based on three pairs of antagonistic processes.

whereas chromatic colours such as red, blue, green, and yellow have hue. Hering invented the **opponent process theory of colour vision** (Hurvich & Jameson, 1957). He imagined that the process of colour vision was based on three pairs of antagonistic colours: yellow–blue, red–green, and white–black, the last being responsible for achromatic colours. In the absence of stimulation, all pairs give rise to the experience of grey, which represents a state of balance between opponent processes. Light acts on each pair so as to yield one of its component colours and inhibit the other. Thus we cannot experience a "reddish-green" because red and green form an antagonistic pair. However, we can experience a "greenish-yellow" or a "reddish-blue," because the colours they are composed of can both be activated at the same time (Hurvich & Jameson, 1957, p. 400). A theory similar to Hering's appears to ground the Berlin–Kay order in the visual system. Perhaps *black*, *white*, *red*, *green*, *yellow*, and *blue* refer not only to basic colours, but also to basic visual processes. If that is the case, these colours will be the first ones that a language will name. Other colours, such as *pink*, are blends of primary visual experiences, and consequently less salient and less likely to be named.

Unfortunately, theories of the Hering type do not appear to be standing up to the test of time. Without denying that opponent process cells exist, Saunders and van Brakel (1997, p. 178) argue that the evidence still does not support the hypothesis that there are "exactly two pairs of opponent hues [or] three pairs of opponent colours." Moreover, the visual system does not appear to process colour separately from other forms of visual information. "There is strong evidence that between retina and cortex, processing of wavelength is intricately mixed with luminosity, form, texture, movement response, and other environmental change" (Saunders & van Brakel, 1997, p. 177). Davidoff (2001, p. 382) concluded that "there is no evidence that neurons respond selectively to any of the four basic colours." In short, there would not appear to be a strong case for the existence of an isomorphism between the Berlin–Kay series and the physiology of the visual system.

Furthermore, there now appears to be some doubt about the universality of the Berlin–Kay series itself. Recall that, in their studies of the Dani, Heider [Rosch] and Olivier (1972) found that the lack of a colour name in their language did not seem to prevent the Dani from remembering the colour. In an attempt to replicate the Heider and Olivier result, Roberson, Davies, and Davidoff (2000) studied the Berinmo, another stone-age tribe from Papua New Guinea. The Berinmo language contains five colour terms:

- *wapa*: *white and pale colours*; also means "European person"
- *kel*: *black*; also means "dirty"
- *mehl*: *red*
- *wor*: spans *yellow/orange/brown/khaki*
- *nol*: spans *green/blue/purple*; also means "live"

The participants—22 Berinmo-speakers and a matched British sample—were asked to name 40 different colour chips. They all took a memory task in which they were shown a colour chip for five seconds, then were asked to pick it out of an array of 40 colour chips. The results did not replicate Heider and Olivier's findings. Rather, the pattern of Berinmo colour memory was different from that of the English-speakers, and was in fact related to Berinmo colour names. These results did not support the hypothesis that "the colour space is universally similar and independent of language" (p. 377).

Davidoff, Davies, and Roberson (1999) took advantage of the fact that the Berinmo language does not distinguish between *blue* and *green*, but does make a distinction that is not made in English. Thus *nol* spans *green/blue/purple* and is categorically different from *wor*, which spans *yellow/orange/brown/khaki*. Participants were shown and then asked to remember a colour for 30 seconds. They were then shown a pair of colours and asked to identify the one they had been shown previously. Suppose the participants were first shown a blue colour and then tested with a blue/green pair. This should have been more difficult for the Berinmo than for the English participants, because blue and green are in the same language category for the former but in different categories for the latter. In general, pairs of colours within a category should be more difficult to choose between than pairs of colours from two different categories. This turned out to be true. English participants made relatively more errors when they had to choose between *nol* and *wor* colours, but the Berinmo made relatively more errors when they had to choose between *blue* and *green* colours. What is a qualitative distinction for one culture is a different shade for the other.

In a study that examined the acquisition of colour names in two different languages, Roberson, Davidoff, Davies, and Shapiro (2004) provided more evidence for the linguistic relativity hypothesis. They studied the Himba, "a semi-nomadic cattle-herding tribe in northern Namibia" (p. 555). The Himba have five basic colour terms:

- *serandu*: spans *red, orange,* and *pink*
- *dumbu*: spans *beige, yellow,* and *light green*
- *zoozu*: spans all dark colours and *black*
- *vapa*: spans all light colours and *white*
- *burou*: spans *green, blue,* and *purple*

The acquisition of colour terms was studied for both English and Himba. The participants were children, and they were studied for three years beginning at three or four years of age. One finding was that the English children did not necessarily acquire colour words in the Berlin–Kay order. In both languages, the order in which colour terms were acquired varied quite widely. As the children, both Himba and English, acquired colour terms, the pattern of their memory for colours changed and they began showing superior performance for colours that are focal in their language. The conclusion was that colour categories are not the outcome of an innate unfolding of the visual system, but are acquired within a particular culture.

At least as far as colour words are concerned, the evidence is currently tilting towards the linguistic relativity hypothesis. However, Kay and Regier (2003) still maintained that there are "genuine universal tendencies in colour naming" (p. 9085). They acknowledged considerable variability in colour words between languages. However, based on survey data from more than 100 unwritten languages, they concluded that there are "universally privileged points . . . reflected in the basic colour terms of English" (p. 9089). Only time will tell how this long-standing controversy will play out. Regier and Kay (2004, p. 290) suggested that the "universalist–relativist" dichotomy has outlived its usefulness and that "the field might benefit from its abandonment." However, precisely what might replace it remains unclear.

COGNITION IN ACTION BOX 9.4 | Lovely Keys and Sturdy Bridges

Before you read the rest of this box, take a moment to think about how you would describe a *key*. What about a *bridge*?

If you've ever studied a language such as French or Spanish, you will know that nouns in those languages are either masculine or feminine; German even has a third gender (neutral). Could the gender of a noun influence perception of the thing it represents? This is an interesting question, especially in its broad implication that the language we use is capable of influencing our thoughts in general. University of California San Diego researcher Lera Boroditsky asked this question and devised a clever experiment. First, she simply presented Spanish and German speakers with various objects, either verbally or in the form of a picture, and asked them to describe each one. When Spanish speakers were given a key (*la llave*, feminine) they described it as "intricate," "little," and "lovely." However, German speakers describing a key (*der Schlüssel*, masculine) used words such as "hard," "heavy," "jagged," and "metal." By contrast, a bridge (masculine, *el puente*, in Spanish; feminine, *die Brücke*, in German) was described in prototypically masculine terms by Spanish speakers and prototypically feminine terms by German speakers. At this point one might conclude that language does shape the way we think. However, the effect could perhaps be attributed to some sort of cultural phenomenon. To ensure that this was not the case, Boroditsky designed another experiment (see Phillips & Boroditsky, 2003).

Briefly, Boroditsky taught two groups of English-speaking participants about the supposed grammatical distinction in a fictional language called Gumbuzi. First, each group was shown two sets of pictures in which inanimate objects were paired with drawings of either male or female figures. They were then shown two additional sets of the same objects and figures and taught that in Gumbuzi the words for the objects in one set were preceded by *sou* and those in the other by *oos* (soupative vs. oosative). In this way they learned to associate the *sou/oos* distinction with gender. After the participants had mastered the distinction, they were then shown all of the pictures again, one at a time (without any labels), and asked to generate adjectives for the objects. The results were the same as in the experiment with Spanish and German speakers. That is, English speakers now produced stereotypical masculine descriptions for the objects that had been paired with the male pictures, and stereotypical feminine descriptions for the ones that had been paired with the female pictures. For example, a violin was described as artsy, beautiful, creative, curvy, delicate, elegant, interesting, pretty, and wooden in the feminine condition, and chirping, difficult, impressive, noisy, overused, piercing, shiny, slender, voluptuous, and wooden in the masculine condition. This work, and other experiments by Boroditsky, seems to suggest that the gender assigned to objects by a language can indeed influence how they are perceived.

Language and Spatial Frames of Reference

The linguistic relativity hypothesis is still alive and well in the study of spatial frames of reference. The studies we reviewed in Chapter 7 suggested that we imagine ourselves as upright in a spatial framework that can be described by terms such as *above–below, ahead–behind*, and *left–right* (Tversky, 2003). But it's important to note that the *we* in the preceding sentence refers to speakers of English, who are often the only group represented by the participants in psychological studies. What about speakers of other languages? At least three spatial frames of reference can be found in different languages (Levinson, 1996).

The differences between the three can be seen in Figure 9.15a, which is based on an example from Levinson, Kita, Haun, and Rasch (2002, p. 159). If we said that *the man is at the chair's back* we would be using an **intrinsic frame of reference**, based on the relationships between the objects being described. But we could also say that *the man is to the right of the chair*. In that case we would be using a **relative frame of reference**, so-called because the man is to the right of the chair *relative to* our position as observers. The relative frame of reference is the one most familiar to speakers of English. Finally, we could say that *the man is to the north of the chair*. In this case the frame of reference is said to be **absolute**, because the relationships between the objects are described in terms of an invariant set of coordinates. You might find this last example puzzling; isn't the man standing to the *east* of the chair? In fact, we don't know: we are simply accustomed to reading maps, which are typically drawn with north at the top and east on the right *relative to* the observer. In an absolute frame of reference the man could be standing to the north of the chair.

Now imagine yourself walking around behind the picture and looking at it from the other side, as shown in Figure 9.15b. How does this affect the way you describe the relationship between the man and the chair? He is still at the *back* of the chair and to its *north*—but now you would have to say that he is to the *left* of the chair. This illustrates how a change in the observer's position affects the orientation of objects in the relative frame of reference, but leaves the other frames of reference unchanged.

Try to imagine how you would describe spatial relationships if your language did not include a relative frame of reference. In fact, there are languages that use only intrinsic or absolute frames. For example, Tzeltal (a Mayan language) uses the word for *uphill* to mean approximately *south*, and the word for *downhill* to mean approximately *north*. In this language you might say the equivalent of *I left my glasses to the north of the telephone* (Majid, Bowerman, Kita, Haun, & Levinson, 2004, p. 109). Does this different way of speaking correspond to a different way of representing space? In a series of experiments, Levinson and his colleagues (e.g., Levinson, Kita, Haun, & Rasch, 2002; Pederson, Danziger, Wilkins, Levinson, Kita, & Senft, 1998) have demonstrated the effect of language on spatial representation. One example is given in Figure 9.16. Participants are shown a toy figure being moved by the experimenter along the path represented on the viewing table. After a delay of 30 seconds, the participant is then rotated 180° and shown a maze on the testing table. The participant's task is to "choose the path that the toy person . . . followed" (Majid, Bowerman, Kita, Haun, & Levinson, 2004, p. 110). Tzeltal speakers tended to choose a path based on an absolute frame of reference. However, Dutch-speaking participants overwhelmingly chose a path based on a relative frame of reference. The Dutch language, like English, specializes in a relative linguistic framework. Thus each group's responses were consistent with its habitual frame of reference. The conclusion, based on this and similar experiments, was that the particular language we speak imposes a way of representing space that we must use in order to be able to communicate with others in our linguistic community.

Without endorsing its conclusions, Bloom and Keil (2001, p. 358) considered Levinson's line of research to be "one of the most promising attempts to explore the relationship between the linguistic difference and cognitive differences." Some investigators are prepared to conclude that "Whorf's original idea about how language

intrinsic frame of reference
Spatial relationships are based solely on the relationships between the objects being described.

relative frame of reference
Spatial relationships are described relative to an observer's viewpoint.

absolute frame of reference
Spatial relationships are described in terms of an invariant set of coordinates.

(a)

(b)

FIGURE 9.15 | The man is at the chair's back

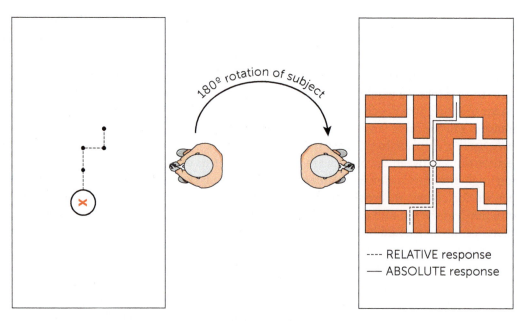

FIGURE 9.16 | The relationship between language and space

Adapted from: Levinson, S.C., Kita, S., Haun, D.B.M., & Rasch, B.H. (2002). p. 165. Copyright 2002. Reprinted by permission of Elsevier.

shapes categories might be right after all" (Yoshida & Smith, 2005). However, there are still some who claim that spatial frames of reference are universal. For example, Gallistel (2002a, 2002b) argued that the brain can represent a number of different spatial frameworks, and that these are available for use quite independent of the language spoken. In a similar vein, Clark (2004) suggested that languages do not obliterate conceptual frameworks that are inconsistent with them. Although different languages highlight certain categories rather than others, we are not fated to think only in the ways that our language provides.

We do not yet know the final verdict on the linguistic relativity hypothesis. Nevertheless, as Barbara Malt has noted, its revival reflects "the kind of cross-cultural work . . . [that] psychologists have traditionally left to linguists and anthropologists." A cognitive psychologist who studies language and thought, Malt went on to express the "hope that [these studies] will inspire more cognitive and developmental psychologists to go into the field and pursue these kinds of comparisons, which are the only way to really find out which aspects of perception and cognition are universal and which are culture and language specific" (Malt, as quoted in Adelson, 2005, p. 26).

Summary

In this chapter we have seen how cognitive psychologists think about language and its basic structure. From the beginning, a relationship between the structure of our experience and the structure of language has been observed. Furthermore, theories of language structure are intimately linked to theories of language acquisition and evolution.

One influential figure in the psychology of language is Noam Chomsky. His concepts of universal grammar, deep structures, and surface structures suggest that a process for learning language is *innate*, or present from birth (i.e., the innateness hypothesis). The alternative theory, championed by B.F. Skinner, suggests that we learn language as children by making use of informative feedback on our utterances. While their veracity remains undetermined, these theories have inspired researchers to demonstrate the surprising richness of the linguistic environment in which children learn language.

Other approaches examine the impact of different contexts on aspects of language. For example, the context in which you receive and understand written/spoken language influences specific modes of communication and comprehension (e.g., code and inferential models, figures of speech). More personal contexts include those in which thought appears to be independent of speech, as with inner speech (i.e., speech for oneself) or literacy (i.e., the influence of language on itself). Finally, cultural contexts provide evidence that some aspects of cognition and perception may not be universal, but rather culture-specific. As such, the different languages we learn and the different words we use may shape how we actually experience and perceive the world (linguistic relativity).

CASE STUDY

Case Study Wrap-Up

We opened this chapter with a look at the McGuffey's series of readers. Clearly, the English that young students were expected to learn 140 years ago was much more complex and difficult than the English that is taught today. Does the simplification of the language that students are exposed to have an impact on adult literacy and general cognitive ability?

That is a tough question to answer. However, several pieces of evidence reviewed in this chapter are relevant to it. For instance, research by Huttenlocher et al. (2002) showed that students' language comprehension ability is influenced by the complexity of their teachers' speech. We also saw that the way parents correct their children's speech affects their speech production (Chouinard & Clark, 2003), and noted that increased exposure to printed language (i.e., reading more) might improve overall intelligence (Stanovich & Cunningham, 1992). Finally, the Nun Study reported by Snowdon (Box 9.3) suggests a strong link between *idea density* early in life and cognitive health in later years.

Together, these findings suggest that (1) language abilities depend on how language is learned early in life, and (2) early language abilities may predict cognitive abilities (and even intelligence) later in life. In the light of these findings, you might want to pick up *McGuffey's Reader* and get to work! You might also want to learn another language: it seems that regular use of two or more languages may stave off the onset of dementia symptoms by roughly four years (see Bialystok, Craik, & Freedman, 2007).

In the Know: Review Questions

1. Outline the development of Chomsky's various approaches to language, including his views on the evolution of language.
2. Review evidence bearing on the innateness hypothesis, paying particular attention to the "poverty of the stimulus" argument.

3. Discuss the process of communication and comprehension, using figurative language to illustrate the process.
4. Discuss evidence for and against the linguistic relativity hypothesis. Which side of the debate are you on? Why?

Key Concepts

absolute frame of reference

articulation

basic colour terms hypothesis (Berlin–Kay order)

code model of communication

competence vs performance

concealing function hypothesis

conversational maxims

co-operative principle (Grice)

deep and surface structure

diacritical marks

dual route theory

dyslexia

egocentric speech (Piaget)

figurative language

given–new contract

grammatical transformations

hesitation pauses

idea density

inferential model of communication

innateness hypothesis

inner speech (Vygotsky)

intrinsic frame of reference

language

language acquisition device (LAD) and universal grammar hypothesis

linguistic relativity

literacy

metalinguistic awareness

minimalism

mirror neurons

morphemes

opponent process theory of colour vision (Hering)

parameter–setting hypothesis

parental reformulations

phonemes

phonological dyslexia

phrase structure rules

polysemy

"poverty of the stimulus" argument

pretense theory of irony

psycholinguistics

recursion

relative frame of reference

Sapir–Whorf hypothesis

semantics

speech

surface dyslexia

syntactic development

syntax

tree diagram

zone of proximal development (Vygotsky)

Links to Other Chapters

frames of reference
Chapter 7 (egocentric frame of reference)

innateness hypothesis
Chapter 4 (domain-specific modules)
Chapter 5 (evolution of memory systems)
Chapter 12 (musical intelligence)

language acquisition device
Chapter 12 (evolution of *g*)

recursion
Chapter 11 (paradoxes, reasoning, and recursion)

Further Reading

D. Bickerton advanced an influential version of the hypothesis that a specific innate faculty contains a model of language. Much of his work is based on fascinating studies of pidgin and creole languages. (A pidgin is a rudimentary language that develops among people who need to communicate but don't share a common language; a creole is a more formal and structured language that develops from a pidgin when children begin to acquire it as their native language.) See Bickerton, D. (1984); Bickerton, D.J. (1988); and Bickerton, D. (2000).

Judgments of grammaticality often rest on the intuitions of native speakers of the language—a rather elusive criterion. Carroll, Bever, and Pollack (1981) spell out just how problematic those intuitions can be.

For a study of individual differences in the use of irony see Ivanko, Pexman, and Olineck (2004).

Eskritt, Lee, and Donald (2001) bring out an intriguing aspect of literacy. More effects of language on categorization are discussed in Sera, Elieff, Forbes, Burch, Rodríguez, and Dubois (2002).

Bickerton, D. (1984). The language bioprogram hypothesis. *Behavioral and Brain Sciences, 7,* 173–221.

Bickerton, D.J. (1988). A two-stage model of the human language faculty. In S. Straus (Ed.), *Ontogeny, phylogeny and historical development* (pp. 86–105). Norwood, NJ: Ablex.

Bickerton, D. (2000). Resolving discontinuity: A minimalist distinction between human and non-human minds. *American Zoologist, 40,* 862–873.

Carroll, J.M., Bever, T.G., & Pollack, C.R. (1981). The non-uniqueness of linguistic intuitions. *Language, 57,* 368–383.

Eskritt, M., Lee, K., & Donald, M. (2001). The influence of symbolic literacy on memory. *Canadian Journal of Psychology, 55,* 39–50.

Ivanko, S., Pexman, P.M., & Olineck, K.M. (2004). How sarcastic are you? *Journal of Language and Social Psychology, 23,* 244–271.

Sera, M.D., Elieff, C., Forbes, J., Burch, M.C., Rodríguez, W., & Dubois, D.P. (2002). When language affects cognition and when it does not: An analysis of grammatical gender and classification. *Journal of Experimental Psychology: General, 131,* 377–397.

10

Problem-Solving

Chapter Contents

Chapter Objectives

- To describe the Gestalt approach to insight and problem-solving.
- To consider functional fixedness and how it can hinder problem-solving.
- To examine artificial intelligence approaches to problem-solving and how they resemble the ways humans solve problems.
- To discuss the various approaches to the study of problem-solving in science.

Vaccinating in the Wake of Wakefield

The largest outbreak of measles in the Americas since 2002 occurred in Quebec in 2011, with a total of 776 cases. Of the people involved 79 per cent had not been vaccinated against measles. Fortunately, no deaths were reported from the Quebec outbreak. But that doesn't mean that measles isn't an extremely dangerous disease. In 2013, 145,700 people around the world died of measles (World Health Organization, 2015)—a figure that works out to approximately 16 deaths every hour. And while that number is alarming, it pales in comparison to the 2.6 million deaths caused by measles in 1980, the year when widespread vaccination against the disease began. It has been estimated that the measles vaccine prevented approximately 15.6 million deaths between 2000 and 2013 alone (World Health Organization, 2015).

Nevertheless, a number of people today advocate against giving children vaccinations. A large part of this anti-vaccination movement can be attributed to a paper published in 1998 by Andrew Wakefield, in which he claimed to have identified a link between the measles, mumps, and rubella (MMR) vaccination and autism. You may have noticed that we have not included a citation for this paper: that is because it was retracted in 2010, after Wakefield was found to have had falsified portions of the study. He has since been barred from practising medicine in the United Kingdom. While he continues to be a voice for the anti-vaccination movement, his findings have never been replicated, and no study has found any relationship between the (MMR) vaccine and autism (see for example, Jain et al., 2015). Even though this information has been widely publicized, there are still numerous parents who elect not to vaccinate their children. In so doing, they put not only their own children at risk, but anyone who for any reason has not been immunized against measles, mumps, and rubella—including infants too young to have received the two required inoculations.

While this is a very short description of a much larger global issue, it's easy to see that the Wakefield paper has created problems for many people besides parents. For example, how should healthcare workers approach the issue? How might the public be better educated about such issues? Should schools turn away students who haven't been vaccinated? And how should scientists respond? Does it make sense to continue investing time, money, and effort on research that fails to show a link between the MMR vaccine and autism, or would it be more beneficial to focus on developing better autism treatments and (hopefully) prevention strategies? Meanwhile, of course, many new parents still struggle with the vaccination decision. If you had an infant, would you give her the MMR vaccine? Even if the answer seems obvious to you, it could be a serious issue for your partner. So what would you do? In the next two chapters we will explore a number of ideas central to problem-solving as well as reasoning and decision-making processes, which might help you deal with difficult questions in the future.

FIGURE 10.1 | Andrew Wakefield

Insight Problems and the Gestalt Theory of Thinking

We referred briefly to Gestalt theory in Chapters 2 and 3. Gestalt psychologists argue that consciousness tends to be organized into a coherent whole or *Gestalt* (form or configuration). If you take a look at Figure 10.2, you will probably see either an old woman with a large nose and thin lips, or a young woman looking over her shoulder. This ambiguous image is an example of a bi-stable figure. Although your perceptions may alternate from one moment to the next, at any given moment you will see only one configuration as whole and complete—never both at the same time. The experience you have when a bi-stable figure suddenly changes from one stable configuration (the young woman) to the other (the old woman) is called a Gestalt switch (Hanson, 1958; Kuhn, 1970; Searle, 2000; Wright; 1992).

Gestalt switches can also occur in response to verbal material. Consider the following example, from Koffka (1935, p. 640):

> Swimming under a bridge came two ducks in front of two ducks, two ducks behind two ducks, and two ducks in the middle. How many ducks were there in all?

DISCOVERY LAB

Gestalt switch
A sudden change in the way information is organized.

FIGURE 10.2 | A bi-stable figure

If you're like most people, your spontaneous answer will be *six*, because your representation of the ducks is organized like this.

O   O
O   O
O   O

The phrase "two ducks" makes you think of a *pair*. But suppose you were told that the ducks were swimming in single file. Now you may realize there is another organization that fits the description just as well, but is simpler. The answer is that that there were *four* ducks, organized like this:

O

O

O

O

When you realize that *four ducks* is a simpler solution to the problem, you may experience the sort of Gestalt switch that is characteristic of **insight problems**. An insight problem typically gives us all the information we need to solve it: no additional information is required. However, the way the problem is posed makes it difficult to see the solution; therefore we need to look at in a different way. An insight problem may be defined as one that requires "a re-structuring of the way in which it is represented [i.e., framed in the mind] before [a] solution is possible" (Gilhooly, 2003, p. 478; Weisberg, 1995, p. 161). Not all problems are insight problems, of course, and we will explore other problem types as we go along. To begin with, however, we will concentrate on insight problems.

The Gestalt theory of insight has been very controversial, but it is still central to problem-solving research. Before we can evaluate contemporary research on insight, we need to be as clear as we can about what the Gestalt psychologists meant by the term *insight*. To that end, let's review some examples of Gestalt psychologists' work on this topic.

Köhler and the Mentality of Apes

Köhler was marooned on the island of Tenerife during the First World War. While there he studied the process of problem-solving in chimpanzees, specifically "whether they do not behave with intelligence and insight under conditions which require such behavior" (Köhler, 1925/1956, p. 3). Chimpanzees were useful participants because they could be placed in an experimental situation and presented with problems that they might never have faced before. Köhler described the behaviour of a chimpanzee named Sultan, who was in a cage with fruit outside it, beyond his reach (Figure 10.3). There was a short stick *in* the cage, and a longer stick just *outside* the bars. The longer stick was out of reach, but the short one could be used to drag it nearer. After vainly trying to use first the short stick and then a bit of wire, Sultan studied the whole scene. Finally he used the short stick to obtain the large stick and then used the latter to get the banana. "From the moment his eyes fall upon the long stick, his procedure forms one consecutive whole … [and] follows, quite suddenly on an interval of hesitation and doubt" (Köhler, 1925/1956, pp. 155–156). To Köhler, Sultan's behaviour displayed insight, by which he meant the ability to understand how the parts of a situation are related to one another. Insight occurs spontaneously and suddenly, and involves a perceptual restructuring of the situation. The chimpanzee suddenly saw how to solve the problem. Insightful problem-solving was all-or-nothing: either he saw the solution or he did not.

FIGURE 10.3 | Sultan performing a problem-solving task

Kohler, W. (2013). The mentality of apes. London: Routledge.

Wertheimer and Productive Thinking

Wertheimer (1959) is often considered the founder of Gestalt psychology. His book on problem-solving was called *Productive Thinking*. To get a handle on what productive thinking entails, let's consider Wertheimer's (1959, p. 266) *altar window problem*.

The problem is as follows (see also Figure 10.4). A circular altar window is to be surrounded with gold paint. The area to be painted gold is bounded by two parallel vertical lines tangent to the circle and equal in length to the diameter of the circle. These lines are joined by semicircles. To figure out how much paint is required, you need to know the size of the area inside the lines but outside the window.

Wertheimer described several attempts to solve this problem. The accounts from some of his adult participants are particularly instructive. They interpreted the problem in terms of what they had learned from similar problems in the past. Some of them felt certain that they could solve such an apparently simple problem. However, they attempted to apply solution procedures blindly, without any real conception of what the problem required. Thus it was easy for them to find the area of the window itself because they already knew the formula for finding the area of a circle. Similarly, it was easy to see how the area of the semicircles at the top and the bottom of the figure could be calculated, but they couldn't remember any formulas for calculating the area of "the four funny remainders" (Wertheimer, 1959, p. 267).

Enter a child with no mathematical training. His first reaction to the problem is to say that, of course, he doesn't know enough to solve it. (Humility in the face of a problem is always a good way to begin.) Then he looks at the figure for a moment and realizes that the two top and bottom semicircles fit inside the window. Thus the area required is simply the area of a square with sides the same size as the diameter of the circle.

The child is not constrained to any specific way of thinking, unlike the adults who attempted to solve this problem. Later in the chapter we will discuss functional fixedness and how children are less susceptible to this barrier to problem-solving. Thus the child is capable of seeing the relationships between the parts of the whole figure, and that's all he

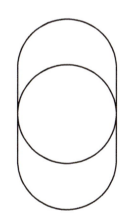

FIGURE 10.4 | The altar window problem

From *Productive Thinking* by Max Wertheimer and edited by Michael Wertheimer. Copyright © 1945, 1959 by Valentin Wertheimer; renewed © 1987 by Michael Wertheimer. Reprinted by permission of HarperCollins Publishers.

needs to see the solution. Too often, as with Wertheimer's educated participants, superficial learning interferes with the ability to see what might be obvious to someone more naive. As Alexander Pope observed, "a little learning is a dangerous thing."

The altar window example shows why Wertheimer argued that there are two types of thinking. **Productive thinking** reflects a grasp of the general principles that apply in the situation at hand. **Structurally blind thinking** is the kind of thinking shown by those adult participants who reproduced thinking they had done before in other situations, which was inappropriate for this particular situation. More recently this has been referred to as **reproductive** thinking (Cunningham & MacGregor, 2014). Instead of thinking reproductively, the child was sensitive to the structural requirements of the actual problem that he was asked to solve.

In order to think productively, you need to go beyond having a little knowledge that you can misapply: you need to look at the situation with fresh eyes in order to recognize and apply the general principles that are relevant to it. To illustrate, here are some insight problems.

Look at Figure 10.5. Suppose that a is 5 inches long and b is 5½ inches long. The problem is to find the area of the square plus the strip (Wertheimer, 1967b, p. 279). The productive approach to such a problem is to ask, "What general truths do I know that might fit a situation like this?" In order to discover them, you need to perceptually restructure this situation and recognize that the figure can be decomposed into two triangles of base b and height a. Now you can see that the general principle you need is the formula for finding the area of a triangle, which is $\frac{1}{2}(a \times b)$. Because there are two triangles, the required area is $(2 \times \frac{1}{2})(a \times b)$, or just $a \times b$. Thus formulas you have learned in the past can be very useful, but they need to be applied with an understanding of the structural requirements of the situation. That is, they need to be used with insight into the problem's structure.

The tendency to apply previous learning blindly can sometimes lead you to the right answer without your understanding why it is right. Consider the following problem (Wertheimer, 1967b, p. 280). Is the number below divisible by nine?

$$1,000,000,000,000,000,000,000,000,000,000,008$$

Suppose you try dividing 9 into the first two digits and notice that the remainder is 1, so that the same result will recur for all of the division steps up to the final digit. The remainder of 1 at the penultimate step produces a final dividend that is divisible evenly by 9: hence the entire number is evenly divisible by 9. A calculator will confirm this conclusion. To have insight into the problem, however, you need to see that this number can be decomposed into two numbers. Thus:

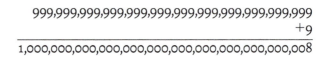

Because both numbers are divisible by nine, their sum must also be divisible by nine. This insight will hold for any number of the same form.

---

productive thinking (Wertheimer)

Thinking based on a grasp of the general principles that apply in the situation at hand.

structurally blind/ reproductive thinking

The tendency to use familiar or routine procedures, reproducing thinking that was appropriate for other situations, but is not appropriate for the current situation.

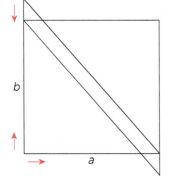

FIGURE 10.5 | Find the area of the square plus the strip

From: Wertheimer, M. (1925/1967). p. 279. Copyright 1967 by Routledge & Kegan Paul.

Karl Duncker's seminal monograph "On Problem-Solving" (1945) has become a classic of the problem-solving literature. In it he presents numerous interesting problems and analyzes how people solve them. Among them is what Duncker calls the "familiar match problem in which four equilateral triangles are to be constructed out of six matches" (1945, p. 26). Can you come up with a solution? If you do, try to relate your problem-solving process to the concepts in this chapter.

Duncker and Functional Fixedness

Duncker (1945) was particularly interested in the effect that previous experience has on problem-solving. When we have a problem, often our first impulse is to ask ourselves, "What did I do in similar situations in the past?" Duncker called this activity **analysis of the situation**, and it involves determining what functions the objects in the situation have and how they could be used to solve the problem. Each object can be seen as potentially capable of performing several different functions. Sometimes, though, we are unable to see beyond the most common function of a particular object and recognize that it could also perform the function we need to solve a problem. When that happens, we have fallen into the trap of **functional fixedness**.

Here is an example of functional fixedness called the coin problem (Simmel, 1953). Suppose you have eight coins and a balance. One of the coins is counterfeit and therefore lighter than the others. How can you find the counterfeit coin by using the balance only twice?

Most people initially think of dividing the coins into two groups of four coins each. One of the two groups will be lighter and so must contain the counterfeit coin. Then you can take the four coins from that group and weigh them two against two. Of course, one of the groups of two will be lighter. But you can't determine which of the two remaining coins is the counterfeit one because you have already used the balance twice.

Before we consider how to approach this problem correctly, let's analyze the previous solution attempt. Why do we initially divide the coins into two groups of four? One reason is that we know that eight things can be evenly divided into two groups of four. One of the functions of the number eight is that it can be divided that way. The fact that $4 + 4 = 8$ is a highly available bit of knowledge for us. Because this property of the number eight is so well known, it's the first thing we think of. In fact, when people try to solve this problem, they often keep coming back to the four versus four division. When the obvious way of using materials keeps us from seeing the most appropriate way for the situation at hand, then we are functionally fixed. Imposing this unnecessary constraint on the problem makes it very difficult to arrive at the correct solution.

The solution to Simmel's coin problem can be very difficult to see, because it lies in dividing the coins in a way that is far from obvious: in three groups of three, three, and two

analysis of the situation

Determining what functions the objects in the situation have and how they can be used to solve the problem.

functional fixedness (Duncker)

The inability to see beyond the most common use of a particular object and recognize that it could also perform the function needed to solve a problem; also, the tendency to think about objects based on the function for which they were designed.

coins. First you weigh three versus three. If they balance, the counterfeit coin must be in the group of two coins, which you then weigh them one against one. Alternatively, if the first weighing shows that one group of three coins is lighter than the other, you can take any two of the three coins from the lighter group and weigh them against each other. If they balance, then the third (unweighed) coin must be the counterfeit one. If they don't balance, then you will know that the lighter one is counterfeit. This procedure is guaranteed to find the solution. However, it's much more complex and less familiar than the four-against-four approach.

Finding solutions to problems often requires you to overcome functional fixedness. It may be only after you've realized that the obvious ways of tackling a problem don't work that you will be open to a reorganization of the problem that will allow you to see the solution. Variables that may determine the presence or absence of functional fixedness will be considered later in this chapter.

Maier and the Concept of Direction

N.R.F. Maier was not one of the original Gestalt psychologists, but he adopted many of their ideas in his approach to the study of thinking. He is usually credited with introducing one of the most difficult of all insight problems, known as the nine-dot problem (see Figure 10.6). It requires you to connect all the dots with four straight lines without lifting your pencil from the paper (the solution is given in the second part of the figure). Notice that the solution requires that you extend two lines outside the square formed by the dots. Now that you know how to solve the nine-dot problem with four lines, can you do it with three?

What keeps many people from seeing the solution is the assumption that all their lines must be drawn within the square. A Gestalt psychologist might say that they are fixated by this unnecessary assumption, and that once this fixation is overcome, the problem can be solved. To test this view, Weisberg and Alba (1981) decided to tell participants

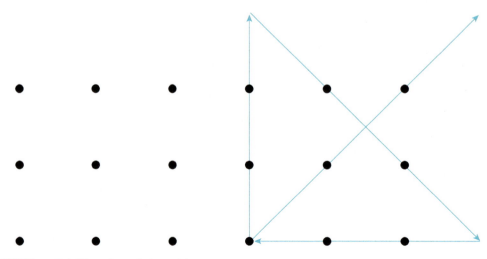

FIGURE 10.6 | The nine-dot problem

that they could draw lines outside the square area, reasoning that this hint should enable them to solve the problem more easily. Even with the hint, however, many participants still did not solve the problem. "The Gestalt view holds that once fixation is broken, the solution either appears whole in a flash of insight or is produced smoothly as one step leads to another" (Weisberg, 1986, p. 45). Because this was not what happened, Weisberg and Alba concluded that there was no evidence to support the Gestalt theory of problem-solving. Weisberg and Alba's conclusion led to a controversy over the nature of insight (e.g., Dominowski, 1981; Ohlsson, 1984). Ellen (1982) tried to show that Weisberg and Alba's account of Gestalt theory was incorrect. To do this he relied on Maier's (1931/1968; 1970) classic explorations of problem-solving in the Gestalt tradition. One of Maier's best-known problems is the two-string problem shown in Figure 10.7. There are two strings hanging from the ceiling. The task is to tie the two strings together, but they are too short for the participant to reach one while holding onto the other. The productive solution is to tie a weight to one of the strings, set it swinging, go and get the second string, walk over to the middle of the room, and wait for the first string to swing over to you. Then you can tie them together.

If participants did not see the solution spontaneously, Maier gave them a hint. He brushed past one of the strings, setting it swinging. After this hint, many participants solved the problem. For several of them the solution appeared suddenly, as a whole. However, few of the latter attributed their discovery to the hint that Maier had given them. Maier (1931/1968) interpreted these results in the Gestalt way:

> Changes in meaning and organization are experienced suddenly . . . it is not surprising to find that the very thing which sets off this combination is unexperienced. Before the solution is found there is disharmony. The reasoner cannot quite see the relation of certain things in the room to the solution of the problem. The next experience is of having an idea. The "transformation" or "organization" stage is not experienced in reasoning any more than in a reversible perspective. The new organization is suddenly there. It is the dominant experience and covers any factor that just preceded it (p. 26).

In other words, an insightful experience can mask the hint that gave rise to it.

Maier argued that, in order to be effective, a **hint** must be consistent with the direction that the person's thinking is taking. It can't be useful unless it responds to a difficulty that the person has already experienced: otherwise it will not be recognized as relevant to the

hints (Maier's view)
A hint must be consistent with the direction that the person's thinking is taking, and cannot be useful unless it responds to a difficulty that the person has already experienced.

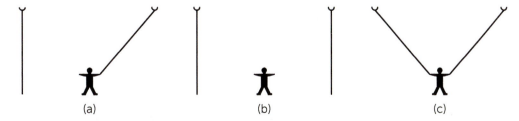

FIGURE 10.7 | **Maier's two-string problem**

problem. Ellen argued that the hint given by Weisberg and Alba was useless to participants because it was irrelevant to the direction of their thought.

Insight Is Involuntary

Metcalfe and Wiebe (1987) attempted to clarify the distinction between problems that require insight to solve and those that do not. They pointed out that one of the essential characteristics of an insight problem is that the solution appears suddenly, without warning; we have already considered several examples of this type. By contrast, other problems are solved gradually in a stepwise progression. Metcalfe and Wiebe suggested that many arithmetic and algebra problems are of this type. For example, finding the square root of 16 requires not insight but the application of a stepwise solution procedure.

Metcalfe and Wiebe reasoned that people working on a non-insight problem should be able to tell when they are getting closer to the solution: that is, they should have a growing **feeling of "warmth"** as they approach the solution. This is because non-insight problems are solved step-by-step, and with each step they feel they are "getting warmer." If participants are asked to solve a non-insight problem in a four-minute interval, and to rate their feelings of "warmth" at 15-second intervals, those ratings should gradually rise as the solution is approached. By contrast, with insight problems participants should not feel that they are getting warmer until the solution actually appears; thus the feeling-of-warmth with insight problems should stay more or less level until the solution is reached, at which time it should rise dramatically. In their experiments, Metcalfe and Wiebe found that feeling-of-warmth ratings for insight and non-insight problems were largely consistent with their hypothesis (Figure 10.8).

Metcalfe and Wiebe also examined ratings for **feeling of knowing**. In this case, participants were asked to rank in order the set of problems they would be working on, from those they thought would be the easiest to handle to those they thought they might not be

feeling of "warmth"
The feeling that many people have as they approach the solution to a problem (i.e., "getting warm").

feeling of knowing
The feeling that you will be able to solve a particular problem.

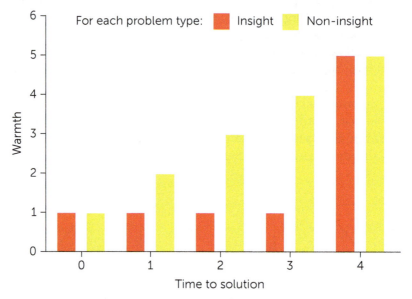

FIGURE 10.8 | Feeling-of-warmth ratings as a function of time spent solving the problem

Data from: Metcalfe, J., & Wiebe, D. (1987).

If you want to see some hilarious examples of creative problem-solving, take a look at *The Red Green Show*, starring the award-winning Canadian comedian Steve Smith. Red is the leader of a men's lodge located somewhere in northern Canada, and almost every episode of his show includes a segment called "Handyman Corner." Here Red demonstrates improbable do-it-yourself projects, virtually all of which involve a roll (sometimes many rolls) of duct tape. One early project was a beer cooler made of duct tape and an old toilet tank. A list of the episodes and links to videos of all 300 episodes can be found at www.redgreen.com/watch.html. You won't have to watch many episodes to realize that duct tape is not the only key to Red's success at comedic problem-solving: another is his ability to overcome *structurally blind thinking* and *functional fixedness*.

FIGURE 10.9 | Red Green

able to solve. They then tried to solve the problems. For non-insight problems, participants were able to predict fairly accurately which ones they would be able to solve and which ones they would not. For insight problems, however, there was no such predictability. These results are consistent with the hypothesis that participants are aware of the procedures they can use to solve non-insight problems, and therefore can predict which ones they will be able to solve, based on whether or not they possess the relevant knowledge. By contrast, insight problems are solved by the sudden emergence of knowledge that the participant was not aware of before attempting to solve the problem.

Feelings of knowing and feelings of "warmth" reflect judgments that participants make about their own knowledge. Such judgments are examples of metacognition, or what you know about what you know—how accurately you can assess your own cognitive processes. Metcalfe and Wiebe showed that participants' metacognitive assessments of their performance on non-insight problems were quite accurate. However, their metacognitive assessments of their performance on insight problems were not accurate, because an insight is not something that can be planned. An insight is something that happens to you, not something that you decide to have.

Current Approaches to Insight Problems

Jones (2003) observed that there are two contrasting approaches to the study of insight problems, which he called the progress monitoring theory and the representational change theory. Let's look at each of them in turn.

Progress Monitoring Theory

progress monitoring theory

The theory that we monitor our progress on a problem, and when we reach an impasse we are open to an insightful solution.

Progress monitoring theory is represented by the work of MacGregor, Ormerod, and Chronicle (2001; Ormerod, MacGregor, & Chronicle, 2002; Chronicle, MacGregor, & Ormerod, 2004). Participants in their research took what seemed to be the most straightforward route to a solution, but with insight problems this approach often led to failure. It was only when the participants realized that they had gone down a blind alley that they considered alternative possibilities. The participants monitored their progress on a problem, and when they reached an impasse they were open to an insightful solution.

In one experiment participants were given the nine-dot problem (p. 312) with one correct line already drawn. One group was given the problem with a line connecting three dots horizontally and extending outside the area of the square. Another group was given the problem with a diagonal line that did not extend outside the area of the square. Since drawing lines outside the square is crucial to the solution, you might think that the horizontal line would be more effective. However, it was the diagonal line that led to the greatest percentage of participants solving the problem.

The reason the diagonal line was more effective was that it led participants to reach an impasse more quickly. Participants typically look ahead only one or two moves at a time and try to connect the most dots possible with each line. Given the diagonal line, they can more easily see that if they follow that strategy they will run out of moves before reaching the solution. This realization prompts them to consider alternative strategies, increasing the likelihood that they will reach a solution.

Representational Change Theory

representational change theory

The theory that insight requires a change in the way participants represent the problem to themselves.

constraint relaxation

An aspect of representational change theory: the removal of assumptions that are blocking problem solution.

chunk decomposition

An aspect of representational change theory: parts of the problem that are recognized as belonging together are separated into "chunks" and thought about independently.

Representational change theory is represented by the work of Knoblich, Ohlsson, Haider, and Rhenius (1999; Knoblich, Ohlsson, & Raney, 2001). Like the Gestalt psychologists, they argued that insight requires a change in the way we represent the problem to ourselves. Their unique contribution was to hypothesize that achieving representational change depends on two processes: constraint relaxation and chunk decomposition. **Constraint relaxation** is the removal of whatever assumptions are blocking problem solution; for example, the assumption that lines may not extend outside the square area is a constraint that may prevent solution of the nine-dot problem. **Chunk decomposition** means separating the problem into the "chunks" that belong together and thinking about them independently. As an example, Knoblich et al. (1999, p. 1536) pointed to highly skilled chess players who see familiar patterns in the arrangement of chess pieces on the board but can decompose these patterns into smaller chunks when necessary.

The role of these two processes in insight problems can be illustrated by way of *matchstick arithmetic problems*. These are equations composed of Roman numerals formed with matchsticks. Here is an example.

$$VI = III + III$$

The equation says that 6 (VI) equals 3 (III) plus 3 (III). Now consider the following:

$$IV = III + III$$

This equation is clearly incorrect, since 4 (IV) does not equal 3 (III) plus 3 (III). However, it can be made correct by moving a single matchstick. Can you tell which one? If not, look again at the first example.

To solve problems of this kind, people familiar with ordinary arithmetic need to relax constraints that they have learned. For example, in ordinary arithmetic you can't simply change one number (e.g., 4) into another (e.g., 6). However, as we have just seen, in matchstick arithmetic you *can* change IV into VI simply by moving the matchstick on the left of the V to the right of the V. Another condition for solving matchstick arithmetic problems is that you must be able to decompose chunks. For example, the configuration V is a chunk. Now consider the following equation. What do you need to do to make both sides equal?

$$V = II$$

The V is composed of two matchsticks. If you make both of them vertical, then you will have II = II. Alternatively, you could make the right-hand side of the equation into V by tilting the vertical matchsticks obliquely to one another, which would give you V = V.

Both constraint relaxation and chunk decomposition promote insight by facilitating the construction of novel representations. In one study, Knoblich, Ohlsson, and Raney (2001; see also Grant & Spivey, 2003) monitored eye movements as participants solved matchstick arithmetic problems. Presumably eye movements indicate which parts of the problem the participant is thinking about. The fact that successful solvers spent more time looking at the parts of the problem that required constraint relaxation and/or chunk decomposition supports the hypothesis that these processes lead to changes in the way the problem is represented.

Jones (2003, p. 1026) noted that the progress monitoring and representational change theories are not contradictory. The former focuses on the process by which reaching an impasse forces the participant to seek an insightful solution, while the latter focuses on the process that makes it possible to reach an insightful solution. In other words, the two theories address different parts of the problem-solving process and therefore should be seen as complementary.

Insight and the Brain

In Chapter 4, on attention, we discussed evidence that the anterior cingulate cortex (ACC) detects conflicting response tendencies and facilitates the process whereby we become aware of such conflicts. Luo and Niki (2003; Luo, Niki, & Philips, 2004; Mai, Luo, Wu, & Luo, 2004) have found evidence for ACC involvement in the insight process using both functional magnetic resonance imaging (fMRI) and event-related potential (ERP) techniques. Participants in their studies were given riddles such as *What can move heavy logs but cannot move a small nail?* Most participants came up with answers that they suspected to be incorrect, such as *a crane*. If they could not think of an answer, they were given it. In this case the answer was *a river*. Participants reported having an *Aha!* experience on learning the answer. Corresponding to these insight experiences was activation in the ACC. The authors suggested that the ACC may be involved in detecting the conflict between the way we have been thinking about the problem and the correct way to solve it.

Luo and Niki (2003) also reported hippocampal involvement in the insight process. We discussed the importance of the hippocampus for the consolidation of memories in Chapters 5 and 6, on memory. Luo and Niki (2003, p. 321) believe that this function of the hippocampus helps to explain its role in insight. "From an evolutionary perspective, the property of responding to the 'insightful' experiences and fixing them in long-term memory can greatly enhance the possibility of an animal's survival. . . . [T]his property of the hippocampus enables the organism to preserve" the sort of information that may facilitate survival sometime in the future. The relationship between the hippocampus and insight is also explored in the studies we will examine next.

Insight and Sleep

When you have a problem and are uncertain of the solution, you may decide to "sleep on it." Wagner, Gais, Haider, Verleger, and Born (2004) have shown that this may be an excellent strategy. To investigate the relationship between sleep and insight, they gave participants a *number reduction task*. This is a demanding task that requires close attention to detail. Participants are given a string of eight numbers, all composed of only three numbers: 1, 4, and 9. They then have to generate a series of responses using two rules. The first, called the *same rule*, stipulates that if there is a sequence of two *identical* numbers, then the response must be one of those numbers. Thus for the sequence 4 4 the response is 4. The second rule, called the *different rule*, stipulates that for a sequence of two different numbers, the response is the third number. For example, the response to the sequence 1 4 would be 9. The response to the first two numbers in a string is then compared with the third number in the string. Thus if the first two numbers are 4 and 4, for which the response is 4, this response (4) is then compared to the next number in the string. If that next number is 9, then the correct response is 1. How this works can be seen in the diagram on the next page.

Comparing 1 and 9, by the second rule, gives you 4 as the first response; then comparing 4 to 1 gives you 9 as the second response, by the same rule; 9 is then compared with 4 so that 1 is the next response, again by the same rule; 1 compared with 9 gives 4, by the same rule. Then 4 compared with 4 gives 4; this is the first time that the first rule comes into play. You can complete the response sequence for yourself. The participant's task is to find the last number in the response sequence. In this case, the last response is 9, and so that is the answer to the problem. Participants are not required to provide any other number: only the last one.

Now examine the response sequence for this sequence of numbers: 4 9 1 4 4 1 9. Notice that the last three numbers are the mirror image of the numbers in the second, third, and fourth positions: 4 1 9 is the mirror image of 9 1 4. The second, third, and fourth responses are the mirror image of the last three responses for all the problems the participant is asked to solve. This means that the required response, which is the last one, is always the same as the second response. Consequently the participant has only to generate the second response in order to have the response the problem requires. This is the insightful solution: you don't need to generate seven responses to find the required response; all you need to find is the second response.

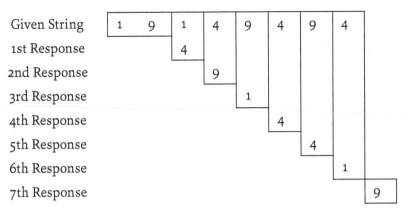

Even after solving many such problems, few of the participants in the Wagner et al. study achieved an insightful solution, although they did become faster with practice. However, once they gained insight into the problems' structures, their behaviour changed dramatically. They would no longer produce a string of responses, but simply announce the required response immediately after determining the second response. Three groups of participants were given a training period consisting of several number reduction problems, followed by an interval of eight hours during which one group slept and the others did not; then they were tested on additional number reduction problems. One group *slept* between 11 p.m. and 7 a.m.; the second remained *awake* between 11 p.m. and 7 a.m.; and the third remained *awake* between 11 a.m. and 7 p.m. The interesting result was that 59 per cent of the participants who had slept produced insightful solutions when tested. Across both groups of those who had remained awake, only 22 per cent of participants produced insightful solutions. The conclusion drawn by Wagner et al. was that sleep promotes insight. The results of the experiment are shown in Figure 10.10.

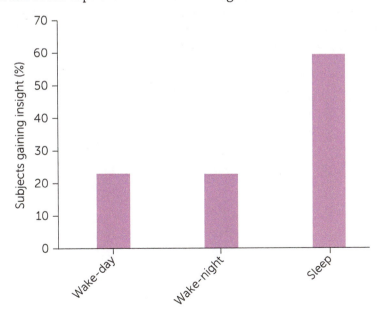

FIGURE 10.10 | **Insight with and without sleep: results of an experiment by Wagner et al.**

From: Wagner, U., Gais, S., Haider, H., Verleger, R., & Born, J. (2004). Reprinted by permission from Macmillan Publishers Ltd: *Nature*, 427, 352–5, copyright (2004).

This finding dovetails with Luo and Niki's (2003) findings suggesting hippocampal involvement in the process of solving insight problems. That is, the restructuring process that occurs as a result of sleep may be similar to memory consolidation during sleep, "resulting in delayed learning without the need for further practice or task engagement" (Stickgold & Walker, 2004, p. 192). Wagner et al. (2004, p. 354) suggested that, partly through interaction with other neural structures, the hippocampus "not only strengthens memory traces quantitatively, but can also catalyze mental restructuring, thereby setting the stage for the emergence of insight."

Functional Fixedness and the Design of Tools

Although the use of tools is not unique to humans, it is so common among us that we can justifiably be called "the ultimate tool users" (Defeyter & German, 2003, p. 134). Most of the tools we use as adults in a technologically advanced society have only one function. For example, lawnmowers, garlic presses, and staplers are generally used solely for the purposes they were designed to serve. As we saw in our earlier discussion of Duncker and functional fixedness, we are often unable to think of a use for an object other than its intended function.

In a series of experiments, German and Defeyter (2000; Defeyter & German, 2003) have demonstrated that young children may be less functionally fixed than older children. In one study, five-, six-, and seven-year-olds were divided into two groups at each age level and presented with a task that required them to discover that a box they had been given could be used not just as a container but as something to stand on. One group was presented with the *pre-utilization condition*, and the other was presented with the *no-pre-utilization condition*. In the pre-utilization condition, the box was full of things, demonstrating its conventional function as a container. In the no-pre-utilization condition, the box was empty. The amount of time taken by those children who solved the problem is shown in Figure 10.11. Notice that the five-year-olds were equally fast regardless of whether the boxes were full or empty.

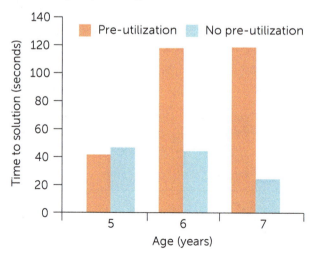

FIGURE 10.11 | Effect of pre-utilization on functional fixedness as a function of age

Data from: German, T.P., & Defeyter, M.A. (2000). p. 710

However, the six- and seven-year-olds performed much worse under the pre-utilization condition.

German and Defeyter (2000; Defeyter & German, 2003) interpreted these and similar results as pointing to the development of a tendency to perceive the function of a tool in terms of the use for which it was designed. By age six or thereabouts, children believe that the function of an object is the one for which it was created, and have difficulty seeing any other use for it. By contrast, children who are five or younger see the function of an object as determined by the goal of the *user* rather than that of the *designer*. If the goal is to find something to stand on, then, to the five-year-old mind a box will do perfectly well.

Is functional fixedness acquired solely in technologically advanced countries where many objects are designed for a single purpose? To explore this question, German and Barrett (2005) examined functional fixedness in the Shuar of the Amazon region in Ecuador. These people have been "exposed only to a small set of manufactured artifacts, and the set of artifacts to which they are exposed tends to be 'low tech'" (p. 2). The participants were adolescents and young adults, ranging in age from 12 to 25 years old. One of the tasks they were given was similar to the box problem described above, with one group in the pre-utilization condition and the other in the no-pre-utilization condition. The Shuar participants showed the same effect of pre-utilization as the older children in the earlier experiment. That is, it took them longer to solve the problem when the box's function as a container had been shown to them than when it had not. The researchers' conclusion was that even in a technologically sparse culture, people will develop the idea that an object's function is the one for which it was designed. This leads to the broader conclusion that there may be a universal tendency to think about objects "based on design rather than current use" (German & Barrett, 2005, p. 4). This way of thinking may have evolved because most problems are solved by using tools in the way they were designed to be used. It's usually not necessary to think of alternative uses for a lawnmower, for example. Functional fixedness would then come about as a "costly side effect" of an otherwise efficient system (Defeyter & German, 2003, p. 152).

The Flexibility–Rigidity Dimension

The experiments of Luchins and Luchins (1942, 1950, 1994a, 1994b) are among the most interesting demonstrations of the way repeating a particular approach to solving a problem can leave us unable to see alternative approaches. One of the ways the Luchinses showed this was with *water jar problems*. Imagine that you have three jars, labelled A, B, and C, and a supply of water. Your task is to use the jars to obtain a specific amount of water. For example, suppose the three jars had capacities of 21, 127, and 3 litres, respectively. How could you use them to obtain 100 litres of water? Think about it.

The solution to this problem involves four steps. First, fill up the 127-litre jar (B). Second, pour out 21 litres into jar A. Third, pour 3 litres into jar C. Fourth, dump out jar C and pour 3 litres into jar C again. You are left with 100 litres in jar B, and the problem is solved. Now consider this problem. Jar A has a capacity of 14 litres, B a capacity of 163 litres, and C a capacity of 25 litres. Your task is to get 99 litres. This problem can be solved in the same way as the first. Fill jar B, subtract jar A, and subtract jar C twice.

In the Luchinses' experiments, participants were given a series of water jar problems just like the two we have considered. All of them could be solved using the same formula: *B minus A minus 2C*. After solving five problems using that formula, participants had developed a *rigid set*, or Einstellung effect. As we saw in Chapter 4, a set facilitates some responses while inhibiting others. In the water jar situation, participants developed a particularly rigid set as shown by their responses to the following problem, which was given next in the series. A, B, and C have capacities of 23, 49, and 3 litres, respectively, and the required amount is 20 litres. Participants typically use the *B minus A minus 2C* formula on this problem, even though a simpler procedure would work just as well. The required amount can be obtained simply by filling A and emptying 3 litres out of it into C. So the simpler formula, *A minus C*, would work, but participants don't see it because of the Einstellung they have developed on the previous trials.

The Luchinses administered this kind of test to more than 5000 participants. Einstellung effects were very reliable findings. In one of their experiments (Luchins & Luchins, 1950, experiment 3), with sixth-graders, the effects were quite dramatic. The children were told to work as quickly as possible. After initially solving the problems using the same method throughout, they were told there was a simpler method for some of the problems and were instructed to find it. However, it was difficult for them to change their approach, and most of them persisted in following the more complicated procedure. There was evidence that the children found the demands of the situation quite stressful. Under pressure to perform quickly, they were locked into a rigid pattern and unable to be flexible.

Woltz, Gardner, and Bell (2000) tested the generality of the Luchinses' findings using a version of the number reduction task that we looked at earlier in this chapter. Recall that number reduction problems have two rules, a *same* rule and a *different* rule. In the problems used by Woltz et al., the three numbers were always 1, 2, and 3, and the given string was four numbers long (e.g., 3213). Participants were trained on number sequences that required them to follow the same sequence of rules over and over. For example, they might be asked to solve problems in which the rules had to be applied in the sequence *same–different–same* or *different–same–different*. They were then tested on problems that required the use of new rule sequences, such as *same–different–different* or *different–same–same*. Those participants who had the most practice during training showed the greatest negative transfer when tested with problems requiring a new rule sequence. That is, they kept responding with previously learned rule sequences and their performance levels dropped as a result. Indeed, among highly practised participants, errors increased from 20 per cent during training to 60 per cent during testing. Less practised participants also showed negative transfer, but the increase in their error rate was not so dramatic: from 20 per cent errors to 35 per cent. These results clearly showed an Einstellung effect resulting from repetitive practice.

Woltz et al. relate their study to other research into common errors made in everyday life. The Einstellung effect resembles the kinds of errors we all make when we have overlearned a particular routine and continue to follow it when we should do something new. Perhaps you can think of an example from your own life where you have been stuck using the same (incorrect) strategies only to fail repeatedly at a problem. Reason (1990) describes such routines as strong but wrong (Reason, 1990). For example, suppose that you always take the bus to and from work but one day you drive instead. There's a good chance that you'll end up leaving your car in the parking lot and taking the bus home.

Flexibility–Rigidity and the Brain

In Chapter 4, on attention, we noted that prefrontal areas of the brain are thought to provide "a top-down bias that favours the selection of task-relevant information. . . . [S]uch a bias is especially important for exerting control when task-irrelevant information can effectively compete with task-relevant information for priority in processing" (Milham, Banich, & Barad, 2004, p. 212). Then we discussed the fact that the left dorsolateral prefrontal cortex (DLPFC) has been singled out as playing a particularly important role in selecting between alternative response tendencies. In Chapter 5, on memory systems, we reviewed evidence suggesting that the left DLPFC should be seen as an integral part of working memory, monitoring and controlling alternative courses of action.

Colvin, Dunbar, and Grafman (2000) have extended this picture of the role of the left DLPFC in a study of water jar problems done with patients with prefrontal lesions. Solving water jar problems requires a counterintuitive move—one that appears to take the solver farther away from the goal rather than closer to it. In order to make the counterintuitive move, the solver must inhibit the most obvious one. For example, in the first of the Luchinses' problems discussed above, the most obvious strategy is to find a way to put 100 litres *into* the 127-litre jar. The counterintuitive strategy is to find a way to empty 27 litres *out of* the 127-litre jar.

Both frontal lobe lesion patients and normal controls were given water jar problems. The patients solved fewer problems than the controls, and also made fewer counterintuitive moves. When patients were categorized according to the sites of their lesions, those with damage to the left frontal lobe showed the most impairment. It appeared that "intact left

---

CONSIDER THIS
BOX 10.3

Self-Control and Problem-Solving

Have you ever noticed that making a hard decision can drain you mentally and even make you feel physically tired? In *Willpower: Rediscovering the Greatest Human Strength* (2011), the social psychologist Roy F. Baumeister and the well-known journalist John Tierney develop the idea that certain demanding tasks can deplete the reserves of willpower that are needed for exercising self-control. They also review recent studies showing that, conversely, performance on demanding tasks (e.g., problem-solving tasks) can be impaired when the resources needed for self-control are depleted.

A good example of how depletion of those resources can lead to poorer problem-solving is provided by Baumeister, Bratslavsky, Muraven, and Tice (1998). In their study, these researchers depleted some participants' self-control resources by having them hold back their emotions while viewing emotionally impactful videos; then they had them complete a problem-solving task (unscrambling sequences of letters to make meaningful words within a predetermined time limit). Strikingly, those participants who had had to control their emotions formed fewer meaningful words in the allotted time frame than did a control group that had watched the same video without trying to control their emotions. Apparently, exerting self-control drained a resource needed for problem-solving. What is that resource? Evidence suggests that it could be the amount of glucose available to fuel successful brain function (see Baumeister & Tierney, 2011; Gailliot, Baumeister, DeWall, Maner, Plant, Tice, Brewer & Schmeichel, 2007).

dorsolateral prefrontal cortex function is critical for successful" performance on water jar problems (Colvin et al., 2000, p. 1136). Without that function the person is unable to inhibit obvious moves in order to make counterintuitive ones.

Mindlessness

Langer (1989, 2000; Langer & Piper, 1987) proposed that the flexibility–rigidity distinction could be conceptualized in terms of **mindfulness** and **mindlessness**. People who are experiencing Einstellung effects behave *mindlessly* in assuming that there is only one way to interpret a situation. By contrast, to behave *mindfully* means to actively seek new possibilities. As Langer pointed out, once you have mindfully created a new way of doing something, then you may later use that way mindlessly. This is what happened to the participants in the Luchinses' experiments. After mindfully discovering the "B minus A minus 2C" rule, those participants proceeded to mindlessly apply it to subsequent problems.

Langer and Piper reasoned that one way of preventing the development of mindlessness is to encourage people to think about things in a tentative rather than absolute way. For example, describing objects in terms that allowed participants to see that they could have alternative uses might encourage mindfulness, whereas describing them in terms of single uses might not. Langer and Piper did an experiment in which participants were shown three objects: a dog's rubber chew toy, a polygraph pen, and a hairdryer attachment. For half the participants, the objects were described unconditionally as one thing only, as in, "This is a dog's chew toy." For the other half of the participants, the objects were described conditionally, as in, "This could be a dog's chew toy." The experimenter then pretended to need an eraser and asked participants what to do. A mindful response would have been to suggest that the chew toy could be used as an eraser. If the chew toy had been described conditionally, then participants were much more likely to make the mindful response than when it had been described unconditionally.

Responding to new objects and events conditionally appears to be an important aspect of mindfulness. Conditional understanding allows people to avoid rigidity in responding. Although unconditional description offers an economical way of categorizing things, it does so by blinding us to new possibilities.

Artificial Intelligence Approaches to Problem-Solving

Might it be possible to program a computer so that the way it does things is indistinguishable from the way that a person does them? If so, then the computer program might be a good model of human behaviour. Computer simulation approaches to problem-solving have been extremely influential, in large measure because of the work of Nobel Prize winner Herbert Simon. As we shall see, there are computer programs that solve problems in ways that resemble the intelligent human approach to problem-solving. These programs are examples of **artificial intelligence**. Let's look at some examples and see how computer simulation and artificial intelligence work.

The relationship between artificial intelligence approaches and other approaches to problem-solving is well illustrated by Newell's (1983) discussion of the work of George

Polya. Polya wrote a famous guide to problem-solving called *How to Solve It* (1945/1957) based on **heuristics**: problem-solving procedures (typically rules of thumb or shortcuts) that can often be useful but do not always work.

Polya (1945/1957, p. xvi) outlined his heuristic methods as follows. First, to understand the problem you need to formulate it in a way that will allow you to begin thinking about it. For example, you might draw a diagram. Once you think you understand what the problem requires, then you can move on to the second stage and devise a plan. For example, you might try to find a similar problem that you know how to solve, and then see if the same method will work for the present problem. The third stage is to carry out the plan, with careful attention to detail. Finally, you need to examine the result to make sure that it is the right one, and determine whether or not the method you used in this case could be used to solve other problems.

As Newell (1983, p. 202) observed, Polya's description of problem-solving has much in common with later artificial intelligence techniques. Artificial intelligence requires as clear and precise a formulation of the problem as possible. In order to make a computer program work, we can't rely on vague hunches and intuitions; we must be able to specify a procedure. Polya's heuristic approach was designed to be clear, precise, and explicit. It is this kind of method—the direct opposite of the insight that the Gestalt approach emphasizes—that people working on artificial intelligence are interested in.

In programming heuristic problem-solving methods, artificial intelligence researchers use unambiguous solution procedures called **algorithms** (Dietrich, 1999). The rules governing long division are a common example: they are unambiguous, and a computer can easily be programmed to follow them. Algorithms may be divided into two classes: *systematic* and *non-systematic*. "A systematic algorithm is guaranteed to find the solution if one exists . . . [but] non-systematic algorithms . . . are not guaranteed to find a solution" (Korf, 1999, p. 373). Since Polya's heuristic method is not guaranteed to find a solution, it is an example of a non-systematic algorithm.

A Simple Example of Artificial Intelligence

Computer programs that play games invented by humans are useful examples of artificially intelligent systems. For example, there are excellent programs that play games such as checkers, Scrabble, backgammon, chess, and bridge, and that solve crossword puzzles (Schaeffer & van den Herik, 2002). A tipping point in the history of artificial intelligence occurred in 1997 when the chess-playing program called *Deep Blue* defeated world chess champion Garry Kasparov in a six-game match (Campbell, Hoane, & Hsu, 2002). In fact, early research in artificial intelligence centred on creating a chess-playing program (Newell, Shaw, & Simon, 1958; Newell & Simon, 1972, Chap. 11). Since chess is a very intricate game, and the programs written to play it are correspondingly complicated, in the discussion below we will look at a much simpler game called Go-Moku, which has also been explored by psychologists (e.g., Eisenstadt & Kareev, 1977).

Go-Moku is played on a lattice, a portion of which is shown in Figure 10.12, and is similar to tic-tac-toe and Connect Four. One player tries to place five *X*s in a line, while the other tries to place five *O*s in a line. The situation in Figure 10.12 is such that the person playing *X*s is in an unstoppable position. No matter where the person playing *O*s moves, *X* will win on the following move. This situation is called an *open four*, and is obviously

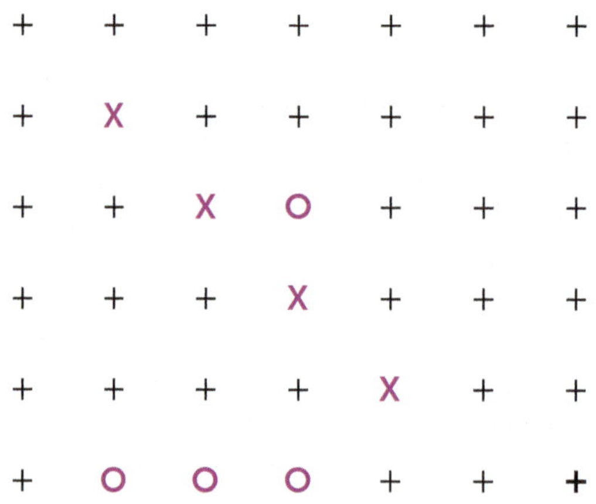

FIGURE 10.12 | A portion of the Go-Moku playing surface

one that both players try to create. Meanwhile, the person playing *Os* has created a situation called an *open three*. If you can create two open threes, then you will be in a better position, because if your opponent blocks one of them you can turn the other into an open four on your next move. Thus in addition to the overall goal of making five in a row there are various **subgoals**, such as creating open fours and threes.

If you were writing a computer program to play Go-Moku against an opponent, what sorts of characteristics would your program need to have? First it would need a data structure and an **evaluation function**. The data structure corresponds to what Polya called "understanding the problem." It consists of a representation of the playing board and the possible states of each position on the board, whether *X*, *O*, or empty. The evaluation function handles all the elements that Polya referred to as "creating a plan, carrying out the plan and evaluating the plan" (Polya, 1945/1957, p. xvi). Given a particular position on the board, the program works out all the possible moves. Each of the possibilities is evaluated. For example, a move that makes five in a row has the highest value; one that makes four in a row the next highest; and so on. Defensive moves can also be given a value: blocking five in a row gets the most points; blocking four in a row gets the next most; and so on. The move with the highest value is the one that the program will make.

The Problem Space

In the case of a simple game like Go-Moku, it's possible to have the program evaluate all possible moves at any stage of the game. Thus a successful computer program uses a systematic algorithm to calculate which of all the possible moves would be the best. Current Go-Moku programs will win every time, provided they are allowed to make the first move (Allis, van der Herik, & Huntjens, 1996; Muller, 2001). However, Go-Moku programs typically don't do the sorts of things that more complicated games must. The term **problem space** refers to the representation of the problem, including the goal to be reached and the various ways of transforming the given situation into the solution (Newell & Simon, 1972, p. 59; Keren, 1984). Go-Moku's problem space is very simple, but more complex games such as chess have extremely complicated problem spaces, and they must be analyzed at least two moves in advance. Good chess players need to be able to anticipate not only what their opponents might

subgoal
A goal derived from the original goal, the solution of which leads to the solution of the problem as a whole.

evaluation function
The process whereby a plan is created, carried out, and evaluated.

problem space
The representation of a problem, including the goal to be reached and the various ways of transforming the given situation into the solution.

do in response to their next move, but what moves they might make then, how their opponent might respond, and so on. Thus the possibilities have to be examined two, three, or even more moves in advance. This makes it very difficult to create a systematic algorithm for chess, as we shall see.

A **search tree** represents all the possible moves branching out from the initial state of the problem. As Newell, Simon, and Shaw (1962) pointed out, solving a problem is a bit like making your way through a maze. In a maze such as the one shown in Figure 10.13, you must get from the start (S) to the goal (G), and avoid taking a path that leads to a dead end. From the starting point you are faced with a series of choices, or branches, in the maze. Finding your way through the maze requires you to make the right decision at each choice point. The search tree for a game like chess is enormous, since there are 30 or even 40 legal moves that can be made at any point in the game. If you were to evaluate each alternative to see where it would lead, you would have to examine another 30 or 40 alternatives for each of the first 30 or 40 alternatives.

You can begin to see where this will lead. "If we undertake to look ahead only 5 moves, with 30 legal alternatives at each step, we must consider 1015 positions in order to evaluate a single move" (Newell & Simon, 1972, p. 97). The extremely rapid increase in the number of alternatives that must be considered as you explore the problem space for a complex problem is called a *combinatorial explosion*. Such an explosion cannot be effectively managed by a systematic algorithm. "Even if a computer could examine a million possibilities per second, examining 1015 possibilities would take 31.7 years" (Korf, 1999, p. 372). Since you can't consider all the alternatives, you need non-systematic methods to find the best route through the problem space.

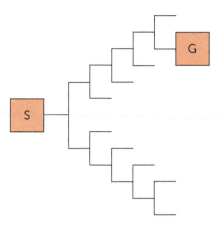

FIGURE 10.13 | A maze in which you must get from the start (S) to the goal (G)

General Problem Solver (GPS) and the Tower of Hanoi

One of the most frequently cited computer programs designed to perform that kind of heuristic search was Newell and Simon's (1972; Simon, 1979) **General Problem Solver (GPS)**. To model problem-solving, it's often useful to analyze the structure of **toy problems**. As the name suggests, these are not real-life problems, but the sort of thing you might find in a toy shop. They are useful because they have a known structure and interesting data can be collected from participants as they try to solve them. One of the problems extensively explored by Simon and his co-workers is a game invented by French mathematician Édouard Lucas in 1883 called the *Tower of Hanoi* (e.g., Anzai & Simon, 1979; Simon, 1975); see Figure 10.14. In one version of this problem, three concentric rings (small, medium, and large) are placed around one of three posts and the task is to move all the rings from the post labelled A to the post labelled C. The constraints are that only one ring may be moved at a time and no ring may be placed on a ring smaller than itself. Thus you can move the smallest ring to B, but then you can't place the medium-sized ring on top of it.

Before looking at Figure 10.14, which shows the solution to a three-ring problem, try solving it yourself. Although the final goal is to move all the rings from A to C, this goal can be decomposed into a series of subgoals. One subgoal is to move the small and medium rings to post B. This subgoal can be achieved by moving the small ring to C, then the medium ring to B, and finally placing the small ring on top of the medium ring on B. This allows the large ring to be moved to C. The next subgoal is to move the small and medium rings from B to C. First move the small ring to A, then the medium ring to C, and finally move the small ring to C.

search tree
A representation of all the possible moves branching out from the initial state of the problem.

General Problem Solver (GPS)
A computer program used to perform non-systematic searches.

toy problems
Problems used to analyze the problem-solving process.

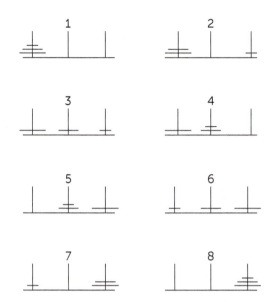

FIGURE 10.14 | Solution for the three-ring version of the Tower of Hanoi problem

How can you program a procedure like that on a computer? GPS does it by means of **production rules** (Eisenstadt & Simon, 1997; Simon, 2000). A production rule consists of a condition and an action. The notation that Simon used is C→ A, where *C* stands for a condition and *A* stands for an action. Thus one obvious production rule is:

Problem solved→ halt

If the condition of solving the problem is met, then the problem-solving process is halted. How is it determined that the problem is solved? A problem is solved if there is no difference between the state that has been reached and the goal that was sought. The analysis of differences between the current state and the goal state is an essential part of GPS. At the beginning of the problem-solving process there is a large difference between the current and goal states. This is in fact the definition of a problem: being in one state and attempting to reach another state (the goal). The heuristic procedure that GPS uses to reduce differences between current and goal states is known as **means–end analysis**.

In order for the problem-solving process to advance, subgoals may have to be substituted for the original goal. For example, if there is no action that would follow from the current condition and lead directly to the goal, there may be a subgoal that can be reached directly from the current state. Once that is accomplished, then the difference between the initial state and the goal state will have been reduced. If necessary, another subgoal can then be formulated, and once that is reached, the difference between initial and final states will be further reduced. In analyzing a problem, GPS creates a **goal stack**. The final goal to be reached is on the bottom of the stack, with the subgoals piled on top of it in an order that is the reverse of the one in which they are to be attained. Thus the first subgoal to be reached is on the top of the stack, followed by the next subgoal, and so on.

Notice that the description we have just given is a more general formulation of the specific procedure for solving the Tower of Hanoi problem. Simon (1975) argued that GPS is, as its name implies, a general problem-solving procedure that can be applied to particular problems such as the Tower of Hanoi. The condition–action pairs that would be used to solve the Tower of Hanoi would include rules that recognize when a goal cannot be directly achieved and would then substitute another goal for it, until a legal move can be made. This procedure is applied over and over until the problem is solved.

Thinking Aloud as a Method for Studying Human Problem-Solving

One of the goals of Simon's research was to write computer programs that mimic the procedures participants actually use when solving problems such as the Tower of Hanoi. In order to find out what those procedures are, a technique called **thinking aloud** has often been used (Ericsson & Simon, 1980, 1993; Newell, 1977). Ericsson and Simon referred to the thinking-aloud method as *concurrent verbalization*: the verbalization of information as the participant is attending to it. By contrast, in *retrospective verbalization* the participant is asked about cognitive processes that occurred at an earlier point in time. Concurrent verbalization relies on short-term memory, whereas retrospective verbalization relies on long-term memory. When participants think aloud, they put into words a process that normally takes place non-verbally. This verbal description of the solution process is called a *protocol*. Although there may be omissions in these protocols, they still contain a great deal of useful information.

> **thinking aloud**
> Concurrent verbalization: the verbalization of information as the participant is attending to it.

Here is a typical example of a protocol generated by a participant while solving the Tower of Hanoi problem, taken from Anzai and Simon (1979, p. 138). The participant is trying to solve a *five*-disk version of the Tower of Hanoi puzzle. You might find it instructive to try this yourself.

1. I'm not sure, but first I'll take 1 from A and place it on B.
2. And I'll take 2 from A and place it on C.
3. And then, I take 1 from B and place it on C. (The interrogator asks, "If you can, tell me why you placed it there.")
4. Because there was no place else to go, I had to place 1 from B to C.
5. Then, next, I placed 3 from A to B.
6. Well . . . , first I had to place 1 to B, because I had to move all disks to C. I wasn't too sure though.
7. I thought that it would be a problem if I placed 1 on C rather than B.
8. Now I want to place 2 on top of 3, so I'll place 1 on A.
9. Then I'll take 2 from C, and place it from A to B.
10. And I'll take 1 and . . . place it from A to B.
11. So then, 4 will go from A to C.
12. And then . . . , um . . . , oh . . . , um . . .

As you can see, there is a lot of information in these protocols. In conjunction with observing the actual behaviour of the participant, these protocols can give the experimenter a reasonably complete description of a psychological process. Obviously, the raw protocol needs to be analyzed carefully. Newell (1977) recommended taking a series of steps to clarify the protocol. First, the protocol should be divided into phrases (descriptions of single acts). Then the experimenter constructs a problem behaviour graph: a concrete description of the way the participant moves around in the problem space. This description can be used as the basis for a production system designed to model the participant's behaviour. Generalizing across a number of participants' descriptions makes it possible to model the kind of system that is eventually embodied in a computer simulation.

Although concurrent verbalization is very widely used, there is evidence suggesting that it may interfere with some aspects of the problem-solving process (Schooler, Ohlsson, & Brooks, 1993). In order to determine the usefulness of thinking-aloud protocols, Fleck and Weisberg (2004) conducted a detailed analysis and comparison of problem-solving behaviour in both verbalization and non-verbalization conditions. They concluded that "instructing participants to verbalize did not adversely affect their thought processes" (p. 1003). It's important that the participants "talk to themselves" rather than to the experimenter. This produces a useful record of the problem-solving process without requiring the participant to communicate to anyone other than him/ herself. Protocols obtained in this way resemble inner speech, and may capture some aspects of the process whereby speech regulates thought (Benjafield, 1969a).

Can Computer Programs Experience Insight?

Michael Wertheimer (1985), the son of the Max Wertheimer who wrote *Productive Thinking*, criticized computer simulations of problem-solving from a Gestalt perspective. He argued, as have many others, that insight is nowhere to be found in a computer program. "Missing in such work is the crucial step of *understanding*, that is, grasping both what is crucial in any given problem and why it is crucial. Classical Gestalt analyses of productive thought emphasized precisely this phenomenon of insight" (Wertheimer, 1985, p. 19).

In a reply, Simon (1986, p. 253) argued that there were really two parts to Wertheimer's critique. The first issue is empirical. Can computer programs "represent, and thereby explain, the rich range of learning and problem solving behaviors with which Gestalt psychology has been centrally concerned"? The second issue is whether the concepts of Gestalt psychology can be "sharpened up and made useful to experimental psychology." We'll address each of these issues in turn.

Programming Insight

Kaplan and Simon (1990) showed that even a very difficult insight problem can be analyzed in terms compatible with an artificial intelligence approach. The problem they focused on is called the *mutilated checkerboard problem* (see below). There is a standard 8-by-8 checkerboard, from which two corners have been removed. Participants are asked to imagine placing dominoes on the board. Each domino covers two vertical or two horizontal squares. Dominoes cannot be placed diagonally. There are 62 squares. Can 31 dominoes be placed to cover the 62 squares exactly? If not, why is it not possible for 31 dominoes to cover the 62 squares? Spend a few minutes thinking about this problem.

The way that the typical participant initially represents the problem cannot lead to a solution. Participants can imagine placing tiles on the checkerboard for several hours without reaching a solution. At that point the participant will have reached an impasse. The participant may realize "a need to look at the problem in a new way" (Simon, 1995, p. 944).

A restructuring of the problem's representation can occur if the participant begins to focus on the number of black and white squares. Notice that both the missing squares are white. This means that there are 32 black squares and 30 white ones. Each domino must cover one black and one white square, and there are 31 dominoes. After covering 30 black and 30 white squares with 30 dominoes, there will still be two black squares left over. Remember that a domino must cover one black and one white square. Therefore, no matter where the two black squares are, they cannot be covered by the single remaining domino. It is not possible for 31 dominoes to cover the 62 squares.

The mutilated checkerboard problem has all the features of an insight problem. First, the way the problem is initially represented leads the solver nowhere. Reaching an impasse, the solver is forced to restructure the problem, focusing on previously unattended elements. This leads the solver to the insight that the problem cannot be solved.

Simon (1995, pp. 943–944) constructed a computational model of insight that was intended to explain the process of restructuring. The program begins searching for a problem solution, following a path that leads to a dead end. When it has been unsuccessful for a certain period of time, a *stop rule* will cause the program to pause and abandon the problem space it has been searching. When the program resumes, it will begin by attending to previously neglected aspects of the problem and represent the problem in a new way. As a result the program takes a new direction, which is more likely to be successful.

This model of insight reflects the behaviour of human problem-solvers. Yet those sympathetic to Gestalt psychology might still say that the program does not capture the richness of the insight experience. This brings us to Simon's second issue: can the concepts of Gestalt psychology be "sharpened up and made useful to experimental psychology"? In Simon's theory of insight, all the explanatory concepts have a definite meaning, and *insight*, insofar as it is a scientific concept, can be modelled just as any other cognitive process can. To modern proponents of the Gestalt perspective who might argue that computer simulation of *insight* and *understanding* requires "twisting these terms out of all semblance to their intended meaning," Simon responds that their concepts may be too distant from empirical science to be meaningful (1986, p. 253–254). In his view, it might be necessary to abandon the language of Gestalt psychology in order to achieve truly scientific explanations.

Solving Problems in Science

Although Simon found it "reasonable that research on human thinking should begin with relatively contentless tasks" such as the Tower of Hanoi, "research in both cognitive psychology and artificial intelligence has been turning more and more to … domains that have substantial, meaningful content" (1981, p. 102). Among those domains is problem-solving in science. Klahr and Simon (1999, 2001) observed that there are four complementary approaches to the study of problem-solving in science: **historical accounts**, **observation of ongoing scientific investigations**, **laboratory studies**, and **computational models**.

Historical Accounts

Simon (1992, p. 157) recommended studying the history of science as a source of hypotheses concerning the ways in which knowledge is acquired. However, it was Nersessian

historical accounts, observation of ongoing scientific investigations, laboratory studies, and computational models

Different methods for studying problem-solving in science.

cognitive history of science

The study of historically important scientific discoveries in a framework provided by cognitive science.

Zeigarnik effect

The "quasi-need" to finish incomplete tasks.

(1995) who coined the phrase **cognitive history of science**. This endeavour combines "case studies of historical scientific practices" with "scientific investigations of how humans reason, judge, represent, and come to understand" (Nersessian, 1995, p. 195). In other words, case studies of working scientists are informed by the framework that cognitive science provides.

A landmark in cognitive historical studies was Gruber's (1974/1981; Gruber & Wallace, 2001) reconstruction of the process by which Darwin arrived at his theory of evolution through natural selection. Gruber spent 20 years studying Darwin's notebooks to understand the thinking that led to evolutionary theory. Scientists are often meticulous record-keepers, and this was especially true of Darwin. His notebooks trace the development of his ideas over more than 50 years. Gruber observed that Darwin's enterprise illustrated the strength of the **Zeigarnik effect**: the "quasi-need" to finish incomplete tasks (Zeigarnik, 1927/1967). Although this effect can be detected in a laboratory, its true significance is revealed only when we see someone working on a problem over many years or even decades. This is precisely the sort of lifelong problem-solving that many successful scientists engage in. Giving up is not an option for them, and without such persistence complex scientific problems might never be solved.

Another important strand of research in cognitive history is Tweney's (1991, 1999) analysis of the diaries of the nineteenth-century English physicist Michael Faraday. Faraday's "work revolutionized physics and led directly to both classical field theory and relativity theory" (Williams, 1991, p. 278). Tweney shows that the diaries themselves played an essential role in Faraday's scientific problem-solving. Faraday understood that keeping detailed records of his work was essential because he could not rely on his memory. One reason he could not rely on memory was that he was extraordinarily productive, completing over 30,000 experiments. We have already seen how unreliable memory can be, and Faraday was acutely aware of its failings. Farady's diary served as an external memory aid. However, the diary entries themselves needed to be organized. One way of understanding this necessity is to imagine yourself with an enormous number of files stored on your computer. You need an indexing system not only to find files, but also to remember what the files contain (Tweney, 1991, p. 303). Faraday used a version of the *method of loci*, which we reviewed in Chapter 7, to help him keep track of diary entries. More important, he used paper slips much in the way we might use Post-it notes now. These slips were reminders of diary entries, and he would arrange and rearrange them, looking for patterns, "in effect constructing a larger whole from the separate bits and pieces" (Tweney, 1991, p. 305). The larger whole he sought was the body of scientific laws he eventually came to discover. In Faraday's diaries we can see how important memory is to the process of scientific problem-solving.

Observation of Ongoing Scientific Investigations/ Laboratory Studies

in vivo/in vitro method (Dunbar)

In the case of scientific problem-solving, *in vivo* research involves the observation of ongoing scientific investigations, while *in vitro* research involves laboratory studies of scientific problem-solving.

Dunbar (2000, 2001; Dunbar & Blanchette, 2001; Fugelsang, Stein, Green, & Dunbar, 2004) pioneered what he called the *in vivo/in vitro* **method** for studying problem-solving in science. *In vivo* means "in the living" and *in vitro* means "in glass." This distinction comes from biology, where it refers to studies of the living organism (*in vivo*) versus studies in an artificial environment (*in vitro*). In psychology it refers to the distinction between ecologically valid research (*in vivo*) and laboratory research (*in vitro*). In the case of scientific problem-solving, *in vivo* research involves the observation of ongoing scientific investigations, while *in vitro* research involves laboratory studies of scientific problem-solving. "A key feature of the *in vivo/in vitro* method is that we can investigate a question in a naturalistic situation and then go back to the psychological laboratory and conduct controlled experiments on what has been identified in the naturalistic settings" (Dunbar, 2001, p. 118).

To set up an *in vivo* study, the investigator needs to find research settings in which successful scientific problem-solving is likely to occur. Dunbar chose to investigate the field of molecular biology because of its attraction for ambitious and high-achieving scientists. By interviewing outstanding figures in the field, including a Nobel Prize winner, Dunbar was able to identify a number of laboratories involved in important and innovative research, and eventually selected eight of them to study (Dunbar, 2000, p. 51). He found that each laboratory held weekly meetings, attended by the head of the lab, post-doctoral and graduate students, and lab technicians. Since a great deal of scientific problem-solving took place at these meetings, Dunbar made extensive video and/or audiotape recordings of them, and these recordings became part of the data with which he and his colleagues worked. They also built their own molecular genetics laboratory, where participants were first taught about molecular genetics using computer models and then given tasks such as "discovering how genes control other genes" (Dunbar, 2000, p. 50). (The *in vivo/in vitro* method is extremely time-consuming.) These laboratory studies provided a complementary data set. Several findings emerged from Dunbar's studies, but we have space here to deal with only two of them.

Unexpected Findings

Most people resist accepting information that is inconsistent with their expectations. This is a phenomenon we will examine at length in the next chapter, on reasoning. Even now, however, you can easily see that ignoring **unexpected findings** would be fatal to successful scientific problem-solving. Although scientists may initially resist information that disconfirms favoured hypotheses, successful problem-solvers don't persist in trying to confirm their original hypotheses: instead, they set themselves a new goal of explaining the unexpected findings. This is an adaptive strategy in science because unexpected results are so common: Dunbar (2000, p. 52) found that unexpected results occurred 40 to 60 per cent of the time in experiments done across all the laboratories studied. Always being right is not the hallmark of successful scientists. Rather, success reflects the extent to which unexpected findings are made a primary focus of research. This focus leads to the reformulation of scientific models, which can themselves be tested in turn.

Distributed Reasoning

Scientists in earlier times, including Darwin, may have solved problems largely in isolation, but today successful scientific problem-solving is usually the product of a group effort. Weekly team meetings provide a wealth of information concerning **distributed reasoning** (reasoning done by more than one person). Distributed reasoning is particularly effective in changing problem representations because different people reach different conclusions

unexpected findings
Although scientists may initially resist information that disconfirms favoured hypotheses, successful problem-solvers attempt to explain surprising results.

distributed reasoning
Reasoning done by more than one person.

even when all of them are dealing with the same evidence (Dunbar, 2000, p. 55). Consequently, distributed reasoning is a way of avoiding Einstellung effects and promoting novel lines of investigation instead.

Computational Models

Scientific problem-solving can be studied by creating computer programs that simulate well-known discoveries. These programs can derive scientific laws from the relevant data (Simon, Valdéz-Pérez, & Sleeman, 1997). One example is BACON, a program that incorporates very general heuristics (Langley, Simon, Bradshaw, & Zytkow, 1987). For example, it searches for patterns in the relationships between two variables, such as whether they increase together, or one increases while the other decreases. BACON has "discovered" several well-known scientific laws. Among them was Kepler's third law of planetary motion, which expresses the relationship between the length of time it takes a planet to orbit the sun and the distance of that planet from the sun. The closer to the sun a planet is, the less time it takes to complete an orbit. Kepler's third law describes this relationship precisely. Since it was originally derived using data that Kepler got from others, and Kepler did not make detailed records of his discovery process, the heuristics of BACON cannot be compared with it to see if they are similar. However, Qin and Simon (1990) compared BACON's heuristics with the procedures that students used when confronted with data similar to those used by Kepler. All their participants had experience with physics, calculus, and chemistry. They were told that the experimenters were interested in how scientific laws were discovered. The participants' problem was to "build a formula describing the relationship between two groups of data" (p. 283). Although none of the participants realized that what they had to discover was Kepler's third law, some discovered it nonetheless. The heuristics used by the successful participants were similar to those used by BACON. This research shows that scientific problem-solving may be entirely data-driven, since everything that both BACON and the participants did was determined solely by the data they were given, without any theoretical framework.

Klahr and Simon (1999) noted that each approach to scientific problem-solving has its own strengths and weaknesses. For example, studies of historical records have face validity in that they are obviously about scientific problem-solving and not something else. Laboratory studies are not obviously face valid, since true scientific problem-solving cannot be carried out in the short time span of a psychological laboratory experiment. However, these studies can provide rigour and precision through control over variables that are hypothesized to be important determinants of scientific problem-solving. Direct observation of ongoing scientific work not only has face validity but may expose new phenomena as well as social factors that other methods may not reveal. Computational modelling is low in face validity, but allows for rigorous testing of models of problem-solving that have been derived from the other methods (Klahr & Simon, 1999, p. 531). No method can replace any other, but all are complementary.

Summary

In this chapter we have discussed how cognitive psychologists approach problem-solving and looked at contemporary research in the field. First we considered how Gestalt psychologists conceptualize *insight*: as the sudden, often involuntary, understanding of a complex situation. The Gestalt approach to solving *insight problems* stresses the importance of

---

BACON
A computer program that has been able to "discover" several well-known scientific laws.

---

face validity
Methods that clearly measure what they are supposed to measure are said to be "face valid."

understanding how the parts of a situation are related to the whole. *Productive thinking* requires us to move beyond *structurally blind (reproductive) thinking* and *functional fixedness*.

We also considered two approaches to the study of insight problems: *progress monitoring* and *representational change*. Although these theories stand in contrast to one another, they both reflect the idea that solving an insight problem requires a change in the way a problem is represented.

After a brief look at research into the involvement of the *anterior cingulate cortex* and the *hippocampus* in the insight process, we considered the evidence that sleep promotes insight.

Research on functional fixedness suggests that after the age of about six, people tend to become less flexible in their approaches to problem-solving: for example, to perceive tools only in terms of their intended functions. This tendency towards rigidity, which is found in primitive as well as technologically advanced societies, leads us to repeatedly take the same approach to solving a problem, rather than to consider alternative approaches.

We also looked at the use of computer programs to model human problem-solving behaviour, focusing on Newell and Simon's *General Problem Solver* as an example. Gestalt psychologists have criticized computer simulations of problem-solving for failing to address the experience of insight. However, Simon and colleagues have pointed to the *mutilated checkerboard problem* as an example of an insight problem that can in fact be analyzed in ways that are compatible with an artificial intelligence approach. They have also thrown the problem back to the Gestalt psychologists, suggesting that they need to redefine their conceptualization of insight in terms that are more conducive to empirical research.

Finally, we considered four complementary approaches to studying problem-solving in science: *historical accounts*, *observation of ongoing scientific investigation*, *laboratory studies*, and *computational models*. All these methods are valuable because they highlight different aspects of the problem-solving process.

CASE STUDY

Case Study Wrap-Up

At the beginning of this chapter we discussed a problem that many new parents face: whether or not they should vaccinate their children. While we hope that the answer is obvious, many parents still seem to ignore the evidence. In the next chapter, on reasoning, we will discuss in more depth how people can tend to ignore information that goes against their beliefs or expectations. In a sense, this tendency is an example of *rigid thinking*, or perhaps even *functional fixedness*. Regardless of your own answer to the vaccination question, it highlights two important points. First, when confronted with a problem it is important that we look at it with as much *flexibility* as possible, so

as to avoid imposing unnecessary *constraints* on our ability to solve it. This is true whether the problem is ecologically valid (as in the case of the vaccination question), or more academic in nature (as in the case of the problems used to study problem-solving in the laboratory). Second, the majority of research into problem-solving has involved relatively constrained laboratory studies using problems that are arguably unrealistic (e.g., insight problems, the Tower of Hanoi). The fact that it isn't easy to apply the concepts learned from these studies to everyday problem-solving only underlines the need for more ecologically valid research in this area.

In the Know: Review Questions

1. What is insight? What is responsible for its occurrence? What can be done to facilitate it?
2. What is functional fixedness? Why does it occur?
3. Outline the basic features of GPS, using the Tower of Hanoi problem to illustrate your answer.
4. Discuss methods for studying problem-solving in science.

Key Concepts

algorithms

analysis of the situation

artificial intelligence

BACON

chunk decomposition

cognitive history of science

computational models

constraint relaxation

distributed reasoning

Einstellung effect (Luchins)

evaluation function

face validity

feeling of knowing

feeling of "warmth"

functional fixedness (Duncker)

General Problem Solver (GPS)

Gestalt switch

goal stack

heuristic

hints (Maier's view)

historical accounts

insight problem

in vivo/in vitro method (Dunbar)

laboratory studies

means–end analysis

mindfulness vs mindlessness (Langer)

negative transfer

observation of ongoing scientific investigations

problem space

production rules

productive thinking (Wertheimer)

progress monitoring theory

representational change theory

search tree

strong but wrong routines

structurally blind/reproductive thinking

subgoal

thinking aloud

toy problems

unexpected findings

Zeigarnik effect

Links to Other Chapters

feeling of knowing

Chapter 5 (butcher-on-the-bus phenomenon)

Gestalt switch

Chapter 2 (isomorphism)

heuristics

Chapter 8 (commitment heuristic)

Chapter 11 (heuristics and biases, representativeness, availability, recognition)

insight

Chapter 12 (creativity and problem-finding)

metacognition

Chapter 6 (elaboration and distinctiveness)

problem space

Chapter 11 (importance of the problem space)

Chapter 12 (creativity and problem-finding)

sleep

Chapter 6 (sleep, memory, and false memory)

Further Reading

Gick and Lockhart (1995) proposed a simple technique for constructing insight problems that you might like to try yourself. They noted that the key to composing a riddle is to get the problem-solver to initially interpret information incorrectly. One way to do this is to use a word that can be interpreted in more than one way. For example, most people interpret the word *lake* to refer to a liquid body of water, but a lake can also be frozen. A riddle can be constructed by requiring the problem-solver to come up with the less common meaning in order to make sense of the situation that the riddle describes. An example of a riddle solution given by Gick and Lockhart is "The stone rested on the surface of the lake for three months, after which it sank to the bottom some 10 metres below." Only when the problem-solver realizes that the lake was initially frozen does the solution to the riddle become clear.

Some criticisms of computer simulation approaches to thinking go even further than the Gestalt critique, arguing that the activities of computer programs don't count as thinking. People who express this belief often ally themselves with the German philosopher Heidegger (1968). For Heidegger, the ability of computer programs to represent the chain of inferences leading from one state to another would not have been the essence of thinking. Computer programs are good at simulating processes such as reasoning and calculation. However, the essence of thinking lies *behind* these processes; it is not reducible to them. Computer programs don't capture the subjective origin of thinking—the concern with the fundamental problem of being alive in the world. Although Heidegger is often difficult to follow, and even more difficult to paraphrase, his ideas about thinking may resonate with many people who have reservations about artificial intelligence.

Computer simulation approaches to psychological processes have often been criticized for what they appear to leave out. Even some cognitive psychologists have suggested that to design a computer program that would simulate emotion would not be a very meaningful exercise; among them is Neisser (1964). Although Simon (1967) attempted to deal with this problem, most work in this area has specialized in cognition, and it is perhaps fair to say that the role of emotion in mental life has been neglected. See also Simon (1995).

For a wonderful example of the cognitive history of science see Netz (1999).

Gick, M., & Lockhart, R.S. (1995). Cognitive and affective components of insight. In R.J. Sternberg & J.E. Davidson (Eds.), *The nature of insight* (pp. 197–228). Cambridge, Mass.: MIT Press.

Heidegger, M. (1968). *What is called thinking?* (J. Glen Gray, Trans.). New York: Harper & Row.

Neisser, U. (1964). The multiplicity of thought. *British Journal of Psychology, 54*, 1–14.

Netz, R. (1999). *The shaping of deduction in Greek mathematics: A study in cognitive history.* Cambridge: Cambridge University Press.

Simon, H.A. (1967). Motivational and emotional controls of cognition. *Psychological Review, 74*, 29–39.

Simon, H.A. (1995). The information-processing theory of mind. *American Psychologist, 50*, 507–508.

11

Reasoning, Judgment, and Choice

Chapter Contents

Chapter Objectives

- To describe various understandings of syllogistic reasoning.
- To identify various heuristics and biases that affect people's judgments.
- To understand ecological rationality.
- To explore the importance of training in statistical reasoning.

The (In)famous Hockey Stick

In 1998, just before global warming became a major issue in the public sphere, researchers Michael Mann, Raymond Bradley, and Malcolm Hughes published what soon became one of the most widely discussed papers in the climate change debate. Using tree-ring measurements as proxies for historical temperatures, Mann, Bradley, and Hughes (1998) tracked northern hemisphere temperatures from the year 1400 AD onwards. The resulting graph (Figure 11.1) shows that temperatures remained within a more or less stable range until about a century ago, when they began rising steadily. The shape of the graph—like a horizontal hockey stick with its blade in the air—led many to dub it the "hockey stick." Mann et al. (1998) examined various possible causes of the hockey-stick pattern, and ultimately concluded that the rise was due to "anthropogenic factors": specifically, the steady increase in human-caused carbon dioxide emissions that has accompanied industrialization since the early 1900s.

Responses to the paper were mixed, to say the least. Those who were predisposed to believe the authors' conclusion that humans are responsible for global warming hailed the paper as an example of outstanding scientific research. The hockey-stick reconstruction was featured as groundbreaking evidence for anthropogenic global warming in a major report by the Intergovernmental Panel on Climate Change (IPCC).

Others, however, took a completely different view. Skeptics argued that there were problems with both the authors' modelling technique and their selection of tree rings; for details, see climateaudit.org and wattsupwiththat.com. Among the leading critics of the anthropogenic warming theory are two Canadians: mining consultant Stephen McIntyre and economist Ross McKitrick (McIntyre & McKitrick, 2005; 2009; see also Montford, 2010).

How is it possible that exactly the same scientific evidence can be evaluated so differently? Well, in many cases, scientific methods are based on assumptions, and assumptions can always be questioned. Whether we accept any assumption is a matter of individual judgment. The conflicting evaluations of Mann et al.'s findings and conclusions are a good example of what researchers on reasoning and judgment call **motivated reasoning**. Motivated

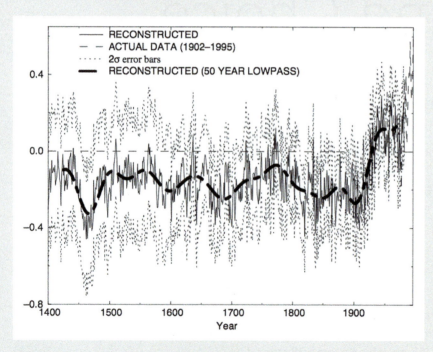

FIGURE 11.1 | Northern hemisphere temperatures (°C) from 1400 to 1995 as reconstructed by Mann et al.

The "zero line corresponds to the 1902–80 calibration mean of the quantity [and] uncertainty limits are shown by the light dotted lines surrounding the solid reconstruction. . . ."

From: Mann et al., 1998, p. 783. Reprinted by permission from Macmillan Publishers Ltd, *Nature*, 392, 779–87, copyright (1998).

reasoning is the implicit inclination to evaluate evidence in a way that fits with our prior views and beliefs. According to Scurich and Shniderman (2014, p. 2), "This dynamic is more than simply making self-serving attributions; it unknowingly affects the way in which information is processed." The influence of motivated reasoning is thought to be largely unconscious.

To demonstrate the impact of motivated reasoning, Scurich and Shniderman (2014) collected participants' views on the death penalty. Then they randomly assigned participants to two groups, each of which was shown a different version of a supposed newspaper article. Both versions purported to describe a recent study (actually fictional) examining the brain activity of violent offenders just after they had watched a video of a prisoner either undergoing execution or "being held in solitary confinement" (Scurich & Shniderman, 2014, p. 2). According to both versions of the article the offenders' brain activity depended on the film they had watched. The reported difference in brain activation involved the frontal lobe, which would sound impressive to someone with no knowledge of neuroscience, and reasonable even to someone with some cursory knowledge. Importantly, the experimental data reported were exactly the same in both versions; however, the reported

interpretations were radically different: in one case the researchers were said to have concluded that the death penalty would prevent crime (the "is-a-deterrent" version); in the other, that it would not (the "is-not-a-deterrent" version). After reading the article, participants were asked about the quality of the neuroscientific study it described. The results of the study are shown in Figure 11.2.

As you can see, participants' evaluation of the quality of the neuroscientific study strongly depended on the interaction of the conclusion drawn from the study and their own pre-existing attitudes towards the death penalty. Specifically, the quality of the study was rated highest when the conclusion drawn from it matched the participant's pre-existing view, and lowest when it did not. It seems that we tend to be more skeptical of studies that lead to conclusions that are inconsistent with our views than those that are consistent with them. Views about global warming research are no exception.

Research on motivated reasoning suggests the general conclusion that our evaluation of evidence can be heavily influenced by our prior experiences. In this chapter we will discuss the various factors that influence our reasoning, judgments, and choices.

> **motivated reasoning**
> Biased evaluation of evidence, in accordance with one's prior views and beliefs.

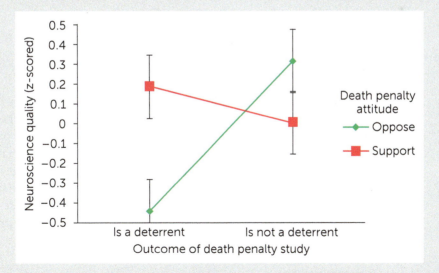

FIGURE 11.2 | Participants' judgments of the quality of neuroscientific findings as a function of (a) whether the results were interpreted to imply that the death penalty is or is not a deterrent to crime and (b) participants' own views regarding the death penalty (for or against)

From Scurich, N., & Shniderman, A. (2015).

Reasoning

Syllogistic Reasoning

There has been a veritable explosion of research on reasoning in recent years, "turning logic and reasoning into a major field of cognitive psychology" (Evans, 2002, p. 978). **Reasoning** has been defined as "a process of thought that yields a conclusion from percepts, thoughts, or assertions" (Johnson-Laird, 1999, p. 110). Those "percepts, thoughts, or assertions" are called *premises.* Exactly what makes a conclusion follow logically from the premises is not always an easy question to answer, because there are different systems of logic (Evans, 2002, p. 985). The oldest of those systems, Aristotelian or syllogistic logic, has been the subject of much psychological research.

A **syllogism** consists of two premises and a conclusion. Each of the premises specifies a relationship between two categories. Consequently, *syllogistic reasoning* is sometimes called *categorical reasoning.* Each premise in a syllogism can take any of four different forms (see Table 11.1).

Let's briefly consider each of these premise forms. The *universal affirmative* premise can be represented diagrammatically as shown below for the premise "All A are B." Notice that this premise might refer to a situation in which "All A are B, but some B are not A" (see below left). This would be the case for a premise such as "All cows are animals," because some animals are not cows. However, sometimes a universal affirmative premise refers to a situation in which "All A are B, and all B are A" (see below right). This would be true for a statement such as "All right angles are 90-degree angles" (Chapman & Chapman, 1959, p. 224). Thus a universal affirmative premise may be understood in different ways, even though from a logical point of view all possible ways of understanding a premise are equally important.

reasoning
A thought process that yields a conclusion from premises.

syllogism
A syllogism consists of two premises and a conclusion. Each of the premises specifies a relationship between two categories.

TABLE 11.1 | Four Forms of Syllogistic Reasoning

Form	Examples
Universal affirmative	All A are B.
	All cows are animals.
	All right angles are 90-degree angles.
Universal negative	No A are B.
	No tomatoes are animals.
	No acute angles are 90-degree angles.
Particular affirmative	Some A are B.
	Some animals are dangerous.
	Some pigeons are clever.
Particular negative	Some A are not B.
	Some animals are not cows.
	Some pigeons are not clever.

The diagrammatic representation for "No A are B" is completely different (see below). The two circles are separate, meaning that no member of one class is also a member of the other class. An important property of a *universal negative* premise is that its converse also is true. A premise may be converted by reversing the order of the subject and predicate. The converse of "No A is B" is "No B is A." Thus "No tomatoes are animals" also means that "No animals are tomatoes."

For the *particular affirmative* case illustrated below, in which "Some A are B," there are several possible depictions. Notice that, although "Some A are B," it may still be true that "Some A are not B," or that "Some B are not A." Thus it is true that "Some animals are not dangerous" and that "Some dangerous beings are not animals." Nevertheless, particular affirmative premises may be converted. If "Some A are B," then it is also true that "Some B are A." Finally, as counterintuitive as it may seem, in logic *some* means at least one, and *possibly* all (Ruby, 1960, p. 194); we will explore the challenge that this poses a little later. To reiterate, it's important to recognize that premises such as these may be interpreted in a variety of ways.

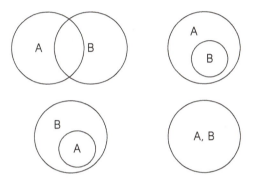

The *particular negative* case is diagrammed below as overlapping circles; however, like the other premise forms, "Some A are not B" is open to a number of specific interpretations. For example, the converse of "Some A are not B" is "Some B are not A." This is an inference that people often accept (Chapman & Chapman, 1959), although it is not necessarily true. It is true that "Some animals are not cows," but it does not follow that "Some cows are not animals." Similarly, people often infer that "Some A are not B" means that "Some A are B" (Ruby, 1960, p. 195). In everyday language, the latter is often the intended meaning. In the case of "Some animals are not cows," it's also empirically true that "Some animals are cows." But consider a statement such as "Some Saudi Arabians are not ice hockey players." Perhaps some Saudi Arabians *are* ice hockey players: we don't know. However, it isn't logically necessary for *some* Saudi Arabians to be ice hockey players just because some of them are not; it may also be the case that *none* of them are.

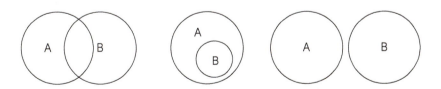

As we have seen, it's possible to interpret the premises of a syllogism in a variety of ways. From the standpoint of logic, all possible ways of understanding a premise are equally important. This situation becomes more complicated when premises are combined to arrive at a conclusion, especially since a valid syllogism requires that the conclusion follows for every possible scenario. Even one exception will render the syllogism invalid.

Logicism

At least since Aristotle, many have believed that logical reasoning is an essential part of human nature. This belief is called **logicism**. To illustrate it, logicists point to the practical syllogism (e.g., Thornton, 1982). A **practical syllogism** is one in which two premises point to a conclusion that calls for action (see Henle, 1962/1968, p. 103). Here is an example:

Premise 1:   I need to understand psychology as a whole.
Premise 2:   The only way to understand psychology as a whole is through the study of cognition.
Conclusion: Therefore I need to study cognition.

If you accept the premises, then you will agree that you need to study cognition. Some (e.g., Henle, 1962/1968) have argued that the practical syllogism is a common feature of everyday life. For example: "People who have a virus should act so as not to infect others. I have a virus. Therefore I should act so as not to infect others." Once again, if you accept the premises, then you will act so as not to infect others. For those who believe in the importance of logic in everyday life, the practical syllogism is not an abstraction studied in a cognition course, but "the natural mode of functioning of the conscious mind" (Henle, 1962/1968, p. 103). From this perspective, the ability to reason is what most distinguishes human beings from other forms of life.

One problem for logicism is that untrained participants make logical errors when asked to evaluate the validity of syllogistic arguments. This suggests that processes other than logic determine the conclusions that participants reach. However, it is also true that the same participants do not always make logical errors. In fact, they make logically correct deductions at a level greater than chance (Evans, 2002, p. 992). Consequently, a central concern in reasoning research is to determine the conditions under which participants will reason logically as well as the conditions under which they will reach conclusions in some other way.

The Effect of Content on Syllogistic Reasoning

Consider the following syllogism:

All Canadians love snow.
All Mounties are Canadians.
Therefore, all Mounties love snow.

You might object to this syllogism if you happen to know a Canadian who doesn't love snow, and so determine that the first premise is empirically incorrect. However, when it comes to judging the validity of a syllogism, the truth or falsehood of the premises is irrelevant. The validity of a syllogism depends only on whether or not the conclusion necessarily follows from the premises. People often find it difficult to separate the validity of a syllogism from the issue of whether the syllogism is consistent with their experience or beliefs. Thus they may accept an invalid syllogism if they believe that the conclusion is true in the real world (Galotti, 1989, p. 336). However, the effect of believability is greater if the syllogism is invalid (Newstead, Pollard, Evans, & Allen, 1992). For example, consider the following invalid syllogisms (from Evans, Handley, and Harper, 2001, p. 932).

Premise 1	No addictive things are inexpensive.	No millionaires are hard workers.
Premise 2	Some cigarettes are inexpensive.	Some rich people are hard workers.
Conclusion	Therefore, some addictive things are not cigarettes.	Therefore, some millionaires are not rich people.

Believable but invalid syllogisms like the one on the left were accepted as valid by 71 per cent of participants, while unbelievable and invalid syllogisms like that on the right were accepted by only 10 per cent. The difference in acceptance rates—61 per cent—shows how powerful the believability effect can be for some invalid syllogism types. Now examine the following valid syllogisms (also from Evans, Handley, and Harper, 2001, p. 932).

Premise 1	No police dogs are vicious.	No nutritional things are inexpensive.
Premise 2	Some highly trained dogs are vicious.	Some vitamin tablets are inexpensive.
Conclusion	Therefore, some highly trained dogs are not police dogs.	Therefore, some vitamin tablets are not nutritional.

Believable and valid syllogisms like the one on the left were accepted as valid by 89 per cent of participants, while unbelievable but valid syllogisms like that on the right were accepted as valid by 56 per cent. The difference in acceptance rates here—only 33 per cent—indicates that believability has a much smaller effect for valid syllogisms. These data are presented graphically in Figure 11.3.

What accounts for the difference in acceptance rates? Evans, Handley, and Harper (2001, p. 955) suggest that participants in a syllogistic reasoning task initially determine whether the conclusion is believable or unbelievable. If it's unbelievable, they then try to find some flaw in the premises that renders the conclusion invalid. However, if the conclusion is believable, they don't try to establish that the syllogism is invalid: instead, they try to find some way of thinking about the premises that renders the conclusion valid. In other words, they set themselves the goal of discovering a syllogism to be invalid only if the conclusion is unbelievable.

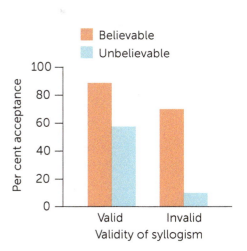

FIGURE 11.3 | Differences in acceptance rates for four different types of syllogism

Data from: Newstead, S.E., Pollard, P., Evans, J. St B.T., & Allen, J.L. (1992). p. 262. With permission from Elsevier.

The Interpretation of "Some"

The fact that premises are often open to alternative interpretations creates another serious difficulty for people who are asked to judge the validity of syllogisms. In order to judge whether or not a conclusion is valid, we must consider only those inferences that are consistent with all possible interpretations of a set of premises. Yet we don't always work out *all* the possible interpretations of a set of premises. Consequently, we reason according to the specific way we interpret the premises (Begg, 1987, p. 63; Begg & Harris, 1982; Ceraso & Provitera, 1971). The way we interpret premises that contain the word *some* provides a good example.

Consider the statement "Some people are human." Although it is a meaningful (and empirically true) statement, it violates our feelings about the proper use of *some* and may even be offensive. The statement "Some people are human" seems to imply that "Some people are not human." Although that is not a logically necessary implication, it seems necessary because we ordinarily interpret *some* to mean "some but not all" (Feeney, Scrafton, Duckworth, & Handley, 2004). Thus according to our usual understanding of *some*, the statement "Some people are human" means that "*Not all* people are human." If you use *some* in this way, you are not using it strictly in the way dictated by logic, in which *some* means "at least one, and *possibly* all" (Ruby, 1960, p. 194). A study by Begg (1987) showed how ubiquitous the ordinary, non-logical use of *some* may be.

In Begg's (1987) experiment, participants were given a description of a set of people and their occupations. For example, they might have been told that a group of people consisted of 20 artists and 80 writers. Half of each subgroup were men, and the other half were women. Thus subsets of the group could be described using statements such as:

Some men are artists; some men are writers.
Some women are artists; some women are writers.

In one part of the experiment, participants were asked to rate certain statements using the word *some* in terms of how misleading they felt them to be. Statements in which *some* referred to a minority of the group were felt to be less misleading than those that referred to a majority of the group. Thus statements such as "Some men are artists" were considered more easily believed and less misleading than statements such as "Some men are writers," because there were fewer male artists (10) than male writers (40). In other words, for many people the word *some* carried with it the connotation of "less than the whole amount under consideration." The same result was found for "Some women are artists" and "Some women are writers." The former statement was seen as more believable than the latter.

Feeney, Scrafton, Duckworth, and Handley (2004) found that children use *some* in the conversational manner by age seven or eight.

Mental Models and Deductive Reasoning

A very influential current theory of syllogistic reasoning is Philip Johnson-Laird's (1983, 1988, 2001; Johnson-Laird & Byrne, 1993; Johnson-Laird & Steedman, 1978). According to Johnson-Laird (1988, pp. 277ff.), we construct a mental model of the situation to which a set of premises refers and then draw conclusions that are consistent with the model. There may be several mental models that can be derived from a given set of premises. If a conclusion is consistent with all the models that are constructed, then it is accepted.

What does a mental model look like? From Johnson-Laird's viewpoint, the details of the model, such as whether it makes use of vivid imagery, are irrelevant. The important thing is how the parts of the model go together. A mental model is a mental structure. Let's see how this might work for a premise such as "All whales are strong." We will use the kind of notation employed by Johnson-Laird (1983, Chap. 5; 1988, p. 228). You might first imagine a set of whales, like this:

whale
whale

You might form your model from images of whales. You can then add to your mental model the information that *whales are strong*.

whale = strong
whale = strong
          [strong]

The brackets around the third *strong* above is to represent the fact that your model may contain strong things that are not whales. If you then think of Moby Dick (a famous fictional whale) you can add him to your model:

Moby Dick = whale = strong
              whale = strong
                        [strong]

Having constructed this model, you are in a position to make an inference. You can now see that Moby Dick is strong, a relationship that might not have occurred to you before you constructed your model.

What makes a syllogism difficult is that there may be several alternative mental models. To see why this matters, consider these premises:

No camels are whales.
All whales are endangered animals.

Three mental models can be constructed from these premises. Let's begin with the first model and the first premise, which can be represented like this:

camel
camel
_____
          whale
          whale
          [whales]

In Johnson-Laird's notation, the line represents the fact that camels and whales belong to different sets. "The two groups are, as it were, fenced off from each other" (Johnson-Laird, 1983, p. 96). The second premise can be incorporated into the model as follows:

camel
camel
_____
          whale = endangered animal
          whale = endangered animal
          whale = endangered animal
                    [endangered animals]

If the reasoner stops here, having constructed only one model, then the most likely conclusion is that "No camels are endangered animals." In fact, Johnson-Laird (1988, p. 229) noted that this as a very common response when participants are given this particular type of premise pair. However, there is a second mental model that can be constructed from these premises, incorporating the possibility that *camels* might be *endangered animals*, too.

camel
camel = endangered animal
————————————————————
$\quad\quad$ whale = endangered animal
$\quad\quad$ whale = endangered animal
$\quad\quad\quad$ [endangered animals]

Johnson-Laird reported that this kind of model can lead to the conclusion that *Some camels are not endangered animals*. However, this conclusion also looks risky if you construct the third mental model:

$\quad\quad$ camel = endangered animal
$\quad\quad$ camel = endangered animal
————————————————————
$\quad\quad$ whale = endangered animal
$\quad\quad$ whale = endangered animal
$\quad\quad\quad$ [endangered animals]

At this point you might want to give up without drawing any conclusion from this pair of premises. Johnson-Laird (1983, Table 5.1; 1988, p. 229) reported that no participants in his experiments drew the valid conclusion that "Some endangered animals are not camels." Drawing this conclusion requires the inspection of the three models from the bottom up, as it were, to see that it is valid in each case. Johnson-Laird's model seems to fit nicely as an explanation for the difficulty that can arise in deductive reasoning.

Relational Reasoning

The scope of mental models theory has expanded considerably over the years (Johnson-Laird, 2001). A good example of its range of applicability is **relational reasoning** (Goodwin & Johnson-Laird, 2005). Of particular interest are *transitive relations* (Strawson, 1952, p. 46), which are usually expressed by comparative sentences such as *A is taller than B*. The relation *taller than* is transitive because if *A is taller than B*, and *B is taller than C*, then *A must also be taller than C*. There are a great many transitive relations; other examples include *wider than* and *deeper than*. Transitive relations typically come in pairs, one of which is the opposite of the other (Clark & Card, 1969; Harris, 1973). Thus *narrower than* is the opposite of *wider than* and *shallower than* is the opposite of *deeper than*.

A widely investigated form of reasoning is the *linear syllogism*, or **three-term series problem** (Wason & Johnson-Laird, 1972, Ch. 9). These problems consist of two comparative sentences from which a conclusion must be drawn. Suppose you were told that "B is smaller than A" and "B is larger than C," and then were asked "Which is smallest?" In response to such questions, many people construct a mental model consisting of a horizontal or

relational reasoning
Reasoning involving premises that express the relations between items (e.g., *A is taller than B*).

three-term series problem
Linear syllogisms consisting of two comparative sentences from which a conclusion must be drawn.

vertical spatial array (DeSoto, London, & Handel, 1965; Johnson-Laird, 1972). A vertical array could be built by first placing B in the array, and then A above it, like this:

A
|
B

Then you could deal with the second premise by putting C below B.

A
|
B
|
C

By inspecting this imaginary array, you can see that C is the smallest. The conclusion is not required in order to construct the array. Rather, the conclusion emerges once the array has been constructed out of the two premises (B < A; B > C).

This example illustrates the iconic nature of mental models: the relations between the parts of the model correspond to the relations between the parts of the situation it represents (Goodwin & Johnson-Laird, 2005, p. 475). It also shows that you can get more out of a mental model than you put into it. Goodwin and Johnson-Laird (2005, p. 476) call this the principle of emergent consequences. Once you have constructed a mental model, you can see relationships that were not evident before you constructed it.

Another principle is that of parsimony, whereby people tend to construct only one mental model if possible, and the simplest one at that. For example, what mental model would you construct given the following premises? *Ann is a blood relative of Chris* and *Chris is a blood relative of Gordon*. If you're like most people, you will construct a mental model something like this:

Ann
|
Chris
|
Gordon

> **iconic**
> A characteristic of mental models, according to Johnson-Laird's theory: the relations between the parts of the model correspond to the relations between the parts of the situation it represents.
>
> **emergent consequences**
> A principle of Johnson-Laird's theory: you can get more out of a mental model than you put into it.
>
> **parsimony**
> A principle of Johnson-Laird's theory: people tend to construct the simplest mental model possible.

This mental model leads to the conclusion *Ann is a blood relative of Gordon*. However, treating *blood relative* as a transitive relation leads to an overly simple mental model. It is overly simple because it fails to consider the possibility that Gordon and Ann are the parents of Chris, and thus not blood relatives of one another. Participants given linear syllogisms based on such *pseudotransitive relations* drew the logically incorrect conclusion most of the time. However, when encouraged to think about more complicated examples, such as relationships based on marriage, participants can see the error of their thinking. Once again we see that people may at first behave less than logically, but later can think in a more complex manner.

An Alternative to the Mental Models Approach

Another approach to reasoning is based on the idea that there are natural deduction systems (Braine, 1978; Gentzen, 1964; Rips, 1983, 1988, 1994). To begin to understand this approach, let's consider a problem from Smullyan (1978, p. 22). The problem is cast in the form of statements made by the inhabitants of an island, each of whom is either a knight or a knave. Knights always tell the truth, while knaves always lie. Suppose you are told the following (Rips, 1989, p. 86):

> We have three inhabitants, A, B, and C, each of whom is a knight or a knave. Two people are said to be of the same type if they are both knights or both knaves. A and B make the following statements:
> A: B is a knave.
> B: A and C are of the same type.
> What is C?

Knight–knave problems always have solutions. What do you think the solution to this one is? We know that A is either a knight or a knave. If we assume that A is a knight, and is therefore telling the truth, "B is a knave" must be a true statement. And since knaves are liars, B's statement that A and C are of the same type is false. A and C must be of different types. If A is a knight, then C must be a knave. What happens if we begin by assuming that A is a knave and therefore lying? That means that "B is a knave" is a false statement and B is a knight. Because knights tell the truth, B's statement that A and C are of the same type must be true. If A is a knave, then C must be a knave as well. Thus if we begin by assuming that A is a knight, then we conclude that C is a knave, and if we begin by assuming that A is a knave, then we also conclude that C is a knave. C must be a knave.

Other reasoning problems only look as if they have solutions. We can waste a lot of time trying to solve those insoluble problems. This issue is explored in Box 11.1.

CONSIDER THIS
BOX 11.1

Paradoxes, Reasoning, and Recursion

A process that refers to itself is called *recursive*. Recursion can have interesting effects on reasoning. The first thing to recognize about recursion is that it can sometimes lead to awkward forms of thought. The most famous example is the liar paradox (P. Hughes & Brecht, 1975). There is a very old story about Epimenides the Cretan, who is supposed to have said that *All Cretans are liars*. Because Epimenides is a Cretan, he is including himself when he says that *All Cretans are liars*. Suppose that Epimenides is telling the truth. That means that *All Cretans are liars* and that Epimenides, being a Cretan, is himself a liar. But if Epimenides is a liar, then he cannot be telling the truth and all Cretans are not liars. Thus the assumption that he is telling the truth leads to the conclusion that he is not telling the truth.

What happens if we begin by assuming that Epimenides is lying? That means that his statement *All Cretans are liars* is a lie. If some Cretans tell the truth, then Epimenides' behaviour is merely one example of the state of affairs on Crete. Thus the assumption that he is a liar leads to the conclusion that he exemplifies the truth while lying. We may conclude that if Epimenides exemplifies truth when he lies, then in some sense when he is lying he is expressing a truth. As Hughes and Brecht pointed out, this kind of reasoning can make your head swim.

Natural Deduction Systems

When Rips (1989) asked undergraduate participants to think aloud while solving knight–knave problems, he found that they appeared to follow what he called natural deduction rules. A natural deduction system makes use of propositions stored in working memory. Propositions are statements structured around connectives such as *if . . . then*, *and*, *or*, and *not*. The system uses deduction rules to draw conclusions from these propositions. When one proposition follows from another, the first proposition can be said to *entail* the second. Among the rules belonging to a natural deduction system are the following, where *p* and *q* are propositions (Rips, 1989, p. 94):

> 1. *p* AND *q* entail *p*, *q*

This rule means that if you have a proposition of the form *p* AND *q* in working memory, then you can derive *p* and *q* as separate propositions. Thus from the proposition "A is a knight AND B is a knight" you can infer the two propositions "A is a knight" and "B is a knight."

> 2. *p* OR *q* and NOT *p* entails *q*

For example, if you have the propositions "A is a knight OR B is a knight" and "A is NOT a knight" in working memory, then you can infer the proposition "B is a knight."

These are not the only rules in the system, but they are probably enough to give you the general idea. A natural deduction system consists of psychologically basic inference rules. These are "elementary inference principles" (Rips, 1989, p. 94) that participants rely on to solve reasoning problems. Rips showed that the number of errors and the time taken to solve the knight–knave problem depend on the number of inferences required.

The natural deduction approach to reasoning is different from Johnson-Laird's mental models approach. "According to the natural deduction model, people carry out deduction tasks by constructing mental proofs. They represent the problem information, make further assumptions, draw inferences, and come to conclusions on the basis of this derivation" (Rips, 1989, p. 107).

Johnson-Laird and Byrne (1990; Johnson-Laird, 1997a, 1997b) proposed a mental models alternative to Rips's theory. However, Rips (1990, 1997) argued that his data showed no evidence that people construct mental models to solve reasoning puzzles such as knight–knave problems. Gallotti, Baron, and Sabini (1986) studied the solution procedures of participants who had been asked to solve a set of syllogisms and concluded that some of them seemed to take a mental models approach, whereas others used strategies that were more consistent with the sort of rule-following theory suggested by Rips. Nevertheless, it's unlikely that the two approaches can be easily reconciled (e.g., Johnson-Laird, 1997a, 1997b; Rips, 1997).

> **natural deduction system**
> A reasoning system made up of propositions and deduction rules that are used to draw conclusions from these propositions.

Wason's Puzzles

Syllogisms were not invented for the purpose of psychological research. Studies of syllogistic reasoning are just one example of research that focuses on a task familiar to a discipline other than psychology in the hope that it will shed light on psychological processes.

Another approach is to invent reasoning tasks that directly tap interesting aspects of reasoning. No one was more inventive in the design of psychologically interesting reasoning tasks than Wason (Evans & Johnson-Laird, 2003). His puzzles have been used in hundreds of studies. We will review research springing from two of his inventions: the generative problem and the card selection task.

The Generative Problem

According to Wason (1960, 1977a, 1978; Wason & Johnson-Laird, 1972), a generative problem is one that requires us to actively generate (rather than passively receive) the information needed to solve it. Wason apparently discovered his original generative problem (1966) in a dream. Participants in an experiment using it were told that "the three numbers 2, 4, 6 conformed to a simple relational rule which the experimenter had in mind, and that their task was to discover the rule by generating sequences of three numbers, the experimenter telling them each time whether the rule held" (p. 139) for the sequence they generated. At each trial, participants would also write down a hypothesis about the rule. When they felt highly confident that they had discovered the rule, they were allowed to propose it. If they were not correct, they were told so and then would continue with the task until they discovered the rule.

Participants in such experiments tend to think that the task is more straightforward than it often turns out to be. For example, one of Wason's (1966, p. 140) participants generated the numbers 8, 10, 12, and was told that this sequence was consistent with the rule that Wason had in mind. At that point, the participant had the hypothesis that two are added to each previous number. Then the participant generated another sequence, 14, 16, 18, and was told that it too was consistent with the rule. After generating some other sequences, such as 20, 22, 24, and 1, 3, 5, and learning that they too were consistent with the rule, the participant proposed that *starting with any number, two is added each time to form the next number*—but this was not the rule Wason had in mind. The participant went on to propose several other sequences, such as 2, 6, 10, and other rules, such as *the difference between two numbers next to each other is the same*. This was not the correct rule either. Many of Wason's participants gave up before discovering the rule.

The rule Wason had in mind was *any increasing series of numbers*. Thus all the sequences proposed in the preceding paragraph were consistent with it (as are 1, 2, 3, or 1, 4, 9; in fact, the number of possible sequences is infinite). If you are ever a participant in a similar experiment, you might want to keep in mind that proposing sequences that are consistent with your hypothesis is not an effective strategy: rather, you should propose a sequence that is *inconsistent* with your hypothesis.

To see why this is so, consider the following example. Suppose you believe that *starting with any number, two is added each time to form the next number*. What will happen if you propose a sequence such as 1, 2, 3, which is inconsistent with your hypothesis? You will be told that it is consistent with the rule that the experimenter has in mind. You can then conclude that your hypothesis is false.

Finding out that your hypothesis is false may not strike you as particularly useful, but in fact that is all you can ever discover with certainty in this task. The appropriate strategy is to attempt to falsify your hypotheses, and thus eliminate incorrect beliefs. In other words, you can arrive at the correct rule by means of what Wason (1966, p. 141) called an **eliminative strategy**.

As influential philosophers of science (e.g., Popper, 1959) have pointed out, formulating a hypothesis and then attempting to falsify it is a key aspect of scientific inquiry. However, Wason's participants did not behave like scientists. Instead they persisted in seeking confirmatory evidence for their hypotheses. As we noted in the last chapter, even successful scientists may at first resist evidence that disconfirms a favourite hypothesis. Certainly Wason's experiments show that ordinary people are prone to a **confirmation bias**. We will explore this subject in more detail as we go along.

Wason's (1966, p. 145; Wason & Evans, 1975) most influential invention was his **selection task**, which has given rise to an enormous amount of research. Like the generative problem, it can appear deceptively simple, leading participants to believe that they know the answer when in fact they are mistaken. If you have not seen this problem before, you might like to try it yourself. Participants are shown four cards, each of which has a number on one side and a letter on the other side. Suppose you were shown the cards below and told by the experimenter that if a card has a vowel on one side, then it has an even number on the other side. Which cards must you turn over in order to determine whether or not the experimenter is telling the truth?

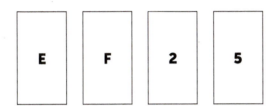

If you concluded that you need to turn over the E and the 2, or just the E, then you are in good company. Those are the most common types of response to this task. Johnson-Laird and Wason (1970) reported that of 128 participants given the selection task, 59 chose the alternatives corresponding to turning over the E and the 2, and another 42 participants chose just the alternative corresponding to turning over the E. However, these responses are not entirely correct. In order to see why there is another answer, we must explore the logical structure of this task more carefully.

Think again about the rule given by the experimenter: if a card has a vowel on one side, then it has an even number on the other side. Suppose that the backs of the four cards you have already seen were as follows:

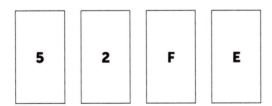

Thus if you turned over the E, you would find the number 5. This discovery clearly falsifies the rule and tells you that the experimenter was not telling the truth. Therefore you would have been correct to want to turn over the E, because the odd number on its back would tell you that the rule was false. Now consider the second card. Because F is not a vowel, it doesn't matter that there is an even number on the other side. Whatever might be on the

confirmation bias
The tendency to seek confirmatory evidence for a hypothesis.

selection task (Wason)
A four-card problem based on conditional reasoning.

other side, it can't tell you anything about the rule, so you don't need to turn this card over. The result for the third card is also irrelevant, because the rule does not say that an even number on one side *requires* a vowel on the other. If there were a vowel on the other side it would be consistent with the rule, but a consonant does not falsify the rule. So you don't need to turn over the third card either. The result for the fourth card, however, is particularly informative. If you turn over the 5, you find the letter E on the other side. Notice that this falsifies the rule, because there is a card with a vowel on one side and an odd number on the other. In general, you need to turn over cards displaying odd numbers, because they can falsify the rule.

Initially, the results of experiments using the selection task were taken to support the operation of a confirmation bias. If participants choose a card showing a vowel and a card showing an even number, they are deliberately choosing cards that could confirm the rule rather than disconfirm it. Oakhill and Johnson-Laird (1985) argued that actively seeking information that will disconfirm a rule is one of the characteristics of rational thought:

CONSIDER THIS
BOX 11.2

Conditional Reasoning

conditional reasoning

Reasoning that uses conditional ("if . . . then") statements.

truth tables

A way of presenting the various combinations of the constituents of logical statements.

Wason's selection task illustrates what is called **conditional reasoning**. Conditional reasoning uses conditional statements—that is, statements with an IF . . . THEN . . . form: IF one condition occurs, THEN another condition occurs. A conditional statement has two parts, the *antecedent* and the *consequent*. The antecedent comes after the word "if," and the consequent comes after the word "then." The rule in the selection task is an example of a conditional statement: *IF a card has a vowel on one side, THEN it has an even number on the other side*. The antecedent of this rule comes after IF, as in: *IF a card has a vowel on one side*. The consequent comes after the word THEN, as in: *THEN it has an even number on the other side*. In general, we can say that conditional statements have the form *IF p, THEN q*, where *p* refers to the antecedent, and *q* refers to the consequent.

Truth tables were invented by Wittgenstein (1921/1974, p. 32) as a way of presenting the various combinations of the constituents of logical statements. In the truth table

below are listed the possible truth values for an antecedent (*p*) and a consequent (*q*). The truth value of *p* can be either true (T) or false (F), as can the truth value of *q*. When both *p* and *q* are true, then obviously the conditional statement *IF p THEN q* is also true. When *p* is true but *q* is false, then *IF p THEN q* is false. This case corresponds to a card with a vowel on one side but an odd number on the other. If *p* is false but *q* is true, then *IF p, THEN q* is still true. This case corresponds to a card with a consonant on one side and an even number on the other; it does not falsify the rule. To drive this point home, consider a statement such as *If it rains, then the match will be cancelled* (Strawson, 1952, p. 82). The match might be cancelled for a variety of reasons other than rain, and that would not falsify the statement. Finally, if both *p* and *q* are false, then that does not falsify *IF p, THEN q*. If it does not rain, and the match is not cancelled, then the rule still stands.

p	q	If p then q
T	T	T
T	F	F
F	T	T
F	F	T

Rationality depends on the search for counterexamples. If, say, you hold the prejudice that women are bad drivers, and your curiosity is only provoked by cases of bad driving, then you will never be shaken from your bias; if a bad driver turns out to be a woman, your prejudice is confirmed; if a bad driver turns out to be a man your prejudice is not disconfirmed since you don't believe that only women are bad drivers. Unless you somehow are able to grasp the potential relevance of *good* drivers to your belief, then the danger is that you will never be disabused of it, and will never understand the force of counterexamples (p. 93).

However, subsequent research has shown that the selection task is heavily influenced by the content of the cards (Johnson-Laird, 1983, pp. 31ff.). For example, Wason and Shapiro (1971) showed that a more realistic version of the task was much easier to solve. Suppose that the rule is: *Every time I go to Toronto, I travel by plane.* In a task such as this, the majority of participants see that they need to turn over the card with *car* on it. This is because (as you should have guessed by now) if they turn over the *car* card and it has *Toronto* on the other side, then the rule will have been falsified.

DISCOVERY LAB

The Selection Task and Domain-Specific Reasoning

Cosmides (1989) pointed out that there is little evidence to support the hypothesis that people reason in accordance with the rules of a single logical system. If we did use a single system, our reasoning processes should not be affected by the content of the problem. However, as we have just seen, performance on logical tasks such as Wason's selection task is heavily influenced by content. The inferences that people make with a concrete version of the task are different from the inferences they make with an abstract version. According to Cosmides, the evidence is compelling that people do not use the same reasoning processes across different tasks, and consequently there is no single "psychologic" that we use when we reason.

Cosmides (1989; Cosmides & Tooby, 1994; Fiddick, Cosmides, & Tooby; 2000) proposed an evolutionary account of human reasoning. "It is advantageous to reason adaptively, instead of logically, when this allows one to draw conclusions that are likely to be true but cannot be inferred by strict adherence" to formal logic (Cosmides, 1989, p. 193). Natural selection would tend to produce inference procedures for solving "important and recurrent adaptive problems" (Cosmides, 1989, p. 193). What constitutes adaptive reasoning may differ from one type of problem to another. Consequently, different types of problem may require the use of different, *domain-specific* inference procedures.

One kind of adaptive problem that humans must solve involves "social exchange—co-operation between two or more individuals for mutual benefit" (Cosmides, 1989, p. 195). People make social contracts. They agree to arrangements in which they give something up in order to gain something else. A social contract specifies the relation between the costs and the benefits of such an arrangement. It would be very important to be able to detect cheaters—individuals who violate social contracts—because they would attempt to have the benefit without paying the cost (Cosmides, 1989, p. 197). Cosmides hypothesized that inference procedures have evolved that allow us to pay particular attention to such cases.

social contract theory
The theory that inference procedures have evolved to deal with social contracts in which people give something up in order to gain something else.

With this background in mind, consider the inferences required in the Wason selection task. This task can be used to represent a social contract, as shown below. The standard social contract can be stated in the form of the rule *If you take the benefit, then you pay the cost*. Obviously, in order to see if the rule is being followed, you would choose the *Cost not paid* and *Benefit accepted* cards. The other two cards are irrelevant to the detection of rule violations.

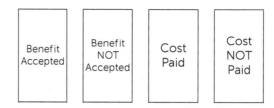

A "switched" social contract has a different structure: *If you pay the cost, then you take the benefit*. How would you detect violations of this rule? If you are behaving logically, then you must choose the *Benefit not accepted* and the *Cost paid* cards. For a switched social contract, the logically correct choices are the two cards that should not be chosen for a standard social contract. Yet Cosmides hypothesized that people will tend to follow a procedure for detecting cheaters (i.e., violators of a social contract). In order to detect cheaters, you should choose the *Cost not paid* and *Benefit accepted* cards even in the switched version of the social contract problem. In this case the logically correct choice and the social contract choice are not the same. Cosmides presented evidence that participants given social contract and switched social contract problems make choices that are consistent with social contract theory.

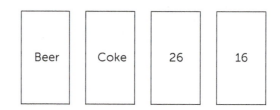

In general, Cosmides argued that in a selection task that has the content of a social contract, people will make inferences consistent with social contract theory. However, a selection task that does not have such content does not elicit such inferences. Thus the abstract version of the Wason selection task does not embody a social contract, and does not elicit the same inferences as the concrete social contract version shown above, which was invented by Griggs and Cox (1982). In this example, each card has a beverage on one side and an age on the other side. The rule is: *If a person is drinking beer, then he must be over 21 years old*. The benefit, such as it is, is permission to drink beer. The cost is waiting until one is 21. In order to detect cheaters, you should turn over the Beer card and the 16 card, and this is in fact what participants do when asked to solve this problem.

DISCOVERY LAB

Cosmides' results were replicated with similar problems by Gigerenzer and Hug (1992). They have also been replicated in a culture quite remote from Harvard, where Cosmides (1989) gathered her original data. Sugiyama, Tooby, and Cosmides (2002) studied the Shiwiar, who are hunter-horticulturalists living in the Ecuadorian Amazon. Sugiyama et al. (2002) hypothesized that a domain-specific reasoning process such as cheater detection would be a cross-cultural universal, since natural selection would have ensured that such a functional process could not be disrupted by "cultural or environment variability" (p. 11538). Because most tests of the existence of a domain-specific cheater detection module had been conducted in literate, industrialized societies, it was important to see if the same sort of reasoning process existed in a much more isolated cultural context. Of course, a selection task involving legal drinking age was not an appropriate research tool for the Shiwiar, and so the task was modified to be culturally relevant. The standard social contract was *If you eat an aphrodisiac, then you must be married*. The switched social contract was *If you give me a basket of fish when you return from fishing, then you may use my motorboat*. Given these tasks, the Shiwiar chose the cheater detection response at a rate almost identical to that of Harvard students. Sugiyama et al. (2002, p. 11541) concluded that the reasoning governing social contracts is "a reliably developing, universal feature of the human cognitive architecture, functioning as an evolutionarily stable strategy."

Cosmides' theory of reasoning holds that there are specialized inference procedures that we use to think about different kinds of problems, although precisely how many inference procedures there may be is an open question. Cosmides argued against the view that people use the same reasoning procedures across all domains. Rather, there may be several different *domain-specific modules* that operate in different ways on problems with different content (Cosmides & Tooby, 1994).

Judgment and Choice

Thus far we have looked at reasoning tasks that involve evaluating or arriving at a conclusion based solely on given information. In what follows we look at what happens when we are forced to go beyond the given information and make judgments and choices between possible, often uncertain, outcomes.

Judgment and choice are two sides of the same coin. Good judgment is a prerequisite for good decision-making. Someone who is able to make good judgments will be able to choose appropriately between alternative courses of action. The circumstances under which we make good or bad judgments have been extensively explored. A parallel line of investigation concerns the nature of good judgment itself.

Heuristics and Biases

The study of judgment and choice has been strongly influenced by the collaboration of Amos Tversky and Daniel Kahneman, who established a research program devoted to heuristics and biases (Gilovich & Griffin, 2002). A heuristic, as we noted in Chapter 10, is a rule of thumb or shortcut that works in some situations but can mislead us in others, while a **bias** is a predisposition to see a particular type of situation in a particular way. Psychologists such as Tversky and Kahneman have uncovered several biases associated with particular heuristics. In what follows we examine some of the biases that arise in situations that require us to make judgments and/or decisions.

bias
A predisposition to see a particular type of situation in a particular way.

Intuitive Statistics

What happens when people try to estimate the chances that a particular event will occur? Suppose someone asked you to predict how often an unbiased coin will come up heads in a series of four tosses. Obviously, the best guess would be two out of four: since the coin is unbiased, you would expect it to come up heads 50 per cent of the time. However, you would probably not be surprised to see no heads at all in any particular series of four tosses. In general, the events that make up a particular sample can't be expected to mirror the proportions of those events in the total population. Thus an unbiased coin will come up heads 50 per cent of the time in the long run, but may come up heads in other proportions in the short run. This fact is called the **law of large numbers**.

One of the misconceptions surrounding the law of large numbers is its relation to what is commonly called the law of averages (Newman, 1956, pp. 1450ff.). The law of large numbers allows us to believe that a particular proportion will obtain in the long run. Now suppose that after 10 tosses a coin still has not come up heads. The common belief in the **law of averages** may lead you to believe that it's now more likely that the next toss will come up heads. People appear to believe that because there will be an equal number of heads and tails in the long run, at some point there must be more heads to compensate for the tails that have already come up.

That this conclusion is incorrect can be seen from the following hypothetical example, adapted from Schuh (1968, pp. 211ff.). It could be that after an initial run of 10 tails there are even numbers of heads and tails over the next 1000 tosses. This would mean that there were 510 tails and 500 heads after 1000 tosses of the coin. This is pretty close to a 50–50 split; in fact, it is a 50–50 split to two decimal places. All the law of large numbers requires is that the proportion of heads or tails increasingly approximate 0.50 after a sufficiently large number of tosses. The law of large numbers does not require that this proportion actually be 0.50 after some arbitrary number of tosses (say, 1000). At no point in the sequence of tosses, regardless of how many there are, do the odds of throwing a head or a tail differ from 50–50. The odds on any particular coin toss are independent of any other coin toss. To believe otherwise is to accept what is called the **gambler's fallacy**. In reality, your chances of throwing heads are no better after a sequence of tails than after any other sequence.

Representativeness and the Belief in the Law of Small Numbers

We noted above that the events that make up a particular sample may not reflect the proportions of those events in the entire population. Suppose that half the students at a university are men, the other half women. That does not mean that a small, random sample of ten students will contain five men and five women. Nevertheless, people often seem to believe in what Tversky and Kahneman (1971) called the **law of small numbers**. This is the belief that a small sample should be representative of the population from which it is drawn. This belief is reflected in use of the **representativeness heuristic**, a rule of thumb according to which we make inferences on the assumption that small samples resemble one another and the population from which they are drawn. The following example comes from Kahneman & Tversky (1972):

> There are two programs in a high school. Boys are a majority (65 per cent) in program A, and a minority (45 per cent) in program B. There are equal numbers of classes in each of the two programs.

---

law of large numbers
The larger the sample, the closer a statistic will be to the true value.

law of averages
A fallacy based on the assumption that events of one kind are always balanced by events of another kind.

gambler's fallacy
The mistaken belief that an event that has not occurred on several independent trials is more likely to happen on future trials.

law of small numbers
The mistaken belief that a small sample should be representative of the population from which it is drawn.

representativeness heuristic
Making inferences on the assumption that small samples resemble one another and the population from which they are drawn.

You enter a class at random, and observe that 55 per cent of the students are boys. What is your best guess—does the class belong to program A or program B? (p. 431)

People will tend to guess that the class belongs to program A, because it has a majority of boys and is therefore more *representative* of program A than of program B.

The same kind of representativeness heuristic operates when people are asked to judge whether or not a particular sequence of events was produced by a random process. Tversky and Kahneman discussed research showing that a sequence of coin tosses such as T T H H T T H H does not strike us as truly random because it has a pattern, and patterns are intuitively unlikely if a process is not operating according to some rule.

Lopes (1982) pointed out that even very sophisticated thinkers with a lot of mathematical training have difficulty specifying what distinguishes random from non-random processes. She noted that there is a difference between a random process and a random product.

COGNITION IN ACTION
BOX 11.3

Is There a Hot Hand in Basketball?

A controversial example of the way the representativeness heuristic works was presented by Gilovich, Vallone, and Tversky (1985). Many fans of men's professional basketball perceive a player who has shot a run of baskets as having a hot hand. In fact, Gilovich et al. (1985) found that 91 per cent of fans believed that a player has "a better chance of making a shot after having just made his last two or three shots than he does after having just missed his last two or three shots" (p. 297). In other words, most fans believe that success on any particular shot is not random.

Gilovich et al. analyzed 48 home games played by the Philadelphia 76ers in the 1980–1 season. They could find no evidence that players were more likely to shoot a basket after making one, two, or three baskets than they were after missing one, two, or three. Thus the chance of hitting a shot was not greater after a sequence of hits than it was after a sequence of misses. For example, if a player made 50 per cent of his shots, then the probability of his hitting a shot was not greater than 50 per cent after a hit, nor was it lower than 50 per cent after a miss. There was no evidence that either hits and/or misses were clustered. Sequences of hits and misses occurred no more frequently than would be expected on a purely random basis.

Another interesting finding was that most of the Philadelphia 76ers the researchers interviewed appeared to share their fans' belief that hits were more likely following hits than following misses. Players and fans alike tended to perceive any sequence of shots as a "streak," even though the probability of making a basket is completely independent of the outcome of preceding shots.

Many people disputed Gilovich et al.'s conclusion, and the **hot-hand belief** may actually be true for some sports (e.g., Gilden & Wilson, 1995). In fact, even though statistically sophisticated observers now generally accept that the hot-hand belief is false in the case of basketball, it may still be useful for players to behave as if it were true. Burns (2004) distinguishes between hot-hand belief and **hot-hand behaviour** and points out that even if the belief is false, it may benefit the team if it means that better shooters get the ball more often. Hence, Burns (2004) concludes, it is not always the case that a belief must be true in order to lead to adaptive behaviour.

hot-hand belief
The belief that a player who has just made two or three shots is on a streak and will likely make the next shot.

hot-hand behaviour
A bias that leads the teammates of a player who has just scored a basket to let him take the next shot.

A random process, such as tossing an unbiased coin, may generate sequences that don't appear to be random. Thus even though it is perfectly possible for an unbiased coin to generate the sequence T T H H T T H H, most of us will feel that this sequence is not one we would choose to represent randomness.

Adjustment and Anchoring

Which of the following produces the larger number?

$$8 \times 7 \times 6 \times 5 \times 4 \times 3 \times 2 \times 1$$
$$1 \times 2 \times 3 \times 4 \times 5 \times 6 \times 7 \times 8$$

Students who were given five seconds to come up with an estimate consistently judged the second sequence to yield a much smaller product than the first (Tversky & Kahneman, 1974). The average estimate for the first sequence was 2250; for the second, 512. In fact, both sequences yield 40,320. Why even the higher estimate was so far off the mark would be interesting to explore; however, what concerns us here is the difference between the two estimates. This discrepancy arose because the participants **adjusted** their estimates depending on the starting value of the sequence. Because the first sequence started with a larger number than the second, it appeared to yield a larger product than the second. In other words, the two sequences were **anchored** by different values, and those anchors created the illusion that the sequences yielded different outcomes.

In general, when people are asked to judge the magnitude of something, their judgment will be biased by the initial value to which they are exposed (Chapman & Johnson, 2002, p. 121). In another study cited by Kahneman and Tversky (1974), different groups of participants were asked to estimate the percentage of African countries in the United Nations. Before answering, each group was given a random number and instructed to indicate whether that number was higher or lower than their estimate. Those participants initially given a low number (e.g., 10) subsequently estimated the percentage of African countries in the UN to be significantly lower than did those who were given a higher number (e.g., 65). This result suggests that our judgment is not simply a function of what we know, or think we know. Rather, judgment can be biased by aspects of the situation in which the judgment is made.

Availability

Some experiences are more easily recalled than others. We could say that those experiences are more *available* than others (Asch & Ebenholtz, 1962). In general, **availability** refers to the ease with which something can be brought to mind (Horowitz, Norman, & Day, 1966; Tversky & Kahneman, 1974; Schwartz & Vaughn, 2002). Obviously, availability plays a central role in the way we recall previous experiences. There may be many things we have experienced that do not come readily to mind. Tversky and Kahneman have shown how availability influences our judgment.

For example, suppose you were asked to judge how frequently an event of a particular class occurs. Tversky and Kahneman (1973a) asked people to judge the relative frequency with which the letter *R* occurs in different positions in words—specifically, whether it occurs more frequently as the first letter or the third. They found that approximately 69 per cent

adjustment and anchoring
People's judgments of magnitude are biased (i.e., adjusted) by the initial value to which they are exposed (i.e., the anchor).

availability
The ease with which something can be brought to mind.

What a Pain!

Over the course of his distinguished career, Kahneman made numerous important contributions to research on attention and perception, many of them while he was a professor at the University of British Columbia from 1978 to 1986 (see www.publicaffairs.ubc.ca/services-for-media/ubc-facts-figures/). In collaboration with his long-term colleague Amos Tversky, Kahneman applied ideas from the fields of attention and perception to the fields of judgment and decision-making, creating an influential research program that ultimately garnered him the 2002 Nobel Prize in Economics (see Kahneman, 2002).

One of Kahneman's studies (Redelmeir & Kahneman, 1996), which reveals an interesting aspect of the way we formulate judgments, is elegantly and lucidly described in his latest book, *Thinking, Fast and Slow* (Kahneman, 2011, p. 378–381). Redelmeir and Kahneman (1996) asked patients who were undergoing colonoscopy without anesthesia to report on the level of pain they were feeling at one-minute intervals throughout the procedure. Patients rated their pain using a scale that ranged from "0" meaning "no pain" to "10" meaning "extreme pain" (see p. 4). Then, following the procedure, they were also asked to retrospectively assess the overall level of pain they had felt. Redelmeir and Kahneman (1996) centred their discussion on the results from two patients (Patient A and Patient B); Figure 11.4 shows their minute-by-minute pain ratings. As you can see, Patient B experienced more pain overall than Patient A. Interestingly, however, their retrospective judgments of discomfort did not show the same pattern. How was that possible?

The data strongly suggested that the patients did not base their retrospective judgments on the sum of their moment-to-moment experiences of pain. Rather, they formed those judgments by averaging (1) the highest level of pain experienced during the procedure and (2) the level of pain experienced at the end of the procedure. This finding reflects what Kahneman (2011) called the **peak–end rule**. What's even more interesting is that the retrospective judgments of discomfort did not reflect the total duration of the colonoscopy, a phenomenon referred to as **duration neglect**

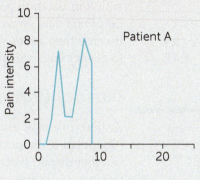

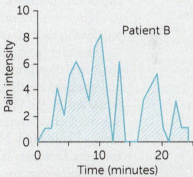

FIGURE 11.4 | Moment-to-moment judgments of pain from two patients undergoing colonoscopy

From: Redelmeier, D. A., & Kahneman, D. (1996).

(Kahneman, 2011). These findings led to the counterintuitive conclusion that people will retrospectively feel better about a painful procedure if its duration is extended until the pain has begun to subside (Kahneman, 2011; see also Kahneman, Frederickson, Schreiber, & Redelmeier, 1993). One explanation for the tendency to base judgments of overall pain on the peak and ending levels could be that these are the levels most available to memory.

peak–end rule

Retrospective judgments of the total painfulness of an event are formed by averaging the pain experienced during the most painful moment of the event and that felt at the end of the event.

duration neglect

The finding that retrospective judgments of the total painfulness of an event are unrelated to the event's duration.

of participants judged *R* to occur more frequently in the first position. In fact, *R* is more often the third letter.

Why do so many people believe that *R* occurs more frequently in the first position than in the third? In order to judge the frequency of the two classes of words, you might try to recall words of each type. But the letter *R* is a better cue for words beginning with *R* than for words with *R* in the third position. Thus you would be more likely to think of a word such as *runner* or *rain* than *carpet* or *berry*. In this situation, words beginning with *R* are more available. Because they are more easily recalled, we believe there are more of them. We confuse the frequency with which we can remember something with how frequently it actually occurs.

DISCOVERY LAB

Illusory Correlation

Availability may also be responsible for the phenomenon called **illusory correlation** (Chapman & Chapman, 1969). Sometimes people believe that events go together when in fact they do not. Tversky and Kahneman (1974) suggested that judgments of how frequently two events occur together depend on availability. If thinking of one kind of event makes you remember the other kind of event, then you may infer that the two kinds tend to occur together in the real world.

Shweder (1977) conducted an extensive review of this kind of thinking. As he pointed out, correlation is not an intuitive concept. **Intuitive concepts** are relatively easy to acquire, and are used by almost all adults. Among Shweder's examples were the concept of an external world, the idea that one thing can be a part of something else, and the notion that one word can be synonymous with another. No formal education is needed to acquire concepts of this kind. However, many other concepts are not so easily learned. Statistical concepts, for example, are not acquired without formal instruction and willingness to learn. Often the proper use of such non-intuitive concepts requires fairly detailed calculations. Consider the following problem: "A piece of paper is folded in half. It is folded in half again, and again.... After 100 folds, how thick will it be?" (Shweder, 1977, p. 638). When you first hear this problem, you might intuitively think of a large book and estimate a thickness of 3 or 4 inches. In fact, the thickness is over 200,000 *miles*. You have to actually work out what happens when you fold the paper in order to see why the thickness becomes so great.

Correlation is a very good example of a non-intuitive concept. To explain why the concept of correlation is so difficult to acquire, Shweder used an example taken from Smedslund (1963). Consider the data in Table 11.2.

Smedslund's participants, who were nurses, generally inferred from those data that there was a connection between having the symptom and having the disease. The reason most often given for this conclusion was that the largest number of cases occurs in the cell showing the presence of both the disease and the symptom. That is, the nurses focused on instances that were consistent with the hypothesis that the disease and the symptom are correlated. This experiment is important in part because it is another illustration of confirmation bias. However, it also shows how the tendency to pay attention to confirming instances and ignore disconfirming instances facilitates illusory correlation.

TABLE 11.2 | Relationship between a Symptom and a Disease in a Sample of 100 Cases

Symptom	Disease		
	Present	Absent	Total
Present	37	33	70
Absent	17	13	30
Total	54	46	100

Source: Shweder, R.A. (1977). Likeness and likelihood in everyday thought. *Current Anthropology, 18*, 637–658. Copyright 1977 by the University of Chicago. Reprinted by permission.

In order to properly determine whether or not the data in Table 11.2 demonstrate a correlation between the symptom and the disease, you must also consider those cases in which the symptom is absent but the disease is present. In fact, the data show that of the 70 people who have the symptom, only 37 (53 per cent) have the disease, whereas of the 30 who do not have the symptom 57 per cent have the disease. Thus you can see that the symptom is not a very good predictor of who has the disease and who does not. Therefore you should not say that the symptom and the disease are correlated. On the contrary, on the basis of these data you should conclude that the two events—symptom and disease—are unrelated.

Redelmeier and Tversky (1996) provided a good example of a common, real-world illusory correlation. The belief that arthritis pain is correlated with changes in the weather goes back thousands of years. Many doctors as well as patients still believe in this relationship. However, research on the subject has failed to find good evidence for it. Redelmeier and Tversky obtained data for 18 arthritis patients twice a month for 15 months. Sixteen of those patients believed in the weather/arthritis pain correlation. Patients' assessments of their pain on particular days were correlated with the local weather as measured by barometric pressure, temperature, or humidity. The average of these correlations was .01. Since correlations can vary from −1 to +1, with .00 denoting a complete absence of correlation, this result means that there is no evidence whatsoever that arthritis pain and the weather are related. Some patients believed that there might be a lag between the weather and their symptoms, so correlations were also computed between arthritis pain and the weather on two days before and two days after the day on which pain data was recorded. The average of these correlations was .00.

Given that it is extremely unlikely that weather and arthritis pain actually have anything to do with one another, what is it that prompts so many people to believe in a causal relation? Redelmeier and Tversky suggest that people may focus on days when they experience extreme pain and look for changes in the weather at those times, ignoring times when the weather changes but their pain remains the same. "A single day of severe pain and extreme weather might sustain a lifetime of belief in a relation between them" (Redelmeier & Tversky, 1996, p. 2896).

Regression towards the Mean

Another way in which the concept of correlation is sometimes misused involves the phenomenon of regression towards the mean. To understand how this works, consider two variables that are in fact correlated: the average height of parents and the average height of their children. However, the correlation is not perfect. For purely mathematical reasons, whenever two variables are not perfectly correlated, extreme values on one variable tend to yield less extreme values on the other variable. Thus very tall parents tend to have somewhat shorter offspring, and very short parents tend to have somewhat taller offspring. The relationship between these two variables in a sample gathered by Galton (1886) is shown in Figure 11.5. The average, or mean, values for both parents and children are about the same (roughly 68 inches). The figure can be used to predict the height of children on the basis of their parents' height. Notice how, for any value of parents' height, the predicted value of children's height is closer to the average, or mean, than is that of their parents. Thus parents whose combined heights average out to less than 65 inches tend to have children who are almost 66 inches tall, whereas parents whose heights average to 72 inches tend to have children who are less than 71 inches tall. This phenomenon is called **regression to the mean**.

regression to the mean
For purely mathematical reasons, whenever two variables are not perfectly correlated, extreme values on one variable tend to be related to values on the other variable that are closer to (i.e., regressed to) the mean of that variable.

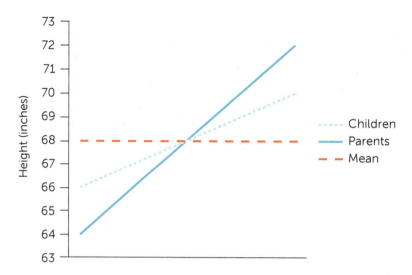

FIGURE 11.5 | Relationship between the height of parents and their children

To regress means to return: thus parents (the "extreme value" variable) tend to have children (the less extreme variable) who regress to the mean.

In general, for two variables that are not perfectly correlated, high values on the first variable are related to lower values on the second, and low values on the first are related to higher values on the second. This means that when you use the values of one variable to predict the values of the other, you will find that the predicted values of the second variable are somewhat closer to the mean, or average, of the second variable. Keep in mind that this occurs for purely mathematical reasons. Galton (1889, as cited by Walker, 1943, and Senders, 1958), who first discovered regression to the mean, put it this way:

> The law of Regression tells heavily against the full hereditary transmission of any gift. Only a few out of many children would be likely to differ as widely as the more exceptional of the two parents. The more bountifully the Parent is gifted by nature, the more rare will be his good fortune if he begets a son who is endowed yet more largely. But the law is even-handed: it levies an equal succession-tax on the transmission of badness as of goodness. If it discourages the extravagant hopes of a gifted parent that his children will inherit all his powers, it no less discountenances extravagant fears that they will inherit all his weakness and disease (p. 106).

Regression to the mean occurs in a great many situations beyond the one that intrigued Galton. Tversky and Kahneman (1974) gave several examples. Suppose that some students perform much better on a particular examination than would normally be expected of them. What would you predict for their next examination? If you follow the logic of regression towards the mean, you would predict that their next examination would be closer to their average level of performance. Similarly, a dismal score on an exam should predict a better outcome next time.

There is no need for causal explanations of this variability. Yet a causal explanation is often precisely what we want. After a poor performance is succeeded by a better one, we may attribute the difference to the fact that we worked harder the second time, or that the exam was easier. Such explanations may account for some of the variability in our performance, but some variability will remain unexplained. It is just this uncertainty that people find hard to accept. Because we are anxious to understand the reasons for our successes and failures, we sometimes impose unwarranted interpretations.

Tversky and Kahneman pointed out the relevance of regression to the mean for understanding the role that reward and punishment may, or may not, play in changing behaviour.

THINK TWICE
BOX 11.5

Assessing Your Own Reasoning Abilities

How good are your reasoning and decision-making skills? One popular test was developed by Frederick (2005). Known as the Cognitive Reflection Test, or CRT, it consists of the three problems shown in Figure 11.6. Without looking at the answers below, try to answer them as quickly as you can.

The answers are as follows: (1) 5 cents; (2) 5 minutes; and (3) 47 days. Chances are that you missed at least one of them. Why? Although the questions look easy, they are actually the sort of "trick questions" you hope never to see on a test or exam. Each one is designed in such a way as to lead you to think of an "intuitive" answer very quickly. For instance, when answering the third question, you think about covering *half* the lake, and this immediately leads you to think it should take *half* the time. Half the patch, half the time, right? Wrong! What often gets missed is the fact that it would have taken 47 days of doubling for the patch to reach half of its final extent: on day 47 it would have been half the size that it would be on the final, 48th day.

According to Frederick (2005, p. 27):

The three items on the CRT are "easy" in the sense that their solution is easily understood when explained, yet reaching the correct answer often requires the suppression of an erroneous answer that springs "impulsively" to mind.

Frederick (2005) notes that to be successful on questions like these, you have to (a) recognize that the first answer you think of is wrong, (b) ignore it, and (c) continue to apply rigorous reasoning to solve the problem. This test is often used to distinguish between decision-making done by a fast, intuitive system (which in this case gives you the wrong answer), and a much slower, more effortful rational system (which in this case provides the right answer). This distinction is captured in the title of Daniel Kahneman's book—*Thinking Fast and Slow*.

---

(1) A bat and a ball cost $1.10 in total. The bat costs $1.00 more than the ball. How much does the ball cost? ____cents

(2) If it takes 5 machines 5 minutes to make 5 widgets, how long would it take 100 machines to make 100 widgets? ____minutes

(3) In a lake, there is a patch of lily pads. Every day, the patch doubles in size. If it takes 48 days for the patch to cover the entire lake, how long would it take for the patch to cover half of the lake? ____days

---

FIGURE 11.6 | The three-question CRT

From: Frederick, S. (2005).

For example, if a child performs exceptionally well on some task, then it's tempting for parents to offer praise. Those same parents might be disappointed when, on a subsequent occasion, the child's performance is not so good. If they punish the child and (as is likely) the performance improves the next time around, the parents may be tempted to credit the punishment. Yet these varying results may have nothing to do with the fact that the child's behaviour was rewarded or punished: they may come about purely as a consequence of regression to the mean. As Tversky and Kahneman (1973b) observed, "the human condition is such that, by chance alone, one is most often rewarded for punishing others and most often punished for rewarding them" (p. 251).

Ecological Rationality

Tversky and Kahneman's work has not gone unchallenged. According to Gigerenzer and Goldstein (1996, p. 651), for instance, heuristics and biases research suggests that people are "hopelessly lost in the face of real-world complexity, given their supposed inability to reason according to the canon of classical rationality, even in simple laboratory experiments." By contrast, Gigerenzer and Goldstein proposed that people usually make good decisions by using simple heuristics that rely on ecologically valid cues. For example, consider what Goldstein and Gigerenzer (2002) call the recognition heuristic:

> When choosing between two objects (according to some criterion), if one is recognized and the other is not, then select the former. For instance, if deciding at mealtime between Dr Seuss's famous menu choices of green eggs and ham (using the criterion of being good to eat), this heuristic would lead one to choose the recognized ham over the unrecognized odd-colored eggs (Todd & Gigerenzer, 2000, p. 732).

The recognition heuristic relies on the fact than people are very good at telling the difference between events they have experienced previously and those they have not. The classic demonstration of this discriminatory behaviour was an experiment by Shepard (1969), who allowed participants to examine 612 photographs for as long as they liked. They were then given 68 pairs of photographs. One member of each pair was from the previous set and one was new. Participants were able to tell which was which about 99 per cent of the time. But the recognition heuristic will not work unless two conditions are met. First, the person must recognize some of the alternatives between which a choice must be made, but not all of them. Second, the alternatives that are recognized must also be the correct choices. Under those conditions the recognition heuristic is ecologically valid, and using it is **ecologically rational**. A heuristic is ecologically rational if it "produces useful inferences by exploiting the structure of information in the environment" (Todd, Fiddick, & Krauss, 2000, p. 375).

Gigerenzer and his colleagues (Goldstein & Gigerenzer, 2002) have shown how the recognition heuristic works in a series of demonstrations. One such demonstration required participants to decide which of two US cities was larger. When the two cities were San Diego and San Antonio, American students correctly chose San Diego two-thirds of the time. However, German students correctly chose San Diego 100 per cent of the time. This result is counter-intuitive because we would expect that American students would know more about

recognition heuristic
When choosing between two objects (according to some criterion), if one is recognized and the other is not, then select the former.

ecological rationality
A heuristic is ecologically rational if it produces useful inferences by exploiting the structure of information in the environment.

American cities than would German students. The explanation is that the American students recognized both San Antonio and San Diego as American cities, and therefore were unable to use the recognition heuristic to distinguish between them. Thus American students could not know which city was larger unless they had that knowledge in their memory to be recalled. The German students, however, didn't need to know which city was larger in order to make the correct choice: they simply picked San Diego because they recognized it and rejected San Antonio because they did not recognize it. Recognition is ecologically valid in a situation like this because people are more likely to have heard of large cities than small ones. Therefore the recognition heuristic is *ecologically rational* in this case.

This example illustrates the difference between the recognition heuristic and the *availability heuristic*, which we considered earlier in this chapter. The availability heuristic inclines the participant to decide in favour of the most easily recallable alternative. By contrast, the recognition heuristic doesn't require participants to recall anything. They don't need to *recall* the population of San Diego or San Antonio. All they need to do is *recognize* one of the two choices.

One of the implications of the recognition heuristic is that people who know less may sometimes be able to make better judgments than people who know more. Here is an example modelled on one used by Goldstein and Gigerenzer (2002, p. 79). Imagine three American sisters, each of whom must take a test on the relative size of Canadian cities. One of the Americans is housebound and knows nothing about Canada. The second knows only what she has read in the press and seen on television. The third has been studying Canadian geography and history. Who will do better on the test? Goldstein & Gigerenzer would predict that the second sister would do better than the others, because "she is the only one who can use the recognition heuristic" (2002, p. 79). The third sister knows *too much* to be able to use it, and the first sister knows *too little*. This outcome is called the **less-is-more effect**.

Criticisms of the Ecological Rationality Approach

Gigerenzer and his colleagues have proposed the existence of an *adaptive toolbox* containing a variety of heuristics, of which the recognition heuristic is usually a component. However, some have argued that the recognition heuristic is much more limited in its generality than Gigerenzer and his group suggest (e.g., Oppenheimer, 2003; Newell, 2005). Others have suggested that while simple heuristics might work well for some relatively unimportant decisions, they can't be applied to truly important decisions such as choosing a mate or raising a child:

> Mate selection does not just involve the self and the partner. It usually also involves the interests of parents, friends, members of reference groups, and so forth. A career decision, too, often involves many different parties, as do union–management negotiations, international negotiations, and the like. . . . I suspect that many others seeking decision rules for the high stakes decisions they encounter in their lives will not find that [these] rules . . . make their decisions all that easy (Sternberg, 2000a, p. 764).

For their part, Kahneman and Tversky (1996) argued that Gigerenzer had exaggerated the difference between his work and theirs. There is no reason why the recognition heuristic couldn't be studied within the framework of heuristics and biases research (Kahneman &

less-is-more effect
Sometimes the person who knows less is able to make a better judgment than the person who knows more but is unable to use that knowledge in the situation at hand.

Frederick, 2002, pp. 58–59). It's possible that, over time, these two approaches will become more complementary than antagonistic.

Training in Statistical Reasoning

We considered the problem space within which reasoning takes place in Chapter 10. As we noted then, the problem space consists of the way the problem is represented, including the goal to be reached and the various ways in which the situation might be transformed into the solution (Newell & Simon, 1972, p. 59). Keren (1984) has analyzed how misunderstanding of the problem space leads to the use of inappropriate heuristics. Consider the following problem:

> Three coins are to be given to two children (Dan and Mike) using the following rule. An ordinary deck of cards is shuffled and cut. If the top card is red, Dan gets a coin, but if it is black, Mike gets a coin. The deck is shuffled again, and the next coin is assigned using the same procedure. Finally, the third coin is allocated, again following the same method. What is more likely to occur:
>
> a.   One child will get three coins; the other will get none.
> b.   One child will get two coins; the other one.
> c.   Both possibilities (a) and (b) are equally likely.

The correct answer is (b), but more than 40 per cent of participants chose the incorrect but intuitively reasonable alternative (c). In order to see why (b) is correct, examine Figure 11.7: a tree diagram of the various possible outcomes. Notice that there are eight possibilities, and that in six of them one child gets two coins and the other child gets one. Thus alternative (b) is the most likely outcome. If you think through the problem in this way, you will get the right answer.

However, there is at least one other way of thinking about the problem, which leads to the wrong answer. Participants might imagine only the possible ways in which the coins

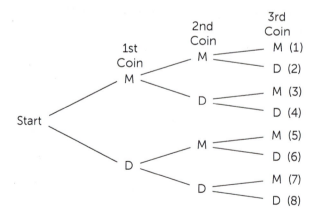

FIGURE 11.7 | Problem space for the Keren coin problem

From: Keren, G. (1984). Copyright 1984 by Elsevier Science Publishers. Reprinted by permission.

could be divided, without considering how these divisions come about. When the problem is so construed, there appear to be only four possible outcomes. Mike could get 3, and Dan 0; Mike could get 2 and Dan 1; Mike could get 1 and Dan 2; and Mike could get 0 and Dan 3. If the participant assumes that all these alternatives are equally likely, then alternative (c) appears to be correct. Half the time one child gets 3 coins and the other 0; and the other half of the time one child gets 2 coins and the other gets 1.

By thinking about the different ways in which participants can represent a problem, we can understand why some answers seem more reasonable than others. Different problem spaces provide different *frames* within which a problem can be understood or misunderstood (Kahneman & Tversky, 1984). As Tversky and Kahneman (1983) have noted, "because we normally do not have adequate formal models for computing the probabilities of such events, intuitive judgment is often the only practical method for assessing uncertainty" (p. 293). In the Keren coin problem above, people who don't think through the problem may rely on the more intuitive solution procedure and end up making an incorrect inference. However, as Nisbett, Krantz, Jepson, and Kunda (1983) have observed, proper training in statistics may enable us to think more appropriately about problems like these.

As Nisbett et al. pointed out, some situations make it more likely that even untrained people will use the appropriate reasoning procedures. Nisbett et al. proposed that three factors determine when people will use the appropriate reasoning procedures:

1. *Clarity of the problem space.* In the Keren problem it's important to be aware of all the alternatives. This is true of any problem that calls for statistical reasoning. Some problem spaces are easier to grasp than others. When the problem space is poorly understood, errors may result.

2. *Recognition of the operation of chance.* It's easier to see chance at work in some situations than in others. In sports the operation of chance factors such as weather and injuries is relatively obvious, and the effect these factors have on the outcome of games is clear. Yet as we saw in our discussion of the hot-hand fallacy, people often perceive chance phenomena as orderly even when they know better. Nevertheless, we may be more likely to use sound reasoning procedures when we are aware that chance is a factor.

3. *Cultural prescription.* People may reason better if they come from a culture that values statistical reasoning and provides the appropriate training.

In one of their studies Nisbett et al. (1983) gave participants two problems. The first involved a football coach who typically identifies two or three exciting prospects at the beginning of each season, but finds that they seldom go on to perform as well as he had expected. Participants were asked to explain why the coach has to revise his opinion of players he originally thought were brilliant.

The second problem involved a director of a theatre company who is initially enthusiastic about the stage presence of some novice actors but is eventually disappointed by their performances. Participants were asked to explain why the director has to revise her opinion of actors who showed such promise at first.

Both these problems require at least an intuitive understanding of the concept of regression to the mean, and the explanation is the same in both cases: the novices performed at an exceptionally high level at the tryouts, but eventually their performance returned to its usual level. Causal explanations such as "The boys who did well at tryout slacked off to avoid making their teammates jealous" were not relevant.

Nisbet et al. (1983) found that participants who had some experience with the field of activity mentioned in the problem were more likely to reason appropriately about it. Thus people who had played team sports in high school or college were more likely to recognize a regression effect in the first problem than were those who did not have such experience. Similarly, participants with acting experience were more likely to recognize a regression effect in the second problem.

As Nisbett et al. pointed out, becoming an expert in a particular area means becoming a member of its subculture (e.g., football players, actors), and the process of enculturation may require the acquisition of the reasoning procedures appropriate to that domain. In that case, some of the heuristics that people use may be *domain-specific*. Nevertheless, the fact that we can learn to use the correct inference procedures in specific areas suggests that we can be trained to use statistical reasoning in almost any context. Nisbett et al. (1983) believed that such training was becoming the norm in our culture, and that in time we might see a general rise in the ability to reason statistically.

It's important to remember, however, that training in the methods of one field doesn't tell you anything about appropriate reasoning procedures in other fields. Lehman, Lempert, and Nisbett (1988) reviewed the reasoning ability of people in various fields who had received training in the reasoning procedures specific to their disciplines. Graduate students in psychology who had been trained in statistical reasoning were able to generalize their training to problems in everyday life. However, training in chemistry did not provide that kind of benefit: "chemistry provides no improvement in statistical or methodological reasoning. . . . [T]here is little need to differentiate among the various types of causal relations because chemistry deals primarily with necessary-and-sufficient causes. . . . [T]he luxury of not being confronted with messy problems that contain a substantial uncertainty and a tangled web of causes means that chemistry does not teach some rules that are relevant to everyday life" (Lehman, Lempert, & Nisbett, 1988, p. 441). Thus training in a discipline such as psychology may help a student cope with reasoning problems in everyday life in a way that training in a discipline such as chemistry cannot. Mill, Gray, and Mandel (1994, p. 247) further explored Lehman and Nisbett's (1990) claim that "undergraduate training in the social sciences, particularly psychology, does lead students to apply statistical and methodological reasoning skills to a range of everyday situations." Mill, Gray, and Mandel (1994) recruited participants from undergraduate research methods and statistics courses in psychology and tested their ability to apply what they were being taught to situations in everyday life. For example, they were asked to evaluate the claim of a pharmaceutical company that its new drug led to recovery from illness in 75 per cent of patients who received it. Of course, such a claim is meaningless unless you know what percentage of people recover without taking the drug. It turned out that students who had taken methods and statistics courses did no better on "critical thinking" items than students who had not taken such courses. Only students who had taken additional tutorials in critical thinking showed improvement. Thus undergraduate training in research methods does not necessarily mean that students will be able to apply what they have been taught. Recall Kahneman's (2002, p. 451) observation that reason is not very vigilant, and "allows many intuitive judgments to be expressed, including some that are erroneous." To apply what you have learned about statistical reasoning to problems in everyday life is hard work, and sometimes you may not be inclined to make the effort.

Summary

In this chapter we have seen how logic and reasoning can shed light on psychological processes. Different systems of logic vary in their answers to the question of what makes a conclusion follow logically from a set of assertions or *premises*.

Syllogistic or categorical reasoning examines the relationship between two premises and a conclusion and takes several forms. One influential theory of syllogistic reasoning proposes that we construct a *mental model* of the situation to which a set of premises refers, and then draw conclusions that are consistent with the model. Another, *natural deduction systems* theory, holds that we use deduction rules to draw conclusions from various propositions—statements structured around connectives such as *if . . . then, and, or*, and *not*—that are stored in working memory. *Wason's puzzles* represent an alternative approach, focusing not on syllogistic reasoning but on a variety of tasks that directly tap interesting aspects of reasoning (*generative problem, eliminative strategy, the selection task*).

All three of the above research approaches examine the more or less formal reasoning we do when we are given certain information and draw conclusions from it. When the information required for that kind of reasoning isn't available, however, we must rely on judgment. The evidence suggests that many of our judgments are based not on reason, but rather on rules of thumb (*heuristics*), which are susceptible to *biases*. *Anchoring* and *availability* are just two of the many heuristics we use when making judgments under conditions of uncertainty. While some researchers hold that relying on heuristics often leads to poor judgments, others believe that in many real-world situations, the use of heuristics is both effective and *ecologically rational*. Interestingly, reasoning under uncertainty can be improved through training. It seems that training in the kind of statistical reasoning that is commonly used in psychology can improve the judgments we make in everyday life.

CASE STUDY

Case Study Wrap-Up

We began this chapter with a discussion of how widely people's views on the merits and implications of scientific studies can vary. In particular we highlighted the contrasting responses to Mann et al.'s report on the hockey-stick temperature reconstruction as examples of the *motivated reasoning* that can prevent us from evaluating evidence in an objective and dispassionate manner. As we noted throughout the chapter, much of our thinking is based on heuristics rather than rational thought. Instead of applying logical reasoning, we make judgments on the fly, based on fragments of information, and often give less weight to the validity of an argument than to its fit with our own biases. As Kahneman (2011, p. 45) notes, failure to do the slow, deliberate work of rational thinking can sometimes lead to "embarrassing" results.

In the Know: Review Questions

1. Discuss possible sources of difficulty in syllogistic reasoning, paying particular attention to content bias and the meaning of *some*.
2. Outline Johnson-Laird's mental models approach to syllogistic reasoning. Compare it to natural deduction theory.
3. What do experiments conducted using Wason's puzzles suggest about what makes a reasoning problem difficult?
4. Define and give examples of each of the following: representativeness; adjustment and anchoring; availability. In each case, briefly describe a relevant experiment.
5. Do you believe in the hot hand? Give reasons for your answer. In what other situations might the hot hand be a true or a false belief?
6. What is rational about the recognition heuristic? Can you think of any situations other than those identified in the text in which it might work?

Key Concepts

adjustment and anchoring

availability

bias

conditional reasoning

confirmation bias

duration neglect

ecological rationality

eliminative strategy

emergent consequences

gambler's fallacy

generative problem

hot-hand behaviour

hot-hand belief

iconic

illusory correlation

intuitive concept

law of averages

law of large numbers

law of small numbers

less-is-more effect

logicism

motivated reasoning

natural deduction system

parsimony

peak–end rule

practical syllogism

reasoning

recognition heuristic

relational reasoning

regression to the mean

representativeness heuristic

selection task (Wason)

social contract theory

syllogism

three-term series problem

truth tables

Links to Other Chapters

mental models

Chapter 7 (cognitive maps and mental models)

emergent properties

Chapter 2 (Sperry)

Chapter 7 (images and ambiguous figures)

heuristics

Chapter 8 (commitment heuristic)

Further Reading

Suppose that the following assertions apply to a specific hand of cards:

> If there is a king or a queen in the hand, then there is an ace in the hand.
> There is a king in the hand.
> What, if anything, follows?

Anyone who thinks there *must* be an ace in the hand should read Johnson-Laird and Savary (1999). If you find paradoxes interesting, read Sainsbury (1988). For a novel approach to the study of reasoning based on the centrality of linguistic processes, see Polk and Newell (1995).

Research interest in the selection task has been intense. As a consequence, there are too many alternative explanations to fully cover in this text. For an account of the selection task based on relevance theory, see Sperber and Girotto (2002). For a connectionist approach, see Leighton and Dawson (2001). Atran (2001) argues that the selection task does not require a domain-specific interpretation.

Josephs, Giesler, and Silvera (1994) proposed a heuristic called the *quantity principle.* In one experiment, participants were asked to write an essay that they believed would earn them a very high grade. Those who used a small font for their essays tended to write more than those who chose a larger font, even though no restrictions were placed on the length of the essay. Since a small font requires more words to produce the same number of pages as a larger font, it appeared that quantity was the important variable influencing participants' judgment of the quality of their essays. The saying "more is better" describes the principle that is consistent with the *quantity principle*, a heuristic that tends to make us confuse quality with quantity. Have you known any professors who seemed to believe that good essays have more pages than poor ones?

For some marvellous illustrations of how meaningful coincidences can mislead us, see Eco (1989).

Over (2000) provides a good brief critique of the ecological rationality issue.

Atran, S. (2001). A cheater detection module? Dubious interpretations of the Wason selection task and logic. *Evolution and Cognition, 7*, 1–7.

Eco, U. (1989). *Foucault's pendulum.* New York: Knopf.

Johnson-Laird, P.N., & Savary, F. (1999). Illusory inferences: A novel class of erroneous deductions. *Cognition, 71*, 191–229.

Josephs, R.A., Giesler, R.B., & Silvera, D.H. (1994). Judgment by quantity. *Journal of Experimental Psychology: General, 123*, 21–32.

Leighton, J.P., & Dawson, M.R.W. (2001). A parallel distributed processing model of Wason's selection task. *Journal of Cognitive Systems Research, 2*, 207–231.

Over, D.E. (2000). Ecological issues: A reply to Todd, Fiddick, & Krauss. *Thinking and Reasoning, 6*, 385–388.

Polk, T.A., & Newell, A. (1995). Deduction as verbal reasoning. *Psychological Review, 102*, 533–566.

Sainsbury, R.M. (1988). *Paradoxes.* Cambridge: Cambridge University Press.

Sperber, D., & Girotto, V. (2002). Use or misuse of the selection task? Rejoinder to Fiddick, Cosmides, and Tooby. *Cognition, 85*, 277–290.

12

Intelligence and Creativity

Chapter Contents

Chapter Objectives

- To examine the various ways in which cognitive psychologists have conceptualized intelligence and how these conceptualizations have changed over time.
- To describe the Flynn effect and look at possible explanations for it.
- To review and evaluate Robert Sternberg's theory of successful intelligence.
- To critically consider Howard Gardner's theory of multiple intelligences.
- To identify the factors related to the development of expertise.
- To explain the processes involved in creativity.

© Mira/Alamy Stock Photo

A Child Prodigy

A prodigy may be defined as a person with outstanding ability in some capacity. Child prodigies display abilities well beyond those of the average adult, let alone child. They are extremely rare, but they do exist. One example is the chess player Sergey Karjakin (b. 1990), who was awarded the title of Grandmaster—the second highest honour in the chess world—when he was just 12. More recently, Tristan Pang (b. 2001) was doing high school math at the age of 2 and earning top marks at the University of Auckland before he was a teenager.

Another outstanding child prodigy, Kim Ung-Yong, was listed in the *Guinness Book of World Records* as having an IQ of 210—the world's highest at the time. (An average IQ is 100, and to be considered a genius you would need an IQ of at least 130—although researchers still have not agreed on the exact definition of that term.) Born in 1962, he began speaking at the age of 2 months and was able to converse fluently by 6 months. By contrast, most children only begin to produce simple words such as *dada* around their first birthday, and don't start forming two- or three-word sentences until about 18 months. By the time he turned 4 Kim was able to read not only in his own language (Korean), but also in Japanese, German, and English, and less than a year later he demonstrated his proficiency in these languages as well as Chinese, Spanish, Vietnamese, and Tagalog on Japanese television.

Kim's talents were not limited to languages. Whereas most kids in North America only begin learning algebra around the age of 13, Kim was able to understand algebraic concepts before his first birthday, and his television appearance included a segment in which he solved complicated calculus problems. At 8, after auditing physics courses from the age of 4, he was invited by NASA to study in the United States, where he completed his doctorate in physics at 15 and began working with NASA. In 1978, however, he chose to return to Korea. We will look at the reasons behind that decision at the end of this chapter.

FIGURE 12.1 | Kim Ung-Yong

The Concept of Intelligence: Historical Background

Perhaps no concept has been more central to the development of psychology as a discipline than the concept of intelligence. For more than a century, intelligence has typically been measured using intelligence tests (Anastasi, 1965).

The Binet–Simon Test

Despite variations in form and content, most intelligence tests today are still patterned on the one devised by Alfred Binet and Théophile Simon (Binet & Simon, 1905a/1965) in response to a request from French educational authorities who wanted a way of assessing the benefit of schooling for children. The test they created was designed to distinguish between children of normal and subnormal intelligence. Binet and Simon (1905b/1965) defined intelligence as:

> a fundamental faculty, the alteration or lack of which is of the utmost importance for practical life. This faculty is judgment, otherwise called good sense, practical sense, initiative, the faculty of adapting oneself to circumstances. To judge well, to comprehend well, to reason well, these are the essential activities of intelligence (p. 38).

Notice the *practical* emphasis of that definition: intelligence is "practical sense," "the faculty of adapting oneself to circumstances," and consists of "activities" such as reasoning and comprehension. Some examples from the Binet and Simon (1911/1915) test are given in Table 12.1. Binet and Simon were careful to base their scale on a substantial body of empirical research, arranging their items "in a real order of increasing difficulty" (Binet & Simon, 1908/1965), to permit comparison in terms of *mental age*. Of "203 children studied individually" 103 performed at "exactly the mental level that we attribute[d] to their age"; 44 were advanced and 56 were below their age level (Binet & Simon, 1908/1965, p. 44).

The Binet–Simon scale seemed to be just the sort of thing that many people in the United States were looking for. Lewis M. Terman (1877–1956) developed the most successful adaptation of the scale for the American context. Because Terman did this work at Stanford University, his version of the Binet test was called the *Stanford–Binet*. Based on a suggestion by the German psychologist William Stern (1912/1967, p. 453) that a useful measure of intelligence could be obtained by dividing a child's mental age (MA) by his or her chronological age (CA), Terman proposed the following equation for what came to be known as the intelligence quotient (IQ):

$$IQ = \frac{MA}{CA} \times 100$$

This formula means that a "normal" child will have an IQ of 100. Terman (1916/1948, p. 489) obtained Stanford–Binet IQ scores for 905 children between the ages of 9 and 14, and reported that their distribution was approximately normal. The fact that there was a significant relationship between IQ and variables such as teachers' estimates of children's intelligence suggested that the test had some validity. Partly for this reason, the Stanford–Binet test came to be very widely accepted.

Charles Spearman

It's not easy to decide whether the word *intelligence* should be taken to refer to one ability or to many different abilities. If the latter, it's not easy to determine precisely how these abilities are related to one another. We can begin to appreciate some of these problems if we consider the work of Charles Spearman (1863–1945), who laid the groundwork for what became factor analysis (Lovie & Lovie, 1993). Factor analysis begins with a set of correlations between several measures, such as different mental tests. Then statistical procedures

intelligence (Binet and Simon's 1905 definition) A fundamental faculty, the alteration or lack of which is of the utmost importance for practical life.

factor analysis A statistical procedure that derives a number of underlying factors that may explain the structure of a set of correlations.

TABLE 12.1 | Example of Binet and Simon's Items

Age	Item
3	Give family name
4	Repeat three numbers
5	Compare two weights
6	Distinguish morning and afternoon
7	Describe a picture
8	Give a day and date
9	Name months of the year in order
10	Criticize absurd statements
12	Describe abstract words
15	Give three rhymes for a word in one minute
Adult	Give three differences between a president and a king

are used to derive a number of underlying variables ("factors") that may explain the structure of the set of correlations. As a result of his analysis of the pattern of correlations between different tests of mental abilities, Spearman (1904, 1927/1965) proposed what came to be called the *two-factor theory of intelligence*. This theory held that:

> every individual measurement of every ability . . . can be divided into two independent parts. . . . The one part has been called the "general factor" and denoted by the letter *g*; it is so named because, although varying freely from individual to individual, it remains the same for any one individual. . . . The second part has been called the "specific factor" and denoted by the letter *s*. It not only varies from individual to individual, but even for any one individual from each ability to another (Spearman, 1932/1970, p. 75).

general intelligence (g)
The part of intelligence that is common to all abilities.

The two-factor theory is illustrated in Figure 12.2. As you can see, it's a hierarchical model in which **general intelligence (*g*)** is the primary factor on which various specific factors (*s*) depend. In Figure 12.2, those specific factors are represented by abilities in four specific school subjects (French, English, mathematics, and music). Spearman found that those specific abilities were all correlated with each other, such that people who did well in one specific area tended to do well in the others, and vice versa. Still, the inter-correlation between specific abilities was not perfect. Each specific ability was seen as determined in part by *g* and in part by circumstances specific to that ability. Thus someone could have a high level of *g*, but varying specific abilities. This formulation continues to be a subject of controversy. When it came to estimating the effect of education on intelligence, Spearman concluded that heredity was more important in determining *g*, but that the specific factors could be shaped by schooling.

Spearman was able to devise a statistical criterion that allowed him to estimate the amount of *g* that contributed to each specific ability. Spearman believed that *g* represented the amount of *mental energy* available to an individual. This was a general, non-specific

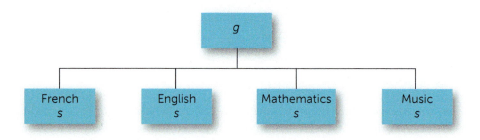

FIGURE 12.2 | Spearman's two-factor theory of intelligence

Table is based on work of Charles Spearman (1863–1945).

energy that could be directed towards the specific abilities, which were seen as engines driven by *g*.

Spearman exercised considerable influence on the way succeeding generations of psychologists have regarded intelligence. Despite the controversy that surrounds his view, it is widely supported (e.g., Johnson, Bouchard, Krueger, McGue, & Gottesman, 2004). Many would agree with Jensen (1972, p. 77) that "when the term intelligence is used it should refer to *g*, the factor common to all tests of complex problem solving."

General Intelligence (*g*)

In a review of research done over the 100 years since Spearman (1904), Lubinski (2004) argued that, if anything, general intelligence is more important in the twenty-first century than ever before. General intelligence predicts academic achievement and work performance. However, it accounts for only about half of the variability in performance. As Lubinski points out, even highly intelligent people must work hard if they are to fulfill their goals, and they must work even harder if they are to become outstanding in their field. On this point Lubinski cites Simonton (1994), whose work we will consider later in the chapter. Ambitious students would do well to heed Simonton's words:

> Making it big [becoming a star] is a career. People who wish to do so must organize their whole lives around a single enterprise. They must be monomaniacs, even megalomaniacs, about their pursuits. They must start early, labor continuously, and never give up the cause. Success is not for the lazy, procrastinating or mercurial (1994, p. 181).

Fluid Intelligence and g

A distinction is often made between fluid and crystallized intelligence. **Crystallized intelligence** consists of things we have learned, and may increase throughout life. By contrast, **fluid intelligence** is the ability to think flexibly, and although it may increase while we are young, it levels off as we mature. Fluid intelligence and general intelligence are often thought to be highly similar if not identical (Lubinski, 2004, p. 98). Thus tests of general intelligence typically assess the ability to grasp unfamiliar relationships, rather than the content of a person's knowledge. Spearman's word for the ability that underlies *g* was **eduction**, from the Latin meaning *to draw out*. Thus general intelligence may be measured by the ability to draw out the known relationships that apply in a novel situation. A set of measures known as the **Raven Progressive Matrices** (Carpenter, Just, & Shell, 1990; J.C. Raven, Styles, & J. Raven, 1998) was explicitly designed to measure a central aspect of what Spearman meant by general intelligence (J. Raven, 2000).

For examples of problems similar to those in the Raven test, see Figure 12.3. Each matrix contains nine configurations, the last of which is left blank. You must decide which of the eight alternatives presented under each matrix is the correct one to fill in the blank. Make a note of your answer to each of the three matrix problems in the figure before you read the answers at the end of the chapter. You will see that the reasoning required can be quite subtle and varied. Spearman called this sort of reasoning *eduction*

crystallized intelligence
The body of what someone has learned; may continue to increase throughout life.

fluid intelligence
The ability to think flexibly; may increase in youth but levels off as we mature.

eduction (Spearman)
Literally, *drawing out*. General intelligence may be the ability to draw out the relationships that apply in a novel situation.

Raven Progressive Matrices
A set of problems that constitutes the most widely accepted test of *g*.

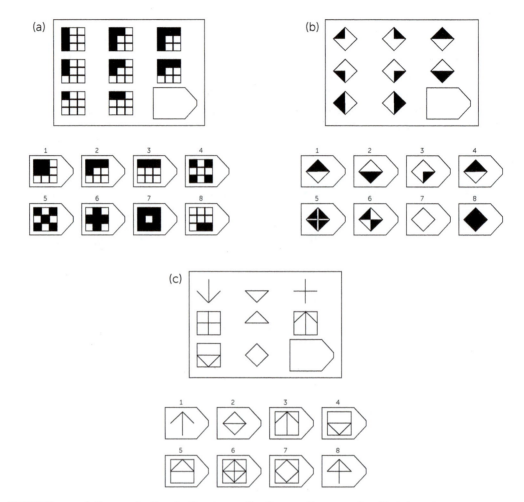

FIGURE 12.3 | Items similar to those on the Raven Progressive Matrices test

From: Carpenter, P.A., Just M.A., & Shell, P. (1990). p. 409. Copyright 1990 by the American Psychological Association. The use of APA information does not imply endorsement by APA.

of relations and correlates: the ability to grasp how things are related to one another and what goes with what.

Working Memory and g

working memory capacity

The theory that working memory capacity and *g* are closely related.

It has been suggested that working memory capacity may be not only an important aspect of *g*, but even synonymous with it (Conway, Kane, & Engle, 2003; Engle, Tuholski, Laughlin, & Conway, 1999). One reason is that Spearman's concept of *mental energy* is intuitively similar to the *central executive function* of working memory (Ackerman, Beier, & Boyle, 2005). As you may recall from Chapter 5, the central executive selects and integrates information, constituting a workspace within which solutions to problems are formulated (Baars, 2002). Now look again at Figure 5.6, which distinguishes between *fluid* and *crystallized* systems. As Baddeley (2000b) put it, the former are "themselves unchanged by learning," while the latter are "cognitive systems capable of accumulating long-term knowledge" (p. 421). Thus the central executive appears to perform a function similar to that ascribed to fluid intelligence and, by extension, to *g*.

Even so, the fact that there seems to be an intuitive relationship between general intelligence and the central executive function of working memory doesn't mean that there is an empirical one. If there were an empirical relationship, then scores on a test of individual differences in working memory capacity would be correlated with scores on a test of *g*. One way of testing working memory capacity is to have people continue to work on a task in the face of distraction (Conway, Kane, & Engle, 2003, p. 551). For example, the *operation span task* measures the ability to remain goal-oriented and not allow extraneous information to interfere with the problem at hand (Engle, Tuholski, Laughlin, & Conway, 1999, p. 315). Participants are shown an arithmetic problem that requires a yes/no answer; for example, "Does (8/4) − 1 = 1?" Once the participants have responded, a word (e.g., *tree*) appears on the screen and they read it aloud. Then another arithmetic problem is presented, followed by another word. This sequence may be repeated as many as six times. During the testing phase, the participants are shown the arithmetic problems again and asked to pair each one with the word that had followed it. Thus they must not only solve arithmetic problems, but at the same time keep track of the relationship between each problem and the corresponding word. The participant's score is the number of words correctly recalled in the correct order.

Tests of working memory capacity do correlate positively with tests such as the Raven. But the correlation is far from perfect. After reviewing dozens of studies, Ackerman et al. (2005, p. 51) concluded that working memory capacity and *g* are not the same. In fact, measures of working memory capacity show some correlation not only with *g* but with many different measures of intellectual ability. Barrett, Tugade, and Engle (2004) argued that working memory capacity is related to the ability to regulate attention. If that is the case, it would play an important role in bringing cognitive processes under voluntary control.

DISCOVERY LAB

Neural Plasticity and g

Garlick (2002, 2003) pointed out that Spearman's concept of *mental energy* is no longer a useful explanatory concept in the context of current neuroscientific theories. Rather, he advanced the hypothesis that neural plasticity underlies *g*. *Plasticity* is the ability of an organism to adapt to changes in the environment; *neural plasticity* refers to changes in brain circuitry. This kind of change occurs over the course of one's life, but (as one might suspect) the greatest changes occur between infancy and adolescence.

Individual differences in neural plasticity reflect differences in the ability to adapt to a changing environment by forming and/or altering connections between neurons. Individual differences in neural plasticity are likely due to genetic variation (Petrill et al., 2004, p. 811), although the precise mechanisms whereby genes determine plasticity are not yet known. Garlick (2002, p. 121) has hypothesized that people vary in the extent to which their brains were "able to adapt their neural circuitry to environmental stimulation during childhood." The hallmark of neural plasticity is the ability to adapt to any circumstances with which we are confronted, although there are obvious limits to this ability. Such a mechanism would not only "mean that children would be able to learn to read and write" even if their ancestors lacked those skills, but would also "allow the person to adapt and function intelligently no matter what the environmental requirements" (Garlick, 2002, p. 120). However, children low in neural plasticity would be less able to adapt to environmental change, and even children high in neural plasticity would develop intellectually only to the extent that they were exposed to appropriate environmental stimulation.

neural plasticity
Changes in neuronal circuitry often associated with maturation, environmental adaptation, and modulation by experience which may lead to learning and behavioural modification.

The Evolution of g

A theory of the evolution of *g* has been advanced by Kanazawa (2004). Central to this theory is a distinction made by Cosmides and Tooby (2002) between dedicated intelligence and improvisational intelligence. They associate the former with the domain-specific modules that are hypothesized to have evolved to solve recurring problems; two examples that we have considered in this book are the *cheater detection module* (Chapter 11) and the *language acquisition device* (Chapter 9). By contrast, improvisational intelligence would have evolved to deal with relatively unique, unpredictable problems. The ability to deal with surprises such as a bush fire or a flash flood may have enabled survival and thus been selected for. As Kanazawa pointed out, unexpected problems by definition cannot be solved by dedicated, preprogrammed mechanisms. Rather, what is required is the flexibility that general intelligence affords. Thus Kanazawa argues that *g* and improvisational intelligence are the same.

As we have seen, our current circumstances are radically more novel and complex than those faced by prehistoric people. Kanazawa (2004, p. 515) pointed out that very few things in the environment of a technologically advanced society "existed 10,000 years ago . . . virtually everything you see around you today in your natural environment (books, computers, telephones, televisions, automobiles, etc.) is evolutionarily novel." Dedicated mechanisms are of limited use in such an environment. What is required is general intelligence (Gottfredson, 1997).

One implication of Kanazawa's theory is that general intelligence is valuable only in evolutionarily novel situations. For example, mating is certainly not an evolutionarily novel situation, and so we would not expect high *g* to be advantageous in that context. Not only do people high in general intelligence not have more children than those low in *g*, but in our era *g* is *negatively* correlated with number of offspring (Kanazawa, 2004, p. 517). One possible explanation might be that the use of contraceptive methods varies with *g*. Birth control may help to solve the evolutionarily novel problem of no longer being able to rely on infant mortality to control the number of our dependents (Kanazawa, 2004, p. 521).

The Flynn Effect

J.R. Flynn (1984, 1987, 1999, 2003) created a firestorm of controversy when he discovered that IQ scores had been rising over time in every industrialized country he examined. These increases were not trivial. For example, Americans had gained 14 IQ points between 1932 and 1978. Samples of members of the military of the Netherlands, Israel, Norway, and Belgium show an average gain of six IQ points per decade between 1952 and 1982 (Flynn, 1999, p. 6). This last result is particularly noteworthy because it is based on Raven scores. Since the Raven is acknowledged to be the best measure of *g* (Neisser, 1997a, p. 441), it would appear that *g* has been increasing over time. A few decades are far too short a time for evolution to have worked its magic. Consequently, the rapid rise in *g* must be due to environmental factors. Notice that this does not mean that *g* is completely determined by environmental factors, for the following reason. Suppose that *g* depends on neural plasticity. Variations in neural plasticity may be inherited. However, as we observed earlier, neural plasticity requires environmental stimulation in order to actualize its potential. An individual's actual level of *g* will depend on the interaction of neural plasticity with environmental conditions (Garlick, 2003, p. 188). Thus the Flynn effect could be the result of an enriched environment that enables potential *g* to become actual *g* (cf. Dickens & Flynn, 2001).

A great deal of attention has been devoted to trying to figure out which environmental changes have produced the Flynn effect (e.g., Neisser, 1998). Among the possible candidates are improvements in nutrition and health (Lynn, 1998), education (Blair, Gamson, Thorne, & Baker, 2005), and environmental complexity. With regard to this last factor, Green and Bavelier (2003) studied the effects of playing video games in a group of 18–23-year-olds who had played games such as *Grand Theft Auto* and *Halo* for at least one hour per day for the previous six months. This group showed superior performance on a number of standard attention tasks when compared with a group that had no video game experience. Moreover, training naive participants on video games for as little as 10 days led to gains on standard attention tasks such as the flanker task and the attentional blink (AB) task (both of which we encountered in Chapter 4). Although this study did not investigate the possibility that intelligence increases as a result of complex visual experience, it did show that such experience may enhance basic cognitive processes.

Whether any or all of these variables are crucial to the Flynn effect is presently unknown. Several other variables could also have played a role in the rise in IQ. What do you think some of those variables might be?

Sternberg's Theory of Successful Intelligence

There are other approaches to intelligence that de-emphasize the importance of *g* in order to highlight alternative aspects of intelligence. Two of the most influential are those of Robert J. Sternberg and Howard Gardner. We will consider Sternberg's theory first.

Instead of analyzing intelligence in terms of factors, Sternberg focused on what have been referred to as intellectual components. Whereas factors define the *structure* of intelligence, components describe the *processes* of intelligence. A component is "an elementary information process that operates upon internal representations of objects or symbols" (Sternberg, 1980, p. 574). We represent events to ourselves by means of cognitive processes such as perception and memory. We then manipulate these representations in a variety of ways. We can think about things, imagine them from different perspectives, remember similar things, and so on. The different ways in which we transform cognitive representations are the components of intelligence. For example, you can represent the object in which you are now sitting as a chair and then think of the superordinate category for that concept (*chair* is a member of the class *furniture*). People vary in the speed and accuracy with which they can carry out such operations, and these variations are part of what we recognize as individual differences in intelligence.

Sternberg (1984b) identified three kinds of components: *metacomponents*, *performance components*, and *knowledge acquisition components*. These components are found in all aspects of intelligence, and so may be said to be universal (Sternberg, 1998, 1999a, 1999b).

Flynn effect
An increase in IQ scores over historical time.

intellectual components (Sternberg)
Elementary information processes that operate on internal representations of objects or symbols.

Metacomponents

Metacomponents are "higher order processes used in planning, monitoring, and decision making in task performance" (Sternberg, 2009, p. 57). These are the components that control the execution of other components. Before you attempt to solve a problem, you must make some decisions about the kind of problem it is and how you will tackle it; it's at this stage that metacomponents come into play. Many intelligence test items are timed, and in that context a speedy response is often taken to be more indicative of intelligence than a slow, considered one. Yet the most intelligent approach to solving a particular problem may not be the fastest one. In many situations, careful consideration of the nature of the problem, thorough planning of the solution procedure, and monitoring of that operation as it proceeds will lead to better results than "shooting from the hip." Emphasizing the distinction between reflective and impulsive approaches to problem-solving, Sternberg suggested that in most situations what matters is not speed but "intelligent allocation of one's time to the various . . . problems at hand" (2009, p. 60).

Performance Components

Performance components—"the processes that are used in the execution of a task" (Sternberg, 1984a, p. 166)—are used at every stage of the solution process. These stages include encoding the various aspects of the problem situation, comparing the different parts of the problem, and generating the appropriate response. The running example used by Sternberg (e.g., 1980, p. 576) is the procedure for solving analogies. When asked to solve the analogy *fish is to water as worm is to: (a) earth or (b) hook*, you must first encode each term to determine its meaning. Then you can compare the parts of the analogy to find similarities (e.g., *fish* and *worm* are both living creatures). Mapping is a very important process whereby past knowledge is related to ("mapped onto") the present situation. You already know the relationship between fish and water: fish live in the water. You can then map this relationship onto the pairs *worm, earth* and *worm, book*. The relationship of "lives in" certainly fits the first pair better than the second. Worms live in the earth, but they die on hooks. After finding the solution you can then give the appropriate response (*earth*).

Knowledge Acquisition Components

As the name suggests, **knowledge acquisition components** are the processes used for "learning new information and storing it in memory" (Sternberg, 1983, p. 5). The key aspect of these components is selectivity. It's impossible to learn everything; you must be able to filter out the irrelevant and pick up the relevant information. Information so acquired must then be retained in a meaningful form so that it can be used later. An expert is someone who has acquired and is able to use information specific to a particular class of tasks.

The Triarchic Theory

The components just described are universal in that they enter into all intelligent behaviour. However, intelligent behaviour has three different content areas: analytical, creative, and practical. All three make use of the same components, but they vary with respect

COGNITION IN ACTION
BOX 12.1

Can Colour Help Us Solve Problems?

When we want to get to know someone, we'll ask a variety of questions: Where are you from? Where did you go to school? Do you have any siblings? And so on. As we get to know the person better we'll start to ask more intimate questions about things like childhood memories or favourite colours. Remarkably, psychologists have only recently begun to study the relationship between colours and human cognition. Recent research suggests that simply viewing a particular colour can either enhance or diminish performance on simple tasks. For example, Stone (2003) claimed to show evidence that performance on an easier task diminished over time in a blue environment but remained steady in a red environment However, the advantage for red over blue was reversed in other research (see Elliot, Maier, Moller, Friedman, & Meinhardt, 2007). To address these contradictory findings, Mehta and Zhu (2009) explored how different colours could affect cognitive performance on a number of tasks (see Elliot & Maier, 2014 for a recent review).

You might be wondering how it is possible that a change of colour could lead to a change in performance. One reason could be that we learn to make associations between colours and certain experiences (e.g., environments, ideas, tasks, moods). For example, you might have learned to associate red with danger or mistakes (what colour does your professor use to highlight errors on papers and exams?). By contrast, blue is often associated with peace and relaxation (think of a calm sea or a cloudless sky). Mehta and Zhu used this framework to propose that red could be associated with *avoidance* of danger and mistakes, together with heightened vigilance and enhanced performance on tasks requiring attention to detail. The reverse was hypothesized for blue, which should be associated with *approach* and lead to enhanced performance on tasks requiring innovative solutions to problems.

Using tasks designed to test their conceptualizations of avoidance (red) and approach (blue), Mehta and Zhu (2009) found that these colours did in fact have the hypothesized effects. Their procedure was relatively straightforward: participants were asked to complete different tasks on a computer with the background coloured either red or blue (or a neutral control condition). In one of the experiments participants were required to solve a series of 12 anagrams. For 6 of these the target words related to either approach (e.g., *adventure*) or avoidance (e.g., *prevent*), and for 6 the target words were neutral. As hypothesized, response times were fastest when the background colour matched the orientation associated with the target word (approach or avoidance). A second study required participants to rate various brands of products such as toothpaste that were described in terms that emphasized either positive aspects (whitens teeth: approach) or negative aspects (cavity prevention: avoidance). Again, when accompanied by the blue background the approach condition was favoured over the avoidance condition, and vice versa.

While these first two studies are interesting, neither really tested whether the background colour for a particular type of task—red for detail-oriented (avoidance) tasks; blue for creative tasks (approach)—enhanced performance. This was precisely what the remaining experiments in the Mehta and Zhu (2009) study were designed to do. The first, a word-recall task performed against either a red or a blue background, showed that performance was better in the red condition (i.e., participants were able to remember more words). The final experiment gave participants one minute to list as many uses for a brick as they could think of (see p. 397). Although participants came up with equal numbers of uses, regardless of colour condition, the uses suggested by those in the blue condition were judged to be more creative.

What can we learn from this research? We may not yet fully understand the relationship between art and human cognition, but research such as Mehta and Zhu's shows that we are making significant strides towards understanding the influence of colour. Perhaps you should try changing the background colour on your computer, depending on the kind of assignment you're working on?!

*triarchic theory
of intelligence*

Sternberg's theory
consisting of analytic,
practical, and creative
intelligence.

analytical intelligence

The ability to solve
relatively straightforward
problems; considered to be
general intelligence.

creative intelligence

The ability to reason using
novel concepts.

*entrenched vs non-
entrenched concepts*

Entrenched concepts strike
us as natural and easy to
reason with, whereas non-
entrenched concepts strike
us as unnatural and difficult
to reason with.

practical intelligence

The ability to find problem
solutions in real-world,
everyday situations.

to the "mental contents and representations" they use (Sternberg, Castejón, Prieto, Hautamäki, & Grigerenko, 2001, p. 2). As you will see in Box 12.2, Sternberg's **triarchic theory** has a surprising parallel with another, much older theory of intelligence.

Analytical Intelligence

For Sternberg, **analytical intelligence** is the closest to what conventional intelligence tests measure. To the extent that g is important, it is with respect to analytical intelligence. Tests such as the Raven are good measures of analytical intelligence.

Creative Intelligence

Creative intelligence is the ability to reason using novel concepts (Sternberg, 1999a, p. 304). A familiar situation allows people to use what Sternberg (1982) called **entrenched concepts**; these strike us as natural and are easy to reason with. By contrast, unfamiliar or novel situations may require the use of **non-entrenched concepts** that strike us as unnatural and are difficult to reason with. Following are examples of these two types of concept, which Sternberg adapted from Goodman (1955). The colour concepts *blue* and *green* are natural concepts. Robins' eggs have been blue ever since we can remember, and we expect that they will remain blue forever. Emeralds are always green, and we expect them to remain so in the future. However, we do not ordinarily possess colour concepts that refer to objects that change colour over time. For example, freshly picked bananas are often green and turn yellow only as they ripen. We could invent a concept called *grellow* to describe objects that are green now, but later turn yellow. Similarly, there could be a novel concept *bleen* to describe objects that are blue now, but will turn green later. To reason with concepts such as *grellow* and *bleen* would be to reason in a novel conceptual system.

Sternberg invented several problems to measure people's ability to think with novel concepts such as *grellow* and *bleen*. For example, can there be an object to which the concept *blue* was applied in the year 2000, but to which the concept *green* properly applies in 2013? It's tempting to answer "Yes," but what do you think? The proper answer, given the possibility of *bleen*, is "No." If an object changes colour from green to blue, then it must be a *bleen* object in the year 2013. Conceptualizing it as *blue* in 2000 turns out to have been a mistake. When the object turns green in the year 2013, it becomes clear that it was really a *bleen* object all along.

The ability to reason with novel concepts allows us to explore problem spaces that otherwise would remain closed to us. This increases the range of problems we can approach successfully.

Practical Intelligence

Sternberg (1999a, p. 305; Sternberg & Wagner, 1986, 1994) saw **practical intelligence** as important in familiar situations of a non-academic sort. He stressed the necessity of studying intelligence in real-world settings. To illustrate the difference between practical intelligence and IQ, Sternberg (1998, p. 494) cited the work of Silvia Scribner (1986, 1993; Herman, 1993). Scribner used the *ethnographic method* in her investigations, approaching

An Ancient Parallel to Sternberg's Theory of Intelligence

The similarity of Sternberg et al.'s theory to Aristotle's classical theory of intelligence was pointed out by Tigner and Tigner (2000). They observed that Aristotle (384–323 BC) also recognized three kinds of intelligence. The first, theoretical intelligence, corresponds to what most people now think of as "intelligence." It was the ability to understand subjects such as mathematics and science and to acquire and analyze various metalanguages such as those involved in language analysis, literary criticism, or the analysis of history and government (what we now call political science). Aristotle's second kind of intelligence was practical; here, the focus was on the ability to choose a wise course of action. Finally, productive intelligence was reflected in the ability to make things (perhaps best exemplified in the arts).

As Tigner and Tigner (2000) pointed out, Aristotle's system has strong similarities to the triarchic theory of intelligence proposed by Sternberg (1988). Although Sternberg used different labels for them (analytical, practical, and creative), his three kinds of intelligence

are essentially the same as Aristotle's. Sternberg did not copy Aristotle's system, but arrived at it using the empirical methods of contemporary psychology. Thus one reason for believing that Aristotle's system has merit is that it has been independently verified by an investigator using different methods in a very different era.

Sternberg (2000b) made the sage observation that the similarity between his theory and Aristotle's illustrates the importance of revisiting historically important approaches to psychology:

> If both philosophical and psychological analysis support an idea, the idea gains credibility by virtue of the overlap in substantive findings across methods of analysis. . . . Tigner and Tigner's (2000) analysis shows how important it is to study the history and philosophy of psychology. There are many alternative paths to knowledge and understanding about the human mind (Sternberg, 2000b, p. 178).

the study of practical cognition in the same way that an anthropologist would approach the study of a particular culture or subculture. This method relies on naturalistic observation in the field, and should be seen as a part of the ecological approach to psychology (Scribner, 1993). A good example of the ethnographic method in action is Scribner's (1986) study of dairy workers.

A common stereotype of work in highly mechanized contexts such as assembly lines (Figure 12.4) is that it does not engage the worker's cognitive processes at a very high level. There may be some truth to this, but perhaps not as much as is commonly believed. Scribner (1986, p. 15) defined practical thinking as "mind in action . . . thinking that is embedded in the larger purposive activities of daily life and that functions to achieve the goals of these activities." One of the contexts she investigated was a modern dairy. "The dairy is a prototypical industrial system in which many occupational activities involve standardized and repetitive duties performed under highly constrained conditions" (Scribner, 1986, p. 21).

Scribner observed workers performing a variety of functions. For example, delivery truck drivers developed their own ways of working out the cost of a delivery. Scribner reported that experienced drivers made virtually no computational errors in on-the-job calculations. However, they made many errors in pencil and paper tests of arithmetic. It may

FIGURE 12.4 | Assembly-line worker

be concluded that the pencil and paper test, which was similar to the sort of test that might be given in school, did not predict their on-the-job behaviour very well.

Sternberg and Kaufman (1998, p. 495) argued that Scribner's study shows the independence of practical intelligence from "measures of academic skills, including intelligence test scores, arithmetic test scores, and grades."

The Sternberg Triarchic Abilities Test

Sternberg, Castejón, Prieto, Hautamäki, and Grigorenko (2001) collected data from three international samples to validate the Sternberg Triarchic Abilities Test (STAT). This test contains items intended to measure the three content areas of intelligence identified in the triarchic theory. Sternberg et al. argued that the data supported the hypothesis that the three content areas were distinct factors. However, the results were not unambiguous, and (as we shall see below) they lend themselves to alternative interpretations.

Successful Intelligence

For Sternberg (1999a, 1999b; Sternberg & Kaufman, 1998, pp. 493–496), all three aspects of intelligence are important, each in its own way. Seldom will an individual be strong in all three. People need to make the most of their individual strengths while at the same time recognizing their weaknesses. Someone strong in analytical intelligence may find the most success in an academic career. Someone high in creative intelligence may become a successful entrepreneur. Practical intelligence may enable someone to "work effectively in an environment" without being "explicitly taught" what is required (Sternberg, 1999a, p. 305). People who are strong in all these intelligences will perform well in a greater variety of contexts than those who are not.

Criticisms of Sternberg's Theory

Although Sternberg's approach has been extremely influential, it is not without its critics. For example, Brody (2003a, 2003b) observed that the STAT measures of analytical, practical, and creative intelligences are correlated; he concluded that the three are "substantially related to one another" (p. 341). In a similar vein, Gottfredson (2003a, 2003b) argued that there was no evidence unequivocally supporting the independent existence of a practical intelligence. Indeed, Gottfredson suggested that Sternberg underplayed the importance of g in practical affairs. The thrust of these criticisms is that the STAT adds nothing to existing measures of g, and that the triarchic theory is superfluous, given the wealth of evidence supporting g theory. In response to his critics, Sternberg (2003a, 2003b) observed that the triarchic theory is relatively recent compared to g theory and expressed the hope that future research will fulfill its promise.

Howard Gardner and the Theory of Multiple Intelligences

For Gardner (1983, 1993a) intelligence is not one thing but many. Rejecting the idea that there is an underlying ability common to all intelligent activity, he argued that there are **multiple intelligences**, or "relatively autonomous human intellectual competences" (1983, p. 8). He played down the importance of general intelligence (g), arguing that it emerges only as a result of sampling too narrow a range of abilities (Walters & Gardner, 1986, p. 177).

Gardner traced his approach in part to the nineteenth-century phrenology of Gall and Spurzheim, which we discussed in Chapter 2. The basic idea behind phrenology was that particular areas of the brain have unique functions, similar to the faculties we considered in Chapter 2. The phrenologists proposed that basic differences in abilities between people arose because the areas of the brain that were responsible for controlling these functions were differentially developed. If we translate the basic phrenological insight about brain organization into a statement about intelligence, then we could say, with Gardner (1983, p. 55), that there are several distinctive intelligences, each of which is supported by specific parts of the brain. Although a complex task, such as playing the violin, may draw on several parts of the brain, not all parts are equally involved in all forms of intelligence. In fact, this is one of Gardner's arguments for the existence of separate intelligences: "To the extent that a particular faculty can be destroyed, or spared in isolation, as a result of brain damage, its relative autonomy from other human faculties seems likely" (Gardner, 1983, p. 63). Research with neuroimaging techniques has lent some support to Gardner's "distinction among domains in terms of the separable anatomical networks they activate" (Posner, 2004, p. 25). However, these networks do not operate in complete isolation: they interact with one another.

In all, Gardner (1983, p. 63) listed eight criteria for the identification of a separate intelligence. Three of the most interesting are as follows. First, a separate intelligence will have a **symbol system** for representing what we know. Usually we think of knowledge as being represented in a language of some kind. For instance, this textbook uses English to

multiple intelligences (Gardner)
The hypothesis that intelligence consists not of one underlying ability but of many different abilities.

symbol systems
Different forms of representation, such as drawing, music, and mathematics, that express different forms of intelligence.

represent information about cognitive psychology, while a calculus textbook would use, in addition to English, mathematical formulae. But these are not the only symbolic forms available to us.

If you had to tell someone how to get to your place, for instance, you could use words to describe the route; in that case you would be creating a cognitive map. But you could also use a pencil and paper to draw a literal map. Similarly, if someone asked you to describe your mood, you could use words to explain; but you might also play a piece of music that you feel expresses your state of mind. So here we have, in drawing and music, at least two additional *symbolic forms* (Cassirer, 1953–1959), or ways of representing events. Language, pictures, music, and mathematics are examples of symbol systems that are used around the world and are all, in different contexts, important for adaptation and survival. Gardner investigated the possibility that each of these symbolic forms expresses a separate intelligence.

Gardner's second "sign" of a separate intelligence is an association with exceptional individuals such as *prodigies*. The existence of these rare cases cannot be easily explained by a general theory of intelligence. Furthermore, why is it that prodigies appear in certain disciplines, such as mathematics and chess, and rarely if ever in others, such as literature (Gardner, 1983, p. 29)? The symbolic forms in which prodigies specialize may be the separate intelligences that underlie competence in other areas. By contrast, competence in a discipline such as history may require the interplay of several specific intelligences, as well as long-term study.

Third, a separate intelligence will have a distinctive *developmental history* (Gardner, 1983, p. 64). There should be a characteristic way in which expertise develops, with everyone beginning in the same way and some, though not all, reaching very high levels of competence. To describe an intelligence in this way is to assume that it is possible to objectively define what constitutes the expert use of a particular symbolic form. The study of the development of expertise is a significant part of the study of specific intelligences.

Here is Gardner's original list of intelligences, with one or two outstanding examples of each type: musical intelligence (Mozart, Louis Armstrong), bodily–kinesthetic intelligence (Babe Ruth, Sidney Crosby), linguistic intelligence (Shakespeare, T.S. Eliot), logico-mathematical intelligence (Isaac Newton, Albert Einstein), spatial intelligence (London taxi drivers; Polynesian sailors who navigate over vast distances), and personal intelligence (Annie Sullivan, the teacher who found a way to communicate with the young Helen Keller). Gardner (2004) did not consider this list to be final, and other candidates are always considered. Gardner's unique contribution has been to focus our attention on symbol systems that are not always seen as central to the concept of intelligence.

Gardner's (1980, 1982) work has had the salutary effect of drawing attention to neglected but extremely important aspects of intelligence. In the next two sections we will look at the typical developmental patterns in two symbol systems, visual and musical.

Drawing

Our ability to make pictures is one facet of what Gardner (1983) called *spatial intelligence*. The development of this ability is not linear: it's not as if the preschool child were a bad artist, the school-age child a better artist, and the trained adult a superior artist. Rather, Gardner and Winner (1982; Winner, 1982, p. 175) suggest that artistic skills, and perhaps many others, follow a pattern of U-shaped development in which "aesthetic pleasingness" is initially quite high, then declines for a time before rising again (see Figure 12.5). As Siegler (2004) observed, U-shaped development is particularly interesting because it contradicts the widespread assumption that performance always improves with age. In U-shaped development, "performance is initially relatively good, . . . subsequently becomes worse, and . . . eventually improves" (p. 3).

A child's early drawings are relatively high in what might be called *aesthetic pleasingness* because of their vitality (Gardner, 1980, pp. 94ff.). Preschoolers' artwork is called *preconventional* for several reasons. There are only passing attempts to use realistic colour or to organize objects in the way they are actually organized in space; objects appear to float on top of the page (Winner, 1982, p. 152), and there is no attempt at perspective. According to Winner (1982, p. 169) the "golden age of children's drawing" is characterized by use of bright colours, freedom from the constraints of realism, absence of stereotyped forms, and willingness to explore and experiment.

When children go to school, however, their artwork enters a *conventional period*. According to Gardner and Winner, the dip in the U comes about not so much because children have lost the freedom of self-expression as because they are preoccupied with learning the rules and conventions that underpin expertise in drawing. Ultimately, those who master the rules will be able to use them in a creative way. When they are no longer entirely bound by convention, their work can move into a *postconventional* phase in which it may be admired for its vitality as well as its mastery. A well-known example is the work of Picasso.

Many professional artists have admired preschoolers' art. Mature artists' work often shows the freedom from constraint by conventional norms that characterizes young children's art. But they are doing something very different from what preschoolers do. They are trying to achieve what children achieve, but in a skillful way. The mature artist knows how to achieve intentionally what the child achieves without thinking (Winner, 1982, p. 175).

> **U-shaped development**
> The hypothesis that the development of many symbolic forms initially is delightfully pre-conventional, then descends to the merely conventional, but ultimately may achieve the integration of the post-conventional.

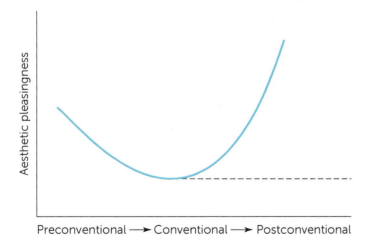

FIGURE 12.5 | U-shaped development

However, Winner emphasizes that it is rare to advance this far along the developmental curve, at least in our culture. Once we descend to the conventional level (the dotted line in Figure 12.5), most of us are content to stay there.

Music

The development of musical intelligence is similar in some respects to the development of drawing. During the first few years of life, children spontaneously do a number of musical things. "Toddlers commonly invent songs before they can reproduce conventional songs" (Trehub, 2003, p. 669). They sing tunes and beat rhythmic patterns. Dowling and Harwood (1986, pp. 144ff.) have reviewed some of the musical phenomena of the preschool years. The emergence of early musical activity, such as singing, may require that the child have older models, such as parents and siblings, to imitate. In any case, when children reach their second year, they begin to produce what adults will accept as something resembling singing.

Some theorists, notably Bernstein (1976, p. 16), have argued that young children typically produce a particular melodic pattern spontaneously, and that this pattern is evidence of an innate musical knowledge. Bernstein maintained that the kinds of sound patterns that children use to tease each other ("Nya-Nya-Nya-Nya-Nya") or call each other by name ("A-lice," "Tom-my") reflect this innate musical knowledge.

Gardner (1982, pp. 144ff.) examined the possibility that there is a basic melody that all children would spontaneously sing as their first song. He concluded that there is not much evidence that such an *ur-song* (*ur* means original or earliest) actually exists, but it is an intriguing speculation all the same (see also Dowling & Harwood, 1986, p. 147).

By the end of the third year, children begin reproducing conventional, culturally provided song models such as the "Alphabet Song," "Twinkle, Twinkle Little Star," or "Old MacDonald Had a Farm." Like drawing, singing does not typically develop during the school years the way that linguistic skills do; the latter, of course, are honed through schooling. But Gardner (1983, p. 111) observed that there are wide cross-cultural variations in this respect. In cultures that put a higher value on musical competence than North America does, musical intelligence typically progresses much further. Here again we can see the role that culture plays in encouraging the development of particular intelligences.

There has been widespread speculation concerning the possibility that music lessons enhance IQ. One of the most persuasive studies was done by Schellenberg (2004). For one year, four different groups of six-year-olds were exposed to keyboard lessons, voice lessons, drama lessons, or no lessons. The IQ scores of all groups improved, probably as a result of starting schooling in general. However, the two groups exposed to music lessons showed greater IQ gains than the other two groups. This suggests that particular kinds of music in school curricula might have beneficial effects on IQ. Schellenberg speculates that chess lessons or science lessons might also have a beneficial effect. Such activities may provide instruction in a wide range of abilities (e.g., spatial, mathematical) that are transferrable to other contexts.

Bamberger's (1982, 1986) studies of the development of musical knowledge indicate that it varies along the implicit–explicit dimension, which we considered in our Chapter 8 discussion of concepts. When we reviewed Reber's work we noted that

ur-song
The hypothetical first song that all children would spontaneously sing.

people can have tacit knowledge without being able to say what it is that they know. Bamberger's observations of musically gifted children suggest that their knowledge is initially of this implicit kind. For example, a child's ability to imitate a well-known older performer appears to reflect a feeling for the task as a whole, rather than a careful analysis of the model.

About the tacit nature of young people's musical ability, Bamberger (1986) said, "Indeed, exposing it to scrutiny is almost to be feared: . . . 'it won't work if you think about it'" (p. 393). However, as these students become adolescents, they inevitably become more reflective about their music, as they do about other aspects of their life. They feel an inconsistency between their increasingly explicit understanding of music and the earlier, spontaneous, non-reflective understanding (and love) of music they had as children. Bamberger referred to this phase as the mid-life crisis of the musician because gifted musicians typically begin studying music very early in their lives (often before the age of five), and so are well into their musical careers by adolescence. Winner (2000) observed that gifted children may feel they are studying music more for their parents or teachers than for themselves. She noted that many music students give up their studies at this point.

Bamberger's analysis may hold true for less than gifted music students as well. How many people do you know who stopped taking music lessons around the age of 14? How many of them loved the music, but hated the lessons? Integrating the implicit and explicit aspects of music is a difficult task, but necessary if the student is to achieve adult mastery of this symbolic form (Gardner, 1982, p. 111).

Criticisms of Multiple Intelligence Theory

Walters and Gardner (1986) reviewed some of the early objections to the theory of multiple intelligences. One criticism was that what the theory calls "intelligences" are more properly called "talents" or "gifts." But Walters and Gardner saw no reason to reserve "intelligence" for the kind of logical/mathematical or linguistic skills that are most valued by our culture. Certainly, Gardner's approach has had considerable influence on parents' and educators' belief that "people differ in their abilities to solve problems and make contributions to society in diverse ways" (Cuban, 2004).

A persistent criticism is that the theory of multiple intelligences is not grounded in scientific data (Chen, 2004). This criticism has much truth to it. However, the theory does have support from case studies (e.g., Gardner, 1993b). Gardner (1999, 2004) has consistently argued that the study of intelligence is by nature interdisciplinary and should be approached from a variety of perspectives, including those of the humanities and the arts as well as the sciences.

Expertise

We noted that one of Gardner's criteria for a separate intelligence was that it be possible to define what constitutes expertise in that area. Independent of Gardner's theory, there has been a great deal of interest in understanding what it takes to make someone an expert. The classic study of expertise was undertaken by Chase and Simon (1973), who extended

mid-life crisis of musicians (Bamberger)

As music students become adolescents, they may feel a tension between their increasingly explicit understanding of music and the spontaneous love of music they had as children.

earlier work by de Groot (1965). They compared the ability of chess masters and novices to remember the positions of chess pieces they had been shown arranged on a chessboard. Memory was tested by having participants reproduce the positions they had seen. Chess masters remembered the positions better than novices, particularly if the arrangement they were shown was one that had been reached in an actual game. The relations between the pieces in such an arrangement are meaningful to chess experts, whereas a random placement of pieces is relatively meaningless to experts and novices alike. Experts are only slightly superior to novices in their ability to remember a random arrangement of pieces (Gobet & Simon, 1996).

Chase and Simon suggested that experts perceive game position arrangements in larger units, or chunks, than novices, who don't know enough to recognize the meaning of pieces' positions. Because novices are not able to "chunk" the information, they must remember the position of each individual piece, and this constraint makes the task more difficult for them than for the experts, particularly when the situation to be remembered is one that could occur in an actual game. Gobet and Simon (1996, p. 31) observed that "chess players have seen thousands of positions, and for expert players, most positions they see readily remind them of positions or types of positions they have seen before."

Ericsson and Charness (1994) reviewed the literature on expert performance and concluded that its most important determinant is *practice*. They downplayed the importance of innate talent and emphasized the degree to which becoming a world-class expert in any area depends on "extended intense training" (p. 730). Whether the goal is to become a chess master or an Olympic medallist, at least 10 years of full-time practice are required. This **10-year rule** (Rossano, 2003, p. 210) works out to roughly 10,000 hours. The quality of the practice also matters: in music, for instance, morning practice appears to be best. At the same time it is important not to practise too much, to avoid the risk of "burn-out" (Ericsson & Charness, 1994, p. 742).

No evidence has been found to suggest that there are anatomical differences between the brains of novices and experts, at least in the case of expert memorizers. Maguire, Valentine, Wilding, and Kapur (2003) compared top-level participants at the World Memory Championships with a group of non-expert participants matched for age and intelligence. MRI images revealed no structural differences in the brains of the two groups. However, the expert memorizers reported using the *method of loci* for tasks such as remembering strings of digits. As we saw in Chapter 7, this method involves a mental walk through a series of images, and in fact fMRI scans revealed that parts of the brain associated with navigation, such as the hippocampus, were more active in the expert memorizers than in the novices. In other words, although there was no *anatomical* difference between the two groups, there was a *functional* difference in the parts of the brain that were active. By contrast, the brain scans of London taxi drivers and a control group (Chapter 7) did show an *anatomical* difference (enlargement of the posterior part of the hippocampus). The difference between expert memorizers and taxi drivers probably reflects the fact that the memorizers had learned to employ the same strategy—the method of loci—for different materials, whereas the taxi drivers had had to acquire their knowledge of London's streets by sheer repetition. Ericsson (2003) noted that the Maguire et al. study (2000) supports the view that there is nothing innately different about the brains of experts. Rather, years of practice shape the brain and make true expertise possible.

10-year rule
The hypothesis that roughly 10 years of intense practice is necessary in order to become an expert in a domain.

Creativity

It's no easier to find a consensus concerning the meaning of creativity than it is to find a consensus for the meaning of *intelligence*. However, one definition that has been widely accepted holds that creativity involves "the production of novel, socially valued products" (Mumford & Gustafson, 1988, p. 28). The reference to social value suggests that creativity entails not just originality but what Vinacke (1974) called appropriateness (p. 354). To qualify as creative, a product must not only be original: it must also provide a "solution to a significant social problem" (Mumford & Gustafson, 1988, p. 28). This definition is quite broad, and allows for a variety of research approaches. Some studies have focused on the processes responsible for original behaviours, without really addressing the question of appropriateness. Others have more thoroughly explored the social context within which creative behaviour is evaluated.

> **creativity**
> The production of novel, socially valued products.

Creativity and Problem-Finding

Psychologists exploring creativity and original thinking have been especially interested in problem-finding (Runco, 2004, p. 675). The best-known researcher associated with this topic was Getzels (1975). He observed that problem-finding may strike some people as a luxury. Aren't there already enough problems to go around? Why would we need more people finding problems? The answer is that the quality of a solution often depends on the way the problem is formulated. To make this point Getzels (1975) quoted Einstein:

> **problem-finding (Getzels)**
> The ability to discover new problems, their methods and solutions.

> The formulation of a problem is often more essential than its solution, which may be merely a matter of mathematical or experimental skill. To raise new questions, new possibilities, to regard old questions from a new angle, requires creative imagination and marks real advance in science (p. 12).

However, science is not the only context in which problem-finding is valuable. Getzels (1975, p. 15) gave the following example of problem-finding in the real world. Suppose you have a flat tire on a deserted country road. You need to change the tire, but you don't have a jack, and so you define the problem as getting a jack. In that case you would probably start walking back to town. However, someone else might define the problem as raising the car. This is a more productive approach because it allows you to see the potential relevance of things other than jacks to the solution of your problem. In Getzels's example, the person who defines the problem as raising the car notices that there is a pulley attached to the hay loft of a nearby barn. If you push the car over to the barn, you can use the pulley to raise it while you change the tire. The creative solution is made possible by the way the problem is formulated.

Getzels (1975) contrasted problem-finding with other forms of cognition in three respects: the way the problem is stated, the method used to solve the problem, and the solution itself. In many cognitive processes all three of these elements are simply given to us. For example, suppose a group of students have been asked to multiply 1232 by 54,762. In this case (a) the problem is provided by the teacher to the students; (b) the solution procedure is known by the teacher (and, we hope, by the students); and (c) the students simply generate a solution, which the teacher can evaluate as either right or wrong. In this case the students do not discover anything in the course of solving the problem: they simply apply the rules they have already learned. Of course, it is possible to present students with problems in a way that allows them to discover something in the course of problem-solving. Sometimes the teacher knows the correct method for approaching a problem, but allows the students to discover the method on their own. Many of the "insight" problems (e.g., the nine-dot problem) that we considered in Chapter 10 are of this sort. The person to whom the problem is given does not know how to solve it initially, but discovers the correct method in the course of attempting a solution.

Even in this case, however, the person does not discover the problem: rather, it is given to him or her. True problem-finding does not occur unless the same person formulates the problem, devises the method, and reaches the solution, all of which are unknown to anyone else. This kind of problem-finding occurs in all areas of endeavour. According to Csikszentmihalyi (2002), Getzels's

> most generative idea has been the concept of "problem finding"—the notion that whereas most approaches to understanding creativity focus on its problem-solving aspects, what really differentiates a creative thought from a less original one is that it deals with an issue no one had seen as problematic before. Thus, it is the formulation of a hitherto unperceived problem, rather than its solution, that is the hallmark of creativity (Csikszentmihalyi, 2002, p. 290).

Creativity as Evolution in Miniature

An influential theory of the creative process was advanced by Campbell (1960), who applied Darwinian evolutionary theory to the process of knowledge acquisition. As Campbell saw it, there are two key aspects to the evolutionary process. One is **blind variation**, in which we explore alternatives without knowing in advance which one will have the desired consequences. An example of blind variation is trial and error, of the sort that was perhaps first described by the comparative psychologist C. Lloyd Morgan (1894). Morgan noted that his dog had learned how to escape from the fenced-in yard by lifting the latch on the gate. This was not the product of any insight on the dog's part: rather, it was the result of a process in which the animal explored his environment and by chance hit on an action that would free him.

Other forms of blind variation allow the organism to pick up information from the environment without actually moving around in it. As an example Campbell pointed to *echolocation*—the system that species such as bats use to navigate and find prey. The bat will emit a sound that bounces off objects in the environment, producing an echo that serves as a cue to the location of objects. The animal can then behave appropriately on the basis of the feedback it gets from the sound it emits. People can also learn to echolocate, and it seems that many blind people do so.

Campbell's point about echolocation is that it is a *blind* process, both literally and figuratively: the sound that is emitted is not sent in any particular direction. In order for echolocation to work properly, all locations must have an equal chance of being sampled. It's the feedback from the environment that tells us which direction is the correct one. The environment provides the selection criterion for a correct action. Without blind

blind variation (Campbell)

The generation of alternative problem solutions without foresight.

variation, we won't get any information from the environment, and we won't learn anything new.

Creative thinking, from Campbell's viewpoint, involves blind variation on a symbolic level. We can imagine various alternative courses of action, as well as the selection criterion for an appropriate action. We may have a fairly clear idea of the sort of solution that a given problem requires, and may then vary our thinking until an idea occurs that fits the requirements. The variation is *blind* in that we have no idea what the answer will be, so that any idea is a potential candidate. There is no restriction on the ideas this process may generate. Of course, most of the ideas generated will be of little or no value (Campbell, 1960, p. 393). But eventually the process of generating alternative ideas may result in a successful one. The key mechanism of creative thinking is *serendipity*—accidental discovery. Alternatives that turn out to meet the selection criteria, whatever they happen to be, are then retained for future use in similar contexts.

All the foregoing can be summarized in terms of Simonton's (1984, 2003) version of Campbell's theory. Simonton stated three "core propositions":

1. Creative solutions to problems require some process of variation. These variations are **chance permutations** of mental elements. Permutations are different combinations of cognitive units such as ideas and concepts.
2. Variations are selected on the basis of a set of criteria.
3. Variations that meet the criteria are retained.

> **chance permutations**
> Different combinations of mental elements produced according to no set rule.

Creativity and Remote Associations

One characteristic of creative individuals is the ability to generate remote (i.e., uncommon) associations. Given a word association task, most adults will produce common associations. For example, when asked to name the first word they think of when they hear "chair," they will tend to say "table"; and when they hear "body," they will most often say "mind" (Deese, 1965). We may think of words and objects as having a hierarchy of associations attached to them. In the case of objects, these associations involve possible uses. An example of such a hierarchy is given in Figure 12.6. This kind of structure is sometimes called a *divergent hierarchy* because it consists of a set of associations that diverge from a single object (Berlyne, 1965, p. 88). Associations that are low in the hierarchy are less obvious and less available to most of us as responses. The availability of responses is related to the frequency of their occurrence in the person's experience: the most frequently used sit at the top of the hierarchy.

One of the difficulties that may arise when we want to solve a problem is that the response we need is low in the hierarchy of associations available to us. If I want to build a bookcase and have a supply of bricks at hand, but don't think of bricks as possible components of a bookcase, then I will miss one possible solution to the problem. As we saw in Chapter 10, it's easy to be functionally fixed: that is, to be unable to see anything beyond the familiar or obvious uses for things. Functional fixedness is the opposite of originality. In fact, a widely used test of original thinking is the **alternate uses test** (Barron, 1963; Vartanian, Martindale, & Kwiatkowski, 2003), in which people are asked to list

> **alternate uses test (Barron)**
> A test that asks people to list uncommon uses for common objects.

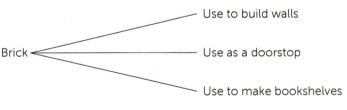

FIGURE 12.6 | A hierarchy of responses to a brick

as many uses as possible for common objects. The more unusual the uses suggested, the higher the score.

Mednick (1962) suggested that an individual's creativity is a reflection of his or her **associative hierarchy**. Most of us have only a few associations arranged in a steep hierarchy and therefore see only the most obvious uses for things. By contrast, creative people have many associations arranged in a "flat" hierarchy and hence are just as likely to see unusual uses as more obvious ones. As Simonton (2003, p. 483) observed, "a flat associative hierarchy means that for any given stimulus, the creative person has many associations available, all with roughly equal probabilities of retrieval." As a consequence, the associations of creative people are relatively unpredictable (cf. Mohr, Graves, Gianotti, Pizzagalli, & Brugger, 2001). This variability leads creative people to generate a wide variety of ideas that can be subjected to selection criteria.

Mednick (1967) invented a widely used test of originality called the **remote associations test (RAT).** It requires the person to come up with a single association to link three apparently unrelated words. Consider these three words: *soda, buffalo, fall*. Can you think of one word that is associated with all three of them? How about *water* (*soda water, water buffalo, water fall*)? Here are a number of other examples that are similar to RAT items, although they are not taken from the RAT. Some are much easier than others, depending on how strongly associated the answer is with one or more of the three words. (Answers are at the end of the chapter.)

worm	juice	blossom
fish	gun	up
head	sick	port
blood	grass	eyes
guard	blow	some
log	ship	boy
sugar	man	hard
foot	rat	course
time	end	fare
new	good	leap
craft	broom	hunt
carrier	air	black
chase	work	news
name	poison	pig

The RAT purports to measure the individual's ability to produce associations between words that at first do not appear to be strongly related. However, it has been criticized on the grounds that its results do not correlate well with those of independent measures of the ability to produce remote associations (Perkins, 1981, p. 252). The role of remote associations in creative thinking remains unclear, especially if we define creativity in terms of the production of material that is not only novel, but socially valued. Remote associations may play a part in the production of novel ideas, but their role in the production of socially relevant ideas is less obvious.

associative hierarchy

The idea that the associations used for problem-solving are arranged in a hierarchy, and that creative people not only have more associations than most, but have them arranged in "flatter" hierarchies: thus they are more likely than most to recognize alternative possibilities.

remote associations test (RAT; Mednick)

A test that asks the participant to come up with a single association to link three apparently unrelated words.

What is the hallmark of a highly intelligent person? Is it just the ability to remember large numbers of facts? Could the ability to think creatively be linked to intelligence? These are questions that many researchers have addressed, and it does appear that creativity and intelligence are linked. Some of you may remember the TV series called *MacGyver* (Selma and Patty's favourite show on *The Simpsons*). In every episode MacGyver would face some seemingly impossible predicament, yet he would always find a solution by using nearby materials in unorthodox ways. For example, in one episode he managed to create a "rocket-powered" harpoon gun and zip line using only materials found in an old attic: cleaning fluid, a telescope, moth balls, rope, and a pulley. The capacity for creative problem-solving is not limited to humans. For example, chimpanzees will use different-sized sticks to dig out an ant or termite nest, and crows will drop nuts on the road, then wait for a car to drive by and crack open the shells.

Today more than ever, creative thinking is seen as central to intelligence. In many situations we actually have all the information we need to solve a problem stored in our long-term memory, but can't access it because of the way the problem is framed. It takes flexible and creative thinking to come up with the right answer. Are you interested in testing your own ability to think creatively? One common test involves thinking of unusual ways to use a brick (see p. 397). Another takes familiar phrases involving numbers and asks you to identify them on the basis of the numbers and the first letters of the words: thus *24 H in a D* would mean *24 hours in a day*. Here are a few more examples (answers are at the end of the chapter):

5 T on a F

9 L of a C

12 M in a Y

52 C in a D (WJs)

13 L in a B D

From: http://www.experts-exchange.com/other/puzzles_riddles/q_21793289.html.

Summary

This chapter has discussed the ways in which psychologists have conceptualized *intelligence*. Many conceptualizations rest on the notion of a single *general intelligence* (*g*) that is common to all types of intelligence and underlies more specific abilities. General intelligence appears to be a useful construct, as research has shown that it can predict academic achievement and work performance. We also considered the importance of working memory, neural plasticity, and evolution in relation to general intelligence.

An important finding in research on intelligence is the *Flynn effect*, which indicates that IQ scores have been increasing in industrialized nations over time. Since increases in IQ have been occurring too quickly for evolution to account for them, researchers have looked to environmental factors such as improvements in nutrition, health, and education, and increasing environmental complexity.

While many theories emphasize the importance of general intelligence, several others focus on different aspects of intelligence. Robert Sternberg's theory of *successful intelligence* proposes that three different types of components or processes underlie all aspects of intelligence: *metacomponents*, *performance components*, and *knowledge acquisition components*. Sternberg also outlined three different content areas of intelligence—*analytical*, *creative*, and *practical*—and suggested that individuals will vary across the three types. Similarly, Howard Gardner's theory of *multiple intelligences* proposes that intelligence does not consist of one ability but rather of many different abilities. An important contribution of this theory is the emphasis it places on the use of *symbol systems*, such as drawing and music, in intelligent behaviour.

Research on *expertise* indicates that practice is the most important factor in the development of expertise. Innate talent or anatomical differences in brain structure do not appear to play a critical role in the development of expertise.

Like intelligence, *creativity* has been conceptualized in numerous ways; nevertheless, cognitive psychologists agree that creativity involves the production of novel, socially valued products. Concepts such as *problem-finding*, *blind variation*, and *remote associations* are considered instrumental to understanding creativity.

CASE STUDY

Case Study Wrap-Up

Kim Ung-Yong, the child prodigy who was the subject of the case study that opened this chapter, was estimated by the Stanford–Binet test to have an IQ of 210. How Kim would score on the Raven test of *g* (general intelligence) we don't know, but according to Spearman's two-factor theory of intelligence (Figure 12.2) he would probably have a very high *g*. We can likely make the same assumption with respect to Sternberg's concept of analytical intelligence, since it has been argued that *g* and analytical intelligence are largely the same. Where Kim would score on Spearman's variable *s* (specific ability: the variable ability within an individual for different abilities) or Sternberg's practical intelligence is not clear. However, we may find a partial answer in Kim's own reflections on his life.

As we saw, Kim completed his PhD in the US at the age of 15 and then went to work for NASA. But by 1978 the loneliness of his life there led him to move back to Korea. Although he eventually established a successful career in business planning, the choice to return attracted considerable attention, and some media critics judged him a failure. In 2010 Kim told the *Korea Herald* that "People expected me to become a high-ranking official in the government or a big company, but I don't think just because I chose not to become the expected it gives anyone a right to call anyone's life a failure."

Fortunately, Kim now says he is happy. Although his exceptional intelligence has helped him in life, he feels that too much importance is attached to a high IQ: "If there is a long spectrum of categories with many different talents, I would only be a part of the spectrum. I'm just good in concentrating on one thing, and there are many others who have different talents." Thus by his own assessment it seems likely that Kim would have a relatively high *g*, but varying specific abilities.

As you have probably noticed, one of the messages of this chapter is that there are many kinds of intelligence. Kim's story may lend credence to Gardner's theory of multiple intelligences. But a high *g* does not necessarily mean that someone will be intelligent across all domains, or act in the most intelligent manner in all situations. There could be many supposed geniuses who don't have a creative bone in their bodies. In any event, Kim's modest appraisal of his own abilities may give hope to the rest of us. Even if you aren't an expert in calculus, as he was, there are likely some other types of intelligence in which you excel.

In the Know: Review Questions

1. Discuss the nature and evolution of general intelligence.
2. What is the Flynn effect? Which explanation of it do you find most plausible? Why?
3. First discuss the triarchic theory of intelligence and then briefly assess Sternberg's approach to the study of intelligence.
4. Discuss Gardner's criteria for identifying a separate intelligence. Then outline his approach to the study of a particular symbol system, such as drawing or music. Briefly discuss the merits and limitations of this approach.
5. Do you prefer Sternberg's or Gardner's approach? Why?
6. What makes someone an expert? Take into account the properties of expertise outlined in the text.
7. What is problem-finding? Why is it an important part of the creative process?
8. What role do associations play in the creative process? In your answer, discuss at least two measures of creativity.

Key Concepts

alternate uses test (Barron)
analytical intelligence
associative hierarchy
blind variation (Campbell)
chance permutations
creative intelligence
creativity
crystallized intelligence
dedicated intelligence
eduction (Spearman)
entrenched vs non-entrenched concepts
factor analysis
fluid intelligence
Flynn effect
general intelligence (*g*)
improvisational intelligence
intellectual components (Sternberg)

intelligence (Binet and Simon)
knowledge acquisition components (Sternberg)
metacomponents (Sternberg)
mid-life crisis of musicians (Bamberger)
multiple intelligences (Gardner)
neural plasticity
performance components (Sternberg)
practical intelligence
problem-finding (Getzels)
Raven Progressive Matrices
remote associations test—RAT (Mednick)
symbol systems
10-year rule
triarchic theory of intelligence
ur-song
U-shaped development
working memory capacity

Links to Other Chapters

fluid and crystallized intelligence
Chapter 5 (working memory)

working memory capacity
Chapter 5 (working memory)

creativity and problem-finding
Chapter 10 (insight problems)

Further Reading

For a wealth of material associated with the study of intelligence, go to www.intelltheory.com/

There is not enough room in a textbook to discuss the challenges of studying group differences in intelligence. If you wish to investigate this topic in the context of American culture, you could begin by reading Chapter 5 of Ciancialo & Sternberg (2004). Herrnstein & Murray (1994) took a contentious approach to the topic, touching off a controversy that is the subject of Jacoby and Glauberman (1995). For an alternative to Herrnstein and Murray's viewpoint see Gould (1996).

Sternberg and Lubart (1992) explore the relationship between problem-finding and risk-taking.

Both Gardner and Winner belong to Project Zero, the mission of which "is to understand and enhance learning, thinking, and creativity in the arts, as well as humanistic and scientific disciplines, at the individual and institutional levels"; for more information go to www.pz.harvard.edu/.

For a useful overview of multiple intelligences theory see Shearer (2004). And for more on the psychology of music see Lewis (2002) and Moore, Burland, and Davidson (2003). The evolution of intelligence is further explored by Roth and Dicke (2005).

Ciancialo, A.T., & Sternberg, R.J. (2004). *Intelligence: A brief history*. Oxford: Blackwell.

Gould, S.J. (1996). *The mismeasure of man* (2nd ed.). New York: Norton.

Herrnstein, R.J., & Murray, C. (1994). *The bell curve: Intelligence and class structure in American life*. Glencoe, Ill.: Free Press.

Jacoby, R., & Glauberman, N. (1995). *The bell curve debate*. New York: Times Books. Ill.: Free Press.

Lewis, P.A. (2002). Musical minds. *Trends in Cognitive Sciences, 6*, 364–366.

Moore, D.G., Burland, K., & Davidson, J.W. (2003). The social context of musical success: A developmental account. *British Journal of Psychology, 94*, 529–549.

Roth, G., & Dicke, U. (2005). Evolution of the brain and intelligence. *Trends in Cognitive Sciences, 9*, 250–257.

Shearer, B. (2004). Multiple intelligences theory after 20 years. *Teacher's College Record, 106*, 2–16.

Sternberg, R.J., & Lubart, T.I. (1992). Buy low and sell high: An investment approach to creativity. *Current Directions in Psychological Science, 1*, 1–5.

Answers to Problems

Raven Progressive Matrices problems.

Problem a: The number of black squares in the top of each row increases by one from the first to the second and the second to the third column. The number of black squares along the left stays the same within a row but changes between rows from 3 to 2 to 1. Answer: 3.

Problem b: The figures in the first two columns (or rows) combine to form the figure in the third column (or row). Answer: 8.

Problem c: In each row, look for three elements—for example, horizontal line, vertical line, and V—each of which occurs only twice in that row. Answer: 5.

Answers to the remote association items on p. 398: *apple, blow, air, blue, body, cabin, candy, race, zone, year, witch, mail, paper, pen*.

Answers to the creative thinking items in Box 12.3: 5 toes on a foot, 9 lives of a cat, 12 months in a year, 52 cards in a deck (without jokers), 13 loaves in a baker's dozen.

13

Consciousness

Chapter Contents

Chapter Objectives

- To understand and be able to distinguish different levels of consciousness.
- To look at unconscious perception.
- To explore meta-consciousness, as illustrated by mind-wandering and lucid dreaming, and how it relates to consciousness.
- To discuss the relationship between consciousness and the brain.
- To explain various deficits of consciousness.

Blindsight

Imagine you are suffering from excruciating migraine headaches. The pain is so bad that you have to see a neurosurgeon. The doctor conducts a series of tests and concludes that there is a problem with some blood vessels at the back of your brain, near an area involved in visual perception. Since the only hope of relief lies in removal of the blood vessels and a small amount of brain tissue serviced by them, you agree to go under the knife. When you wake up after the surgery, the migraine is mostly gone, but you are unable to see anything in the lower left quadrant of your visual field. Although the area affected becomes somewhat smaller over time, the problem does not go away. Sometime later, while examining your perception, your doctor places a series of objects in the blind area of your visual field and asks you to identify their orientation. Certain that you don't see anything, you can only guess. However, to your astonishment, the doctor tells you that most of your "guesses" were correct.

In what is now considered to be a classic case study, Weiskrantz (1986) describes just such a patient. DB had undergone a surgery that left him with a blind area in his lower visual field. What was striking about this case was that even though DB could not consciously see the objects presented in his blind area, his guesses about their properties were impressively accurate. For instance, Weiskrantz (1986, p. 26) reported that DB was able to point to and reach for objects presented in his blind area with a high degree of accuracy. As another example, Weiskrantz (1986) described an informal test in which DB was shown a short stick in his blind area. Of course, he reported not seeing anything. Yet when asked to guess at the stick's orientation, his answers were very accurate. Weiskrantz (1986, p. 24) reported the following discussion with DB, which took place after he had correctly identified the orientation of the stick on multiple trials without seeing the stick itself:

> "Did you know how well you had done?" he was asked. "No," he replied, "I didn't—because I couldn't see anything; I couldn't see a darn thing." "Can you say how you guessed—what it was that allowed you to say whether it was vertical or horizontal?" "No, I could not because I did not see anything; I just don't know." Finally, he was asked, "So you really did not know you were getting them right?" "No," he replied, still with something of an air of incredulity.

Weiskrantz and his colleagues dubbed this condition **blindsight**.

Blindsight brings up a number of interesting questions about consciousness. While DB claimed that he was in no way aware of the objects in his blind visual field, he nevertheless was able to answer correctly when asked about the orientation of those objects. How does this fit in with your notion of what *consciousness* is? In fact, the question of consciousness is a very tricky one, especially in the context of experimental methodology. How do you design an experiment when it is so difficult to operationally define exactly what consciousness is? In this chapter we will delve into the unresolved debate about what consciousness is, how to define it, and how it can be studied from a number of different perspectives.

blindsight

A condition in which patients with damage to the primary visual cortex are able to make accurate judgments about objects presented to their blind area even though they report no conscious experience of the objects and believe they are only guessing.

Distinguishing among Different Levels of Consciousness

The field of philosophy has had a deep interest in consciousness for centuries. From the classic work of Descartes (1644/1911) to more contemporary philosophers and psychologists such as Dennett (1991), Gazzaniga (2011), and Searle (1990, 1992), consciousness has been a central question in investigations of the human mind. Over the years, many have suggested that there might be different levels of consciousness, each with different characteristics and qualities. In this section we will consider several ways of thinking about how the various levels of consciousness could be distinguished.

Autonoetic, Noetic, and Anoetic Consciousness

As we saw in Chapter 5, Tulving's (1985) research has made immense contributions to our understanding of memory. In addition, it directly relates different divisions of memory to different levels of consciousness, as shown in Table 13.1.

As the table indicates, Tulving (1985) suggested that each of the three systems of memory is associated with a different kind of consciousness. For example, procedural memory can be described as anoetic (non-knowing) because it does not go beyond itself; it stays in the here and now. When I'm riding a bike, I'm concerned only with the immediate situation, focused on responding appropriately to a particular vehicle (the one I am on) in a particular situation (the one I am in) at a particular time (now). By contrast, semantic memory is noetic (knowing) because when we use it we are aware not only of our immediate surroundings, but also of things that lie beyond it. If I'm riding my bike and remember that Polanyi (1958) wrote about the sort of skill that bike-riding requires, then my memory will be accompanied by noetic consciousness. Finally, episodic memory is autonoetic (self-knowing) because it involves remembering personal experiences.

Tulving (2001, 2002a, 2002b) has been especially interested in episodic memory and autonoetic consciousness. Normal adults are able to see themselves as having a past and a future as well as a present. Their individual experiences are located in time, and they are able to engage in "mental time travel" (Tulving, 2002a, p. 2). Although remembering a personal past is a crucial aspect of episodic memory, so is the ability to project ourselves into the future and imagine what we might find there. It is this ability that enables us to set goals and plan future actions (Atance & O'Neill, 2001).

Autonoetic awareness requires healthy functioning of the frontal lobe. Among the most important sources of evidence for this relationship was the now-abandoned medical practice of prefrontal leucotomy (also known as prefrontal lobotomy; see Figure 13.1). This was a surgical procedure, invented by Moniz (1954/1968; Freeman & Watts, 1950/1968), in which the connections between the prefrontal lobes and other parts of the brain were severed. One goal of the procedure was to calm patients who ruminated excessively about themselves and their problems: "Frontal leucotomies change patients so that they are no longer interested in the sorts of past, present, and future problems that were so absorbing and incapacitating before the operations" (Wheeler, 2000, p. 602).

anoetic, noetic, and autonoetic Three levels of consciousness corresponding to the procedural, semantic, and episodic memory systems.

prefrontal leucotomy A surgical procedure, now abandoned, in which the connections between the prefrontal lobes and other parts of the brain were severed; also known as prefrontal lobotomy.

TABLE 13.1 | The Relationship between Memory Systems and Consciousness

Memory System	Consciousness
episodic	autonoetic
semantic	noetic
procedural	anoetic

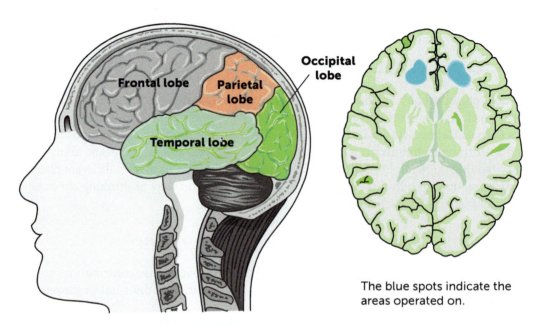

Frontal lobe

Parietal lobe

Occipital lobe

Temporal lobe

The blue spots indicate the areas operated on.

FIGURE 13.1 | Prefrontal leucotomy

This procedure was used to control symptoms such as excessive anxiety and self-absorption, but was discontinued because of side effects such as apathy and listlessness.

Tulving (2002b) has argued that autonoetic consciousness is not only uniquely human, but a crucial factor in the evolution of human culture and civilization. He has called our sense of subjective time **chronesthesia**, and considers it a cognitive capacity as important in its own way as the capacity to see or hear. "The development of civilization and culture was, and its continuation is, critically dependent on human beings' awareness of their own and their progeny's *continued existence* in time that includes not only the past and the present but also the future" (Tulving, 2002b, p. 321). This capacity has enabled humans to contemplate changing the environment to suit them better, rather than simply adapting to it. The consequence has been the emergence of a human culture that has altered the environment in many ways. Autonoesis and chronesthesia depend on the prefrontal lobes, as we have seen. "The conclusion follows that the human prefrontal cortex, undoubtedly in collaboration with other areas of the brain, is directly responsible for the cultured world as it exists today" (Tulving, 2002b, p. 321).

Non-conscious, Conscious and Meta-conscious Experiences

As interesting as Tulving's perspective is, there are other ways of conceptualizing consciousness that may have broader applications. For instance, Schooler (2002) distinguished between three levels of consciousness: non-conscious (unexperienced), conscious (experienced), and meta-conscious (re-represented). Although the terms are fairly self-explanatory, it's important to define them, as we will use these distinctions in the rest of this chapter. First, the **non-conscious** or unconscious dimension of consciousness

chronesthesia
Our subjective sense of time.

non-conscious
The level of consciousness that operates without our attention, continuously monitoring and changing the contents of thought, and tracking and changing behaviour to address goals.

monitors and changes the contents of thought, tracking and changing behaviour to address immediate goals; it resembles Tulving's anoetic consciousness in that we are not aware of it while it is at work (Schooler, 2002). **Conscious**, in Schooler's framework, means simply aware (of whatever we are experiencing in the moment, our surroundings, thoughts, etc.); it refers to the basic level that Tulving called noetic consciousness. Finally, the third or **meta-conscious** level comes into play whenever we focus conscious attention on our own state of mind.

We will look at all three of these levels, beginning with unconscious processes.

Unconscious Perception

As we have seen, Weiskrantz's (1986) studies of blindsight suggest that we may be able to perceive visual objects even when we have no conscious experience of them. In fact, William James (1890/1983, p. 275) observed more than a century ago that people are not actually aware of everything in their environment. Why do different students describing the same lecture give different accounts of it? There are two reasons: first, because none of us can be aware of every component of an event; and, second, because we encode events in different ways. As Reber (1985) pointed out, words arrive at your ear as a sequence of physical, acoustic events; then you have to transform those events into meaningful words. The process of transforming information into one or more forms of representation is known as **encoding**.

Information can be encoded in several ways. Consider how we might encode a word. In an influential paper, D.D. Wickens (1970) used this example: "When a person hears the word *horse*, it is encoded into the broader categories of beasts of burden, four-legged creatures, mammals, warm blooded animals, and finally of animals in general" (p. 1). How does this encoding process take place? Wickens suggested that it is largely automatic: in a world with so much information available at any moment, the task of encoding it would be impossibly complex if we had to be aware of what we were doing. As an analogy, Wickens pointed to a major league baseball player who is able to hit or catch a ball without paying attention to what he is doing. In fact, there is evidence that if highly skilled performers do try to pay attention to what they are doing, their performance declines (Baumeister, 1984; Beilock, Carr, McMahon, & Starkes, 2002; Gray, 2004; Schlenker & Leary, 1982).

Wickens suggested that the process of encoding is not only unconscious but also very fast. Moreover, an event can be encoded along several different dimensions simultaneously. Thus a single word might be encoded in terms of multiple dimensions: frequency of occurrence, how we feel about it, as well as its physical characteristics, such as its length and sound. This process is called multidimensional encoding.

Wickens's point of view is consistent with the existence of a phenomenon called subliminal perception (N.F. Dixon, 1971; Lazarus & McCleary, 1951). **Subliminal or unconscious perception** (also referred to as perception without awareness) operates when a stimulus has an effect on behaviour even though it has been exposed too rapidly, or at too low an intensity, for the person to be able to identify it. For example, suppose that a word (the stimulus) is presented to a participant for an interval so brief that it is below the participant's threshold for reporting the occurrence of an event. (Another word for threshold is **limen**, and so a stimulus that is "below threshold" is called *subliminal*.) Even when the participant

conscious
The basic level of awareness.

meta-conscious
The level of consciousness at play when you direct your attention to your own state of mind.

encoding
The process of transforming information into one or more forms of representation.

subliminal or unconscious perception
Perception without awareness; occurs when the stimulus is too weak to be consciously recognized, but still has an impact on your behaviour.

limen
Threshold.

does not identify the stimulus, it may still have an effect. Wickens reviewed experiments in which participants have been able to say whether the stimulus word is pleasant or unpleasant, without reporting that they have actually seen it (e.g., Eriksen, Azuma, & Hicks, 1959).

Subliminal perception effects often involve semantics (the study of meaning; see Chapter 9). Two words that are similar in meaning are said to be semantically related. Thus *duck* and *swan* are semantically related in that both refer to water birds (Eagle, Wolitzky, & Klein, 1966). In some early subliminal perception experiments, participants would report seeing a word that was semantically related to the stimulus word, but would not report seeing the word they were actually shown (Postman, Bruner, & McGinnis, 1948).

Experiments like the ones we have just described were often criticized. For one thing, they appear to have serious methodological problems. How can we be sure that a stimulus presented below the threshold of awareness was not actually seen? If the stimulus was attended to, however briefly, then we should not be surprised if it had some effect on behaviour. In the late 1970s and early 1980s, however, novel experimental techniques revived the notion that information is extensively encoded below the threshold of awareness. Among the most influential studies were those that employed a technique called "backward masking."

Backward Masking

backward masking
Presenting a stimulus, called the target, to the participant and then covering, or masking, the target with another stimulus.

Backward masking involves presenting a stimulus, called the target, to the participant and then covering, or masking, the target with another stimulus. As we saw in Chapter 4, the time difference between the first stimulus and the masking stimulus is called the stimulus onset asynchrony, or SOA.

In one early experiment (Marcel, Katz, & Smith, 1974), participants were briefly shown a single word that was then masked by a pattern. The participants were asked to report whatever they could. Sometimes participants reported words that they had not been shown but that were semantically related to the stimulus word (e.g., *queen* instead of *king*, or *apple* instead of *orange*). This phenomenon is sometimes called priming, by analogy with the activity of priming a pump. The stimulus acts as a *prime* that makes a semantically related response more likely.

COGNITION IN ACTION | Backward Masking and the Brain
BOX 13.1

What brain mechanisms are involved in backward masking? We noted in Chapter 3 that conscious visual perception depends on both feedforward processing, in which information from the primary visual cortex travels to regions in the inferior temporal lobe, and feedback (or re-entrant) connection, in which information from the inferior temporal cortex is sent to primary visual areas. The available evidence suggests that the re-entrant feedback connections are involved in backward masking (Lamme & Roelfsema, 2000).

Figure 13.2 (from Lamme & Roelfsema, 2000) shows the important role of feedback connections in backward masking. The bottom of the figure shows a timeline of stimulus presentation, with a stimulus presented at time zero that is followed by the mask presented 40 ms later. The presentation time of the stimulus is shown in

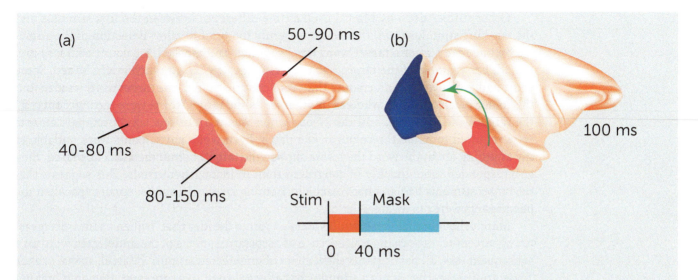

FIGURE 13.2 | **The brain mechanisms involved in backward masking when a mask is presented 40 ms after the onset of an initial stimulus**

Panel (a) shows the areas involved in the initial feedfoward flow of processing at various time points after stimulus onset. Panel (b) shows how, roughly 100-ms after stimulus onset, feedback information about the stimulus from the inferior temporal cortex (shown in red) conflicts with the processing of the mask in primary visual cortex (shown in blue).

Figure from Lamme, V.A.F., & Roelfsema, P.R. (2000), The distinct modes of vision afforded by feedforward and recurrent processing, *Trends in Neurosciences, 23*, 571–579, Figure 3, p. 577. Copyright (2011), with permission from Elsevier.

red and the presentation time of the mask in blue. Panel (a) shows the brain areas involved in the initial feedforward processing of the stimulus. As you can see, the stimulus is first processed by the primary visual cortex (within 40 to 80 ms after stimulus onset), then by the inferior temporal lobe (within 80 to 150 ms after onset), and also by an area above the eyes known as the frontal eye field (within 50 to 90 ms after stimulus onset). Remember from Chapter 3 that the inferior temporal cortex typically processes the stimulus (including its meaning) as a whole and is involved in conscious perception of the stimulus.

Importantly, a single feedforward sweep of the visual information might not be enough to lead to a conscious experience of the stimulus. So, within 100 ms after the stimulus onset, areas in the inferior temporal lobe send information back to the primary visual cortex. Normally, if the stimulus is not masked, this feedback information would combine with continued processing of the stimulus in the primary visual cortex, sending even a stronger message about the stimulus forward

to the inferior temporal cortex, ultimately leading to a conscious experience of the stimulus.

The impact of the mask on neural processing is shown in Panel (b). Notice that when the feedback pathways are activated (roughly 100 ms after stimulus onset), sending information about the stimulus (shown in red) back to the primary visual cortex, the latter is no longer processing the stimulus, but the mask (shown in blue). Now the feedback information no longer matches the information being processed in the primary visual cortex, and so the initial processing of the stimulus is not strengthened. Instead, new information about the mask is fed to later processing areas. Because the mask is the last stimulus presented, subsequent feedback and feedforward processing brings the mask into consciousness. The end result is conscious experience of the mask and failure to consciously perceive the initial stimulus. However, the initial feedforward sweep did carry information about the stimulus to the inferior temporal cortex, creating the opportunity for perception without awareness (i.e., subliminal perception).

Other studies done by Marcel used a time difference between the first stimulus and the masking stimulus (SOA) that was apparently too brief to allow detection of the stimulus. In one study, after a target word was presented and masked, a colour patch was presented. For example, if the target was the word *blue*, the colour patch might be red. Some trials had target words and colours that were congruent (e.g., the target word was *red* and the colour patch was red), whereas in other trials the target words were incongruent (e.g., the target word was *blue*, and the colour patch was red). In one condition, participants were required to name the colour of the patch. Even when participants were not able to say anything about the word they were shown (the target) before the mask appeared, they still responded more quickly in congruent than in incongruent trials. This suggests that the target stimulus had an effect on colour-naming latency (response time) even when the participants were not aware of it.

Marcel thought that these studies lent support to the idea that "[w]hen an indirect measure of perceptual processing is used, such as associative effects of the undetected word on a subsequent task, all participants show effect of undetected stimuli" (Marcel, 1983a, p. 232). To determine whether or not a stimulus has affected cognitive processes, then, it might not be necessary to rely on **direct measures** of cognitive processes, such as participants' verbal reports that they have not seen the stimulus; **indirect measures** of perceptual processes could be used instead. Masking a stimulus so that it is not reported by the participant does not mean that it has no effect: it may be processed anyway and thus influence that person's subsequent behaviour.

Inattentional Blindness and Unconscious Perception

In Chapter 4 we introduced the experimental paradigm that Mack and Rock (1998; Mack, 2003) used to study inattentional blindness (see Figure 4.5). Among the issues addressed by that paradigm is the question of whether unattended stimuli are nevertheless registered by the system and able to influence behaviour. To answer it, Mack and Rock presented a word in one of the quadrants defined by the cross and later asked participants to perform a word completion task. They hypothesized that if a priming effect was observed for a word to which participants were inattentionally blind, that "would indicate that the unseen word was registered and encoded below the level of conscious awareness" (p. 176).

For example, Mack and Rock would present a word such as *chart* in one of the quadrants of the cross and sometime later they would ask participants to complete the word stem *cha– –*. The fact that so many common words begin with *cha—chair, chase, charm*, and so on—made it very unlikely that anyone would choose to create the word *chart* by chance. However, participants who had been shown the word *chart* and claimed not to have seen it were much more likely than those who had not been shown it to use the letters *rt* to complete the word-stem. These results were evidence "of the processing, registration and encoding of the unseen and unidentified words presented under conditions of inattention" (Mack & Rock, 1998, p. 179).

Merikle, Smilek, and Eastwood (2001) observed that Mack and Rock's technique for studying attention is more **ecologically valid** than techniques used to investigate unconscious perception that rely on masking or manipulation of the quality of the stimulus. The Mack and Rock paradigm reflects the very common situation in which there are many unattended stimuli outside [an individual's] immediate focus of attention which are not consciously experienced. In these situations, the unattended stimuli could be consciously experienced if the person's focus of attention changed so that it was directed toward the relevant spatial locations. For this reason, the experimental conditions in studies in which unattended stimuli are presented at spatial locations removed from the current focus of attention more closely resemble the conditions under which visual stimuli are perceived in everyday situations (p. 121).

Objective and Subjective Thresholds

Backward-masking experiments such as Marcel's (1983a) are examples of the **dissociation paradigm**: an experimental strategy designed "to demonstrate that it is possible to perceive stimuli in the complete absence of any conscious awareness of these stimuli" (Merikle & Reingold, 1998, p. 304). Merikle (1992) described its general form:

> First, a measure of conscious perceptual experience (C) is selected. Second, a measure that is sensitive to unconscious perceptual processes (U) is identified. Third, experimental procedures are initiated to ensure that C exhibits no sensitivity to the critical perceptual information. If U can then be shown to exhibit some sensitivity to the same perceptual information that C is insensitive to, then it is concluded that perception without awareness has been demonstrated (p. 792).

However, this paradigm still does not eliminate the threshold problem. Merikle and his colleagues (Cheesman & Merikle, 1986; Merikle, Smilek, & Eastwood, 2001) have pointed out the importance of distinguishing between **objective** and **subjective thresholds**. The objective threshold is the level at which people detect a target stimulus no more often than would be expected by chance. For example, suppose that participants are presented with a series of stimuli and asked to indicate in each case whether or not they have detected the stimulus: if someone is correct only half the time, then it seems reasonable to conclude that he or she is only guessing and is not in fact aware of the presence or absence of the stimulus. The participant's results are no better than "would be obtained by a blind observer" (Erdelyi, 2004, p. 75). The subjective threshold can be determined by degrading "the stimulus conditions until the quality of the stimulus information is so poor that observers claim not to be able to perceive the stimuli" (Merikle & Daneman, 2000, p. 1296). In other words, the stimulus may be presented so quickly, or at such a low intensity, that participants will *say* they have not perceived it.

In backward-masking experiments, the objective threshold refers to an SOA at which a participant can detect the target stimulus only at a chance level. The subjective threshold refers to an SOA at which a participant claims not to be able to detect the stimulus. The subjective threshold has been used to distinguish between conscious and unconscious processes. However, it is far from obvious that perception without awareness has in fact occurred when participants "do not believe any useful stimulus information was perceived" (Merikle & Joordens, 1997, p. 111). One problem is the impossibility of demonstrating "in a completely convincing fashion" that "no relevant information was consciously perceived"

dissociation paradigm
An experimental strategy designed to show that it is possible to perceive stimuli in the absence of any conscious awareness of them.

objective and subjective thresholds
The point at which participants can detect a stimulus at a chance level versus the point at which they say they did not perceive it.

(Merikle & Joordens, 1997, p. 111). To rule out this possibility would require a complete assessment of the contents of the participants' consciousness (Merikle & Reingold, 1998). Rather than try to make a sharp distinction between conscious and unconscious effects, a better research strategy might be to investigate the relative contributions of each (Merikle & Joordens, 1997, p. 112).

One study often cited as an example of just such a strategy was conducted by Debner and Jacoby (1994), who used a **process dissociation procedure**. This technique requires participants *not* to respond to items they have seen previously. If participants are aware of having previously seen an item, then they can exclude it. If they are not aware of having previously seen an item, however, there is no reason for them to exclude it. Items were masked and presented for short (50 milliseconds) or long (500 milliseconds) durations. Then a word stem appeared on the screen, consisting of the first three letters of a five-letter word. An example would be *tab– –*, which could be completed with different letter combinations such as *table*, *tabby*, or *taboo* (Debner & Jacoby, 1994, p. 308). Participants were easily able to exclude the items they had seen for the longer duration. Thus, shown *table* for 500 milliseconds and then shown *tab– –*, they chose a word other than *table* to complete the word stem. This shows that participants had perceived the item and were able to control their response on the stem-completion task.

However, if participants were shown *table* for only 50 milliseconds, they were much less likely to exclude it as a solution to the stem-completion task. In fact, they were much more likely to choose *table* than they would have been by chance alone. The fact that they were unable to exclude the word *table* suggests that they did not perceive the word when it was shown to them. However, it also suggests that their behaviour was influenced by an event of which they were unaware. In short, participants were not in conscious control of their own behaviour.

Mindful of the controversies surrounding perception without awareness, Kihlstrom (2004) proposed using the term **implicit perception** for the phenomenon we have reviewed in this section. "Implicit perception" refers to "the effect on the subject's experience, thought or action of an object in the current stimulus environment in the absence of, or independently of, conscious perception of that event" (Kihlstrom, 2004, p. 94). This definition is intended to link unconscious perception to similar phenomena in other areas of cognition.

Unconscious Perception: Summary

Although Marcel's (1983a, 1983b) experiments have been superseded, the conclusions he drew from them are still valuable. His studies and the others we have reviewed point to the importance of the distinction between conscious and unconscious mental processes. People are not always aware of perceptual processes. Importantly, what studies of unconscious perception reveal is that a conscious percept is not always the goal of perception. Recall the blindsight patient DB, who was unable to consciously perceive an object presented in his blind area, but could accurately point at it. This suggests that one key aspect of perception is that it allows us to behave appropriately in our environment.

---

process dissociation procedure

An experimental technique that requires participants *not* to respond with items they have observed previously.

---

implicit perception

The effect on a person's experience, thought, or action of an object in the current stimulus environment in the absence of, or independent of, conscious perception of that event.

Consciousness and the Grand Illusion

When we look at the world around us, the picture we see appears to be sharp, detailed, and complete. Indeed, consciousness seems to have the qualities of completeness, fullness and relatively seamless continuity. But what if this was an illusion? Let's consider this possibility in the context of visual consciousness, or conscious visual perception.

As we saw in Chapter 3, our perceptual experiences can be influenced by our knowledge and the context in which objects appear, through re-entrant (feedback) connections in our perceptual system. In fact, prior knowledge and context can have a significant effect on our conscious perceptions. What if, instead of having a true and accurate visual representation of the world, we were actually processing only fragments of our visual field and representing only one or two objects in detail at a time, with the rest of consciousness being filled (or completed) by our prior knowledge? Though this sounds far-fetched, there is considerable evidence that it may be the case.

Change Detection

A change detection study conducted by Rensink, O'Regan, and Clark (1997) compellingly demonstrated that our experience of a picture-like visual world may be an illusion. They showed participants two pictures of the same scene on a computer screen. The two pictures were almost identical, except for one object or region, which was altered in one of the pictures. For instance, one view of an airport scene showed the engine of an airplane and the other omitted it. Images of the two versions were flashed on the screen for a few hundred milliseconds each in alternation, separated by a blank interval of a few hundred milliseconds. As the two photos switched back and forth (with the blank screen in between), participants had to detect the change. Many researchers in the field were surprised to find that in most cases it took many alternations of the photos before the change was finally detected. You can experience the same effect just by looking at an original photo and an altered version of it presented side by side, as in Figure 13.3. Can you see the difference?

FIGURE 13.3 | An original image and a slightly altered version of it

Can you see the difference? Hint: focus on the pumpkins.

change blindness

Failure to consciously detect an obvious change in a scene.

grand illusion of conscious perception

The illusion that what we see in our visual field is a clear and detailed picture of the world.

Shifting your eyes back and forth between images simulates the condition (alternating images with a brief interval in between) that Rensink and colleagues created.

One of the main points raised by change blindness is that our internal representation of the world is not as rich as we think. We feel that we perceive all the information in our visual field with high resolution. However, the fact that we fail to detect and be consciously aware of very large changes across scenes suggests that this feeling may be largely an illusion. In fact, the illusion of a rich and detailed representation of the external world has been called the grand illusion of conscious perception (see Enns, 2004; Noë, Pessoa, & Thompson, 2000). Rensink and colleagues (1997) argued that, contrary to our subjective experience, we likely process only one or two objects in detail at any given moment. It seems that the grand illusion is the result of the combination of very fragmentary visual information with our prior knowledge of the world.

In light of the research on change blindness, you might wonder how it is that we are able to get around in the world safely and efficiently. The change detection experiment reported by Rensink and colleagues suggests one possible answer to that question. In addition to presenting two photographs with a brief temporal interval in between (the condition that led to change blindness), they included a condition in which they removed the interval and presented the photographs back-to-back. They found that under this condition the change was often noted immediately. The change was easily detectable in this case because switching directly from one image to the other, without a temporal interval, created a flicker or motion signal that attracted the participants' attention. The same mechanism likely operates in the real world. We become aware of important changes that occur while we are driving, for example, because they create motion signals that attract our attention.

Change blindness is not restricted to static images (for a review of the literature on this subject, see Simons & Rensink, 2005). In fact, people often fail to perceive change in everyday life. For instance, Simons and Levin (1998) have shown that people can even fail to notice that their conversation partner has changed—at least when the latter is a stranger and the change occurs while he or she is briefly outside of view. Viewers have even been known to miss very unusual or surprising events (e.g., a figure in a gorilla suit walking across the scene) when their attention is focused on other activities on the screen (e.g., people passing a ball; see Simons & Chabris, 1999). For examples, take a look at www.youtube.com/watch?v=IGQmdoK_ZfY.

The Constraints of the Visual System

If you still don't believe that your conscious experience of a detailed and complete visual world is an illusion, consider the characteristics of the primary visual system and the physical limits of the eye. In an influential paper published in the *Canadian Journal of Psychology*, vision researcher Kevin O'Regan (1992) made a strong case for the idea that a high-fidelity percept of the world is not possible for several reasons. First, O'Regan noted that visual information is degraded as it moves through the visual organs to the brain. It might come as a surprise to you that there are several layers of cells between the light coming into the eyes and the photoreceptors that receive the light information. This means that the light information is inevitably degraded as it is absorbed and reflected by this intervening tissue.

Second, O'Regan noted that information from all areas of viewed space is not equally represented in the brain. This means that your visual acuity is not going to be the same across your whole field of vision. At the levels of both the retina at the back of the eye and the primary visual cortex, there is a progressive decrease in visual processing for information away from the centre of vision and towards the periphery. Recall that, even at the level of the retina, detailed visual processing occurs only in the very small region known as the fovea, which is densely packed with photoreceptors; the photoreceptors that process peripheral information are fewer and more widely spaced. This difference in the processing of central and peripheral information is further magnified in the primary visual cortex. The decline in visual acuity for objects in the visual periphery is demonstrated in Figure 13.4. Assuming the viewer is focusing on the centre of the image, this figure shows how much the letters outside the fovea would have to be enlarged in order to be equally perceptible across the visual field. Even at a physiological level, then, we can process detailed information from only a very small region of visual space. The conscious experience of uniform detail across our field of view appears to be nothing more than an illusion.

In addition to these points raised by O'Regan, it is also worth noting that our visual experiences are frequently interrupted by eye blinks and eye movements. Every time your eye moves, which is roughly every quarter of a second, the information hitting your retina changes too fast for it to be processed effectively. However, your visual system suppresses visual processing during this time of *retinal blur*, rendering you unaware of it, through a process known as *saccadic suppression* (see Ridder III & Tomlinson, 1997). In the same way, we are typically not consciously aware that our visual field goes blank every time we

retinal blur
The blurring of information on the retina that occurs during fast eye movements.

saccadic suppression
The halting of visual processing during an eye movement.

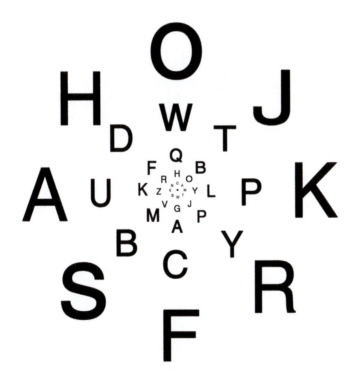

FIGURE 13.4 | How objects would have to vary in size in order to be equally discernible for an observer who is focusing on the dot in the centre

blink suppression

The halting of visual processing during an eye blink.

blind spot

A region in the eye that does not contain any photoreceptors; therefore the visual system cannot process visual stimuli that fall in that region.

blink because we suppress visual processing during the blink; this phenomenon is known as **blink suppression** (see Ridder III & Tomlinson, 1997). During moments of saccadic and blink suppression, our brain simply fills in the "blind" interval based on information perceived before and after the suppressed moments to give us a smooth, continuous visual experience.

Perceptual Filling-In

You might think that a non-uniform retina would be problematic enough for our conscious experience of a perfectly clear percept, but it turns out that each eye has a region in which there are no photoreceptors (light receptors) at all. If you look back at Figure 3.1, you will notice that there is an area at the back of the eye to which the optic nerve is connected. In this area, known as the **blind spot** (see Pessoa, Thompson, & Noe, 1998; Palmer, 1999),

THINK TWICE
BOX 13.2
Can You Find Your Blind Spot?

In his book *Vision Science: Photons to Phenomenology*, vision scientist Stephen Palmer (1999, p. 34) outlines an excellent exercise that you can do to detect your blind spot. A version of this exercise is reproduced in Figure 13.5. The figure shows an "X" and a dot. To experience your blind spot, focus your left eye on the "X." It is very important that you use your left eye for the exercise and keep the other (right) eye closed. While you fix your left eye on the "X", you should also be able to see the dot out of the corner of your eye. Keeping your right eye closed, slowly move the page towards or away from you. As you move the page and the dot enters the area of your blind spot, it will suddenly vanish. Make sure you move the page slowly so that you don't miss the experience. You might have to try this several times to get the desired effect. As you move the page back and forth, you will notice that the dot vanishes only when the page is a specific distance away from your face. Moving the page too close or too far away from your face will move the dot out of your blind spot, revealing it to the visual cells around the blind spot. For a demonstration of the blind spot in both eyes see Pessoa et al. (1998, p. 725).

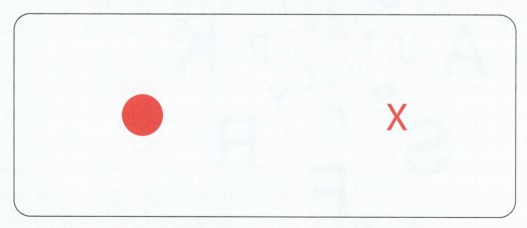

FIGURE 13.5 | A demonstration of the blind spot

there is a complete absence of photoreceptors: since the light that falls on this region is not processed, you are essentially blind to stimuli presented in the corresponding area of your visual field. "But," you say, "I don't experience an empty hole in my field of view!" Although the blind spot is there, you typically do not experience it because your brain compensates for the missing information with the information it receives both from the receptors surrounding the blind spot and from the other eye; this process is called *filling-in*. Pessoa, Thompson, and Noë (1998, p. 723) define filling-in as the subjective experience that "something is present in a particular region of visual space when it is actually absent from that region, but present in the surrounding area." Pessoa et al. (1998) call this process **perceptual completion**.

The Grand Illusion: Summary

Demonstrations of change blindness, the nature of the eye and the primary visual system, saccadic and blink suppression and the filling-in phenomenon all indicate that much of our conscious subjective visual experience is a construction. The evidence suggests that our conscious experience of a clear, detailed view is composed of (at most) a couple of the objects in our visual field at any one time. Thus the idea that we experience a richly detailed world of perceptual objects seems to be a grand illusion. This illusion is created in part by the way information travels back and forth between the higher and lower visual areas, via feedforward and feedback pathways: our conscious visual experience of the world is constructed through successive iterations, each building on the previous one. What allows us to function effectively in the world, even though we see only one or two objects at a time, is the fact that we have built-in mechanisms (such as rapid detection of motion signals) that direct our attention to important objects and events around us (see Chapter 4).

Meta-Consciousness

Having discussed unconscious processes and consciousness, we now turn to Schooler's (2002) third level of consciousness: meta-consciousness. In *The Oxford Companion to Consciousness*, Schooler and Smallwood (2009, p. 439) define **meta-consciousness** or meta-awareness as "the metacognitive process of consciously appraising and thereby explicitly re-representing the current contents of thought." In other words, meta-consciousness comes into play when "consciousness is turned on itself" (Schooler and Smallwood, 2009, p. 439) and examines its own contents. Here we will discuss two phenomena that illustrate how meta-consciousness differs from consciousness: mind-wandering and lucid dreaming.

Mind-Wandering

As an example of the distinction between consciousness and meta-consciousness, Schooler (2002) points to the experience of **mind-wandering** (or "zoning out") while reading. Undoubtedly, you have found this happening to you (perhaps even while reading parts of this textbook): you realized that your thoughts had wandered to some entirely unrelated topic, and couldn't remember much of what you'd "read" during that time. According to Schooler,

perceptual completion (filling-in)
The incorrect impression that a stimulus occupies a section of the visual scene when in fact it occupies only the region around it.

meta-consciousness
Conscious awareness of what is occurring in one's consciousness.

mind-wandering
The state in which your thoughts wander from a particular task without your realizing that this has occurred; also referred to as zoning out.

Reichle, and Halpern (2004, p. 203), the moment when you realize that you have "zoned out" is a moment of meta-consciousness:

> The disassociation between the experience of zoning out while reading and the awareness that one has been zoning out illustrates the value of distinguishing between experiential consciousness, corresponding to the contents of experience, and what we alternatively refer to as "metaconsciousness" or "meta-awareness" . . . corresponding to one's explicit awareness of the contents of consciousness.

Schooler et al. (2004) assessed participants' tendencies to mind-wander while they read a long passage from a book on a computer screen. Episodes of mind-wandering were indexed in two ways. First, participants were instructed to report whenever they noticed that their mind had wandered from the reading material to task-unrelated matters. Episodes detected using this **self-caught method** (see also Smallwood & Schooler, 2006) reflected instances in which the meta-consciousness spontaneously became engaged and recognized that the participant's mind had wandered. In addition, the researchers used an intermittent probe, asking participants whether they had been mind-wandering just the probe was presented. This **probe-caught method** (see also Smallwood & Schooler, 2006), in which participants were reminded to become meta-conscious, is an example of a technique called **experience sampling**, which involves asking people to introspect and report on their conscious experiences at specific moments in time.

If participants were always meta-conscious—always aware of the contents of their consciousness—they would presumably self-catch all their mind-wandering episodes, leaving none to be detected by the probe-caught method. However, this is not what Schooler and his colleagues found. Even though participants were consciously trying to monitor their mental activity, the probes still caught a substantial number of mind-wandering episodes. This indicated that meta-consciousness was suspended at times, allowing consciousness to drift to task-unrelated thoughts without the participants' noticing it. These lapses of meta-consciousness, or **temporal dissociations** between meta-consciousness and consciousness (Schooler, 2002, p. 340; Schooler & Smallwood, 2009, p. 440), occur quite frequently. It's even possible that they are the norm and meta-consciousness is the exception, engaged only intermittently throughout our conscious lives. At this point, the triggers that engage meta-consciousness remain largely unknown.

Lucid Dreaming

Some consciousness researchers focus exclusively on conscious states during the waking hours (e.g., Koch, 2004, pp. 11–12), but it seems reasonable to include dreaming in the category of conscious states as well. After all, some dreams are so vivid that, even after waking, their contents can be mistaken for events that actually took place in waking life.

As we sleep, we typically cycle through several distinct stages. Dreams occur during the stage known as **rapid eye movement (REM) sleep**. This stage is also characterized by increased activity in the cerebral cortex (relative to the other stages of sleep) and inhibition of motor activity except in the eyes, which move rapidly from side to side. You can tell when a sleeper is in the REM stage by observing the eyes: even with the eyelids closed, the cornea

self-caught method

A technique used to catch episodes of mind-wandering in which participants are asked to monitor their consciousness and report anytime their mind has wandered.

probe-caught method

A technique used to catch episodes of mind-wandering by presenting participants with a probe asking them whether they were mind-wandering just before the probe was presented.

experience sampling

The general technique of asking people to comment on the contents of their consciousness at specific moments.

temporal dissociation

The temporary disengagement of meta-consciousness, resulting in lack of awareness of the contents of consciousness.

rapid eye movement (REM) sleep

The stage characterized by dreaming, increased brain activity relative to other stages of sleep, and the inhibition of motor activity except in the eyes, which move rapidly back and forth.

(the surface on which contact lenses are placed) makes a distinct bulge, which can be seen moving back and forth.

During regular dreams, we are typically conscious only of the events we are "living out" in the dream: we aren't aware that we are dreaming. In other words, dreams usually unfold without the engagement of meta-consciousness. However, a state known as lucid dreaming is characterized by a distinct awareness that one is experiencing a dream (Gackenbach, 1991; Kahan & LaBerge, 1994; Voss, Holzmann, Tuin & Hobson, 2009). That is, lucid dreaming is dreaming with meta-consciousness, or what some researchers call "reflective awareness" (e.g., Kahan & LaBerge, 1994). In a lucid dream state, we are not only aware that we are dreaming, but can actually guide how the dream unfolds. What's more, we can learn to be better at lucid dreaming (Voss et al., 2009).

To study lucid dreaming, researchers can increase the likelihood that participants will experience lucid dreams by instructing them before they go to sleep to monitor their consciousness for unusual events and use those events as triggers to become lucid. To signal to the researcher that they are lucid, participants are trained to make a sequence of predetermined eye movements: for instance, to move their eyes to the left, then to the right, then to the left again, and finally back to centre, and to repeat this pattern after a short pause. (Since other types of movement will be inhibited during REM sleep, the eyes will be the only body parts that the lucid dreamer can move.) To monitor eye movements, researchers place electrodes near the eye to generate an electrooculogram (EOG): a record of changes in the electrical potentials generated by eye movements, created by placing electrodes near the eyes.

Electrical potentials from the movement of the eyes (EOG) over time are shown in Figure 13.6. The three panels show data from a person who is awake with eyes closed (WEC), in a state of lucid dreaming (lucid) and during non-lucid REM sleep (Voss et al., 2009). The figure also shows data collected from an electromyogram (EMG), which records muscle activity of the body. In this case, the EMG was recorded by placing an electrode on the chin (Voss et al., 2009).

The top panel of the figure shows the EOG and EMG records of a participant who is awake with eyes closed and voluntarily moving to the left, to the right, back to the left, then to centre, and repeating this sequence once. You can tell the participant is awake because of the large amount of muscle activity revealed by the EMG record shown below the EOG record. The next panel shows the EOG and EMG records of the same participant in a lucid dreaming state, following the instruction to move the eyes back and forth voluntarily. Although this EOG record strongly resembles the waking EOG record, we know that the participant is actually in REM sleep because the EMG record shows very limited muscle activity. Finally, the last panel shows EOG and EMG activity associated with REM sleep and presumably regular non-lucid dreaming. Notice that in a regular non-lucid REM state, the EOG shows evidence of the eye movement that is the characteristic of REM sleep, but none of the clear and systematic eye movement control associated with lucid and awake states. As expected, the EMG record in this instance shows almost no muscle activity.

Based on findings such as this, as well as other measurements of brain activity, Voss et al. (2009) conclude that lucid dreaming is a "hybrid" state in which the engagement of meta-consciousness allows the dreamer to become aware that the current state of consciousness includes a dream. As Voss et al. put it (2009, p. 1197), "In lucid dreaming, self-reflection arises . . . so that the dreamer recognizes that he is not awake but asleep." The difference

lucid dreaming
A dream state in which we are aware that we are dreaming.

electrooculogram (EOG)
A record of the changes in electrical potentials generated by the movements of the eye.

electromyogram (EMG)
A record of the changes in muscle activity of the body.

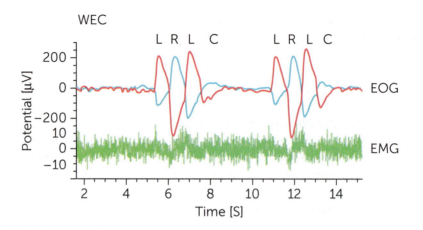

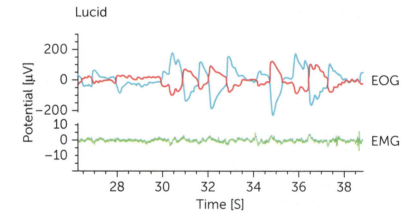

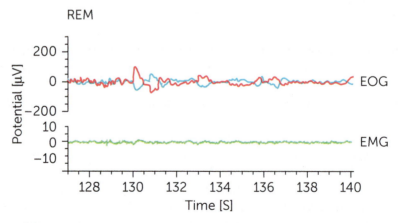

FIGURE 13.6 | Changes in electrical potentials over time associated with eye movements (EOG) and muscle movements (EMG) from an individual who is (from top) awake with eyes closed (WEC); in a state of lucid dreaming; and in non-lucid rapid eye movement sleep (REM)

From Voss, U., Holzmann, R., Tuin, I., & Hobson, J.A. (2009), Lucid dreaming: A state of consciousness with features of both waking and non-lucid dreaming, *SLEEP, 32*, 1191–1200. Figure 1, p. 1193.

between regular and lucid dreaming is another interesting example of the distinction between consciousness and meta-consciousness.

Consciousness and the Brain

Many cognitive neuroscientists believe that consciousness is a product of brain activity. For instance, Christof Koch (2004, p. 10) holds that "consciousness emerges from the neuronal features of the brain." Thus a widespread corollary assumption is that consciousness can be understood and explained by understanding the neural activity that gives rise to it.

While this assumption seems straightforward and reasonable, understanding the relationship between consciousness and the brain might be more challenging than it initially appears. In a seminal contribution to the study of consciousness, the philosopher David Chalmers (1995) distinguished two types of problems regarding the relationship between consciousness and the brain: easy and hard. According to Chalmers (1995), the easy problems of consciousness are those that can be answered using the standard methods of cognitive neuroscience: for example, which brain areas are active when one is conscious of a visual object. By contrast, the hard problems of consciousness involve understanding the specific subjective qualities of an individual's consciousness. For example:

> Why is it that when our cognitive systems engage in visual and auditory information-processing, we have visual or auditory experience: the quality of deep blue, the sensation of middle C? How can we explain why there is something it is like to entertain a mental image, or to experience an emotion? It is widely agreed that experience arises from a physical basis, but we have no good explanation of why and how it so arises. Why should physical processing give rise to a rich inner life at all? It seems objectively unreasonable that it should, and yet it does (1995, p. 201).

At present, cognitive neuroscience does not have any solid solutions to the hard problems of consciousness; however, it has made considerable headway in understanding the easy problems. In this section we will focus on findings pertaining to the easy problems, exploring what we know about the neural correlates of consciousness. Our specific focus will be on visual consciousness, as this continues to be the most widely studied aspect of consciousness (see Koch, 2004, and Rees, Kreiman & Koch, 2002 for reviews).

You may recall from Chapter 3 that visual object recognition involves the activation of neurons in the inferior temporal lobe of the brain (see Figure 3.2). Thus it might not surprise you to learn that the neurons in the inferior temporal lobe are also involved in visual consciousness. A particularly compelling demonstration of this involvement was reported by Tong, Nakayama, Vaughan and Kanwisher (1998), who used a stimulus presentation technique known as binocular rivalry. An example of a visual stimulus used in their binocular rivalry study is shown at the top of Figure 13.7. As you can see, the stimulus is composed of two images, one superimposed on the other. Notice that one of these images is presented in red (a house) and the other in green (a face). Participants in these studies are given special glasses that selectively filter the colours associated with each image.

easy problems of consciousness
Understanding what types of conscious states relate to what types of neural activity.

hard problems of consciousness
Understanding why the brain gives rise to subjective experiences that have the specific qualities they have.

binocular rivalry
When a different image is presented to each eye, the viewer becomes conscious of only one of the images at a time.

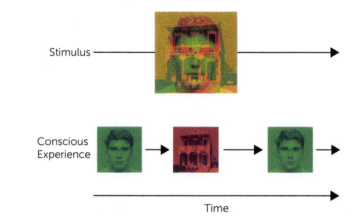

FIGURE 13.7 | **A stimulus presentation demonstrating binocular rivalry**

The initial stimulus is composed of two images in different colours, and participants wear special glasses that allow for each coloured image to be projected to only one eye. Participants are consciously aware of only one of the images at a time.

Image (modified) from Tong, F., Nakayama, K., Vaughan, J.T., & Kanwisher, N. (1998), Binocular rivalry and visual awareness in human extrastriate cortex, *Neuron, 21*, 753–759, Figure 1a, p. 754. Copyright (1998) National Academy of Sciences, USA.

CONSIDER THIS
BOX 13.3

Beyond Human Consciousness

Many cognitive neuroscientists and philosophers believe that consciousness is not exclusive to humans. For instance, Christof Koch (2004, p. 12) writes:

> It is possible that some species of animals—mammals, in particular—possess some, but not necessarily all, of the features of consciousness; that they see, hear, smell, and otherwise experience the world. Of course, each species has its own unique sensorium, matched to its ecological niche. But I assume that these animals have feelings, have subjective states.

This general assumption has led researchers to explore the neural correlates of consciousness in species other than humans, especially monkeys (e.g., Sheinberg & Logothetis, 1997).

While some scholars would be content to see consciousness restricted to a limited number of species, others cast their net much more broadly. For instance, David Chalmers (see above) currently holds that in fact everything has some form of consciousness. Troubled by the roaring failure of modern cognitive neuroscience to solve the hard problems of consciousness, Chalmers now postulates that material processes in the brain cannot explain consciousness because consciousness is a fundamental property of matter itself. In fact, he has suggested that all matter has some form of consciousness: this view is called **panpsychism**. Chalmers suggests that consciousness varies in complexity in direct proportion to the complexity of the material system with which it is associated: the human brain is a complex neural system and so it is associated with complex consciousness, whereas a rock is very simple and so has a very basic consciousness (see Oizumi, Albantakis & Tononi, 2014). You can watch Chalmers discuss his views in this widely viewed TED talk: www.ted.com/talks/david_chalmers_how_do_you_explain_consciousness?language=en

panpsychism
The view that everything has some form of consciousness.

In the example presented in Figure 13.7, the lens in front of one of the eyes would filter out red light and allow green to pass through, whereas the lens in front of the other eye would filter out green light and allow red to pass through. The end result is that the green stimulus (in this case, the face) stimulates the retina of one eye and the red stimulus (in this case, the house) stimulates the retina of the other eye.

What do people consciously see in such a situation? It turns out that they are aware of only *one* of the images presented in the two eyes at a time. As they view the stimulus, their conscious perception switches from the stimulus in one eye to the stimulus in the other eye. This oscillation is depicted in the bottom of Figure 13.7. It is as if the two different images perceived by the two eyes fight for access to consciousness, which is why researchers have used the term binocular (two eyes) rivalry (fighting for awareness) to describe this situation. Binocular rivalry is a powerful tool for studying visual consciousness because during such experiments both of the images presented to the eyes are processed by the visual system, but only one of the images makes it into consciousness at any single point in time. Another reason for its utility is that participants can reliably report when each switch in awareness occurs, making it possible for researchers to relate specific brain activity to participants' consciousness of each image.

The selection of a house and a face as the superimposed stimuli in Tong et al.'s (1998) experiment was not random. Houses and faces were selected because, as we saw in Chapter 3, there are distinct areas in the inferior temporal lobe that process places (the parahippocampal place area, or PPA) and faces (the fusiform face area, or FFA). Using fMRI, it is therefore possible to track activity in these two brain areas that correspond to participants' oscillating awareness of the house and face under conditions of binocular rivalry. The brain activations (% MR signal; higher numbers mean more brain activation) from the PPA and the FFA are shown in Figure 13.8. The left side of the figure shows how activation

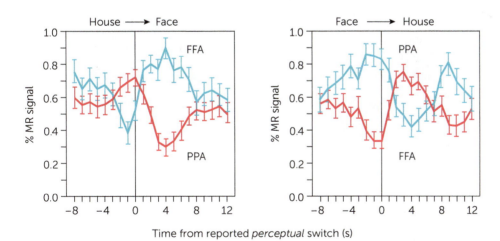

FIGURE 13.8 | **Changes in brain activation as measured by fMRI in the fusiform face area (FFA) and the parahippocampal place area (PPA) during binocular rivalry of superimposed images of a face and a house**

The left side shows how brain activation changes when a person first perceives the house and then the face, while the right side shows the reverse situation.

Image (modified) from Tong, F., Nakayama, K., Vaughan, J.T., & Kanwisher, N. (1998), Binocular rivalry and visual awareness in human extrastriate cortex, *Neuron, 21*, 753–759, Figure 4a, p. 756. Copyright (1998) National Academy of Sciences, USA.

changes when the participant is first conscious of the house and then spontaneously switches to being conscious of the face. The point at which consciousness switches between the two images is depicted as the zero point on the y-axis. Notice that as consciousness switches from the house to the face, activation in the PPA (place area) decreases, whereas activation in the FFA (face area) increases. Thus, the amounts of activation in the PPA and FFA correspond to the conscious experience of the houses and the faces, such that consciousness of an image is associated with more activation in the brain area that processes that image. A similar pattern can be seen on the right side of the figure, which shows changes in brain activation when the participant is first conscious of the face and then switches to become conscious of the house (the reverse of the previous scenario). In this case, when consciousness switches from the face to the house, activation in the PPA increases and activation in the FFA decreases. We can be confident that the difference in activations is specific to consciousness of one particular image because both images are available to and processed by the visual system: in other words, all processing other than that related to consciousness is tightly controlled across changes in conscious perception.

Other evidence that neurons in the temporal lobe are involved in conscious perception comes from studies that monitor brain activity as the contents of consciousness are varied using a technique known as **flash suppression** (e.g., Kreiman, Fried & Koch, 2002). Examples of stimuli used in a flash suppression study reported by Kreiman et al. (2002) are shown in Figure 13.9a; the conscious experiences associated with the stimuli are shown in Figure 13.9b. The left and right sides of the figures show slightly different flash suppression scenarios, so let's consider the left side first. In this scenario, the right eye is shown a picture of former US president Bill Clinton and the left eye is shown a blank screen, which results

flash suppression
When different images are presented to each eye and one of the images is replaced, the new image enters consciousness and the image presented to the other eye is suppressed from consciousness.

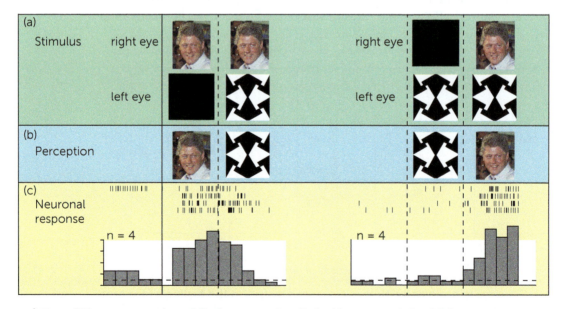

FIGURE 13.9 | **Two different scenarios of flash suppession (left side versus right side)**

The figure shows the stimuli shown to a patient (Panel a), the corresponding conscious perceptual experience (Panel b), and the corresponding response of a neuron in the temporal lobe measured on four occasions (n=4; Panel c).

Image from Kreiman, G., Fried, I., & Koch, C. (2002), Single-neuron correlates of subjective vision in the human medial temporal lobe, *Proceedings of the National Academy of Science USA*, 99, 8378–8383, Figure 1, p. 8380. Copyright (2002) National Academy of Sciences, USA.

in the conscious perception of the face of Bill Clinton; this is shown in the first column of the left side of Figures 13.9a and 13.9b. To avoid confusion, notice that in the figure the image presented to the right eye is shown *above* the image shown to the left eye, and the resulting conscious experience is shown below it (in Panel b). Shortly afterwards, the blank screen presented to the left eye is changed to a geometric pattern. The flash onset of the geometric pattern causes it to enter consciousness, suppressing the face of Bill Clinton from consciousness—hence the term "flash suppression." This is shown in the second column of the left side of Figures 13.9a and 13.9b.

Flash suppression follows the same principle as binocular rivalry: when two different images are presented to the two eyes, only one of them enters consciousness. However, flash suppression gives the experimenter more control over the switching of the contents of consciousness (in this case, from Bill Clinton to the geometric pattern) because the onset of the new image viewed by one eye (in this case, the geometric pattern in the left eye) reliably triggers the switch in consciousness. In standard studies using binocular rivalry, the switch in consciousness between the images presented to the eyes occurs spontaneously and so is under less experimental control.

Now let's consider the scenario shown on the right side of Figures 13.9a and 13.9b. The first column on the right side of the figure shows a case in which the right eye is shown a blank screen and the left eye is shown a geometric pattern, which results in the conscious perception of the geometric pattern. The second column shows how the viewer's conscious percept changes to that of Bill Clinton when the image of Bill Clinton is suddenly flashed to the right eye, suppressing the geometric shape from consciousness.

Having seen how flash suppression can change the contents of consciousness, we can now consider the neural correlates of those changes. Kreiman et al. (2002) recorded the activity of single neurons from the temporal lobes (in a specific area known as the amygdala) of patients who suffered from **epilepsy**. Epilepsy is the uncontrolled firing of neurons in the brain that can result in debilitating seizures (mental disruptions and uncontrolled muscle contractions). These patients had recording electrodes placed in their brain's temporal lobes so that doctors could detect the exact locations where the uncontrolled brain activity began at the onset of their seizures. Since the insertion of recording electrodes was medically necessary, Kreiman et al. (2002) took the opportunity to conduct a flash suppression study and record the activity of single neurons to see if any of them were selectively active during conscious awareness of a stimulus. Having implanted electrodes in the brain, the researchers showed the patients a large set of images to determine whether any of the neurons from which they were recording were activated by any of the images. The reason we have been talking about images of Bill Clinton is that a neuron adjacent to one of the electrodes implanted in one patient happened to be selectively responsive to images of him.

Figure 13.9c shows the activity of the "Clinton neuron" and how it changed as the patient's consciousness changed during the flash suppression study. The activity of the neuron, measured over four episodes (n = 4), is shown in two ways: first in the form of vertical lines, each corresponding to a firing of the neuron, and then in the form of a histogram, with higher bars depicting more activity. You can think of the x-axis (horizontal axis) of the histogram as depicting the time course of a trial in which the flash suppression stimuli were presented.

Let's look first at the scenario on the left side of the image, in which conscious perception changed from Bill Clinton to a geometric shape. The baseline activity of the neuron is shown to the left of the first vertical dashed line, showing that before the flash suppression

epilepsy
The uncontrolled overactivity of neurons in the brain that can cause mental disruptions and uncontrolled muscle contractions.

stimuli were presented, the neuron was not very active. Importantly, notice that when the person was conscious of Bill Clinton at the beginning the trial, the neuron fired vigorously and that this activity dropped off considerably once his image was suppressed from consciousness by the flash onset of the geometric pattern. Now consider the scenario on the right side of the image, in which the participant was first conscious of the geometric shape and then of Bill Clinton once his image was flashed to the right eye. Notice that in this case, the relatively low baseline activity of the neuron (shown to the left of the vertical dashed line) continued when the patient was conscious of the geometric shape, but that the neuron's activity increased greatly once Bill Clinton entered consciousness. These results compellingly suggest that the specific neuron in the patient's temporal lobe responded selectively to the conscious perception of Bill Clinton.

The foregoing studies clearly demonstrate that neurons in the temporal cortex of the brain are involved in visual consciousness of objects we perceive. But that is not the only area associated with conscious experience. In their review of the neural correlates of consciousness—which were discovered in studies using binocular rivalry and similar techniques to vary conscious experience—Rees et al. (2002) noted that the parietal and prefrontal cortices (Figure 13.10)

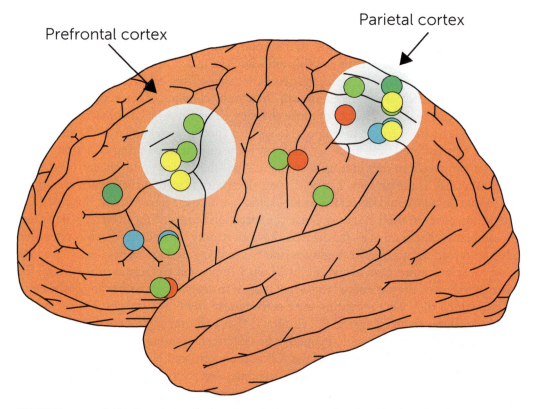

FIGURE 13.10 | Each coloured dot represents a study showing activation associated with changes in conscious experience

The fact that the dots seem to cluster in the prefrontal cortex and the parietal cortex suggests that these areas are involved in the process of transitioning between images in consciousness.

Image (modified) from Rees, G., Kreiman, G., & Koch, C. (2002), p. 268. Adapted by permission from Macmillan Publishers Ltd: *Nature Reviews Neuroscience*, 3, 261–70, copyright (2002).

Is Consciousness a Unitary Entity?

Consciousness has generally been considered a unitary entity. However, vision scientist Semir Zeki has suggested an alternative view: according to his **theory of microconsciousness**, "instead of a single, unified, visual consciousness, there are many different visual consciousnesses that are distributed in time and space" (Zeki, 2009, p. 442). In Chapter 3 we saw that different areas along the visual pathways are responsible for different aspects of visual perception. For instance, if an area known as vision area 4 (V4) is damaged, then colour perception will be compromised. Similarly, damage to areas involved in processing motion will impair conscious perception of motion. According to Zeki (2009), the various areas involved in visual perception are responsible for distinct microconsciousnesses, which combine to give us the sense of a single unified consciousness. If Zeki is correct, then one might wonder how many microconsciousnesses there are in all.

theory of microconsciousness (Zeki)
The view that each individual has "many different visual consciousnesses that are distributed over space and time."

seem to be particularly active at the moments during which conscious experience switches between stimuli in situations of binocular rivalry. This observation led them to suggest that "activity in frontal and parietal cortex might be causally associated with the generation of transitions between different percepts" (Rees et al. 2002, pp. 267–268).

Finally, we should also consider the possibility that consciousness involves not only activation in specific brain areas, but also some degree of *coordinated activity* between various brain areas (see Ward, 2003, for a review). Along these lines, there is some evidence suggesting that consciousness is associated with increased synchronous firing of neurons in multiple brain areas. When many neurons fire synchronously, they create a strong signal that can be measured by placing electrodes on the scalp and recording the data using electroencephalography (see Chapter 2). The synchronous firing of neurons produces spikes in the electroencephalogram at a (high) frequency of roughly 40 cycles per second (see Rees et al., 2002, p. 266; Ward, 2003, p. 555): a frequency known as the **gamma frequency**. The available evidence suggests that a large signal at the gamma frequency is associated with conscious experience (Ward, 2003).

gamma frequency
Spikes in the electroencephalogram that occur at roughly 40 cycles per second.

Studies like the ones discussed here have gone a long way towards improving our understanding of the relationship between consciousness and the brain. However, there are still many unknowns about the neural correlates of consciousness. Although this research addresses only what David Chalmers calls the "easy problems" of consciousness, it seems that even these problems aren't so easy after all.

Deficits of Consciousness

As we noted in Chapter 1, brain injuries can be informative for the study of human cognition. They can also contribute to our understanding of consciousness. The case study of blindsight, for instance, demonstrated that people can still act on objects that are outside their consciousness, and we have seen how the brain "fills in" the blind spots in our visual field. As remarkable as these examples are, however, they concern fairly small, circumscribed regions of vision.

By contrast, the disorder known as **visual hemispatial neglect** affects half of the individual's whole visual field. Thus someone who has suffered an injury (often a stroke) to the right parietal lobe will be unaware of the entire region of space on the left (contralateral) side. Although right spatial neglect can occur following a left hemisphere injury, left neglect is far more common, whether because the right hemisphere is more involved in spatial processing than the left, or because the language problems associated with a left-hemisphere stroke, such as aphasia (impaired speech production and/or comprehension), overshadow any problems associated with right-sided spatial attention.

Whatever the reason for the unequal distribution of left and right spatial neglect, the consequences of this disorder are profoundly interesting. For instance, patients with spatial neglect may not be conscious of anything in their contralesional visual field: thus they may shave or apply makeup to only half their face, or eat only half the food on their plate. When asked to draw a clock face, they may cram all the numerals onto one side of the circle, or simply enter six numerals and then report that the task is complete (see Figure 13.11).

Finally, spatial neglect can extend beyond vision: for example, a patient may fail to detect touches to the half of the body on the neglected side. Interestingly, when a neglected part of the body (say, the left hand) is moved into the intact area (i.e., to the right), it is no longer neglected. That said, neglect is not always relative to the environmental reference frame (the overall environment). It can also be specific to an object: thus a patient with left neglect may be unable to place numbers on a clock face correctly even when the entire face is moved into the preserved field.

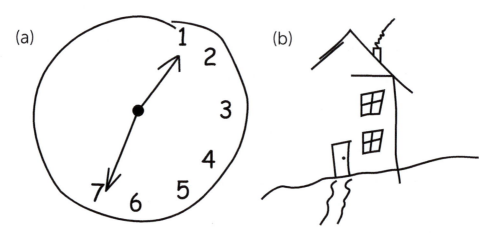

FIGURE 13.11 | A clock and a house drawn by an individual with visual hemi-neglect

All the numbers on the left side of the clock are missing (a), as is much of the left side of the house (b).

From Abdullaev, Y., & Posner, M.I. (2005), How the brain recovers following damage, *Nature Neuroscience 8*, 1424–25, Figure 1. Reprinted by permission from Macmillan Publishers.

Split-Brains and Consciousness

We first encountered split-brain patients in Chapter 2. As you may recall, their condition is a consequence of surgery to control severe epilepsy by severing the corpus callosum (the major fibre tract connecting the left and right hemispheres) in the hope of isolating the seizures to a single hemisphere. Now, while language skills are usually isolated to a single hemisphere, typically the left, in a small percentage of the population those skills exist in both hemispheres, and a small fraction of these individuals have had their hemispheres surgically disconnected. When these individuals are tested, however, remarkable behaviours can emerge. For instance, consider the following case reported by Gazzaniga, Nass, Reeves, and Roberts (1984). A split-brain patient named JW is seated before a computer screen, when one word ("ten") is flashed to one hemisphere and another word ("clock") is flashed simultaneously to the other hemisphere. When JW is asked was he saw, he says "ten" because his left hemisphere, but not the right hemisphere, controls speech. Asked if he saw anything else, he says "No, just 'ten.'" However, much later these words are flashed again to JW, and this time he is asked to draw what he saw using his left hand (right hemisphere). He picks up a pen and draws a picture of a clock, revealing that the right hemisphere saw and understood that it had been presented with a clock. Most remarkably, he proceeds to draw hands on the face, setting it to 10 o'clock!

For decades researchers have interpreted findings of this type as evidence that each hemisphere can be conscious of the meaning of words presented to the other hemisphere (e.g., Seymour, Reuter-Lorenz, & Gazzaniga, 1994). However, that does not appear to be the case. When split-brain patients are given word-pairs like "rain-bow" or "fire-arm" or "sky-scraper," with one half of each pair going to one hemisphere and the other going to the other hemisphere, they never draw a rainbow, or a gun, or a tall building: instead, they draw a literal combination of the two words: for instance, a scraper against the sky (see Figure 13.12). These findings indicate that neither hemisphere is conscious of the meaning of the word presented to the other hemisphere. Rather, each hemisphere is drawing an image of its word and integrating them on the same piece of paper. The only thing that is shared is control of the drawing hand.

FIGURE 13.12 | A scraper against the sky

From Kingstone, A., & Gazzaniga, M.S. (1995), Figure 2, p. 325. Copyright © 1995 by the American Psychological Association. Reproduced with permission. The use of APA information does not imply endorsement by APA.

Phantom Limbs and Consciousness

A **phantom limb** occurs when a body part, such as an arm or a leg, is suddenly lost (e.g., through amputation). The person *feels* that the missing body part is "still there" even though he knows that it is not (Simmel, 1956). "Many patients awake from an anaesthetic after an amputation feeling certain that the operation has not been performed. They feel the lost limb so vividly that only when they reach out to touch it, or peer beneath the bed sheets to see it, do they realize that it has been cut off" (Katz, 1993, p. 336). The phantom limb is a vivid but in a sense false memory (a concept that we discussed in Chapter 6). The phantom develops immediately after an amputation in approximately 75 per cent of patients, and incidence rises to 85 per cent eight days after such surgery (Katz, 1993; Ramachandran & Hirstein, 1998). There is often intense pain associated with the phantom limb; in fact, "more than 70 per cent of amputees continue to experience phantom limb pain of considerable intensity as long as 25 years after amputation" (Katz, 1993, p. 336). Can this acute awareness of pain in a limb that no longer exists tell us anything about consciousness?

Phantom limbs occur as a consequence of the way the **body schema** represents the parts of our bodies and their relationships. If the loss of a body part, such as a finger, occurs slowly, as it does in people with leprosy, then there is much less likelihood of experiencing a phantom (Simmel, 1956; Ramachandran & Hirstein, 1998, p. 1625); perhaps it's easier for the schema to adjust when the change is gradual. In any event, the schema does change, even in cases of sudden and devastating loss.

To understand how the schema changes, however, we must first look at how the various parts of the body are represented in the sensory cortex under normal conditions. The image in Figure 13.13 is a version of the **Penfield homunculus**. Named after Wilder Penfield, the neuroscientist who developed the concept, the "homunculus" is a map of the sensory cortex that shows where the various parts of the body are represented. The area of each body part in the map is proportional to the area of the cortex that represents it. Notice that the hands are represented next to the face.

The significance of this location can be seen in the case of a man who developed a phantom limb after his arm was amputated just above the left elbow (Ramachandran, 2004, p. 10; Ramachandran, 1993; Ramachandran, Rogers-Ramachandran, & Cobb, 1995). Amazingly, when stimulated with a cotton swab on the surface of his face, he felt as if parts of his missing hand were being stimulated. There have been several reports of similar cases. Why does this happen? Recall that the face is next to the hand in the Penfield homunculus. Ramachandran (2004, p. 13) explains the phenomenon as follows:

When an arm is amputated, no signals are received by the part of the brain's cortex corresponding to the hand. It becomes hungry for sensory input and the

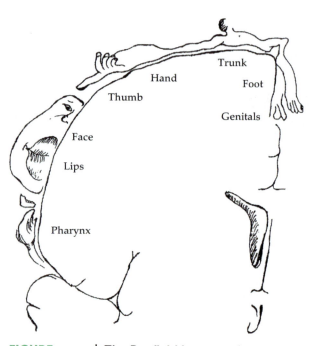

FIGURE 13.13 | The Penfield homunculus

sensory input from the facial skin now invades the adjacent vacated territory corresponding to the missing hand.

Brain-imaging techniques have supported this hypothesis, showing that for the sort of patient just described, "input from the face and upper arm could now activate the hand area" of the brain (Ramachandran & Hirstein, 1998, p. 1616). The body schema is not fixed, but shows considerable plasticity (i.e., flexibility). This flexibility is well illustrated by an ingenious technique used to ameliorate phantom pain. Sometimes a patient feels as if the phantom hand is clenching, with the fingernails digging painfully into the skin. If the person could unclench the phantom hand, perhaps the pain would go away. Now look at Figure 13.14. This apparatus allows the patient to see the mirror image of the remaining hand in such a way that the missing hand appears to have returned. If the patient unclenches the real hand, the phantom hand will feel as if it too is unclenching; in fact, the pain goes away in many patients (Jackson & Simpson, 2004). Nothing could better demonstrate the dynamic way in which the body schema, and schemata generally, are organized and reorganized (Ramachandran & Hirstein, 1998, p. 1622).

You can experience an analog of a phantom limb by setting up a variant of the procedure illustrated in Figure 13.14. You will need a plastic hand or a glove. Put your left hand in your lap, and your right hand flat on a table. Your right hand must be hidden from your view by some sort of screen (e.g., a pile of books). Then put the fake hand on the table in front of you, as shown in Figure 13.14. Have a confederate "repeatedly tap and stroke your concealed right hand in a random sequence. Tap, tap, tap, stroke, stroke, tap, stroke, stroke. At the same time, while you watch, he must also tap and stroke the visible dummy in perfect synchrony" (Ramachandran & Rogers-Ramachandran, 2005). After a while, you will feel as if *you* are being touched on the dummy hand.

plasticity
Flexibility. As used here it refers to the notion that brain areas typically used for one function can be recruited and used for other purposes.

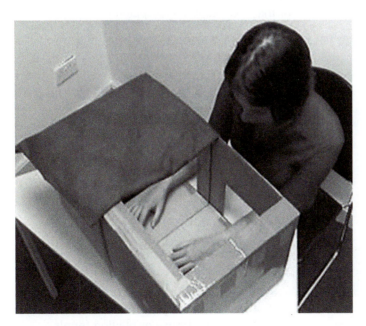

FIGURE 13.14 | **The phantom limb mirror box**

Brain Imaging Reveals Consciousness in a Patient Diagnosed as Being in a Vegetative State

In the disorders of consciousness discussed so far—spatial neglect, split-brain, phantom limb—consciousness has been equated with our ability to communicate that we are self-aware through a behavioural response. But what if the ability to speak, mouth a word, smile, move a hand, or just blink one's eyes was absent? If you were conscious but unable to communicate this fact to others, then by definition you would not be considered conscious. In short, if the opportunity to self-report awareness is lost, it is impossible to determine if consciousness exists. Until now, patients with "locked-in syndrome" following acute brain injury or disease have been considered to be in a vegetative state in that they show "no evidence of awareness of environment or self." However, this positive diagnosis (vegetative state) is dependent on a negative finding (no signs of consciousness) and therefore is vulnerable to a false-negative result (what scientists call a Type II error).

Professor Adrian Owen, a researcher formerly at Cambridge University in the UK, now at the University of Western Ontario, has recently used some of the neuroimaging techniques discussed in Chapter 2 to solve this problem. Owen reasoned that if a measurable brain response could be used as a proxy for a motor response, then locked-in patients would have the opportunity to communicate to others that they were conscious. In his original paper, published in *Science* (Owen et al., 2006), he studied a 23-year-old woman, Sharleen, who had suffered a severe brain injury in a traffic accident. Because she was unresponsive to outside stimulation and did not exhibit any spontaneous intentional behaviours, Sharleen was diagnosed as being in a vegetative state. Using fMRI, however, Owen and his team asked Sharleen to engage in two mental imagery tasks: (1) walking around rooms in her home, and (2) playing tennis. Each task produced a classic pattern of brain activity that was indistinguishable from that produced by conscious control subjects. Imagining walking around her house yielded brain activations in the navigation network (the parahippocampal gyrus and parietal cortex), and imagining playing tennis resulted in activations in brain regions that control motor responses (supplementary motor areas). Owen et al.

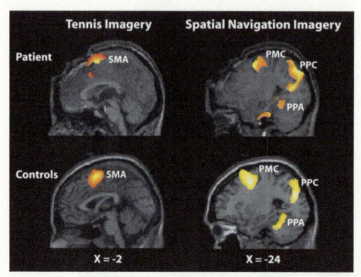

FIGURE 13.15 | Brain imaging results demonstrated similar activity patterns between Sharleen and conscious controls when instructed to imagine walking around the house or playing tennis

From Owen, A. M., Coleman, M.R., Boly, M., Davis, M.H., Laurey, S., & Pickard, J.D. (2006), Detecting awareness in the vegetative state, *Science, 313*, 1402.

concluded that Sharleen had made a "decision to coop-erate" that "represent[ed] a clear act of intention" to con-sciously imagine playing tennis and exploring a house. In short, though she met the clinical criteria for a vegetative state diagnosis, she was in fact conscious. It now ap-pears that approximately 40 per cent of patients with similar conditions are misdiagnosed. Vital research is now underway in this exciting new area of investigation.

Summary

In this chapter we have tackled the difficult and important question of what consciousness is. Some researchers define consciousness only in operational terms, as the ability to com-municate verbally what was experienced or presented. However, this definition fails to ac-count for other levels of non-conscious and unconscious perception, as seen in phenomena such as blindsight and subliminal perception.

Perhaps one of the greatest illusions in cognitive psychology is that of conscious percep-tion. Since change blindness research has robustly demonstrated that we are often unaware even of large changes in our environment, it now seems that our perception of the world is nowhere near as clear and detailed as we tend to think. Meta-consciousness is conscious awareness of our own consciousness. One example that most of us are familiar with is the experience of suddenly realizing that we have been mind-wandering. Research has suggested that participants often fail to notice that they have zoned out in this way. In fact, this kind of temporal dissociation may be the norm. Another form of meta-consciousness comes into play during lucid dreaming: that is, when you are aware of your dreams while you are having them.

Finally, we turned to the relationship between consciousness and the brain, beginning with a review of some studies exploring the neural correlates of visual consciousness and concluding with a look at some deficits of consciousness that are associated with damage to specific areas of the brain. Individuals with hemispatial neglect fail to report the presence of items in the visual space that is contralateral to their brain injury, even when they do not have any sensory deficits. Studies of split-brain have made invaluable contributions to our understanding of human consciousness. Nevertheless, a great many questions remain to be answered in this area, let alone in the far broader area of interest to David Chalmers—the philosopher who has suggested that all matter has some form of consciousness.

CASE STUDY

Case Study Wrap-Up

We began this chapter with the story of DB, who had undergone a surgery that left him with a blind area in his lower visual field. Even though he was not consciously aware of stimuli presented to his blind field, he was sur-prisingly accurate when questioned about the proper-ties of those objects. This suggests that blindsight could be considered a form of subliminal perception—a form of non-conscious perception in which the stimulus is presented so quickly or faintly that the observer is un-aware of it. The fact that the stimulus nevertheless af-fects the individual's behaviour indicates that it must have been perceived to some degree.

In the Know: Review Questions

1. What brain areas are specifically involved in visual consciousness?
2. Describe the anoetic, noetic, and autonoetic levels of consciousness. How do they relate to different memory systems?
3. Differentiate between the "easy" and the "hard" problems of consciousness.
4. What are the similarities and differences between binocular rivalry and flash suppression?
5. Explain subliminal perception and describe how backward masking and stimulus onset asynchronies are used in empirical tests of subliminal perception.

Key Concepts

anoetic consciousness

autonoetic consciousness

backward masking

binocular rivalry

blindsight

blind spot

body schema

change blindness

chronesthesia

conscious, non-conscious, and meta-conscious

direct vs indirect measures

dissociation paradigm

easy and hard problems of consciousness

ecologically valid

electromyogram (EMG)

electrooculogram (EOG)

encoding

epilepsy

experience sampling

flash suppression

gamma frequency

grand illusion of conscious perception

implicit perception

limen

lucid dreaming

meta-conscious

mind-wandering

noetic consciousness

objective and subjective thresholds

panpsychism

Penfield homunculus

perceptual completion (filling-in)

phantom limb

plasticity

prefrontal leucotomy

probe-caught method

process dissociation procedure

rapid eye movement (REM) sleep

retinal blur

saccadic and blink suppression

self-caught method

subliminal perception

temporal dissociation

theory of microconsciousness (Zeki)

visual hemispatial neglect

Links to Other Chapters

memory and consciousness
Chapter 3 (visual perception)
Chapter 5 (episodic, semantic and procedural memory)

the grand illusion of visual perception
Chapter 4 (attention)

deficits in consciousness
Chapter 2 (brain injuries)

split-brain patients
Chapter 2 (methodologies in cognitive science)

Further Reading

Christof Koch is one of the leading figures into the scientific study of consciousness. For a very thorough and relatively up-to-date review of the neuroscientific understandings of consciousness, see Koch (2004).

An interesting synthesis between the neural correlates to consciousness and philosophical understandings of consciousness is provided in Block (2005).

The *Oxford Companion to Consciousness* (edited by T. Bayne, A. Cleeremans and P. Wilkens) is a particularly useful resource for those interested in the scientific study of consciousness.

Two journals that have many useful papers on consciousness are *Consciousness and Cognition*, and *The Journal of Consciousness Studies*.

So-called subliminal perception has great commercial potential, as Kihlstrom (1987) observes. One way of exploiting that potential has been through the marketing of self-help audiotapes designed to improve memory or self-esteem by means of subliminal messages. Greenwald, Spangenberg, Pratkanis, and Eskenazi (1991) devised a clever study to determine the actual effects of such products. They found that participants believed the labels (e.g., "improves memory") on the tapes they were given, even when they had been deliberately mislabelled. After five weeks of listening to them, all participants—including those who had actually received self-esteem tapes—believed that their memories had improved; however, tests showed no change whatsoever in their performance. Studies such as this suggest that we should be skeptical about the claims made by manufacturers of such aids. See also Moore (1995).

Bayne, T., A. Cleeremans, & P. Wilken (Eds.). The Oxford companion to consciousness. Oxford, UK: Oxford University Press.

Block, N. (2005). Two neural correlates of consciousness. *Trends in Cognitive Sciences, 9*, 46–52.

Greenwald, A.G., Spangenberg, E.R., Pratkanis, A.R., & Eskanazi, J. (1991). Double-blind tests of subliminal self-help audiotapes. *Psychological Science, 2*, 119–122.

Kihlstrom, J.F. (1987). The cognitive unconscious. *Science, 237*, 1335–1552.

Koch, C. (2004). *The quest for consciousness.* New York.

Moore, T.E. (1995). Subliminal self-help audiotapes: An empirical test of auditory consequences. *Canadian Journal of Behavioural Science, 27*, 9–20.

Glossary

absolute frame of reference Spatial relationships are described in terms of an invariant set of coordinates.

abstraction The hypothesis that we tend to remember only the gist, not the specifics, of what we experience.

achromatopsia A visual deficit characterized by inability to perceive colour because of damage to the area of the brain that processes colour information.

action slips The kind of behavioural errors that often occur in everyday life.

adjustment and anchoring People's judgments of magnitude are biased (i.e., adjusted) by the initial value to which they are exposed (i.e., the anchor).

affordances The potential functions or uses of stimuli (i.e., objects and events) in the real world.

akinetopsia (motion blindness) An inability to perceive the motion of objects.

algorithm An unambiguous solution procedure (e.g., the rules governing long division).

alternate uses test (Barron) A test that asks people to list uncommon uses for common objects.

ambient optical array (AOA) All the visual information that is present at a particular point of view.

analog form of representation hypothesis The hypothesis that a mental image embodies the essential relationships of the thing it represents.

analysis of the situation Determining what functions the objects in the situation have and how they can be used to solve the problem.

analytical intelligence The ability to solve relatively straightforward problems; considered to be general intelligence.

anoetic, noetic, and autonoetic Three levels of consciousness corresponding to the procedural, semantic, and episodic memory systems.

anterior cingulate cortex (ACC) An area of the brain that may detect conflicting response tendencies of the sort that the Stroop task elicits.

apoptosis Programmed pruning of neurons.

apparent-distance theory An explanation for the moon illusion based on the idea that the perceived size of the moon depends on the assumptions the visual system makes about the distance of the moon from the observer.

articulation The production of a language's sounds.

artificial intelligence The "intelligence" of computer programs designed to solve problems in ways that resemble human approaches to problem-solving.

associative deficit hypothesis The hypothesis that older adults have a deficiency in creating and retrieving links between single units of information.

associative hierarchy The idea that the associations used for problem-solving are arranged in a hierarchy, and that creative people not only have more associations than most, but have them arranged in "flatter" hierarchies: thus they are more likely than most to recognize alternative possibilities.

atomistic Focusing on the components of objects.

attention capture The diversion of attention by a stimulus so powerful that it compels us to notice it even when our attention is focused on something else.

attentional blink (AB) Failure to notice the second of two stimuli presented within 550 milliseconds of each other.

auditory imagery The experience of sound in your mind that is not caused by stimulation of the receptive cells in your ears.

autobiographical memories Episodic memories of events recalled in terms of the time in our life when they occurred.

autobiographically consequential experiences (ACEs) Pivotal experiences in a person's life, typically occurring between the ages of 18 and 35.

availability The ease with which something can be brought to mind.

backward masking Presenting a stimulus, called the target, to the participant and then covering, or masking, the target with another stimulus.

BACON A computer program that has been able to "discover" several well-known scientific laws.

basic colour terms hypothesis (Berlin–Kay order) The hypothesis that there is an invariant sequence regulating the emergence of colour terms in any language.

bias A predisposition to see a particular type of situation in a particular way.

binocular rivalry When a different image is presented to each eye, the viewer becomes conscious of only one of the images at a time.

bit Short for "binary digit"; the most basic unit of information. Every event that occurs in a situation with two equally likely outcomes provides one "bit" of information.

blind spot A region in the eye that does not contain any photoreceptors; therefore the visual system cannot process visual stimuli that fall in that region.

blind variation (Campbell) The generation of alternative problem solutions without foresight, and the retention of those that work in a particular context.

blindsight A condition in which patients with damage to the primary visual cortex are able to make accurate judgments about objects presented to their blind area even though they report no conscious experience of the objects and believe they are only guessing.

blink suppression The halting of visual processing during an eye blink.

body schema The individual's schematic representation of his or her body.

bottom-up influences The feedforward influence of the external environment on the resulting perceptual experience.

Broca's aphasia A deficit in the ability to produce speech as a result of damage to Broca's area.

Broca's area The area of the brain's left hemisphere that is responsible for how words are spoken.

Brown–Peterson task An experimental paradigm in which subjects are given a set of items and then a number. Subjects immediately begin counting backward by threes from the number and, after a specific interval, are asked to recall the original items.

butcher-on-the-bus phenomenon The feeling of knowing a person without being able to remember the circumstances of any previous meeting or anything else about him or her.

capacity model The hypothesis that attention is like a power supply that can support only a limited amount of attentional activity.

catch trials Trials of a detection task in which a target is not presented.

categorical distance The number of units traversed during mental scanning: for instance, landmarks on an island map, rooms in a building, or counties in a state.

category-specific deficits Selective deficits in knowledge, resulting from brain damage.

central bottleneck The hypothesis that there is only one path along which information can travel, and it is so narrow that the most it can handle at any one time is the information relevant to one task.

central cueing paradigm An experimental method in which a central cue (e.g., arrow) points to a location in which a target might subsequently appear.

central executive The component of working memory that coordinates information from the three subsystems.

chance permutations Different combinations of mental elements produced according to no set rule.

change blindness Failure to consciously detect an obvious change in a scene.

channel capacity The maximum amount of information that can be transmitted by an information-processing device.

childhood amnesia The general inability to retrieve episodic memories from before the age of about 3.

chromesthesia Coloured hearing.

chronesthesia Our subjective sense of time.

chunk decomposition An aspect of representational change theory: parts of the problem that are recognized as belonging together are separated into "chunks" and thought about independently.

chunking A strategy used to increase the capacity of STM by arranging elements in groups (chunks) that can be more easily remembered.

cocktail party phenomenon The ability to attend to one conversation when many other conversations are going on around you.

code model of communication A model of communication based on the information-processing theory.

cognitive dedifferentiation Fusion of perceptual processes that typically function independently.

cognitive demon A feature detector in the pandemonium model that decides whether the stimulus matches its pattern.

cognitive ethology A new research approach that links real-world observations with laboratory-based studies.

cognitive history of science The study of historically important scientific discoveries in a framework provided by cognitive science.

cognitive map Information from the environment that is "worked over and elaborated . . . into a tentative, cognitive-like map . . . indicating routes and paths and environmental relationships" (Tolman).

cognitive unconscious hypothesis The hypothesis that implicit learning represents an evolutionarily primitive form of unconscious cognition.

commission error Failure to withhold a response to the infrequent digit in the SART.

commitment heuristic A strategy in which we commit ourselves to the belief that something is true when it is only likely to be true.

competence vs performance We may have an internalized system of rules that constitutes a basic linguistic competence, but this competence may not always be reflected in our actual use of the language (performance).

concealing function hypothesis The hypothesis that language is a kind of code, and that the parameters set for one language serve to conceal its meanings from the speakers of another language.

conceptual modules Modules responsible for domain-specific knowledge.

concreteness The degree to which a word refers to something that can be experienced by the senses (i.e., heard, felt, smelled, or tasted).

concurrent The synesthetic response itself.

conditional reasoning Reasoning that uses conditional ("if . . . then") statements.

confirmation bias The tendency to seek confirmatory evidence for a hypothesis.

connectionism A theory that focuses on the way cognitive processes work at the physiological/neurological (as opposed to information-processing) level. It holds that the brain consists of an enormous number of interconnected neurons and attempts to model cognition as an emergent process of networks of simple units (e.g., neurons) communicating with one another.

conscious The basic level of awareness.

conservative focusing A concept formation strategy of actively formulating hypotheses and selecting instances to see if your hypotheses are correct by focusing on one attribute at a time and by selecting instances that vary only in that attribute.

consolidation theory The classic theory that memory traces of an event are not fully formed immediately after that event, but take some time to consolidate.

consolidation The process through which memory traces are stabilized to form long-term memories. See Chapter 6 for a full discussion.

constraint relaxation An aspect of representational change theory: the removal of assumptions that are blocking problem solution.

context effects The change in perception of a visual component of a scene based on the surrounding information in the scene and the observer's prior knowledge.

contrast energy The relative ease with which a stimulus can be distinguished from the background against which it is displayed.

controlled vs automatic processes Processes that demand attention if we are to carry them out properly versus processes that operate without requiring us to pay attention to them.

conversational maxims Say no more than is necessary (*maxim of quantity*); be truthful (*maxim of quality*); be relevant (*maxim of relation*); and avoid ambiguity (*maxim of manner*).

co-operative principle The assumption that the speaker intends to say something concise, truthful, relevant, and unambiguous.

cornea The outer tissue of the eye and the first layer that light passes through on its way to the back of the eye.

correlated attributes The hypothesis that some combinations of attributes tend to occur more frequently than other combinations.

covert attention Attending to something without eye movement.

creative intelligence The ability to reason using novel concepts.

creativity The production of novel, socially valued products.

criterial attribute An attribute that is required in order for something to qualify as an instance of a concept.

cross-modal effects The ability to appreciate that the sensations of one modality can be similar to those in another modality.

crystallized intelligence The body of what someone has learned; may continue to increase throughout life.

crystallized systems Cognitive systems that accumulate long-term knowledge.

cueing effect Faster responses on cued compared to uncued trials in the cueing task.

decay The term used to refer to the time course of forgetting.

decision demon A feature detector in the pandemonium model that determines which pattern is being recognized.

declarative memory One of two major divisions of memory, also known as explicit memory; the memory system that contains knowledge that can be stated.

dedicated intelligence Intelligence associated with domain-specific modules that would have evolved to solve recurring problems.

deep and surface structure The sequence of words that make up a sentence constitutes a surface structure that is derived from an underlying deep structure.

default network A set of brain areas that are active when an individual does not have a specific task to do and is absorbed in internal thought.

déjà vu The impression that you have already experienced the situation in which you find yourself, accompanied by the sense that this is not actually the case.

denotivity The degree to which an object is meaningful and familiar to an individual observer.

diacritical marks Symbols that indicate the correct pronunciation of letters in a particular word.

dichotic listening Participants are presented with two verbal messages simultaneously, typically one to each ear, and are asked to focus on (i.e., attend to) only one of them. They are then asked to respond to a series of questions about what they heard, most often about the message played to the unattended ear.

diffusion tensor imaging (DTI) An MRI-based neuroimaging technique that makes it possible to visualize the white-matter tracts within the brain.

direct vs indirect measures Participants' reports that they have seen a stimulus, as opposed to the effects of an undetected stimulus on a subsequent task.

disconnection syndrome Amnesic patients may be able to acquire new information and yet not be aware that learning has taken place.

dissociation paradigm An experimental strategy designed to show that it is possible to perceive stimuli in the absence of any conscious awareness of them.

distinctiveness The precision with which an item is encoded.

distinctiveness hypothesis The hypothesis that the more distinctive the item is, the easier it will be to recall.

distributed reasoning Reasoning done by more than one person.

divided attention The ability to attend to more than one thing at a time.

domain-specific modules The hypothesis that parts of the brain may be specialized for particular tasks, such as recognizing faces.

dorsal ("where") pathway The stream of visual processing in the brain that is responsible for determining object location and motion, and which guides action.

dorsolateral prefrontal cortex (DLPFC) An area of the brain that may exert a top-down bias that favours the selection of task-relevant information.

double-function words Words that refer to both physical and psychological properties (e.g., *warmth*).

dual route theory The theory there are two separate pathways for reading, one for comparing words to a mental dictionary and another for converting letters to sounds and stringing the sounds together to make words.

dual-coding theory The theory that there are two ways of representing events, verbal and non-verbal.

duration neglect The finding that retrospective judgments of the total painfulness of an event are unrelated to the event's duration.

dyslexia A reading disorder, ranging from difficulty learning to read and spell to the loss of those abilities.

early selection The hypothesis that attention prevents early perceptual processing of distractors.

earworm A conscious experience of sound—typically a short phrase of catchy music—that seems to get stuck on replay in your head.

easy problems of consciousness Understanding what types of conscious states relate to what types of neural activity.

echo When a probe goes out from primary to secondary memory, memory traces are activated to the extent that they are similar to the probe.

ecological approach A form of psychological inquiry that reflects conditions in the real world.

ecological approach to the study of memory An approach that emphasizes real-world complexities in its investigations to discover general principles.

ecological rationality A heuristic is ecologically rational if it produces useful inferences by exploiting the structure of information in the environment.

ecologically valid Generalizable to conditions in the real world.

eduction (Spearman) Literally, *drawing out*. General intelligence may be the ability to draw out the relationships that apply in a novel situation.

egocentric frame of reference Using information available from our current perspective to orient ourselves.

egocentric perspective transformations You imagine yourself moving, while the objects in the environment remain still.

egocentric speech Speech that does not take the listener's perspective into account.

eidetic imagery Images projected onto the external world that persist for a minute or more even after a stimulus (e.g., a picture) is removed.

Einstellung effect (Luchins) The tendency to respond inflexibly to a particular type of problem; also called a *rigid* set.

elaboration Adding to or enriching information by relating it to other information.

electromyogram (EMG) A record of the changes in muscle activity of the body.

electrooculogram (EOG) A record of the changes in electrical potentials generated by the movements of the eye.

eliminative strategy A strategy based on attempting to falsify your hypotheses, in order to eliminate incorrect beliefs.

embodied Existing within a body; the term reflects the general view that cognition depends not only on the mind but also on the physical constraints of the body in which the mind exists.

embodied cognition The role of cognition is to facilitate successful interaction with the environment.

emergent causation In Sperry's sense, causation brought about by an emergent property. Once the "mind" emerges from the brain, it has the power to influence lower-level processes.

emergent consequences A principle of Johnson-Laird's theory: you can get more out of a mental model than you put into it.

emergent properties New properties that emerge when a mental image is constructed.

emergent property (Sperry) In Sperry's sense, a property that "emerges" as a result of brain processes, but is not itself a component of the brain. In the case of the mind, this means that consciousness is neither reducible to, nor a property of, a particular brain structure or region.

empirical theory of colour vision The theory that colour perception is influenced by prior experience with the way different illuminations affect colour.

encoding The process of transforming information into one or more forms of representation.

endogenous shifts Voluntary movements of attention.

entrenched vs non-entrenched concepts Entrenched concepts strike us as natural and easy to reason with, whereas non-entrenched concepts strike us as unnatural and difficult to reason with.

entry points The locations to which we direct our eyes before starting to read a section in a piece of complex material such as a newspaper.

epilepsy The uncontrolled over-activity of neurons in the brain that can cause mental disruptions and uncontrolled muscle contractions.

epiphenomenalism "Mind" is a superfluous by-product of bodily functioning.

episodic buffer The mechanism that moves information to and from long-term memory.

episodic memory The subdivision of declarative memory concerned with personal experience.

errorless learning Participants in a learning situation are taught in such a way that they never have the opportunity to make errors.

evaluation function The process whereby a plan is created, carried out, and evaluated.

event-related potential (ERP) An electrical signal emitted by the brain after the onset of a stimulus.

excitatory and inhibitory connections Connections that either enhance or diminish the associations between the units that make up a neural network.

exogenous shifts Involuntary movements of attention triggered by external stimuli.

experience sampling The general technique of asking people to comment on the contents of their consciousness at specific moments.

extrastriate body area (EBA) An area in the ventral stream that is involved in processing non-facial body parts.

face validity Methods that clearly measure what they are supposed to measure are said to be "face valid."

factor analysis A statistical procedure that derives a number of underlying factors that may explain the structure of a set of correlations.

family resemblance Instances of concepts that possess overlapping features, without any features being common to all.

feature A component or characteristic of a stimulus.

feature detection theory Detecting patterns on the basis of their features or properties.

feedforward sweep The propagation of visual information from the primary visual cortex down the "what" and "where" pathways.

feeling of knowing The feeling that you will be able to solve a particular problem.

feeling of "warmth" The feeling that many people have as they approach the solution to a problem (i.e., "getting warm").

figurative language Various figures of speech, such as metaphor and irony.

figure–ground segmentation (segregation) The separation of a scene such that one component of the scene becomes a figural object and the other component(s) become(s) the backdrop.

filter A hypothetical mechanism that would admit certain messages and block others.

filter model A theory based on the idea that information processing is restricted by channel capacity.

fixation Holding the eye relatively still in order to maintain an image on the fovea.

flanker task An experiment in which participants may be influenced by an irrelevant stimulus beside the target.

flash suppression When different images are presented to each eye and one of the images is replaced, the new image enters consciousness and the image presented to the other eye is suppressed from consciousness.

flashbulb memories Vivid, detailed memories of significant events.

fluid intelligence The ability to think flexibly; may increase in youth but levels off as we mature.

fluid systems Cognitive processes that manipulate information.

Fynn effect An increase in IQ scores over historical time.

focus gambling The concept formation strategy of selecting instances that vary from the first positive instance in more than one attribute.

folk biology The concepts that ordinary people use to understand living things.

folk psychology An umbrella term for various assumptions and theories based on the everyday behaviour of ourselves and others.

folk taxonomy A classification system composed of a hierarchy of groups.

forgetting curve Ebbinghaus's finding that the rate at which information is forgotten is greatest immediately after the information has been acquired, and declines more gradually over time.

fovea The region of the retina where photoreceptors are most densely packed.

functional fixedness (Duncker) The inability to see beyond the most common use of a particular object and recognize that it could also perform the function needed to solve a problem; also, the tendency to think about objects based on the function for which they were designed.

functional magnetic resonance imaging (fMRI) A non-radioactive, magnetic procedure for detecting the flow of oxygenated blood to various parts of the brain.

fusiform face area (FFA) An area in the inferior temporal cortex that is responsible for the conscious recognition of faces.

Galton's number The number of autobiographical episodes available to participants from the preceding 20 years, as calculated by Crovitz, Schiffman, and Apter (1991): 224.

gambler's fallacy The mistaken belief that an event that has not occurred on several independent trials is more likely to happen on future trials.

gamma frequency Spikes in the electroencephalogram that occur at roughly 40 cycles per second.

general intelligence (g) The part of intelligence that is common to all abilities.

general problem solver (GPS) A computer program used to perform non-systematic searches.

generative problem Participants are told that the three numbers 2, 4, 6 conform to a simple relational rule that the experimenter has in mind, and that their task is to discover the rule by generating sequences of three numbers. The experimenter tells them each time whether the rule has been followed.

geons The set of 36 basic three-dimensional shapes from which all real-world objects can be constructed.

Gestalt switch A sudden change in the way information is organized.

given–new contract A tacit agreement whereby the speaker agrees to connect new information to what the listener already knows.

goal stack The final goal to be reached is on the bottom of the stack, with the subgoals piled on top of it in the reverse of the order in which they are to be attained.

goal-derived category A category invented for a specific purpose on a particular occasion.

graded structure Describes a concept in which some members of the category are better examples of it than others.

gradient of texture density Incremental changes in the pattern on a surface, which provide information about the slant of the surface.

grammatical transformations Rules operating on entire strings of symbols to convert them to new strings.

grand illusion of conscious perception The illusion that what we see in our visual field is a clear and detailed picture of the world.

grouping The combination of individual components to form a percept of a whole object.

hard problems of consciousness Understanding why the brain gives rise to subjective experiences that have the specific qualities they have.

Hebb rule A connection between two neurons takes place only if both neurons are firing at approximately the same time.

hesitation pauses Pauses in speech, often characterized by disfluencies such as *um* or *uh*.

heuristic A problem-solving procedure (typically a rule of thumb or shortcut); heuristics can often be useful, but do not guarantee solutions.

hints (Maier's view) A hint must be consistent with the direction that the person's thinking is taking, and cannot be useful unless it responds to a difficulty that the person has already experienced.

hippocampus A site in the brain that plays a crucial role in the consolidation of memory traces.

historical accounts, observation of ongoing scientific investigations, laboratory studies, and computational models Different methods for studying problem-solving in science.

Höffding function The process whereby an experience makes contact with a memory trace, resulting in recognition.

holistic Focusing on the entire configuration of an object.

hot-hand behaviour A bias that leads the teammates of a player who has just scored a basket to let him take the next shot.

hot-hand belief The belief that a player who has just made two or three shots is on a streak and will likely make the next shot.

icon The initial, brief representation of the information contained in a visual stimulus.

iconic A characteristic of mental models, according to Johnson-Laird's theory: the relations between the parts of the model correspond to the relations between the parts of the situation it represents.

iconic and echoic sensory memory The visual and auditory sensory memory systems, respectively. Sensory memory has the ability to register a large amount of information, although it typically decays quickly: iconic memory has an upper limit of one second; echoic memory has a limit of two seconds.

idea density The number of distinct ideas present in a sentence or paragraph.

illusory correlation The mistaken belief that events go together when in fact they do not.

image as anticipation hypothesis The hypothesis that an image is a readiness to perceive something.

imagens The units containing information that generate mental images; the components of the non-verbal system.

imagery (Paivio's sense) The ease with which something such as a word can elicit a mental image.

implicit perception The effect on a person's experience, thought, or action of an object in the current stimulus environment in the absence of, or independent of, conscious perception of that event.

implicit vs explicit learning Learning that takes place unintentionally versus learning that takes place intentionally.

improvisational intelligence Flexible intelligence that would have evolved to deal with relatively unique, unpredictable problems.

inattentional blindness Failure to attend to events that we might be expected to notice.

inducer The cue that elicits a synesthetic experience.

inferential model of communication A model of communication based on Grice's inferential theory.

information pickup The process whereby we perceive information directly.

information theory The theory that the information provided by a particular event is inversely related to the probability of its occurrence.

inhibition of return (IOR) Slower responses to cued than to uncued trials in the cueing paradigm.

innateness hypothesis The hypothesis that children innately possess a language acquisition device that comes equipped with principles of universal grammar.

inner speech Speech for oneself that regulates thought.

insight problem A problem that we must look at from a different angle before we can see how to solve it.

integration The hypothesis that we abstract the meaning of an event and then put that meaning together with the rest of our knowledge to form a coherent, consistent whole.

intellectual components (Sternberg) Elementary information processes that operate on internal representations of objects or symbols.

intelligence (Binet and Simon's 1905 definition) A fundamental faculty, the alteration or lack of which is of the utmost importance for practical life.

intentional binding effect Events that take place after one has taken some action are perceived as occurring sooner than they actually did.

interactionism Mind and brain are separate substances that interact with and influence each other.

interhemispheric transfer Communication between the brain's hemispheres, enabled in large part by the corpus callosum.

interpretation The hypothesis that we interpret information by making inferences, and then remember the inferences as part of the original information.

intrinsic frame of reference Spatial relationships are based solely on the relationships between the objects being described.

introspection "Looking inward" to observe one's own thoughts and feelings.

intuitive concept A type of concept that is easily acquired and used by almost all adults.

in vivo/in vitro method (Dunbar) In the case of scientific problem-solving, *in vivo* research involves the observation of ongoing scientific investigations, while *in vitro* research involves laboratory studies of scientific problem-solving.

involuntary semantic memory ("mind popping") A semantic memory that pops into your mind without episodic context.

iris The tissue that surrounds the pupil and is responsible for the distinct colour of the eye.

isomorphism Mental events and neural events share the same structure.

Jost's law of forgetting Of two memory traces of equal strength, the younger trace will decay faster than the older one.

jumbled word effect The ability to raed wdors in steentnces evne wnhe smoe of the ltteers rea mexid up.

knowledge acquisition components (Sternberg) Processes concerned with learning and storing new information.

Korsakoff's syndrome A form of amnesia affecting the ability to form new memories, attributed to thiamine deficiency and often (though not exclusively) seen in chronic alcoholics.

lab-based approach to memory research An approach that emphasizes controlled laboratory (as opposed to real-world) research in the search for general principles.

language Open-ended verbal communication that consists of all possible sentences.

language acquisition device (LAD) and universal grammar hypothesis The hypothesis that children possess a language acquisition device containing general principles that apply to any natural language (universal grammar).

late selection The hypothesis that we perceive both relevant and irrelevant stimuli, and therefore must actively ignore the irrelevant stimuli in order to focus on the relevant ones.

law of averages A fallacy based on the assumption that events of one kind are always balanced by events of another kind.

law of equipotentiality Although some areas of the cortex may become specialized for certain tasks, any part of an area can (within limits) do the job of any other part of that area.

law of large numbers The larger the sample, the closer a statistic will be to the true value.

law of mass action Learning and memory depend on the total mass of brain tissue remaining rather than the properties of individual cells.

law of progressions and pathologies A "last in, first out" principle referring to the possibility that the last system to emerge is the first to show the effects of degeneration.

law of small numbers The mistaken belief that a small sample should be representative of the population from which it is drawn.

left and right hemispheres theory The theory that the left hemisphere of the brain controls speech and is better at processing verbal material than is the right hemisphere, which is better at non-verbal tasks.

lens The transparent tissue in the eye that refracts light and focuses it on the back of the eye.

less-is-more effect Sometimes the person who knows less is able to make a better judgment than the person who knows more but is unable to use that knowledge in the situation at hand.

levels of processing A continuum that ranges from registering an event purely in terms of its physical characteristics to analyzing it in terms of its relationship to other things that you know.

lexical decision task (LDT) A task requiring participants to determine whether a presented string of letters is a word or not.

life script A cultural narrative that prescribes the age norms for important events in an individual's life.

limen Threshold.

linguistic relativity The notion that two languages may be so different from each other as to make their native speakers' experience of the world quite different from each other.

literacy The ability to read and write; sometimes extended to include the metalinguistic ability to talk or write about text.

localization of function The idea that there is a direct correspondence between specific cognitive functions and specific parts of the brain.

location-suppression hypothesis A two-stage explanation for the Quiet Eye phenomenon: in the preparation stage, the Quiet Eye maximizes information about the target object; then, during the location stage, vision is suppressed to optimize the execution of an action or behaviour.

logicism The belief that logical reasoning is an essential part of human nature.

logogens The units containing the information underlying our use of a word; the components of the verbal system.

lucid dreaming A dream state in which we are aware that we are dreaming.

magnetoencephalography (MEG) A non-invasive brain imaging technique that directly measures neural activity.

McGurk effect The auditory experience of the syllable "da" when seeing a mouth silently saying "ga" while at the same time hearing a voice say "ba."

means—end analysis The procedure used by General Problem Solver to reduce differences between current and goal states.

memory bump An increase in the number of memories between 10 and 30 years of age over what would be expected if memories decayed smoothly over time.

memory trace The trace that an experience leaves behind in memory.

mental model theory The theory that we construct a mental model of a given situation, on the basis of which we understand, reason, and draw conclusions about it.

mental rotation Imagining an object in motion and viewing it from different perspectives.

metacognition Knowledge about the way that cognitive processes work; understanding of our own cognitive processes.

metacomponents (Sternberg) Executive processes used in planning, monitoring, and decision-making in task performance.

meta-conscious The level of consciousness at play when you direct your attention to your own state of mind.

meta-consciousness Conscious awareness of what is occurring in one's consciousness.

metalinguistic awareness The ability to talk about language itself, without worrying about what it refers to.

metamemory Beliefs about how memory works.

method of loci A mnemonic technique based on places and images.

method of opposition Pits conscious (explicit) and unconscious (implicit) tendencies against one another.

method of repeated reproduction One participant is given multiple opportunities to recall a story over time.

method of serial reproduction One participant, A, writes down what he or she can recall of a previously read story. A's version is given to a second participant, B, who reads it and then tries to reproduce it. B's version in turn is given to C, and so on.

method of vanishing cues A way of teaching amnesic patients the meaning of computer commands by presenting them with definitions of the commands and fragments of the commands' names. Additional letters are presented until the patient guesses the word. Then letters are progressively removed until the patient is able to give the name of the command when presented with its definition.

mid-life crisis of musicians (Bamberger) As music students become adolescents, they may feel a tension between their increasingly explicit understanding of music and the spontaneous love of music they had as children.

mind wandering A shift of mental resources away from the task at hand and towards internal thoughts.

mindfulness vs mindlessness (Langer) Openness to alternative possibilities versus the tendency to behave as if the situation had only one possible interpretation.

mind-wandering The state in which your thoughts wander from a particular task without your realizing that this has occurred; also referred to as zoning out.

minimalism The belief that linguistic competence has only those characteristics that are absolutely necessary.

mirror neurons Neurons that fire not only when performing an action, but also when observing an action. Broca's area in monkeys contains mirror neurons that fire not only when the animal makes grasping movements, but also when it observes other animals making those movements.

misaligned hierarchies Judgments made at one level suggest one conclusion while judgments made at another level suggest a contrasting conclusion.

misinformation effect The hypothesis that misleading post-event information can become integrated with the original memory of the event.

mnemonic techniques Procedures used to aid memory.

modal model of memory A memory model proposed by Atkinson and Shiffrin (1968), consisting of sensory memory, short-term memory, and long-term memory.

modality appropriateness hypothesis The hypothesis that different senses are better at processing different stimuli, and therefore that different sensory modalities dominate at different times, depending on circumstances.

modules Different parts of the brain, each of which is responsible for particular cognitive operations.

mood congruence The idea that mood might cause selective learning of affective material.

mood-dependent recall The hypothesis that mood congruence between learning and recall sessions should facilitate recall.

moon illusion The tendency for the moon to appear different in size depending on whether it is near the horizon or high in the night sky.

morpheme The smallest unit in language that carries meaning.

motivated reasoning Biased evaluation of evidence, in accordance with one's prior views and beliefs.

moving window technique A method of determining how much visual information can be taken in during a fixation, in which the reader is prevented from seeing information beyond a certain distance from the current fixation.

multiple intelligences (Gardner) The hypothesis that intelligence consists not of one underlying ability but of many different abilities.

multiple-trace memory model Traces of each individual experience are recorded in memory. No matter how often a particular kind of event is experienced, a memory trace of the individual event is recorded each time.

mystic writing pad model A model of memory based on a toy writing tablet that retains fragments of old messages even after they have been "erased." In time, these fragments accumulate and begin to overlap, so that they become increasingly hard to read.

natural deduction system A reasoning system made up of propositions and deduction rules that are used to draw conclusions from these propositions.

negative transfer The tendency to respond with previously learned rule sequences even when they are inappropriate.

neural network Neurons that are functionally related or connected.

neural plasticity Changes in neuronal circuitry often associated with maturation, environmental adaptation, and modulation by experience which may lead to learning and behavioural modification.

non-conscious The level of consciousness that operates without our attention, continuously monitoring and changing the contents of thought, and tracking and changing behaviour to address goals.

non-declarative memory The other major division of memory, also known as implicit memory; the memory system associated with behaviour that does not require conscious thought.

nonsense syllables Nonsense "words" consisting of a consonant followed by a vowel followed by a consonant.

Now Print! theory The theory that especially significant experiences are immediately "photocopied," preserved in long-term memory, and resistant to change.

number forms Automatically generated images of numbers in various spatial layouts external to an individual.

nystagmus Small but continuous eye movements during fixation.

objective and subjective thresholds The point at which participants can detect a stimulus at a chance level versus the point at which they say they did not perceive it.

objective distances The true distances between objects in the real world, which are preserved in our mental images.

opponent process theory of colour vision The hypothesis that colour vision is based on three pairs of antagonistic processes.

optic ataxia A condition characterized by a deficit in the ability to successfully reach for objects, especially when they are presented in the periphery of vision, with unimpaired ability to identify them.

optic flow field The continually changing (i.e., transforming) pattern of information that results from the movement of either objects or the observer through the environment.

organizational principles The rules (or laws) that govern the perception of whole objects or events from a collection of individual components or features.

overload view The view that performance on vigilance tasks declines over time because such tasks are so demanding.

overt attention Attending to something with eye movement.

pandemonium A model of pattern recognition consisting of three levels: data, cognitive demons, and decision demon.

panpsychism The view that everything has some form of consciousness.

parahippocampal place area (PPA) An area in the ventral stream that is responsible for the conscious recognition of places.

parallel mental activity Thinking about something other than the task at hand.

parallel processing Many neural connections may be active at the same time.

parallelism "Mind" and brain are two aspects of the same reality, and they operate in parallel.

parameter-setting hypothesis The hypothesis that language acquisition involves the setting of various parameters contained within a universal grammar (e.g., position of verb in relation to object). A parameter is a universal aspect of language that can take on one of a small set of possible values.

parental reformulations Adult reformulations of children's speech. They are negative in that they inform children that they have made a mistake and positive in that they provide examples of correct speech.

parsimony A principle of Johnson-Laird's theory: people tend to construct the simplest mental model possible.

partist strategy A concept formation strategy, used in reception tasks, in which you initially hypothesize that only some attributes are members of the concept.

path integration The process whereby our position in relation to an important location is continuously updated as we move through the environment.

pattern recognition The ability to recognize an event as an instance of a particular category of event.

peak–end rule Retrospective judgments of the total painfulness of an event are formed by averaging the pain experienced during the most painful moment of the event and that felt at the end of the event.

Penfield homunculus A map of the sensory cortex that shows where the various parts of the body are represented; the size of each part is proportional to the area of the cortex that represents it.

percept The visual experience of sensory information.

perception The processing of sensory information in such a way that it produces conscious experiences and guides action in the world.

perceptual completion (filling-in) The incorrect impression that a stimulus occupies a section of the visual scene when in fact it occupies only the region around it.

perceptual cycle The process whereby our schemas guide our exploration of the world and in turn are shaped by what we find there.

perceptual representation system (PRS) A memory system containing very specific representations of events that is hypothesized to be responsible for priming effects.

perceptual symbols Aspects of perceptual memories that stand for events in the world and enter into all forms of symbolic activity.

performance components (Sternberg) The processes that are used in the execution of a task.

peripheral cueing paradigm A test in which a light (i.e., the cue) flashes in the periphery and is followed by a target either in the same (cued) location or a different (uncued) one.

permastore Bahrick's term for the state of relative permanence in which he found that some kinds of memory can be retained over very long periods of time.

phantom limb The feeling, following the sudden loss of a body part, that it is still present.

phoneme The smallest unit in language. Phonemes are combined to form morphemes.

phonological dyslexia A form of dyslexia affecting only the ability to read letter-by-letter; the ability to recognize words as entire units remains intact.

phonological loop Temporary store of linguistic information.

photoreceptors Cells that transduce light energy into a neural signal.

phrase structure rules Rules describing the way symbols can be rewritten as other symbols.

phrenology The study of the shape, size, and protrusions of the cranium in an attempt to discover the relationships between parts of the brain and various mental activities and abilities.

plasticity Flexibility. As used here it refers to the notion that brain areas typically used for one function can be recruited and used for other purposes.

polysemy The existence of multiple meanings for one word.

positron emission tomography (PET) An imaging technique in which a participant is injected with a radioactive substance that mingles with the blood and circulates to the brain. A scanner is then used to detect the flow of blood to particular areas of the brain.

"poverty of the stimulus" argument The argument that the linguistic environment to which a child is exposed is not good enough to enable language acquisition on its own.

practical intelligence The ability to find problem solutions in real-world, everyday situations.

practical syllogism One in which two premises point to a conclusion that calls for action.

prefrontal leucotomy A surgical procedure, now abandoned, in which the connections between the prefrontal lobes and other parts of the brain were severed; also known as prefrontal lobotomy.

pretense theory of irony When speaking ironically, people are only pretending to mean what they say.

primary memory A memory system proposed by William James (1890); thought to be the area where information is initially stored so that it is available for consciousness, attention, and general use. (Chapter 5)

primary memory What we are aware of in the "immediately present moment"; often termed "immediate memory" or "short-term memory." (Chapter 1)

primary metaphor A pairing of subjective experience with sensorimotor experience

primary visual cortex The area at the back of the brain that is primarily responsible for the basic processing of visual information.

prime The item that is presented first in a priming experiment. Later response times to this or related items are generally faster.

priming The unconscious process through which recognition of a particular item is facilitated by previous exposure to an identical or related item.

principle of common movement Visual features that move simultaneously and follow the same path are perceived to form a whole entity.

principle of encoding specificity The way an item is retrieved from memory depends on the way it was stored in memory.

principle of experience Visual components are grouped together based on the prior experience and knowledge of the observer.

principle of parallelism Lines that are parallel or similar in orientation are perceived as going together.

principle of proximity Visual components that are close to one another are grouped to form a whole.

principle of similarity Visual features that have a high degree of visual similarity are combined.

principle of symmetry Symmetrical lines are perceived as going together.

probe A "snapshot" of information in primary memory that can activate memory traces in secondary memory.

probe or target The second item presented in a priming experiment; may be identical, related, or unrelated to the prime.

probe-caught method A technique used to catch episodes of mind-wandering by presenting participants with a probe asking them whether they were mind-wandering just before the probe was presented.

problem space The representation of a problem, including the goal to be reached and the various ways of transforming the given situation into the solution.

problem-finding (Getzels) The ability to discover new problems, their methods and solutions.

procedural memory The memory system concerned with knowing how to do things.

process dissociation procedure An experimental technique that requires participants *not* to respond with items they have observed previously.

production rules A production rule consists of a condition and an action $(C \rightarrow A)$.

productive thinking (Wertheimer) Thinking based on a grasp of the general principles that apply in the situation at hand.

progress monitoring theory The theory that we monitor our progress on a problem, and when we reach an impasse we are open to an insightful solution.

propositional knowledge hypothesis The hypothesis that knowledge about the world is represented and stored in the form of propositions.

prosopagnosia A selective deficit in the ability to consciously recognize faces resulting from damage to the FFA.

prospective memory The intention to remember to do something at some future time.

prototypical Representative of a pattern or category.

Proust effect The power of odours as autobiographical memory cues.

psycholinguistics The branch of cognitive psychology interested in how we comprehend, produce, acquire, and represent (in the mind) language.

pupil The space through which light passes on its way to the back of the eye; adjusted in size by the iris; to an observer the pupil appears black.

quiet eye Sustained and steady eye gaze prior to an action or behaviour.

rapid eye movement (REM) sleep The stage characterized by dreaming, increased brain activity relative to other stages of sleep, and the inhibition of motor activity except in the eyes, which move rapidly back and forth.

rapid serial visual presentation (RSVP) The presentation of a series of stimuli in quick succession.

rationalization The attempt to make memory as coherent and sensible as possible.

Raven Progressive Matrices A set of problems that constitutes the most widely accepted test of *g*.

reappearance hypothesis Neisser's term for the now rejected idea that the same memory can reappear, unchanged, again and again.

reasoning A thought process that yields a conclusion from premises.

recency bias vs primacy bias A tendency to recall experiences from the recent past versus a tendency to recall experiences from the relatively distant past.

reception task A concept formation task in which the instances presented to the participant are chosen by the experimenter.

recognition by components (RBC) The theory that we recognize objects by breaking them down into their fundamental geometric shapes.

recognition heuristic When choosing between two objects (according to some criterion), if one is recognized and the other is not, then select the former.

reconsolidation The hypothetical process whereby a memory trace is revised and reconsolidated.

recursion The capacity of any one component (e.g., phrase or sentence) to contain any number of similar components.

re-entrant (feedback) connections Connections between brain areas that allow the propagation of visual information from the endpoints of the "what" and "where" pathways back to the primary visual cortex.

regression to the mean For purely mathematical reasons, whenever two variables are not perfectly correlated, extreme values on one variable tend to be related to values on the other variable that are closer to (i.e., regressed to) the mean of that variable.

regressions Right to left movements of the eyes during reading, directing them to previously read text.

rehearsal The process through which information in short-term memory is maintained.

relational reasoning Reasoning involving premises that express the relations between items (e.g., *A is taller than B*).

relative frame of reference Spatial relationships are described relative to an observer's viewpoint.

remote associations test (RAT; Mednick) A test that asks the participant to come up with a single association to link three apparently unrelated words.

representational change theory The theory that insight requires a change in the way participants represent the problem to themselves.

representativeness heuristic Making inferences on the assumption that small samples resemble one another and the population from which they are drawn.

resource depletion account A version of the overload view according to which performance declines over time as attentional resources become depleted.

retina The tissue at the back of the eye that contains light receptors.

retinal blur The blurring of information on the retina that occurs during fast eye movements.

retinotopic A principle of organization of the primary visual cortex, whereby information falling on adjacent areas of the retina is processed in adjacent areas of the cortex.

retroactive interference A decline in recall of one event as a result of a later event.

Ribot's law of retrograde amnesia Older memories are less likely to be lost as a result of brain damage than are newer memories.

saccades The rapid, jerky movements made as the eye scans an image.

saccadic suppression The halting of visual processing during an eye movement.

Sapir–Whorf hypothesis The hypothesis that two languages may be so different from one another as to make their native speakers' experience of the world qualitatively different.

scatter-reflection The degree to which light scatters when reflected from a surface.

schema An expectation concerning what we are likely to find as we explore the world (plural *schemas* or *schemata*).

schema (Bartlett) An active mass of organized past reactions that provides a setting that guides our behaviour.

script A set of expectations concerning the actions and events that are appropriate in a particular situation.

search tree A representation of all the possible moves branching out from the initial state of the problem.

secondary memory A memory system proposed by William James (1890); thought to be the long-term storage area for memories. (Chapter 5)

secondary memory Knowledge acquired at an earlier time that is stored indefinitely, and is absent from awareness; also called "long-term memory." (Chapter 1)

selection The hypothesis that we select information both as we receive it and as we recall it.

selection task A concept formation task in which the participant selects instances from those presented by the experimenter.

selection task (Wason) A four-card problem based on conditional reasoning.

selective attention Attending to relevant information and ignoring irrelevant information.

selective looking Occurs when we are exposed to two events simultaneously, but attend to only one of them.

self-caught method A technique used to catch episodes of mind-wandering in which participants are asked to monitor their consciousness and report anytime their mind has wandered.

semantic memory The subdivision of declarative memory concerned with general knowledge (e.g., facts, words, and concepts).

semantics The meaning of words and sentences.

sensory system A system that links the physical and perceptual worlds via the nervous system; composed of sensory receptors, neural pathways, and distinct regions of the brain preferentially dedicated to the perception of information.

sequential attention hypothesis The hypothesis about the relationship between overt and covert attention that posits a tight relationship between the two, whereby covert attention is shifted first and overt eye movement follows.

serial processing Only one neural activity may take place at any one time.

set A temporary, top-down organization in the brain that facilitates some responses while inhibiting others in order to achieve a certain goal; also referred to as a "mental set."

shadowing task A task in which the subject is exposed to two messages simultaneously and must repeat one of them.

simultaneous scanning The concept formation strategy of keeping in mind all possible hypotheses and trying to eliminate as many as possible with each instance selection.

smooth pursuit movements Movements of the eye that, because they are not jerky, enable the viewer to maintain fixation on a moving object.

social contract theory The theory that inference procedures have evolved to deal with social contracts in which people give something up in order to gain something else.

source monitoring framework The theory that some errors of memory are caused by mistaken identification of the memory's source.

spatial attention The process of selecting visual information for conscious awareness in specific regions of space.

spatial framework An imaginary space with one vertical (*above–below*) and two horizontal dimensions (*ahead–behind* and *left–right*).

special places strategy Choosing a storage location that other people will not think of; the problem is that when the time comes to retrieve the item, you may not think of it either.

specific and general levels of representation As people age they tend to forget specific details but to remember deeper, more general meanings.

speech Those sentences that are actually spoken; only a small subset of language.

split brain A condition created by severing the corpus callosum.

spotlight metaphor The idea that spatial attention is like a spotlight that we shine on an object when we select it for more complex and conscious processing.

spreading activation The idea that activation of the paths that make up a semantic network spreads from the node at which the search begins.

squelching The tendency of the nervous system to inhibit the processing of unclear features.

stimulus onset asynchrony (SOA) The time difference between the onset of one stimulus and the onset of a subsequent stimulus.

stimulus An entity in the external environment that can be perceived by an observer.

strong but wrong routines Overlearned response sequences that we follow even when we intend to do something else.

strong synesthetes People for whom an inducer in one sensory modality (e.g., a sound) produces a concurrent image in another sensory modality (e.g., a colour).

Stroop task A naming task in which colour names are printed in colours other than the colours they name.

structural limits The hypothesis that attentional tasks interfere with one another to the extent that they involve similar activities.

structurally blind/reproductive thinking The tendency to use familiar or routine procedures, reproducing thinking that was appropriate for other situations, but is not appropriate for the current situation.

subgoal A goal derived from the original goal, the solution of which leads to the solution of the problem as a whole.

subliminal or unconscious perception Perception without awareness; occurs when the stimulus is too weak to be consciously recognized, but still has an impact on your behaviour.

successive scanning The concept formation strategy of formulating a single hypothesis and testing it by selecting instances until the correct hypothesis emerges.

superordinate, basic, and subordinate levels (Rosch) Levels of inclusiveness of a concept, as in *tree*, *oak*, and *live oak*.

supervenient In Sperry's sense, describes mental states that may simultaneously influence neuronal events and be influenced by them.

surface dyslexia A form of dyslexia affecting only the ability to recognize words as entire units; the ability to read words letter-by-letter remains intact.

sustained attention The act of maintaining attention focused on a single task for a prolonged period of time.

sustained attention to response task (SART) A continuous response task in which digits (e.g., 0 to 9) are sequentially presented on a computer screen and participants are asked to press a button in response to all but one of them (e.g., the infrequent digit 3); response to this infrequent digit is supposed to be withheld (see Robertson et al., 1997).

switch cost The finding that performance declines immediately on switching tasks.

syllogism A syllogism consists of two premises and a conclusion. Each of the premises specifies a relationship between two categories.

symbol systems Different forms of representation, such as drawing, music, and mathematics, that express different forms of intelligence.

synesthesia The condition in which a stimulus appropriate to one sense (e.g., a sound) triggers an experience appropriate to another sense (e.g., a colour).

syntactic development Development of the ability to organize words into grammatical sentences.

syntax The rules that govern how words and sentences are structured.

tacit knowledge Knowing how to do something without being able to say exactly what it is that you know.

task-related knowledge An observer's knowledge of the goals and the task at hand as it guides the eyes during a visual task.

task switching Changing from working on one task to working on another; usually studied in situations in which the switch is involuntary.

template-matching theory The hypothesis that the process of pattern recognition relies on the use of templates or prototypes.

temporal dissociation The temporary disengagement of meta-consciousness, resulting in lack of awareness of the contents of consciousness.

10-year rule The hypothesis that roughly 10 years of intense practice is necessary in order to become an expert in a domain.

theory of ecological optics The proposition that perception results from direct contact of the sensory organs with stimulus energy emanating from the environment and that an important goal of perception is action.

theory of microconsciousness (Zeki) The view that each individual has "many different visual consciousnesses that are distributed over space and time."

thinking aloud Concurrent verbalization: the verbalization of information as the participant is attending to it.

three-term series problem Linear syllogisms consisting of two comparative sentences from which a conclusion must be drawn.

time spaces The visual experience of time units such as days of the week or months of the year as occupying spatial locations outside the body.

tip-of-the-tongue phenomenon (TOT) Knowing that you know something without quite being able to recall it.

top-down influences The feedback influence of context and the individual's knowledge, expectations, and high-level goals on perceptual experience.

topological breakage The discontinuity created by the intersection of two textures.

toy problems Problems used to analyze the problem-solving process.

transformation Gibson's (1966) term for the changes in the optical information hitting the eye that occur as the observer moves through the environment.

tree diagram A description of a process that proceeds from one level at which a number of relationships are simultaneously present to other levels at which those relationships are ordered serially.

triarchic theory of intelligence Sternberg's theory consisting of analytic, practical, and creative intelligence.

truth tables A way of presenting the various combinations of the constituents of logical statements.

underload view The view that performance on vigilance tasks declines over time because such tasks are not stimulating enough to hold people's attention.

unexpected findings Although scientists may initially resist information that disconfirms favoured hypotheses, successful problem-solvers attempt to explain surprising results.

ur-song The hypothetical first song that all children would spontaneously sing.

u-shaped development The hypothesis that the development of many symbolic forms initially is delightfully pre-conventional, then descends to the merely conventional,

but ultimately may achieve the integration of the post-conventional.

ventral ("what") pathway The stream of visual processing in the brain that is responsible for determining object shape, colour, and meaningful identity.

vigilance decrement The decline in performance over time in vigilance tasks.

vigilance Sustained attention as an externally imposed requirement.

visual agnosia An inability to identify objects visually even though they can be identified using other senses (e.g., touch).

visual hemispatial neglect Lack of visual awareness of objects located in the contralesional field.

visual prepotency effect The hypothesis that the visual system dominates the other senses when it comes to perceptual processing.

visuo-spatial sketchpad Temporary store of non-linguistic (visual) information.

vividness of visual imagery The degree to which an image is clear and lively, and resembles an actual percept.

von Restorff effect If one item in a set is different from the others, it is more likely to be recalled.

weak synesthetes People who can appreciate cross-modal associations without having strong synesthetic experiences.

Wernicke's aphasia A deficit in the ability to comprehend speech as a result of damage to Wernicke's area.

Wernicke's area Area of the brain's left hemisphere that is responsible for processing the meaning of words.

wholist strategy A concept formation strategy, used in reception tasks, in which you initially hypothesize that all attributes are members of the concept.

word superiority effect It's easier to identify a letter (e.g., *p*) if it appears in a word (e.g., *warp*) than if it appears alone.

working memory The system that allows for the temporary storage and manipulation of information required for various cognitive activities.

working memory capacity The theory that working memory capacity and *g* are closely related.

Zeigarnik effect The "quasi-need" to finish incomplete tasks.

zone of proximal development Defined by Vygotsky as "the distance between the actual developmental level as determined by independent problem-solving and the level of potential development as determined through problem-solving under adult guidance or in collaboration with more capable peers."

References

Abraham, C. (2004, Dec. 4). Marooned in the moment. *Globe and Mail*, pp. F1, F4–F5.

Ackerman, P.L., Beier, M.E., & Boyle, M.O. (2005). Working memory and intelligence: The same or different constructs? *Psychological Bulletin, 31*, 30–60.

Adelson, R. (2005). Hues and views: A cross-cultural study reveals how language shapes color perception. *Monitor on Psychology, 36*. Retrieved 23 March 2005 from www.apa.orgmonitor/feb05/hues.html.

Alaimo, C. (1996a, December 2). No ordinary sales pitch. *St. Catharines Standard*, p. B1.

Alaimo, C. (1996b, November 4). A rags to fishes story. *St. Catharines Standard*, p. D1.

Alba, J.W., & Hasher, L. (1983). Is memory schematic? *Psychological Bulletin, 93*, 203–231.

Allen, R., & Reber, A.S. (1980). Very long term memory for tacit knowledge. *Cognition, 8*, 175–186.

Allis, L.V., van den Herik, H.J., & Huntjens, H.J. (1996). Go-Moku solved by new search techniques. *Computational Intelligence, 12*, 7–23.

Allport, D.A. (1980). Attention and performance. In G. Claxton (Ed.), *New directions in Cognitive Psychology* (pp. 26–64). London: Routledge & Kegan Paul.

Allport, D.A., Styles, E.A., & Hsieh, S. (1994). Shifting intentional set: Exploring the dynamic control of tasks. In C. Umiltà & M. Moscovitch (Eds.), *Attention and Performance XV: Conscious and Unconscious Information Processing* (pp. 421–452). Cambridge, MA.: MIT Press.

Alsius, A., Navarra, J., Campbell, R., & Soto-Faraco, S. (2005). Audiovisual integration of speech falters under high attention demands. *Current Biology, 15*, 9, 839–843.

Altmann, G.T.M. (2001). The language machine: Psycholinguistics in review. *British Journal of Psychology, 92*, 129–170.

Anastasi, A. (1965). *Individual differences*. New York: Wiley.

Anderson, C.A., & Bushman, B.J. (1997). External validity of "trivial" experiments: The case of laboratory aggression. *Journal of General Psychology, 1*, 19–41.

Anderson, J.R. (1976). *Language, memory and thought*. Hillsdale, NJ: Erlbaum.

Anderson, J.R. (1978). Arguments concerning representations for mental imagery. *Psychological Review, 85*, 249–277.

Anderson, J.R. (1983). *The architecture of cognition*. Cambridge, MA: Harvard University Press.

Anderson, J.R. (1984). Spreading activation. In J.R. Anderson & S.M. Kosslyn (Eds.), *Tutorials in learning and memory* (pp. 61–90). San Francisco: Freeman.

Anderson, J.R., Bothell, D., & Douglass, S. (2004). Eye movements do not reflect retrieval processes. *Psychological Science, 15*, 225–231.

Anderson, J.R., & Bower, G.H. (1973). *Human Associative Memory*. Washington: Hemisphere Press.

Anderson, D.C., & Buyer, L.S. (1994). Is imagery a functional component of the "bizarre imagery" phenomenon? *American Journal of Psychology, 107*, 207–222.

Anderson, J.R., & Reder, L.M. (1999). The fan effect: New results and new theories. *Journal of Experimental Psychology: General, 128*, 186–197.

Anderson, R.C., & Pichert, J.W. (1978). Recall of previously unrecallable information following a shift in perspective. *Journal of Verbal Learning and Verbal Behavior, 17*, 1–12.

Andrews, P.W., Gangestad, S.W., & Matthews, D. (2002). Adaptationism—how to carry out an exaptationist program. *Behavioral and Brain Sciences, 25*, 489–553.

Anstis, S.M. (1974). A chart demonstrating variations in acuity with retinal position. *Vision Research, 14*, 589–592.

Anzai, Y., & Simon, H.A. (1979). The theory of learning by doing. *Psychological Review, 86*, 124–140.

Armstrong, S.L., Gleitman, L.R., & Gleitman, H. (1983). What some concepts might not be. *Cognition, 13*, 263–308.

Arrington, C.M., & Logan, G.D. (2004). The cost of a voluntary task switch. *Psychological Science, 15*, 610–615.

Asch, S.E. (1946). Forming impressions of personality. *Journal of Abnormal and Social Psychology, 41*, 258–290.

Asch, S.E. (1955). On the use of metaphor in the description of persons. In H. Werner (Ed.), *On expressive language* (pp. 29–38). Worcester, MA.: Clark University Press.

Asch, S.E. (1958). The metaphor: A psychological inquiry. In R. Tagiuri & L. Petrillo (Eds.), *Person perception and interpersonal behavior* (pp. 86–94). Stanford, CA: Stanford University Press.

Asch, S.E. (1969). A reformulation of the problem of associations. *American Psychologist, 24*, 92–102.

Asch, S.E., & Ebenholtz, S.M. (1962). The principle of associative symmetry. *Proceedings of the American Philosophical Society, 106*, 135–163.

Asch, S.E., & Nerlove, H. (1960). The development of double function terms in children. In H. Wapner & B. Kaplan (Eds.), *Perspectives in psychological theory* (pp. 41–60). New York: International Universities Press.

Asch, S.E., & Zukier, H. (1984). Thinking about persons. *Journal of Personality and Social Psychology, 6*, 1230–1240.

Ashby, F.G., & Casale, M.B. (2003). A model of dopamine modulated cortical activation. *Neural Networks, 16*, 973–984.

Ashby, F.G., Isen, A.M., & Turken, A.U. (1999). A neuropsychological theory of positive affect and its influence on cognition. *Psychological Review, 106*, 529–550.

Atkinson, R.C., & Shiffrin, R.M. (1968). Human memory: A proposed system and its control processes. In K.W. Spence & J.T. Spence (Eds.), *The psychology of learning and motivation*. (Vol. 2, pp. 89–105). New York: Academic Press.

Atkinson, R.C., & Shiffrin, R.M. (1971). The control of short-term memory. *Scientific American, 225*, 82–90.

Atran, S. (1999). Folk biology. In R. Wison & F. Keil (Eds.), *The MIT encyclopedia of the cognitive sciences* (pp. 316–317). Cambridge, MA.: MIT Press.

Atran, S. (2005). Adaptationism for human cognition: Strong, spurious or weak? *Mind and Language, 20*, 39–67.

Atance, C.M., & O'Neill, D.K. (2001). Episodic future thinking. *Trends in Cognitive Sciences, 5,* 533–539.

Atran, S., Medin, D., & Ross, N. (2004). Evolution and evolution of knowledge: A tale of two biologies. *Journal of the Royal Anthropological Institute, 10,* 395–420.

Azzopardi, P., & Cowey, A. (1993). Preferential representation of the fovea in the primary visual cortex. *Nature, 361,* 719–721.

Baars, B.J. (1986). *The cognitive revolution in psychology.* New York: Guilford Press.

Baars, B.J. (1992). *Experimental slips and human error: Exploring the architecture of volition.* New York: Plenum Press.

Baars, B.J. (2002). The conscious access hypothesis: Origins and recent evidence. *Trends in Cognitive Sciences, 6,* 47–52.

Bach, P., & Tipper, S.P. (2006). Embodying the motor skills of famous athletes. *Quarterly Journal of Experimental Psychology, 59,* 2033–2039.

Baddeley, A.D. (1978). The trouble with levels: A re-examination of Craik and Lockhart's framework for memory research. *Psychological Review, 85,* 139–152.

Baddeley, A.D. (1986). *Working memory.* Oxford: Oxford University Press.

Baddeley, A.D. (1987a). Amnesia. In R.L. Gregory (Ed.), *The Oxford companion to the mind* (pp. 20–22). Oxford: Oxford University Press.

Baddeley, A.D. (1987b). Memory and context. In R.L. Gregory (Ed.), *The Oxford companion to the mind* (pp. 463–464). Oxford: Oxford University Press.

Baddeley, A.D. (1989). The psychology of remembering and forgetting. In T. Butler (Ed.), *Memory: History, culture and mind* (pp. 36–60). Oxford: Blackwell.

Baddeley, A.D. (2000a). Short-term and working memory. In E. Tulving & F.I.M. Craik (Eds.), *The Oxford handbook of memory* (pp. 77–92). New York: Oxford University Press.

Baddeley, A.D. (2000b). The episodic buffer: A new component of working memory? *Trends in Cognitive Sciences, 11,* 417–423.

Baddeley, A.D. (2001). The concept of episodic memory. *Philosophical Transactions of the Royal Society (Series B), 356,* 1345–1350.

Baddeley, A.D. (2002a). Fractionating the central executive. In D.T. Stuss and R.T. Knight (Eds.), *Principles of frontal lobe function* (pp. 246–260). New York: Oxford University Press.

Baddeley, A.D. (2002b). Is working memory still working? *European Psychologist, 7,* 85–97.

Baddeley, A.D. (2003a). Working memory and language: An overview. *Journal of Communication Disorders, 36,* 189–203.

Baddeley, A.D. (2003b). Working memory: Looking back and looking forward. *Nature Reviews Neuroscience, 4,* 829–839.

Baddeley, A.D., & Andrade, J. (2000). Working memory and the vividness of imagery. *Journal of Experimental Psychology: General, 129,* 126–145.

Baddeley, A.D., & Hitch, G.J. (1974). Working memory. In G. Bower (Ed.), *Recent advances in learning and motivation* (Vol. 8, pp. 47–89). New York: Academic Press.

Bahrick, H.P. (1984). Semantic memory in permastore: Fifty years of memory for Spanish learned in school. *Journal of Experimental Psychology: General, 113,* 1–31.

Bahrick, H.P. (2000). Long-term maintenance of knowledge. In E. Tulving & F.I.M. Craik (Eds.). *The Oxford handbook of memory* (pp. 347–362). New York: Oxford University Press.

Bahrick, H.P., & Hall, L.K. (1991). Lifetime maintenance of high school mathematics content. *Journal of Experimental Psychology: General, 120,* 20–33.

Bahrick, H.P., & Hall, L.K. (2005). The importance of retrieval failures to long-term retention: A metacognitive explanation of the spacing effect. *Journal of Memory and Language, 52,* 566–577.

Bahrick, H.P., Hall, L.K., & Berger, S.A. (1996). Accuracy and distortion in memory for high school grades. *Psychological Science, 5,* 265–271.

Bailey, M.E.S., & Johnson, K.J. (1997). Synaesthesia: Is genetic analysis feasible? In S. Baron-Cohen & J.E. Harrison (Eds.), *Synaesthesia: Classic and contemporary readings* (pp. 182–207). Oxford: Blackwell.

Baker, M.C. (2003). Linguistic differences and language design. *Trends in Cognitive Sciences, 7,* 349–353.

Baldwin, J.M. (1897). *Mental development of the child and the race* (2nd ed.). New York: Macmillan.

Ballard, P.B. (1913). Oblivescence and reminiscence. *British Journal of Psychology Monograph Supplements, 1,* 1–82.

Bamberger, J. (1982). Growing up prodigies: The mid-life crisis. In D.H. Feldman (Ed.), *Developmental approaches to giftedness* (pp. 61–77). San Francisco: Jossey-Bass.

Bamberger, J. (1986). Cognitive issues in the development of musically gifted children. In R.J. Sternberg & J. Davidson (Eds.), *Conceptions of giftedness* (pp. 388–413). New York: Cambridge University Press.

Banaji, M.R., & Crowder, R.G. (1989). The bankruptcy of everyday memory. *American Psychologist, 44,* 1185–1193.

Bar, M. (2004). Visual objects in context. *Nature Reviews Neuroscience, 5,* 617–629.

Barber, P. (1988). *Applied cognitive psychology.* New York: Methuen.

Barnard, P.J., Scott, S., Taylor, J., May, J., & Knightley, W. (2004). Paying attention to meaning. *Psychological Science, 15,* 179–186.

Barrett, L.F., Tugade, M.M., & Engle, R.W. (2004). Individual differences in working memory capacity and dual-process theories of mind. *Psychological Review, 130,* 553–573.

Barron, F. (1963). The disposition toward originality. In C.W. Taylor & F. Barron (Eds.), *Scientific creativity: Its recognition and development* (pp. 139–152). New York: Wiley.

Barron, S. (2005, July 24). R we D8ting? *New York Times.* Accessed 24 July 2005.

Barsalou, L.W. (1983). Ad hoc categories. *Memory & Cognition, 11,* 211–227.

Barsalou, L.W. (1987). The instability of graded structure: Implications for the nature of concepts. In U. Neisser (Ed.), *Concepts and conceptual development* (pp. 101–140). Cambridge: Cambridge University Press.

Barsalou, L.W. (1999). Perceptual symbol systems. *Behavioral and Brain Sciences, 22,* 577–660.

Barsalou, L.W. (2003). Abstraction in perceptual symbol systems. *Philosophical Transactions of the Royal Society of London (Series B), 358,* 1177–1187.

Barsalou, L.W., Simmons, W.K., Barbey, A.K., & Wilson, C.D. (2003). Grounding conceptual knowledge in modality-specific systems. *Trends in Cognitive Sciences, 7,* 84–91.

Barsalou, L.W., Solomon, K.O., & Wu, L.L. (1999). Perceptual simulation in conceptual tasks. In M.K. Hiraga, C. Sinha, & S. Wilcox (Eds.), *Cultural, typological, and psychological perspectives in cognitive linguistics: The proceedings of the 4th conference of the International Cognitive Linguistics Association: Vol. 3* (pp. 209–228). Amsterdam: John Benjamins.

Barton, J.J.S., Press, D.Z., Keenan, J.P., & O'Connor, M. (2002). Lesions of the fusiform face area impair perception of facial configuration in prosopagnosia. *Neurology, 58,* 71–78.

Bartlett, F.C. (1932). *Remembering.* Cambridge: Cambridge University Press.

Bartlett, F.C. (1958). *Thinking: An experimental and social study.* New York: Basic Books.

Baumeister, R.F. (1984). Choking under pressure: Self-consciousness and paradoxical effects of incentives on skillful performance. *Journal of Personality and Social Psychology, 46,* 610–620.

Baumeister, R.F., Bratslavsky, E., Finkenhauer, C., & Vohs, K.D. (2001). Bad is stronger than good. *Review of General Psychology, 5,* 323–370.

Baumeister, R. F., Bratslavsky, E., Muraven, M., & Tice, D. M. (1998). Ego depletion: Is the active self a limited resource? *Journal of Personality and Social Psychology, 74,* 1252–1265.

Baumeister, R.F., & Tierney, J. (2011). *Willpower.* Penguin Press: New York.

Bavelier, D., Corina, D., Jezzard, P., Padmanabhan, S., Clark, V.P., Karni, A., Prinster, A., Braun, A., Lalwani, A., Rauschecker, J.P., Turner, R., & Neville, H. (1997). Sentence reading: A functional MRI study at 4 Tesla. *Journal of Cognitive Neuroscience, 9,* 664–686.

Beck, J. (Ed.). (1982). *Organization and representation in perception.* Hillsdale, NJ: Erlbaum.

Beckers, G., & Zeki, S. (1995). The consequences of inactivating areas V1 and V5 on visual motion perception. *Brain, 118*(1), 49–60.

Begg, I. (1982). Imagery, organization and discriminative processes. *Canadian Journal of Psychology, 36,* 273–290.

Begg, I. (1987). Some. *Canadian Journal of Psychology, 41,* 62–73.

Begg, I., & Denny, J.P. (1969). Empirical reconciliation of atmosphere and conversion interpretations of syllogistic reasoning errors. *Journal of Experimental Psychology, 81,* 351–354.

Begg, I., & Harris, G. (1982). On the interpretation of syllogisms. *Journal of Verbal Learning and Verbal Behavior, 21,* 595–620.

Beilock, S.L., Carr, T. H., MacMahon, C., & Starkes, J.L. (2002). When paying attention becomes counterproductive: Impact of divided versus skill-focused attention on novice and experienced performance of sensorimotor skills. *Journal of Experimental Psychology: Applied, 8*(1), 6.

Beilock, S.L., & Holt, L.E. (2007). Embodied preference judgments: Can likeability be driven by the motor system? *Psychological Science, 18,* 51–57.

Benjafield, J. (1969a). Evidence that "thinking aloud" constitutes an externalization of inner speech. *Psychonomic Science, 15,* 83–84.

Benjafield, J. (1969b). Logical and empirical thinking in a problem-solving task. *Psychonomic Science, 14,* 285–286.

Benjafield, J. (1983). Some psychological hypotheses concerning the evolution of constructs. *British Journal of Psychology, 74,* 47–59.

Benjafield, J. (1987). An historical, social analysis of imagery and concreteness. *British Journal of Social Psychology, 26,* 155–164.

Benjafield, J., & Adams-Webber, J. (1976). The Golden Section hypothesis. *British Journal of Psychology, 67,* 11–15.

Benjafield, J., & Giesbrecht, L. (1973). Context effects and the recall of comparative sentences. *Memory & Cognition, 1,* 133–136.

Benjafield, J., & Green, T.R.G. (1978). Golden Section relations in interpersonal judgement. *British Journal of Psychology, 69,* 25–35.

Benjafield, J., & Segalowitz, S. (1993). Left and right in Leonardo's drawings of faces. *Empirical Studies of the Arts, 11,* 25–32.

Benjamin, A.S., Bjork, R.A., & Schwartz, B.L. (1998). The mismeasure of memory: When retrieval fluency is misleading as a metamnemonic index. *Journal of Experimental Psychology: General, 127,* 55–68.

Benson, D.F., & Greenberg, J.P. (1969). Visual form agnosia: A defect in visual discrimination. *Archives of Neurology, 20,* 82–89.

Bergman, E.T., & Roediger, H.L. (1997). Can Bartlett's repeated reproduction experiments be replicated? *Memory & Cognition, 27,* 937–947.

Berk, L.E. (1994, November). Why children talk to themselves. *Scientific American, 271,* 78–83.

Berlin, B., Breedlove, D.E., & Raven, P.H. (1973). General principles of classification and nomenclature in folk biology. *American Anthropologist, 89,* 914–920.

Berlin, B., & Kay, P. (1969). *Basic color terms: Their universality and evolution.* Berkeley: University of California Press.

Berlyne, D.E. (1965). *Structure and direction in thinking.* New York: Wiley.

Berlyne, D.E. (1971). *Aesthetics and psychobiology.* New York: Appleton-Century-Crofts.

Bernstein, L. (1976). *The unanswered question.* Cambridge, MA: Harvard University Press.

Berntsen, D., & Rubin, D.C. (2002). Emotionally charged autobiographical memories across the life span: The recall of happy, sad, traumatic, and involuntary memories. *Psychology and Aging, 17,* 636–652.

Berntsen, D., & Rubin, D.C. (2004). Cultural life scripts structure recall from autobiographical memory. *Memory & Cognition, 32,* 427–442.

Berry, D.C., & Dienes, Z. (1991). The relationship between implicit memory and implicit learning. *British Journal of Psychology, 82,* 359–373.

Best, J.B. (2001). Conditional reasoning processes in a logical deduction game. *Thinking and Reasoning, 7,* 235–254

Betsch, T., Haberstroh, S., Molter, B., & Glöckner, A. (2004). Oops, I did it again—relapse errors in routinized decision-making. *Organizational Behavior and Human Decision Processes, 93,* 62–74.

Bialystok, E., Craik, F.I.M., & Freedman, M. (2007). Bilingualism as a protection against the onset of symptoms of dementia. *Neuropsychologia, 45,* 459–464.

Bianchi, M. (2002). Novelty, preferences, and fashion: When goods are unsettling. *Journal of Economic Behavior & Organization, 47,* 1–18.

Biederman, I. (1987). Recognition-by-components: A theory of human image understanding. *Psychological Review, 94*(2), 115–147.

Biederman, I., Ju, G., & Clapper, J. (1985). The perception of partial objects. Unpublished manuscript, State University of New York at Buffalo.

Bielock, S.L., Carr, T.H., MacMahon, C., & Starkes, J.L. (2002). When paying attention becomes counterproductive: Impact of divided versus skill-focused attention on novice and experienced performance of sensorimotor skills. *Journal of Experimental Psychology: Applied, 8,* 6–16.

Bigelow, P. (1986). The indeterminability of time in "Sein und Zeit." *Philosophy and Phenomenological Research, 46,* 357–379.

Binet, A., & Simon, T. (1965). New methods for the diagnosis of the intellectual level of subnormals. In A. Anastasi (Ed.), *Individual differences* (pp. 35–41). New York: Wiley. (Original work published 1905b.)

Binet, A., & Simon, T. (1965). The development of intelligence in the child. In A. Anastasi (Ed.), *Individual differences* (pp. 41–44). New York: Wiley. (Original work published 1908.)

Binet, A., & Simon, T. (1965). Upon the necessity of establishing a scientific diagnosis of inferior states of intelligence. In A. Anastasi (Ed.), *Individual differences* (pp. 30–34). New York: Wiley. (Original work published 1905a.)

Binet, A., & Simon, T. (1915). *A method of measuring the development of the intelligence of young children* (C.H. Town, Trans.). Chicago: Chicago Medical Books. (Original work published 1911.)

Binkofski, F., Amunts, K., Stephan, K.M., Posse, S., Schormann, T., Freund, H.J., Zilles, K., & Seitz, R.J. (2000). Broca's region subserves imagery of motion: A combined cytoarchitectonic and fMRI study. *Human Brain Mapping, 11*, 273–285.

Birnbaum, M.H., & Mellers, B.A. (1979). Stimulus recognition may mediate exposure effects. *Journal of Personality and Social Psychology, 37*, 391–394.

Birnboim, S. (2003). The automatic and controlled information-processing dissociation: Is it still relevant? *Neuropsychology Review, 13*, 19–31.

Bjork, R.A., & Richardson-Klavehn, A. (1989). On the puzzling relationship between environmental context and memory. In C. Izawa (Ed.), *Current issues in cognitive processes* (pp. 313–344). Hillsdale, NJ: Erlbaum.

Black, M. (1962). Linguistic relativity: The views of Benjamin Lee Whorf. In M. Black (Ed.), *Models and metaphors* (pp. 244–257). Ithaca, NY: Cornell University Press.

Blair, C., Gamson, D., Thorne, S., & Baker, D. (2005). Rising mean IQ: Cognitive demand of mathematics education for young children, population exposure to formal schooling, and the neurobiology of the prefrontal cortex. *Intelligence, 33*, 96–106.

Blaney, P.H. (1986). Affect and memory: A review. *Psychological Bulletin, 99*, 229–246.

Block, N. (2005). Two neural correlates of consciousness. *Trends in Cognitive Sciences, 9*, 46–52.

Bloom, A. (1981). *The linguistic shaping of thought*. Hillsdale, NJ: Erlbaum.

Bloom, P., & Keil, F.C. (2001). Thinking through language. *Mind & Language, 16*, 351–367.

Blumenthal, A.L. (1970). *Language and psychology*. New York: Wiley.

Blumenthal, A.L. (1977). *The process of cognition*. Englewood Cliffs, NJ: Prentice-Hall.

Bodner, G.E., & Masson, M.E.J. (2003). Beyond spreading activation: An influence of relatedness proportion on masked semantic priming. *Psychonomic Bulletin & Review, 10*, 645–652.

Bohannon, J.N. (1988). Flashbulb memories for the space shuttle disaster: A tale of two theories. *Cognition, 29*, 179–196.

Bohannon, J.N., & Symons, V.L. (1992). Flashbulb memories: Confidence, consistency, and quantity. In E. Winograd & U. Neisser (Eds.), *Affect and accuracy in recall: Studies of "flashbulb" memories* (Vol. 4, pp. 65–91). New York: Cambridge University Press.

Borges, B., Goldstein, D.G., Ortmann, A., & Gigerenzer, G. (1999). Can ignorance beat the stock market? In G. Gigerenzer, P.M. Todd, & the ABC Research Group (Eds.), *Simple heuristics that make us smart* (pp. 59–72). New York: Oxford University Press.

Borges, J. (1966). *Other inquisitions*. New York: Washington Square Press.

Bornstein, R.F. (1989). Exposure and affect: Overview and meta-analysis of research, 1968–1987. *Psychological Bulletin, 106*, 265–289.

Bornstein, R.F., & D'Agostino, P.R. (1992). Stimulus recognition and the mere exposure effect. *Journal of Personality and Social Psychology, 63*, 545–552.

Boucher, J., & Osgood, C.E. (1969). The Pollyanna hypothesis. *Journal of Verbal Learning and Verbal Behavior, 8*, 1–8.

Bourne, L.E. (1966). *Human conceptual behavior*. Boston: Allyn & Bacon.

Bouvier, S.E., & Engel, S.A., (2006). Behavioral deficits and cortical damage loci in cerebral achromatopsia. *Cerebral Cortex, 16*, 183–191.

Bower, G.H. (1970a). Analysis of a mnemonic device. *American Scientist, 58*, 496–510.

Bower, G.H. (1970b). Imagery as a relational organizer in paired-associate learning. *Journal of Verbal Learning and Verbal Behavior, 9*, 529–533.

Bower, G.H. (1981). Mood and memory. *American Psychologist, 26*, 129–148.

Bower, G., Black, J., & Turner, T. (1979). Scripts in memory for text. *Cognitive Psychology, 11*, 177–220.

Bower, G.H., & Morrow, D.G. (1990). Mental models in narrative comprehension. *Science, 247*, 44–48.

Boylin, W., Gordon, S.K., & Nehrke, M.F. (1976). Reminiscing and ego integrity in institutionalized elderly males. *Gerontologist, 16*, 118–124.

Bradley, D.R., & Petry, H.M. (1977). Organizational determinants of subjective contour: The subjective Necker cube. *American Journal of Psychology, 90*, 253–262.

Braine, M.D.S. (1978). On the relation between the natural logic of reasoning and standard logic. *Psychological Review, 85*, 1–21.

Brandimonte, M.A., & Gerbino, W. (1993). Mental reversal and verbal recoding: When ducks become rabbits. *Memory & Cognition, 21*, 23–33.

Bransford, J.D., & Franks, J. (1971). The abstraction of linguistic ideas. *Cognitive Psychology, 2*, 331–350.

Brefczynski, J.A., & Yoe, E.A. (1999). A physiological correlate of the "spotlight" of visual attention. *Nature Neuroscience, 2*, 370–374.

Bregman, A.S. (1977). Perception and behavior as compositions of ideals. *Cognitive Psychology, 9*, 250–292.

Brentano, F.C. (1874). *Psychologie von dem Empirischen Standpunkt* [Psychology from an empirical standpoint]. Leipzig: Duncker & Humblot.

Broadbent, D.E. (1954). The role of auditory localization in attention and memory span. *Journal of Experimental Psychology, 47*, 191–196.

Broadbent, D.E. (1956). Successive responses to simultaneous stimuli. *Quarterly Journal of Experimental Psychology 8*, 145–52.

Broadbent, D.E. (1957). A mechanical model for human attention and immediate memory. *Psychological Review, 64*, 205–215.

Broadbent, D. (1958). *Perception and Communication*. London: Pergamon Press.

Broadbent, D.E. (1980). Donald E. Broadbent. In L. Gardner (Ed.), *A history of psychology in autobiography* (vol. 7, pp. 39–73). San Francisco: W.H. Freeman.

Broadbent, D.E. (1980). The minimization of models. In A.J. Chapman & D.M. Jones (Eds.), *Models of man* (pp. 113–128). Leicester: British Psychological Society.

Broadbent, D.E. (1984). The Maltese cross: A new simplistic model for memory. *Behavioral and Brain Sciences, 7,* 55–94.

Broadbent, D.E. (1990). A problem looking for solutions. *Psychological Science, 1,* 240–246.

Broadbent, D.E. (1992). Listening to one of two synchronous messages. *Journal of Experimental Psychology, General, 121,* 51–55. (Original work published 1952).

Broca, P. (1966). Paul Broca on the speech center. In R. Herrnstein & E. Boring (Eds.), *A source book in the history of psychology* (pp. 223–229). Cambridge, MA: Harvard University Press. (Original work published 1861.)

Brockmole, J.R., Wang, R.F., & Irwin, D.E. (2002). Temporal integration between visual images and visual percepts. *Journal of Experimental Psychology: Human Perception and Performance, 28,* 315–334.

Brody, N. (2003a). Construct validation of the Sternberg Triarchic Abilities Test: Comment and reanalysis. *Intelligence, 31,* 319–324.

Brody, N. (2003b). What Sternberg should have concluded. *Intelligence, 31,* 339–342.

Brokate, B., Hildebrandt, H., Eling, P., Fichtner, H., Runge, K., & Timm, C. (2003). Frontal lobe dysfunctions in Korsakoff's syndrome and chronic alcoholism: Continuity or discontinuity? *Neuropsychology, 17,* 420–428.

Brooks, J.O., & Watkins, M.J. (1989). Recognition memory and the mere exposure effect. *Journal of Experimental Psychology: Learning, Memory, and Cognition, 15,* 968–976.

Brooks, L.R. (1968). Spatial and verbal components of the act of recall. *Canadian Journal of Psychology, 22,* 349–368.

Brown, A.S. (1991). A review of the tip-of-the-tongue experience. *Psychological Bulletin, 109,* 204–223.

Brown, A.S. (2003). A review of the déjà vu experience. *Psychological Bulletin, 129,* 394–413.

Brown, A.S., Bracken, E., Zoccoli, S., Douglas, K. (2004). Generating and remembering passwords. *Applied Cognitive Psychology, 18,* 641–651.

Brown, J. (1958). Some tests of the decay theory of immediate memory. *Quarterly Journal of Experimental Psychology, 10,* 12–21.

Brown, R. (1958). *Words and things.* New York: Free Press.

Brown, R. (1968). *Words and things.* New York: Free Press.

Brown, R. (1973). *A first language.* Cambridge, MA: Harvard University Press.

Brown, R., & Hanlon, C. (1970). Derivational complexity and the order of acquisition in child speech. In J.R. Hayes (Ed.), *Cognition and the development of language* (pp. 11–53). New York: Wiley.

Brown, R., & Kulik, J. (1977). Flashbulb memories. *Cognition, 5,* 73–99.

Brown, R., & Lenneberg, E. (1956). A study in language and cognition. *Journal of Abnormal and Social Psychology, 49,* 454–462.

Brown, R., & McNeill, D. (1966). The "tip of the tongue phenomenon." *Journal of Verbal Learning and Verbal Behavior, 5,* 325–337.

Brown, S.C., & Craik, F.I.M. (2000). Encoding and retrieval of information. In E. Tulving & F.I.M. Craik (Eds.), *The Oxford handbook of memory* (pp. 93–107). New York: Oxford University Press.

Bruce, D. (1985). The how and why of ecological memory. *Journal of Experimental Psychology: General, 114,* 78–90.

Bruce, D. (1986). Lashley's shift from bacteriology to neuropsychology, 1910–1917, and the influence of Jennings, Watson, and Franz. *Journal of the History of the Behavioral Sciences, 22,* 27–43.

Bruce, D., & Bahrick, H.P. (1992). Perceptions of past research. *American Psychologist, 47,* 319–328.

Bruner, J.S. (1983). *Child's talk.* New York: Norton.

Bruner, J.S. (1985). Vygotsky: A historical and conceptual perspective. In J. Wertsch (Ed.), *Culture, communication and cognition* (pp. 21–34). Cambridge: Cambridge University Press.

Bruner, J.S., Goodnow, J.J., & Austin, G.A. (1956). *A study of thinking.* New York: Wiley.

Brunswik, E. (1956). *Perception and the representative design of experiments.* Berkeley: University of California Press.

Bruyer, R., Laterre, C., Seron, X., Feyereisen, P., Strypstein, E., Pierrard, E., & Rectem, D. (1983). A case of prosopagnosia with some preserved covert remembrance of familiar faces. *Brain and Cognition, 2,* 257–284.

Bryant, D.J., Tversky, B., & Franklin, N. (1992). Internal and external spatial frameworks for representing described scenes. *Journal of Memory and Language, 31,* 74–98.

Bryson, B. (2003). *A short history of nearly everything.* New York: Broadway Books.

Burke, D.M., MacKay, D.G., Worthley, J.S., & Wade, E. (1991). On the tip of the tongue: What causes word finding failures in young and older adults? *Journal of Memory and Language, 30,* 542–579.

Burns, B.D. (2004). Heuristics as beliefs and behaviors: The adaptiveness of the "hot hand." *Cognitive Psychology, 48,* 295–331.

Burns, B.D., & Weith, M. (2004). The collider principle in causal reasoning: Why the Monty Hall dilemma is so hard. *Journal of Experimental Psychology: General, 133,* 414–449.

Cabeza, R., & Nyberg, L. (2003). Special issue on functional neuroimaging of memory. *Neuropsychologia, 41,* 241–244.

Cacioppo, J.T., Berntson, G.G., Lorig, T.S., Norris, C.J., Rickett, E., & Nusbaum, H. (2003). Just because you're imaging the brain doesn't mean you can stop using your head: A primer and set of first principles. *Journal of Personality and Social Psychology, 85,* 650–661.

Calvo-Merino, B., Glaser, D.E., Grezes, J., Passingham, R.E., & Haggard, P. (2005). Action observation and acquired motor skills: An fMRI study with expert dancers. *Cerebral Cortex, 15,* 1243–1249.

Calvo-Merino, B., Grezes, J., Glaser, D.E., Passingham, R.E., & Haggard, P. (2006). Seeing or doing? Influence of visual or motor familiarity in action observation. *Current Biology, 16,* 1905–1910.

Campbell, D.T. (1960). Blind variation and selective retention in creative thought as in other knowledge processes. *Psychological Bulletin, 67,* 380–400.

Campbell, M., Hoane, A.J., & Hsu, F. (2002). Deep Blue. *Artificial Intelligence, 134,* 57–83.

Caplan, D., Alpert, N., Waters, G., & Olivieri, A. (2000). Activation in Broca's area by syntactic processing under conditions of concurrent articulation. *Human Brain Mapping, 9,* 65–71.

Card, S.K., English, W.K., Burr, B.J. (1978). Evaluation of mouse, rate controlled isometric joystick, step-keys, and text keys for selection on a CRT. *Ergonomics, 21,* 601–613.

Carpenter, P.A., Just, M.A., & Shell, P. (1990). What one intelligence test measures: A theoretical account of the processing in the Raven Progressive Matrices Test. *Psychological Review, 97,* 404–431.

Carroll, J.B. (1953). *The study of language.* Cambridge, MA: Harvard University Press.

Carroll, J.M. (1997). Human-computer interaction: Psychology as a science of design. *International Journal of Human-Computer Studies, 46,* 501–522.

Carroll, J.M., Bever, T.G., & Pollack, C.R. (1981). The non-uniqueness of linguistic intuitions. *Language, 57,* 368–383.

Carroll, J.M., Kellogg, W.A., & Rosson, M.B. (1991). The task-artifact cycle. In J.M. Carroll (Ed.), *Designing interaction: Psychology at the human-computer interface* (pp. 74–102). New York: Cambridge University Press.

Carter, J.R., & Irons, M.D. (1991). Are economists different, and if so, why? *Journal of Economic Perspectives, 5,* 171–177.

Casselden, P.A., & Hampson, S.E. (1990). Forming impressions from incongruent traits. *Journal of Personality and Social Psychology, 59,* 353–362.

Cassirer, E. (1953–1959). *The philosophy of symbolic forms* (3 vols.). New Haven: Yale University Press.

Castles, A., & Coltheart, M. (1993). Varieties of developmental dyslexia. *Cognition, 47,* 149–180.

Cattell, J. McK. (1903). Statistics of American psychologists. *American Journal of Psychology, 14,* 310–328.

Cazden, C.B. (1976). Play with language and metalinguistic awareness. In J.S. Bruner, A. Jolly, & K. Sylva (Eds.), *Play: Its role in development and evolution* (pp. 603–608). London: Penguin.

Ceraso, J., & Provitera, A. (1971). Sources of error in syllogistic reasoning. *Cognitive Psychology, 2,* 400–410.

Chalmers, D.J. (1995). Facing up to the problem of consciousness. *Journal of Consciousness Studies, 2,* 200–19.

Chalmers, P.A. (2003). The role of cognitive theory in human computer interface. *Computers in Human Behavior, 19,* 593–607.

Chambers, D., & Reisberg, D. (1985). Can mental images be ambiguous? *Journal of Experimental Psychology: Human Perception and Performance, 11,* 317–328.

Chambers, D., & Reisberg, D. (1992). What an image depicts depends on what an image means. *Cognitive Psychology, 24,* 145–174.

Chang, T.M. (1986). Semantic memory: Facts and models. *Psychological Bulletin, 99,* 199–220.

Chapman, G.B., & Johnson, E.J. (2002). Incorporating the irrelevant: Anchors in judgments of belief and value. In T. Gilovich, D. Griffin, & D. Kahneman (Eds.), *Heuristics and biases: The psychology of intuitive judgment* (pp. 120–138). Cambridge: Cambridge University Press.

Chapman, L.J., & Chapman, J.P. (1959). Atmosphere effect re-examined. *Journal of Experimental Psychology, 55,* 220–226.

Chapman, L.J., & Chapman, J.P. (1969). Illusory correlation as an obstacle to the use of valid psychodiagnostic signs. *Journal of Abnormal Psychology, 74,* 271–280.

Chase, W.G., & Simon, H.A. (1973). Perception in chess. *Cognitive Psychology, 4,* 55–81.

Chaytor, N., & Schmitter-Edgecomb, M. (2003). The ecological validity of neuropsychological tests: A review of the literature on everyday cognitive skills. *Neuropsychological Review, 13,* 181–197.

Cheesman, J., & Merikle, P.M. (1986). Distinguishing conscious from unconscious perceptual processing. *Canadian Journal of Psychology, 40,* 343–367.

Chen, J.-Q. (2004). Theory of multiple intelligences: Is it a scientific theory? *Teacher's College Record, 106,* 17–23.

Cherniak, C. (1984). Prototypicality and deductive reasoning. *Journal of Verbal Learning and Verbal Behavior, 23,* 625–642.

Cherry, E.C. (1953). Some experiments on the recognition of speech with one and with two ears. *Journal of the Acoustical Society of America, 25,* 975–979.

Chomsky, N. (1957). *Syntactic structures.* The Hague: Mouton.

Chomsky, N. (1959). Review of Skinner's verbal behavior. *Language, 35,* 26–58.

Chomsky, N. (1965). *Aspects of the theory of syntax.* The Hague: Mouton.

Chomsky, N. (1966). *Cartesian linguistics.* New York: Harper & Row.

Chomsky, N. (1967). The formal nature of language. In E. Lenneberg, *Biological foundations of language* (pp. 397–442). New York: Wiley.

Chomsky, N. (1968). *Language and mind.* New York: Harcourt, Brace & World.

Chomsky, N. (1972). *Language and mind* (Enlarged ed.). New York: Harcourt Brace Jovanovich.

Chomsky, N. (1980a). *Rules and representations.* New York: Columbia University Press.

Chomsky, N. (1980b). Rules and representations. *Behavioral and Brain Sciences, 3,* 1–61.

Chomsky, N. (1981). *Lectures on government and binding.* Dordrecht, the Netherlands: Fortis.

Chomsky, N. (1995). Language and nature. *Mind, 104,* 1–61.

Chomsky, N. (2005). Three factors in language design. *Linguistic Inquiry, 36,* 1–22.

Chomsky, N. (2006). Noam Chomsky: you ask the questions. Interview in *The Independent,* 28 Aug. Retrieved 22 Oct. 2015 from www.independent.co.uk/news/people/profiles/noam-chomsky-you-ask-the-questions-5330371.html.

Chouinard, M.M., & Clark, E.V. (2003). Adult reformulations of child errors as negative evidence. *Journal of Child Language, 30,* 637–669.

Christian, J., Bickley, W., Tarka, M., & Clayton, K. (1978). Measures of free recall of 900 English nouns. *Memory & Cognition, 6,* 379–390.

Christoff, K., Gordon, A.M., Smallwood, J., Smith, R., & Schooler, J.W. (2009). Experience sampling during fMRI reveals default network and executive system contributions to mind wandering. *Proceedings of the National Academy of Sciences, 106* (21), 8719–8724.

Chronicle, E.P., MacGregor, J.N., & Ormerod, T.C. (2004). What makes an insight problem? The roles of heuristics, goal conception, and solution recoding in knowledge-lean problems. *Journal of Experimental Psychology: Learning, Memory, and Cognition, 30,* 14–27.

Chu, S., & Downes, J.J. (2000). Long live Proust: The odour-cued autobiographical memory bump. *Cognition, 75,* B41–B50.

Chwilla, D.J., & Kolk, H.H.J. (2002). Three-step priming in lexical decision. *Memory & Cognition, 30,* 217–225.

Claparède, E. (1951). Recognition and "meness." In D. Rapaport (Ed.), *Organization and pathology of thought* (pp. 58–75). New York: Columbia University Press. (Original work published 1911.)

Clark, A. (1999). An embodied science? *Trends in Cognitive Sciences, 3,* 345–351.

Clark, E.V. (2004). How language acquisition builds on cognitive development. *Trends in Cognitive Sciences, 8,* 472–478.

Clark, H.H. (1969). Linguistic processes in deductive reasoning. *Psychological Review, 76*, 387–404.

Clark, H.H. & Card, S.K. (1969). The role of semantics in remembering comparative sentences. *Journal of Experimental Psychology, 82*, 545–553.

Clark, H.H., & Clark, E. (1977). *The psychology of language*. New York: Harcourt Brace Jovanovich.

Clark, H.H., & Fox Tree, J.E. (2002). Using *uh* and *um* in spontaneous speaking. *Cognition, 84*, 73–111.

Clark, H.H., & Gerrig, R. (1984). On the pretense theory of irony. *Journal of Experimental Psychology: General, 113*, 121–126.

Clark, H.H., & Haviland, S.E. (1977). Comprehension and the given-new contract. In R.O. Freedle (Ed.), *Discourse production and comprehension* (pp. 1–40). Norwood, NJ: Ablex.

Clark, J.M., & Paivio, A. (1989). Observational and theoretical terms in psychology: A cognitive perspective on scientific language. *American Psychologist, 44*, 500–512.

Clayton, N.S., & Dickinson, A. (1998). Episodic-like memory during cache recovery by scrub jays. *Nature, 395*, 272–278.

Cleeremans, A., Destrebecqz, A., & Boyer, M. (1998). Implicit learning: News from the front. *Trends in Cognitive Sciences, 2*, 406–416.

Clifford, B.R. (2004). Celebrating levels of processing. *Applied Cognitive Psychology, 18*, 486–489.

Cofer, C. (1973). Constructive processes in memory. *American Scientist, 61*, 537–543.

Cole, W.G., & Loftus, E.F. (1979). Incorporating new information into memory. *American Journal of Psychology, 92*, 413–425.

Collins, A.M., & Loftus, E.F. (1975). A spreading-activation theory of semantic processing. *Psychological Review, 82*, 407–428.

Collins, A.M., & Quillian, M.R. (1972). Experiments on semantic memory and language comprehension. In L.W. Gregg (Ed.), *Cognition in learning and memory* (pp. 117–137). New York: Wiley.

Colman, A.M. (2003). Cooperation, psychological game theory, and limitations of rationality in social interaction. *Behavioral and Brain Sciences, 26*, 139–198.

Coltheart, M., Rastle, K., Perry, C., Ziegler, J., & Langdon, R. (2001). DRC: A dual route cascade model of visual word recognition and reading aloud. *Psychological Review, 108*, 204–256.

Colvin, M.K., Dunbar, K., & Grafman, J. (2000). The effects of frontal lobe lesions on goal achievement in the water jug task. *Journal of Cognitive Neuroscience, 13*, 1129–1147.

Conway, A.R.A., Kane, M.J., & Engle, R.W. (2003). Working memory capacity and its relation to general intelligence. *Trends in Cognitive Sciences, 7*, 547–552.

Conway, M.A., Cohen, G., & Stanhope, N. (1991). On the very long-term retention of knowledge acquired through formal education: Twelve years of cognitive psychology. *Journal of Experimental Psychology: General, 120*(4), 395.

Conway, M.A., & Pleydell-Pearce, C.W. (2000). The construction of autobiographical memories in the self-memory system. *Psychological Review, 107*, 261–288.

Corballis, M.C. (1997). Mental rotation and the right hemisphere. *Brain and Language, 57*, 100–121.

Corballis, M.C. (2003). From mouth to hand: Gesture, speech and the evolution of right handedness. *Behavioral and Brain Sciences, 26*, 199–260.

Corballis, M.C. (2004a). The origin of modernity: Was autonomous speech the critical factor? *Psychological Review, 111*, 543–552.

Corballis, M.C. (2004b). FOXP2 and the mirror system. *Trends in Cognitive Sciences, 8*, 95–96.

Coren, S., & Girgus, J.S. (1980). Principles of perceptual organization and spatial distortion: The Gestalt illusions. *Journal of Experimental Psychology: Human Perception and Performance, 6*, 404–412.

Cosmides, L. (1989). The logic of social exchange: Has natural selection shaped how humans reason? Studies with the Wason selection task. *Cognition, 31*, 187–276.

Cosmides, L., & Tooby, J. (1994). Origins of domain specificity: The evolution of functional organization. In L.A. Hirschfeld & S.A. Gelman (Eds.), *Mapping the mind: Domain specificity in cognition and culture* (pp. 85–116). New York: Cambridge University Press.

Cosmides, L., & Tooby, J. (2002). Unraveling the enigma of human intelligence: Evolutionary psychology and the multimodular mind. In R.J. Sternberg & J.C. Kaufman (Eds.), *The evolution of intelligence* (pp. 145–198). Mahwah, NJ: Erlbaum.

Cowan, N. (1988). Evolving conceptions of memory storage, selective attention, and their mutual constraints within the human information-processing system. *Psychological Review, 104*, 163–191.

Cowan, N. (2001). The magical number 4 in short-term memory: A reconsideration of mental storage capacity. *Behavioral and Brain Sciences, 24*, 87–114.

Craik, F.I.M. (1980). *Cognitive views of human memory* (Cassette Recording). Washington: American Psychological Association.

Craik, F.I.M. (2002). Levels of processing: Past, present . . . and future? *Memory, 10*, 305–318.

Craik, F.I.M., & Grady, C.L. (2002). Aging, memory, and frontal lobe functioning. In D.T. Stuss and R.T. Knight (Eds.), *Principles of frontal lobe function* (pp. 528–540). New York: Oxford University Press.

Craik, F.I.M., & Lockhart, R.S. (1972). Levels of processing: A framework for memory research. *Journal of Verbal Learning and Verbal Behavior, 11*, 671–684.

Crawford, L.E., & Cacioppo, J.T. (2002). Learning where to look for danger: Integrating affective and spatial information. *Psychological Science, 13*, 449–453.

Cree, G.S., & McRae, K. (2003). Analyzing factors underlying the structure and computation of the meaning of *Chipmunk, Cherry, Chisel, Cheese,* and *Cello* (and many other such concrete nouns). *Journal of Experimental Psychology: General, 132*, 163–201.

Crovitz, H.F. (1970). *Galton's walk*. New York: Harper & Row.

Crovitz, H.F., & Schiffman, H. (1974). Frequency of episodic memories as a function of their age. *Bulletin of the Psychonomic Society, 4*, 517–518.

Crovitz, H.F., Schiffman, H., & Apter, A. (1991). Galton's number. *Bulletin of the Psychonomic Society, 29*, 331–332.

Csikszentmihalyi, M. (1990). *Flow: The psychology of optimal experience*. New York: Harper & Row.

Csikszentmihalyi, M. (2002). Jacob Warren Getzels (1912–2001). *American Psychologist, 57*, 290–291.

Csikszentmihalyi, M., & Beattie, O.V. (1979). Life themes: A theoretical and empirical exploration of their origins and effects. *Journal of Humanistic Psychology, 19*, 46–63.

Csikszentmihalyi, M., & Getzels, J. (1973). The personality of young artists: An empirical and theoretical exploration. *British Journal of Psychology, 64*, 91–104.

Cuban, L. (2004). Assessing the 20-year impact of multiple intelligences on schooling. *Teacher's College Record, 106*, 140–146.

Cui, X., Jeter, C.B., Yang, D., Montague, P.R.,& Eagleman, D.M. (2007). Vividness of mental imagery: Individual variability can be measured objectively. *Vision Research, 47*, 474–478.

Cunningham, J.B., & MacGregor, J.N. (2014). Productive and re-productive thinking in solving insight problems. *Journal of Creative Behavior, 48*, 44–63.

Cupchik, G.C. (1988). The legacy of Daniel E. Berlyne. *Empirical Studies of the Arts, 6*, 171–186.

Curran, T. (2001). Implicit learning revealed by the method of opposition. *Trends in Cognitive Sciences, 5*, 503–504.

Curtis, C.E., & D'Esposito, M. (2003). Persistent activity in the prefrontal cortex during working memory. *Trends in Cognitive Sciences, 7*, 415–423.

Cytowic, R.E. (2002). *Synaesthesia: A union of the senses* (2nd ed.). Cambridge, MA: MIT Press.

Daley, T.C., Whaley, S.E., Sigman, M.D., Espinosa, M.P., & Neumann, C. (2003). IQ on the rise: The Flynn effect in rural Kenyan children. *Psychological Science, 14*, 215–219.

Damasio, A.R., & Benton, A.L. (1979). Impairment of hand movements under visual guidance. *Neurology, 29*, 170.

D'Andrade, R. (1987). A folk model of the mind. In D. Holland & N. Quinn (Eds.), *Cultural models in language and thought* (pp. 112–148). Cambridge: Cambridge University Press.

Darwin, C. (1859). *On the origins of species by means of natural selection*. London: Murray.

Davidoff, J. (2001). Language and perceptual categorization. *Trends in Cognitive Sciences, 5*, 382–387.

Davidoff, J., Davies, I., & Roberson, D. (1999). Colour categories in a stone-age tribe. *Nature, 398*, 203–204.

Dawes, R.M. (1988). *Rational choice in an uncertain world*. San Diego: Harcourt Brace Jovanovich.

Dawes, R.M. (1993). Prediction of the future versus understanding of the past: A basic asymmetry. *American Journal of Psychology, 106*, 1–24.

Dawes, R.M. (1994). *House of cards: Psychology and psychotherapy built on myth*. New York: Free Press.

Dawes, R.M. (1999). A message from psychologists to economists: Mere predictability doesn't matter like it should (without a good story appended to it). *Journal of Economic Behavior & Organization, 39*, 29–40.

Dawkins, R. (1976). *The selfish gene*. Oxford: Oxford University Press.

Dawkins, R. (1988). *The blind watchmaker*. London: Penguin.

Dawson, M.R.W. (2005). *Connectionism: A hands-on approach*. Malden, MA: Blackwell.

Debner, J.A., & Jacoby, L.L. (1994). Unconscious perception: Attention, awareness, and control. *Journal of Experimental Psychology: Learning, Memory, and Cognition, 20*(2), 304–317.

DeDreu, C.K.W., & Boles, T.L. (1998). Share and share alike or winner take all? The influence of social value orientation upon the choice and recall of negotiation heuristics. *Organization Behavior and Human Decision Processes, 76*, 253–276.

Deese, J. (1965). *The structure of associations in language and thought*. Baltimore: Johns Hopkins University Press.

Deese, J. (1970). *Psycholinguistics*. Boston: Allyn & Bacon.

Deese, J. (1984). *Thought into speech: The psychology of a language*. New York: Prentice-Hall.

Deese, J., & Hamilton, H.W. (1974). Marking and propositional effects in associations to compounds. *American Journal of Psychology, 87*, 1–15.

Defeyter, M.A., & German, T.P. (2003). Acquiring an understanding of design: Evidence from children's insight problemsolving. *Cognition, 89*, 133–155.

de Haan, E.H.F., & Cowey, A. (2011). On the usefulness of "what" and "where" pathways in vision. *Trends in Cognitive Neuroscience, 15*, 460–466.

Dehaene, S. (2003). The neural basis of the Weber-Fechner law: A logarithmic mental number line. *Trends in Cognitive Science, 7*, 145–147.

Dehaene, S., et al. (1998). Imaging unconscious semantic priming. *Nature, 395*, 597–600.

De Lisi, R., & Wolford, J.L. (2002). Improving children's mental rotation accuracy with computer game playing. *Journal of Genetic Psychology, 163*, 272–282.

Denis, M., & Kosslyn, S.M. (1999). Scanning visual mental images: A window on the mind. *Current Psychology of Cognition, 18*, 409–465.

Dennett, D. (1991). *Consciousness explained*. Boston: Little, Brown.

Dennett, D. (1995). *Darwin's dangerous idea*. New York: Simon & Schuster.

Dennett, D. (2003). The Baldwin effect: A crane, not a skyhook. In B.H. Weber & D.J. Depew, *Evolution and learning: The Baldwin effect reconsidered* (pp. 69–80). Cambridge, MA: MIT Press.

Depew, D.J. (2003). Baldwin and his many effects. In B.H. Weber & D.J. Depew, *Evolution and learning: The Baldwin effect reconsidered* (pp. 3–31). Cambridge, MA: MIT Press.

de Saussure, F. (1916). *Cours de linguistique generale* [Course in general linguistics]. Paris: Bally & Sechehaye.

Descartes, R. (1644/1911). *The principles of philosophy*. E. Haldane and G. Ross (Trans.). Cambridge: Cambridge University Press.

DeSoto, C.B., London, M., & Handel, S. (1965). Social reasoning and spatial paralogic. *Journal of Personality and Social Psychology, 2*, 513–521.

Di Carlo, A., Baldereschi, M., Amaducci, L., Lepore, V., Bracco, L., Maggi, S., Bonaiuto, S., Perissinotto, E., Scarlato, G., Farchi, G., & Inzitari, D. (2002). Incidence of dementia, Alzheimer's disease, and vascular dementia in Italy. The ILSA Study. *Journal of the American Geriatric Society, 50*, 41–48.

Dickens, W.T., & Flynn, J.R. (2001). Heritability estimates versus large environmental effects: The IQ paradox resolved. *Psychological Bulletin, 108*, 346–369.

Dietrich, E. (1999). Algorithm. In R.A. Wilson, & F.C. Keil, (Eds.), *The MIT encyclopedia of the cognitive sciences* (pp. 11–12). Cambridge, MA: MIT Press.

DiLiilo, V., Kawahara, J.-I., Zuvic, S.M., & Visser, T.A.W. (2001). The preattentive emperor has no clothes: A dynamic redressing. *Journal of Experimental Psychology: General, 130*, 479–492.

Di Pellegrino, G., Fadiga, L., Fogassi, L., Gallese, V., Rizzolatti, G. (1992). Understanding motor events: A neurophysiological study. *Experimental Brain Research, 91*, 176–189.

Di Pellegrino, G., Rafal, R., & Tipper, S.P. (2005). Implicitly evoked actions modulate visual selection: Evidence from parietal extinction. *Current Biology, 15*, 1469–1472.

DiSessa, A. (1983). Phenomenology and the evolution of intuition. In D. Gentner & A.L. Stevens, (Eds.), *Mental models* (pp. 15–33). Hillsdale, NJ: Erlbaum.

Dixon, M.J., Smilek, D., Cudahy, C., & Merikle, P.M. (2000). Five plus two equals yellow. *Nature, 406*, 365.

Dixon, N.F. (1971). *Subliminal perception: The nature of a controversy*. London: McGraw-Hill.

Dixon, R.M.W. (1982). *Where have all the adjectives gone?* Berlin: Walter de Gruyter.

Dominowski, R.L. (1981). Comment on "An examination of the alleged role of 'fixation' in the solution of several 'insight' problems by Weisberg and Alba." *Journal of Experimental Psychology: General, 110*, 199–203.

Dowling, W.J., & Harwood, D.L. (1986). *Music cognition*. New York: Academic Press.

Downing, P.E., Bray, D., Rogers, J., & Childs, C. (2004). Bodies capture attention when nothing is expected. *Cognition, 93*, B27–B38.

Downing, P.E., Jiang, Y., Shuman, M. & Kanwisher, N. (2001). A cortical area selective for visual processing of the human body. *Science, 293*, 2470–2473.

Downs, R.M., & Stea, D. (1977). *Maps in minds: Some reflections on cognitive mapping*. New York: Harper & Row.

Dreisbach, G., & Goschke, T. (2004). How positive affect modulates cognitive control: Reduced perseveration at the cost of increased distractibility. *Journal of Experimental Psychology: Learning, Memory, and Cognition, 30*, 343–353.

Dudai, Y. (2004). The neurobiology of consolidations, or, how stable is the engram? *Annual Review of Psychology, 55*, 51–86.

Dulany, D., Carlson, R., & Dewey, G. (1984). A case of syntactical learning and judgment: How conscious and how abstract? *Journal of Experimental Psychology: General, 113*, 541–555.

Dulany, D., Carlson, R., & Dewey, G. (1985). On consciousness in syntactic learning and judgment: A reply to Reber, Allen and Regan. *Journal of Experimental Psychology: General, 114*, 25–32.

Dunbar, K. (2000). How scientists think in the real world: Implications for science education. *Journal of Applied Developmental Psychology, 21*, 49–58.

Dunbar, K. (2001). What scientific thinking reveals about the nature of cognition. In K. Crowley & C.D. Schunn (Eds.), *Designing for science: Implications from everyday, classroom, and professional settings* (pp. 115–140). Mahwah, NJ: Erlbaum.

Dunbar, K., & Blanchette, I. (2001). The *in vivo/in vitro* approach to cognition: The case of analogy. *Trends in Cognitive Sciences, 5*, 334–339.

Duncker, K. (1945). On problem-solving. *Psychological Monographs, 58* (5, Whole No. 270).

Dupré, J. (1987). *The latest on the best: Essays on evolution and optimality*. Cambridge, MA: MIT Press.

Durgin, F.H. (1999). The (illusory) perception of visual detail: Texture and faces. *Perception, 28* (Suppl.), 43.

Eacott, M.J., & Crawley, R.A. (1998). The offset of childhood amnesia: Memory for events that occurred before age 3. *Journal of Experimental Psychology: General, 127*, 22–33.

Eagle, M., Wolitzky, D.L., & Klein, G.S. (1966). Imagery: The effect of a concealed figure in a stimulus. *Science, 151*, 837–839.

Ebbinghaus, H. (1964). *Memory: A contribution to experimental psychology*. New York: Dover. (Original work published 1885.)

Eco, U. (1989). *Foucault's pendulum*. New York: Knopf.

Edgerton, S. (1975). *The Renaissance rediscovery of linear perspective*. New York: Basic Books.

Edmonds, E.A., & Green, T.R.G. (Eds.). (1984). Ergonomics of the user interface (Special Issue). *Behaviour and Information Technology, 3*(2).

Edwards, D., & Potter, J. (1992). The Chancellor's memory: Rhetoric and truth in discursive remembering. *Applied Cognitive Psychology, 6*, 187–215.

Egan, J.P., Carterette, E.C., & Thwing, E.J. (1954). Some factors affecting multichannel listening. *Journal of the Acoustical Society of America, 26*, 774–782.

Eich, E. (1984). Memory for unattended events: Remembering with and without awareness. *Memory & Cognition, 12*, 105–111.

Eich, E. (1995). Searching for mood dependent memory. *Psychological Science, 6*, 67–75.

Eich, E., & Forgas, J.P. (2003). Mood, cognition, and memory. In A.F. Healy & R.W. Proctor (Eds.), *Handbook of psychology: Vol 4. Experimental psychology* (pp. 61–83). Hoboken, NJ: Wiley.

Eich, E., & Macaulay, D. (2000). Are real moods required to reveal mood-congruent and mood-dependent memory? *Psychological Science, 11*, 244–248.

Eich, E., Macaulay, D., & Ryan, L. (1994). Mood-dependent memory for events of the personal past. *Journal of Experimental Psychology: General, 123*, 201–215.

Eich, E., & Metcalfe, J. (1989). Mood-dependent memory for internal versus external events. *Journal of Experimental Psychology: Learning, Memory, and Cognition, 15*, 443–455.

Eich, J.E., Weingartner, H., Stillman, R.C., & Gillin, J.C. (1975). State-dependent accessibility of retrieval cues in the retention of a categorized list. *Journal of Verbal Learning & Verbal Behavior, 14*(4), 408–417.

Einstein, G.O., & McDaniel, M.A. (1987). Distinctiveness and the mnemonic benefits of bizarre imagery. In M.A. McDaniel & M. Pressley (Eds.), *Imagery and related mnemonic processes: Theories, individual differences and applications* (pp. 78–102). New York: Springer-Verlag.

Einstein, G.O., McDaniel, M.A., & Lackey, S. (1989). Bizarre imagery, interference, and distinctiveness. *Journal of Experimental Psychology: Learning, Memory, and Cognition, 15*, 137–146.

Einstein, G.O., McDaniel, M. A., Smith, R.E., & Shaw, P. (1998). Habitual prospective memory and aging: Remembering intentions and forgetting actions. *Psychological Science, 9*, 284–288.

Einstein, G.O., McDaniel, M.A., Williford, C.L., Pagan, J.L., & Dismukes, R.K. (2003). Forgetting of intentions in demanding situations is rapid. *Journal of Experimental Psychology: Applied, 9*, 147–162.

Eisenstadt, M., & Kareev, Y. (1977). Perception in game playing. In P.N. Johnson-Laird & P.C. Wason (Eds.), *Thinking* (pp. 548–564). Cambridge: Cambridge University Press.

Eisenstadt, S.A., & Simon, H.A. (1997). Logic and thought. *Minds and Machines, 7*, 365–385.

Ekman, P.D. Facial expressions. (1999). In T. Dalgleish & M. Power (Eds.), *Handbook of cognition and emotion* (pp. 45–60). New York: Wiley.

Ellen, P. (1982). Direction, past experience, and hints in creative problem-solving. *Journal of Experimental Psychology: General, 111*, 316–325.

Elliot, A.J., & Maier, M.A. (2014). Color psychology: Effects of perceiving color on psychological functioning in humans. *Annual Review of Psychology, 65*, 95–120.

Ellis, H.C. (1990). Depressive deficits in memory: Processing initiative and resource allocation. *Journal of Experimental Psychology: General, 119*, 60–62.

Ellis, M.B., & Lewis, H.D. (2001). Capgras delusion: A window on face recognition. *Trends in Cognitive Sciences, 5*(4), 149–156.

Emerson, M.J., & Miyake, A. (2003). The role of inner speech in task switching: A dual-task investigation. *Journal of Memory and Language, 48*, 148–168.

Engle, R.W., Tuholski, S.W., Laughlin, J.E., & Conway, A.R.A. (1999). Working memory, short-term memory, and general fluid intelligence: A latent variable approach. *Journal of Experimental Psychology: General, 128*, 309–331.

Enns, J.T. (2004). *The thinking eye, the seeing brain: Explorations in visual cognition.* New York: Norton.

Enns J.T., & Di Lollo, V. (2000). What's new in visual masking? *Trends in Cognitive Sciences, 4*, 345–352.

Epstein, R., Harris, A., Stanely, D. & Kanwisher, N. (1999). The parahippocampal place area: Recognition, navigation, or encoding? *Neuron, 23*, 115–125.

Erdelyi, M.H. (1970). Recovery of unavailable perceptual input. *Cognitive Psychology, 1*, 99–113.

Erdelyi, M.H. (1985). *Psychoanalysis: Freud's cognitive psychology.* New York: Freeman.

Erdelyi, M.H. (2004). Subliminal perception and its cognates: Theory, indeterminacy, and time. *Consciousness and Cognition, 13*, 73–91.

Erdelyi, M.H., & Becker, J. (1974). Hypermnesia for pictures: Incremental memory for pictures but not for words in multiple recall trials. *Cognitive Psychology, 6*, 159–171.

Erdelyi, M.H., & Kleinbard, J. (1978). Has Ebbinghaus decayed with time? The growth of recall (hypermnesia) over days. *Journal of Experimental Psychology: Human Learning and Memory, 4*, 275–289.

Erdmann, E., & Stover, D. (2000). *Beyond a world divided: Human values in the brain-mind science of Roger Sperry.* San Jose, CA: Authors Choice Press. (Originally published 1991.)

Erickson, T.D., & Mattson, M.E. (1981). From words to meaning: A semantic illusion. *Journal of Verbal Learning and Verbal Behavior, 20*, 540–551.

Ericsson, K.A. (2003). Exceptional memorizers: Made, not born. *Trends in Cognitive Sciences, 7*, 233–235.

Ericsson, K.A., & Charness, N. (1994). Expert performance: Its structure and acquisition. *American Psychologist, 49*, 725–747.

Ericsson, K.A., & Simon, H.A. (1980). Verbal reports as data. *Psychological Review, 87*, 215–251.

Ericsson, K.A, & Simon, H.A. (1993). *Protocol analysis.* Cambridge, MA: MIT Press.

Eriksen, C.W., Azuma, H., & Hicks, R. (1959). Verbal discrimination of pleasant and unpleasant stimulus prior to specific identification. *Journal of Abnormal and Social Psychology, 59*, 114–119.

Erikson, E.H. (1959). Identity and the life cycle. *Psychological Issues, 1*, 50–100.

Erikson, E.H., Erikson, J., & Kivnick, H.Q. (1986). *Vital involvement in old age.* New York: Norton.

Evans, G.W. (1980). Environmental cognition. *Psychological Bulletin, 88*, 259–287.

Evans, J. St B.T. (1980). Current issues in the psychology of reasoning. *British Journal of Psychology, 71*, 227–239.

Evans, J. St B.T. (1982). *The psychology of deductive reasoning.* London: Routledge & Kegan Paul.

Evans, J. St B.T. (2002). Logic and human reasoning: An assessment of the deduction paradigm. *Psychological Bulletin, 128*, 978–996.

Evans, J. St B.T. (2003). In two minds: Dual process accounts of reasoning. *Trends in Cognitive Sciences, 7*, 454–459.

Evans, J. St B.T., & Johnson-Laird, P.N. (2003). Editorial obituary: Peter Wason (1924–2003). *Thinking and Reasoning, 9*, 177–184.

Evans, J. St B.T., Handley, S.J., & Harper, C.N.J. (2001). Necessity, possibility and belief: A study of syllogistic reasoning. *Quarterly Journal of Experimental Psychology, 54*, 935–958.

Falk, R. (1989). Judgment of coincidences: Mine versus yours. *American Journal of Psychology, 102*, 477–493.

Farah, M.J. (1989). Mechanisms of imagery-perception interaction. *Journal of Experimental Psychology: Human Perception and Performance, 15*, 203–211.

Farah, M.J. (1990) *Visual agnosia: Disorders of object recognition and what they tell us about normal vision.* Cambridge, MA: MIT Press.

Farah, M.J. (1996). Is face recognition "special"? Evidence from neuro-psychology. *Behavioural Brain Research, 76*, 181–189.

Farah, M.J. (2005a). Neuroethics: The practical and the philosophical. *Trends in Cognitive Sciences, 9*, 34–40.

Farah, M.J. (2005b). Reply to Jedliça: Neuroethics, reductionism and dualism. *Trends in Cognitive Sciences, 9*, 173.

Farah, M.J., & McClelland, J.L. (1991). A computational model of semantic impairment: Modality specificity and emergent category specificity. *Journal of Experimental Psychology: General, 120*, 339–357.

Farah, M.J., & Rabinowitz, C. (2003). Genetic and environmental influences on the organization of semantic memory in the brain: Is "living things" an innate category? *Cognitive Neuropsychology, 20*, 401–408.

Faulkner, X., & Culwin, F. (2005). When fingers do the talking: A study of text messaging. *Interacting with Computers, 17*, 167–185.

Fechner, G.T. (1876). *Vorschule der Aesthetik.* Leipzig: Breitkopf und Hartel.

Feeney, A., Scrafton, S., Duckworth, A., & Handley, S.J. (2004). The story of *some*: Everyday pragmatic inference by children and adults. *Canadian Journal of Experimental Psychology, 58*, 121–132

Feldman, D.H. (1986). *Nature's gambit.* New York: Basic Books.

Feldman, J. (2003). The simplicity principle in human concept learning. *Current Directions in Psychological Science, 12*, 227–232.

Fellbaum, C., & Miller, G.A. (1990). Folk psychology or semantic entailment? *Psychological Review, 97*, 565–570.

Fendrich, R., Wessinger, C.M., & Gazzaniga, M.S. (1992). Residual vision in a scotoma: Implications for blindsight. *Science, 258*, 1489–1491.

Feng, J., Spence, I., & Pratt, J. (2007). Playing an action video game reduces gender differences in spatial cognition. *Psychological Science, 18*, 850–855.

Ferber, S., Humphrey, G.K., & Vilis, T. (2003). The lateral occipital complex subserves the perceptual persistence of motion-defined groupings. *Cerebral Cortex, 13*, 716–721.

Fernandez-Duque, D., & Johnson, M.L. (2002). Cause and effect theories of attention: The role of conceptual metaphors. *Review of General Psychology, 6*, 153–165.

Fiddick, L., Cosmides, L., & Tooby, J. (2000). No interpretation without representation: The role of domain-specific representations and inferences in the Wason selection task. *Cognition, 77*, 1–79.

Fiebach, C.J., & Friederici, A.D. (2003). Processing concrete words: fMRI evidence against a specific right hemisphere involvement. *Neuropsychologia, 42*, 62–70.

Findlay, C.S., & Lumsden, C.J. (1988). Thinking creatively about creative thinking. *Journal of Social and Biological Structures, 11*, 165–175.

Findlay, J.M. & Gilchrist, I.D. (2003). *Active vision: The psychology of looking and seeing*. Oxford: Oxford University Press.

Finger, S. (1994). *Origins of neuroscience: A history of explorations into brain function*. New York: Oxford University Press.

Finger, S. (2000). *Minds behind the brain: A history of the pioneers and their discoveries*. New York: Oxford University Press.

Finke, R.A. (1996). Imagery, creativity, and emergent structure. *Consciousness and Cognition, 5*, 381–393.

Finke, R.A., Pinker, S., & Farah, M.J. (1989). Reinterpreting visual patterns in mental imagery. *Cognitive Science, 13*, 51–78.

Fitts, P.M. (1992). The information capacity of the human motor system in controlling the amplitude of movement. *Journal of Experimental Psychology: General, 121*, 262–269. (Original work published 1954.)

Fivush, R., & Hayden, C.A. (Eds.). (2003). *Autobiographical memory and the construction of a narrative self*. Mahwah, NJ: Erlbaum.

Fivush, R., & Nelson, K. (2004). Culture and language in the emergence of autobiographical memories. *Psychological Science, 15*, 573–577.

Flavell, J. (1979). Metacognition and cognitive monitoring. *American Psychologist, 34*, 906–911.

Fleck, J., & Weisberg, R.W. (2004). The use of verbal protocols as data: An analysis of insight in the candle problem. *Memory & Cognition, 32*, 990–1006.

Flynn, J.R. (1984). The mean IQ of Americans: Massive gains 1932 to 1978. *Psychological Bulletin, 95*, 29–51.

Flynn, J.R. (1987). Massive IQ gains in 14 nations: What IQ tests really measure. *Psychological Bulletin, 101*, 171–191.

Flynn, J.R. (1999). Searching for justice: The discovery of IQ gains over time. *American Psychologist, 54*, 5–20.

Flynn, J.R. (2003). Movies about intelligence: The limitations of *g*. *Current Directions in Psychological Science, 12*, 95–99.

Fodor, J.A. (1983). *The modularity of mind: An essay in faculty psychology*. Cambridge, MA: MIT Press.

Fodor, J.A. (2000). *The mind doesn't work that way*. Cambridge, MA: MIT Press.

Fowler, H.W. (1965). *A dictionary of modern English usage* (2nd ed.). Oxford: Oxford University Press.

Fraisse, P., & Piaget, J. (1963). *Experimental psychology: History and method*. New York: Basic Books.

Frank, H. (1959). *Grundlagenprobleme der Informations-sthetik und erste Anwendung auf die mime pure*. Schnelle: Quickborn.

Frank, H. (1964). *Kybernetische Analysen Subjektiver Sachverhalte*. Schnelle: Quickborn.

Frank, R.H., Gilovich, T., & Regan, D.T. (1993). Does studying economics inhibit cooperation? *Journal of Economic Perspectives, 7*, 159–171.

Frank, R.H., Gilovich, T., & Regan, D.T. (1996). Do economists make bad citizens? *Journal of Economic Perspectives, 10*, 187–192.

Franklin, N., & Tversky, B. (1991). Searching imagined environments. *Journal of Experimental Psychology: General, 119*, 63–76.

Franz, S.I. (1912). New phrenology. *Science, 35*, 321–328.

Frase, L.T., & Kamman, R. (1974). Effects of search criterion upon unanticipated free recall of categorically related words. *Memory & Cognition, 2*, 181–184.

Frazer, J.G. (1959). *The golden bough* (abridged). New York: Doubleday (Ed. T.H. Gaster, 1922). (Original work published 1911.)

Frederick, S. (2005). Cognitive reflection and decision making. *Journal of Economic Perspectives, 19*, 25–42.

Freeman, W., & Watts, J.W. (1968). Prefrontal lobotomy. In W.S. Sahakian (Ed.), *History of psychology: A source book in systematic psychology* (pp. 377–379). Itaska, Ill.: Peacock. (Originally published 1950.)

French, C.C., & Richards, A. (1993). Clock this! An everyday example of a schema-driven error in memory. *British Journal of Psychology, 84*, 249–253.

French, R.M. (2000). The Turing test: The first 50 years. *Trends in Cognitive Sciences, 4*, 115–122.

Frenda, S.J., Patihis, L., Loftus, E.F., Lews, H.C., & Fenn, K.M. (2014). Sleep deprivation and false memories. *Psychological Science, 25 (9)*, 1674–1681.

Frenkel, K.A. (1989). The next generation of interactive technologies. *Communications of the ACM, 32*, 872–881.

Freud, S. (1961). A note upon the mystic writing pad. In J. Strachey (Ed. & Trans.), *The standard edition of the complete psychological works of Sigmund Freud* (Vol. 19). London: Hogarth Press. (Original work published 1925.)

Freud, S. (1977). *Introductory lectures on psychoanalysis* (J. Strachey, Trans.). New York: Norton. (Original work published 1916.)

Fugelsang, J.A., Stein, C.B., Green, A.E., & Dunbar, K.N. (2004). Theory and data interactions of the scientific mind: Evidence from the molecular and the cognitive laboratory. *Canadian Journal of Experimental Psychology, 58*, 86–95.

Gackenbach, J. (1991). Frameworks for understanding lucid dreaming: A review. *Dreaming, 1*, 109–128.

Gailliot, M.T., Baumeister, R.F., DeWall, C.N., Maner, J.K., Plant, E.A., Tice, D.M., Brewer L.E., & Schmeichel, B.J. (2007). Self-control relies on glucose as a limited energy source: Willpower is more than a metaphor. *Journal of Personality and Social Psychology, 92*, 325–336.

Gallistel, C.R. (2002a). Language and spatial frames of reference in mind and brain. *Trends in Cognitive Sciences, 6*, 321–322.

Gallistel, C.R. (2002b). Conception, perception and the control of action. *Trends in Cognitive Sciences, 6,* 504.

Gallotti, K.M. (1989). Approaches to studying formal and everyday reasoning. *Psychological Bulletin, 105,* 331–351.

Gallotti, K.M., Baron, J., & Sabini, J. (1986). Individual differences in syllogistic reasoning: Deduction rules or mental models? *Journal of Experimental Psychology: General, 115,* 16–25.

Galton, F. (1879a). Psychometric experiments. *Brain, 2,* 148–160.

Galton, F. (1879b). Psychometric facts. *The Nineteenth Century,* 425–433.

Galton, F. (1886). Regression toward mediocrity in hereditary stature. *Journal of the Anthropological Institute, 15,* 246–263.

Galton, F. (1908/1973). *Inquiries into human faculty and its development.* New York: E.P. Dutton.

Gardiner, J.M. (2001). Episodic memory and autonoetic consciousness: A first-person approach. *Philosophical Transactions of the Royal Society (Series B), 356,* 1351–1361.

Gardiner, J.M., & Richardson-Klavehn, A. (2000). Remembering and knowing. In E. Tulving & F.I.M.Craik, (Eds.), *The Oxford handbook of memory* (pp. 229–244). New York: Oxford University Press.

Gardner, H. (1980). *Artful scribbles.* New York: Harper & Row.

Gardner, H. (1982). *Art, mind and brain.* New York: Basic Books.

Gardner, H. (1983). *Frames of mind: The theory of multiple intelligences.* New York: Basic Books.

Gardner, H. (1985). *The mind's new science.* New York: Basic Books.

Gardner, H. (1993a). *Multiple intelligences: The theory in practice.* New York: Basic Books.

Gardner, H. (1993b). *Creating minds.* New York: Basic Books.

Gardner, H. (1999) *The disciplined mind: What all students should understand.* New York: Simon & Schuster.

Gardner, H. (2004). Audiences for the theory of multiple intelligences. *Teacher's College Record,* 212–220.

Gardner, H., & Winner, E. (1982). First intimations of artistry. In S. Straus (Ed.), *U-shaped behavioral growth* (pp. 147–168). New York: Academic Press.

Garlick, D. (2002). Understanding the nature of the general factor of intelligence: The role of individual differences in neural plasticity as an explanatory mechanism. *Psychological Review, 109,* 116–136.

Garlick, D. (2003). Integrating brain science research with intelligence research. *Current Directions in Psychological Science, 12,* 185–192.

Garner, W.R. (1962). *Uncertainty and structure as psychological concepts.* New York: Wiley.

Gauthier, I., Curran, T., Curby, K.M., & Collins, D. (2003). Perceptual interference supports a non-modular account of face processing. *Nature Neuroscience, 6,* 428–432.

Gauthier, I., Skudlarski, P., Gore, J.C., & Anderson, A.W. (2000). Expertise for cars and birds recruits brain areas involved in face recognition. *Nature Neuroscience, 3,* 191–197.

Gazzaniga, M. (2011). *Who's in charge? Free will and the science of the brain.* New York: Harper Collins.

Gazzaniga, M.S., Fendrich, R., & Wessinger, C.M. (1994). Blindsight reconsidered. *Current Directions in Psychological Science, 3,* 93–96.

Gazzaniga, M.S., Nass, R., Reeves, A., & Roberts, D. (1984). Neurologic perspectives on right hemisphere language following surgical section of the corpus callosum. *Seminars in Neurology, 4,* 126–135.

Gelman, S.A. (2004). Psychological essentialism in children. *Trends in Cognitive Sciences, 8,* 404–409.

Gelman, S.A., & Welman, H.M. (1991). Insides and essences: Early understandings of the non-obvious. *Cognition, 38,* 213–244.

Gentner, D. (1983). Structure-mapping: A theoretical framework for analogy. *Cognitive Science, 7,* 155–170.

Gentner, D. (2002). Mental models. In N.J. Smelser & P.B. Bates (Eds.), *International Encyclopedia of the Social and Behavioral Sciences* (pp. 9683–9687). Amsterdam: Elsevier Science.

Gentner, D., & Gentner, D.R. (1983). Flowing waters or teeming crowds: Mental models of electricity. In D. Gentner & A.L. Stevens (Eds.), *Mental models* (pp. 99–129). Hillsdale, NJ: Erlbaum.

Gentzen, G. (1964). Investigations into logical deduction. *American Philosophical Quarterly, 1,* 288–306.

German, T.P., & Barrett, H.C. (2005). Functional fixedness in a technologically sparse culture. *Psychological Science, 16,* 1–5.

German, T.P., & Defeyter, M.A. (2000). Immunity to functional fixedness in young children. *Psychonomic Bulletin & Review, 7,* 707–712.

Getzels, J.W. (1975). Problem finding and the inventiveness of solutions. *Journal of Creative Behavior, 9,* 12–18.

Getzels, J.W., & Csikszentmihalyi, M. (1972). Concern for discovery in the creative process. In A. Rothenberg & C. Hausman (Eds.), *The creativity question* (pp. 161–165). Durham, NC: Duke University Press.

Getzels, J.W., & Csikszentmihalyi, M. (1976). *The creative vision: A longitudinal study of problem finding in art.* New York: Wiley.

Ghiselin, M.T. (1981). Categories, life and thinking. *Behavioral and Brain Sciences, 4,* 269–313.

Gibbs, R.W. (1986). On the psycholinguistics of sarcasm. *Journal of Experimental Psychology: General, 115,* 3–15.

Gibbs, R.W. (1996). Why many concepts are metaphorical. *Cognition, 61,* 309–319.

Gibbs, R.W. (2004). Metaphor is grounded in embodied experience. *Journal of Pragmatics, 36,* 1189–1210.

Gibson, E.J., & Spelke, E.S. (1983). The development of perception. In P.H. Mussen (Ed.), *Handbook of child psychology, vol. 3, Cognitive development* (pp. 1–76). New York: Wiley.

Gibson, J.J. (1941). A critical review of the concept of set in contemporary experimental psychology. *Psychological Bulletin, 38,* 781–817.

Gibson, J.J. (1950). *The perception of the visual world.* Boston: Houghton Mifflin.

Gibson, J.J. (1959). Perception as a function of stimulation. In S. Koch (Ed.), *Psychology, a study of a science: Sensory, perceptual, and physiological formulations.* New York: McGraw-Hill.

Gibson, J.J. (1961). Ecological optics. *Vision Research, 1,* 253–262.

Gibson, J.J. (1966). *The senses considered as perceptual systems.* Boston: Houghton Mifflin.

Gibson, J.J. (1969). Outline of a theory of direct visual perception. Paper presented at the Conference on the Psychology of Knowing, Edmonton, Alberta.

Gibson, J.J. (1977). The theory of affordances. In R. Shaw & J. Bransford (Eds.), *Perceiving, acting and knowing* (pp. 67–82). Hillsdale, NJ: Erlbaum.

Gibson, J.J. (1979). *The ecological approach to visual perception*. Boston: Houghton Mifflin.

Gigerenzer, G., & Edwards, A. (2005). Simple tools for understanding risks: From innumeracy to insight. *British Medical Journal, 327,* 741–744.

Gigerenzer, G., & Goldstein, D.G. (1996). Reasoning the fast and frugal way: Models of bounded rationality. *Psychological Review, 103,* 650–669.

Gigerenzer, G., & Hug, K. (1992). Domain-specific reasoning: Social contracts, cheating, and perspective change. *Cognition, 43,* 127–171.

Gilden, G.L., & Wilson, S.G. (1995). Streaks in skilled performance. *Psychonomic Bulletin & Review, 2,* 260–265.

Giles, G.M., & Clark-Wilson, J. (1988). Functional skills training in severe brain injury. In I. Fussey & G.M. Giles (Eds.), *Rehabilitation of the severely brain-injured adult* (pp. 69–101). London: Croom Helm.

Gilhooly, K. (2003). Problems in problem-solving. *Trends in Cognitive Science, 7,* 477–478.

Gilligan, S.G., & Bower, G.H. (1984). Cognitive consequences of emotional arousal. In C. Izard, J. Kagan, & R. Zajonc (Eds.), *Emotions, cognition and behavior* (pp. 547–588). New York: Cambridge University Press.

Gillihan, S.J., & Farah, M.J. (2005). Is self special? A critical review of evidence from experimental psychology and cognitive neuroscience. *Psychological Bulletin, 131,* 76–97.

Gilovich, T., & Griffin, D. (2002). Introduction—heuristics and biases: Then and now. In T. Gilovich, D. Griffin, & D. Kahneman (Eds.), *Heuristics and biases: The psychology of intuitive judgment* (pp. 1–19). Cambridge: Cambridge University Press.

Gilovich, T., Mevec, V.H., & Chen, S. (1995). Commission, omission, and dissonance reduction: Coping with regret in the "Monty Hall" problem. *Personality and Social Psychology Review, 21,* 182–190.

Gilovich, T., Vallone, R., & Tversky, A. (1985). The hot hand in basketball: On the misperception of random sequences. *Cognitive Psychology, 17,* 295–314.

Gil-White, F. (2001). Are ethnic groups biological "species" to the human brain? *Current Anthropology, 42,* 515–554.

Giroux, L., & Larochelle, S. (1988). *The cognitive ergonomics of computer systems.* Laval, Que.: Canadian Automation Research Centre.

Glenberg, A. (1997). What memory is for. *Behavioral and Brain Sciences, 20,* 1–55.

Glenberg, A., Smith, S.M., & Green, C. (1977). Type I rehearsal: Maintenance and more. *Journal of Verbal Learning and Verbal Behavior, 16,* 339–352.

Glicksohn, J., Steinbach, I., & Elimalac-Malmilyan, S. (1999). Cognitive dedifferentiation in eidetics and synaesthesia: Hunting for the ghost once more. *Perception, 28,* 109–120.

Glisky, E.L., & Schacter, D.L. (1989). Extending the limits of complex learning in organic amnesia: Computer training in a vocational domain. *Neuropsychologia, 27,* 107–120.

Glosser, G., & Friedman, R.B. (1991). Lexical but not semantic priming in Alzheimer's disease. *Psychology and Aging, 6,* 522–527.

Glucksberg, S (2003). The psycholinguistics of metaphor. *Trends in Cognitive Sciences, 7,* 92–96.

Godden, D., & Baddeley, A.D. (1975). Context-dependent memory in two natural environments: On land and underwater. *British Journal of Psychology, 66,* 325–331.

Goffman, E. (1978). Response cries. *Language, 54,* 787–815.

Gold, I., & Stoljar, D. (1999). A neuron doctrine in the philosophy of neuroscience. *Behavioral and Brain Sciences, 22,* 809–869.

Goldinger, S.D. (1998). Echoes of echoes? An episodic theory of lexical access. *Psychological Review, 105,* 251–279.

Goldman-Eisler, F. (1968). *Psycholinguistics: Experiments in spontaneous speech.* London: Academic Press.

Goldstein, D.G., & Gigerenzer, G. (2002). Models of ecological rationality: The recognition heuristic. *Psychological Review, 109,* 75–90.

Gonsalves, B., Reber, P.J., Gitelman, D.R., Parrish, T.B., Mesulam, M.-M., & Paller, K.A. (2004). Neural evidence that vivid imagining can lead to false remembering. *Psychological Science, 15,* 655–660.

Goodale, M.A., Milner, A.D., Jakobson, L.S., & Carey, D.P. (1991). A neurological dissociation between perceiving objects and grasping them. *Nature, 349,* 154–156.

Goodale, M.A., & Westwood, D.A. (2004). An evolving view of duplex vision: Separate but interacting cortical pathways for perception and action. *Current Opinion in Neurobiology, 14,* 203–211.

Goodman, N. (1955). *Fact, fiction and forecast.* Cambridge, MA: Harvard University Press.

Goodwin, D.W., Powell, B., Bremer, D., Hoine, H., & Stern, J. (1969). Alcohol and recall: State dependent effects in man. *Science, 163,* 1358–1360.

Goodwin, G.P., & Johnson-Laird, P.N. (2005). Reasoning about relations. *Psychological Review, 112,* 468–493.

Gordon, I.E. (1974). Left and right in Goya's portraits. *Nature, 249,* 197–198.

Gordon, P.C., & Holyoak, K.J. (1983). Implicit learning and the "mere exposure" effect. *Journal of Personality and Social Psychology, 45,* 492–500.

Gorfein, D.S., & Hoffman, R.R. (1987). *Memory and learning: The Ebbinghaus centennial conference.* Hillsdale, NJ: Erlbaum.

Gorman, M.E. (1986). How the possibility of error affects falsification on a task that models scientific problem-solving. *British Journal of Psychology, 77,* 85–96.

Gorman, M.E. (1989). Error, falsification and scientific evidence. *Quarterly Journal of Experimental Psychology, 41 A,* 385–412.

Gottfredson, L.S. (1997). Why g matters: The complexity of everyday life. *Intelligence, 24,* 79–132.

Gottfredson, L.S. (2003a). Dissecting practical intelligence theory: Its claims and evidence. *Intelligence, 31,* 343–397.

Gottfredson, L.S. (2003b). On Sternberg's "Reply to Gottfredson." *Intelligence, 31,* 415–424.

Gottschaldt, K. (1967). Gestalt factors and repetition. In W.D. Ellis (Ed.), *A source book of Gestalt psychology* (pp. 109–135). New York: Humanities Press. (Original work published 1926.)

Gould, S.J. (1985). *The flamingo's smile.* New York: Norton.

Gould, S.J., & Lewontin, R.C. (1979). The spandrels of San Marco and the Panglossian paradigm: A critique of the adaptationist programme. *Proceedings of the Royal Society of London (Series B), 205,* 581–98.

Gould, S.J., & Vrba, E.S. (1982). Exaptation: A missing term in the science of form. *Paleobiology, 8,* 4–15.

Graf, P., & Schacter, D.L. (1985). Implicit and explicit memory for new associations in normal and amnesic subjects. *Journal of Experimental Psychology: Learning, Memory, and Cognition, 11*, 501–518.

Grainger, J., & Whitney, C. (2004). Does the human mind raed wrods as a wlohe? *Trends in Cognitive Sciences, 8*, 58–59.

Grant, E.R., & Spivey, M.J. (2003). Eye movements and problem-solving. *Psychological Science, 14*, 462–466.

Gray, R. (2004). Attending to the execution of a complex sensorimotor skill: Expertise differences, choking, and slumps. *Journal of Experimental Psychology: Applied, 10*, 42–54.

Green, B. G. (2001). Psychophysical measurement of oral chemesthesis. In S.A. Simon & M.A.I. Nicolelis (Eds.). *Methods in chemosensory research* (pp. 3–20). Boca Raton, FL: CRC Press.

Green, C.S., & Bavelier, D. (2003). Action video game modifies visual selective attention. *Nature, 423*, 534–537.

Green, T.R.G. (1982). Pictures of programs and other processes, or how to do things with lines. *Behaviour and Information Technology, 1*, 3–36.

Green, T.R.G., & Payne, S. (1982). The wooly jumper: Typographic problems of concurrency in information display. *Visible Language, 16*, 391–403.

Green, T.R.G., & Payne, S.J. (1984). Organization and learnability in computer languages. *International Journal of Man-Machine Studies, 21*, 7–18.

Green, T.R.G., Payne, S.J., & van der Veer, G.C. (Eds.). (1983). *The psychology of computer use*. London: Academic Press.

Greenberg, D.L. (2004). President Bush's false "flashbulb" memory of 9/11/01. *Applied Cognitive Psychology, 18*, 363–370.

Greenberg, J.H. (1966). *Language universals*. The Hague: Mouton.

Greene, J. (1972). *Psycholinguistics: Chomsky and psychology*. Baltimore: Penguin.

Greene, R.L. (1987). Effects of maintenance rehearsal on human memory. *Psychological Bulletin, 102*, 403–413.

Greeno, J.G. (1994). Gibson's affordances. *Psychological Review, 101*, 336–342.

Greenstein, J.S., & Arnaut, L.Y. (1987). Human factors aspects of manual computer input devices. In G. Salvendy (Ed.), *Handbook of human factors* (pp. 1450–1489). New York: Wiley.

Greenwald, A.G., Spangenberg, E.R., Pratkanis, A.R., & Eskanazi, J. (1991). Double-blind tests of subliminal self-help

audiotapes. *Psychological Science, 2*, 119–122.

Grice, H.P. (1971). Meaning. In D. Steinberg & L. Jakobovits (Eds.), *Semantics: An inter-disciplinary reader* (pp. 53–59). Cambridge: Cambridge University Press. (Original work published 1957).

Grice, H.P. (1975). Logic and conversation. In P. Cole & J.P. Morgan (Eds.), *Syntax and semantics: Vol. 3. Speech acts* (pp. 41–58). New York: Academic Press.

Grice, H.P. (1978). Further notes on logic and conversation. In P. Cole (Ed.), *Syntax and semantics: Vol. 9. Pragmatics*. New York: Academic Press.

Grier, R A., Warm, J.S., Dember, W.N., Matthews, G., Galinsky, T.L., Szalma, J.L., & Parasuraman, R. (2003). The vigilance decrement reflects limitations in effortful attention, not mindlessness. *Human Factors, 45*, 349–359.

Griggs, R.A., & Cox, J.R. (1982). The elusive thematic materials effect in Wason's selection task. *British Journal of Psychology, 73*, 407–420.

Griggs, R.A., & Newstead, S.E. (1983). The source of intuitive errors in Wason's THOG problem. *British Journal of Psychology, 74*, 451–459.

Groen, G.J., & Parkman, J.M. (1972). A chronometric analysis of simple addition. *Psychological Review, 79*, 329–342.

Gross, L. (1983, March). Why Johnny can't draw. *Arts Education*, 74–77.

Gross, S.R., & Miller, N. (1997). The "golden section" and bias in perceptions of social consensus. *Personality and Social Psychology Bulletin, 1*, 241–271.

Grossenbacher, P.G., & Lovelace, C.T. (2001). Mechanisms of synesthesia: Cognitive and physiological constraints. *Trends in Cognitive Sciences, 5*, 36–41.

Gruber, H.E. (1981). *Darwin on man: A psychological study of scientific creativity* (2nd ed.). Chicago: University of Chicago Press. (Original work published 1974).

Gruber, H.E., & Wallace, D.B. (2001). Creative work: The case of Charles Darwin. *American Psychologist, 56*, 346–349.

Grudin, J. (1989). The case against user interface consistency. *Communications of the ACM, 32*, 1164–1173.

Guastello, S.J., Traut, M., & Korienek, G. (1989). Verbal versus pictorial representations of objects in a human-computer interface. *International Journal of Man-Machine Studies, 31*, 99–120.

Guiard, Y., & Beaudoin-Lafon, M. (2004). Fitts' law 50 years later: Applications and contributions from human-computer interaction. *International Journal of Human-Computer Studies, 61*, 747–750.

Guilford, J. (1967). *The nature of human intelligence*. New York: McGraw-Hill.

Haber, R.N. (1979). Twenty years of haunting eidetic imagery: Where's the ghost? *Behavioral and Brain Sciences, 2*, 583–629.

Haber, R.N. (1983). The impending demise of the icon: A critique of the concept of iconic storage in visual information processing. *Behavioral and Brain Sciences, 6*, 1–13.

Haggard, P., Clark, S., & Kalogeras, J. (2002). Voluntary action and conscious awareness. *Nature Neuroscience, 5*, 382–385.

Haines, R.F. (1991). A breakdown in simultaneous information processing. In G. Obrecht & L.W. Stark (Eds.), *Presbyopia research* (pp. 171–175). New York: Plenum Press.

Halper, F. (1997). The illusion of *The Future*. *Perception, 26*, 1321–1322.

Halpern, A.R., & Bartlett, J. C. (2011). The persistence of musical memories: A descriptive study of earworms. *Music Perception, 28*, 425–431.

Halpern, S. (2002, Aug. 15). Heart of darkness. *New York Review of Books, 49*, 16–22.

Hamilton, H.W., & Deese, J. (1971). Does linguistic marking have a psychological correlate? *Journal of Verbal Learning and Verbal Behaviour, 10*, 707–714.

Hampson, S.E. (1998). When is an inconsistency not an inconsistency? Trait reconciliation in personality description and impression formation. *Journal of Personality and Social Psychology, 74*, 102–117.

Hampton, R.R., & Schwartz, B.L. (2004). Episodic memory in nonhumans: What, and where, is when? *Current Opinion in Neurobiology, 14*, 192–197.

Hancock, P.A. (2013). In search of vigilance: The problem of iatrogenically created psychological phenomena. *American Psychologist, 68*, 97–109.

Hanson, N.R. (1958). *Patterns of discovery*. Cambridge: Cambridge University Press.

Hanson, N.R. (1969). *Perception and discovery: an introduction to scientific inquiry*. San Francisco: Freeman, Cooper & Co.

Harle, S.K., & Vickers, J.N. (2001). Training quiet eye improves accuracy in the basketball free throw. *Sport Psychologist, 15*, 289–305.

Harris, J. (1984). Methods of improving memory. In B.A. Wilson & N. Moffat (Eds.), *Clinical management of memory problems* (pp. 46–62). Rockville, Md: Aspen Publications.

Harris, R.J. (1973). Answering questions containing marked and unmarked adjectives and adverbs. *Journal of Experimental Psychology, 97*, 399–401.

Harrison, J. (2001). *Synaesthesia: The strangest thing.* Oxford: Oxford University Press.

Harshman, R.A., & Paivio, A. (1987). "Paradoxical" sex differences in self-reported imagery. *Canadian Journal of Psychology, 41*, 287–302.

Hatfield, G. (1992). Empirical, rational, and transcendental psychology: Psychology as science and as philosophy. In P. Guyer (Ed.), *The Cambridge companion to Kant* (pp. 200–227). Cambridge: Cambridge University Press.

Hatfield, G. (1998). Kant and empirical psychology in the 18th century. *Psychological Science, 9*, 423–428.

Hatfield, G., & Epstein, W. (1987). The status of the minimum principle in the theoretical analysis of visual perception. *Psychological Bulletin, 97*, 155–186.

Hauser, M.D., Chomsky, N., & Fitch, W.T. (2002). The faculty of language: What is it, who has it, and how did it evolve? *Science, 298*, 1569–1579.

Hayman, C.A., & Tulving, E. (1989). Contingent dissociation between recognition and fragment completion: The method of triangulation. *Journal of Experimental Psychology: Learning, Memory, and Cognition, 15*, 228–240.

Hazeltine, E., Teague, D., & Ivry, R.B. (2002). Simultaneous dual-task performance reveals parallel response selection after practice. *Journal of Experimental Psychology: Human Perception and Performance, 28*, 527–545.

Heath, S.B. (1986). The functions and uses of literacy. In S. de Castell, A. Luke, & K. Egan (Eds.), *Literacy, society and schooling* (pp. 15–26). Cambridge: Cambridge University Press.

Heath, S.B. (1989). Oral and literate traditions among black Americans living in poverty. *American Psychologist, 44*, 367–373.

Hebb, D.O. (1949). *The organization of behavior.* New York: Wiley.

Heckhausen, H., & Beckmann, J. (1990). Intentional action and action slips. *Psychological Review, 97*, 36–48.

Heider, E.R. [Eleanor Rosch]. (1971a). Focal color area and the development of color names. *Developmental Psychology, 4*, 447–455.

Heider, E.R. [Eleanor Rosch]. (1971b). On the internal structure of perceptual and semantic categories. Paper presented at the Conference on Developmental Psycholinguistics, Buffalo, NY.

Heider, E.R. [Eleanor Rosch], & Olivier, D. (1972). The structure of the color space in naming and memory for two languages. *Cognitive Psychology, 3*, 337–354.

Heider, F. (1958). *The psychology of interpersonal relations.* New York: Wiley.

Heim, S., Opitz, B., Friederici, A.D. (2003). Distributed cortical networks for syntax processing: Broca's area as the common denominator. *Brain and Language, 85*, 402–408.

Heinrichs, R.W. (1984). Verbal responses to human figure paintings: A test of the uncertainty hypothesis. *Canadian Journal of Psychology, 38*, 512–518.

Hejmadi, A.H., Rozin, P., & Siegal, M. (2004). Once in contact, always in contact: Contagious essence and conceptions of purification in American and Hindu Indian children. *Developmental Psychology, 40*, 467–476.

Helton, W.S., & Russell, P.N. (2011). Working memory load and the vigilance decrement. *Experimental Brain Research, 212*, 429–437.

Helton, W.S., & Russell, P.N. (2013). Visuospatial and verbal working memory load: Effects on visuospatial vigilance. *Experimental Brain Research, 224*, 429–436.

Henderson, J.M. (1992). Object identification in context: The visual processing of natural scenes. *Canadian Journal of Psychology, 46*(3), 319–341.

Henderson, J.M. (2003). Human gaze control during real-world scene perception. *Trends in Cognitive Sciences, 7*, 498–504.

Henderson, J.M., Pollatsek, A., & Rayner, K. (1989). Covert visual attention and extrafoveal information use during object identification. *Perception & Psychophysics, 45*, 196–208.

Henle, M. (1968). Deductive reasoning. In P.C. Wason & P.N. Johnson-Laird (Eds.), *Deductive reasoning* (pp. 93–107). Baltimore: Penguin. (Original work published 1962).

Henle, M. (1987). Koffka's principles after fifty years. *Journal of the History of the Behavioral Sciences, 25*, 14–21.

Hering, E. (1961). Principles of a new theory of the color sense. In R.C. Teevan & R.C. Birney (Eds.), *Color vision* (pp. 28–31). New York: Van Nostrand. (Original work published 1878.)

Herrmann, D.J. (1993). The ethnographic method and the investigation of memory. *Applied Cognitive Psychology, 7*, 184.

Herrmann, D.J., & Neisser, U. (1979). An inventory of everyday memory experiences. In M.M. Gruneberg & P.E. Morris (Eds.), *Applied problems in memory.* London: Academic Press.

Hertel, P.T., & Gerstle, M. (2003). Depressive deficits in forgetting. *Psychological Science, 14*, 573–578.

Hertel, P.T., & Hardin, T.S. (1990). Remembering without awareness in a depressed mood: Evidence of deficits in initiative. *Journal of Experimental Psychology: General, 119*, 45–59.

Hertel, P.T., & Rude, S.S. (1991). Depressive deficits in memory: Focusing attention improves subsequent recall. *Journal of Experimental Psychology: General, 120*, 301–309.

Heyes, C. (2003). Four routes of cognitive evolution. *Psychological Review, 110*, 713–727.

Hick, W.E. (1952). On the rate of gain of information. *Quarterly Journal of Experimental Psychology, 4*, 11–26.

Hilgard, E.R. (1980). The trilogy of mind: Cognition, affection and conation. *Journal of the History of the Behavioral Sciences, 16*, 107–117.

Hilgard, E.R. (1987). *Psychology in America: An historical survey.* New York: Harcourt Brace Jovanovich.

Hintzman, D.L. (1986). "Schema abstraction" in a multiple-trace memory model. *Psychological Review, 93*, 411–428.

Hintzman, D.L., Curran, T., & Oppy, B. (1992). Effects of similarity and repetition on memory: Registration without learning? *Journal of Experimental Psychology: Learning, Memory, and Cognition, 18*(4), 667–690.

Hirschfeld, L.A., & Gelman, S.A. (1994). *Mapping the mind: Domain specificity in cognition and culture.* Cambridge: Cambridge University Press.

Hirschfeld, L.A., & Gelman, S.A. (1997). What young children think about the relationship between language variation and social difference. *Cognitive Development, 12*, 213–238.

Hirst, W. (1986). The psychology of attention. In J. LeDoux and W. Hirst (Eds.), *Mind and brain: Dialogues in cognitive neuroscience* (pp. 105–141). New York: Cambridge University Press.

Hirst, W., & Kalmar, K. (1987). Characterizing attentional resources. *Journal of Experimental Psychology: General, 116*, 68–81.

Hirst, W., & Levine, E. (1985). Ecological memory reconsidered: A comment on Bruce's "The how and why of ecological memory." *Journal of Experimental Psychology: General, 114*, 269–271.

Hirst, W., Neisser, U., & Spelke, E. (1978). Divided attention. *Human Nature, 1*, 54–61.

Hirst, W., Spelke, E.S., Reaves, C.C., Caharack, G., & Neisser, U. (1980). Dividing attention without alteration or automaticity. *Journal of Experimental Psychology: General, 109*, 98–117.

Hoc, J.M. (2001). Towards ecological validity of research in cognitive ergonomics. *Theoretical Issues in Ergonomic Science, 2*, 278–288.

Hodges, J.R. (2000). Memory in the dementias. In E. Tulving & F.I.M. Craik (Eds.), *The Oxford handbook of memory* (pp. 645–648). New York: Oxford University Press.

Hodges, J.R., Salmon, D.P., & Butters, N. (1992). Semantic memory impairment in Alzheimer's disease: Failure of access or degraded knowledge? *Neuropsychologia, 30*, 301–314.

Hoegg, J.W., & Alba, J.W. (2007). Taste perception: More than meets the tongue. *Journal of Consumer Research.* 490–498.

Hoff, E. (2004). Progress, but not a full solution to the logical problem of language acquisition. *Journal of Child Language, 31*, 923–926.

Hoffman, R.R., & Deffenbacher, K.A. (1992). A brief history of applied cognitive psychology. *Applied Cognitive Psychology, 6*, 1–48.

Hofstadter, D. (1979). *Godel, Escher, Bach: An eternal golden braid.* New York: Basic Books.

Hofstadter, D. (1982). Meta-font, metamathematics, and metaphysics: Comments on Donald Knuth's "The concept of a meta-font." *Visible Language, 16*, 309–338.

Hollins, M. (1985). Styles of mental imagery in blind adults. *Neuropsychologia, 23*, 561–566.

Holloway, C. (1978). *Cognitive psychology: Units 22–23.* Milton Keynes, UK: Open University.

Holmberg, N., Holsanova, J., & Holmqvist, K. 2006. Using eye movement measures to describe readers' visual interaction with newspapers. Proceedings, EARLI SIG 2 conference, "Text and Graphics Comprehension," University of Nottingham, 30 Aug.–1 Sept.

Hoptman, M.J., & Davidson, R.J. (1994). How and why do the two cerebral hemispheres interact? *Psychological Review, 116*, 195–219.

Horowitz, L.M., Norman, S.A., & Day, R.S. (1966). Availability and associative symmetry. *Psychological Review, 73*, 1–15.

Horstmann, G. (2002). Evidence for attentional capture by a surprising color singleton in visual search. *Psychological Science, 13*, 499–505.

Howard, D.V., Fry, A., & Brune, C. (1991). Aging and memory for new associations: Direct versus indirect measures. *Journal of Experimental Psychology: Learning, Memory, and Cognition, 17*, 779–792.

Howard, I.P., & Templeton, W.B. (1966). *Human spatial orientation.* London: Wiley.

Howe, M.L., & Courage, M.L. (1993). On resolving the enigma of infantile amnesia. *Psychological Bulletin, 113*, 305–326.

Hubbard, T. L. (2010). Auditory imagery: Empirical findings. *Psychological Bulletin, 136*, 302–329.

Hubel, D.H., & Wiesel, T.N. (1962). Receptive fields, binocular interaction and functional architecture in the cat's visual cortex. *Journal of Physiology, 160*, 106–154.

Huettel, S.A., Mack, P.B., & McCarthy, G. (2002). Perceiving patterns in random series: Dynamic processing of sequence in prefrontal cortex. *Nature Neuroscience, 5*, 485–490.

Hughes, G. (1988). *Words in time.* Oxford: Blackwell.

Hughes, P., & Brecht, G. (1975). *Vicious circles and infinity.* New York: Penguin.

Humphrey, G. (1963). *Thinking: An introduction to its experimental psychology.* New York: Wiley. (Original work published 1951.)

Humphrey, N.K., & McManus, C. (1973). Status and the left cheek, *New Scientist, 59*, 437–439.

Hunt, E.B., & Agnoli, F. (1991). The Whorfian hypothesis: A cognitive psychology perspective. *Psychological Review, 98*, 377–389.

Hunt, E.B., & Hovland, C.I. (1960). Order of consideration of different types of concept. *Journal of Experimental Psychology, 59*, 220–225.

Hunt, R.R. (1995). The subtlety of distinctiveness: What von Restorff really did. *Psychonomic Bulletin and Review, 2*, 105–112.

Hunt, R.R., & Lamb, C.A. (2001). What causes the isolation effect? *Journal of Experimental Psychology: Learning, Memory, and Cognition, 27*, 1359–1366.

Hunter, I.M.L. (1977). An exceptional memory. *British Journal of Psychology, 68*, 155–164.

Hunter, I.M.L. (1979). Memory in everyday life. In M.M. Gruneberg & P.E. Morris (Eds.), *Applied problems in memory.* London: Academic Press.

Hurvich, L., & Jameson, D. (1957). An opponent-process theory of color vision. *Psychological Review, 64*, 384–390.

Hutchins, E. (1983). Understanding Micronesian navigation. In D. Gentner & A.L. Stevens (Eds.), *Mental models.* Hillsdale, NJ: Erlbaum.

Huttenlocher, J., & Higgins, E.T. (1971). Adjectives, comparatives and syllogisms. *Psychological Review, 78*, 487–504.

Huttenlocher, J., Vasilyeva, M., Cymerman, E., & Levine, S. (2002). Language input and child syntax. *Cognitive Psychology, 45*, 337–374.

Hyams, N.M. (1986). *Language acquisition and the theory of parameters.* Dordrecht, the Netherlands: Reidel.

Hyman, I.E., & Neisser, U. (1991). *Reconstructing mental images: Problems of method* (Emory Cognition Project Tech. Rep. No. 19). Atlanta: Emory University.

Hyman, R. (1953). Stimulus information as a determinant of reaction time. *Journal of Experimental Psychology, 45*, 188–96.

Iacoboni, M., Freedman, J., Kaplan, J., Jamieson, K.H., Freedman, T., Knapp, B., & Fitzgerald, K. (2007, Nov. 11). This is your brain on politics. *New York Times* Op-Ed.

Indian and Northern Affairs Canada (2000). *Nunavut, Canada's third territory "North of 60."* Retrieved 21 March 2005 from Indian and Northern Affairs Canada. www.ainc-inac.gc.ca/ks/pdf/nunavu_e.pdf.

Innocence Project (2009). Reevaluating lineups: Why witnesses make mistakes and how to reduce the chance of a misidentification. Benjamin N. Cardozo School of Law, Yeshiva University. Retrieved 23 Oct. 2015 from www.innocenceproject.org/news-events-exonerations/reevaluating-lineups-why-witnesses-make-mistakes-and-how-to-reduce-the-chance-of-a-mis-identification.

Innocence Project (2015). DNA exonerations nationwide. Retrieved 15 Oct. 2015 from www.innocenceproject.org/free-innocent/improve-the-law/fact-sheets/dna-exonerations-nationwide.

Inoue, S. & Matsuzawa, T. (2007). Working memory of numerals in chimpanzees. *Current Biology, 17*(23).

Isen, A.M. (1984). Toward understanding the role of affect in cognition. In R.S. Wyer & T.K. Srull (Eds.), *Handbook of social cognition* (pp. 174–236). Hillsdale, NJ: Erlbaum.

Isen, A.M., Daubman, K.A., & Nowicki, G.P. (1987). Positive affect facilitates creative problem-solving. *Journal of Personality and Social Psychology, 52,* 1122–1131.

Ivry, R., & Knight, R.T. (2002). Making order from chaos: The misguided frontal lobe. *Nature Neuroscience, 5,* 394–396.

Jack, A.I., & Shallice, T. (2001). Introspective physicalism as an approach to the science of consciousness. *Cognition, 79,* 161–196.

Jack, A.I., & Roepstorff, A. (2002). Introspection and cognitive brain mapping: From stimulus-response to script report. *Trends in Cognitive Sciences, 6,* 333–339.

Jackson, M.A., & Simpson, K.H. (2004). Pain after amputation. *Continuing Education in Anaesthesia, Critical Care & Pain, 4,* 20–23.

Jacoby, L.L. (1999). Ironic effects of repetition: Measuring age-related differences in memory. *Journal of Experimental Psychology: Learning, Memory, and Cognition, 25,* 3–22.

Jacoby, L.L., & Dallas, M. (1981). On the relationship between autobiographical memory and perceptual learning. *Journal of Experimental Psychology: General, 110,* 306–340.

Jacoby, L.L., & Hollingshead, A. (1990). Reading student essays may be hazardous to your health. *Canadian Journal of Psychology, 44,* 345–358.

Jacoby, L.L., & Kelley, C.M. (1994). A process-dissociation framework for investigating unconscious influences: Freudian slips, projective tests, subliminal perception, and signal detection theory. *Current Directions in Psychological Science, 1,* 174–179.

Jacoby, L.L., & Witherspoon, D. (1982). Remembering without awareness. *Canadian Journal of Psychology, 36,* 300–324.

Jakobson, L.S., Archibald, Y.M., Carey, D.P., & Goodale, M.A. (1991). A kinematic analysis of reaching and grasping movements in a patient recovering from optic ataxia. *Neuropsychologia, 29,* 803–809.

James, T., Soroka, L., & Benjafield, J. (2001). Are economists rational, or just different? *Social Behavior and Personality, 29,* 359–364.

James, W. (1983). *Principles of psychology.* Cambridge, MA: Harvard University Press. (Original work published 1890.)

Jarick, M., Dixon, M.J., Stewart, M.T., Maxwell, E.C., & Smilek, D. (2009). A different outlook on time: Visual and auditory month names elicit different mental vantage points for a time-space synaesthete. *Cortex, 45*(10), 1217–1228.

Jaynes, J. (1977). *The origins of consciousness in the breakdown of the bicameral mind.* Boston: Houghton Mifflin.

Jaynes, J. (1979). Paleolithic cave paintings as eidetic images. *Behavioral and Brain Sciences, 2,* 605–607.

Jedlièa, P. (2005). Neuroethics: Reductionism and dualism. *Trends in Cognitive Sciences, 9,* 172.

Jenkins, J.G., & Dallenbach, K.M. (1924). Obliviscence during sleep and waking. *American Journal of Psychology, 35,* 605–612.

Jenkins, J.J. (1974). Remember that old theory of memory? Well, forget it! *American Psychologist, 29,* 785–795.

Jensen, A.R. (1972). *Genetics and education.* New York: Harper & Row.

Jersild, A. (1927). Mental set and shift. *Archives of Psychology, 14* (Whole No. 89), 5–82.

Johnson, C.J., Paivio, A., & Clark, J.M. (1996). Cognitive components of picture naming. *Psychological Bulletin, 120,* 113–139.

Johnson, M., & Lakoff, G. (2002). Why cognitive linguistics requires embodied realism. *Cognitive Linguistics, 13,* 245–263.

Johnson, M.K. (1985). The origin of memories. In P.C. Kendall (Ed.), *Advances in cognitive-behavioral research and therapy* (Vol. 4, pp. 1–27). New York: Academic Press.

Johnson, M.K. (1988). Reality monitoring: An experimental phenomenological approach. *Journal of Experimental Psychology: General, 117,* 390–394.

Johnson, M.K., Hashtroudi, S., & Lindsay, D.S. (1993). Source monitoring. *Psychological Review, 114,* 3–28.

Johnson, M.K., & Raye, C.L. (1981). Reality monitoring. *Psychological Review, 88,* 67–85.

Johnson, M.K., & Raye, C.L. (1998). False memories and confabulation. *Trends in Cognitive Sciences, 2,* 137–145.

Johnson, W., Bouchard, T.J., Krueger, R.F., McGue, M., & Gottesman, I.J. (2004). Just one *g*: Consistent results from three test batteries. *Intelligence, 32,* 95–107.

Johnson-Laird, P.N. (1972). The three-term series problem. *Cognition, 1,* 57–82.

Johnson-Laird, P.N. (1983). *Mental models.* Cambridge, MA: Harvard University Press.

Johnson-Laird, P.N. (1988). *The computer and the mind.* Cambridge, MA: Harvard University Press.

Johnson-Laird, P.N. (1997a). Rules and illusions: A critical study of Rips's *The psychology of proof. Minds and Machines, 7,* 387–407.

Johnson-Laird, P.N. (1997b). An end to the controversy: A reply to Rips. *Minds and Machines, 7,* 425–432.

Johnson-Laird, P.N. (1999). Deductive reasoning. *Annual Review of Psychology, 50,* 109–135.

Johnson-Laird, P.N. (2001). Mental models and deduction. *Trends in Cognitive Sciences, 5,* 434–442.

Johnson-Laird, P.N., & Byrne, R.M.J. (1990). Meta-logical problems: Knights, knaves, and Rips. *Cognition, 36,* 69–84.

Johnson-Laird, P.N., & Byrne, R.M.J. (1993). Precis of "deduction." *Behavioral and Brain Sciences, 16,* 323–380.

Johnson-Laird, P.N., Herrmann, D.J., & Chafin, R. (1984). Only connections: A critique of semantic networks. *Psychological Bulletin, 96,* 292–315.

Johnson-Laird, P.N., Legrenzi, P., Girotto, V., Legrenzi, M.S., & Caverni, J.P. (1999). Naïve probability: A mental model theory of extensional reasoning. *Psychological Review, 106,* 62–88.

Johnson-Laird, P.N., & Steedman, M. (1978). The psychology of syllogisms. *Cognitive Psychology, 10,* 64–99.

Johnson-Laird, P.N., & Wason, P.C. (1970). A theoretical analysis of insight into a reasoning task. *Cognitive Psychology, 1,* 134–148.

Johnston, E.B. (2001). The repeated reproduction of Bartlett's "Remembering." *History of Psychology, 4,* 341–366.

Johnston, W.A., & Dark, V.J. (1986). Selective attention. In M. Rosenzweig & L. Porter (Eds.), *Annual Review of Psychology* (pp. 43–75). Palo Alto, CA: Annual Reviews.

Jones, G. (2003). Testing two cognitive theories of insight. *Journal of Experimental Psychology: Learning, Memory, and Cognition, 29,* 1017–1027.

Jones, W.P., & Hoskins, J. (1987, October). Back propagation: A generalized delta learning rule. *Byte Magazine,* pp. 155–162.

Jonides, J. (1981). Voluntary versus automatic control over the mind's eye's movement. In J.B. Long & A.D. Baddeley (Eds.), *Attention & performance IX* (pp. 187–203). Hillsdale, NJ: Lawrence Erlbaum Associates.

Jonides, J., Badre, D., Curtis, C., Thompson-Schill, S.L., & Smith, E.E. (2002). Mechanisms of conflict resolution in prefrontal cortex. In D.T. Stuss & R.T. Knight (Eds.), *Principles of frontal lobe function* (pp. 233–245). New York: Oxford University Press.

Jorgenson, J., Miller, G.A., & Sperber, D. (1984). Test of the mention theory of irony. *Journal of Experimental Psychology: General, 113,* 112–120.

Judson, H.F. (1984). Century of the sciences. *Science 84,* 41–43.

Jung, C.G. (1950). Foreword. *The I Ching or book of changes* (C.F. Baynes, Trans.). Princeton, NJ: Princeton University Press.

Jung, C.G. (1973). *Synchronicity: An acausal connecting principle.* Princeton, NJ: Princeton University Press.

Kadosh, R. C., Henik, A., Catena, A., Walsh, V., and Fuentes, L.J. (2009). Induced cross-modal synaesthetic experience without abnormal neuronal connections. *Psychological Science, 20,* 258–265.

Kahan, T.L., & LaBerge, S. (1994). Lucid dreaming as metacognition: Implications for cognitive science. *Consciousness and Cognition, 3,* 246–264.

Kahneman, D. (1973). *Attention and effort.* Englewood Cliffs, NJ: Prentice-Hall.

Kahneman, D. (2002). Maps of bounded rationality: A perspective on intuitive judgment and choice. In Tore Frängsmyr (Ed.), *Les Prix Nobel/The Nobel Prizes 2002.* Stockholm: Nobel Foundation. Retrieved 2 May 2005, from http://nobelprize.org/economics/laureates/2002/kahnemann-lecture.pdf.

Kahneman, D. (2003). A perspective on judgment and choice: Mapping bounded rationality. *American Psychologist, 58,* 697–720.

Kahneman, D., & Frederick, S. (2002). Representativeness revisited: Attribute substitution in intuitive judgement. In T. Gilovich, D. Griffin, & D. Kahneman (Eds.), *Heuristics and biases: The psychology of intuitive judgment* (pp. 49–81). Cambridge: Cambridge University Press.

Kahneman, D., & Miller, D.T. (1986). Norm theory: Comparing reality to its alternatives. *Psychological Review, 93,* 136–153.

Kahneman, D., & Treisman, A. (1984). Changing views of attention and automaticity. In R. Parasuraman & D.R. Davies (Eds.), *Varieties of attention* (pp. 29–61). Orlando, Fla: Academic Press.

Kahneman, D., & Tversky, A. (1972). Subjective probability: A judgment of representativeness. *Cognitive Psychology, 3,* 430–454.

Kahneman, D., & Tversky, A. (1979). Prospect theory: An analysis of decision under risk. *Econometrica, 47,* 263–271.

Kahneman, D., & Tversky, A. (1984). Choices, values, and frames. *American Psychologist, 39,* 341–350.

Kahneman, D., & Tversky, A. (1996). On the reality of cognitive illusions. *Psychological Review, 103,* 582–591.

Kanazawa, S. (2004). General intelligence as a domain-specific adaptation. *Psychological Review, 111,* 512–523.

Kanizsa, G. (1979). *Organization in vision: Essays on Gestalt perception.* New York: Praeger.

Kanouse, D.E., & Hanson, L.R. (1971). Negativity in evaluations. In E.E. Jones (Ed.), *Attribution: Perceiving the causes of behavior.* Morristown, NJ: General Learning Press.

Kant, I. (1929). *Critique of pure reason* (N.K. Smith, Trans.). New York: St Martin's Press. (Original work published 1781.)

Kanwisher, N., McDermott, J., & Chun, M. (1997). The fusiform face area: A module in human extrastriate cortex specialized for face perception. *Journal of Neuroscience, 17,* 4302–4311.

Kaplan, C.A., & Simon, H.A. (1990). In search of insight. *Cognitive Psychology, 22,* 374–419.

Kapur, N., Glisky, E.L., & Wilson, B.A. (2002). External memory aids and computers in memory rehabilitation. In A.D. Baddeley, M.D. Kopelman, & B.A. Wilson (Eds.), *The handbook of memory disorders* (pp. 757–783). New York: Wiley.

Katz, A.N., Blasko, D.G., & Kazmerski, V.A. (2004). Saying what you don't mean: Social influences on sarcastic language processing. *Current Directions in Psychological Science, 13,* 186–189.

Katz, A.N., Paivio, A., Marschark, M., & Clark, J.M. (1988). Norms for 204 literary and 260 non-literary metaphors on 10 psychological dimensions. *Metaphor and Symbolic Activity, 3,* 191–214.

Katz, D. (1951). *Gestalt psychology: Its nature and significance.* London: Methuen.

Katz, J. (1993). Phantom limb experience in children and adults: Cognitive and affective contributions. *Canadian Journal of Behavioural Science, 25,* 335–354.

Kaufman, L., & Kaufman, J.H. (1999). Explaining the moon illusion. *Proceedings of the National Academy of Sciences, 97,* 1, 500–505.

Kaufman, L., & Rock, I. (1962). The moon illusion. Part I. *Science, 136,* 953–961.

Kay, P., & McDaniel, C.K. (1978). The linguistic significance of the meanings of basic color terms. *Language, 54,* 610–646.

Kay, P., & Regier, T. (2003). Resolving the question of color naming universals. *Proceedings of the National Academy of Sciences, 100,* 9085–9089.

Kay, R.H. (1989). A practical and theoretical approach to assessing computer attitudes: The Computer Attitude Measure (CAM). *Journal of Research on Computing Education, 21,* 456–463.

Kay. R.H. (1993). An exploration of theoretical and practical foundations for assessing attitudes towards computers: The Computer Attitude Measure (CAM). *Computers in Human Behavior, 9,* 371–386.

Kelley, C.M., & Jacoby, L.L. (2000). Recognition and familiarity; process dissociation. In E. Tulving & F.I.M. Craik (Eds.), *The Oxford handbook of memory* (pp. 215–228). New York: Oxford University Press.

Kennedy, H., Batardiere, A., Dehay, C., & Barone, P. (1997). Synaesthesia: Implications for developmental neurobiology. In S. Baron-Cohen & J.E. Harrison (Eds.), *Synaesthesia: Classic and contemporary readings* (pp. 243–256). Oxford: Blackwell.

Keren, G. (1984). On the importance of identifying the correct "problem space." *Cognition, 16,* 121–128.

Kihlstrom, J.F. (1987). The cognitive unconscious. *Science, 237,* 1335–1552.

Kihlstrom, J.F. (1995). Memory and consciousness: An appreciation of Claparède and "Recognition et Moitié." *Consciousness and Cognition, 4,* 379–386.

Kihlstrom, J.F. (2004). Availability, accessibility, and subliminal perception. *Consciousness and Cognition, 13,* 92–100.

Kinder, A., Shanks, D.R., Cock, J., & Timney, R.J. (2003). Recollection, fluency, and the explicit/implicit distinction in artificial grammar learning. *Journal of Experimental Psychology: General, 132*, 551–565.

Kingstone, A., & Gazzaniga, M.S. (1995). Subcortical transfer of higher order information: More illusory than real? *Neuropsychology, 9*, 321–328.

Kingstone, A., & Klein, R.M. (1993). "Visual offsets facilitate saccadic latency—Does predisengagement of visuospatial attention mediate this gap effect?," *Journal of Experimental Psychology: Human Perception and Performance, 19*(6), 1251–65.

Kingstone, A., Smilek, D., Eastwood, J.D. (2008). Cognitive ethology: A new approach for studying human cognition. *British Journal of Psychology, 99*(3), 317–345.

Kingstone, A., Smilek, D., Ristic, J., Friesen, C.K., & Eastwood, J.D. (2003). Attention researchers! It's time to take a look at the real world. *Current Directions in Psychological Science, 12*, 176–180.

Kinsbourne, M., & Wood, F. (1975). Short-term memory processes and the amnesic syndrome. In D. Deutsch & J.A. Deutsch (Eds.), *Short-term memory*. New York: Academic Press.

Kirasic, K. (1991). Spatial cognition and behavior in young and elderly adults: Implications for learning new environments. *Psychology and Aging, 6*, 10–18.

Klahr, D., & Simon, H.A. (1999). Studies of scientific discovery: Complementary approaches and convergent findings. *Psychological Bulletin, 125*, 524–543.

Klahr, D., & Simon, H.A. (2001). What have psychologists (and others) discovered about the process of scientific discovery? *Current Directions in Psychological Science, 10*, 75–79.

Klatzky, R.L., Clark, E.V., & Macken, M. (1971). Asymmetries in the acquisition of polar adjectives. *Journal of Experimental Child Psychology, 16*, 32–46.

Klauer, K.C., Mierke, J., & Musch, J. (2003). The positivity proportion effect: A list context effect in masked affective priming. *Memory & Cognition, 31*, 953–967.

Klein, G.A. (1993). A recognition-primed decision (RPD) model of rapid decision making. *Decision making in action: Models and methods, 5*(4), 138–147.

Klein, R.M. (2000). Inhibition of return. *Trends in Cognitive Neuroscience, 4*(4), 138–147.

Klein, R.M., & Pontefract, A. (1994). Does oculomotor readiness mediate cognitive control of visual attention? Revisited! In C. Umiltà and M. Moscovitch (Eds.). *Attention and performance 15: Conscious and nonconscious information processing* (pp. 333–350). Cambridge, MA: MIT Press.

Klein, S.B., Cosmides, L., Tooby, J., & Chance, S. (2002). Decisions and the evolution of memory: Multiple systems, multiple functions. *Psychological Review, 109*, 306–329.

Klein, S.B., Loftus, J., & Kihlstrom, J.F. (1996). Self-knowledge of an amnesic patient: Toward a neuropsychology of personality and social psychology. *Journal of Experimental Psychology: General, 125*, 250–260.

Knoblich, G., Ohlsson, S., Haider, H., & Rhenius, D. (1999). Constraint relaxation and chunk decomposition in insight problem-solving. *Journal of Experimental Psychology: Learning, Memory, and Cognition, 25*, 1534–1555.

Knoblich, G., Ohlsson, S., & Raney, G.E. (2001). An eye movement study of insight problem solving. *Memory & Cognition, 29*, 1000–1009.

Koch, C. (2004). *The quest for consciousness: A neurobiological approach*. Englewood, CO: Roberts and Company.

Koenig, C.S., & Griggs, R.A. (2001). Elementary my dear Wason: The role of problem representation in the THOG task. *Psychological Research, 65*, 289–293.

Koenig, C.S., & Griggs, R.A. (2004a). Analogical transfer in the THOG task. *Quarterly Journal of Experimental Psychology, 57A*, 557–570.

Koenig, C.S., & Griggs, R.A. (2004b). Facilitation and analogical transfer in the THOG task. *Thinking and Reasoning, 10*, 355–370.

Koffka, K. (1922). Perception: An introduction to the Gestalt-Theorie. *Psychological Bulletin, 19*(10), 531–585.

Koffka, K. (1935). *Principles of Gestalt psychology*. New York: Harcourt, Brace.

Köhler, W. (1925). *The mentality of apes*. London: Routledge & Kegan Paul.

Köhler, W. (1929). *Gestalt psychology*. New York: Liveright.

Köhler, W. (1940). *Dynamics in psychology*. New York: Liveright.

Köhler, W. (1956). *The mentality of apes*. New York: Vintage. (Original work published 1925.)

Köhler, W. (1969). *The task of Gestalt psychology*. Princeton, NJ: Princeton University Press.

Komatsu, L.K. (1992). Recent views of conceptual structure. *Psychological Bulletin, 112*, 500–526.

Koneçni, V.J. (1996). Daniel E. Berlyne (1924–1976): Two decades later. *Empirical Studies of the Arts, 14*, 129–142.

Koppen, C., Alsius, A., Spence, C. (2008) Semantic congruency and the Colavita visual dominance effect. *Experimental Brain Research, 184*, 533–546.

Korf, R. (1999). Heuristic search. In R.A. Wilson & F.C. Keil (Eds.), *The MIT encyclopedia of the cognitive sciences* (pp. 372–373). Cambridge, MA: MIT Press.

Koriat, A. (2000). Control processes in remembering. In E. Tulving & F.I.M. Craik (Eds.), *The Oxford handbook of memory* (pp. 333–346). New York: Oxford University Press.

Koriat, A., & Bjork, R.A. (2005). Illusions of competence in monitoring one's knowledge during study. *Journal of Experimental Psychology: Learning, Memory, and Cognition, 31*, 187–194.

Koriat, A., & Goldsmith, M. (1996). Memory metaphors and the real life/laboratory controversy: Correspondence versus storehouse conceptions of memory. *Behavioral and Brain Sciences, 19*, 167–228.

Koriat, A., Goldsmith, M., & Pansky, A. (2000). Toward a psychology of memory accuracy. *Annual Review of Psychology, 51*, 481–537.

Kornmeier, J., & Bach, M. (2004). Early neural activity in Necker-cube reversal: Evidence for low-level processing of a gestalt phenomenon, *Psychophysiology, 41*, 1–8.

Korsakoff, S.S. (1899). Étude médico-psychologique sur une forme des malades de la mémoire [Medical-psychological study of a form of diseases of memory]. *Revue Philosophique, 28*, 501–530.

Kosslyn, S.M. (1980). *Image and mind*. Cambridge, MA: Harvard University Press.

Kosslyn, S.M. (1983). *Ghosts in the mind's machine*. New York: Norton.

Kosslyn, S.M., Ball, T.M., & Reiser, B.J. (1978). Visual images preserve metric spatial information: Evidence from studies of image scanning. *Journal of Experimental Psychology: Human Perception and Performance, 4*, 47–60.

Kosslyn, S.M., Ganis, G., & Thompson, W.L. (2003). Mental imagery: Against the null hypothesis. *Trends in Cognitive Sciences, 7*, 109–111.

Kosslyn, S.M., Ganis, G., & Thompson, W.L. (2001). Neural foundations of imagery. *Nature Reviews Neuroscience, 2,* 635–642.

Kosslyn, S.M., Thompson, W.L., & Ganis, G. (2002). Mental imagery doesn't work like that. *Behavioral and Brain Sciences, 25,* 198–201.

Kraemer, J.M., Macrae, C.N., Green, A.E., & Kelley, W.M. (2005). Sound of silence activates auditory cortex. *Nature, 434,* 158.

Kraus, S., & Wang, X.T. (2003). The psychology of the Monty Hall problem: Discovering psychological mechanisms for solving a tenacious brain teaser. *Journal of Experimental Psychology: General, 132,* 3–22.

Krech, D. (1962). Cortical localization of function. In L. Postman (Ed.), *Psychology in the making.* New York: Wiley.

Krech, D., & Crutchfield, R.S. (1958). *Elements of psychology.* New York: Knopf.

Kreiman, G., Fried, I., & Koch, C. (2002). Single-neuron correlates of subjective vision in the human medial temporal lobe. *Proceedings of the National Academy of Science USA, 99,* 8378–8383.

Kreitler, H., & Kreitler, S. (1972). *The psychology of the arts.* Durham, NC: Duke University Press.

Kreuz, R.J., & Glucksberg, S. (1989). How to be sarcastic: The echoic reminder theory of verbal irony. *Journal of Experimental Psychology: General, 118,* 374–386.

Kristol, A. (1980). Color systems in southern Italy: A case of regression. *Language, 56,* 137–145.

Kuhn, D. (1989). Children and adults as intuitive scientists. *Psychological Review, 96,* 674–689.

Kuhn, D. (1991). Thinking as argument. *Harvard Educational Review, 62,* 155–178.

Kuhn, T.S. (1970). *The structure of scientific revolutions* (2nd ed.). Chicago: University of Chicago Press.

Kunda, Z., & Nisbett, R.E. (1986). The psychometrics of everyday life. *Cognitive Psychology, 18,* 195–224.

Kvavilashvili, L., & Mandler, G. (2004). Out of one's mind: A study of involuntary semantic memories. *Cognitive Psychology, 48,* 47–94.

LaBerge, D.L. (1990). Attention. *Psychological Science, 1,* 156–162.

Lachter, J., & Bever, T.G. (1988). The relationship between linguistic structure and associative theories of language learning: A constructive critique of some connectionist learning models. *Cognition, 28,* 195–247.

Lagnado, D.A., & Shanks, D.R. (2003). The influence of hierarchy on probability judgement. *Cognition, 89,* 157–178.

Lakatos, I. (1970). Falsification and the methodology of scientific research programmes. In I. Lakatos & A. Musgrave (Eds.), *Criticism and the growth of knowledge* (pp. 91–195). Cambridge: Cambridge University Press.

Lakoff, G. (1987). *Women, fire and dangerous things.* Chicago: University of Chicago Press.

Lakoff, G., & Johnson, M. (1980). *Metaphors we live by.* Chicago: University of Chicago Press.

Lakoff, G., & Johnson, M. (1999). *Philosophy in the flesh.* New York: Basic Books.

Lamme, V.A.F., & Roelfsema, P.R. (2000). The distinct modes of vision afforded by feedforward and recurrent processing. *Trends in Neurosciences, 23,* 571–579, Figure 3, p. 577.

Langer, E.J. (1989). *Mindlessness/mindfulness.* Reading, MA: Addison-Wesley.

Langer, E.J. (2000). Mindful learning. *Current Directions in Psychological Science, 9,* 220–223.

Langer, E.J., & Piper, A.I. (1987). The prevention of mindlessness. *Journal of Personality and Social Psychology, 53,* 280–287.

Langley, P., Simon, H.A., Bradshaw, G.L., & Zytkow, J.M. (1987). *Scientific discovery: Computational explorations of the creative process.* Cambridge, MA: MIT Press.

Lappin, S. Levine, R., and Johnson, D.E. (2000). The structure of unscientific revolutions. *Natural Language and Linguistic Theory 18,* 665–771

Lashley, K.S. (1929). *Brain mechanisms and intelligence.* Chicago: University of Chicago Press.

Lashley, K.S. (1978). Basic neural mechanisms in behavior. In E.R. Hilgard (Ed.), *American psychology in historical perspective* (pp. 265–283). Washington: American Psychological Association. (Original work published 1930.)

Lasnik, H. (2002). The minimalist program. *Trends in Cognitive Sciences, 6,* 432–437.

Laughlin, P., Lange, R., & Adamopoulos, J. (1982). Selection strategies for "Mastermind" problems. *Journal of Experimental Psychology: Learning, Memory, and Cognition, 8,* 475–483.

Lavery, J.J. (1962). Retention of simple motor skills as a function of type of knowledge of results. *Canadian Journal of Psychology, 16,* 300–311.

Lavie, N., Hirst, A., Fockert, J.W. de, & Viding, E. (2004). Load theory of selective attention and cognitive control. *Journal of Experimental Psychology: General, 133,* 339–354.

Lavie, N., Ro, T., & Russell, C. (2003). The role of perceptual load in processing distractor faces. *Psychological Science, 14,* 510–515.

Lazarus, R.S. (1984). On the primacy of cognition. *American Psychologist, 39,* 124–129.

Lazarus, R.S., & McCleary, R. (1951). Autonomic discrimination without awareness: A study of subception. *Psychological Review, 58,* 113–122.

LeDoux, J. (2003). *Synaptic self.* New York: Penguin.

Lee, D.N. (1980). The optic flow field: The foundation of vision. *Philosophical Transactions of the Royal Society B, 290,* 169–179.

Lefebvre, V.A. (1985). The Golden Section and an algebraic model of ethical cognition. *Journal of Mathematical Psychology, 29,* 289–310.

Lefebvre, V.A., Lefebvre, V.D., & Adams-Webber, J. (1986). Modeling an experiment on construing self and others. *Journal of Mathematical Psychology, 30,* 317–330.

Lehar, S. (2003). Gestalt isomorphism and the primacy of subjective conscious experience: A gestalt bubble model. *Behavioral and Brain Sciences, 26,* 375–444.

Lehman, D.R., & Nisbett, R.E. (1990). A longitudinal study of the effects of undergraduate training on reasoning. *Developmental Psychology, 26,* 952–960.

Lehman, D.R., Lempert, R.O., & Nisbett, R.E. (1988). The effects of graduate training on reasoning. *American Psychologist, 43,* 431–442.

Lemmons, P. (1982, November). A short history of the keyboard. *Byte Magazine,* pp. 386–387.

Levine, L.J., & Pizarro, D.A. (2004). Emotion and memory research: A grumpy overview. *Social Cognition, 22,* 530–554.

Levinson, S.C. (1996). Language and space. *Annual Review of Anthropology, 25,* 353–382.

Levinson, S.C., Kita, S., Haun, D.B.M., & Rasch, B.H. (2002). Returning the tables: Language affects spatial reasoning. *Cognition, 84,* 155–188.

Levy, D.A., Stark, C.E.L., & Squire, L.R. (2004). Intact conceptual priming in the absence of declarative memory. *Psychological Science, 15,* 680–686.

Lévy-Schoen, A. (1981). Flexible and/or rigid control of oculomotor scanning behavior. In D.F. Fisher, R.A. Monty, & J.W. Senders (Eds.), *Eye movements: Cognition and visual perception* (pp. 299–314). Hillsdale, NJ: Erlbaum.

Lewis, M.P., Simons, G.F., & Fennig, C.D. (eds.). 2015. *Ethnologue: Languages of the World* (18th edition). Dallas, Texas: SIL International. Online version: http://www.ethnologue.com.

Leyens, J.-P., & Corneille, O. (1999). Asch's social psychology: Not as social as you may think. *Personality and Social Psychology Review, 3*, 345–357.

Libet, B., Gleason, C.A., Wright, E.W., Pearl, D.K. (1983). Time of conscious intention to act in relation to onset of cerebral activity (readiness-potential). *Brain 106*(3): 623–42.

Liebowitz, S., & Margolis, S.E. (1996). Typing errors. *Reason, 28*, 28–36.

Lightfoot, D. (1982). *The language lottery: Toward a biology of grammars.* Cambridge, MA: MIT Press.

Lindsay, D.S. (1993). Eyewitness suggestibility. *Current Directions in Psychological Science, 2*, 86–88.

Lindsay, D.S., & Johnson, M.K. (1989). The eyewitness suggestibility effect and memory for source. *Memory & Cognition, 17*, 349–358.

Lindsay, D.S., & Johnson, M.K. (2001). False memories and the source monitoring framework: Reply to Reyna and Lloyd (1997). *Learning and Individual Differences, 12*, 145–161.

Lindsay, D.S., Hagen, L., Read, J.D., Wade, K.A., & Garry, M. (2004). True photographs and false memories. *Psychological Science, 15*, 149–154.

Link, S. (1994). Rediscovering the past: Gustav Fechner and signal detection theory. *Psychological Science, 5*, 335–340.

Lissauer, H. (1890/1988). A case of visual agnosia with a contribution to theory (M. Jackson, Trans.). *Cognitive Neuropsychology, 5*, 153–192.

Livingston, R. (1967). Reinforcement. In G. Quarton, T. Melenchuk, & F. Schmidt (Eds.), *The neurosciences: A study program* (pp. 499–514). New York: Rockefeller University Press.

Lockhart, R.S., & Craik, F.I.M. (1990). Levels of processing: A retrospective commentary on a framework for memory research. *Canadian Journal of Psychology, 44*, 87–112.

Loehlin, J.C. (1989). Partitioning environmental and genetic contributions to behavioral development. *American Psychologist, 44*, 1285–1292.

Loehlin, J.C. (1992). *Latent variable models: An introduction to factor, path and structural analysis* (2nd ed.). Hillsdale, NJ: Erlbaum.

Loftus, E.F. (1991). The glitter of everyday memory . . . and the gold. *American psychologist, 46*, 16–18.

Loftus, E.F. (1992). When a lie becomes memory's truth: Memory distortion after exposure to misinformation. *Current Directions in Psychological Science, 1*, 121–123.

Loftus, E.F. (2003). Make-believe memories. *American Psychologist, 58*, 867–873.

Loftus, E.F. (2004). Memories of things unseen. *Current Directions in Psychological Science, 13*, 145–147.

Loftus, E.F., & Hoffman, H.G. (1989). Misinformation and memory: The creation of new memories. *Journal of Experimental Psychology: General, 118*, 100–104.

Loftus, E.F., & Loftus, G.R. (1980). On the permanence of stored information in the human brain. *American Psychologist, 35*, 409–420.

Loftus, E.F., & Palmer, J.C. (1974). Reconstruction of automobile destruction: An example of the interaction between language and memory. *Journal of Verbal Learning and Verbal Behavior, 13*, 585–589.

Loftus, E.F., & Yuille, J.C. (1984). Departures from reality in human perception and memory. In H. Weingartner & E.S. Parker (Eds.), *Memory consolidation: Psychobiology of cognition* (pp. 163–184). Mahwah, NJ: Erlbaum.

Lopes, L.L. (1982). Doing the impossible: A note on induction and the experience of randomness. *Journal of Experimental Psychology: Learning, Memory, and Cognition, 8*, 626–636.

Lorayne, H., & Lucas, J. (1976). *The memory book.* London: Allen.

Lovie, A.D., & Lovie, P. (1993). Charles Spearman, Cyril Burt, and the origins of factor analysis. *Journal of the History of the Behavioral Sciences, 29*, 308–321.

Lowenstein, G. (1994). The psychology of curiosity: A review and reinterpretation. *Psychological Bulletin, 116*, 75–98.

Lubart, T.I. (2001). Models of the creative process: Past, present and future. *Creativity Research Journal, 13*, 295–308.

Lubinski, D. (2004). Introduction to the special section on cognitive abilities: 100 years after Spearman's (1904) "'General intelligence' objectively determined and measured." *Journal of Personality and Social Psychology, 86*, 96–111.

Luce, R.D. (2003). Whatever happened to information theory in psychology? *Journal of General Psychology, 7*, 183–188.

Luchins, A.S. (1942). Mechanization in problem-solving. *Psychological Monographs, 54*, Whole No. 248.

Luchins, A.S., & Luchins, E.H. (1950). New experimental attempts at preventing mechanization in problem-solving. *Journal of General Psychology, 42*, 279–297.

Luchins, A.S., & Luchins, E.H. (1994a). The water jar experiments and einstellung effects. Part I: Early history and surveys of textbook citations. *Gestalt Theory, 16*, 101–121.

Luchins, A.S., & Luchins, E.H. (1994b). The water jar experiments and einstellung effects. Part II: Gestalt psychology and past experience. *Gestalt Theory, 16*, 205–270.

Luncageli, D., Tressoldi, P.E., Bendotti, M., Bonaomi, M., & Siegel, L.S. (2003). Effective strategies for mental and written arithmetic calculation from the third to the fifth grade. *Educational Psychology, 23*, 507–520.

Luo, J., & Niki, K. (2003). Function of hippocampus in "insight" of problem-solving. *Hippocampus, 13*, 316–323.

Luo, J., Niki, K., & Philips, S. (2004). Neural correlates of the "Aha!" reaction. *Neuroreport, 15*, 2013–2017.

Luria, A.R. (1961). *The role of speech in the regulation of normal and abnormal behavior.* New York: Liveright.

Luria, A.R. (1976). *Cognitive development: Its cultural and social foundations.* Cambridge, MA: Harvard University Press.

Lyddy, F. (2002). Interpreting visual images, individually. *Trends in Cognitive Sciences, 6*, 500.

Lynch, K. (1960). *The image of the city.* Cambridge, MA: MIT Press.

Lynn, R. (1998). In support of the nutrition theory. In U. Neisser (Ed.), *The rising curve* (pp. 207–218). Washington: American Psychological Association.

Lynott, D., Corker, K.S., Wortman, J., Connell, L., Donnellan, M.B., Lucas, R.E., & O'Brien, K. (2014). Replication of "Experiencing physical warmth promotes interpersonal warmth" by Williams & Bargh (2008, *Science*). *Social Psychology, 45*, 216–222.

Maas, S. (1983). Why systems transparency? In T.R.G. Green, S.J. Payne, & G.C.

van der Veer (Eds.), *The psychology of computer use*. London: Academic Press.

McClelland, J.L. (1979). On the time relations of mental processes: An examination of systems of processes in a cascade. *Psychological Review, 86*, 287–330.

McClelland, J.L. (1981). Retrieving general and specific knowledge from stored knowledge of specifics. Proceedings of the Third Annual Conference of the Cognitive Science Society, Berkeley, CA.

McClelland, J.L. (2000). Connectionist models of memory. In E. Tulving & F.I.M. Craik (Eds.), *The Oxford handbook of memory* (pp. 583–596). New York: Oxford University Press.

McClelland, J.L., & Rumelhart, D.E. (1981). An interactive activation model of context effects in letter perception. Part I. An account of basic findings. *Psychological Review, 88*, 375–407.

McClelland, J.L., & Rumelhart, D.E. (1986a). A distributed model of memory. In J.L. McClelland & D.E. Rumelhart (Eds.), *Parallel distributed processing* (Vol. 2, pp. 170–215). Cambridge, MA: MIT Press.

McClelland, J.L., & Rumelhart, D.E. (Eds.). (1986b). *Parallel distributed processing: Explorations in the microstructure of cognition: Vol. 2. Psychological and biological models*. Cambridge, MA: MIT Press.

McClelland, J.L., & Rumelhart, D.E. (1988). *Explorations in parallel distributed processing: A handbook of models, programs and exercises*. Cambridge MA: MIT Press.

McClelland, J.L., Rumelhart, D.E., & Hinton, G.E. (1986). The appeal of PDP. In D.E. Rumelhart & J.L. McClelland (Eds.), *Parallel distributed processing* (Vol. 1, pp. 33–44). Cambridge, MA: MIT Press.

McCloskey, M., Wible, C.G., & Cohen, N.J. (1988). Is there a special flashbulb-memory mechanism? *Journal of Experimental Psychology: General, 117*, 171–181.

McConkie, G.W., & Rayner, K. (1975). The span of the effective stimulus during a fixation in reading. *Perception and Psychophysics, 17*(6), 578–586.

McCormack, P.D. (1958). Performance in a vigilance task as a function of length of inter-stimulus interval and interpolated rest. *Canadian Journal of Psychology, 12*, 242–260.

McDaniel, M.A., DeLosh, E.L., & Merritt, P. (2000). Order information and retrieval distinctiveness: Recall of common versus bizarre material. *Journal of Experimental Psychology: Learning, Memory, and Cognition, 26*, 1045–1056.

McDaniel, M.A., Einstein, G.O., DeLosh, E.L., May, C.P., & Brady, P. (1995). The bizarreness effect: It's not surprising, it's complex. *Journal of Experimental Psychology: Learning, Memory, and Cognition, 21*, 422–435.

MacGregor, J.N., Ormerod, T.C., & Chronicle, E.P. (2001). Information processing and insight: A process model of performance on the nine-dot and related problems. *Journal of Experimental Psychology: Learning, Memory, and Cognition 27* (1), 176.

McGurk, H., & MacDonald, J. (1976). Hearing lips and seeing voices. *Nature, 264*, 746–748.

McIntyre, S., & McKitrick, R. (2005). The M&M critique of the MBH98 northern hemisphere climate index: Update and implications. *Energy & Environment, 16*, 69–100.

McIntyre, S., & McKitrick, R. (2009). Proxy inconsistency and other problems in millennial paleoclimate reconstructions. *Proceedings of the National Academy of Sciences, 106*, E10.

Mack, A. (2003). Inattentional blindness: Looking without seeing. *Current Directions in Psychological Science, 12* (5), 180–184.

Mack, A., Pappas, Z., Silverman, M., & Gay, R. (2002). What we see: Inattention and the capture of attention by meaning. *Consciousness and Cognition, 11*, 488–506.

Mack, A., & Rock, I. (1998). *Inattentional blindness*. Cambridge, MA: MIT Press.

Mackavey, W.R., Malley, J.E. & Stewart, A.J. (1991). Remembering autobiographically consequential experiences: Content analysis of psychologists' accounts of their lives. *Psychology and Aging, 6*, 50–59.

McKeefry, D., & Zeki, S. (1997). The position and topography of the human colour centre as revealed by functional magnetic resonance imaging. *Brain, 120*, 2229–2242.

McKelvie, S.J. (1995). *Vividness of visual imagery: Measurement, nature, function and dynamics*. New York: Brandon House.

McLean, J.R., & Hoffman, E.R. (1973). The effects of restricted preview on driver steering control and performance. *Human Factors, 15*, 421–430.

MacLeod, C.M. (1991). Half a century of research on the Stroop effect: An integrative review. *Psychological Bulletin, 109*, 163–203.

MacLeod, C.M. (1992). The Stroop task: The "gold standard" of attentional measures. *Journal of Experimental Psychology: General, 121*, 12–15.

MacLeod, C.M., & MacDonald, P.A. (2000). Interdimensional interference in the Stroop effect: Uncovering the cognitive and neural anatomy of attention. *Trends in Cognitive Sciences, 4*, 382–391.

MacLeod, C.M., & Sheehan, P.W. (2003). Hypnotic control of attention in the Stroop task: A historical footnote. *Consciousness and Cognition, 12*, 347–353.

McManus, I.C. (1983). Basic colour terms in literature. *Language and Speech, 26*, 247–252.

Macmillan, M. (2002). *An odd kind of fame: Stories of Phineas Gage*. Cambridge, MA: MIT Press.

McNamara, T.P. (1992). Priming and constraints it places on theories of memory and retrieval. *Psychological Review, 99*, 650–662.

McNamara, T.P., Rump, B., & Werner, S. (2003). Egocentric and geocentric frames of reference in memory of large-scale space. *Psychonomic Bulletin & Review, 10*, 589–595.

McNeill, D. (1970). *The acquisition of language*. New York: Harper & Row.

McNeill, D. (1980). *Conceptual basis of language activity* (cassette recording). Washington: American Psychological Association.

McNeill, D. (1985a). Language viewed as action. In J. Wertsch (Ed.), *Culture, communication and cognition* (pp. 258–270). Cambridge: Cambridge University Press.

McNeill, D. (1985b). So you think gestures are nonverbal? *Psychological Review, 92*, 350–371.

McNeill, D. (1989). A straight path—to where? Reply to Butterworth and Hadar. *Psychological Review, 96*, 175–179.

McRae, K., & Boisvert, S. (1998). Automatic semantic similarity priming. *Journal of Experimental Psychology: Learning, Memory, and Cognition, 24*, 558–572.

MacWhinney, B. (2000). *The CHILDES project: Tools for analyzing talk*. Mahwah, NJ: Erlbaum.

MacWhinney, B. (2004). A multiple process solution to the logical problem of language acquisition. *Journal of Child Language, 31*, 883–914.

Mackworth, N. (1965). Originality. *American Psychologist, 20,* 51–66.

Mackworth, N.H. (1948). The breakdown of vigilance during prolonged visual search. *Quarterly Journal of Experimental Psychology, 1,* 6–21.

Mackworth, N.H. (1964). Performance decrement in vigilance, threshold, and high-speed perceptual motor tasks. *Canadian Journal of Psychology, 18,* 209–223.

Maess, B., Koelsch, S., Gunter, T.C., & Friederici, A.D. 2001. Musical syntax is processed in Broca's area: An MEG study. *Nature Neuroscience, 4,* 540–545.

Maguire, E.A., Gadian, D.G., Johnsrude, I.S., Good, C.D., Ashburner, J., Frackowiak, R.S.J., & Frith, C.D. (2000). Navigation-related structural change in the hippocampi of taxi drivers. *Proceedings of the National Academy of Science, 2000,* 4398–4403.

Maguire, E.A., Valentine, E.R., Wilding, J.M., & Kapur, N. (2003). Routes to remembering: The brains behind superior memory. *Nature Neuroscience, 6,* 90–95.

Mai, X.-Q., Luo, J., Wu, J.-H., & Luo, Y.-J. (2004). "Aha!" effects in a guessing riddle task: An event-related potential study. *Human Brain Mapping, 22,* 261–270.

Maier, N.R.F. (1968). Reasoning in humans: II. The solution of a problem and its appearance in consciousness. In P.C. Wason & P.N. Johnson-Laird (Eds.). *Thinking and reasoning* (pp. 17–27). (Original work published 1931.)

Maier, N.R.F. (1970). *Problem-solving and creativity in individuals and groups.* Belmont, CA: Wadsworth.

Majid, A., Bowerman, M., Kita, S., Haun, D.B.M., & Levinson, S.C. (2004). Can language restructure cognition? The case for space. *Trends in Cognitive Sciences, 8,* 108–114.

Mann, M.E., Bradley, R.S., & Hughes, M.K. (1998). Global-scale temperature patterns and climate forcing over the past six centuries. *Nature, 392,* 779–787.

Mandler, G. (2002). Organization: What levels of processing are levels of. *Memory, 10,* 333–338.

Marcel, A.J. (1983a). Conscious and unconscious perception: Experiments on visual masking and word recognition. *Cognitive Psychology, 15,* 197–237.

Marcel, A.J. (1983b). Conscious and unconscious perception: An approach to the relations between phenomenal experience and perceptual processes. *Cognitive Psychology, 15,* 238–300.

Marcel, A.J., Katz, L., & Smith, M. (1974). Laterality and reading proficiency. *Neuropsychologia, 12,* 131–139.

Marcer, V.L., Zihl, J., & Cowey, A. (1997). Comparing the visual deficits of a motion blind patient with the visual deficits of monkeys with area MT removed. *Neuropsychologia, 35,* 1459–1465.

Marian, V., & Neisser, U. (2000). Language-dependent recall of autobiographical memories. *Journal of Experimental Psychology: General, 129,* 361–368.

Marks, D.F. (1972). Individual differences in the vividness of visual imagery and their effect on function. In P.W. Sheehan (Ed.), *The function and nature of imagery* (pp. 83–108). New York: Academic Press.

Marks, D.F. (1999). Consciousness, mental imagery and action. *British Journal of Psychology, 90,* 567–585.

Marks, L.E. (1978). *The unity of the senses: Interrelations among the modalities.* New York: Academic Press.

Marks, L.E. (1982). Bright sneezes and dark coughs, loud sunlight and soft moonlight. *Journal of Experimental Psychology: Human Perception and Performance, 8,* 177–193.

Marschark, M., Richman, C.L., Yuille, J.C., & Hunt, R.R. (1987). The role of imagery in memory: On shared and distinctive information. *Psychological Bulletin, 102,* 28–41.

Marshall, J.C., & Fink, G.R. (2003). Cerebral localization, then and now. *NeuroImage, 20,* S2–S7.

Martin, A., & Caramazza, A. (2003). Neuropsychological and neuroimaging perspectives on conceptual knowledge: An introduction. *Cognitive Neuropsychology, 20,* 195–212.

Martin, L. (1986). Eskimo words for snow: A case study in the genesis and decay of an anthropological example. *American Anthropologist, 88,* 418–423.

Martindale, C. (1981). *Cognition and consciousness.* Homewood, Ill.: Dorsey Press.

Martindale, C. (1984). The pleasures of thought: A theory of cognitive hedonics. *Journal of Mind and Behavior, 5,* 49–80.

Martindale, C., Moore, K., & West, A. (1988). Relationship of preference judgments to typicality, novelty, and mere exposure. *Empirical Studies of the Arts, 6,* 79–96.

Martino, G., & Marks, L.E. (2001). Synesthesia: Strong and weak. *Current Directions in Psychological Science, 10,* 61–65.

Maslow, A.H. (1946). Problem-centering versus means-centering in science. *Philosophy of Science, 13,* 326–331.

Massaro, D.W. (1998). *Perceiving talking faces: From speech perception to a behavioral principle.* Cambridge, MA: MIT Press.

Mast, F.W., and Kosslyn, S.M. (2002) Visual mental images can be ambiguous: Insights from individual differences in spatial transformation abilities. *Cognition, 86,* 57–70.

Matsukawa, J., Snodgrass, J.G., & Doniger, G.M. (2005). Conceptual versus perceptual priming in incomplete picture identification. *Journal of psycholinguistic research, 34(6),* 515–540.

Maurer, D. (1997). Neonatal synaesthesia: Implications for the processing of speech and faces. In S. Baron-Cohen & J.E. Harrison (Eds.), *Synaesthesia: Classic and contemporary readings* (pp. 224–242). Oxford: Blackwell.

Mayer, E. (1991). The ideological resistance to Darwin's theory of natural selection. *Proceedings of the American Philosophical Society, 135,* 123–139.

Mayer, R.E. (2004). Teaching of subject matter. *Annual Review of Psychology, 55,* 715–744.

Mayer, U. (2004). Conflict, consciousness and control. *Trends in Cognitive Sciences, 8(4),* 145–148.

Medin, D.L. (1989). Concepts and conceptual structure. *American Psychologist, 44,* 1469–1481.

Medin, D.L., & Atran, S. (2004). The native mind: Biological categorization and reasoning in development and across cultures. *Psychological Review, 111,* 960–983.

Mednick, S.A. (1962). The associative basis of the creative process. *Psychological Review, 69,* 220–227.

Mednick, S.A. (1967). *The remote associations test.* Boston: Houghton Mifflin.

Mehta, R., & Zhu, R.J. (2009). Blue or Red? Exploring the Effect of Color on Cognitive Task Performances. *Science, 323,* 1226–1229.

Mehler, J. (1963). Some effects of grammatical transformations: On the recall of English sentences. *Journal of Verbal Learning and Verbal Behavior, 2,* 560–566.

Meiran, N., Hommel, B., Bibi, U., & Lev, I. (2001). Consciousness and control in task switching. *Consciousness and Cognition, 11*, 10–33.

Merikle, P.M. (1992). Perception without awareness: Critical issues. *American Psychologist, 47*, 792–795.

Merikle, P.M., & Daneman, M. (2000). Conscious vs. unconscious perception. In M.S. Gazzaniga (Ed.), *The new cognitive neurosciences* (2nd ed.) (pp. 1295–1303). Cambridge, MA: MIT Press.

Merikle, P.M., & Joordens, S. (1997). Measuring unconscious influences. In J.D. Cohen & J.W. Schooler (Eds.), *Approaches to consciousness* (pp. 109–123). Hillsdale, NJ: Erlbaum.

Merikle, P.M., & Reingold, E.M. (1998). On demonstrating unconscious perception: Comment on Draine and Greenwald. *Journal of Experimental Psychology: General, 127*(3), 304–310.

Merikle, P.M., Smilek, D., & Eastwood, J.D. (2001). Perception without awareness: Perspectives from cognitive psychology. *Cognition, 79*, 115–134.

Messick, D.M. (1987). Egocentric biases and the golden section. *Journal of Social and Biological Structures, 10*, 241–247.

Metcalfe, J. (1998). Cognitive optimism: Self-deception or memory-based heuristics? *Personality and Social Psychology Review, 2*, 100–110.

Metcalfe, J. (2002). Is study time allocated selectively to a region of proximal learning? *Journal of Experimental Psychology: General, 131*, 349–363.

Metcalfe, J., & Kornell, N. (2003). The dynamics of learning and allocation of study time to a region of proximal learning. *Journal of Experimental Psychology: General, 132*, 530–542.

Metcalfe, J., & Kornell, N. (2005). A region of proximal learning model of study time allocation. *Journal of Memory and Language, 52*, 463–477.

Metcalfe, J., & Wiebe, D. (1987). Intuition in insight and non-insight problem-solving. *Memory & Cognition, 15*, 238–246.

Meyer, D.E., & Schvaneveldt, R.W. (1976). Meaning, memory structure, and mental processes. In C. Cofer (Ed.), *The structure of human memory* (pp. 54–89). San Francisco: Freeman.

Meyer, G.E. & Hilterbrand, K. (1984). Does it pay to be "Bashful"? The seven dwarfs and long-term memory. *American Journal of Psychology, 97*, 47–55.

Milgram, R.M., & Rabkin, L. (1980). Developmental test of Mednick's associative hierarchies of original thinking. *Developmental Psychology, 16*, 157–158.

Milham, M.P., Banich, M.T., & Barad, V. (2003). Competition for processing increases prefrontal cortex's involvement in top-down control: An event-related fMRI study of the Stroop task. *Cognitive Brain Research, 17*, 212–222.

Milivojevic, B., Johnson, B.W., Hamm, J.P., & Corballis, M.C. (2003). Non-identical neural mechanisms for two types of mental transformation: Event-related potentials during mental rotation and mental paper folding. *Neuropsychologia, 41*, 1345–1356.

Mill, D., Gray, T., & Mandel, D.R. (1994). Influence of research methods and statistics courses on everyday reasoning, critical abilities, and belief in unsubstantiated phenomena. *Canadian Journal of Behavioural Science, 26*, 246–258.

Miller, D.R. (1999). The norm of self-interest. *American Psychologist, 54*, 1053–1060.

Miller, G.A. (1953). What is information measurement? *American Psychologist, 8*, 3–11.

Miller, G.A. (1956). The magical number seven, plus or minus two. *Psychological Review, 63*, 81–97.

Miller, G.A. (1986). Dictionaries in the mind. *Language and Cognitive Processes, 1*, 171–185.

Miller, G.A., Galanter, E., & Pribram, K. (1960). *Plans and the structure of behavior.* New York: Holt, Rinehart & Winston.

Miller, M.B., & Kingstone, A. (2005). Taking the high road on subcortical transfer. *Brain and Cognition, 57*, 162–164.

Milner A.D., & Goodale, M.A. (1995). *The visual brain in action.* Oxford: Oxford University Press.

Milner, P. (2003). A brief history of the Hebbian learning rule. *Canadian Psychology, 44*, 5–9.

Minsky, M., & Papert, S. (1969). *Perceptrons.* Cambridge, MA: MIT Press.

Mischel, T. (1967). Kant and the possibility of a science of psychology. *The Monist, 51*, 599–622.

Mischel, T. (1969). Scientific and philosophical psychology: An historical introduction. In T. Mischel (Ed.), *Human action* (pp. 1–40). New York: Academic Press.

Mitchell, D.B. (1989). How many memory systems are there? Evidence from aging. *Journal of Experimental Psychology: Human Learning and Memory, 15*, 31–49.

Mitchell, D.B., & Bruss, P.J. (2003). Age differences in implicit memory: Conceptual, perceptual or methodological? *Psychology and Aging, 18*, 807–822.

Mitchell, G. (2004). Case studies, counterfactuals, and causal explanations. *University of Pennsylvania Law Review, 152*, 1517–1608.

Mitchell, K.J., & Johnson, M.K. (2000). Source monitoring: Attributing mental experiences. In E. Tulving & F.I.M. Craik (Eds.). *The Oxford handbook of memory* (pp. 179–195). New York: Oxford University Press.

Moeser, S.D. (1982). Memory integration and memory interference. *Canadian Journal of Psychology, 36*, 165–188.

Mohr, C., Graves, R.E., Gianotti, L.R.R., Pizzagalli, D., & Brugger, P. (2001). Loose but normal: A semantic association study. *Journal of Psycholinguistic Research, 30*, 475–483.

Monin, B. (2003). The warm glow heuristic: When liking leads to familiarity. *Journal of Personality and Social Psychology, 85*, 1035–1048.

Moniz, E. (1968). Prefrontal leucotomy. In W.S. Sahakian (Ed.), *History of psychology: A source book in systematic psychology* (pp. 372–377). Itaska, Ill.: Peacock. (Original work published 1954.)

Monsell, S. (2003). Task switching. *Trends in Cognitive Sciences, 7*, 134–140.

Montero, B. (1999). The body problem. *Noûs, 33*, 183–200.

Montford, A.W. (2010). *The hockey stick illusion.* London: Stacey International.

Moore, J.W. & Obhi, S.S. (2012). Intentional binding and the sense of agency: A review. *Consciousness and Cognition, 21*, 546–561.

Moore, T.E. (1995). Subliminal self-help audiotapes: An empirical test of auditory consequences. *Canadian Journal of Behavioural Science, 27*, 9–20.

Moray, N. (1959). Attention and dichotic listening: Affective cues and the influence of instructions. *Quarterly Journal of Experimental Psychology, 11*, 56–60.

Moreland, R.L., & Zajonc, R.B. (1977). Is stimulus recognition a necessary condition for the occurrence of exposure effects? *Journal of Personality and Social Psychology, 35*, 191–199.

Moreland, R.L., & Zajonc, R.B. (1979). Exposure effects may not depend on stimulus recognition. *Journal of Personality and Social Psychology, 37*, 1085–1089.

Morgan, C.L. (1894). *Introduction to comparative psychology*. London: Walter Scott.

Morris, N., & Jones, D.M. (1990). Memory updating in working memory: The role of the central executive. *British Journal of Psychology, 81*, 111–121.

Morris, P.E., Jones, S., & Hampson, P. (1978). An imagery mnemonic for the learning of people's names. *British Journal of Psychology, 69*, 335–336.

Morton, J. (1969). Interaction of information in word recognition. *Psychological Review, 76*, 165–176.

Morton, J. (1976). On recursive reference. *Cognition, 4*, 309.

Muller, M. (2001). Global and local tree game searches. *Information Sciences, 135*, 187–206.

Mullin, P., & Egeth, H.E. (1989). Capacity limitations in visual word processing. *Journal of Experimental Psychology: Human Perception and Performance, 15*, 111–123.

Mumford, M.D., & Gustafson, S.B. (1988). Creativity syndrome: Integration, application and innovation. *Psychological Bulletin, 103*, 27–43.

Murphy, G.L. (2003). The downside of categories. *Trends in Cognitive Sciences, 7*, 513–514.

Murray, D.J. (1993). A perspective for viewing the history of psychophysics. *Behavioral and Brain Sciences, 16*, 115–186.

Nadel, L., & Hardt, O. (2004). The spatial brain. *Neuropsychology 18*(3), 473–476.

Nader, K. (2003). Memory traces unbound. *Trends in Neurosciences, 26*, 65–72.

Nappe, G.W., & Wollen, K.A. (1973). Effects of instructions to form common and bizarre mental images on retention. *Journal of Experimental Psychology, 100*, 6–8.

Natsoulas, T. (1978). Consciousness. *American Psychologist, 33*, 906–914.

Naveh-Benjamin, M. (2000). Adult age differences in memory performance: Tests of an associative deficit hypothesis. *Journal of Experimental Psychology: Learning, Memory, and Cognition, 26*, 1170–1187.

Naveh-Benjamin, M., Guez, J., Kilb, A., & Reedy, S. (2004). The associative memory deficit of older adults: Further support using face-name associations. *Psychology and Aging, 19*, 541–546.

Naveh-Benjamin, M., Hussain, Z., Guez, J., & Bar-On, M. (2003). Adult age differences in episodic memory: Further support for an associative deficit hypothesis. *Journal of Experimental Psychology: Learning, Memory, and Cognition, 29*, 826–837.

Necker, L.A. (1964). On an apparent change of position in a drawing or engraved figure of a crystal. In W. Dember (Ed.), *Visual perception: The nineteenth century* (pp. 78–83). New York: Wiley. (Original work published 1832.)

Neisser, U. (1962). Cultural and cognitive discontinuity. In T.E. Gladwin & W. Sturtevant (Eds.), *Anthropology and human behavior*. Washington: Anthropological Society of America.

Neisser, U. (1963). Decision-time without reaction-time: Experiments in visual scanning. *American Journal of Psychology, 76*, 376–385.

Neisser, U. (1967). *Cognitive psychology*. New York: Appleton-Century-Crofts.

Neisser, U. (1970). Visual imagery. In J. Antrobus (Ed.), *Cognition and affect* (pp. 159–178). Boston: Little, Brown.

Neisser, U. (1976). *Cognition and reality: Principles and implication of cognitive psychology*. New York: W.H. Freeman/Times Books/Henry Holt & Co.

Neisser, U. (1978a). Anticipations, images, and introspection. *Cognition, 6*, 169–174.

Neisser, U. (1978b). Memory: What are the important questions? In M.M. Gruneberg, P.M. Morris, & R.N. Sykes (Eds.), *Practical aspects of memory* (pp. 3–24). London: Academic Press.

Neisser, U. (1979). Tracing eidetic imagery. *Behavioral and Brain Sciences, 2*, 612–613.

Neisser, U. (1980). *Toward a realistic cognitive psychology* (cassette recording). Washington: American Psychological Association.

Neisser, U. (1981). John Dean's memory: A case study. *Cognition, 9*, 1–22.

Neisser, U. (1982a). Snapshots or benchmarks? In U. Neisser (Ed.), *Memory observed: Remembering in natural contexts* (pp. 43–48). San Francisco: Freeman.

Neisser, U. (Ed.). (1982b). *Memory observed: Remembering in natural contexts*. San Francisco: Freeman.

Neisser, U. (1983). Components of intelligence or steps in routine procedures? *Cognition, 15*, 189–197.

Neisser, U. (1985). The role of theory in the ecological study of memory: Comment on Bruce. *Journal of Experimental Psychology: General, 114*, 272–276.

Neisser, U. (Ed.). (1986). *The school achievement of minority children*. Hillsdale, NJ: Erlbaum.

Neisser, U. (1988). Five kinds of self-knowledge. *Philosophical Psychology, 1*, 35–59.

Neisser, U. (1988). What is ordinary memory the memory of? In U. Neisser & E. Winograd (Eds.), *Remembering reconsidered: Ecological and traditional approaches to the study of memory* (pp. 356–373). New York: Cambridge University Press.

Neisser, U. (1991). A case of misplaced nostalgia. *American Psychologist, 46*, 34–36.

Neisser, U. (1993). The self perceived. In U. Neisser (Ed.), *The perceived self* (pp. 3–21). New York: Cambridge University Press.

Neisser, U. (1997a). Rising scores on intelligence tests. *American Scientist, 85*, 440–447.

Neisser, U. (1997b). The ecological study of memory. *Proceedings of the Royal Society of London (Series B), 352*, 1697–1701.

Neisser, U. (Ed.). (1998). *The rising curve*. Washington: American Psychological Association.

Neisser, U. (2003). New directions for flashbulb memories: Comments on the *Applied Cognitive Psychology* special issue. *Applied Cognitive Psychology, 17*, 1149–1155.

Neisser, U. (2004). Memory development: New questions and old. *Developmental Review, 24*, 154–158.

Neisser, U., & Becklen, R. (1975). Selective looking: Attending to visually specified events. *Cognitive Psychology, 7*, 480–494.

Neisser, U., Boodoo, G., Bouchard, T.J., Boykin, A.W., Brody, N., Ceci, S.J., et al. (1996). Intelligence: Knowns and unknowns. *American Psychologist, 51*, 77–101.

Neisser, U., & Weene, P. (1962). Hierarchies in concept attainment. *Journal of Experimental Psychology, 64*, 640–45.

Nelson, K., & Gruendel, J. (1981). Generalized event representations: Basic building blocks of cognitive development. In M.E. Lamb & A.L. Brown (Eds.), *Advances in developmental psychology* (pp. 131–158). Hillsdale, NJ: Erlbaum.

Nersessian, N.J. (1995). Opening the black box: Cognitive science and the history of science. *Osiris, 10,* 194–211.

Newell, A. (1977). On the analysis of human problem-solving protocols. In P.N. Johnson-Laird & P. Wason (Eds.), *Thinking: Readings in cognitive science* (pp. 46–61). Cambridge: Cambridge University Press.

Newell, A. (1983). The heuristic of George Polya and its relation to artificial intelligence. In R. Groner & M. Groner (Eds.), *Methods of heuristics* (pp. 195–243). Hillsdale, NJ: Erlbaum.

Newell, A. (1985). Duncker on thinking: An inquiry into progress in cognition. In S. Koch & D. Leary (Eds.), *A century of psychology as science: Retrospections and assessments* (pp. 392–419). New York: McGraw-Hill.

Newell, A., & Simon, H.A. (1972). *Human problem-solving.* Englewood Cliffs, NJ: Prentice-Hall.

Newell, A., Shaw, J.C., & Simon, H.A. (1958). Chess-playing programs and the problem of complexity. *IBM Journal of Research and Development, 2,* 320–335.

Newell, A., Simon, H., & Shaw, J.C. (1962). The processes of creative thinking. In H.E. Gruber, G. Terrell, & M. Wertheimer (Eds.), *Contemporary approaches to creative thinking* (pp. 63–119). New York: Atherton.

Newell, B.R. (2005). Re-visions of rationality? *Trends in Cognitive Sciences, 9,* 11–15.

Newman, J.R. (1956). *The world of mathematics.* New York: Simon & Schuster.

Newstead, S.E., Pollard, P., Evans, J. St B.T., & Allen, J.L. (1992). The source of belief bias effects in syllogistic reasoning. *Cognition, 45,* 257–284.

Ngo, M.K., Sinnett, S., Soto-Faraco, S., & Spence, C. (2010). Repetition blindness and the Colavita effect. *Neuroscience Letters, 480,* 186–190.

Ngo, M.K., Cadieux, M.L., Sinnett, S., Soto-Faraco, S., & Spence, C. (2011). Reversing the Colavita visual dominance effect. *Experimental Brain Research, 214*(4), 607–18.

Nicholls, M.E.R., Clode, D., Wood, S.J., & Wood, A.G. (1999). Laterality of expression in portraiture: Putting your best cheek forward. *Proceedings of the Royal Society of London (Series B), 266,* 1517–1522.

Nicholls, M.E.R., Wolfgang, B.J., Clode, D., & Lindell, A.K. (2002). The effect of left and right poses on the expression of facial emotion. *Neuropsychologia, 40,* 1662–1665.

Nichols, S. (2004). Folk concepts and intuitions: From philosophy to cognitive science. *Trends in Cognitive Science, 8,* 514–518.

Nickerson, R.S. (1996). Ambiguities and un-stated assumptions in probabilistic reasoning. *Psychological Review, 120,* 410–433.

Nicolson, R.I., & Gardner, P.H. (1985). The QWERTY keyboard hampers schoolchildren. *British Journal of Psychology, 76,* 525–531.

Nisbett, R.E., Krantz, D.H., Jepson, C., & Kunda, Z. (1983). The use of statistical heuristics in everyday inductive reasoning. *Psychological Review, 90,* 339–363.

Noble, C.E. (1952). An analysis of meaning. *Psychological Review, 59,* 421–430.

Noë, A., Pessoa, L., & Thompson, E. (2000). Beyond the grand illusion: What change blindness really teaches us about vision. *Visual Cognition, 7,* 93–106.

Noë, A., & Thompson, E. (2004). Are there neural correlates of consciousness? *Journal of Consciousness Studies, 11,* 3–28

Noice, H. (1991). The role of explanations and plan recognition in the learning of theatrical scripts. *Cognitive Science, 15,* 425–460.

Noice, H. (1992). Elaborative memory strategies of professional actors. *Applied Cognitive Psychology, 6,* 417–427.

Noice, H. (1993). Effects of rote versus gist strategy on the verbatim retention of theatrical scripts. *Applied Cognitive Psychology, 7,* 75–84.

Norman, D.A. (1981). Categorization of action slips. *Psychological Review, 88,* 1–15.

Norman, D.A. (1983). Some observations on mental models. In D. Gentner & A.L. Stevens (Eds.), *Mental models* (pp. 7–14). Hillsdale, NJ: Erlbaum.

Norman, D.A. (1992). *Turn signals are the facial expressions of automobiles.* Reading, MA: Addison-Wesley.

Norman, D.A. (1993). *Things that make us smart.* Reading, MA: Addison-Wesley.

Norman, D.A. (1998). *The invisible computer.* Cambridge, MA: MIT Press.

Norman, D.A. (2002). *The psychology of everyday things.* New York: Basic Books. (Original work published 1988.)

Norman, D.A., & Bobrow, D.G. (1976). Active memory processes in perception and cognition. In C. Cofer (Ed.), *The structure of human memory* (pp. 114–132). San Francisco: Freeman.

Norman, D.A., & Draper, S.W. (1986). *User-centered system design.* Hillsdale, NJ: Erlbaum.

Norman, D.A., & Fisher, D. (1982). Why alphabetic keyboards are not easy to use: Keyboard layout doesn't much matter. *Human Factors, 24,* 509–519.

Noveck, I.A. (2001). When children are more logical than adults: Experimental investigations of scalar implications. *Cognition, 78,* 165–188.

Noyes, J., & Garland, K. (2005). Students' attitudes toward books and computers. *Computers and Human Behavior, 21,* 233–241.

Nyberg, L. (2002). Levels of processing: A view from functional brain imaging. *Memory, 10,* 345–348.

Oakhill, J.V., & Johnson-Laird, P.N. (1985). Rationality, memory and the search for counterexamples. *Cognition, 20,* 79–94.

Oakhill, J.V., Johnson-Laird, P.N., & Garnham, A. (1989). Believability and syllogistic reasoning. *Cognition, 31,* 117–140.

O'Brien, D.P., Noveck, I.A., Davidson, G.M., Fusch, S.M., Lea, R.B., & Freitag, J. (1990). Sources of difficulty in deductive reasoning: The THOG task. *Quarterly Journal of Experimental Psychology, 42A,* 329–351.

O'Brien, E.J., & Wolford, C.R. (1982). Effect of delay of testing on retention of plausible versus bizarre mental images. *Journal of Experimental Psychology: Learning, Memory, and Cognition, 8,* 148–152.

O'Connor, N., & Hermelin, B. (1972). Seeing and hearing in space and time. *Perception & Psychophysics, 11,* 46–48.

Ogilvie, J. (2002). Turn the other cheek. *Trends in Cognitive Sciences, 6,* 234.

Ohlsson, S. (1984). Restructuring revisited. *Scandinavian Journal of Psychology, 25,* 65–78.

Oizumi, M., Albantakis, L., & Tononi, G. (2014). From the phenomenology to the mechanisms of consciousness: Integrated information theory 3.0. *PLOS Computational Biology, 10,* 1–25.

O'Kane, G., Kensinger, E.A., Corkin, S. (2004). Evidence for semantic learning in profound amnesia: An investigation with patient H.M. *Hippocampus, 14,* 417–425.

O'Keefe, J., & Nadel, L. (1978). *The hippocampus as a cognitive map.* Oxford: Oxford University Press.

Olivers, C.N.L., & Nieuwenhuis, S. (2005). The beneficial effect of concurrent task-irrelevant mental activity on temporal attention. *Psychological Science, 16*, 265–269.

Olson, D.R. (1977). From utterance to text: The bias of language in speech and writing. *Harvard Educational Review, 47*, 257–281.

Olson, D.R. (Ed.). (1985). *Literacy, language and learning: The nature of reading and writing.* New York: Cambridge University Press.

Olson, D.R. (1986). The cognitive consequences of literacy. *Canadian Psychology, 27*, 109–121.

Olson, D.R. (1996). Towards a psychology of literacy: On the relations between speech and writing. *Cognition, 60*, 83–104.

Olson, D.R., & Astington, J.W. (1986a). Children's acquisition of metalinguistic and metacognitive verbs. In W. Demopoulos & A. Marras (Eds.), *Language learning and concept acquisition* (pp. 184–199). Norwood, NJ: Ablex.

Olson, D.R., & Astington, J. (1986b). Talking about text: How literacy contributes to thought. Paper presented to the Boston University Conference on Language Development, Boston.

Olson, G.M., & Olson, J.S. (2003). Human-computer interaction: Psychological aspects of the human use of computing. *Annual Review of Psychology, 54*, 491–516.

Oppenheimer, D.M. (2003). Not so fast! (and not so frugal!): Rethinking the recognition heuristic. *Cognition, 90*, B1–B9.

O'Regan, J.K. (1992). Solving the "real" mysteries of visual perception: The world as an outside memory. *Canadian Journal of Psychology, 46*, 461–488.

Ormerod, T.C., MacGregor, J.N., & Chronicle, E.P. (2002). Dynamics and constraints in insight problem-solving. *Journal of Experimental Psychology: Learning, Memory, and Cognition, 28*, 791–799

Osgood, C.E. (1979). From Yang and Yin in cross-cultural perspective. *International Journal of Psychology, 14*, 1–35.

Osgood, C.E., & Richards, M.M. (1973). From Yang and Yin to "and" or "but." *Language, 49*, 380–412.

Ost, J., & Costall, A. (2002). Misremembering Bartlett: A study in serial reproduction. *British Journal of Psychology, 93*, 243–255.

Owen, A.M., Coleman, M.R., Boly, M., Davis, M.H., Laurey, S., & Pickard, J.D. (2006). Detecting awareness in the vegetative state. *Science, 313*, 1402.

Paige, J.M., & Simon, H.A. (1966). Cognitive processes in solving algebra word problems. In B. Kleinmuntz (Ed.), *Problem-solving* (pp. 51–119). New York: Wiley.

Paivio, A. (1965). Abstractness, imagery and meaningfulness in paired-associate learning. *Journal of Verbal Learning and Verbal Behavior, 4*, 32–38.

Paivio, A. (1969). Mental imagery in associative learning and memory. *Psychological Review, 76*, 241–263.

Paivio, A. (1971). *Imagery and verbal processes.* New York: Holt, Rinehart & Winston.

Paivio, A. (1983). The empirical case for dual coding. In J. Yuille (Ed.), *Imagery, memory and cognition: Essays in honor of Allan Paivio* (pp. 307–332). Hillsdale, NJ: Erlbaum.

Paivio, A. (1986). *Mental representations.* Oxford: Oxford University Press.

Paivio, A. (1991). Dual coding theory: Retrospect and current status. *Canadian Journal of Psychology, 45*, 255–287.

Paivio, A., & Begg, I. (1981). *The psychology of language.* Englewood Cliffs, NJ: Prentice-Hall.

Paivio, A., Khan, M., & Begg, I. (2000). Concreteness and relational effects on recall of adjective-noun pairs. *Canadian Journal of Experimental Psychology, 54*, 149–159.

Paivio, A., Walsh, M., & Bons, T. (1994). Concreteness effects on memory: When and why? *Journal of Experimental Psychology: Learning, Memory, and Cognition, 20*, 1196–1204.

Paivio, A., Yuille, J., & Madigan, S. (1968). Concreteness, imagery and meaningfulness values for 925 nouns. *Journal of Experimental Psychology Monograph Supplement, 76*(1), Pt. 2.

Palmer, C.F., Jones, R.K., Hennessy, B.L., Unze, M.G., & Pick, A.D. (1989). How is a trumpet known? The "basic object level" concept and the perception of musical instruments. *American Journal of Psychology, 102*, 17–37.

Palmer, S.E. (1992). Common region: A new principle of perceptual grouping. *Cognitive Psychology, 24*, 436–447.

Palmer, S.E. (1999). *Vision science: Photons to phenomenology.* Cambridge, MA: MIT Press.

Pani, J.F., & Chariker, J.H. (2004). The psychology of error in relation to medical practice. *Journal of Surgical Oncology, 88*, 130–142.

Papanicolauo, A.C. (1998). *Fundamentals of functional brain imaging.* Lisse: Swets & Zeitlinger.

Paprotte, W., & Sinha, C. (1987). A functional perspective on early language development. In M. Hickmann (Ed.), *Social and functional approaches to language and thought* (pp. 203–222). New York: Academic Press.

Parker, A.J., Krug, K., & Cumming, B.G. (2003). Neuronal activity and its links with the perception of multistable figures. In A. Parker, A. Derrington, & C. Blakemore (Eds.), *The physiology of cognitive processes* (pp. 139–156). Oxford: Oxford University Press.

Parkin, A.J., & Hunkin, N.M. (2001). British memory research: A journey through the 20th century. *British Journal of Psychology, 92*, 37–52.

Pashler, H. (1994). Dual-task interference in simple tasks: Data and theory. *Psychological Bulletin, 116*(2), 220–244.

Pashler, H. (1998). *The psychology of attention.* Cambridge, MA: MIT Press.

Pashler, H., Johnston, J.C., & Ruthruff, E. (2001). Attention and performance. *Annual Review of Psychology, 52*, 629–651.

Pattyn, N., Neyt, X., Henderickx, D. & Soetens, E. (2008). Psychophysiological investigation of vigilance decrement: Boredom or cognitive fatigue? *Physiology & Behavior, 93*, 369–378.

Paul, I.H. (1967). The concept of schema in memory theory. In R.R. Holt (Ed.), *Motives and thought: Psychoanalytic essays in honor of David Rapaport* (pp. 215–258). New York: International Universities Press.

Payne, S.J., & Green, T.R.G. (1989). The structure of command languages: An experiment on task-action grammar. *International Journal of Man-Machine Studies, 30*, 213–234.

Peabody, D. (1990). The role of evaluation in impressions of persons. In I. Rock (Ed.), *The legacy of Solomon Asch* (pp. 57–75). Hillsdale, NJ: Erlbaum.

Pederson, E., Danziger, E., Wilkins, D., Levinson, S., Kita, S., & Senft, G. (1998). Semantic typology and spatial conceptualization. *Language, 74*, 557–589.

Peelen, M.V., Heslenfeld, D.J., & Theeuwes, J. (2004). Endogenous and exogenous attention shifts are mediated by the same large-scale neural network. *NeuroImage, 22*, 822–830.

Peeters, G., & Czapinski, J. (1990). Positive-negative asymmetry in evaluations: The distinction between affective and informational negativity effects. In W. Stroebe & M. Hewstone (Eds.), *European Review of Social Psychology* (Vol. 1). Chichester: Wiley.

Pelli, D.G. (1999). Close encounters—An artist shows that size affects shape. *Science, 285*, 844–846.

Pelli, D.G., Farell, B., & Moore, D.C. (2003). The remarkable inefficiency of word recognition. *Nature, 423*, 752–756.

Penn, D.C., Holyoak, K.J., & Povinelli, D.J. (2008). Darwin's mistake: Explaining the discontinuity between human and nonhuman minds. *Behavioral and Brain Sciences, 31*(2), 109–130.

Perkins, D.N. (1981). *The mind's best work.* Cambridge, MA: Harvard University Press.

Perner, J. (2000). Memory and theory of mind. In E. Tulving & F.I.M. Craik (Eds.), *The Oxford handbook of memory* (pp. 297–312). New York: Oxford University Press.

Pessoa, L., Kastner, S., & Ungerleider, L.G. (2003). Neuroimaging studies of attention: From modulation of sensory processing to top-down control. *Journal of Neuroscience, 23*, 3990–3998.

Pessoa, L., Thompson, E., & Noë, A. (1998). Finding out about filling-in: A guide to perceptual completion for visual science and the philosophy of perception. *Behavioral and Brain Sciences, 21*(6), 723–802.

Peterson, L.R., & Peterson, M.J. (1959). Short-term retention of individual verbal items. *Journal of Experimental Psychology, 58*, 193–198.

Peterson, M.A., & Gibson, B.S. (1993). Shape recognition inputs to figure–ground organization in three-dimensional displays. *Cognitive Psychology, 25*, 383–429.

Peterson, M.A., Kihlstrom, J.F., Rose, P.M., & Glisky, M.L. (1992). Mental images can be ambiguous: Reconstruals and reference-frame reversals. *Memory & Cognition, 20*, 107–123.

Petrill, S.A., Lipton, P.A., Hewitt, J.K., Plomin, R., Cherny, S.S., Corley, R., & Defries, J.C. (2004). Genetic and environmental contributions to general cognitive ability through the first 16 years of life. *Developmental Psychology, 40*, 805–812.

Petry, S., & Meyer, G. (1987). *The perception of illusory contours.* New York: Springer.

Pheasant, S. (1986). *Bodyspace: Anthropometry, ergonomics and design.* London: Taylor & Francis.

Phillips, W., & Boroditsky, L. (2003). Can quirks of grammar affect the way you think? Grammatical gender and object concepts. *Proceedings of the 25th annual meeting of the Cognitive Science Society*, pp. 928–933.

Piatelli-Palmarini, M. (1989). Evolution, selection and cognition: From "learning" to parameter setting in biology and in the study of language. *Cognition, 31*, 1–44.

Pikas, A. (1966). *Abstraction and concept formation.* Cambridge, MA: Harvard University Press.

Pike, G., & Edgar, G. (2005). Perception. In Braisby, N., & Gellatly, A. (Eds.). *Cognitive psychology.* Oxford: Oxford University Press.

Pillemer, D.B. (1990). Clarifying the flashbulb memory concept. *Journal of Experimental Psychology: General, 119*, 92–96.

Pinker, S. (1988). Learnability theory and the acquisition of a first language. In F. Kessel (Ed.), *The development of language and language researchers: Essays in honor of Roger Brown* (pp. 97–119). Hillsdale, NJ: Erlbaum.

Pinker, S. (1994). *The language instinct.* London: Penguin.

Pinker, S. (1997). *How the mind works.* New York: Norton.

Pinker, S. (1999). *Words and rules.* New York: HarperCollins.

Pinker, S., & Finke, R.A. (1980). Emergent two-dimensional patterns in images rotated in depth. *Journal of Experimental Psychology: Human Perception and Performance, 6*, 244–264.

Pinker, S., & Jackendoff, R. (2005). The faculty of language: What's special about it? *Cognition, 95*, 201–236.

Pirolli, P. (2005). Rational analyses of information foraging on the web. *Cognitive Science, 29*, 343–373.

Pirolli, P., & Card, S. (1999). Information foraging. *Psychological Review, 106*, 643–675.

Podgorny, P., & Shepard, R.N. (1978). Functional representations common to visual perception and imagination. *Journal of Experimental Psychology: Human Perception and Performance, 4*, 21–35.

Poeppel, D., & Hickock, G. (2004). Introduction: Towards a new functional anatomy of language. *Cognition, 92*, 1–12.

Poincaré, H. (1960). *Science and method.* New York: Dover. (Original work published 1924.)

Polanyi, M. (1958). *Personal knowledge.* Chicago: University of Chicago Press.

Pollio, H.R., Barlow, J.M., Fine, H.J., & Pollio, M.R. (1972). *Psychology and the poetics of growth.* Hillsdale, NJ: Erlbaum.

Pollio, H.R., Smith, M.K., & Pollio, M.R. (1990). Figurative language and cognitive psychology. *Language and Cognitive Processes, 5*, 141–167.

Polya, G. (1957). *How to solve it.* New York: Anchor. (Original work published 1945.)

Poort, J., Raudies, F., Wannig, A., Lamme, V.A.F., Neumann, H., & Roelfsema, P.R. (2012). The role of attention in figure-ground segregation in Area V1 and V4 of the visual cortex. *Neuron, 75*, 143–156.

Popper, K.R. (1959). *The logic of scientific discovery.* New York: Basic Books.

Posner, M. (1978). *Chronometric explorations of the mind.* Hillsdale, NJ: Lawrence Erlbaum Associates.

Posner, M. (1980). Orienting of attention. *Quarterly Journal of Experimental Psychology, 32*, 3–25.

Posner, M.I., & Cohen, Y. (1984). Components of visual orienting. In H. Bouma & H. Bouwhuis (Eds.), *Attention and Performance, X* (pp. 531–556). Hillsdale, NJ: Lawrence Erlbaum Associates.

Posner, M.I. (1969). Abstraction and the process of recognition. In G.H. Bower & J.T. Spence (Eds.), *The psychology of learning and motivation* (Vol. 3, pp. 44–100). New York: Academic Press.

Posner, M.I. (1973). *Cognition: An introduction.* Glenview, Ill.: Scott, Foresman.

Posner, M.I. (1986). *Chronometric explorations of mind.* Oxford: Oxford University Press.

Posner, M.I. (2004). Neural systems and individual differences. *Teacher's College Record*, 24–30.

Posner, M.I., Goldsmith, R., & Welton, K.E., Jr. (1967). Perceived distance and the classification of distorted patterns. *Journal of Experimental Psychology, 73*(1), 28–38.

Posner, M.I., & Keele, S.W. (1968). On the genesis of abstract ideas. *Journal of Experimental Psychology, 77*, 353–363.

Posner, M.I., & Keele, S.W. (1970). Retention of abstract ideas. *Journal of Experimental Psychology, 83*, 304–308.

Posner, M.I., Nissen, M.J., & Klein, R.M. (1976). Visual dominance: An information-processing account of its origins and significance. *Psychological Review, 83*, 157–171.

Postman, L., Bruner, J., & McGinnis, E. (1948). Personal values as selective factors in perception. *Journal of Abnormal and Social Psychology, 43*, 142–154.

Price, D. (1963). *Little science, big science.* New York: Columbia University Press.

Puente, A.E. (1995). Roger Wolcott Sperry (1913–1994). *American Psychologist, 50*, 940–941.

Pullum, G.K. (1991). *The great Eskimo vocabulary hoax, and other irreverent essays on the study of language.* Chicago: University of Chicago Press.

Pullum, G.K., & Scholz, B.C. (2002). Empirical assessment of stimulus poverty arguments. *Linguistic Review, 19*, 9–50.

Purves, D., & Lotto, R.B. (2003). *Why we see what we do: An empirical theory of vision.* Sunderland, MA: Sinaur Associates.

Pylyshyn, Z.W. (1973). What the mind's eye tells the mind's brain: A critique of mental imagery. *Psychological Bulletin, 80*, 1–24.

Pylyshyn, Z.W. (2002). Mental imagery: In search of a theory. *Behavioral and Brain Sciences, 25*, 157–238.

Pylyshyn, Z.W. (2003a). Explaining mental imagery: Now you see it, now you don't. *Trends in Cognitive Sciences, 7*, 111–112.

Pylyshyn, Z.W. (2003b). Return of the mental image: Are there really pictures in the brain? *Trends in Cognitive Sciences, 7*, 113–118.

Qin, Y., & Simon, H.A. (1990). Laboratory replication of scientific discovery processes. *Cognitive Science, 14*, 281–312.

Quillian, R. (1969). The teachable language comprehender: A simulation program and theory of language. *Communications of the ACM, 12*, 459–476.

Quinlan, P.T. (2003). Visual feature integration theory: Past, present, and future. *Psychological Bulletin, 129*, 643–673.

Rabbitt, P. (1990). Applied cognitive gerontology: Some problems, methodologies and data. *Applied Cognitive Psychology, 4*, 225–246.

Radvansky, G.A., Gibson, B.S., & McNerney, M.W. (2011). Synesthesia and memory: Color congruency, von Restorff, and false memory effects. *Journal of Experimental Psychology: Learning, Memory and Cognition, 37*, 219–229.

Raichle, M.E. (2003). Functional brain imaging and human brain function. *Journal of Neuroscience, 23*(10), 3959–3962.

Raichle, M.E. (2008). A brief history of human brain mapping. *Trends in Neurosciences, 32*, 118–126

Raichle, M.E. (2010). The origins of functional brain imaging in humans. In *History of Neurology.* S Finger, F Boller, KL Tyler (Eds). In *Handbook of Clinical Neurology, 95* (3rd series). Elsevier, Amsterdam.

Raichle, M.E., & Snyder, A.Z. (2007). A default mode of brain function: A brief history of an evolving idea. *Neuroimage, 37*(4), 1083–1090.

Ramachandran, V.S. (1993). Filling in gaps in perception: Part II: Scotomas and phantom limbs. *Current Directions in Psychological Science, 2*, 56–65.

Ramachandran, V.S. (2004). *A brief tour of consciousness.* New York: Pi Press.

Ramachandran, V.S., & Hirstein, W. (1998). The perception of phantom limbs: The D.O. Hebb lecture. *Brain, 121*, 1603–1630.

Ramachandran, V.S., & Rogers-Ramachandran, D. (2005). *Scientific American: Mind, 14(5),* 99–100.

Ramachandran, V.S., Rogers-Ramachandran, D., & Cobb, S. (1995). Touching the phantom limb. *Nature, 377*, 489–490.

Rasch, B., & Born, J. (2013). About sleep's role in memory. *Physiological Reviews, 93*(2): 681–766.

Rastle, K.G., & Burke, D.M. (1996). Priming the tip of the tongue: Effects of prior processing on word retrieval in young and older adults. *Journal of Memory and Language, 25*, 586–605.

Ratliff, F. (1976). On the psychophysiological bases of universal color terms. *Proceedings of the American Philosophical Society, 120*, 311–330.

Ratneshwar, S., Barsalou, L.W., Pechmann, C., & Moore, M. (2001). Goal-derived categories: The role of personal and situational goals in category representations. *Journal of Consumer Psychology, 10*, 147–157.

Raven, J. (2000). The Raven's progressive matrices: Change and stability over culture and time. *Cognitive Psychology 41*, 1–48.

Raven, J.C., Styles, I., & Raven, M.A. (1998). *Raven's progressive matrices: SPM plus test booklet.* Oxford: Oxford Psychologists Press/San Antonio, Tex.: Psychological Corporation.

Rawson, K.A., & Kintsch, W. (2005). Rereading effects depend on time of test. *Journal of Educational Psychology, 97*, 70–80.

Rayner, K. (1998). Eye movements in reading and information processing: 20 years of research. *Psychological Bulletin, 124*(3), 372–422.

Rayner, K., Rotello, C.M., Stewart, A.J., Keir, J., & Duffy, S.A. (2001). Integrating text and pictorial information: Eye movements when looking at print advertisements. *Journal of Experimental Psychology: Applied, 7*(3), 219–226.

Rayner, K., White, S.J., Johnson, R.L., & Liversedge, S.P. (2006). Raeding wrods with jumbled lettres: There is a cost. *Psychological Science, 17*(3), 192–193.

Raz, A., Landzberg, K.S., Schweizer, H.R., Zephrani, Z.R., Shapiro, T., Fan, J., & Posner, M.I. (2003). Posthypnotic suggestion and the modulation of Stroop interference under cycloplegia. *Consciousness and Cognition, 12*, 332–346.

Reason, J. T. (1979). Actions not as planned: The price of automatization. In G. Underwood & R. Stevens (Eds.), *Aspects of consciousness, Vol. 1: Psychological issues.* London: Wiley.

Reason, J.T. (1984). Lapses of attention in everyday life. In R. Parasuraman & D.R. Davies (Eds.), *Varieties of attention* (pp. 515–549). Orlando, Fla: Academic Press.

Reason, J.T. (1990). *Human error.* New York: Cambridge University Press.

Reber, A.S. (1967). Implicit learning of artificial grammars. *Journal of Verbal Learning and Verbal Behavior, 5*, 855–863.

Reber, A.S. (1985). *The Penguin dictionary of psychology.* London: Penguin.

Reber, A.S. (1989). Implicit learning and tacit knowledge. *Journal of Experimental Psychology: General, 118*, 219–235.

Reber, A.S. (1990). On the primacy of the implicit: Comment on Perruchet and Pacteau. *Journal of Experimental Psychology: General, 119*, 340–342.

Reber, A.S. (1997). Implicit ruminations. *Psychonomic Bulletin & Review, 4*, 49–55.

Reber, A.S., & Allen, R. (1978). Analogy and abstraction strategies in synthetic grammar learning: A functionalist interpretation. *Cognition, 6*, 189–221.

Reber, A.S., Allen, R., & Regan, S. (1985). Syntactical learning and judgment, still unconscious and still abstract: Comment on Dulany, Carlson and Dewey. *Journal of Experimental Psychology: General, 114,* 17, 24.

Reber, A.S., Allen, R., & Regan, S. (1985). Syntactical learning and judgment, still unconscious and still abstract: Comment on Dulany, Carlson, & Dewey. *Journal of Experimental Psychology: General, 114,* 17–24.

Reber, A.S., Kassin, S.M., Lewis, S., & Cantor, G. (1980). On the relationship between implicit and explicit modes in the learning of a complex rule structure. *Journal of Experimental Psychology: Human Learning and Memory, 8,* 492–502.

Reber, A.S., & Lewis, S. (1977). Implicit learning: An analysis of the form and structure of a body of tacit knowledge. *Cognition, 5,* 333–362.

Reber, A.S., Walkenfeld, F.F., & Hernstadt, R. (1991). Implicit and explicit learning: Individual differences and IQ. *Journal of Experimental Psychology: Human Learning and Memory, 17,* 888–896.

Rebok, G.W. (1987). *Life-span cognitive development.* New York: Holt, Rinehart & Winston.

Redelmeier, D. A., & Kahneman, D. (1996). Patients' memories of painful medical treatments: Real-time and retrospective evaluations of two minimally invasive procedures. *Pain, 66,* 3–8.

Redelmeier, D.A., & Tversky, A. (1996). On the belief that arthritis pain is related to the weather. *Proceedings of the National Academy of Sciences, 93,* 2895–2896.

Reder, L. (1980). The role of elaboration in the comprehension and retention of prose. *Review of Educational Research, 50,* 5–53.

Reder, L.M., & Kusbit, G.W. (1991). Locus of the Moses illusion: Imperfect encoding, retrieval or match? *Journal of Memory and Language, 30,* 385–406.

Rees, G., Kreiman, G., & Koch, C. (2002). Neural correlates of consciousness in humans. *Nature Reviews Neuroscience, 3,* 261–270.

Regan, D. (2000). *Human perception of objects.* Sunderland, MA: Sinauer Associates.

Regier, T., & Kay, P. (2004). Color naming and sunlight. *Psychological Science, 15,* 289–290.

Reicher, G.M. (1969). Perceptual recognition as a function of meaningfulness of stimulus material. *Journal of Experimental Psychology, 81,* 275–280.

Reisberg, D., Pearson, D.G., & Kosslyn, S.M. (2003). Intuitions and introspections about imagery: The role of imagery experience in shaping an investigator's theoretical views. *Applied Cognitive Psychology, 17,* 147–160.

Rensink, R.A., O'Regan, J.K., & Clark, J.J. (1997). To see or not to see: The need for attention to perceive changes in scenes. *Psychological Science, 8,* 368–373.

Rhodes, G., Byatt, G., Michie, P.T., & Puce, A. (2004). Is the fusiform face area specialized for faces, individuation, or expert individuation? *Journal of Cognitive Neuroscience, 16,* 189–203.

Rice, M.L. (1989). Children's language acquisition. *American Psychologist, 44,* 149–156.

Richeson, J.A., et al. (2003). An fMRI investigation of the impact of interracial contact on executive function. *Nature Neuroscience, 6,* 1323–1328.

Richman, C.L. (1994). The bizarreness effect with complex sentences: Temporal effects. *Canadian Journal of Experimental Psychology, 48,* 444–450.

Rickles, W., Cohen, M.J., Whitaker, C.A., McIntyre, K.E. (1973). Marijuana induced state-dependent verbal learning. *Psychopharmacologia, 4,* 349–354.

Ridder III, W.H., & Tomlinson, A. (1997). A comparison of saccadic and blink suppression in normal observers. *Vision Research, 37,* 3171–3179.

Rigdon, M.A., & Epting, F. (1982). A test of the Golden Section hypothesis with elicited constructs. *Journal of Personality and Social Psychology, 43,* 1080–1087.

Rinck, M., & Denis, M. (2004). The metrics of spatial distance traversed during mental imagery. *Journal of Experimental Psychology: Learning, Memory, and Cognition, 30,* 1211–1218.

Rips, L.J. (1983). Cognitive processes in propositional reasoning. *Psychological Review, 90,* 38–71.

Rips, L.J. (1988). Deduction. In R.J. Sternberg & E.E. Smith (Eds.), *The psychology of human thought* (pp. 116–152). Cambridge: Cambridge University Press.

Rips, L.J. (1989). The psychology of knights and knaves. *Cognition, 31,* 85–116.

Rips, L.J. (1990). Paralogical reasoning: Evans, Johnson-Laird, and Byrne on liar and truth-teller puzzles. *Cognition, 36,* 291–314.

Rips, L.J. (1994). *The psychology of proof: Deductive reasoning in human thinking.* Cambridge, MA: MIT Press.

Rips, L.J. (1997). Goals for a theory of deduction: Reply to Johnson-Laird. *Minds and Machines, 7,* 409–424.

Rips, L.J., & Conrad, F.G. (1989). Folk psychology of mental activities. *Psychological Review, 96,* 187–207.

Rips, L.J., & Conrad, F.G. (1990). Parts of activities: Reply to Fellbaum and Miller. *Psychological Review, 97,* 571–575.

Risko, E., Anderson, N., Sarwal, A., Engelhardt, M., & Kingstone, A. (2012). Everyday attention: Variation in mind wandering and memory in a lecture. *Applied Cognitive Psychology, 26,* 234–42.

Ristic, J. & Kingstone, A. (2006). Attention to arrows: Pointing to a new direction. *Quarterly Journal of Experimental Psychology, 59,* 1921–1930.

Rizzolatti, G., Riggio, L., Dascola, I., & Umiltà, C. (1987). Reorienting attention across the horizontal and vertical meridians: Evidence in favor of a premotor theory of attention. *Neuropsychologia: Special Issue: Selective Visual Attention, 25(1-A),* 31–40.

Rizzolatti, G., Riggio, L., & Sheliga, B.M. (1994). Space and selective attention. In C. Umiltà and M. Moscovitch (Eds.), *Attention and Performance 15: Conscious and Nonconscious Information Processing* (pp. 232–265). Cambridge, MA: MIT Press.

Ro, T., Russell, C., & Lavie, N. (2001). Changing faces: A detection advantage in the flicker paradigm. *Psychological Science, 12,* 94–99.

Roberson, D., Davidoff, J., Davies, I.R.L., & Shapiro, L.R. (2004). The development of color categories in two languages: A longitudinal study. *Journal of Experimental Psychology: General, 133,* 554–571.

Roberson, D., Davies, I., & Davidoff, J. (2000). Color categories are not universal: Replications and new evidence from a stone-age culture. *Journal of Experimental Psychology: General, 129,* 369–398.

Roberts, R.M., & Kreuz, R.J. (1994). Why do people use figurative language? *Psychological Science, 5,* 159–163.

Robertson, I.H., Manly, T., Andrade, J., Baddeley, B.T., & Yiend, J. (1997). "Oops!": Performance correlates of everyday attentional failures in traumatic brain injured and normal subjects. *Neuropsychologia, 35, 6,* 747–758.

Robinson, D. A. (1965). The mechanics of human smooth pursuit eye movements. *The Journal of Physiology, 180,* 569–591.

Rock, I. (1983). *The logic of perception.* Cambridge, MA: MIT Press.

Rock, I. (1984). *Perception.* New York: Freeman.

Rock, I. (Ed.). (1990). *Legacy of Solomon Asch: Essays in cognition and social psychology.* Hillsdale, NJ: Erlbaum.

Rock, I., & Ceraso, J. (1964). A cognitive theory of associative learning. In C. Scheerer (Ed.), *Cognition* (pp. 110–146). New York: Harper & Row.

Rock, I., & Kaufman, L. (1962). The moon illusion. Part II. *Science, 136* (3521), 1023–1031.

Rock, I., Wheeler, D., & Tudor, L. (1989). Can we imagine how objects look from other viewpoints? *Cognitive Psychology, 21,* 185–210.

Roediger, H.L. (1997). Remembering. *Contemporary Psychology, 42,* 488–492.

Roediger, H.L., III, & Blaxton, T.A. (1987). Effects of varying modality, surface features, and retention interval on priming in word fragment completion. *Memory & Cognition, 15,* 379–388.

Roediger, H.L., Gallo, D.A., & Geraci, L. (2002). Processing approaches to cognition: The impetus from the levels-of-processing framework. *Memory, 10,* 319–332.

Roediger, H.L., & McDermott, K.B. (1993). Implicit memory in normal human subjects. In F. Boller & J. Grafman (Eds.), *Handbook of neuropsychology* (Vol. 8, pp. 63–131). Amsterdam: Elsevier.

Roelfsema, P.R., Lamme, V.A.F., Spekreijse, H., & Bosch, H. (2002). Figure–ground segregation in a recurrent network architecture. *Journal of Cognitive Neuroscience, 14,* 525–537.

Ronan, K.R., & Kendall, P.C. (1997). Self-talk in distressed youth: States of mind and content specificity. *Journal of Clinical Child Psychology, 26,* 330–337.

Rosch, E.H. (1975). Cognitive representations of semantic categories. *Journal of Experimental Psychology: General, 104,* 192–233.

Rosch, E.H. (1978). Principles of categorization. In E. Rosch & B. Lloyd (Eds.), *Cognition and categorization* (pp. 27–48). Hillsdale, NJ: Erlbaum.

Rosch, E.H. (1988). Coherences and categorization: A historical view. In F. Kessel (Ed.), *The development of language and language researchers: Essays in honor of Roger Brown* (pp. 373–392). Hillsdale, NJ: Erlbaum.

Rosch, E.H., & Mervis, C.B. (1975). Family resemblances: Studies in the internal structure of categories. *Cognitive Psychology, 7,* 573–605.

Rosch, E.H., Mervis, C.B., Gray, W.D., Johnson, D.M., & Boyes-Braem, P. (1976). Basic objects in natural categories. *Cognitive Psychology, 8,* 382–439.

Rosenholtz, R., & Malik, J. (1997). Surface orientation from texture: Isotropy or homogeneity (or both)? *Vision Research, 37,* 2283–2293.

Rosnow, R.L., & Rosenthal, R. (1989). Statistical procedures and the justification of knowledge in psychological science. *American Psychologist, 44,* 1276–1284.

Rossano, M.J. (2003). Expertise and the evolution of consciousness. *Cognition, 89,* 207–236.

Rouse, W.B., & Morris, N.M. (1986). On looking into the black box: Prospect and limits in the search for mental models. *Psychological Bulletin, 100,* 349–363.

Rozin, P., & Fallon, A.E. (1987). A perspective on disgust. *Psychological Review, 94,* 23–41.

Rozin, P., Fallon, A., & Augustoni-Ziskind, M. (1985). The child's conception of food: The development of contamination sensitivity to "disgusting" substances. *Developmental Psychology, 21,* 1075–1079.

Rozin, P., Markwith, M., & Ross, B. (1990). The sympathetic magical law of similarity, nominal realism and neglect of negatives in response to negative labels. *Psychological Science, 1,* 383–384.

Rozin, P., Millman, L., & Nemeroff, C. (1986). Operation of the laws of sympathetic magic in disgust and other domains. *Journal of Personality and Social Psychology, 50,* 703–712.

Rozin, P., & Nemeroff, C. (2002). Sympathetic magical thinking: The contagion and similarity "heuristics." In T. Gilovich, D. Griffin, & D. Kahneman (Eds.), *Heuristics and biases: The psychology of intuitive judgment* (pp. 201–216). Cambridge: Cambridge University Press.

Rozin, P., & Royzman, E.B. (2001). Negativity bias, negativity dominance, and contagion. *Personality and Social Psychology Review, 5,* 296–320.

Rubens, A.B., & Benson, D.F. (1971). Associative visual agnosia. *Archives of Neurology, 24*(4), 305–316.

Rubin, D.C. (1975). Within word structure in the tip-of-the-tongue phenomenon. *Journal of Verbal Learning and Verbal Behavior, 14,* 392–397.

Rubin, D.C. (2000). The distribution of early childhood memories. *Memory,* 265–269.

Rubin, D.C. (2002). Autobiographical memory across the lifespan. In P. Graf & N. Ohta (Eds.), *Lifespan development of human memory* (pp. 159–184). Cambridge, MA: MIT Press.

Rubin, D.C. (2005). A basic-systems approach to autobiographical memory. *Current Directions in Psychological Science, 11,* 79–83.

Rubin, D.C., & Berntsen, D. (2003). Life scripts help to maintain autobiographical memories of highly positive, but not highly negative, events. *Memory & Cognition, 31,* 1–14.

Rubin, D.C., & Friendly, M. (1986). Predicting which words get recalled: Measures of free recall, availability, goodness, emotionality, and pronounceability for 925 nouns. *Memory & Cognition, 14,* 79–94.

Rubin, D.C., Rahhal, T.A., & Poon, L.W. (1998). Things learned early in adulthood are remembered best. *Memory & Cognition, 26,* 3–19.

Rubin, D.C., Wetzler, S.E., & Nebes, R.D. (1986). Autobiographical memory across the lifespan. In D.C. Rubin (Ed.), *Autobiographical memory* (pp. 202–221). Cambridge: Cambridge University Press.

Ruby, L. (1960). *Logic: An introduction.* New York: Lippincott.

Rugg, M.D. (1995). Event-related potential studies of memory. In M.D. Rugg & M.G.H. Coles (Eds.), *Electrophysiology of mind* (pp. 132–170). New York: Oxford University Press.

Rugg, M.D. (2002). Functional neuroimaging of memory. In A.D. Baddeley, M.D. Kopelman, & B.A. Wilson (Eds.), *The handbook of memory disorders* (pp. 57–80). Chichester: Wiley.

Rugg, M.D., Otten, L.J., & Henson, R.N.A. (2003). The neural basis of episodic memory: Evidence from functional neuroimaging. In A. Parker, A. Derrington, & C. Blakemore (Eds.), *The physiology of cognitive processes* (pp. 211–233). Oxford: Oxford University Press.

Rumelhart, D.E., & McClelland, J.L. (Eds.). (1986). *Parallel distributed processing: Explorations in the microstructure of cognition: Vol. I Foundations.* Cambridge, MA: MIT Press.

Runco, M.A. (2004). Creativity. *Annual Review of Psychology, 55,* 657–687.

Rundus, D. (1977). Maintenance rehearsal and single-level processing. *Journal of Verbal Learning and Verbal Behavior, 16,* 665–681.

Ruthruff, E., Johnston, J.C., Van Selst, M., Whitsell, S., & Remington, R. (2003). Vanishing dual-task interference after practice: Has the bottleneck been eliminated or is it merely latent? *Journal of Experimental Psychology: Human Perception and Performance, 29,* 280–289.

Ruthsatz, J., & Detterman, D.K. (2003). An extraordinary memory: The case of a musical prodigy. *Intelligence, 31,* 509–518.

Ryle, G. (1949). *The concept of mind.* London: Hutchison.

Sachs, J. (1967). Recognition memory for syntactic and semantic aspects of connected discourse. *Perception and Psychophysics, 2,* 437–442.

Sacks, O., 1995. *An anthropologist on Mars: Seven paradoxical tales.* New York: Knopf.

Sadoski, M., & Paivio, A. (2001). *Imagery and text: A dual-coding theory of reading and writing.* Mahwah, NJ: Erlbaum.

Sahakian, B., & Morein-Zamir, S. (2007). Professor's little helper. *Nature, 450,* 1157–1159.

Sainsbury, R.M. (1988). *Paradoxes.* Cambridge: Cambridge University Press.

Salmon, D.P., Butters, N., & Chan, A.S. (1999). The deterioration of semantic memory in Alzheimer's disease. *Canadian Journal of Experimental Psychology, 53,* 108–116.

Samson, D., & Pilon, A. (2003). A case of impaired knowledge for fruit and vegetables. *Cognitive Neuropsychology, 20,* 373–400.

Sapir, E. (1949). *Selected writings of Edward Sapir.* Berkeley: University of California Press.

Sarter, M., Berntson, G.G., & Cacioppo, J.T. (1996). Brain imaging and cognitive neuroscience. *American Psychologist, 51,* 13–21.

Saslow, M.G. (1967). Effects of components of displacement-step stimuli upon latency for saccadic eye movement. *Journal of the Optical Society of America, 57,* 1024–1029.

Saunders, B.A.C., & van Brakel, J. (1997). Are there nontrivial constraints on colour categorization? *Behavioral and Brain Sciences, 20,* 167–228.

Schactel, E. (1947). On memory and childhood amnesia. *Psychiatry, 10,* 1–26.

Schachter, S.S., Christenfeld, N., Ravina, B., & Bilous, F. (1991). Speech disfluency and the structure of knowledge. *Journal of Personality and Social Psychology, 60,* 362–367.

Schachter, S.S., Rauscher, F., Christenfeld, N., & Crone, K.T. (1994). The vocabularies of academia. *Psychological Science, 5,* 37–41.

Schacter, D.L. (1987). Implicit memory: History and current status. *Journal of Experimental Psychology: Learning, Memory, and Cognition, 13,* 501–518.

Schacter, D.L. (1992). Understanding implicit memory. *American Psychologist, 47,* 559–569.

Schacter, D.L. (1999). The seven sins of memory: Insights from psychology and cognitive neuroscience. *American Psychologist, 54,* 182–203.

Schacter, D.L., & Dodson, C.S. (2001). Misattribution, false recognition and the sins of memory. *Philosophical Transactions of the Royal Society (Series B), 356,* 1385–1393.

Schacter, D.L., & Graf, P. (1986). Effects of elaborative processing on implicit and explicit memory for new associations. *Journal of Experimental Psychology: Learning, Memory, and Cognition, 12,* 432–444.

Schacter, D.L., & Tulving, E. (1994). What are the memory systems of 1994? In D.L. Schacter & E. Tulving (Eds.), *Memory systems 1994* (pp. 1–38). Cambridge, MA: MIT Press.

Schacter, D.L., Wagner, A.D., & Buckner, R.L. (2000). Memory systems of 1999. In E. Tulving & F.I.M. Craik (Eds.). *The Oxford handbook of memory* (pp. 627–643). New York: Oxford University Press.

Schaeffer, J., & van den Herik, H.J. (2002). Games, computers, and artificial intelligence. *Artificial Intelligence, 134,* 1–7.

Schank, R.C. (1982a). Depths of knowledge. In B. de Gelder (Ed.), *Knowledge and representation* (pp. 170–216). London: Routledge & Kegan Paul.

Schank, R.C. (1982b). *Dynamic memory.* New York: Cambridge University Press.

Schank, R.C., & Abelson, R.P. (1975). *Scripts, plans and knowledge.* Proceedings of the Fourth International Joint Conference on Artificial Intelligence. Tbilisi, USSR.

Schank, R.C., & Abelson, R.P. (1977). *Scripts, plans, goals and understanding.* Hillsdale, NJ: Erlbaum.

Schellenberg, E.G. (2004). Music lessons enhance IQ. *Psychological Science, 15,* 511–514.

Schlenker, B.R., & Leary, M.R. (1982). Social anxiety and self-presentation: A conceptualization and model. *Psychological Bulletin, 92,* 641–669.

Schlosser, Eric (2001). *Fast food nation: The dark side of the all-American meal.* Boston: Houghton Mifflin.

Schmidt, E. A., Schrauf, M., Simon, M. Fritzsche, M., Buchner, A. & Kincses, W.E. (2009). Drivers' misjudgement of vigilance state during prolonged monotonous daytime driving. *Accident Analysis and Prevention, 41,* 1087–1093.

Schmidt, R.A., & Bjork, R.A. (1992). New conceptualizations of practice: Common principles in three paradigms suggest new concepts for training. *Psychological Science, 3,* 207–217.

Schmidt, S.R. (2002). The humour effect: Differential processing and privileged retrieval. *Memory, 10,* 127–138.

Schmidt, S.R., & Williams, A.R. (2001). Memory for humorous cartoons. *Memory & Cognition, 29,* 305–311.

Schmuckler, M.A. (2001). What is ecological validity: A dimensional analysis. *Infancy, 2,* 419–436.

Schneider, W. (1987). Connectionism: Is it a paradigm shift for psychology? *Behavior Research Methods, Instruments, & Computers, 19,* 73–83.

Schneider, W., & Chein, J.M. (2003). Controlled and automatic processing: Behavior, theory, and biological mechanisms. *Cognitive Science, 27,* 525–559.

Scholz, B.C., & Pullum, G.K. (2002). Searching for arguments to support linguistic nativism. *Linguistic Review, 19,* 185–223.

Schooler, C. (1998). Environmental complexity and the Flynn effect. In U. Neisser (Ed.), *The rising curve* (pp. 67–79). Washington: American Psychological Association.

Schooler, J.W. (2002). Re-representing consciousness: Dissociations between experience and meta-consciousness. *Trends in Cognitive Sciences, 6(8),* 339–344.

Schooler, J.W., Ohlsson, S., & Brooks, K. (1993). Thoughts beyond words: When language overshadows insight. *Journal of Experimental Psychology: General, 122*(2), 166.

Schooler, J.W., Reichle, E.D. & Halpern, D.V. (2004). Zoning-out during reading: Evidence for dissociations between experience and metacognition. In D.T. Levin (Ed.), *Thinking and seeing: Visual metacognition in adults and children.* Cambridge, MA: MIT Press.

Schooler, J.W., & Smallwood, J. (2009). Metacognition. In Bayne, T., Cleeremans, A., & Wilken, P. (Eds.). *The Oxford companion to consciousness.* Oxford: Oxford University Press.

Schubotz, R.I., & von Cramon, D.Y. 2001. Interval and ordinal properties of sequences are associated with distinct premotor areas. *Cerebral Cortex, 11*, 210–222.

Schuh, F.C. (1968). *The masterbook of mathematical recreations.* New York: Dover.

Schwartz, N., & Vaughn, L.A. (2002). The availability heuristic revisited: Ease of recall and content of recall as distinct sources of information. In T. Gilovich, D. Griffin, & D. Kahneman (Eds.), *Heuristics and biases: The psychology of intuitive judgment* (pp. 103–119). Cambridge: Cambridge University Press.

Schwartz, R.M. (1997). Consider the simple screw: Cognitive science, quality improvement, and psychotherapy. *Journal of Consulting and Clinical Psychology, 65*, 970–983.

Schwartz, R.M., & Garamoni, G.L. (1986). A structural model of positive and negative states of mind: Asymmetry in the internal dialogue. In P.C. Kendall (Ed.), *Advances in cognitive-behavioral research and therapy* (Vol. 5, pp. 1–62). New York: Academic Press.

Schwartz, R.M., & Michelson, L. (1987). States of mind model: Cognitive balance in the treatment of agoraphobia. *Journal of Consulting and Clinical Psychology, 55*, 557–565.

Schweich, M., van der Linden, M., Bredart, S., Bruyer, R., Nelles, B., & Schils, J.-P. (1992). Daily life difficulties reported by young and elderly subjects. *Applied Cognitive Psychology, 6*, 161–172.

Scott, S.K. (2004). The neural representation of concrete nouns: What's right and what's left? *Trends in Cognitive Sciences, 8*, 151–153.

Scribner, S. (1986). Thinking in action: Some characteristics of practical thought.

In R.J. Sternberg & R.K. Wagner (Eds.), *Practical intelligence* (pp. 13–30). New York: Cambridge University Press.

Scribner, S. (1993). An activity theory approach to memory. *Applied Cognitive Psychology, 7*, 185–190.

Scurich, N., & Shniderman, A. (2015). The selective allure of neuroscientific explanations. *PLOS One, 9*, 1–6.

Searle, J.R. (1990). Consciousness, explanatory inversion and cognitive science. *Behavioral and Brain Sciences, 13*, 585–642.

Searle, J. (1992). *The rediscovery of the mind.* Cambridge, MA: MIT Press.

Searle, J. (2000). Consciousness. *Annual Review of Neuroscience, 23*, 557–578.

Sedgwick, H.A. (1980). The geometry of spatial layout in pictorial representation. In M.A. Hagen (Ed.), *The perception of pictures* (pp. 33–90). New York: Academic Press.

Sekuler, R., Sekuler, A.B., Lau, R. (1997). Sound alters visual motion perception. *Nature, 385*, 308.

Selfridge, O. (1959). Pandemonium: A paradigm for learning. In *Symposium on the mechanization of thought processes* (513–526). London: Her Majesty's Stationery Office.

Semon, R. (1923). *Mnemic psychology* (B. Duffy, Trans.). London: George Allen & Unwin. (Original work published 1909.)

Senders, V.L. (1958). *Measurement and statistics.* New York: Oxford University Press.

Sévigny, S., Cloutier, M., Pelletier, M.-F., & Ladouceur, R. (2005). Internet gambling: Misleading payout rates during the "demo" period. *Computers in Human Behavior, 21*, 153–158.

Seymour, S.E., Reuter-Lorenz, P.A., & Gazzaniga, M.S. (1994). The disconnection syndrome: Basic findings reaffirmed. *Brain, 117*, 105–115.

Shafto, M., & MacKay, D.G. (2000). The Moses, mega-Moses, and Armstrong illusions: Integrating language comprehension and semantic memory. *Psychological Science, 11*, 372–378.

Shalit, B. (1980). The Golden Section relation in the evaluation of environmental relations. *British Journal of Psychology, 71*, 39–42.

Shams, L., Kamitani, Y., & Shimojo, S. (2001). Sound modulates visual evoked potentials in humans. *Journal of Vision, 1*(3), 479–479a.

Shams, L., Kamitani, Y., & Shimojo, S. (2004). Modulations of visual perception by sound. In G. Calvert, C. Spence, & B.E. Stein (Eds.), *The Handbook of Multisensory Processes* (pp. 26–32). Cambridge, MA: MIT Press.

Shanks, D.R. (2004). Implicit learning. In K. Lamberts & R. Goldstone (Eds.), *Handbook of cognition* (pp. 202–220). London: Sage.

Shannon, C.E. (1948). A mathematical theory of communication. *Bell System Technical Journal 27*, 379–423, 623–656.

Shannon, C.E., & Weaver, W. (1949). *The mathematical theory of communication.* Urbana: University of Illinois Press.

Shapiro, K.L., Arnell, K.M., & Raymond, J.E. (1997). The attentional blink. *Trends in Cognitive Sciences, 1*, 291–296.

Sheinberg, D.L., & Logothetis, N.K. (1997). The role of temporal cortical areas in perceptual organization. *Proceedings of the National Academy of Science USA, 94*, 3408–3413.

Shepard, R.N. (1966). Learning and recall as organization and search. *Journal of Verbal Learning and Verbal Behavior, 5*, 201–204.

Shepard, R.N. (1967). Recognition memory for words, sentences, and pictures. *Journal of Verbal Learning and Verbal Behavior, 6*, 156–163.

Shepard, R.N. (1978). The mental image. *American Psychologist, 33*, 125–137.

Shepard, R.N. (1984). Ecological constraints on internal representation: Resonant kinematics of perceiving, imagining, thinking, and dreaming. *Psychological Review, 91*, 417–447.

Shepard, R.N. (1990). *Mind sights: Original visual illusions, ambiguities, and other anomalies, with a commentary on the play of mind in perception and art.* New York: W.H. Freeman and Co.

Shepard, R.N., & Cooper, L.A. (1982). *Mental images and their transformations.* Cambridge, MA: MIT Press.

Shepard, R.N., & Metzler, J. (1971). Mental rotation of three-dimensional objects. *Science, 171*, 701–703.

Shettleworth, S.J. (2004). Review of B.H. Weber & D.J. Depew, "Evolution and learning: The Baldwin effect reconsidered." *Evolutionary Psychology, 2*, 105–107.

Shiffrin, R.M., & Atkinson, R.C. (1969). Storage and retrieval processes in long-term memory. *Psychological Review, 76*, 179–193.

Shiffrin, R.M., & Schneider, W. (1977). Controlled and automatic human information processing: II. Perceptual learning, automatic attending and a general theory. *Psychological Review, 84,* 127–190.

Shimojo, S., & Shams, L. (2001). Sensory modalities are not separate modalities: Plasticity and interactions. *Current Opinion in Neurobiology, 11*(4), 505–509.

Shipp, S. (2004). The brain circuitry of attention. *Trends in Cognitive Sciences, 8,* 223–230.

Shneiderman, B. (1998). *Designing the user interface* (3rd ed.). Reading, MA: Addison-Wesley.

Sholl, M.J. (1987). Cognitive maps as orienting schemata. *Journal of Experimental Psychology: Learning, Memory, and Cognition, 13,* 615–628.

Shrauf, R.W., & Rubin, D.C. (2003). On the bilingual's two sets of memories. In R. Fivush & C.A. Hayden (Eds.), *Autobiographical memory and the construction of a narrative self* (pp. 121–146). Mahwah, NJ: Erlbaum.

Shweder, R.A. (1977). Likeness and likelihood in everyday thought. *Current Anthropology, 18,* 637–658.

Siegler, R.S. (2004). U-shaped interest in U-shaped development—and what it means. *Journal of Cognition and Development, 5,* 1–10.

Silvia, P.J. (2005). What is interesting? Exploring the appraisal structure of interest. *Emotion, 5,* 89–102.

Sime, M.E., & Coombs, M.J. (Eds.). (1983). *Designing for human computer communication.* London: Academic Press.

Simmel, M.L. (1953). The coin problem: A study in thinking. *American Journal of Psychology, 66,* 229–241.

Simmel, M.L. (1956). Phantoms in patients with leprosy and in elderly digital amputees. *American Journal of Psychology, 69,* 529–545.

Simmons, W.K., & Barsalou, L.W. (2003). The similarity in topography principle: Reconciling theories of conceptual deficits. *Cognitive Neuropsychology, 20,* 451–486.

Simon, H.A. (1969). *The sciences of the artificial.* Cambridge, MA: MIT Press.

Simon, H.A. (1975). The functional equivalence of problem-solving skills. *Cognitive Psychology, 7,* 268–288.

Simon, H.A. (1979). *Models of thought.* New Haven: Yale University Press.

Simon, H.A. (1981). *The sciences of the artificial* (2nd ed.). Cambridge, MA: MIT Press.

Simon, H.A. (1986). The information-processing explanation of Gestalt phenomena. *Computers in Human Behaviour, 2,* 241–255.

Simon, H.A. (1992). What is an "explanation" of behavior? *Psychological Science,* 150–161.

Simon, H.A. (1995). Explaining the ineffable: AI on the topics of intuition, insight and inspiration. *Proceedings of the Fourteenth International Joint Conference on Artificial Intelligence,* 939–948.

Simon, H.A. (2000). Artificial intelligence. In A.E. Kazlin (Ed.), *American Psychological Association encyclopedia of psychology* (vol. 1, pp. 248–255). New York: Oxford University Press.

Simon, H.A., Valdéz-Pérez, R.E., & Sleeman, D.H. (1997). Scientific discovery and simplicity of method. *Artificial Intelligence, 91,* 177–181.

Simons, D.J. (2000). Attentional capture and inattentional blindness. *Trends in Cognitive Sciences, 4,* 147–155.

Simons, D.J., & Chabris, C.F. (1999). Gorillas in our midst: Sustained inattentional blindness for dynamic events. *Perception, 28,* 1059–1074.

Simons, D.J., & Levin, D.T. (1997). Change blindness. *Trends in Cognitive Science, 1*(7), 261–267.

Simons, D.J., & Levin, D.T. (1998). Failure to detect changes to people during a real-world interaction. *Psychonomic Bulletin & Review, 5*(4), 644–649.

Simons, D.J., & Rensink, R.A. (2005). Change blindness: Past, present, and future. *Trends in Cognitive Sciences, 9*(1), 16–20.

Simonton, D.K. (1984). *Genius, creativity and leadership.* Cambridge, MA: Harvard University Press.

Simonton, D.K. (1988). *Scientific genius.* New York: Cambridge University Press.

Simonton, D.K. (1993). Genius and chance: A Darwinian perspective. In J. Brockman (Ed.), *Creativity* (pp. 176–201). New York: Simon & Schuster.

Simonton, D.K. (1994). *Greatness: Who makes history and why.* New York: Guilford.

Simonton, D.K. (2003). Scientific creativity as constrained stochastic behavior: The integration of product, person, and process perspectives. *Psychological Bulletin, 129,* 475–494.

Sinha, P. (2002). Recognizing complex patterns. *Nature Neuroscience Special Issue: Beyond the Bench: The Practical Promise of Neuroscience, 5,* 1093–1097.

Sinnett, S., Hodges, N., Chua, R., & Kingstone, A. (2011). Embodiment of motor skills when observing expert and novice athletes. *Quarterly Journal of Experimental Psychology, 64,* 657–658.

Skinner, B.F. (1957). *Verbal behavior.* New York: Appleton-Century-Crofts.

Skinner, B.F. (1964). Behaviorism at fifty. In T.W. Wann (Ed.), *Behaviorism and phenomenology* (pp. 79–97). Chicago: University of Chicago Press.

Skinner, B.F. (1989). The origins of cognitive thought. *American Psychologist, 44,* 13–18.

Slamecka, N. (1985). Ebbinghaus: Some associations. *Journal of Experimental Psychology, 11,* 414–435.

Slamecka, N., & Graf, P. (1978). The generation effect: Delineation of a phenomenon. *Journal of Experimental Psychology: Human Learning and Memory, 4,* 592–604.

Sloboda, J. (1981). Space in musical notation. *Visible Language, 15,* 86–110.

Sloman, S.A. (1996). The empirical case for two systems of reasoning. *Psychological Bulletin, 119,* 3–22.

Sloman, S. A., Hayman, C. A., Ohta, N., Law, J., & Tulving, E. (1988). Forgetting in primed fragment completion. *Journal of Experimental Psychology: Learning, Memory, and Cognition, 14*(2), 223.

Sluckin, W., Colman, A.M., & Hargreaves, D.J. (1980). Liking words as a function of the experienced frequency of their occurrence. *British Journal of Psychology, 71,* 163–169.

Smallwood, J. & Schooler, J.W. (2006). The restless mind. *Psychological Bulletin, 132,* 946–958.

Smedslund, J. (1963). The concept of correlation in adults. *Scandinavian Journal of Psychology, 4,* 165–173.

Smilek, D., Callejas, A., Dixon, M.J., & Merikle, P.M. (2007). Ovals of time: time-space associations in synaesthesia. *Consciousness and Cognition, 16,* 507–519.

Smilek, D., Dixon, M.J., Cudahy, C., & Merikle, P.M. (2002). Synesthetic color experiences influence memory. *Psychological Science, 13,* 548–552.

Smilek, D., Rempel, M.I., & Enns, J.T. (2006). The illusion of clarity: Image segmentation and edge attribution without filling-in. *Visual Cognition, 14,* 1–36.

Smith, N.K., Cacioppo, J.T., Larsen, J.T., & Chartrand, T.L. (2003). May I have your attention, please: Electrocortical responses to positive and negative stimuli. *Neuropsychologia, 41,* 171–183.

Smith, V.L., & Clark, H.H. (1993). On the course of answering questions. *Journal of Memory and Language, 32,* 25–38.

Smullyan, R.M. (1978). *What is the name of this book? The riddle of Dracula and other logical puzzles.* Englewood Cliffs, NJ: Prentice-Hall.

Smyth, M.M., & Clark, S.E. (1986). My half-sister is a THOG: Strategic processes in a reasoning task. *British Journal of Psychology, 77,* 275–287.

Snowdon, D. (2001). *Aging with Grace: What the Nun Study Teaches Us About Leading Longer, Healthier and More Meaningful Lives.* New York: Bantam.

Sohn, M., Anderson, J.R., Reder, L.M., & Goode, A. (2004). Differential fan effect and attentional focus. *Psychonomic Bulletin and Review, 11,* 729–734.

Sokal, M. (2001). Practical phrenology as psychological counseling in the 19th-century United States. In C. Green, M. Shore, & T. Teo (Eds.), *The transformation of psychology: The influences of 19th-century natural science, technology, and philosophy* (pp. 21–44). Washington: American Psychological Association.

Soukoreff, R.W., & Mackenzie, I.S. (2004). Toward a standard for pointing device evaluation, perspectives on 27 years of Fitts' law research in HCI. *International Journal of Human-Computer Studies, 61,* 751–789.

Sparrow, B., Liu, J., and Wegner, D.M. (2011). Google effects on memory: Cognitive consequences of having information at our fingertips. *Science 333* (6043), 776–778.

Spearman, C. (1904). "General intelligence" objectively determined and measured. *American Journal of Psychology, 15,* 201–292.

Spearman, C. (1965). The abilities of man: Their nature and measurement. In A. Anastasi (Ed.), *Individual differences* (pp. 51–57). New York: Wiley. (Original work published 1927.)

Spearman, C. (1970). *The abilities of man: Their nature and measurement.* New York: AMS Press. (Original work published 1932.)

Spelke, E., Hirst, W., & Neisser, U. (1976). Skills of divided attention. *Cognition, 4,* 215–230.

Spence, D.P. (1973). Analog and digital descriptions of behavior. *American Psychologist, 28,* 479–497.

Spence C (2009) Explaining the Colavita visual dominance effect. *Experimental Brain Research, 214,* 607–618. *Prog Brain Res 176:*245–258.

Spence, C. (2015). Multisensory flavor perception. *Cell, 161,* 24–35.

Spence, C., Nicholls, M. E. R., & Driver, J. (2001). The cost of expecting events in the wrong sensory modality. *Perception & Psychophysics, 63,* 330–336.

Sperber, D. (2002). In defense of massive modularity. In E. Dupoux (Ed.), *Language, brain and cognitive development: Essays in honor of Jacques Mehler* (pp. 47–57). Cambridge, MA: MIT Press.

Sperber, D., & Hirschfeld, L.A. (2004). The cognitive foundations of cultural stability and diversity. *Trends in Cognitive Sciences, 8,* 40–48.

Sperber, D., & Wilson, D. (1995). *Relevance: Communication and cognition* (2nd ed.). Oxford: Blackwell.

Sperber, D., & Wilson, D. (2002). Pragmatics modularity and mind-reading. *Mind & Language, 17,* 3–23.

Sperling, G. (1960). The information available in brief visual presentations. *Psychological Monographs, 74,* No. 11.

Sperry, R. (1987). Consciousness and causality. In R.L. Gregory (Ed.), *The Oxford companion to the mind* (pp. 164–166). Oxford: Oxford University Press.

Sperry, R. (1988). Psychology's mentalist paradigm and the religion/science tension. *American Psychologist, 43,* 607–613.

Sperry, R.W. (1964, January). The great cerebral commissure. *Scientific American, 210,* 42–52.

Squire, L.R. (2004). Memory systems of the brain: A brief history and current perspective. *Neurobiology of Learning and Memory, 82,* 171–177.

Squire, L.R., & McKee, R. (1992). Influence of prior events on cognitive judgments in amnesia. *Journal of Experimental Psychology: Learning, Memory, and Cognition, 18,* 106–115.

Srivastava, I. (2005). Mobile phones and the evolution of social behavior. *Behavior and Information Technology, 24,* 111–129.

Stanfield, R.A., & Zwaan, R.A. (2001). The effect of implied orientation derived from verbal context on picture recognition. *Psychological Science, 12*(2), 153–156.

Stanovich, K.E. (2004). *The robot's rebellion: Finding meaning in the age of Darwin.* Chicago: University of Chicago Press.

Stanovich, K.E., & Cunningham, A.E. (1992). Studying the consequences of literacy within a literate society: The cognitive correlates of print exposure. *Memory & Cognition, 20,* 51–68.

Stanovich, K.E., & West, R.F. (1998). Individual differences in rational thought. *Journal of Experimental Psychology: General, 127,* 161–188.

Stanovich, K.E., & West, R.F. (2000). Individual differences in reasoning: Implications for the rationality debate? *Behavioral and Brain Sciences, 23,* 645–726.

Stanovich, K.E., & West, R.F. (2003a). The rationality debate as a progressive research program. *Behavioral and Brain Sciences, 26,* 531–534.

Stanovich, K.E., & West, R.F. (2003b). Evolutionary versus instrumental goals: How evolutionary psychology misconceives human rationality. In D.E. Over (Ed.), *Evolution and the psychology of thinking: The debate.* Hove, UK: Psychology Press.

Steering Committee of the Physicians' Health Study Research Group. (1988). Preliminary report: Findings from the aspirin component of the ongoing physicians' health study. *New England Journal of Medicine, 318,* 262–264.

Stein, B., Bransford, J., Franks, J., Owings, R., Vye, N., & McGraw, W. (1982). Differences in the precision of self-generated elaborations. *Journal of Experimental Psychology: General, 111,* 399–405.

Stein, B.E., London, N., Wilkinson, L.K., & Price, D.D. (1996). Enhancement of perceived visual intensity by auditory stimuli: a psychophysical analysis. *Journal of Cognitive Neuroscience, 8*(6), 497–506.

Stern, W. (1966). On the mental quotient. In R.J. Herrnstein & E. Boring (Eds.), *A source book in the history of psychology* (pp. 450–453). Cambridge, MA: Harvard University Press. (Original work published 1912.)

Sternberg, R.J. (1980). Sketch of a componential subtheory of intelligence. *Behavioral and Brain Sciences, 3,* 573–614.

Sternberg, R.J. (1982). Natural, unnatural, and supernatural concepts. *Cognitive Psychology, 14,* 451–488.

Sternberg, R.J. (1983). Components of human intelligence. *Cognition, 15,* 1–48.

Sternberg, R.J. (1984a). Mechanisms of cognitive development: A componential approach. In R.J. Sternberg (Ed.), *Mechanisms of cognitive development* (pp. 163–209). San Francisco: Freeman.

Sternberg, R.J. (2009). Toward a triarchic theory of human intelligence. In J.C. Kaufman and E.L. Grigorenko (Ed.), *The Essential Sternberg* (pp. 33–70). New York: Springer. .

Sternberg, R.J. (1988). *The triarchic mind: A new theory of human intelligence.* New York: Viking.

Sternberg, R.J. (1992). Ability tests, measurements, and markets. *Journal of Educational Psychology, 84,* 134–140.

Sternberg, R.J. (1999a). The theory of successful intelligence. *Review of General Psychology, 3,* 292–316.

Sternberg, R.J. (1999b). Successful intelligence: Finding a balance. *Trends in Cognitive Sciences, 3,* 436–442.

Sternberg, R.J. (2000a). Damn it, I still don't know what to do! *Behavioral and Brain Sciences, 23,* 764.

Sternberg, R.J. (2000b). Cross-disciplinary verification of theories: The case of the triarchic theory. *History of Psychology, 3,* 177–179.

Sternberg, R.J. (2003a). Issues in the theory and measurement of successful intelligence: A reply to Brody. *Intelligence, 31,* 331–337.

Sternberg, R.J. (2003b). Our research program validating the triarchic theory of successful intelligence: Reply to Gottfredson. *Intelligence, 31,* 399–413.

Sternberg, R.J., Castejón, J.L., Prieto, M.D., Hautamäki, J., & Grigorenko, E.L. (2001). Confirmatory factor analysis of the Sternberg triarchic abilities test in three international samples. *European Journal of Psychological Assessment, 17,* 1–16.

Sternberg, R.J., & Kaufman, J.C. (1998). Human abilities. *Annual Review of Psychology, 49,* 479–502.

Sternberg, R.J., Powell, C., McGrane, P., & Grantham-McGregor, S. (1997). Effects of a parasitic infection on cognitive functioning. *Journal of Experimental Psychology: Applied, 3,* 67–76.

Sternberg, R.J., & Wagner, R.K. (1986). *Practical intelligence.* New York: Cambridge University Press.

Sternberg, R.J., & Wagner, R.K. (1994). *Mind in context: Interactionist perspectives on human intelligence.* New York: Cambridge University Press.

Stevens, A., & Coupe, P. (1978). Distortions in judged spatial distances. *Cognitive Psychology, 10,* 422–437.

Stevens, G.C. (1983). User-friendly computer systems? A critical examination of the concept. *Behaviour and Information Technology, 2,* 3–16.

Stevenson, R.J. & Case, T.I. (2005). Olfactory imagery: A review. *Psychonomic Bulletin & Review, 12,* 244–264.

Stevenson, R.J., Prescott, J., & Boakes, R.A. (1999). Confusing tastes and smell: How odours can influence the perception of sweet and sour tastes. *Chemical Senses, 24,* 627–635

Stich, S. (1983). *From folk psychology to cognitive science: The case against belief.* Cambridge, MA: MIT Press.

Stickgold, R., & Walker, M. (2004). To sleep, perchance to gain creative insight? *Trends in Cognitive Sciences, 8,* 191–192.

Stone, N.J. (2003). Environmental view and color for a simulated telemarketing task. *Journal of Environmental Psychology, 23,* 63–78.

Stone, L., & Lindell, R. (2013). Passengers aboard fatal Ottawa bus crash left to wonder why driver didn't stop. Global News. Retrieved 23 Oct. 2015 from http://globalnews.ca/news/854557/passengers-aboard-fatal-ottawa-bus-crash-left-to-wonder-why-driver-didnt-stop/.

Stover, D., & Erdmann, E. (2000). *A mind for tomorrow: Facts, values, and the future.* Westport, Conn.: Praeger.

Strawson, P.F. (1952). *Introduction to logical theory.* London: Methuen.

Strayer, D.L., Cooper, J.M., Turrill, J., Coleman, J., Medeiros-Ward, N., & Biondi, F. (2013). Measuring cognitive distraction in the automobile. AAA Foundation for Traffic Safety.

Strayer, D.L., Turrill, J., Coleman, J. R., Ortiz, E.V., & Cooper, J.M. (2014). Measuring cognitive distraction in the automobile II: Assessing in-vehicle voice-based. *Accident Analysis & Prevention, 372,* 379.

Strayer, D., & Drews, F. (2007) Cell-phone-induced driver distraction. *Current Directions in Psychological Science, Vol. 16, No. 3,* 128-131.

Strayer, D.L., Drews, F.A., & Johnston, W.A. (2003). Cell phone-induced failures of visual attention during simulated driving. *Journal of Experimental Psychology: Applied, 9,* 23–52.

Strayer, D.L., & Johnston, W.A. (2001). Driven to distraction: Dual-task studies of simulated driving and conversing on a cellular phone. *Psychological Science, 12,* 462–466.

Strohmeyer, C.F. (1982). An adult eidetiker. In U. Neisser (Ed.), *Memory observed: Remembering in natural contexts* (pp. 399–404). San Francisco: Freeman. (Original work published 1970.)

Stroop, J.R. 1935. Studies of inference in serial verbal reactions. *Journal of Experimental Psychology, 18*(6), 643–662. Reprinted 1992 in *Journal of Experimental Psychology: General, 121,* 15–23.

Suddendorf, T., & Busby, J. (2003). Mental time travel in animals? *Trends in Cognitive Sciences, 7,* 391–396.

Sugiyama, L.S., Tooby, J., & Cosmides, L. (2002). Cross-cultural evidence of cognitive adaptations for social exchange among the Shiwiar of Ecuadorian Amazonia. *Proceedings of the National Academy of Sciences, 99,* 11537–11542.

Suzuki, R., & Arita, T. (2004). Interactions between learning and evolution: The outstanding strategy generated by the Baldwin effect. *BioSystems, 77,* 57–71.

Swanson, L.W. (2003). *Brain architecture: Understanding the basic plan.* New York: Oxford University Press.

Talarico, J.M., & Rubin, D.C. (2003). Confidence, not consistency, characterizes flashbulb memories. *Psychological Science, 14,* 455–461.

Talland, G.A. (1968). *Disorders of memory and learning.* Baltimore: Penguin.

Tammet, D. (2009). *Embracing the wide sky: A tour across the horizons of the mind.* Free Press: New York.

Taylor, H.A., & Tversky, B. (1992). Descriptions and depictions of environments. *Memory & Cognition, 20,* 483–496.

Taylor, J.G. (1966). Perception generated by training echolocation. *Canadian Journal of Psychology, 20,* 64–81.

Terman, L.M. (1948).The measurement of intelligence. In W. Dennis (Ed.), *Readings in the history of psychology* (pp. 485–496). New York: Appleton-Century-Crofts. (Original work published 1916.)

Terrace, H.S. (1985). In the beginning was the "Name." *American Psychologist, 40,* 1011–1028.

The Oxford English Dictionary [compact disk] (1992). Oxford: Oxford University Press.

The Right Stuff. (1983). *Psychology Today, 17*(12), 58–63.

Thomas, J.C., Jr. (1974). An analysis of behaviour in the hobbits-orcs problem. *Cognitive Psychology, 6,* 257–269.

Thomson, D.R., Seli, P., Besner, D., & Smilek, D. (2014). On the link between mind wandering and task performance over time. *Consciousness and Cognition, 27,* 14–26.

Thompson, C.P. (1997). Schematic and social influences on memory. *Contemporary Psychology, 42,* 492–493.

Thorndike, E.L. (1898). Animal intelligence: An experimental study of the associative processes in animals. *Psychological Review Monograph Supplement, 2(8).*

Thornton, M.T. (1982). Aristotelian practical reason. *Mind, 91,* 57–76.

Tibbetts, P.E. (2001). The anterior cingulate cortex, akinetic mutism, and human volition. *Brain and Mind, 2,* 323–341.

Tierney, J. (1991, July 21). Behind Monty Hall's doors: Puzzle, debate and answer? *New York Times,* pp. 1, 20.

Tigner, R.B., & Tigner, S.S. (2000). Triarchic theories of intelligence: Aristotle and Sternberg. *History of Psychology, 3,* 168–176.

Titchener, E.B. (1966). From "A text-book of psychology." In R.J. Herrnstein & E. Boring (Eds.), *A source book in the history of psychology* (pp. 599–605). Cambridge, MA: Harvard University Press. (Original work published 1910.)

Todd, P.M., Fiddick, L., & Krauss, S. (2000). Ecological rationality and its contents. *Thinking and Reasoning, 6,* 375–384.

Todd, P.M., & Gigerenzer, G. (2000). Précis of "Simple heuristics that make us smart." *Behavioral and Brain Sciences, 23,* 737–780.

Todd, P.M., & Gigerenzer, G. (2003). Bounding rationality to the world. *Journal of Economic Psychology, 24,* 143–165.

Toglia, M., & Battig, W. (1978). *Handbook of semantic word norms.* Hillsdale, NJ: Erlbaum.

Tolman, E.C. (1948). Cognitive maps in rats and men. *Psychological Review, 55,* 189–208.

Tolman, E.C. (1959). Principles of purposive behavior. In S. Koch (Ed.), *Psychology: A study of a science* (pp. 92–157). New York: McGraw-Hill.

Tong, F., Nakayama, K., Vaughan, J.T., & Kanwisher, N. (1998). Binocular rivalry and visual awareness in human extrastriate cortex. *Neuron, 21,* 753–759.

Toppino, T.C. (2003). Reversible-figure perception: Mechanisms of intentional control. *Perception & Psychophysics, 65,* 1285–1295

Toth, J.P. (2000). Nonconscious forms of human memory. In E. Tulving & F.I.M. Craik (Eds.), *The Oxford handbook of memory* (pp. 245–261). New York: Oxford University Press.

Townsend, J.T. (1990). Serial vs. parallel processing: Sometimes they look like Tweedledum and Tweedledee but they can and should be distinguished. *Psychological Science, 1,* 46–54.

Trachtenberg, L., Streumer, J., & van Zolingen, S. (2002). Career counseling in the emerging post-industrial society. *International Journal for Educational and Vocational Guidance, 2,* 85–99.

Tranel, D., & Damasio, A.R. (1985). Knowledge without awareness: An autonomic index of facial recognition by prosopagnostics. *Science, 228*(4706), 1453–1454.

Trehub, S.E. (2003). The developmental origins of musicality. *Nature Neuroscience, 6,* 669–673.

Treisman, A. (1969). Strategies and models of selective attention. *Psychological Review, 76,* 282–299.

Treisman, A. (1986). Features and objects and visual processing. *Scientific American, 255*(5), 114–125.

Treisman, A. (1996). The binding problem. *Current Opinion in Neurobiology, 6,* 171–178.

Treisman, A. (1996). Selection for perception for selection for action. *Visual Cognition, 3*(4), 353–357.

Treisman, A., & Gelade, G. (1980). A feature-integration theory of attention. *Cognitive Psychology, 12,* 97–136.

Treisman, A., & Gormican, S. (1988). Feature analysis in early vision: Evidence from search asymmetries. *Psychological Review, 95,* 15–48.

Tucker, M., & Ellis, R. (1998). On the relations between seen objects and components of potential actions. *Journal of Experimental Psychology-Human Perception and Performance, 24*(3), 830–846.

Tucker, M., & Ellis, R. (2001). The potentiation of grasp types during visual object categorization. *Visual Cognition, 8,* 769–800.

Tucker, M. & Ellis, R. (2004). Action priming by briefly presented objects. *Acta Psychologica, 116,* 185–203.

Tulving, E. (1972). Episodic and semantic memory. In E. Tulving & W. Donaldson (Eds.), *Organization of memory* (pp. 382–403). New York: Academic Press.

Tulving, E. (1983). *Elements of episodic memory.* Oxford: Clarendon Press.

Tulving, E. (1984). Relations among components and processes of memory. *Behavioral and Brain Sciences, 7,* 257–268.

Tulving, E. (1985). Memory and consciousness. *Canadian Psychology, 26,* 1–12.

Tulving, E. (1986). What kind of a hypothesis is the distinction between episodic and semantic memory? *Journal of Experimental Psychology: Learning, Memory, and Cognition, 12,* 307–311.

Tulving, E. (2000). Concepts of memory. In E. Tulving & F.I.M. Craik (Eds.), *The Oxford handbook of memory* (pp. 33–43). New York: Oxford University Press.

Tulving, E. (2001a). The origin of autonoesis in episodic memory. In H.L. Roediger, J.S. Nairne, I. Neath, & A.I. Surprénant (Eds.), *The nature of remembering* (pp. 17–34). Washington: American Psychological Association.

Tulving, E. (2001b). Episodic memory and common sense: How far apart? *Philosophical Transactions of the Royal Society (Series B), 356,* 1505–1515.

Tulving, E. (2002a). Episodic memory: From mind to brain. *Annual Review of Psychology, 53,* 1–25.

Tulving, E. (2002b). Chronesthesia: Conscious awareness of subjective time. In D.T. Stuss and R.T. Knight (Eds.), *Principles of frontal lobe function* (pp. 311–325). New York: Oxford University Press.

Tulving, E., & Donaldson, W. (Eds.). (1972). *Organization of memory.* New York: Academic Press.

Tulving, E., & Schacter, D. (1990). Priming and human memory systems. *Science, 247,* 301–306.

Tulving, E., Schacter, D. L., & Stark, H. A. (1982). Priming effects in word-fragment completion are independent of recognition memory. *Journal of Experimental*

Psychology: Learning, Memory, and Cognition, 8(4), 336.

Tulving, E., & Thomson, D.M. (1973). Encoding specificity and retrieval processes in episodic memory. *Psychological Review, 80*, 352–373.

Tulving, E., & Wiseman, S. (1975). Relation between recognition and recognition failure of recallable words. *Bulletin of the Psychonomic Society, 6*, 79–82.

Tunney, R.J., & Shanks, D.R. (2003). Subjective measures of awareness and implicit cognition. *Memory & Cognition, 31*, 1060–1071.

Tuohy, A.P. (1987). Affective asymmetry in social perception. *British Journal of Psychology, 78*, 41–51.

Tuohy, A.P., & Stradling, S.G. (1987). Maximum salience vs golden section proportions in judgemental asymmetry. *British Journal of Psychology, 78*, 457–464.

Tuohy, A.P., & Stradling, S.G. (1992). Positive-negative asymmetry in normative data. *European Journal of Social Psychology, 22*, 483–496.

Turing, A. (1950). Computing machinery and intelligence. *Mind, 59*, 433–450.

Tversky, A., & Kahneman, D. (1971). Belief in the law of small numbers. *Psychological Bulletin, 76*, 105–110.

Tversky, A., & Kahneman, D. (1973a). Availability: A heuristic for judging frequency and probability. *Cognitive Psychology, 5*, 207–232.

Tversky, A., & Kahneman, D. (1973b). On the psychology of prediction. *Psychological Review, 80*, 237–251.

Tversky, A., & Kahneman, D. (1974). Judgement under uncertainty: Heuristics and biases. *Science, 185*, 1124–1131.

Tversky, A., & Kahneman, D. (1983). Extensional versus intuitive reasoning: The conjunctive fallacy in probability judgement. *Psychological Review, 90*, 293–314.

Tversky, A., & Kahneman, D. (2000). Rational choice and the framing of decisions. In D. Kahneman & A. Tversky (Eds.), *Choices, values, and frames* (pp. 209–223). Cambridge: Cambridge University Press.

Tversky, B. (2003). Structures of mental spaces: How people think about space. *Environment and Behavior, 35*, 66–80.

Tweedy, J. R., Lapinski, R. H., & Schvaneveldt, R. W. (1977). Semantic-context effects on word recognition: Influence of varying the proportion of items presented in an appropriate context. *Memory & Cognition, 5*(1), 84–89.

Tweney, R.D. (1991). Faraday's notebooks: The active organization of creative science. *Physics Education, 26*, 301–306.

Tweney, R.D. (1999). Toward a cognitive psychology of science: Recent research and its implications. *Current Directions in Psychological Science, 7*, 150–154.

Uhr, L. (1966). Pattern recognition. In L. Uhr (Ed.), *Pattern recognition* (pp. 365–381). New York: Wiley.

Ullmann, S. (1957). *The principles of semantics: A linguistic approach to meaning* (2nd ed.). Cambridge, MA: MIT Press.

UNESCO (2015). Endangered languages. Retrieved 23 Oct. 2015 from www.unesco.org/new/en/communication-and-information/access-to-knowledge/linguistic-diversity-and-multilingualism-on-internet/atlas-of-languages-in-danger/.

Urgesi, C., Berlucchi, G., & Aglioti, S.M. (2004). Magnetic stimulation of extrastriate body area impairs visual processing of nonfacial body parts. *Current Biology, 14*, 2130–2134.

Uriagereka, J. (1998). *Rhyme and reason: An introduction to minimalist syntax*. Cambridge, MA: MIT Press.

Usher, J.A., & Neisser, U. (1993). Childhood amnesia and the beginnings of memory for four early life events. *Journal of Experimental Psychology: General, 122*, 155–165.

Uttal, W.R. (2001). *The new phrenology: The limits of localizing cognitive processes in the brain*. Cambridge, MA: MIT Press.

Van der Henst, J.B., Carles, L., & Sperber, D. (2002). Truthfulness and relevance in telling the time. *Mind and Language, 17*, 457–466.

Van Ormer, E.B. (1933). Sleep and retention. *Psychological Bulletin, 30*, 415–439.

Vartanian, O., Martindale, C., & Kwiatkowski, J. (2003). Creativity and inductive reasoning: The relationship between divergent thinking and performance on Wason's 2–4–6 task. *Quarterly Journal of Experimental Psychology, 56*, 1–15.

Vendler, Z. (1972). *Res cogitans: An essay in rational psychology*. Ithaca, NY: Cornell University Press.

Vicente, K.J., & Brewer, W.F. (1993). Reconstructive remembering of the scientific literature. *Cognition, 46*, 101–128.

Vickers, J.N. (1996). Visual control when aiming at a far target. *Journal of Experimental Psychology: Human Perception and Performance, 22*, 342–354.

Vickers, J.N. (2004). The Quiet Eye: It's the difference between a good putter and a poor one, here's proof. *Golf Digest* (Jan.), 96–101.

Vinacke, W.E. (1974). *The psychology of thinking*. New York: McGraw-Hill.

von Restorff, H. (1933). Über die Wirkung von Bereichsbildungen im Spurenfeld. *Psychologische Forschung, 18*, 299–342.

Vos Savant, M. (1990a, September 9). Ask Marilyn. *Parade Magazine*, p. 15.

Vos Savant, M. (1990b, December 2). Ask Marilyn. *Parade Magazine*, p. 25.

Vos Savant, M. (1991, February 17). Ask Marilyn. *Parade Magazine*, p. 12.

Voss, U., Holzmann, R., Tuin, I., & Hobson, J.A. (2009). Lucid dreaming: A state of consciousness with features of both waking and non-lucid dreaming. *SLEEP, 32*, 1191–1200. Figure 1, p. 1193.

Vygotsky, L.S. (1978). *Mind in society*. Cambridge, MA: Harvard University Press. (Original work published 1935).

Vygotsky, L.S. (1986). *Thought and language* (A. Kozulin, Trans.). Cambridge, MA: MIT Press. (Original work published 1934.)

Wagemans, J., Elder, J.H., Kubovy, M., Palmer, S.E., Peterson, M., Singh, M., & von der Heydt, R. (2012). A century of Gestalt psychology in visual perception: I. Perceptual grouping and figure-ground organization, *Psychological Bulletin, 138*: 1172–1217.

Wagenaar, W.A., Hudson, P.T.W., & Reason, J.T. (1990). Cognitive failures and accidents. *Applied Cognitive Psychology, 4*, 273–294.

Wagner, U., Gais, S., Haider, H., Verleger, R., & Born, J. (2004). Sleep inspires insight. *Nature, 427*, 352–355.

Wainer, H., & Velleman, P.F. (2001). Statistical graphics: Mapping the pathways of science. *Annual Review of Psychology, 52*, 305–335.

Walker, H.M. (1943). *Elementary statistical methods*. New York: Holt.

Wallas, G. (1926). *The art of thought*. London: Cape.

Walters, J.M., & Gardner, H. (1986). The theory of multiple intelligences: Some issues and answers. In R.J. Sternberg (Ed.), *Practical intelligence* (pp. 163–182). New York: Cambridge University Press.

Wang, R.F., & Spelke, E.S. (2000). Updating egocentric representations in human navigation. *Cognition, 77*, 215–250.

Wang, R.F., & Spelke, E.S. (2002). Human spatial representation: Insights from animals. *Trends in Cognitive Sciences, 6,* 375–382.

Ward, J., & Simner, J. (2003). Lexical gustatory synaesthesia: Linguistic and conceptual factors. *Cognition, 89,* 237–261.

Ward, L.M. (2003). Synchronous neural oscillations and cognitive processes. *Trends in Cognitive Sciences, 7,* 553–559.

Warm, J.S., Parasuraman, R., & Matthews, G., (2008). Vigilance requires hard mental work and is stressful. *Human Factors, 50,* 433–441.

Warrington, E., & Weiskrantz, L. (1982). Amnesia: A disconnection syndrome? *Neuropsychologia, 20,* 233–248.

Warrington, E.K., & Shallice, T. (1984). Category specific semantic impairments. *Brain, 107,* 829–854.

Wason, P.C. (1960). On the failure to eliminate hypotheses in a conceptual task. *Quarterly Journal of Experimental Psychology, 12,* 129–140.

Wason, P.C. (1966). Reasoning. In B.M. Foss (Ed.), *New horizons in psychology* (pp. 135–151). Harmondsworth, UK: Penguin.

Wason, P.C. (1977a). "On the failure to eliminate hypotheses . . .": A second look. In P.N. Johnson-Laird & P.C. Wason (Eds.), *Thinking: Readings in cognitive science* (pp. 307–314). Cambridge: Cambridge University Press.

Wason, P.C. (1977b). Self-contradictions. In P.N. Johnson-Laird & P.C. Wason (Eds.), *Thinking: Readings in cognitive science* (pp. 114–128). Cambridge: Cambridge University Press.

Wason, P.C. (1978). Hypothesis testing and reasoning. In *Cognitive Psychology* (Block 4, Unit 25, pp. 17–56). Milton Keynes, UK: Open University Press.

Wason, P.C., & Brooks, P.G. (1979). THOG: The anatomy of a problem. *Psychological Research, 41,* 79–90.

Wason, P.C., & Evans, J. St B.T. (1975). Dual processes in reasoning? *Cognition, 3/2,* 141–154.

Wason, P.C., & Johnson-Laird, P.N. (1972). *Psychology of reasoning: Structure and content.* London: Batsford.

Wason, P.C., & Shapiro, D. (1971). Natural and contrived experience in a reasoning problem. *Quarterly Journal of Experimental Psychology, 23,* 63–71.

Watson, J. M. & Strayer, D.L. (2010). Supertaskers: Profiles in extraordinary multi-tasking ability. *Psychonomic Bulletin & Review, 17,* 479–485.

Waugh, N.C., & Norman, D.A. (1965). Primary memory. *Psychological Review, 72,* 89–104.

Weaver, C.A. III. (1993). Do you need a flash to form a flashbulb memory? *Journal of Experimental Psychology: General, 122,* 39–46.

Webster, J.C., & Thompson, P.O. (1953). Some audio considerations in air control towers. *Journal of the Audio Engineering Society, 1*(2), 171–175.

Webster, J.C., & Thompson, P.O. (1954). Responding to both of two overlapping messages. *Journal of the Acoustical Society of America 26*(3), 396–402.

Wegner, D.M. (2003). The mind's best trick: How we experience conscious will. *Trends in Cognitive Sciences, 7,* 65–69.

Weidman, N. (1994). Mental testing and machine intelligence: The Lashley-Hull debate. *Journal of the History of the Behavioral Sciences, 30,* 162–180.

Weisberg, R.W. (1986). *Genius, creativity and other myths.* New York: Freeman.

Weisberg, R.W. (1994). Genius and madness? A quasi-experimental test of the hypothesis that manic-depression increases creativity. *Psychological Science, 5,* 361–367.

Weisberg, R.W. (1995). Prolegomena to theories of insight in problem-solving: A taxonomy of problems. In R.J. Sternberg & J. Davidson (Eds.) *The nature of insight.* Cambridge, MA: MIT Press.

Weisberg, R.W., & Alba, J.W. (1981). An examination of the role of fixation in the solution of several insight problems. *Journal of Experimental Psychology: General, 110,* 169–192.

Weiskrantz, L. (1986). *Blindsight: A case study and implications.* Oxford: Oxford University Press.

Weiskrantz, L. (2000). Epilogue: The story of memory and the memory of a story. In E. Tulving & F.I.M. Craik (Eds.), *The Oxford handbook of memory* (pp. 645–648). New York: Oxford University Press.

Weitzenhoffer, A.M., & Hilgard, E.R. (1962). *Stanford Hypnotizability Scale Form C.* (Revised by J. Kihlstrom). Retrieved 5 October 2004 from http://ist-socrates.berkeley. edu/~kihlstrm/PDF files/Hypnotizability/SH SSC%20Script .pdf.

Welch, R. B., & Warren, D. H. (1986). Intersensory interactions. In K.R. Boff, L. Kaufman, & J.P. Thomas (Eds.), *Handbook of perception and performance, Vol. 1: Sensory processes and perception* (pp. 25-1–25-26). New York: John Wiley and Sons.

Werner, H. (1961). *Comparative psychology of mental development.* New York: Science editions. (Original work published 1948.)

Werner, H., & Kaplan, B. (1963). *Symbol formation.* New York: Wiley.

Wertheimer, M. (1959). *Productive thinking.* New York: Harper.

Wertheimer, M. (1967a). Laws of organization in perceptual forms. In W.D. Ellis (Ed.), *A source book of Gestalt psychology* (pp. 71–88). New York: Humanities Press. (Original work published 1923.)

Wertheimer, M. (1967b). The syllogism and productive thinking. In W.D. Ellis (Ed.), *A source book of Gestalt psychology* (pp. 274–282). New York: Humanities. (Original work published 1925.)

Wertheimer, Michael (1985). A Gestalt perspective on computer simulations of cognitive processes. *Computers in Human Behaviour, 1,* 19–33.

Wertsch, J.V. (Ed.). (1985). *Vygotsky and the social function of mind.* Cambridge, MA: Harvard University Press.

Wertsch, J.V., & Stone, C. (1985). The concept of internalization in Vygotsky's account of the genesis of higher mental functions. In J.V. Wertsch (Ed.), *Culture, communication and cognition* (pp. 162–179). Cambridge: Cambridge University Press.

Wetzler, S.E., & Sweeney, J.A. (1986). Childhood amnesia: An empirical demonstration. In D.C. Rubin (Ed.), *Autobiographical memory* (pp. 191–201). Cambridge: Cambridge University Press.

Wheeler, M.A. (2000). Episodic memory and autonoetic awareness. In E. Tulving & F.I.M. Craik (Eds.), *The Oxford handbook of memory* (pp. 597–608). New York: Oxford University Press.

Wheeler, M.E., Petersen, S.E., Buckner, R.L. (2000). Memory's echo: Vivid remembering reactivates sensory-specific cortex. *Proceedings of the National Academy of Sciences USA, 97,* 11125–11129.

Wheeler, M.A., Stuss, D.T., & Tulving, E. (1997). Toward a theory of episodic memory: The frontal lobes and autonoetic consciousness. *Psychological Bulletin, 121,* 331–354.

White, P.A., & Milne, A. (1999). Impressions of enforced disintegration and bursting in the visual perception of collision events. *Journal of Experimental Psychology: General, 128,* 499–516.

Whitehead, D. (2003). Review of Sadoski & Paivio, "Imagery and text: A dual coding theory of reading and writing." *Reading and Writing: An Interdisciplinary Journal, 16,* 159–262.

Whorf, B.L. (1956). *Language, thought and reality.* Cambridge, MA: MIT Press.

Wickelgren, W.A. (1979). *Cognitive psychology.* Englewood Cliffs, NJ: Prentice-Hall.

Wickens, C.D. (1984). Processing re-sources in attention. In R. Parasuraman & D.R. Davies (Eds.), *Varieties of attention* (pp. 63–102). Orlando, Fla: Academic Press.

Wickens, D.D. (1970). Encoding categories of words: An empirical approach to meaning. *Psychological Review, 77,* 1–15.

Wiggins, M.W. (2011). Vigilance decrement during a simulated general aviation flight. *Applied Cognitive Psychology, 25,* 229–235.

Williams, L.E., & Bargh, J. A. (2008). Experiencing physical warmth influences interpersonal warmth. *Science, 322,* 606–607.

Williams, L.P. (1991). Michael Faraday's chemical notebook: Portrait of the scientist as a young man. *Physics Education, 26,* 278–283.

Williams, R. (1976). *Keywords: A vocabulary of culture and society.* New York: Oxford University Press.

Williams, W.M. (1998). Are we raising smarter children today? School and home-related influences on IQ. In U. Neisser (Ed.), *The rising curve* (pp. 125–154). Washington: American Psychological Association.

Wilson, B.A. (2002). Management of remediation of memory problems in brain-injured adults. In A.D. Baddeley, M.D. Kopelman, & B.A. Wilson (Eds.), *The handbook of memory disorders* (pp. 655–682). New York: Wiley.

Wilson, B.A., & Moffat, N. (1984). *Clinical management of memory problems.* Rockville, Md: Aspen Publications.

Wilson, B.A., & Patterson, K. (1990). Rehabilitation for cognitive impairment: Does cognitive psychology apply? *Applied Cognitive Psychology, 4,* 247–260.

Wilson, M. (2002). Six views of embodied cognition. *Psychonomic Bulletin & Review, 9,* 625–636.

Winner, E. (1982). *Invented worlds.* Cambridge, MA: Harvard University Press.

Winner, E. (2000). The origins and ends of giftedness. *American Psychologist, 55,* 159–169.

Winograd, E., & Soloway, R. (1986). On forgetting the locations of things stored in special places. *Journal of Experimental Psychology: General, 115,* 366–372.

Winograd, T., & Flores, F. (1986). *Understanding computers and cognition: A new foundation for design.* Norwood, NJ: Ablex.

Witkowski, S.R., & Brown, C.H. (1983). Marking reversals and cultural importance. *Language, 59,* 569–582.

Witt, J.K. (2011). Action's effect on perception. *Current Directions in Psychological Science, 20,* 201–206.

Witt, J.K., & Proffitt, D.R. (2005). See the ball, hit the ball: Apparent ball size is correlated with batting average. *Psychological Science, 16,* 937–938.

Wittgenstein, L. (1953). *Philosophical investigations.* Oxford: Blackwell.

Wittgenstein, L. (1974). *Tractatus logico-philosophicus.* London: Routledge & Kegan Paul. (Original work published 1921.)

Wixted, J.T. (2004a). The psychology and neuroscience of forgetting. *Annual Review of Psychology, 55,* 235–269.

Wixted, J.T. (2004b). On common ground: Jost's (1897) law of forgetting and Ribot's (1881) law of retrograde amnesia. *Psychological Review, 111,* 864–879.

Wolfe, J.M. (2003). Moving towards solutions to some enduring controversies in visual search. *Trends in Cognitive Sciences, 7,* 70–76.

Wolff, P., Medin, D.L., & Pankratz, C. (1999). Evolution and devolution of folk biological knowledge. *Cognition, 73,* 177–204.

Woltz, D.J., Gardner, M.K., & Bell, B.G. (2000). Negative transfer errors in sequential cognitive skills: Strong-but-wrong sequence application. *Journal of Experimental Psychology: Learning, Memory, and Cognition, 26,* 601–625.

Wong, C.K., & Read, J.D. (2011). Positive and negative effects of physical context reinstatement on eyewitness recall and identification. *Applied Cognitive Psychology, 25* (1), 2–11.

Wood, N., & Cowan, N. (1995). The cocktail party phenomenon revisited: Attention and memory in the classic selective listening procedure of Cherry (1953). *Journal of Experimental Psychology: General, 124,* 243–262.

Woodworth, R.S. (1940). *Psychology* (4th ed.). New York: Holt.

World Health Organization (2015). Measles fact sheet. Retrieved 16 Oct. 2015 from www.who.int/mediacentre/factsheets/fs286/en/.

Wright, E. (1992). Gestalt switching: Hanson, Aronson, and Harre. *Philosophy of Science, 59,* 480–486.

Wundt, W. (1970). The psychology of the sentence. In A.L. Blumenthal (Ed.), *Language and psychology* (pp. 9–33). New York: Wiley. (Original work published 1890.)

Yaden, D.B., & Templeton, S. (Eds.). (1986). *Metalinguistic awareness and beginning literacy: Conceptualizing what it means to read and write.* Portsmouth, NH: Heinemann.

Yamamoto, S., and Kitizawa, S. (2001). Reversal of subjective temporal order due to arm crossing, *Nature Neuroscience,* 4(7), 759–765.

Yang, C.D. (2004). Universal grammar, statistics or both? *Trends in Cognitive Sciences, 8,* 451–456.

Yarbus, A.L. (1967). *Eye movements and vision.* Trans. L.A. Riggs. New York: Plenum Press.

Yates, F.A. (1966). *The art of memory.* Chicago: University of Chicago Press.

Yeung, N., & Monsell, S. (2003). The effects of recent practice on task switching. *Journal of Experimental Psychology: Human Perception and Performance, 29,* 919–936.

Yoshida, H., & Smith, L.B. (2005). Linguistic cues enhance the learning of perceptual cues. *Psychological Science, 16,* 90–95.

Young, M., Robinson, S., & Alberts, P. (2009). Students pay attention!: Combating the vigilance decrement to improve learning during lectures. *Active Learning in Higher Education, 10,* 41–55.

Yovel, G., & Paller, K.A. (2004). The neural basis of the butcher-on-the-bus phenomenon: When a face seems familiar but is not remembered. *NeuroImage, 21,* 789–800.

Yuille, J. (1968). Concreteness without imagery in PA learning. *Psychonomic Science, 11,* 55–56.

Zacks, J.M., Mires, J., Tversky, B., & Hazeltine, E. (2000). Mental spatial transformations of objects and perspective. *Spatial Cognition and Computation, 2,* 315–332.

Zago, S., Lorusso, L., Ferrucci, R., & Priori, A. (2012). Functional neuroimaging: A historical perspective. In P. Bright (Ed.), *Neuroimaging—Methods.* INTECH Open

Access Publisher. Available from: www.intechopen.com/books/neuroimaging-methods/the-origins-of-functional-neuroimaging-techniques.

Zajonc, R.B. (1968). Attitudinal effects of mere exposure. *Journal of Personality and Social Psychology Monograph, 9* (2, Pt. 2), 1–28.

Zajonc, R.B. (1980). Feeling and thinking: Preferences need no inferences. *American Psychologist, 35*, 151–175.

Zajonc, R.B. (1984). On the primacy of affect. *American Psychologist, 39*, 117–123.

Zajonc, R.B. (2001). Mere exposure: A gateway to the subliminal. *Current Directions in Psychological Science, 10*, 224–228.

Zampini, M., and Spence, C. (2004). The role of auditory cues in modulating the perceived crispness and staleness of potato chips. *Journal of Sensory Science, 19*, 347–363.

Zangwill, O.L. (1972). Remembering revisited. *Quarterly Journal of Experimental Psychology, 24*, 123–138.

Zatorre, R. J., & Halpern, A.R. (1993). Effect of unilateral temporal-lobe excision on perception and imagery of songs. *Neuropsychologia, 31*, 221–232.

Zeigarnik, B. (1967). On finished and unfinished tasks. In W.D. Ellis (Ed.), *A source book of Gestalt psychology* (pp. 300–315). New York: Humanities Press. (Original work published 1927.)

Zeki, S. (2009). Microconsciousness. In T. Bayne, A. Cleeremans, & P. Wilken (Eds.), *The Oxford companion to consciousness*. Oxford: Oxford University Press.

Zeki, S., & Marini, L. (1998). Three cortical stages of colour processing in the human brain. *Brain, 121*, 1669–1685.

Zhai, S., Kristensson, P.O., & Smith, B.A. (2005). In search of effective text input interfaces for off the desktop computing. *Interacting with Computers, 17*, 229–250.

Zihl, D., Von Cramon, D., & Mai, N. (1983). Selective disturbance of movement vision after bilateral brain damage. *Brain, 106*, 313–340.

Zimler, J., & Keenan, J. (1983). Imagery in the congenitally blind: How visual are visual images? *Journal of Experimental Psychology: Learning, Memory, and Cognition, 9*, 269–282.

Zizak, D.M., & Reber, A.S. (2004). Implicit preferences: The role(s) of familiarity in the structural mere exposure effect. *Consciousness and Cognition, 13*, 336–362.

Zwaan, R.A. (2004). The immersed experiencer. Toward an embodied theory of language comprehension. In B.H. Ross (Ed.), *The psychology of learning and motivation: Advances in research and theory* (Vol. 44, pp. 35–62). New York: Academic Press.

Zwaan, R.A., Madden, C.J., Yaxley, R.H., & Aveyard, M.E. (2004). Moving words: Dynamic representations in language comprehension. *Cognitive Sciences, 28*, 611–619.

Photo Credits

Fig. 1.1: © Twentieth Century Fox/Photofest, Inc.; Fig. 1.2: © Sean Barnard; Fig. 1.9: Science Photo Library; Fig. 1.12: Copyright © Philippa Griffith-Jones/Alamy Stock Photo; Fig. 1.14: Halper, F. (1997). The illusion of The Future. *Perception*, 26, pp. 1321–2. Reprinted with permission of the author; Fig. 2.1: Muhammad Ali—AP Photo/Ross D. Franklin; Ronald Reagan—Shutterstock/Joseph Sohm; Margaret Thatcher—AP Photo/Lefteris Pitarakis; Fig. 2.2 (a): US National Library of Medicine/Science Photo Library; Fig. 2.2 (b): Reuters/Ricardo Moraes; Fig. 2.3: © dpa picture alliance archive/Alamy Stock Photo; Fig. 2.4: © Mark Strozier/iStockphoto; Fig. 2.5: Will & Deni McIntyre/Science Source; Fig. 2.7: University of Wisconsin and Michigan State Comparative Mammalian Brain Collections, the National Museum of Health and Medicine. Preparation of all images and specimens have been funded by the National Science Foundation and the National Institutes of Health; Fig. 2.14: JAMES KING-HOLMES/HENRY LUCKHOO/SCIENCE PHOTO LIBRARY; Fig. 2.15: JAMES KING-HOLMES/SCIENCE PHOTO LIBRARY; Fig. 2.16: Simon Fraser/Science Source; Fig. 2.17: From "Brave Gabby Gives Thumbs Up To Doctors" by Richard Huff and Corky Siemaszko (01/11/11). © Daily News, L.P. (New York). Used with permission; Fig. 3.13: http://swiked.tumblr.com/; Fig. 4.1: Transportation Safety Board of Canada; Fig. 5.1: Columbia/The Kobal Collection/Art Resource; Fig. 5.5: http://www.jensenwalker.com/contact/; Fig. 5.10: Courtesy Professor Laszlo Seress; Fig. 5.9: Photo of H.M. Copyright © by Suzanne Corkin, used by permission of The Wylie Agency; Fig. 5.11: By permission of The Wylie Agency LLC; Fig. 5.18: Google.com; Fig. 5.19: © Ocean/Corbis; Fig. 6.1: Scott Witter; Fig. 6.4: © Dennis Hallinan/Alamy; Fig. 6.5: © Laperruque/Alamy; Fig. 8.1: AP Photo/Paul Sakuma; Fig. 8.4: CREATISTA/Shutterstock.com; Fig. 9.4: Arleco Producciones/Blogitravel.com; Fig. 10.2: © David Howells/Corbis; Fig. 10.3: Library of Congress LC-DIG-ds-00175 (digital file from original print); Fig. 12.4: © Brasil2/iStockphoto

Index

ONWARD, DEAR BOYS

Onward, Dear Boys

A FAMILY MEMOIR OF THE GREAT WAR

Philippe E. Bieler

McGill-Queen's University Press

Montreal & Kingston • London • Ithaca

ISBN 978-0-7735-4468-0 (cloth)
ISBN 978-0-7735-9670-2 (ePDF)
ISBN 978-0-7735-9671-9 (ePUB)

Legal deposit fourth quarter 2014
Bibliothèque nationale du Québec

Printed in Canada on acid-free paper that is 100% ancient forest free
(100% post-consumer recycled), processed chlorine free

McGill-Queen's University Press acknowledges the support of the
Canada Council for the Arts for our publishing program. We also
acknowledge the financial support of the Government of Canada
through the Canada Book Fund for our publishing activities.

LIBRARY AND ARCHIVES CANADA CATALOGUING IN
PUBLICATION

Onward, dear boys : a family memoir of the Great War / [edited by]
Philippe E. Bieler.

Includes bibliographical references and index.
Issued in print and electronic formats.
ISBN 978-0-7735-4468-0 (bound).–ISBN 978-0-7735-9670-2 (ePDF).–
ISBN 978-0-7735-9671-9 (ePUB)

1. Bieler, Philippe E., 1933– – Family. 2. Buhl family. 3. World War,
1914–1918 – Personal narratives, Canadian. 4. World War, 1914–1918
– Québec (Province) – Montréal. 5. Soldiers – Québec (Province) –
Montréal – Biography. 6. Brothers – Québec (Province) – Montréal
– Biography. 7. Swiss Canadians – Québec (Province) – Montréal –
Biography. 8. Protestants – Québec (Province) – Montréal – Biogra-
phy. 9. Immigrants – Québec (Province) – Montréal – Biography.
I. Bieler, Philippe E., 1933–, editor

D640.A2B53 2014   940.4'8171   C2014-904877-7
                                     C2014-904878-5

Set in 10.5/13 Sina Nova and Bulmer MT with Avenir Next
Book design & typesetting by Garet Markvoort, zijn digital

Dedicated to my grandmother Blanche

who is at the heart of this book

CONTENTS

ABBREVIATIONS

AHQ	Army Headquarters
BB	Blanche Bieler
BEF	British Expeditionary Force
Brig. Gen.	Brigadier General
CB	Charles Bieler
CBD	Canadian Base Depot
CCS	Casualty Clearing Station
CFA	Canadian Field Artillery
CLI	Canadian Light Infantry
CMG	Companion of the Order of the St. Michael and St. George
CO	Commanding Officer
CRA	Commanding Royal Artillery
Capt.	Captain
Col.	Colonel
DSO	Companion of the Distinguished Service Order
FOO	Forward Observation Officer
GHQ	General Headquarters
HMS	His Majesty's Ship
HQ	Headquarters
KCB	Knight Commander of the Order of the Bath
KCMG	Knight Commander of the Order of the St. Michael and St. George
Lieut or Lt	Lieutenant
MVO	Member of the 4th or 5th Class of the Royal Victorian Order
NCO	Non-Commissioned Officer
OC	Officer Commanding
OP	Observation Post
PPCLI	Princess Patricia's Canadian Light Infantry
Princess Pats	Princess Patricia's Canadian Light Infantry
Pte	Private
RA	Royal Artillery
RAF	Royal Airforce
RE	Royal Engineers
YMCA	Young Men's Christian Association

The Bieler Family, Geneva, June 1908

PREFACE

In 1908, my Swiss-born paternal grandparents, Pastor Charles Bieler and his wife, Blanche Merle d'Aubigné Bieler, sailed to Montreal with their family. At the time, their five sons ranged in age from sixteen to seven. A mere seven years later, three of their sons, Jean, Etienne, and André, volunteered for duty in World War I. The fourth son, Philippe, enlisted in 1916 as he turned eighteen. The youngest, Jacques, remained at home with his parents throughout the war.

This book is about the experience of building a new life in Canada in the pre-War years, of war, as recorded through the voice of a mother who penned a manuscript entitled "Nos Origines," of a father who supplemented his wife's writings in her text and in letters, and of sons who sent letters to their parents from various corners of the European theatre of battle. I occasionally insert my own voice, as "editor," in order to tie the various narratives together and to offer context concerning places and events at home and at war.

In her manuscript, Blanche, my grandmother, mentions with pride and fondness her "crown of sons." The photograph on the facing page visually captures this sentiment. As a result of war she lost one of those sons, and a decade later a second. And yet she and my grandfather "soldiered" on, participating in the intellectual life of McGill University, enjoying the successes of their three remaining sons, welcoming grandchildren into the world, and becoming part of the fabric of Quebec and Canada. They lived on the sidelines of a second war, but not without worry. Their eldest son, Jean, and his family, who were residing in Geneva, had to find a way to escape Europe in 1941.

My grandparents and their five sons were newcomers to Canada. But their decision to emigrate, to move "onward" to a different continent and new horizons, was itself rooted in family tradition. The families of both my grandparents were a European blend of Swiss, French, Polish, and Irish blood, bound together historically in the French language and in Protestant faith.

In the years before their departure for Canada, my grandparents themselves had moved from Switzerland to Paris, where my grandmother's brother "Oncle Charles" and her sister "Tante Julia" had settled. Little did they know that four of

Family Reunion at La Clairière in 1935.
Top, left to right: André, Jacques, and Jean; middle: Blanche, Jeanette with Nathalie,
Charles, and Raymonde; bottom: friend, Philippe (author of this book), and friend

their sons would make that trip back across the Atlantic to participate in what was supposed to be the "war to end all wars."

IN 1958, AT THE AGE OF NINETY-FOUR, my grandmother died, having outlived my grandfather by twelve years. It was a sad moment, and the transition was punctuated by the sale of their much-loved Laurentian property, La Clairière. I can remember the gathering of the entire family to hear the reading of her will. My father, Jean, was willed furniture, and, as eldest grandson, I received the family book, "Nos Origines." I had a feeling that it was their hope that I would take it one step further.

My grandparents had recorded the details of their life, and in particular the years of World War I, in "Nos Origines." It was handwritten in French and contained over five hundred pages of text, pictures, and other family records. It was an arduous task to decipher the cramped writing on the thin, almost transparent, paper, but it was read by many, and it influenced my immediate generation. Over the years, I wondered whether I could add anything. One day, the Vimy

Charles Bieler at La Clairière

Trust approached me about writing an article about my family during World War I. One thing led to another, and finally I accepted the challenge of writing this book. The book is largely a compilation of excerpts from "Nos Origines" and from the hundreds of letters that my grandparents, uncles, and father left behind.

My grandparents were both highly educated intellectuals, fluent in French, German, and English. My grandfather was a well-known and eloquent speaker, and my grandmother a prolific writer. She published, in 1929, a history of the Merle d'Aubigné family, including the official biography of her father, Jean Henri. French was their language, but they were first of all devout Protestants and enthusiastic evangelists. It was no surprise, therefore, that in coming to Quebec they would choose a Protestant milieu, which in Montreal was mostly English.

"Nos Origines" was written during a period from about 1925 to 1940. It deals briefly with the lives of my grandparent's ancestors, and in much greater detail with their lives and those of their immediate family. Each of my grandparents wrote in French, composing their own chapters, and some of these dealt with the same periods.

"Nos Origines" quotes excerpts from many of the boys' letters, but an important part of the text is in the form of "memoires" written by my grandparents. They were derived from conversations that they had with their sons after the war, visits from friends and relatives, other letters, and public sources. It is important to remember that my grandmother spent over a year with André during his recuperation from his serious gas exposure during the battle of Passchendaele. He would have told her many things that would never have passed the censors. During the war all the soldiers' letters were censored by senior officers.

I translated and edited the letters and my grandparents' memoirs, attempting to eliminate repetitive family details and to cut from the memoirs subjects that were dealt with better in the letters. In the text, excerpts from the memoirs are signed (BB) for Blanche, and (CB) for Charles. The letters are signed and dated by their author.

There were two categories of letters. The first being the many hundreds written by my father and his brothers in France and England during the war. The second were the much rarer ones written by my grandparents to their sons.

I'm told that most of the letters written by parents to their boys were lost in the mud of Flanders. My grandmother, having the time-consuming task of writing to four boys, decided to stencil copies to each one. She also felt sorry for their good friend, Jacques Grellet, who couldn't be contacted by his parents in neutral Switzerland, so she made an extra copy for him. Two years ago, as I was searching for information, a cousin called me to say that she had received a bundle of World War I letters from an unknown lady. It turned out that Grellet drowned in the Great Slave River after the war, and his possessions were sent to his brother's wife. Her daughter was cleaning the attic, found the bundle, and traced the Bieler family in Paris. Grellet had volunteered into Canada's "Railway Regiment," which stayed behind the Front during all of 1917 and 1918. His copies of the letters will join those of the other three boys at the archives of Queen's University.

Another anecdote concerns the picture of a château in the Pas de Calais region, located near the boys' battlefields. I chose it haphazardly to illustrate the kind of place they sometimes enjoyed during their rest days. When I sought permission to use the photograph from the current owner, he responded with enthusiasm, explaining that British Field Marshal John French and some of his men had slept there in 1915.

Etienne was the most prolific writer of the four boys, but there were blanks during two periods. The first was after his minor wound just before the battle of Passchendaele through until his return to the Lens Front. My grandmother must have mislaid them. The second was during his year with the Antisubmarine Division, where absolute secrecy was mandated. André may have written as many letters as his brother, but they were usually brief and less regular. Philippe, who

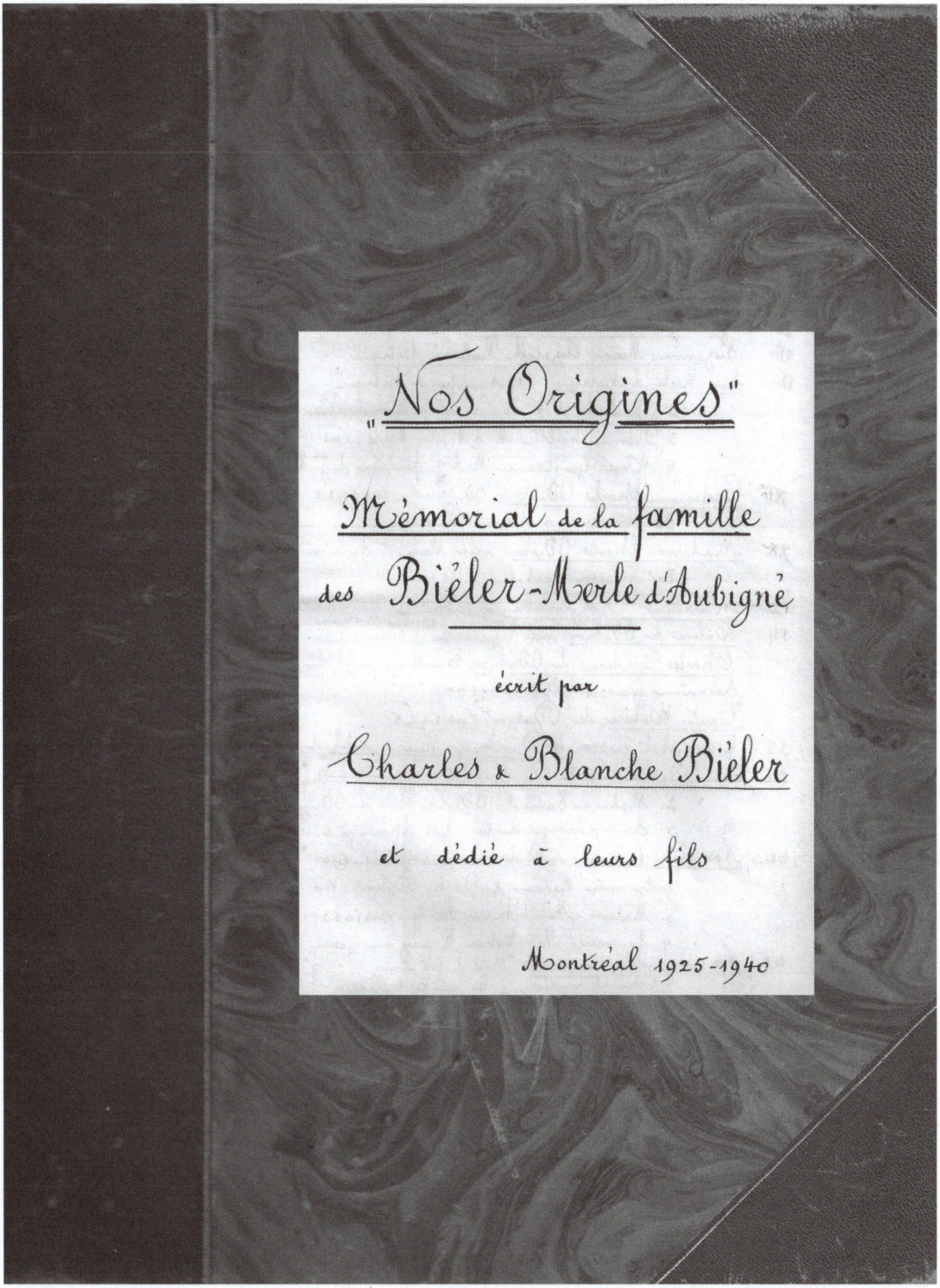

"Nos Origines"

Mémorial de la famille

des Biéler-Merle d'Aubigné

écrit par

Charles & Blanche Biéler

et dédié à leurs fils

Montréal 1925-1940

"Nos Origines"

arrived later, wrote the most focused and poetic letters. There are very few letters from my father, Jean. I believe that Tante Jeanette, André's well-organized wife, filed all of André's, Etienne's, and Philippe's letters and sent them to the Queen's archives, whereas my parents left me with an incomplete box of papers, and I often had to rely on my grandparents for information about my father.

I have included the major part of almost all their letters. I attempted to keep all the non-repetitive material that told the story. A major exception is the volume of letters from Etienne during his many months recovering at the Camberwell Hospital. He would go on at some length about the nursing care and the visits from Lady Bunting and a myriad other titled and untitled visitors. My comments with regard to the editing and translation of my grandparents' "memoirs" also applies to the letters.

This book records the events of World War I, and the lives of my family at home and at war, in chronological order. The war years are divided into twelve chapters, ranging from periods of three months to six months. The "backbone" is the overall events of the war, which I sourced from a number of books and articles. The most important contributions came from Colonel G.W.L. Nicholson's *Canadian Expeditionary Force, 1914–1919*, Ralph Hodder-Williams's *Princess Patricia's Canadian Light Infantry, 1914–1919*, Grandson Michael's online *Canadian Great War Project: Canadian Field Artillery*, and A.J.P. Taylor's *The First World War: An Illustrated History*.

A weakness of attempting to write a detailed historical account often comes from lack of information. This is especially true in writing about wars where those who have the facts are not permitted to divulge them. I tried to circumvent that by reviewing and quoting some of the official war diaries.

Etienne was a lieutenant in the Canadian Field Artillery. From February 1916 to June 1916 he was with the 3rd Brigade; from July 1916 to March 1917, he was with the 12th Brigade; and finally in April 1917 with the 1st Brigade. He fought in the battles of Sanctuary Wood, Courcelette, and Vimy. The daily activity of the Brigades was recorded in the Canadian Corp's war diaries, which were archived in Canada's Library and Archives and later reorganized by Grandson Michael in his Canadian Great War Project. Given the strict censorship, as Etienne was not permitted to write about his daily war activities, some of these diaries are included in the narrative. It is very likely that Etienne was there as they were being written and even that he wrote some of them himself. He is mentioned in many of them.

However, the heart of the book is "Nos Origines," the letters, blended within a matrix of the memoirs, and the actual events of the war. There are therefore three voices: those of the boys, those of my grandparents, and my own voice, relating the news of the day as I have derived it from numerous sources.

Philippe E. Bieler

ONWARD, DEAR BOYS

CHAPTER ONE

Onward

1908

On board the SS *Parisian*, 5 September 1908 (in front, from left, Jacques,
Philippe, André; Jean, standing at far right, next to Etienne)

YEARS AGO, ON MY WAY TO GENEVA, I used to stay at my Oncle Robert's apartment in Paris. We used to talk about the fun he and his brothers and sisters had with my father and uncles. He liked to tell the story about my grandfather's decision to immigrate. Apparently, one day, my grandfather, Charles, met with his brother-in-law, Oncle Charles, and explained to him that he had had enough of the too-frequent trips, often third class, which his mission as general agent of the Sunday Schools of France imposed on him, and he was hoping to find a new activity of a more intellectual character, perhaps overseas, where the cost of educating his children would be more reasonable. He presented him with a printed sheet of paper, listing three positions available at McGill University. My grandfather said proudly that he had decided to choose America, and he felt that he could apply for all three: "I would be well suited to take on the Theology job at the Presbyterian College; I'm good at maths, so the Math job would be great; and geography is my passion, I could sure do that!" Oncle Charles was reading the paper carefully and suddenly said: "Charles! McGill is not in America. It's in Canada!"

"What's the difference!" replied my grandfather in a loud voice.

McGill University was a leading English-speaking university in Canada, but it was already conscious of its role in educating French-speaking citizens of the Province of Quebec. My grandfather's background fitted well. They were looking for a French-speaking gentleman with an ecclesiastical background to head the French department of their Presbyterian college. Before he had much of a chance to have second thoughts, he and my grandmother, Blanche, were packing their bags. Little did they know the adventures that they were about to face.

BUT YOU WERE GROWING UP, my dear sons, and your future would not be secure without our help. I had not taken the steps to be naturalized in France, and, as foreigners, you did not have a clear future in the country. Half the careers at least would not be available for you … what could we do? At one time I was tempted to become the pastor of the Église Libre Française in Strasbourg. Happily for us, this post wasn't offered to me. Your mother asked herself whether you might not consider finding careers in America; which would have resulted in a separation. Instead of a separation could we not perhaps go over together? But how could we?

In 1907, I heard that two gentlemen had come from Canada to search for a successor to Professor Coussinat of the Presbyterian College in Montreal. I would have liked to have met them, but they left without my being able to. Nevertheless, they had been given my name, and, in the spring of 1908, when the professor whom they had hired for a period of three months decided that he did not want the job for the long term, they offered it to me. We had very little time to dispose of our furniture,

Bieler House, Levallois-Perret, near Batignolles in northwest Paris

pack our things, send our luggage, and say goodbye to our family and our friends. I am still a little surprised that we had the courage to undertake such an adventure!

It wasn't easy for our whole family, and our luggage, to leave Europe. Your mother more than I organized the move from the rue Gide in Levallois-Perret, and the Maison Blanche on the Lac de Bret. We had to sort, pack, sell, and buy. We had no experience with a long-distance voyage; we were going to a country that we didn't know, to people that we had never seen. Everything for us was new, and a little daunting. It took determination and a good deal of faith to cast off so many ties that could have kept us in Europe. Many people didn't understand, and one of our neighbours at Lac de Bret sighed as she thought of us going to a country of cannibals!

You will remember that, at the end of August 1908, we made a trip to London, arranged by Tante Julia. We were taking advantage of some special travel arrangement,

Batignolles Boulevard, St Ouen, Paris

which allowed us to visit this great Anglo-Saxon metropolis and to view the huge Franco-British Exhibition, in which Canada had an important place.

We were emotional on the afternoon of 5 September 1908, as the SS *Parisian* lifted her anchor and we left Le Havre, and we broke our link with our countries and our families. Two of our good friends had expressed their love with two memorable receptions. The first one, on an evening in May at the Union Chrétienne de Paris, in the heart of the noisy metropolis, where the representatives of the École du Dimanche expressed their regrets and their wishes and had assembled a lovely volume of parables by Bunand. The second, a charming garden party, held on the Thomas estate in Frontenac, left us with a souvenir of sunflowers, and affection from these genevois friends. With all those impressions fresh in our minds, and Tante Julia, who came on board to say goodbye, how could we leave without tears in our eyes?

However, despite the emotion, as parents, we felt a sudden relief. There would be ten days of rest to look forward to, and the joy of leaving together, as opposed to leaving in Europe our poor mother, who was tired and almost at the point of collapsing. We were also filled with this incurable optimism, this spark of adventurous spirit that was bringing us to Canada, where we would work to plant deep roots. We would water them with a few tears, strengthen them mostly from the sun, our good humour, and our Father in heaven, who had protected us until now, and hopefully, would continue to bless us.

SS *Parisian*

So, in fact, everything was smiling at us: the calm of the first days, the saline air that was restoring our strength, the courteous Canadians, prepared to tell us about their country, and finally the service on our *Parisian* (not inferior to those of current transatlantic steamers).

Lying comfortably on my deck chair, I was comparing this passage with our trips in Europe. Those trips between our homes in Paris and Lac de Bret, where we disembarked in Dijon with a pile of half-awake children and a stack of suitcases on the platform open to the weather. Then a long wait and, at 1 o'clock, a shrill whistle throwing us into a frenetic chase towards the crowded carriages with their hard seats. They were less hard than the voices of the passengers complaining about the arrival of this large family with their boxes and endless items!

Despite the increasing swell, and the moments of seasickness, we were well off. First Class on the Allan Line was better than Third Class on the PLM.

We felt the cold of the Strait of Belle Isle, and then the calm and the sun of the St Lawrence. My boys were excited and fought for my binoculars to look along the green shore at the rows of little white houses and small villages with tin steeples. It was not far from Quebec, with its promise of a few hours' stop. We improvised a picnic under the old fort, and spent a fortune on postcards. Finally, we arrived in Montreal in the afternoon of the following day, in tropical temperatures. A group of clergymen were waiting for us, and quite surprisingly old Mr. Provost, formerly a student of the Oratoire, had recognized us from afar with his opera glasses, because of Blanche's resemblance to her brother. "That's Mrs Bieler, surrounded by her husband and her five sons." —Charles Bieler (CB)

CHAPTER TWO

Quebec

1908 to 1914

Jacques Cartier Square, Montreal, 1908

*T*he shores of the St Lawrence gave us our first impression of Canada. During our brief stop in Quebec, we were struck by its magnificent site, as well as by the strange accent of the population. Our reception in Montreal on 15 September could not have been more encouraging. Professor Morin offered us his hospitality, which was the beginning of a lifelong friendship. A few days later, in their drawing room, he introduced us to the French clergymen and their wives. We were introduced to the congregation of the St Jean church two Sundays later.

Meanwhile our furniture, which had been sent by cargo, was held back in England, so that we could neither settle in nor end the generous hospitality of our friends, the Morins. The family needed to be split in two, with Father staying in Montreal with the two eldest, and Mother leaving with the three youngest to spend several weeks in the United States. It was a good omen to renew, soon after our arrival, the good relations that we continued to have with the descendants of our Oncle Guillaume. We were also grateful to be with our dear cousin Charles Carhart, who opened wide the doors of their charming rectory in Vermont. Then there was our lovely cousin Hortense Dufourg, welcoming us in her house on 85th Street in New York, and Addie and John Darrow, receiving us at the Peekskill boarding house where they were spending their elderly years. Finally, our good Quaker friends, Walter and Julia Wood, in their family home on Locust Street in Philadelphia. She had visited us in Geneva many years before. Speaking of them, let's not forget John, the black butler that little Jacques admired so much.

Having left André and Philippe in Dorset [Vermont] to work on their English at the village school, and, accompanied only by Jacques, we left the rolling hills of Vermont, to follow the Hudson River right up to Peekskill. From there I could see in the distance the property of my Oncle Guillaume on Lake Mohegan, and we got to see the skyscrapers of New York, as well as Independence Hall and the Liberty Bell of Philadelphia. That was an interesting and beautiful detour, confirming the marvels of the industrial and the secular history of the United States. I was to often see these places in the future, but nothing surpasses the impressions of the first visit. I returned to Montreal to preside over our move to Parc Lafontaine, followed the next year to Columbia Street. Father and sons were already weary of their teaching and studying.

You will remember how we got to know Montreal, by going from east to west and north to south in search of a lodging, and how much we admired the Maison Charboneau, at 666 Sherbrooke Street East, opposite Parc Lafontaine. A charming house, with a wonderful view, but it was unfortunately a little too expensive for us.

At the beginning of October, Dad met his principal, Doctor Scrimger, and his colleagues. He became close to all of them. The principal was gracious, but reserved: he maintained a certain distance! The registrar, Professor Fraser, was a scholar. We were also fond of the distinguished Alexander Gordon, renowned for literature. All that Professor Welsh and his colleagues were asking was to welcome us and to celebrate our arrival. As Scots, for us they represented "Old Europe."

Guillaume

The French-language students were of two groups: those that were registered in theology, very keen to be prepared to give French sermons; and some who came from the Cours Préparatoire, former students of Pointe-aux-Trembles, who wished to learn about French literature, psychology, and history. They were solid chaps, woodsmen, who were more familiar with manual labour than exercises of the spirit, but very keen to learn.

We were greeted kindly, despite a little mistrust with respect to our European reputation for having an overly sharp and critical outlook. However, we admired this vast and beautiful Canada and appreciated its importance and attraction, at a time when the country seemed to be moving rapidly towards a fantastic prosperity. Canadians were happy with the increase in the population, and boasted about the rapid progress of the West, which they described as a paradise.

You remember your early days at school. For the two eldest at the High School of Montreal, where everything was difficult at the beginning, and then easier and easier as you worked conscientiously with that desire of surpassing your new comrades. André and Philippe at that moment were working on their English under the shadow of the belfry in Dorset, near the wonderful Charles Carharts, and Jacques was learning "I see a cat" at the Aberdeen School.

New Presbyterian College, Montreal

The first winter seemed terribly severe, and in fact it was. We learned about frozen ears, and also how to skate and snowshoe. On Sunday afternoon we went to admire the ice palace built on Fletcher's Field. We, the parents, not being as sporting as our sons, joined the intellectual and religious community, visiting especially the various French churches and the missionary schools. At Pointe-aux-Trembles, where a position as a member of the committee was reserved for Dad, we were surprised to see in the classes men and women of marriageable age learning the basics, along with young schoolchildren as classmates. The school offered to young people, who had not had the opportunity in their distant woods, the chance to be educated, and hence to improve their status. We were impressed with the Sunday congregation, which listened intently and sang with gusto.

We were also surprised with the brevity of the academic year, which had not even started at the beginning of the month of October. At Christmas, we had enjoyed more than fifteen days of holidays, and already, in mid March, they talked about the final exams and the termination of the courses, with the convocation in the first week of April. We learned that this short academic year corresponded with the needs of the country. All the theological students, even those taking preparatory courses, had to spend at least twenty-four weeks at evangelical camps. The professors had a much-appreciated period of leisure, when they could prepare their courses for the following winter.

There was an important change in our life in 1909. Our apartment on Sherbrooke Street was much too small; we needed to move on. We were advised to consider the

Les Colombettes

English section of Montreal, or Westmount, where we could mingle in an English-speaking milieu. Not finding a suitable apartment, we decided to put together all our available funds and buy a house at 98 Columbia Avenue, a house we called "les Colombettes." The building was elegant on the exterior, with a red-grey front and a small tower, but it had many failings that we discovered later. It was especially difficult to heat, but we were at last going to be at home, with lots of room and a huge basement where we could install a woodworking shop, and a veranda giving onto a tiny garden. It was complete enough that we could avoid finding a country place for the summer, as our boys could be initiated in the Canadian woods at Powters Camp in Saint-Donat-de-Montcalm.

As it turned out, the new house was only half-successful. Westmount is very hot in the summer. Perhaps it was because we were in a sixteen-year climatic period in which one suffocates in summer and then freezes in winter. In fact, already in the summer of 1909 our family became unfaithful to the city. I had accepted from Miss de Nottbeck, the friend and admirer of André and Philippe in Dorset, Vermont, an offer to come with our entire gang to spend the holidays in a house on her property.

Dad had already left in May for Europe, to occupy Oncle Charles's pulpit in Neuilly, and afterwards to be present on 12 August at the golden wedding of his parents. The celebration was at the Champ-de-l'Air agricultural college, which his father had created and helped to build over the last thirty years. Meanwhile, Jean, who had been accepted at the preparatory courses at the Presbyterian College, passed the McGill matriculation exam at age seventeen, with good marks, even in English.

As we were all together after that brief separation, it was time to review our family, and for good or bad paint the picture of our boys. Their physical appearance had been very happily recorded in a photograph by Boissonas in Geneva that summer. Their moral character was probably more difficult to capture by a mother who couldn't pretend to be perfectly objective, nor have any scientific knowledge. Nevertheless, it appeared that Jean was honest, conscientious, and excellent with his youngest brothers, and had a strong sense of devotion to others. That was a serious problem for us when he went to England for a brief exchange. Jean did not have the same linguistic difficulties as his brothers and succeeded very rapidly at the High School, where he was able to do two years in one.

However, if at the beginning my boys had certain difficulties in adapting to their new environment, what was the cause? The language differences certainly, as French education being Catholic in Canada, it was necessary to send them to English schools. Then, the racial differences: their friends, Anglo-Saxons or Scottish almost exclusively, were less complicated, while our sons were a combination of Latin, Germanic, and Slav blood, making them a little more adaptable and less harsh than their peers. In addition, the two eldest had undergone the more rigid French school program, based on French culture, that allowed them to develop a critical sense at an earlier age. Their classmates were more interested in sports and also in the friends of their sisters. All this made my boys a little more timid at the beginning, but they soon developed excellent friendships: Jean with Dewey, Mathewson, Pedley, Bruneau, and others, and Etienne with a group with scientific tastes, of which the leader was the dear and eccentric George Douglas.

It is difficult to speak of Etienne indifferently, as he was an inspiring character who was hard to criticize. His brothers, his teachers, his friends, even his enemies agreed that he was gentle, energetic, intelligent, and polite, and of course no one found it strange that his mother was of the same opinion. I had never had any

Blanche Bieler

complaints about this exceptional son, nor had any concerns about him. Everyone, from the chambermaid to the leaders of the university, recognized his qualities. It was only he, it seemed, that ignored them. In July 1910, the newspapers were boasting of his scholastic success, and his picture was in everyone's hands, but he retired in the background. Later, during the final examinations, he often spent more time preparing his rivals to beat him than in training himself to beat them. A hard worker, he also brought inspiration to others. His playmates later said of him: "If we were a happy and uncomplicated crowd of youngsters, we owed it in good part to Etienne's influence."

André was a special "personality" that one should have brought up exclusively. There was in him a tireless physical activity, despite often frail health, a great inventive intensity, and constant effort towards the realization of his ideas. There were sometimes moments of dreamy distraction, already indicating an artistic nature more sensitive to forms and colours and motion than to the abstractions of grammar. André advanced in his life outside the well-beaten paths, always being himself without the dryness and egotism that often degrades eccentric individuals.

Philippe Bieler

Philippe was a very attractive child, with his round face, his lovely eyes, and his laughing mouth. He wasn't always well-behaved or a serious worker, but was for-given his few bad humours and disagreements, as we couldn't bear to be angry with him for very long. In his good moments, his courtesy was perfect. Never will I forget his charming reception, when I visited him at St-Pie on the banks of the Yamaska, where we had sent him to be looked after with Jacques while his brothers became "coureurs de bois" at Powters Camp. He had the same joyful greeting during my visits to Stanstead College, where we had sent him as an apprentice, with the hope that he would become serious about his studies. Later, at the beginning of the war, what a reputation he gained with the neighbours at 16 Island Lake, who knew this devoted and helpful young man, who was always available. Philippe had what it took to be a perfect gentleman.

Does Jacques deserve any praise for having been a polite and well-behaved child, or do his attributes come from a particularly bright star that shone the night he was born on that 17 April 1901, at the Maison Blanche? Delightful baby, gracious little boy, pleasant schoolboy, who grew up with no setbacks or inhibitions in a sunny atmosphere, because he was himself an optimist and a peacemaker, with an instinctive horror of conflicts. This pleasant nature could have become a weakness, but he proved later that, if his glove was soft and supple, the hand inside it was very firm. What an attractive Boy Scout, exemplified the day he received the Canadian Cup for his dexterity in all fields. That dexterity was tested over the years as he produced a series of ingenious electrical gadgets for his mother. His ideas pleased everyone.

Youth can be easily transplanted, whereas adults have more difficulty in starting again. Dad had considerable difficulties with the English language at the beginning. He conquered it for day-to-day conversation, but nevertheless always suffered. He was passionate about language. For him it was disappointing not to be able to use in his courses and sermons the rich vocabulary, the fluidity of expression, and the mastery of words, which in his mother tongue came so easily. Fortunately, the greater part of his work was in French.

One also had to adapt to a foreign mentality, and with enormous patience conquer any jealousies and prejudices. I mention it, as it would be wrong to pretend that we were always warmly received and enjoyed immediate success. Up until our arrival, we often had to deal with adversities, but never against hostile people. Now, quite to the contrary, the material conditions were easier but the human obstacles were often greater. Fortunately, at the Presbyterian College the atmosphere reflected the good nature and integrity of its staff. We had such a charming reception from everyone, and they very quickly became our friends, and often came to visit us. Relations with the students were also excellent.

Being used to sharing a few of my husband's tasks, I would have been quite disoriented if I had been unable to pursue such activities. Happily, I found an opportunity in developing a student-relations program.

DURING THE MONTH OF JULY 1911, the family rented an attractive holiday cottage belonging to Pastor Masse on the shore of Long Lake in the 16 Island Lake area in the Laurentians. The boys found the area so pleasant that they begged Dad to consider the possibility of buying what Jacques described as a little point of land, with a little house and a little boat, which would really be ours. To start with, the idea seemed to be beyond our means, but it happened to coincide with a comment that Pastor Scott, from Perth, had made to Dad while he was at the annual meeting of our church in Ottawa. "Professor, as I understand it you came to Canada with your sons. Let me give you some advice: buy yourself – it won't ruin you – a farm where you can spend your summers, and where your sons can learn to handle the tools of the carpenter and the gardener." The opportunity presented itself one Sunday as we were questioning a neighbour about a picturesque corner of their property. Her husband, a John Morrow, was quick to respond, "I can't sell you a parcel of my property. If you wish to settle here, buy the whole farm." The farm had 143 acres of land, with reasonable buildings that could be renovated. He was asking eight hundred dollars. We took our time to reflect and to consult several friends.

Dad's father – it was his last letter – wrote to him to encourage him to buy it. He regretted not having attempted such an adventure. The deal was done, and that's why, a quarter of a century later, I can write these words in a large, comfortable room, which had been John Morrow's stable. It was of humble origins but couldn't be better today.

We named the property La Clairière, and during the following winter the most audacious plans were conceived. We would have a farmer who would have cows, pigs, and chickens. We prepared to buy some lovely Swiss bells for the herd. But luckily, very luckily, the farmer that we had in mind backed out at the last minute. The fact is that he would not have succeeded and we would have sunk with him, as Laurentian farms aren't worth much, and their upkeep requires more money than they generate. So events forced us to abandon our plans, and attack the log cabin that old Cassy had built twenty-five years earlier, and John Morrow had expanded.

I WAS CLEARLY NOT VERY USEFUL for my husband's professional duties, and also not much help in the preparation of my sons' homework, which doesn't play an important role in Canadian education. I had originally spent a good deal of time helping them with their English, but as they began to play sports with their friends, the family playtime also became less frequent. There remained, of course, our meals, gay and noisy, our evenings around our lamp, and our "Sundays," which in Canada, in the good old days before the war, were still sought after.

Having been relieved of a part of my usual duties, I gained a little more time to spend on my household, which was necessary, as we now had only one housemaid. In Paris we had added a temporary to our full-time servant. And what faithful servants have I had during my lifetime: Pauline, Louise, Amélie, Berthe Joli, Ellen Morrow, Rose Fluckinger, and many others.

I was president during twenty-five consecutive years of the Societé Missionaire des Dames Françaises de Montréal. In addition I undertook many activities involving the poor, the unhappy, and the unemployed, but I could perhaps be criticized for not having found, prior to the war effort, a useful community activity using my talents. Unfortunately, as everything in Canada seemed to be done in committees, there was little room for the enterprising housewife.

SEEING LA CLAIRIÈRE TODAY, still rustic but so attractive and comfortable, one couldn't imagine what was once a log cabin when we bought it. The big room looked like a stable, with its many half-high partitions. The bedroom was far worse, with its ugly flooring and its rotten walls, beneath the large, square beams covered with decomposing plaster and old rags. The gallery was shaky, the house was surrounded with stumps and old boards, the garden filled with thistles, and all around it was a bare clearing, denuded of any shade or vegetation. Yet our collective optimism was such that none of us doubted that the oil from our elbows, more reliable than a magician's wand, would be able to transform it.

Family working at La Clairière

It was a bit of a strange project, considering that our talents were more suited to cooking blackberry tarts than building log cabins! Our truck driver, arriving on the first day with a stove, a mattress, and a bunch of fruit bushes, thought we were crazy. We were there, on this crisp day of May, and we lost no time moving in. The mattress was stretched out on the floor for sleeping, the stove with its pipe through the window was lit, and we found two stumps for tables and a candle in a bottle as a lamp. With this extensive installation in place, we ran to the garden to plant our blackberries. It was for Dad and I our first very brief stay at La Clairière.

The future blackberry pies a reality, we needed to start building, and that's exactly what we did during the summer holiday. Dad was the supervisor and carpenter. The bedboards and various objects started to appear from his shop. Etienne was the architect and foreman, and his brothers took turns as apprentice carpenters, roofers, floor men, and plumbers. Jean would have preferred to be with us, but it was already the fourth summer since our arrival in Canada, and, as a student at McGill, he was spending his summer holidays, as is common in this country, at a salaried job. The jobs varied between salesman, tutor, or office boy, but he learned about business and was able to participate in paying his university fees. In addition, he began to familiarize himself with the different regions of the province, as well as penetrating the different classes of the population. It was an interesting initiative for the observant and broad-minded boy that he was.

We needed first of all to transform the big room, and what a charming room it became, with its original rose-coloured pine walls, a solid parquet floor, and, in the evening, the crackling of the burning pine and maple logs in the Franklin stove. Larger windows, a bookcase, rustic armchairs, André's paintings on the walls, a big carpet, a large sofa, and in the middle, the family table. A big lamp focused on the family and gave the walls and beams rose-coloured reflections and a sense of intimacy. In the daytime there were superb views, of the garden on one side, and on the other towards the lawn, the lake, the hills, and the woods.

Upstairs, we were transforming our bedroom. We built a kitchen, and added a room in the barn next door, as well as a veranda at each end of the house. Later we created the sweet and rustic small dining room, with a communicating larder. And so, each spring, the work inside and out restarted with renewed vigour. Outdoors was important, and we planted bushes, fir trees, larches to frame the house, and an orchard that was to suffer from all the problems of Canadian winters. Then there was the creation of a vegetable garden, flowerbeds, a rock garden, the seeding of a lawn, and later, even a large excavation on the slope to locate a future tennis court.

All this work, undertaken without the help of any specialists, was crowned in 1915 when Philippe and Jacques, with the help of pipes, parts of old motors, and an enormous beer barrel, succeeded in installing running water. After many delays and failures, all of a sudden, one morning, a piercing cry was heard. It was Philippe, throwing his arms in the air and exclaiming: "The water is rising, the water is rising," just as triumphant as Christopher Columbus years ago when he had cried "Land, land."

Often, when I turn on what we call here a *champelure* and witness the abundant clear water, I think of Philippe. Meanwhile, the completed house was rendered in white, with wood trimmings, unifying all the connections and additions in the same tint. We had, on the shores of Lake Long, a house like the one we had left in the Swiss countryside, and inside were all the beds, couches, bookcases, stools, benches, and twelve tables of different sizes that Dad had built.

NARRATIVES AND ANECDOTES OF LA CLAIRIÈRE

OUR NEIGHBOUR: Johnny Morrow, the previous owner of La Clairière, was six feet tall, with angular features, a Celtic humour, and a strong local accent. He was energetic with his axe, but relaxed at rest, as he smoked slowly his old pipe. He came from an Irish Protestant background, a tiny clan lost in the French–Catholic population. Without a doubt, he was the most colourful character of the area!

Brunette

In 1911, when we spent our first holidays in the Laurentians at the Maison Masse, we liked to row to the end of 16 Island Lake area, to buy milk at the Morat farm of Lake Long. We then had a chat with Johnny, while his wife, always with a baby on her hip, worked in her kitchen, and the little Violette, with blue eyes and bright blonde hair, milked the cows of the milk we were to take away.

It was at the end of one of those trips that we had made that rather innocent remark about his property. We had asked him: "Mr. Morrow, we admire your place so much that we are just wondering if you would sell us a small lot, just big enough to build a bungalow and a boathouse?"

"Well, Mrs.," was his answer, "it's this way. I have a mind to buy a farm in Laurel, where my children could get some education, 'cause I know no more than signing my name, and that's not enough nowadays. But don't you people ask me to sell a bit of me land. It would be like asking me to sell a limb of me cow. It's the whole cow, or no cow. It's the whole 150 acres of Johnny Morrow's farm, or it's not a square foot."

The next year the Morrows moved, and we replaced them. To our stupefaction, we learned that our friend, completely illiterate, was named president of the Laurel Protestant School Commission!

However, Johnny was nostalgic about Lake Long, and sometimes came to wander in the fields that he had created, and where he had embellished the place in his own fashion by cutting the trees right up to the house. "When I bought the house from old Cassy," he would say, "the front room was too low, so I chopped the beams and saved the boards and lifted the ceiling about sixteen inches. A feller should not have to stoop when he enters is own home. The right thing for the master is to hold his head up, and keep his hat on his head, says I."

The famous day when Brunette, our own cow, strayed, the former proprietor was making one of his nostalgic wanderings. Hearing the poor animal moving in the brush, he ran in and disengaged her horns from the branches and returned her to the house, saying to Tante Julia, who had been visiting from France, "Remember, Miss, that our cows are all right as long as you treat them well. But they are awfully fond of their independence, so never again try to tie down a Canadian cow!"

SEVERAL YEARS LATER, we heard one day that our good neighbour, Father Millette, was in negotiations with a Frenchman desiring to buy a lovely point of land, with its magnificent pine tree. It jutted out in our lake and formed, on both sides, bays with deep green water. In answer to our questions, the old man answered that he owned this land, while Morrow insisted that it belonged to us. It was finally decided in a friendly manner that Millette would interrupt the negotiations until such time as an official surveyor came to settle the issue. That was done, and here is what Johnny Morrow, the following spring, told us about the arbitration.

"Father Millette, the surveyor, and I were to meet on the frozen lake on a Tuesday at 10 o'clock. So I gets up early, eats my breakfast, puts on a warm sweater and a muffler, for it looked like a North wind, and off I goes through the fresh snow, saying to misself, says I: 'Johnny Morrow, you're in Professor Bieler's shoes today, so you must behave just right and do him honour.' Suddenly I stop and sez I to misself, 'Why Johnny, you've forgotten the most important thing, that is your Bible.' So back I turn, fetch the old book, puts it into my breast pocket, and goes off again. But what do I see standing on the ice in front of the cottage? Quite a crowd waiting for me. The surveyor of course, and Father Millette, but also three of his sons! That will never do says I. I could have brought along my three sons just as well, but what's the use, measurements are measurements? 'Father Millette, send your three boys back home, we three men can settle the thing between us, and we'll begin by swearing on this here Bible that we are going to be fair and honest on the job.' So we swore, then took up the chain and made straight for the old spruce on tother side of the point, which I had marked with me axe long ago. The surveyor found it was correct, Father Millette had to give in, and I goes back home thinking I had earned my dinner, and had stood firm and straight in the Professor's shoes, sure enough!"

The friendship of the Morrows during all these years had been a real benediction and had resulted in a series of exchanges and good deals.

Are these hollow spots in the floor of the big room worrying? Johnny arrives with a pipe in his mouth, axe on his shoulders. He slides under the house and, with the help of a jack, straightens out in no time the problem undulations. Does the garden need to be completely dug out? Bertie arrives with his pleasant smile and finishes the digging in one day. Would it be exciting to have a grand trip in a carriage? Stanley appears with his old cart harnessed with two half-wild horses, and there we are bumping along through the potholes on our way to a picnic at the Rivière Perdue. Are we short of butter and cream at La Clairière? Violette with blue eyes brings us fresh products from her creamery. Are we short of help at home? Ellen Morrow, Johnny's sister, comes to give us a hand, and becomes our dear and faithful servant for several years, until death takes her away.

Winter doesn't interrupt these good relations. The Morrows seem to be in good health, but hereditary goiter is a problem and brings them sometimes to Montreal for an operation. For the mother it was serious and took a long time. Her husband decided to undertake the great adventure of a trip to Montreal, and arrived with large ambitions and very modest means. He would eat his meals with us, but where would he live? He thought about the Windsor Hotel, which had been highly recommended. "I went there to see if it would suit me," said he. "It seemed right enough: smart and comfortable, but just a bit too noisy for me, so I decided to stay at the Immigrant's Home round the corner, and we sure had a jolly night in that dormitory: A Scotsman danced a jig, a Welshman gave us some rousing songs, an Englishman prayed and sang hymns, and I told them some of me old yarns until they roared and roared with laughing. We had a better time than them folks at that Windsor place, let alone the big money it costs."

EACH SUMMER TWO GET-TOGETHERS END THE SEASON: a tea at the Morrows, where we feast on cream and fresh bread with delicious jams, and then the party at our house. One arrives on the famous team that we have harnessed as best we could. One inspects the improvements that we have made to the property, where our friends recognize every rock. One takes the risk of a rowboat ride – except for Johnny, who swears that he has never had a bath in his life and that he was too old to start now! One has tea outside and one leaves wishing for another happy reunion the next year.

OUR RELATIONS WITH OUR CLOSEST NEIGHBOURS, the Millettes, swarming on one of the shores of the lake, was just as excellent. The Patriarchs, across the way, had sixteen beautiful children, all married now. They would on their own prevent the Canadian race from disappearing, as they stopped counting grandchildren and great-grandchildren when they reached the imposing total of seventy-five. At the present time, the number has apparently increased substantially. When we have the time to chat, the old pioneer tells us about his work as a lumberman creating new pastures for his farm. The dear old lady, with her remaining lovely Lorraine accent, talks about her childhood memories: the invasion of her native village by the Prussians in 1870, the shells that exploded, the bodies in the streets, the wailing in the houses, and all the horrors of war. Then she faced the daring immigration of her courageous mother with her two young children, the passage, and the miserable life in the Laurentian forests. Finally everything works out when her lovely fourteen-year-old daughter marries Adonias Millette, the pioneer of Lake Long. With hard work, thrift, and common sense, the valiant couple little by little attained the ease that they enjoy today.

ONE MUST SAY THAT THESE PEASANTS, a cross between Normans and Lorraines, know how to deal with opportunities. We saw it in the Pointe deal. We had already witnessed this talent one Sunday in the early years when Father Millette, very impressive in his formal attire, walked up slowly towards our house with a serious and diplomatic expression. He had the sense to begin his conversation with a chat about the rain and the sunshine, before getting to his subject, which he presented more or less as follows:

"My eldest son, Adonius, is married, and quite rightly he has asked for a concession from the Province of Quebec. They gave him twenty-five acres that borders your lot. That's where there is the Petit Lac and the cottage where they will live for the official three years. So, you will understand, he will need a road to get there, and the Quebec law states that it's the closest neighbour that must build this road. It will be necessary to locate, dig, ballast, transport, level, and build two bridges over the stream. This is why I have come to arrange this matter with you and to propose that I and my boys do the job for 150 dollars. It's a bargain at that price."

We were floored. We had found the eight hundred dollars for the land, and several hundred dollars worth of boards, beams, tools, nails, paint, furniture, boats – so much that we wondered how we would pay for it – and on top of this, where would we find it? Another 150 dollars in order for the Millette son to move into the neighbouring forest? Are they taking advantage of our being foreigners and city dwellers? … We will not get caught in the trap!

We sent home our negotiator as politely as our indignation allowed, and as soon as our little man in his Sunday best disappeared beyond the corner of the barn, there was a family conclave. We took the decision to profit from Jean's apprenticeship at Maître Lafleur's law office, to confuse our plaintiff somewhat. Jean did the research that was asked, but he found no laws on this subject. It was therefore necessary to consider common law, very powerful in Quebec, and research it at our expense. Johnny Morrow and his sons undertook the task at a reasonable cost. It was in this way, with our financial help, that they studied the regulations of the road network of Argenteuil County, that we stayed in good terms with our first neighbours, and that the Morrows were able to buy the separator that allowed them to sell us delicious cream and send butter to Lachute.

OTHER NEIGHBOURS ARE IN less pleasant businesses. The first arrivals, often during our gardening visit of 24 May, are the mosquitoes and the blackflies. Tante Julia from time to time seeing the cheeks and the arms of her nephews covered in blood (that was during the worst season in May and June), ran after them with a smoking pot, hoping to scatter the enemy with a barrage of smoke. At the beginning of August, we were relieved by applying citronella oil, and soon these nasty battalions disappeared of their own accord.

Other neighbours also difficult to dislodge are those who without permission choose to live under the house: amateur whistlers, skunks, very knowledgeable in culinary delights, who penetrated into the cellar, leaving everything upside-down, as well as their special perfume. It was necessary to eliminate them using traps or gunshots. What a gallop we did across the field chasing one of these lovely, furry animals, dragging behind her long majestic tail, and, while running, using without any hesitation the defensive weapon that Providence had given her. If one succeeds in killing her, one of our neighbours will have a scarf and a fur almost as beautiful as one from the silver fox.

Certain years when the winter is long and harsh, the wolves and the bears approach the farms, hoping to find food. My plan to eat fresh lamb and economize on our budget was thwarted, as the following summer we found bloody pieces of wool hanging on the fences, proof that the relationship between wolves and lambs hadn't changed since the good La Fontaine. Sometimes a friendly bear competed with us in the picking of raspberries, and we shot one a few metres from the house in the upper woods.

The Millettes' horses are welcomed when they bring us a cart filled with resinous bark for our stove, or they delight the children in a cart ride. They are real pests when they wander and graze at night around the house. Mr Bieler then jumps out of bed, puts on his nightgown, and chases them, carrying a lamp in one hand and brandishing a cane with the other. It's a real theatrical comedy and funnier for us than for him!

However the horses are the most polite and most honest creatures in comparison with Mrs Cow, who is capable of playing every trick possible. You know the tale of Brunette written by André. She was an angel as compared to the misdeeds of our neighbours' cows. Listen to this:

One Sunday when no one was guarding the house, a whole herd, following the lakeshore behind the bushes, succeeded in getting right onto our lawn. When we returned from a walk, the cows were chewing the remainder of a meal that seemed to us to be suspect. In fact, the buckets used to soak next day's washing, sitting near the lake, were upside down, the sheets, tablecloths, pillow cases, and napkins were on the ground in shreds, while these greedy animals were enjoying the soapy water that they had drunk – and my best towel, which they had swallowed.

We had had a first sample of their appetite the day that Philippe tied our rowboat to the wharf at 16 Island Lake, leaving at the bottom of the boat rolls of cardboard destined to insulate the ceiling of one of our mansard-roofed windows. Having left early the next day with a small cart to fetch the rolls, he returned distressed, saying that they had disappeared! There were animal footprints everywhere on the shore, but all that remained of the cardboard was the wire and the metal pins that held it together. How to explain this robbery? The next day Mr Millette was passing on the road.

"Tell me neighbour," asked Father, "are your cows feeling well today?"

"Not so well," was the answer. "They must have eaten something that didn't agree with them. They are all moaning and haven't produced any milk."

"Nothing surprising," replied Father, "judging from their extraordinary appetite for my ceiling. It's the marine algae contained in the cardboard that tempted them. You have lost your milk, my rolls have disappeared, which means, I guess, that we are even."

If the upstairs room was particularly warm during the hot spell it was the fault of the Millette cows!

If there are animals that are rude and bothersome, there are some that are charming: yellow goldfinches, bluebirds, robins, thrushes calling with a flute-like voices, and these adorable hummingbirds with their long beaks, sucking the sugar from the roses at the edge of the veranda. There are also these lovely brown squirrels that come to pick up the crumbs under our lunch table.

To whom will we pass on La Clairière when we are no longer here? That's what we often ask ourselves when we think of all the effort, of all the work that was accomplished.

THE PRE-WAR YEARS

THERE IS NOTHING OF GREAT IMPORTANCE to say about our 1909–10, 1910–11 winters. The family was all there and well-unified. I ran the household, and was happy in the evening to welcome the family in the Les Colombettes salon. On Sunday I had begun to invite students, a custom I maintained, which brought me great popularity amongst the students.

Dad preached sometimes in one and sometimes in another of our French churches. His ordinary theology and philosophy courses were taken by a limited number of students, and our young French pupils were finding the demands of the authorities of the college to be excessive. They were asked to undertake the same English studies as their English friends, on top of their French program. Dad also gave some lessons in French literature to a group of ladies, and from time to time a conference at the Alliance Française. We were interested in the meetings of the Cercle Français, where literature and music were discussed, and where we had made many friends. We appreciated especially the polite and distinguished secretary, Madame Sophie Cornu. She had retired from her teaching at Macdonald College, and had found a place for Dad's sister, Hélène, who came from Paris to join us in 1910.

The summer of 1911 was for a number of reasons to become important in our life. It was, to start with, at the end of that spring that we had the glorious success of Etienne's entrance exams to McGill. The principal, Mr. Dixon, said that his results were unprecedented, and would never be repeated. Then, Dad's departure for Nova Scotia, where he was bold enough to accept the pulpit of the Presbyterian Church of Stellarton during the month of July. This was a unique opportunity to get into contact with these jolly and very intelligent Scottish groups in Pictou County. This visit to Stellarton introduced him to the Halifax Presbyterian College, known as Pine Hill, which two years later honoured him with a doctorate in theology, *honoris causa*.

AFTER THE STORIES OF OUR NEIGHBOURS, human, four-footed, or winged, it's appropriate to consider our boys. They were certainly worthy of considerable praise for their skilful and steadfast work, for the harmony that had never ceased to rule between them, and for their joy as they went from play to work. We are proud to think that they grew up in an environment with a healthy work ethic, a measure of cheerfulness, and a basis of profound happiness.

There were little clashes. Etienne's precision made it difficult for him to compromise; he didn't accept a straight line not drawn with a plumb line. There was adversity: like the time our second-hand motors didn't work, and we were forced to transport all the construction equipment by rowboat, and pulled by our brave rowers. It suddenly capsized, with the contents disappearing in the water. There were other misadventures that were so amusing that we laughed instead of crying.

Jacques, despite being just eight years old, was already very talented at nailing the roof tiles, but found the hours up there all by himself long and hot, and he wanted his little friend to join him. This new worker was lifted onto the beams that covered the big veranda, and soon our two friends banged hard and in rhythm. But at that moment the dinner bell rang, and at the same time there was a formidable clap of thunder, and soon the rain flowed down the roof and poured directly into our soup bowl, bubbling away in the kettle below. It appeared that Jacques's friend had not sealed the joints properly. Here on in the amateurs would be excluded!

IN 1913 WE WENT TO EUROPE WITH ETIENNE AND JACQUES. We saw parents and friends, fascinated to hear our tales: we told them about the endless frontier and the opportunity for millions of Europeans to come and seek their fortune. To their ears it sounded like the Eldorado, dreamt and sung about by the ancient poets.— Blanche Bieler (BB)

Westmount, 6 April 1913

To my children,

As your mother and I leave for Europe, we are feeling the need to leave you a few helpful words in the event of a tragedy or an accident in Europe that would leave you without our care. These things happen, and one needs to be ready for anything.

If such a development did happen, it wouldn't be us that would suffer. We are leaving our trust and our confidence to Him, who never abandons his own. We are also asking Him for his grace and His goodness in overseeing your needs.

We are asking that the four youngest accept their eldest brother, Jean's, affection and authority, to ensure their moral and material needs. We expect that the youngest would do their best to remain unified. Etienne would share the responsibility with Jean.

Your resources would be very modest. Mother's assets are about $20,000, to which is added the premium from two life insurance policies, one of $2,000 from the London Union (see attached document), and the other for $2,000 from the Mutual Life of Waterloo. These two policies are intended to cover the loan of $4,000 that I gave to your mother for the purchase of Les Colombettes. Certain better investments with these funds would have allowed her to generate $1,200 to $1,400 per year.

I own Les Colombettes. It would have to be sold or let. If let, it should generate about $700 to $800 per year, but $100 in taxes needs to be deducted.

I have a special insurance of $2,000, covering travel accidents in steamships or railways (see attached documents).

La Clairière is an asset, but we have to consider the $400 of further costs for property improvements, as well as $40 for Etienne's trip to Europe. Once finished, the property could generate $100 per year. You also have a little money at the Caisse d'Epargne Fatio in Geneva.

These small investments, well administered, could generate about $1,800 per year. That's an almost secure daily bread, during your years of education. I think that your Tante Julia, so faithfully attached to all of you, would agree to come and share your life until Jacques is of age. You would set yourselves up in a modest lodging, and each one would do his best to share his possessions.

Jean could take a part of his share to fund his law degree. Etienne also, for his engineering degree. André, once he has graduated from his technical school, should seek a job in an architectural firm. Philippe, once he has passed his matriculation, could think about becoming a businessman. Jacques seems to be well suited to become an engineer.

It would be good if your small inheritance remained intact, other than for necessary expenditures, right up to the time that Jacques is of age, and that Tante Julia is still with you.

Dr Scrimger, Professor Morin, and Mr Eugene Lafleur would give you necessary advice. The latter would be invited to assist you with regard to all legal matters. Tante Hélène would, of course, help.

I would like Tante Julia to be your official guardian, if the laws of Quebec permit it. If not, Professor Morin could be considered.

Pray that God bless you dear children, and that He teaches you to serve and love Him.

Charles

THE PRE-WAR HOLIDAYS WERE WONDERFUL. As the renovations advanced, there was more time for entertainment: swimming in the lake, climbing the minor summits of the area, trips by canoe to explore the lakes and portages, and long walks. Jacques's birthday was a big occasion, and he invited the whole neighbourhood for a vast picnic. After the baseball game, we picked up the provisions and we finished the evening by a huge bonfire, telling stories and singing many songs. Then another party in September, decorated by autumn colours and filled with lovely surprises.

In 1914 we lived once again at La Clairière, braving the great horde of mosquitoes and blackflies. Dad had come in the spring with Etienne and André to complete the installations left in a quite rudimentary state in 1912, and they installed panelling and flooring, while Jacques Grellet, a relative of our cousin Virst, was planting a garden with every possible vegetable.—(BB)

EARLY THAT SUMMER IT WAS THE ANNUAL LAKE FRASER PICNIC, a good two-hour walk from La Clairière. It was a splendid afternoon, and the family certainly didn't think that this party might be uniting them all for the last time. Since they were bringing the food, and Blanche wasn't feeling very energetic, they stopped at the Morrows to pick up some supplies. Johnny decided to drop out, because the barley needed to be harvested and he was concerned about leaving his animals. They didn't seem to be in a rush, but all of a sudden Blanche felt a push, and landed in the bottom of the hay cart. Four strong men dressed in white picked up the tow bar, and, despite her cries and protests, they took off at full speed along the sandy shore. Three miles later, they arrived at Laurel on the shore of Lake Fraser. Her horses recovered their breath and they built a huge bonfire, followed by a picnic, perfumed with smoke and the scent of blackberries. Later still, as an Egyptian Princess, but at a more moderate rate, they returned her home on the lower road.—(CB)

La Clairière

Lunch at La Clairière

CHAPTER THREE

1914

Princess Patricia inspecting the Princess Patricia's Canadian Light Infantry

BLANCHE AND CHARLES WERE AT LA CLAIRIÈRE on that fateful day in late June when they heard that Archduke Franz Ferdinand had been shot. They had been following the developments and were concerned about the growing tensions between Germany and its neighbours, but like most everybody else in Canada, they didn't think that the assassination would have much impact on their lives.

They returned to Montreal in early August, much earlier than usual. They had taken the train back to make their usual appearance at the ceremony for Swiss National Day. Jean was in Paris at Neuilly at the Merle d'Aubigné family reunion. On 1 August, Germany declared war on Russia, and on 3 August on France. On 30 July, Britain's foreign secretary, Sir Edward Grey, had received a proposal from the German chancellor, asking Britain to remain neutral, but admitting that Germany intended to violate Belgium's neutrality. The House of Commons had previously strongly voted in favour of staying out of the war, but now could not breach the pact that had been signed between Britain, France, and Belgium. Thus, on 3 August, Britain was also at war with Germany.

On a very hot and stormy 1 August, with weary limbs and heavy hearts, the family headed to a restaurant to celebrate the Swiss National Day. The mood was far from joyful, faces were anxious, plates were hardly touched, and wine remained in the glasses. The younger ladies discussed in low voices the probable departure of their husbands. When Henri Martin, the Swiss consul, got up to toast the homeland, he was so emotional that he could hardly speak. There was no applause, no singing, and they all went home early, as one does after a funeral.

The month of August was otherwise quite pleasant. It was nice to wake up to that faint red haze in the distance, and to feel the breath of still-cool night air streaming through the window. And, now that the period of uncertainty was past, a great wave of loyal demonstrations surged across Canada. The crowds in the streets of Montreal were enthusiastic, and the singing of "La Marseillaise" and "Rule, Britannia" was accompanied by impromptu parades, flag-waving, speech-making, and the honking of colourful automobiles. Sir Wilfrid Laurier, the former prime minister, joined his successor, Sir Robert Borden, in his enthusiasm for joining Britain in the conflict. Although Canada had only three thousand trained soldiers, another sixty thousand had been training under the auspices of a citizens' army, and were anxious to join in. There was no lack of enthusiasm, but the reality was that the equipment and the training programs left a lot to be desired. There were few uniforms and rifles, what boots there were leaked like sieves, and the cavalry was in the same proportion to the total army as it had been during the Boer War. Meanwhile, by mid-August the Germans had marched through Belgium and were within fifty miles of Paris.

At the beginning, Charles thought that the only concern for the boys would be the threat of recruitment. Even if the Kaiser was to start shooting his guns, how could that have an effect on a totally neutral Swiss family that had immigrated to a country with pacific designs, and whose interests were entirely

North American? Events were to prove him wrong. Already, the advances by the German army and the inability of the Allies to do much about it were becoming increasingly worrying. Jean hadn't been concerned about leaving for Europe only a few weeks before, and hadn't had difficulty in finding an Italian ship on its way to Marseille. But would he now find one to take him back? They wondered where it would stop. If the Germans walked into Paris, who was going to stop them from crossing the Channel? Hopefully, it was a better barrier than the fence at the Belgian border. A lot of Etienne's class was British, and they had only one thought: that was to pack a rifle and bayonet and get on a boat as soon as possible

Their next-door neighbour, Mrs Cook, was German, and when they told her about the successes of the Allies, she would pull out a German paper that was telling another story: a rapid invasion of Belgium, a push into France right up to the Marne, the eternal "nach Paris" of the Prussians. Who was one to believe? A friend of hers at the German embassy was worried about rumours that the Canadian government was going to send them home. "Which side am I on?"

AS SOON AS THE FAMILY RETURNED TO MONTREAL PERMANENTLY, at the start of the university classes, they were under no illusion about what was going to happen. As honourable and dutiful citizens, there would ·be nothing to hold back the boys. Already two of them were almost always in khaki, and spending all their spare time in military drill. Another worry was Jean's difficulty in finding a way back to Canada, particularly as he wrote that the Swiss Army wanted to meet with him, given his dual citizenship as a Swiss Canadian. Fortunately, the transatlantic ships were more heavily booked in the opposite direction, and he hadn't lived in Switzerland since he was a baby.

A new Montreal regiment was being created. Apparently, the day before Britain officially declared war, Captain Andrew Hamilton Gault, a Montreal veteran of the South African War, approached the government about the creation of a regiment funded in part by his donation of $100,000. It was to be named, after Princess Patricia, the daughter of the Governor General, the Duke of Connaught. Volunteers, mostly former British citizens from across Canada, joined within days, and were to leave for France at the end of August. Given Captain Gault's association with Montreal and McGill, the boys concluded that they were likely to hear more about this development in the weeks to come.

The news about the Princess Pats spread quickly along the corridors of McGill. The Minister of Militia and Defence, Sam Hughes, was pleased with the rapid execution of the decision to enlist as many men as possible. He was also actively putting together a first Canadian contingent to follow the Princess Pats to the Front. However, there had been no provision for replacing the future Princess Pat casualties. Two graduates of McGill, Percival Molson and George McDonald, suggested to the minister that an infantry company be recruited from university men and their friends, to become the basis of reinforcing the Princess Pats. The

(*above*) Les Colombettes 1914. (Left to right) Jean, Etienne, and André;
(*facing page*) André's Attestation Paper, confirming his agreement to volunteer

University Companies would come into being in early 1915, and lose no time in beginning to recruit. Recruiting officers at the principal universities collected men and sent them forward to Montreal. The McGill buildings were used as a mobilization centre, and the training was initially conducted by Major A.S. Eve, a McGill Physics professor.

By mid-September 1914 Jean suddenly reappeared, ready to start his second year at the law faculty. He had finally been able to book a transatlantic passage and a way to get from Paris to the coast. Etienne was completing his last year in undergraduate Physics. In his spare time, he had created a scientific club, where he and a group of fellow physicists did certain experiments not usually done at the university lab. He was an avid botanist, and often accompanied an old pastor in long walks in the mountains. He also took his religious education with his father seriously, and its influence was important and helped to develop his sense of humility and perseverance. André entered the Institut Technique de Montréal, where he developed his skills in mechanics and drawing, in preparation for the courses in architecture that he would take at McGill in the future. The two youngest were less affected by the events, and went to school in Westmount, as before.

Between the regular training exercises, and the establishment of the mobilization centre, McGill became more and more a hub of military activity. Etienne was particularly closely involved, as Major Eve was also one of his physics professors. In January 1915, the 1st University Company was being organized, and in mid-March both Etienne and André volunteered. Jean, because of his poor eyesight,

Original

ATTESTATION PAPER.

No. *A10963*

Folio. *B.10*

CANADIAN OVER-SEAS EXPEDITIONARY FORCE.

QUESTIONS TO BE PUT BEFORE ATTESTATION.

(ANSWERS).

1. What is your name? .... *André Charles Bieler*
2. In what Town, Township or Parish, and in what Country were you born? .... *Lausanne Switzerland*
3. What is the name of your next-of-kin? .... *Charles Bieler*
4. What is the address of your next-of-kin? .... *98 Columbia Ave Westmount P.Q.*
5. What is the date of your birth? .... *Oct 8 1897 1896*
6. What is your Trade or Calling? .... *Student*
7. Are you married? .... *No*
8. Are you willing to be vaccinated or re-vaccinated? .... *Yes*
9. Do you now belong to the Active Militia? .... *No*
10. Have you ever served in any Military Force? .. *as Cadet at school*
    If so, state particulars of former Service.
11. Do you understand the nature and terms of your engagement? .... *Yes*
12. Are you willing to be attested to serve in the CANADIAN OVER-SEAS EXPEDITIONARY FORCE? .... *Yes*

A. Bieler (Signature of Man).

E.M. Nope (Signature of Witness).

DECLARATION TO BE MADE BY MAN ON ATTESTATION.

I, *André Charles Bieler*, do solemnly declare that the above answers made by me to the above questions are true, and that I am willing to fulfil the engagements by me now made, and I hereby engage and agree to serve in the Canadian Over-Seas Expeditionary Force, and to be attached to any arm of the service therein, for the term of one year, or during the war now existing between Great Britain and Germany should that war last longer than one year, and for six months after the termination of that war provided His Majesty should so long require my services, or until legally discharged.

Date *15th March* 1915

A. Bieler (Signature of Recruit)

E.M. Nope (Signature of Witness)

OATH TO BE TAKEN BY MAN ON ATTESTATION.

I, *André Charles Bieler* do make Oath, that I will be faithful and bear true Allegiance to His Majesty King George the Fifth, His Heirs and Successors, and that I will as in duty bound honestly and faithfully defend His Majesty, His Heirs and Successors, in Person, Crown and Dignity, against all enemies, and will observe and obey all orders of His Majesty, His Heirs and Successors, and of all the Generals and Officers set over me. So help me God.

A. Bieler (Signature of Recruit)

Date *15 March* 1915

J. G. Hall (Signature of Witness)

CERTIFICATE OF MAGISTRATE.

The Recruit above-named was cautioned by me that if he made any false answer to any of the above questions he would be liable to be punished as provided in the Army Act.

The above questions were then read to the Recruit in my presence.

I have taken care that he understands each question, and that his answer to each question has been duly entered as replied to, and the said Recruit has made and signed the declaration and taken the oath before me, at *Montreal* this *15th* day of *March* 1915.

A.N. Grier J.P. (Signature of Justice)

I certify that the above is a true copy of the Attestation of the above-named Recruit.

Gregor Barclay (Approving Officer)

A Dulmage Lt Col

M. F. W. 23.
150 M.—12-14.
H.Q. 1772-30-341.

was not considered eligible for the front lines, and could legitimately have stayed in Canada. However, he was intent on serving, and managed to join, as a secretary, an ambulance unit created and equipped by the Faculty of Medicine. André was eighteen, too young and not physically strong, but he was influenced by his two elder brothers' decision. By law he wasn't able to volunteer without the authorization of his parents, and they felt that giving two sons was already enough. Charles and Blanche finally agreed, hoping that he wouldn't pass the physical exam. Unfortunately, however, he was found to be in good health, and he volunteered, even a few days before his brothers. Etienne and André were immediately enrolled in the 1st University Company, which was later absorbed by the Princess Patricia's Canadian Light Infantry.

CHAPTER FOUR

The Front

January to July 1915

Lancashire Fusiliers in a trench

Blanche, Charles, and the five boys celebrated Easter of 1915 together at the Béthanie church, for the last time. Shortly after, Etienne and André left for Camp Niagara to undertake two months of training. It was while they were at the camp that Etienne received from McGill, in absentia, the gold medal and the diploma of Bachelor of Arts. After that, they would be going abroad to the Canadian Training Camp at Shorncliffe, Kent. Jean left for France, this time in uniform, on 11 May 1915, only six weeks later.

ETIENNE AND ANDRÉ'S FIRST LETTERS, written at the Shorncliffe Camp in England, started to arrive in early May. For Etienne, they would be at intervals of eight, ten, or fifteen days, right up to his return on 20 January 1919, which totals 116 letters during his forty-five-month absence. His letters were so lively, so fresh, so optimistic, so affectionate, so much the faithful image of this exceptionally gifted person. It's important to remember, however, that, if the tone is fun, if the accent suggests the pleasant aspects of this military experience, it's because of censorship, and also Etienne's fear of alarming his parents. Like most of the other soldiers, he is silent about the horrors he has witnessed, and tries to talk about the more pleasant aspects of the war.—(BB)

Camp Niagara, 2 May 1915

My dear mother

We have arrived safely at this camp that seems quite nice, after a rather long but pleasant trip. Soon after our departure we laid down, André and Calder on a bench that is transformed into a deck chair, a little hard but okay, and for me on the wood of the upper bunk. We slept a fair amount, being woken up from time to time by cries like "keep them 'ands behind the seams of them trousers"... imitating the sergeant major.

We were shocked on arrival in Toronto with the news of the Canadians' huge losses in France. We left, with the band ahead of us, from the North Toronto station to the harbour. Two hours later our boat docks at Niagara-on-the-Lake. We have a round tent, 12 feet in diameter, with a wooden floor. We are six, each of us with a rubber sheet and a blanket. The first meal at the camp wasn't too bad. Can you imagine that André bruised his hand while playing baseball, and won't be able to use his gun for one or two days? Bad luck!

Etienne

Easter 1915

Camp Niagara, May 1915

My dear parents

Here is the first letter that I am writing to you since my departure.
We are beginning our real military life. We have worked hard today demolishing all the tents that remained and were no longer useful. I am feeling very well, and Etienne is also.

André

IN EARLY MAY WE WERE AT HOME AT LES COLOMBETTES, and heard that the University boys were preparing to leave Canada. We began to prepare for our soldiers' first leave, including the treats that we would give them. Then, towards the end of the month, we were disappointed to learn that they would not be given a leave, and that the train would bring them straight to the docks, where they would board immediately for England.

We had no choice but to accept, and at least pack the famous treats: the fresh strawberries with cream and sugar, cakes, biscuits, and chocolates were wrapped and brought to the harbour by the four of us (Jean had already left several weeks earlier). A tense wait, and then a whistle and a loud metallic rumble … it was the

Exercising at Camp Niagara (André front, centre, in lighter shirt)

train, where minutes later groups of joyful and noisy khaki shapes flowed out. As soon as we recognized our first dear face, we wanted to jump into his arms! It wasn't to be. Sentiments were not the order of the day. The soldiers lined up in several ranks, waiting for the order to climb the gangplank to the waiting steamship, which was already belching torrents of smoke. Then, breaking all the rules, the mothers, paying no attention to the instructions, broke through the ranks and hugged frantically their sons, and dumped their gifts at their feet. The soldiers, touched by the mothers' emotion, explained that, regrettably, the order was official: furthermore the commanding officer was adamant that they were not allowed to take even the smallest parcel! The families were upset and left with their baskets, and the troops marched up the frail gangplank and were soon swallowed within the big ship.

Then, thoroughly upset by the horrible image of this hasty departure, and the sour feeling about the unnecessary provisions, one of the mothers went to hide behind a pile of crates to cry … and cry! All of a sudden, two muscled arms squeezed her from behind … it was André, who, having refused to comply, had mysteriously escaped to seek a last kiss and the famous baskets. "Please don't cry, dear Mother, we will come back shortly. I will send you Etienne, via this same coal chute." But the propellers began to spin, and soon, to the cries of the soldiers and the waving goodbyes of the assistants, the ship slipped away towards the blue waters of the St Lawrence.—(BB)

SHORNCLIFFE CAMP

7 July 1915

My dear mother,

We arrived in Plymouth yesterday, Tuesday morning, with beautiful weather, after a relatively good crossing that would have been delicious in first class. But we can't complain, as we had a good cabin, while the others were in horrible dormitories in the hold.

We took the train at about noon, and it was only around nine that we arrived at the completely debilitated Shorncliffe station. We are in a camp with wooden huts, quite spacious, and covered with galvanized tin. We each have a little wooden bed with a good mattress and two blankets. We eat our meals in the same hut. Every evening we receive our allotment of bread for the next day. The rest comes before each meal.

You can imagine how happy and surprised we were to see Jean arrive in our hut, all of a sudden, this morning. He's in the same camp, a few paces away. In six weeks or two months, we must be ready to leave. Have we been given a good daily schedule? We get up at 5:30, gymnastics at 8, drill at 9, grenade throwing at 10, bayonet fighting at 11, from 2 to 5 marching and field operations. We dig trenches three times a week, and there are some night exercises from 7 to 10.

Apparently it's not too difficult to get a promotion. I will therefore try.

Etienne

HAVING ARRIVED IN SHORNCLIFFE ON 8 JULY 1915, Etienne and André had only five weeks to enjoy the charm of the English countryside and the games of bowls before embarking to join their regiment at the Front.—(BB)

Shorncliffe, July 1915

My dear mother,

We had Saturday afternoon off, so we took the opportunity to go to Canterbury. At each turning, one runs into a war wounded who has returned from the war, and each one has a story to tell. The officers give us brief lectures when we are resting following a long and fast uphill run, with boots weighing ten pounds on each foot. They say that this war is the least strategic war in history.

We have refilled all the beautiful trenches that we sweated so hard to dig.

André

Etienne (standing) and André

July 1915

My dear father,

At our return from Folkestone, yesterday evening, we were very surprised to find out that we should get ready to leave at 4 p.m. this afternoon. I presume that we will still stay several weeks in the rear before going to the Front, but everything seems to indicate that we will leave for France this afternoon. The only annoyance is that, of our six officers, only the two captains will leave with us. Officers who have had more experience will replace the others. Other than that, we are leaving all together and will become a complete company, as far as we know. I think that I told you that my request for a promotion has been sent to Ottawa.

Etienne

ARRIVAL AT THE FRONT

THE CANADIANS WERE SOON ON ACTIVE DUTY. The 1st Division was the first, and in late February 1915, each brigade, along with its field artillery and engineer, as well as its signal and service men, joined one of two British divisions for a week at the Front. The Canadians were allotted a section that was initially some fifteen kilometres south of Ypres, a few miles north of Armentières. The indoctrination was practical and thorough. The 1915 Battles of Ypres were in full swing.

The first Princess Patricias had landed in France at the end of December 1914, at about the same time as Canada's First Contingent. The force included volunteers from across Canada, who had joined soon after the declaration of war. During the first three months of 1915, the Canadian Forces had served in the St Éloi sector, in the southern part of the Ypres Salient, where there were some particularly fierce battles. In May, the soldiers of the PPCLI distinguished themselves at the Battle of Bellewaarde Ridge. They managed to successfully defend the ridge against a massive attack by the Germans. However, at the conclusion, they were left with only four officers and 150 men, out of their initial strength of 550. The 1st University Company of the PPCLI Regiment was due to arrive shortly thereafter, and Etienne and André were there. They must have been apprehensive about the challenge that they were about to face.

THE 1ST UNIVERSITY COMPANY ARRIVED at Petit Moulin in the neighbourhood of Armentières, very near to Belgian Flanders. This humid and flat plain, which went right up to the shore of the English Channel, still had a certain charm during these summer days, before the war had completely disfigured it. The sails of windmills were still seen turning in the distant hazy horizon, bales of straw were lying near the large farms, shaded by hedges and large trees, while the chimneys of Armentières marked the huge industrial expanse of Flanders.

After the bloody days of Mont St Eloi, the Princess Pats regiment was reorganized, blending the fresh recruits with the old "grumps" of the permanent army. These old-timers loved to talk about their impressive feats to these naïve volunteers, who were eager to learn about the tricks of warfare.—(BB)

Rest Camp, 23 July 1915

My dear mother,

Here we get up at 7, then we have breakfast and tidy up for the 9 o'clock inspection. We then march for two or three hours. We are always followed by women with baskets, who try to sell us mediocre fruit and okay chocolates at crazy prices; it would seem that it's their only source of income, and seeing the crowds of children who beg for pennies at the outskirts of the camp, it seems that the entire country is living off the English and Canadian soldiers.

In the afternoon there is often a cricket match. This afternoon it's between the officers and subalterns and the men of our company. We have supper at 5 p.m. and we go to bed at 9, which gives us 10 hours of sleep, which we sometimes add to during the day. We need to catch up now, as we won't be able to have as much in the trenches.

There are several changes in the Company since we left England. I think that I already told you that only two of our officers came with us: Captains Barclay and McDougall, as platoon commanders. The other two platoons are under the two lieutenants Martin and Stewart, who are in charge of the company. The other three have had experience at the Front. Stewart Forbes is now the sergeant of our platoon. He is certainly one of the best subalterns of the company, but he's not very popular. Our section also has a new corporal, a big and strong student from Queen's called Harvey, who will be damn good.

I forgot to tell you how surprised we were Wednesday afternoon to see Jean arrive. He had gotten a special leave from the colonel, and had been able to stay about an hour. He's about 15 miles from here. It's amusing that we were so close at Shorncliffe, and once again here.

Etienne

29 July 1915

My dear father,

Here we are finally at our regiment's base, a few miles from the Front, and nothing reminds us that we are so close to the enemy lines, except for

*the German planes that venture above us, but at a great height, and the
German bombs that we see explode as soon as our airplanes get close to the
enemy batteries.*

*It was a long night spent in a pile of soldiers, with all their arms
and baggage, in one of these vehicles that the good Vaudois call so
appropriately, "bôites à cailloux." We arrived at 6 in the morning at a
small station, where we were asked to get out. Before they directed us to
our new camping ground, we had the time to have a cup of coffee and
toast at a farm a few yards from the station. A one-hour-and-a-half
march with all our equipment brought us to a camp such as I had never
seen. Instead of parallel lines of white tents with pointed roofs, there were
a few wooden and canvas huts painted in the strangest way to mislead
the enemy airplanes and some small shelters for two, made of rubberized
canvas and branches. We are twenty-five in a low hut, about the size of
the Les Colombettes living room. André preferred to build a shelter with
his friend Stewart.*

*While the rest of our company were going to spend half the night
digging reserve trenches, we, the new arrivals, went to bed, early, to rest
from the previous night. This morning we had an inspection from the
regimental colonel, and this afternoon was again free. We went to the
river a few paces from here to take a good bath. You will be reassured that
we are in an area little exposed to the Front. The trenches are said to be
spacious, healthy, and well maintained, and don't suffer from enemy
artillery fire. We will do seven-day shifts in the front lines, fourteen days
in reserve, then we will return for seven days at the base.*

Etienne

THE BOYS' SITUATION BECAME much more serious: camouflaged huts, thorough
inspections, enemy airplanes, exploding shells and bombs. They were in fact not
very far from the action. Trench warfare required many activities: pails of sand to
fill, trenches to dig, night guards to be set up. The best moment was when the mail
arrived, especially if a good letter was accompanied by some tasty parcels. They
enjoyed cooking the contents with groups of friends, as a change from the daily
rations. Water often needed to be pumped from a far-away abandoned farm, and
the wood, including broken fence posts, old boxes, etc., was picked up as best they
could! It was fortunate that this part of Armentières was fairly quiet and that the
countryside became idyllic only a few miles from the trenches: the setting sun would
light up the old farms, the young poplars turned golden, and the wheat fields were
illuminated with rays of sunlight.—(BB)

Petit Moulin
Armentières, 30 July 1915

My dear Philippe,

We are resting this evening watching the airplanes being shot at by anti-aircraft guns, both German and British. It's very exciting. Apparently the planes are not often hit.

What we call the base is the camp of the PPCLI or a field with a few huts made by the soldiers from rubber sheets and all kinds of branches of every description. The officers have the Bell tents, all smeared with paint to render them invisible for the airplanes. Another guy and I have made a tent with our two rubber sheets, and we have had the good luck of finding a blanket.

This afternoon we went swimming in a river a few steps away from the camp. There's a springboard made from all the odds and ends possible and imaginable. It seems funny to be swimming with the sound of the guns and watched vigilantly by an observation balloon.

André

NO. 3 CANADIAN GENERAL HOSPITAL

IT WAS PERHAPS FITTING that Jean, the eldest of the five boys, was the first to arrive in France. In his case, his stay in England was very brief, and he and his colleagues wasted no time to begin to set up temporary hospital facilities on the shores of the Channel. The ambulance, I should say McGill's hospital, officially called the No. 3 Canadian General Hospital, was initially camped in tents and quite basic barracks at Camiers, near Boulogne. Jean, particularly in the beginning, had to accept living conditions that were far from comfortable, and often within a tent on two blankets laid on the ground. He was initially an assistant in the registrar's office.—(BB)

YMCA, Field Branch
NO. 3 General Hospital (McGill)
Canadian Expeditionary Force
22 June 1915

My dear parents,

Having left Southampton on the 17th, we arrived here last Saturday. We then travelled all night on a cattle boat that brought us to a port in Northern France, very early the following morning. We were well escorted, so that there were no concerns about submarines. We had to sleep on deck, but as it wasn't cold, we didn't suffer.

Camiers Hospital, 1915

As the boat was quite slow it was only early the following day that we landed. After the disembarking of the five hundred horses that we had on board, we began to unload our cars, food supplies, comfortable beds, tents, etc. There was a well-organized group of cranes, which loaded our open vans directly. The ambulances were waiting to transport us to the high ground behind the town, where a rest camp for the soldiers coming to and from the Front was located. The next morning, the train took us to an unknown destination. After a forty-minute trip on the train/bus, we arrived at a station located between two tiny French villages. It was a typical coastal countryside, with few trees and numerous hills between the sea and the sand dunes. We were ordered to immediately unload the twenty vans filled with all our equipment. The Army Service Corp. from a nearby base had given us a dozen huge cars, so that the job was quickly completed. I think that we were all disappointed to see that we weren't the only hospital in the area. Four other hospitals are in the process of being established here, and we are only separated by the width of the many roads that criss-cross our huge camp. There is only one that is ready to receive the wounded; the others will be opened in due course. Obviously, this arrangement has also

Blanche Bieler; Charles Bieler

certain big advantages; we will soon have water just about everywhere, and electricity will also be connected in the near future. The YMCA is building a huge wooden barrack, and the canteen is well-furnished with all sorts of equipment. Our camp is on a slight slope descending towards the railway. Since the beginning of the week we have moved into our permanent tents. My mates are very pleasant, including: Henry Fry, one of my classmates, Elder, the trumpet player, and Rankin, one of the office employees.

In total, we will have about two hundred tents, and the hospital wards will contain twenty beds. The only buildings are the kitchens, the operating rooms, and the showers. The camp is square, with the hospital in the centre, offices to the west, nurses, soldiers, and junior officers to the south, and, to the north, soldiers that have been sent back from the Front to do the heavy work.

I don't think that my French is very useful, as the wounded are now carefully sorted before being sent to the various hospitals.

Jean

THE CANADIAN FAMILY

MEANWHILE, BACK AT HOME, the twelve months that elapsed from March 1915 to March 1916 marked an especially rich and emotional period. At the moment that

Philippe Bieler

the war eliminated the moral support of the eldest boys, God gave us Philippe, and soon Jacques, a wonderful compensation: two real friends, sharing our worries and doubling all our joy. Philippe was transformed. It was like a return to all the charming qualities of his childhood, with, on top of it, a nice virility, a new sense of helpfulness, and a mysterious depth. The family chores included looking after the two boys, and Camille Chazeaud, who was also often there, as well as mailing the overseas parcels. Philippe's presence helped to make it happen. With him, our large house, despite all its empty places, didn't seem too gloomy, but it was at La Clairière, which we all loved so much, that he particularly displayed his ingenuity and his energy. Our cavalier's role as service engineer wasn't restricted to home. He was in charge of delivering all the messages to those who lived around the lake, as the war had eliminated the mothers' usual messengers. His boat was in constant use, free of charge, as postal van, taxi to the train station, delivery boat, or church carriage. He did all that, even the hauling of the weeds from our vegetable garden, with a smile.

Philippe was starting his second year at McGill in the Faculty of Commerce, and became deeply involved in the traditional student initiations. At one point they did a mock battle in the Mount Royal woods. It was a fun story to describe to our boys,

Jacques Bieler

who were fighting the real war, and their laughter could be heard across the ocean! Jacques was also growing up, and became quite adept at the various trades required at La Clairière. He and Philippe had engineered the water installation there, a useful initiation into his future profession.

But it was wartime, which was difficult at the beginning and strange and uncertain as the years progressed. We were threatened once again with Philippe's approaching departure. I tried to console myself by cutting fabric and rolling bandages in the Red Cross rooms at McGill, but that wasn't enough to satisfy my emotions. I needed more and better activity than that. I eventually was to find it with my war relief activity.

For your father, it was a constantly changing scene. The house was depopulated, but so were the classes at the college. He would have risked remaining idle if the sudden death of Principal Scrimger hadn't abruptly changed his position. Professor Fraser became interim principal of the Presbyterian College, and a year later, principal. They asked your father to replace him as registrar, and this function put him in a close and constant relationship with all the students of the college, English as well as French.—(BB)

CHAPTER FIVE

Training

August 1915 to January 1916

St Martin's Plain, Shorncliffe Camp

THE SPRING OF 1915, one of the bloodiest periods on the Western Front, was followed during the balance of the year without a major battle involving the Canadians.

FIRST DAYS AT THE FRONT

OUR YOUNG SOLDIERS LOOKED FORWARD to their summer rest periods: they called them "glorious picnics," which were often quite exciting. They built huts and tents. André, with his friend Stewart, built a very comfortable shelter. They swam in the Lys, a small lazy river that wasn't bothered by the war and continued to flow peacefully towards the Escaut, and they played games in the fields, now dried by the good weather.—(BB)

9 August 1915

My dear mother,

I want first of all to reassure you about our security. Here we are in the trenches, but everything is so quiet that one feels almost at home. In fact, everything is organized for the best. I think that you can also count on us not to expose ourselves unnecessarily to a bombardment, but even in a relatively quiet Front there can be accidents. You will have heard about the death of Bill Lester. It was a terrible shock for all of us, as he was one of the most loved in the company, always so jovial, and in good humour, and he is up until now the only one who has received even a scratch. But I think that, if I were to die, like him, I would be ready. I am counting on the Lord's pardon.

You will be happy to know that André and I are together, and both of us perfectly well. We do our little cooking with Bruneau and Stewart and with the addition of what we have bought in town before leaving, and a few surprises from Tante Julia, we are coping very well.

Etienne

10 August 1915

Dear Jacques,

We are thinking of you during your birthday, while hearing the "Wisbangs" whistling over our heads.

It's not something that one likes to tell his mother, but we are a little flea-ridden, which is not very pleasant for those not used to it. We wash in water, which is not of a quality even equal to the contents of the pail under the kitchen sink, but what can you do, that's life in the trenches! It's quite funny to be there after having heard so much about it.

André

The Lys River

PPCLI A.10963
19 August 1915

My dear mother,

We have had a lot of rain these last few days, and we naturally enjoy the inevitable mud in our sleeping holes. However, since we don't sleep very often nor for very long, having had only two hours of rest last night, and the two hours weren't all in a row, you can imagine that I was in a great mood, while cooking our breakfast with wet wood and kneeling in the mud!

We are completing our period in the saphead, a kind of passageway leading towards the German trenches. The other night when I was on guard, I almost thought that I was at 16 Island Lake, as the machine guns looked so much like speedboats. The German machine guns are absolutely like Millette's speedboat, while the British ones look like an old two-cylinder motorboat.

If you think that you are the only ones who eat well, you are completely wrong. How would you like a good dish of potatoes, cooked in bacon grease and topped up with cheese, or an excellent dish of roast potatoes cooked in bacon and sprinkled with tomatoes?

André

26 August 1915

My dear mother,

Here is André returning from the rear. He hadn't been feeling well, and the doctor sent him there for two days. He's come back with a flourishing expression, on foot, with a bag on his back and gun on his shoulder, saying that he had enjoyed a little rest in a nearby village schoolroom, surrounded by a nice garden and a few trips in a motorized ambulance to distract him. Let's hope he doesn't have to go to a hospital for something more serious.

Like the last time, André and I are in an advanced position, a "sap," which is about sixty metres ahead of the first-line trenches. We get a little less sleep than in the other positions. With twelve men and a corporal, we need to furnish two guards all night long for three positions, but on the other hand we have more time to rest during the day. While the others spend a good part of the day digging and filling sand bags, all we have to do is deliver these two guards, while the others read, write, cook, and sleep. Sydney Bruneau, André, and I have adopted the system of two meals a day at about 10 a.m. and 5 p.m. We prefer to have a good sleep from sunrise to about 9 o'clock. That's when one of us gets up to prepare the 10 a.m. meal. The first problem is water. We need to walk ten minutes zigzagging in the trenches right up to the yard of a ruined farm to procure the precious liquid. In addition, it looked as though the Germans would cut our water supply for good when one day we saw that they had located a machine gun there to protect it. Fortunately, they moved on, so we can once again go there to get the water for our coffee and cocoa. The chef's second problem is to find wood. Our rations are received raw, and all that we get to cook them is coke that doesn't burn in an open fire. We have to steal what we can, maybe a box, or a board, or a fence post. In the evening, the same process to prepare the dinner. The rations consist of bacon, bread, cheese, jam, tea, sugar, and from time to time condensed milk, butter, or tinned stew. I'm not counting the boxes of meat from Chicago, the "bully beef" that no one eats if he can find something else.

The morning and evening meals are interrupted by two inspections that we could well do without. In the morning it's the sanitary service, "Corporal Chloride" as we call him. He passes with a pail of chloride that he spreads amply on the floor of the trenches and the dugouts, and is furious with a red face when he sees uncovered food or dirty plates. The poor guy, I think we frustrate him. In the evening, it's the inspection of the rifles. An officer comes along with the sergeant major and a sergeant. Each rifle must shine both inside and out, and horrors for someone whose rifle is not absolutely clean, even if it's one speck of dust.

Etienne

3 September 1915

My dear father,

Our battalion has left the trenches and here we are once again all reunited
at the rest camp where we had rejoined our regiment six weeks ago. In our
absence they have built many new tents, which means that we can all be
sheltered, as well as the 2nd University Company, who have joined us here.

Yesterday afternoon, André and I and two others got a leave to go to
the nearby village. As we went by the old Gothic church, the sound of the
organ attracted us, and we sat and listened for a few minutes to the old
Highlander playing the organ. Afterwards, I continued alone right up to
the next town. The town is almost abandoned by the civilians as a result of
the bombardment, but I think that the absent are more than replaced by the
British soldiers.

I have just heard that my name was mentioned in Shorncliffe's promotion
announcements.

Etienne

6 September 1915

My dear parents,

Briefly, our battalion spent the month in trenches quite close to Armentières,
in an especially secure section of the Front. The Germans are more than
three hundred metres from our trenches at this place, and don't seem to
want to do anything much. After a fifteen-day rest, the Patricias have to
enter other trenches nearby. I don't think that they will be more dangerous
or more uncomfortable than the last ones. Since the arrival of the 2nd
Company the regiment has been reorganized. André is in the 2nd platoon
of the 2nd Company. His lieutenant is M. Trevin, who we have had since
the beginning, and his sergeant McClean, who you will have seen at the
departure in Montreal. McClean is a much-loved sergeant. He is firm
and soft, a combination that you don't often find. Unfortunately, the
reorganization has divided our section. They have put some new men and
some veterans in the four sections of the platoon. However André is still in
the same section as Stewart, and is never very far from his former friends of
the old Section 5.

Etienne

7 September 1915

My dear mother,

We are still the two of us together, and nothing indicates that we are to
be separated soon. You seem to think, dear mother, that it's only at La

Clairière that one can have beautiful quiet evenings, but one couldn't imagine a countryside as charming as this old farm in the midst of the wheat fields, where the golden bunches are waiting to be picked, and with these tall poplars along the side of the roads that zigzag through this fertile plain. Only the sound of an airplane circling overhead and the spanking new reserve trench, which hopefully will never be used, reminds us that we are fighting a war.

Etienne

OFFICER TRAINING

ONE MORNING, Etienne and three mates are called by the warrant officer. The command is to leave immediately for an officer training school in England. Mostly good news, but it isn't without some regret that the two brothers leave in different directions from the small train station in Steenwerck. Being together was like being at home away from home!

The officer school is in Shorncliffe, and everything seemed quite charming to a private coming from the trenches: a dry and stylish uniform rather than the wet khaki, a ceremonial mess replacing a dirty shelter, clean, comfortable beds after the mud and the vermin over there, intellectual stimulation instead of passive obedience. It was new, stimulating, and was to last five months that went by quickly, as the days were full with the theory, the exercises, the equitation, then, during the breaks, with sports and walks in the lovely English countryside in all its autumn glory. There were also the charming visits to the Penrose-Fitzgerald cousins in Folkestone, and some interesting weekends in London. The clubs, the theatres, the friends, the welcome at the Swiss church, all of it attracted Etienne.—(BB)

Folkestone, 8 September 1915

My dear father,

I can't believe my eyes, but here I am in a hotel room in Folkestone, instead of waking up in my tent corner near Armentières. You will have learned from the telegram that I sent you that I have finally gotten this famous promotion, but it seems as though it's not in the artillery. I need to meet this morning with the colonel.

Yesterday morning at 9:30 we were all lined up in the camp's exercise field for the inspection of our equipment when the sergeant major called my name and asked me to see the adjutant. There, I met three others who had been called in the same way. He tells us that he has the order to send us immediately to England to receive our promotion.

André accompanied me right up to the Steenwerck station.

Etienne

10 September 1915

My dear mother,

I have a nice little room in one of the huts reserved for officers. It has a galvanized tin roof, quite nice furniture, and varnished white wood walls. I have a batman to shine my shoes, do my room, prepare my morning bath, etc. You can imagine, my dear mother, how funny this seems to me.

At 6:30 p.m. the bugle blows for dinner. It is a fairly formal gathering: the officers are placed in order of rank around a big table of a T-shape and sit when the colonel has said grace. The meal is very good and well served, but beware about arriving late, as one has to excuse oneself to the colonel. After dessert there is always a toast to the king, made by the colonel.

Thursday morning, my friend H.S. and I went to London, with only a three-day leave to order our uniforms and all that we need. The government is generous for that, but it seems to me that it's the tailors and the stores who profit the most. We receive £50 for our equipment. That seems to be a lot of money when one needs to spend £1 for a cap, and £4 for a tunic.

As I left the Paymaster's office and walked down Whitehall, I saw a familiar face, and sure enough it was Sergeant H. Mathewson, who had just come from Shorncliffe for a few days in London. He is one of those that joined the so-called Mounted Rifles, an infantry regiment who are currently in Shorncliffe.

Etienne

17 September 1915

My dear father,

I'll try to send you one or two photographs of our huts. There are four huts for sleeping, divided into little rooms of about thirteen feet by nine, and a larger hut for the mess and the kitchen. They are set in a half-circle on the edge of a plateau covered with soldiers' huts and overlooking the sea. Wednesday afternoon I went to have tea at the Fitzgeralds', who were surprised to see me back so soon from the Front. While I have time I will go and see a few of my friends in the nearby camps. The Montreal Rifles, with Paul Black and Nicholson, are very close to here. Jean also asks me to see Arthur Mathewson at the Highlanders, who are in the same section of Shorncliffe as us.

Etienne

BLANCHE'S FIRST COUSIN had married Admiral Charles Fitzgerald, and they lived in Folkestone, a few miles from the Shorncliffe Camp. Etienne developed a close relationship with them during his long visits to Shorncliffe.

Admiral Charles Fitzgerald was for many years second-in-command of the Admiralty's China Station. He is best known for the controversy that arose following a poorly translated version of an article he wrote for the *Deutsche Review*. The Germans interpreted it as saying that Britain would be better served by a war sooner rather than later, when the German navy would be larger. Partly in order to regain his image in Britain, he organized a group of women in Folkestone to distribute white feathers to men not in uniform. It was reported in the press and rapidly spread across the country.

26 September 1915

My dear mother,

I am very lucky to be able to take this course that is both complete and interesting, but I think that at the end of the three months I will have had enough of this easy life here, and that I will look forward to going back to the Front and to doing something useful as soon as possible. I wonder when my turn will come up. There are so many officers ahead of me on the list that something would need to happen if my turn was ever to materialize.

Etienne

15 October 1915

Dear Philippe,

André wrote about how the French took the German prisoners and replaced them with men from his battalion in the trenches and how they were bombarded by German shells of poor quality that for the most part didn't explode.

My day starts at 6:15 a.m. when my batman comes to wake me. He also takes my shoes to shine them and my belt to burnish it. At 9 we must be on our horses and lined up in front of the stables of the cavalry school. During an hour and a half we do equitation exercises. We have then two courses until 12:30. The afternoon courses are from 2 to 5:30, and from time to time a course of topography in the field.

On Sunday I attended a service at the small Anglican church. The clergyman was an amusing old man who told us quietly that he would read us the sermon he had prepared eleven years ago!

Etienne

Otter Pool

20 October 1915

My dear Philippe,

Saturday afternoon, Robertson, one of the officers in our battalion, and I had the good idea to ride for more than three hours, right up to the Otter Pool camp, about five miles from here, and had tea in a well-kept little inn on the side of the road. Robertson, who was leading, wearing a raincoat, looked like a major or a colonel, followed by a lieutenant carrying an order. In any case that's how we interpreted the salute that we received from the officers that we passed.

Etienne

25 October 1915

My dear mother,

You ask if I have some good friends? ... Yes, certainly. I see mostly the ten that are at the military school with me. They may not all have the same ideas as me, but there are many great guys amongst them, and I have good relations with everyone.

You then tell me that, according to Mr Roussel, one finds in France that the English officers could have a more complete and more scientific preparation. That's absolutely true and quite inevitable in a completely new

*army. But, since we have the opportunity to spend a little time to prepare,
it's up to us to make sure that we don't merit this reproach.*

*I'm sure that you will be happy to receive these few letters received in
Jean's last letter. It's curious that a French officer had the right to give
such complete details of the operation of his battery as described in Cousin
Emile's letter.*

*As reported by various people who have come back from the trenches, I
hear that André is now in the rear, at a rest camp about twelve miles behind
the lines. The regiment certainly deserves a little rest after three weeks in the
trenches.*

Etienne

31 October 1915

My dear father,

*Yesterday we had to stay inside and waste the greater part of the day.
But Thursday and Friday of last week, we were building bridges across
the Hythe Canal, like those built by the English at the time of Napoleon's
projected invasion, where he could have easily landed on a dry lowland.
First of all we built two sections of a bridge of about the same style as
Caesar's bridge across the Rhine, and then a gangway for the pedestrians,
lying on barrels. It's an interesting job, but I don't think that we would ever
have to build such bridges at the Front.*

Etienne

AT THE BEGINNING OF THE AUTUMN, when Etienne left for England, it seemed
as though there was adversity in all directions. In the trenches, during the endless
bombardments, the soldiers began living like cavemen. There were vermin attacks,
continuous rain that soaked them from head to foot, and greasy sticky mud from
the waist down. Night-time brought little relief, with only a wet blanket to protect
them from the cold and damp environment. The sunny carefree days were few and
far between. We guess about all this in reading between the lines of André's letters.
However, he doesn't exaggerate the dangers and deprivations, trying on the contrary to show the acceptable sides of the situation.—(BB)

10 September 1915

My dear parents,

*I have just received your good letter of 21 August that made me very happy,
especially as a replacement for the sudden departure of my secretary,
Etienne, who was suddenly called back to England. This was very sad for
me, but I was expecting it.*

We are finishing our rest camp, and will go back to the trenches next week. We each received a blanket the other day, which I can assure you wasn't too much, as we have had to continually get up and run in the fields to warm up.

Mother sends some lovely descriptions of your sitting room, which must be very pleasant and comfortable, but that doesn't approach the standards in our small huts. It is true that one can't stand up in them, and that there are more holes than canvas at both ends, but in the evening we aren't so badly off, lying on the hard ground or, when it's raining, in the mud, with a candle on the lunch box to read, or one of the veterans telling us stories about his various wars. We also discuss this war, which isn't always very pleasant, except today where we have had rumours about victory in Russia.

The local villagers are very amusing with their strange accents and expressions, some blacks from Africa, and the usual French and English, many of whom are talented singers. The old Negro ballads from their ancient wars are great.

André

⊰——————————⊱

BACK AT THE HOSPITAL, Jean is busy in the registrar's office …

Army Post Office S/L BEF France
27 October 1915

My dear mother

Half our wards are closed, as we needed the workers outside to prepare for winter, and in any case the ones that are still open are not close to being full. Last Friday we received two hundred wounded and sick, and since then, none. Wake-up time here is at 6 a.m., and I usually head for my office at 7:30, where I await the arrival of my captain. I currently spend the day at the Corps Office, where I'm involved in a multitude of tasks. You will have seen that, according to the correspondent of the Star, *what annoys Colonel Birkett, the commanding officer of the hospital, the most is the huge quantity of French administrative paperwork. For example, every Saturday we need to send five lists of the Corps's officers with their different qualifications. We work until 6 p.m., and twice a week I am on duty in the evening. In addition, obviously, we need to work at night when the ambulance trains arrive, etc.*

I have, naturally, less opportunity to see the wounded than those that work in the hospital. I have often talked to them when I saw them in the

The staff at the administration hut. Colonel Birkett (centre)
and Jean (second from left at the rear)

The administration hut

camp. Most of them like to talk about their exploits at the Front, but they rarely talk about what they did themselves. There haven't been any attacks for some time, so almost half the men that are sent to us are sick and not wounded.

I'm very sad not to be able to send you photos of our camp, but as I think I already told you, all those who were found to have cameras after our arrival in France were punished and had their cameras confiscated.

We will here on in only be given one leave per week. That's too bad, because I very much enjoyed the opportunity to visit the area.

I have just torn the little wreath that you have sent me. I don't know any of these young people nor the Miss? They don't interest me a lot. I don't collect photographs of young girls that I know and even less of young girls that I only know by name.

Jean

A TRIP TO THE SOMME

IN OCTOBER 1915, the Princess Pats, were sad to leave the Armentières region, where they had enjoyed several pleasant months in the company of the local residents. From there they took the train to a small town in the Somme valley called Guillancourt.

AT THE BEGINNING OF OCTOBER, the long column advances towards the Somme. The weather is beautiful and cold. André, with his friends, Malcolm Stewart, Jim Mosley, Bill Calder, and Sydney Bruneau, make some important archaeological excavations in the ruins of a village. They discover a stove, some bed frames, and some excellent wool mattresses in the ruins of a bombarded house. Their shelter becomes very comfortable! Bruneau even finds many pictures and interesting books in a collapsed farmhouse. To what rustic intellectual would they have belonged? André meanwhile chooses an oak plate in the ruins of a chapel … Then, sitting on the bank of a canal, with only his penknife and his agile hands, he sculpts for us the crest of the Princess Pats, almost perfect in every detail. This first present from the Front was a sensation in Westmount.—(BB)

FROM GUILLANCOURT the Patricias marched along the banks of the Somme Canal to a hut bivouac near Bray, where the British Third Army was headquartered. They then went into front-line trenches lying south of the River near Frise, with

The Somme

supports at Eclusier-Vaux and reserves at the village of Cappy. The trenches were excellent, as the marl sub-soil of Picardy was ideal for the construction of trenches and other fortified earthworks. It was a particularly pleasant stay, without otherwise anything special to report.

L'Eclusier
Somme, 23 September 1915

My dear mother,

We have travelled a great deal this week and we are located in a very beautiful part of France, a countryside that is much more mountainous than Flanders. You asked me about the meals. In the trenches we cook the meals ourselves, with bacon, cheese, corned beef, and potatoes sometimes, and what we bring ourselves: Quaker Oats, chocolate, condensed milk, and dried fruit. But when we aren't in the trenches we are in reserve, and there the chefs cook the meals in their mobile kitchens.

I'm pleased to say that I have some good friends that are replacing Etienne.

André

2 October 1915

My dear parents,

We are very happy when at dawn we can go into our dugouts, light our little stove (found on a lot where there had been a house, in a big village that we

André (centre) and friends

*occupy), and make some tea, and our meal, before having a sleep on the
pile of straw at the bottom of the trench, almost until lunch, or in one of
the dugouts where we have installed some real beds with springs and very
comfortable wool mattresses that we found in a nearby ruin.*

*Before entering these trenches we lived in a village with only three
inhabitants, an old couple of about ninety years of age and a young girl who
received the Legion of Honour and the Military Medal for having opened the
dam and flooded the Germans when they were here.*

*Last night the Germans set fire to some hay bales with their shells, and
it was magnificent to see them burn, with the steeple of an old church
illuminated in the distance.*

*We rarely shoot, and the Germans even less, and it's very quiet, other
than for the artillery duels. I am annoyed at not being able to give you a
more complete breakdown of our day, but during the day we have about four
hours of sentry duty and one at night, with hours of rest, until the morning.*

*During the day, between sentry duties, we need to dig trenches and do
various other jobs.*

*At around four o'clock in the morning we receive our rations for the day:
a piece of bacon, a piece of frozen meat, a half a pound of bread, a little jam,
and some cigarettes.*

André

The dam that was opened to flood the Germans

5 October 1915

Dear Etienne,

Our trenches aren't too bad, and we have a few very big dugouts, with a stove in almost all of them. There are even some with doors and windows, all of that picked up from the village right behind us; all the wonderful bed springs are obviously used.

We have been bombarded this morning with about ten shells, and about half didn't explode, which shows the quality of the German munitions. We have a super Captain. He's very active and intelligent, and a very good sniper. He has already killed a German with a new rifle with a periscope that he brought with him. I understand that we are now going to do longer trench periods, of about fifteen days. I'm quite pleased, as this will result in less marching, and the opportunity to improve our set-up.

You haven't yet told us what battalions were in Shorncliffe, or where you will probably be transferred? Don't forget to tell your riding instructor that you have a lot of riding experience, since you rode a pony in Dorset! I envy your position a little, but as you seem to envy mine, we should be satisfied where we are. Tell me your thoughts about the advances on the Western Front, and whether this will affect the end of the war. I don't know if I told you that when we arrived in this district I saw my first Germans. They weren't very dangerous, as they were prisoners of the French that we were replacing. These poor guys looked as though they had had enough of the war,

*especially one seventeen or eighteen years old that had a pretty depressed
expression.*

André

                                                                    7 October 1915

My dear mother,

*You ask me to describe one of my days. There are so many different types that
it's difficult to say. On some days, when we have worked all night, we don't
do anything the next day. Other times they ask us to do drill and parades for
hours. Finally, from time to time we try to finish the war!*

André

                                                                    15 October 1915

My dear family,

*When I'm on guard duty during the day, and I look through the periscope
(that has about the same dimensions as a photo), I see the two lines of the
Germans cut out of the chalk. In the foreground is our barbed-wire fence,
about ten yards wide, which looks impenetrable. All this accompanied by the
thunder of the terrible bombardment of Arras. And then I glance for a couple
of minutes at these wonderful photographs of La Clairière, especially the
one of the dining room with its cups, tablecloths, and the comforting smile
of all those faces, and that makes me feel good. Meanwhile, I tell myself that
the quicker we cut the Kaiser's, and little Willy's, heads off, and stopped this
terrible destruction, the better it will be.*

*Here's my usual day: between 5:30 and 6 we receive our rations for the
day. The rations include meat, bread, jam, sometimes butter, cheese, tea,
sugar, and a half-inch candle per week. As soon as we receive the rations,
we have our breakfast: bacon, tea, bread, jam, and a little something extra
from our parcel. After breakfast, which finishes at about eight, we sleep for
two or three hours. From the moment we get up right up to supper, at about
3:30, there's lots to do, including fetching water and wood. The water is
quite close, from a pump in a beautiful ruined farm, and the farmer wasn't
just anybody, judging by his library. Bruneau had even found a number of
books that would have had considerable value at McGill. In a pile of rubble
I found a lovely collection of prints of Rome and its ruins. With regard to the
wood, the best I could find I ripped off the old Gothic pulpit in the church.
There were some beautiful pieces of oak, engraved and sculpted. Having
done all that, a quick wash is required. We take what the British call a
sunbath; I don't know if the British sector has an influence here. As well
as the bath, soldiers can be seen sitting in the sun, doing a very thorough*

inspection of their shirts. I don't want to go on and on with these details, but it is a fact that this process takes about an hour and that the victims add up to over fifty. For supper, we prepare a meat-and-potato stew, accompanied by chocolate and cake given by you. Following the washing up and the cleaning of the dugout, it's 5:30, and the twelve hours of night work begin. I am usually able to sleep uninterrupted for three hours. The rest of the time we search in the darkness of no man's land, to make sure that the Germans don't take us by surprise.

The other day it was dark at around six o'clock, and all of a sudden we got the order to put on our gas masks. You should have seen how fast the order was executed. Everyone climbs up on the shooting platform with his bayonets clipped on. We even started to shoot towards the German trenches, until we were told that it was a false alarm. We had felt sure that the Germans were about to attack.

We were bombarded a little the other day, and a few people were wounded. The Germans attempted revenge, after three of our bombers trapped one of their squads as they marched four-by-four ... all those that could, scattered.

André

1 November 1915

My dear mother,

The other day McKeeken, the one that was in the Niagara group, and I, went to visit the town, the first one that I have visited since Boulogne that isn't a ruin, or about to be one. We left after lunch through some beautiful, very French, woods, with all the branches and logs neatly piled, and the little woodcutters huts were like the ones near Paris. Two hours across woods, fields, and roads brought us to the end of the line of the electric tram, with drivers who either had white beards or were fourteen or fifteen years old. Twenty minutes zigzagging along small, winding streets, and through some lovely modern squares, brought us to what I believe is the most beautiful thing I have ever seen in my life: the Amiens Cathedral. It was too bad that all of the base was encased in sandbags as a protection from the German bombs, but fortunately they weren't piled high enough to cover the saints lined up about halfway up, and the incredible mosaic, which is reputed to be the most beautiful in the world. The interior was even better than the exterior, and it was the great height that impressed me the most. After another visit in town, we went to a restaurant and sat down at a table with plates, knives, forks, and the whole works; it was the first time that I had eaten at a table in four months. I think that I did all right, and I'm not

Amiens Cathedral

ashamed to say that we ate everything that there was on the menu, right to the last crumb.

André

⸎ ——————— ⸎

THE PRINCESS PATS LEFT THE SWAMPS of the Somme and marched westwards through Amiens to Flexicourt. They remained there for several weeks, where they taught fresh British recruits that had been sent to reinforce the Third Army.

❧ ———————— ❧

IN THE ARMY ONE KEEPS MOVING. In Anglo-Black slang it was: "always walking." Soldiers ignore the passing of time as they move from Flanders to the Somme, from the Somme to Artois or to Picardy, only knowing that somewhere there's a need for their bodies as a shield, or for their courage as a tank. Sometimes, at the end of the road it is hell, and sometimes a rather pleasant stop, like at Flexicourt, where the company had the good fortune to stay in a ballroom, behind closed doors, gaily decorated by the village artist, and with the opportunity to tinkle on one of the three pianos and play billiards. Except when they were training Kitchener's new army.—(BB)

9 November 1915

Dear Etienne,

I don't know if I told you that my friend Stewart and I are in the machine-gun section. We are given several training sessions per week, and the work is very interesting.

Since I wrote to you last, we have moved again. We are now in a big village where they manufacture canvas. We are here as a teaching battalion for some new battalions of Kitchener's army.

I wish that you could come and visit our lodging! It's not an old barn surrounded by rocks, with almost no walls. It is a first-class café, and we are housed in the ballroom. There are two or three pianos and a very colourful decor done by the village painter! We have taken advantage of the situation to have a concert this evening, and I must rush to finish, as it will soon start.

André

Flexicourt, 21 November 1915

Dear Philippe,

I congratulate you for having played on your class team; you must have had a very good time. We have a corporal in our platoon who played for the Hamilton Tigers last year, and he was telling me the other day that he was more interested in reading about Canadian football than any war stories in any of the world papers.

We are here as battalion instructors for one of Kitchener's new army's NCO schools. We have lots of ceremonies and parades with our flag unfurled, three sergeants and one lieutenant to guard it. I was on guard duty the other day, and I can tell you that it wasn't warm between midnight and 2 a.m., with snow on the ground since last week.

André

TOWARDS THE END OF 1915, there were some modifications within the structure of the military organization in the Western Front. General Joffre remained the supreme commander of the French forces, and Lt General Douglas Haig was named Commander-in-Chief of the British Army, replacing General Sir John French. The Canadian Expeditionary Force was created, with Lt General Alderson as Commanding Officer. The fast-rising Major General Arthur Currie was promoted to Commanding Officer of the 1st Canadian Division, and, on 27 November, the Princess Patricia's Canadian Light Infantry was merged with the 7th Brigade, under the helm of the 3rd Canadian Division.

Christmas 1915 was quiet, prior to their move to the Front at Kemmel, at the south end of the Ypres Salient.

ANDRÉ WAS SENT TO ROUEN and Harfleur for several weeks, on sick leave.—(BB)

26 November 1915

My dear mother,

Here I am in the hospital for a few days, with some pains in my back. With the application of hot compresses, they are now almost cured. About twenty-five of us are lodged in a big tent, with a coal-burning stove and electric lights. We don't do much all day long. We sit around the stove to read and chat; there is with us a funny old English tramp, who tells us about his adventures on the road and in jail!

André

11 December 1915

My dear parents,

Address my letters here, as I will be at the convalescent camp for a while before returning to the regiment. I thank Dad a lot for his letter and for his word of introduction to the wife of the Amiens pastor, but the letter unfortunately arrived too late, because there are several other towns with cathedrals in France, in addition to Amiens.

I am sending you a little present of no great value.

André

25 December 1915

My dear mother,

I was released from the hospital, as I was almost completely recovered from my problem. I arrived at the convalescent camp in the evening and the next day, after an inspection by the doctor, they told me to leave that evening for Le Havre, which is our base.

We sleep in round tents that aren't at all what could be called waterproof. It might interest you to know how I spent my Christmas. As one of the old boys, I was free for the rest of the day. We had an excellent lunch, served by the sergeants: ham and potatoes, turkey with pudding, roast beef, cake, and candies. At dessert, the colonel entered with a bunch of officers, and drank to our health.

André

Canadian Base Depot
Le Havre, 10 January 1916

My dear mother,

Life is quite monotonous here: we get up at five or six, depending on the days, and the days are spent sometimes in repairing the roads or other jobs in the training camp. It seems quite peculiar to be walking in a French town; everything is so different! If Canada wasn't so far away, I would love to send you a little bit of that wonderful French pastry that I tasted in one of these "patisseries."

André

BEF France, 24 January 1916

My dear mother,

Here I am, as you can see from my address, back with my battalion. Despite the fact that there is more mud and other minor inconveniences, I am glad to be back and to find my friends.

André

4 February 1916

My dear mother,

My comrades did finally get their parcels, as well as mine. In that I wasn't there, rather than sending it back, they consumed it. I am quite well, although I have a cold, but I'm not the only one: the lack of heating is of not much help.

You talk about my long period of inactivity. I don't really know what that's like since my arrival in France. Don't talk to me about a diet, that's of no interest, and in any case it isn't useful. I can assure you that no one presents me with a menu before each meal.

André

TRAINING AT THE FRONT

22 November 1915

My dear mother,

You can imagine my surprise, and obviously my joy, when the director of the military school, during the Saturday-morning exams, hands me a typewritten note that I need to sign. It's an order for my departure to France, Wednesday next week, for fifteen days of on-site instruction. I couldn't imagine what brought me this unexpected opportunity. Twenty-one of us out of a class of fifty are going. It's strange that they chose me, who has already been to the Front. In any case, don't worry. Things have been very calm these days, and in fact I don't think I'll be in the trenches for long. I'll probably already be back here when you receive this letter. I hope to be able to see Jean, but I don't dare hope to go and do a tour as far as the Princess Patricias.

Etienne

29 November 1915

My dear father,

I'm writing to you from my dugout somewhere along the firing line. It's about the only place where one can escape from this terrible mud. I don't have time to send a long letter today, as I'm quite busy here. I'm at the Canadian 27th Battalion for a few days. At our arrival near the firing line, Fife and I were sent to this battalion. We were first of all invited for supper by the quartermaster, who fed us and found us a bed. Then we left the next morning for the trenches, he in one company and me in another. I was well-received by the captain and the officers of my company. It's a pleasure to work with them. The first night I didn't have much to do other than to have a good sleep, but last night, I was up all night. I was asked, with a sergeant, to do the rounds of the guards, at regular intervals, and to make sure everything was going well. It seemed to me at first to be rather incredible to be alone in charge of the whole trench, but it went much better than I had imagined.

I was telling you that the mud was terrible. I think that someone who hasn't seen the trenches during a rainy day could not imagine the reality. It's only by wearing a huge pair of leather boots of over a foot above the knee that one can risk it. But the mud is not the only problem during this rainy weather. The rain soaks the trench walls, which collapse into the trenches, and the men are rebuilding them from morning till night. However, according to the letters that I censored last night, they don't seem to be complaining at all, taking all the little problems in their stride.

N.B. It's nonsense to remind you at the end of a letter like this one, but now that I think about it, I could get into some serious trouble if ever you allowed the publication of any part of this letter.

Etienne

10 December 1915

My dear mother,

I can at last settle a little bit more comfortably to write a letter. We are now in some huts a few miles behind the lines. The six officers of our company have a big hut with a good fire, bunks that are a little hard, but dry, where we don't have the company, more or less desirable, of rats and mice (the rats and mice have found a way to share the leather buttons of my vest while I was in the trenches). It was during some awful weather that we left the trenches. The battalion that was taking our place arrived only one hour after nightfall. Once they were settled in, we zigzagged along the communication trench. Despite having worked all week on the draining, we had water right up to our calves. After the trench, a muddy road, then the big paving stones of the Belgian roads. Finally, after maybe a two-and-a-half-hour walk, we arrived here. Fortunately, one of our officers was here in advance to see to it that the company found a good fire and straw on the bunks on arrival.

This morning it is the same wet weather as yesterday, with a fine rain that makes you appreciate the spot next to the fire. Most of the men went down to the nearby village to take a bath. I hope to do the same this afternoon, but it's not always easy to get permission to leave one's lodging, as the battalion can be called at any time. While we are here, we will have to take the men a little bit in every direction to do all sorts of work in the trenches. The mud, the water, as well as the German shells destroy everything, and one has to continuously rebuild and repair, as well as starting new projects.

I hope to see André. He mustn't be very far from here. I haven't had any news from him for quite a long time. I hope that he has completely recovered. The letter from Jean told me that he hadn't been well.

Etienne

19 December 1915

My dear mother,

It seems that Philippe also wants to leave, to join us here. I can only tell him that I would be very happy to be in his place, sitting by the fire at Les

Colombettes. Is it his friend Gordon Nicholson who enrolled in the 5th University Company?

It was Thursday morning that I left the Front, a little sad to leave this regiment where I had made some good friends. We got on the bus that was to take us to Boulogne, taking with us pieces of shells, German barbed wire, etc., souvenirs to send from England to our parents and the friends of a few officers. They even wanted to load us with a German drum that fortunately wasn't wrapped at the time of our departure.

On my arrival in Boulogne at 5 p.m., I dash over to the hospital to inquire about Jean. A disappointing result: he's still at Dannes-Camiers. I have two friends who were transferred to the artillery, and I think that the colonel of the reserve brigade would admit me also. I would much prefer to be in the artillery, and I think that I would be more useful there.

Etienne

1 January 1916

My dear father,

I see that Gordon Nicholson has enlisted. Tell Philippe that it's not necessary for him to follow. Tommy Dunton, the son of the former Montreal notary, with whom I am here, was telling me this morning when we were talking about Philippe: "There is no need of his enlisting. There are enough of you fellows here already!"

Etienne

IT WAS THEN THAT ETIENNE HEARD THE GOOD NEWS: that in view of his proficiency in mathematics, he was to be given a position in the artillery. Intensive and rapid preparations were required, as they were looking for artillery to be in place at the Front within four weeks.—(BB)

11 January 1916

My dear mother,

As you can see, here I am finally transferred to the artillery. You know that I had always wanted to join the artillery, but I didn't know that it was possible. It was on the 30th of December that I made my request. The adjutant announced to me on Sunday afternoon that I was transferred. Monday afternoon I met my new colonel, and I was taken by the adjutant to my new quarters.

Obviously, artillery is not learnt in one day, and I have several months of hard work prior to being sent to the Front. We are divided into groups of

*six, one group per gun, and under the direction of a sergeant major we get
the gun into position, load, unload, etc. Each person has a specific task, and
everything is done absolutely systematically.*

Etienne

20 January 1916

My dear father,

*Has Philippe then enlisted? Or is that only a prediction? Here I am well
established in the Ross Barracks. It seems that I will find some excellent
friends. I had my first exam this afternoon. It was topography. One of the
questions consisted of translating certain French terms often shown on
maps, including: auberge, barrière, and nacelle!*

Etienne

30 January 1916

My dear mother,

*One mustn't only lead the men, like in the infantry, but also the horses,
and a lot of equipment. My colonel, from the imperial artillery, Colonel
Battiscombe, who gives the main part of our courses, told us the other day:
"It takes a lifetime to learn all there is to know about a horse, and if you
were to get another lifetime after, you could spend it profitably on the same
subject."*

*What a surprise I had, to read the McGill Daily and see, "A fourth son of
Professor Bieler enlists!" How is it that you didn't tell me that Philippe was
going to enlist in the 5th University Company? Anyway, one had to expect it,
as Gordon Nicholson had already enlisted. I am wondering when I will see
Philippe here at Shorncliffe? I guess he should be arriving soon.*

*I had a letter from Jean this week, asking me if I could inquire about a
promotion for him in the Army Service Corps. I went to see the colonel, and
he told me that he couldn't do anything for Jean here.*

Etienne

CHAPTER SIX

The Salient

February to May 1916

The front line at Ypres, 1916

JANUARY 1916 PRESENTED A PRETTY BLEAK PICTURE for the Allies. Most of Belgium and a large part of France were occupied by the Germans, and the Germans had conquered some further key positions in the Salient. In 1914 and 1915, the French had lost some two million men, and were incapable of making any important headway without the British. The German defence tactics were far superior to those of the Allies. Their barbed wire was virtually impassable, and their underground fortresses could accommodate an entire garrison at the Front, while neither the French nor the British had anything in comparison. They also had more and superior rifles, grenades, and mortars.

Both the Allies and the Germans were developing more efficient and more useful aircrafts, and 1916 promised further advances. At the outset of 1916, there was also an increasing use of mines to destroy the enemy positions on both sides.

The Canadian troops at the Western Front in January 1915 already numbered over fifty thousand. They were stationed along a Front running six miles south of the Ypres Salient, where their first winter had brought thigh-deep mud and bitterly cold winds. The soldiers usually undertook a six-day rotation, going from support trenches, to trenches at the front line, and finally to reserve locations. The accommodations during their rest periods in the nearby village ruins were meagre to say the least. These weary soldiers would enjoy some basic refreshments and a few luxuries, like laundry facilities, hot baths, and occasionally a showing of films, improvised by enterprising engineers and commanders.

A YOUNG ARTILLERY OFFICER

10 February 1916

My dear mother,

As we are about a hundred officers, it's difficult to find the instructors and the guns to give us a real course. I had a possibility of being sent to France for fifteen days of instruction in the middle of this month, but on Saturday night, when the list of those that were elected was published, I wasn't included. It will be the next time. In the meantime, I hope to have several days of holiday when André returns from the Front around the 18th of this month, judging from what he says. That means in eight days. I am wondering what we could do together.

Etienne

13 February 1916

My dear father,

On Friday afternoon I saw two of my friends with jubilant expressions, who greeted me with "Here is the third one." In fact twenty-one officers from here must leave for action as soon as possible to be attached to the Canadian

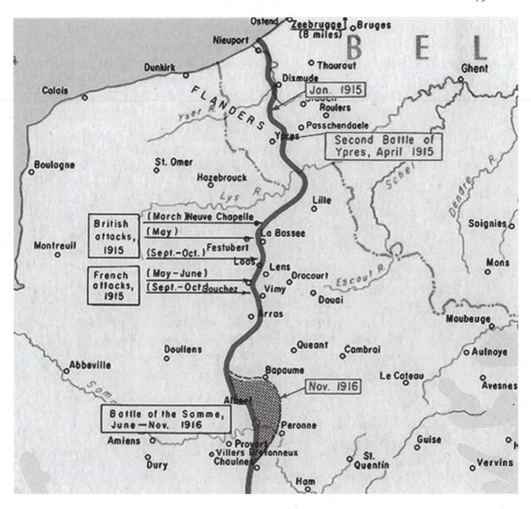

Map of the Western Front, 1915–16

brigades at the Front, and by some extraordinary chance I am one of them.
A week ago, I got a word from André, who was hoping that he would have a
few days break around the 16th of this month. I had planned a motorcycle
trip with him. Now, I think that we must cancel it.

Etienne

A SEA OF MUD BETWEEN Poperinghe and Outerdam, was awaiting Etienne! Snow
and freezing mud, added to the autumn rain, combined to make an indescribable
muck on the land, already tormented by machine-gun craters.

But one is not discouraged by minor details when one has just been promoted
and the rumour is that we will soon chase the Germans all the way to Berlin! As we

await this great day, we must faithfully accomplish our daily tasks: supervise the storage of the shells, these small fiery tubes piled up here and there in the trenches, or accompany on horseback the convoys of munitions passing through the remains of the Great Plain of Ypres, and avoiding if possible the enemy shells aimed at destroying our explosives. Etienne is very happy with his role as the leader of his mobile unit. He feels like a real artillery officer.

We received a letter from Jean, describing his visit with Etienne and their discussion about Philippe's projects, which don't really appeal to him. "Why is he in such a rush to go to the Front as an ordinary private? He should do better than that by taking a course in artillery in Kingston, for example, and in any case delay his departure while we try to hold him in Canada!"—(BB)

14 February 1916

My dear father,

It was at 9:45 on Sunday that the colonel arrived at the service and that the chaplain began. The brigade formed a square, with the officers in front of their men. We had created a choir of the best singers, directed brilliantly by a colonel. It's not in every brigade that the colonel and the majors would stand like this in the melting mud during a half-hour service. Good sermon based on Revelation 21:16. Then the colonel took the whole brigade for a three-quarter-hour march. He had a need to stretch his legs and thought that the men had the same need!

This afternoon I will be an interpreter for an hour or two. Ours left on holiday and isn't back. We had to make the rounds of the houses in the village with the paymaster to arrange for the payment of the men's and horses' lodgings. The cleanliness of all the houses we went in struck me. One couldn't find one grain of dust on the kitchen tiles, and that is during a time of melting and mud.

Since my return to France I haven't yet seen André. I hope to soon have the opportunity.

Etienne

February 24th 1916
EXTRACTS FROM ROUTINE ORDERS BY MAJOR GENERAL A.W. CURRIE
COMMANDING OFFICER 1st CANADIAN DIVISION
OFFICERS
Under authority War Office letter 121/overseas/1660 (A.C.6.) dated 17.2.16 the following officers are permanently attached to the 3rd Canadian Artillery Brigade, supernumerary to establishment and posted as follows:
Lieut. DG Higgins to 9th Battery; Lieut. NI Patterson to 10th Battery; Lieut. RH Deane to 11th Battery; Lieut. ES Bieler to 12th Battery

1796 CAMERAS
From sentences which have lately been awarded by Court-Martial in the case of
men tried for being in possession of a camera it is evident that officers do not
realize the gravity of this offense. Stringent and repeated orders have been issued
by G.H.Q. that no officer or man is to have a camera or similar photographic
apparatus in his possession. Disobedience of these orders is a serious offense and
all such cases are to be tried by Court-Martial and in case of a finding of guilty,
severely punished.

12th Battery, 3rd Brigade. C.F.A.
List of Casualties Feb. 10th 1915 to Feb. 29th 1916
4 men killed or died of wounds
28 men wounded
1 officer wounded

February 29th 1916
A gun of the 12th Battery was hit during the second battle of Ypres by a German
5.9' shell, blowing off a wheel. This wheel was shipped to London, Canada, by
Major EW Leonard. Photograph, attached to original sheet of War Diary, is self-
explanatory.

9 March 1916

My dear mother,

*I must say that I've had an extraordinary bit of luck to be sent to this
battery, one of the best of the division. The major is a real soldier, with
many years of experience in this field, and he wants everything to work
perfectly.*

*After about ten days at the place where I joined the battery, we left
one morning to make our first stop on the way to the Front, a distance of
about twenty-five miles. It's no minor business with an artillery battery.
Thankfully the weather was radiant, and we left enthusiastically.
Unfortunately, after an hour the sky darkened and soon, as is often the case
in March, a wet and cold snow began to fall. The snow and the good weather
went back and forth during the rest of the journey. At 12:45 it was the halt
to feed and water the horses, and to have the snacks and sandwiches that we
had brought. At 6:30 we arrived at the farm that was to shelter us for the
night, that is to say, the officers and the men, the poor horses had to put up
with being tied in a field of mud.*

*Since then we have travelled a short distance to the farm where we now
are. We were received a little like a cat in a bowling game. There was a
crowd of sergeants from the Army Service Corps. These men live more*

comfortably than the colonels of battle divisions, and the farmer's wife was firmly against us throwing them out. Her husband is soft and encouraging, but she creates a scene about everything we ask her, and it's naturally me that is in charge of most of the discussions with the local people.

Etienne

12th Battery 3rd Brigade CFA
March 13th 1916
At 12:45 two German planes passed over the diagonal coming from our rear. They were fired upon but escaped safely to their own lines. About 25% of enemy shells particularly 4.1 Howrs. fired in this vicinity today were blind. The batteries of the Brigade in conjunction with the heavies fired in retaliation from 2:40 PM to 3:00 PM today. The shooting of our batteries was very effective and the shooting of the heavies was also very good. Many direct hits were obtained by our guns on enemy first line and also by the heavies on FACTORY FARM MARK 2. The enemy fire in reply was slight.

March 14th 1916
12th battery reports at 10:10 AM 3 German planes appeared from the direction of MESSINES, They were flying in a South Westerly direction over trenches 14 and 15. Later they flew N.W. over LINDENHOCK and dropped a red rocket about N.27.c One white rocket was dropped by these planes over Mont Kemmel tower and later in the day KEMMEL VILLAGE was shelled. At 12:35 PM smoke of a train was observed travelling N.E. of MESSINES. The train appeared to be proceeding very slowly.

March 18th 1916
Morning rather misty, clearing up about 10:30 AM. Enemy aircraft very active this morning and more or less during the day. Enemy opened up heavy fire with 4.1, 5.9 and 77mm guns on our C and D trenches and points in rear, also on Shell Farm and R.E. Farm. The batteries of the brigade retaliated with 100 rounds on target "H" in conjunction with the heavies. The shooting is reported to have been very good, many direct hits having been made.

March 19th 1916
At 3 PM a German was seen near a dugout at N.36.a.9.2. The battery fired on this point and scored a direct hit. The dugout appears to be very strongly constructed, as no apparent damage was noticed. There is a white tape on two stakes about 50 yards apart at N.30.d.4.6 probably marking the ground for a new trench. A pile of sandbags can be seen at N.30.d.2.7 Communication trench at N.36.b.3.3 has been newly re-vetted and dug out. There is a suspected M.G., emplacement at N.36.a.91/2.2.

German infantryman hauling a 7.58-cm. minenwerfer

20 March 1916

My dear mother,

It's during the evening of a beautiful Sunday that I am writing to you. It's not exactly a rest day, as there are tasks to be done on Sunday like every day in the profession we are in. This morning a torrential rain prevented us from having a service, then the weather lifted, the sun broke through, and the afternoon has been radiant. After lunch I went out with the men to give the horses one hour of exercise, and it was a real pleasure to have a short ride. One doesn't dare go too far from one's lodging, as we can be called at any time. However, yesterday I got permission to have a ride on the horse I have just adopted. It's not a bad animal, and with some care, he will be great.

Etienne

12th Battery 3rd Brigade CFA
March 20th 1916
During the afternoon battery fired upon and dispersed working party at
N.30.d.21/2.6. This party was evidently repairing a German trench. F.O.O. 10th
battery reports at 9 AM heavy artillery and rifle fire heard to the South apparently
near ARMENTIERS, rifle fire ceased about 10 AM but shelling continued at

intervals all day. F.O.O. 12th battery reports at 10:30 PM 19th inst. 2 enemy MINENWERFERS very active, one 97 degrees Mag. and the other 107 degrees Mag. Bearing as observed from N.29.c.8.3 Battery fired on both and fire of MINENWERFERS appreciably diminished. Enemy seems anxious to conserve artillery fire.

OFF ON THE SIDE OF THE ROAD, Etienne sees an infantry battalion having a break. "I'll be damned if it isn't André's unit, maybe I can find him." His friends search, and soon the two brothers, sitting on the side of the road, talk about their recent and future leaves, as well as the news from home: "Mom and Dad are celebrating their silver wedding anniversary, Philippe has apparently volunteered … Why? Isn't it enough for the three of us to be in this never-ending war? It seems that Jacques is an excellent young scout."—(BB)

20 March 1916

My dear mother,

After two or three weeks in the 12th battery, here I am temporarily transferred to the ammunition column. It's the habit here that we begin the work that we do here in this fashion. It won't do me any harm. I need to know a little more about the horses, and learn to ride a little better. Here is how we spend the day: The morning at 6:50 stable parade. We get up for that every three days when one is orderly officer. For forty minutes the men brush, water, and feed the horses. At eight we have breakfast. We get together for the meals in the wooden hut, which is also used as a bedroom. The chaplain, in his role as mess secretary, presides at the table. We have the major, the vet, the paymaster, and the three subalterns, Bell, who was French Master at Montreal High School, and me. The morning is spent exercising the horses, and then cleaning the harnesses. During the afternoon we clean the harnesses again. It's always the same routine, except when we need to transport the munitions to the batteries.

Yesterday morning, I was listening to a conversation between two men. One was recounting an imaginary conversation with his son in 1930: "Father, where did you get that ribbon – at the great war my child – but what did you do in the great war, Father? – Well, child, I cleaned harness in the morning, I cleaned stables in the afternoon, and sometimes I cleaned ammunition."

After this morning's church parade, I asked for permission from the major to leave until 6 p.m., in order to see André. So I left at 11:30 and arrived at the Princess Pats' location at 3 p.m., after having stopped for lunch at a village hall. – I easily found the farm where the No 2 Company was. The first familiar face that I saw was Stewart's, André's friend, and then I saw André. He almost fell down when he saw me. It seems that half of my letters never reached him, and he didn't know where I was. I had a short walk with him. Unfortunately the hour that I had to be with him was quickly over. He continues to look happy with the Patricias and has some very good friends. The poor guy has not yet received his pass for Paris. He had gotten his leave and passport but had not been able to go.

Etienne

3rd Brigade Ammunition Column
March 21st 1916
3 PM smoke observed coming from a dugout at N.36.a.9.2
4:15 PM smoke observed coming from a building at N.30.d.9.7.
This building is probably used as a cook house as smoke appears only at meal times.
F.O.O. 11th battery reports about 5 AM our heavy guns and 18 pdrs fired on trenches and hills about WYTSCHAETE. This firing lasted about 20 minutes. F.O.O. 12th battery reports the same firing by our guns and that 3 shells exploded in WYTSCHAETE and the remainder too far over to be observed. No reply.

March 22nd 1916
F.O.O. 12th battery reports that at 4:30 PM our STOKES gun fired on enemy lines to the left of SPANBROEKMOLIN. Enemy retaliated with 4.1" bursting in air and 77 mm guns. These batteries were firing from 15 degrees and 18 degrees respectively left of MESSINE CHURCH from sound bearing taken from S.P.8 (N.29.0.8.2.). This fire did not silence our STOKES gun.

March 25th 1916
Brigade order No. 126 issued today:
Lieut. RH Harcourt transferred from Amm. Col. to 12th Battery
Lieut. ES Bieler transferred from 12th Battery to Amm. Column.
F.O.O. 12th battery reports at 3:30 PM an enemy Trench Mortar fired about 12 rounds on Trench D.4 Our Trench Mortars and Stokes gun retaliated with good effect, breaching the enemy parapet opposite d.4.

March 26th 1916
Our bombardment gradually silenced enemy and caused considerable damage to his works. The bombardment by the batteries of the brigade was very effective and there was little retaliation for this shooting.

March 31 1916
In accordance with op order no 128 one-half of the brigade's Amm. Column and one section per battery moved out today on relief and proceeded to billets near EECKE.

ANDRÉ IN THE SALIENT

29 February 1916

My dear father,

You will have heard the news of the death of Laddie Millen, that will be a terrible hit for his family. A few hours before I was speaking to him and he was telling me about his trip to Scotland.

The Germans are very good marksmen; they destroyed four of our periscopes the last time, and one of the guys almost lost an eye from the flying glass from one of the mirrors. We were hit with a sausage the other day (a big bomb projected by a mortar). It's very exciting to see them come; if one watches them come they can generally be avoided.

André

20 March 1916

My dear parents,

I am ashamed to have been silent all this time, but I wait and put off day by day hoping that I will receive a short message from you. It was a terrible disappointment for me when all of a sudden, in fact the day I was to leave for Paris, they stopped all leaves without much of a chance that it will start again prior to the summer, but the army is the army!

André

25 March 1916

My dear parents,

I'm sure that you would have trouble in guessing to whom I passed your letter no 9: Etienne, who came to see me the other day. I found him much fatter and taller; he is magnificent in his officer's uniform. I hope to see him from time to time now that he is in Belgium.

Mother described so well how she had obtained socks for Tante Julia's soldiers, but there's a little Canadian soldier who would also like to have some.

André

P.S. If mother could find me some pills to relieve my back, I would be very grateful.

3 April 1916

Dear Dad,

What pains me in your letters, is to see that Mom has almost abandoned the wonderful plan of coming to Europe this summer. I hope that she has

Canadian troops passing through Ypres, showing the
Halle aux Draps (Cloth Hall) and the cathedral

*been reassured about the dangers of the submarines, and that she will
decide to come all the same. The newspapers of the last few days say that the
Germans are changing their minds about sinking all ships, whether enemy
or otherwise, that dare to enter the area near the North Sea. And Philippe?
André, who I saw yesterday, tells me that he heard it said that the company
is expected in England.*

*Unfortunately André and I were only together for a few minutes. I had
heard that he was in this area and even that a Great Russian Duke was
to inspect the regiment one of these days. It was only last night that I could
arrange to see him a few moments while I was transporting munitions. He
was radiant at the idea of finally being able to go on leave.*

Etienne

3 April 1916

Dear Dad,

*The mud is drying beautifully, but the dust is already beginning to show its
face. Our new general, who replaced the one who was killed in the trenches a
few weeks ago, inspected us this morning.*

*On our return from the trenches a few days ago we went through the town
of Ypres. What a ruin, not one house still upright, and the monuments even*

worse than that shown in the pictures. Only the tower remains of the Halle aux Draps, and there's not much left of that.

You perhaps know that we have lost Bruneau; because of his eyes, he's thinking of not returning. I have heard that Phil is in quarantine in England. If you are able to pull some strings to help me get into the "Flying Corps," I would appreciate it, another eight months in the Front is quite enough for any man.

André

THE CANADIAN FRONT LINE was almost continually bombarded during 4 and 5 April 1916. A veteran British artillery officer described it as the most violent bombarding that he had ever experienced.

3 April 1916

My dear mother,

Did I tell you that we have, with our officers of the Ammunition Column, a large very amusing Englishman, a Mr Steel, who taught French at the High School during the last three or four years, and had Laddie Millen in his classes. He was shocked to hear of his death and had gone the other day to place several stones around the cross over his grave.

Since our arrival here, we have worked to prepare for the long-awaited visit of our Corps Commander. This morning, woken up at 5:30, everyone is working like mad to clean himself, to shine the harness hardware, to break in the leather, to brush his horses, and to prepare everything else. We have selected a guard of honour made up of older soldiers who handle their rifles so well that they would have made the guards at Buckingham Palace jealous. You can therefore imagine everybody's disappointment when it was announced that the Corps Commander couldn't come, and that we had to accept a brief inspection by one of his subordinates.

Yesterday, Sunday, as you can imagine, we didn't have much of a break the day before this visit. We had, however, a brief service out of doors, given by Canon Scott from Quebec, a good-looking man but doesn't seem to be much of an orator.

Etienne

15 April 1916

Dear mother,

Finally, here is the news of my leave that you have been waiting for. I am now back in the battalion after my little stay in Paris.

I left at 10 p.m. on Friday, I arrived in Paris at 10 a.m. after a quite tiring trip in the third-class carriages of the "poilus," surrounded by others on leave like me. It didn't take me long to find the Metro to the Porte Maillot ... I must have looked quite peculiar with my rifle, my bags, and my overcoat covered with mud ... it felt quite funny, as it was the first time in a long time that I sat at a dinner table ... Unfortunately I had to meet with the British Police that morning, so I missed the church service ... we got back in time for dinner, and who shows up but Camille Chazeaud in his French uniform! He doesn't seem very happy with his regiment and envies my khakis!

The next day I had to leave, as I was recalled all of a sudden. Once again a long voyage, and here I am back in my trenches! I will remember for a long time this little trip to Paris that brought back so many good memories. I sent a package to Jacques; I hope that he'll get it, the content exploded very close to me.

André

28 April 1916

My dear parents,

I have received your two letters, but stop worrying about me, I feel fine and I don't know why you think that I'm in the hospital.

There's a little lake just in front, and I swim in it almost every day. I presume that Etienne told you about our day together. I was really happy to see him and to be able to talk together about home.

About the room above the kitchen: the best way is to build it yourselves, trench style in sandbags, with a rubber sheet as a roof. It's both economical and more or less healthy.

André

18 May 1916

My dear parents,

I'm back in Paris! Without having any expectations, the other day while I was in the front line, the sergeant told me to get my passport and head for Paris. You can imagine that it didn't take me long to leave, particularly as the Germans were bombarding us very energetically. I was also lucky, as that same morning a shell hit the cubbyhole where I had spent the morning. After a long walk, I arrived at the train thoroughly soaked, covered with mud. I must have looked pretty peculiar as I arrived in Neuilly just in time for dinner. Naturally I couldn't warn them, and they weren't at all expecting me. It didn't take me very long to improve my appearance and have a good meal. The next day, on hearing that the entire family was in

André Bieler

Orleans, I asked the mission for permission to go, but they replied that I was not permitted to leave Paris.

Monday I met Tante Julia for lunch near the station, and then left for Boulogne. After a night on the train, I find myself not far from Napoleon's monument, and find Jean's hospital. He has a good college-like set-up in the Registrar's Office. I found that he hadn't changed as much as Etienne, and seemed to be very well. After visiting the hospital and having dinner at a good restaurant, we made a good trip to the countryside and the seacoast. The weather was perfect, and I can't remember ever having a more enjoyable trip (it was at Wimereux). That evening, as I was going to the train, I found out that I had another day with Jean. I visited the hospital more thoroughly and met a few wounded men from our company. It is not as pleasant to return to the Battalion as the leave has been, but I am happy at re-joining my friends.

André

PHILIPPE VOLUNTEERS

MEANWHILE, PHILIPPE TRAINED every day after the lectures, and then completed his training at Camp Niagara, where the marching order, near the end of March, surprised them. He announced that they would have one day's leave before leaving for Halifax, and that if that didn't disturb Maman too much, he would like to bring to lunch all his friends that didn't have family in Montreal.

We add all the extensions to the dining-room table, about twenty place settings, and lay out a lot of tasty delicacies, and flowers on the white tablecloth. Then, the sound of military boots, voices and laughter, filters down the street and fills the house. We sit down, and the boys gulp down with considerable appetite the big and small dishes, and when the dessert comes, Philippe's parents and the soldiers together toast this happy day, and hope to meet again at Les Colombettes after their victorious return! … But tragically, of this group, only one was to survive the war. We had the heart-rending privilege in 1920 to hug this dear badly wounded comrade at the Vancouver military hospital, and to receive from his deathbed a tray that he had made.

Before breaking up, the joyful group met at Strathcona Hall, where the university had organized a goodbye reception for the company. We then sat in the drawing room with our families to enjoy quietly this last intimate afternoon. The rooms at the university were attractive with flowers and a generous buffet surrounded by several khaki coloured groups, contrasting with the bright colours of the young ladies waiting on their gallant cavaliers. The parents, less happy than their children, were at the periphery, talking to the officers. We would have all so much wished to prolong this moment, but military orders being what they are, they had to march off instead.

Philippe on his departure from Montreal

All of a sudden, Philippe's mother felt an arm around her waist. It was he, and he said: "What would you say, Maman, if we went together to a little hiding place? There behind this door there's a very low radiator, where we could talk so comfortably!" We sat down, just as if we were playing hide-and-seek, and hand-in-hand we looked straight into each other's eyes, without saying much … Words are a little childish in moments like that! Then, we cried, as the bugle played some particularly emotional notes. We embraced frantically, and the long khaki column lined up and began to file out, and disappeared into the melting snow and darkness. They were off to their barracks, and would leave the next morning at the break of day. Jacques and his father intended to be there for a final embrace and to witness the long convoy move off, with each window crowded with laughing faces and frenetic waves of their caps.

What weeks these were at the beginning of the war, and what strange years were to follow! Up until then, these developments had not affected our private lives, but we are now weighed down by world solidarity, with its combination of both indignation, and enthusiasm. Our sons … they are no longer ours and belong to the grand cause, and all that we know is that they are "somewhere in France"! Our time, our ability … we are no longer in control, we all belong to the same cause, aiming towards this same victory for which they will fight.

The first and most important thing to do is to uphold the morale of our sons. That's what we are trying to do with frequent letters, by parcels, and by our prayers. Without an exact address, without complete instructions, our hearts and our eyes search for them on the maps of the Front, but because of the censorship, it is only a long time afterwards that we know where they passed. We think of them a lot, and they certainly don't forget us: Jean, always alert in his hospital in Boulogne, is in an excellent information centre, and writes to us or sends us telegrams.

Philippe's first letters were not important enough for us to transcribe. The details of their train trip from Montreal to Halifax can be summarized in three words: rest, cigarettes, and maps. The countryside was nothing but fields of snow, with here and there a small spruce forest. At the stops, a swarm of young girls often swooped onto the train to sell sweets. Then it was the sea, the Halifax harbour, a little walk around the city, and the embarkation on the *Olympic* on 1 April 1916. Philippe, looking forward to lounging on deck and playing games, was very disappointed at being condemned to the infirmary with acute laryngitis, and he suffered right up to his arrival in Liverpool.

What a contrast to travel across a green and pleasant countryside in a minuscule train, as compared to the passage through the depressing Canadian deep freeze, and then to arrive finally at the West-Sandling camp. There were rows of attractive barracks on the slope of a sand dune. Each one housed about thirty soldiers, and Philippe settled in quickly and proceeded to polish the leather and buttons in preparation for the great inspection the next day.—(BB)

ETIENNE'S FINAL MONTHS IN THE AMMUNITION COLUMN

3rd Brigade Ammunition Column
April 15th 1916
At 2:30 PM enemy fired a number of Trench Mortars into our trenches South of the Canal. The Mortar used by the enemy is a new one shaped like a rum bottle but just a trifle larger having a fuse at the top. It is made of sheet steel and has a wooden handle attached to the base which disappears when it is fired. The bomb is estimated to weigh about 80 lbs.
At 3:45 PM a number of Germans were seen in the enemy front line trench at 0.4.a.5.6 apparently observing their fire South of the Canal. One had a cap on with a red band around it and a red vertical band running through the centre of the peak of the cap.

17 April 1916

My dear mother,

I only have the time to write a short note today, as I am leaving this evening for a brief stay in the trenches. The officer who directs the trench mortars has asked for an officer to spend several days to help him, and I think that it will be an experience that I won't regret. Obviously I am not thinking of going in there forever. I much prefer the artillery in the countryside, pure and simple.

Our life here these days is not very tiring. We are well set up in a farm with good stables for the horses, a good number of huts and tents for the men. The officers are in huts that aren't too bad at all. I share my compartment with Steel, about whom I talked in my last letter, and with the veterinarian. A wooden frame with bags nailed across makes a perfectly comfortable bed, and our sleep proves it.

We are very hospitable here at the Front, always happy to see a new face and to hear the news and the rumours they may have heard. Yesterday morning, Sunday, we had a brief service here given by our padre. During the afternoon I left on horseback to see André. The camp where I thought I would find him is only three or four miles from here. Having gotten there, I find out that André had finally left for Paris. Thursday night they came to wake him up at 11 o'clock to tell him he could leave, but that he had to be back on Tuesday. It's a little short, but better than nothing. I still have nothing from Philippe. I wonder if he's in England.

Etienne

3rd Brigade Ammunition Column
April 18th 1916
An Infantry officer of the 26th battalion who is in the trenches on the opposite side of the canal informs me that enemy used a pontoon bridge on the canal at a point about 0.4.a.8.7 and 0.4.a.8.8 at night. I had a look at these points and I find the enemy have a foot bridge under construction about 0.4.a.8.6. This must have been put up during the night as I have not noticed any work about that point before.
Signed Lieut. Colonel J.H. Mitchell, O.C. 3rd Canadian Artillery Brigade

28 April 1916

My dear mother,

I am here for several days' rest before returning to the Ammunition Column. It's wonderful to have absolute freedom for a few days. The second evening, I had an experience that was quite unusual for a poor lieutenant like me – I had dinner with General Appleby at the Canadian Headquarters, where I had been held back on a business matter. Being the only guest, I was sat on the right of the general, who was perfectly courteous, and I can assure you that the menu didn't displease me after the "popote" of the trenches.

Yesterday afternoon I had the pleasant surprise of seeing André arrive. He seemed to be still beaming after his visit to Paris. As André was free for the afternoon, we went on a tour of the neighbouring town together. It was during a beautiful warm afternoon, real summer weather. Also the first thing I did was to take a bath. Then we had tea together, and then to a movie organized by one of the divisions.

André seemed to be in great health. He looked very well, even after a night digging in the trenches. He showed me your photograph of the four soldiers. Who was ingenious enough to include Philippe? It's very well done.

Etienne

Belgium, 9 May 1916

My dear father,

Here I am once again in the Ammunition Column since Sunday after Easter. After several days of complete rest in the French Mortar rest billet, I wasn't unhappy to start an active life again, but it's apparently not for long. I have just received the order to go on Sunday to a military school not far from here.

Etienne

3rd Brigade First Division, 21 May 1916

My dear mother,

Here I am at the beginning of the last week of this course, and I think that we would all like it to continue for a long time. The work is interesting and not overwhelming, and the countryside is so lovely during these beautiful spring days that we almost forget that we are at war. A sign in the yard says: "It is forbidden to speak Flemish," indicates that we are in France!

Etienne

3rd Brigade, 1st Divison CFA
May 27th 1916
At 10:35 AM this date the 11th and 12th Batteries 458th Howr. Battery assisted by the 461 Howr, Battery of the Left Group and 128 Heavy Battery fired on suspected gun emplacement at I.36.b.3.7 A gun at this supposed point has been firing on our trenches. The enemy retaliated at 10:45 AM in rear of our trenches about 400 yards left of the DUMP with 20 rounds from 5.9" Howrs.
Considerable airplane activity during the afternoon in which our planes maintained a decided ascendancy. Several enemy balloons up during the afternoon.

May 30th 1916
O. C's 10th, 11th, and 12th Batteries and O.C. C Battery (49th) will rearrange the personnel of the four subsections of their Batteries so as to absorb the newly

posted N.C.O.s and men into the various subsections while maintaining a uniformity in trained men in each. The same principle will be followed by O.C.'s Batteries at their Wagon Lines.

Lieut ES Bieler is hereby transferred for duty to C. Battery (49th), on organization.

CHAPTER SEVEN

Sanctuary Wood

June to August 1916

Sanctuary Wood. A lone soldier makes his way through the remains of
trees, mud, and water in what was the battlefield.

THE MILITARY PROSPECTS IN MAY WERE PARTICULARLY GLOOMY, but fortunately the weather was beautiful and the mud was drying. The Germans were transferring a huge number of troops to the West, but the Allies still enjoyed a superiority of men, and the command of the sea. General Joffre and General Haig disagreed on the overall Allied strategy on the Western Front, but given the huge French losses further south, they finally compromised and began to plan a combined major thrust in the Somme Valley.

THE BATTLE OF SANCTUARY WOOD

The British and Canadians had been allocated what Haig considered to be a critical section of the northern Front. This salient, which had been carved out around Ypres, was the barrier between the German and British Fronts. If the enemy conquered the entire highland, the Allies would likely be forced to withdraw. In addition, such a conquest would hinder the transfer of Allied troops to the Somme. It appeared that the Germans had heard about the plans for the Somme, and were therefore preparing to attack as soon as possible.

Troops were being transferred from the north to the Somme, including a large part of the British Army and the artillery. As a result, the Canadian Forces became a significant part of what was left in the Salient. The Canadians were getting ready for the inevitable. General Currie's 1st Division, which included Etienne's 3rd Artillery Brigade was to be located near the top of Mt Sorrel. The 7th Brigade was to be located in front of Sanctuary Wood, and was to be manned by the Princess Pats. The Germans, meanwhile, were transferring new troops to assure their conquest of Mt Sorrel and the trenches to the north of Sanctuary Wood.

A LITTLE TO THE EAST OF Ypres are these small wooded hills, and it was here that André on his return from Paris found his comrades digging trenches night and day in anticipation of an attack from the enemy. The Germans had been strengthened by the arrival of fresh troops from Wurtemberg. Their officers were particularly ambitious and eager to succeed; they wanted a victory. The Canadians held Mont Sorrel and Sanctuary Wood – ironic to be called by such a peaceful name! – Can a wood be so called when that entire region is about to be left desolate with huge holes, naked and burned, and soon reduced to shreds. Nevertheless there were here and there in the shade of a bush a few poppies, showing their red petals that seemed already to look like bloodstains.—(BB)

THE GERMAN ARTILLERY BEGAN bombarding at 6 a.m. on 2 June. A veritable tornado of fire hit the Canadians for four hours. It was almost impossible for the Canadian artillery to react. The Patricias had raked the Germans with machine-gun fire, but it was insufficient to prevent the complete destruction of the Allied trenches and the annihilation of the garrisons in their midst.

> 12th Brigade, 1st Division CFA
> June 2 1916
> 7 PM Received orders to take over our old guns and equipment again and proceed back into action in our old position at H.23.d and cover the Zillebeke switch as the enemy had attacked our front after a four-hour heavy bombardment and succeeded in occupying it between Hill 60 and Hodge for a depth of about 1,000 yards. Battery in action at 2 AM 3rd inst. and had a section of the 8th Battery under Lieut. Gordon attached. Battery is now an emergency defence unit. Gun emplacements had to be altered to allow required switch to left from our old zone.

It wasn't long before the Patricias were so badly hit that there were very few survivors. At midday, the Germans taking advantage of the situation advanced slowly through the woods, where there was nothing but the dead, throwing hand grenades and spreading liquid fire. All night long, a sergeant with a few of his surviving men did their utmost to hold back the enemy by spraying them with machine-gun fire, but they were unable to halt the Germans' onslaught. As dawn drew near on 3 June 1916, the headquarters sent a message to retreat. There were no more officers, almost no men, no more ammunition, no more food, and in fact, no more of anything.

ANDRÉ HAD SPENT THE EVENING before 1 June with a friend in one of these bomb craters where they were setting up an advanced sentry line. Then, at daybreak, the projectiles began arriving with a long moaning sound. Then a shrill whistling before the final terrific explosion. Everything is falling over; the ground is trembling, the wounded are screaming, the dying are moaning. It's death in the trenches, and hell all around. André, having deposited a souvenir next to him, sees it thrown in the air and reduced to rubble by a shell, and it's a miracle that he hadn't shared the same fate as his package! He didn't even have the time to regret the loss of that lovely piece of stained glass from the "Halle aux Draps," that he was hoping to keep as a souvenir, when another shell explodes and dumps on him an avalanche of chunks of earth, scraps of bags, and broken branches. The furious swirling from the bombardment didn't send him hurtling in the air, but, quite to the contrary, buried him prematurely. Fortunately some kindly gravediggers pull him out of his tomb, unharmed, and he is reborn in the brilliant light of the barricade. Tac-tac-pan-boum! Up above, all around, everywhere, it continues to crackle in long gusts or by individual bangs, the shrapnel with their furious detonation, and the big ones crashing with their racket of a racing locomotive suddenly hitting a wall. "The gusts of fire and thunder unleashes such a terrific boom that one feels annihilated, with the stink of sulphur turning our stomachs, eyes blink, are blinded and dripping with tears." It was an honourable feat for André to have fought with the Princess Pats for three days and three nights in that absolutely desperate situation. He had told himself: "They will not come through."

"But why this massacre? What was our artillery doing?" (We learned later that many artillery brigades had been sent to the Somme, and it was the infantry's blood that paid for this error.) The Sanctuary Wood battle cost the Princess Patricias more than 400 casualties, including 150 killed, including the commanding officer, Lt-Col H.C. Buller. Though they inflicted substantial casualties, they could not halt the advance, but credit for temporarily checking the enemy's right wing belongs to the Patricias.—(BB)

THE PRINCESS PATS HAD PLAYED a critical role on 2 June. Despite their isolation, or the hope of any immediate support, they had neither retired or failed to guard their rear. One will never know whether an enterprising enemy might not have changed the course of the Western Front. The well-trained young German soldiers, supported by their mighty artillery, might have been able to advance through the mud of Flanders and so jeopardize the communications that General Haig would not have been able to pursue his Somme offensive or prevent the breakdown of the headquarter's communications with the Ypres Front. If the media had not been more preoccupied with the naval battle in Jutland, the battle of Sanctuary Wood would have been in the headlines. In any case, Canada records it as one of its most glorious military operations, and as long as World War I is talked about, the courage of the Patricias will be remembered. Their defence of the Ypres Salient continued during July and August.

ANDRÉ IS WOUNDED

AS SOON AS THE SENTRIES RETURNED to the trenches the next morning, they began to clean up one of the most cruel bombardments of the war. "The operation isn't easy, as there are so many wounded to transport! As far as the dead are concerned, we leave them to the enemy." André has a thigh wound, and he lifts Captain Irvine, who has been seriously hit, and with three friends they carry him to the rear. Then with his hands, that aren't in any way antiseptic, he manages to extract the bits of shrapnel from his leg and clippety-clop arrives at the black hole, where the overworked doctors give first aid to the wounded. Then, as he descends into the underground shelter, he is greeted with a "Hello, André." It is Erroll Amaron, who will look after him and arrange for his transport by car right up to Poperinghe, from where he will be directed to Camiers. After hell it is purgatory, as he waits for the paradise of the hospital.

On 2 June, when the terrible battle of Sanctuary Wood was in full force, Etienne worried about how he could get any news of André, who must have been in the centre of that furnace.

In Boulogne, Jean received the ambulances carrying the endless number of wounded soldiers, and was hence always the first to know about all the battles. If possible, he would telegraph his parents reassuring news, and those messages invariably arrived before the newspaper, before the "Whizz-bang" of the wounded, and before the official letter from Ottawa. Of course, this time, he was particularly interested in finding his brother. He did, and what a pleasant moment it was for both of them to talk and to share a few delicacies from the hospital's kitchen.—(BB)

4 June 1916

Dear Dad,

I have just sent you a telegram that may have somewhat surprised you at first, but I hope that it has relieved you of any anxiety about André. I suppose that the newspapers will have written horrific reports about these last two nights. I was myself quite worried about André when yesterday morning I heard the first rumours of what happened to his battalion. In the evening I made as many enquiries as I could, without any success. This afternoon, I saw one of André's friends returning with a wounded soldier. He told me that he had seen André at four this morning in good health and out of danger. "He stuck to it like a young hero and an old trooper," he said. We can all be proud of him.

I hadn't seen André for over five weeks. This artillery course just coincided with a rest period for him behind the lines, so I had missed him. Incidentally, I often have news from Jean by one or the other returning from leave in England. All Montrealers that have a couple of hours in Boulogne don't miss going to the McGill Hospital, and many see Jean.

Etienne

6 June 1916

My dear mother,

After having gotten fuller information about André, I found out that, after all, he hadn't escaped completely intact from this battle the other day. After having been subjected to a long series of bombardments, nothing better could have happened than a couple of weeks of complete rest and care, and that's what he will get. In the afternoon I went to the nearby town and, riding by a big hospital, I decided to see if I could find any traces of André. It was exactly the hospital where he had spent the night, the day before. "Light shell wound in left thigh," is all I could find out there. That night I went to his regiment, which was resting after a few very difficult days. One of his friends told me

that he had gotten a small shrapnel wound and that he had been able to go
to the dressing station on foot. The officers had all accompanied the body of
the colonel right up to the cemetery where the body of their previous colonel
had been buried some twelve months previously.

Etienne

AT CAMIERS AND LE HAVRE, André realized that he had caught the "good wound."
As it wasn't serious, it was to be a pleasant moment. What perfect relaxation! Mus-
cles relaxing in the warmth of a bath, aching limbs brushing against the freshness of
the sheets, a head full of sleep lying softly on the pillow. After the noise, the blinding
flashes, the horrible stench, everything is mellowness and deep calm: the summer
light filtering through the red canvas of the huge tent, the sea breeze, which in the
Boulogne outskirts blows gently from all sides, the muffled footsteps of the nurses,
the musical clicking of the cups, even the hushed groans of the wounded, which are
gradually diminishing, as some are recovering while others are dying.—(BB)

4 June 1916

Dear mother,

What a change after all that to arrive in a white bed with a nurse and
an orderly to serve you, and what a rest! My bed is next to my corporal's,
a super guy. I didn't tell you that the wound I got during the evening of
the battle of 3 June is in my left thigh. I fortunately managed to go to the
emergency station on Menin Road.

André

Camiers Hospital, 6 June 1916

You have probably received my card telling you that I was wounded. It's
happily nothing very serious, and I think that I will be cured in a week.
I don't think that I can describe to you the German attack, but it was
terrible, particularly the bombardment. We felt as though we were on a boat,
such was the turbulence of the ground. I was buried twice, and fortunately I
was rescued. I lost all of my equipment and all of my little souvenirs (except
for a few photos), which a trench mortar sent hundreds of feet into the air.

André

Camiers, 16 June

My dear father,

My wound is looking good. I had the nice surprise of seeing Jean entering
our tent carrying a magnificent basket of strawberries. I really enjoyed

Convalescent Camp. André third from the right

his visit, and he promised to come back when I am in the convalescent camp from where we will be able to walk along Paris Plage. Nothing from Philippe for ages, but good news from Etienne.

André

Le Havre, July 1916

My dear parents,

I'm still at the base waiting to go to the Front one of these days. I'm having a good time at the YM here, where there is something interesting every day: lectures, concerts, or very well-directed services by the chaplain, who is so popular that we clap when he enters the room. I promise you a good letter when I find Phil at the battalion.

Affectionately,
André

Convalescent Camp
Le Havre, 13 August 1916

My dear mother,

Here I am after a week at the convalescent camp, and one really can't complain about the treatment we get. Yesterday I was having a little nap after lunch when, all of a sudden, I was awakened, and was surprised to

*see Oncle Charles at the door of the hut, having come specially, direct from
Paris, to see me. I immediately asked permission to accompany him to town,
and then to the station. He was returning from Mont de Plan and had lots
of news to report. After a good walk at the height of land from which the
view is magnificent, and a little walk along the beach, we had a brief tea
before going to the station.*

André

EACH NEW LETTER FROM ANDRÉ confirmed the speed of his recovery, and in late
July he wrote joyfully from the convalescent camp in Le Havre, where, following
several circumstances, he was to stay quite a while. It's a beautiful time of the year,
and André took the opportunity to swim in the sea, work in the garden, walk in Le
Havre, and see his Basset cousins. There was no lack of entertainment: one day it's
the visit by Oncle Charles, having come especially from Paris to see him. Two or
three times it's Etienne, and when one doesn't have any visitors, the YMCA offers its
reading room, its lectures, and its concerts. However, he was bored with relaxing.
André was looking for something to do, if possible something to create.—(BB)

30 August 1916

My dear mother,

*I am still at the convalescent camp. Tell Jacques not to try to take apart the
base of the shell that I sent him that could have exploded in a Canadian
trench.*

*I have had several visits from Etienne these last few days, but I haven't
yet been able to go out with him. I am drawing quite a bit, and I have
already had several thank yous from people who received a drawing from
"the soldier."*

André

4 September 1916

My dear Philippe,

*About a week ago, while on parade, we were asked whether there were
any artists amongst us, and obviously I gave my name, and they sent it to
headquarters somewhere, so, if I could get an artist's job, I might not see you
at the regiment. I would probably be in the R.E. group. I will therefore wait
here until such time that I'm told to go.*

*We would be very comfortable here if we received a little more money. We
get only 10 francs a month and one pass per week. Etienne has come two or
three times to see me.*

André

Mosaics at the Convalescent Camp. The Corps commander comparing a battalion
cap badge with a model made of coloured chalk and glass.

I DON'T KNOW HOW our convalescent's inventive spirit led him to the activity of
drawing a series of crests of the Canadian regiments on the lawn of the hospital. It
was exactly what he liked to do, and there he was collecting the necessary bits: the
sand and the sea shells for the white, crushed coal for the black, powdered bricks for
the red, crushed glass for the blue and the green. With this original palette, leaning
forward on the lawn, patiently, meticulously, our lawn artist drew, coloured, wrote
symbols and mottos, and everyone at the hospital became interested in his mosaics.
So much so, that one day a senior officer enquired about who had been the artist,
and said he would put in a good word about employing him in the army's artistic
department. This comment nurtured a new hope for André, long ago forgotten.

Meanwhile, his superiors arranged for him to transfer to a service function. He
was given the supervision of the vans, supplying each morning the soldiers who
were training in the hills. Once there, André, an experienced camper, installed a
double row of cauldrons, separated by a long flame element. Soon fifteen hundred
soldiers were drinking their hot tea with their midday meal. The stay in Le Havre
was not unpleasant. It wasn't, however, worth a Paris leave.—(BB)

PHILIPPE GOES TO THE FRONT

PHILIPPE GOT BACK TO his numerous exercises and miscellaneous military duties
with gusto: gymnastics, shooting, bayonet combat, guard duty, Zeppelin attacks,
digging of trenches, kitchen duty. One day, the sergeant asked all the soldiers in
hut No. 4 to step forward and announced that they were in quarantine until further

notice, because of a case of measles. That isolation was later extended, because of an outbreak of mumps. It was a rather strange situation, where they weren't sick, didn't need to join in the military routine, but were nevertheless not entirely free. It was thus that Philippe and his roommates had the good fortune to explore Kent, while their poor comrades had to continue with their military drudgery.

Thanks to the quarantine, everything for Philippe is new and fun. Then on 4 June they embark at Southampton, and life changes suddenly. First of all, there was the terrible news on that day about the casualties at Sanctuary Wood. The rumour was that the entire battalion was destroyed. Fresh troops are required to replace them. Not a wonderful situation, and, more important, what about André?—(BB)

Salient d'Ypres, 4 July 1916

My dear parents,

My last letters described our arrival at the rear of the lines. This time I will talk about our arrival at the trenches. We had been warned one evening about our departure the following morning. Indeed, we wake up and breakfast very early, so that the country kitchens can go ahead. After cleaning our barn and tidying up, we see that the road is black with an endless mobile ribbon. These are the buses that are to take us to the Front. Each vehicle leaves when it is full, and keeps its distance with perfect regularity. Such is the Army Service Corps. The countryside that we are crossing is peaceful and prosperous. The peasants are in the fields, the kids at school. The houses, with their roofs of red tiles, make a lovely contrast with the greenery of the countryside. We pass through villages with their churches, their small inns, and their round cobblestones, which shake the buses and their occupants. Once we parked to allow a grey car to pass, with a general and his aide-de-camp.

After quite a long trip, we turn into a country road, where our lunch is waiting for us. It's a kind of soup-stew with endless ingredients. We then trade in our caps for quite heavy steel helmets; we dump our big bags and keep only the small ones. The rumbling of the guns, lightning flashes, and black smoke on the horizon tells us that we are now very close to the Front.

We leave soon after, on foot this time, sometimes on the road, and sometimes across the fields. All of a sudden, the landscape changes. Instead of beautiful crops, weeds, instead of occupied farms, empty houses. No familiar sounds, no chickens in the courtyards. The air stinks of rot, everywhere are round holes filled with water, and the trees along the road are decapitated. The beams of the demolished roofs are silhouetted against the clear sky of this long summer evening. We cross a bridge and enter a large, partly ruined village. We are allotted the cellars, where we will sleep during the day, so as to work at night. All in silence, no orders, no singing, no lights, except

Philippe

distant lights that glow on the horizon until nightfall. We are beginning our existence of rats in their hole.

Philippe

13 July 1916

Dear Mother,

All in all, our hole is very comfortable. After our first night in the cellar, we got up quite late, then, climbing to the ground floor, we explore our new home. The big room with a tiled floor has two windows looking out to the road. After a thorough cleaning, we move in. Over the fireplace, in gilded frames, the father and mother look at us with unflinching eyes. Poor unknown people, where are they now? On the right is a lovely wardrobe, on the left a washbasin with a mirror above it that by some miracle escaped destruction. We move the beds to the cellar, we set up the tables and chairs in the little back garden, where there are a few daisies and dahlias. It would be perfect without the bombardment that is starting. This is my first impression of firing. A bit of shrapnel and some explosives fall on the village. First of all, one hears a sinister whistling, and then the dull sound of an explosion. All that was falling far away, fortunately. But close enough for us to hear the crumbling of walls, and see the plaster and the dust fly up to the sky.

A little later, it's an airplane duel. Two planes fly in from opposite sides. Machine guns spit and, all of a sudden, one of the planes falls somersaulting head-over-heels before finally dropping straight down and disappearing behind the house across the street. We will never know what happened to the pilot.

During the first evening, it wasn't yet completely dark when we set out towards the trenches, in single file, guns on our shoulders and shells in our belts. After having splashed about in the mud, we are brought to a pile of shovels. A veteran digger tells us what to do and recommends that we stop each time there is a flare in the air. The Germans could possibly see us if we moved.

You ask me to give you my impressions? It's difficult to sort them out. At times, when the bombardment is intense, I have certainly been frightened, but I also have other impressions.

Philippe

24 July 1916

Dear Mother,

One night we were ordered to do a thorough wash prior to entering the trenches ... Then we filed out under the rain, and in the dark of night. Horrors for someone who slips and falls in the ocean of mud that would quickly cover him right up to his neck. I have had the experience of such a bath. Fortunately, the trenches are relatively dry, and I rested while waiting my turn as guard. Soon after, I was perched on a kind of elevated step and could see for the first time a view of no man's land, and I can assure you that it isn't beautiful: barbed wire in every direction, and beyond, bomb craters and more bomb craters, and in the distance the yellow glow of a flare. Our sector is not as exposed as others. We can therefore sleep, if we aren't on guard nor occupied in repairing the wall. We only have two meals: one at 11 a.m., and the other at 5 to 6 p.m., and we are really not badly fed. After some terrible weather, we were able to dry out the last day in the glorious sun. We then marched a long way up to the rest camp. To be thus out of danger is like the removing of a huge weight, and the number of hours that we sleep indicates how tired we were! During our free time, sergeants make us do some idiotic exercises, while our friends are killed very close by. It's ridiculous to spend two hours learning how to salute a colonel!

One night, as I was going to bed, a corporal came to tell me that I was wanted at the officers' hut. As I was putting on my putters I began to wonder what mistakes I could have made, when before me stood Etienne. He was sun-tanned, with red cheeks, and hadn't changed at all. We talked in the corner for a good while, and it was long enough to really catch up. We will see each other again, as he is camped nearby. Sunday afternoon we went to the Bath Parade, which takes place in a covered van where one suspends one's uniform on a cross and is showered in hot water, and watched by the saints in their niche. It's delicious to dress again in clean undergarments and disinfected uniforms!

Philippe

3 August 1916

Dear Mother,

We have been busy recently digging trenches. We sleep behind the lines. Then, every evening at dusk, we cross the fields. Once at the depot we hear about what we will do: Digging party or Carrying party. Depending on our role, we are given shovels or we are to carry loads, sometimes on our shoulders, sometimes pushing small narrow-gauge wagons. The work is hard and, because of machine-gun fire, is often dangerous. As soon as we hear the first bullets' pop-pop-pop, we immediately disappear, some in a bomb crater, the others behind some ruin or simply lying down. No one gets up until the bombardment stops. These experiences are often fun, but other times very sinister. After a week of this grave digging, we rested in a village about a day's walk behind the lines. It was nice to see big trees and wheat fields, and to sleep in a barn.

Philippe

17 August 1916

Dear Mother,

The harvest has started. With its bright yellows, its golds, and its dark yellows, it resembles the paintings of Oncle Ernest. It makes such a pretty contrast with the greenery of the trees and the red of the tiles, and the wings of the windmills! Western friends deplore the primitive methods of the

Digging trenches

local farmers, who are still harvesting with scythes. But what would their
machines accomplish in small fields of less than a few hectares?

Philippe

22 August 1916

Dear Mother,

*We occupied trenches quite close to those of the Germans, so that we could
hear coughing and muffled voices. Our comrades, who we were replacing,
told us such frightening things about their snipers that, when it was my
turn to guard, I thought I wouldn't come through it alive ... The view
that I had was gloomy, and time stood still ... daylight finally comes with
its welcome light, which reveals the sandbags of the Germans' walls. We
are then very happy to regain our dugout and to go to sleep on a pile of
bags. However we find there another enemy: big rats, who always try to
nibble something.*

*One night we suffered from a new type of bombardment. The Germans
used their Minenwerfer, or trench mortar. These bombs look like pails that
spin in the air before falling and exploding with a terrific bang. Watching
for them is one of the sports in the trenches – one sees them very well against
a clear summer sky, as they come in – then running quite fast along the
trench to avoid them. However, we get tired of this game quite quickly, and
we develop a strong desire for an attack and a battle to teach them a lesson.*

Behind our lines there is a little valley, a true valley of the shadow of death. Where there were woods, a small stream, greenery, and flowers, there is now only holes, mud, a few smashed stumps, not a leaf, not a tuft of grass! It is awful at all times, but when it is illuminated by the uncertain greenish light of a flare, it is ten times worse.

Philippe

BEHIND A 28-POUNDER IN BELGIUM

C Battery CFA 1st Division, 3 June 1916

My dear mother,

As you can see, my address has changed once again. I am now in a battery that is being created, and I have at last a permanent position. After the artillery school, I have wandered for a few days from one place to another. First of all, the Ammunition Column for one day, then I was attached to a battery. A few days with the trucks and a few hours in the trenches with this battery – the one where Walter Hyde, the son of Mrs H from Montreal, is – then I was sent here. I am happy to finally have a definitive position, and we are all very interested in the creation of our new battery. Captain Bell, who was with me in the Ammunition Column, is now with us here.

I can't make my letters more detailed or more interesting beyond what I'm permitted to say. Naturally, when one is at war one must from time to time venture where German bombs could hit you, but since I have been here, I have never had one of my men killed or wounded.

I'm in a battery that has no guns, no horses, and almost no men – that is to say, we have about twenty men presently. Since the mess of our Ammunition Column no longer exists, the Captain and I have dinner alone, unless there are visitors. We are very hospitable here at the Front. The other day we hosted a paymaster. Today it was our chaplain, who lives like a hermit in a magnificent tent.

Etienne

14 June 1916

My dear mother,

I'm still behind the lines with the few men in our battery, waiting impatiently for the guns, horses, and additional men. The other day, with a triumphant expression, my French-Canadian batman brought me back a Matin. *He got it from a soldier who had bought it to see the last figures on the numbers of Austrian prisoners, and for whom the text was written in Greek. In fact, with the naval battle, the death of Kitchener, Verdun, the combats on this Front, and finally the glorious Russian advance, the newspaper doesn't miss much news, and it is more and more encouraging.*

Etienne

49th Battery, 3rd Brigade, 1st Division, 25 June 1916

My dear mother,

I don't know if you remember having seen the caricature done by Bain's father: "I am staying at a farm." It shows an officer sitting on a case in front of a pile of bricks and rubble, the only remains of a Flemish farm, construction materials for trench building and empty food tins are piled up on his side. He writes home and starts like this: "I am staying at a farm." This caricature will give you an idea more or less exactly of the place from where I am writing to you. When I entered the cellar this morning, lit only by a single candle that gave a certain glow on two or three men and an officer lying in the corners, I wondered what we would think about sleeping in such a spot in peacetime.

I did a tour in the trenches that we had taken from the Germans two weeks ago, and I brought back some souvenirs: one Mauser rifle, some German shells, and one or two military postcards, one of which I tried to send home. Did it pass the censors? That's what I would like to know.

I have a new address. The 49th Battery is Battery C, which has simply changed name. It is now a real battery in every sense. I returned there this morning, and I enjoyed a "tub" and the complete change enormously.

On my return, I found a ten-line note from Phil, announcing that he is now in France. He seems completely happy with his situation. I will go to see him as soon as I get the chance. As for André, it looks as though he is again in Le Havre.

Etienne

June 22nd 1916
The 12th Brigade C.F.A. commenced its existence today with major SB Anderson CFA in command and Capt JD Armour CFA as Adjutant. The Brigade is composed of 8th Battery CFA Capt FJ Alderson CFA in command; 47th Battery CFA Capt AA Durkee CFA in command; and 49th Battery CFA Capt GH Cook CFA in command. The work of organization of Brigade H.Q. and the three Batteries is to proceed at once.

30 June 1916

My dear mother,

Here we are already at the end of June. The Russians haven't yet been stopped in their triumphant advance; the Italians are winning back their lost territory; the French continue their heroic defence of Verdun; and we are

*ready to help them along the entire Front. It seems to me that we can now
start to think about the end of the war.*

*I'm writing to you from a dugout covered with six feet of bricks and earth,
which we enter through a tiny, twisty passage just large enough to squeeze
through. Once inside, it's perfect calm, and one sleeps like a groundhog.
But we don't always need to be shut into a dugout. We eat in an old country
house, a little dilapidated it's true, but there remains a table, a sufficient
number of chairs, in addition to the thirteen volumes, I think, of the great*
Universal Dictionary of the 19th Century. *The rest of the furniture and
books have long ago disappeared, since it was abandoned twenty months
ago.*

Etienne

49th Battery 12th Brigade 1st Division,
July 15th
Lieut ES Bieler – 49th Battery and 4 O.R. sent to Divisional Anti-Gas School.

19 July 1916

My dear mother,

*I am sending you only a few words to tell you that I'm still in good health,
and all goes well. I haven't had any news in the last few days from either
André or Philippe. I'm wondering if André has already returned to his
regiment.*

Etienne

49th Battery, 12th Brigade 1st Division
July 21st 1916
Major SB Anderson C.O. and Capt JD Armour Adjutant made an inspection of
Battery Wagon lines this morning, At the 8th Battery horses and harness were in
good condition, especially horses. At the 47th the condition of horses showed a
great improvement. The harness was not satisfactory. The 49th also showed a great
improvement in condition of horses, which are rather a poor lot. The harness and
lines showed results of a lot of work.
July 25th 1916
Enemy blew up a mine and 49th battery fired 204 rounds in retaliation. Men
worked all day repairing Brigade Headquarters.

25 July 1916

My dear mother,

*It's been one year and one week since André and I arrived in Boulogne. I
am currently very busy. I spend two days in the trenches, then four behind*

the guns. On one of my free afternoons, I met the vet, who was looking for a riding partner. He's in his forties, great fun, and a good mate, so we rode off together. We were riding along a rocky road, which wasn't very pleasant, when we came up to a railway crossing, and saw a better road a few hundred metres to the left. So we turned onto the railway line, and all of a sudden we hear a whistle behind us. It was a train, and ahead of us was a bridge crossing a stream fifty metres further. There was a fence on both sides of the tracks, but fortunately a few metres of grass before the bridge allowed us to jump out just as the train was closing in. I learned never again to ride along a railway line. Apparently we had crossed into France, and we were pleased to hear French spoken, and not this dreadful Flemish.

I'm sorry if I frightened you a bit with this German postcard. I sent it almost sure that that it would never get there. Yesterday afternoon I met, quite by chance, Chisholm, Jean's old friend. I was pleasantly surprised to see not only the three stars of a captain, but also a Military Cross pinned onto his uniform.

Etienne

30 July 1916

Dear Jacques,

I often think that it would interest you to travel here to come and see the marvels that we use to fight this war: guns of every calibre, from the one that shoots the airplanes and fills the sky with puffs of smoke, right up to the big one that shoots now and again a 1,500-pound projectile more than five miles, before shooting a huge number of stones hundreds of feet in the air and making holes big enough for a house foundation.

There are also the airplanes that, despite the shells and the enemy planes that chase them, venture up to five miles behind the lines. From time to time we see five of ours flying through the air in a perfect V formation. Those are the ones that drop bombs onto enemy territory. There are also the cigar balloons, tied to a cable two or three miles behind the lines, whose sharp eyes see even minor movements that they signal to the artillery. But if you came here, you would wonder where these enormous guns are: the fact is that you can go by one of them at a distance of two hundred metres without seeing anything, and you need to be shown twice before noticing them, as they are so well hidden. Then, if you want to get closer, there's always a guard to stop you. It's no admittance, except on business, even for a general. But I've now said enough. The censor would say that I have revealed state secrets.

If you were here, you would hear all sorts of extraordinary rumours. When the newspapers don't reach us on time, we are satisfied by the many

*sensational news items that come from unknown sources. Six weeks ago it
was the Austrian Army who surrendered to the Russians. Two days ago, it
was von Hindenburg who surrendered, or Hindenberg who took the Tsar
prisoner. But the funniest part is that we believe it.*

*It's been three weeks since seeing either André or Philippe. They must be
together, but I'm not sure.*

Etienne

49th Battery 12th Brigade 1st Division
August 1st 1916
Brig-Gen HC Thacker C.M.G. C.R.A, 1st Canadian Division inspected the horse
lines of the Brigade, The Headquarters and 8th Battery were very satisfactory, the
harness and vehicles being in good shape and the horses and vehicles being in
good shape and the horses were in good condition. The 47th and 49th Batteries
need considerable work yet to bring them up to standard of the 8th Battery.
Weather fine.
The wagon Lines of the 12th Brigade were inspected by the Corps commander Lt
Gen Hon Julian Byng K.C.B. K.C.M.G. M.V.O. accompanied by Brig Gens Burstall
and Hacker and staff.
He expressed himself as very well satisfied with the appearance and condition of
personnel, horses and vehicles, especially those of Headquarters and 8th Battery.

JEAN AND ETIENNE AT THE OFFICERS' HOSPITAL

IT IS UNNECESSARY TO LOOK for a danger that is always present. Etienne realized
this on 3 August, while standing at his periscope trying to determine the whereabouts of an enemy battery, which, from the trenches opposite, viewed continuously
their position. His instrument served as a target for the enemy shells, and one hit
him at the very top of his head. When our wounded officer was lifted and eventually treated in the ambulance, the loud congratulations from the doctors confirmed
that, if the shell had hit one millimetre lower, he would never have thought again!
However, there was a pleasant side to the accident, being the days in the hospital at
Boulogne, not far from Jean, and Le Havre, where he saw André.—(BB)

49th Battery 12th Brigade 1st Division
August 2nd 1916
Lieut ES Bieler, 49th Battery was wounded in the head at the Battery Observing
Point this morning. He was removed to Dressing Station at Railway Dugouts and
afterwards to Casualty Clearing Station.

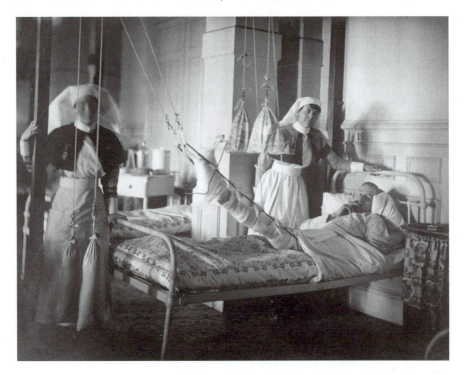

No. 14 General Hospital, Wimereux, Officers' Ward

No. 7 Stationary Hospital
Boulogne, 5 August 1916

Dear Mother,

Before this letter arrives you will have received my telegram of this morning, as well as an official telegram announcing that I am wounded. There is, in fact, nothing to worry about.

    Thursday morning I was studying the enemy lines with a periscope, when, all of a sudden, I felt a kind of burning sensation on the top of my head, and the sound of a gunshot vibrated in my ears. They laid me down at the bottom of the trench, and the stretcher bearers bandaged me. They bandaged me again there, and again one mile further on. The doctor says that it's a minor surface wound, and that the bone is untouched. A car brought me to an ambulance, where, as I was the only wounded officer, I was politely invited to dine with the doctors. After dinner, another car brought me to a big hospital housed in a multitude of large tents and huts, where I spent the night. I was in the area of non-serious injuries. In the room next door there were those too seriously wounded to be able to be moved immediately. It was the next morning that I left there in an ambulance

Jean Bieler

train, as slow as it was comfortable. At 15 km/h it would be difficult to seriously shake the wounded. I arrived last night at 9 p.m. at a huge hotel, recently built, that is superbly arranged for use as a hospital.

We are cared for exceptionally well by pleasant nurses. It's pretty funny to be in a bed with white sheets, in a lovely room overlooking the sea, with a pot of honeysuckle on the table. I don't know how long I'll be here. I could leave this evening for England or stay here until I'm cured. I haven't yet seen Jean. I'm really hoping that he'll be able to come this afternoon.

Etienne

JEAN IS THE MOST DISCREET OF THE FOUR BOYS, and it was finally, in this comfortable hospital setting, that he was able to describe to Etienne in some detail what was happening at Boulogne.

Soon after his arrival in Boulogne, Jean was selected to work in the office of the hospital's registrar. He was slowly promoted to more and more important and time-consuming roles, although remaining a "non-com." He was responsible for the preparation of reports and complicated statements, as well as receiving and

Arrival of wounded at No. 3 Canadian General Hospital (McGill) in France

answering letters, which often resulted in frequent night work. He had to assist in the arrival of convoys of the wounded, which were for the most part subsequently evacuated to hospitals in England. He needed to find out from the doctors their name, age, division, and the seriousness of the wounds, for those who needed to travel on special trains. This meticulous registration lasted often right up to day-break, and nevertheless, at 7:30, he had to be on parade, and right after that, to begin the day's routine once again.

His work lacked both charm and variety. It was the work of a statistician, basically tabulating losses. Filling the pages with names, figures, etc. wasn't very exciting, and brought little intellectual activity. Jean, however, accomplished his task conscientiously, and was appreciated by his superiors. On several occasions, he attempted to apply for a position as an intelligence officer. The hospital managers were not interested in helping him to leave. His recompense was the feeling that he was useful, which somewhat relieved him of the annoyance of being and remaining a "non com."

At the beginning he had accompanied, or found again later, fellow students from McGill that he liked, and his letters showed the attachment he had to his friends. He talked of Harry Fry, George Hobart, and C.K. Mathewson. He enjoyed his evenings or excursions with them. As gradually the numbers declined, when for reasons of health or service they went their way, the isolation weighed on him. There were plenty of new friends, but they weren't like the old ones. In the evening or on

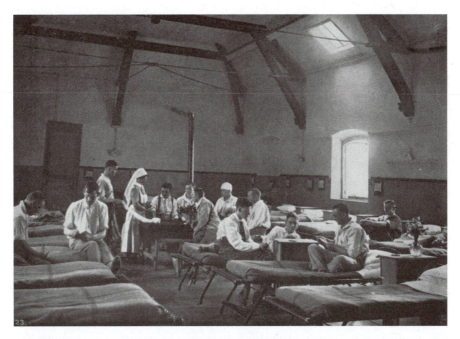

Ward C at "McGill"

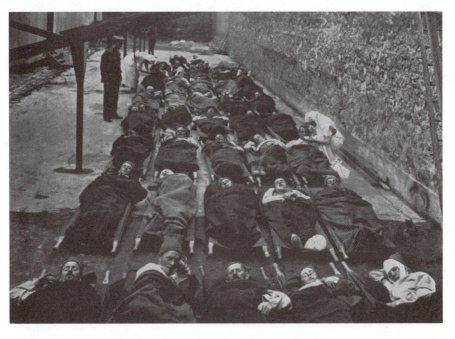

Stretcher cases ready to go to England

Sunday, the office workers could take off and see something less dreary than the barracks. Downtown Boulogne was not far, and he liked to go to Madame Dupré's pastry shop or to Mr. Arbousse Bastide's presbytery. Jean admired the clergyman and his wife for their constant and generous hospitality.

Then there were walks often only in Boulogne, as he had to be back to the barracks quite early. And on other occasions he would walk further away along the coast, to Wimireux, for example. Or, when he found a bicycle, he would pedal towards the countryside to Montreuil or some even-more-distant village. He loved the peace of a picturesque castle, or some hotel where he could have a better dinner than what was offered for the evening tea at the barracks. Jean's circle of friends outside the hospital was on the increase. He talked often of a certain lord of the manor who looked after Canadians particularly well.

However, his favourite moments were when he had the opportunity to see one or another of his three brothers. Boulogne was a crossroad, and also the medical centre. All Canadians came through at one time or another, and Jean watched for these passages. But no one would have thought that they would be spending another three years there; hope fed the necessary courage, and helped to put up with the insufficiencies and the difficulties. He was, of course, constantly reminded how fortunate they were as compared to the poor soldiers living in their muddy trenches, where they were little more than moles.—(BB)

15 August 1916

My dear mother,

The last time I was writing to you from the hospital and was telling you about my conversations and my walks with Jean. That stay in the hospital didn't last long. Monday morning, the doctor, an old, very amusing major, told me during his morning visit: "Temporary base tomorrow." I asked him if that would kill all chances for a leave. He simply answered, "I would not dare put you before a medical board. They would laugh at me if I did." That's to tell you that my wound is healing rapidly.

So it was this morning that I arrived at the Canadian Base, where I presume that I'll be a little while longer. My first task was to find out about André. He had recently spent a couple of days at the hospital with a little bronchitis, and is now in the convalescent camp. If all goes well, I hope to go and see him tomorrow. It's fortunately not very far from here. You will once again be at Les Colombettes when this letter reaches you, about to begin another winter.

I'm afraid that we must be resigned to be again separated during this year, but once winter is behind us, it won't be too many months until we can be sure that the war is happily over.

Etienne

27 August 1916

My dear mother,

On Tuesday the doctor found that my wound was completely healed and that I could go back to the base. Wednesday afternoon, I went to find André. I found him in a lovely camp, surrounded with flowers in the middle of some lovely properties at the top of the hill that looks out over the town. André will have told you in his letters that he was employed to decorate the garden by creating Regimental Crests. He looked very well and very active. He had been offered a job as a draughtsman, and he was waiting for someone to come and take him to the interview. He seems to be very keen on it. I'm leaving tonight, taking a group of reinforcements to the Front, after which I return here until I'm sent back to the Front for good.

Etienne

5 September 1916

My dear mother,

I am back at the Front. They suddenly announced on Friday morning that I was leaving that night. On my way back from the Front last week, I took the narrow-gauge train to Boulogne. It was thus that Tuesday night I ran into Jean at 8:30, which didn't surprise him. I was able to take Jean to dinner in town. We had lots to talk about, and each went his way at 10 p.m. with the intention of continuing the next morning. On my return, I went to see André as early as possible. I found him still at his convalescent camp. He was hopeful to land the draughtsman job, and was impatiently waiting for an interview.

Etienne

14 September 1916

My dear mother,

Did I tell you that, on my return here, I found that my place had been filled, while my name remained on the battery's register. I was therefore sent to the wagon-lines to help the captain look after the horses and the food supplies. Strangely, the captain had been the warrant officer at the Ross Barracks while I was there. Captain Biggar is a large Englishman, full of energy and good humour.

I was in the horse-lines yesterday morning while the horses were being brushed when I heard a pipe band, then a whole battalion started down the hill and passed very close to me. I didn't have much trouble in recognizing that it was Philippe's. I found him a few minutes away from here. He looked very well and saw everything so positively. He had walked many miles in the last few days, but said that he had almost enjoyed the march. They were presumably on their way to a distant destination. We walked here and there together on the outskirts of his camp, talking about this and that, letters from home, what we had done since our last meeting, etc. If you saw him, dear mother, I'm sure that you would have no regrets to have let him leave. It seems to me that he has gained so much in every way since I saw him sixteen months ago at our departure from Montreal.

Etienne

THE MONTH OF AUGUST ended with Etienne's close call, André's recovery in Le Havre, and Philippe's arrival at the Front. Etienne was back on his feet and preparing to join the march towards the Somme.

These pages can't contain the history of the war, nor relate the sentiments of those in the back who followed in thought, in prayers, with worry, with pain, their sons, engaged in a fight which surpassed human strength. And, it seemed that it would never finish. One would never open the newspaper without emotion. One read with a heavy heart the announcements displayed by the magazines, one trembled to see names of people we loved. One tore, with a broken soul, the envelope of the military mail coming from Europe, happy again when it announces a wound and nothing worse. We were living very near other parents, sharing the same anxieties. Relationships were created by common pains. Then, by some message from above, in 1916, we were officially granted Canadian nationality.—(BB)

Les Colombettes, 27 August 1916

My postman told me today that Rumania has entered the fray ... If that's true, I think it's very significant, particularly now when Italy has decided to declare war on Germany. The Rumanians are a sly bunch. If they get into the act, it seems to indicate that the Germans are close to defeat and all that is now required is a good kick. Could be a sign of the end. It seems impossible to me that there won't be a strong reaction in Germany. All that brings some hope.

Charles

CHAPTER EIGHT

The Somme
September to December 1916

The capture of the sugar refinery at Courcelette by the Canadians

ON 4 DECEMBER 1915 THE ALLIES DECIDED to evacuate Gallipoli. Two days later, the Allied generals met at Chantilly, the French military headquarters, to develop the strategy for the defeat of the enemy in 1916. They decided that the Somme was to be the scene of the battle to end all battles. It was of no great geographical significance, but the objective was: to help the Allies in Ypres and other Fronts by preventing the Germans from further troop transfers from the west; to relieve the pressure on the French forces at Verdun; and to maximize the attrition of the German Army.

The commander of the French armies, General Joffre, was increasingly concerned about the French losses at Verdun and felt that a combined offensive with the British at the place where the French and the British lines joined would be ideal. On the other hand, General Haig had always insisted that he preferred to attack near Ypres, and then pursue the enemy northwards. In conclusion, despite the fact that it wasn't a vital centre, and that the Germans had both a communications advantage as well as a shorter line, Haig decided to compromise, and agreed to go ahead.

The Germans attacked Verdun on 21 February, and the assault claimed huge French losses. Time had moved on, and the urgency of the Somme attack intensified. Joffre wanted to attack on 1 July at the latest, but Haig felt that the troops were not fully prepared and the Canadians and a number of other reinforcements were not due until September. Joffre's date was at least a month earlier than Haig desired, but he finally decided to accept.

The Somme was a highly unsuitable place for an Allied attack. They would have to fight their way up to the crest of the hills, where the Germans had dugouts forty feet deep, secure from the worst bombardments. In addition, the Germans had been provoked for months by British raids, and had taken measures to further strengthen their defences. No army could conceivably succeed in breaking through this Front.

THE OLD OR RECENT NEWS in the newspapers fascinates Etienne: the Verdun resistance, the Russian advance, the submarine warfare, the ground regained by the Italians, and the concept of advancing at last, to fight under an open sky, and to be thrust into the great adventure that seemed to be electrifying the Canadian troops. "Can't we foresee an early ending of this war?" However, as they advanced to the Somme, Etienne became more and more concerned about the local news. Was the actual experience of what they were about to witness going to be as horrifying as some were saying?—(BB)

FINALLY, ON 1 JULY AT 7:30 A.M., the Allies attacked the German Front just east of Albert. The Canadians were still two months away. It was a massive beginning with an enormous seven-day bombardment, combined with discharges of gas. The enemy was alert and still mainly underground in their dugouts. Then, the British soldiers went over the top, through the British barbed wire, formed a solid line, and began to advance. The Germans had plenty of time to emerge from underground and man their machine guns. Bullets flew in every direction as the British struggled across no man's land. They sustained the heaviest loss ever suffered in a single day: sixty thousand casualties and twenty thousand killed.

49th Battery 12th Brigade 1st Division
September 1st 1916
During the day Batteries registered further points in anticipation of an attack to be made by 39th & 49th Divisions. Artillery fire on both sides was below normal today. Great difficulty is being experienced by Brigade in obtaining sufficient water for the horses. We applied to 25th Division but could get no satisfaction from them. Each unit is allotted to a certain trough and permission must be obtained for any other units to use these troughs. We were allotted water troughs 300x S. of Cross Roads in Varennes (8 miles N W of Albert), but this is too far away to be of use to us. It takes about 2 ½ hours to make a round trip from wagon lines.

September 2nd 1916
Intense bombardment commenced on a wide front. All Batteries got away fairly well together. 47th Battery reports a counter attack is expected. Huns can be seen in the road by the apple trees at R. 31 b – All Batteries notified to shoot at these troops in the open and some very good sport was indulged in. Our Batteries dispersed two lots of these men who were evidently assembling for a counter attack. No counter attack was delivered. So far no information has been received as to the result of our infantry attack.

September 3rd 1916
49th Battery report enemy reinforcements seen coming up through Thiepval. All batteries ordered to engage these troops. F.O.O. 8th Battery reports about 500 prisoners with white and Red Cross seen coming over to our trenches without arms in direction of Mouquet Farm – The Colonel saw these men himself.

On the road to the Somme
8 September 1916

My dear parents,

The war news is good. The women and children are harvesting everywhere in this beautiful French countryside. They line up their bales with perfect

Brick factory

symmetry. Let's hope that the husbands and fathers will soon return to taste this flour!

Philippe

49th Battery 12th Brigade 1st Division
September 11th 1916
Brigade Headquarters moved from Albert la Boiselle headquarters.
We are in old German front line where there are two deep dugouts. Remainder of shelter will have to be improved.

September 13th 1916
Lieutenant Gilfoy 49th Battery was slightly wounded in the thigh by shell fire.
Orders sent to Batteries for night shooting as above – 33 rounds per Battery per hour to be expended.

THE PATRICIAS AT THE SOMME

THE BRITISH ATTACKED AGAIN ON 14 JULY.
On 7 September the Princess Pats had left Flanders, partly by train and partly on foot, arriving in the Somme battle area at Albert on the 13th, where they bivouacked in a brick quarry. They then marched on towards the village with the lovely name of Courcelette, and halted nearby. German positions solidly established in impregnable trenches blocked the road.—(BB)

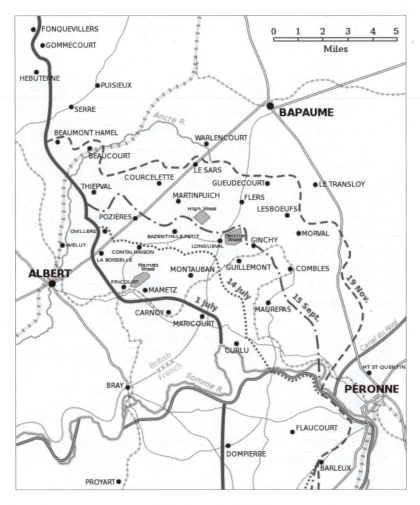

Map of the Somme battlefield, 1916

GIVEN THE DISASTROUS RESULTS AT THE FRONT, General Haig decided to make a particularly strong attack in mid-September using fresh forces, including the Canadian Corps. The German Front had been pushed back to about a mile from the
little village of Courcelette, and he hoped that a breakthrough there would clear
the way for the cavalry to advance northward to the important town of Bapaume.

On 15 September, Etienne, and his Artillery Brigade, were posted at the rear,
and began an intense bombardment. The Canadian Corps was to help secure several points having good views of the enemy trenches. They crushed the Germans'
front-line trenches, but the Princess Pats, meanwhile, lost their way in the broken
ground, where all landmarks had been obliterated. Though raked by rifle and
machine-gun fire as they struggled forward between shell-holes, they eventually

managed to join their fellow British brigades, and in short order captured the trenches.

49th Battery 12th Brigade 1st Division
September 15th 1916
Zero time received from 1st C.D.A, it will be at 6:20 AM today.
Our bombardment started – it was very intense – some bursts appeared to be very high at first. 49th battery reports one gun out of action – the "A" tube being cracked. 1st C.D.A. notified of above and asked if they can procure another gun from us.
From reports received, everything up to now seems to have gone very well.
Party of 152 German prisoners passed our headquarters on their way back – all looked very worn and haggard. As far as is known, our infantry have everywhere gained their objectives. Definite information is not available, as telephone communication forward has been most difficult to maintain.
49th Battery report they are out of ammunition – this is the second time this battery has run out of ammunition today and shows that there is apparently poor management at their wagon lines. Message from 1st C.D.A. "Reduce your rate of fire to 1 round per gun every two minutes." It is reported by our airplanes that our infantry have gained their objective and now hold Courcelette.
49th – Battery's task is to above shoot as the latter is still without ammunition. And don't expect to have any before about 2 AM.
Latest airplane photos taken at 4 PM today show new German trenches as follows … (above information is not much good now as our attack this evening gained all their objectives).
49th Battery advises at 3:50 AM that they now have 700 rounds ammunition on hand … Battery ordered to detail an officer to report to Brigade headquarters as Liaison Officer.

Despite the appearance of the first military tanks ever to be used at war, the infantry was being decimated by enemy fire. They nevertheless advanced during the night in the midst of the flames, the rat-tat-tat of the machine guns, and the explosion of the shells. For three days the battle continued, night and day, and they succeeded in making a significant advance. The village was finally captured, four thousand prisoners were taken, and dozens of enemy trenches were occupied. It had been a bloody massacre, but the Canadians had finally conquered the high ground at the top of the hill. However, all six tanks had eventually broken down, and the cavalry never got the chance to make the famous breakthrough.

September 16th 1916
O.C. 49th Battery reports that the gunman who went with Lt. Kitto this morning to report as Liaison Officer to 25th Brigade has just returned and reports that Lt. Kitto was killed by a sniper on his way up.

Operation order received from 1st C.D.A. for an attack and bombardment this evening commencing at 4:57 PM. Attack will be made by 3rd Canadian Division (including PPCLI).

It wasn't enough to capture the town. There were more attacks during the following evening and the next day in order to advance further and consolidate their victory. Then the trenches and the roads were cleared, and only the ruins and craters remained. Some three hundred Canadians had been either killed or wounded.

"AND PHILIPPE MUST BE IN THERE SOMEWHERE," said Etienne. There was a mysterious telepathy, which often preceded the underwater telegraphy and the military post. Blanche, who was staying in Toronto on the night of 15 September, had felt that one of her sons was facing a dangerous experience. Soon after, she received a cable from Jean: "Philippe safe," and, then a word from Ottawa, announcing that Philippe had been gassed during the battle, and is being cared for in an ambulance.—(BB)

21 September 1916

My dear mother,.

Here is a letter that you will receive very late. I hope that you haven't been too worried about me and that my Whizz-Bang will have reassured you. I'm writing to you from a tent pitched in an orchard, very far back from the Front. It's a Divisional Rest Station.

The newspapers will have informed you about our departure from Ypres and our arrival in the Somme. Our attack the other day succeeded very well. From afar the Germans are good soldiers and know very well how to shoot us. However, when we are on to them with our bayonets, they throw away their guns and act like whipped dogs, shouting: "Kamarade! Gute Englisher," and all that after having killed half our friends. Arriving in the second trench, we all began to cough and were forced to put on our gas masks. That's why they have sent us here to rest. There is nothing serious, only the cough and a tickling of the lungs.

Philippe

29 September 1916

My dear mother,

As soon as we felt sufficiently well, we got bored and decided to go back to the battalion. I am now in the machine-gun company, and I can assure you that it's more interesting and not more dangerous than being an ordinary soldier. They tell me that I have grown and gotten thinner. I'm with Nick and all my friends. In answer to Dad, I would say that I have had a unique experience that I wouldn't have wanted to miss for anything in the world, now that it's over.

Since my first trenches, I have always wondered how the interior of the German trenches compared to ours. My curiosity was more than satisfied the other day during our attack, when we chased out the occupants from an enemy position. They were in such a rush to get out or to be saved, that they had left everything intact. This allowed us to examine in great detail and even to prepare a meal with the remains of their rations: their bread is very black, their butter has a horrible chemical taste, and their meat had a suspicious smell, which led us to believe that it was horse meat. In a package that a poor guy had probably received from his parents, we found some delicious biscuits, some cigars and cigarettes. A few of my mates took away some helmets, but I took a nice ground sheet, bigger and more useful than ours.

The other day, as I was in the rear, I admired an artillery duel. (One doesn't admire them from the first line.) The night was black and there was a great silence. All of a sudden, everything goes wild, it seemed that the terrible sound of guns came from every point on the horizon at the same time. Even at this distance, such a horrible uproar that one couldn't hear one's voice. The intermittent light of the flares, the lightning of that storm, was sufficient to view this terrible scene. Earth cascading from the sky, bits of boards, tracks, posts shot in every direction and falling into this chaotic earthquake. From the trenches come May Day signals, red and green flames flickering in the midst of the black smoke, as well as dust and obscurity. If this isn't hell — where is it?

It was also here that I had an interesting encounter with some German prisoners. We spoke French with one and English with the other. They were happy to be away from the gunfire, but concerned about crossing the channel. Did we take the precaution of labelling those boats filled with war prisoners, so that their submarines didn't attack them? I told them not to worry.

Philippe

❧ ——————————— ❧

THE HUGE SACRIFICE OF THESE LAST THREE MONTHS had resulted in some minor advances, but General Haig was unsatisfied and decided in late September that a concerted effort must be undertaken to push on. The British and Canadians, including Etienne's artillery brigade, were in heavy combat on the Theipval ridge, only a mile northwest of Courcelette. Major General Currie's 1st and 3rd Brigades, and Major General Lipsett's 7th Brigade, including the Patricias, then attacked at Ancre Heights, also a few miles away. Etienne's artillery had helped break up a counterattack by the Germans, but despite much vigour and determination, they had little success, and they were soon back in their original positions. On 8 October there were 1,364 Canadian casualties.

Neuville-Saint Vaast Trenches (Arras-Lens Front)
26 October 1916

Dear parents,

Since my last letter we have marched a long, long way, right up to this area, which is new for me. We are part of our brigade's machine-gun unit, but don't change my address (7th Canadian Machine Gun Company).

Philippe

The final engagement at the Somme for the Canadians was 8 October. On the 9th, the Patricias marched northwards to their position on the Front near Neuville–St Vaast. Etienne's artillery brigade was to march back to Camblain l'Abbé at the end of the month.

FINAL DAYS AT THE SOMME

15 October 1916

My dear mother,

During the wet weeks that followed Courcelette, because of the rain, I often slept with a tin sheet over my head, and I would awake with my feet in the muck. But don't worry, dear mother, I am having them dig a little shelter where I will be completely dry. I will even build a stove from some tin cans. One of my gunners found in one of the enemy's trenches a superb two-man saw, like those we used to build La Clairière.

We pick up wood in the ruins of the village, and then the major and I warm up and count the logs. My commander was on leave, so I have to not only feed forty men, but also four guns, which are at least as hungry as humans. Yesterday, while doing the rounds beyond the firing line, I come accidentally straight into my old battalion the "Princess Pats." Just before the sergeant major blew the two sharp whistles announcing their departure, I had the time to exchange two words with Phil, happy and looking well, and well recovered from his gas attack of last week, which earned him four good days of rest at the hospital.

Etienne

10 *November 1916*

My dear mother,

After the battle and the advance, one had to be resigned for a while to a war in slow motion, which we shared with the rats and the vermin.

Etienne

49th Battery 12th Brigade 1st Division
November 25th 1916
49th Battery reported at Wagon Lines
Our responsibility terminated at 5PM and the event was celebrated by all hands having a drink. Weather very wet all day.
Operation order 128 and March Tables received from 1st C.D.A. The first days destination is Amplier – on the 28th Vacquerie le Bouca – on the 29th Marquay.

26 *November 1916*

My dear mother,

It's working, we are leaving behind us all signs of civilization and are penetrating deeper and deeper into a gloomy desert of ruins, sticky mud, and bomb craters. Bravo! We will perhaps finish this huge clean-up before Christmas.

Etienne

27 *November 1916*

My dear mother,

We passed through Raincheval. Up to this time the traffic was very congested and on the whole very poorly regulated. Marching was very difficult, owing to the many halts occasioned by repeatedly bumping into the Brigade immediately in front of us, and also to the large number of vehicles, which continually got mixed up in the Column. From this time on, conditions were much better, and the column made fairly good time to its destination. On the whole the accommodation was very poor. Everyone was very tired and it was late when the Brigade was able to turn in for the night. The horses, though tired, stood the march well, which was a hard one, owing to the many hills and the adverse conditions mentioned above.

Weather – cold with a heavy fog most of the day.

Etienne

30 November 1916

My dear mother,

We are marching and my bilingualism gives me the opportunity to take off on horseback as a scout, accompanied by a colleague and an escort, to organize the evening's sleeping arrangements: roofs for the men and enclosures for the horses. It's much more interesting than dragging one's feet along the roads. On arriving at our destination, our first visit is always with the mayor, an old farmer very keen to give us the addresses of his councillors, and even to give us a lift. These lovely people are for the most part very happy to be helpful to the soldiers. During these long trips, I became quite attached to my horse, a big skinny animal, who is no beauty, but is always courageous, intelligent, and faithful.

After having crossed the undulating plains of the Artois and of Picardie, one arrives in the coal country near Lens. We had reached our destination and we were installed in luxurious lodgings at the home of a miner: large room with tiled floor, fireplace, electric lights, three rooms upstairs, with beds laid out with sheets and quilts. We are like royalty, and our men are almost as well off.

Etienne

49th Battery 12th Brigade 1st Division
December 5th 1916
Arrived Camblain-Chatelain. Billets are excellent- All under cover and very comfortable. Horses staked in fields. The afternoon was spent in "Shaking Down."

30 December 1916

The Christmas holidays are spent brushing the horses, cleaning the guns, polishing the harnesses in view of the coming inspection. Two chickens were at the heart of our Christmas menu, letters and parcels made for a very pleasant balance of the day. Unfortunately, the banquet that we wanted to organize for our men couldn't be arranged.

Etienne

IN CONCLUSION, the battle of the Somme was strategically a dismal failure. The spirit of the German army had been worn down, but the Canadians and the British were worn out also. There had been such high expectations prior to the battle on 1 July, and now all that could be said was that both sides were at a complete deadlock.

THE YEAR-END AT THE ARRAS-LENS FRONT

3 November 1916

My dear parents,

After our latest turn in the trenches, our unit was located in the cellar of a demolished house. A little staircase descended into an arched cellar, where a hot-water boiler kept us warm. The furniture included metal beds, a table, and some chairs. One of us did the cooking, while the others took turns on guard duty, which wasn't unpleasant, as we were sheltered. In fact the government has dressed us well, with big leather boots that go up above our knees, an insulated leather jacket, a great overcoat, as well as a rubber sheet.

Philippe

1 December 1916

My dear parents,

This letter will bring you my Christmas wishes. I can assure you that, on that day more than ever, my heart will be in Montreal. I will think about the good breakfast at daybreak, the various tricks that we invented to fill the morning, the dinner where there was no lack of turkey or plum pudding. Finally at 4 PM we lit the Christmas tree, and we were ecstatic about all the surprises. And how we liked to prolong this wonderful moment sitting around the fireplace! Don't think that I've become sentimental or that I'm suffering from the blues. But how can one forget Christmas at home, especially when one is so far away? When all this is too much, I then say to myself Why not be happy with the thought that we will be together next year? There's no question that this war will finish, and that we will once again find the joys of Canada!

Philippe

20 December 1916

My dear parents,

The other day two of my friends and I were lunching on eggs and French fries in a small inn in the neighbourhood when a young French soldier appeared at the door. Picture the emotional state of the mother as he walked in: crying, laughing, kissing, not able to believe that her son had returned! I wondered when it would be our turn to give such joy to our parents. Not for only nine days, but forever.

*Last night we left the trenches after a long stint of eighteen days ... I am
feeling better than nine out of ten of my friends ... It is true that it's very
sad to have lost Ferguson. After the confrontation, we had waited for him
on the battlefield, thinking that he might return with the slow ones, but
no trace of our friend. We asked all our friends and learned that a man of
his description had been killed by a sniper at the Front. Can one say that a
super chap like him is better off in heaven than in this awful war?*

Etienne

30 December 1916

My dear parents,

*We had a marvellous Christmas day: blue skies, warm sun, and in the
farm where we were resting, a big table in the most beautiful room for our
banquet. We had roast goose from the bread oven, a great stuffing, mashed
potatoes, and a real plum pudding. Our officers had added some fruit,
some nuts, and some cigarettes. Afterwards I went for a walk on a nearby
hill and, having sat down against the base of a ruined wall of a château,
I reread my letters from home. The day was ended pleasantly at the YMCA
concert. The varied programs that they offer are wonderful. All that,
followed by the trenches with the rain and the mud that has reappeared.
Despite the fact that our rubber boots reach our thighs, we sink so deeply
that the water and the mud enters from above.*

Philippe

AUTUMN WITH ANDRÉ

Canadian Base Depot, 5 October 1916

My dear father,

*I have left the convalescent camp and I am once again at the Canadian
Depot, where I'm still waiting for this job as an artist.*

André

C.B.D., 6 November 1916

My dear mother,

*I have just heard and saw in a paper that Philippe was wounded, but I
don't yet have any details, and you probably already know more. I hope that
he will be able to go to England.*

*I'm working here as a food distributor. We transport it in cars right up to
the training camp four miles from here.*

André

11 December 1916

My dear mother,

I am concerned to see that you are worrying about my job as an artist, but it is true that I'm beginning to think that I may have lost it.

Here I work with the corporal, a good guy. Every morning they send us some twenty men to load a large car, and we walk three kilometres to the place where we make the tea, outside in any kind of weather, for a great number of soldiers.

I'm sad at not being able to write better French, but I hardly speak French any more, and it would be much easier for me to write in English.

André

18 December 1916

My dear parents,

Recently I have visited all the shops in town to see whether I could find something very French to send you for Christmas, but how disappointing, nothing but English books and English things!

I met at the Ruban Bleu an old man who is a great admirer of Father Chiniquy. He's an old rector who has a nephew in Montreal. He's sad at having given to someone his last treatise on Chiniquy, and he would like someone to send it to him. I gave him Dad's address, and I think he'll write to him about that.

André

YMCA, End of December 1916

My dear mother,

After a good stay and rest at Le Havre, here I am once again at the Front.

I wasn't at all expecting to leave for some time yet, when all of a sudden the order came to prepare to leave.

I hope to see Etienne and Phil soon. I haven't yet rejoined my battalion. My address is: Pte. A. Bieler 10962 No. 1 Co. 3rd Batt. BEF.

André

CHAPTER NINE

Crossroad
January to March 1917

Canadian Artillery loading an 18-pounder field gun

SOON AFTER THE ALLIES LEFT THE BATTLEFIELDS of the Somme in November 1916, the Allied generals began to plan a new strategy. The war had been very costly during the last two years, but some believed that there were some positive signs. The Germans had finally failed in Verdun, and despite the cost, the British and French had seriously hurt the Germans at the Somme. Change and new strategies were required.

The three major military leaders felt that no one was taking the necessary strategic leadership. France had decided that General Nivelle's assurances of victory, based on his success at Verdun, were more convincing than those of General Joffre, and he replaced him at the helm. Lloyd George was elected prime minister in Britain, and he promised to run a better war. Both Lloyd George and Germany's Ludendorff insisted that victory could be achieved. Ludendorff despaired about those in Germany seeking peace.

Given the huge French losses in Verdun, the French were having problems defending their southern section of the Western Front, let alone attacking the enemy. In order for General Nivelle's plan of ending the war in one stroke to be successful, it was necessary for the British and the French to operate a joint strategy. General Haig's role was to distract the Germans from General Nivelle's activities. In early 1917, the British pushed the Somme Front some five miles. They then followed with a well-rehearsed offensive near Arras. This was to include the conquest of Vimy Ridge. The Canadian Corps had not been involved in any major operations during that winter.

DESPITE EVERYTHING, Christmas and the New Year hadn't been too bad at the reserve camp of Mont St Eloi. There was the usual exchange of good wishes and presents, in the presence of Princess Patricia of Connaught, the colonel-in-chief of the regiment. There were gala menus, parcels from home, cigarettes, a comedy evening, and on 1 January a grand revue.

Jean wrote on the 26th that he had had a quite busy Christmas, but brightened by some good meals, some friendly moments, all helped by the nurses' efforts to liven up the hospital wards with decorations and concerts. Madame Ladouceur told us yesterday that her son had said that Jean had delivered a very successful speech at a banquet in his hospital on 1 January, given in honour of those boys leaving the hospital to go on active service.

Jacques Grellet had a sad Christmas in quarantine, while waiting to build roads near London to relieve the intense traffic congestion blocking the capital. We will no doubt know tomorrow how André spent his holidays. We are wondering who would have the influence to allow him to leave the kitchens of the soldiers' mess. He is warm and sheltered, but for a soldier it's not very ambitious. Of all of you, Jean seems to be the only one who attended a church service, I hope that the others will have sung a Christmas hymn silently within their heart or have found a few friends with whom to sing an old refrain.—(BB)

Les Colombettes, 28 January 1917

My dear boys,

On Wednesday I spoke at St Andrews in Westmount, tonight at the 1st Baptist, and tomorrow at the YWCA. It's a little too much for one week, but the next one will be quieter. Jacques and I have begun to assemble a little war museum, which we are finding very interesting, and for which "contributions will be thankfully received." Herewith the catalogue so far:

- *Princess Patricia badge, sculpted by André and fixed on a red ribbon*
- *Piece of shell found in Alsace by Mr Roussel*
- *The point of a shell, sent by André*
- *Etienne's identity badge*
- *Philippe's Princess Patricia shoulder strap*
- *A button from a Brandenburg prisoner*
- *A piece of sandbag with authentic trench mud, from Philippe*
- *Dried flowers from the Front, sent by André and Camille*
- *Paper knife made from a shell casing from Tante Julia*
- *Woven article from a blind soldier, sent by Mr Cornu*

Blanche

ON 5 JANUARY, Etienne finally left on his first leave, and arrived that Saturday evening in Paris, to spend ten lovely days in Neuilly under Oncle Charles and Tante Lucy's welcoming roof. A few days later, Jean came to join him, and together the two brothers lunched here, and dined there, spending the evenings elsewhere, loving being together, and for the contact with Tante Julia and those cousins that the war had not dispersed. The service at the Neuilly church falling religiously the day after the arrival and the day before the departure: "How will the young man purify his path? By being careful in accordance with your word."—(BB)

16 January 1917

My dear mother,

It was on Friday evening the 5th that I left the battery. At noon the next day I was lunching with Jean at the Hôtel de Boulogne, and was persuading him not to delay making a request to join me in Paris. That night I slept at the hotel in Boulogne and I arrived in a quiet and grey provincial like Paris on the 7th.

On Sunday Tante Lucy, cousin Idelette, and I went to the Trocadero to hear Vandervelde and Maeterlinck at a big rally protesting the deportations of Belgians to Germany. The oratory talent of one and the sense of humour of the other resonated in the great hall.

Monday there was a little invitation at Miss Wellington's in honour of an airman that was leaving for the Front the next day, after several days' leave.

On Wednesday evening, there was a Zeppelin alert. I saw the firemen zooming along the streets, ringing their alarm bells. All the lights were extinguished, and everyone was waiting for a bomb explosion from one moment to the next. One hour later, the bugle was heard to confirm that the danger had passed. The next day we heard that a projector had seen a strange cloud and that it was likely to have been that bomb, dropped from the supposed Zeppelin.

On Thursday we spent a lovely day with Tante Julia in Fontainebleau. Cousin Guy had no problem getting a day's leave. He put on his blue uniform with red stripes and looked absolutely great. Military life seems to agree with him. He is a junior officer candidate, requiring day and night activity. After lunch, we did a long walk in the woods. The sun appeared, and the forest was superb. We went right up to the shooting range on a large plain surrounded by a pine forest, where we showed Tante Julia a few of the famous 75s practising. From there we returned to the station to catch our train.

I was forgetting to tell you that, the evening prior to my departure, I had the pleasant surprise of finding Jean at the Merles. I was hoping for that, but I didn't dare to expect it. On Saturday, Jean and I went to see the "Bourgeois Gentilhomme." That reminded us of those Wednesday evenings when Dad would read to us the poetry and prose of the great philosophers.

We have been talking about your trip here. You must come and spend a year in Europe, and it's naturally to Paris that you should come. Dad could find thirty-six churches needing a pastor during the war. As for you, please don't come to Paris to kill yourself with work for war charities, but I know you could find interesting and useful work. We could come to see you from time to time, whether to Boulogne or Paris,

Etienne

Les Colombettes, 4 February 1917

My dear boys,

Will this letter get through? Will the navigation continue courageously as before or are we for a while going to be separated from Europe? That's what we are asking ourselves quite naturally the day after the too famous and too *active Bernstorff has finally gotten his passports.* Naturally all thoughts turned towards Washington, as soon as we learned here the Germans' intentions, and we have been in suspense for forty-eight hours, right up to the moment when the Standard appeared in the newsstands last night. And now, what will the future be? Could an intervention by the US precipitate the outcome, or will it simply be another complication?*

The newspapers are announcing the probability of a major offensive with the Germans in your region. Mother is quite preoccupied, as you will no doubt understand. In the case that God preserves you or one of you is taken prisoner, take all possible precautions by having a belt with money hidden in it. You know better than us how to handle these painful eventualities. A guy called Palliser, who I think was your friend at the PPCLI, had a curious adventure in Germany. He must have been made prisoner during his first clash with the Germans. He was seriously wounded, and the parents were told that there was no hope of seeing him again. But it seems that he ran into some German civilians who sympathized, in view of his ability to speak their language. They took care of him, fed him, and when he was cured they arranged for him to escape across the Dutch border. He doesn't understand himself how he could have had such luck. He now lives in Lachute.

Charles

* Count Bernstorff, German ambassador to Washington, announced unrestricted submarine warfare as of 1 February.

A COLD SPRING ON THE WESTERN FRONT

12th Brigade CFA, 17 January 1917

My dear Jean,

It's been a week since I received your letter from the hospital in Wimereux. I presume that you are now out and that you are completely cured from your bout with the measles.

I have just spent another seven days in our section in the middle of the woods. I had, happily, an infantry officer nearby, and we exchanged visits to discuss the rumours. It was thus that he told me that his batman had the other day met the colonel's batman, and that he had said that we had taken quite a bit of the second trenches not far from here. It was unfortunately only a rumour, but it had the same effect as some real news.

Etienne

21 January 1917

My dear mother,

During the night the cold did its thing and created a thick sheet of black ice. On going out to do a tour of the guns, I slipped and hurt my knee. The doctor suggested that I rest the knee, and they sent me here, as I couldn't do my turn in the trenches. It's luckily nothing.

The officer whose place I have taken here has told me a funny story. I told you that we were in the park of a little château. The house is a ruin, but a few yards from it there is still a pond holding a large population of carp and goldfish. A German bomb found its way right into the middle of the pond and exploded, killing the majority of the inhabitants. The fish floated to the surface and were soon frozen into a thick layer of ice. So, quite simply in breaking the ice, our men found enough fish to make three or four good meals and break the monotony of stew and "bully beef."

I have just received this letter from Tante Julia. The Parisians have been hit by the cold harder than us. We can buy coal, or at least what one calls coal. It's not worth shipping, as all it is is a black dust with a hard piece here and there that looks like anthracite, but is more likely a piece of slate. Nevertheless, we get it to burn, and we are kept warm more or less.

Dear mother, don't tire yourself out with lectures and collections. But I know how Tante Julia appreciates the results of your efforts. I will be interested to hear if you have done that planned conference in Ottawa, and to have your impressions of the reception at Rideau Hall.

With this new U-boat campaign, I fear that we won't be able to have you on these shores this summer. In fact, we are optimistic these days and we can hope to see you again in Canada, maybe before the end of the year.

Etienne

25 January 1917

My very dear Dad,

Here I am during the last several days camped with my section in a lovely little corner of the woods and rolling fields that almost remind me of the La Clairière countryside! My shelter isn't too bad. It's a large room, about ten by fifteen feet, built of circular steel sections bolted together. At one end, a lovely big fire is crackling away in an open fireplace, brought there, I presume, from some nearby abandoned houses. We are quite isolated from the men. There is some infantry in nearby shelters.

Etienne

P.S. Tell Mom that I don't want to see any quotes from my letters reproduced in the Daily.

4 February 1917

My dear mother,

Be very careful not to tire yourself too much with all your war work. It will perhaps be finished soon, and you mustn't be sick at our return.

I'm pleased to hear about your lunch at Rideau Hall, and that the Duchess of Devonshire and her distinguished guests appreciated your efforts. That must have been encouraging for you.

Etienne

4 February 1917

My dear mother,

It's almost a Canadian winter, except that we don't have reasonable central heating. These days we are living in a big house that is, to us, like a palace. We have paper to replace the window with one broken pane to let in a little light, and lots of wind, however, it is a real house. The rooms are high, wide, and long, and therefore cold, as the little stove where we make our fires isn't sufficient to heat them. We are lucky to easily get coal, which is not the case everywhere, especially in Paris.

No mud in the trenches, as is usually the case, even in the winter, but instead of the mud there is a thin coating of ice on the trench floors, so that one travels around better on skates than in heavy boots. It's Sunday today. Here, however, it's just another day. We can't give "Fritz" one day's rest.

I met Percy Corbett very near here the other day. He's now in the 13th Battalion. Tell his brother if you see him that he's looking well. I would like to say more but I don't dare.

Etienne

12 February 1917

Dear Tante Julia,

Good news from Jean and Philippe. Jean had measles and was been sent to the Hospital in Wimereux, where he is being cared for in a bathhouse. The second is still at the Front and is feeling well. Please tell me how you found André, and whether you had been able to go to Le Havre to see him.

Etienne

49th Battery 12th Brigade 1st Division
February 10th 1917
Lieut. E.S. Bieler's name was submitted as a candidate for the army Intelligence corps as he had an excellent knowledge of French and knew German fairly well.

16 February 1917

Dear Tante Julia,

You will have read more in the newspapers about what we do than I can tell you. Here we are today in the countryside that only a week ago belonged to the Germans. It was magnificent to hear and, for those that were able, to see this artillery barrage, cutting everything in its wake to allow our infantry to make the biggest one-day advance since the beginning of the war. Already the next day we advanced on enemy soil. We are now in one of these famous German underground apartments with long, steep stairs leading us to a long, narrow panelled gallery sheltered from everything. There are rooms of every description and every size. In every one we see indications of surprise and a hasty escape: meals half-eaten, open lunchboxes, clothes thrown here and there on the bunks. We find all kinds of strange objects, curious or useful, lamps, telephones, pistols, etc.

It's been a long time since I've seen my brothers. André is not far from here, but impossible to have a moment to go and see him. Whereas Philippe must be back in the trenches somewhere.

Etienne

49th Battery 12th Brigade 1st Division
March 1st 1917
The 8th battery fired on four barrages supporting a raid on German trenches carried out by the 14th Canadian Battalion and raid was a very satisfactory one. Ten prisoners were brought back belonging to 22nd Regiment and 10th Reserve Regiment. Dugouts were blown up and casualties inflicted on the enemy. The enemy retaliated for 10 minutes on our trenches they then closed down.

3 March 1917

My dear mother,

I have an officer from another battery sharing my dugout. We read or write, and to help the evenings to go by we roast some snacks on the fire, and then we go to bed early and get ten good hours of sleep, unless we are woken in the middle of the night to send a few pills to "Fritz" to force him to be quiet.

What do you think of this nice little advance in the Somme? I jumped with joy on the 26th when the news was heard on the telephone. We had been almost trapped in the mud for so long in front of these same villages last fall that this success is particularly interesting for us, and my men were just as interested as me when I brought them the news and showed them the advance on the map. Since then, we have gotten the newspaper three times, and it has regularly announced a further advance. Things seem to be moving ahead very fast in Mesopotamia as well. Is this the beginning of the end?

I have heard that Philippe is not far from here now, and I have some hope to see him perhaps one day next week. It's been more than five months since I saw him last.

Nothing from Jean, nor André, nor Philippe. Cousin Emile will soon come on leave; he is passing his officer exams in Orleans.

Etienne

IF THE LETTERS FROM the civilians to the military were longer and the parcels more numerous, there was also a sad trend in the opposite direction: a short note with no address and often without a date, written in the rain on some poor paper. Sometimes more detailed and more easily read letters written in the rear, and even a small package containing an object made at the Front: like a medallion sculpted at the edge of the canal of the Yser, a gun shell, the tip of a bayonet, or a button from a uniform, filed, crimped, and adjusted to make a lovely paper knife. Another time it is the thin wooden strips from a wrecked airplane used to create a little frame prettily decorated with a garland, or a piece of lace bought from an old Flemish worker: "Mom will know what to do with it!"

After his rest at Le Havre, André had rejoined his battalion in the coal-mining area of the Pas de Calais. This was not to be a happy return. First of all, André's best friends are gone. They are demobilized, wounded, dead … Then it's the short sad days of winter in that dreadful climate of the North: it drizzles, it smokes, it rains, and the water drips from the helmet just like a roof during a shower.—(BB)

February 1917

My dear father,

There's a big difference at the battalion since I left it. I meet very few known faces, but I was pleased to meet Biddolph, who I think is in touch with Mom. He reminds me a lot of Etienne.

What bad luck I had with Philippe! Here he is away just as I come to his side; but I am very glad that he went at this time. I thank you for having made some approaches for me, but I fear that they are not of much use, unless I am wounded again and sent back to England.

The mud is incredible, wherever we go. Last week we were in tiny shelters, about three feet high, and just long enough to lie down. We were seven: very super squeezed!

André

31 January 1917

My dear parents,

It's gotten colder, a few inches of snow are covering the ruins and the rubbish, the horrible chocolate cream has hardened, and one can walk on it without sinking.

The sides of the trenches are dry and hard like rock. What a mess in the spring when it melts and collapses. I'm not looking forward to it!

Philippe

Bruay, 17 February 1917

My dear parents,

I am on guard duty today and we are now resting in a small town. About twenty of us are lodged in the attic of a private house on the town square where the market is held. On that day, as of 6 a.m. the carts begin to arrive, and the women, helped by the children, don't take long to install their little boutiques. At 8 a.m. the crowd, civilian and military, gathers together. It's great fun to observe the variety of uniforms. The young French soldiers are in light blue, often quite pale, the old soldiers have funny old tunics, the alpine hunters are well turned out, with their berets down to their ears and their dark-blue jackets that highlight their yellow stripes, the Belgians are in khaki, the colonials are wearing a red fez, and, as for us, we have the dullest uniforms. Meanwhile the children play football in the square.

Philippe

26 February 1917

My dear parents,

Last Sunday I went to the 3 p.m. service at the Protestant church, and I was so glad to find myself in this environment. A nice lady approaches me at the end and invites me to see her the next day. I went and found out that they were the Reverend and Mrs. Lemaitre, of Swiss origin, who had lived in this invaded country for many years, but, given their nationality, they had been able to return from Germany and continue their work on the other side of the Front. As soon as I mentioned my name, we discovered that we had many acquaintances in common. They also very much admire Tante Julia, who, before the war came to organize plays in their church. Mrs. Lemaitre told me many interesting things about her experiences in Germany. I have a nice little home at her place and I intend to benefit from it during my stay here.

Philippe

General Hospital, Etaples, 25 March 1917

My dear parents,

Here's what happened to me: We were resting in the little village I was speaking about, when one morning on the village square during morning gymnastics, I didn't feel well at all. When I went to see the first-aid corporal, he found that I had a temperature of 103 and so sent me to the ambulance and from there to the Casualty Clearing Station. The following day they dress us with cap and gloves and, without further comment, we are loaded onto mobile stretchers and eventually put to bed in a hospital train, where we were in comfortable beds near large windows through which we could admire the sad and monotonous countryside. Due to endless stops, we only arrived at our destination twenty-four hours after our departure. How happy I was after this tiring trip to be stuffed into a fresh white bed and to sleep like a log! I woke up in a beautiful huge tent, where Jean soon arrived for a visit. You can imagine my joy in seeing him after this two-year separation! He was very kind and thoughtful, and, as he left, gave me a nice present.

Because of a minor setback, I am still in Etaples, and I'm working as a junior nurse making beds, as the room's librarian, secretary, sweeper, accountant, handy man, assistant to the sergeant of the Red Cross service. All that makes the time go by. Jean came back to see me.

Philippe

49th Battery 12th Brigade 1st Division
March 15th 1917
A.H.Q, 12-31 received informing us that the Batteries of the 12th Brigade C.F.A.
were to be split up in the following manner:
47th Battery to go to the 1st Brigade
8th Battery to go to the 2nd Brigade
49th Battery to go to the 3rd Brigade

March 20th
Lieut. E.S. Bieler was transferred from 12th Brigade to 1st Brigade

1st Battery CFA, 20 March 1917

My dear mother,

While looking for the last time through the letters and things that were beginning to clutter my files, and overcrowd the limited baggage of a soldier,

I have just found your package of January 11. I must confess that I have lost the pen, and she was so soft that it was a pleasure to write!

I'm giving you a new address on this letterhead: 1st Battery CFA; the 47th has in fact been eliminated. Today one section of two guns has moved to the 3rd, and my section comprising the other two to the 1st. The major leaves to command the 3rd. From three batteries, they have created two of six guns each. And it isn't without tears and gnashing of teeth that the 47th, which had basically been closed thirty months ago, was divided forever. I received the order to prepare for my exit to join the 1st Battery last night. I had previously felt that I was attached to the battery and to my men, of which I took several of the best ones! However, if that had been difficult for me, how much more difficult it must have been for the major, who had recruited the team and led it for thirty months.

But, in the army you have to accept things the way they come. I have only been in the 1st Battery for a few hours, and I think that I feel good about where I am. I knew two of the officers at McGill, and they both greeted me warmly.

Etienne

29 March 1917

My dear mother,

I pick up my letter after a two-hour interruption. I was interrupted a moment to shoot several rounds. We have finished now, and I still have a moment before the food rations arrive and the letters leave.

In your last letter, you were asking me a whole list of questions. I will try to answer as best as I can, given the restrictions of the censors:

I have a section of two guns. They are field guns called 18-pounders that are similar to the French 75s. Each gun has one sergeant, one corporal, two bombardiers, eight gunners, and nine conductors, excluding the cook, the saddler, and the blacksmith. The gun and the two vans each have six horses. In action I only see the gunners and the guns. The rest of the section stays at a certain distance behind. This is what is called the "wagon line." It is that part of the battery that is responsible for supplying us with munitions and food.

I have been in this section since the beginning of January. It has been changed quite a lot since we moved. A few of my best junior officers and men have stayed with the rest of the battery. But the heart is the same, and we have what it takes for the section to be second to none. In action, my job has mostly to do with the battery in general. We each take turns at the observation post for one or two days, depending on the situation. We have

An 18-pounder

a good situation here. We sleep in one of those beautiful courtyards that can only be found in France, and that we were quite pleased to find. There are piles of old wooden building materials in the area. We can make a good fire in our courtyard in the evening, and cook some delicious meals, or at least they seem that way after a cold day in the fresh air. We also each have our turn at the battery and our turn in the trenches with the infantry. That way we lead an ambulant life, rarely two nights in a row at the same place.

I have just heard from Tante Julia that André is once again at the Front. He would maybe be with the "Pats" again; the 3rd Entrenching Battalion was only a reserve for the infantry. The "Pats" are apparently not far from here. I intend to have a look around there the next time I will have a free afternoon, maybe in two or three days.

Etienne

Boston, 4 March 1917

Dear boys,

*Complete change of scene in Boston. I arrived in a very aristocratic section,
at the home of ladies that have travelled a great deal, that went to school
in Lausanne or Dresden, and with whom it was easy to talk of many
interesting things. It's very strange to be in the US at this time. Public
opinion is overexcited, and people think that war with Germany is now
inevitable. Some are sad; they are the confirmed pacifists, and there are
many of those. Others think that courageous sacrifice is a must, in order to
maintain the great reputation of America.*

*I think that I told you that our congress was meant to deal with religious
education in the schools and universities. In fact, we spent our time on
the actual situation and the obligations that the American citizens now
faced. Thus, one of the projects was on this: "Is the obedience to Christ's
laws compatible with the necessities of the modern state?" The one who
presented this thesis, Professor Brown from New York, showed three possible
attitudes: one, as the Germans say, impossible; two, those who pretend that
Christianity necessarily implies non-participation in war, like Bryan;
and finally, those who think that, given the current circumstances, there
are problems even more serious than war, that Christianity itself tries to
avoid. The subject is now much discussed in Canada, but seems new for
the Americans.*

Charles

March 1917

My dear brothers,

*Two of Dad's bookcases were about to collapse, which would have been
catastrophic. It was therefore necessary to repair them, which took a lot
of time. Wednesday afternoon, Harry and I went to visit the ginger-ale
factory. There are a lot of bottles that explode with a big bang when the soda
water is poured in. Friday I went with the Millers to St Anne's. We saw
the greenhouse, the baby chicks, the cows, the pigs, the bulls, and the calves.
We also went to see the maple-sugar production, and we tasted an ample
assortment of the product. We also went to see the military hospital. There
are several huge two-storey houses connected by hallways. We had a good
look, and then found out that it was forbidden to visit.*

Affectionately, your brother
Jacques

"Always marching." Panoramic view of Canadian troops carrying trench mats, interspersed with German prisoners in a wasteland of mud.

NOTHING OF GREAT IMPORTANCE HAPPENED during the spring of 1917. Neither Lloyd George nor Haig were sure how to achieve a victory, but they were nevertheless convinced that they would get there. The Allied leaders were watching the Germans strengthening their positions, and were beginning to be concerned about Nivelle's promise for a definitive victory.

Meanwhile, the Germans were also becoming more aggressive on the high seas, and began to threaten the British Isles with a policy of sending their U-boats to sink all enemy shipping at sight. Their only hesitation was that they knew it could lead the Americans to enter the war. The situation changed dramatically on 31 January, following a sudden announcement from Germany confirming that they would immediately introduce unrestricted submarine warfare: "all shipping, including neutral ships, would be sunk at sight in the War Zone of the Eastern

Atlantic." President Wilson broke off relations with Germany on 2 February, but still hoped to avoid declaring war. The German U-boats immediately went into action.

Etienne's 12th Brigade had a month's rest at Camblain l'Abbé.

CHAPTER TEN

War Relief

1915 to 1918

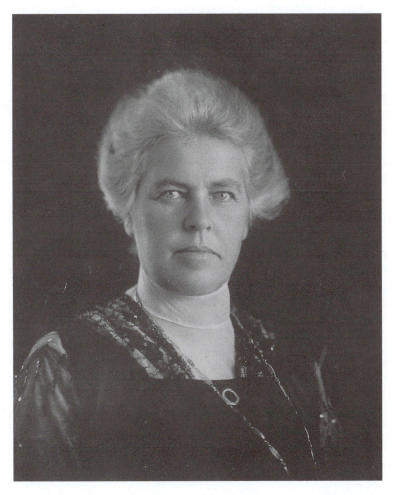

Julia Merle d'Aubigné

BEFORE THE WAR, BLANCHE'S SISTER, Julia Merle d'Aubigné, had been active doing charity work among the homeless and poor in Northern France. As war broke out, she saw the need to create an organization to help the hordes of refugees from the north who had escaped from the horrors of war. Her centre of operation was the Cirque d'Hiver, a circus building built by Napoleon in Paris, which had been turned into a vast refugee camp. She was instrumental in arranging for the French government to take over that operation, so she could concentrate on helping the trainloads of soldiers from the north, who were arriving in Paris devoid of anything. She then created an association called "Les Amis du Soldat." Her brother Charles, pastor of the Neuilly church, along with a few of his colleagues and friends, including the pastor Victor Monod, who was to become chaplain of the French Fleet, and General Robert Nivelle, who led the French Army in 1917, gave her valuable support, but she nevertheless soon faced a serious financial problem. She decided that perhaps her sister could help raise funds in Canada, and she sailed to Montreal to talk to her. Blanche was immediately receptive, but said that it would be impossible unless she left her home and went to seek the funds in the United States.

Blanche was a very energetic, pious woman, who despaired at seeing her boys leaving for the Front, and felt that she too could work hard at making some sacrifice and contribution for the country and the world at large. Julia's request might well be a perfect answer. Despite her sons' dangers and sufferings, they weren't necessarily the most unhappy. Julia had explained to her at long length the plight of millions of French citizens in all walks of life, including soldiers, orphans, refugees, and priests. This was the need that she would be addressing. Canada, in general, was a large, rich country, but Quebec and Ontario were small and geographically far removed from the rest of the nation. The northeastern United States had a huge population, was close by, and was at the centre of the financial world. Her only real contacts, however, were a few relatively distant cousins, living in the New York area. In addition, she had no financial experience, and it would likely be difficult to convince citizens of a neutral country to fund a war that no one wanted. She sought advice from her brother, who she thought might have some good US contacts. Charles suggested that she go to the congress of a McAll Mission in Hartford, which he often attended. It was early May in the second year of the war, and clearly not good timing for her, as the three eldest were getting ready to leave, and she needed to help them prepare. However, she felt that it was her duty to accept.

Blanche concluded that the solution would be to draft a sales pitch that she could present to the US audiences. But what should it be? Perhaps she could come up with it through some sort of divine intervention. She sought it one evening with such gusto that she fell asleep, already relieved and confidant that she would wake up at dawn face-to-face with a finished conference. It came to her in a dream. She had seen the "Little France," born in an oak forest, growing in the

Oncle Charles

religious spirit of cathedrals, embodied in the patriotism of Jeanne d'Arc, and gradually becoming the sovereign of a large kingdom, eventually a vast empire, proud, absolute, and magnificent. Then, following setbacks and revolutions, she is discouraged, unbelieving, and anxious, until the day when an invasion shakes her and her heroism and faith is reborn, as it was in years past. The speech that grew out of this became known as "The Soul of France."

To organize these tours without publicity, without a manager, without the backing of a local committee, it was necessary to have everything at hand: correspondence, timetables, finances, and a multitude of other details. In a matter of weeks, she had a schedule, which began in May 1915 with two tours organized by her new friends at the McAll Mission. Her tours usually lasted about three weeks, and sometimes up to three months. She went from town to town, aiming at very large auditoriums, and collecting just enough to send to Europe: about 4,000 francs per month. On a world scale, it wasn't a great success, but what a joy it was for her to regularly fund "good works," where every cent counted. Best of all, perhaps, was her privilege of making lifelong friends in just about every home she stayed in. Not once was she allowed to sleep in a hotel or eat in a restaurant!

Blanche always started with "The Soul of France," keeping in reserve for other meetings her chats about the "good works" of her sister and her illustrated lecture on Belgium. The money destined for the Belgian orphans was sent via the underground. It was only near the end of the war that their Belgian friends learned about the origins of the miraculous manna that had prevented so many children from dying of hunger.

"The Soul of France" became quite famous, and it wasn't unusual for her to be asked to deliver it a second time on the same day. It opened many doors and many purses from both the educated and the less-educated, at large and small auditoriums, from the north to the south of the United States, and the east to the west of Canada. Basically, the Americans wanted to collaborate, as they hoped that they were helping to ensure that France wouldn't collapse. They were saturated with newspaper articles, and welcomed the rhythmical beat of a poem. Under the varnish of materialism, the Americans had an emotional and idealistic side, easy to touch in this dramatic era. Often before she started to speak, someone would get up, "Please don't forget to tell us about the 'Soul of France.'" Her fifth trip, in April and May 1917, brought her to Washington, Philadelphia, and Baltimore. The news from the Front, however, was a constant worry, and often made it difficult to concentrate.

Philadelphia, 22 April 1917

My dear boys,

I can hardly believe that, having left Montreal almost three weeks ago, I haven't been able until today to find the half day necessary to write my circular letter about my travels, and that I had to resort to sending postcards. You know better than me about the difficulties one faces when away from normal life, and in my case better organized at my writing table than you in your trenches. It is leisure time that is missing, and not the enthusiasm, between the meetings, dinners, and notes to be written. I often don't have a minute from morning till night. Fortunately, all this allows me to work as well as possible for Tante Julia's charities, during this pleasant summer season!

Having left Montreal on 4 April, I headed to Ithaca, a pleasant small town south of the Adirondacks. I was greeted warmly at the home of a lady who was descended from a Wells of the battle of Hastings fame, and for whom Tunbridge Wells was named, an ancestor that the good lady prefers to forget. The next day I met Jacques at the home of our dear cousins the

Carharts, who received us with open arms. There were great conversations that continuously returned to "your dear soldier boys." We walked right up to the "Sound," where it was pleasant to climb up the footpaths and now and again rest in some sheltered corner, away from the wind. Then we had two sessions at their church, with a very friendly audience in a fragrant Easter atmosphere. At 12 on 8 April, I prayed especially for each of you. Did you feel my message?

On Tuesday morning, after Easter, I was off to New York. I presume that Jacques will have told you about his interesting, although somewhat tiring, days. It was fun to see him walking through New York, map in hand, like a very resourceful Yankee, mingling downtown with the old merchants. That's when he wasn't glancing at electric gadgets, lifting his mother to a platform, or dragging her down the subways. He is having fun playing Buffalo Bill, seriously interested in the Natural History Museum, quite intrigued by Billy Sunday, and moved by the superb "Joan of Arc" film. He was fascinated by the great Dutch and French masters, and I tried to teach him about the beautiful works at the Museum of Modern Art. He loved the Zoo, and was intrigued by our friend, Mr. Scheffelin's, chemical experiments! We have two furnished small rooms in their house, and eat our meals here and there, except for their very copious breakfasts. We had a nice, light lunch at the Dufourgs', where we got a thousand things for you. With respect to violence in the streets, all we saw were khaki tents, surrounded by people hanging out. I understand that Wilson believes that conscription will produce a superior army! If the wonderful Carharts had not given me $40, and the Scheffelins $100, New York would have produced only a marginal sum for my fund. I was there mostly for Jacques, who loved his holiday. On Saturday morning the 14th I left for Philadelphia, while he stayed until the evening.

I had an excellent reception at Miss Wood's lovely old house on South Street. She seems to be looking younger, and her brother Walter is more of a businessman than ever. The black servant is greying and sends his best to Jacques, and the nice maids send their wishes to Tante Julia. A thoughtful detail was flowers, a yellow journal containing Tante Julia's article on Madame Nick, and a lovely book on Franco-American relations by Mr. Jusserand. It's interesting to be at this time in a Quaker centre, headquarters of almost all the pacifist societies of the US. These wonderful people, full of common sense, who fought for peace as long as war wasn't declared. As of 6 April, instead of being stubborn, they have all asked themselves how best they could serve their country and humanity, without renouncing their principles. It is their conscience that is the basis of their Quaker doctrine. Some are selling their cars, others are cutting their holidays, simplifying their dress, and meals, and increasing their activities in their numerous good works for France, Belgium, Poland, Serbia,

Armenia, etc. They teach the children not to leave anything on their plates. The grand ladies are planting potatoes. Miss Wood is picking up all the rags, the newspapers, and other scraps of paper, and tries to ensure that her cook should serve the entire salad, not just the heart! All that is so new in such a rich country that it's almost a new sport, full of good taste and charm. The Quakers are calm and not as arrogant as their politicians. Who knows if the approach that they are taking so seriously won't become a principle and a supplement to their way of life. I very much appreciated the service Sunday morning in a Presbyterian church. The clergyman quoted this sentence from a British statesman: "The great need of the age is more spiritually minded men of the world." At five o'clock we left by car with Miss Wood for the beautiful Quaker College of Haverford, where we dined with the principal, prior to a conference in the Church Hall. It was a holiday weekend, and I saw only the families of a few professors and a few neighbours. The service was in a small, well-built auditorium, comfortable, with blank walls and austere bars at the windows, without chairs, without a lectern, not even a table to put my notes. But from those sincere expressions and closed mouths one saw their souls and their sense of duty. There was an amusing moment when I was finishing my meeting. I proposed a verse from a hymn, and a man replied that they would be embarrassed to accept! I responded, "Brave Quaker, continue to fly your spiritual flag as high as possible in spirit and truth," which is something our churches a little too often forget!

On Monday, after settling a few minor details, I had a good meeting with members of the International Committee of Sunday Schools. I gave them a note that they promised to present at their meeting on Thursday in New York. I suggested that they should use a part of the funds for day-to-day purposes, but also set aside a sum to organize an International Congress to help the French and Belgian schools to survive during the war. Let's hope that they will listen!

Tuesday, I spoke to the French War Relief, presided over by the extraordinary and famous friend of our cousins Jordan and Denis, Mrs. Cornelius Stevenson. I was confused when I realized that the lunch to which she had invited me afterwards wasn't the modest snack I expected, but a delicious lunch of six courses, served in the smartest ladies club, and all that in honour of the old relationships of our families. One of the guests was the head of a Belgian fund, another presided over a Polish fund, a third, with a tragic expression, was introduced to me as the president of the "Ice Flotilla." I wondered if it was some sort of fund for polar bears, but I soon curtailed my laughter when I was told that they had been three on the Titanic, her husband died, she was rescued, and her son, who she thought she had lost, was lifted more dead than alive onto a raft. Isn't it surprising that she had no resentment against the iceberg, but that, quite to the contrary, she founded a fund that made and distributed ice for the ambulances at the Front in France!

Wednesday, the usual miscellaneous tasks, and in the afternoon a marvellous car trip to visit Miss Wood's parents, and a friend of Tante Julia, a Mrs. Randolph, that despite her age would like to skewer the Kaiser. We followed the Delaware across an immense park, all exploding in flowering magnolias.

I made another nice trip on Thursday, starting from an area of splendid estates, and then at a Concord ladies place, talking "France" in the morning and stopping at 1 o'clock for a light lunch wherever we might be. I was promised something special at No 53 St Lazare Street. Sure enough, a lovely walk in the park, where I picked flowers, which made me wonder whether there were any left in what used to be the valleys and woods of Picardie and Flanders! Tuesday it was the turn of Bryn Mawr College, where I had a charming and youthful audience. Finally on Saturday my trip was almost finished. On Monday I attended a very interesting ceremony. A lunch for two hundred people, organized by thirteen famous artistic associations both social and philanthropic, to celebrate the seventieth birthday of Mrs. Cornelius Stevenson. There was a short but well chosen menu, served on some thirty tables, and speeches both touching and amusing, of which the most applauded was the toast of Prof. Lanson of the Sorbonne, who had been sent officially by the French ambassador to Washington. Presidents of several leading US universities that had oriental studies departments got up one after the other to make teasing comments about Mrs. Stevenson's influence. They claimed that, through her teaching and her writing, they had been made to appreciate Babylon, and learn about the religion of the Egyptians! My seatmate was an uncle of Mr Paul Leyson, with whom I had a particularly pleasant conversation. During this charming party there was one small problem: a profusion of roses and hors d'oeuvres that was viewed by some as not being appropriate in wartime. The atmosphere as far as I was concerned was sophisticated, as compared to our poor Montreal with old-fashioned customs, where at banquets women were sent behind gallery fences, like a group of common prisoners. I loved this stay in Philadelphia, this town with its historical and slightly austere aroma, despite its luxury and its modern activities. But perhaps my best memory will be the welcome I had in Miss Wood's large, private, and peaceful house. Miss Wood and Miss Cook send you their heartfelt messages, and I end, dear boys, by kissing you, and telling you how much I love you and congratulate you for your courage, you who work for "the Cause."

Blanche

Westmount, 8 May 1917

Dear absents,

Cards and letters written in a rush have kept my soldiers up to date on my spring journey to the United States, from which I returned today, 8 May. Thinking that a more detailed report of my trip might not only interest them, but also other correspondents to which it is impossible to write personally, I will make copies of this circular written by typewriter, in order to send a few beyond the trenches. I'm writing this rough draft in the night train that is bringing me from New York to Montreal.

The bank account to which I transfer some French war funds being empty, or almost so, I decided to accept the invitation of the McAll Mission to their annual meeting in Baltimore, and, as a result, my trip was prepaid, and it was convenient for me to stop on the way for my own collections.

The atmosphere was particularly joyful and peaceful on Easter Monday, and nothing would have suggested that our soldiers were taking part in a dreadful battle.

Jacques had joined me and we spent the weekend with our cousins in Larchmont, on the banks of the Sound. Jacques couldn't wait to see New York, and five days weren't enough to wander around it in every direction. We were particularly intrigued by Billy Sunday. You may be curious to know about my impression of this evangelistic clown. Actually, I'm not sure if I admired more this man's enterprising spirit or the aura that he creates. For a revival campaign of three months, he built a huge auditorium, able to sit twenty-three thousand people with a chorus of several thousand voices. But I was even more surprised and a little scandalized when I witnessed the whole auditorium bursting with laughter, repeated and provoked by his jokes, or clapping with all their might as Billy screamed and did his damnedest to run down the sins of New York. There are surely in this big city some huge gulfs requiring some extraordinary remedies, which aren't to everybody's taste.

The United States declared war four days before our arrival. Did we notice anything special in New York? Hardly, except for the quantities of hats, and by the recruitment tents at every crossroad. The common folk are indifferent, while the leaders are tense and silent.

I had all kinds of interesting experiences in the city of the Quakers. I was impressed with the unity of these people. Despite the traumas that they faced, there seemed to be a strong sense of harmony between the young and the old. After ten days spent in Philadelphia in a friendly home and a pleasant environment, it wasn't without apprehension that I took the train for the capital, where I would have to carve my own way amid strangers.

Washington is not governed by its citizens, but by three commissioners selected by the president. Jacques remembers seeing one at the Cap à

Maréchal Joffre acclaimed in New York, 1917

l'Aigle church. The Andersons gave me an introduction, and Madame Commissioner McFarland offered me a drawing-room meeting in a house so ordinary that it was evident that its owner hadn't enriched herself dishonestly by her important position. She is a member of the Covenant Church, where I had the privilege to speak twice: in total, five meetings in seven days.

Having seen at a distance the parade given for the visiting French delegation on the 27th, I decided the next day to walk over to the French Embassy. Just as I got there, a car did a U-turn to enter the gates, and I waved my handkerchief so frenetically that the Maréchal saluted me with a big smile that illuminated his large handsome face. One day, when grandchildren are climbing on my knees, they will be able to say: "He saluted you, grandmother. He saluted you."

After having seen Joffre, the other attractions weren't very exciting, and in any case I was short of time to visit official buildings and museums. However, I allowed myself to be lifted by elevator within the interior of the monument that rises five hundred feet up from the pavement, from where there is a splendid view, and then I spent a few hours in the House of Representatives to hear a hot debate between the partisans of voluntarism and conscription.

"We want volunteers. George Washington was a volunteer, Abraham Lincoln had been a volunteer, while the two thieves were there by coercion."

"Yet another reason to have an obligatory service," screamed another. "We don't allow for the elite of the Nation to be killed, to save the cowards and those in cushy positions."

You know that it was this last opinion that prevailed!

Having arrived in Washington with apprehension, I left the capital with regret. My rooming house was very comfortable, the weather fresh and beautiful, the greenery and flowers superb, and the population so welcoming. I was particularly happy to celebrate with these great allies, and it renewed my courage at a time when the complications in Russia, and the enormous sacrifices of the Franco-British advance, worried me enormously. The night of 29 April was particularly frightening, and then the next day, the telegram from Jean announcing that Etienne was wounded again. I hope that some entirely reassuring news will soon show us that, after the first shock, we were right to be comfortable that our lieutenant had escaped from a greater danger, and was resting comfortably between two white sheets in a good hospital. But how hard it is to be so far away from our wounded!

Baltimore was my last stop. I was to participate in the annual meeting of the McAll Mission, and to extend my visit for a few days in order to tend to my small business. My quarters couldn't have been more pleasant: A beautiful house of the region, occupied by three Fowler sisters, descendants of an admiral of the French Fleet who accompanied Lafayette. I was reminded of my connection with this aristocratic ancestor, who is so much admired currently! But with all that, what magnificent hospitality, what perfect courtesy, reflecting a breed filled with intelligence, character, and piety.

Despite its Anglo ring, McAll is basically a French charity. There were numerous, reports, speeches, discussions, all reflecting the renewed interest in France brought by the political events. Two Frenchmen began to talk. Mr Marcel Knecht, an English professor at the Lycée de Nancy, who accompanied the Joffre-Viviani group as an interpreter, spoke briefly, followed by a young Arts graduate called Alcide Picard. If I understood properly, he was secretary of the Parliamentary Action Committee, represented in the United States by Honlacque. He is Protestant, has done eighteen months of war service, was repatriated for health reasons, and is to look after and organize the French courses that are to be given in the American recruitment camps. He read his New Testament every evening in the trenches, and this reading, which seemed mysterious to his comrades, constantly provoked some serious discussions. We need to tell Camille that the Colonials are tougher, but that one must continue to move forward without being discouraged.

*I thought that what I had to say was pretty ordinary after the account
of these real soldiers, but the fact that I spoke good English compensated
for my lack of experience at the Front, and my listeners were very attentive
and enthusiastic. Having repeated my stories frequently, I know when the
applause will come! There's the Marne Victory moment, there's the one, a
very long and healthy one, where they applaud the generosity and devotion
of Switzerland, and to finish there's the one where Tante Julia's man from
Lille finds his evacuated wife.*

*The highlight of these two days was the evening meeting, in a huge church
crowded with those wishing to hear the famous Robert Speer. What a cool
breeze when he begins by declaring that he doesn't know either France or the
French or their history. And then it slowly warms up, as he articulates with
great gestures and describes France's place in the past and at the present
time, denying therefore his useless but very sincere introduction.*

*After these very full days I had a drawing-room meeting, and another in
a ladies club. Finally, a day of well earned rest on Sunday, as I was worn
out by these four weeks, complicated by a persistent cough that should have
melted in the southern heat, if it had been a normal spring, but it was fires
in the fireplaces and furs to go out. What a joy to finally head for Montreal
on Monday 7 May, grateful for this excellent tour, but especially so happy to
return home.*

*With respect to my funding, my readers would have thought that, with
the enthusiasm for France that at this moment vibrates America, I would
be bringing back a huge sum. But no, these good Americans with their huge
enterprises are no doubt far greater donors to their charities than to the
"Ami du Soldat." However, my comments may give greater assistance to the
Red Cross and to the National Security than to those that I represent. In
any case, it isn't the point, because Tante Julia receives regularly what she
needs, and France benefits accordingly! I return with $1,000, which is my
average for four weeks.*

*I continue this morning my letter begun last evening. Here is the
St Lawrence, the smoke from Pointe St Charles, and Mont Royal in
the distance. How I'm looking forward to taking up my duties at Les
Colombettes, and to reading the letters that have no doubt arrived from
Europe.*

Blanche

THE NEXT SIX MONTHS weren't particularly eventful, and then we faced the terrible news of Philippe's death. Hurt by this great pain I wasn't able to resume my
travels for some time.

The seventh tour was the most important, as it lasted from May to July 1918. It was lengthened, because this time Dad and I left and returned together, going in the interval separately to some very amusing rendezvous. It was delightful for me to rediscover the charming environment of Baltimore, at Hampton at my friend Mrs. Purvis's, at Richmond, where I tasted the charm of Virginia, at Philadelphia, at Haverford, where it's so wonderful to see Juliana Wood again, at Chambersburg, where I met the hostess of Wilson College, at Clifton Springs where I indulged in a brief cure, and in Rochester where I was received by the famous and very rich Strong family. From there the embarkation on Lake Ontario, the rendezvous with my husband, the navigation on the St Lawrence, and the surprise arrival of Jacques. Finally, the return to La Clairière, and then to Montreal, where we devour the newspapers full of the most encouraging news about the advance of the Allies.—(BB)

THE SUMMER OF 1918 saw us all working to help finish the war. Your mother had resumed her conference work in the United States. Her presentation, "The Soul of France," had become a classic. I had agreed to represent the Protestants of France in the United States. Decidedly we were making headway in all directions. I succeeded several French chaplains, who had been doing this work prior to leaving the country. My job was to awaken the French citizens living in the United States to the Allies' enormous efforts. During three months, directed by the French High Commission in Washington, I toured the Mid-West, giving speeches in Philadelphia, Pittsburgh, Buffalo, Columbus, Cincinnati, Louisville, Indianapolis, as well as many smaller towns. I worked hard, and tried to be eloquent in English. I was told that I succeeded quite well; however it was clearly a temporary gift.—(CB)

CHAPTER ELEVEN

Vimy

April to June 1917

The Battle of Vimy Ridge (after the artist Richard Jack)

THE FIRST FEW DAYS OF APRIL were dramatic for both World War I in general and the Canadian soldiers in particular. President Wilson finally decided that the United States should declare war on Germany. This was announced on 6 April. Then, on 9 April, Vimy was attacked by the Canadian Forces.

THE BATTLE OF VIMY

The First Battle of Arras was intended to tie in with General Nivelle's plan to end the war with a single bold stroke, and to retain some sort of initiative in the Somme. The assault of Vimy Ridge on 9, 10, and 11 April was to be a part of that campaign, and was not intended to stand alone. The ridge dominated the German defences linking their southern line to their main line that led to the Belgian coast. It was strategically therefore a defensive keystone, as well as one of the most important features of the Western Front.

1 April 1917

My dear parents,

We were very close to Vimy, whose minor crest hides the Lens plain and the view of the coalfields of Lens. Up until now, this enemy position had challenged the efforts of the headquarters staff of the successive armies: French, English, and Canadians. For quite some time we had been aiming at the wrong side. The hour had now come to go over the fence on the other side, and be installed on the top!

André

THE WEATHER TURNS COLDER; the frost dries the mud, resonating with a solid thump to their footsteps. The days are longer, and even in some poor defoliated bush, there are birds to sing of spring and bring them courage! But it isn't an easy exercise, and merits a meticulous preparation. That's why the Canadian Corps that had been selected for the attack underwent particularly intensive training, both in the front line and in the nearby villages of Neuville–St Vaast and Souchez. When they are in the rear, groups of a hundred soldiers are trained in temporary trenches to advance, so that each man will know exactly what he will have to do in all the imaginable circumstances. At the Front, they raid and exhaust the enemy by attacks, even in the middle of the day. This thorough preparation is essential to ensure that everything has been studied, and nothing can go wrong.—(BB)

World War I Uncle Sam recruiting poster

THE ATTACK ON VIMY RIDGE was to be launched from the Western Front line, running from two miles north of the Village of Vimy to five miles south of Arras. The Patricias were assigned a central position at the highest part of the ridge. They had been selected because of the precision that they had shown in previous engagements, but there was no doubt that the battle would be quite different than the others. In this battle they knew the trenches intimately, they would attack a battlefield that they had traversed frequently, and they had been rehearsing their attack throughout the winter. They participated in the construction of eleven tunnels, located to allow the final attack preparations to be invisible to the enemy, so that the soldiers would not be interfered with or shelled by the enemy. The main "Grange Tunnel" had three exits and was 750 yards long.

INSTEAD OF AN EASTER WITH FLOWERS, the weather worsens once again. So it's through gusts of wind and hail in an impressive silence on the night of Easter, on 8 April 1917, that the Princess Pats reach the forecasted positions, along a nine-hundred-metre line. The lucky ones were sheltered in the huge caverns of Huguenot origins, which the firemen had enlarged further. They catch a few hours of sleep, prior to the inevitable awakening, which, after a warm shot of rum, would launch them forward towards success or towards death. However, they will be better protected than at Sanctuary Wood, as this time the majority of the Canadian artillery divisions initiated a bombardment with a ferocity and a precision that left nothing to be desired. The barrage of gunfire prepared the infantrymen's assault. And what an assault!—(BB)

> 1st Brigade 1st Division
> April 8th 1917
> Many horses died during the past few days owing to so much hauling of ammunition and cutting down of hay and straw ration. Infantry Commanders of the 5th and 17th Battalions report that there is no more wire on their zones, this confirms our report. The standard gauge railway is now well past 2nd Howitzer Battery and is running through the valley to Ariane Dump.

WITH THE PRINCESS PATS IN THE CENTRE, opposite the crater field, the four Canadian Divisions, for the first time, fought side by side. The advances varied in the different sections. For the Patricias, the first and second distances were, respectively, about seven hundred and five hundred yards. The goals of the entire Brigade were to move through La Folie Wood, and to consolidate a line on the East side of the Ridge. The extensive mining activity made for substantial difficulties in traversing the first ground. There were also many impassable large craters. The depth of the craters, the myriad remnants of obstructions, as well as the ruins of former trenches, added to the misery of these soldiers, who were carrying large, awkward loads on their backs.

Before dawn on 9 April, every soldier had a hot meal and a shot of rum, then, promptly at 4:30 a.m., all the Patricias, officers and men, were in position. The 18-pounders intense shrapnel bombardment started with sudden fury at 5:30 a.m. At exactly that moment, the first wave of Patricias shuffled out of Grange Tunnel and started to climb to the top of the crater line. There was nothing then in their way, as the garrisons and the barbed wire had been blown to pieces by the mortars. Both the German Front and support lines were immediately overrun, so that, by 6 a.m., the entire Brigade had reached its first objective line. Then

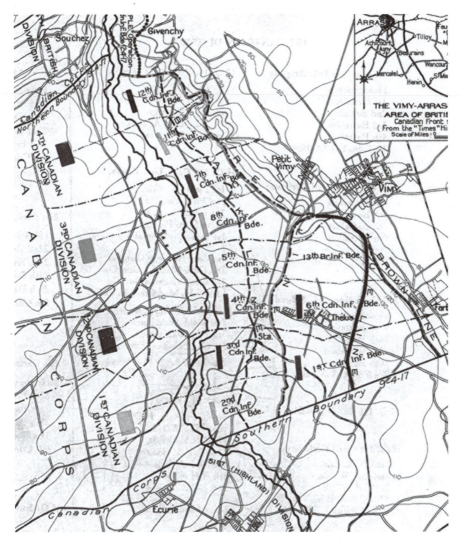

Four Canadian Divisions in line on Vimy Ridge.

the Canadians, in forty minutes, stormed and decimated the German's first line. Despite the continuing resistance of the enemy, they continued to advance. The initial onslaught had been brilliant.

Electrified by the music of the bagpipes, the soldiers, wave after wave, tumbled down real volcanic craters, climbing on the other side, spread the remains of the barbed wire, stepped over the parapets, the trenches, the wounded, the bodies. They stumbled, fell, got entangled in their load, got up and continued to climb the slope steadily, but also calmly, as it's impossible to run in this terrain.

1st Brigade 1st Division

April 9th 1917

At Zero hour (5:30 AM) the big advance on Vimy Ridge commenced. A wonderful series of barrages were put up on the German front and Support line. Our troops had very little trouble in reaching the German front and support lines. The Reserve line was held by a few hostile machine guns, which caused the only serious casualties our troops suffered. This did not stop them however and before dark the whole Ridge of Vimy was in our hands. On the Canadian Corps front alone some 27 hostile guns were captured and over 3,000 prisoners. Our casualties were in the neighbourhood of 2,000.

In the early afternoon Major Durkee O.C. 3rd Battery started his Battery forward and shortly after dark his six guns were reported in action near the Nine Elms. This Battery being the farthest forward in the 1st Army front. Throughout the whole advance very little hostile shelling was reported. Lt. Col. Maclaren DSO and a party of four left the Brigade HQ and made a reconnaissance of the forward area. Battery positions were selected.

15 April 1917

My dear parents,

Here is a letter that you must have been expecting with considerable impatience. My last one was written the day before going into the trenches for the attack, about which you must have seen reports in the newspapers.

We were pretty concerned, to say the least, when we were reminded that, the following day, we were to attack one of the most important and strongest German positions.

Before the big day, we had spent several days in the forward trenches, to see what we could see of the German trenches without being caught by a German marksman. They then gave us one night of rest, and just before dawn we took our positions in the trenches with a huge load on our shoulders: food, a shovel, bombs, etc.

It was still night when a huge bombardment of several minutes began. Our lieutenant, with his cane in the air, gave us the signal to charge, but don't imagine a magnificent charge with shining bayonets and bugles blowing. We advance as best we can, across a terrain completely shattered by several weeks of bombardment. At twenty metres from the German trenches, we see our first Germans with their hands in the air, crying: "Kamerad, Kamerad!" We show them the rear, and, with a little slap on the backside, they are only too happy to run as fast as possible away from their officers.

Moving ahead at the same time as us, there was a magnificent barrage of shrapnel, which resulted in sending the Germans into their dugouts, so, as we advanced, we hardly saw anyone. We caught them by throwing smoke

A machine-gun emplacement on the crest of Vimy Ridge

*bombs into their underground habitations that are often real palaces.
Imagine rooms with electric lights, antique furniture, stolen from nearby
châteaux, armoires of provisions, black bread, honey, mineral water,
champagne, tinned meat. The one we were dealing with was in fact a
brigade headquarters, where there were a dozen officers with about the same
number of Iron Crosses.*

*It took us about one hour to reach our objective, but it felt like five
minutes. The ridge is above a steep hill. When we got to the summit, the
view was magnificent, a town, villages, and some lovely roads, where
we could see the German artillery in full retreat, trapped by our heavy
batteries.*

*But I described the least horrible, as the conquest was not the only part:
there were also the moans of the seriously wounded, but we knew that our
action was necessary if we were to get closer to ending the war.*

*Could you send me a little money in each letter, five or six francs,
that would help me considerably to buy chocolate and other necessary
things for the trenches. Now goodbye, and once again, thank you for your
correspondence, always very much appreciated.*

André

Current view from Vimy Ridge

THE FINAL OBJECTIVE for the Patricias required a five-hundred-yard continued advance. From there they were ordered to push the line northwards, while some were to quickly patrol further down the hill to determine whether the Germans were still in the vicinity. In less than an hour, at 7:45, the second objective had been accomplished. From there, the new front line had a great view towards Vimy, and enemy outposts were reported and quickly dispersed by the artillery. By noon, they passed through the Germans' second line and concluded the capture of the whole area from La Folie to Neuville–St Vaast. The Patricias had fewer than fifty casualties, but during the earlier advance, many officers had fallen. It was a common story: privates replacing their fallen officers, and medics and runners concentrating on their roles, despite their own danger.

MANY YEARS LATER, André was to reflect: "What a view! The vast mining centre, with its chimneys, its worker housing, and its slag heaps magically illuminated by rays of sun piercing through the clouds. On the roads we saw clearly the German artillery retreating, pestered by the Canadian batteries. To see the backs of the enemy running off down the roads confirmed the victory with all its satisfaction. Instead of seeing their square heads and their round eyes over the parapets in front of us, we could look off into the distance and see a distant view. It led us to that marvellous illusion that after this master stroke it would soon be the end of the war! But we never forgot the moans of the wounded, and the best friends that fell beside us. However, we didn't have the time to compile these impressions, as we had to clean the enemy trenches, which criss-crossed the Vimy ridge from Neuville–St Vaast to Bois de la Folie. There was no doubt that there were still soldiers lying in ambush."

André, along with a few friends, had the opportunity to run into the luxurious shelter of the German commander. To find a palace in a hole is like a tale from a *Thousand and One Nights*! The shelter had a floor and partitions, antique furniture, and a piano, tinned food, and many bottles. There was even the wounded general sitting at his table who was semi-conscious. In his state of semi-paralysis, he was no doubt shocked by the rudeness of these Canadians, who quietly began to smoke the best cigars, to empty the best bottles, enjoying the very best delicacies, and to skim through a collection of *Simplicimus*, in which the German editor ridicules President Wilson and the American flag. The invaders, very tired, quite exhilarated by success and by the champagne, then lie down on the comfortable beds and fall into a deep sleep.

Once again, Etienne had helped, with the fire of his guns, to sweep the area in front of the footsteps of his brothers. Philippe fought at Courcelette and André at Vimy. It was often a few soldiers in heroic moments, who, supported by the units in the rear, overturned the enemy positions with guns, machine guns, bayonets, fists, and anything else, as long as the goal was achieved. The brothers had that special advantage where they could commune with each other on the battlefield. Meanwhile, the Germans still held the third line, and it needed to be crushed in its turn. There were multiple clashes, some advances, some reversals, some counterattacks, until finally the objective was achieved.—(BB)

1st Brigade 1st Division
April 10th 1917
Our 1st, 4th, and 2nd Batteries left their old positions and took up positions in the forward area some two hundred yards in advance of the 3rd Battery. Rain prevented registration to any extent today.
1st Brigade HQ established in deep German dugout some 150 yards to the right flank of the Nine Elms. Lieut Turnbull attached to this HQ from this date to be officer in charge of signals, 1st Brigade.

April 11th 1917
Weather partly fair and registration of our 1st, 2nd, and 4th Batteries was completed today. O.Ps. have a splendid view of a large stretch of the flat country east of Vimy Ridge. Our infantry pushed on past Willerval today and arrangements were at once to move the Batteries to more advanced positions. We are still however doing a lot of night firing to prevent the enemy from improving the wire in front of his defensive line which is known as the Oppy line and is just within range.

12 April 1917

My dear mother,

*Here I am again with the machine gunners, after three days of
convalescence, where I was very bored ... It's much more interesting here. We
observe the huge work undertaken in the rear to make possible the activity
of the Front. The view extends towards a village built in a hollow, with
its red roofs, its belfry, its château, and sand dunes spotted with clumps of
pines. The sea in the distance is sometimes blue and calm and other times
dark and menacing. We are taking a machine-gun course and work six
hours each day. I am learning a pile of useful things ... the rest of the time
I take walks, and what interests me the most are the train tracks and the
road. I have never seen such traffic on one railway line. The trains come one
after another without interruption, filled first of all by munitions, others by
merchandise, others by troops, others with more coal and cars. What a lot
of things are required for an army! The road is monopolized by ambulances
and trucks doing the hospital service, and they are mostly driven by women.
It's also fun to meet the colonials: Scots, Irish, Australians, and New
Zealanders. These last ones, like us, don't very much appreciate the strict
discipline of our English instructors.*

Philippe

THE SUCCESSES OF THE 7TH BRIGADE, along with its Princess Pats Regiment, further enhanced the growing reputation of the Canadians. Sir Douglas Haig commented: "To have carried this position with so little lost testifies to soundness of plan, thoroughness of preparation, dash and determination in execution and devotion to duty on the part of all concerned." In the history of World War I it is well-known that, in the critical last hundred days of the war, the British control of Vimy Ridge marked a dividing line between conquest and disaster.

Perhaps in part as a result of the Vimy success, General Haig was promoted to Field Marshal by King George V, and General Currie to Commanding Officer of the Canadian Corps.

During the battle of the Somme, the Germans had learned that the rigid defence of a line was no longer a good military tactic, and they developed a new defence strategy. They put it into practice in the Eastern Somme during the spring of 1917, where it was clearly more efficient and strategically advantageous to retire to the line established by General Hindenberg. They systematically wrecked a desolate area some fifty miles deep. General Nivelle was preparing his attack, and rather than taking the opportunity of attacking a retreating army, he delayed it long enough for the enemy to increase their forces from eighteen to forty-two divisions. On 16 April he did attack, but after a month, the leading French army had not advanced by more than four miles. The French army was near to mutiny and suffered enormous casualties. General Pétain, who had finally also led the French to a victory in Verdun, replaced Nivelle as commander-in-chief of the French Army

While Nivelle was fighting his losing battle, General Haig decided that he should resume the attacks in the Scarpe area. He wished to push the German line opposite Arras by some four miles. It was not to be a successful venture, but there was an exception at the battle of Arleux on 28 April. The Canadian attack succeeded in making a significant advance, and it was during this battle that Etienne was seriously wounded and ended his artillery career.

1st Brigade 1st Division
April 28th 1917
The 1st Canadian Division launched their second attack at 4:25 this morning with great success and obtained all final objectives by 5:25 AM that is to the Eastern edge of Arleux Wood. The 2nd British Division on our right made a successful attack and the enemy were driven back to Oppy Wood. In all some 8 officers and 300 OR were taken prisoners. In the early evening the enemy made a strong counter-attack all along our front and extending to some distance on our right. Our artillery responded very quickly, and the enemy's attack was repulsed and heavy casualties inflicted on him.

1st London General Hospital
Camberwell, London SE, 6 May 1917

My dear mother,

In my last letter I had promised you to write the next day, but it's only today that I pick up my pencil.

I presume that you would like to have the details about the circumstances relative to my wound. It was Saturday 28 April at 6 p.m. The enemy bombs had been falling in the neighbourhood of the battery all afternoon. The captain, a former McGill friend, and the other officers had gone for supper, and I was alone at the battery with several men. All of a sudden, the bombs came closer, and one of them fell a few paces from the dugout where I was. I then called the captain to get his permission to leave the guns for a moment, until the bombardment stopped. I was about to re-enter the cover, preceded by the last man, when a bomb exploded with a large bang a few paces from me and a piece hit me just above the right knee. Two men helped me to enter a dugout, where they laid me on a stretcher. In less than a minute the officers were there, and the captain, armed with a big knife, cut my trousers, then as a good medical student he bandaged me, and I stayed there

*until the bombardment stopped. I wasn't suffering very much. A moment
later, the doctor arrived and rebandaged me, then four men carried me in
the stretcher. A kilometre further on, they deposited me on a small carriage
on the narrow-gauge railway line, and left me in the care of a Canadian
ambulance man and three German prisoners, quite fresh, having done their
work day prior to being sent to the rear.*

*Following the carriage, a motorized ambulance took me around midnight
to a big hospital in a city of huts. There I was undressed and put to bed. I
was woken up early the next day for the cleaning of the wound before they
sent me further. The ambulance train took me to Boulogne at 5 o'clock, and
from the station I was directed towards Wimereux, where I was given a good
bed in a room with a view of the sea. They telephoned Jean immediately,
and he was able to come and see me. He is looking very well and has at last
just received his first stripe. On Tuesday he came to say hello as I boarded the
boat for England.*

Etienne

ETIENNE FINDS THAT HIS ROLE as a wounded soldier is much less interesting
than that of an artillery officer. The broken bones are removed, but the remaining flakes create complications, but how can one complain when you are lying in a
sunlit room, giving onto a park filled with spring flowers and leaves.—(BB)

*No. 1 General Hospital
Etaples, 29 April 1917*

My dear mother,

*I have a moment to myself to write you briefly. On or about the fourteenth of
this month I hurt my foot with an old rusty nail that broke through my boot
and pierced my heel quite deeply. After one week in bed here, I was able to
get up and walk a bit. There's a great deal of work to do, and very few who
can help. We have three or four young amputees and other serious cases. I
enter the names in the register and I help with the bandages. I'm busy from
morning until night.*

*I hope to see Jean in three or four days. One of the orderlies from the No.
3 General Hospital was here this afternoon and told me, but they are so busy
that nothing happens immediately.*

*When I leave here I will once again go to the Canadian Base. I don't
think I'll be there for long.*

*It's quite funny the way we are playing hide-and-seek with Philippe.
We have both been in France for almost one year, and we haven't yet seen
each other.*

André

Les Colombettes, 20 May 1917

My dear boys,

*Let's hope that the conscription will not be delayed and that all those selfish
and cowardly men will soon be dressed in khaki and sent to the Front.
However, we ask ourselves who will be left at the Presbyterian College and
McGill.*

*Mr. Fernand Buisson, the famous creator of the Public Primary Schools
of France, talked about the Sacred Union. I have rarely heard anything
quite as moving. He spoke of the Catholics, the Protestants, the Israelites,
and the Socialists. He was influenced by soldiers' letters, and paid respect
to the sons of clergymen. This evening brought such a satisfying religious
feeling, and gave me an immense uplift. Dear boys, if in our day it is the
Anglo-Saxons that are materialistic, and the French that are spiritualists,
listen good and hard to the Huguenot blood that is in your veins and let it
take the leading role. I think, however, that deep down, the Englishman is
more religious than he looks.*

*Nothing from Philippe since 13 March, when he was training as a
machine-gunner. On the other hand a charming letter from Madame
Lemaitre, who tells us all kinds of nice things about his visit in Bruay.
She found him well-tanned with a confident expression. Good news from
Camille, who has been in the midst of the advance, where he must have done
his duty to perfection, as he was told about a reward that he will no doubt
tell us about in a forthcoming letter.*

Blanche

La Clairière, 24 May 1917

Dear boys,

*Monday morning we will catch a train leaving Montreal at 9:20, according
to the CNR's new timetable, where there is not even one train a day, and
on some days it goes in the morning and on others in the evening, in order
to satisfy everyone's tastes. We met Pastor Bruce Taylor in the train,
who inquired about our soldiers. He is very pleased with Prime Minister
Borden's speech about starting conscription very soon.*

*We have spent a part of our evenings reading Borden's long speech,
followed by a few hours to discuss it. We have been without newspapers*

for three days, and we are now wondering what effect it has had on the population. I have heard that there is a spilt in the ranks of the Liberal Party, and a large group have joined the Nationalists and the left wing of the Conservative Party. Laurier was very embarrassed as he stepped up to the podium on Friday.

Dear boys, we are thinking of you especially, as we remember your collaboration and your perseverance, and I'm thinking of all those things that I would like to do together with you. That God protect you, and give you the strength to go to the conclusion no matter what happens. We hope that André and Philippe have managed to meet.

Charles

ETIENNE GOES TO HOSPITAL

SOME GOOD LETTERS FILLED with lovely details, and some honest enthusiasm, proves to his parents in Canada that Etienne has reason for viewing himself as very privileged. He talks about his weeks in bed, followed by his first steps, leaning on a cane or held up by crutches, or luxuriously pushed in a wheelchair. Installed on the green lawn, he reads the newspapers: Messines, Moscow, Washington! He devours books and magazines. Then, at tea time, a little group of pleasant ladies come and join him. A few of them are titled; others have pretty Irish faces, which further stimulates the eloquence of the group. They are Penroses, Fitzgeralds, Hewsons, Bartons, and even friends from Montreal come to say hello to their cousin or their Canadian friend.—(BB)

> *Ward 35, 1st London General Hospital*
> *Camberwell, 1 June 1917*

My dear father,

I suppose that you are following with interest the controversy with respect to conscription in Canada, and that you are hoping that they will accept what they are proposing to Bourassa and Lavergne. We have a bit of news about what's going on in the newspapers here, and it makes our blood boil to think that one tolerates such traitors.

And finally here are the Americans that are awakened, and none too soon. I hope that their commitment will help shorten this terrible war. With considerable emotion I wonder sometimes if it will finish prior to Jacques's departure. That God saves Mom from this sacrifice. It doesn't seem possible now, but who would have thought that it could have lasted at least three years?

1st London General Hospital, Camberwell

Here I am once again in my pram! ... Miss Bunting made a very pleasant visit, and the next day I had a good visit from Lady Carlyle.

Etienne

8 June 1917

My dear mother,

Like us here, you will also have rejoiced with the good news from the Front. After Vimy it will be Messine's turn, and all that seems to have gone so well. When one has spent several months in the Ypres Salient, haunted by the presence of Vimy ridge, anywhere else would have been insignificant, but it dominated this whole part of our lines, and was a continual danger for our men, one feels even more the importance of that victory. As for the dangers in Lille, I don't think that the time is ripe for Tante Julia to prepare to return to her tasks there.

Here it has been more than five weeks that I have been at the hospital, and I'm beginning to get used to this monotonous life without incidents ... I had once again several visits this week. First of all, on Tuesday afternoon, Lady Bunting came all alone.

Etienne

Camberwell, 14 June 1917

Dear Tante Julia,

This time it's in the shade of a tree in a garden on a beautiful morning. There's next to me a kitchen garden that would be a joy for mother. It is tended by one of the wounded in our ward, an officer who had his jaw crushed, who, having three months of hospital before him, spends most of his time doing gardening.

Etienne

17 June 1917

My dear mother,

There's a particularly lovely little annex for the officers, with a billiard table, some good armchairs, several writing tables, as well as some good books, facing a lovely lawn with multicolour flowers …

Thanks for your letter describing your most interesting trip to the USA, typewritten … as well as a good little letter from Philippe who sounds well. I will send the letter to André tonight.

Etienne

21 June 1917

My dear mother,

I haven't been able to find the circular from Tante Julia that you are asking for, as I don't have much room to keep my things here at the hospital. I have to throw out most of the letters.

But, it's time that I get into my armchair to go to the concert at the YMCA, and that I leave you dear mother.

Etienne

13 July 1917

My dear father,

I have in front of me your good letter of 24 June. Everything you tell me about the discussions that conscription is bringing to Canada interests me very much. Will we be obliged to discount the French Canadians like the Irish? I think that it's difficult to do it otherwise. The other day I went to see in another ward a French Canadian that had been at the Front twenty-six months, and we discussed conscription. He saw in Borden's proposition an attack by England at Canadians' liberty! …

In the afternoon I met my friend Stevens, and we went together to see some German films that are being shown here now. It's propaganda for the

Germans and neutralists. We see the Kaiser, with his best smiles and his
best greetings to the Austrians during his visit to Vienna ...

I presume that you all read about the air display of last week. We were
in the best seats here: twenty-three enormous machines were flying directly
towards us for a moment, when all of a sudden they turned left and
disappeared in the east.

Etienne

As of the end of June, Etienne is allowed a few outings. Despite a much reduced "season," one still sees, in London, horsemen riding by, cars driving along shaded lanes, and boats skimming on the Serpentine. Does he feel a little embarrassed quietly munching on the tearoom's strawberries and cream? In the following days, he visits those in London who had invited him, and wanders to Hornsey Lane to the Hoffmanns, to Blackheath to the Bains, or to Hatfield to the Hart-Dykes.—(BB)

La Clairière, 10 June 1917

My dear boys,

We will remember last Sunday as being particularly bright. As there was
no regular service, we replaced it by a family get-together at the Morrows,
who were waiting for us. We had trouble in speaking of anything else but
"Them Boys." Johnny murmured, "To think of them reared in a palace of
Westmount, such a fine place as never I did see, and now sleepin' in the
mud, and eatin' poor food and doing harder work than any farm labourer,
it makes me just sick to think on it." At around 1 o'clock we left, escorted by
the whole gang, right up to the boat.

The event of the week was the visit of Balfour. Big banquet at the Windsor,
followed by the convocation at McGill, where he and his colleagues, Sir Cecil
Spring-Rice, ambassador in Washington, Lieutenant General Bridges, and
Rear Admiral Sir Dudley de Chair, received various university awards.
Balfour concluded the ceremony with a good speech. But the best was his
warm smile, the purity of his accent, and his pleasant voice.

. Here I am at the end of my news, and my paper, which leaves me to hug
all of you and to recommend that you hurry up to conclude this war, as
it seems that everyone is fed up with it! So as to not lose your new talents,
you will be able to dig some beautiful trenches in the potato field, if you can
finish your job before autumn!

Very affectionately,
Blanche

10 June 1917

My dear brothers,

I promised you in my last letter that I would tell you a little more about my boat. I started it on 10 May, and now all that needs to be done is to paint it and install the motor. It is really classy, and certainly far better than a rowboat. I'm thinking of painting the bottom green, the sides white, grey on the floorboards, and varnish the rest. I should finish this week, as I will be starting my exams. I hope to send it as soon as possible to 16 Island Lake, where I'm sure it's going to be a big hit.

Jacques

Les Colombettes, 17 June 1917

My dear boys,

Little by little, either with the Scouts or his friends, Jacques is becoming a leader. They admire his initiative, and come to help him with his boat. He has gained a little reputation at target shooting, and in a couple of days, apparently, the Star *will publish his picture holding the trophy. I would never have thought that one of my sons would appear in a paper's sporting page!*

Etienne continues in his spare time to write to us some very interesting descriptions of his life in the hospital. If after his pleasant and restful stay at the hospital, and if he is still lucky enough to have a leave in Canada, he would be amongst the most privileged soldiers of this war. I'm sure that each one of you would be delighted to be in his place. It is comforting that you are all quite happy that he had this opportunity granted to him. Camille mentions too briefly in a postcard the ceremony when he was decorated with the "Croix de Guerre," we congratulate him sincerely and would like to have the text of the day's events.

Blanche

1 July 1917

Dear brothers,

If I didn't write to you last Sunday, it was because I was in Hudson at the Ladouceurs. I had a very good time, and I accomplished one of my dreams: to operate a car. I drove their McLaughlin 6 fifteen miles!

I was invited twice to Mrs. Logan's, with some Italian sailors. One time we were ten, of which some spoke English, some French, and some Italian. These sailors came to Montreal to help finish the construction of two submarines at Vickers, and when finished they will sail them to Italy.

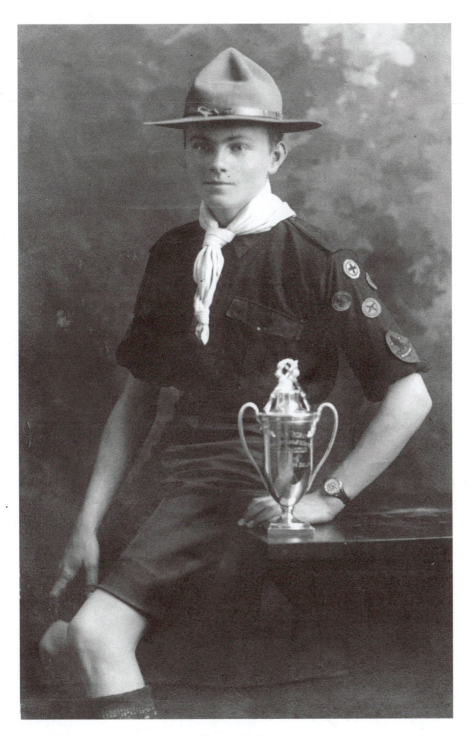

Jacques Bieler

I am sitting on the veranda near the boat, which is almost ready to go to 16 Island Lake. The motor is in its place and was easier to install and adjust than I had thought. We baptized it Friday, and the guests were the two Days and the two Ropers. A cream supper and then the "GREAT CEREMONY"… so "baby" was decorated with flowers and drapes, and the godmother smashed a ginger-ale bottle against the nose, while the parrot on the other side of the lake accompanied with his whistling. There were speeches, and toasts, but the best is its name, "VIMY," in your honour.

Jacques

Westmount, 1 July 1917

Dear boys,

This first of July, as inscribed here above, reminds me of the one three years ago. Etienne had come to join me on the evening of the 30th. The air was stormy, politically speaking. Two days before, the archduke, the future ruler of Austria, had been assassinated in Sarajevo, and the next day the well-informed Montreal papers said that this could lead to a European war. They weren't wrong!

This week we have been pleased to see once again the writing of Philippe and André. Our friend Camille, who also writes to us, finds that those that are sent to the hospital are for the most part lucky. Philippe couldn't tell us much, but we have been pleased to see that his writing is as strong as his character. Dear fighters, we surround you with affection and prayers. That our God supports your courage and gives you that self-assurance, that he loves you and that you will always have a refuge next to him. As Dr Symonds said the other day, we are in an era where often it's the sons that set the example. Please continue to give it to us, and do us good through your endurance and your bravery.

And now, goodbye … the value of the mark is declining, if only that could be a real sign of decline!

Charles

CHAPTER TWELVE

Philippe
July to October 1917

Philippe Bieler

ON 7 JULY, SIR DOUGLAS HAIG ORDERED the Canadian Corps to capture Lens. General Currie convinced him to concentrate on Hill 70 instead. Following some twenty counterattacks, Hill 70 was taken by the British and Canadians. It was one of the finest victories of the war, but with a very high number of casualties. The next few months were relatively quiet for the Canadians.

In early May, British and French leaders met in Paris, and reviewed some new strategies. Emphasis was initially to be given to a policy of attrition, dealt by surprise attacks. It was then Sir Douglas's recurring desire to deliver a blow to the Ypres Front. He wished to attack first of all the dominating ridge at Messines, followed by an eventual objective of securing the Belgian coast.

Meanwhile, few people in the West noticed the first stirrings of a second Russian storm. Lenin had returned to Russia from his Zurich exile in April 1917, and, in the following months, Socialist leaders in Russia began to call for a peace without annexations or indemnities, which culminated at the end of the year with an Armistice between Germany and Russia on considerably harsher terms.

THE RUNNER

Arras-Lens Front, 10 May 1917

My dear mother,

What beautiful weather! A real summer day, intense heat, not a cloud in the sky, but almost no greenery, I suppose because of the war. The trees are too badly wounded or sick to have the courage to grow leaves. Some of them are very badly wounded, their trunks broken, their branches ripped to shreds. Others are corpses, lying on the ground, and the fields are ploughed too much in the Krupp system to bear any crops at all. It's not nature's fault that spring is late ... we are now in a reserve position, set up in a shelter that our dear friend Fritz was kind enough to excavate. He did it well, when he built this concrete roof two- to three-feet thick, which protects us from the bombs. We are four in our shelter: our section's officer, a sergeant, a batman, and I am the runner. I carry the dispatches from the section to the company and do the rounds of the machine guns with my lieutenant. It's a good job, not tiring. While I was nosing around in the local village, now in ruins, I found some rhubarb plants in a little deserted garden. We made some excellent compotes that everyone enjoyed ... next Sunday is Mother's day, and we are all thinking of our mothers. My best wishes and kisses for this day. The 24th of May will remind me of many happy memories. How is the boat coming along? I haven't had any news.

Philippe

15 June 1917

My dear mother,

We are enjoying superb weather. It's so pleasant to be warmed by the sun instead of crowding around a fire in some hole ... The last time we were resting they replaced the afternoon exercise by games and sports. I came third in the obstacle course, fourth in the bag race, and second to last in the hundred yards. I am definitely better built for comfort than for speed! We had a very good time ... Here we are again in some trenches taken from the enemy. We are very comfortable. I went to explore the gardens of an abandoned village, and under the debris and the weeds I found some red currants and some very ripe blackberries. Unfortunately, our friend Fritz saw us, began to shoot at us, and we were unable to have our dessert ... I am sending a little red rose to mother found in this garden ... Things have changed a lot since winter, it is no longer strictly a sit-down war. One leaves one's position and advances!

Philippe

Château de la Haie
Souchez, 20 July 1917

My dear parents,

I am writing to you from a little paradise where we are resting after a stint in the trenches. Our camp is set up in a field completely surrounded by a beautiful forest in the French style, hardly touched by the bombardments. It is so restful to be in a normal corner of the country and forget a bit about the massacres and the barbarism of the Front! I am writing to you from the YMCA. We hear a brass band and the clapping of a concert held in a nearby tent, the doors of the cinema have just opened, and people are queuing to get in. One would think that we were at the Neuilly fair! However, the big event of the week was the meeting with André. Tante Julia had written to me that he had returned to his battalion, so I began to look for him in their rest camp, but he was either at the concert or at the cinema, or at a match, or boxing? As hard to find as the proverbial needle! I resigned myself to wait at the door of the big tent, and it seemed to me that this unfortunate concert would never end. The crowd finally comes out, and there he is! It was good to see each other after twenty-five months of separation! He's grown, he's expanded, and his cheeks are less hollow. Our meeting was very pleasant, but very brief, as we each had to return to our camps. Thank you for your letters. We live from one letter to the next.

Philippe

Lunch with Philippe (at the far left)

28 July 1917

My dear mother,

What a nice surprise to see the arrival of a good package, just as we are in the trenches. How that reminds me of home ... The delicacies wrapped in the bread paper. With the five francs that you sent me I could buy some coffee in a machine and some other goodies.

I had a pleasant surprise the other day as I walked out of a concert given by the YM, and saw, who do you think? It was Philippe, who I hardly recognized with his moustache and his substantial stature. It was late, and he couldn't stay, but I hope to see him soon.

The other day we saw the King go by. He was in a car, and, as he was going very fast, we weren't able to recognize all the generals.

Captains Molson and Biddolph were killed by the same mortar.

André

La Clairière, 15 July 1917

My dear boys,

You will remember how the discussions with Mr Millette with respect to the road ended up with a directive from the commune, obliging Dad to build it this summer. Very annoying, as we had to complete certain repairs at Les Colombettes, and Dad didn't think he had the resources to invest at least a further $150, as well as finding the manpower, much reduced because of the war. Then, everything worked out: John Morrow took charge to immediately undertake the hard work in the woods for $100, and the rest later. After eight days of hard work, the wonderful guy arrived a few moments ago with sweat running down his face and a big smile, asking us to go and inspect his creation. "I want you mister to come and see me job, and pass over Victoria Bridge!" We toasted it with a glass of blackberry syrup, and he left with his cheque, the harnesses, his men, and an expression of extreme satisfaction for the good work, and his money. Dad is also happy, except for the empty purse.

The tricolour flag is flying on the mast in honour of yesterday's Bastille celebration. Dad and I are sitting on the southern veranda, which is now encircled with grape vines. The rock garden is flowering with pansies, everything is peaceful and colourful, but this is not enough to make us forget about the huge hole that your absence causes, dear absent sons. If only our Russian friends could hit firmly and hard in order to bring an end soon!

Blanche

ETIENNE COMES HOME

22 July 1917

My dear mother,

You may have been surprised to receive my Wednesday telegram. Last Sunday I was invited for tea at Mrs. Finley's, and was warmly welcomed. She has a charming small apartment in Bayswater, where she lives with her daughters. Doctor Finley spends most weekends there and happened to be

*there on Sunday. He was kind enough to write to the colonel who manages
the Canadian sick-leaves.*

*I went to see him the following day, and he suggested that I go and see
my doctor at the hospital right away to ask him to arrange a meeting with
the medical council, to certify that I would not be capable to return to the
Front for two months. My doctor was very positive, and sent me Wednesday
to the medical council. It all went very quickly. These gentlemen checked my
wound and immediately recommended two months' leave.*

*I am, therefore, since Wednesday on leave, and all I have to do is wait for
a boat. The doctor told me that I could stay at the hospital, meanwhile, as
long as I wanted.*

Etienne

WE WERE TO ENJOY another several lovely weeks. First of all, an excursion for the
two of us to Northfield. It was good to be together in this beautiful countryside, to
meet the cream of American Christianity, and at sunset to speak simply to a huge
audience sitting on the lawn of the "Round Top."

Etienne is feeling quite well and is awaiting an announcement from the Medical
Council, which he eventually receives. It is an official two-month leave, and he is
free to go to Canada on the first available boat. We must rush back to La Clairière
for this great occasion.—(BB)

31 July 1917

My dear mother,

*I'm finishing this letter Wednesday morning. It never stopped raining
yesterday, a torrential rain that is continuing today. It's horrible to think
of our troops, who are bravely attacking despite the rain and the mud, and
who have already accomplished a brilliant success. From one moment to
the next, we have for a long time been waiting for this attack, and here we
have waited for the bad weather before beginning! I'm almost sure that the
Canadians aren't there, and I'm happy for André and Philippe. The last
wounded Canadians that we have had were from the Lens area.*

Etienne

*Royal Overseas Officers Club
Pall Mall, London, 3 August 1917*

My dear Jean,

*Since I have heard that there won't be a boat within at least one or two
weeks, I have accepted the invitation of Mary Barton to spend a couple*

*of days in Ireland ... so here is two weeks of my leave that I have lost
in Canada.*

*I have met several guys that I knew: first of all Ralph Hayes, the captain
of the 3rd Battery, who is in the hospital here, and is also thinking of going
to Canada, and Greg Masson, poor guy, who lost two brothers in one month,
one in the RFY and the other in the RNAY, and has two months to go and see
his parents. I wasn't able to ask him enough questions about my old Battery.
Can you imagine that they lost fifteen men in two or three days about a
month ago; an entire gun detachment of my section was blown up in one hit.
I also met two guys that I knew who now have their promotions.*

*Have you any news of André? I haven't had any for a long time, and I'm
wondering what's happening to him. I'll write to him. Both he and Philippe
should soon have their leaves. They are really not very lucky.*

*I've received a good letter from Emile, thanking us for our little wedding
present. It cost £2.20. If you give me your share, I will pay André's and
Philippe's.*

My address until my departure:
c/o Mrs. Barton, Farndrey, Dunsdalle, Co. Cork, Ireland

Etienne

YES, THE FAMILY WAS THERE in this lovely August weather and alerted by a joyful cablegram, was waiting impatiently. Every evening with a lantern's glow we went down to the little wharf, hoping that this time we wouldn't return empty-handed. But, no, the motor we heard from afar stopped near a distant house and the long watch, in the darkness and sometimes in the rain, finished with another disappointment. Finally one night, in order to dissipate the autumn mist and to brighten the darkness, we had lit a bonfire on the shore, and at last a boat docks, and our lieutenant descends radiant and alert, despite a little limp. We were ecstatic, and celebrated during fifteen unforgettable days. Endless chats, picnics, work on the rock garden, and even the most fun excursion to Mont Tremblant, in an antique carriage we picked up at Mr Laroze's.—(BB)

THE SUMMER OF 1917

Lapinay près Bethune, 5 August 1917

My dear Jacques,

*I guessed that your boat was called Vimy and that it performed well. I
would like you to send me a plan, showing the location of the motor and the
control system.*

*We are in a training phase currently, and it's very pleasant to sit down
at the end of the day in the farmer's house with a big bowl of milk, and*

André at the "Corner of Blighty"

sometimes a bowl of soup as well. You can be sure that I prefer to spend my few pennies here, as these people sure need it, with everything doubling, even tripling. They are certainly dramatically affected by the war.

The other day we had a bath in one of the big factories around here. It was really well equipped – super hot showers, lockers, etc.

I received a registered letter the other day from Mom, dated 8 May, and I want to thank her a lot for the 10 francs that are helpful for the evening bowls of milk.

André

Paris, 16 August 1917

My dear parents,

And at last here it was. I wanted to see everything that was possible and imaginable. The first day I washed and, with the help of the department stores, I was a bit renewed, and then with a good Turkish bath taken with the Samaritans, I felt completely civilized. The terrible thing was that the bed was so soft that I couldn't sleep, but I quickly adjusted.

As Tante Julia's meeting only finished in the evening, I decided to visit the soldiers' leave club. A "Corner of Blighty" made for Mr Butler, that reminds me so much of mother when she makes her little remarks about her visit of Versailles or the Sunday service, etc. One has tea there, five or six per table, presided over by some ladies and young English or Canadian girls, where the conversation is quite home-like. After a few songs, and reading a few Canadian papers, I went to get Tante Julia and we returned together for a good dinner.

A taxi took us to the Invalides to see the war painters. The paintings were too small, but of places I know, like St Éloi, Neuville–St Vaast, Ypres, etc. Etienne saw them and, according to Tante Julia, found them too colourful. After that, we saw a lovely exposition of objects saved from the bombardments in Ypres, Arras, Reims, etc., and remains from some ruined castles.

A lovely boat ride to St Cloud ended the day and almost the leave, which went much too quickly. On Monday I'll probably go to Versailles and Tuesday another little visit to the Front to check how Fritz is doing, and probably visit the beautiful city of Lens.

André

8 August 1917

My dear mother,

How I would like to tell you what we do in the trenches, but all of that is not permitted. It's lucky that they don't censor your letters, all of them so full of interesting things. I can, however, tell you that we are relishing the tomatoes and fresh vegetables, and even the fruit ... mother's pen makes us live la Clairière!

Philippe

Paris, 29 August 1917

My dear parents,

You will be happy to know that I am at last on leave. It's not necessary to tell you that as soon as we were paid, we ran off, before the authorities had the idea of changing their minds ... A trip not particularly interesting in the midst of a golden August countryside. How nice it is to leave the camps overflowing with soldiers. We arrive in Paris at 9 p.m., and we are directed to the British Army and Navy Leave Club in l'hôtel Moderne,

Neuilly Protestant Church

Place de la Republique. I'm with a Canadian friend, with whom I get along particularly well ... The first night our beds seemed too cosy and our breakfast completely insufficient. We go to three restaurants before having enough, a little ashamed about eating like a horse ... after visiting the military police of the Pepin barracks, I go to 53A rue St Lazare to see Tante Julia. The janitor tells me she's on the fifth floor, and warns me to give my shoes a good wipe, as he had just waxed the stairs! Tante Julia receives me very affectionately. We arrange to meet at the Neuilly church on Sunday, where Oncle Charles is to preach.

What good memories I have of the boulevards Bineau and Inkerman! They have built the famous Lycee-hospital opposite the church. The church hasn't changed, even including the sound of the bell that had stopped just as I walked over the grill. I sit in a corner under the gallery, and here is a gentleman who has recognized me as a Bieler, and who comes to shake my hand. It's the nice Mr Deschamps, but without his lovely red knot with a golden edge of the good old days! Tante Julia joins me as Oncle Charles climbs up to the pulpit. How well he looks up there, always the same, although a little whiter. His glance confirms that he has recognized us. He announces the death of the young Giraudet, his mother and his sister are there, looking very shaken. There's not a man in the audience. That's war

*for you! I don't recognize many people, except for the orphans sitting in front
as usual. That reminds me of the touching goodbyes to my mother by these
children at the time of our departure to Canada. I remember that I almost
cried with them.*

*After the service, Oncle Charles shakes hands with all the parishioners.
All three of us then went to lunch at l'avenue de la Grande Armée, and we
talk about the news from Canada, about his farm, and of the war, and
afterwards I go with Tante Julia to the Invalides: Napoleon's tomb, the
German trophies, the war paintings. I return along the grands boulevards
to observe the crowd, almost entirely military; there are almost no civilians.
First of all French soldiers in varied uniforms: light blue, khaki, dark blue,
a few red trousers, Zouaves, wounded, many decorated with the Croix de
Guerre, the Military Medal, or the Légion d'Honneur. Then the Belgians,
with their police bonnets decorated in the front with a red spot. And the
Russians, short tunics, large shoulder pads, high boots. The Italians are
in green-grey uniforms with big capes, the Serbs are in grey uniforms with
funny caps split in the middle, the Americans aren't too bad with their
tight uniforms and their Stetson hats. Finally there are the English, the
Australians, and the Canadians, with marks on their sleeves that intrigue
the Parisians. Incidentally, everyone is praising our efforts around Lens. I
am allowed to repeat it, as all the newspapers are talking about it.*

*The next day I was invited to Oncle Charles's for lunch. How wonderful
he is, and how quickly time goes by as we talk together! Then, I accompany
him to his courses. First of all at the Union Chrétienne, which reminds me
of the jumble sales at the École du Dimanche, great days in our childhood.
Then to Mr Bassonas's office, who supervises the Foyers du Soldat. He sends
you his greetings. Then to see the Reverend Pfender. I am therefore seeing
all the leaders of the Église Reformée, and everywhere I go I am greeted
as a friend. Not everyone has the good fortune to be a Bieler, immediately
recognized and greeted. We haven't forgotten you, dear Dad and dear
Mother, and we appreciate what you are doing for France. We end our
rounds and pass in front of the YMCA, right on avenue Montaigne, if you
please! The Americans don't take half measures in offering this grand
building to their soldiers ...*

*I spent two days seeing Paris in great detail with my friend. Then on
Friday I went to Neuilly to fetch a bicycle that Oncle Charles wanted to
send to cousin Emile. I leave on the bicycle to do a spin in the forest. It was
wonderful to cycle rapidly along these beautiful avenues, well maintained
and shaded by giant trees. Then back to Oncle Charles's, where Emile
appears. What a super officer in his light blue uniform! We are quickly
reacquainted, and after lunch he invites me to visit l'École Militaire. He
shows me around the magnificent buildings, and, following a pleasant little*

cup of tea, accompanies me to the station, and I return to Paris. The next day I moved to Tante Julia's at Clamart, and it's in the dining room, where I'm feeling right at home, that I'm writing to you. Yesterday, Tante Julia and I went to church at Jouy. Following an excellent sermon, we returned to Chaville and then Paris. I would have liked to leave that same evening and visit Jean, but unfortunately they refused to give me a further leave, and I went straight to the Grande-Roue.

Philippe

IT WAS 8 SEPTEMBER, and the leaves were starting to fall. André's second year of the war was almost over, with seemingly no hope for this employment as a drafts-man. After eleven months of waiting, the authorities must have forgotten, and he would have to resign himself to a new winter in the trenches!—(BB)

Near Vimy Ridge, September 1917

My dear father,

I received your letter from Northfield when we were in the trenches. I had the great pleasure of seeing Phil for three or four hours yesterday. He had just returned from leave, and couldn't say enough about Tante Julia, Emile, and Oncle Charles. It's a great wonder to find relatives that are as welcoming.

The other day my captain said that he received a letter from you, and naturally I asked myself what it could be about. He didn't tell me anything until today. Please don't worry about me. I would certainly love a promotion if that was possible, but it seems that there is a surplus of officers, many of my friends have been waiting such a long time.

André

Mt St Éloi, 12 September 1917

My dear parents,

Here I am again with my company after some great memories from my leave. We are resting behind the lines ... you will no doubt realize that my return to the trenches wasn't joyful. I was homesick for the first time, but that will pass ...

We are lodged in a large old house, called a château around here, and it still has its doors and windows. As soon as I arrived, I went searching for André, and what good moments we had together! He seems to be in perfect health and is so nice and full of smiles. We shared some profound and intimate subjects, including so many souvenirs. It's interesting that our conversations always finish at 16 Island Lake; it must be the centre of the

world! We are wondering if Etienne is there now and we await your news impatiently.

Philippe

Mont St Éloi, 14 September 1917

My dear Jacques,

I am writing to you in a shelter within the trenches. We are not badly off: bunks, a table, some cases as make-believe chairs, a candle stuck in a tin can for lighting. I saw André, but not for long!

Philippe

September 1917

My dear dad,

Thank you for your good parcel containing a real cake. It's something we don't see any more in France.

The day before yesterday, Phil and I were invited by Grellet to his little hut, where he served us an excellent dinner: homemade omelette, buttered potatoes, plum compote, tea, and cigarettes. He's changed a lot since I saw him last. It was a long walk of about twelve kilometres, but it was really worthwhile. We talked a lot about 16 Island Lake.

I saw the director of our division's medical services yesterday, and he thought I was in good shape. Phil speaks constantly of Jacques.

André

Near Jacques Grellet's hut

10 September 1917

To Charles Bieler,

It was Saturday 8 September, as I was travelling, I discovered quite accidentally the Princess Pats, and as they were all doing their exercises, I gave a tiny note to one who was resting, asking him to give it to André.

The next morning I was going to try them again, with the hope of bringing them back to my little hut. As I was arriving at their quarters, the battalion was returning from the church parade. There they were free, and I ask about André. Three or four friends call for him and I see coming towards me this great André, that I had difficulty at first recognizing, as he had changed so much. With his lovely red cheeks, a good head of hair, and his wide shoulders, he is the model of good health, and certainly the military service had done him a lot of good. How can I express to you the joy that I felt in finding myself beside him, and chatting with him. Right away I asked him to come and spend the afternoon at my place with Phil, but all depended on the latter, so off we went to find him in his lodgings. I hid in the ruins of a house and told André to warn him that a friend wanted to see him. When he got to a few feet from my hiding place, I jumped out, and he was so surprised to see me, and both of us were so happy to have found each other. His physique had changed dramatically. He had lost quite a bit of weight, but all for the good, and had a very male look, with his fine black mustache and his round red cheeks, and in his lovely black eyes, whose glance had gone through fire of battle, there was something strong, decisive, and thorough.

As Philippe was not available before four, he promised to come and join us at my place. André and I shared the pitiful lunch of a trooper, eating off the same plate, and we set out talking about all of you, about the Vimy battle, about his leave in Paris, and the work of my battalion. The few kilometres were soon behind us, and we found ourselves in my hut, where my friends were preparing a little supper. Soon after, Philippe arrived, having hitched a ride on a truck. Your parents' circular letter thirty-six had just arrived, and we read it together, and also reviewed all our dearest memories of Canada, and, in chatting about a thousand things, he appeared so happy and so pleased with the little very simple meal, which reminded him a little bit of home.

Jacques Grellet

22 September 1917

My dear parents,

What great mail! Two circulars, one letter from Jacques, and a few lines from Etienne, written on Dad's letter!

I was so much picturing Etienne arriving in his uniform that I was disappointed to think that he was dressed in civilian attire. I hope that he will get an extended leave. It would be so good for all of you ... when one sees so many mothers in Paris walking around with their boys on leave, one realizes how difficult it is for you to have this joy only for the first time since the beginning of the war. I would so much like André to also go to Canada. He has been so brave and he is at the Front for so, so long!

The other day Jacques Grellet came to see André ... He took us to his little hut, and prepared a supper for us up to the likes of a Parisian restaurant: omelette, potatoes, green beans, plum compote. He looks good in his Canadian uniform.

Last night, we went to see Nicholson, who is an officer near here. He is still the same super guy, and I was very pleased to see him again. Bulmer Rutherford has just arrived in France, but I haven't yet been able to see him.

Philippe

30 September 1917

My dear mother,

I have just received your good letter. But why do you think that I am jealous of your happiness? Quite to the contrary, write about all the pleasures you are having with Etienne, and we will enjoy them along with you.

As I told you in my last letter, I am once again separated from Philippe. I won't therefore be able to give him the letter right away. I am from time

to time a gymnastic instructor here; I am going to take a course as "scout,"
given by a South African instructor, a very interesting guy.

André

IT HAD BEEN A MEMORABLE SUMMER. In July, in Bethune, it was a new training period. Andre was living with a peasant family and enjoyed sitting at the kitchen table, in front of an omelette and a few big bowls of milk. In August, the leave was a nice bonus. Finally in September, Andre had run unexpectedly into his brother: a taller Philippe, with a mustache. They had received a lunch invitation from their good friend, Jacques Grellet, who was considered part of the family and worked for Canada's "Railway Regiment."—(BB)

PHILIPPE IS TAKEN AWAY

AROUND 20 SEPTEMBER, we received a last letter from Philippe, describing another period of combat, and he added: "I am sending you a card that I received at the YMCA. I underlined one sentence that is I think true for many of my friends and certainly for me."

This card, entitled: Christ in Flanders, contains verses, very secular in form, but deeply religious in its meaning, with this introduction: "Many men, like the writer of this poem, seem to feel that Christ is nearer and easier to understand at the Front, and so they may, for we are fighting in his cause and He is here."

At the moment that Philippe was sending us this letter, he was apparently in perfect health, and couldn't have thought that he had only several days to live ... That God be blessed for this final message!

Philippe's health started to deteriorate on 28 September, and on 30 September an ambulance took him to a hospital near Aubigny en Artois. On 1 October, his complexion became yellowish, and his temperature increased. The military chaplain wrote: "I saw your son in hospital today, and he asked me to write to you for him. He is patient and plucky, but I am sorry to say very ill" ... On 2 October, he writes: "I am sorry to have to convey to you the sadness that your son Private Philippe Bieler passed away in hospital last night. He will be buried at the cemetery at Aubigny en Artois, a pretty place on the top of the hill, and I will arrange for a cross to be erected."

On 10 October 1917, at our return to Les Colombettes, we found the fatal telegram announcing unceremoniously the terrible news of the death of this much-loved son. Soon letters from Jean, André, the military chaplain, the nurse, and a few officers and friends gave us on the one hand an account of his brief illness and on the other hand expressions of sympathy from all those who had known him.

As André ponders his future in the trenches, a crushing blow finishes him off. He receives the terrible news: Philippe is dead ... Philippe, who, since his earliest childhood had been his playmate, and his classmate. Philippe his confidant, his best friend, almost his twin, so little was their age difference. Philippe, his brother by blood and by warfare. He, so much alive, yesterday still so joyful and so affectionate! When Etienne had left, André had felt a big hole in his life. But when he had heard that Philippe was thinking of volunteering, he had protested strongly. Three was enough in this hell, his junior was too young to be dragged into it. As Philippe wouldn't listen, the only solution was to welcome him as well as possible! Since then, at each of their rare meetings, it had been as they said: "a little home away from home." "We then shared letters, parcels, and souvenirs from home, and our hearts warmed with the most tender and most virile affection. Is it possible that all that is finished, buried under a little wooden cross in an Artois cemetery?" It was too horrible to think about! All of André's letters during this difficult autumn are tinged in black. The letters from home, Philippe's letters now in his possession, even the sympathy from his friends, all of that awakens his grief, despite his intense search for everything that has to do with it.—(BB)

9 October 1917

My dear parents,

I have just received the news of Philippe's death. It's only been one month since I left him, and he seemed to be in perfect health. It was really during these last days spent with him that I best remembered those pre-war days where we were such good friends. All my life, I will remember that lovely day when we went to visit Grellet. It was a long walk, but it seemed very brief as we talked together about home, and especially 16 Island Lake, which he loved so much. He talked to me a lot about Jacques and the leave.

His hospital was only about twenty kilometres from here. The weather is currently very bad. At the first clearing, I'll borrow a bicycle and I'll go and see the chaplain, and the nurse who looked after him at the end.

Take courage. He did his duty.

André

11 October 1917

My dear parents,

It made me feel good to receive something from home; Philippe's news leaves me with a huge hole in my life. Even though we didn't see each other often, I always knew he was nearby. It was such a great joy to talk about home together.

I've already tried twice to go to his hospital, but in vain. I can't get hold of a bicycle. I will try again on Sunday, and I'll then write you a longer letter.

André

No. 3 *Canadian General Hospital* BEF
18 October 1917

My dear parents,

You will wonder first of all what is the cause is of this long silence. While some of the most horrible battles of the war were in progress, two of our clerks were on leave, and the work had to be done anyway. It was only late yesterday evening that I heard about the death of our dear Philippe. This loss cannot be replaced. Tante Julia, who saw him more recently, will be able to tell you more than me, as I spent only a few hours with him since 6 May 1917. These few hours will leave me with an indelible impression for the rest of my life of this dear boy! What energy he had! What good humour, what cheerfulness. I will always remember the pleasant moments we spent in front of the Canadian Red Cross Hut at Etaples, talking about his experiences at the Front, of the period of training he had just had in Bruay, and of the great battle for which he was preparing and thank God he was not a part of, but where so many brave men fell for their country! He was also funnier than ever, and the two nurses, one more or less a relative of Mr. McLennon, who loved him so. War had only changed him physically; otherwise he had remained our good Philippe of yesteryear. I am a little lost as to what were the circumstances that led to his death. It must have been very sudden, as he didn't seem to have written to anyone during his sickness, and very fast and obviously very serious, as he died in a Casualty Clearing Station, that is to say, very close to the Front. We generally only keep the most serious cases there, the others being immediately evacuated to the base, just like Etienne, who, unless I am mistaken, passed through the same hospital.

I am happy, dear parents, to feel that Etienne is in your midst for this difficult ordeal. That will ruin the end of his leave. I know that you are resigned about this great bereavement, as our Father in heaven has decided that our family, up until now so spared, has now seen one of its dearest members make the supreme sacrifice at the age of nineteen. As our Anglican chaplain said at the death of his only son, killed in one of the first trench raids that had ever been tried, and that he had invented, "Promoted to service with God." Like me, the comparisons with the less-fortunate families won't console you completely for the death of our ray of sunshine, of my favourite brother, but it will allow us to put ourselves in the shoes of the less fortunate and to regain our courage despite it all. You probably know that until the end of the war one can't build monuments. A nice wooden cross with the name and R.I.P. on top is all. However, I have seen several English military cemeteries, and I can confirm that one couldn't find anything cleaner and quieter and even more artistic. If I go, I will buy a few flowers.

Sergeant Jean Bieler

You will be pleased to hear that I have been promoted to Lance Sergeant, which is for me the equivalent of full sergeant, as I'm paid more than an ordinary sergeant and I benefit from all of a sergeant's privileges.

Jean

Westmount, 21–23 October 1917

Dear soldiers and dear dispersed family members,

In personal letters to each of you, we have announced our great bereavement, but without being able to add any details. We don't yet have these details. We will perhaps never have them. Two very brief notes, one from the chaplain and one from the nurse who watched over the last moments of our dear child, have however given us certain facts that help us to reconstruct his last days.

Visit of HM The Queen to the hospital, with Colonel Birkett, 1917

I must go back a little so that I can tell you what Philippe had been for us in the last few months before his departure. All his minor character deficiencies had suddenly disappeared, and he became considerate, helpful, tidy, a hard worker, remaining joyful, sometimes hilarious, and very affectionate. On the last day, he brought fifteen friends for lunch, and it was curious to witness to what extent all these people, older than him, seemed to like and respect him and accept his being the life of the party. The best of that group are dead, but no doubt there will be a few that will write to us.

I won't tell you about the emotions of this separation, but let me tell you about a document that you will one day receive. It is in the form of a little volume that he intended later to turn into a war diary. But his accounts have nothing impersonal, there are some charming descriptions, sometimes with inadequate spelling, but not lacking in style, some amusing or sad scenes, taken as they were, and some more intimate comments that show that he was continually thinking of home and his family, and forgetting his minor problems, so as to be better able to think of the others, and always ready to send thanks for the last letter and whatever meagre parcel. I hope that you have reviewed the copies of the letter where he described with such enthusiasm the leave in Paris, the first and only one during the eighteen months he served. After that we received another three letters of 12, 14, and 23 September, and here are a few excerpts:

*"Here I am back in the trenches, and for the first time I felt a little
homesick. What cured me was to see André. What great moments we
had together." "How nice it is to know that mother has at last a lodger,
let's hope that he will be able to stay a long time!" "I was so sad not to
have permission to see Jean in Boulogne."*

*There was also a lovely note for Jacques, so funny and affectionate as
always. You know that it was only on Monday 8 October that we received
the news that he was dangerously ill, and on Wednesday the 10th the news
of his death, resulting from trench fever. The next day, all the newspapers
published the news with some pleasant comments that might normally not
have been seen amongst the numerous others. But no, right after the first
editions, the letters of condolence began arriving in large bundles, very
few cards, often full pages filled with the most heartfelt sympathy. The
most touching ones came from those who knew him best: Morins, Pecks, the
parents of his "bunch," Rutherford, Nicholson, and Taylor, the Carharts,
the Stanstead teachers. Also amongst the humble, the former maids and
charwomen attended the service for him too. All in all about two hundred
letters, that I would like you to read in part, as almost all of them include
an affectionate message to you, and such lovely thoughts about the sacrifice,
and eternal life! If possible read out loud "He giveth His beloved sleep,"
and "Just away." These two made me feel better, and contain several
thoughts that appear in these letters. Various corporations and committees
also expressed their condolences, amongst others: the governor general, the
corporation of McGill University, the Municipality of Westmount, the
Soldiers' Swiss League, etc.*

*All that doesn't bring back our little soldier, but it helps to carry the
weight. I forgot to say that I receive many visits, that I have been sent many
roses, as if one had guessed that it was his favourite flower, which he picked
now and again for me in the ruins of Flanders, or dried rose from Arbois.
These bouquets arrived so fresh, so young, and so beautiful, but after a
few hours these roses leaned over, and died too soon, like our Philippe,
leaving behind, like him, a good memory, and a delicious perfume. All
these emotions will be prolonged, as we receive the letters from Europe. The
first two arrived yesterday, the first one from the chaplain, and one from
the nurse, saying briefly that Phil arrived two days before his death at
Ambulance 42 (the same one where Etienne had his first aid after his first
wound, situated between Arras and St Pol), he was already unconscious, and
they did everything possible to save him. He died 1 October at 10 p.m. and
was buried in the small cemetery of d'Aubigny-en-Artois (Pas de Calais). It
is there that we will go one day to plant some rose bushes around the little
wooden white cross that marks the place of his last sleep, where he finally*

*rests from his great fatigue. He wasn't as tough as he looked, and had not
been able to deal with the exhausting life of a soldier in action. I would like
Tante Julia, Jacques Grellet, and André to write to me how he looked the last
time they saw him. Had he lost weight, did he have dark lines under his eyes,
did he seem worn out, or did he look more or less as he did in the past?*

*The dear child sleeps. It's up to us to work until the day when we will
find him again. Dad has some important new courses, but not as time-
consuming as previous years, which gives him several half-days of work
in his office each week, which do him good. So Etienne has thus gone back
to McGill, and he is working hard, as he has gotten the post of Physics
Demonstrator, left vacant by his Professor King, who was asked to go to
England to work for the Admiralty; this job, added to his studies, makes for
a very busy schedule. Had I told you that the military authorities here have
received the order not to send him back for the moment? There are presently
too many wounded officers in England, resulting from excessive promotions.
Etienne is having a problem in accepting this development. To cast aside his
uniform, to be warm, while his brothers and friends fight, missing maybe
Victory Day! ... But since he doesn't have a choice, he calmly puts up with
the situation, happy to be with us, and to return to his mathematics. For
us, this decision has been excellent news, but we would not have retained
him if his duty was to return. Since Philippe's death, Jacques has become
more serious; he works more, but has become more interested in his manual
activities. His latest acquisition is a marvellous American tool that is a
vice and combines grinding and several other functions, allowing him to
undertake various industrial activities. As for me, I'm up and down. My
sleeping is improving, and I'm regaining my strength, but I suffered a hard
blow that will leave a scar forever. When I deliver my future speeches about
the war I will really know what it cost.*

Affectionately yours,
Blanche

26 October 1917

My dear parents,

*We are very far from where Philippe is buried, and it's impossible for me to
go there. How sad! We will probably soon get back to that area, and I will do
everything possible to get there.*

*My heart trembles each time you mention Philippe. I am now receiving
all his letters; tell me if you want me to send them to you. In the meantime,
I'll keep them here.*

*On my return to the battalion yesterday, I was able to obtain more
details about Philippe's brief illness. He was in the trenches and had a*

small wound in his foot. In passing, the doctor told him that it would be wise for him to be treated. When he arrived at the dressing station, they bandaged him and sent him to the rear, far from the trenches. Once there, he was treated by an old friend of Jean's from the General Hospital, who felt that he didn't look well, and took his temperature, and found it to be very high. He telephoned for an ambulance, and stretcher-bearers, and in the meantime put him to bed and gave him something for the fever. The ambulance arrived shortly after, and Philippe left, concerned about his equipment. The corporal told him "You will be back in a couple of days. It isn't worthwhile to worry about it." That's to show you that it didn't look serious at that time. Jean's friend is to write to the corporal, and you will no doubt get a copy.

André

To André and Etienne,

Poor and very dear boys, it's me that's had all the pleasure to have had you at my hut, and I won't forget those few hours spent on the banks of the little river, where our fraternal affection was revealed …

One felt that Philippe's soul was maturing too quickly, hélas!, during the difficult experiences he had been through, during an hour of danger, he must have met the Father face to face, and that he had given himself to him. His face reflected peace, confidence, and a clear-cut conviction of being directed by a superior force towards the only goal, that of justice, in accepting the sacrifice that was being asked.

Jacques Grellet

7th Canadian Machine Gun Co.
8 October 1917

Dear Sergeant Bieler,

Your brother Private P.A. Bieler was not with me when he went to the hospital, as he was with the Princess Pats at the time, because all attached men had to be sent back to their battalions at the end of last September.

From last winter up until that date, he had been with me, and I may say that I cared more for him than for any other man in the company. Consequently he was a great friend of mine. He had been my runner for a long time, and a more brave, intelligent, and pleasant chap could not be found anywhere. Many a time I gave him the opportunity of going on a gun, for he was a perfectly splendid gunner, but he refused, because he wanted to be my runner, and an ideal runner he was too! There is not a single man

The English Cemetery, D'Aubigny-en-Artois

in the company who did not think a great deal of your brother. Never an unkind word, and always willing to do something for others!

The last fight ... It was a very trying fight indeed, and how proud I was of his conduct! The same applies to every engagement he was in: brave as the bravest, cheerful as the most cheerful, willing as the most willing. The men of my section are terribly upset at losing such a charming companion as "Phil," as he was always called ... There is not a thing that I would not have done for him, as I loved him as a brother. He undoubtedly would have received a commission had he been a little older. All the officers were fond of him, and had spoken of this quite frequently. I can never express my regrets sufficiently for your dear brother's death.

Lieutenant B.J. Mothersill

Paris, 15 November 1917

My dearest Blanche and Charles,

We all enjoyed so much being with André during his recent leave, and it was almost over, when in my office on rue St Lazare I saw a young soldier with a beaming expression. It was our Phil, arriving straight from the battle at

*Lens, where I heard later that he had been particularly heroic. How can I
describe my joy in seeing him again?*

*He was no longer the big boy, cheerful and a joker, of five years ago, but
a big, handsome soldier, slimmed by the deprivations of war, sun-tanned,
with a young mustache and brown eyes, both soft and deep ... the portrait of
his mother! He was ingenious, affectionate, sober, modest, discreet, obliging,
happy with everything, shining forth life, joy, and youth. With all that,
one felt that he was a soldier who the war had helped gain determination,
courage, and mastery of himself.*

*These ten days of leave, his first during twelve months of war, sailed by.
Philippe seemed so happy to renew his relations with his aunt, uncle, and
those of his cousins that he had been able to contact, and that he hadn't seen
for nine years, and also to see Paris again, and the welcoming family homes,
to talk about Canada, his parents and his brothers. We left each other on
3 September at the Gare du Nord after many days filled with happy and
joyful activities.*

Julia

Is it possible that this young life, so full of promise, was already over? For the first
time I felt what it was like to lose the blood of my blood, the skin of my skin, and the
affection from my heart, so soft, so strong, and so fresh!—(BB)

Gravestone of Philippe Bieler. Private Philippe Alfred Bieler,
Princess Patricia's C.L.I., 1st October, 1917, age 19

CHAPTER THIRTEEN

Passchendaele

October to December 1917

Members of Australian 4th Division Field Artillery, 10th Field Artillery Brigade, on a
duckboard track through Château Wood, near Hooge in the Ypres salient, 29 October 1917.
The leading soldier is Gunner James Fulton, followed by Lieutenant Anthony Devine.

IN 1916, SIR DOUGLAS HAIG ORDERED that a plan be prepared for an operation to clear the Flemish coast. The coast was only thirty miles away, and the Germans' key railway could be eliminated. That scheme, dependent essentially on undertaking an offensive north of Armentières, had changed many times. He still thought, however, that from the Ypres Salient he could push through the German lines and roll up the enemy lines from the north. It looked geographically quite attractive, but on closer inspection it was not. The Germans were protected in the north by the flooded dikes. The bombardments near Ypres had churned the plain into an impassable mud bath, and as the years had gone by, the Germans had fortified their lines and transferred many divisions from Verdun to the north. Just about every senior British official, including Lloyd George, was against his plan, but Haig insisted, and the British army marched on.

Haig's plan began at Messines, a village located a few miles south of Ypres, dominated by a 150-foot ridge. It was in the hands of the Germans, and was a key observation point from which they had a perfect view of the British Front. Over a period of several months, millions of pounds of explosives were dug underneath. On 7 June, the pile of explosives was detonated and the enemy's position was decimated. In short order, the British were able to capture the entire ridge. The success did not change the opposing opinion of the leading military and political leaders. However, the war cabinet was badly informed, and many of the vital facts were concealed from them. The civilian ministers were tired, and did not even debate the issue. They eventually gave their whole-hearted support.

General Haig had chosen the Canadians to play a central role in the attack at Passchendaele. General Currie had previously pointed out that it would be a very costly experience, but, given the decision, he prepared elaborate plans for the difficult attack. The Germans were fully aware of the British plans and also prepared. A million soldiers were crammed into the Ypres Salient on each side of the Front. From Messines, the battle moved on towards Passchendaele.

It was soon obvious that it would be a disaster. The British advanced less than a mile and were not even able to reach the German main line. The intense shellfire had churned up the ground and turned it to an impassable mud swamp that swallowed most everything that attempted to get through, sometimes even the tanks. By mid-August the pace slackened, but General Haig insisted that it carry on.

IT'S CERTAINLY NOT WITH GREAT JOY that the Princess Pats head towards Ypres in the autumn of 1917. A continuous fight was raging in a battlefield with a fatal reputation. From 23 to 27 October, they were terribly bombarded among the ruins of Ypres. André remembers these spooky nights among the decapitated columns and broken arches of the Halle aux Draps. At night, these huge ruins, illuminated by the flickering glow of the campfires, etch in the black sky their profiles, their

Manhandling an 18-pounder field gun through the mud near Langemarck, 16 October 1917.

shadows, and their fantastic lights that would have been the joy of Rembrandt or Gustave Doré.—(BB)

THE BATTLE OF PASSCHENDAELE

THE CANADIANS HAD JOINED the British on 18 October, and General Currie was asked to take the lead towards the capture of the village of Passchendaele. The Canadians were to deliver three attacks at intervals of three or more days. Although there was ample evidence of Currie's skill, and of his troops' determination, he knew that the engagement would become very costly.

IN FACT, everything was against the Canadians. First of all the lie of the land: the enemy was firmly in place on the hill; at the foot, a plain so badly torn by the machine guns that the ground had disappeared. It was no more than a vast swamp, irrigated by the rain and by the little Ravebeek River, whose flooding created deep black ponds where the bombs had fallen, and covered the whole area with mud. To these already trying difficulties, wouldn't the bad weather add its additional

Ravebeek swamp. German prisoners and wounded Canadians coming in through the mud

traumas? Torrential rain, the west wind, cold, and fog. At Vimy, it was a wet spring, but, all the same, springtime. At Passchendaele, it's the most pathetic autumn that one has ever seen. At Vimy, the bagpipes had motivated the attackers, and here and there a trench, or a bomb crater, had given an instant of protection. At Passchendaele there isn't any music, other than the roar of the bombardments, nor any protection, other than the frail shelter of the steel helmet. Seven months ago, one could see from whence came the firing, now it comes from everywhere, as the air force had made substantial advances, and added firing from the skies to that of the artillery.

The Vimy crest had been taken with a method and a precision that gave confidence to the combatants. For the attack on the Passchendaele hill there were so many imponderables that all programs had a risk of being useless. This attack seemed to be an insane proposition. Did it warrant the unnecessary sacrifice of several thousand men? Was the project of closing the Porte de Calais so urgent, no matter what price? No one seemed to have the time even to ask these critical questions.—(BB)

4 November 1917

My dear mother,

On the 28th, we leave the camp and cross the Ravebeek Swamp as best we can, to relieve the regiment occupying one of the slope's first spurs. During the day of the 29th, the bombardment increases, and we prepare to attack. Our heavy loads are distributed: each man carries his gun, 170 shells, an airplane signal, rations for three days, three sandbags, two grenades, a map, a box of dry alcohol, and a shovel. Despite the gusts of wind and the downpours, we abandon our coats and move ahead in the torrents of water and in the middle of the night!

André

ANDRÉ WAS INTERVIEWED by the CBC in 1975, and this was his actual experience of the battle:

Passchendaele: I can hardly think about, or even spell, that horrid name. What a horrible place; just a sea of mud. It seemed to have been raining for a month that fall, and the whole place was thick mud in a flat, feature-less plain. A duck walk had been laid down, boards tied together, so that the troops could walk over the mud. Unfortunately, the duck walk was only wide enough for single-file travel; it was impossible to pass soldiers coming the other way.

We began the march toward the Front, and when we met the 42nd Regiment coming away from the Front, they were obliged to step off the duck walk to let us pass. Each soldier held onto another as they stepped onto the mud, in order to keep themselves from falling. We had priority, as we were going to the Front and they were returning. The mules were not so lucky. If they stepped off the duck walk, they could not get back on, the mud was so deep. They were shot immediately, and we saw their rotting, stinking carcasses, stiff legs in the air, all along the way.

We had begun our attack not very far from the place where I was wounded almost two years before, and to get there we had to cross mile after mile of a sea of mud. At dawn, the guns begin a huge bombardment, and here we were crossing the swamps and the barbed-wire fences. As we continued, the Germans sprayed gas and it became very dark. We were of course wearing our masks, and it's very difficult to see through the glass. I tripped, and it took two men to pull me from the mud. You can imagine the difficulty in getting to an attack position, when in addition the Germans were constantly bombarding us.

The Germans, hidden in their blockhouses and their tiny forts, fight tooth and nail, and their machine guns spit death in the ranks of the attackers. Everywhere, dark flames shoot up to the sky, amidst huge explosions. Flares drop from the sky and explosives detonate at our feet. The waves of our men, feet firmly on the ground, anxious and stupefied by the sudden tempest that thunders in every direction, stop for an instant, then a team effort lifts them up and pushes them forward again. We must pass through this fiery whirlwind. We stumble; we hold each other up in

Passchendaele topography: a scene at Garter Point,
on the battlefield near Zonnebeke, in the Ypres sector.

the huge billows of smoke. We see the ground open up under our feet. We move abruptly to avoid gaping holes, the dead lying on the ground, land mines, and the wounded, who are struggling and clinging. The soldiers, and particularly the officers, are falling like flies. If this was to continue, the regiment would be completely annihilated!

Right from the beginning, we lost all our officers, with the exception of one, for which I was the communication agent. Our sergeant rallied several men to charge directly, and having gotten to a few feet of the enemy, he fell from a shot to his heart. How horrible, a man of great courage, married with several children. The position was taken, and the Germans who were shooting at us until the last moment give up with arms in the air crying "Kamarad," but we were no longer taking many prisoners. The German airplanes were very active; they shot at us from a few hundred metres overhead, and telegraphed our positions to their batteries.

The further advance was leading to the most dramatic and fateful incident of the day – the capture of the pillbox on the Meetcheele Spur. The troops had to drive straight up against the fortified positions of Meetcheele Ridge, which spat machine-gun fire unceasingly. In the first advance, all the officers but two were killed. The company sergeant major took command. He rallied the shattered remnant of the company and led it forward. He fell, and a sergeant took over, and before them stood only the pillbox untouched by the artillery and raining death from every loophole.

I saw many fall. One was Papineau of Quebec, a descendant of the celebrated family. He had not been in the Front lines for several years, but, together with others, he had joined the ranks when the regiment, so severely depleted, desperately needed reinforcements and support.

The tide turned when Sergeant Mullins, who was known for his resourcefulness and bravery, ran forward and threw a bomb into the pillbox. The explosion killed everyone inside, and stopped the barrage from the German side. He took prisoner those who surrendered, and installed himself in the blockhouse, pulled a machine gun out of a hole, placed it on the roof as a defence against the counterattacks of the enemy and to consolidate the victory. For this he won the Victoria Cross. But the casualties on our side were much greater than for the German side.

The enemy, however, was far from being entirely defeated; their reserves arrived and pestered us. Four friends and I, all of a sudden, find ourselves separated from the troop. To avoid the bombardment that was starting again, we find a bomb crater and dump the miscellaneous baggage that we had been complaining about. With our shovels, we build a shelter, and cook our food with the alcohol, to satisfy our ravenous appetite. But there's the sound of sliding ... It's our sergeant, who crawled over while trying to reorganize the advance of the remaining soldiers. But six of us crowded together is "too much," he declares. So we then hide two-by-two in some nearby cavities. I spent the night with Captain Tenbrook.

The next day, 1 November, there's an important message to be sent to headquarters. Who will do it? I had a bit of a reputation, because I have a very good sense of direction; I always know where I am, and also I can see in the dark. Because of this, I was asked to deliver the dispatch to headquarters. This meant walking back through the mud and the dark, and, worst of all, through enemy fire. As I approached the barrage, I decided the only thing to do was to take my chances and barge in. I was lucky; I got through.

When I reached the headquarters, which was in the old German blockhouse, I found it in disarray. No one seemed to be in charge, and an

André Bieler in 1975

atmosphere of despair and disorder hung over the place. I hardly knew to whom to give my dispatch; no one seemed ready to receive it. The commanding officer held his head in his hands, and tears were in his eyes. It was clear that the enormous losses suffered by the regiment were almost too much to bear.

I finally found someone who would accept my dispatch, and he explained that this was good timing, as they were looking for a guide to help the moving of the remaining Princess Pats, after the ninety-six hours of combat. I was tired, hungry, and thirsty, but no one offered me food or drink or rest. I'm put in charge, and headed to where I had been told to go, zigzagging across craters and swamps, at the head of three hundred men, whom I steer to the new Canadian position. The enemy, however, won't let go without chasing us with their poisonous gas. We are all exhausted, sleeping standing up, trying to put on our masks, but frequently taking them off to find our way in the midst of the chaos, forgetting that the dreadful gas will get its revenge for our carelessness. And so I retraced my steps through the dark and the mud, which stank of the blood of three years of war. Once again we had to go through the barrage of enemy fire. I got through, but of course, many did not. At the end of the battle, only a handful of us were left, and not a single officer or NCO. In fact I was the senior among those few that remained.

The Passschendaele crest had been captured, but the Patricias had been almost wiped out. The regiment had never before faced such a distressing situation. General Dyer, Commanding Officer of the 7th Division, of which the Patricias were a part, came to thank the regiment at nearby Pommern Castle and said: "The Princess Patricias earned for themselves on that 30 October deathless glory. Fierce in attack, wise in disposition, the work of the whole Battalion on that day was of a calibre that would be hard to excel. Their casualties were very heavy, but all ranks lived up to the high traditions of the Regiment."

There was a final attack at Passschendaele village on 7 November, which left it in ruins. It was the final moment of this horrible battle that caused three hundred thousand British and Canadian casualties and two hundred thousand German casualties. A particularly sad conclusion was that the new British Front protruded into German territory, and when the Germans attacked the following year, the British shortened the line and abandoned those trivial gains of 30 October 1917.

IT IS A LONG WAY, from one destination to another, before finally arriving at Poperinghe, where he can sleep at last, and what a sleep! However, as he woke up the next morning, André felt a burning sensation in his chest, and found it impossible to talk. His vocal cords and his bronchial tubes were so badly burned that he remained dumb for more than ten days, and it took many years before he was cured of the scars of Passschendaele. We soon heard that the victory provoked congratulations from all the newspapers and all the Allied governments. However, for Sir Arthur Currie, these praises had a sour taste, as he had lost 80 per cent of his officers, and 60 per cent of his men. Deep sympathy is expressed to the families; mentions and medals are distributed to many survivors. But what injustice! Such a huge number of officers, who witnessed the courage of their men, carried their secrets to the grave. André's name was certainly amongst those who condemned this injustice. His officer should at least have received the medal that he so much deserved.

André, graduated from the "furnace" safe and sound, and then had a pathetic little accident, in which a rusty nail plunged into his heel, resulting in another stay at the hospital. The wards were full of the badly wounded, arms and legs were amputated, and the better-off hobbled, and served as secretaries and nurses prior to returning to their regiments.

Poperinghe was one of the rare little market towns still standing in the otherwise-ravaged Flanders. It was there that André rejoined the Princess Pats, which were being reorganized after the great battle. Its narrow, old-fashioned streets had all the small inns and shops dear to soldiers. The big church still had its belfry, several of the mill's wings were turning, and many of the farms had conserved their roofs and even their windmills. On the heavy soil of the fields, were old people, women, and children dragging their ploughs in preparation for the harvest they hoped their menfolk would undertake the following year.—(BB)

CANADIAN ARMY CORPS TOPOGRAPHICAL SECTION

5 November 1917

My dear parents,

You will have seen in the newspapers articles on our battle. Our change of Front and different preparations made it completely impossible for me to go and find out more at Philippe's hospital. We will return perhaps further south, and I sincerely hope to be able to go to see his grave.

And here I am, far away from the horrors of war, in a little Flemish village.

André

IT WAS FROM THERE THAT André was waiting to leave once again for the trenches, when one day a friend tells him: "You are the lucky one. There seems to be good news for you in the orderly room." André drops in, receives the details of his promotion to the topographical section, and immediately packs his bag and says his goodbyes. A truck takes him to Camblain l'Abbé, where his new colleagues are camped. Everything on this happy day contributes to the immense joy that beats in his heart. He is given a warm welcome from Captain Flechen. He is to be far from this horrible battlefield, and he joins his mates around a real dining-room table. It's in a quiet country corner, with a series of white wooden huts, a pleasant dormitory with double bunks, almost like home. There is a clean workshop, where a precise and captivating job, involving the tracing on maps of the troop advances, is awaiting. This type of work was brand new for André, but he was excited by the challenge and the prospect of being an apprentice in a function that was in complete accord with his tastes. He learned very quickly, and was soon promoted to the rank of sergeant, in charge of a team of juniors.—(BB)

17 November 1917

My dear parents,

I am taking advantage of a free afternoon to write you a few words.

I think that my last letter was still from the battalion, but I have since changed, and I'm in the topographic section of the Canadian Army Corps. We draw geographical maps and various other jobs for the Intelligence Department. The difference in this battalion is black and white. Our meals are on a table with a tablecloth, and there are two chefs. Finally, the work is very interesting, and I hope to stay as long as possible.

This morning I went to see the hospital and Philippe's grave. I spoke to the very pleasant nurse, but as it's already a month and a half later, she wasn't able to give me much detail.

Her recollection was that Philippe arrived at the hospital at five o'clock in the afternoon, and looked quite happy, despite his very high temperature. They put him to bed with some hot-water bottles, as he was complaining of the cold, and, as he seemed to be a little confused, the nurse asked him his address and if he had any contacts in France. He answered no. After that, he completely lost consciousness until morning, when he seemed better, but he died that evening. We initially thought that he had jaundice, but following an examination, they found that he had a septic poisoning. The nurse told me that a Frenchman had come the previous day, but had not left his name or his address.

I went afterwards to the cemetery to see the grave, and I had no problem in finding a simple wooden cross. I gave ten francs to the guardian, an old English soldier. He will arrange it the best he can, and have it photographed. I'll send you a copy as soon as it's done. A photograph of the hospital ward will also be taken. I'll go again soon to check that everything was arranged at the cemetery.

We work from nine in the morning to ten at night, with one hour free every day, and one afternoon per week. There is one guy from McGill, and others from Western universities. All great guys. We pay twenty francs a month for our meals, and I can assure you that it seems quite amusing to be sitting at a table with a waiter serving you. We are going to do something great at Christmas, for about fifteen francs per person.

I visited the Lemaitres yesterday. It's quite a long way, but I'm hoping to go several times this winter. I immediately felt the great affection they had for Phil. Mrs. Lemaitre showed me his favourite chair and how they recognized his footsteps going up the stairs. It was funny that their maid, as soon as she saw me, went to tell the Lemaitres that Philippe's brother was at the door. Apparently we had the same voice and a lot of mannerisms in common.

André

12 December 1917

My dear parents,

Last Monday I received a brief message from Jean announcing his arrival the same day. I succeeded in freeing myself, and we left to see what is for us the most sacred spot in this country, so devastated by the war. But I waited in vain, turning each time someone opened the door, but it was only the next day, after I had given up waiting, that I see appearing at the door a Jean like Mom would like him to look: red cheeks and a tailor-made uniform. I

*made arrangements with a friend to exchange a free afternoon, and went
out with him for a few minutes to show him the highlights of the village.
Our sergeant offered him the hospitality of their mess for lunch, and then
we set out to go and see Philippe's grave. I am sending you some photos that
I arranged to have taken that have held up this letter from one day to the
next. I will take care of the cross as soon as I can visit our battalion. I will
get something made of better quality, but, after all, it isn't the beauty of the
cross that we will remember most!*

*It was a very emotional moment for us two to see his grave with its little
wooden cross. It was a beautiful day, but the airplanes were flying overhead,
and the guns were rumbling.*

*So, here I am, very late, to wish you my most sincere wishes for Christmas
and the New Year. We have been extremely busy these last few days, and I
also needed to catch up following Jean's visit, so correspondence had to be
set aside.*

André

> *No. 3 Canadian Gen. Hospital APO 3 BEF*
> *France, 28 December 1917*

My dear parents,

*Since my return on night duty, I had a few days at the beginning that
were very hard, then it became lighter around Christmas. These last few
nights have been very busy again. Masses of sick and wounded had been
kept during the holidays, and we had to evacuate them rapidly afterwards.
From all that, there were lengthy written documents and more complicated
statistics.*

*I very much enjoyed my little family reunion with André at the middle
of December. After having waited several days for the return of my staff
sergeant, and the availability of a truck, I set out on 11 December. At the
headquarters of the Red Cross, situated in one of the town's leading hotels,
I found three medical corps officers who were going to the same place as I
was. The two most senior sat in the front with the chauffeur, while a young
captain and I fixed up a spot as well as we could in between cases containing
various supplies. As you know, the Red Cross provides for the ambulances
and the hospitals various extras that the army doesn't supply. We had in
our load Christmas presents, boxed fruit, lemons, and a lot of other goods.
On the way, we stopped for lunch at a big hospital centre with the sergeant
and the chauffeur. The latter is welcomed everywhere, because of the
influence he is supposed to have. We stopped for tea in a small town near the
Front that Etienne knows well. From there, we travelled for one and a half
hours in the black of night. Our chauffeur knew the way very well and, at*

Canadian Headquarters, Camblain-l'Abbé

6:30, we arrived at our destination: a hut built by the French during their occupation of this region, not far from a strategic crossroad. Captain Lan, our former quartermaster, had arranged for me to sleep and have my meals there. It was too late to go and see André.

The next morning we drove to the Canadian Corps Headquarters, located not too far away in a place that you will understand I can't divulge. There was a substantial wall, and a little further a gate, where we explained to the guard the reason for my visit. One of the staff guided me to Captain Lan's office. We found him, one of the richest Montreal merchants, more or less well-established in an attic with a mansard roof. He was very polite and gave me some information and told me to organize to leave the day after tomorrow on the truck that had brought me. I was then taken to the barrack of the Intelligence Draughting Department. I had no trouble in finding André. He had grown quite a bit, but otherwise looked much the same. He still had that candid smile and seemed to be in perfect health. He introduced me to his various colleagues and to the staff sergeant, who arranged for André to be free in the afternoon and evening, and invited me to one of the sergeants' messes for lunch. André came out with me briefly, and then went back to work, while I went for a short walk.

André is currently part of the "attached substaff." The staff is made up of headquarters officers and the substaff of junior officers and soldiers working for the headquarters on a regular basis. The "attached substaff" includes junior officers and soldiers on a temporary assignment from their units. It is probable that a number of the permanent draftsmen from the Intelligence Department will be leaving shortly, and that André and two or three others like him will be trained progressively to eventually take their place. It is likely that, in the next few weeks, if all goes well, he will be transferred to the Canadian Topographical Service and soon after be promoted sergeant. Sergeant Watson tells me that André doesn't have the experience of several of their draftsmen, but he has the ability and the willingness. He has no doubts that all is going well.

Soon after, André and I headed for the place where Philippe had passed his last hours and was buried. We went first of all to the cemetery that overlooks the hamlet. André knew the spot, and led me there immediately. Our dear brother's grave was the only one that had some flowers, and up until now was marked only by a simple white wooden cross. The regiment had made PPCLI crosses, at its expense, for all the soldiers and officers who died at the Front, and André will make arrangements for one to be erected. Despite its fairly elevated position, one doesn't see too much from the cemetery, except for the airplanes flying overhead, as if guarding against any enemy attacks. From there, it's only a hop, skip, and jump to the CCS, where Sister Branett showed me the bed where Philippe died and repeated to me what André and the commanding officer of the hospital had already written. We had supper in town before returning to my depot, where we had another good chat before we each went our own way.

André found that, at the beginning, most of the work was pretty difficult. He is on duty from nine in the morning to ten at night, six days a week; the other day he had the afternoon and evening free. There isn't yet a YMCA, which means that he spends most of his leisure hours in the drafting room. His work is extremely interesting, but of a completely confidential nature; you won't be surprised if his letters are more vague than ever, as he is naturally obliged to be very circumspect. It would be out of question for him, for example, to write to parents in a neutral country.

Jean

Les Colombettes, 5 December 1917

My dear boys,

We are living through a particularly tense period ... Mother is involved in politics, which is new for her, but she is succeeding very well, and obviously, when women have their full voting rights, which will certainly happen, I won't be surprised if she becomes minister of foreign affairs in Ottawa!

She will tell you herself about her experiences on the same stage as John MacNaughton.

The conscription issue is dominating the news. It is clear that the government will lose in our dear Province or in many places. The fight is between so-called liberals; whereas in other provinces the opinions vary a great deal. Today I saw a few very pessimistic men who believe in Laurier's victory, despite the vote of the soldiers, who one says are 100 per cent for the Unionist Party. When you read these words, it will have been decided, so it's useless that I go on about this controversial subject.

As for me, I am less involved in active politics, but I've been involved in the campaign for victory loans. At least in this domain there was agreement. In my speeches I used a letter from Sir Wilfrid Laurier strongly recommending the subscription, which gave me a few congratulations. That was a great Laurier promotion. This campaign allowed me to enter a number of workshops and witness the working conditions. They offered us a few dinners at the Windsor to compensate us for our efforts.

They are talking about uniting St Paul and St Andrew in view of Bruce Taylor's departure to become principal at Queen's. The churches are overly slanted towards warlike sermons, but there are people that are worth listening to. Harry Lauder has uttered some truths to the Canadians. He confirmed that he didn't have any French blood, but instead bastard blood; this has insulted Mayor Martin, who would have liked to arrest him.

Charles

19 December 1917

My dear boys,

While blowing through our fingers, we are preparing for Christmas, with its "bûche de Noël," plum pudding, colourful candles, and quite a few presents. Our absentees for the moment, and our dear absentee for life, will probably not see even the smallest present. It certainly hasn't been a wonderful year, and quite to the contrary a year of war and sacrifice, but Christmas must always spell hope for peace and consolation, don't you think? We must therefore not interrupt the long chain of lovely Christmases, but only reduce everything in such a way that nothing clashes with the family's pain, and the terrible suffering of the entire world!

We barely see Etienne at meals, so Christmas will be an opportunity for him to be more relaxed and brighten the atmosphere with his pink cheeks and big appetite. I'm not involved with his periodic arrangements in the basement, and would prefer that he make a few minor repairs or even join me in a walk up the mountain. What would make me even happier would be to know that all my soldiers are on leave.

Visits to the poor and sick and my correspondence dealing with raising funds is always active, and, as of Saturday, I will have a full house, with Tante Hélène and Pastor Victor Monod, the chaplain of the French Fleet, who is coming to rest at our house for several days. We are really looking forward to having him, and we have invited the Union Missionaire on the Thursday after Christmas, along with a few friends, to meet our distinguished guest.

I am speaking to you of cooking and housekeeping like a diligent "hausfrau" of the past, forgetting that I am now a voter and that it might be the moment to throw pots and pans and brooms into the bushes! Our polling station is in the entrance hall of Dr. Nicols, a French Canadian, who is a heavy smoker and usually in extremely bad humour. The little polling assistant in a petticoat gave me the most engaging smiles, recognizing that I was a most serious voter. I did put my cross at the right place, which didn't prevent our candidate, Sevigny, from losing, while Leduc triumphed. But it was only actually a partial failure, as, for the whole of Canada, the party, pro-union and conscription, won by at least forty-five seats, despite Quebec Province voting 100 per cent for Laurier. You are no doubt aware that the vote had been given to the mothers, wives, sisters, and daughters of the soldiers. There has been a massive political education campaign for women, and I had the opportunity to speak at two of these meetings. It was wonderful to see the enthusiasm of the junior members of the "Union Chrétienne," on the one hand, and the wives of soldiers, on the other hand, preparing seriously for their new electoral functions. Facsimile voting stations had been erected, where they could practise the very simple task of filling their ballot and casting their vote. Let's hope that the cowards and those in cushy appointments, which we had to put up with until the election, will now march with our soldiers!

It's always the good ones that leave. Henri Bourgoin, and Felix Grosjean said goodbye to us on Thursday, taking with them a big basket of goodies. The seats at the Presbyterian College are empty, and the bulletin board of those killed is being filled. We are at the eighth name already! Each family, one after the other, is called to make the supreme sacrifice!

We continue to receive some excellent letters of sympathy. Today's are very touching: One from Douglas, the other is from Walter Pfeiffer! There was also a Christmas card from the Canadian Headquarters, and we felt that we were at the top of the military ladder now that we have a son in such good company!

Dear soldiers, what will your Christmas be like? If it isn't great I hope that at least you will be able to celebrate it in the spirit of these verses:

Then let every heart keep Christmas within,
Christ's pity for sorrow, Christ's hatred for sin,
Christ's care for the weakest, Christ's courage for rights,
Christ's dread of the darkness, Christ's love of the light,
Everywhere, Everywhere, Christmas tonight!

Blanche

31 December 1917

My dear boys,

On 27 December, Mother invited the Missionary Union to come to our house to meet and hear Mr Monod. Charles Rochedieu was also there. For him it was a goodbye supper, as he was leaving for New York two days later, having decided to enroll in the US Medical Corps. Isn't it odd that having submitted his application as a volunteer in a Canadian Corps, they had told him that they weren't enrolling any more volunteers for this corps in Canada. Mr Monod spoke about the unity of the Christian world resulting from the war, with great simplicity, but a firm tone. Christians from all nations are united on the French soil, whether they are from Malagasy, Bastia, Zahir, or China. It is the blacks and the Oceanians with their pious approach that evangelize the French, who have lost their evangelical spirit.

We froze at the Bethanie church, despite the hot pipes! In the evening we read together in the sitting room a lecture by Benjamin Vallotton, given in Paris and published in a review, about the help the Swiss were bringing to the war effort. Unfortunately the exploits of a few pro-German Swiss seem to have made people forget about what Switzerland has done and continues to do with great devotion for the relief of the thousands of unfortunate people who cross the border daily.

Monday we were, with Tante Hélène, invited by Mrs Welsh to a war supper. It was all very good. There was meat that wasn't meat, but no one could guess: it must have been "Welsh Rabbit"! A good speech by Mr Malcolm Campbell on the father of the Canadian railways, George Stephenson's principles: "Do the best with everything, think the best of everybody, hope the best for thyself!"

Mother and I will finish the year crying a little, thinking of our absent boys who will return, if God permits, and of our absent one who will never return. The thoughts of him naturally hit us with greater intensity, and there was a mixture of gentleness and sourness as we went over our memories of him.

Charles

ANDRÉ SPENT CHRISTMAS and 1 January 1918 happily in his pleasant topographic environment. In addition, there were positive signs that could indicate the possibility that the war would end. He observes that his friends take advantage of their leaves to get married, but without the thought of doing the same. He becomes preoccupied with his future after the war, closer than one may think, and he begins to consider the profession of architecture. But what lengthy studies will be required before being able to earn a living, and what a delay relative to his peers who stayed in Canada!—(BB)

THE PRINCESS PATRICIAS enjoyed a relatively quiet year end, initially in the Ypres area, prior to returning to the Lens Front in December.

CHAPTER FOURTEEN

Spring Offensive
January to July 1918

German General Erich Ludendorff

THE BATTLE OF PASSCHENDAELE was a sad finale for 1917. The Allies were apprehensive in early 1918 as they realized that they would likely soon be facing a crisis. They were aware that, throughout the winter, the Germans had been transferring troops from the east to the west. By mid-February they had 178 divisions in the Western Front as compared to the Allies' 173. Military authorities who remembered those unsuccessful offensives when the odds had been three-to-two in the Allies' favour didn't wish to think about the possibility of a German conquest with lesser odds.

There had been a continuous debate between the British and the French about the consolidation of the Allied leadership. During a conference of British and French political and military leaders on 26 March 1918 in Doullens, Field Marshal Haig said that he would accept General Foch as the leader. Foch was promptly promoted to Commander-in-Chief of the Allied Armies.

It was on 21 March, a few miles west of St Quentin, that the Germans launched their first major offensive against the British. At 4:40 a.m., the artillery began the biggest barrage of the entire war, and hit targets over 150 square miles. It had not been a complete surprise, but the size of the attack had not been expected. A dense fog aided the enemy, and allowed their storm troopers, who were leading the attack, to penetrate, undetected, deep into British territory. Early on the first day, the Germans were able to push through the British lines in a number of places, and the British were forced to retreat. As distances were considerable and much of the British territory was not strategically significant, the German infantry became exhausted and had increasing difficulty moving forward. Their advance faltered, and fresh British troops were sent in to strengthen the defence. The Germans eventually gave up. Important strategic positions in Amiens and Arras remained secure, but the Allies lost 255,000 men.

Less than a month later, on 9 April, the Germans attacked near the border of Flanders. They overran both the British and the less-prepared Portuguese defenders. There was considerable concern that in a week they could advance another fifteen miles to the channel ports. Once again the Germans faced technical problems in moving forward, and counterattacks by the Allies stopped them in their tracks. The second offensive was over on 29 April, after only three weeks.

On 27 May, the Germans tried again, this time not too far from Paris, between Soissons and Rheims. Six tired and depleted British divisions and an inept French army attempted to resist, but the Germans managed to reach the Marne River. Fortunately, some fresh US infantry recruits, along with some Senegalese sharpshooters curtailed the enemy advance. Then, in July, a German division from Rheims did manage to cross the Marne, but were intercepted by a major French offensive and forced to evacuate. This final evacuation not only ended the German's third offensive, but also led to the cancellation of their much-heralded final attack in Flanders.

Despite large territorial gains, the German spring offensive was a bitter failure for them. They were now in a number of exposed positions, and their divisions were exhausted and depleted. The British, on the other hand, had been seriously wounded, but were far from broken.

The Canadian Corps, with their able commander, General Currie, were viewed as having one of the strongest divisions in the Western Front. They had fortunately escaped the heavy fighting during the German offensive, and were manning seven miles of the Front, from Hill 70 and Lens in the north to the Avion-Mercourt sector in the south. That Front had become particularly important, as the collieries behind Lens and Vimy were the only ones left that remained accessible to the Germans in the north.

THE SPRING OF 1918

3rd Canadian General Hospital APO3
11 February 1918

My dear parents,

I hope that my long treatise addressed to Etienne from Paris wasn't sunk in the Andania. *We have just learned that a certain number of letters had sunk with this ship, which left England a few days after I wrote to you.*

I hope that Mom didn't go too far in interrupting Jacques's invitations. In ten years it will be of no use for him to have been the first or the tenth of his class, but the relations and the friendships that he will have made will be with him for the rest of his life. If my current life doesn't bring me great joy, it at least doesn't present any deceptions and regrets. I am satisfied with little; all I need is two or three good friends, but I don't think that I will ever be perfectly happy, like most other people. Philippe's death has certainly been very painful, but it seems to me that sometimes, as a brother, I should have felt it more deeply.

Please don't give me a speech on religion. I like a good service, but, on the other hand, I hate to receive a sermon in a letter. I believe in all the essential doctrines of the Christian religion, and I try to confirm them in my life. I don't know if I should have digressed to this extent. It was suggested by Mom's comments on Jacques, about whom I would like my experience to be useful.

It seems to me that Etienne was right not to accept a job where he would have been a subordinate to an unpleasant officer. I was telling him that the last review board classed me "B3" (clerical duties on L of C) because of my eyesight; so, here I am in Boulogne forever, but it's nice meanwhile to be in Paris on my leave.

Bertrand invited me to a very posh restaurant with cousin Louisette. Apparently his business is going very well. I met with the Dalements, who are in the magnetic-tape business, which is also booming. In fact everyone in France seems to be doing well, except for the clergymen, professors, and other civil servants. Everything is very expensive; Hachette is saying that book prices are up 70 per cent since 1 January 1918! The vignerons are making a killing. I was told that a proprietor, who before the war was breaking even, had made a profit of 900,000 francs! It's true that wine is selling at 1.65 F/litre. The Peyrans have found a good buyer for their property. It's the same story in industry, where a worker can earn up to 50 francs a day, and an eighteen-year-old boy often in excess of 20 francs. You can imagine that the bosses are also doing well.

I was able to get both a sugar and a bread token on my last day. In Paris, gasoline is also restricted, but with these exceptions, everything is available. In the best restaurants, nothing has changed except that cakes and pastries are unavailable.

I dropped in to Jeanne's, and found her busier than ever. On top of her Sunday schools and Thursday sessions, she is the link between the American YMCAs and the Girls Colleges. The Americans that want to do it well are installing restaurants, nurseries, etc. within the munition factories in France. Mrs. Sautter, with the help of the American YMCA, is putting together fifteen hundred Soldier Homes.

On the last day, Maurice, who was on leave, arrived. He's feeling much better and expects to return soon to the Tractor Corps at the Front. I found the situation in Boulogne to be particularly calm on my return.

Jean

FEBRUARY BROUGHT André's third leave to Neuilly.—(BB)

3 March 1918

My dear parents,

Here I am back at work, after a leave at Oncle Charles's. I want first of all to thank Mom for the package of cigarettes and prunes that arrived while I was away on leave, and, not unlike the good and ancient customs of the army, was opened in my absence. They left me a package of cigarettes, and they all asked me where the prunes came from ... we are asking for more!

And now, during my leave: I leave here after breakfast on a tiny train like the one at Lion-sur-Mer, that drops me off at a more important station, where I catch a somewhat faster train that gets me to Paris at nine o'clock in the evening. The big army car drives us directly to the barracks, where they stamp the permit and where we are given varying advice about what to do or not to do. Then we get back into the cars and are taken to any one of the hotels recommended by the YMCA. I go to the Leave Club, a modern hotel on the Place de la Republique. An excellent dinner is awaiting us, served by French and English ladies living in Paris. It was, in fact, where Philippe had spent a part of his last leave. A clean bed, with lovely white sheets, is waiting for us upstairs, for the bargain price of two francs fifty! The next day I wake up with a cold, just like all the other soldiers on leave that come to Paris! It's a very damp city. That doesn't prevent me from having a good breakfast and going to find Tante Julia's office, which I locate without any trouble, but unfortunately no aunt: it's the morning when she doesn't come in. So I go to bed early, feeling a bit asthmatic. On Sunday, after breakfast, I arrive in time for church in Neuilly.

I was too early, and I was waiting near the gate when I see advancing towards me a handsome officer in sky-blue uniform. It was Guy, who wasn't quite an officer, but had the right to wear the uniform. Oncle Charles wasn't preaching, as he had exchanged places with another, but it was all the same pleasant to hear the hymns and a sermon in perfect French.

I enjoyed seeing Louisette: we planned a little restaurant lunch with Tante Julia. We then roamed along the grands boulevards and had some tea without cakes (restricted in wartime). We said goodbye and hoped to see each other again during the next leave.

I'm running out of time, and I'm having some memory lapses. I'll tell you more the next time. All goes well here. I have been promoted to sergeant, and I have been transferred to the Canadian Headquarters, which means that I will no longer see the "Pats," which doesn't displease me.

André

14 March 1918

My dear parents,

As I told you in my last letter, I am now a sergeant, and I receive $1.70 per day. That's a tidy little sum, and it will be useful after the war. I therefore no longer need the cash that was so useful when I was in the battalion. We are working as hard as ever, but I'm able to exercise more regularly. My drawing has improved a lot. I can now do all the work that is undertaken here: it's a wonderful situation, and that could be useful if I wanted to continue for a while after the war.

I'm very grateful to Jacques for his brief but interesting note. He's lucky to be going to such an enterprising school as Westmount High.

I hope that Mom is not wearing herself out with her lectures and that her funds aren't only for the Belgians; the French have played a bigger role.

A formal portrait of the Commander-in-Chief of the Canadians,
Lieutenant General Sir Arthur Currie, on his charger

*I will ask Jacques to do me a favour at Hughes Owen in St James Street.
I need him to buy me two "Pazent Pens," No. 4 and No. 6. I'm attaching a
cheque that I believe should cover the expense.*

André

17 April 1918

My dear mother,

*At lunch yesterday there was a Belgian lieutenant, a French corporal,
Maurice, a Canadian sergeant, and Oncle Henri. It was a pleasant
moment with a conversation mostly about the war, where we each perceived
some small differences. After lunch, someone suggested that we sing, and
after that we played board games.*

 *Everyone is quite optimistic here; we feel the end of the war in these huge
battles. I think that we will all be together once again by Christmas perhaps
(not all together, as we will be missing one forever).*

The work continues to be interesting. The other day I was working in General Currie's room. I knock on the door and he opens the door himself, and after I had explained who I was, he shows me the work to be done.

André

Les Colombettes, 13 March 1918

My dear boys,

Today, I will have some unexpected tasks, because the military authorities are taking over our college to turn it into a convalescent hospital. You will be amused to know that I will move into a bathroom in Divinity Hall. That is called a war measure.

I spent one Saturday in Toronto to pacify the Swiss Society, which has become divided into two irreconcilable parts: the success has unfortunately only been temporary.

On 4 March I had to go to New York, where I was asked to replace my principal at the congress of the Religious Education Association. Then, following a call from Washington, I took the night train to go and see the head of the information office at the French Embassy. It is, in fact, possible that I will spend a part of the summer giving lectures as a representative of the French Protestant churches in the US. It is now being organized: please don't speak to anyone about it for the moment. It seemed very strange to find myself one moment in an official French office, to see officers in sky-blue uniforms or in khaki, as those who instruct the American troops have adopted the local colour, and to hear once again the voices of the banks of the Seine. I then went to give my respects to the new Swiss minister, Dr Sulzer, of the famous Sulzer Company in Winterthur.

Charles

Les Colombettes, 10 April 1918

My dear boys,

Those who have lived in the west and who have met only Italians and Germans, think that it's normal for the Canadians to give up their fathers' language.

But you will no doubt find that these are pretty pointless discussions at a time when there are more serious questions to be dealt with. However, things are quite tense in Quebec, and we should not embitter them further in order to soothe other Canadian citizens.

We are following the events of the Great War with considerable interest and wish to be persuaded that General Foch is making the right decisions with regard to this huge campaign.

The "daily saving system" is to be introduced here, and people are realizing that, no matter how small a country is, it should adhere to the principle. In the restaurants, even at the Windsor, both bread and sugar is rationed.

Charles

Les Colombettes, 19 April 1918

My dear boys,

The French High Commissioner in Washington has contacted Dad and told him that the Paris Protestant Committee has confirmed that they would like him to lead a delegation to the US to do a three-month tour. The Montreal Protestant Church, who had wanted to send him to a church in Saskatoon, has given him leave. He is completing in haste his role as registrar, and is preparing three different lectures: "French Reforms in the Modern Era" – "The Two German Invasions" (the 1914 and 1918 battles of the Marne) – "Faith and War in France." He will only have time to pack his bags, as he has promised to be in Chicago on 9 May.

I have had a series of approaches and telephone conversations with regard to our organizing the raising of funds in Canada for the reconstruction after the war of Protestant churches and vicarages that had been destroyed in France and Belgium.

Blanche

ANDRÉ WAS ENJOYING many pleasant interludes, but if the troops gained ground by the battles that marked the last hundred days of the war, it was necessary for the topographers to be constantly ahead of them, and furnish the necessary maps. The normal day went from 7 a.m. to 7 p.m., but when there was greater pressure, they worked a part of the night, with cups of black coffee to stay awake. For a while, André was in charge of a quite interesting project. It consisted of bringing up to date, based on the most recent correspondence and the latest aerial photographs, all of General Currie's military maps. He needed to mark the advances and retreats of the Canadian troops so that the general could plan the critical battle strategies. Every morning, he entered this sacred tent and sat at the great table, surrounded by the intimate details of the general's life: huge slippers, family pictures here and there, favourite books and newspapers.

Unfortunately, the topographers weren't always close to the headquarters. Once, when they were quite far away, André, after having worked very late, received the order to go immediately by motorcycle to carry very urgent maps to the high command. The driver, an unreliable person, drinker, and show-off, was sleeping and refused to move. André insisted, and the other eventually obeyed. Having decided

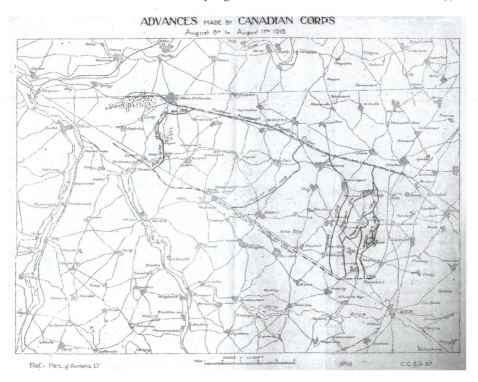

ADVANCES MADE BY **CANADIAN CORPS**
August 8ᵗʰ to August 17ᵗʰ 1918

World War I map found in André Bieler's personal belongings

to take revenge, the guy takes off at a great speed over impossible roads full of pot-holes, trying to provoke some sort of accident. André, frightened to death, grips his briefcase and finally arrives without any broken bones.—(BB)

YMCA, April 1918

My dear father,

We continue to be quite busy, but the work is interesting, and time flies by. Thanks for Phil's photo; it's a good one and, as you can see, he had changed dramatically since he was in France. The last photo taken here was clearly the best. I would have very much liked to attend to the grave for his birthday, but at the present time, it's impossible. I'm already looking forward to my next leave, where I will be able to see Etienne, but that's still a long way off!

At least, I feel that I haven't been completely wasting my time. My drawing has certainly progressed a lot. That will always be useful after the war! All your projects interest me considerably. Jacques, who becomes a summer farmer, and Dad giving lectures! I hope that it won't be too tiring and that you will benefit from all the modern comforts during your trips.

André's rest camp, Le Château de Philiomel

We have loved your parcel No C; the cake was really delicious, and absolutely fresh. One would have thought that it had just been made. Everyone voted that it was the best tea this year. The sugar is just right and I have enough for some time.

André

30 April 1918

My dear mother,

It makes us feel good to receive and taste from time to time things that come from home. In France, at the moment, one only buys what's necessary, and even the civilians have recently had trouble finding bread.

I went to see Nicholson at his battalion. His brother has recently lost his arm; he hopes to see him during his next leave. He sends you his best regards. I hope to see Bulmer Rutherford soon. I wonder if you ever see Maclean's *magazine; there are often pen-and-ink drawings of places we frequent. They are drawn by one of my friends here in this section. He's a particularly talented artist.*

Our mess is in a private house. Going in morning, midday, and evening, one gets a bit of a view of family life, with the husband wounded at Salonica and the baby sick. Life is not easy!

I'm pretty undecided about my future after the war. Architecture might well be a dead profession for quite a long time. If Dad meets architects

*in one of his numerous activities, I would like him to seek their advice.
However naval architecture will certainly become very important. Do you
remember when the secretary of Vickers offered me an apprenticeship there?
It might have been a good idea to accept. The years are going by, and one
will have to make a big effort to find a job when everyone is returning to the
country at the same time.*

André

4 June 1918

My dear mother,

*A lot has happened around here since my last letter. We must hope that it
won't delay too much the big reunion of our family, dispersed in the four
corners of the world.*

*I really feel as though I'm on holiday during the good weather at 16 Island
Lake, except that there isn't a lake! Three of us have a tent in the woods
of a magnificent château belonging to a former French count. At seven in
the morning we get up and do a half-hour of gymnastics with an excellent
instructor, then we have breakfast, followed by a little work and a game of
tennis, baseball, or volleyball (a new game, half tennis, half basketball).
After lunch, it starts all over again – games, walks: in conclusion, I have
never done so much sport in my whole life! We also bathe in an outdoor
swimming pool, fed with pure, clear water from a nearby spring.*

*I went to see Bulmer Rutherford the other day, and he gave me the news
from all of Westmount. He sends you his best wishes. I received Jacques's
package with the Pozent pen, which was an enormous success here. We will
try to get the government to buy us some.*

*I had a visit yesterday by a friend of Jean's, and I was very pleased to
have news from Boulogne. He seemed to like Jean a lot.*

André

Les Colombettes, 5 May 1918

My dear boys,

*I gave a little lecture in Châteaugay, and then stretched out and spent
the night there. I came back feeling great. Tomorrow night I need to say a
few words at a concert in Victoria Hall, organized by Erskine's organist.
It would amuse you to see a poster on the corner of Greene Avenue: "For
Miss d'Aubigné's war relief: Mrs. Charles Bieler will give an address"!
Fortunately, the energetic Mrs. Russell Murray took everything in hand,
and all I had to do was to say a few words during the intermission.*

*It seems that the Americans don't allow parcels to accompany soldiers'
letters. As soon as you can confirm the safe arrival of the cakes, in the*

absence of the maternal oven, I will try to find something else to send you!
Jean made the generous remark that one should first of all think of those who
are less well fed than him. That's a good rule, but if one helps the "poilus"
and the prisoners, we have the right to also send a surprise to our dearest
soldiers, don't you think? If I go to the land of sugar, I should be allowed
to send you some, without displeasing Dr. Raymond! The shippers are in
difficulty only in Montreal where we can only ship one parcel at a time. So,
with these tasty thoughts, I hug you gently and remain your affectionate
mother.

Blanche

La Clairière, 24 July 1918

My dear boys,

And then there's the newspaper that one devours if the news is good,
although the huge headlines don't succeed in fooling us, like they do for
these wonderful Americans! "YANKS TAKE 20 TOWNS," the text itself, more
exactly, shows how the French, helped by the ambulance men, have taken
some twenty villages or hamlets. A little further it's "AMERICANS TURN THE
TIDE OF VICTORY," and in fact, it's a story about a brilliant move by Foch!
What big children these nephews of Uncle Sam are! There are, however,
some more reasonable people who read the sober New York Times, *who*
even shake their heads or smile ironically at the exaggerations of Wilson's
European admirers, this great talker who could after all only be a little
great man!

I won't summarize Dad's news, as I believe that he is keeping you up
to date on his travels. He just sent me a package of newspaper cuttings
that show how much he is understood and appreciated. I don't know if the
American optimism is generated by him, but in any case the headlines about
his talks are very positive: "Great Victory for Allies, Noted Theologian
Expects." And in fact the newspapers are not denying his statements.

Blanche

BY MID-1918, THE ALLIES' OPTIMISM GREW DAILY, but a new threat then appeared. The influenza epidemic was spreading around the world. It had reached the Western Front, where it was to cost the British forces over a hundred thousand casualties. The inadequate diet of the Germans resulted in an even greater number of sufferers on their side. It is likely that this had also contributed to their decision to cancel their major Flanders strategy.

CHAPTER FIFTEEN

Anti-Submarine

January to November 1918

RMS *Lusitania*, 7 May 1915

AT THE OUTBREAK OF THE WAR, the German army was by far the mightiest and best-prepared military force in the world. However, Britain's navy governed the seas, and thereby controlled the world's international trade, as well as the major supply routes to Europe and Germany. The Kaiser was actively developing a strategy to counter the British sea supremacy. It was to be a two-pronged approach.

They developed oil-fed turbines for their warships, to replace the traditional coal-fired ones, which doubled the speed of the ships, as well as eliminating their telltale smoke. Winston Churchill and Jack Fisher, the British Sea Lord, were not far behind, and these developments stimulated their search for oil supplies in Persia. Meanwhile, as Germany didn't have a reliable source of oil, and was blocked by the British in the Persian Gulf, they decided to build a railroad to Baghdad, in partnership with the Ottoman Empire. It was one of the factors that eventually led to World War I.

Concurrently, Germany focused their engineering skills on the development of the submarine. By 1914, Germany already had a fleet of what they called U-boats, which were initially harboured in the Baltic, and subsequently, after the fall of Belgium, began to be based just north of the Western Front. The curtain was raised on 7 May 1915 when a U-boat sank the world's most luxurious ocean liner, the *Lusitania*, off the coast of Ireland. It was a significant event, both in terms of understanding the power of the U-boat strategy, but also in influencing the Americans to begin to think about joining the war, which President Wilson was doing everything to avoid. Britain itself became a realizable target. In April 1917 alone, more than a million tons of British and neutral ships were lost. One ship out of every four leaving British ports never came home. Neutral and American ships refused to sail to British ports. There was no hope of replacing the losses with new ships.

Soon after the outbreak of World War I, the Admiralty had become increasingly concerned about the threat of the German U-boats, and decided in July 1915 to create the Board of Invention and Research (BIR), to research and develop technology to eliminate the threat. Lord Fisher was chosen to become president. A panel, mostly comprised of leading British scientists, was put together. Among those selected were Sir Ernest Rutherford and his good friend, another eminent British scientist, William Bragg. The Board was split into six sections, with Section II, Submarine and Wireless Telegraphy, assuming the greatest importance. Bragg became the senior scientist of that section.

Ernest Rutherford's early research activities had been in related fields to those that challenged the BIR. Following three years at the Cavendish Laboratory at Cambridge, he had accepted in 1898 the position of Professor of Experimental Physics at McGill's new Macdonald Physics Laboratory. Assisted by Robert Boyle and A.S. Eve, he undertook early experiments in what eventually was to become SONAR. Boyle was to receive McGill's first Physics Doctorate, and Eve became a very close friend of Rutherford. Rutherford left McGill in 1907 to chair the

SM U-14 German submarine

Manchester University Physics Department, where he stayed for the following twelve years.

During 1916, the BIR reviewed thousands of suggestions, either developed internally or received from the public at large. They included charming procedures involving the training of sea lions to search under water, or seagulls to leave their excrement on enemy conning towers! The admirals also got into the act, and one came up with the Q-boat procedure, where dummy merchant boats, acting as decoys, would suddenly open fire on surfacing U-boats.

Lord Jellicoe, Supreme Commander of the "Grand Fleet," complained that the BIR was too independent and was not concentrating on the necessary technological developments. In December 1916, Lloyd George was elected prime minister, and one of his first priorities was to address the U-boat threat. He promoted Admiral Jellicoe to First Sea Lord, and he created the Anti-Submarine Division to be headed by Admiral Duff. It was to spearhead the anti-U-boat technology, and oversee the activities of the BIR. Despite considerable friction between the two organizations, the emphasis became technologically oriented, and William Bragg and Section II were at the helm. Hydrophones initially seemed to be the most promising development, but Bragg decided to concentrate on the "Loop" technology that had the dual capacity of both harbour protection and high-seas U-boat elimination. It had been initiated in 1915, but had so far failed. "Loops" rely on the production of an induced current in a stationary loop wire, when a magnet (or, say, a submarine) moved overhead. As early as 1916, cables were laid at the entrance of a number of harbours in Britain, but despite good laboratory results, acoustical disturbances in these large outlays rendered them useless for reliable submarine detection.

At about this time, Etienne had been wounded at the battle of Arleux, and had spent three months at the Camberwell Hospital in London. In August 1917, he had returned to Canada to complete his rehabilitation. He was demobilized in November, and returned to McGill to pursue his MA in Physics. At one point, he joined his friend and mentor, the physicist, Louis King, who was undertaking some experiments on the transmission of sound through fog. They took off by boat and on foot to define the acoustics of different types of sirens, and what modifications resulted during storms or foggy periods. The thick Labrador fog and the big waves sweeping the bridge were a pleasant transition from the foul smells of the trenches. It was good for him, and he returned looking like an old sea captain.

Following the changes of emphasis at the BIR, additional scientists were recruited. Rutherford recommended that three of his former McGill assistants, A.S. Eve, Robert Boyle, and Louis King, be invited. Then, in late 1917, Eve suggested that Etienne should also be approached. Etienne had been offered a position as professor at Princeton University, training American officers in the management of ammunition delivery in the battlefield. Feeling that it was his duty to return to the military, he had accepted the post. Eve was disappointed, but with the help of the McGill chancellor, convinced Etienne that his duty would be even better served in London.

Etienne arrived in London in January 1918. Eve introduced him to William Bragg and described him as "pure gold." Etienne was now surrounded by some of the leading scientists of the day. He was intrigued by the research that Rutherford and Robert Boyle were doing, particularly as Rutherford felt that their ASDIC program (later to be called SONAR), would eventually be superior to the "loops." Several months went by, in which Etienne mingled with the scientists at Kew and Greenwich. They discussed together many of the projects that were in process and they gave him ideas to further his work on solving the "loops" problems.

The eventual decision of the Germans to undertake unrestricted U-boat warfare had pushed the US into the war, and opened the relationship between the British and US navies. Lloyd George, against the opinion of senior admirals, listened to the American advice and introduced convoys. The Americans loaned a number of destroyers to supplement the decimated British fleet. The result was an important decline in shipping losses. There was nevertheless an urgent need to pursue the anti-submarine program. The U-boat sinkings had to be further reduced, the fleet needed to be protected, and the US destroyers were required elsewhere.

By mid May, Etienne and his team were ready to put aside the theory and get on with the practical. Bragg was very keen to try to solve the "loops" dilemma. This would require extensive onsite experimentation. The Admiralty had established its initial Experimental Station near Harwich in January 1917, which was conveniently close to the British Submarine Flotilla, but it could not be considered a

Staff of the McGill Physics faculty, 1926–27.
(Left to right) A.S. Eve, L.V. King, D.A. Keys, and Etienne Bieler

satisfactory deep-water experimental site. Scapa Flow in the Orkney Islands, on the other hand, was ideal. It was the key Royal Navy harbour, and there were a number of deep-water entrances already cabled.

IN EARLY JUNE they embarked on a tiny trawler in the midst of a violent storm. It took them twenty-four hours in unusually heavy seas to reach Kirkwall, the capital and only major settlement on the island. The Orkney countryside is so heavily windswept that no trees or even bushes survive, but when the sun comes out, the soft, hazy light sparkles with the blue of the sea, the purple of the heather, and the red of the rocks. Kirkwall is a strange little capital, more like a fishing village, lost in the midst of the desert. Several trees, protected by the Roman Church, lend a special charm. Nearby, there is a military post, with its empty infirmary. Etienne and his team were warmly greeted by the officers. They lost no time in recruiting a group of local fishermen to help them set up a laboratory, and to plan the laying of additional cables in appropriate locations.

In this country, where in June and July it's possible to read your newspaper at midnight on the beach, there is ample time to get a lot done. There was a lot to do, which did include some very pleasant moments. The clergyman took them out on

HMS *Colossus* at anchor at Scapa Flow with other ships of the Grand Fleet

a miraculous fishing trip, where they caught sixty-two huge fish. Another time the major invited them for tennis. He was a very hospitable fellow, whose place was always open for the local officers. His family came for the summer holidays to enjoy their huge house with its ancient walls and fields of wild flowers.—(BB)

ETIENNE AND HIS TEAM ADDED lengths of cable to a network that had been laid a few years earlier at several entrances to the Scapa Flow harbour. They then undertook a series of experiments, based in good part on the research that Etienne had developed. Eventually, they succeeded in resolving the problems that had plagued the loops ever since their original installation. As their facilities in the Orkneys were not sufficient to complete their work, in early August they moved to the Weymyss Bay Experimental Station, not far from Glasgow.

Bragg was pleased with the result, but, despite the good news from the Front, decided to send Etienne to Hardelot on the French Channel coast, a few miles from Boulogne. The latest plan was to install a loop across the channel from Harderlot to Dungeness, in Kent. There was competition from another approach, necessitating the construction of a dozen ninety-foot-high towers to be sunk in place between Portsmouth and Cap Gris Nez, just north of Boulogne!

On 28 October 1918, with the Royal Navy's Grand Fleet anchored within the Scapa Flow harbour, U-Boat UB-116 was blown up in one of the loop minefields.

An observer had noticed the telltale deflection of a loop's needle, and, seeing that there was no surface ship there, he pressed the button and the line of mines exploded. It was the first recorded use of indicator loops. They became the leading anti-submarine defence system between the two world wars, and were replaced by Boyle's SONAR at the start of World War II.

At war's end, Rutherford was appointed chair of the Cavendish laboratory at Cambridge. He was instrumental in directing Etienne to join him there and submitted his thesis to the Royal Society of London. The thesis had been fundamental for the resolution of the "loops" problems.

On the Currents induced in a Conductor by the Passage of a Mass of Magnetic Material over it.

By E. S. BIELER, M.Sc., 1851 Scholar of McGill University.

(Communicated by Sir E. Rutherford, F.R.S.—Received April 22, 1921.)

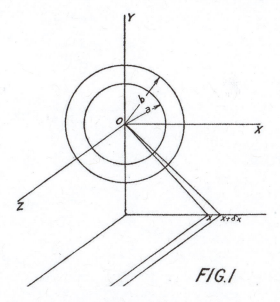

At time t let x be the horizontal distance of the shell from the conductor. In the interval δt, x has increased to $x + \delta x$, and the number N of tubes of induction cut by the conductor in the interval is given by

$$\delta N = \left(\int_{-\infty}^{\infty} \frac{\partial V'}{\partial y} \, dz \right) dx.$$

Magnetic Material graphic

———

THE VIABILITY OF the "loops" and the Armistice were confirmed. Etienne was free to return to the hospital to have a final operation on his leg, and enjoy the Armistice lying on his bed in Camberwell.—(BB)

CHAPTER SIXTEEN

100 Days

August to November 1918

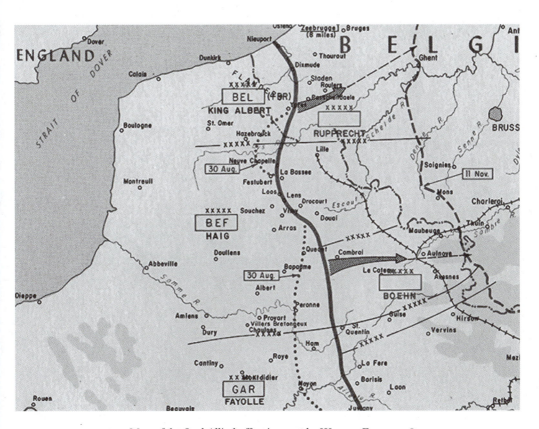

Map of the final Allied offensives on the Western Front, 1918

GENERAL FOCH INVITED THE ALLIED MILITARY LEADERS, Haig, Pétain, and Pershing, to his headquarters on 24 July, a few days after the Germans cancelled their major Flanders attack. They were pleased with the developments. The rout of the Germans' Rheims offensive had been extremely costly for them, both in numbers of casualties and in their confidence. For the first time since earlier in the year, the Allies had a superiority in manpower, and each month twenty-five thousand additional US recruits joined the ranks. It was time for the Allies to take the offensive. He proposed that the British assume the offensive in the extreme north, the French in the centre, and the Americans in the south. Haig requested, however, that they should first attack the Amiens Front, in order to free the railways from there. Foch agreed.

AMIENS

ONE DAY AN OFFICER from the High Command asked André to accompany him and several other officers to a meeting where maps and documents were to be exchanged with a French corps that the Canadians were to relieve in Amiens. He describes it as a quite pleasant expedition, involving a trip in a convertible and the eager reception of the topographic data by some doddering French specialists with their long beards, in their splendid villa. The majority were apparently art teachers in the secondary-school system. While the high-ranking officers were having their meeting, André had lunch with the professors, and they celebrated an "*entente cordiale*." The meeting took place on 24 July at Maréchal Foch's headquarters in the village of Sarcus, ten miles south of Amiens.—(BB)

HAIG PROMPTLY INITIATED the Amiens strategy. He named Currie, once again, to mastermind the attack and ensure that the Canadian troops played a prominent role. As the Germans were conscious that a move of the Canadians to a new sector usually indicated an imminent attack, Currie took extreme measures to keep utmost secrecy. Troop transfers were done at night, and a deception operation was created to misrepresent and conceal the Canadians' position. Much as in Vimy, the Canadian Corps were placed in the middle of the battlefield, with the Patricias at the centre. They would be responsible for striking the critical blow.

A FEW DAYS LATER, another high-ranking officer asked André to undertake an important and very secret mission. He was to go that night by motorcycle, carrying maps and a sealed file. Arriving at a certain crossroad, he found an entire Canadian Brigade waiting for him. He had been asked to then open the file, read the directions

General Foch and his staff at his headquarters, Sarcus, Oise

he was to follow, locate the route from one of the maps, and guide the troops right up to the indicated destination. This was the secret transfer of the 7th Infantry Brigade from their billets in the concentration area towards their battle assembly positions, on 6 August. The program was carried out perfectly, and André reconfirmed his quite unique reputation.—(BB)

THE BATTLE OF AMIENS BEGAN precisely at 4:20 a.m. on 8 August, in the midst of dense fog. The Canadians' 7th Brigade, with the Patricias in the centre, filed over the Luce River on duckboard bridges. The way had been cleared by six hundred British tanks that had cut through the enemy's barbed wire and attacked their positions. The Patricias marched forward in high spirits, as they met an ever-increasing flow of enemy prisoners. By the end of the day, they were eight miles from the start. They went on for three more days, but not with the ease of the first day, as the supporting artillery wasn't able to maintain the pace. Then, only a few weeks later, they were back to Arras to join the Allies' advance to the Hindenberg Line.

German prisoners carrying Canadian wounded to the rear, passing a tank
on the Amiens-Roye road during the Battle of Amiens.

By 10 August, the Germans were forced to retreat from the huge salient that
they had so brilliantly conquered a few months before. General Erich Ludendorff, commander of the German forces, called it "the Black Day of the German
Army." It was an important psychological moment for the Allies. The faith in victory, which had supported the German morale during these last few months, was
shattered. The soldiers were exhausted, and both the politicians and the generals
began to quarrel, with some recommending that an armistice be negotiated.

THE FINAL DAYS

18 August 1918

My dear mother,

You will see in the newspapers what we are doing these days. We are
currently camped outside, and we can't complain, with the beautiful
weather we are now having. We have an excellent chef, who makes us some
magnificent dishes on an old stove found in a nearby village in ruins. We
also have a Ford to fetch the groceries. It's fun the way she crosses the fields as
easily as she runs along the roads. While our officer was on leave, I had quite
a lot of responsibility, and I think I did all right.

I will go to England during my next leave. I need to go there to settle certain matters, and I am also very anxious to see Etienne. Unfortunately the leave is not yet scheduled. It is very difficult to get them these days.

Fruit and vegetables are extremely rare around here this year. The farmers didn't plant anything this spring, because of the Germans. They are sad not to be able to make any cider, as there are no apples.

André

AS THE SUCCESSES OF 1918 started to accumulate, the Canadian Divisions began moving northward to rejoin the British Army's march towards the east. On 26 August the Battle of the Scarpe took place. The 2nd and 3rd Divisions pushed the Germans another five miles, but the casualties were heavy, including Jean's good friend Major Georges Vanier, who lost his leg. Then, the Drocourt-Quéant line, which was viewed as one of Germany's most powerful defence systems, fell into the Allied hands after a very vicious battle.

La Clairière, 29 August 1918

My dear boys,

We will read a few short verses from the big Bible, and pray for the victory that may follow the uninterrupted march that we have just read about, and we pray also for the European families that we love so much, and especially for our soldiers. We are presuming that the Canadian advance is giving the topographers so much work that André finds it impossible to write.

Blanche

Les Colombettes, 17 September

My dear boys,

The memorable events at La Clairière are not as important as the apparently decisive ones in the European battlefields. They can include a successful mushroom-picking expedition, or an unproductive wild-game-shooting expedition.

However, we have had several more important events. On 7 September we raised a slightly creased Swiss flag to salute the arrival of Mr Isele, the official federal representative of Switzerland, who came to spend twenty-four hours with us, along with his wife and son. They seem to be enjoying the countryside, as they have had to spend all summer in town to settle a number of different matters, amongst which is the internship of Germans in Canada.

Charles

20 September 1918

My dear parents,

Let's Go! We aren't yet there, however, but everything is moving and there is nothing more encouraging. The topographic service is always on the lookout and moves often.

At the time of the victorious pressure on Quéant, we had to pack our bags rapidly in order to keep in contact with the great advance. We march, and in the destroyed villages, now evacuated by the enemy, we see refugees wandering, having come on foot from far away, to look in the ruins for the location of the houses where the family had lived for several generations! Groups of poor uprooted people search in the rubble for some revealing item, and are delighted if they find a latch or a window bar that could serve to establish the whereabouts of their property. They think that it will take fifty years to rebuild the village and its gardens.

André

25 September 1918

My dear father,

Your letter of 4 September didn't arrive, because there is no sergeant major to receive it. If I don't write often, don't put all the blame on the torpedoes but more on the insufficient non-military news, and a job as routine as civilian life.

I went to visit my old battalion the other day. Most of my old friends are gone, a few officers, but that's all!

Our greatest privilege is our mess. We have found an excellent chef that helps us to remember our meals at home. Imagine the surprise this evening when we saw on a table with a lovely white wax tablecloth (which cost us thirty francs): two magnificent homemade pies!

It's strange that many of my friends are getting married these days. They must be seeing the approaching end of the war!

André

Then it was the Canal du Nord, perhaps the most formidable barrier on the road to the east. In what was perhaps General Currie's most audacious plan, he proposed to construct a bridge that would have to be built by engineers while under fire. Covered by a massive artillery bombardment, on 27 September, the entire Canadian army crossed the bridge. From there the Corps captured the critical Bourlon Woods. Having lost these many key miles, including the Hindenburg Line, the German army accelerated its retreat. General Ludendorff called Prince Max of Baden, newly appointed German Chancellor, on 29 September to suggest that they negotiate a conditional surrender. The chancellor refused.

Les Colombettes, 6 October 1918

My dear boys,

I wanted to attend a commemoration service for the Westmount soldiers killed in the last year, but the weather was so bad that the ceremony was cancelled. It is also possible that the real reason for the cancellation was the Spanish flu that is beginning to ravage the city. One doesn't want, with reason, to frighten the population, and the newspapers are not very clear on this point, but we are taking precautions.

The news from Europe is incredibly interesting these days. We vibrate with you as we read about these marvellous details of the advance all along the line, when for so long we were marking time. And Bulgaria! What a collapse! And what about Turkey? The people here are complaining that there's a shortage of turkeys for thanksgiving dinner!

Charles

Cambrai was captured on 9 October, after another difficult and costly Canadian offensive. It was to be General Currie's final battle in the series that had begun in Arras six weeks before. He had an imposing record: he had fought forward twenty-three miles and liberated fifty-four towns and villages, but at the horrific cost of over thirty thousand casualties.

The further Allied victories in October, and more recent bad news from the Western Front, had badly shaken the Germans. On 4 October, Germany wrote to President Wilson, requesting an armistice. Wilson conferred with his colleagues, and they insisted that it be an unconditional surrender. The Germans refused.

THE EARLY SIGNS of the victory to come, gave both heart and energy to the soldier. The leaves are beginning to fall, the days are getting shorter, and the cold autumn wind is blowing on the backs of the fleeing German army.—(BB)

HRH THE PRINCE OF WALES, General Currie, and the officers of the 3rd Division attended the burial of its former commander, Major General Lipsett, on 15 October. A few days later, the Canadians liberated the town of Denain, and the group took the occasion to celebrate with the population. They were given a heroes' welcome and were greeted with cheers and shouts of "Vive la France." French tricolours, long hidden, appeared as if by magic along the route of the marching troops. The Prince of Wales, General Currie, and the others later attended a triumphant celebration that was held in the town square.

HRH The Prince of Wales (second left) with General Currie (left) and the
Canadian divisional general whose men captured Denain, standing outside
the town's church, 19 October 1918

2 November 1918

My dear father,

*What do you think of the news – an armistice may be signed as you receive
this letter! It's wonderful that the four-year effort has finally come to an end.*

*We are lodging in a house belonging to a lady who only a few weeks ago
was lodging Germans in our room. She has talked to me in detail about the
suffering they had endured under the helm of the Germans. The women had
to work in the fields for the Germans, and in several instances, she had seen
the German officers slap her neighbours for insignificant trivialities. She
hasn't seen any meat for three years, and the American flour was blended
with sawdust before being distributed to the population.*

*Last Sunday, 20 October, I assisted at the mass and great celebration
in honour of the liberation of Denain, a small town near here. We had
a beautiful drive by car through the village, decorated with French flags,
hidden and sewn into their mattresses since the beginning of the war. What
joy there was reflected in every face!*

*We arrived much too late to go into the church, but saw the distribution
of flowers to the generals that were there. Then we walked in the streets,
when all of a sudden a lovely lady runs after us and invites us to her house.
The hot chocolate is on the stove, and she does everything possible to show us
her appreciation, despite telling more terrible martyr stories.*

She had a great sense of humour, in the classical French style. She showed off her patriotism by crying "Vive la France! Down with the enemy!" ... and she was proud to say that she had hidden the hens, and the Germans hadn't had one single egg!

Then she showed us the small dirty stable where she had lived for five long winter months while the Germans occupied her house. The French newspaper was stuck onto the front door, and the crowd read thoroughly every word with surprise. It no longer mentioned the great German victory that they had been accustomed to read about.

There's a procession in the main street, the troops march in an impeccable formation, the civilians raise their hats, but they have suffered too much to be able to shout their cries of joy. A gap in the procession, and here marching are ten old veterans, at least seventy years old, carrying their dear flag, which had been buried for many years. The crowd welcomes them and applauds them with great gusto. At the foot of the statue to Maréchal de Villars, officers of all ranks are grouped around General Currie and the Prince of Wales. Then the mayor gives his speech. Or, in fact, he is supposed to speak, but in reality it's Madam the mayor's wife who does and says everything, while the mayor, a little bit behind, approves by nodding his head.

Lots of love to all. Haven't yet received the pipe, but thanks for the birthday package.

André

THE CANADIANS COULDN'T be delayed by the festivities. They then resume their march, constantly pestered by the stubborn enemy, and the topographers followed. On 10 November, they arrive at Valenciennes, that former lace-manufacturing centre, now the city of steel. The soldiers are lodged as best they can be in the municipal buildings, and André's office is in a deserted school, humid and freezing. The next day, André, feeling the first shivers of the flu, all the same joins in to the wild rejoicing that bursts in every direction as the liberation is announced. He wrote: "Celebrations, parades, speeches, flag presentations, nothing was missing at the ceremony where the civil authorities were given back the governing of their town. It was a magnificent victory day." The Canadians then crossed the Belgian border and advanced towards Mons, where an unforgettable reception was waiting for them.—(BB)

GERMANY FINALLY ACCEPTED President Wilson's conditions for a military armistice on 20 October. It was received with dismay by many in Germany, and it was only

Canadian troops marching through the streets of Mons
on the morning of 11 November 1918

on 8 November that General Foch met with the German Armistice Commission in a railway carriage parked in the woods of Compiègne. The Canadian troops meanwhile had marched to Mons, in Belgium, where the war had started in 1914.

On 11 November at 6:30 a.m., a message was sent to the Canadian Corps Headquarters, announcing that hostilities would cease at 11 a.m. that day. The world rejoiced, and work stopped for the rest of the day for all who had heard the good news.

AT THE BEGINNING OF SEPTEMBER 1918, Etienne had once again the pleasure of working a little while as a technical consultant in a naval station near Boulogne, and to see Jean, before going to the hospital to have a further operation on his inadequately healed leg. On 11 November, it's from his bed in Camberwell that Etienne sees the waving of the hats, the light of the torches, and the joyous sound of cries, songs, and band music. Despite the flu that dominated the room, despite this annoying quarantine, the sick were just as joyous, but less noisy than those on the street.—(BB)

CHAPTER SEVENTEEN

Homeward

1919

Charles and Blanche Bieler

AT THE MOMENT WHEN VICTORY AND PEACE WERE FINALLY ASSURED, it was very traumatic for thousands upon thousands of Allied soldiers, after having escaped all the dangers of the war, to find themselves vanquished by the Spanish flu bug. Another final horror to face! André, along with many other sick soldiers, had the disappointment of being in Valenciennes when their victorious friends advanced through Belgium. The sudden end of the hostilities didn't bring much change in Jean's situation; the McGill Hospital didn't receive any more wounded, but it was being filled with Allied prisoners returning from Germany with their health in tatters. The office work therefore continued at the same level of intensity right through the spring of 1919.

IN 1919 OUR SONS RETURNED one after the other. First of all Etienne in January, delighted with his scientific experiences in the Orkney Islands, and his very interesting contacts with Dr. Eve and other British physicists; then André's arrival on 11 April at La Clairière; and in August a new celebration to welcome Jean, our last soldier to return, as sadly, sadly! Philippe would never come back!—(BB)

Camiers, 1 December 1918

My dear mother,

It has been a while since my pencil has done any work, or written any letters. I had, unfortunately, caught a bad bronchitis while we were stationed in a huge empty school with no heating. It was 11 November when I had to stop, following a morning of celebrations and parades, as we passed on the management of Valenciennes to the civilian population. There were speeches and presentations of flags; it was a magnificent victory morning!

That afternoon, I felt very stuffed up and I had a high temperature, and the doctor sent me to the hospital in the city's new school, which had been used as a German hospital for four years. They put me to bed and I stayed a few days before being sent here.

I had the pleasure of seeing Jean again. He's always the same, and we spent a good afternoon together. When you receive this, I will probably be in England, and it may not be so long before I see you all again. In any case, it will be this spring. As far as life goes here, there's nothing to say except for the medicine four times a day, and a good bed every night!

I'm thinking a lot about future projects, but it's impossible to decide anything in advance. What will the entrance exams for McGill be like? One talks a lot about farms in the West.

The asthma has unfortunately not gone, as it comes back each time that I go to a big city; in the country, I feel like a spring chicken. All that gives me a lot to think about.

André

No. 3 Canadian General Hospital APO S91 BEF
6 December 1918

My dear mother,

For the last time, I hope, or I'm sure, that I will be communicating by letter my best Christmas and New Year's wishes.

Who would have thought four months ago that we could win the war so quickly, even before the arrival of huge numbers of American troops? We must be very thankful for this great relief, and thank God to have brought an end to this horrible war. I don't know what peace will bring. As for us, we have had a lot of trouble believing it, and it's only after several days that we realized that the armistice had really been signed, and that we were really the winners!

Since the signing of the armistice, we have rarely been so busy, and I wasn't able to celebrate in town like the majority of the soldiers. I was finally able to go out at 8 p.m. and I saw the parades and the fireworks, but I missed the music and the torchlight retreat. Everyone was ecstatic, although there were some that were a little less exuberant, as though they had attended an excellent McGill Theatre night. Naturally, everyone had removed their hats, and the big game was to exchange your headgear; I saw a French sailor with an Australian hat, holding hands with an American wearing a German cap, while an artillery soldier with his spurs had a beret with a red pompon.

Up to now, peace hasn't brought us any relief. Quite the contrary, we still have as many sick and quite a few wounded. The organization at the base has had to be changed and modified in view of the arrival of the repatriated prisoners, which complicates many things. The leaves were relaxed, so that my best secretaries disappeared one after the other. Since my return at the end of October, I got out only three times before 7:30 p.m. (Sunday included of course).

With respect to what Mom refers to as my projects! I hope to go on leave (a regular one this time) to Paris at the beginning of February! I hope to do a quick side trip to Nice, as I might as well benefit from the army travel rates while they last. I won't be surprised to be released in the spring or at the beginning of the summer at the latest. I had thought of going to Paris for several months, but I think that, when the demobilization starts, it will

happen much more quickly than we had thought several months ago, and
that all the wonderful plans of Khaki College will fall apart.

They created a branch of the Khaki College here; naturally it started with
huge classes, but that initial enthusiasm didn't last long.

André would have told you that I went to see him in Camiers two weeks
ago. Given my contacts, I found out that he is still there, and I'm planning
to go and see him tomorrow if that can be arranged. I found that he was in
fact not so well. It looked as though his asthma was better, but he was still
suffering considerably from bronchitis. He was in bed, and was waiting
from one day to the next to go to England. He has not yet left, but please
don't worry. Once he's in England he will be sent to Canada quickly. His
sickness started during the evening of Armistice Day, as the Canadian
Headquarters was going to move once again, and he didn't feel well enough
to go any further. He was sent to the hospital in Valenciennes and from
there to Camiers. He has had a fascinating summer, undertaking various
projects. A leisurely May and June in a beautiful château. In July he worked
for the RAF with the assistance of several draftsmen; then the Amiens battle
and a one-day visit to a French headquarters to deliver maps. From there a
trip to Arras (as usual in a side-car), where he stayed for quite a while. His
final itinerary took him to Quéant, Denain, and Valenciennes, where he
saw Poincaré, just before he collapsed. He had some great experiences that
will interest you a lot. But it's getting late, and I must stop.

Jean

INITIALLY EVACUATED TO Camiers, where he saw Jean, André embarked for England and was treated in Birmingham, in the beautiful university buildings. It was
now almost the fourth Christmas since his mobilization! Time had appeared to
move more quickly than the reality of these four difficult years.—(BB)

1st Southern General Hospital, Birmingham
15 December 1918

My dear parents,

Here we are just before Christmas, which brings back memories of so many
family celebrations in Neuilly, with all its preparations of hymns and
readings, or at Les Colombettes, with the little tree and the presents. But, at
last, here is the last one I hope for a long time to come that will take place
without the complete family, where the only one that will be missing is the
one that will no longer light the candles on the tree! Sunday is visitors' day
at the hospital; it doesn't make you feel good to see all those other fathers,
mothers, and friends! However it won't be long now.

It was a long trip from Etaples to here. It took us twenty-four hours: by ambulance, then a train up to Calais, then a boat on a rough Channel (but I wasn't sick). Finally, at Dover, I boarded another train to Edgbaston. We are in a university building built in 1907, thus almost new. It's amusing, as I'm in the machine room, almost identical with the one at the École Technique in Montreal.

Most of the English will go on leave for Christmas, but I think I will have a better Christmas here than walking the streets of London. In any case, I can't go to Paris. We have had a bit of music this evening. We have a good piano and guys who sing very well.

André

ANDRÉ WAS CONVALESCING in Birmingham, and Etienne longed to see his brother after almost two years of separation. On 1 January, his repatriation having been confirmed at long last, he arranges to spend several days in these university buildings where several hundred convalescents are being treated, of which the greatest in his opinion, is that former cadet who had so many interesting things to tell.

Etienne, buttoned up in his officer's uniform, with a fresh complexion, and suntanned by the sea air, had, despite his little limp, nothing but happy things to talk about. André, having lost a lot of weight after forty-one months of danger and deprivation, being wounded in the great battles and poisoned by the asphyxiating gas, was not looking quite as rosy. The contrast between the military careers of the two brothers might have been a sore point, but André was proud to think that Etienne had been able to apply his mathematics and his physics to the common good, and on the other hand, Etienne admired André's bravery and ingenuity. André, more frail than him, had been able to do almost three long years at the Front, and a year making the maps that eventually helped the Canadians to push the enemy back to Berlin.

How happy they were, huddled together in a corner of the lounge or walking in the park! They talked about home, the beginning of the Princess Pats, their war adventures, the friends that they won't see again, and future projects. Then the brothers separated once again, but only for a short time.—(BB)

1 January 1919

My dear mother,

Etienne will have told you about our day in rainy London, which would have been better if it had been Montreal or Winnipeg. While we were inspecting the magnificent Canadian war posters, which I hope will be shown in Montreal before long, I began to feel my asthma. Then, while visiting with the Douglas girls, I began to feel really badly. Finally, I had to return as quickly as possible to Epsom. On our arrival at the camp, I was examined by a doctor who sent me immediately to the hospital, to be examined by a real doctor, the first time since my arrival in England.

André

ETIENNE IS GREETED WITH OPEN ARMS on his arrival at Les Colombettes on 30 January 1919, and the stories are boundless.—(BB)

Epsom, 26 January 1919

My dear mother,

I deeply regret leaving the Survey Section in November; everything is so monotonous here. I am almost thinking of taking the four-month course at the Khaki University.

  I very much enjoyed Etienne's visit when I was in Birmingham, and we had a beautiful Christmas at the hospital, with a Christmas tree and a pleasant celebration.

  I have saved about $900 during the war. That will be useful on my return. We are so badly paid here, almost not enough to buy tobacco. I must be careful that the money saved during the war is spent in Canada, and not here.

André

THE REPATRIATION OF THE Canadian troops took time. André spent many weeks at Epsom, and then a few weeks at a convalescent camp at Taplow. In March, as the lawns were turning bright green and spotted with snowdrops and primroses, he walked the footpaths of the Astor Manor.—(BB)

18th General Hospital, 6 March 1919

My dear mother,

Finally, I am classified ITC (Invalid to Canada) with three months' of treatment in the outdoors. I will have one month at home before beginning the treatment. Now we must wait – wait for a boat (the Germans almost sank them all).

  As you can see from the address, I am in a Canadian Hospital built on the magnificent property of the multi-millionaire Astors. One can understand the situation of the British working class when a man can own such a property. The countryside around here is covered with properties like this – all this land, whose only use is for walking. We have visited the house,

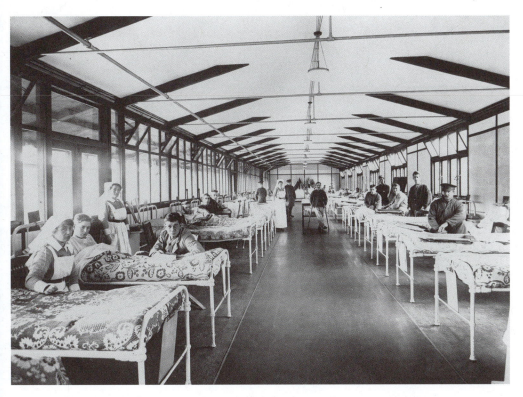

Wounded: Nurses and patients at the New Brunswick ward of the Duchess of Connaught's
Canadian Red Cross Hospital at the Astor estate, Cliveden, in Berkshire

*or should I say château, as it would be called in France. It's wonderful but
it isn't a home: a Louis XV dining room transported from France, bought
from a family that had more ancestors than money. I don't think that, with
all that gold trimming, one could have much of a rest, these mirrors and
the painted ceiling done by I don't know which famous artist! The walls are
covered with Romneys and Joshua Reynoldses as though they were bought at
the 5-, 10-, and 15-cent stores! There are also incredible Gobelin tapestries.*

*I'm hoping to visit Windsor Castle before leaving. A dozen guys go
together and are received by a few members of the Royal Family: the Princess
Mary or others.*

André

NOT BEING ABLE to put up with it any longer, André pursues all the possible medical
and military avenues, and eventually obtains his repatriation ticket. Then finally, another few weeks of lodging in a not-very-attractive "workhouse" in Liverpool.—(BB)

André Bieler's boat home

Liverpool, 14 March 1919

My dear father,

I went to see the adjutant on my own, who straightened everything out and told me that he would try to send me on the next boat. I hope things move ahead as fast here on in.

The hospital here is in an old workhouse "No. 6 General Hospital," L. Ward, Kirkdale, Lancs. I am tired after this non-stop trip of seven hours.

André

ANDRÉ FINALLY EMBARKS FOR Canada and arrives in Montreal on 11 April 1919. How he has grown! He left as an adolescent, and here he is, a man, matured by his efforts and his ordeals. Unfortunately, his privations, the fatigues, and especially the poisonous gas have seriously affected his health. The unpredictable Montreal spring goes from ice to sun, between snow and greenery. There are mixed emotions, between the grief for the missing, and the immense joy over the return of two soldiers. For Jean it will eventually be only a moment, and Philippe will never return! However, gratitude moves into first place, and we organize at Les Colombettes a big reception, for all those friends eager to welcome our two soldiers. Then, on 24 May we get together with all the young people of La Clairière for a picnic and several bonfires. André plunges back into that former environment, which he had so often talked about during these four years of war, now all over.

Jean went on leave to the Riviera, and on his return he finally left Boulogne and headed for Ripon in Northern England, a region less sunny than the South of France, where Canada had located its Khaki University. It was a very strict military atmosphere, which he described as almost pedantic.—(BB)

Khaki University, April 1919

My dear father,

As you will see from the above address, I have finally arrived at the KU, where you were the first to encourage me to go. My first impression is mostly favourable, as I had not expected to find something marvellous.

I spent some very pleasant last days at Boulogne. On Friday the 28th my office colleagues invited me to dinner. The following evening, we had our usual party, then on Sunday I went to say goodbye to my friends at the château. Tuesday afternoon, I went to say goodbye to Mrs. Dupré, the owner of the pastry shop, and finally to A.B.'s. Their eldest son, who had been a prisoner in Germany, was there on leave.

I once again did the rounds of the hospital; the colonel was particularly polite and thanked me for my services. The ship left punctually on time: I stayed in the stern to view the French shoreline disappear slowly, and to think of the four long years (they seemed short to me) that I have spent on this French soil that I love so much. I wonder when I will see it again!

There's a parade every Wednesday and PT every morning. Other than that, the KU allows you to do what you want. To tell the truth I was a little disappointed to learn that there was a law faculty; I had kind of hoped that I would be sent off to a real university. I start my courses on Monday: I am looking forward to it in every respect.

Jean

HOWEVER, the leaves, although rarely given, brought some variety to Jean's monotonous existence. He was eventually authorized at Easter to go to London to meet with his former registrar in Boulogne, Dr Francis, who introduced him to Sir William Osler, McGill's most famous living graduate. For Jean, this was like an oasis in the desert. He spent almost eight days in the warm and hospitable atmosphere of this distinguished man's home. The house was like an enormous library. Jean was treated like a son, and he was invited to come again. It was a revelation for him to witness the likes of this learned, Christian, hospitable, and generous gentleman.—(BB)

Khaki University, 28 April 1919

My dear mother,

I have wondered whether I wouldn't have been better off to have tried to be sent to a real university instead of going to the Khaki College, which looks more like a camp than a university. I am annoyed to note that Dad seems to think that I am in the process of spending my assets! I understand that the senior staff of the KU only recommends those students for Oxford and Cambridge who have $500 in the bank, in addition to their pay and daily indemnity.

During my last morning at the Oslers', Sir William came into the little sitting room in a dressing gown where I was reading, and, despite Lady Osler's protests, he began rummaging in his bookcases to find for me the work of Lavanter, a famous Zurich gentleman. He finally brought me an enormous volume in German, and two smaller ones in French on the study of Physiognomy, which he asked me to read. He also gave me an essay to read that he had written on Michel Servet. Although he lost his only son during the war, Sir William is very preoccupied with the food supply of the Central Empires, in the event that we don't urgently supply them with protein. He was discussing the subject at dinner when Johnston, Etienne's friend, exclaimed, "Let them starve, they started the war." Sir William, who is normally calm, became angry and said, "Haven't you any Christian Principles?" Johnston, who always has something to say, shut up this time. Johnston is a good guy, but a little too sure of himself and of his accomplishments.

Saturday morning, I went into town to do some comparative pricing at the tailors, which confirmed some very high prices:

- *1 blue suit*   £9 9sh
- *1 grey suit*   £7 7sh
- *1 morning suit*   £13 13sh

I arrived here yesterday morning without much enthusiasm.

Jean

13 Warwick Rd, London SW5, 29 June 1919

Dear André,

On Wednesday 18th I heard that my request to be sent to do a course at the Inns of Court in London had been accepted, and that I should be ready to leave that evening with thirteen friends. Our courses are at the Inner Temple, and we can use the magnificent library. We need to pass our Ripon exams at the same time, which doesn't leave me much leisure time.

I went to Cousin Jack's at Wimbledon last week. I've been invited to
Lady Macdonell's on Monday and I hope to go to Oxford next Saturday. I
didn't find Lady Stowel, as the address given by Tante Julia as Notting Hill
Square hasn't existed for years!
  Our courses finish on the 11th, and we should be leaving Ripon on about
20 July, but our departure may be delayed. I'm sorry not to have spent the
whole time in London. With the six-shilling daily living allowance, I could
have easily lived there without going bankrupt.

Jean

IN JULY, Jean passed an exam that was to give him his LLB at McGill. It was only in August that he joined us at La Clairière. Tante Julia had also arrived to celebrate and rejoice in the return of our boys.

Charles and Blanche were relieved and overjoyed to finally welcome back four of their five boys, but they were obviously still weighed down by Philippe's death. As the boys relaxed in their home environment, Charles and Blanche were still on duty in the United States and Canadian provinces. Two of Blanche's tours were yet begun, and Charles hadn't completed his evangelical itinerary. Their next challenge was to ensure that the boys settled happily and usefully within the Canadian environment that they had left behind in 1914.

Jean, the eldest, was probably the least Canadian, but he had been the only one who had set foot into the professional arena, and it seemed that an opportunity was presenting itself. Etienne was an integral part of the McGill Physics Department, with which he had continued to associate in his position at the British Admiralty in 1918. Jacques had grown up as a Canadian, and was about to graduate from Westmount High School. André, on the other hand, had no university training, was a World War I invalid, and was concerned as to what to do next.—(BB)

CHAPTER EIGHTEEN

Memorial

Lens Church

*W*e travelled to Europe to attend the inauguration of the Lens Church held on 28 June 1925. The French Reformed Church, various Protestant committees friendly with foreign countries, and several officers representing the President of France and the Minister of Defence, were in attendance. After having gallantly saluted the important visitors, Mr Paul Frezier, State Councillor, turned towards us and said:

"Please allow me, in the name of my committee, to say a few words to you, Professor Bieler, and to you, Mrs Bieler. It is appropriate for us to remember what you did from the bottom of your heart, for your second home. At the beginning of the war you set an example for all Canadians: your four sons left the country as volunteers, to defend and to free occupied France. We all salute your sacrifice, and we recognize why the soil of the province of Quebec has become sacred for you.

While your sons were doing their duty, you were also being enlisted. You, Mrs Bieler, stimulated positively the thoughts of Canadian Protestants, and English-speaking Canadians, towards the soldiers in the invaded regions of France and Belgium, miners in the Pas de Calais, factory workers in the North, the poor soldiers deprived of letters, parcels, and other comforting missiles. With your sister, Miss Merle d'Aubigné, you created a charity aimed at both the military and the refugees in the invaded provinces, where you sent them the fruit of your resources. You also found time to help discreetly but efficiently our pastors' wives, especially those who were alone in their parishes, and in their homes. Your sympathy was always for France.

Canada was not big enough for the extent of your zeal, and you, Mr Bieler, accepted a French propaganda mission across the United States. We know that you have thrilled many audiences. Your official mission, dear Professor, has received heartfelt congratulations from our Washington embassy. The war being over, you deserved a long rest, but you sought the help of Christian brethren to help raise the funds necessary for the building of this church. It is appropriate to repeat in a loud voice that you deserve great applause from our country."—(BB)

CHAPTER NINETEEN

Professional Challenge

1920 to 1950

Montage of (clockwise from upper left) Jean, Etienne, Jacques, and André Bieler

JEAN

JEAN SELDOM TALKED about his professional life, but finally, urged by his two brothers, he typed up a brief life story a few years before his death in 1976. This is the part dealing with his years at the League of Nations between 1919 and 1941.

AT MY RETURN HOME IN August 1919, my mother announced that she had a big secret that she would only divulge at the end of the meal! It was that Sir Herbert Ames, the Member of Parliament for Westmount, was looking for a bilingual secretary to accompany him overseas. I met with Sir Herbert, and he explained rather coolly that it was a job in the League of Nations administration, but that I wouldn't be qualified because of my lack of stenographic competence. I was very much surprised a few days later, to hear that Sir Eric Drummond, Secretary General of the League of Nations, had wired that it was a private secretary that he required, not a stenographer. I accepted their offer.

In hindsight it's difficult to describe my most vivid impressions during these first and most-important phases of my career. The meetings of the League of Nations, structured in a strict and unchanging fashion, fade in my memory. I assisted probably at the opening and the closing of all of the sessions and a great many council meetings. I was present during the historic sessions, during which the procedures were adopted, Germany was elected to the League, the Disarmament Conference was created, China was left to its own future, the sanctions against Italy were voted, and finally the USSR was excluded from the Institution. I can remember the moving speech when Guiseppe Motta, during the first meeting in the Reformation Hall, called for the universalization of the League and the admission of Germany; of the forceful calls by Ramsay MacDonald and Edouard Herriot presented in the same Hall in favour of the procedures; the conciliatory speech from Gandhi at the opening of the Disarmament Conference; the unconvincing explanations by Sir John Simon to justify the negative attitude of the Leading Nations towards China; and the noisy entry of Goebbels, at the Electoral Palace, surrounded by bodyguards, during the 1933 Assembly. I was also always present at the debates between Albert Thomas and Carl Hambro in the cramped and overheated chamber at the Quai Wilson, where the Finance Commission met. I remember the great discouragement resulting from the world crisis presented by Albert Thomas at the Control Commission, three days before the death of the director of the Bureau International du Travail; the courteous and always satisfying meetings with Sir Eric Drummond in his plain office in the old building, and much more frightening ones with his successor, Joseph Avenol, in his luxurious office in the New Palais des Nations.

I also remember a trip to Rome in May 1920, for the Council's fifth session, which had been delayed by the Wagons Lits strike, and we had been forced in the

League of Nations, Geneva, 1921. Front row, left to right: Dr. Nansen, Secretary, Refugee Affairs; Sir Herbert Ames, Finance Secretary. Back row, left to right: Sir Eric Drummond, Secretary General; Jean Bieler, Deputy Finance Secretary

League of Nations session. Jean Bieler, fourth from left at the head table

Palais des Nations

waiting room to join the dignitaries of the Church on their way to the beatification of Jeanne d'Arc. We arrived in Rome the next day, where the revolution seemed about to erupt. We were nevertheless able to create the secretariat, ratify the nominations, and sketch the organization of the Justice Department prior to meetings at the Senate and at the Agricultural Institute. On Sunday it was the beatification at St Peter's and a magnificent reception at the French Embassy, where I wore a white tie borrowed from a hotel clerk!

On 14 February 1930, I married Raymonde de Candolle, a descendant of the botanist, Augustin Pyramus de Candolle.

Time went on, and the League grew. The Quai Wilson building became too small, and plans were made to build something more substantial. My pessimism was such that I found the plans too grandiose and too ambitious. However, in my capacity of Deputy Treasurer and a member of the building committee, I was involved with all the complications. We moved in 1936, but it wasn't until 1938 that the final Assembly Hall was finished. The inauguration was particularly depressing. Bruno Walter directed the Orchestre de la Suisse Romande for the opening concert, where the various pieces, particularly "Eine Kleine Nachtmusik," will remain imprinted in the memory of the audience. Two days later, the Agha Khan, the president of the Assembly, whose candidacy depended on his extreme wealth, received the guests in the Great Green Marble Gallery. The fifteen hundred guests were in a state of anxiety, and were thinking more about Hitler's Machiavellian plans than the questions

Quebec premier, Maurice Duplessis, giving a speech

listed in the Assembly's agenda. During the dinner given by the British Delegation, we were shocked to hear about a visit to Berchtesgaden, and relieved to talk about one at Godesberg. The anxiety and concerns increased as the session terminated in a spirit of intense pessimism. The few diplomats still in Geneva were preparing to leave, and we were already assuming that, in the days ahead, Paris would be flattened by German bombs.

The 1939 Assembly was held under the auspices of war. Help for Finland was the main subject on the agenda, and Switzerland was granted her wish that the European conflict would not be discussed on its neutral territory. A massive reduction of employment in the secretariat was also voted.

The months go by; Holland, Belgium, and France are invaded. The secretariat prepares to move to Vichy. But despite the Germans' rapid advance, the decision is taken to leave the secretariat in Geneva. Mr. Avenol, devastated by the fall of his country, quits after some unpleasant discussions, in which I am involved. The direction of the secretariat is given to Sean Lester, who is instructed to manage the transition of the League, as agreed in the Versailles Agreement, and the new organization that will be born from the United Nations victory. Given my position of secretary of the Finance Commission, I was asked to partake in the closing meetings of the League of Nations. Reduced to a minimum, the secretariat did its best. The meeting that was to be held in Lisbon to settle a few problems was blocked by the Germans, and I returned to Geneva to manage the secretariat. In April 1941, my old friend Arthur Mathewson asked me to come to Quebec and assist him with the finances of the Province. I accepted, and resigned from the League of Nations in 1941.—(Jean)

JEAN SERVED, AS DEPUTY MINISTER OF FINANCE OF THE PROVINCE OF QUEBEC, under five premiers: Adélard Godbout, Maurice Duplessis, Paul Sauvé, Antonio Barrette, and Jean Lesage.

ETIENNE

ETIENNE RETURNED TO CANADA IN FEBRUARY 1919, and immediately went back to McGill, as both a student and an assistant in the Physics Laboratory, under the able guidance of Dr L.V. King. Since the family had sold Les Colombettes, and as Blanche was leaving for Florida with André, Etienne moved in with Jacques in his basement lodgings at the Presbyterian College. At the end of the semester, Etienne was awarded an MA in Science, with distinction.

Meanwhile, in 1920, Sir Ernest Rutherford had been appointed to the Chair of the Cavendish Laboratory at Cambridge, and was looking for some of his former students to join him. One was James Chadwick, with whom he had worked during his tenure at Manchester University. Another was Etienne, whom he had known at the British Admiralty. The Chancellor at McGill conveniently helped to arrange for Etienne to receive the "1851 Exhibition" Scholarship, with which he entered Caius College, Cambridge, and became a Research Student at the Cavendish Laboratory. It was a time when the inner citadel of the atom was assaulted by bombardment with the alpha particles of radium, and Rutherford had shown that the mass or weight of an atom is concentrated in a relatively small nucleus.

James Chadwick, who was later to prove the existence of neutrons, and was a key player in the US's Manhattan Project, had this to say about his colleague:

> Etienne joined me in an investigation of the collisions of alpha particles
> with hydrogen nuclei, which I had just begun. From our observations,
> Bieler and I were able to show that at large distances the force between
> the particles was given by Coulomb's law, and to fix with fair accuracy the
> point of departure from this law. Bieler then took over the natural develop-
> ment of these experiments. I think that the chief conclusions eventually
> reached by Bieler may be put thus: that the collisions of alpha particles
> with light atoms disclose the complex structure of the nuclei and that the

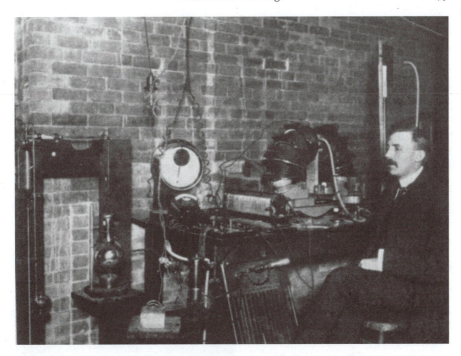

Ernest Rutherford in his laboratory

effective sizes of the nuclei may be determined in this way; and that at very small distances the force between two charged particles is no longer given by Coulomb's Law, but a new force, varying very rapidly with the distance, comes into action.

It is perhaps unnecessary to point out the importance of Bieler's contribution to our knowledge of the atomic nucleus.

Cambridge 1929

In his spare time Etienne enjoyed the company of his colleagues and quite often his brothers, whether it was André in Paris or Jean in Geneva. At Cambridge he ran with the "Hare and Hounds Club." This group of geniuses would sprint through the fields and the woods, sliding under the hedges, leaping over streams and fences, and at dusk, soaking wet, covered in mud, and out of breath, they would arrive at an old inn and have a big meal in a jolly atmosphere filled with laughter and singing.

His trips were sometimes more serious. He had worked with Bohr, Bragg, and Rutherford, who introduced him to the Duke of Broglia, to whom he talked about his relationship with the Noailles and the d'Aubignés, and the problems of Theoretical Physics. On one occasion he met Madame Currie. She was in mourning and looked worn-out. One would not have guessed that this little woman was

Sir James Chadwick

the great lady who had been heaped with honours. "She spoke," wrote Etienne, "in a soft, unassuming voice, as she introduced me to one of her technicians, who was in the process of condensing radium residues for hospitals."

Etienne's research, with Rutherford and Chadwick at his side, was time-consuming, particularly as he was concurrently preparing his PhD thesis. In June 1923, he presented his thesis, "The Law of Force in the immediate Neighbour-hood of the Atomic Nuclei," and was awarded a PhD. He returned to Montreal in the summer of 1923 and was appointed Assistant Professor of Physics at McGill. His new assignment was to be director of studies of the faculty of Physics.

University administration began to absorb most of his time, so that it was only in the evening and weekends that he could tend to his beloved research. Having become an authority on radioactivity, he began to be interested in the theory of magnetism. It was during this time that he also began to think that practical ap-plications of scientific discovery might in the long term be more useful than pure theory. He thought of the untapped resources of Canadian geography. McGill had been approached by the Alderson and MacKay mining company about find-ing a physicist who might be interested in inventing a piece of equipment to generate better information on the location of ore bodies. They suggested it to Etienne and H.J. Watson.

This was Etienne's opportunity to explore the field of geophysics. Watson and he evolved a scheme for exploration within a large insulated loop laid on the ground, through which passed an alternating current of a few amperes. By induction, the conducting ore bodies out of sight beneath the ground responded with a secondary current, allowing for the joint electro-magnetic field to be explored with suitable receiving coils and headphones. This work took them to some of the famous mines in the Rouyn district in northern Quebec. The outdoor life, the stimulation of a new problem, and the association with mining men and geophysical prospectors brought a new zest to life, and produced a conflict between his love of pure physics and the attraction of a lively practical problem.

IN 1916, the chairman of the Australian Development and Migration Commission made inquiries in London, which led to an agreement being arrived at between the Empire Marketing Board and the Commonwealth government for an Imperial geophysical survey to be conducted in Australia over a period of two years from 1928. McGill was approached, and Dr. Eve was consulted. Eve was quite keen to be involved but, following conversations with McGill's chancellor, Etienne was chosen as the candidate to direct the survey, to be supervised by Broughton Edge, a London physicist. The object was to try out the best physical methods as thoroughly as possible in the course of two years' fieldwork, and at the same time to instruct young Australian scientists in the theory and practice of the methods and in the correct use of the various delicate instruments involved. The primary purpose of the survey was to test the methods, rather than to open new fields.

Etienne, as Deputy Director of the Imperial Geophysical Experimental Survey, arrived in Australia in July 1928. He had complete charge of the work in the absence from the country of Mr Broughton Edge. He came armed with his magneto-electric device, now called the Bieler–Watson Radiometer, which was to be compared with the various other current devices.

To supervise teams spread out not just in a province, nor a country, but also over an entire continent, is quite different than going down the stairs to McGill's lecture hall and into the students' laboratory. In addition, due to the differences in the gauge of the rails, he had to change trains six times while travelling across the country. In the deserts it was usually on foot through soft sand, dragging a caravan, carrying tents, equipment, and all other items required by nomads. After each of these long trips, he faced the extensive administrative details, as well as side trips to the University of Melbourne to analyze and prepare reports and conclusions. In March 1929, he wrote: "As time goes by, we begin to realize the immensity of the job that we need to squeeze into these two years. The practical work will finish at the beginning of 1930, and we still have several far-off

Etienne Bieler in Australia

regions to explore. Then we will have to coordinate this mass of information and prepare the final report."

In Tasmania in the early summer of 1929, he wrote to his mother about the evolution of his religious beliefs: "You are right, I am not in a religious atmosphere on this continent, but that fact allows me perhaps to think out these questions more independently. As I study the modern scientific viewpoint, with its confirmation of the organic unity of creation, and of the gradual evolution of inanimate nature towards life, as one of the natural results of the laws of matter and energy, some of the old biblical beliefs fail to satisfy me, and I tend towards a conception of God that is less personal, but no less real, and certainly not less noble. And still, when I think of the personalities whose lives and actions are inspired by biblical ideas, when I think of the legacy, which they have left behind, a heritage of noble example and sturdy moral traditions, I realize that conceptions can never replace convictions, and I ask myself how this treasure can be preserved for our descendants. I see two sides to the revelation of God in the world, one involving the physical the other involving the soul: it seems to me that it should be possible to find a synthesis of these two."

In July in Australia Etienne headed for the Western beaches, where his team was waiting for him. He started to shiver during the train journey. They would have liked him to stay in Perth, but he insisted on going on to the setting sun.

Portrait of Ernest Rutherford (left); General Currie,
Commander of the Canadian troops in France (right)

At Geraldton, a tiny port on the shores of the Indian Ocean, the fever halted
him. He was transported to the hospital, where the doctor concluded that it was
pneumonia and worked hard to save him. After thirty-two hours of great despair,
Etienne, who has already conquered the hearts of all those around him, says
that he's feeling better and appears to want to sleep. When the nurse came in a
little later, Etienne's dear face appeared illuminated, but he was very pale and
strangely immobile.

In Geraldton, not only the geophysical team, but also the church and the civic
leaders, deeply touched at the thought of the sacrifice of this young life, led him
to his last home, and erected a monument on his grave. At McGill, on 27 October,
the hall was jammed for a solemn service in his memory.

(An excerpt from a letter Sir Ernest Rutherford wrote to Blanche Bieler in October
1929)

His work with me in Cambridge was of fundamental importance and gave
us the first evidence of the laws of force around a nucleus.

Sir Ernest Rutherford

(An excerpt from a letter General Sir Arthur Currie wrote to Blanche Bieler in October 1929)

I was drawn to him first when I recognized in him a comrade in the great adventure. When I came to know more about him, to learn his gentleness, his kindly nature, his love of the good and the beautiful, his attachment to his home and his family, I realized that he, for one, had not been dazzled, even momentarily, by what some may call the glamour of war, that it was only his strong sense of duty, his just appreciation of the issues involved, for he had a mind above his fellows and could detect those issues clearly, his hatred of shams and hypocrisies, his sense of what was at stake, that led him to enlist when freedom's trumpet called her sons to battle.

General Sir Arthur Currie

ANDRÉ

ANDRÉ WAS VERY ILL when he finally arrived back in Canada in April. His lungs had been badly burnt by the gas. He was classified as a war invalid, with a pension, who could not begin any professional activity. It was summertime at La Clairière, where his family and the Laurentian air compensated for his constant pains. Come the fall, the most important next step was to go to a warm climate.

André and Blanche left for Daytona Beach in October, equipped with a suitcase full of artist's supplies. Blanche was a talented lady, but by year-end she had taught him everything she knew about art. She enrolled him at Stetson University, where he pursued his education with a more qualified teacher. From there, he wandered northward, staying for a while at a US veterans' hospital, prior to enrolling at the Woodstock Summer School. It was an important moment for André. There he met his future art teacher, Charles Rosen, and was surrounded with an enthusiastic group of fellow artists, many also veterans. On his return to Montreal, in the family's new house, located in downtown Montreal, just across the street from McGill, André's health declined.

In February 1921, Blanche and André left for Bermuda. It was a relaxing and beautiful few months. He was anxious to get back to the Woodstock Summer School, while Blanche was actively planning his future. She felt that he should go back to his roots in Switzerland, where he could work with his uncle, the well-known Valais artist Ernest Bieler, and perhaps spend some time in the warm climate of Provence. André sailed to Europe in late 1921, and headed for "Courmette," a convalescent home in the Provençal Alps. Blanche and Etienne joined him there in April 1922, and they travelled together in Italy prior to his joining Oncle Ernest in the Valais.

André Bieler assisting his uncle, Ernest Bieler

Oncle Ernest had a major commission to paint a fresco in a church a few miles from Sion in the Valais. André joined in, and, in the following three years, he spent the majority of his time with his uncle, learning the intricacies of his profession. At one point Oncle Ernest suggested that he study in Paris. He spent five months in the spring of 1923 at the Académie Ranson, and the École des Beaux Arts. He was excited by the atmosphere and the people, sometimes seeing some of the greats, like Gauguin. Unfortunately, the climate didn't suit him, and he returned to Oncle Ernest, Lac Leman, and the Valais. There were several trips: one with Etienne to Italy, where he admired the classics as well as the scenery, and of course the people. He had seen many specialists about his health, and with their

Les Berlines, Quebec, 1928, by André Bieler

help, and considerable patience on his part, he began to feel better. In December 1925 he joined Jean in his new apartment at the Cour St Pierre in Geneva. He was painting actively and, as usual, making many friends. He had his first one-man show in Montreal, and then one also in Geneva. In the summer of 1926, André began to show a real sense of joyous anticipation of his return to Canada. There was a greater self-confidence in his work, but he was eager to find the right milieu, where he could relate his humanist interest to the Canadian habitant. He returned to Canada on 26 September 1926.

After so many trips back and forth across the ocean, it was heartening to witness a reconstitution of at least a part of the Bieler family: Etienne seemed to be in Montreal permanently, André was setting up a kind of studio in the annex to the Methodist College, and Jacques was soon to return from England. André, however, was keen to find a place in the relative isolation of a community where he could continue the sort of creative exploration of the land and the people that he had found so rewarding in Switzerland. He sought it first of all in the

André at the market

Gaspé, but soon discovered the ideal location: the village of Ste-Famille, on the Île d'Orléans. It seemed perfect in every sense, the population with their ancient customs, a virginal countryside, the gracious hills, and the distant views of the St Lawrence and the mountains. He didn't hesitate, and rented an old house at the edge of the village.

Montreal art critic Robert Ayre said of André, "Humanity is André Bieler's subject ... he isn't any kind of missionary: he is a painter." André did just that during his four years on the Île d'Orléans. He painted the churches, he painted the landscapes, but his main subject was always the people. In many ways, he carried on with his uncle's tradition, where he had specialized in portraits that the Canadian artists of the day avoided. André felt that a landscape with no figures was often incomplete.

Wanting to rejoin the mainstream of art and renew friendships, André decided to return to Montreal in 1930. His return was to a city already scarred by the Depression. The unemployed used to flow like two rivers along St Catherine Street; artists were to struggle equally against apathy and the prevailing attitude that art was a luxury. The artists all knew each other, and all thought that they were going to change the world. André was nicknamed "the artist."

In 1931, André married Jeanette Meunier, who was in charge of Eaton's "l'intérieur Moderne." Together, they designed modern steel furniture that wasn't known in North America. With a few of their artist friends, they created the "Atelier," an art school that they were forced to close in 1933. André made posters for the Canadian Celanese Company. He was recognized for several unique achievements in the early 1930s, including what was probably the first true fresco in Canada. It is a striking portrait of St Christopher carrying the infant Christ on his shoulders, painted on the outside wall of a house owned by André's brother Jacques.

In 1936, Queen's University established a Chair of Fine Arts. Later that year, André was appointed as resident artist. At that time, only two other universities in Canada offered courses in art for degree credit. In 1940, curious to discover more of his country, André obtained a position to teach painting at the Banff Summer School. But during these years, André's paintings remained centred on the life and land of rural Quebec, to which he returned in the summer for sketching sessions,

In October 1940, F.P. Keppel, president of the Carnegie Corporation, visited R.C. Wallace, principal of Queen's and together they made an unexpected call on André in his studio. They invited him to sketch out his idea of a meeting between artists of the east and west, to discuss their mutual problems and to learn about modern developments in the profession. Following a series of talks, more-detailed plans were drawn up, and Keppel concluded that this could be a really significant meeting, and that he would help to fund it.

The structure of the conference was André's plan. His concern for the position of the artist in society in North America had some basis in his experiences in Switzerland, when he worked with his uncle on the fresco in Le Locle. The conference was open to all Canadian artists of professional standing, to art critics, and to educators. The National Gallery arranged for an exhibition of Canadian art. The conception of the conference was both idealistic and practical. It was attended by over 150 delegates; the list of participants read like a catalogue of Canadian art history of the early twentieth century. It was the instigator in the establishment of the Canada Council in 1957.

In 1969 André was awarded an honorary doctor of laws degree by Queen's University at the convocation on 31 May, and was invited to give the convocation address. Earlier he had been awarded the Order of Canada

JACQUES

BACK IN MONTREAL, in the spring of 1918, the YMCA had launched a farming program for young students, and Jacques had convinced his principal to schedule the exams early so that he and his mates could enrol. He endured long and tiring hours of farm labour, then, in the fall of 1918, as Jean and Etienne were making their final contribution to World War I, Jacques entered McGill. This was a year devoted to pre-engineering, and Jacques was not impressed with the courses or the professors.

During the summer of 1920, he began more serious occupations. As a junior engineer, he helped to supervise the construction of a new factory for the Canadian Fur Company, which was conveniently located near La Clairière. Two years later, he spent his holidays in Cleveland at the Bailey Motor Company, prior to receiving his engineering degree. With his degree in hand, while wondering what he should do, he got an offer from the Bailey Company, and he moved to a pleasant suburb of Cleveland. Mr. Bailey was a hard-working Puritan, and the privilege of working on his projects demanded a type of slavery, but Jacques recognized the value of the apprenticeship, and was devastated when US immigration forced him to return to Canada.

A friend then told him, "Go and see the International Paper Company." He followed the advice, and was soon in the Gatineau helping to survey the limits of a huge dam and reservoir the size of Lake Geneva. It was a great opportunity to be in a lovely corner of the Laurentians, working with a team of colourful lumberjacks. He remembers that Christmas Eve, when they left in a long line of red sleds on a layer of white snow, shaken by the holes and the ruts, along narrow roads towards a lunch stop, only to take off again at great speed to a wonderful Christmas feast at home.

As the winter activities were less exciting, and he longed to be in Europe, he decided to join his old friends at the Bailey Company in London. He enjoyed his work there as a junior engineer involved in various foreign operations, although he found that the English engineers lacked the culture of the Germans and the French. There was some wonderful compensation during his travels. On one occasion he joined Etienne and André in a few hilarious days in Paris, and on another occasion he spent time in Italy with his friend Crawford Wright.

On his return to Montreal in 1929, given his experiences at the Bailey Company, he had little trouble in landing a job at the Dominion Oilcloth Company.

Jacques Bieler in 1925

Jacques Bieler in 1935

La Maison Rose

During the Depression, Jacque's activities were reduced and became somewhat monotonous. However, as business picked up, everything changed, and he played a key role as a senior engineer in charge of implementing the installation of a new power plant. He was to work there for almost twenty years.

During his university years, Jacques had been active in the Student Christian Movement, and he and his friends had been influenced by J.S. Woodsworth, whose theme was "Socialism, the Gospel of the Working Class." Later, in London, he was active in the International Club, where Anglo-Saxons, Latins, Germans, and others discussed world affairs. Then, back in Montreal, a group of young professors and intellectuals, including Jacques, created the League for Social Reconstruction. Their goal was to create a society where production and distribution were more equally shared. Frank Scott, Eugene Forsey, and others got together and published a manifesto. Jacques joined his friends at regular evening meetings to study how Canada could build, on the ruins of the war and the Depression, a more just and less selfish society. It wasn't a political party or a revolutionary cell, but simply a study group looking for ways to replace "laissez-faire" with a measure of progress. The league itself eventually disappeared, but was an instigator of the formation of the CCF Party, forerunner of the NDP, in which Jacques became quite active.

St Christopher fresco at the entrance of La Maison Rose

Unlike his brothers, Jacques had been too young to participate in the horrors of World War I, and he was almost forty in 1939, when the last hopes for peace with the Nazis crashed. As soon as war was declared, he decided to offer his engineering knowledge to the Allied cause. He moved to Ottawa and was the organizer and director of the Department of Munition's rocket-manufacturing division. It was there that he met Zoe Brown-Clayton, his future wife, and a future editor of the *Montreal Star*.

But it wasn't only work and politics. Jacques was an avid outdoorsman, and particularly enjoyed skiing. He was one of the founders of the Red Bird Ski Club, which produced a number of the leading Canadian Olympic skiers in the 1930s and 1940s. In conjunction with that, he and André rebuilt La Maison Rose, that well-known landmark in St Sauveur, with André's fresco of St Christopher painted on the wall facing main street.

CHAPTER TWENTY

History

Agrippa d'Aubigné

The Bielers

MY EARLY BIELER ANCESTORS were woodcutters in the Aare valley in northern Switzerland. They were devout, hardworking, ambitious people, who in the seventeenth century moved to the Canton de Vaud on the shores of Lake Geneva. We suspect that they moved in order to be closer to the heart of the Protestant movement. My great-great-grandfather, François, served in Napoleon's army in Italy, and after the fall of the empire became a *traiteur-patissier* (caterer) of some renown in Geneva, which was becoming rich and influential with the return of peace and its admission to the Swiss Confederation in 1815. At one time he was maître d'hôtel to Madame de Staël at the Château de Coppet.

My great-grandfather, Samuel, had worked as a veterinarian, and had subsequently attended a veterinary college near Paris, which was in part a military school. There, he found himself in the middle of the 1848 revolution, mounting guard at the barricades of the Paris Hôtel de Ville. He returned to Switzerland as the officer in charge of the army's horses in Suisse Romande. He was a leader in Swiss agriculture, and founded and directed l'Institut agricole du Canton de Vaud. He married Nathalie de Butzow, the daughter of a Protestant member of the rural Polish nobility. They had ten children and my grandfather Charles was the eldest. Samuel was a religious man and spent most of his Sundays with the congregation of the "Réveil," the religious movement founded by the father of the future wife of one of his sons!

The Merle d'Aubignés

IN THE SIXTEENTH CENTURY, the teachings of Luther in Germany, followed by those of Calvin in France, were at the root of the Protestant Reformation and the years of Religious Wars. Agrippa d'Aubigné, a very early ancestor, was a friend of Henri IV, and collaborated with him in the drafting of the Edict of Nantes, which was an effort to protect the Protestants. It was revoked by Louis XIII, and Agrippa was sentenced to death and fled to Geneva. Switzerland, and in particular Geneva, became the hub of a vast missionary enterprise. Protestant citizens of neighbouring countries flocked to the safety, and the fascination, of the evangelical movement there.

Many years later, Agrippa's descendant, my great-great-grandfather Aimé Robert Merle d'Aubigné, collaborated with Napoleon. In about 1789, he had established an international postal and courier service, operating from neutral Geneva. The system was accepted by the Committee for Public Safety of the Republic, and for a number of years, important and confidential dispatches from all directions passed through his hands. It was a curious anomaly that this Genevese should be directing a confidential service of the French Republic, that this so-called aristocrat should be carrying out the affairs of the Jacobins, and that those "sans-culottes" should trust their correspondent without flinching! Aimé Robert's adventurous life in a Europe torn by revolution and strife ended mysteriously in 1799 when he left his family again to search for important dispatches, which had been intercepted by the advancing armies of Austria and Russia. He was last heard of near Schaffhausen, on his way to the distant war zone.

Aimé Robert's son, Jean Henri Merle d'Aubigné, my grandmother's father, was instrumental in the evolution of the Protestant doctrine. Along with several other religious leaders, including Robert Haldane from Scotland, and César Malan from Geneva, they created the "Réveil" movement. The main aim was to move even further away from Catholicism, towards an emphasis on the New Testament, and in particular the work of St Paul. In 1817, having just graduated from university, he was appointed pastor of the French Protestant Church in Hamburg. He wrote from there: "I would like to write a history of the Protestant Reformation. I would like this history to be a scholarly document that presents facts that are not yet known." He began a lifelong journey throughout Europe, preaching his beliefs and his vision of unifying Christians. His base was nevertheless in Geneva, where he would be seen lecturing at the Theology School that he founded, preaching on Sundays at St Pierre's Cathedral, or hidden in his library on the shore of Lake Geneva, researching and writing his epic. The book earned a foremost place among modern French ecclesiastical historians, and was translated into most European languages.

Jean Henri was close to his two brothers, Guillaume and Ami. Unlike their brother, they were entrepreneurs, and they decided to go to America to seek their fortune. Guillaume became an important merchant in New York City. Ami ran his brother's subsidiary in New Orleans, but became disenchanted, and, to the horror of all of Geneva, returned there with his group of slaves.

OUR IMMEDIATE FAMILY

Charles

MY GRANDFATHER WAS BORN in 1860 in Rolle, a small town on the shore of Lake Geneva. He graduated from the College de Genève in 1878, where, in addition to the thirty-two hours of regular courses per week, another three of religious education was mandated. His parents urged him to undertake a theological education, but he felt that he should seek a more gainful occupation. He eventually compromised and accepted a three-month course at the Faculté de Théologie de l'Académie de Lausanne. His professors and his courses impressed him so much that he abruptly changed his mind and decided to follow his parents' advice.

Charles was interested in Luther, and decided to spend a few years in Germany as a tutor, prior to enrolling and receiving a degree in Lausanne, at the Ecole de Théologie de l'Eglise Libre. It was time to begin a career. He chose to join his brother Ernest, who was studying painting in Paris, and attempt to enrol at the Ecole de Théologie de Batignolles, which was viewed as the top school for aspiring French pastors. The position of Sous Directeur (Deputy Director) was vacant, and he was fortunate to land the job, quite an honour for a young clergyman. He later said, "For three years I breathed in the glory of this austere institution that was as exacting as a sheet of music." It was during these years, in 1889, that an old school friend introduced him to his sister, Blanche Merle d'Aubigné.

Blanche

MY GRANDMOTHER WAS BORN in Geneva in 1864. Her father, a widower in middle age, had remarried Frances Hardy, the daughter of John Hardy, an Irish clergyman who lived and preached in Kilcullen in County Kildare. He was the son of Captain Hardy, a career officer, attached to a British regiment.

Blanche was brought up in the splendour of the Merle d'Aubigné estate on the shore of Lake Geneva. It was nevertheless a very Calvinistic environment, which was subdued as compared to what she termed, "the ecstatic devotion of the Catholics." One of her most vivid early recollections was that of her father standing tall in the pulpit of the St Pierre Cathedral. Her headmistress was of a similar style, with rigid discipline combined with fascinating teaching. She reflected many years later, "If I had been born fifty years later, I might have been tempted to become a doctor or a teacher, but unfortunately I let myself be influenced by the ideas of the times where those of our milieu studied music or painting, took some university courses, and learned a few useful languages."

Blanche was very close to her sister, Julia. She also travelled extensively with her brothers. Henri was a pastor in Belgium, and Charles's pulpit was in Germany. The two both moved to Paris and were close friends in the years ahead. She went quite frequently to Ireland to visit her mother's family, who were active in politics, the armed forces, and the church. She met an interesting crowd of English gentlemen in Geneva, and she was intrigued by the work done by the evangelists Moody and Booth, but quite concerned about the ideas of Darwin and Huxley.

She had enjoyed social and intellectual pursuits, but her principal occupation during these prenuptial years was helping her mother, and enjoying her sister and sisters-in-law. She was proud of becoming the director of a large Sunday school, which she felt was perfect training for the future. Then, one morning during the summer of 1889, at the foot of the fountain in the main square of the alpine village of Gryon, her brother Charles introduced her to his friend Charles Bieler.

Charles and Blanche

IN 1891, MY GRANDPARENTS were married in the Chapel of the Oratoire. A grand reception, attended by "le tout Genève" followed at La Graveline, the Merle d'Aubigné residence. The marriage brought together four families of diverse origins and traditions that all experienced, within a few generations, the political, military, religious, and intellectual ferment of Europe in the eighteenth and nineteenth centuries.

The previous year, my grandfather had been approached by Mr J.L. Gaillard to succeed him as proprietor and director of the college he had founded in Lausanne some forty years previously. It had an excellent reputation, offering a complete education for boys between the ages of twelve and twenty. Charles and Blanche moved into its magnificent apartment soon after the wedding. Jean was born the following year, and the next three followed: Etienne in 1895, André in 1896, and Philippe in 1898. (Jacques was born at the Maison Blanche near Lausanne in 1901.) It was a comfortable, but most challenging, eight years. Blanche was occupied with her four babies, and Charles was learning the business, and coping with the college's inadequate financing. Finally, in 1898, the school was closed and integrated into the Geneva school system.

My grandfather had heard that the job as director of the French Protestant Sunday Schools was available, and given the circumstances he didn't hesitate. It was an opportunity to return to a life more closely associated with the ministry and the teaching of theology, as well as returning to a Paris that he had enjoyed in the past and where most of Blanche's brothers and sisters now lived. It was nevertheless a courageous step to leave their country of origin, with a growing family and slender resources. The return was, in one sense, a reversal of the Huguenot emigration.

The family first settled in a small house in the chic district of Neuilly, not far from Oncle Charles's church. He was the pastor, and the church became their religious centre. Oncle Charles was conveniently well off, and lived in a large house nearby, full of cousins. My grandmother explained: "Our relationship with my brothers, sisters, sisters-in-law, and their children was also excellent. Soon the cousins began to form groups: Louisette, Emile, and Jean were already absorbed in serious studies; Idelette and Etienne were always good friends, especially since the day of a gallant rescue of a doll that had fallen into the wrong hands; André, Philippe, and Guy, the three responsible for this nasty act, and many others; and finally Robert and Jacques, who would have become great friends if circumstances had allowed it. They all went to the same schools, first of all to École Nicolet, and afterwards to the Lycée Carnot. The school days were long and tiring, and usually followed by my helping Jean prepare his essays, while Philippe was preparing his future role by machine-gunning his cardboard soldiers. Fortunately, I didn't have to deal with Etienne's times tables!"

Meanwhile my grandparents found time to pursue various other activities. "For my husband it involved his increasing interest in his publications and his reports. For me it was the satisfaction of collaborating a little with his work and undertaking some practical endeavours, including the direction of the nursery class of the Neuilly school." Their time together was precious, as my grandfather was very often away doing his rounds of Sunday schools, right across the country.

As some of the children were reaching secondary-school age, they decided to move closer to the centre of town. Neuilly was in any case too expensive. They found a pleasant small house in Levallois-Perret, a nearby suburb, which was closer to both transportation and the shops.

Before leaving Geneva, eight years before, my grandmother had decided to try and maintain, during the summer holidays, some close ties with the Swiss countryside. They found a lovely old house, la Maison Blanche, next to a lake, at the edge of a forest in the foothills of the Alps, and not far from Oncle Charles's farm. To make this economically feasible, she organized a summer camp for boys, a pioneering venture in the Switzerland of the early days of the twentieth century. There were various courses for those who needed to repeat their exams, manual work, swims, hikes, etc. The boys were international, and my grandfather was proud to point out that some of the boys did well in life: Claude Elliott became Provost of Eton College and Alfred Roth chief of Clemenceau's cabinet. My grandmother was more likely to talk about the house becoming a local religious and social centre.

THE DEPARTURE

WHAT WERE THE MOTIVATIONS that brought my family to Canada in 1908? My grandfather recorded that he had not become a French citizen, and he realized that, as his five sons grew, their future in France might be precarious, and that some avenues and opportunities would be closed to them. He had experienced this problem himself. Perhaps the cost of educating his children overseas would be helpful. They had been in Paris since 1898: undoubtedly they were influenced by the political ambiance of France at that period. It was a time of economic stagnation and a growing fear of the organizational strength of Germany, as focused in Paul Valéry's essay "La Conquete Allemande," published in 1897. The Panama Canal project had evolved into a political scandal, with the exposure of corruption, and brought no less than financial ruin for many of the bourgeoisie. Above all, the political and intellectual "cause célèbre" of the Dreyfus affair had radically reduced the international prestige of France. The pardon of Dreyfus in 1899, associated with the threat of boycott by foreign countries of the great Exposition of 1900, was at best a compromise. Zola saw the exposition (and the pardon) as "strangling truth and justice," in his play "La Verité en Marche." The innocence of Dreyfus was not declared until 1906.

These events were of deep concern to my grandparents, as evidenced by their diaries. In the spring of 1908, he was offered the position to succeed Professor Coussinat, then back in France, for the post of teaching theology to the French-speaking students at the Presbyterian College of Montreal. The principal, John Scrimger, confirmed the offer: "At a meeting of the Presbyterian College Board held yesterday 23 May 1908, I was authorized by a unanimous vote to offer you the position as French Professor." This was a particularly timely development.

They were about to make yet another move. My grandfather was forty-eight, and my grandmother forty-four. My father, Jean, was sixteen and was completing his French matriculation. His brother Etienne was thirteen, and already an accomplished mathematician. André was twelve and intrigued by all things artistic. Philippe was a joyful and handsome ten-year-old, and Jacques was what his parents described as the perfect toddler.

BIELER FAMILY

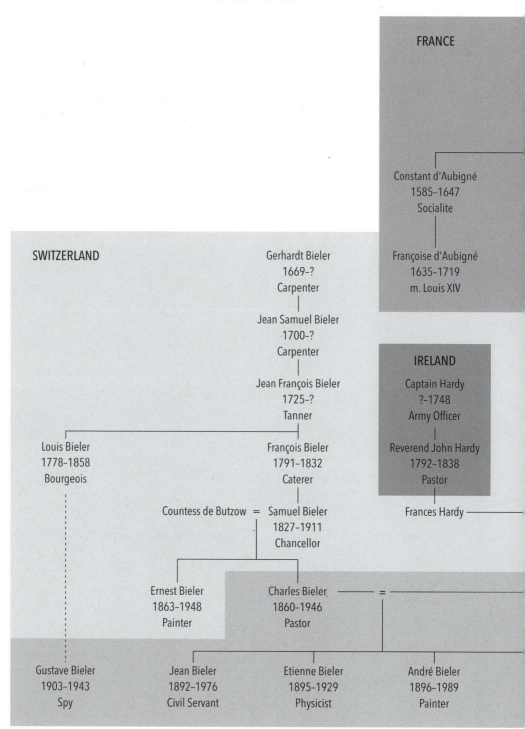

FRANCE

Constant d'Aubigné
1585–1647
Socialite

Françoise d'Aubigné
1635–1719
m. Louis XIV

SWITZERLAND

Gerhardt Bieler
1669–?
Carpenter

Jean Samuel Bieler
1700–?
Carpenter

Jean François Bieler
1725–?
Tanner

IRELAND

Captain Hardy
?–1748
Army Officer

Reverend John Hardy
1792–1838
Pastor

Louis Bieler
1778–1858
Bourgeois

François Bieler
1791–1832
Caterer

Countess de Butzow = Samuel Bieler
1827–1911
Chancellor

Frances Hardy

Ernest Bieler
1863–1948
Painter

Charles Bieler =
1860–1946
Pastor

Gustave Bieler
1903–1943
Spy

Jean Bieler
1892–1976
Civil Servant

Etienne Bieler
1895–1929
Physicist

André Bieler
1896–1989
Painter

D'AUBIGNÉ FAMILY

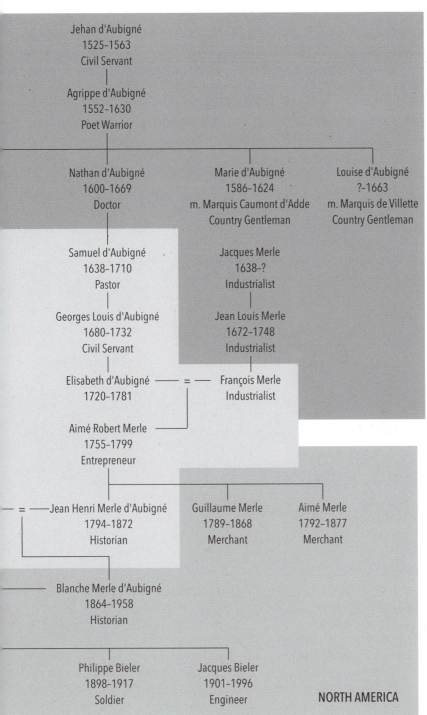

Jehan d'Aubigné
1525–1563
Civil Servant

Agrippe d'Aubigné
1552–1630
Poet Warrior

Nathan d'Aubigné
1600–1669
Doctor

Marie d'Aubigné
1586–1624
m. Marquis Caumont d'Adde
Country Gentleman

Louise d'Aubigné
?–1663
m. Marquis de Villette
Country Gentleman

Samuel d'Aubigné
1638–1710
Pastor

Jacques Merle
1638–?
Industrialist

Georges Louis d'Aubigné
1680–1732
Civil Servant

Jean Louis Merle
1672–1748
Industrialist

Elisabeth d'Aubigné —— = —— François Merle
1720–1781   Industrialist

Aimé Robert Merle
1755–1799
Entrepreneur

= ——Jean Henri Merle d'Aubigné
1794–1872
Historian

Guillaume Merle
1789–1868
Merchant

Aimé Merle
1792–1877
Merchant

Blanche Merle d'Aubigné
1864–1958
Historian

Philippe Bieler
1898–1917
Soldier

Jacques Bieler
1901–1996
Engineer

NORTH AMERICA

Martin Luther 1517

Edict Nantes 1598

17th Century

Westphalia Treaty 1648

18th Century

19th Century

Protestant Reformation

ACKNOWLEDGMENTS

Painting by André

THIS WAS A STORY ABOUT THE COURAGE of my grandparents and their five boys during World War I. I wish, in conclusion, to acknowledge my grandparents for having written the greater part of the book, while they played their role in their new country.

It goes without saying that the book would not have been possible without the considerable support of many others, and I list some hereunder:

My wife and children for being awakened at 5 a.m. as I scrambled down the stairs. Nathalie Sorenson for her special relationship with our grandmother. Carol Brettell, for teaching me how to write an introduction. Jacques, Sylvie, and Philippe Baylaucq for having discovered the pile of letters. Ted Bieler for having found the pictures to replace my father's missing letters. Andy Powell, Desmond Morton, and Philip Cercone for encouraging me to keep going. Erskine Holmes for pointing out that many of my assumptions were incorrect. Carles Riba for having transformed the words into something more or less readable. Mandi O'Neill for finding photographs that met the publisher's specifications. Marilyn Timmerman for insisting that the letters were the key. Thalia Field for introducing me to Mr. Scrivener's magic formula, and Adwoa Hinson for her administrative skills. Susie Forbath for having helped me discard the unimportant. And the horde of brilliant writers at the Hay Festival who confirmed that I was an unlikely author.

Philippe Bieler

ILLUSTRATION CREDITS

167 http://en.wikipedia.org/wiki/File:Unclesamwantyou.jpg

169 Library and Archives Canada/First World War map collection/e000000519-
000000520

171 Library and Archives Canada/Credit: W.I. Castle/Department of National Defence
fonds/PA-00110

194 Observatoire du Patrimoine Religieux

204 *No. 3 Canadian General Hospital (McGill) in France (1915, 1916, 1917),*
views illustrating life and scenes in the hospital: With a short description of its
origin, organisation, and progress. http://www.iwm.org.uk/collections/item/
object/205195977

208 http://www.archives.pe.ca/peiain/sousfondsdetail.php3?fonds=Acc4225&series=
Series10&subseries=Subseries2. No. 27.

211 © Imperial War Museums, E(AUS) 1220

213 © Imperial War Museums, Q 3007

214 © Imperial War Museums, CO 2190

216 Australian War Memorial, E01121

229 Bundesarchiv-Bildarchiv, Bild 146-2013-0089

234 © Imperial War Museums, CO 2120

238 Claire and Frédéric Devys

241 Bundesarchiv-Bildarchiv, DVM 10 Bild-23-61-17

243 Library of Congress, LC-DIG-ggbain-17779

245 Physics Department, McGill University

246 © Imperial War Museums, SP 1680

249 http://en.wikipedia.org/wiki/File:Western_front_1918_allied.jpg

251 Photographer: Albert Moreau, ECPAD, SPA 292 M 5194

252 CWM 19930012-421 George Metcalf Archival Collection © Canadian War Museum

256 The National Library of Scotland

258 © Imperial War Museums, CO 3660

265 © Imperial War Museums, Q 53611

277 Library and Archives Canada/Canadian Broadcasting Corporation fonds/
PA-178340

279 Rutherford Museum, McGill University

280 Sir James Chadwick © National Portrait Gallery, London

283 Rutherford Museum, McGill University

283 Library and Archives Canada/Department of National Defence fonds/PA-001370

287 Musée de Québec

All other illustrations are from the Bieler family collection.

SELECTED BIBLIOGRAPHY

Bercuson, David. *The Patricias: The Proud History of a Fighting Regiment*. Toronto: Stoddart, 2001.

Ferguson, Niall. *The Pity of War, 1914–1918*. New York: Basic Books, 1999.

Hodder-Williams, Ralph. *Princess Patricia's Canadian Light Infantry, 1914–1919*. 2 vols. London, Toronto: Hodder and Stoughton, 1923.

Michael, Grandson. *Canadian Great War Project. Canadian Field Artillery* (online). http://www.canadiangreatwarproject.com/warDiaryLac/wdLacMain.asp.

Nicholson, Colonel G.W.L. *Canadian Expeditionary Force, 1914–1919: Official History of the Canadian Army in the First World War*. Ottawa: Queen's Printer, 1962.

Taylor, A.J.P. *The First World War: An Illustrated History*. London: Hamish Hamilton, 1963.

Williams, Jeffrey. *Princess Patricia's Canadian Light Infantry*. London: Leo Cooper, 1972.

Wikipedia. Arthur Currie. en.wikipedia.org/wiki/Arthur_Currie.

INDEX